The Writings of Herman Melville

The Northwestern-Newberry Edition

VOLUME FOURTEEN

Correspondence

This volume edited and annotated, with Historical Note, by
LYNN HORTH

Revised and augmented from
The Letters of Herman Melville (*1960*)
edited by
MERRELL R. DAVIS
and WILLIAM H. GILMAN

Correspondence

HERMAN MELVILLE

NORTHWESTERN UNIVERSITY PRESS
and
THE NEWBERRY LIBRARY
Evanston and Chicago
1993

PUBLICATION OF *this edition of* THE WRITINGS OF HERMAN MELVILLE *has been made possible through the financial support of Northwestern University and its Research Committee and The Newberry Library. The research necessary to establish the text was initially undertaken under the Cooperative Research Program of the U.S. Office of Education, and preparation of this volume has been supported by the National Endowment for the Humanities, a federal agency which supports the study of such fields as history, philosophy, literature, and languages. Use of the 1960 edition of* The Letters of Herman Melville *was arranged with William H. Gilman and Laura Davis, and also with permission of Yale University Press. Northwestern University Press produced and published this revised and augmented edition and reserves all rights.*

LIBRARY OF CONGRESS CATALOG CARD NUMBER 92–085490

PRINTED IN THE UNITED STATES OF AMERICA

Cloth Edition, ISBN 0–8101–0981–6
Paper Edition, ISBN 0–8101–0995–6

CENTER FOR EDITIONS OF
AMERICAN AUTHORS

AN APPROVED TEXT

MODERN LANGUAGE
ASSOCIATION OF AMERICA

In 1960 The Letters of Herman Melville *was dedicated thus by its editors:*

For Melville scholars of three generations

STANLEY T. WILLIAMS
LEON HOWARD
HARRISON HAYFORD

In 1993 this Correspondence *volume of Melville's* Writings, *revised and augmented from that landmark volume in a still later generation, pays dedicatory honor in turn to those editors:*

MERRELL R. DAVIS
WILLIAM H. GILMAN

Contents

EDITORIAL APPENDIX

ABBREVIATIONS AND SHORT TITLES

For an explanation of the documentation used throughout this volume, see the section on "Sources," pp. 810–11 below. For terms, symbols, and recording methods used in the textual reports that follow each letter, see pp. 839–40 below.

ALS/LS/AL/TLS	Autograph letter signed / letter signed (not autograph) / autograph letter (not signed) / typed letter signed
Bercaw [followed by entry number]	Mary K. Bercaw, *Melville's Sources*. Evanston: Northwestern University Press, 1987.
Birss, "A Mere Sale to Effect"	John H. Birss, " 'A Mere Sale to Effect,' with Letters of Herman Melville." *New Colophon* I (July 1948), 239–55.
Davis	Merrell R. Davis, *Melville's MARDI: A Chartless Voyage*. New Haven: Yale University Press, 1952.
Davis-Gilman	*The Letters of Herman Melville*, ed. Merrell R. Davis and William H. Gilman. New Haven: Yale University Press, 1960 [with illustrations not present in later printings].
ESM	Elizabeth Shaw Melville
Gilman	William H. Gilman, *Melville's Early Life and REDBURN*. New York: New York University Press, 1951.
Hayford-Davis	Harrison Hayford and Merrell R. Davis, "Herman Melville as Office-Seeker." *Modern Language Quarterly* 10 (1949), 168–83, 377–88.
HCL	The Houghton Library (Harvard College Library) of Harvard University
HCL-D	Dix Collection
HCL-M	Melville Collection
Journals	*The Writings of Herman Melville*, vol. 15, ed. Howard Horsford with Lynn Horth. Evanston and Chicago: Northwestern University Press and The Newberry Library, 1989.
Leyda, *Portable Melville*	Jay Leyda, ed., *The Portable Melville*. New York: Viking, 1952.
Log	Jay Leyda, *The Melville Log: A Documentary Life of Herman Melville*. 2 vols. New York: Harcourt, Brace, 1951. Reprinted, with supplement, New

York: Gordian Press, 1969. See also *New Log* (below).

M   Herman Melville

Metcalf   Eleanor Melville Metcalf, *Herman Melville: Cycle and Epicycle.* Cambridge: Harvard University Press, 1953.

MHS   Massachusetts Historical Society, Boston
MHS-D   Dana Collection
MHS-S   Shaw Collection

Minnigerode   Meade Minnigerode, *Some Personal Letters of Herman Melville and a Bibliography.* New York: Brick Row Book Shop, 1922.

Murray   Archives of the John Murray publishing firm, London.

New Log   *The New Melville Log*, ed. Jay Leyda and Hershel Parker. New York: Gordian Press, forthcoming.

NN   Northwestern-Newberry Edition

NYPL   Rare Books and Manuscripts Division, The New York Public Library, Astor, Lenox, and Tilden Foundations
NYPL-B   Berg Collection
NYPL-D   Duyckinck Family Papers
NYPL-GL   Gansevoort-Lansing Collection

Paltsits   *Family Correspondence of Herman Melville, 1830–1904*, ed. Victor Hugo Paltsits. New York: New York Public Library, 1929. Earlier published in the *Bulletin of the New York Public Library* 33 (July 1929), 507–25; and 33 (August 1929), 575–625.

Parker, *Gansevoort Melville's London Journal and Letters*   *Gansevoort Melville's 1846 London Journal and Letters from England, 1845*, ed. Hershel Parker. New York: New York Public Library, 1966. Earlier published in the *Bulletin of the New York Public Library* 69 (December 1965), 633–54; 70 (January 1966), 36–49; 70 (February 1966), 113–31.

Sealts [followed by entry number]   Merton M. Sealts, Jr., *Melville's Reading.* Columbia: University of South Carolina Press, 1988. See also: "A Supplementary Note to *Melville's Reading* (1988)," *Melville Society Extracts* 80 (February 1990), 5–10.

Sealts, *Early Lives*	Merton M. Sealts, Jr., *The Early Lives of Melville: Nineteenth-Century Biographical Sketches and Their Authors.* Madison: University of Wisconsin Press, 1974.
Sealts, *Melville as Lecturer*	Merton M. Sealts, Jr., *Melville as Lecturer.* Cambridge: Harvard University Press, 1957; Folcroft, Pa.: Folcroft, 1973.
Thorp	*Herman Melville: Representative Selections*, ed. Willard Thorp. New York: American Book Company, 1938.
UCLA-Leyda	Leyda Collection, University Research Library, University of California at Los Angeles
UV-Barrett	Herman Melville Collection, Clifton Waller Barrett Library, Manuscripts Division, Special Collections Department, University of Virginia Library
Weaver	Raymond M. Weaver, *Herman Melville: Mariner and Mystic.* New York: George H. Doran, 1921.

NOTES ON THE ILLUSTRATIONS

530   Letter to William J. Bok, 24 November 1890. Courtesy of the Rare
      and Manuscript Collections, Cornell University Library.

Principal Persons and Places
542   Melvill[e] and Gansevoort genealogical tables: prepared for the pres-
      ent edition with the assistance of the Berkshire County Historical
      Society and with the benefit of earlier tables published in Metcalf
      (endpapers), Gilman (endpapers), and Merton M. Sealts, Jr., "The
      Melvill Heritage," *Harvard Library Bulletin* 34 (1986), 337–61.
544   Melville and Gansevoort families: courtesy of the Rare Books and
      Manuscripts Division, The New York Public Library, Astor, Lenox
      and Tilden Foundations (Gansevoort-Lansing Collection).
546   Lemuel Shaw and Hope Savage Shaw: courtesy of the Rare Books
      and Manuscripts Division, The New York Public Library, Astor,
      Lenox and Tilden Foundations (Gansevoort-Lansing Collection).
      Elizabeth Shaw Melville: courtesy of the Houghton Library, Har-
      vard University (Melville Collection).
      The Melville children: courtesy of the Department of Special Collec-
      tions, University Research Library, University of California at Los
      Angeles (Leyda Collection).
547   Richard T. Greene ("Toby"): 1846, courtesy of the Houghton
      Library, Harvard University (Melville Collection).
      Nathaniel Hawthorne: steel engraving, 1851, from the Cephas
      Thompson portrait, 1850, presented by Sophia Hawthorne to Mel-
      ville in 1851; courtesy of the Houghton Library, Harvard University
      (Melville Collection).
      Sarah Huyler Morewood: portrait by Henry Luman, 1861, courtesy
      of the Berkshire County Historical Society.
      Richard Henry Dana, Jr.: frontispiece to Charles Francis Adams,
      Richard Henry Dana: A Biography (Boston and New York: Hough-
      ton, Mifflin, 1890).
      W. Clark Russell: *The Book Buyer* N.S. 7 (April 1890), facing p. [95].
      Edmund C. Stedman: Laura Stedman and George M. Gould, *Life
      and Letters of Edmund Clarence Stedman* (New York: Moffat, Yard,
      1910), II, facing p. 314.
548   Evert A. Duyckinck: courtesy of the Miriam and Ira D. Wallach
      Division of Art, Prints and Photographs, The New York Public
      Library, Astor, Lenox and Tilden Foundations (Print Collection).
      Richard Bentley: *Extracts from LE LIVRE* (Edinburgh: Clark, 1886),
      facing p. 1.
      John Murray III: F. Espinasse, "The House of Murray," *Harper's
      New Monthly Magazine* (September, 1885), p. 520.

George L. Duyckinck: frontispiece to vol. II of *Cyclopædia of American Literature*, rev. ed. (Philadelphia: Zell, 1875).

The Harper brothers: photograph by Mathew Brady, c. 1850, courtesy of the Library of Congress.

Charles F. Briggs: *The Knickerbocker Gallery* (New York: Hueston, 1855), facing p. [481].

George William Curtis: *Knickerbocker Gallery*, facing p. [329].

George P. Putnam: frontispiece to George Haven Putnam, *A Memoir of George Palmer Putnam*, vol. 1 (New York and London: Putnam's [privately printed], 1903).

549 Arrowhead: *Cyclopædia of American Literature*, ed. Evert and George Duyckinck (New York: Scribner's, 1856), II, 674.

Melville's 1860 drawing of Arrowhead: formerly in the collection of Eleanor Melville Metcalf (now unlocated; see the NN *Journals*, p. 643).

550 The Gansevoort family mansion: pencil sketch by E. L. Henry, 1874, courtesy of the Rare Books and Manuscripts Division, The New York Public Library, Astor, Lenox and Tilden Foundations (Gansevoort-Lansing Collection).

Broadhall in the 1870's: courtesy of the Berkshire Athenaeum.

Letters Received

568 Letter from Allan Melville, 17 October 1844, p. 4. Formerly in the collection of Henry A. Murray. Courtesy of Nina Murray.

607 Letter from Nathaniel Hawthorne and Sophia Peabody Hawthorne, 27 March 1851, p. 1. Courtesy of the Rare Books and Manuscripts Division, The New York Public Library, Astor, Lenox and Tilden Foundations (Gansevoort-Lansing Collection).

632 Letter from Maria Gansevoort Melville, 10 February 1854. Courtesy of the Rare Books and Manuscripts Division, The New York Public Library, Astor, Lenox and Tilden Foundations (Gansevoort-Lansing Collection).

638 Letter from George P. Putnam, 13 May 1854. Courtesy of the Houghton Library, Harvard University (Melville Collection).

645 Letter from Richard T. Greene, 16 June 1856, p. 1. Courtesy of the Houghton Library, Harvard University (Melville Collection).

702 Letter from T. Apoleon Cheney, 7 December 1869, p. 1. Courtesy of the Houghton Library, Harvard University (Melville Collection).

739 Prospectus (1888) for "A Library of American Literature." Courtesy of the Houghton Library, Harvard University (Melville Collection).

Correspondence

My dear Aunt

You asked me to write you a letter but I thought tht I could not write well enough before this. I now study Spelling, Arithmetic, Grammar, Geography, Reading, and Writing. I past a very pleasant vacation, at Bristol. give my love to Grandmamma, Grandpapa, and all my aunts.

Your dear Nephew,
Herman, Melvill.

To Lucy Melvill, on or before 11 October 1828 (reduced). Courtesy of Cody Memorial Library, Southwestern University (Osborne Collection).

Melville's Letters

1828

TO UNKNOWN
ON OR BEFORE 11 OCTOBER 1828 · NEW YORK

Unlocated. Melville began his letter-writing career by the age of nine with what appears to have been a writing exercise, as he indicates in "the third letter that I ever wrote," dated 11 October 1828, to his maternal grandmother, Catherine Van Schaick Gansevoort, below. His first letter may have been this unlocated one, presumably also to a relative, or it may have been the one to his aunt Lucy Melvill, just below. Davis-Gilman Unlocated 273.

TO LUCY MELVILL
ON OR BEFORE 11 OCTOBER 1828 · NEW YORK

At the age of six in 1825, Melville entered the New-York Male High School, which his older brother Gansevoort (1815–46) also attended until 1829, when they both left to attend Columbia Grammar School. This undated letter, evidently written in the fall term after his August 1828 vacation spent with his uncle John D'Wolf and aunt Mary Melvill D'Wolf in Bristol, Rhode Island, may be one of the first two letters he "ever wrote" (see the letter of 11 October 1828 to his maternal grandmother, Catherine Van Schaick Gansevoort, just below). Melville remained a favorite of his aunt Lucy (1795–1877), the second youngest of his father's five surviving sisters, to whom this letter is addressed. In a 23 July 1847 reply to Lemuel Shaw's invitation to Melville's wedding, her second husband, Amos Nourse,

3

wrote: "I have no need to speak of the interest we both feel in the event & ceremony which you so kindly invite us to witness — Lucy has always felt a peculiar attachment to her nephew" (HCL-M). The four other Melvill aunts were Mary Melvill D'Wolf (1778–1859), Priscilla (1784–1862), Jean (1788–1866), and Helen (1798–1864). At this time Lucy was still living in Boston with her parents, Melville's "Grandmamma" and "Grandpapa," Priscilla Scollay Melvill (1755–1833) and Major Thomas Melvill (1751–1832), with whom Melville had stopped briefly on his way to Bristol during the summer of 1828. The family name was then spelled without a final "e," as Melville signs his name here. It was not until after the death of Melville's father, Allan Melvill (1782–1832), that his wife, the former Maria Gansevoort (1791–1872), and her children altered the spelling of their name.

My dear Aunt

You asked me to write you a letter but I thought tht I could not write well enough before this. I now study Spelling, Arithmetic, Grammar, Geography, Reading, and Writing. I past a very pleasant vacation at Bristol. give my love to Grandmamma, Grandpapa, and all my aunts.

> Your dear Nephew,
> Herman, Melvill.

ALS on a 30 × 15.75 cm part-sheet (torn along both sides and also cut and torn unevenly at the top), folded in half, of white wove paper, watermarked with the partial initials "J W &". Melville inscribed the first page, in ink, and addressed the fourth page "To) | Miss Lucy Melvill. | Boston." Davis-Gilman Unlocated 272.

LOCATION: Osborne Collection, Cody Memorial Library, Southwestern University.

PUBLICATION: (simultaneous) T. Walter Herbert, Jr., "The Osborne Collection," *Melville Society Extracts* 61 (February 1985), 8–9 (with reproduction), and T. Walter Herbert, Jr., and Jon D. Swartz, *The Osborne Collection of Melville Materials at Southwestern University* (Georgetown, Texas: Cody Memorial Library, 1985), pp. 2, 8 (also with reproduction).

TEXTUAL NOTE: Aunt] *possibly before* Lucy *where a piece of manuscript is now torn out*

TO CATHERINE VAN SCHAICK GANSEVOORT
11 OCTOBER 1828 · NEW YORK

Melville's "third letter" gives a slightly fuller account of his studies at the New-York Male High School. His "class book" has been identified as Levi Leonard's *The Literary and Scientific Class Book* (Sealts 325a). His enclosed drawing is unlocated. By "Grandmamma," Melville may have slipped and meant his mother, who had taken her younger children to Albany to visit her mother—Melville's grandmother, Catherine Van Schaick Gansevoort (1751–1830), to whom the letter is addressed. (Melville's grandfather, General Peter Gansevoort [b. 1749], had died in 1812.) Also in Albany were "Uncle Peter," Peter Gansevoort (1788–1876), his mother's third oldest living brother, and "Aunt Mary," Mary Ann Chandonette Gansevoort (1789–1851), widow of Peter's and Maria's brother Leonard (1783–1821). Melville's sisters were Helen Maria (1817–88), Augusta ("Gus," 1821–76), Catherine ("Kate," 1825–1905), and Frances Priscilla ("Fanny," 1827–85). Allan (1823–72) was Melville's only younger brother at this time; Thomas (1830–84) was born two years later.

11th of October, 1828.

Dear Grandmother

This is the third letter that I ever wrote so you must not think it will be very good. I now study Geography, Gramar, Arithmetic, Writing, Speaking, Spelling, and read in the Scientific class book. I enclose in this letter a drawing for my dear Grandmother. Give my love to Grandmamma Uncle Peter, and Aunt Mary. And my Sisters and also to allan.

Your affectionate Grandson,
Herman Melvill.

ALS on a part-sheet (unevenly cut along the left edge and torn along the top) of white wove paper, 20.1 cm in length and 14.5 cm wide at the top and 15.2 cm wide at the bottom. Melville inscribed only one side of the leaf, in ink.

LOCATION: HCL-M.

PUBLICATION: Weaver, p. 68. Davis-Gilman 1.

TEXTUAL NOTES: third] h *inserted above caret* • class] *added* • Give] G *altered from* g

1832

TO MARIA GANSEVOORT MELVILLE
BEFORE 7 AUGUST 1832 · ALBANY

Two unlocated letters. When Melville's father, Allan Melvill, suffered financial reverses in 1830, he moved his family to Albany, where Melville attended the Albany Academy from October 1830 to October 1831 (it is not known why he was abruptly withdrawn in the fall of 1831; David Titus in "Herman Melville at the Albany Academy," *Melville Society Extracts* 42 [May 1980], 7, speculates that it may have been due to illness). After Allan Melvill's death in January 1832, Melville's older brother Gansevoort managed the fur and hat store his father had started and Melville worked in the New York State Bank in Albany. During a cholera epidemic in Albany in the summer of 1832, Maria Melville left the city with her eight children and visited relatives in Pittsfield, Massachusetts. Only Herman, almost thirteen years old at this time, returned to his job in Albany, at the insistence of his uncle Peter Gansevoort. From Albany he apparently forwarded the family mail to his mother, who later went to stay in Boston. Two letters from him to her during this period are cited in her 7 August 1832 letter to Peter Gansevoort: "The letter which Herman thought was from a Cousin in Maine was from Miss [Caroline] Yates at Long Island, it was dated 18th July & required an immediate answer . . . . Her Grandfathers Widow, who I beleive is near sixty, has married a country Youth of 25 . . . my best love to Herman. His last letter was much praise'd, for its superiority over the first, the hand writing particularly, he must practise often, & daily" (NYPL-GL). Davis-Gilman Unlocated 274 and 275.

TO HELEN MARIA MELVILLE
AFTER 8 AUGUST 1832 · ALBANY

Unlocated. In an 8 August 1832 letter to their uncle Peter Gansevoort, Melville's oldest sister Helen strongly remonstrated, "I am sorry that my brother Herman cannot find time to answer my last, but tell him I am expecting a letter every day and shall be sadly disappointed if I return to Albany before he writes" (NYPL-GL). Though there is no evidence that Melville answered the last letter Helen sent to him while he was in Albany and she was in Pittsfield during the cholera epidemic, her insistence makes it likely that he did finally reply (see LETTERS RECEIVED, p. 551).

1837

TO CHARLES VAN LOON
[SUMMER?] 1837 · PITTSFIELD

Unlocated. In 1835 Melville had returned to school—first at the Albany Classical School for a year and then from September 1836 to March 1837 in the Latin section at the Albany Academy, which he had attended earlier. In January of 1835 he joined the Albany Young Men's Association, and at some point a debating club associated with it called the Philo Logos Society. But his membership in that society was apparently unwelcome to some members, if a letter signed "R." published in the 15 April 1837 *Albany Microscope* can be taken seriously (see LETTERS RECEIVED, pp. 551–53). It accused the "bohun upus melvum" of a lack of "fixed principles" and of having been the "principle destroyer" of the "Ciceronian Debating Society." Charles Van Loon was president of the Philo Logos Society and a contemporary of Melville at the Albany Academy, which he later left to become apprenticed to an apothecary. In 1837, however, he was preparing to become a Baptist minister (Gilman, p. 91). In the midst of a later controversy over the presidency of the society carried on in the columns of the *Microscope* (see the headnote to Melville's 24 February 1838 letter, below), Van Loon referred to a letter he had received from Melville written while Melville was "called from town for a few months." Assuming that Melville actually wrote such a letter (and that Van Loon did not invent it for rhetorical purposes), he probably did so after he left Albany for Pittsfield in June 1837 to help run the farm of his uncle Thomas (see the headnote to his 30 December 1837 letter to Peter Gansevoort, just below). Challenging a statement Melville had made, that he " '*left the society in an apparently healthy and prosperous condition,*' " Van Loon wrote: "The following extract of a letter received from you during that absence and now in my possession will stamp false upon the declaration." He then quoted from Melville's now unlocated letter: " '*but I have been digressing from the beginning of my letter my object is to know the existing situation of the society; whether it is on the rapid decline I left it in, or whether like the Phoenix it hath risen from its ashes, &c., &c.*' " For the full text of Van Loon's printed letter in which this excerpt appeared, see LETTERS RECEIVED, pp. 557–61, and for fuller discussions of Melville's correspondence in print with Van Loon, see the headnotes to his three published letters of February and March 1838, below. Davis-Gilman 3.

TO PETER GANSEVOORT
30 DECEMBER 1837 · PITTSFIELD

During the summer of 1837 Melville went to Pittsfield, Massachusetts, to help run the farm of his uncle Thomas Melvill, Jr. (1776–1845). He then remained in the Pittsfield area to teach school for a term in the Sikes district. Recalling this period after an excursion in the spring of 1852, Melville's sister Augusta noted: "visited the old school house of Washington Mountain where the Author once taught the young idea how to Shoot" (see Merton M. Sealts, Jr., *Early Lives*, p. 126, and " 'An utter idler and a savage': Melville in the Spring of 1852," *Melville Society Extracts* 79 [November 1989], 2–3, and corrections in 80 [February 1990], 15). As this end-of-year letter records, Melville visited his family in Albany at least twice—once in the fall, returning to Pittsfield with his cousin Robert (1817–81), Thomas Melvill's son, and again in November, probably at Thanksgiving, when his uncle Peter gave him a book described by Robert S. Forsythe as "Self Teacher — 1834" (Sealts 456a, unlocated), inscribed "Herman G. Melville from his aff Uncle Peter Gansevoort Albany Nov. 1837." (The book Melville praises in this letter, J. Orville Taylor's *The District School* [Sealts 497, unlocated], was also probably presented to him by his uncle Peter at the same time.) The middle initial "G." in the inscription is not confirmed by any other evidence and may have been derived from associating Melville with Herman Gansevoort (1779–1862), the uncle for whom Melville had been named and to whom Melville sends his greetings at the close of this letter. He also sends his greetings to "Aunt Mary"—Peter Gansevoort's first wife, Mary Sanford Gansevoort (1814–41)—and their son, Henry Sanford Gansevoort (1834–71). Although Melville dates his letter 31 December, it was postmarked in Pittsfield on 30 December.

Pittsfield Dec 31st 1837

My Dear Uncle

At my departure from Albany last fall with Robert you expressed a desire that I should write you when my school should have gone into operation, — but, when in a few weeks I again returned, you did not repeat your request; still, however, I considered my promise binding — & it is with pleasure that I now proceed to redeem it.

I should have taken up my pen at an earlier day had not the variety & importance of the duties incident to my vocation been so numerous and pressing, that they absorbed a large portion of my time.

But now, having become somewhat acquainted with the routine of buisness, — having established a systim in my mode of instruction, — and being familiar with the charactars & disposions of my schollars: in short, having brought my school under a proper organization — a few intervals of time are afforded me, which I improve by occasional writting & reading

My scholars are about thirty in number, of all ages, sizes, ranks, charaters, & education; some of them who have attained the ages of eighteen can not do a sum in addition, while others have travelled through the Arithmatic: but with so great swiftness that they can not recognize objects in the road on a second journey: & are about as ignorant of them as though they had never passed that way before.

My school is situated in a remote & secluded part of the town about five miles from the village, and the house at which I am now boarding is a mile and a half from any other tenement whatever — being located on the summit of as savage and lonely a mountain as ever I ascended. The scenery however is most splendid & unusual, — embracing an extent of country in the form of an Ampitheatre sweeping around for many miles & encircling a portion of your state in its compass.

The man with whom I am now domicilated is a perfect embodiment of the traits of Yankee character, — being shrewd bold & independant, carrying himself with a genuine republican swagger, as hospitable as "mine host" himself, perfectly free in the expression of his sentiments, and would as soon call you a fool or a scoundrel, if he thought so — as, button up his waistcoat. He has reared a family of nine boys and three girls, 5 of whom are my pupils — — and they all burrow together in the woods — like so many foxes.

The books you presented me (and for which I am verry gratefull) I have found of eminent usefulness, particularly John O Taylors "Dristict School" — an admirable production by the by, which if generally read is calculated to exert a powerful influence and one of the most salutary & beneficial charactar.

I have given his work a diligent and attentive perusal: and am studying it, to the same advantage, — which a scholar traveling in a country — peruses its hystory, — being surrounded by the scenes it describes.

I think he has treated his theme in a masterly manner, and displays that thourough knowledge of his subject — which is only to be obtained by Experience.

Had he been perfectly familiar with the circumstances of this school, — the difficultys under which it labours, and in short with every thing pertaining to it, — he could not have sketched it in a more graphic manner, than he has, in his description of the style in which schools of this species are genneraly conducted.

Intimatly am I acquainted with the prevalence of those evils which he alledges to exist in Common-Schools.

Orators may declaim concerning the universally-diffused blessings of education in our Country, and Essayests may exhaust their magazine of adjectives in extolling our systim of Common School instruction, — — but when reduced to practise, the high and sanguine hopes excited by its imposing appearance in *theory* — are a little dashed.

Mr Taylor has freely pointed out its defects, and has not been deterred from reproving them, by any feelings of delicasy. If he had, he would have proved a traitor to the great Cause, in which he is engaged. But I have almost usurped the province of the Edinburgh Reveiw — so as I am approaching the confines of my sheet I will subscribe myself

Your affectionate nephew
Herman Melville

My love to Aunt Mary, & a kiss to Henry. Remember me to Uncle Herman   H M

ALS on a 39.5 × 24.6 cm sheet, folded in half, of pink wove paper. Melville inscribed the first three pages, in ink, and addressed the fourth page "Peter Gansevoort Esq | Albany"; it was postmarked in Pittsfield on 30 December.

LOCATION: NYPL-GL.

PUBLICATION: Paltsits, pp. 5–7. Davis-Gilman 2 (with partial reproduction).

TEXTUAL NOTES: house at which I am] *before* (over) • however] how-|ever • Ampitheatre] *originally* Amphitheatre *then first* h *canceled* • as hospitable] as *inserted above caret* • an admirable] an *originally* and *then* d *canceled* • acquainted with] *before canceled* those • Essayests] *before canceled* made • adjectives] tives *added in another hand below an area torn off in unsealing the letter where it had presumably been written by M* • little] *before canceled word-start* • Mr] *miswritten* My • been deterred] *after canceled* refrained

1838

TO THE EDITOR OF THE *ALBANY MICROSCOPE*
PUBLISHED 24 FEBRUARY 1838 · ALBANY

Melville's career as a schoolteacher in the Sikes district was short-lived (see his 30 December 1837 letter, just above), and by early 1838 he was back in Albany with his family. On 13 February 1838 the *Albany Evening Journal* listed the following officers of the Philo Logos Society as "unanimously elected to serve for the following year": president, Herman Melville; vice president, Lotus Niles; secretary, Daniel E. Bassett; and treasurer, Alfred Greene. This announcement introduced a brouhaha in print over the legitimacy of Melville's election. A total of eight letters touching on this matter (three of them by Melville) appeared between February and April of 1838 in the *Albany Microscope*, a paper "devoted to popular tales, history, legends and adventures, anecdotes, poetry, satire, humour, sporting, and the drama"—as its masthead proclaimed (the only known copy is in the New York State Library). Just how serious this controversy was is hard to judge. Quite possibly, these letters were written simply to give the participants an opportunity to practice their rhetorical skills and attract attention to the Philo Logos debating society with its flagging membership (see Melville's 1837 letter to Charles Van Loon, above). The letter that inaugurated the whole debate in print was published in the *Microscope* on 17 February 1838 (see LETTERS RECEIVED, pp. 553–54) and signed "Sandle Wood," whom Melville identified as the former president of the society, Charles Van Loon—although Van Loon denied writing the letter. Here is Melville's response, as the newly elected president, to "Sandle Wood," written for publication in the *Microscope* and signed—like all three of his letters—"Philologian [or Philologean]." (Although Melville does not identify himself in this first letter, he does so in his second one [17 and 24 March], as does Van Loon in his 10 March reply [see LETTERS RECEIVED, pp. 554–57].)

The meeting place of the society, Stanwix Hall, was one of the investments of Melville's uncles, Peter and Herman Gansevoort. Completed in 1833, it contained not only meeting rooms, but also offices, shops, a restaurant, a ballroom, and "bedrooms for single gentlemen" (see Alice P. Kenney, *The Gansevoorts of Albany* [Syracuse: Syracuse University Press, 1969], p. 200; for the financial consequences of this investment for Maria Melville and her children, see pp. 207–13).

Mr. Editor: — In every community there is a class of individuals, who are of so narrow-minded and jealous a disposition that deserving merit when developed in others, fills their bosoms with hatred and malice: and where a number of men having labored in the erection of some commendable institution are tendered the applause which their actions deserve, their breasts swell with envy, and they endeavor to villify and abuse what, if they could partake the admiration paid these, they would be as extravagant in eulogising and applauding as they were before clamorous in traducing and decrying.

Fortunate is it, however, for society, that their malignant efforts are generally powerless and feeble, and are not accompanied with that gratifying success, which in the accomplishment of a good object, is the source of the highest felicity.

Indeed, in the majority of instances the world is supremely indifferent as to which side of a cause they espouse, since they are frequently more annoying to their friends than troublesome to their enemies. They may be considered as a band of moral outlaws, the interdicted weapons they employ are falsehood and deceit, but so blunted and dulled by long service and ill-usage, that it is with extreme difficulty they can be made to inflict a serious injury. Truly, so harmless have they become, that society with a mildness and lenity quite praiseworthy, tolerates them in all their inoffensive doings and smiles with derision at their ineffectual attempts to wound the sanctity of private reputation, or to plunge their wooden daggers in the side of public virtue.

Nor does their impotency proceed from the lack of ingenuity to plan, or the will to perform, but from their utter destitution of the ability to do. Surely were their weapons as sharp as their purpose, the number of murdered reputations would exactly correspond with the stabs of their slanderous poignards.

In the *van* of these notable worthies stands pre-eminent, that silly and brainless *loon* who composed the article in your last week's paper, denying the existence of the Philo Logos Society, the legality of its recent election, and its alleged possession of a room in Stanwix Hall.

I have only to remark in relation to this interesting production, that it is not more inelegant in style than wanting in truth and veracity. It is a complete tissue of infamous fabrications, and is as destitute of a single fact as is the author of parts. I refrain from enlarging upon what probable motives induced the writer to the publication of his miserable effusion. I will not say it proceeded from the pique of mortified pride, or from an unhallowed and foolish envy, but will merely remark that from whencesoever it derived its origin, it is contemptible, dastardly and outrageous.

Any individual calling at No. 9 Gallery, Stanwix Hall, next Friday evening at 7 o'clock, will receive indubitable evidence of the utter fallacy of "Sandle Wood's" statement, and will see the society in full operation, the officers (of whose election the public was notified in the Evening Journal,) in the act of discharging their respective duties, and as well furnished a room as is "owned, rented, or any manner used," by the most flourishing debating institution of which old Gotham may boast.

Philologian.

Original document not located. Text from first publication, emended by NN.

PUBLICATION: *Albany Microscope*, 24 February 1838. Gilman, pp. 251–52. Davis-Gilman 4.

TEXTUAL NOTES: deserve, their] NN; deserve. Their • smiles] NN; smile

TO THE EDITOR OF THE *ALBANY MICROSCOPE* AND CHARLES VAN LOON
PUBLISHED 17 AND 24 MARCH 1838 · ALBANY

This is the second of Melville's letters to appear in the *Microscope* in the Philo Logos controversy. In his first letter in the *Microscope* (24 February 1838), Melville had assumed that his opponent in print—"Sandle Wood"—was Charles Van Loon; in this letter Van Loon was certainly Melville's addressee. After Melville's earlier letter with its personal attacks on "that silly and brainless *loon*," Van Loon had responded in the 10 March issue denying his authorship of the "Sandle Wood" letter, but championing its attack on the legitimacy of Melville's presidency (see LETTERS RECEIVED, pp. 554–57). This answer from Melville was printed in two parts, the first signed "Philologian" and the second "Philologean." For the next installment in this controversy, Van Loon's two-part response (31 March and 7 April), see LETTERS RECEIVED, pp. 557–61.

The invective of Melville's long letter and its attention to wordplay give some clue as to the debating skills and modes of rhetoric familiar to members of the Philo Logos Society, and again raise the possibility that these letters were written in part as rhetorical exercises designed to attract attention to the club. The full title of the book Melville accuses Van Loon of drawing upon for his "vulgar" rhetoric is *Slang. A Dictionary of the Turf, the Ring, the Chase, the Pit, of Bon-Ton, and the Varieties of*

Life, Forming the Completest and Most Authentic Lexicon Balatronicum Hitherto Offered to the Notice of the Sporting World, For Elucidating Words and Phrases that are necessarily, or purposely, cramp, mutative, and unintelligible, outside their respective Spheres. Interspersed with Anecdotes and Whimsies, with Tart Quotations, and Rum-Ones; with Examples, Proofs, and Monitory Precepts, Useful and Proper for Novices, Flats, and Yokels. It was compiled by "Jon Bee" [John Badcock], Editor of the *Fancy, Fancy Gazette, Living Picture of London,* "and the like of that" (London: Hughes, 1823). While the editor prided himself on omitting many of the indecent words in his model, Grose's *Classical Dictionary of the Vulgar Tongue* (1785), he defined and glossed enough slang words, cant, and vulgarisms to be useful to emulators of Peter Porcupine (i.e., William Cobbett, 1762–1835), the quarrelsome British journalist, or of Junius, pseudonym of the anonymous author of a series of invective letters that appeared in the London *Public Advertiser* from 1769 through 1771.

Mr. Editor: — I had not intended again to obtrude myself upon your columns, when I penned my last communication, but circumstances which I need not mention having altered my determination, I beg of you to excuse the liberty I take, when I request you to insert the following epistle, which, if it be rather long you must not demur, as it is the last I shall inflict upon your patience. I am at a loss to account for the avidity with which Mr. C*****s V*n L**n seeks to drag before the public a distorted narrative of the transactions of a private society; unless it be a mere feint or stratagem, under which he advances towards the overthrow of my reputation. However, as he lays down many grave and serious charges, I am constrained to reply thereto, in the hope of exculpating myself from allegations the most unfounded and malignant. I am aware that my communication is somewhat long and tedius, but as Mr. C*****s V*n L**n intimates his design of publishing a series of articles upon the subject, and being unwilling to parade myself before the public in a subsequent number — I have seen fit to obviate the necessity alluded to by giving a faithful account of the affair, together with a few reflections thereon, in one comprehensive survey.

*To Mr. "Sandle Wood" alias "Ex-President" alias C*****s V*n L**n.*

Sir, — Without venturing to criticise the elegance of your composition, the absurd vagaries of your imagination, or impeaching the taste you have displayed in the abundance, variety and novelty of your tropes and figures, or calling into question the accuracy of your mode of Latinising English substantives, I shall without further delay, proceed to consider the merits of your late most fanciful performance. And I cannot but sincerely deplore the rashness with which you have published a production evidently composed in the heat and turmoil of passion, and which must remain without the sanction of your cooler judgement, and the approval of your otherwise respectable understanding. To no other cause can I impute that vile scurrility, that unholy defamation, and that low and groveling abuse which are the distinguishing characteristics of your late unfortunate attempt to asperse, through its chief officer, the institution over which I have the honor to preside. In all your ribaldry and villification there lurks a spirit of implacable rancour and hate, which afford the most delightful commentaries upon the dignity of your christian character. Alas! that your discretion should have been so little consulted when this evidence of the rabidness of your vindictive nature should have been suffered to escape in the moment of your unguarded wrath, which must ever remain to demonstrate the hollowness of your religious professions of meekness, forbearance and love. Nor can I pass over without comment, the multitude of those blackguard epithets, which dance in sweet confusion throughout the whole extent of your recent production. *Here*, sir, are you upon vantage ground! I will not contend with you for the palm of vulgarity, nor seek to emulate the Billingsgate volubility of abuse in which you practice to perfection. Ah! what toilsome hours of study, what turning over of the leaves of Bee's Slang Dictionary, what studious attention to the lessons of the most accomplished masters of this divine art must have been required, ere you could have made way to that wonderful proficiency, which you seem to have attained in your late most brilliant communication. I have understood that the fish-women of Paris and the Thames were considered as the models of a regular blackguard style, as the standard and criterion by which all excellence in that department of polite literature was to be judged; and that for a readier flow of insolence, shamelessness and scurrility they proudly challenged the world. But I doubt whether the annals of Billingsgate itself, the posthumous papers of the renowned Peter Porcupine, or any of those interesting works which have been burned by the hands of the common hangman can match in purity of style and delicacy of phraseology, that valuable article which if it be destitute of every other excellence, must still be considered as the *chef-d'ouvre* of loafer eloquence. In this respect, I renounce, if ever I cherished all claims to superiority; and surely if laurels are to be reaped in such encounters — your brow is crowned with many a sprig. In regard to the hatred which you express towards me — I return it with no kindred detestation, but contemplate it with that mild and frigid contempt which it so richly deserves, and in common with the few who perused your performance, smiled at the folly which could prompt the utterance of personal dislike, and commiserate the headlong inconsiderateness which hurried you prematurely on to so public an avowal. If, however, you flatter yourself that you have bullied me into silence, or that the menaces which hang in terrorum over my devoted head, are objects of annoyance; I pray you to undeceive yourself, and rest assured, that I hold your abusive calumnies to be the outpourings of a causeless animosity, and your threats of defiance, as an idle and empty bravado. Under the dominion of temper and transported with fury, you have indulged in a vein of remarks, which with all the malice and acrimony of Junius, possess nought of that brilliancy of wit, that pugnancy of satire and force, and beauty of expression which redeemed him from the charge of vulgarity. His malevolence, his rancour and vindictiveness, were in a manner assuaged by the polished elegance of his style and the splendor of his diction. Instead of knocking down his man with savage ferocity, he skillfully parries his furious lounges, watches his opportunity, and runs him through the body, to the satisfaction of every beholder. But you have neither the bravery nor the strength to perform the one, nor the address and dexterity to achieve the other. Again, sir, I beg of you to accept my condolements upon your pitiable failure to substantiate your infamous allegations; my regret that so much good stationary should have been squandered in the prosecution of your charges; and my utter and profound indifference to all your professions of hatred, hostility and revenge. May these truly christian attributes cling around the sacred lawn with which you are hereafter to be invested, and your angelic nature be a fit illustration of the peaceful spirit of the gospel you profess.

Philologian.

Startle not, most amiable sir, when I inform you of what you are already apprised, that in your animadversions upon the relations which subsist between myself and the Philologos Society, you have shown yourself a stranger to veracity, to the truth of genuine narrative, and utterly disregardful of the feelings of my fellow members, and careless of the best and truest interests of the institution which you ostensibly defend. Now, therefore in behalf of the society, its members and myself, I feel bound by imperative necessity, to undertake your many fallacious positions, and to tear up and destroy that puny breast-work of sophistry and error, behind which you entrench the poverty and nothingness of your pretensions. At the solicitation of several of the Philologos Society, I became a member. Things proceeded with the utmost tranquility and order, until yourself indulging in a train of bitter and caustic personalities, drew upon yourself the bolts of my indignation, whereas frantic with rage, and burning with resentment, you moved that "the conduct of H——— M——— be considered as disgraceful to himself, &c." — Abortive attempt! Your motion was rejected, *viva voce* and yourself condemned to the pangs of mortified pride and foiled ambition. And yet with a hardihood, unparallelled and barefaced, you endeavor to palm upon the public a palpable misrepresentation of the facts of this transaction, if mention whereof be made, it must redound to your lasting discredit. Thus much for the vote of censure which you allege was passed upon my conduct by the P.L.S. Called from town for a few months, I left the society in an apparently healthful and prosperous condition; on my return, however, my astonishment was unlimited, when I beheld our institution, which whilom flourished like a young cedar, in the last stages of a rapid decline. Immediately I instituted vigorous efforts for its resuscitation, in which I was assisted by several prominent members, who all co-operated in the laudable design of reviving the ancient spark; we succeeded; obstacles were brushed aside, difficulties surmounted, and our labors crowned with gratifying success. In the midst of our generous endeavors, yourself being president of the P.L.S. was repeatedly importuned to unite with us in our operations — and having uniformly held yourself aloof — hereby showing none of that interest for the society which was to be expected from its chief officer, was tacitly and virtuously deposed and the few who then stood by the Assistant, resolved, to hold a new election; to that end they called meeting after meeting, but in vain! so few attended that the project was almost thrown up in despair. As a last attempt, however, it was decided, that if a certain number should be present at the next session, hereafter ensuing — the election should be proceeded with. Our expectations were realized, and at the first meeting of the society, subsequent to its restoration, the present incumbent was unanimously preferred to the presidency. — Through my endeavors, a large and elegant room was obtained in Stanwix Hall, together with suitable furniture to the same, free from all expenses to the society. By virtue of my office, I convened the Ass. at an early day, to adopt measures for the future course of the institution. My invitation was responded to, with alacrity by all the members of the society, which mustered in strong force as to a grand military review. The meeting progressed with the utmost harmony and good feeling, when yourself stung with disappointment, smarting with envy, and boiling with wrath, sailed with all the majesty of offended pride into the midst of the assemblage, and pronounced his recent election to have been unconstitutional and corrupt, becoming, however, rather unruly, you were called to order, and mildly requested to resume your seat; deeming this an outrage upon your dignity, with stentorian lungs you bellowed forth an appeal from the decision of the chair; when the society, disgusted with your insolence, by a large and triumphant majority vindicated the course of its president, ratified his election, and freely censured your intemperate and ungentlemanly behavior.

Frustrated then in your every endeavor to gratify the pique of private hostility — in order still to accomplish your iniquitous designs, you published under the signature of "Sandle Wood" a vile calumny upon the Ass., to which I indignantly rejoined, denying the slanderous accusations preferred, and insinuating yourself to be the author of the malignant effusion. Detected then, where you had every reason to suppose entire secresy would be observed, your anger knew no bounds, and disdaining all concealment and throwing off the mask entirely you hastened to give free vent to it, through the columns of the *Microscope*, in a tirade of obscenity and abuse, in which it is your peculiar province to excel.

It has not been, I can assure you, without reluctance that I have been drawn into any public disputation with one of your stamp, but a regard for my own reputation impelled me to expose the malevolence of your intentions; my only motive being then removed, I

cheerfully bid a long good night to any further newspaper controversy with you, and subscribe myself,

> Very respectfully
> Your obedient servant
> Philologean.

N.B. Your incoherent ravings may be continued if you choose;
they remind me of the croakings of a Vulture when disappointed of
its prey.

Original document not located. Text from first publication, emended by NN.

PUBLICATION: *Albany Microscope*, 17 and 24 March 1838. Gilman, pp. 254–58. Davis-Gilman 5.

TEXTUAL NOTES (for symbols used, see p. 840): distorted narrative] NN; distorted nara-
tive · overthrow] over-|throw · tropes] NN; scopes · substantives] NN; substantive · hate,
which] NN; ~. ~ · unguarded] NN; ungaurded · shamelessness] NN; shameless-
nes · eloquence.] NN; ~, · Philologian.] *before editor's note:* To be concluded next
week. · Startle] *after editor's italicized note:* [Concluded.] · unparallelled] NN; unparrellel-
led · resuscitation] NN; resusitation · I convened the Ass.] NN; I convened the
As · disappointment] NN; dissapointment · accusations preferred] NN; accusations prefered

TO THE EDITOR OF THE *ALBANY MICROSCOPE*
PUBLISHED 31 MARCH 1838 · ALBANY

This final letter by Melville under the pseudonym "Philologean" appeared in the
same issue of the *Albany Microscope*, on 31 March, as the first installment of Charles
Van Loon's response to Melville's letter published 17 and 24 March (see above and
LETTERS RECEIVED, pp. 557–59). Unlike his earlier two, this letter—headed
"YOUNG MENS' ASSOCIATION."—is not a response to Van Loon but a calm-
ly reasoned letter to the editor soliciting support for the Philo Logos Society and
making no mention whatsoever of the controversy. Melville apparently never answered Van Loon's strongly worded letter, printed on 31 March and 7 April. Although two more letters appeared in the *Microscope* concerning the controversy, it
was no longer a matter of heated debate. On 7 April, along with the conclusion of
Van Loon's letter, one signed "Americus" urged the reconciliation of Melville and
Van Loon. On 14 April, a letter by Van Loon signed "Ex-President" declared the
controversy settled (see LETTERS RECEIVED, pp. 563–64). In any case, Melville's in-
volvement with the society was shortly to end. In May the Melville family, in
severe financial straits after the failure of Gansevoort's fur and hat business the previous spring, moved to Lansingburgh, a dozen miles north on the other side of the
Hudson River.

Mr. Editor: — Aware that your paper is read by a large portion of the young men of Albany, I have been induced to solicit a small space, for the purpose of directing their attention to an institution, with which their honor as well as interest is deeply involved, I allude to the debating society attached to the Young Mens' Association. It is unnecessary to say that the Association, (as a whole) is sustained in a manner highly creditable to the young men of this city. The public spirit and laudable ambition that effected its organization, has increased with its onward progress, and we feel fully assured that the Young Mens' Association, is destined to awaken deeper and deeper interest, as years more and more develop its happy and benign influences. But we regret that what can be told of the whole cannot be said of its parts; the debating society does not receive that attention which its importance demands. It is unnecessary to speak of its advantages; they must be familiar to all, what doth it avail a man? though he possesses all the knowledge of a Locke or a Newton, if he know not how to communicate that knowledge. What? though he holds in his hand, "the sword of his country's defence" if he know not how to wield the "trusty steel." The former would be often of more practical use, than a true honored volume reposing in eternal obscurity, and the latter of no greater prowess than a man of straw. We ask no higher testimony in favor of its advantages, than the recorded opinions of all great men, Burke, the English Orator and Statesman acknowledged that the first spring which moved him on in a career of fame and honor, was the fostering encouraging effect of a literary club, our own Clay had revealed to him the latent powers of a giant mind in a like institution, and Franklin the philosopher and sage attributed the early development of his natural resources to the same mind stirring soul animating cause, but why specify? The learned are as one man, in their opinion of the importance of debating societies in developing the mind, and prompting to greater and higher efforts, may we not entertain then a confident hope that the young men of Albany, true to their interest and jealous of their honor, will devote that attention to this branch of the Association, which its importance so richly deserves; and may we not confidently anticipate the uniform attendance and efficient co-operation of our newly elected managers in reviving the society, and multiplying its usefulness.

Philologean.

Original document not located. Text from first publication, emended by NN.

PUBLICATION: *Albany Microscope*, 31 March 1838. Gilman, pp. 262–63. Davis-Gilman 6.

TEXTUAL NOTES: laudable] NN; laupable • assured] NN; assnred • influences] NN; inflnences • said] NN; sail • though he possesses] NN; thhough he possesses • often of more] NN; often more • volume] NN; volumn • eternal] NN; eternat • reviving] NN; revieving

TO MARY ELEANOR PARMELEE
AFTER MAY 1838 · LANSINGBURGH

An indeterminate number of unlocated letters, reportedly destroyed, were written by Melville to Mary Parmelee of Lansingburgh, New York. According to Mrs. Frances G. Wickes in a 21 August 1947 letter to William H. Gilman: "Melville was in love with my Grandmother [Mary Eleanor Parmelee, a granddaughter of Cornelius Lansing (b. 1752), one of the founders of Lansingburgh Academy]. The reports about their reading Tennyson together, his letters to her etc. are quite true." See Gilman, pp. 104, 326, and Metcalf, p. 23.

TO AUGUSTA MELVILLE [AND FAMILY?]
BEFORE 4 OCTOBER 1838 · PITTSFIELD

Unlocated. On 17 September 1838 Melville attended the wedding in Pittsfield of his cousin Robert Melvill to Susan Bates (1814–85). A possible letter from Melville to his family at the time of the wedding can be inferred, since Robert's sister Julia Melvill (1820–46) wrote to Augusta Melville in Lansingburgh on 4 October 1838 from Cleveland, Ohio, where she was with her family en route to Galena, Illinois, stating: "Herman wrote you all about the wedding I suppose" (NYPL-GL).

TO ALLAN MELVILLE
10 NOVEMBER 1838 · LANSINGBURGH

Two days after this letter to Allan was written, Melville was enrolled at the Lansingburgh Academy to study surveying and engineering. Melville appended his message, written with the large flourishes of a clerk, to a letter of the same date from their mother, Maria Melville, which Melville wryly addressed on the outside to "Master Allan Melville." Their mother's letter concerned various items of family news, including Melville's new course of study at the academy. Only Allan had remained in Albany, serving as a clerk in his uncle Peter Gansevoort's law office. Also serving as a clerk in the same office was Melville's friend from the Albany Academy, Eli James Murdock Fly (1817–54). Two years later in the spring of 1840, Fly may have accompanied Melville on a fruitless job hunt to Galena, Illinois (Gilman, p. 151). Fly certainly accompanied Melville in the fall of 1840 to New York City, where Gansevoort Melville, then beginning his law career there, supported them both while they looked for work, as a 26 November 1840 letter from

Gansevoort to Allan states (Berkshire Athenaeum). Fly later worked for a time in Gansevoort Melville's law office, as Allan's 17 October 1844 letter to Melville indicates (see LETTERS RECEIVED, pp. 565–71). This is Melville's only known written message to Fly, even though it seems likely there was correspondence between them, since they remained friends as adults (see the headnote to Melville's 26 March 1851 letter to Evert Duyckinck for more about that friendship).

Nov 10th 1838

Allan Melville
Sir
    I am with the profoundest regard

Your obdt Servt
Herman Melville

PS. My complements to Eli James Murdock tell him I shall be down in a few days

Herman Melville

ALS on a 39.8 × 25.4 cm sheet, folded in half, of white wove paper. Maria Melville inscribed the first two pages and Melville the third; both are in ink. Melville addressed the fourth page "Master Allan Melville | (Care of Gen Peter Gansevoort) | Albany" and wrote the word "Single" in the upper left corner.

LOCATION: Berkshire Athenaeum, Pittsfield, Massachusetts. *Provenance*: Agnes Morewood.

PUBLICATION: Gilman, p. 104. Davis-Gilman 7.

TEXTUAL NOTES: Murdock] ock *obscured by wax seal* · PS.] S *partially torn in unsealing the letter*

1839

TO WILLIAM J. LAMB
BEFORE 20 APRIL 1839 · LANSINGBURGH

Unlocated. In early April 1839 an abortive effort was made with the help of Peter Gansevoort to place Melville in the engineering department of the state canal system. Meanwhile Melville was beginning his writing career in the local *Democratic Press, and Lansingburgh Advertiser*. On 20 April 1839 a notice in that paper stated: "*To Correspondents*. The communication of 'L. A. V.' is received. An interview with the writer is requested" (see LETTERS RECEIVED, p. 564). This "communication" may have been a letter from Melville to the editor, William J. Lamb, proposing his two "Fragments from a Writing Desk," which were published on 4 and 18 May 1839 in the *Democratic Press* under the initials "L. A. V." See the NN *Piazza Tales* volume, pp. 191–204, 622–25. Davis-Gilman Unlocated 276.

TO [GANSEVOORT MELVILLE?]
AFTER 25 MAY 1839 · LANSINGBURGH

Melville wrote this brief message on the inner margin of a copy of the 4 May 1839
Democratic Press, and Lansingburgh Advertiser, in which the first of his "Fragments
from a Writing Desk" had appeared. The message (and the paper) were probably
intended for his brother Gansevoort, who recently had been in Lansingburgh recuperating from an illness. In a 23 May 1839 letter to her son Allan, Maria Melville
reported that "Gansevoort feels well enough to go about, & will leave for New
York in a few days" (NYPL-GL). Presumably Melville wrote this note to his
brother after his return to New York. For more about Melville's "Fragments from
a Writing Desk," see the NN *Piazza Tales* volume, p. 623.

When I woke up this morning, what the Devel should I see but your
cane along in bed with me
I shall keep it for you when you come up here again

AL, inscribed in ink on the inner margin of the *Democratic Press, and Lansingburgh Advertiser* (4
May 1839), on the back of the page on which the first of Melville's "Fragments from a Writing Desk" appeared.

LOCATION: HCL-M.

PUBLICATION: *Log*, I, 85. Davis-Gilman 8.

TO MARIA GANSEVOORT MELVILLE
9 JULY 1839 · LIVERPOOL

Unlocated. In the spring of 1839 Gansevoort helped arrange for Melville to join the
crew of a Liverpool packet, the *St. Lawrence*, which sailed from New York on 5
June 1839 and returned to that port the following September. One letter from Melville during this voyage is cited in Maria Melville's 25 September 1839 letter to
Allan: "I should have written you last week, that we had receiv'd a letter from
Herman, dated Liverpool 9th July — he writes that he is well, very anxious to see
home, and to prove it, says he would give all the sights of Liverpool to see a corner
of home — he appears to think the St Lawrence will not return to New
York — this trip, but put Sail for Charlston, or one of the New England ports, it
was still unsettled, depending on their Cargo — " (Berkshire Athenaeum). Davis-
Gilman Unlocated 276a.

TO ALLAN MELVILLE
7 DECEMBER 1839 · LANSINGBURGH

After Melville returned from Liverpool, he once again taught for several months,
this time at the Greenbush & Schodack Academy in Greenbush, New York. On

6 December, Melville went to Lansingburgh with his friend Eli James Murdock
Fly to spend several days with his family. While there, he appended a note to a
letter his mother wrote on 7 December 1839 to his brother Allan, still working
in Albany. In her letter, Maria Melville commented that she felt "cheered by
Hermans prospects — he appears to be interested in his occupation — he has a
great charge, & deep responsibility is attached to the education of 60 Scholars,
which I understand is the number usual during the greater part of the year — "
(Berkshire Athenaeum).

Melville's mock dialect in his note may have been inspired partly by the opening of his mother's letter, which chided Allan for his poor spelling. He may have
signed himself "Tawney" (colloquial for Indian) not only because of the deep tan he
must have acquired in his four months as a sailor on his voyage to and from Liverpool in the preceding summer, but also because there was a running joke in the
family about Allan's dread of tanning (see New Log, August 1834 and 4 March
1835). The title "Sergeant" that Melville gives to Allan may have been in reference
to Allan's position as a law clerk (but then again Melville's youngest brother
Thomas is called "general" in a 28 January 1843 letter from Helen to Augusta Melville [see the New Log]). Maria Van Schaick Peebles (1782–1865), mentioned at the
end of Melville's note, a first cousin of Maria Melville, lived two streets away in
Lansingburgh.

My Dear Sergeant
    How is you? Am you very well? How has you been? — As to
myself I haint been as well as husual. I has had a very cruel cold for
this darnation long time, & I has had and does now have a werry
bad want of appetisement. — I seed Mrs Peebles tother day and she
did say to me to not to fail to tell you that she am well
                                                No more at present
                                                from you friend
                                                Tawney

ALS, "Tawney", on a 40.2 × 25.1 cm sheet, folded in half, of white wove paper, faintly
embossed with the manufacturer's circular stamp. Maria Melville inscribed the first two and a
half pages and Melville the bottom half of the third page; both are in ink. Maria Melville
addressed the fourth page "Mʳ Allan Melville. | Stanwix Hall. | Albany." Another hand noted
in pencil above the signature "H M".

Location: Berkshire Athenaeum, Pittsfield, Massachusetts. Provenance: Agnes Morewood.

Publication: Gilman, p. 148. Davis-Gilman 9.

1840

TO MARIA GANSEVOORT MELVILLE
BEFORE 5 FEBRUARY 1840 · GREENBUSH

Unlocated. Having written a single-page letter to her son Allan on 5 February 1840, Maria Melville added below the seal on the outside an instruction for him: "Put yours & Hermans letters on the outside of the packet. You must not loose it" (Berkshire Athenaeum). Her letter, primarily concerning a carpet bag and a fur cap, gives no indication of the significance of Melville's letter, apparently written to her from Greenbush, New York, where he was teaching. Davis-Gilman Unlocated 277.

1841

TO MARIA GANSEVOORT MELVILLE
ON OR BEFORE 3 JANUARY 1841 · FAIRHAVEN

Unlocated. On 3 January 1841 Melville sailed from Fairhaven, Massachusetts, as an ordinary seaman on the whaler *Acushnet* under Captain Valentine Pease. A letter home written from aboard ship just before sailing is cited in Maria Melville's Lansingburgh letter (misdated 8 December for 8 January 1841) to her daughter Augusta, then visiting in Albany: "Last week I received a long letter from Herman, who has embarked for a long Voyage to the Pacific, under the most favorable auspices, and feeling perfectly happy, Gansevoort was with him to the last and assisted with his more matured Judgement in supplying him with every comfort, Gansevoort says he never saw him so completely happy, as when he had determined upon a situation and all was settled, he sends much love and affectionate remembrance to his Sisters" (NYPL-GL).

TO MARIA GANSEVOORT MELVILLE AND FAMILY
BEFORE 15 MARCH 1841 · RIO DE JANEIRO

Unlocated. A shipboard letter is cited in Gansevoort Melville's 14 August 1841 letter to Lemuel Shaw, which states: "We have rec^d only one letter from Herman. That was from Rio Janeiro into which port the Accushnet had put, for the purpose of selling two hundred barrels of oil which she had taken off the Bahama banks — " (Social Law Library). Since the consular returns report that the *Acushnet* came into port in Rio de Janeiro on 13 March and left on 15 March, Melville's letter must have been sent during this period.

TO GANSEVOORT MELVILLE
BETWEEN 23 JUNE AND 2 JULY 1841 · PERU

Unlocated. Another shipboard letter (see the entry just above) is cited in Gansevoort Melville's 22 July 1842 letter to Lemuel Shaw, which states: "I am in receipt of a letter from my brother Herman dated August 1841 at Santa Martha, coast of Peru — He was then in perfect health, and not dissatisfied with his lot — The fact of his being one of a crew so much superior in morals and early advantages to the ordinary run of whaling crews affords him constant gratification. By the papers I see that his ship — The Acushnet — Pease — was spotted in Dec last — at sea — all well — " (MHS-S). (Since the Abstract Log of the *Acushnet* records coming to anchor in Santa Martha Harbor on 23 June and leaving on 2 July 1841, the August date given by Gansevoort for Melville's letter is evidently mistaken.) Davis-Gilman Unlocated 278.

1842

TO GEORGE LEFEVRE, FOR HENRY SMYTH
25 SEPTEMBER 1842 · TAHITI

On 9 July 1842 Melville deserted the *Acushnet* with Richard Tobias (Toby) Greene at the Marquesas Islands, and spent a little less than four weeks with the natives of the Typee Valley. He escaped a month later to serve on the Australian whaler *Lucy Ann*, then sailed in early November for a six-month cruise on a third whaler, the *Charles and Henry*, and finally, after spending three months ashore on the Hawaiian Islands, signed as an ordinary seaman with the U.S.S. *United States*. No letters written during this period have been located; however, one penciled letter (identified by the handwriting) that Melville wrote on behalf of a shipmate on the *Lucy Ann* was found among the British consular records at Tahiti when they were transferred to the Mitchell Library in Sydney, Australia (see the Hendricks House edition of *Omoo*, ed. Harrison Hayford and Walter Blair [New York, 1969], pp. 309 and 315–16).

   The letter was written during a shipboard revolt that occurred while the *Lucy Ann* was anchored at Tahiti. Henry Smyth (spelled both "Smith" and "Smyth" in the consular records) had been judged too ill to serve and Melville was off duty when other members of the crew began refusing to do their duty on 22 September 1842. Melville later joined the revolters, but Smyth, also an ordinary seaman, did not—although as this letter indicates he had earlier refused to do his duty. Smyth's friend George Lefevre, formerly a crew member of the *Lucy Ann*, was now imprisoned aboard the French frigate *Reine Blanche*, also anchored at Tahiti, for his part in an earlier revolt (on the crew list, only his name was followed by the notation "mutiny"). Their other two companions, "Peter" and "Young Smith," are unidentified. For more about the revolt in which Melville was involved, see the Hendricks House *Omoo*, pp. 309–39.

On Board the Lucy Ann
September 25th 1842

Dear George

   On arriving here the other day I was sorry to hear that you were verry ill on board the French Frigate. — I should like verry much to go and see you but I cannot possibly as I can not be allowed to; — so I take the liberty to write you a few lines.

— You know we all agreed to hang out on your account when we came aboard from the Corvette — but it so happened that those who talked loudest were the first to return to their duty. I was the last one that went forward, and would not have turned to at all, but that I found it was of no use, — so after being in double irons some time I thought it best to go forward & do my duty as usual

You must remember me to Peter

I do not know that I have any thing further to say to you

I often think of you & I & Young Smith have often talked about you during the night watches at sea

— Good bye

My Dear George

Hoping you will be soon at liberty

I remain Yours &c

Henry Smyth

George Lefevre
On Board the French Frigate

Original document not examined. Text from photograph (in The Newberry Library) of the LS (2 pp.). Melville addressed the letter on a separate sheet "For | George Lefevre | On Board | The French Frigate".

LOCATION: Mitchell Library, Sydney, Australia.

PUBLICATION: (partial) *Log*, I, 146. Harrison Hayford and Walter Blair, eds., *Omoo* (New York: Hendricks House, 1969), pp. 315–16.

TEXTUAL NOTES: who talked] *after canceled* yo · usual] *before* (over) *in bottom margin* · Good] G *written over* Y

1843

TO THE MELVILLE FAMILY
JUNE 1843 · HAWAII

Unlocated. An undetermined number of letters is cited in Allan Melville's 17 October 1844 letter to Melville (see LETTERS RECEIVED, pp. 565–71): "Your letters written in June 1843 were rec^d as also a package once before that." No other reference to letters of this date, when Melville was in Hawaii after being discharged from the *Charles and Henry*, or to the earlier package has been located.

1844

TO ALLAN MELVILLE
13 OCTOBER 1844 · BOSTON

Unlocated. A letter from Melville, written the day before he was discharged from the crew of the U.S.S. *United States* and announcing his arrival in Boston, is cited in Allan Melville's delighted reply of 17 October 1844 (see LETTERS RECEIVED, pp. 565–71). Allan briefly quotes Melville's letter as stating that " 'the circumstances connected with the ship' " had prevented his immediate reunion with his family. Melville's letter failed to specify what the delaying circumstances were, and Allan's letter anxiously inquires as to their exact nature. Probably it was simply that Melville had not yet been discharged on 13 October (see the 14 October entry in the log of the *United States*: "Completed breaking out & clearing out ship. Paid off her crew & turned her over to the officers of the yard" [*Log*, I, 186]). Whether Allan went to Boston to greet his brother, as he proposed in his letter, or whether Melville made his own way to New York or directly to Lansingburgh is not known; however, on 21 October Allan wrote to their mother: "Herman has arrived & you may expect him every hour after tomorrow" (NYPL-GL). Similarly an unsigned and unaddressed message from this period, but not in Allan's hand, states simply: "Herman has arrived & you may expect him every moment" (NYPL-GL). It is on a part-sheet with the message in blue ink and the date, October 1844, below in black ink, possibly by a different hand. Hershel Parker, noting the similarities of the handwriting in this note with Melville's in the *Typee* manuscript fragment (NYPL-GL), speculates that this second note was written by Melville himself, imitating Allan's note, just before returning home for the first time in nearly four years.

1845

TO AUGUSTA MELVILLE
BEFORE 20 JANUARY 1845 · NEW YORK

Unlocated. A letter to his sister Augusta is cited in Melville's letter of 20 January 1845 to his sister Catherine, just below. Davis-Gilman Unlocated 279.

TO CATHERINE MELVILLE
20 JANUARY 1845 · NEW YORK

In early January 1845 Melville had come down from Lansingburgh to visit his brothers Gansevoort and Allan ("the Sergeant"), both now pursuing their legal careers in New York. This letter praising the name Kate may have been inspired by the fact that Melville's nineteen-year-old sister Catherine (or Kate), to whom he writes, was visiting relatives in Albany where at least two other Kates were to be found: (1) Maria Melville's cousin Catherine Gansevoort Van Vechten (1789–1853), whose husband, Teunis Van Vechten (1785–1859), was twice mayor of Albany (1837–39 and 1841–42) and who lived at this time on Montgomery Street in Albany, where Melville's sister was staying; and (2) Catherine Van Vechten (b. 1826), the Van Vechtens' daughter and second cousin to Melville and his sister. With three Kates in the household, Melville's high-blown praise of the name could be enjoyed by several members of the "Clan-Kate." Although this is one of only two references to the Van Vechtens in Melville's known letters (see his 5 September 1877 letter to Catherine Gansevoort Lansing), there were many associations between the two families. Melville's sisters, particularly Augusta and Helen, both mentioned in this letter, maintained a correspondence with their Albany cousins and visited them regularly, as did their mother. Melville's brother Allan made a point of taking his first wife Sophia to visit the Van Vechtens in July 1848, and Melville's youngest brother, Thomas, was an almost exact contemporary and a close friend of Cuyler Van Vechten (1830–75), Catherine Van Vechten's younger brother. Also it was Catherine Van Vechten's husband, Elisha P. Hurlbut, who initiated a petition to President Lincoln in 1861 recommending Melville for appointment as U.S. consul at Florence (National Archives).

New York, Jany 20th 1845

My Dear Sister: — What a charming name is yours — the most engaging I think in our whole family circle. — I dont' know how it is precisely, but I have always been very partial to this particular appellative & can not avoid investing the person who bears it, with certain quite captivating attributes; so, when I hear of Kate Such a One — whether it be Kate Smith or Kate Jones, or Kate Any Body Else I invariably impute to the said Kate all manner of delightfull characteristics. — Not, that terms of general admiration will do at all, when applied to the Clan-Kate — for the Kates, D'you see, are a peculiar race, & are distinguished by peculiar attributes — Thus, the Kates as a general rule are decidedly handsome, but if we may not speak of their beauty in terms of unqualified admiration, they still will be found to incline towards good looks, and at any rate, they are never positively ugly. — But, "Fine feathers dont' make fine birds" & "Handsome is, that handsome does" & all that sort of thing; — & so if the Kates were only distinguishable by their beautiful plumage, why, I would not give a fig for a Kate, any more than I would for a Gloriana Arabella Matilda — Not I, — for mere beauty is among the least of the manifold merits of the Kates. Besides loveliness of form & face, the Kates are always amiable, with fine feelings, a little too modest at times, but wondrous sly, always in good humor, sometimes in regular mad-cap spirits, & once in a while (I

am *sorry* to say it) rather given to romping & playing Miss
Billy — But then I love them all the better for that, for they romp
with such grace & vivacity, that I verily beleive they are more dangerous then, than at other times; tho' to say truth, Kate demure, in a
neat little apron & sitting in the corner marking a pocket-
handkerchief — for all her hypocritical pretensions — is as murderous a little elf as the biggest of the Tom-Boys — Now, I saw a girl
in Broadway yesterday, & I'll lay you a rose-bud her name was
Kate — Why, I'm sure of it. — Did'nt she have two sweet merry
eyes & a round merry face, and a merry smile, & even a kind of a
merry little walk — and then it was just as plain as day that she was
amiable, kind-hearted, full of sensibility & all that — & it was just as
plain that her name was Kate. — But I suppose you laugh & cry
Pooh! at my theory of the Kates, & say it is all nonsense, a mere
whim, a notion — Well, suppose it is — it is not the less true, & if
you deny that, I will adduce an argument in proof, that will fairly
make you blush, it is so forcible & to the point, — For, will I not
bring your own sweet self in evidence? to prove my doctrine. And,
say, Do you not possess all the qualities I have ascribed to this particular class, — & then, pray Miss, what is your name but
Kate? — Oh, Now! In Heaven's name — Dont' look so abashed!
What! Face, neck & bosom all bathed in glowing floods of vermil-
lion! — Verily, Modesty is the cheifest attributes of the
Kates — Come, Come, up with those drooping eye-lids & that
down cast head, and confess that the Kates are better than the Pol-
lies, & you the best of the Kates.
I was overjoyed to hear My Dear Kate (Now, is it not a pretty
name) that your visit to Albany has been productive of the most
beneficial results to your health — I predicted as much — & knew
that when I laid my commands upon your cousin-friend Miss Kate
Van Vecthen to restore the rose to your cheeck, that she would accomplish the behest. — I congratulate you upon your recovery, &
hope that you will not permit inattention to diet & exercise to bring
on a relapse. — I got a long & delightful letter from Augusta the
other day — the morning previous to receiving it, I had sent one to
her, & could not avoid thinking, when I read her communication,
what a poor thing she received in exchange for it. — This morning
Gan^st got a letter from Helen — They are all well. — Gan^st is well, &
so is the Sergeant. They send much love. — Oh, I want you to find

out — but never mind = Now I want you to write me a long letter, dont' take pattern after mine & fill it with nonsence, but send me a sober sheet like a good girl

— You know you can· put this letter of mine, among your things — Can't you? My respects to all the Van Vecthens.

Your loving brother

Herman

ALS on a 42.6 × 27.2 cm sheet, folded in half, of blue wove paper. Melville inscribed the first three pages, in ink, and addressed the fourth page "Miss Catherine Melville | Care of Teunis Van Vechten Esq | Albany | /N° 11. Montgomery Street./"; it was stamped paid.

LOCATION: NYPL-GL.

PUBLICATION: Paltsits, pp. 7–9. Davis-Gilman 10.

TEXTUAL NOTES: sometimes] some-|times • elf as] s *written over* n • that her name] *after canceled* as day • much —] *before* I *and another word-start canceled* • you will . . . a relapse] ou *and a* were *written in a torn-off area on the second leaf of the letter where the seal was attached* • Helen] *miswritten* Hellen

TO GANSEVOORT MELVILLE
BEFORE 1 SEPTEMBER 1845 · [LANSINGBURGH?]

Unlocated. On 31 July 1845 Melville's older brother, Gansevoort, had left for London to become the new secretary of legation at the American ministry there, probably taking with him Melville's recently completed draft of *Typee*. A letter can be inferred from Gansevoort's 16 September 1845 letter to their mother, in which he states that he had received a number of letters by the "steamer of the 1st" and that on 15 September he had written a letter "to Herman" about his personal expenses in London and "also as to 'Typee' " (NYPL-GL; see Parker, *Gansevoort Melville's London Journal and Letters*, pp. 62–63; see also LETTERS RECEIVED, p. 572). The implication is that Gansevoort was writing in response to a letter from Melville that had come on the 1 September steamer. Presumably Melville's letter had included some discussion of the manuscript. Davis-Gilman Unlocated 280.

TO GANSEVOORT MELVILLE
BEFORE 18 NOVEMBER 1845 · LANSINGBURGH

Unlocated. Just when Gansevoort Melville offered the manuscript of *Typee* to John Murray III (1808–92) is unclear. Not until 17 October 1845 did Murray write to Gansevoort expressing interest in the pages of the manuscript he had been given to read, along with some suspicion that it seemed the work of "a practised writer" rather than an authentic sailor-narrative (Murray's unlocated letter is cited in

Gansevoort's reply on 21 October). In answering Murray, Gansevoort wrote: "The Author will doubtless be flattered to hear that his production seems to so competent a judge as yourself that of 'a practised writer' — the more so as he is a mere novice in the art" (Murray).

A possible letter from Melville concerning the book can be inferred from Gansevoort Melville's comment in an 18 November 1845 letter to his brother Allan: "I shall write Herman a note as to 'Typee', in regard to which I am estopped from making any movement until I hear from him again & receive the additional Mss chapters" (NYPL-GL). Whether or not Melville's earlier letter was recent is unclear; nor is it clear whether "the additional Mss chapters" had been long discussed or were a new development announced in this inferred letter. (In either case, as Hershel Parker argues in "Evidences for 'Late Insertions' in Melville's Works" [*Studies in the Novel* 7 (Fall 1975), 409–13], it is likely that Melville himself rather than his publisher Murray called for the additions.) Gansevoort received the additional chapters from his brother before 6 December 1845 (see the next entry). Davis-Gilman Unlocated 282.

TO GANSEVOORT MELVILLE
BEFORE 3 DECEMBER 1845 · LANSINGBURGH

Unlocated. On 3 December 1845 John Murray wrote to Gansevoort Melville offering one hundred pounds "at Six Months from the day of publication" for the English copyright of Melville's first book (letterbook, Murray). An earlier letter from Melville to his brother about the book is cited in Gansevoort's 4 December reply to Murray: "At a late hour last eve^g (having been at the Legation all day) I received your note too late to communicate its contents to the author of the Mss, by the steamer of to-day, which tho' desirable, is the less important because I have a recent letter from him giving me carte blanche in the premises" (Murray). This "recent" letter possibly accompanied the "additional Mss chapters" that Gansevoort had also received by early December, as his subsequent 6 December letter to Murray states: "In my last conversation I stated that the last steamer from the U.S, brought to me some corrections & additions to the Mss in your hands. I have the pleasure of sending them herewith for perusul. The bulk of the new matter consists of three new chapters, numbered respectively 20 — 21 — & 27" (Murray). Davis-Gilman Unlocated 283.

TO GANSEVOORT MELVILLE
BEFORE 20 DECEMBER 1845 · LANSINGBURGH

Unlocated. Gansevoort Melville, who had evidently had the manuscript pages of *Typee* in his possession in order to make corrections, returned the bulk of them (retaining chaps. 11 and 12) to John Murray on 20 December 1845. He explained in an enclosed letter that he had included "four or five pages & slips of paper cont'g for the most part corrections by the author accompanying it. He seems to regard them as of importance & I should be sorry to have them overlooked" (Murray).

Since these corrections and additions were not included in Gansevoort Melville's earlier packet of 6 December 1845 (see the entry just above) sent to Murray, it can be inferred that Melville sent these to Gansevoort later, accompanied by a letter urging their inclusion. The book appeared at the end of February 1846 in England as Numbers 30 and 31 of Murray's Colonial and Home Library, under the title *Narrative of a Four Months' Residence among the Natives of a Valley of the Marquesas Islands; or, A Peep at Polynesian Life.* Not until Murray issued the British "Revised Edition" of the book at the end of 1846 was "Typee" prefixed to the title.

1846

TO GANSEVOORT MELVILLE
BEFORE 16 JANUARY 1846 · LANSINGBURGH

Unlocated. At least one letter and possibly more are indicated by Gansevoort Melville's diary entry for 16 January 1846: "The mails by the Acadia arrived — all well at home — I rec^d letters from Mother, Helen, Herman" (NYPL-GL; see Parker, *Gansevoort Melville's London Journal and Letters*, p. 25). Davis-Gilman Unlocated 285 (misdated 3 January 1846).

TO HELEN MARIA MELVILLE
23 FEBRUARY 1846 · LANSINGBURGH

Unlocated. After receiving a letter from his brother Allan on the morning of 23 February 1846 indicating that it was uncertain whether Wiley & Putnam would publish *Typee* in their "Library of Choice Reading" and that it was also uncertain whether the English edition of the book had actually arrived on the *Cambria*, Melville left that evening for New York to confer with his publishers (see LETTERS RECEIVED, p. 574). Before leaving he wrote to his sister Helen, who was visiting the Shaw family in Boston. As Maria Melville's 28 February 1846 letter from Lansingburgh to her daughter Augusta, who was visiting in Albany, reports: "Herman wrote Helen before he left here that as he was going on to New York, she had better remain a week or more longer until his return when he would take Boston in his way back and escort her home" (NYPL-GL). Hope Savage Shaw, the second wife of Lemuel Shaw (Melville's future father-in-law; see Melville's 19 March letter to him, below), recorded in her diary that Melville arrived in Boston on 4 March 1846 (MHS-S).

TO GANSEVOORT MELVILLE
28 FEBRUARY 1846 · NEW YORK

Unlocated. A letter from Melville is cited in Gansevoort Melville's 3 April 1846 reply: "Yours of Feb 28 was rec^d a few days ago . . . . I am happy to learn by it that the previous intelligence transmitted by me was 'gratifying enough.' I am glad that you continue busy, and in my next or the one after that will venture to make some suggestions about your next book" (see LETTERS RECEIVED, pp. 575–77). According to Gansevoort's 1846 London journal, he had "transmitted" his "previous intelligence" to his brother on 3 February 1846 (see Parker, *Gansevoort Melville's London Journal and Letters*, p. 33). In replying, Melville must have consulted his brother about some of the family's financial decisions since Gansevoort writes: "As to Fanny [Frances Priscilla] — when I receive the accounts I will write fully. Tom's matter has not been forgotten." Gansevoort never did write more "fully," however. His 3 April letter was the last to Melville before his death in London a month later. Davis-Gilman Unlocated 286.

TO LEMUEL SHAW
19 MARCH 1846 · LANSINGBURGH

Lemuel Shaw (1781–1861), Chief Justice of the Massachusetts Supreme Court (1830–60), was for years a friend and adviser of the Melvill family. He had been engaged to Allan Melvill's sister Nancy Wroe Melvill, who died in 1813. He subsequently married Elizabeth Knapp (1784–1822) and then five years after her death Hope Savage (1793–1879), the "Mrs Shaw" referred to in this letter. He remained a friend of Allan Melvill's and served with John D'Wolf as co-executor of the estate of Allan's father, Thomas Melvill. As such he remained in regular communication with Allan's siblings, including Priscilla Melvill in Boston. Shaw and D'Wolf found it necessary after Allan's death to sue Maria Melville and her children on behalf of his siblings in order to protect their inheritances from Allan's creditors. This indicated no personal animosity on the part of Shaw or of the Melvill heirs, but he seems to have had no contact with Maria Melville or her children from soon after Allan's death until January 1841, when Gansevoort apparently called on Shaw in Boston and recultivated the relationship. That winter Melville's oldest sister Helen spent the first of many winters with the Shaws in Boston.

In 1847 Judge Shaw became Melville's father-in-law, when his only daughter (by his first wife) "Miss Elizabeth" (1822–1906), to whom Melville sends his warm remembrances here, married the young author who had dedicated *Typee* to him. Melville's comment on the dedication in this letter may cast light on its change in wording from "affectionately" in the English edition to "gratefully" in the American edition. Leon Howard, in the NN *Typee,* speculates that it was Gansevoort who supplied "affectionately" in the English edition (p. 284). Presumably the copy of the American edition of *Typee* inscribed "Chief Justice Shaw With the sincere respects of the author. March 19th 1846." (HCL-M) is the one Melville sent to him with this letter.

Lansingburgh March 19. 1846

My Dear Sir — Herewith you have one of the first bound copies of "Typee" I have been able to procure. —— The dedication is very simple, for the world would hardly have sympathised to the full extent of those feelings with which I regard my father's friend and the constant friend of all his family.

I hope that the perusal of this little narrative of mine will afford you some entertainment. Even if it should not possess much other merit your knowing the author so well, will impart some interest to it.

— I intended to have sent at the same time with this, copies of "Typee" for each of my aunts — but have been disappointed in receiving as many as I expected. — I mention, however, in the accompanying letter to my Aunt Priscilla that they shall soon be forthcoming.

Remember me most warmly to Mrs Shaw & Miss Elizabeth, & to all your family, & tell them I shall not soon forget that agreeable visit to Boston.

With sincere respect, Judge Shaw,
I remain gratefully and truly Yours
Herman Melville

Chief Justice Shaw,
Boston.

ALS on a 41.6 × 26.9 cm sheet, folded in half, of green wove paper, embossed with the manufacturer's square stamp enclosing a ship above the word "PARIS". Melville inscribed the first two pages, in ink. Lemuel Shaw later noted on it in ink "Herman Melville | 19 March 1846".

LOCATION: HCL-M.

PUBLICATION: Weaver, p. 258. Davis-Gilman 11.

TEXTUAL NOTES: possess] *miswritten possesss* • been] *inferred word; M's word was on a small portion torn from the top edge of the leaf*

TO PRISCILLA MELVILL
19 MARCH 1846 · LANSINGBURGH

Unlocated. A letter to his aunt Priscilla announcing the imminent arrival of a copy of *Typee* is cited in Melville's 19 March 1846 letter to Lemuel Shaw, just above. Priscilla Melvill of Boston was one of the five Melvill aunts (see the headnote to Melville's 1828 letter to his aunt Lucy Melvill), to whom he promised copies of *Typee*, as he mentioned in his letter to Judge Shaw. His other Melvill aunts had all married by this time. Mary Melvill D'Wolf was now in Dorchester, Massachusetts; Jean Melvill Wright in Boston; Lucy Melvill Nourse in Hallowell, Maine; and Helen Melvill Souther in Hingham, Massachusetts. Melville is also known to have sent a copy of *Typee* to his uncle Peter Gansevoort's second wife, Susan Lansing Gansevoort (1804–74), in Albany, one to his mother's cousin Maria Peebles in

Lansingburgh, and one to Gansevoort Melville's close friend and political ally William E. Cramer (see *New Log*, 20 March 1846). It is not known, however, whether Melville also sent letters either announcing or accompanying these copies. Davis-Gilman Unlocated 287.

TO GANSEVOORT MELVILLE
[26?] MARCH 1846 · LANSINGBURGH

Unlocated. Only the postmarked folded blank sheet Melville used as the envelope for a letter has been located. He addressed it: "Gansevoort Melville Esq | U.S. Secretary of Legation | London. | For the | Boston Steamer". It was postmarked in Lansingburgh on 27 March and later stamped "AA 15 Ap 15 1846" as well as with a large "5" (NYPL-GL). Davis-Gilman Unlocated 288.

TO THE EDITOR OF THE *ALBANY ARGUS*
BEFORE 21 APRIL 1846 · LANSINGBURGH

Unlocated. The authenticity of *Typee* was a recurrent issue in its reviews. Beginning with the first known British review in the *Athenæum* of 21 February 1846, critics repeated John Murray's initial skepticism about the book—that it seemed the work of "a practised writer" rather than a common sailor. Two early American reviews that raised this issue were in the *New York Evangelist* (9 April 1846) and the *Morning Courier and New-York Enquirer* (17 April 1846). These may have prompted Melville to request—presumably by letter—that a communication be placed in the *Albany Argus*, edited by Gansevoort's friend Edwin Croswell (see Melville's 4 July 1846 and 2 April 1847 letters to him, below). The resulting article, titled "Herman Melville's Book," printed in the 21 April 1846 *Argus* (and reprinted in that paper three days later), began by stating that *Typee* "is having a deservedly great run. It is a book of unusual interest, both in the incidents and in the style. There seems to be an impression in some quarters that the events are too strange to be true, and the book has been designated as a beautiful fiction." Then apparently either quoting or paraphrasing Melville, it reported: "The author desires to state to the public, that Typee is a true narrative of events which actually occurred to him. Although there may be moving incidents and hairbreadth escapes, it is scarcely more strange than such as happen to those who make their home on the deep." The article then concluded by quoting an extract from the London *Critic* (which Gansevoort Melville had sent to Croswell; see Parker, *Gansevoort Melville's London Journal and Letters*, p. 53) praising the "vivid and forcible" writing of Melville's book. Davis-Gilman Unlocated 289.

TO WILEY & PUTNAM
7 MAY 1846 · LANSINGBURGH

While the pages of Melville's manuscript were being set in type for Murray in January 1846, Gansevoort gave the first 107 pages of the proof sheets of *Typee* to

George P. Putnam of Wiley & Putnam, having been introduced by Washington Irving, who was then in London. Putnam quickly accepted the book for American publication in the firm's "Library of Choice Reading" (ultimately publishing it in their "Library of American Books" in March 1846, titled *Typee: A Peep at Polynesian Life. During a Four Months' Residence in a Valley of the Marquesas*). (For more on Putnam, see the entry for Melville's letter written to Putnam's publishing firm after 1 October 1852.) Although Melville, under pressure from John Wiley, was later forced to make so many substantial excisions to *Typee* that it was issued as a "revised edition" on 6 August 1846, the "slight alterations" he is discussing in this letter to his publishers were apparently earlier minor changes and corrections of his own. There is no evidence to indicate that any such minor changes were incorporated in the American edition prior to the revised edition; see G. Thomas Tanselle, " 'Typee' and De Voto Once More," *Papers of the Bibliographical Society of America* 62 (1968), 601–4.

Lansingburgh May 7, 1846

Gentlemen — Herewith you have a corrected copy of Typee. Besides correcting mere typographical errors, I have made two or three slight alterations.

— I do not know exactly to what extent you can, without incurring much expence, alter the plates — But I hope that you will see, that all my alterations are attended to, except such as would be attended with any considerable trouble or expence. Of course, all the mere verbal corrections can be easily made.

I remain, Gentlemen, respectfully
Your Obt Sevt
Herman Melville

Mess Wiley & Putnam
Broadway

ALS on a 38.2 × 23 cm sheet, folded in half, of white wove paper, watermarked with the manufacturer's name "HUDSON BATH" and embossed with its stamp (a circular device surmounted by feathers and enclosing a crown). Melville inscribed the first page, in ink, and wrote on the fourth page "Mesrs Wiley & Putnam". Another hand, presumably a clerk's, later noted on the fourth page in ink "H Melville | May 7 — 1846" and yet another hand, probably a librarian's, noted on that page in pencil "Herman Melville | 1819 — | Poet and novelist. | See Drake, & Appleton".

LOCATION: Gratz Collection, Historical Society of Pennsylvania, Philadelphia. *Provenance*: Simon Gratz.

PUBLICATION: Davis-Gilman 12.

TO ALEXANDER W. BRADFORD
23 MAY 1846 · LANSINGBURGH

As Melville's communication in the *Albany Argus* on 21 April 1846 (see above) indicates, he felt compelled to contest some of the reviews that had cast doubt on the authenticity of *Typee*. Alexander Warfield Bradford (1815–67) appears to have encouraged Melville to publish a reply to the "obnoxious" review that had appeared on 17 April 1846 in the "C & Enquirer"—the *Morning Courier and New-York Enquirer* (no reprintings of the "malicious notice" in "papers in the Western part of the state" have been located; see *Checklist of Melville Reviews*, ed. Kevin J. Hayes and Hershel Parker [Evanston: Northwestern University Press, 1991]). Bradford, a classmate of Gansevoort's at the Albany Academy, was the son of the Reverend John M. Bradford, the Melvilles' minister in Albany. He was admitted to the bar in 1837, shortly after his marriage to Marianne Gray (d. 1875). When Gansevoort was first starting his law practice in 1842, he joined Bradford in the same offices at 51 William Street in New York, and Allan studied law in Bradford's office at that same time. Bradford was active in Whig politics, and published—as Allan mentioned in his welcoming 17 October 1844 letter to Melville (see LETTERS RECEIVED, pp. 565–71)—one of the earliest studies of American ethnology, *American Antiquities and Researches into the Origin and History of the Red Race* (Boston: Saxton & Pierce; New York: Dayton & Saxton, 1841). In 1839 before sailing for Liverpool, Melville along with his brothers Gansevoort and Allan stayed with the Bradfords in New York for a few days (Gilman, p. 128). Although no other correspondence between Melville and Bradford has been located, they evidently remained in touch after Gansevoort's death, as indicated by a letter Bradford wrote to President Lincoln in March 1861 recommending Melville for a consulship (National Archives; he also signed at this time a joint letter of recommendation with Elisha P. Hurlbut and others). In 1846 his particular value as an adviser to Melville lay in his capacity as coeditor of the *American Review: A Whig Journal of Politics, Literature, Art and Science*. Though Melville makes no mention of it here, a month earlier, on 3 April 1846, this New York journal had published a favorable review of *Typee*, praising the book's "air of truthfullness and fidelity" (pp. 415–16). Another pair of reviews written in this same vein that Melville does mention were those that had appeared in *Chambers's Edinburgh Journal* (5 [25 April 1846], 265–69, and 5 [2 May 1846], 282–84). They treated the book as a documentary account, the first providing simply a straightforward summary of *Typee* and the second offering an anonymous factual description of the "Marquesas and the Marquesans" as a "sequel to the Adventure of Herman Melville." Melville apparently hoped that Bradford had enough influence at the New York *Courier and Enquirer* to get his rebuttal to its earlier review challenging the documentary character of *Typee* published there anonymously. However, Melville's article, which was enclosed with this letter to Bradford, has not been located and may not have been published.

Lansingburgh — May 23, 1846
Dear Sir — Herewith you have the article we spoke of. I have endeavored to make it appear as if written by one who had read the
book & beleived it — & moreover — had been as much pleased with
it as most people who read it profess to be. Perhaps, it may not be
exactly the right sort of thing. The fact is, it was rathar an awkward
undertaking any way — for I have not sought to present my own
view of the matter (which you may be sure is straitforward enough)
but have only presented such considerations as would be apt to suggest themselves to a reader who was acquainted with, & felt freindly
toward the author. — Indeed, I have moddled some of my remarks
upon hints suggested by some reviews of the book. — Bye the by, I
received to day among other papers, a number of Chambers's Edinburgh Journal containing an abridged account of the adventure — &
I could not but feel heartily vexed, that while the intelligent Editors
of a publication like that should thus endorse the genuineness of the
narrative — so many numskulls on this side of the water should
heroically avow their determination not to be "gulled" by it. The
fact is, those who do not beleive it are the greatest "gulls". — full
fledged ones too. —
     What I have written embodies some thoughts which I think will
tell with the public if they are introduced thro' the proper channel.
— That channel is the C & Enquirer, as it contained the obnoxious
review. — I feel confident that unless something of this kind appears
the success of the book here as a genuine narrative will be seriously
impaired. I am told that, that malicious notice (for it certainly has
that sort of edge to it) has been copied into papers in the Western
part of the state. — It will do mischief unless answered. —— But I
need say no more on this head, since you are as well aware of this as
I can be. You have been so kind as to express your willingness to do
what you can in this matter, & I rely so fully upon you having the
ability to do all that is requisite that I will not add a word
more. — Now that I think of it, however, if they should demur at
inserting the accompanying article on account of its contradicting a
previous notice, you might in that case procure its insertion as a
communication. But you understand how to manage it best.
     Will you have the kindness to write me a single line as soon as
you shall make any arrangements? Present my renewed comple-

ments to Mrs Bradford for the honor of her letter, and beleive me to be

Yours Truly
Herman Melville

As you know best in what sort of style such an article as is needed ought to be written — I beg of you, that you will make any alterations you see fit in the accompanying document. — I am wholly unused to this sort of work — & therfore, if it be not asking too much, I hope you will prepare it to suit yourself. — But what I have written contains the substance of what, I think, ought to appear

H M.

ALS on a 39.6 × 25.2 cm sheet, folded in half, of blue wove paper with lines, faintly embossed with the manufacturer's oval stamp. Melville inscribed the first three pages, in ink. The letter was once tipped to another sheet along the left edge of the folded sheet.

LOCATION: Boston Public Library. *Provenance*: Mellen Chamberlain.

PUBLICATION: Zoltán Haraszti, "Melville Defends *Typee*," *More Books: The Bulletin of the Boston Public Library* 22 (June 1947), 203–8. Davis-Gilman 13.

TEXTUAL NOTES: fact is, it was] *miswritten* fact is, it | it was • awkward] *miswritten* awkard • themselves] *miswritten* themslves • Editors] s *added* • not add] not *miswritten* nod

TO GANSEVOORT MELVILLE
29 MAY 1846 · LANSINGBURGH

Unaware that his brother Gansevoort had died nearly three weeks earlier in London, on 12 May 1846, Melville wrote him this letter on Friday, 29 May, misdating it June (Melville's error is indicated by the cancellation stamp on the back of the envelope). Gansevoort had become ill in March, written his last letters home to Augusta and to Melville on 3 April (see LETTERS RECEIVED, pp. 575–77), and made the last entry in his diary the following day. Shortly thereafter he turned his duties as secretary of legation over to McHenry Boyd (see Louis McLane to James Buchanan, 18 May 1846 [National Archives], and Parker, *Gansevoort Melville's London Journal and Letters*, p. 60). It was not until early June that the family learned of Gansevoort's death; a notice was placed in the *Albany Argus* on 4 June.

This 29 May letter, clearly intended to distract Melville's ailing brother, contains a miscellany of news from Lansingburgh. "Miss C. Van. R." was Cornelia Paterson Van Rensselaer (1823–97), a second cousin and a particular friend of Augusta Melville. As the daughter of General Stephen Van Rensselaer (1789–1868), she held a privileged social position; her 10 June 1846 wedding in Albany was to

Nathaniel Thayer (1808–83), a Boston merchant (Cuyler Reynolds, *Genealogical and Family History of Southern New York and the Hudson River Valley* [New York: Lewis Historical Publishing Co., 1913], I, 26). (The news of Gansevoort's death may have prevented Augusta's participation.) "General Veile" was probably Major General J. J. Viele, who delivered the welcome address at the ceremony in Troy, New York, celebrating the triumphant homecoming of General John E. Wool from the Mexican War in August 1848 (Arthur J. Weise, *History of the City of Troy* [Troy: Young, 1876], p. 202). War had been officially declared on 11 May 1846 and would have been of great interest to Gansevoort in his diplomatic capacity. The quotation Melville uses to describe the war fervor is not in Proverbs; he is probably thinking of James 3.5: "Behold, how great a matter a little fire kindleth." His postscript about a "second edition" of *Typee* refers to the second printing of the first American edition of his book—news that Gansevoort would have welcomed.

Lansingburgh Friday, June 29ᵗʰ 1846

My Dear Gansevoort — I look forward to three weeks from now, & think I see you openning this letter in of those pleasant hamlets roundabout London, of which we read in novels. At any rate I pray Heaven that such may be the case & that you are mending rapidly. Remember that composure of mind is every thing. You should give no thought to matters here, until you are well enough to think about them. As far as I know they are in good train.

Mr Boyd's second letter announcing your still continued illness was a sad disappointment to us. Yet he seemed to think, that after all you were in a fair way for recovery — & that a removal to the country (then it appears intended shortly) would be attended with the happiest effects. I can not but think it must be; — & I look for good tidings by the next arrival. — Many anxious enquiries have been made after you by numerous friends here. ——

The family here are quite well — tho' very busy dressmaking. Augusta is one of the bridesmaids to Miss C. Van. R. & her preperations are now forwarding.

People here are all in a state of delirium about the Mexican War. A military arder pervades all ranks — Militia Colonels wax red in their coat facings — and 'prentice boys are running off to the wars by scores. — Nothing is talked of but the "Halls of the Montezumas" And to hear folks prate about those purely figurative apartments one would suppose that they were another Versailles where our democratic rabble meant to "make a night of it" ere long. — The redoubtable General Veile "went off" in a violant war paraoxysm to Washington the other day. His object is to get a commission for raising volunteers about here & taking the feild at their head next fall. — But seriously something great is impending. The Mexican War (tho' our troops have behaved right well) is nothing of itself — but "a little spark kindleth a great fire" as the well known author of the Proverbs very justly remarks — and who knows what all this may lead to — Will it breed a rupture with England? Or any other great powers? — Prithee, are there any notable battles in store — any Yankee Waterloos? — Or think once of a mighty Yankee fleet coming to the war shock in the middle of the Atlantic with an English one. — Lord, the day is at hand, when we will be able to talk of our killed & wounded like some of the old Eastern conquerors reckoning them up by thousands; — when the Battle of Monmouth will be thought child's play — & canes made out of the Constitution's timbers be thought no more of than bamboos. — I am at the end of my sheet — God bless you My Dear Gansevoort & bring you to your feet again.

Herman Melville

Typee is coming on bravely — a second edition is nearly out. — I need not ask you to send me *every notice of any kind* that you see or hear of.

ALS on a 38.4 × 23 cm sheet, folded in half, of white wove paper, watermarked with the manufacturer's name "HUDSON BATH" and embossed with its stamp (a circular device surmounted by feathers and enclosing a crown). Melville inscribed all four pages, in ink. He addressed the envelope *"For the Boston Steamer.* | Gansevoort Melville Esq | U.S. Secretary of Legation | London"; it was canceled on 15 June 1846.

LOCATION: Berkshire Athenaeum, Pittsfield, Massachusetts. *Provenance*: Agnes Morewood.

PUBLICATION: (partial) *Log*, I, 214, 215–16. Leyda, *Portable Melville*, pp. 340–41. Davis-Gilman 14.

TEXTUAL NOTES: in of] *intervening word lacking (presumably "one")* • roundabout] ro *written over a previous word-start* • delirium about the Mexican] M *rewritten* • volunteers] *miswritten* voulunters • there] *written over* their • Atlantic] *miswritten* Alantic • talk] *corrected from* tak • conquerors] *inserted with caret* • Typee . . . of.] *written vertically in the left margin of p. 3; placed here editorially* • kind] *miswritten* kink *(underlined)*

TO JAMES K. POLK
6 JUNE 1846 · LANSINGBURGH

Unlocated. A two-paragraph extract from a letter to President Polk concerning Gansevoort's political service and untimely death is quoted in Melville's 6 June 1846 letter to James Buchanan, just below. The letter has not been found to survive among Polk's papers in the Library of Congress. For more information about Gansevoort Melville's political career, see Hershel Parker, "Gansevoort Melville's Role in the Campaign of 1844," *New-York Historical Society Quarterly* 49 (April 1965), 143–73. Davis-Gilman Unlocated 290.

TO JAMES BUCHANAN
6 JUNE 1846 · LANSINGBURGH

On 18 May 1846 Louis McLane (1786–1857), American minister to the Court of St. James's, wrote James Buchanan (1791–1868), then secretary of state under President Polk, about Gansevoort's illness and death (National Archives). He enclosed copies of letters from two of those in attendance, Edward Moore and Dr. W. F. Chambers, stated the arrangements he had made for the remains to be returned to the United States on the packet-ship *Prince Albert*, under Captain Sebor, to sail on 20 May, and gave a financial accounting. Gansevoort's total assets at his death consisted of the balance of his salary from 30 April to 12 May, "in the hands of the bankers, £19.0.6, £1.10.0 in his house, and the proceeds of the Court-costume £8.0.0 amounting in all to £28.10.6." The outstanding expenses included bills of the physicians (£26.16.0) and of placing the remains aboard ship (£24.9.0), and the anticipated cost of "freight out (not supposed to exceed £2.0.0) and the expense of final interment in the United States to be provided for." Since interment in London "could not have been less than £50" and since the government had no provision for such a calamity, McLane recommended that the government pay a "quarter's salary" (as customary for a minister or chargé d'affaires in such a situation) or pay the funeral and medical expenses, "provided they do not in the whole exceed one hundred pounds."

Melville's effort in writing to Buchanan was simply to reinforce McLane's recommendation and to remind Buchanan of his own as well as President Polk's political debt to Gansevoort, who, as a young and ardent New York Democrat, had campaigned for them through Tennessee, Kentucky, Ohio, and New York. For Buchanan's 9 June reply affirming that fifty pounds would be provided for the expenses related to Gansevoort's death, see LETTERS RECEIVED, pp. 577–78.

Lansingburgh Rensselaer Co. New York,
June 6th 1846.

The Honorable
James Buchanan
Secretary of State,

Sir — You have ere this, I presume received a letter from the Hon Louis McLane referring to certain urgent pecuniary claims upon government connected with the sudden decease of my brother Mr Gansevoort Melville late Secretary of Legation in London. — In

a most friendly letter to the family of the deceased M^r McLane refers
to having written such a communication. I earnestly hope, Sir, that
this is not only so, but that you have favorably considered the subject to which M^r McLane alludes. ——

Permit me Sir, here to submit to you an extract from a letter,
addressed by me this day to the President.

"Our family are in exceedingly embarrassed circumstances, and
"unless the measure which M^r McLane reccommends is carried out,
"a great part of the expenses attendant on my brother's last illness
"and funeral will have (for some time at least) to remain un-
"paid. — The claims of a widowed mother, four sisters, and a
"younger brother, are paramount even to the duties we owe the
"dead. —— I should feel most bitterly the reproach, to which the
"country in some measure, and the memory of my poor brother
"would be subjected, should these debts remain long uncancelled.
"But I can not think that this will be the case.

"The services which so many of my family in many ways have
"rendered the country — my noble brother's own short but brilliant
"public career, and the universally-acknowledged and signal ser-
"vices he rendered the Democratic party in the last memorable gen-
"eral election — all these, Sir, will surely lend great weight to the
"urgent claims of the case itself."

I hardly think Sir, that I need say one word more. I rely upon
the justice of government, and upon Mr Buchanan's giving his
favorable consideration to a subject, so peculiarly deserving of it.

I have the honor to be, Sir,

Most Respectfully

Herman Melville.

ALS on a 38.2 × 23 cm sheet, folded in half, of white wove paper, watermarked with the
manufacturer's name "HUDSON BATH" and embossed with its stamp (a circular device surmounted by feathers and enclosing a crown). Melville inscribed the first three pages, in ink.
Another hand, presumably a clerk's, noted at the top of the first page, in ink, "rec^d June 9",
and still another hand added in pencil, "H. Melville | June 6 — | Answ. 9th June" and "M^r
Riddall | Mr Derrick". The letter is now bound in with the "Miscellaneous Letters of the
Department of State" of 1 April–30 June 1846.

LOCATION: National Archives.

PUBLICATION: Hayford-Davis, pp. 169–71. Davis-Gilman 15.

TEXTUAL NOTES: M^r McLane refers] McLane *written* McLanee *with second* e *wiped* • Sir, that this]
after wiped word-start

TO WILLIAM L. MARCY
6 JUNE 1846 · LANSINGBURGH

In his effort to obtain financial assistance in settling Gansevoort's affairs, Melville also turned to another New York politician, William Learned Marcy (1786–1857), secretary of war under President Polk. Marcy had been one of the original members of the New York state political machine known as the "Albany Regency," which had included Martin Van Buren and with which Melville's uncle Peter Gansevoort was associated. In 1844 Marcy had broken with Van Buren to become a leader of the "Hunkers," the conservative wing of the New York Democrats, and it appears that in appointing Marcy over the candidates recommended by Van Buren, President Polk had taken the word of young New York Democrats, like Gansevoort Melville, who were opposed to Van Buren and the radicals (see Glyndon G. Van Deusen, *The Jacksonian Era* [New York: Harper & Row, 1959], pp. 193–94, and Hershel Parker, "Gansevoort Melville's Role in the Campaign of 1844," *New-York Historical Society Quarterly* 49 [April 1965], 151–73). The enclosed extracts of letters mentioned by Melville are unlocated, as are the letters themselves.

Lansingburgh June 6th 1846

The Hon W L Marcy
Secretary of War
Sir,

Your personal acquaintance with my late brother Mr Gansevoort Melville will I think justify me in addressing you on a subject, very nearly concerning his memory, and with regard to which, your official influence can not but be of great service.

Accompanying this is an extract from a letter of the Hon Louis McLane to the relatives of the deceased. — As also an extract from a letter written by me this day to the President. —— After perusing these extracts you will clearly perceive my object in writing you.

I need not enlarge upon the claims of the case itself — they are most obvious. Nor need I allude to the powerful claims my late brother's family have upon the best consideration of government. His own short but distinguished public career is familiar to you, as well as the noble service he rendered the Democratic Party. ——

I have sought to secure no parade of influence in this matter, for I firmly beleive, that its nature is such as to insure its receiving the earnest attention & prompt action of government. — But Sir, I can not but hope, that this personal appeal of a mourning family, to

whom Providence has brought unspeakable & peculiar sorrows, will
not be without effect upon you

I have the Honor to be, Sir
Most Respectfully
Herman Melville

M^r McLane has written to the Secretary of State on the subject. I have
myself taken the liberty to address that officer as well as the President.

ALS on a 38.4 × 23 cm sheet, folded in half, of white wove paper, watermarked with the
manufacturer's name "HUDSON BATH" and embossed with its stamp (a circular device surmounted by feathers and enclosing a crown). Melville inscribed the first three pages, in ink.

LOCATION: Collection of Maurice Sendak. *Provenance*: American Art Association, Anderson
Galleries, sale 3916, 20 October 1931, lot 132 (with reproduction); Estelle Doheny; St. John's
Seminary; Doheny sale, Christie's, 17–18 October 1988, lot 1481 (with reproduction).

PUBLICATION: (partial) *Log*, I, 217. Davis-Gilman 16.

TEXTUAL NOTES: Accompanying] *miswritten* Accompaning • address] *after wiped* do

TO LOUIS McLANE
BEFORE 13 JUNE 1846 · LANSINGBURGH

Unlocated. A letter of instruction to Louis McLane, the American minister in
London, is cited in Melville's 13 June 1846 letter to his uncle Peter Gansevoort,
below. For more on McLane see the headnote to Melville's 6 June 1846 letter to
James Buchanan, above, and also John A. Munroe, *Louis McLane: Federalist Jackso-
nian* (New Brunswick: Rutgers University Press, 1973), pp. 515, 519, 535. Davis-
Gilman Unlocated 291.

TO McHENRY BOYD
BEFORE 13 JUNE 1846 · LANSINGBURGH

Unlocated. A letter of instruction to Gansevoort Melville's associate McHenry Boyd is
cited in Melville's 13 June 1846 letter to his uncle Peter Gansevoort, just below. During
Gansevoort's illness, Boyd took over his duties at the American legation in London and
carried out the final settlement of his affairs. Davis-Gilman Unlocated 292.

TO PETER GANSEVOORT
13 JUNE 1846 · LANSINGBURGH

Melville's request in his letters to President Polk, Secretary of State Buchanan, and
Secretary of War Marcy (see above) was granted, as Melville states in this letter to

his uncle Peter Gansevoort. On 6 June 1846 (probably before receiving Melville's letter of that date), Buchanan wrote Louis McLane at the American legation that £50 could be charged to the expenses of the legation to pay for Gansevoort's funeral expenses (including the cost of shipping his remains home aboard the *Prince Albert*) and his unpaid medical bills (National Archives). On 9 June he wrote Melville the same information (see LETTERS RECEIVED, pp. 577–78). After all bills were paid, the amount left as a gift for Mrs. Mansfield, probably Gansevoort's rooming-house owner, and the "colored man" would have been something under £20.

The various relatives mentioned at the close of this letter all belonged to the Gansevoort side of the family. Anthony Augustus Peebles (1822–1905), a second cousin of Melville's, was engaged to Augusta Melville between August 1847 and March 1848. His mother was Maria Van Schaick Peebles, Maria Melville's cousin, who lived near the Melvilles in Lansingburgh. Robert Hewson Pruyn (1815–82)—at this time judge advocate for the state of New York—had in 1841 married Jane Ann Yates, a niece of Peter Gansevoort's second wife, Susan Lansing Gansevoort, to whom Melville sends his greetings in the postscript. Peter Gansevoort's only surviving children, Henry (1834–71) and Catherine ("Kate" or "Kitty," 1839–1918), to whom Melville also sends his greetings, were both from his first marriage to Mary Sanford, who died in 1841.

Lansingburgh June 13. 1846

My Dear Uncle — Yesterday I received a letter from the Secretary of State — stating that M^r McLane was authorized to charge £50 ($250) to the contingent expences of the Legation for the funeral expences of Gansevoort. — This will cover every thing, & leave enough to bestow some testimonial of our esteem upon Mrs Mansfield, & to remunerate the colored man who tended Gansevoort during his illness. — So that all that matter, I rejoice to think is happily settled. — I have written to M^r McLane & Mr Boyd instructing the latter as to the disposal of the amount which will remain after paying the bills mentioned in his letter to us. — I have also strongly acknowledged our gratitude to both for their many attentions to the deceased.

Augustus Peebles told me yesterday by your request that Mr Pruyn was leaving for Europe — We have nothing to send, as the letters spoken of above were sent by mail. ——

— I think it more than probable that the Prince Albert will not arrive before the latter part of next week. — I shall defer my departure for New York until Wednesday P.M. — Of course I shall see you before I go ——

Beleive Me Dear Uncle
Affectionately
Herman

My Love to Aunt Susan, and the children. Mama & the girls send their love to them.

ALS on a 23 × 18.7 cm part-sheet (cut along both sides and the bottom), folded in half, of white wove paper, watermarked with the manufacturer's name "HUDSON" and faintly embossed with its stamp (a circular device surmounted by feathers and enclosing a crown) sideways in the upper right corner. Melville inscribed the first three pages, in ink, and addressed the envelope "Gen' Peter Gansevoort | Albany"; it was postmarked in Lansingburgh on 13 June.

LOCATION: NYPL-GL.

PUBLICATION: Paltsits, pp. 10–11. Davis-Gilman 17.

TEXTUAL NOTES: to charge] *miswritten* to | to charge • yesterday] *before canceled* that • Mr Pruyn] M *written over* P

TO PETER GANSEVOORT
22 JUNE 1846 · NEW YORK

When the *Prince Albert* arrived in New York, Melville saw to the placing of Gansevoort's remains aboard the *Hendrik Hudson* and on 27 June accompanied them to Albany for the burial from Peter Gansevoort's house on 28 June (*Albany Argus*, 29 June 1846, and the diaries of Susan and Peter Gansevoort, NYPL-GL). The "Mr Ten Eyck" referred to in this letter was one of the five sons of Melville's great-uncle Leonard Gansevoort's oldest daughter Magdalena Gansevoort Ten Eyck (1777–1863), who had, with her husband Jacob Ten Eyck, inherited the famous mansion Whitehall, near Albany, bought from the British general Bradstreet by Leonard Gansevoort.

New York June 22ᵈ 1846

My Dear Uncle — On Friday afternoon last I called at your office three times, but without seeing you. My only object was, to tell you that I was going down that afternoon to New York, & that I would write you as soon as I heard of the ship's arrival. —— Up to this hour the Prince Albert has not been reported at the Exchange. — She may be looked for now every moment, as she has been due now several days. — I shall remain here until she arrives, & until I can ascertain when the remains can be got ashore, & a day is fixed for removing them to Albany. — I shall then go up the river at once (so as to avoid the possibility of a letter's miscarrying) & final arrangements can be made for receiving the body at your house. — In all probability I shall arrive the morning preceeding that, on which the remains will.

I beleive that nothing can be done until the remains arrive.

Mama asked me to tell you that she intends to come down after dinner of the day on which the funeral takes place, & go up the same evening.

I saw Mʳ Ten Eyck on Friday, & he said that every thing necessary for the funeral could be arranged the morning of the day on which it takes place. ——

I hope the ship may arrive soon as this delay is most unpleasant every way.

Remember me to Aunt Susan, and
Beleive Me, My Dear Uncle
Yours
Herman Melville

ALS on a 38.2 × 23 cm sheet, folded in half, of white wove paper, watermarked with the manufacturer's name "HUDSON BATH" and embossed with its stamp (a circular device surmounted by feathers and enclosing a crown). Melville inscribed the first three pages, in ink.

LOCATION: Beinecke Library, Yale University. *Provenance*: Adrian H. Joline sale, Anderson Galleries, sale 1132, 23–24 February 1915, in lot 348; Jean Hersholt sale, Parke-Bernet Galleries, sale 1503, 23–24 March 1954, lot 601 (misdated 23 June 1846); Edwin J. Beinecke.

PUBLICATION: Davis-Gilman 18.

TEXTUAL NOTES: ascertain] *miswritten as* certain • after dinner] *inserted with caret above canceled* the morning

TO RICHARD T. GREENE
[2 OR 3] JULY 1846 · LANSINGBURGH

Unlocated. A letter to Richard Tobias Greene (1819–92), the "Toby" of *Typee*, is cited in Melville's 3 July 1846 letter to Evert A. Duyckinck, just below. Greene had sailed on the *Acushnet* with Melville in January 1841, jumped ship with him at the Marquesas in July of that year, and was at this time a house and sign painter in Buffalo, New York. In response to charges that *Typee* lacked authenticity (see the letter just below), he placed a communication in the 1 July 1846 *Buffalo Commercial Advertiser* that concluded with a request for Melville to write to him (see LETTERS RECEIVED, pp. 578–79). Melville, as his 3 July letter to Duyckinck reports, quickly complied after seeing the paper "last night" (2 July). This was the beginning of a correspondence between the former shipmates that continued sporadically for many years.

Greene went on to become, among other things, a telegraph operator, an occasional columnist for the Sandusky, Ohio, *Mirror*, and later a "physician" and journalist in Chicago (for an account of some of these careers, see Clarence Gohdes, "Melville's Friend 'Toby,'" *Modern Language Notes* 59 [January 1944], 52–55). He died less than a year after Melville on 23 August 1892 and was survived by his wife, Mary J. Greene, and a son, Melville's namesake, Herman Melville Greene.

None of Melville's letters to Greene has been located. In a 14 November 1892 letter to Elizabeth Melville (HCL-M), Greene's widow lamented the fact that the "few copies of the old edition [of *Typee*] we had were destroyed in the great fire of 1871" in Chicago—a fact which suggests that Melville's letters to his friend were destroyed as well. For the six letters from Greene to Melville that were handed down to Melville's granddaughter Eleanor Melville Metcalf and are now in the Melville Collection of the Houghton Library of Harvard University, see LETTERS RECEIVED, pp. 644–46, 660–61, 678–80, 681–82, 685–86, and 693–94. Davis-Gilman Unlocated 293.

TO EVERT A. DUYCKINCK
3 JULY 1846 · LANSINGBURGH

Melville first became acquainted with Evert Augustus Duyckinck (1816–78) early in 1846 at Wiley & Putnam's, where Duyckinck was the editor of their "Library of Choice Reading" and "Library of American Books" (the series in which *Typee* was published). As this letter indicates, Melville talked with him sometime between 19 and 26 June 1846, while waiting in New York for the arrival of Gansevoort's remains on the *Prince Albert*. The tone of the letter suggests that they had rapidly become friends, despite Duyckinck's reservations about the veracity of *Typee*. Not long after their talk and much to Melville's delight, the *Buffalo Commercial Advertiser* published on 1 July the brief article that identified Melville's companion "Toby" in *Typee* as a Buffalo "house and sign painter," Richard Tobias Greene, whose father was a farmer in Darien, Genesee County, New York, and that included a communication signed "Toby" offering to "testify to the entire accuracy of the work [*Typee*]" (see LETTERS RECEIVED, pp. 578–79). As Melville predicts here, the article was reprinted; it appeared in the *Albany Evening Journal* on 3 July 1846, in the *Albany Argus* on 4 July, and in the *New York Morning News* on 9 July 1846 (enough publications, perhaps, to have brought it to the attention of the "man" of "little faith" at the *New York Evangelist*, author of the skeptical 9 April 1846 review that had prompted Toby Greene to come forward). On 11 July 1846 Greene published in the *Buffalo Commercial Advertiser* a fuller account of his adventures with Melville entitled "Toby's Own Story" (LETTERS RECEIVED, pp. 579–84), and subsequently Melville wrote up his own account—as he proposes to do in this letter—of what "befell" his companion; it was published with the title "The Story of Toby" as a postscript to the American revised edition of *Typee* and by John Murray first as a separate pamphlet, and then as a postscript to later English printings (see Melville's letters to Duyckinck and Murray, both probably written on 15 July 1846, below).

Lansingburgh July 3ᵈ 1846

There was a spice of civil scepticism in your manner, My Dear Sir, when we were conversing together the other day about "Typee" — What will the politely incredulous Mʳ Duyckinck now say to the true Toby's having turned up in Buffalo, and written a letter to the Commercial Advertiser of that place, vouching for the truth of all that part (what has been considered the most extraordinary part) of the narative, where he is made to figure. — Give ear then, oh ye of little faith — especially thou man of the Evangelist — and hear what Toby has to say for himself. —

Seriously, My Dear Sir, this resurrection of Toby from the dead — this strange bringing together of two such places as Typee & Buffalo, is really very curious. — It can not but settle the question of the book's genuineness. The article in the C.A. with the letter of Toby can not possibly be gainsaid in any conceivable way — therefore I think it ought to be pushed into circulation. I doubt not but that many papers will copy it — Mʳ Duyckinck might say a word or two on the subject which would tell. — The paper I allude to is of the 1ˢᵗ Inst. I have written Toby a letter & expect to see him soon & hear the sequel of the book I have written (How strangely that sounds!)

Bye the bye, since people have always manifested so much concern for "poor Toby", what do you think of writing an account of what befell him in escaping from the island — should the adventure prove to be of sufficient interest? — I should value your opinion very highly on this subject. —

I began with the intention of tracing a short note — I have come near writing a long letter

Beleive me, My Dear Sir
Very Truly Yours
Herman Melville

Pardon me, if I have unintentionally translated your patronymick into the Sanscrit or some other tounge — "What's in a name"? says Juliet — a strange combination of vowels & consonants, at least in Mʳ Duyckinck's, Miss, is my reply.

H M

P.S. N° 2. Possibly the letter of Toby might by some silly ones be regarded as a hoax — to set you right on that point, altho' I only saw the letter last night for the first — I will tell you that it alludes to things that no human being could ever have heard of except Toby. Besides the Editor seems to have seen him.

ALS on a 23 × 19.1 cm part-sheet (torn along the top) of white wove paper, watermarked with the manufacturer's name "HUDSON". The sheet was folded in half (and is now split along the fold); Melville inscribed all four pages, in ink, and addressed the envelope "Mr Duyck-incke | — Care of Wiley & Putnam — | New York."; it was postmarked in Lansingburgh on 3 July.

LOCATION: NYPL-D.

PUBLICATION: (partial—omits first postscript) Minnigerode, pp. 14–16. Thorp, pp. 368–69. Davis-Gilman 19.

TEXTUAL NOTES: I think] *before canceled* they • How] H *rewritten* • unintentionally] *miswritten* unintently • Editor] *inserted with caret above canceled* Edintor

TO EDWIN CROSWELL
4 JULY 1846 · ALBANY

Edwin Croswell (1797–1871), an original member of the "Albany Regency," the New York state political machine, was also the editor of the Regency's paper, the *Albany Argus*, from 1823 to 1853. As a political ally, Gansevoort Melville had kept in touch with him from London, writing him and sending him English newspapers and copies of English reviews of *Typee*. As a result, the *Argus* became a staunch supporter of Melville's books. On 26 March 1846 Croswell printed a favorable notice of *Typee* in the *Argus* and on 21 April 1846 a communication from Melville about his book (see the entry for the unlocated letter associated with this article, above). After news arrived of Gansevoort's death, Croswell published on 5 June 1846 an extended obituary, which included a reference to *Typee*, and when Richard Tobias (Toby) Greene came forward to attest to the authenticity of *Typee* in the *Buffalo Commercial Advertiser* communication of 1 July, Croswell reprinted it on 4 July 1846 under the heading "A Veritable Witness" (see LETTERS RECEIVED, pp. 578–79). Then, after receiving this 4 July letter from Melville, Croswell placed yet another notice in the 7 July *Argus*: "We have a note from the author of 'Typee,' saying that the 'Toby' of the Buffalo Commercial Advertiser, is all that he claims to be, and that this admits of no mistake. Mr. MELVILLE says that he can readily account for what may seem to be inexplicable in 'Toby's' statement, viz: the five dollars paid the Irishman for assisting him on board the ship: and he adds, 'I have written to my old comrade, and expect soon to hear from him and see him.'"

The "inexplicable" matters of the "$5 & the Irishman" are explained in Melville's "Story of Toby," printed as the sequel to *Typee* (see the NN edition, pp. 261–71).

Albany July 4th 1846

My Dear Sir — I have called at your office without seeing you (as I have previous to this) and now write this note to inform you that the "Toby" of the Buffalo Commercial Advertiser is all that he says he is. — Of this there is no mistake — allusions are made in his letter to matters which no one else could know anything about except himself.
— What may appear somewhat strange or even perhaps inexplicable in his statement I can readily account for — ie — the $5 & the Irishman. — — I have seen the Irishman — an old rover settled at the bay of Nukuheva — & heard that he was a "taboo" man in other vallies. — Probably Toby gave him the money after shipping in some vessel in the bay of Nukuheva. It is the custom to pay a man thus shipping his advance in Spanish dollars. —— I have written to my old comrade & expect soon to hear from him — & see him —
— Of course this is only a few lines scrawled to you privately — The information here given, however, may be used by you as you see fit. —

Yours Very Truly
Herman Melville

ALS, formerly attached to the verso of the free endpaper and the recto of the following leaf of a first American edition of *Typee* with Edwin Croswell's bookplate, in the Melville collection of The Newberry Library. The margins of the letter were unevenly trimmed to make the letter fit into Croswell's copy of the book. The letter, now measuring approximately 14.7 × 18 cm, is inscribed in ink on only one side of a blue wove sheet with lines. At the top is pasted a 6.8 × 2 cm segment of the same blue, lined paper with the address "Edwin Croswell Esq | Albany" written by Melville across the lines.

LOCATION: The Newberry Library, Chicago. *Provenance*: Elliot's Books (1967).

TEXTUAL NOTES: 1846] 6 *written over* 7 • allusions] ns *cut off when the margin was trimmed* • vessel] *before wiped* la

TO EVERT A. DUYCKINCK
[15?] JULY 1846 · NEW YORK

John Wiley, the more conservative partner in Wiley & Putnam, had been uneasy from the start about Melville's portrayal of the missionaries in the Pacific islands as well as about some of the political and sexual references in *Typee* (see the NN edition, pp. 283–84). As a result of pressure from Wiley, after many reviewers also objected, Melville deleted or revised in the early summer of 1846 many of his comments on these matters, excising the Appendix and nearly all of the third chapter, as well as substantial passages in eight other chapters and the preface. Richard Tobias (Toby) Greene's reappearance allowed him to add "The Story of Toby"—the "proposed Sequel"—to which he also refers here. The resulting "Revised Edition" came out on 6 August 1846.

Although Melville headed his note to Duyckinck simply "Wednesday Afternoon," it can be tentatively dated 15 July 1846, since it was written from New York "6 or 7 days" before Melville expected to return to New York with the sequel to *Typee* after seeing Greene (probably around 22 July, when his brother Allan sent a letter to Duyckinck on his behalf stating that he would not return until 27 July; see the entry for Melville's unlocated letter to Allan written between 15 and 22 July for a further discussion of the probable chronology of this period). Melville's letter to John Murray, just below, verifies that he was in New York on Wednesday, 15 July.

Wednesday Afternoon

Mʳ Melville is sorry that he goes out of town this evening without again seeing Mʳ Duyckinck.

Typee has come out measurably unschathed from the fiery ordeal of Mʳ Wiley's criticisms. I trust as it now stands the book will retain all those essential features which most commended it to the public favor.

I shall see Toby before I return & obtain all the materials for the proposed Sequel; which with the new preface, & the notices of the book which are proposed to be prefixed to it — will have to remain to be settled until my return in the course of 6 or 7 days.

Very Truly Yours
My Dear Mʳ Duyckinck
Herman Melville

ALS on a 13.4 × 20.7 cm sheet of white wove paper. Melville inscribed only one side of the leaf, in ink; it was mounted on a larger leaf for insertion in Duyckinck's extra-illustrated copy of his *Cyclopædia of American Literature* (New York: Scribner's, 1856; NYPL-D) and placed before p. 675 in the middle of the article on Melville (II, 672–76). It has now been removed (though it remains mounted) and placed with Melville's other letters to Duyckinck.

LOCATION: NYPL-D.

PUBLICATION: (partial) *Log*, I, 222 (dated July 8?). Davis-Gilman 20.

TEXTUAL NOTES: to be settled] *inserted above caret* • Truly] *miswritten* Truyly

TO JOHN MURRAY
15 JULY 1846 · NEW YORK

Without Gansevoort to act as a liaison with his British publisher, John Murray, Melville had to take up direct communication with him. Well aware of Murray's early doubts about the authenticity of his first book, Melville put the news accounts of the reappearance of Richard Tobias (Toby) Greene to full use in this letter. The papers he lists as sending were ones that had reprinted or mentioned Greene's initial communication printed in the *Buffalo Commercial Advertiser* on 1 July 1846: the *Morning Courier and New-York Enquirer* (9 July); the *New York Morning News* (9 July); and the *Albany Argus* (4 July). Similarly the statement he cites—" 'Truth is stranger than Fiction' "—appeared in a 6 July 1846 retraction Melville elicited from Thurlow Weed, the editor of the *Albany Evening Journal*, who had initially cast doubt on the report of Toby Greene's reappearance (see the headnote to Melville's 15 August 1846 letter to Weed, below). The "draught of a letter" Melville says he received from Greene probably refers to an earlier letter-version of "Toby's Own Story" sent to Melville before its publication (*Buffalo Commercial Advertiser*, 11 July 1846; see LETTERS RECEIVED, pp. 579–84).

Besides authenticating his narrative, Melville wanted to lay the basis for further publishing ventures with Murray, beginning with the text of *Typee* as he had revised it for Wiley & Putnam. His letter points out that the revisions to *Typee* would mollify critics, such as the reviewer for the London *Spectator* (28 February 1846), who had commented on "certain sea freedoms" in the book "that might as well have been removed before issuing it." The "enclosed paper" (now unlocated) Melville refers to was presumably a version of his new preface. Although he sent the revised text of *Typee* to England, Murray published only its postscript or "Sequel," "The Story of Toby"; for more on the revision of the English edition, including its title—as Melville requests here—see his letters to Murray on 30 July and 2 September, below. The following year Murray published the English edition of Melville's second book, *Omoo: A Narrative of Adventures in the South Seas*, based in part on Melville's experiences on the *Lucy Ann* of Sydney, Australia—the work described at the end of this letter as "nearly completed." For a record of Murray's 3 August 1846 reply to this letter, see LETTERS RECEIVED, p. 584.

New York July 15th 1846

Mr John Murray,

Dear Sir — The decease of my brother Mr Gansevoort Melville leaving me without any correspondant in London thro' whom to communicate with you, I waive cerimony & address you at once by letter. — My object in so doing, is to inform you of certain matters connected with "Typee" which you ought to be made acquainted with, & to allude briefly to one or two other subjects.

In the first place I have to inform you that "Toby" who figures in my narrative has come to life — tho' I had long supposed him to be dead. I send you by this steamer several papers (N.Y. Courier & Enquirer, N.Y. Morning News, & Albany Argus) containing allusions to him. Toby's appearance has produced quite a lively sensation here — and "Truth is stranger than Fiction" is in every body's mouth. — In Buffalo where he "turned up" the public curiosity was so great that "Toby" was induced to gratify it by publishing the draught of a letter which he had originally sent to me. This is not the letter however, which appears in the papers I send you. — I was sorry for this on some accounts, but it could not be helped. However the impression which Toby's letter has produced is this — ie — that every thing about it bears the impress of truth. — Indeed, the whole Typee adventure is now regarded as a sort of Romance of Real Life. — You would be greatly diverted to read some of the comments of our Western Editors and log-cabin critics. —— But to the point. — I am now preparing a short Sequel to Typee containing a simple account of Toby's escape from the valley as related to me by himself. This Sequel will be bound up with all subsequent editions of the book here. — The curiosity of all readers has been awakened as to what became of him — & now that he has appeared & his story is so interesting, it naturally belongs to the narrative that a sequel like this should be supplied. At any rate the public are apprised of Toby's resurrection & are looking for it. — Besides, it is so strange, & withal so convincing a proof of the truth of my narrative *as I sent it to London* that it can not be gainsaid. ——

Were it not for the long delay it would occasion, I should take no steps towards the publication of any Sequel until I had sent the M.S.S. to you. But as matters are, this can not be done — for there is a present demand for the book which the publishers can not supply — a new edition is in preperation — & after what has happened, this can not come out very well without the story of Toby. — Still, if you publish the Sequel (which as a matter of course I suppose you will) no one will interfere with the publication, since it will be quite brief (perhaps not exceeding eight or ten pages) & depends altogether upon the narrative which precedes it. — Besides, I shall take care that you receive a copy of it by the earliest possible oportunity.

—— I have just said that a new edition of the book was forthcoming — This new edition will be a Revised one, and I can not but
think that the measure will prove a judicious one. — The revision
will only extend to the exclusion of those parts not naturally connected with the narrative and some slight purifications of style. I am
pursuaded that the interest of the book almost wholly consists in the
intrinsick merit of the narrative alone — & that other portions, however
interesting they may be in themselves, only serve to impede the
story. The book is certainly calculated for popular reading, or for
none at all. — If the first, why then, all passages which are calculated to offend the tastes, or offer violance to the feelings of any large
class of readers are certainly objectionable. — Proceeding on this
principle then, I have rejected every thing, in revising the book,
which refers to the missionaries. Such passages are altogether foreign to the adventure, & altho' they may possess a temporary interest *now*, to some, yet so far as the wide & permanent popularity of
the work is conserned, their exclusion will certainly be beneficial,
for to that end, the less the book has to carry along with it the better. — Certain "sea-freedoms" also have been modifyed in the expression — but nothing has been done to effect the general character
& style of the book — the narrative parts are untouched — In short
— in revising the work, I have merely removed passages which
leave no gap, & the removal of which imparts a unity to the book
which it wanted before. — The reasons which will be given to the
public for this step are set forth in the enclosed paper — Something
like this will be published in the shape of a "Preface to the Revised
Edition." —

The new edition containing the Sequel of Toby will be out soon.
This day the printers take it in hand & will hurry it. A copy of it will
be forwarded to you by the first steamer through the house of Wiley
& Putnam. I would send you the M.S.S of the Sequel, but it is by no
means yet finished.

From the widely extended notices of "Typee" which have appeared in England I am led to suppose that it has met with the most
flattering success there. If this be so — it can not be deemed premature in me to remind Mr Murray, of his having assured my deceased
brother that in case the book met with "unusual success" he would
still further remunerate the author. — Therefore, if you feel every
way warranted in so doing (of which of course you are left sole

judge) your early consideration of this subject will for special reasons be most gratifying to me.

— As for the matter of the revised edition — if you publish one from the copy I shall send to you, I leave it to yourself to decide, whether I should be considered as entitled to any thing on account of it. — But however that part of the matter may appear to you — I earnestly trust that you will issue a Revised Edition. Depend upon it Sir, that it will be policy so to do. Nor have I decided upon this revision without much reflection and seeking the advice of persons every way qualifyed to give it, & who have done so in a spirit of candor.

— I entertain no doubt but that the simple story of Toby will add very much to the interest of the book, especially if the public are informed of the peculiar circumstances connected with it. — If you publish it, you will reap this benefit, whatever it may be in a pecuniary way; and altho' you will not be bound to pay me any thing for the Sequel, still, should you make use of it, I rely not a little upon your liberality.

— I had almost forgotten one thing — the title of the book. — From the first I have deeply regretted that it did not appear in England under the title I always intended for it — "Typee" It was published here under that title & it has made a decided hit. Nor was any thing else to be expected — that is, if the *book* was going to succeed at all, for "Typee" is a title *naturally suggested by the narrative itself*, and not farfetched as some strange titles are. Besides, its very strangeness & novelty, founded as it is upon the character of the book — are the very things to make "Typee" a popular title. The work also should be known by the same name on both sides of the water. — For these and other reasons I have thought that in all subsequent editions of the book you might entitle it "Typee" — merely prefixing that single but eloquent word to the title as it now stands with you. If you bring out the revised edition with the Sequel — that would be the time to make this very slight but most important alteration. — I trust that Mr Murry will at once consider the propriety of following this suggestion.

This is an unconscionable letter for a first one, but I must elongate it a little more.

I have another work now nearly completed which I am anxious to submit to you before presenting it to any other publishing house.

It embraces adventures in the South Seas (of a totally different character from "Typee") and includes an eventful cruise in an English Colonial Whaleman (A Sydney Ship) and a comical residence on the island of Tahiti. The time is about four months, but I & my narrative are both on the move during that short period. This new book begins exactly where Typee leaves off— but has no further connection with my first work. — Permit me here to assure Mr Murray that my new M.S.S. will be in a rather better state for the press than the M.S.S. handed to him by my brother. A little experience in this art of book-craft has done wonders.

— Will you be so good as to give me your views about this proposed publication (it will be ready the latter part of the fall — *autumn* I beleive it is with you) as early as possible.

— Mr Murray must pardon the evident haste in which this long letter has been written — it was unavoidable. — With much respect & esteem, Dear Sir, Beleive me

Very Truly Yours
Herman Melville

ALS on two 38.2 × 23 cm sheets of white wove paper, embossed with the "HUDSON BATH" manufacturer's stamp (a circular device surmounted by feathers and enclosing a crown). Both sheets were folded in half; Melville inscribed all eight pages, in ink. Another hand, presumably a clerk's, noted at the top of the first page in ink "July 15. 1846 | Melville H".

LOCATION: Murray.

PUBLICATION: (partial) *Log*, I, 222–23. Davis, pp. 201–4. Davis–Gilman 21.

TEXTUAL NOTES: This is not the letter . . . I send you.] *inserted above caret* • of any Sequel] *second* e *rewritten* • think that] *before canceled* it will • and some slight purifications of style] *inserted above caret* • to some,] *inserted above caret* • no gap] no *written over word-start* • as entitled] as *inserted above caret after canceled* to be • and seeking] and *before a redundant ampersand on the following page* • doubt] *before wiped word-start* • at all,] *inserted above caret* • thought that] *before canceled* if • Tahiti] *after canceled* Tahiti • press than] *before canceled* the one

TO ALLAN MELVILLE
BETWEEN 15 AND 22 JULY 1846 · LANSINGBURGH

Unlocated. A letter from Melville is cited in Allan Melville's 22 July 1846 letter to Evert A. Duyckinck. Allan, who as a lawyer in New York had begun handling his brother's legal affairs, wrote to Duyckinck: "My brother desires me to see Mr Duyckinck & say that he has reached home after having seen 'Toby' & that he will be in town on Monday [27 July] with the sequel. He further more wished me to say to Mr Duyckinck that the advertizing the Revised Edition had better be delayed until his arrival in town for reasons (very good ones I suppose) which he was in too great a hurry to enumerate" (NYPL-D). Melville met with Richard Tobias (Toby) Greene at some time between 3 July (when he wrote Duyckinck that he expected to see Greene "soon") and 22 July (when Allan's letter reported that they had met). Since Melville's letter to Murray on 15 July emphasizes Toby Greene's reappearance and the newspaper reprintings of his 1 July letter in the *Buffalo Commercial Advertiser* but does not offer a description of their meeting, presumably it occurred after that date and before 22 July. Davis-Gilman Unlocated 294.

TO WILLIAM B. SPRAGUE
24 JULY 1846 · LANSINGBURGH

This letter is the first known of those Melville would write throughout the rest of his life for autograph collectors. *Typee* had made Melville suddenly famous, as *Childe Harold* had made Byron ("I awoke one morning and found myself famous"). In this case, the collector was a local clergyman, the Reverend William Buell Sprague (1795–1876), minister of the Second Presbyterian Church of Albany (1829–69).

Dr Sprague,

 Dear Sir — Being told that you particularly desired my autograph I cheerfully send it. — And the author of Typee looks forward with complacency to his joining that goodly fellowship of names which the taste and industry of Dr Sprague have collected. But beleive me, Dear Sir, I take you to be indeed curious in these autographs, since you desire that of

          Herman Melville

Lansingburgh July 24, '46

 Now that I think of it I was charged to write two of them — You remember some one woke one morning and found himself famous — And here am I, just come in from hoeing in the garden, writing autographs.

        Again Yours, Dear Sir
         Herman Melville

ALS on a 22.4 × 18.2 cm sheet, folded in half, of white wove paper, faintly embossed with the manufacturer's stamp, an oval surmounted by two lions and a shield, and watermarked with the name "J. WHATMAN | TURKEY MILL | 1841". Melville inscribed the first three pages, in ink. Both occurrences of the name "Dr Sprague" were later partially rubbed out by another hand.

LOCATION: Collection of David Shneidman. *Provenance*: Dauber & Pine, catalogue 100, December 1931; Edward and Betty Marcus Foundation; Christie's, 22 November 1985, lot 82 (with reproduction).

PUBLICATION: T. O. Mabbott, *Notes & Queries* 162 (27 February 1932), 151–52. Davis-Gilman 22.

TO EVERT A. DUYCKINCK
[30?] JULY 1846 · NEW YORK

As Melville promised in his earlier note to Duyckinck of [15?] July 1846, he returned to New York—arriving on Monday, 27 July 1846—after seeing Richard Tobias (Toby) Greene and preparing the postscript or "Sequel" to be appended to the revised edition of *Typee*. Melville dated his letter written to Duyckinck during this visit Thursday, 28 July, but Thursday fell on 30 July in 1846. That date is a more likely one for this letter since Melville probably did not leave town (as he announces he is about to do) before the thirtieth, which was the date of his letter to John Murray also written from New York and also concerning the revised edition of *Typee* (see below).

Melville and his publishers were concerned about piracy because Toby Greene's reappearance and story had been so widely publicized following his first communication in the *Buffalo Commercial Advertiser* on 1 July. Since the "Story of Toby" was to be the key selling point of the revised edition, a piracy of that material based on what had already appeared in the press could have been damaging to sales (Davis, p. 25). Probably for this reason, Melville had Allan convey to Duyckinck his wish to delay advertising the revised edition until his arrival in town (see the entry for Melville's unlocated letter to Allan, pp. 58–59 above).

It seems to be understood (from what has happened heretofore) that I should leave a little legacy of a note for Mr Duyckinck every time I leave town — In conformity with which understanding, I now bequeath you these few lines, on the eve of my departure for another, & I trust, a cooler land. —

You remember you said something about anticipating the piracy that might be perpetrated on the "Sequel", by publishing an extract or two from it — which you said you would attend to. — I meant to speak to you again about it — but forgot so to do. — However, be so good, as to consider yourself now reminded of it by these presents. — I take this to be a matter of some little moment.

The *Revised* (Expurgated? — Odious word!) Edition of Typee ought to be duly announced — & as the matter (in one respect) is a little delicate, I am happy that the literary tact of Mr Duyckinck will be exerted on the occasion. ——

Do forgive this boring you forever, and Beleive me My Dear M^r
Duyckincke

> Very Faithfully Yours
> Herman Melville

Thursday Afternoon
July 28th '46

ALS on a 23 × 18.9 cm part-sheet (torn along the top), folded in half, of white wove paper, faintly embossed (on the second leaf) with the Hudson Bath manufacturer's stamp (a circular device surmounted by feathers and enclosing a crown). Melville inscribed the first three pages, in ink.

LOCATION: NYPL-D.

PUBLICATION: (partial) Minnigerode, p. 19. Davis-Gilman 23.

TEXTUAL NOTES: meant] *after canceled* ment • Beleive] *miswritten* Beileve

TO JOHN MURRAY
30 JULY 1846 · NEW YORK

Before this letter reached London, John Murray had already replied on 3 August 1846 to Melville's earlier letter of 15 July 1846 ("a week or two since") that had proposed that Murray publish the revised edition of *Typee*. In his reply, Murray offered Melville fifty pounds for that edition (see LETTERS RECEIVED, p. 584). It is unclear when Melville found the "first possible oportunity" to send Murray the sheets for the "book as revised." According to the Wiley & Putnam statement for 30 July through 1 October 1846 (HCL-M), five hundred copies of the revised edition were printed on 31 July, the day after this letter was written. The edition was formally published seven days later on 6 August, but Melville may have waited until 2 September to send the sheets with his letter to Murray of that date (see below).

Mr Murray
Dear Sir

By this Steamer I forward you the Sequel to "Typee" alluded to in my last. The Steamer sails on the 1st August, & the sequel will not be published here, until at least ten days hence — owing to the backwardness in getting out the Revised Edition in which the Sequel will first appear. For the same reason, I am now unable to forward you a copy complete of the book as revised — which I would much wish to do. However, I will see that it is forwarded by the first possible oportunity.

Trusting that you will consider the subjects treated of in the letter I wrote you a week or two since, and write me your views as soon as you conveniently can, I remain, Mr Murray

Very Truly Yours
Herman Melville

New York July 30. 1846.

I am more than ever impressed with the thought, that the permanent reputation as well as the present popularity of Typee will be greatly promoted by the revision to which it has just been subjected. This remark applies equally to both countries.

ALS on an 18.9 × 23 cm part-sheet (torn along the left edge) of white wove paper, embossed with the Hudson Bath manufacturer's stamp (a circular device surmounted by feathers and enclosing a crown). Melville inscribed both sides of the leaf, in ink. Another hand, presumably a clerk's, noted in ink at the top of the first page "July 30. 1846 | Melville Herman".

LOCATION: Murray.

PUBLICATION: (partial) Log, I, 224. Davis, p. 205. Davis-Gilman 24.

TEXTUAL NOTES: which the] after canceled word-start • I will] ink smeared • and write] w written over u

TO THURLOW WEED
15 AUGUST 1846 · ALBANY

Thurlow Weed (1797–1882), a journalist and later a leading figure in the Republican party, was at this time editor of the Albany Evening Journal. On 3 July Weed had reprinted the 1 July Buffalo Commercial Advertiser announcement of Richard Tobias (Toby) Greene's reappearance, with a skeptical note that Greene's "testimony tends to increase rather than to resolve our doubts. There is a dreaminess—an etheriality about [Melville's] story, which raises it above any mere matter of fact relation. . . . We do not believe, therefore, that the mysterious, and mysteriously absent 'Toby,' is a Sign Painter at Buffalo!" According to a 6 July article in the Evening Journal, Melville met with Weed in Albany on 4 July 1846 and told him that he had "no doubt but that the Buffalo Sign Painter" was his "veritable Ship-mate and Companion 'Toby.'" Weed printed this brief report of Melville's visit, concluding, "if this be so, it furnishes a strong exemplification of the seeming contradiction that 'Truth is stranger than Fiction.'" (Melville later quoted that statement in his letter to John Murray on 15 July 1846.) A week later on 13 July the Evening Journal reprinted

Toby Greene's fuller account of his adventures, "Typee—Toby's Own Story," that had appeared on 11 July 1846 in the *Buffalo Commercial Advertiser*. Apparently Melville had won Weed over.

Mr Melville takes great pleasure in presenting to Mr Weed the accompanying copy of Typee — and much regrets not seeing him this morning.

Albany Aug 15. 1846.

ALS, third person, "Mr Melville", on a 24.8 × 19.8 cm part-sheet (torn along the top), folded in half, of blue wove paper, embossed with the manufacturer's small oval stamp enclosing the initials "P & S". Melville inscribed the first page, in ink, and addressed the fourth page "Thurlow Weed Esq"; another hand, probably Weed's, noted on that page in ink "Herman Melville | ('Tommo') | August 15th 1846".

LOCATION: NYPL-B.

PUBLICATION: Davis-Gilman 25.

TO MELVIN O. BRADFORD, PHILEMON FULLER, AND OTHERS
BEFORE 2 SEPTEMBER 1846 · LANSINGBURGH

Unlocated. A letter to the owners of the *Acushnet* (Melvin O. Bradford, Philemon Fuller, and others, of Fairhaven) is cited in Melville's 2 September 1846 letter to John Murray, just below. When Murray expressed renewed concern about the authenticity of Melville's work in his letter to Melville on 3 August 1846 (see LETTERS RECEIVED, p. 584), Melville must have thought it necessary to obtain an affidavit of his desertion with Richard Tobias (Toby) Greene in the Marquesas. Melville's letter to Murray on 19 June 1848 suggests that he did receive some proof to this effect, but from what source is unclear. Davis-Gilman Unlocated 295.

TO JOHN MURRAY
2 SEPTEMBER 1846 · LANSINGBURGH

This reply to Murray's letter of the "3^d Ult" (see LETTERS RECEIVED, p. 584) continues the various topics of Melville's earlier correspondence with his British publisher—the revised edition of *Typee*, the book's authenticity, and "the book on the stocks," *Omoo*. A "copy complete of the book [*Typee*] as revised" probably accompanied this letter (see the headnote to Melville's earlier letter of 30 July 1846). Murray, however, made use of only the new material about Toby in the "Sequel," publishing it first as a separate threepenny pamphlet (16 pp.) in an edition of 1250 copies in September or October 1846 (see John H. Birss, "The Story of Toby, A Sequel to *Typee*," *Harvard Library Bulletin* 1 [1947], 118–19). In January 1847 Murray issued a "New Edition" of the book printed from the plates of the first edition, but with Melville's new short preface added at the opening, the sequel appended (with continuous pagination), and the book's title revised in accordance with Melville's wishes in his earlier letter of 15 July 1846. Murray prefixed *Typee; Or, A* to the original title of the English edition—*Narrative of a Four Months' Residence among the Natives of a Valley of the Marquesas Islands; Or, A Peep at Polynesian Life.*

To meet Murray's concern about authenticity (evidently voiced in his 3 August letter of which only a letterbook notation has been located; see LETTERS RECEIVED, p. 584), Melville cites three new pieces of evidence: the daguerreotype of Richard Tobias (Toby) Greene (Buffalo, 1846, now in HCL-M [see p. 547 below]); an application to the owners of the *Acushnet* for proof of his and Greene's desertion from the ship (see the entry just above); and what was probably a copy of Greene's 11 July 1846 article—"Toby's Own Story"—that had been reprinted in the *New York Mirror* on 1 August. (The former editor of the *Mirror*, N. P. Willis, mentioned by Melville, had been friendly with Gansevoort in London when *Typee* was going through the press and became friends with Melville after returning to the United States in 1846; see the entry for Melville's unlocated letter to Willis of 14 December 1849.) There is no evidence, however, that he sent to Murray "by the next Steamer" an account of his meeting with Greene.

Several of the periodicals Melville mentions at the end of this letter carried more than one notice of *Typee*. Those Melville may have seen include the London *Athenæum* (21, 28 February), the *Spectator* (28 February), *John Bull* (7 March), the *Critic* (7, 14, 28 March), *Examiner* (9 March), *Eclectic Review* (April), *Simmonds' Colonial Magazine* (April), *Douglas Jerrold's Shilling Magazine* (April), *Tait's Edinburgh Magazine* (April), the London *Times* (6 April), the *Sun* (14, 29 April), and the *Gentleman's Magazine* (July), all of which were excerpted in the "Publisher's Advertisement" in the first American edition of *Omoo*.

Lansingburgh Sept 2ᵈ 1846

My Dear Sir — Your very friendly and welcome letter of the 3ᵈ Ult was forwarded to me from New York a few days since — Before alluding to any thing else I can not forbear expressing to you how sensible I am of the sincere sympathy you express in the decease of my noble and lamented brother.

I am extremely happy that you acquiese in the propriety of the revision of Typee, and only fear that possibly you may not fully approve the extent to which it has been carried. Nevertheless I think I have done right. —

The Preface is very short — I made it so purposely — I could not go into particulars without being prosy & egotistic, & so I settled the matter in one or two compendius paragraphs.

— As to the Sequel, I only fear that your expectations, might have been too high — of its interest — & hence you may be disappointed — However, more than to satisfy the reader's curiosity as to Toby's escape could not be expected from it — & it is written as simply as possible.

— The introductory note is brief. Aside from the consideration that Toby's resucitation had been bruited over the country here, so as to render any particular statement needless — I considered that were I to make any such statement it would lead me into divers disenchanting and unromantic details, which at the very close of the story would show as awkwardly as the clumsy frame of a scene peeping into view just as the curtain falls on the last act of the drama.

— I have seen Toby. have his darguerreotype — a lock of those ebon curls. — I had intended by this steamer to write & send you a brief account of my manner of hearing of him — our interview &c — I shall do so by the next Steamer.

Rejoiced am I, My Dear Sir, that the magic, cabilistic, *tabooistic* "Typee" will hereafter grace the title-page of all subsequent English editions of the book — Its judiciousness will be justifyed by the result.

With reference to the payment you promise me at the end of the year I have no doubt it is a fair compensation and I will add that circumstances will make it peculiarly acceptable — You will perhaps some sort of receipt for the money — any thing of that kind I will send you on its reception.

— Concerning the book on the stocks (which bye the by must'nt fall to peices there, since I have not done much to it lately) I will forward you enough of it to enable you to judge therof. — (Perhaps the whole) — However, you must not Dear Sir expect another Typee — The fates must send me adrift again ere I write another adventure like that exactly. —— You ask for "documentary evidences" of my having been at the Marquesas — in Typee. — Dear Sir, how indescribably vexatious, when one really feels in his very bones that he has been there, to have a parcel of blockheads question it! — Not (let me hurry to tell you) that Mr John Murray comes under that category — Oh no — Mr Murray I am ready to swear stands fast by the faith, beleiving "Typee" from Preface to Sequel — He only wants something to stop the mouths of the senseless sceptics — men who go straight from their cradles to their graves & never dream of the queer things going on at the antipodes. —

I know not how to set about getting the evidence — How under Heaven am I to subpeona the skipper of the Dolly who by this time is the Lord only knows where, or Kory-Kory who I'll be bound is this blessed day taking his noon nap somewhere in the flowery vale of Typee, some leagues too from the Monument.

Seriously on the receipt of your welcome favor, Dear Sir, I addressed a note to the owners of the ship, asking if they could procure for me, a copy of that part of the ship's log which makes mention of two rascals running away at Nukuheva — to wit Herman Melville and Richard T Greene. As yet I have nothing in reply — If I think of any other kind of evidence I will send it, if it can be had & despatched.

— Typee however must at last be beleived on its own account — they beleive it here now — a little touched up they say but *true*.

— Accompanying this you will receive a paper (formerly conducted by N P Willis) which contains an article with regard to the genuineness of Typee which I wish you to observe. —

I wish you would send me any further notices of the book you may see — I have no other mode of getting them. I have only seen the Spectator, Times, Sun, John Bull, Athenaeum, Critic, Eclectic, Simmons, Shilling Magazine & one or two others — Possibly there may be a stray one that I have not seen. —

You must pardon this terrific scrawl — I write fast, to save the mail for Boston which leaves now within 20 minutes. — Address me Care of Allan Melville Wall Street New York City.

And now with many thanks for your friendly letter, and cordial wishes for your health & prosperity Beleive me, My Dear Mr Murray

Very sincerely Yours
Herman Melville.

ALS on two 38.2 × 23 cm sheets of white wove paper, embossed with the Hudson Bath manufacturer's stamp (a circular device surmounted by feathers and enclosing a crown). Both sheets were folded in half; Melville inscribed all eight pages, in ink. Another hand, presumably a clerk's, noted in ink at the top of the first page "Sep. 2. 1846 | Melville H."

LOCATION: Murray.

PUBLICATION: (partial) *Log*, I, 226–27. Davis, pp. 205–7. Davis-Gilman 26.

TEXTUAL NOTES: Sept] S *written over wiped* A • go into] *after canceled* and • too high] *miswritten* to high • disappointed] a *written over* p • which at] wh *written over another word-start* • story would] ou *corrected* • scene] *miswritten* scence • no doubt] *after canceled* litt • compensation and] *before canceled* one • perhaps some] *intervening word lacking (presumably "want")* • adventure] *before canceled* such • cradles to] to *inserted above caret after canceled* of • know not] not *inserted above caret* • set] *after canceled* under • subpeona] b *written over canceled* p • they say] *inserted above caret* • Accompanying] *miswritten* Accompany *or* Accompaning • health] l *added* • Very] V *rewritten*

TO THE TROY YOUNG MEN'S ASSOCIATION
BEFORE 28 NOVEMBER 1846 · NEW YORK

Unlocated. In an announcement dated 28 November 1846, the Troy Young Men's Association advertised in the *Troy Budget* the lecturers for the coming season. Among the names listed was that of "Herman Melville, Esq., of Lansingburgh." Melville's 19 January 1847 letter to Hooper Van Vorst explains, however, that he had responded to the Troy invitation only conditionally and suggests that he did not plan to "lecture anywhere, or at all" in 1847. A search of the Troy newspapers uncovered no report of a lecture by Melville during that year (see Warren F. Broderick, "An Early Speaking Engagement," *Melville Society Extracts* [November 1992], 16). Davis-Gilman Unlocated 297.

TO EVERT A. DUYCKINCK
8 DECEMBER 1846 · NEW YORK

During October of 1846 Elizabeth Shaw—Melville's future wife—had visited the Melville family in Lansingburgh. Then from 28 November to 7 December, Melville visited her and her family in Boston. This letter requesting Duyckinck's professional advice about Melville's new book was written in New York on Tuesday, 8 December, the day after his return. According to it, Melville had left the manuscript of the recently completed *Omoo* with an unidentified "particular lady acquaintance" while passing through New York on his way to Boston. Presumably Melville saw Duyckinck at the time appointed here, but gave him only the early chapters of his new book (see the letter just below).

My Dear Mr Duyckinck

    I arrived in town last evening from the East. As I hinted to you some time ago I have a new book in M.S. — Relying much upon your literary judgement I am very desirous of getting your opinion of it & (if you feel disposed to favor me so far) to receive your

hints. — I address you now not as being in any way connected with
Mess W & P. but presume to do so confidentially & as a friend.

In passing thro' town some ten days since I left the M.S. with a
particular lady acquaintance of mine; at whose house I intend calling
this evening to obtain it. The lady resides up town. On my way
down I will stop at your residence with the M.S. & will be very
much pleased to see you — if not otherwise engaged. — I will call,
say at 8½.

With sincere regard
Beleive Me, My Dear Sir
Very Truly Yours
Herman Melville

Wall Street, Tuesday Morning.

If you are to be engaged this evening pray inform me by the bearer.

ALS on a 24.3 × 18.4 cm sheet, folded in half, of white wove paper. Melville inscribed the
first three pages, in ink. Duyckinck noted in pencil on the fourth page "Dec 8. 1846".

LOCATION: NYPL-D.

PUBLICATION: (partial) Minnigerode, pp. 28–29. Davis-Gilman 27.

TEXTUAL NOTES: opinion] *possibly* opinions • not otherwise] *after canceled* at le

TO EVERT A. DUYCKINCK
10 DECEMBER 1846 · NEW YORK

Dated only "Thursday Afternoon," this letter accompanied chapters of *Omoo* that
Melville had apparently not given Duyckinck on 8 December (see above). It was
presumably written two days later, on Thursday, 10 December, the date Duyckinck placed on the first page. The letter shows that Melville made some extensive
last-minute excisions to the book; however, to what extent he actually followed
through with them is unclear. He states that he is rejecting three early chapters, but
the subsequent missionary chapters, listed here by their unaltered numbers, appeared in print as Chapters 32, 33, etc., that is, each only one number lower than in
the letter. It would appear from this that Melville ultimately rejected only one full
chapter; for a further discussion, see the NN *Omoo*, p. 328.

Dear Sir

Herewith you have the remaining chapters Those marked in the
Table of Contents as Nᵒˢ V. VII. & XVII. have been rejected

altogether — but this does not break the continuity of the book. I have not as yet altered the numbers of the chapters as thus affected.

I beg you to pay particular attention to the following chapters — Chapters 33. 34 — & 45. 46. 47. 48. 49. 50. — They all refer more or less to the missions & the condition of the natives.

Very Faithfully Yours
Herman Melville

Thursday Afternoon.

ALS on a 24.8 × 19.9 cm part-sheet (torn along the top) of blue wove paper, faintly embossed on the second leaf of the folded sheet with the manufacturer's small oval stamp enclosing the initials "P & S". Melville inscribed the first two pages, in ink, and addressed the fourth page "Evart A Duyckincke Esq | Clinton Place." Duyckinck wrote the date "Dec 10./ 46" in pencil above the salutation on the first page and also noted in pencil on the fourth page "?Doctor Diddled Writing" ("Writing" is conjectural).

LOCATION: NYPL-D.

PUBLICATION: Charles Roberts Anderson, *Melville in the South Seas* (New York: Columbia University Press, 1939), pp. 238–39. Davis-Gilman 28.

TEXTUAL NOTES: refer] *miswritten* refere • Thursday Afternoon.] *blotted*

TO MARIA GANSEVOORT MELVILLE AND FAMILY
BEFORE 25 DECEMBER 1846 · NEW YORK

Unlocated. A letter from Melville is reported in a series of notes added in postscript by Maria Melville to her daughter Helen's 25 December 1846 letter written from Lansingburgh to Augusta Melville, then visiting in Albany. Maria Melville writes, "We heard from Herman & Allan this morning — Herman is very busy correcting Omoo — and, at the same time endeavoring to procure employment in the CH — " (NYPL-GL). In his efforts to obtain a Custom House appointment or some other government post, Melville traveled to Washington, D.C., in February 1847 (see his letters for that month). Maria Melville also noted that Melville included a request for Augusta: "Herman wishes you to make his most sincere regrets to Mrs Thayer, that he was unable to see her before leaving town — he call'd the Evg previous — she was out — ." Cornelia Van Rensselaer Thayer, the daughter of Maria Melville's cousin, Stephen Van Rensselaer, was an intimate friend of Augusta Melville (see the headnote to the 29 May 1846 letter to Gansevoort), who after her marriage had moved to Mt. Vernon Street in Boston near the Shaws, with whom Melville had been visiting. As she wrote to Augusta on 22 December [1846], she had planned a dinner for Melville, inviting "Mr Prescott, Professor Jackson & some of the distinguished & agreeable literary characters to meet him" (NYPL-GL), but

Melville, concerned about the publication of *Omoo*, left for New York on 7 December, missing the dinner.

TO JOHN R. BRODHEAD
30 DECEMBER 1846 · NEW YORK

John Romeyn Brodhead (1814–73), born in Philadelphia, was a nephew of Harmanus Bleecker, a friend of Melville's uncle Peter Gansevoort. He had been a childhood acquaintance of Melville and his brothers—particularly Gansevoort, as indicated here. He practiced law in New York from 1835 to 1837; subsequently he succeeded Gansevoort as secretary of legation in London (1846–49) under George Bancroft. As a lawyer and family friend, Brodhead was an obvious choice for Melville to light upon when searching for an agent to act on his behalf in England. Melville had already negotiated an agreement with Harper & Brothers—signed on 18 December 1846—to publish "Omoo: A Narrative of Adventure in the South Seas" (HCL-M). According to the endorsement on this letter, Brodhead both received and answered it on 14 January 1847, agreeing to act as agent for the sale of *Omoo* in England. The book was published in March 1847 in London, and in May in New York.

New York Dec 30th 1846

John Romeyn Brodhead Esq

Dear Sir: — The long-standing acquaintance between our families, and particularly that between my late brother Mr Gansevoort Melville and yourself, induce me to solicit a favor which my own slight acquaintance with you would not perhaps warrant. By granting it, as I think you will, you will confer that which I shall not forget.

I have recently made an arrangement with the Harpers to bring out a new work of mine. But altho' it has just gone to press, they are to defer publication until I have concluded arrangements to bring out the work in England. This is for the express purpose, as you will perceive, of securing a copyright there. — Now, I have no correspondent in London who can act for me — is it too much to solicit your friendly offices? — There is little to be done — a mere sale to effect — that accomplished, the rest remains with the publisher.

Presuming that you will not refuse what I ask, permit me, Dear Sir, to take it for granted.

Mr Murray of Albemarle Street has by letter informed me, that upon receiving the proof sheets of my new book he would make me a liberal offer therefore. — I, of course, guarenteeing the integrity of the copyright for England, which I will do.

Now, relying upon your friendly consent to do what I ask of you, I shall write Mr Murray to the effect, that I shall empower Mr Brodhead to treat with him for the sale of the book, & that I will also send the proof sheets under cover to you by the steamer of the 1st of February, & that you will upon their arrival at once submit them to him for an offer.

Do not, I pray you, entertain the slightest apprehension or delicacy as to any responsibility you may think you will assume by acting for me in this matter. For by the steamer which carries over the proof sheets I will give you such instructions as will remove all scruples upon this head.

I will write you fully by the steamer of the 1st of February.

You see, I rely upon your granting this favor — Your declining so to do will not only place me in a very unplesant predicament, but will occasion me no small pecuniary loss.

With high consideration and true regard,

> Beleive Me, Dear Sir
> Your obedient Servant
> Herman Melville

Should there be any probability of your being out of town upon the arrival of the proof sheets, I must beg of you to leave directions for having them forthwith forwarded to Mr Murray. I shall write him to this effect.

ALS on a 39.8 × 24.8 cm sheet, folded in half, of blue wove paper, faintly embossed with the manufacturer's small oval stamp enclosing the initials "P & S". Melville inscribed all four pages, in ink. Brodhead noted in ink above the dateline "Recd & ansd | *14 Jany 1847*".

LOCATION: at present unknown. *Provenance*: H. Bradley Martin sale, Sotheby's, New York, sale 5971, 30–31 January 1990, in lot 2167; 19th Century Shop, catalogue 17 (September 1990), in item 151.

PUBLICATION: Birss, "A Mere Sale to Effect," pp. 240–41. Davis-Gilman 29.

TEXTUAL NOTES: long-standing] long-|standing • induce me to solicit] *before wiped* it • the copyright] *miswritten* the copright • I shall write] write *inserted above caret* • place me in] in *inserted above caret*

TO JOHN MURRAY
30 DECEMBER 1846 · NEW YORK

On 15 July ("Sometime ago") Melville had proposed his second book, *Omoo*, and Murray had promised (in a now unlocated reply) "a liberal offer therefore" (see Melville's 30 December letter to John R. Brodhead, just above). By assuring Murray in this letter that *Omoo* would not be published in America until either on or after the date of publication in England, Melville was recommending the procedure followed with *Typee* and the accepted practice of Cooper, Emerson, and other American writers. Although England had extended its national copyright law in 1838, the United States Congress did not authorize reciprocal copyright agreements with other nations until 1891. Thus, to prevent piracies the accepted practice for British publishers was to bring out their editions of works by American writers in advance of the American editions. As mentioned in his letter of the same day to Brodhead, Melville here writes Murray "to the effect, that I shall empower M[r] Brodhead to treat with him for the sale of the book." The letter Melville expected from Murray on the 4 January steamer (with the payment for the sequel) had not yet arrived by 29 January 1847, when Melville did "write more fully" in sending the proof sheets.

New York December 30th '46

My Dear Sir — The new work which I Sometime ago informed you I was employed upon is at length finished. I have made an arrangement with the house of Harper & Brothers to stereeotype & publish the same. But it is an express condition that after furnishing me with a complete proof, they shall defer publication until I have time to make arrangements to bring out the book in England. They are not to publish until I notify them so to do. Thus the English copyright can be secured.

The work has gone to press; and by the steamer of the 1st of February (the next after that of the 1st of January) I shall send the proof sheets in the U.S. Despatch Bag to M[r] John Romyn Brodhead (with whom I am acquainted) the present American Secretary of Legation. I will also empower him to treat for the sale of the book.

Of course I should much prefer your publishing it, & I think that as it has a certain connection with "Typee" you will be desirous of so doing. The two books will sell together.

M[r] Brodhead will at once submit the proof sheets to you, and I trust that no difficulty will be in the way of making an arrangement satisfactory to all concerned.

My purpose in writing you *now* is merely to apprise you that the proof sheets are forthcoming. By the steamer of the 1st of February I shall write more fully if necessary.

On this point you may rely: that the work will not be published here except simultaniously with its publication abroad.

I expect to have the pleasure of hearing from you by the steamer which leaves England on the 4th January next.

With much regard

Beleive Me, Dear Sir,

Yours

Herman Melville

Mr John Murray
Albemarle Street.

P.S. Should, by any chance Mr Brodhead be out of town upon the arrival of the proof sheets, he will by my directions cause them to be at once forwarded to you unconditionally. To provide for which contingency I will write you further by the steamer of the 1st of February.

ALS on a 39.8 × 24.8 cm sheet, folded in half, of blue wove paper, embossed with the manufacturer's small oval stamp enclosing the initials "P & S" (upside down at the bottom of both leaves). Melville inscribed the first three pages, in ink. Another hand, presumably a clerk's, noted in ink on the fourth page "Dec 30. 1846 | Melville H."

LOCATION: Murray.

PUBLICATION: (very partial) *Log*, I, 231. Davis, pp. 207–8. Davis-Gilman 30.

TEXTUAL NOTES: Harper] *final* s *wiped* · publication] *written over an earlier word-start* · send] *inserted above caret* · write] *added in the margin* · here] *before canceled* until a day or two · town] *before canceled* at · contingency] *miswritten* contigency

1847

TO THE SCHENECTADY YOUNG MEN'S ASSOCIATION
BEFORE 19 JANUARY 1847 · NEW YORK

Unlocated. From Melville's 19 January 1847 letter to Hooper Van Vorst, just below, it can be inferred that Melville declined, presumably by letter, the invitation to lecture that he had received from the Young Men's Association in Schenectady (see LETTERS RECEIVED, p. 585). Davis-Gilman Unlocated 298.

TO HOOPER C. VAN VORST
19 JANUARY 1847 · NEW YORK

Hooper Cummings Van Vorst (1817–88), an Albany lawyer, was president of the Albany Young Men's Association, to which Melville had belonged from 1835 to 1838. Despite Melville's past connection with the society, it is unlikely that he later consented to lecture there in 1847. It is also unlikely that he lectured in Troy (see the entry for his reply to the Troy Young Men's Association written before 28 November 1846, above).

Hooper C Van Vorst Esq
&c &c &c

Dear Sir — Yours of the 14 Inst was forwarded to me from Lansingburgh. —— The Troy Association received a conditional promise from me, upon the strength of which they have advertised my name. — The invitation from Schenectady I declined.

It will be impossible for me to be in Albany on the 29ᵗʰ Inst (the day you mention). But in case I lecture anywhere, or at all, I shall be most happy to lecture before your association in Albany.

I shall be in your city in the early part of next month
Very Faithfully Yours
Herman Melville

New York Jan 19, '47.

ALS on a 49.8 × 24.8 cm sheet, folded in half, of blue wove paper. Melville inscribed the first two pages, in ink. Another hand, possibly Van Vorst's, noted in ink on the fourth page "Herman Melville | Author of Typee". Still another hand, probably a librarian's, later made the notation on the fourth page in pencil "Herman Melville | 1819 — | Poet and novelist. | See Drake, & Appleton".

LOCATION: Gratz Collection, Historical Society of Pennsylvania, Philadelphia. *Provenance*: Simon Gratz.

PUBLICATION: (partial) *Log*, I, 233. Davis-Gilman 31.

TEXTUAL NOTE: Albany.] *before* (over) *in bottom margin*

TO EVERT A. DUYCKINCK
21 JANUARY 1847 · NEW YORK

Evert Duyckinck had signed a contract on 15 January 1847 with the publishers Appleton and Wiley & Putnam to edit, with his younger brother George Long Duyckinck (1823–63), a new weekly, the *Literary World*. They were to have an allotment, as Evert reported to George in a letter of that same day, of a thousand dollars for contributors (NYPL-D). One of Evert Duyckinck's first requests for contributions must have gone to Melville, asking for advance chapters of *Omoo*, but this letter suggests that Melville thought it best to wait, and no extracts of the book appeared in the magazine until the 24 April issue.

From Duyckinck's endorsement on this letter, Melville's "Thursday Morning" can be dated as 21 January 1847. Melville may have written this letter at Allan's residence, which was at 533 Broadway, or he may have written it at the offices of Wiley & Putnam, which were also on Broadway.

My Dear Sir
Upon reflection I question the propriety of publishing any part of the book I am about bringing out so long previous to the publication of the whole.

However, this will not prevent your publishing a chapter or so at a more suitable time, should you desire to —

Yours Truly
Herman Melville

Thursday Morning — Broadway.

ALS on a 25.3 × 20.1 cm part-sheet (torn along the top) of blue wove paper with lines, embossed with the manufacturer's square stamp enclosing the initials "W C & Co" on the second leaf of the folded sheet. Melville inscribed the first page, in ink, and addressed the fourth page "Evart A Duyckinke". Duyckinck noted in ink on that page "H Melville | Recd Jan 21. 1847".

LOCATION: NYPL-D.

PUBLICATION: *Log*, I, 233. Davis-Gilman 32.

TO HARPER & BROTHERS
[23 OR 30?] JANUARY 1847 · [NEW YORK?]

Although Melville headed it only "Saturday morning," this letter can be dated on the basis of the copyright records for *Omoo*. On 18 December 1846 Melville signed the contract with Harper & Brothers for his second book, which stated that the copyright was the author's "sole property" (HCL-M). On 30 January 1847 either Melville or the Harpers on his behalf deposited the title of *Omoo* at the court for the Southern District of New York. It was probably that initial step in the copyright process that Melville was referring to in this letter. The district court ledger records that the published book was deposited on 5 May, only four days after it was announced in the 1 May *Literary World* as "now ready." This was well within the specified six-month time-limit for making the deposit (see G. Thomas Tanselle,

"Copyright Records and the Bibliographer," *Selected Studies in Bibliography* [Char-
lottesville: The University Press of Virginia], p. 102). Thus, there would have been
no reason for Melville to have been concerned about the copyright after the book's
actual appearance. (The catalogue description of the letter [see below], mistakenly
dating it as late April or early May 1847, apparently assumes it to be associated with
the publication of the book.) But between 18 December 1846, when he signed the
contract, and 30 January 1847, just before he mailed the proof sheets to John Murray aboard the 1 February *Hibernia*, Melville had good reason to be concerned that
the American copyright had not yet been taken out. This letter could have been
written on any Saturday during that period, but, given its urgent tone, was most
likely written toward the end of January, either on Saturday, the twenty-third, or
the thirtieth—the same day that the title was deposited.

Saturday morning

Gentlemen — The copyright has not yet been taken out for *Omoo*.
— I rely upon your taking it out immediately; & trust, that you will
attend to all that is necessary.

Truly yours,
Herman Melville

Original document not located. Text from catalogue transcription.

LOCATION: at present unknown. *Provenance*: Edward and Betty Marcus Foundation; Christie's, 22 November 1985, lot 83.

PUBLICATION: "Herman at Christie's: On the Block—Again," *Melville Society Extracts* 63 (September 1985), 10.

TO JOHN MURRAY
29 JANUARY 1847 · NEW YORK

The day after writing this letter to Murray, Melville signed the legal papers em-
powering John R. Brodhead to sell the English copyright of *Omoo* (formerly in the
collection of H. Bradley Martin). He sent them, the American proof sheets, and
this letter by the *Hibernia*, which sailed from New York on 1 February 1847. Since
Murray still had not formally accepted *Omoo*, this letter is in part a reiteration to
him of the book's authenticity and an explanation of its peculiarities (e.g., chap. 63,
which had been reworked from a chapter rejected from *Typee*), but it is also in part
a set of instructions to Murray, based on the assumption that he would publish the
book. When he did so, Murray, in accord with these instructions, did not alter the
title of *Omoo*, as he had that of *Typee*; he also retained the map Melville enclosed
and the dedication to Melville's uncle Herman Gansevoort, of Gansevoort, Saratoga County, New York.

New York January 29th 1847.

My Dear Sir — I presume that before this you have received my letter by the steamer of the 1st of January. By the steamer which carries you this, I send to M[r] John Romeyn Brodhead of the American Legation the proof sheets of my new work. He will immediately cause them to be placed in your hands; and I have fully authorised him to treat in my behalf for the sale of the book. In case you would like to publish it, I anticipate no difficulty in M[r] Brodhead's making an arrangement with you satisfactory to all concerned. I preferred having some one to act for me in London, thinking that it would be much better, all round. ——

I beleive that I informed you in my last that I had made it a positive condition with the Harpers — my publishers here — that the work should not be published by them until I advise them so to do. Of course, this is with the view of securing a copyright for the English publisher. And I shall not instruct them to publish until I hear definitively from England as to the day upon which publication will take place in that country. It is most important, however, that the work should be published as soon as possible. The stereeotype plates are cast, & publication held *here* in suspence. — The steamer which carries out the proof sheets to M[r] Brodhead, will arrive about the 20th of February — perhaps before that time — leaving ample time for arrangements for publication to be made in London, so as to send me definite advices by the steamer which leaves your shores on the 4th of March next. — Should you come to an understanding with M[r] Brodhead, & agree to publish, I confidently rely upon hearing from you by that opportunity — & that you will then *name the day* upon which publication will take place — so that as little delay as possible may be occasioned in bringing the work out here. — I deem it proper to state that every possible precaution has been taken to prevent the getting abroad of any of the proof sheets — & that not the slightest apprehension is to be entertained that it will come out *here* before it does in London. —— Of course, owing to the before-mentioned understanding with the Harpers, the proof sheets which I send to London, are as valuable to a publisher there, as the M.S.S of the book would have been, transmitted to England direct, & previous to making any arrangements here for publication. —— I send M[r] Brodhead a power of attorney, which makes him, in this matter, my authorized agent. —

Of the book itself, of course, you will judge for yourself. So I will not say, what opinions of it have been given here by persons competent to judge of its merits as a work calculated for popular reading. — But I think you will find it a fitting successor to "Typee"; inasmuch as the latter book delineates Polynisian Life in its primitive state — while the new work, represents it, as affected by intercourse with the whites. It also describes the "man about town" sort of life, led, at the present day, by roving sailors in the Pacific — a kind of thing, which I have never seen described anywhere. — The title of the work, may be thought a curious one — but after reading the narrative no one will doubt its propriety as explained in the Preface. — It might, however, be advisable to add to the title as it now stands, the following: — "Including Some Account of a Sojourn on the Island of Tahiti" — But whether this be added or not, I desire the title (as it now appears) to remain untouched — its oddity, or uniqueness, if you please conveys some insight into the nature of the book. It gives a sort of Polynisian expression to its "figure-head." — At any rate, no one questions the right of a parent to dub his offspring as he pleases; — the same should be accorded to an author.

— You will perceive that there is a chapter in the book which describes a dance in the valley of Tamai. This discription has been modified & adapted from a certain chapter which it was thought best to exclude from Typee. In their dances the Tahitians much resembled the Marquesans (the two groups of islands are not far apart) & thus is the discription faithful in both instances.

— In the early part of the work, I make free use of nautical terms without, in all cases, explaining their use. But I am well warranted in so doing by the practice of the most successful writers — Marryatt, Cooper, Dana &c. —— With the proof sheets, I send a map, a draught of the one which will appear with the book here. I have had it drawn expressly for the work. — I think it essential. The dedication, of course, I wish to appear in the English edition. —— I am desirous that the book shall appear in England, just as I send it: altho' there may be some minor errors — typographical — as the plates have been hurried in order to get them ready in time for the steamer. They will be gone over & corrected before publication here. — However, there is no error, which any proof reader might not correct. — the omitting of a figure in the pageing &c. —— In case any thing unforseen should prevent Mr Brodhead from acting in my behalf, the proof sheets will be placed in your hands, unconditionally — in which case, as prompt action is imperative, I rely upon your at once going forward with the publication of the book (should you be pleased with it) & giving me (to use the language of your letter to me) "as liberal an offer as you can" which offer, under the circumstances, you will have to consider accepted, should the above contingency occur. —

Very Truly Yours
Herman Melville

I expected to have heard from you by the last steamer (4th Jan.) but have not heard from you.

You may address me at New York "Care of Allan Melville N° 10 Wall Street."

ALS on a 39.8 × 24.8 cm sheet, folded in half, of blue wove paper, embossed with the manufacturer's small oval stamp enclosing the initials "P & S". Melville inscribed all four pages, in ink. Another hand, presumably a clerk's, noted in ink at the top of the second page "Jan. 29. 1847 | Melville H".

Location: Murray.

Publication: (partial) Log, I, 233–34. Davis, pp. 208–10. Davis-Gilman 33.

Textual Notes: And] originally As • publication will] will inserted with caret above canceled can • little] before canceled day • my authorized] a written over another letter • also describes] es rewritten • figure-head] figure-|head • pageing] eing written over wiped ing • the proof] written over wiped he will • case,] before canceled I rely upon your • an offer] before a wiped closing double quotation mark • I expected . . . from you.] added in the left margin of the fourth page; placed here editorially • You may . . . Wall Street."] added in the left margin of the first page; placed here editorially

TO JOHN R. BRODHEAD
BEFORE 1 FEBRUARY 1847 · [NEW YORK?]

Unlocated. A letter can be inferred from Melville's 30 December 1846 letter to Brodhead, in which he had stated that he would write "fully by the steamer of the 1st of February" when sending the proof sheets for Omoo. In his letter Melville may have instructed Brodhead to get an immediate cash settlement, an arrangement Brodhead requested as soon as Murray accepted the book. On 1 March Murray in a note to Brodhead agreed to pay at once after "deducting the customary interest" (formerly in the collection of H. Bradley Martin; for more on Brodhead's negotiations with Murray see the headnote to Melville's 31 March 1847 letter to Brodhead, below). Davis-Gilman Unlocated 299.

TO EVERT A. DUYCKINCK
2 FEBRUARY 1847 · NEW YORK

This note, written while Melville was in New York overseeing the shipment of the proof sheets of *Omoo* to Murray, can be dated the "Tuesday Morning" of 2 February 1847—the day before 3 February 1847 when Duyckinck received it, according to his endorsement. The "article" Melville mentions here was his review of John Ross Browne's *Etchings of a Whaling Cruise, with Notes of a Sojourn on the Island of Zanzibar. To Which Is Appended a Brief History of the Whale Fishery; Its Past and Present Condition* (New York: Harper, 1846). This note was at one time fastened to the first leaf of the manuscript of the review (NYPL-D). The review appeared in the *Literary World* on 6 March 1847, pp. 105–6 (see the NN *Piazza Tales* volume, pp. 205–11, 464–65, 625–36). It provoked an "expostulatory letter"—now unlocated—from Browne to Frederick Saunders at Harper & Brothers about an "error" in the review. Saunders in turn gave Allan Melville a copy of that letter—also unlocated—and wrote to Duyckinck about publishing a correction of the unspecified error (NYPL-D). No correction, however, was published (see R. D. Madison, "Melville's Review of Browne's *Etchings*," *Melville Society Extracts* 53 [February 1983], 11–13).

The opera Melville saw was Donizetti's *Lucia di Lammermoor*, sung by Ferdinando Beneventano and Clotilde Barili, at Palmo's Opera House (for Melville's later use of Beneventano's name in "Cock-A-Doodle-Doo!" see the NN *Piazza Tales* volume, pp. 282–83, 694). Melville probably attended the sixth and final performance held on Monday, 1 February.

My Dear Sir

I sincerely regret that an unforseen circumstance should have prevented me from being at your house at the time appointed. I should have called at some other time during the evening, but I had previously engaged to go to the Opera.

I have procured the book you spoke of from the Harpers — & shall find much pleasure in making it the basis of an article for your paper

Yours Very Truly
Herman Melville

Tuesday Morning.

ALS on a 24.8 × 19.9 cm part-sheet (torn along the bottom), folded in half, of blue wove paper. Melville inscribed the first page, in ink, and addressed the fourth page "Evart A Duyckincke Esq. | At Wiley & Putnam's". Duyckinck later noted in ink on that page "Herman Melville | recd Feb. 3. 1847." Some penciled calculations are also on the fourth page.

LOCATION: NYPL-D.

PUBLICATION: *Log*, I, 234 (dated 1 February). Davis-Gilman 34.

TEXTUAL NOTES: Opera] O *written over* o • it] *inserted above caret*

TO PETER GANSEVOORT
3 FEBRUARY 1847 · NEW YORK

The New Loan Bill of January 1847, authorizing an issuance of Treasury notes to the amount of $23,000,000 at six percent for government expenses, was expected to create new jobs, one of which Melville was hoping to obtain (see also the entry for the letter he wrote his mother before 25 December 1846). As Melville requested here, his uncle Peter Gansevoort supplied him a letter to John Adams Dix (1798–1879), a senator from New York and a personal friend of his uncle. Any efforts Dix made on Melville's behalf at this time, however, were overshadowed by the feud then raging between the "Barnburner" or radical faction of the New York Democrats, of which Dix was a member, and the "Hunkers" or conservative wing of the party, headed by Secretary of War William L. Marcy—also known to Melville's uncle Peter—over the defeat of Silas Wright for governor of New York. For this and other reasons, Melville failed to obtain a government post; for a further discussion of the other factors working against him, see Hayford-Davis, p. 171. For Peter Gansevoort's reply, see LETTERS RECEIVED, pp. 586–87.

My Dear Uncle

I hear that by the passage of the New Loan Bill a number of additional officers are to be at once created in the Treasury Department at Washington. — I have determined upon going on there, with a view of making an application for one — or, if I do not succeed in this specific object, to press such claims as I have upon some other point.

I have obtained several strong letters from various prominant persons here to the most influential men at the seat of government. And my purpose in writing you is to obtain from you another letter to Gen: Dix, which would be of great service to me. —— As I leave here tomorrow, if you will immediately write & enclose the letter to my address at Washington it will reach me there very shortly after my arrival. ——

My best rememberances to my Aunt & cousins, and Beleive
Me, Very Sincerely, Yours

Herman Melville

New York Feb 3ᵈ '47

ALS on a 20 × 24.9 cm part-sheet (torn along the left edge) of blue wove paper, embossed
with the manufacturer's small oval stamp enclosing the initials "P & S". Melville inscribed
only one side of the leaf, in ink. He addressed the envelope "Gen: Peter Gansevoort | Albany."
and wrote *"Paid"* in the upper left corner; it was postmarked in New York on 4 February.
The envelope is also covered with numerous penciled calculations.

Location: NYPL-GL.

Publication: Paltsits, p. 11. Davis-Gilman 35.

Textual Note: Treasury] *written over another word*

TO EDWIN CROSWELL
[3?] FEBRUARY 1847 · NEW YORK

Unlocated. A letter to Edwin Croswell, Gansevoort Melville's former political ally
(see the headnote to Melville's 4 July 1846 letter to Croswell), is cited in Maria
Melville's 8 February letter quoted in the entry just below. Melville apparently
wrote to Croswell for advice or assistance in obtaining a government post (see also
Melville's letter to his uncle Peter on this subject, just above).

TO MARIA GANSEVOORT MELVILLE
[4?] FEBRUARY 1847 · [WASHINGTON, D.C.?]

Unlocated. Either on his way or after arriving in Washington, D.C., on 4 February
1847, Melville wrote to his mother in Lansingburgh. Her 8 February 1847 addendum
to a 6 February letter of Helen's to Augusta, who was visiting in Albany, reports: "I
had a long letter from Herman without date postmark'd the 4ᵗʰ however. He has gone
on to Washington there are many new offices to be created forthwith under a recent act
of Congress, in the [']Treasury department,' say nothing on the subject, but he has
written to Uncle Peter for an introductory letter to Gen Dix, to Mʳ Crosswell also, he
seems to be in good spirits, has provided himself with many good letters from prominent men at New York to influential Characters at Washington.

"He seems to feel that if he succeeds at all in getting an appointment it will be
brought about by his own *personal exertions* at head quarters. I am glad that he is at
last convinced of this important truth.

"It is worth a fortune to any man to understand this, and act it out, it is a
lesson Herman has been long in learning but he is young enough to profit by it still.
I hope *God* will see fit to bless his endeavours, and if it is for his & our good that he
may succeed.

"Lizzie wrote that Herman was expected at Boston if only for one day. — on his way home so this visit to Washington must be a very sudden affair, he writes his prospects of success are good, but if he do not succeed he would not be surprized but that there will be no lack of exersion on his part, 'the hopes is well 'Dutty,' ['] and the Ledger & day book are getting on bravely. He has not heard from Mr Murray by the Hibernia. Herman writes that he was shewn a very pretty volume of Poetry by M^r W^m E Chaning of Boston they are now published for the first time, one is call'd the 'Island of Nukehiva'[.] It is poetically descriptive of Tipee and is very pretty. Allan will send up the volume together with the remainder of the proof Sheets of Omoo, the first opportunity" (NYPL-GL). The volume of poetry was William Ellery Channing's *Poems*, Second Series (Boston: Munroe, 1847; Sealts 131a).

TO RICHARD T. GREENE
BEFORE 19 FEBRUARY 1847 · LANSINGBURGH

Unlocated. Sometime after the middle of July 1846, when Melville traveled to Buffalo to see his shipboard friend Richard Tobias (Toby) Greene, he apparently received a letter from him requesting some share in the profits of *Typee*, probably prompted by the appearance of "The Story of Toby" in the revised edition. In his response, Melville must have handled the situation deftly because Greene then replied with an apologetic letter. The only present documentation of this correspondence is a letter from Helen Melville, then in Lansingburgh, to her sister Augusta, visiting in Albany, on 19 February 1847. She indicates that Greene's letter of apology arrived "by to-days mail." For her description of the contents of this letter as well as Greene's earlier letter, see LETTERS RECEIVED, p. 588. She concludes by giving some hint of the nature of Melville's letter to Greene that elicited the apology: "I could not bear that a cloud should come between such old and tried friends. Herman's reply to his letter, so beautifully gentle & noble, without any spice or anger of contempt for his unworthy conduct, has brought him to his senses and the result really rejoices me" (NYPL-GL). There is no indication whether Melville wrote a letter to Greene acknowledging the apology.

TO MARIA GANSEVOORT MELVILLE
BEFORE 19 FEBRUARY 1847 · WASHINGTON, D.C.

Unlocated. While Melville was still in Washington, fifty pounds arrived from John Murray, the payment he had promised for the revised edition of *Typee*. Maria Melville's Lansingburgh letter of 19 February 1847 to Augusta, visiting in Albany, reports: "I heard from Herman dated Washington, he has received letters from Messrs Murray & Broadhead, the former with the £50, enclosure, he desires me to get Dr Nelsons [unidentified] bill against him 'individually,' and to have the amount sent to me and it shall immediately be paid, he also wishes me to divide forty dollars between his Sisters as a small 'very slight testimonial of his love & remembrance of them', 'very kind'. 'He also says let them do with the money as they will'[.] This money enables dear Herman to pay all his little debts, to retain fifty dollars for himself and the remainder, I am to

have, of course deducting the beautiful gift of forty — to his belove'd Sisters — he
hopes I will say 'no restraint whatever on the disposition of it.'

"The whole sum of £50, is small, but the proper disposition thereof is beautiful, it at once showing his love of justice in paying his debts, his affection and
gratitude to his Sisters, and his filial love to his Mother — Herman said not a word
about the contents of Mr Broadheads missive" (NYPL-GL). The "missive" Maria
Melville refers to was probably the now unlocated letter that John R. Brodhead
wrote in London on 14 January 1847 in response to Melville's letter of 30 December
1846 (see LETTERS RECEIVED, pp. 585–86).

TO JOHN R. BRODHEAD
31 MARCH 1847 · NEW YORK

As Melville's agent in London, Brodhead proved indispensable. When the proof
sheets of *Omoo* arrived in England on the *Hibernia*, they were "wrongfully seized"
as a piracy by the Liverpool customs officer, who thought they were "an American
reprint of an English Author, entitled '*a Narrative of a voyage to the north seas, by
Melville*' "—as indicated by a draft of Brodhead's 18 February 1847 letter to the
customs officials (formerly in the collection of H. Bradley Martin; published in
Birss, "A Mere Sale to Effect," p. 242). After obtaining the release of the proof
sheets, Brodhead had them delivered to Murray via John Miller, the dispatch agent
at the American legation, to whose services Melville alludes here.

According to Brodhead's diary, Murray on 25 February 1847 offered £150 for
the book, "payable £100. by note at eight months from the day of publication, &
£50. by cheque at 12 months date from the first publication." Brodhead commented, "I think the terms not liberal enough, & yet I shall have to take them I suppose." The next day Murray convinced him that "so far from Melville's first Book
helping the sale of the second, he [Murray] hoped the reverse would be true, for he
had not yet sold enough of the first to pay expenses" (Alexander Library, Rutgers
University). On 28 February Brodhead noted in his diary that he accepted Murray's
offer but asked that it be paid in cash. Replying by letter on 1 March, Murray
agreed to pay "at once, on the publication £144..3..4 in cash," thus deducting the
customary interest (formerly in the collection of H. Bradley Martin). This letter is
Melville's response to Brodhead's now unlocated letter of 3 March 1847, reporting
these arrangements and enclosing copies of his correspondence with Murray (also
unlocated). For more on the sale of *Omoo* and Brodhead's London diary entries and
correspondence concerning it, see the NN *Omoo*, pp. 331–33.

N° 10 Wall Street, New York

March 31st 1847

My Dear Sir — Your letter by the Hibernia of the 3^d of March
enclosing copies of notes between Mr Murray & yourself & informing me of the sale of "Omoo" was duly received.

You authorise me to draw on you for £144.3.4 as the proceeds of the sale. I have accordingly, thro' the house of Prime Ward & Co, drawn bills on you at one day's sight (payable at Barings) for £140 — thus deducting from the original sum a small item for the expences you were put to in rescuing from the Vandals of the Liverpool Custom House "The American pirated copy of "Typee" — & also to provide for any little outlay which may be occasioned by your granting me a little favor I have yet to beg of you.

The precise pecuniary value of most unpublished works is so uncertain & hard to be estimated (especially, under the circumstances, with respect to my new work) that I hardly (between you & me) know how liberal to consider Mr Murray's offer which you accepted áfter due consideration. — At any rate, I have a high opinion of his general liberality in these matters; — and, My Dear Sir, you may beleive me, when I assure you, that I have no doubt you have done all that you could do — for which I need hardly add, you have my best & sincerest thanks.

The book will be out here about the 10th or 12th of april.

You may naturally suppose that I have much curiosity to see how "Omoo" will be received by the sagatious Critics of the English press; & as I have not, now, that intimate correspondence with London which I had not very long since, may I beg of you the favor, to have an eye, occasionaly, upon the Reviews, & to cause to be collected & sent me, in their original form, whatever notices may appear of the book. — Mr Miller, I beleive, used to assist my late brother in these matters. —— In a letter, which I am just about to address to Mr Murray I am going to request him to put up a package for me of several copies of his edition of the book — & I have taken the liberty to suggest that he might send the same to the office of the Legation to be, thence, forwarded to me. — I shall also tell Mr Murray that if there is any thing to be paid, you will attend to it.

Once more, permit me, My Dear Mr Brodhead to tender you my hearty thanks for your friendly agency in my behalf — & to express the hope that I may hear from you whenever your diplomatic engagements admit of epistolary recreation.

With great consideration
& True Regard
I am Yours
Herman Melville.

J Romeyn Brodhead Esq.
Secretary of Legation.

ALS on a 39.8 × 24.8 cm sheet, folded in half, of blue wove paper, embossed with the manufacturer's small oval stamp enclosing the initials "P & S". Melville inscribed the first three pages, in ink. Brodhead noted in ink on the upper left corner of the first page "Ansd 19 Apl", with two lines, one above and one below this note.

LOCATION: at present unknown. *Provenance*: H. Bradley Martin sale, Sotheby's, New York, sale 5971, 30–31 January 1990, in lot 2167; 19th Century Shop, catalogue 17 (September 1990), in item 151.

PUBLICATION: Birss, "A Mere Sale to Effect," pp. 244–45. Davis-Gilman 36.

TEXTUAL NOTES: "The] T *written over* t • "The . . . "Typee"] *second closing double quotation mark lacking* • outlay] *before canceled* you may • I have no doubt] *inserted above caret* • have much] *after canceled* am

TO JOHN MURRAY
31 MARCH 1847 · NEW YORK

This letter to Murray, like the one above written on the same day to John R. Brodhead—both from Allan Melville's law office on Wall Street—was occasioned by Brodhead's now unlocated letter of 3 March 1847 announcing the arrangements he had made with Murray for the publication of *Omoo*. As usual in his letters to Murray, Melville is quick to defend himself against charges of inauthenticity. In this case, the London *Literary Gazette* (12 December 1846) had good-humoredly reproved reviewers for treating *Typee* as "real and authentic" and by way of apology for not "noticing this clever and entertaining production" invited Melville "to dine with us on the 1st of April next: we intend to ask only a small party,—Messrs. Crusoe, Sinbad, Gulliver, Munchausen, and perhaps Pillet, Thiers, Kohl, and a few others."

Murray's note on this letter indicates that at Brodhead's request he later sent six copies of *Omoo* to Melville through Wiley & Putnam.

Nº 10 Wall Street, New York.
March 31ˢᵗ 1847.

Dear Sir — By the steamer of the 4ᵗʰ Inst Mʳ Brodhead informed me that he had disposed of the English copyright of "Omoo" to you for £150, subject, however, to a deduction on account of a cash payment. — As Mʳ Brodhead advises me that the money will be paid over to him on the day of publication (April 1ˢᵗ) I have accordingly (at his suggestion) drawn bills on him at one day's sight. I suppose that this will be all right. — The book will not be out here until about the 10ᵗʰ or 12ᵗʰ of April — thus securing your copyright effectually.

— I trust that the reception which has been predicted for "Omoo" may be verified by the event. If it succeed, the two books can not fail to sell together, & thus assist each other. At any rate, I hope that the sagatious Critic of the London Literary Gazette will hereafter abate something of his incredulity. I can assure him, that I am really in existance. Bye the by, will you be so good as to send me the reviews which may appear of "Omoo" — also, if it be not too much trouble, a few copies — say six — of your edition of the book. Mr Brodhead will defray all expences & the package, if you please, may be sent to his care at the office of the Legation, & so come to me by the Despatch Bag. You may likewise enclose in the package, if convenient, some of your monthly circulars announcing the book as forthcoming. ——

If "Omoo" succeeds I shall follow it up by something else, immediately. — I trust you will not fail to write me should any thing of interest to me turn up.

With Sincere Regard
Beleive Me, Dear Sir
Yours
Herman Melville

Mr John Murray
Albemarl Street.

ALS on a 19.9 × 24.8 cm part-sheet (torn along the left edge) of blue wove paper, embossed with the manufacturer's small oval stamp enclosing the initials "P & S". Melville inscribed both sides of the leaf, in ink. Another hand, possibly Murray's, noted in pencil across the top of the first page (with a penciled line beneath) "I have sent 6 copies thro' Wiley & P. by request of Mr Broadhead". A different hand, presumably a clerk's, noted in ink on the second page "March 31 1847 | Melville Herman".

LOCATION: Murray.

PUBLICATION: (partial) *Log*, I, 239–40. Davis, p. 211. Davis-Gilman 37.

TEXTUAL NOTES: verifyed] y *written over* i • hereafter] *inserted above caret* • assure] *after canceled* assure • really] *miswritten* realley • send me] me *inserted above caret* • your edition] *after canceled* the • Despatch] t *written over another* c

TO EDWIN CROSWELL
2 APRIL 1847 · NEW YORK

On 3 April 1847 the first advertisement announcing *Omoo* appeared in the *Literary World*. With publication imminent, Melville again enlisted the support of Gansevoort's former associate, Edwin Croswell, editor of the *Albany Argus*. As on previous occasions (see Melville's 4 July 1846 letter to Croswell and the entry for his unlocated letter to the *Argus* written before 21 April 1846, above), Croswell's paper promoted Melville's books. On 7 April it issued an announcement of the forthcoming work, which concluded: "We anticipate for this work, equal popularity with that to which it forms the interesting sequel. We infer this not only from its authorship, but from the high price readily paid for the copy-right by the great London publisher." On 3 May, two days after the American publication of *Omoo*, it published a favorable notice. Subsequently, the *Argus* reprinted on 18 June 1849 a review from the 15 June *Boston Daily Advertiser*, which was in turn a synopsis and partial translation of the complimentary and semi-biographical article on Melville and *Omoo* that had appeared in the 15 May 1849 Paris *Revue des deux mondes*. The "note" from Murray to Brodhead praising the new work is now unlocated.

Nº 10 Wall Street, New York.
April 2ᵈ 1847.

My Dear Sir — After considerable unavoidable delay I have completed arrangements for the simultaneous publication of a new work in this country & in England. — I will direct to be sent to your address this day from the office of publication a number (marked "Private") of the "Literary World" announcing in an advertisement the book as forthcoming. — Glance at the advertisement, if you please, & do me the honor of saying something, editorially, in your paper. — Mʳ Murray (who has purchased the copyright for England) speaks of the book in a very high strain of compliment in a note to Mʳ Brodhead of the Legation. But he paid the work a still better & more satisfactory compliment in the offer he made for it.

With high consideration & true regard, Beleive me,

Yours,
Herman Melville

Edwin Croswell, Esq.
Albany

ALS on a 12.4 × 19.9 cm part-sheet (torn along the left edge) of blue wove paper, faintly embossed with the manufacturer's small circular stamp enclosing a shield. Melville inscribed both sides of the leaf, in ink.

LOCATION: The Newberry Library, Chicago. *Provenance*: Elliot's Books (1967).

PUBLICATION: *Log*, I, 237, 240. Davis-Gilman 38.

TO HARPER & BROTHERS
[23?] APRIL 1847 · NEW YORK

Although Melville expected the Harpers to publish *Omoo* on 10 or 12 April 1847—as his 31 March letter to John R. Brodhead had stated—and an announcement appeared in the *Literary World* on 10 April that the book was "just ready," delay of the publication date had become a matter of some entertainment. *Yankee Doodle* announced (10 April): "Important If True—Mr. Herman Melville's forthcoming work, OMOO." Advance extracts did not appear until 24 April and the book itself was not announced as "now ready" until 1 May.

This brief note to the Harpers, dated only "Friday morning," is clearly associated with this period and was probably written on 23 April 1847—the Friday prior to 26 April, when Melville wrote to his second cousin Augustus Van Schaick, enclosing a presentation copy of the book (see below). A second presentation copy went to Melville's uncle Herman Gansevoort, dated 31 April 1847 (now in the Rosenbach Museum & Library).

Dear Sir — Will you put up a couple of bound copies of Omoo for the bearer — of course they are ready by this time

Yours Truly
Herman Melville

Friday morning.

ALS on a 12.1 × 18.4 cm part-sheet (torn along the left edge) of white wove paper. Melville inscribed only one side of the leaf, in ink; it was later pasted to another sheet but has since been detached.

LOCATION: NYPL–Ford Collection. *Provenance*: Gordon Lester Ford; J. P. Morgan.

PUBLICATION: *Log*, I, 241. Davis-Gilman 39.

TO AUGUSTUS P. VAN SCHAICK
26 APRIL 1847 · NEW YORK

Augustus Platt Van Schaick (1822–47), the grandson of John Gerritse Van Schaick, brother to Melville's maternal grandmother, was Melville's second cousin. An immediate link between the two was Maria Melville's cousin and neighbor, Maria Van Schaick Peebles, Augustus's aunt, to whom, as Melville indicates here, Augustus often wrote. The mutual friend or relative "Topping" mentioned at the beginning of Melville's letter is unidentified. Augustus graduated from Rensselaer Polytechnic Institute in 1839, then worked as an engineer on the Erie Canal and on the Troy & Schenectady Railroad. For a period he was a grain-dealer in Lansingburgh. As early as April 1846 Augusta Melville noted how miserable he was looking and feared that his constitution could not stand the voyage to China he was reported to be planning for his health. He went instead to Rio de Janeiro—where Melville sent him this letter. He did not live to "send a challenge" to the English prizefighter "Bendigo"—William Thompson (1811–80) of Nottingham—who on 9 September 1846 had won a ninety-three-round bout and the champion's belt from Benjamin Gaunt. On 10 September 1847 Augustus died at sea on his way home. He is said to have been "the author of many figurative pieces, descriptive, religious, and

*prove to be the case in my
Queen of present wish. If you
will take the advice of one who
does you you will keep up
a radiant heart — 'Nil Desperandum
— so as to come back
to us again & send to
challenge across the lake to
fight Bendigo for the
Champion's Belt of all
England. — All whom
I see desire much happiness
for you & send regard
With true regard*

I am yours

Norman Melville

To Augustus P. Van Schaick, 26 April 1847, p. 3. Courtesy of Clifton Waller Barrett Library, Manuscripts Division, Special Collections Department,
the University of Virginia Library (Herman Melville Collection, #6252-A).

humorous," but there is no record of published work, though it may have appeared, like Melville's juvenilia, in the Lansingburgh or other local papers. See Cuyler Reynolds, *Hudson-Mohawk Genealogical and Family Memoirs* (New York: Lewis Historical Publishing Co., 1911), III, 994; *Biographical Record of the Officers and Graduates of the Rensselaer Polytechnic Institute, 1824–86*, ed. Henry B. Nason (Troy: Young, 1887), pp. 236–37; Augusta Melville to Catharine Van Schaick, 6 April 1846, and Augustus Van Schaick to Catharine Van Schaick, 16 June 1843, in Van Schaick-Baldwin-Walter Papers, New York State Library.

As Augustus Van Schaick's endorsement on its fourth page indicates, this letter accompanied a presentation copy of *Omoo*, now unlocated. Before the book arrived on 6 July, Van Schaick had already made inquiries about it in a 20 May 1847 letter to a friend identified only as "Dutch," asking "has Melville been broaching his brain again, or what is 'Omoo' " (UV-Barrett). Van Schaick's 6 July reply to Melville is now unlocated.

New York April 26. 1847

My Dear Augustus

Topping told me the other day that a ship was about to sail for Rio to day or tomorrow — & thereupon I gave orders to the Harpers to prepare a copy of my new work for you in anticipation of the day of regular publication. — I now take great pleasure in sending it to you & trust its perusal may afford you some pleasure.

When I was last in Lansingburgh Cousin Maria read me a considerable portion of one of your last letters & I was much pleased to see that you had by no means lost that pleasantry of humor you had when here — From this I infer that you are not quite cast-down & indeed I think you have no reason to be, seeing that the beautiful climate of Rio must reinvigorate you & make you a robust fellow after all. That this will prove to be the case is my sincere & fervent wish. If you will take the advice of one who loves you you will keep up a valiant heart — Nil Desperandum — so as to come back to us again & send a challenge across the water to fight Bendigo for the Champion's Belt of all England. — All whom I see desire much happiness for you & send regard

With true regard
I am yours
Herman Melville

ALS on a 39.8 × 24.8 cm sheet, folded in half, of blue wove paper, embossed with the manufacturer's small oval stamp enclosing the initials "P & S". Melville inscribed the first three pages, in ink. Van Schaick noted on the verso in ink "Herman Melville | with copy of

'Omoo' | Recd July 6. 47 | per 'L. Ruig' | Ans^d July 6. 47 — " ("L. Ruig" is a conjectural reading) and also in the same ink made a calculation.

LOCATION: UV-Barrett. *Provenance*: Victor Hugo Paltsits; Howard S. Mott catalogue (1948); Joseph E. Fields; Goodspeed's Book Shop.

PUBLICATION: (partial) *Log*, I, 241–42. Davis-Gilman 40.

TEXTUAL NOTE: water] *miswritten* wate

TO AUGUSTUS P. VAN SCHAICK
11 JUNE 1847 · LANSINGBURGH

Throughout Augustus Van Schaick's stay in Rio de Janeiro, family members wrote him encouraging letters. This hurriedly written 11 June letter and the earlier letter of 26 April 1847, just above, were part of the campaign, as was that of Melville's sister Helen written on the same day as this one and probably enclosed with it (UV-Barrett). In it she reported on her brother's recent return from Boston, where he had made "arrangements to take upon himself the dignified character of a married man some time during the summer"; she went on to mention the successful sales of *Omoo*: "In one week after it was issued the whole edition of 3000; or 3,500 was disposed of and another was put in progress. It has been more highly spoken of on both sides of the Atlantic than its predecessor even, as containing more instructive matter. He bears himself very meekly under his honors however, and to prove it to you, I may mention casually, that he is now at work in the garden, very busy hoeing his favorite tomatoes" (UV-Barrett).

The "gruff" captain, whose son was evidently the bearer of both letters, was George Washington Storer (1789–1864), who had married Mary S. Blount and had four children. The son may have been the midshipman Robert B[lount?]. Storer, who died at sea, 4 July 1847 (*General Navy Register, 1775–1900*), and thus did not complete the delivery of this letter to Van Schaick or provide the companionship Melville anticipated. George Washington Storer was commissioned a captain 9 February 1837, commanded the receiving ship *Constellation* (Boston, 1839), later the *Potomac* (Brazil station, 1840–42), was then stationed at the navy yard, Portsmouth (1843–46), and was appointed Commander in Chief of the Brazil squadron (1847–50) at exactly the time of this letter. He retired in 1862 with the rank of rear admiral. See Malcolm Storer, *Annals of the Storer Family* (Boston, 1927), p. 56.

Lansingburgh
June 11th '47

My Dear Fellow — I have but time to write you a single line — I hear that young Storer leaves to day for New York. — Cousin Maria read me good part of your last letter home. I was much amused with your account of the delightfully according terms upon which you lived with your invalid friend.

I have heard many of your letters read — & your descriptions & the names of various localities you mention are quite familiar to me. Preya Grande &c &c. — Rio harbor you must certainly confess the most glorious sheet of water in the universe. As a sailor "I can not sufficiently admire it"
— What think you of tropical climes My Dear Augustus? But you are a little too far South (on the very border indeed of the South Temperate Zone) to feel the full genial warmth of the Torrid Zone — I envy you your retreat in the country, tho I must acknowledge that if you had an acquaintance — a countryman — to accompany you in your excursions you would find it still more pleasant. You will no doubt, hail with extreme joy the arrival of a friend from Lansingburgh in the person of the gruff Captain's son. — Pray write me without fail & beleive me

  With earnest prayers for your recovery

Very Faithfully
Herman Melville

ALS on a 39.4 × 25 cm sheet, folded in half, of blue wove paper, faintly embossed with the manufacturer's small oval stamp enclosing the initials "P & S". Melville inscribed the first three pages, in ink, and addressed the envelope "Augustus Van Schaick Esq | Rio di Janerio." Van Schaick noted on the envelope, in ink, "Herman Melville | Helen ———"; this suggests that Helen Melville's 11 June 1846 letter in its smaller envelope was enclosed within her brother's letter.

LOCATION: UV-Barrett. *Provenance*: Victor Hugo Paltsits; Howard S. Mott catalogue (1948); Joseph E. Fields; Goodspeed's Book Shop.

PUBLICATION: (partial) *Log*, I, 247. Davis-Gilman 41.

TEXTUAL NOTES: me good] *intervening word lacking (presumably "a")* • find it] t *later crossed with long stroke* • prayers] *miswritten* prays

TO RICHARD BENTLEY
19 JUNE [1847?] · NEW YORK

This letter to Richard Bentley (1794–1871), who succeeded John Murray as Melville's British publisher, is headed only "New York June 19th." With Bentley's initial letter of "the 17 Ult:" unlocated, the dating of Melville's reply in this letter can be only tentative. Melville also gave the same heading to a letter to Murray for which there is positive evidence supporting the year 1848 (see below). However the year 1847 best fits the full evidence of Melville's negotiations with his British publishers. Earlier in that year—on 31 March—Melville had written Murray that he would "follow it [*Omoo*] up by something else, immediately," thus establishing a "partial understanding" with Murray. After his honeymoon and removal to New York, he wrote Murray again on 29 October 1847 (see below), stating: "In anticipation of any movement on my part, I have recently received overtures from a house in London concerning the prospective purchase of the English copyright of a third book," which he described as "another book of South Sea Adventure"; he then assured Murray that he had remained loyal to his original publisher. The phrase "a new work of South Sea adventure" is also more appropriate to Melville's concept of *Mardi* in June 1847 than in June 1848. Finally, on 4 February 1848 Elizabeth Melville could already write to her stepmother, Hope Savage Shaw, that he "has had communications from London publishers with very liberal offers for the book in hand [*Mardi*]" (HCL-M). No offers from any other London publishers have been located. (A further supporting factor in the 1847 dating is the paper, which matches that of Melville's July 1847 letter to Duyckinck, just below.)

Melville's correspondence with Bentley eventuated in his publication of *Mardi*, *Redburn*, *White-Jacket*, and *The Whale*. Unlike Murray, Bentley had early recognized the importance of fiction—hiring Dickens, for example, as the editor of *Bentley's Miscellany* in 1837. Moreover, American authors figured prominently in his publishing ventures. He began his successful "Standard Novels" series in 1831 with Cooper's *The Pilot*, and also published such other contemporaries of Melville as Longfellow, Parkman, and Bancroft. (For more about Melville's publishing relation with Bentley, see Lynn Horth, "Richard Bentley's Place in Melville's Literary Career," *Studies in the American Renaissance 1992*, pp. 229–45.)

New York June 19th

Dear Sir — I am much obliged to you for your note of the 17 Ult: and its friendly overtures; and I regret that at present I am not at liberty to meet them — a partial understanding with another publisher forbidding.

—— Should any thing occur, however, to alter my present views and arrangements, I will not fail to write you; or perhaps, communicate with you thro' the agency of a freind.

Yours Very Truly
Herman Melville

Richard Bentley Esq.

P.S. If you see fit, I would be obliged to you, if you would inform me at what value you would hold the English copy right of a new work of South Sea adventure, by me, occupying entirely fresh ground.

H. M.

I would receive such a communication in confidence, as, of course, you receive this.

ALS on a 19.9 × 15.8 cm sheet, folded in half, of white wove paper, embossed with the manufacturer's small circular stamp enclosing a crown with feathers above the name "DOBBS". Melville inscribed the first three pages, in ink.

LOCATION: University of Illinois Library, Urbana-Champaign.

PUBLICATION: Bernard R. Jerman, " 'With Real Admiration': More Correspondence between Melville and Bentley," *American Literature* 25 (November 1953), 307–8. Davis-Gilman 42.

TEXTUAL NOTES: overtures] *miswritten* overturers • Sea] S *rewritten*

TO EVERT A. DUYCKINCK
[10 OR 31?] JULY 1847 · NEW YORK

Allusions in this letter to reviews of *Omoo* and to "associations" affecting Melville's "personal liberty" (presumably preparations for his coming marriage) suggest July 1847 as its date. The favorable English notice ("frankincense") of *Omoo* that Duyckinck enclosed with his now unlocated letter was probably that of *Blackwood's Edinburgh Magazine*, which appeared in June, was widely quoted in American papers, and received considerable attention from Melville and his family (see Melville's letter to Murray of 29 October 1847, below); unfavorable American notices included the severe attack initialed by G. W. Peck in the July *American Review* and the earlier review in the *New York Evangelist* on 27 May 1847. Duyckinck's diary (NYPL-D) records in an entry of 11 July a visit from Melville (probably on Saturday, 10 July) and also in an entry for Saturday, 31 July, an Astor House dinner with him, the earlier date being the more likely occasion of the informal "visit" proposed in this letter.

My Dear Sir

Day before yesterday I received your friendly note & the paper with frankincense enclosed. Upon my soul, Duyckinck, these English are a sensible people. Indeed to confess the truth, when I compare their reception of Omoo in particular, with its treatment here, it begets ideas not very favorable to one's patriotism. But this is almost being too frank.

Your note should have received an answer sooner — but my associations just now, trench much upon my personal liberty.

With pleasure I comply with your invitation to call upon you — will you be in this evening? for I meditate a visit.

Yours Truly
Herman Melville

Saturday Morning.

ALS on a 20 × 15.8 cm sheet, folded in half, of white wove paper, embossed with the manufacturer's small circular stamp enclosing a crown with feathers above the name "DOBBS". Melville inscribed the first three pages, in ink.

LOCATION: NYPL-D.

PUBLICATION: *Log*, I, 250 (dated early July). Davis-Gilman 43.

TO LEMUEL SHAW
6 AUGUST 1847 · CENTER HARBOR

On 4 August 1847 Melville married Elizabeth (Lizzie) Shaw, daughter of Lemuel Shaw, Chief Justice of Massachusetts. They toured the White Mountains and then Montreal and Quebec on their honeymoon, returning to Lansingburgh at the end of August. This note by Melville was added to Lizzie's first letter of the trip to her stepmother, Hope Savage Shaw, written from Center Harbor, New Hampshire, on Lake Winnipesaukee. Her letter also describes the ride from Franklin, the nearby mountain named Red Hill, the rainy weather, and the plans they had made to take the stage the next day—all of which suggests that Melville may not have read her letter before writing his own. After leaving Center Harbor, they traveled northeast to Conway, New Hampshire, on the Saco River (for Melville's brief descriptive reference to the "romantic landscape" in the "valley of the Saco" see *Moby-Dick*, chap. 1, p. 4).

Friday Morning

My Dear Sir. At my desire Lizzie has left a small space for a word or two. — We arrived here last evening after a pleasant ride from Franklin the present terminus of the Northern Rail Road. The scenery was in many places very fine, & we caught some glimpses of the mountain region to which we are going. Centre-Harbor where we now are is a very attractive place for a tourist, having the lake for boating & trouting, & plenty of rides in the vicinity, besides Red-Hill, the view from which is said to be equal to any thing of the kind in New England. A rainy day however, has thus far prevented us from taking an excursion, to enjoy the country. —— To morrow, I think we shall leave for Conway & thence to Mt Washington. & so to Canada. — I trust in the course of some two weeks to bring Lizzie to Lansingburgh, quite refreshed & invigorated from her rambles. — Remember me to Mrs Shaw & the family, & tell my Mother that I will write to her in a day or two.

Sincerely Yours
Herman Melville

Letters directed, within four or five days from now, will probably reach us at Montreal or Quebec

ALS on a 39.6 × 24.9 cm sheet, folded in half, of white wove paper with lines, faintly embossed with the manufacturer's oval stamp. Elizabeth Melville inscribed the first two and one-half pages to her stepmother, in ink, dating her letter "Centre Harbor. Aug. 6ᵗʰ 1847.", and Melville added his letter to Judge Shaw on the bottom half of the third page and on the top and bottom of the fourth (leaving room for the address in the middle), in ink. He addressed the letters "Mrs. Lemuel Shaw | Boston."; she later noted in ink next to the address "Answered — | August 8 47".

LOCATION: HCL-M.

PUBLICATION: Weaver, p. 262. Davis-Gilman 44.

TEXTUAL NOTE: Quebec] ec *written over* ek

TO MARIA GANSEVOORT MELVILLE
AFTER 6 AUGUST 1847 · NEW HAMPSHIRE

Unlocated. In his note of 6 August to Lemuel Shaw, just above, Melville promised to write his mother "in a day or two." He probably wrote his letter from Conway or near Mt. Washington, New Hampshire. Davis-Gilman Unlocated 300.

TO LEMUEL SHAW
BEFORE 10 OCTOBER 1847 · NEW YORK

Unlocated. In late September Melville and his wife—along with his younger brother Allan and his bride, as well as Melville's mother and all four of his sisters—set up housekeeping in New York at 103 Fourth Avenue with the help of Judge Shaw and Allan's mother-in-law, Mrs. C. M. Thurston, who together advanced the Melvilles several thousand dollars toward the purchase of the house. Sometime during this period Melville wrote to Judge Shaw concerning their financial arrangements, as indicated by a letter of 10 October 1847 that Shaw, then in Worcester, Massachusetts, wrote to his wife, Hope Savage Shaw: "I received your letter last evening and also, your other note, enclosing the letter of Herman. He seems not very well to have understood me, but I believe there will be no difficulty. If any body calls at the house to present a bill of exchange drawn by Herman on me, I wish you to ask the person to call on Mr Clark, cashier of the New England Bank. I have written to him on the subject" (HCL-M). Davis-Gilman Unlocated 301.

TO JOHN MURRAY
29 OCTOBER 1847 · NEW YORK

With a wife and a new household to help support, Melville was concerned about his finances. He wrote this letter to Murray requesting a higher premium for his books on the strength of the June 1847 review of *Omoo* in *Blackwood's Edinburgh Magazine*—or "Old Maga" as the magazine was familiarly called—and of the inquiries made by another publisher about his future works. Although the *Blackwood's* review had been humorously skeptical of the authenticity of *Omoo* and of "the reality of Mr Melville's avuncular relatives," especially "Uncle Gansevoort, of Gansevoort, Saratoga County," it had proclaimed the book "excellent, quite first-rate, the 'clear grit,' as Mr. Melville's country-men would say." This praise, coupled with the "overtures" of another London publisher, perhaps Richard Bentley, who later published *Mardi*, provided Melville with a strong basis for his request. It is also possible that Bentley had responded to Melville's confidential query of 19 June as to "what value" he would put on the "English copy right of a new work of South Sea adventure," perhaps naming a sum higher than any of Murray's previous offers, thus prompting Melville to complain here that he cannot say with Shylock " 'I am content' " (*Merchant of Venice,* 4.1.394). (This speculation, however, turns on the 1847 dating of Melville's 19 June reply to Bentley; see the headnote to that letter.) For Murray's 3 December response, see LETTERS RECEIVED, pp. 590–91.

New York Oct: 29th 1847.

Dear Sir — I beleive we have not communicated since Omoo was published. I have therefore to express to you my gratification at the reception it has been honored with in England. But I can hardly conceal my surprise & diversion at the solemn incredulity respecting the author which would seem to obtain so widely. — Old Maga — God bless his cocked hat! — shakes his venerable head sagatiously, notwithstanding his keen relish for the humorous. Verily, could he survey the portly figure & substantial Dutch bearing of "mine honored Uncle" he would, perforce, confess that a little flesh & blood entered into the composition of my "avuncular relative" — whom Heaven preserve! ―――― As you may possibly imagine, I am engaged upon another book of South Sea Adventure (continued from, tho' wholly independent of, "Omoo") — The new work will enter into scenes altogether new, & will, I think, possess more interest than the former; which treated of subjects comparatively trite.

— In anticipation of any movement on my part, I have recently received overtures from a house in London concerning the prospective purchase of the English copyright of a third book. From this house the offer would be a liberal one, I am confidant. But I have declined trammeling myself in any way — &, from considerations of courtesy, address you now, to learn what you may feel disposed to offer in advance for the book in question. — The signal success of two books, & other considerations peculiar to the case, leave little doubt as to the success of a third: — a fact evidenced by the overtures I have received. — I can not but be conscious, that the feild where I garner is troubled but with few & inconsiderable intruders (in my own peculiar province I mean) — that it is wide & fresh; — indeed, I only but begin, as it were, to feel my hand.

—— I can not say certainly when the book will be ready for the press — but probably the latter part of the coming Spring — perhaps later — possibly not until Fall — but by that time, certainly. — However, I am very desirous of arranging for the sale of the book *now*, (since I perceive it can be done) so as to preclude delay when the M.S. is in readiness. —— Permit me, here, frankly to say, that I was disappointed at the pecuniary value you set upon "Omoo" — tho' from the circumstances of the negotiation, I could not very well — or very courtiously to my friend Mr Brodhead — express my disappointment at the time. — Surely, if the probable sale of Omoo in England is to be estimated by the notices of it which have appeared there, & also by its known sale *here*, you can not be surprised, that to say the least, the book in my estimation brought less than it has proved to be worth, in a merely business point of view. — Under the circumstances I can hardly say with Shylock that "I am content" — nor would it be a happy allusion, while thus upon money matters, likening myself to a Jew. —— Nevertheless, in the sale of the book — Omoo — there was no reservation for the benefit of the author as in "Typee" — unless there was one in your own mind — I have therfore nothing further to say on the subject. —— Now that it strikes me, do you not think that a third book would prove more remunerative to both publisher & author, if got up independent of your library, in a different style, so as to command, say, double the price. Afterwards it might be incorporated into your series of cheap books — a mere suggestion, which may go for what it is worth.

With regard to the new book, let me say that my inclinations lead me to prefer the imprimatur of "John Murray" to that of any other London publisher; but at the same circumstances paramount to every other consideration, force me to regard my literary affairs in a strong pecuniary light.

Yours, My Dear Sir, Very Truly
Herman Melville

John Murray Esq.

ALS on a 37.4 × 23.4 cm sheet, folded in half, of white laid paper, embossed with the manufacturer's oval stamp enclosing the name "SUPERFINE SATIN". Melville inscribed all four pages,
in ink. Another hand, presumably a clerk's, noted in ink at the top of the first page "Ans^d Dec^r
3 / 47. See Letterbook" and on the fourth page "Octr 29 1847 | Melville Herman".

LOCATION: Murray.

PUBLICATION: (partial) *Log*, I, 259, 263–64. Davis, pp. 212–13. Davis-Gilman 45.

TEXTUAL NOTES: enter into] into *added* • a third book] a third *added after canceled* the • overtures
I] *miswritten* ovetures I • very desirous] very *added* • you can not] not *inserted above caret* • to say
on the] the *added after canceled* that • both] b *written over another letter* • so as] as *written over*
at • same circumstances] *intervening word lacking (presumably "time")*

1848

TO JOHN MURRAY
1 JANUARY 1848 · NEW YORK

To Melville's letter of 29 October 1847, John Murray had replied politely but firmly on 3 December 1847 that Melville's books were not as remunerative as he
imagined. Murray provided an accounting of the sales of *Typee* and *Omoo* to dis-
miss Melville's suspicion that his profits on those two books were "immense." For
Melville's new work, he offered to pay one hundred guineas on publication and
one-half the profits on its sales (see LETTERS RECEIVED, pp. 590–91). This 1 January
reply indicates that Melville had greater hopes for his third book. (Murray's 17
January reply to this letter is unlocated.)

New York Jan: 1st '48
Dear Sir — I duly received your letter of the 3^d ult: and am obliged
to you for the frankness of its tenor. The arrangement you propose
for my next book is not altogether satisfactory to me. At the least, I
should want the advance doubled. — I do not think — permit me to
say — that you can very well judge of the merits of the work in
question — Very naturally indeed, you may be led to imagine that
after producing two books on the South Seas, the subject must necessarily become somewhat barren of novelty. But the plan I have
pursued in the composition of the book now in hand, clothes the
whole subject in new attractions & combines in one cluster all that is
romantic, whimsical & poetic in Polynisia. It is yet a continuous
narrative. I doubt not that — if it makes the hit I mean it to — it will
be counted a rathar bold aim; but nevertheless, it shall have the right

To John Murray, 1 January 1848, p. 2 (reduced).
Courtesy of John Murray, Ltd., London.

stuff in it, to redeem its faults, tho' they were legion.

All this to be sure, is confidential — & egotistical — decidedly the latter.

Upon the whole, allow me to suggest, that possibly, you may not form as high an idea of the book *now*, as you may, when you see it.

And therefore, unless something unforseen occurs, I may decide to allow the whole matter to rest where it is. And without seeking the *direct* offers of any other London publisher, wait till the book is completed — then forward it to you, & see whether your offer is not increased by the sight — materially. Thus much is due to you in courtesy, & I will cheerfully do as I say should nothing intervene. But should your views of the book, not coincide with mine in reference to its pecuniary value, of course, I shall then pursue such other course as may seem advisable.

In Some Haste
Very Truly Yours, Dear Sir
Herman Melvill

John Murray Esq
Albemarle Street.

ALS on a 39.8 × 24.8 cm sheet, folded in half, of blue wove paper, embossed with the manufacturer's small oval stamp enclosing the initials "P & S". Melville inscribed the first three pages, in ink, and addressed the fourth page "John Murray Esq | Albemarle Street | London."; it was postmarked in Liverpool on 16 January 1847—the year being an error. Another hand, presumably a clerk's, noted in ink on that page "Jan 1. 1848 | Melville H".

LOCATION: Murray.

PUBLICATION: (partial) *Log*, I, 269. Davis, pp. 213–14. Davis-Gilman 46.

TEXTUAL NOTES: composition of] of *added* • Polynisia] *M's usual spelling; miswritten* Polynusia • aim;] *before canceled* & its authentic • All this] All *added before indented* This (*vestigial capital*) • you may,] *after canceled* when • should nothing intervene] *inserted above caret after* say.

TO A BERLIN PUBLISHER
BEFORE 4 FEBRUARY 1848 · NEW YORK

Unlocated. On 4 February 1848 Elizabeth Shaw Melville mentioned in a letter to her stepmother, Hope Savage Shaw, a "communication" Melville had received "from Berlin to translate from the first sheets into German" his third book. She added that he had not yet "closed" with them, and would not do so "in a hurry"

(HCL-M). At least one and perhaps two letters may be inferred here, since Melville probably acknowledged the communication immediately, and then may have made further enquiries at a later date. Leland R. Phelps and Kathleen McCullough in *Herman Melville's Foreign Reputation* (Boston: G. K. Hall, 1983) report German translations of *Typee* and *Omoo* published in 1847 by G. Mayer in Leipzig, but report no German *Mardi* from this period. Davis-Gilman Unlocated 302.

TO HOPE SAVAGE SHAW
ON OR AFTER 4 FEBRUARY 1848 · NEW YORK

Unlocated. Elizabeth Shaw Melville's 4 February letter to her stepmother, cited in the entry just above, also included an acknowledgment of various presents Hope Savage Shaw had sent. Of Melville's she wrote: "Herman was much gratified with your remembrance of him — and intends to make his acknowledgements for himself" (HCL-M). Thus a thank-you letter to his mother-in-law can perhaps be inferred.

TO WILEY & PUTNAM
12 FEBRUARY 1848 · NEW YORK

Since Melville's contract agreement with Wiley & Putnam had specified that he would receive half-profits from the sales of *Typee*, he continued to receive statements from his first American publisher until the Harpers took over the book early in 1849. The account that Melville had received when he wrote this letter was dated 11 February 1848 and covered the costs and sales of *Typee* through 1 January 1848, recording a balance due to Melville of $154.36—followed by the statement that it was "Subject to Corrections" (HCL-M). When Allan Melville presented this letter from Melville, John Wiley wrote him a check for $154.37, as indicated by Allan's endorsement on the back of the letter. The publication of *Omoo* by the Harpers had boosted the sales of *Typee*, prompting Wiley & Putnam to print another fifteen hundred copies in late 1847 and five hundred in early 1848 (see the NN *Typee*, p. 295, for further discussion of the sales of Melville's first book).

Saturday Feb 12th

Gentlemen

　　I have rec^d your account — but have had no time to examine it; & I see that it is "subject to corrections" — You will have the goodness to pay over to my brother the balance due as appears from the acc^t for which he will give you a receipt on account. — If you can not pay me the cash deducting three months interest which I should prefer; I suppose you will give me your note at 3 mos from Jany 1st

Yours Truly
Herman Melville

If you settle by note please have the note payable to my brother's order.

H. M.

ALS on a 24.8 × 20 cm sheet, folded in half, of blue wove paper. Melville inscribed the first two pages, in ink, and addressed the fourth page "Mess Wiley & Putnam | Broadway". Allan Melville noted in ink on that page "H M's note to | Wiley & Putnam | Feby 12. 1848 | shewed to Wiley | & rec^d check for | $154 37".

LOCATION: HCL-M.

PUBLICATION: *Log*, I, 271. Davis-Gilman 47.

TEXTUAL NOTES: balance] an *rewritten and blotted* · deducting three months interest] *inserted above caret*

TO EVERT A. DUYCKINCK
[8 MARCH 1848?] · NEW YORK

Settled in New York, Melville became a member of Evert Duyckinck's literary circle and contributed reviews to his *Literary World*. This letter was later attached to the manuscript of Melville's review of *The Sea Lions*, entitled "Cooper's New Novel" and printed anonymously on 28 April 1849 in the *Literary World*, although its relation to that review is not apparent. It can possibly be dated Wednesday, 8 March 1848, through a comment Evert Duyckinck made in a 9 March 1848 letter to his brother George: "Melville the other night brought me a few chapters of his new book which in the poetry and wildness of the thing will be ahead of Typee & Omoo. I played the longest rubber of whist last night at his house I ever encountered. It was like his calm at sea — in the new book. What a punishment for a gambler in the next world — an interminable game of whist. — " (NYPL-D). Thus Chapter 2 of *Mardi*, "The Calm," was probably one of the chapters Melville gave Duyckinck.

Wednesday Morning

My Dear Duyckinck

If you happen to be disengaged this evening, come round and make up a rubber of whist — about ½ past seven.

Yours Truly
Herman Melville

ALS on an 8.8 × 13.4 cm sheet, folded in half, of white wove paper, embossed with the manufacturer's small circular stamp enclosing a crown underneath the name "DOBBS". Melville inscribed the first page, in ink. It was later pasted to the manuscript of Melville's *Literary World* review entitled "Cooper's New Novel" (see the headnote above).

LOCATION: NYPL-D.

PUBLICATION: (partial) *Log*, I, 273. Davis-Gilman 48.

TO JOHN MURRAY
25 MARCH 1848 · NEW YORK

Melville had begun work on *Mardi* in the spring of 1847 and had continued to work on it through the early months of 1848. In describing the book in his previous letter of 1 January 1848 to Murray he had canceled the phrase "& its authentic" in favor of the equivocal statement "but nevertheless, it shall have the right stuff in it" (see the reproduction and textual notes). Murray's 17 January 1848 reply is unlocated and was not recorded in his letterbook for this period, but it most likely contained another request for documentary evidence of Melville's travels at sea. This 25 March response, like Melville's earlier letter of 1 January, continues to reject Murray's insistence upon authenticity in the books he published, even to the point of satirizing that insistence in the opening paragraph. Walter E. Bezanson called it Melville's "virtual declaration of literary independence" ("*Moby-Dick*: Document, Drama, Dream," in *A Companion to Melville Studies*, ed. John Bryant [New York: Greenwood Press, 1986], p. 176). The quotation of Hamlet's " 'no more' " (3.1.61) in the first paragraph suggests that Melville was somewhat acquainted with Shakespeare at this time even though he did not read the plays closely until the following year, as his letter of 24 February 1849 to Evert Duyckinck indicates.

New York March 25th 1848

My Dear Sir — Nothing but a sad failing of mine — procrastination — has prevented me from replying ere this to yours of the 17 Jany last, which I have just read over. — Will you still continue, Mr Murray, to break seals from the Land of Shadows — persisting in carrying on this mysterious correspondence with an imposter shade, that under the fanciful appellation of Herman Melvill still practices upon your honest credulity? — Have a care, I pray, lest while thus parleying with a ghost you fall upon some horrible evel, peradventure sell your soul ere you are aware. —— But in tragic phrase "no more!" — only glancing at the closing sentence of your letter, I read there your desire to test the corporeality of H— M— by clapping eyes upon him in London. —— I beleive that a letter I wrote you some time ago — I think my last but one — gave you to understand, or implied, that the work I then had in view was a bona-fide narrative of my adventures in the Pacific, contin-

ued from "Omoo" — My object in now writing you — I should have
done so ere this — is to inform you of a change in my determinations.
To be blunt: the work I shall next publish will in downright earnest a
"Romance of Polynisian Adventure" — But why this? The truth is,
Sir, that the reiterated imputation of being a romancer in disguise has
at last pricked me into a resolution to show those who may take any
interest in the matter, that a *real* romance of mine is no Typee or
Omoo, & is made of different stuff altogether. This I confess has been
the main inducement in altering my plans — but others have operated.
I have long thought that Polynisia furnished a great deal of rich poetical material that has never been employed hitherto in works of fancy;
and which to bring out suitably, required only that play of freedom &
invention accorded only to the Romancer & poet. — However, I
thought, that I would postpone trying my hand at any thing fanciful of
this sort, till some future day: tho' at times when in the mood I threw
off occasional sketches applicable to such a work. — Well: proceeding
in my narrative of *facts* I began to feel an invincible distaste for the
same; & a longing to plume my pinions for a flight, & felt irked,
cramped & fettered by plodding along with dull common
places, — So suddenly abandoning the thing alltogether, I went to
work heart & soul at a romance which is now in fair progress, since I
had worked at it with an earnest ardor. — Start not, nor exclaim
"Pshaw! Puh!" — My romance I assure you is no dish water nor its
model borrowed from the Circulating Library. It is something new I
assure you, & original if nothing more. But I can give you no adequate
idea, of it. You must see it for yourself. — Only forbear to prejudge
it. — It opens like a true narrative — like Omoo for example, on ship
board — & the romance & poetry of the thing thence grow continuously, till it becomes a story wild enough I assure you & with a meaning too.
— As for the policy of putting forth an acknowledged *romance* upon
the heel of two books of travel which in some quarters have been received with no small incredulity — that, Sir, is a question for which I
care little, really. — My *instinct* is to out with the Romance, & let me
say that instincts are prophetic, & better than acquired wisdom — which alludes remotely to your experience in literature as an
eminent publisher. — Yet upon the whole if you consider the thing, I
think you will unite with me in the opinion, that it is possible for me
to write such a romance that it shall afford the strongest presumptive

evidence of the truth of Typee & Omoo by the sheer force of contrast — not that the Romance is to sink in the comparison, but shall be
better — I mean as a literary acheivement, & so essentially different
from those two books. — But not to multiply words about it, I shall
forward the proof sheets to you, & let you judge of it for yourself, for
I have the utmost confidence in you. — Supposing that you should
decide to undertake the publication of this work; — if you rec^d the
sheets by the middle of July next, could you have it out in thirty days
from that time? And would you, under the circumstances, deem it
advisable to publish at that season of the year, — bearing in mind, that
there are reasons that operate with me to make as early a publication as
possible, a thing of much pecuniary importance with me? — If you say
yea to these questions, then I think I should be ready to propose the
following arrangement: — that upon the receipt of the sheets & your
decision to publish, you substitute £150 for the 100 guineas set down
in your letter of Dec ^3d '47 — forwarding upon publication the former
sum, & agreeing to pay me ½ the profits of all future editions (should
there be any) when *all* expences of outlay on your part shall have been
defraid by the book itself; & remitting me some specific memorandum
to that effect, in case of accidents. — If upon the receipt of the sheets
you should agree to this, then, without waiting to communicate with
me, you might consider the matter closed at once & proceed to business at once; — only apprising me immediately of the very earliest day
upon which I could publish here. This would save time. In your next,
will you point out the safest method of forwarding to you my book;
seeing that Omoo met with such adventures at your atrocious Custom
Houses
— By the way, you ask again for "documentary evidence" of my
having been in the South Seas, wherewithall to convince the unbe-
lievers — Bless my soul, Sir, will you Britons not credit that an
American can be a gentleman, & have read the Waverly Novels, tho
every digit may have been in the tar-bucket? — You make miracles
of what are commonplaces to us. — I will give no evidence — Truth
is mighty & will prevail — & shall & must.

In all sincerity Yours
Herman Melville.

ALS on a 39.8 × 24.8 cm sheet, folded in half, of blue wove paper, embossed with the
manufacturer's small oval stamp enclosing the initials "P & S". Melville inscribed all four

pages, in ink. Another hand, presumably a clerk's, noted in ink in the margin of the fourth page "March 25. 1848 | Melville Herman".

LOCATION: Murray.

PUBLICATION: (partial) *Log*, I, 274–75. Davis, pp. 214–16. Davis-Gilman 49.

TEXTUAL NOTES: Shadows] S *written over* s · in downright] in *written over* be · earnest a] *intervening word lacking (presumably "be")* · great] *miswritten* gret · proceeding in] in *added* · feel] *possibly* find · invincible] *possibly* incurible · abandoning] *conjectural reading* · romance which] which *miswritten* whi · prejudge] *after canceled* predjuge · continuously] *possibly* continually · assure you] you *inserted above caret* · to multiply] to *added* · substitute] *miswritten* substite · tar-bucket] tar-|bucket · commonplaces] common-|places

TO HENRY WILLCOX
BEFORE 1 MAY 1848 · NEW YORK

Unlocated. In 1846, at age sixteen, Melville's youngest brother, Thomas, sailed as a green hand aboard the whaleship *Theophilus Chase*. (The ship had initially left the harbor on 18 March 1846, but damage suffered in a gale forced it to return to port; Thomas joined the crew when it left the harbor for the second time on 6 May 1846.) A letter from Melville to the ship's owner, Henry Willcox, in Westport Point, Massachusetts, is reported by Elizabeth Shaw Melville in a letter to her stepmother, Hope Savage Shaw, dated 5 May 1848: "We are looking out for Tom to return every day his ship has been reported in the papers several times lately as homeward bound and Herman wrote to the owner at Westport and received answer that he looked for the ship the first of May. that has already past and we are daily expecting a letter to announce her actual arrival. Then Herman will have to go over to Westport for Tom and see that he is regularly discharged and paid, and bring him home" (HCL-M). In fact, the day before Elizabeth Melville wrote her letter, the ship had returned on 4 May 1848 with fifty barrels of sperm oil. Davis-Gilman Unlocated 303.

TO DANIEL P. PARKER
BEFORE 6 JUNE 1848 · NEW YORK

Unlocated. On 6 June 1848 Elizabeth Shaw Melville wrote to her stepmother, Hope Savage Shaw, that Melville was helping his youngest brother find a new position: "Mother [Maria Melville] feels very uneasy because Tom wants to go to sea again — he has been trying for a place in some store ever since he came home but not succeeding, is discouraged, and says he must go to sea immediately — Herman has written Mr Parker — (Daniel P.) to see if he can send him out in one of his ships. I hope he will, if Tom must go, for Mr Parker would be likely to take an interest in him and promote him. — " In the postscript to her letter, Elizabeth Melville added, "If father should chance to see Mr Parker I wish he would speak to him about Tom" (HCL–M). *Adams's Boston Directory* for 1846 and 1847 lists Daniel P. Parker as residing at 40 Beacon Street with offices at 40 State Street in Boston. Parker was a merchant who had been a friend of Melville's father and who had accompanied twelve-year-old Gansevoort and eight-year-old Herman when they went to Boston and Bristol, Rhode Island, in 1828 to spend their respective summer vacations (see the headnote to Melville's 1828 letter to his aunt Lucy). Davis-Gilman Unlocated 304.

TO JOHN MURRAY
19 JUNE 1848 · NEW YORK

John Murray's letter of 20 May 1848 (to which Melville replies here) is unlocated, but its disapproving response to Melville's letter of 25 March 1848, proposing a " 'Romance of Polynisian Adventure,' " reflected his policy of not publishing poetry or fiction. Murray's "Antarctic tenor" seems to have led Melville to abandon his defiant response of 25 March to the request for " 'documentary evidence' " ("I will give no evidence — Truth is mighty & will prevail — & shall & must") and to promise in this letter to furnish "original documents," possibly affidavits from the owners of the *Acushnet*, for which he had written earlier, according to his 2 September 1846 letter to Murray.

New York June 19th
My Dear Sir — Yours of the 20th May last was duly received. And I should apologise for so long postponing a reply. — In spite of the Antarctic tenor of your epistle, I still adhere to my first resolution of submitting the sheets of my new work to your experienced eye. — I fear you abhor romances; But fancy nevertheless that possibly you may for once relent. — By this mail I purposed sending you one or two original documents, evidencing the incredible fact, that I have actually been a common sailor before the mast in the Pacific. But most unfortunately, this morning I am unable to lay hand on the most important of the documents alluded to. It has been mislaid. But with the rest I will remit it to you as soon as I recover it.

Beleive Me My Dear Sir
Yours Truly
Herman Melville

John Murray Esq.
Albemarle Street.

The "documentary evidence" above mentioned very recently came into my possession (all but one) Hence the change in my decision respecting furnishing you with any thing of that sort.

H. M.

ALS on a 39.8 × 24.8 cm sheet, folded in half, of blue wove paper, embossed with the manufacturer's small oval stamp enclosing the initials "P & S". Melville inscribed the first two pages, in ink, and addressed the fourth page "*Boston Steamer* | John Murray Esq | 50 Albemarle Street | London."; it was postmarked "AV | JY | 1848". Another hand, presumably a clerk's, noted in ink on that page "June 19. 1848 | Melville H."

LOCATION: Murray.

PUBLICATION: (partial) *Log*, I, 278. Davis, pp. 216–17. Davis-Gilman 50.

TEXTUAL NOTES: in the Pacific.] *inserted above caret over a period* • important of] of *written over* one • with the rest] *inserted above caret*

TO WILEY & PUTNAM
19 AUGUST 1848 · NEW YORK

Shortly after receiving his August 1848 statement from Wiley & Putnam, Melville exercised the option in his contract that allowed him to sever his relations with them at sixty days' notice. This letter survives in a copy made by Allan Melville for record; Melville presented the original, according to Allan's notation on his copy, to John Wiley on 19 August. Six months later, in January of 1849, Melville bought out the Wiley & Putnam interest in the stereotype plates of *Typee* and in February transferred the book to the Harpers, who did not issue their reprint until 15 June 1849. Despite what Melville may have hoped to gain by this transfer, the book earned relatively little under the Harpers' distribution (see the NN *Typee*, pp. 295–96, for a further discussion).

John Wiley Esq or
Wiley & Putnam.
    The terms of the agreement by which Typee is published by your house containing the proviso that sixty days notice proceeding from either party to the agreement may at any time at the expiration of the sixty days be terminated, I hereby give you such notice to take effect from this date. At the expiration of the sixty days I will be obliged to you for a full account to that date of all matters growing out of the above mentioned agreement

                                                                Yours &c
                                                                H. Melville

New York 19. Aug 1848.

Original document not located. Text from manuscript copy, in Allan Melville's hand, on a 31.5 × 20.2 cm sheet of blue wove paper with lines, embossed with the manufacturer's square stamp enclosing its name "OWEN & HURLBUT | SO. LEE | MASS". On the verso is a memorandum, also in Allan's hand: "Copy of a notice | to Wiley to | discontinue present | arrange-ment in | sixty days. [from *canceled*] | Aug 19ᵗʰ 1848 — | H. M. served the [the *written over* an] | original of this | notice on Wiley | Aug 19ᵗʰ 1848 in | my presence." In pencil Elizabeth Shaw Melville added "Aug 19 – 1848".

LOCATION (of copy): HCL-M.

PUBLICATION: *Log*, I, 280. Davis-Gilman 51.

TEXTUAL NOTES: or] *added* • Wiley &] *after canceled* Late • proviso that] *before canceled* at

TO EVERT A. DUYCKINCK
14 NOVEMBER 1848 · NEW YORK

The subject of this letter is Joseph C. Hart's *The Romance of Yachting: Voyage the First* (New York: Harper, 1848; Sealts 242), which Duyckinck apparently asked Melville to review for the *Literary World*. The subtitle, "Voyage the First," suggests a second voyage or continuation, as Melville assumes, but in fact the book had no sequel. As Melville complains, the book is largely a series of digressions. In the first two chapters Hart discusses the advantages of living in Knickerbocker New York over Puritan New England, including a contrast between the municipal privileges of New York and the restrictive Puritan laws of New England (a "disgrace" to the age) and cites as authority "Dr. O'Callaghan, an able historian of New-York." This was Edmund Bailey O'Callaghan (1797–1880), physician and historian, whose study of the Dutch land grants in the Albany anti-rent disputes led to his two-volume *History of New Netherland* (New York: Appleton, 1846–48). After introduc-ing the reader to "yachting" as the "true Dolce far Niente," Hart presents a "Log" of his voyage to Spain aboard the *J. Doolittle Smith*, which Melville ironically refers to as the log of Noah's ark. Then, in the chapter "Yachting to Port St. Mary," Hart describes three "Bull Fyttes" and among other digressions discusses the failure of English commentators in their attempt to build Shakespeare's reputation (Hart was one of the first to express doubts that Shakespeare was the author of the plays at-tributed to him; see H. N. Gibson, *The Shakespeare Claimants* [London: Methuen, 1962], p. 18). Melville ends his summary with Chapter 16, a little more than half way through the second of the two volumes in which Harpers published the book. There Hart describes his visit at festival time to the vaults of "Duff Gordon" in "the land of Sherry," Puerto de Santa María, on the bay of Cádiz. This is immediately followed by a title heading, "ST. ANTHONY'S NOSE," and a digressive section ("But of that more anon.") which describes a steersman, "Antonio," and the agreement of Hart and his companions to meet again "on top of *St. Anthony's nose*, upon the Hudson: And while astride of that fine and striking resemblance to his eminent proboscis" to "crack a bottle of righteous Sherry from the foundation butt of St. Peter, in honor of St. Antonio the immaculate." (In referring to this episode Mel-ville uses "North River"—the nautical name for the Hudson; St. Anthony's nose was a summit and well-known landmark on the east bank of the river in the Hud-son Highlands, nearly opposite Bear Mountain.)

On 2 December 1848 an anonymous review of Hart's book appeared in the *Literary World*, presumably by Evert Duyckinck. It stopped short of recommending that the book be burnt "in a fire of Asafetida" (an antispasmodic), but it criticized the book along much the same lines: "No one, certainly, can complain of a want of variety in this volume, or of any of that old fashioned dignity and reserve which formerly attended the making a book. Mr. Hart is a modern decidedly, and, of all moderns, the most modern, helter-skelter, and slap-dash. His book is as capricious as his yacht, tumbling about in all seas and before all winds. We question whether Addison would have allowed it to be literature at all."

Headed only Tuesday morning, the letter can be dated 14 November, a Tuesday in 1848, on the basis of Duyckinck's endorsement. Melville's undated letter acknowledging the receipt of a book from Duyckinck for review (see pp. 533–34 below) may have been written when Hart's book was first sent to him, as Leyda conjectured in the *Log*. See the headnote to that letter for a further discussion. An earlier book by Hart, *Miriam Coffin*, published without the author's name on the title page of any of the three separate editions in 1834 and 1835, was later both cited and quoted by Melville in *Moby-Dick*, probably without knowing it was Hart's book (see the NN edition, pp. xxiii, xxviii, 135, 823, 829, and 856).

Tuesday Morning

What the deuce does it mean? — Here's a book positively turned wrong side out, the title page on the cover, an index to the whole in more ways than one. — I open at the beginning, & find myself in the middle of the Blue Laws & Dr O'Callaghan. Then proceeding, find several extracts from the Log Book of Noah's Ark — Still further, take a hand at three or four bull fights, & then I'm set down to a digest of all the commentaries on Shakspeare, who, according "to our author" was a dunce & a blackguard — Vide passim.

Finally the book — so far as this copy goes — winds up with a dissertation on Duff Gordon Sherry & St Anthony's Nose, North River. ——

You have been horribly imposed upon, My Dear Sir. The book is no book, but a compact bundle of wrapping paper. And as for Mr Hart, pen & ink, should instantly be taken away from that unfortunate man, upon the same principle that pistols are withdrawn from the wight bent on suicide.

— Prayers should be offered up for him among the congregations. and Thanksgiving Day postponed untill long after his "book" is published. What great national sin have we committed to deserve this infliction?

— Seriously, Mr Duyckincke, on my bended knees, & with tears in my eyes, deliver me from writing ought upon this crucifying Romance of Yachting

— What has Mr Hart done that I should publicly devour him? — I bear that hapless man, no malice. Then why smite him?

— And as for glossing over his book with a few commonplaces, — *that* I can not do. — The book deserves to be burnt in a fire of Asafetida, & by the hand that wrote it.

Seriously again, & on my conscience, the book is an abortion, the mere trunk of a book, minus head arm or leg. —— Take it back, I beseech, & get some one to cart it back to the author

Yours Sincerely

H. M.

ALS on a 22.4 × 17.9 cm sheet, folded in half, of white wove paper, embossed with the manufacturer's circular stamp enclosing three flowers. Melville inscribed all four pages, in ink. Duyckinck later noted in pencil on the first page "Herman Melville Nov 14. 1848"; another hand, possibly a librarian's, added the penciled notation "[14 Nov. 1848]".

LOCATION: NYPL-D.

PUBLICATION: (partial) Minnigerode, pp. 30–31 (dated received November 11). Thorp, pp. 369–70. Davis-Gilman 52.

TEXTUAL NOTES: does] *miswritten* dose • & find] & *written over* I • blackguard] ck *written over another letter* • commentaries] *miswritten* commentars • the book] book *miswritten* books • Anthony's] 's *added* • bundle] *miswritten* bundl • the wight] the *written over* a *and* wight *before canceled* who • Mr Duyckincke] ^r *rewritten* • knees] *miswritten* keens

1849

TO JOHN MURRAY
28 JANUARY 1849 · NEW YORK

On 18 November 1848 the *Literary World* reported that "Herman Melville, Esq., Author of 'Typee' and 'Omoo' is about putting to press a new work, which, it is expected, from peculiar sources of interest, will transcend the unique reputation of his former books." Only three days earlier, on 15 November, Melville had signed the contract with Harper & Brothers for *Mardi*, which granted him a five hundred dollar advance on half-profits. Melville's Harper account statement covering this period (HCL-M) shows that the following day he used his discount with the Harpers to order another copy of *Webster's Dictionary* (Sealts 552), mentioned here, presumably to use in correcting the proofs. By the end of January 1849 the proofs were finished. Augusta Melville, who had worked on them throughout that month, announced the good news, quoting (chap. 180, p. 601) and alluding to the book in a 27 January letter to Elizabeth Melville, then in Boston: "The last proof sheets are through. 'Mardi's' a book! — 'Ah my own Koztanza! child of many prayers.' Oro's blessing on thee" (HCL–M).

In this letter to Murray, written the next day, Melville requests double Murray's original offer of 3 December 1847, and reiterates his confidence that his reputation has reached the status of "guinea author," deserving of publication in a more expensive format. Nine days later, on 6 February, Allan Melville sent the proof sheets to John R. Brodhead at the American legation in London and sent a letter to Murray explaining that fact (Murray). After delivering the proof sheets, however, Brodhead noted in his diary on 24 February that Murray had declined the book: "It is a *fiction* & Mr Murray says it don't suit him" (Alexander Library, Rutgers University). Brodhead subsequently offered it to the publisher Richard Bentley, who quickly accepted it (see the headnote to Melville's 26 March 1849 letter to Harper & Brothers, below).

New York January 28th 1849

My Dear Sir:

Herewith you will receive the sheets of "Mardi." After full consideration, I must explicitly state, that I can hardly consent to dispose of the book for less than 200 guineas, in advance, on the day of publication, & half the profits of any editions which may be sold after the book shall have paid for itself — of course, including the outlay of the 200 guineas — Upon these terms should you feel disposed to undertake it, I should feel exceedingly gratified to continue our connection, & should equally regret to be obliged to leave you. — Should you publish, you will, of course, write me at once formally notifying your acceptance of the terms; stating the earliest day upon which publication could take place here without interfering with your interests; & authorizing me to draw on you for the above-mentioned sum.

It would form part of our agreement, also, that your edition is to be an exact transcript of the copy forwarded you; — unless, you should see fit to alter the spelling of a few words (spelt according to Webster) in conformity with some other standard. — I swear by no particular creed in orthography; but my printers here "go for" Webster. — I would here beg to remind you of your own suggestion: — that it would be advisable to publish the book in handsome style, & independently of any series. — Unless you should deem it *very* desirable do not put me down on the title page as "the author of

Typee & Omoo". I wish to separate *"Mardi"* as much as possible
from those books.

Should you decline publication, I trust you will loose no time in
placing the sheets of the book into Mr Brodhead's hands, at the
"United States Legation"

I earnestly hope that we shall join hands in this matter.

Sincerely Yours
H Melville.

John Murray, Esq.

ALS on a 39.8 × 24.8 cm sheet, folded in half, of blue wove paper, embossed with the
manufacturer's small oval stamp enclosing the initials "P & S" (upside down at the bottom of
both leaves). Melville inscribed the first two pages, in ink. Another hand, presumably a
clerk's, noted in ink on the fourth page "Jan 28. 1849 | Melville H".

LOCATION: Murray.

PUBLICATION: (partial) *Log*, I, 286–87. Davis, pp. 217–18. Davis-Gilman 53.

TEXTUAL NOTES: guineas, in advance,] *inserted above caret after canceled* pounds · guineas] *inserted above canceled* pounds · which] *added* · no particular] *after canceled word-start*

TO ALLAN MELVILLE
20 FEBRUARY 1849 · BOSTON

In early January 1849, while the final proof sheets of *Mardi* were being prepared,
Melville took his wife to the home of her father, Chief Justice Shaw, at 49 Mount
Vernon Street in Boston, to await the birth of their first child. Melville returned to
New York to oversee the final corrections of *Mardi* and then went back to Boston
at the end of the month, leaving Allan to send the proof sheets to Murray in
London. According to Hope Shaw's diary, "Mr Herman Melvilles son" (named
Malcolm) was born on 16 February, at "half past 7 o'clock in the morning" (MHS-
S). Two days later in New York Allan Melville's wife, Sophia Thurston Melville
(1827–58), gave birth to their first child, Maria Gansevoort. For a full discussion,
see Hennig Cohen and Donald Yannella, *Herman Melville's Malcolm Letter: "Man's
Final Lore"* (New York: Fordham University Press and The New York Public Li-
brary, 1992).

    This letter of celebration is linked—through its references to Barnum and "Old
Zack"—to a series of comic articles by Melville entitled "Authentic Anecdotes of
'Old Zack'" that appeared (anonymously) in *Yankee Doodle* between 24 July and 11
September 1847 (see the NN *Piazza Tales* volume, pp. 212–29 and 465–68). These
satires had capitalized on overblown press accounts of both "Old Zack"—General
Zachary Taylor (1784–1850), shortly to become the twelfth U.S. president—and
the impresario P. T. Barnum (1810–91).

Tuesday Morning
Feb 20th

I have yours of yesterday. I am rejoiced that Sophia is well after her happy delivery.

Lizzie is doing well, also the phenomenon, which weighs I know not how many pennyweights, — I would say, hundred-weights. —— We desired much to have him weighed, but it was thought that no hay-scales in town were strong enough. It takes three nurses to dress him; and he is as valiant as Julius Cesear. —— He's a perfect prodigy. —— If the worst comes to the worst, I shall let him out by the month to Barnum; and take the tour of Europe with him. I think of calling him Barbarossa – Adolphus – Ferdinand – Otho – Grandissimo Hercules – Sampson – Bonaparte – Lambert. —— If you can suggest any thing better or more characteristic, pray, inform me of it by the next post. —— There was a terrible commotion here at the time of the event. — I had men stationed at all the church bells, 24 hours before hand; & when the Electric Telegraph informed them of the fact — such a ding–donging you never heard. — All the engines came out, thinking the State-House was on fire.

Of course the news was sent on by telegraph to Washington & New Orleans. — When Old Zack heard of it — he is reported to have said — "Mark me: that boy will be President of the United States before he dies." —— In New Orleans, the excitement was prodigious. Stocks rose & brandy fell. —— I have not yet heard from Europe & Pekin. But doubtless, ere this, they must have placed props against the Great-Wall. —— The harbor here is empty: — all the ships, brigs, schooners & smacks having scattered in all directions with the news for foreign parts. — The crowd has not yet left the streets, gossiping of the event. — The number of calls at 49 Mt Vernon Street is incalculable. Ten porters suffice not to receive the cards; and Canning the waiter, dropped down dead last night thro' pure exhaustion. —— Who would have thought that the birth of one little man, when ten thousands of other little men, & little horses, & little guinea-pigs & little roosters, & the Lord only knows what, are being born — that the birth of one little phenomenon, should create such a panic thro' the world: — nay, even in heaven; for last night I dreampt that his good angel had secured a seat for him above; & that the Devel

month to Barnum; and
take the tour of Europe with
him. I think of calling
him Barbarossa — Adolphus —
Ferdinand — Otho — Grandissimo
Hercules — Sampson — Bonaparte
— Lambert. —— If you
can suggest any thing better
or more characteristic, pray,
inform me of it by the next
post. —— There was
a little commotion here
at the tour of the event.
—— I had men stationed
at all the church bells,
24 hours beforehand; &
when the Electric Telegraph
informed them of the fact —
such a ding-donging you
never heard. — All the

To Allan Melville, 20 February 1849, p. 2 (reduced). Courtesy of the Rare
Books and Manuscripts Division, The New York Public Library, Astor,
Lenox and Tilden Foundations (Duyckinck Family Papers).

roared terribly bethinking him of the lusty foe to sin born into this
sinful world. —

H Melville.

The Reverend Father in Wedlock, Allan Melville.

ALS on a 25.3 × 20.3 cm part-sheet (torn along the top), folded in half, of blue laid paper,
partially watermarked with an ornate design above the letter "M". Melville inscribed all four
pages, in ink.

LOCATION: NYPL-GL. *Provenance:* Lyrical Ballad Bookstore.

PUBLICATION: Hennig Cohen and Donald Yannella, *A Perfect Prodigy: Melville on the Birth of
Malcolm* (New York: New York Public Library, 1986).

TEXTUAL NOTES: Barbarossa . . . Lambert] *hyphenation of names possibly intended (see the reproduction)* · Hercules] er *rewritten* · doubtless] *miswritten* doubtles · having] *altered from*
have · foreign] *miswritten* foregin · streets] ts *rewritten* · seat] at *rewritten* · terribly] *miswritten*
terrbily · Allan Melville.] *written below* The . . . Wedlock, *and connected by a line*

TO EVERT A. DUYCKINCK
24 FEBRUARY 1849 · BOSTON

While still at his father-in-law's home after Malcolm's birth, Melville wrote a series
of letters to Evert Duyckinck that provide an index to his reading and interests at
this period. (Unfortunately all of Duyckinck's replies remain unlocated.) In this
first letter Melville is known to have sent him from Boston, dated only "Feb 24th"
but clearly belonging to 1849, he alludes to both contemporary and established
figures.

Among contemporaries, William Allen Butler (1825–1902), "the poet" Melville mentions at the beginning and end of the letter, was a New York lawyer and
one of the frequent guests at Duyckinck's home. His column, "The Colonel's
Club," which usually included at least one satirical poem, had just begun in the 3
February 1849 issue of the *Literary World*. (Its appearance was probably what had
sparked Melville's "curiosity.") Later Butler wrote a number of books, including
biographies of Evert Duyckinck, Samuel Tilden, and Martin Van Buren (see William Allen Butler, *A Retrospect of Forty Years* [New York: Scribner's, 1911]).

Melville also refers to two other figures of the time: Ralph Waldo Emerson
(1803–82) and Fanny Kemble Butler (1809–93). On 5 February Emerson delivered
the fourth in a course of five lectures on "Mind and Manners in the Nineteenth
Century" at the Freeman Place Chapel on Beacon Street, and it is probable that this
fourth lecture was the one Melville attended (see Merton M. Sealts, Jr., *Pursuing
Melville, 1940–1980* [Madison: University of Wisconsin Press, 1982], pp. 257–61).
Fanny Kemble Butler had given readings from *Macbeth* and *Othello* on 12 and 19
February at the Masonic Temple in Boston. The daughter of the English actor

Charles Kemble, she was herself a celebrated Shakespearean actress. Pierce Butler's successful attempt to divorce her for abandonment was a *cause célèbre* in 1848 and 1849. For Melville's later knowledge of her in the Berkshires and possible caricature of her in *The Confidence-Man*, see the NN edition, pp. 287 and 290.

Vital to Melville's development as a writer was his encounter with Shakespeare, while, as he relates here, "lounging" on a sofa "a la" the eighteenth-century poet Thomas Gray. Melville's allusion is to Gray's self-confessed "spirit of laziness" and "indolence" at Cambridge—in sharp contrast with the intensity with which he was reading "the divine William" (see Gray's letters to Dr. Wharton, 11 December 1746, and 25 April and 8 August 1749, in *Correspondence of Thomas Gray*, ed. Paget Toynbee and Leonard Whibley [Oxford: Clarendon, 1935], I, 255, 317, 322; see also "The Encantadas," in the NN *Piazza Tales* volume, p. 145, for another allusion by Melville to this standard image of Gray upon his sofa). Melville's edition in "glorious great type" was presumably *The Dramatic Works of William Shakspeare* (7 vols., Boston: Hilliard, Gray, 1837), which he extensively scored and annotated (HCL-M; Sealts 460); see the NN *Moby-Dick*, pp. 955–56.

Feb 24th

Dear Duyckinck

Thank you for satisfying my curiosity. M[r] Butler's a genius, but between you & me, I have a presentiment that he never will surprise me more. — I have been passing my time very pleasurably here. But chiefly in lounging on a sofa (a la the poet Grey) & reading Shakspeare. It is an edition in glorious great type, every letter whereof is a soldier, & the top of every "t" like a musket barrel. Dolt & ass that I am I have lived more than 29 years, & until a few days ago, never made close acquaintance with the divine William. Ah, he's full of sermons-on-the-mount, and gentle, aye, almost as Jesus. I take such men to be inspired. I fancy that this moment Shakspeare in heaven ranks with Gabriel Raphael and Michael. And if another Messiah ever comes twill be in Shakespere's person. —— I am mad to think how minute a cause has prevented me hitherto from reading Shakspeare. But until now, every copy that was come-atable to me, happened to be in a vile small print unendurable to my eyes which are tender as young sparrows. But chancing to fall in with this glorious edition, I now exult over it, page after page. ——

I have heard Emerson since I have been here. Say what they will, he's a great man. Mrs Butler too I have heard at her Readings. She makes a glorious Lady Macbeth, but her Desdemona seems like a boarding school miss. — She's so unfemininely masculine that had she not, on unimpeachable authority, borne children, I should be curious to learn the result of a surgical examination of her person in private. The Lord help Butler — not the poet — I marvel not he seeks being amputated off from his matrimonial half.

My respects to Mrs Duyckinck & your brother

Yours

H Melville

Evert A Duyckinck Esq

ALS on a 23.4 × 18.3 cm part-sheet (torn along the bottom) of white wove paper, faintly embossed with the manufacturer's stamp of a branch-like design on the second leaf of the folded sheet. Melville inscribed the first three pages, in ink, and addressed the envelope "Evert A Duyckinck Esq | New York."; it was postmarked in Boston on 24 February. Duyckinck later noted in pencil on the top of the first page "Boston".

LOCATION: NYPL-D.

PUBLICATION: Thorp, pp. 370–71. Davis-Gilman 54.

TEXTUAL NOTES: pleasurably] *miswritten* pleasbaly · la] a *written over* as · twill] i *added* · cause] *before canceled word-start* · every] *possibly* any · unimpeachable] *miswritten* unimpeackable · children] *miswritten* childern

TO EVERT A. DUYCKINCK
3 MARCH 1849 · BOSTON

Duyckinck's letter in answer to Melville's 24 February letter, just above, is unlocated. It evidently accused Melville in that 24 February letter of "oscillat[ing] in Emerson's rainbow" and of irreverence toward the archangels in describing Shakespeare as belonging among their ranks. Melville's rejoinder contains a number of oblique topical references. "Emerson's rainbow" alludes to a satirical cartoon that had appeared in the *New-York Tribune* on 6 February, portraying Emerson swinging in an inverted rainbow (see Merton M. Sealts, Jr., *Pursuing Melville, 1940–1980* [Madison: University of Wisconsin Press, 1982], p. 252). "Putnam's store" was the bookshop of G. P. Putnam & Co., at 155 Broadway in New York. Galena, Illinois—where Melville visited his uncle Thomas in the summer of 1840—was named for its lead mines. And the monument to Major General Sir Isaac Brock (1769–1812), erected at Queenston, Ontario, to commemorate a British victory in the War of 1812, was blown up by an Irish-American fanatic on Good Friday, 1840.

The references to Sir Thomas Browne (1605–82) and to Zachary Taylor would have had particular significance for Duyckinck. Melville had borrowed from Duyckinck's library in February 1848 two volumes of the *Works* of Sir Thomas Browne (4 vols., London: William Pickering, 1835–36; Sealts 89, Bercaw 83). Zachary Taylor's defeat of a Mexican force three times the size of his own at Palo Alto in 1846 had figured in Melville's "Authentic Anecdotes of 'Old Zack,'" published in *Yankee Doodle* (24 July to 11 September 1847), a magazine with which

Duyckinck was involved at the time (see the NN *Piazza Tales* volume, pp. 212–29 and 465–66).

As Melville came to the end of the last page of this letter, having driven his horse "so hard" already, he had to tighten his spacing and lengthen his lines in order to fit in his final comments (see the illustration on p. 842 below).

Mount Vernon Street

Saturday, 3ᵈ

Nay, I do not oscillate in Emerson's rainbow, but prefer rather to hang myself in mine own halter than swing in any other man's swing. Yet I think Emerson is more than a brilliant fellow. Be his stuff begged, borrowed, or stolen, or of his own domestic manufacture he is an uncommon man. Swear he is a humbug — then is he no common humbug. Lay it down that had not Sir Thomas Browne lived, Emerson would not have mystified — I will answer, that had not Old Zack's father begot him, Old Zack would never have been the hero of Palo Alto. The truth is that we are all sons, grandsons, or nephews or great-nephews of those who go before us. No one is his own sire. — I was very agreeably disappointed in Mʳ Emerson. I had heard of him as full of transcendentalisms, myths & oracular gibberish; I had only glanced at a book of his once in Putnam's store — that was all I knew of him, till I heard him lecture. — To my surprise, I found him quite intelligible, tho' to say truth, they told me that that night he was unusually plain. —— Now, there is a something about every man elevated above mediocrity, which is, for the most part, instinctively perceptible. This I see in Mʳ Emerson. And, frankly, for the sake of the argument, let us call him a fool; — then had I rather be a fool than a wise man. — I love all men who *dive*. Any fish can swim near the surface, but it takes a great whale to go down stairs five miles or more; & if he dont attain the bottom, why, all the lead in Galena can't fashion the plummet that will. I'm not talking of Mʳ Emerson now — but of the whole corps of thought-divers, that have been diving & coming up again with blood-shot eyes since the world began.

I could readily see in Emerson, notwithstanding his merit, a gaping flaw. It was, the insinuation, that had he lived in those days when the world was made, he might have offered some valuable suggestions. These men are all cracked right across the brow. And never will the pullers-down be able to cope with the builders-up.

And this pulling down is easy enough — a keg of powder blew up
Brock's Monument — but the man who applied the match, could
not, alone, build such a pile to save his soul from the shark-maw of
the Devil. But enough of this Plato who talks thro' his nose. To one
of your habits of thought, I confess that in my last, I seemed, but
only *seemed* irreverent. And do not think, my boy, that because I,
impulsively broke forth in jubillations over Shakspeare, that, therefore, I am of the number of the *snobs* who burn their tuns of rancid
fat at his shrine. No, I would stand afar off & alone, & burn some
pure Palm oil, the product of some overtopping trunk.
— I would to God Shakspeare had lived later, & promenaded in
Broadway. Not that I might have had the pleasure of leaving my
card for him at the Astor, or made merry with him over a bowl of
the fine Duyckinck punch; but that the muzzle which all men wore
on their souls in the Elizebethan day, might not have intercepted
Shakspere's full articulations. For I hold it a verity, that even Shakspeare, was not a frank man to the uttermost. And, indeed, who in
this intolerant Universe is, or can be? But the Declaration of Independence makes a difference. — There, I have driven my horse so
hard that I have made my inn before sundown. I was going to say
something more — It was this. — You complain that Emerson tho' a
denizen of the land of gingerbread, is above munching a plain cake in
company of jolly fellows, & swiging off his ale like you & me. Ah,
my dear sir, that's his misfortune, not his fault. His belly, sir, is in his
chest, & his brains descend down into his neck, & offer an obstacle to
a draught of ale or a mouthful of cake. But here I am. Good bye —
                                                                    H. M.

ALS on a 34 × 21.7 cm sheet, folded in half, of white wove paper with gilt edges. Melville
inscribed all four pages, in ink, and addressed the envelope "Evert A Duyckinck Esq | 'Literary
World' Office | New York."; it was postmarked in Boston on 3 March. Duyckinck later noted in
ink on the envelope "March 3. 1849" and in pencil on the top of the first page "March 1849".

LOCATION: NYPL-D.

PUBLICATION: (partial) Minnigerode, pp. 32–34. Thorp, pp. 371–73. Davis-Gilman 55.

TEXTUAL NOTES: hero] r *added* • heard him] heard *miswritten* herd • unusually] *miswritten*
unusullily *with the final* l *written over another letter and the* y *added* • dont] *before canceled* not • It
was,] *before canceled* that • insinuation] *after canceled* covert • talks] l *added* • jubillations] *before
canceled* at discovering • might not] not *inserted above caret* • Shakspere's] *miswritten* Shakspere • full] *possibly* free • hard] r *added* • is in his chest] is *inserted above caret*

TO HARPER & BROTHERS
26 MARCH 1849 · NEW YORK

When John Murray refused *Mardi* because it was "fiction," John R. Brodhead immediately negotiated the sale of the book to Richard Bentley for two hundred guineas, Melville's asking price, and within three weeks it was advertised as "published this day" on 17 March 1849 in various British publications, including the London *Examiner* and the London *Literary Gazette*.

With British publication secured, Harper & Brothers had only to be notified to proceed with their edition. This notification was written by Allan for his brother, who, apart from traveling to New York on 3 March for a brief visit, remained in Boston with his family until 10 April. On 14 April 1849 the Harper edition of *Mardi*, dedicated to Allan Melville, was published in two volumes.

New York. March. 26th 1849.

Messrs Harper & Brothers.
Gen^{tl}.

Mr Bentley who publishes "Mardi" in England having informed me by note dated 5th inst that he proposed to publish that work on the 15th inst nothing can prevent your publishing here immediately — I notify you accordingly

Respect Yours
Herman Melville
per Allan Melville

LS on a 20.4 × 25.5 cm sheet of blue wove paper, embossed with the manufacturer's square stamp enclosing a crown above the name "BATH". Allan Melville inscribed only one side of the leaf, in ink. Another hand, presumably a clerk's, noted in ink on the verso "Herman Melville | Mar. 26th, 1849 — ".

LOCATION: The Pierpont Morgan Library, New York. MA 1950, the Harper Collection.

PUBLICATION: Davis-Gilman 56.

TEXTUAL NOTE: March] *written over wiped* Feby

TO HARPER & BROTHERS
27 MARCH 1849 · BOSTON

Unlocated. A note requesting that proof sheets of *Mardi* be sent to Evert Duyckinck is cited in Melville's 28 March 1849 letter to Duyckinck, just below. Davis-Gilman Unlocated 305.

TO EVERT A. DUYCKINCK
28 MARCH 1849 · BOSTON

As Melville promised in this letter, the Harpers sent Duyckinck the proof sheets of the first volume of *Mardi*. They arrived on 29 March along with a note from J. W. Harper, Jr., saying that Melville wished no extracts to be published in advance "except in the 'Literary World' "(NYPL-D). Shortly thereafter Duyckinck received the second volume, and on 7, 14, and 21 April he printed substantial extracts in the *Literary World*.

March 28th Boston

Dear Duyckinck — When last in New York, you expressed a desire to be supplied in advance with the sheets of that new work of mine. Yesterday in a note to Cliff Street I requested them to furnish you with the sheets, as ere this they must have been printed. They are for your private eye. I suppose the book will be published now in two or three weeks. Mr Bentley is the man in London. —— Rain, Rain, Rain — an interminable rain that to seek elsewhere than in Boston would be utterly vain — Rhyme by Jove, and spontaneous as heart-beating. — This is the Fourth Day of the Great Boston Rain, & how much longer it is to last the ghost of the last man drowned by the Deluge only knows. I have a continual dripping sensation; and feel like an ill-wrung towel — my soul is damp, & by spreading itself out upon paper seeks to get dry.

Yours well saturated

H Melville

ALS on a 40.4 × 25.1 cm sheet, folded in half, of blue wove paper, embossed with the manufacturer's rectangular stamp enclosing the initials "P & S" within a design of flourishes. Melville inscribed the first page, in ink, and addressed the fourth page "Evert A Duyckinck Esq | New York."; it was postmarked in Boston on 28 March. Duyckinck later noted in pencil on the first page "1849".

LOCATION: NYPL-D.

PUBLICATION: Thorp, p. 373. Davis-Gilman 57.

TEXTUAL NOTES: Bentley is] s *written over* n · Fourth] F *written over* f

TO RICHARD BENTLEY
3 APRIL 1849 · BOSTON

Bentley's "frank & friendly" letter to which Melville responds here is unlocated and was not recorded in Bentley's letterbook for this period (see LETTERS RECEIVED,

March 28th Boston

Dear Duyckinck — When last in New York, you expressed a desire to be supplied in advance with the sheets of that new work of mine. Yesterday in a note to Cliff Street I requested them to furnish you with the sheets, as ere this they must have been printed. They are for your private eye. I suppose the book will be published now in two or three weeks. Mr Bentley is the man in London. — Rain, Rain, Rain — an interminable rain that to seek elsewhere than in Boston would be utterly vain — Rhyme by Jove, and spontaneous as heart-beating. — This is the fourth Day of the Great Boston Rain, & how much longer it is to last the ghost of the last man drowned by the Deluge only knows. I have a continual dripping sensation; and feel like an ill-wrung towel — my soul is damp, & by spreading itself out upon paper seeks to get dry.

Yours well saturated
H Melville

To Evert A. Duyckinck, 28 March 1849 (reduced). Courtesy of the Rare Books and Manuscripts Division, The New York Public Library, Astor, Lenox and Tilden Foundations (Duyckinck Family Papers).

pp. 594–95, for what is known about Bentley's letter). Bentley had initially agreed to publish *Mardi* in two volumes and had so advertised it on 3 March 1849, but two days later he wrote a letter to John R. Brodhead stating that he "thought it best to issue it in three volumes instead of two" (Bentley's letter is attached by a wax seal to a "Memorandum of an Agreement" for *Mardi*, which was prepared by Bentley's firm and signed by Brodhead; the letter's presence in the Melville papers donated to Harvard by Melville's granddaughter Eleanor Metcalf indicates that Brodhead later forwarded it and the contract to Melville).

Boston April 3ᵈ 1849

Dear Sir — By the last steamer letters from yourself & Mʳ Brodhead apprised me of the arrangements having been concluded for the publication of "Mardi." I assure you it is with pleasure that I enter into this connection with you.

As authorised, I have drawn upon you at sixty & ninety days.

I am indebted to you for your frank & friendly letter, & trust you will not fail to write me again, should anything interesting turn up.

Very Truly Yours, Dear Sir,

H Melville

ALS on a 40.2 × 25.1 cm sheet, folded in half, of blue wove paper, embossed with the manufacturer's rectangular stamp enclosing the initials "P & S" within a design of flourishes. Melville inscribed the first page, in ink, and addressed the fourth page "*For the New York Steamer* | Richard Bentley Esq | New Burlington Street | London". It was stamped "Paid" and postmarked (date and place are undeciphered). Another hand noted in pencil on the envelope "For Mardi" and "NY". Still another hand at the top of the first page noted in pencil "Author of Typee' 'Omoo' Mardi &c" and added at the bottom of that page, below Melville's signature, "Herman", also in pencil.

Location: Beinecke Library, Yale University. *Provenance*: James Grant Wilson sale, Merwin-Clayton, 13 April 1905, lot 214; Owen Franklin Aldis (tipped into an American first edition of *Mardi*).

Publication: (partial) *Log*, I, 295–96. Davis, p. 224. Davis-Gilman 58.

Textual Note: your] r *added*

TO JOHN R. BRODHEAD
ON OR AFTER 3 APRIL 1849 · BOSTON

Unlocated. As Melville's 3 April 1849 letter to Richard Bentley, just above, indicates, a communication from Brodhead, now unlocated, had arrived by the same steamer that brought Bentley's letter. Presumably Melville replied to it along lines similar to his reply to Bentley. Davis-Gilman Unlocated 306.

TO EVERT A. DUYCKINCK
5 APRIL 1849 · BOSTON

This last surviving letter in the series written to Duyckinck from Boston again gives an indication of some of Melville's reading. The poem first cited by Melville—" 'Smoking Spiritualised' "—was one of the few secular pieces written by the Reverend Ralph Erskine (1685–1752), whose *Gospel Sonnets* (1720), a kind of versified theology, went through twenty-five editions by 1797. In its 31 March 1849 issue the *Literary World* had reprinted the poem in a review of an American 1849 edition of Erskine's book published by Carter & Brothers in New York.

Melville owned two editions of *The Anatomy of Melancholy* by "*Old* Burton" or Robert Burton—the first a selection (which he had purchased without realizing that it had formerly belonged to his father) and the second a full edition bought in 1848 (Sealts 102, 103; Bercaw 100). Melville's set of Pierre Bayle's *An Historical and Critical Dictionary* has not been located (Sealts 51), nor has any edition of Plato's *Phaedon* that he may have owned; however, a new edition of Madame Dacier's translation of Plato's *Phaedon* (New York: Gowans, 1849) was reviewed in the *Literary World* (3 February 1849). Although Duyckinck's notebook of "Books Lent" does not list the loan at this time, Melville may have borrowed Sir Thomas Browne's works again from him as he had in 1848, for he is not known to have bought a copy until December 1849, when he was in London (*Journals*, p. 44; Sealts 90). Finally, Melville's reference to his own "affair" is to his recently published *Mardi*.

Since Duyckinck's letter in answer to Melville's 3 March letter is unlocated, it is unclear whether Melville learned of the derangement of "Poor Hoffman"—Charles Fenno Hoffman (1806–84)—from it or from a notice that appeared in *Literary America* on 17 March 1849. Hoffman had been the editor of the *Literary World* during a time when Melville was a contributor (May 1847 through September 1848) and had been a member of Duyckinck's literary and social set. Except for a brief interlude in 1849, Hoffman spent the rest of his life in the state hospital at Harrisburg, Pennsylvania. See also Melville's undated letter quoting from a poem by Hoffman, pp. 540–41 below.

Boston April 5th 1849

Dear Duyckinck — Thank you for your note, & the paper which came duly to hand. By the way, that "Smoking Spiritualised" is not bad. Doubtless it has improved by age. The quaint old lines lie in coils like a sailor's pigtail in its keg.

— Ah this sovereign virtue of age — how can we living men attain unto it. We may spice up our dishes with all the condiments of the

Spice Islands & Moluccas, & our dishes may be all venison & wild boar — yet how the deuce can we make them a century or two old? — My Dear Sir, the two great things yet to be discovered are these — The Art of rejuvenating old age in men, & oldageifying youth in books. — Who in the name of the trunk-makers would think of reading *Old* Burton were his book published for the first to day? — All ambitious authors should have ghosts capable of revisiting the world, to snuff up the steam of adulation, which begins to rise straightway as the Sexton throws his last shovelfull on him. — Down goes his body & up flies his name.

Poor Hoffman — I remember the shock I had when I first saw the mention of his madness. — But he was just the man to go mad — imaginative, voluptuously inclined, poor, unemployed, in the race of life distanced by his inferiors, unmarried, — without a port or haven in the universe to make. His present misfortune — rather blessing — is but the sequel to a long experience of morbid habits of thought. —— This going mad of a friend or acquaintance comes straight home to every man who feels his soul in him, — which but few men do. For in all of us lodges the same fuel to light the same fire. And he who has never felt, momentarily, what madness is has but a mouthful of brains. What sort of sensation permanent madness is may be very well imagined — just as we imagine how we felt when we were infants, tho' we can not recall it. In both conditions we are irresponsible & riot like gods without fear of fate. — It is the climax of a mad night of revelry when the blood has been transmuted into brandy. — But if we prate much of this thing we shall be illustrating our own propositions. —

I am glad you like that affair of mine. But it seems so long now since I wrote it, & my mood has so changed, that I dread to look into it, & have purposely abstained from so doing since I thanked God it was off my hands. — Would that a man could do something & then say — It is finished. — not that one thing only, but all others — that he has reached his uttermost, & can never exceed it. But live & push — tho' we put one leg forward ten miles — its no reason the other must lag behind — no, *that* must again distance the other — & so we go till we get the cramp & die. — I bought a set of Bayle's Dictionary the other day, & on my return to New York intend to lay the great old folios side by side & go to sleep on them thro' the summer, with the Phaedon in one hand & Tom Brown in the other. — Good bye I'm called. — I shall be in New York next week — early part.

H Melville

ALS on a 40.2 × 25.1 cm sheet, folded in half, of blue wove paper, embossed with the manufacturer's rectangular stamp enclosing the initials "P & S" within a design of flourishes. Melville inscribed the first three pages, in ink, and addressed the fourth page "Evert A Duyckinck Esq | New York."; it was postmarked in Boston on 5 April.

LOCATION: NYPL-D.

PUBLICATION: (partial) Minnigerode, pp. 8–9. Thorp, pp. 373–75. Davis-Gilman 59.

TEXTUAL NOTES: morbid] *conjectural reading; miswritten* morbib *with second* b *written over a wiped letter* · permanent] *miswritten* permant · thing we] thing *possibly* why · God] G *written over* g

TO LEMUEL SHAW
23 APRIL 1849 · NEW YORK

Returning to New York on 10 April 1849 from their extended stay in Boston, the Melvilles had brought with them Ellen Sullivan, who had been a domestic in the Shaw household for some time, to assist Elizabeth (Lizzie) with the baby. On her return to Boston, as its envelope indicates, Mrs. Sullivan carried this letter, headed only 23 April, to Judge Shaw. Whether Elizabeth's half-brother Samuel Savage Shaw (1833–1915) in turn joined the Melvilles during his vacation—as Melville proposes here—is not known. Samuel Shaw graduated from the Boston Latin School in the spring of 1849 and entered Harvard in July.

Turning from domestic news, Melville surveys a number of the British and American reviews of *Mardi.* The reviewer for the London *Athenæum* (24 March 1849) "cut into" *Mardi,* as Melville writes, calling it a "strange book" in which were "mingled many madnesses" compounded of Carlyle, Emerson, and the "vapid philosophy of Mr. Fenimore Cooper's 'Monikins,'" adding that the opening scenes were the only "good pages of this provoking book." The *Boston Post* (18 April 1849) considered *Mardi* a disappointment after Melville's earlier "graceful, fascinating and vivacious books," concluding that it was "not only tedious but unreadable."

The London *Examiner* (31 March 1849) and the London *Literary Gazette* (24 March 1849) were both more favorably disposed. The *Examiner* recognized the "sly hits at mortal absurdities" in the conversations of the characters and complimented the major digressions in the book as "examples of thoughtful writing, and very extensive reading, much in the manner of Sir Thomas Browne, and with a dash of old Burton and Sterne." The *Literary Gazette* found in the book an "allegorical theme, singularly dressed up with those pieces of scenic and personal description, of which the author is master in regard to this part of the world, and yet allusive (though we must say, to our apprehension, too vaguely) to matters of universal note and the business of life."

New York April 23^d

My Dear Sir — Mrs Sullivan returns to Boston conveying the intelligence of Lizzie's improving strength, & Malcolm's precocious growth. Both are well.

We all expect Samuel to honor us with his presence during the approaching vacation; and I have no doubt he will not find it difficult to spend his time pleasantly with so many companions.

I see that Mardi has been cut into by the London Atheneum, and also burnt by the common hangman in the Boston Post. However the London Examiner & Literary Gazette; & other papers this side of the water have done differently. These attacks are matters of course, and are essential to the building up of any permanent reputation — if such should ever prove to be mine. — "There's nothing in it!" cried the dunce, when he threw down the 47th problem of the 1st Book of Euclid — "There's nothing in it! — " — Thus with the posed critic. But Time, which is the solver of all riddles, will solve "Mardi."

I trust that you will be able so to arrange your affairs as to afford us a more lengthened visit this summer than you did last year.

All the family beg to be kindly remembered.

Sincerely Yours

H Melville

ALS on a 32.2 × 20.3 cm sheet, folded in half, of blue wove paper. Melville inscribed the first two pages, in ink, and addressed the fourth page "Chief Justice Shaw | Boston | Mrs Sullivan." Lemuel Shaw later noted in ink on that page "Herman Melville | 23 April." Another hand noted in pencil on the first page "(1849)".

LOCATION: HCL-M.

PUBLICATION: (partial) *Log*, I, 300. Metcalf, p. 62. Davis-Gilman 60.

TEXTUAL NOTE: approaching] *miswritten* approching

TO RICHARD BENTLEY
5 JUNE 1849 · NEW YORK

Although by the time of this letter Melville had received "assurances" that *Mardi* had "not been written in vain" from favorable reviews in such American periodicals as the *Literary World* (14 April 1849) and the *Home Journal* (21 April 1849) as well as from such British periodicals as the *New Monthly Magazine and Humourist* (April) and the London *Morning Post* (30 April 1849), other early reviews in both

England and America were not as appreciative. Unfavorable reviews from England (some more hostile than others) that would have had time to cross the Atlantic by early June included those in the London *Athenæum* (24 March; see the headnote to the letter just above), *John Bull* (April), the London *Weekly Chronicle* (1 April), the *Spectator* (21 April), *Sharpe's London Journal* (15 May), and possibly the *Morning Chronicle* (19 May). Even the reviewer in Bentley's own *Miscellany* (April) had reservations about the book and could only advise that it was one which "the reader will probably like very much or detest altogether, according to the measure of his own imagination."

Following King Media's command to Babbalanja in *Mardi*—"Away with your logic and conic sections" (chap. 181, p. 606)—Melville proposes in this letter to Bentley a "plain, straightforward, amusing narrative." When it was published by Bentley late in September, this book—*Redburn*—was longer, rather than "a fraction smaller," than *Typee* (see his next letter to Bentley on 20 July 1849 in which he explains that he has "enlarged it somewhat"). Despite his assurances that it would attract a popular audience, Melville received fifty pounds less than he here asked for it.

Although Bentley in his reply of 20 June 1849 (see LETTERS RECEIVED, pp. 595–97) promised to expedite Melville's request for copies of *Mardi*, Melville's subsequent letter of 20 July 1849 to Bentley indicates that none had arrived, and Melville may not have received any until he called personally on Bentley in London in December 1849, as suggested by the fact that two of the surviving presentation copies—those to Allan Melville (NYPL–Autograph Collection) and to Evert Duyckinck (NYPL–Collections of the Rare Book Room)—are both dated 2 February 1850, after he arrived home (see also Melville's accompanying letter to Duyckinck on that date, below).

New York June 5th 1849

Dear Sir — The critics on your side of the water seem to have fired quite a broadside into "Mardi"; but it was not altogether unexpected. In fact the book is of a nature to attract compliments of that sort from some quarters; and as you may be aware yourself, it is judged only as a work meant to entertain. And I can not but think that its having been brought out in England in the ordinary novel form must have led to the disappointment of many readers, who would have been better pleased with it, perhaps, had they taken it up in the first place for what it really is. — Besides, the peculiar thoughts & fancies of a Yankee upon politics & other matters could hardly be presumed to delight that class of gentlemen who conduct your leading journals; while the metaphysical ingredients (for want of a better term) of the book, must of course repel some of those who read simply for amusement. — However, it will reach those for whom it is intended; and I have already received assurances that "Mardi", in its higher purposes, has not been written in vain.

You may think, in your own mind that a man is unwise, — indiscreet, to write a work of that kind, when he might have written one perhaps, calculated merely to please the general reader, & not provoke attack, however masqued in an affectation of indifference or contempt. But some of us scribblers, My Dear Sir, always have a certain something unmanageable in us, that bids us do this or that, and be done it must — hit or miss.

I have now in preparation a thing of a widely different cast from "Mardi": — a plain, straightforward, amusing narrative of personal experience — the son of a gentleman on his first voyage to sea as a sailor — no metaphysics, no conic-sections, nothing but cakes & ale. I have shifted my ground from the South Seas to a different quarter of the globe — nearer home — and what I write I have almost wholly picked up by my own observations under comical circumstances. In size the book will be perhaps a fraction smaller than "Typee"; will be printed here by the Harpers, & ready for them two or three months hence, or before. I value the English Copyright at one hundred & fifty pounds, and think it would be wise to put it forth in a manner, admitting of a popular circulation.

Write me if you please at your earliest leisure; and as you have not yet sent me any copies of your edition of "Mardi" — (which of course I impute to the fact of the prodigious demand for the book with you) — I will thank you to forward me three copies. A note dropped to my friend Mr Brodhead of the Legation, will be the means of informing you whether he can send them to me in the Despatch Bag. If he cannot, the parcel would reach me by Harnden's Express, — addressed to Care of Allan Melville N° 14 Wall Street, New York.

Very Faithfully, Dear Sir,

Herman Melville

Richard Bentley Esq
New Burlington Street.

ALS on a 39.4 × 25 cm sheet, folded in half, of blue wove paper, faintly embossed with the manufacturer's small oval stamp enclosing the initials "P & S". Melville inscribed the first three pages, in ink.

LOCATION: at present unknown. *Provenance*: Hodgson & Co., sale 13, 27–28 April 1939, lot 564; Scribner's Book Store; H. Bradley Martin sale, Sotheby's, New York, sale 5971, 30–31 January 1990, in lot 2167; 19th Century Shop in partnership with other book dealers.

PUBLICATION: Birss, "A Mere Sale to Effect," pp. 245–47. Davis-Gilman 61.

TEXTUAL NOTES: higher] *miswritten* higer • may think,] *before canceled* that a • affectation] *after canceled* aff • hundred] *miswritten* hundread • it would] would *written over* will • reach me by] *originally* reach by me *then* me *wiped and the word inserted above caret after* reach

TO RICHARD BENTLEY
20 JULY 1849 · NEW YORK

Despite Melville's "flattering unction" (*Hamlet*, 2.4.143) in this response to Bentley's discouraged letter of 20 June 1849 (see LETTERS RECEIVED, pp. 595–97), a late "goodly harvest" was not realized. *Mardi* never became a profitable book for Bentley. His "Profit & Loss" statement (formerly in the collection of H. Bradley Martin), sent to Melville in March 1852, listed *Mardi* with a deficit of £68.7.6 and Melville's four books, *Mardi*, *Redburn*, *White-Jacket*, and *The Whale*, as having at that time a deficit of £453.4.6 and a "Probable eventual loss" of £350.

Bentley's 20 June letter had also reported the recent ruling on 5 June 1849 in the case of *Boosey v. Purday* that made it even more difficult for foreigners to be protected by copyright laws in Great Britain (see the headnote to Bentley's letter for more about this ruling). Melville's contention in this reply that "ere long, doubtless, we shall have something of an international law" turned out not to be the case. He along with Cooper, Bryant, Irving, Putnam, Griswold, and others signed a petition calling for an international copyright agreement that was belatedly submitted to the Senate in 1852, but such efforts remained unsuccessful until the 1891 bill authorizing reciprocal copyright agreements with foreign nations was passed by Congress. (For more on the copyright issue see James J. Barnes, *Authors, Publishers, and Politicians: The Quest for an Anglo-American Copyright Agreement, 1815–54* [Columbus: Ohio State University Press, 1974], pp. 167, 227.)

Despite both the copyright situation and the poor showing of *Mardi*, Bentley was willing to proceed with *Redburn*. On 2 July 1849 the Harpers had accepted the book and had gone to press immediately. The final title—*Redburn: His First Voyage. Being the Sailor-Boy Confessions and Reminiscences of the Son-of-a-Gentleman, in the Merchant Service*—was deposited for copyright in New York on 18 August 1849. Soon after, a set of the Harper proofs was sent to John R. Brodhead for submission to Bentley, who went to press immediately to avoid any possible piracy, publishing the book on 29 September 1849 in a two-volume edition.

New York July 20th '49

Dear Sir — I am indebted to you for yours of the 20th June. — Your report concerning "Mardi" was pretty much as I expected; but you know perhaps that there are goodly harvests which ripen late, especially when the grain is remarkably strong. At any rate, Mr Bentley, let us by all means lay this flattering unction to our souls, since it is so grateful a prospect to you as a publisher, & to me as an author. — But

I need not assure you how deeply I regret that, for any period, you should find this venture of "Mardi" an unprofitable thing for you; & I should feel still more greived, did I suppose it was going to eventuate in a positive loss to you. But this can not be in the end. — However, these considerations — all, solely with respect to yourself — prevail upon me to accept your amendment to my overtures concerning my new work: — which amendment, I understand to be this — £100 down on the receipt of the sheets, on account of half profits; & that you shall be enabled to publish a few days previous to the appearance of the book in America — and this, I hereby guarantee.

The work is now going thro' the press, & I think I shall be able to send it to you in the course of three weeks or so. It will readily make two volumes got up in your style, as I have enlarged it somewhat to the size of "Omoo" — perhaps it may be a trifle larger.

Notwithstanding that recent decision of your courts of law, I can hardly imagine that it will occasion any serious infringement of any rights you have in any American book. And ere long, doubtless, we shall have something of an international law — so much desired by all American writers — which shall settle this matter upon the basis of justice. The only marvel is, that it does not now exist.

The copies of "Mardi" have not yet come to hand, tho' I sent to the Harnden & Co, to inquire.

Yours Sincerely
H Melville.

Richard Bentley Esq
New Burlington Street

ALS on a 39.6 × 25 cm sheet, folded in half, of blue wove paper. Melville inscribed the first three pages, in ink.

LOCATION: at present unknown. *Provenance*: Hodgson & Co., sale 13, 27–28 April 1939, lot 565; Scribner's Book Store; H. Bradley Martin sale, Sotheby's, New York, sale 5971, 30–31 January 1990, in lot 2167; Lion Heart Autographs, catalogue 22 (January 1991), item 63 (with reproduction).

PUBLICATION: Birss, "A Mere Sale to Effect," pp. 247–48. Davis-Gilman 62.

TEXTUAL NOTES: there] *miswritten* threre • especially] *miswritten* especilly • positive] *miswritten* possitive • a few days] *inserted above caret* • America] *miswritten* Amerca • American] *miswritten* Amercian *with* A *rewritten* • American] *miswritten* Amercan • have not yet] not *inserted above caret*

TO THE SECRETARY OF LEGATION, LONDON
AUGUST 1849 · NEW YORK

Melville wrote this letter to accompany the proofs of *Redburn*; he addressed it simply to the office of the secretary of legation because he knew that John R. Brodhead was to be succeeded by John Chandler Bancroft Davis (1822–1907), but did not know when. Davis was the son of Senator John Davis of Massachusetts and the nephew of George Bancroft. He served as secretary of legation under Abbott Lawrence, minister to the Court of St. James's (see the entry for Melville's unlocated letter of 22 November 1849), succeeding Brodhead on 31 August 1849. Melville met Davis at the legation not long after arriving in London in November 1849 (*Journals*, p. 22).

New York, August

Dear Sir — If this letter is opened by Mr Brodhead, he will be at no loss to know what it means; since he has most kindly furthered some affairs of mine in London. In the present case, however, *all* I desire, is, that the accompanying parcel for Mr Bentley the publisher, be retained at the Legation, till that gentleman calls or sends for it; which will be immediately; as he is advised of its transmission, & through what channel. —

If, however, Mr Davis should open this letter (and I do not know, exactly, which gentleman will hold the seals at the time it reaches its destination) I have then to beg a favor, of a gentleman, who is personnally unacquainted with me. — Will Mr Davis be so kind, as simply to take care of the parcel, & deliver it to Mr Bentley when he calls?

To Mr Brodhead, it would be unnecessary to state, that my reason for sending the parcel through the Despatch Bag (as in previous cases) is the apprehension, that if forwarded by Express, it would be almost certain of seizure, or protracted detention at the Custom House.

Very Truly
Herman Melville.

The Secretary of the
American Legation
London.

ALS on a 15.8 × 20.1 cm part-sheet (torn along the bottom) of blue wove paper. Melville inscribed both sides of the leaf, in ink. Another hand later added the year "1849" in the dateline of the letter.

LOCATION: at present unknown. *Provenance*: Dudley Olcott; Parke-Bernet Galleries, sale 863, 21–22 April 1947, lot 518; H. Bradley Martin sale, Sotheby's, New York, sale 5971, 30–31 January 1990, in lot 2167; 19th Century Shop in partnership with other book dealers.

PUBLICATION: Birss, "A Mere Sale to Effect," p. 248. Davis-Gilman 63.

TEXTUAL NOTES: *all*] ll *rewritten* • till] t *over wiped* w • beg a] a *inserted above caret after canceled* the

TO LEMUEL SHAW
BEFORE 10 SEPTEMBER 1849 · NEW YORK

Unlocated. A letter written "the other day concerning the letters of introduction" is cited in Melville's subsequent letter of 10 September 1849 to Lemuel Shaw, just below. By September 1849, Melville had completed in a matter of weeks his fifth book, *White-Jacket*. The New York lawyer A. Oakey Hall in one of his "Croton" letters in the *New Orleans Commercial Bulletin* reported that Melville had "dashed" the book off "in a score of sittings" (see the *New Log*, 9 April 1850). Harper & Brothers accepted it and advanced him five hundred dollars, but in order to secure the best terms for British publication Melville apparently waited to negotiate the sale in person when he went to London at the end of 1849. This letter to Shaw, like the 10 September one, was evidently a request for letters of introduction to take with him on his projected trip to England and the Continent. Davis-Gilman Unlocated 308.

TO LEMUEL SHAW
10 SEPTEMBER 1849 · NEW YORK

At Lemuel Shaw's request Edward Everett (1794–1865), the renowned orator, former minister to the Court of St. James's, and current president of Harvard, wrote letters of introduction to Samuel Rogers and Richard Monckton Milnes in London, and Gustave de Beaumont in Paris (see *Journals*, pp. 610–14, for Everett's drafts of these letters as well as his reply to Shaw's letter of request). Melville records making use of only one of these letters—that to Samuel Rogers—during his 1849–50 trip abroad (*Journals*, p. 22). There is no evidence whether Shaw requested or received from Emerson either the letter to Carlyle or any other letters, and Melville did not meet Carlyle in England. Although this letter is headed only with the month and day, it clearly belongs to 1849 because of its association with Melville's trip to England.

Monday Sep^t 10th

My Dear Sir — In writing you the other day concerning the letters of introduction, I forgot to say, that could you conveniently procure me one from Mr Emerson to Mr Carlyle, I should be obliged to you. —— We were concerned to hear that you were not entirely well, some days ago; but I hope you will bring the intelligence of your better health along with you, when you come here on that promised visit, upon which you set out the day after tomorrow. Lizzie is most anxiously expecting you — but Malcolm seems to await the event with the utmost philosophy. — The weather here at present is exceedingly agreeable — quite cool, & in the morning, bracing.

My best rememberances to Mrs Shaw & all.

Most Sincerely Yours
H Melville

If, besides a letter to M͏ʳ Carlyle, M͏ʳ Emerson could give you *other* letters, I should be pleased.

The Board of Health have ceased making reports — the Cholera having almost entirely departed from the city.

ALS on a 32 × 20.4 cm part-sheet (torn along the bottom), folded in half, of blue wove paper, faintly embossed with the manufacturer's square stamp at the bottom of the first leaf. Melville inscribed the first three pages, in ink, and addressed the fourth page "Chief Justice Shaw | Boston." and wrote on it "*Paid*"; it was postmarked in New York on 11 September. Lemuel Shaw noted in ink on that page "Herman | Sept 10".

LOCATION: MHS-S.

PUBLICATION: (partial) *Log*, I, 312–13. Davis-Gilman 64.

TEXTUAL NOTES: hear] *after canceled word-start* · that you] you *miswritten* your · bring] n *added*

TO LEMUEL SHAW
6 OCTOBER 1849 · NEW YORK

Five days before his delayed sailing on Thursday, 11 October, Melville wrote this letter to his father-in-law thanking him for his efforts in obtaining letters of introduction. The additional letter of introduction mentioned by Melville (now unlocated), presumably solicited by Judge Shaw, from a "M͏ʳ Baldwin" may have possibly been from Roger Sherman Baldwin (1793–1863), a senator from Connecticut from 1847 to 1851 and later governor of that state. Another "M͏ʳ Baldwin" later known to Melville through Shaw's niece, Ellen Marett Gifford, was Simeon Baldwin (see Melville's 17 November 1889 letter to him, below). Since he was a contemporary of Melville, and hence too young to have a grown son in Paris, the letter may have been to his father. Finally a Mr. and Mrs.

William Baldwin of Guilford, Connecticut, were among the guests invited by the Shaws to Melville's wedding (HCL-M). In any case Melville does not in his journal record using any letter from Baldwin.

Although Melville gives 25 September as the publication date of *Redburn*, the date was 29 September according to the official report of Richard Bentley's firm—*A List of the Principal Publications Issued from New Burlington Street during the Year 1849*. Harper & Brothers published it in the United States on 15 or 16 November. As this letter indicates, the Harpers also had already prepared proof sheets for Melville's "other book"—*White-Jacket*—for him to take with him to England.

For Mrs. Sullivan, to whom Melville sends his farewell, see the headnote to his letter of 23 April 1849.

New York Oct 6th 1849

My Dear Sir —

On Monday or Tuesday next the ship is to sail, and I must bid you the last good-bye.

On looking over the letters of introduction again, I am more than ever pleased with them; & would again thank you for your kindness. A few days ago, by the way, I received a letter of introduction (thro' the post) from Mr Baldwin to his son in Paris.

Lizzie is becoming more reconciled to the idea of my departure, especially as she will have Malcolm for company during my abscence. And I have no doubt, that when she finds herself surrounded by her old friends in Boston, she will bear the temporary separation with more philosophy than she has anticipated. At any rate, she will be ministered to by the best of freinds.

It is uncertain, now, how long I may be absent; and, of course, my travels will have to be bounded by my purse & by prudential considerations. Economy, however, is my mottoe.

"Redburn" was published in London on the 25th of last month; & will come out here in the course of two weeks or so. The other book I have now in plate-proofs, all ready to go into my trunk.

For Redburn I anticipate no particular reception of any kind. It may be deemed a book of tolerable entertainment; — & may be accounted dull. — As for the other book, it will be sure to be attacked in some quarters. But no reputation that is gratifying to me, can possibly be achieved by either of these books. They are two *jobs*, which I have done for money — being forced to it, as other men are to sawing wood. And while I have felt obliged to refrain from writing the kind of book I would wish to; yet, in writing these two

books, I have not repressed myself much — so far as *they* are concerned; but have spoken pretty much as I feel. — Being books, then
written in this way, my only desire for their "success" (as it is
called) springs from my pocket, & not from my heart. So far as I am
individually concerned, & independent of my pocket, it is my earnest desire to write those sort of books which are said to "fail."
— Pardon this egotism.

Mama has quite recovered from her temporary indisposition; &
all the family are well. They beg to be most kindly remembered to
yourself, & Mrs Shaw, & all. Add my own best rememberances to
theirs, and beleive me, My Dear Sir,

Sincerely Yours
H Melville.

Chief Justice Shaw.

If you please, bid Mrs Sullivan good bye for me.

ALS on a 32 × 20.4 cm part-sheet (torn along the top), folded in half, of blue wove paper.
Melville inscribed all four pages, in ink. Lemuel Shaw noted in ink on the fourth page "Her-
man Melville | Oct 6." For the signet Melville used to seal this letter, see p. 812 below.

LOCATION: MHS-S.

PUBLICATION: (partial) *Log*, I, 316. Metcalf, pp. 67–68. Davis-Gilman 65.

TEXTUAL NOTES: the ship] t *written over* I • friends in] *after canceled* friends • deemed] *before
canceled* an • felt] *after canceled* not • please] *miswritten* plase

TO R. H. DANA, JR.
6 OCTOBER 1849 · NEW YORK

Melville first met his "sea-brother" Richard Henry Dana, Jr. (1815–82) in 1847 at a
tea arranged by Dana's cousin, Ida Russell (see her 8 July 1847 invitation to Dana
[MHS-D] and *The Journal of Richard Henry Dana, Jr.*, ed. Robert F. Lucid [Cam-
bridge: Harvard University Press, 1968], p. 336). Now, two years later, Melville
thanks Dana for writing, on 12 September 1849 at Lemuel Shaw's request, a letter
of introduction to the publisher Edward Moxon (1801–58). (Moxon had published
Dana's *Two Years before the Mast* in London in 1840; for his "connection with
Lamb," see Melville's 1 May 1850 letter to Dana, written after Melville met Moxon.) Although Melville did not record in his London journal making use of the
letter, he probably did present it when he went to see Moxon on 20 November
1849 (see *Journals*, pp. 23 and 312, and pp. 614–15 for Dana's draft version of his
letter to Moxon).

It is apparent from this letter that Dana had written Melville encouraging him to use his experiences aboard the frigate *United States* as the basis for a "man-of-war book"—something he had already done. The "printed copy" that Melville mentions here is a reference to the proof sheets of the American edition of *White-Jacket* (not published until March 1850). Since a British publisher had not yet been secured, the book was particularly open to piracy there—hence Melville's request for confidentiality. There is no record of any public comment from Dana on *White-Jacket* after its publication, nor was there any great need for his endorsement since the reviews were generally quite favorable (see the NN edition, pp. 430–34); moreover, as it turned out, Melville was not away when *White-Jacket* was published, as he anticipated in this letter. Dana did, however, write Melville a letter, now unlocated, which praised *White-Jacket* and *Redburn* (see Melville's reply of 1 May 1850, below).

New York Oct 6th 1849.

My Dear Mr Dana — If I have till now deferred answering your very kind letter by Judge Shaw, it has been only, that I might give additional emphasis to my reply, by leaving it to the eve of my departure. Your letter to Mr Moxon is most welcome. From his connection with Lamb, & what I have chanced to hear of his personal character, he must be a very desirable acquaintance. — Your hint concerning a man-of-war has, in anticipation, been acted on. A printed copy of the book is before me. As it will not appear for some two or three months, may I beg of you, that you will consider this communication confidential? The reason is obvious.

This man-of-war book, My Dear Sir, is in some parts rathar man-of-*warish* in style — rathar aggressive I fear. — But you, who like myself, have experienced in person the usages to which a sailor is subjected, will not wonder, perhaps, at any thing in the book. Would to God, that every man who shall read it, had been before the mast in an armed ship, that he might know something himself of what he shall only read of. — I shall be away, in all probability, for some months after the publication of the book. If it is taken hold of in an unfair or ignorant way; & if you should possibly think, that from your peculiar experiences in sea-life, you would be able to say a word to the purpose — may I hope that you will do so, if you can spare the time, & are generous enough to bestow the trouble? — Your name would do a very great deal; but if you choose to keep that out of sight in the matter, well & good. — Be not alarmed, — I do not mean to bore you with a request to do any thing in this thing — only this: if you feel so inclined, do it, & God bless you.

Accept my best thanks for your kindness & beleive me fraternally Yours — a sea-brother —

H Melville.

Richard H Dana Jr Esq.

A little nursery tale of mine (which, possibly, you may have seen advertised as in press) called "Redburn" is not the book to which I refer above.

ALS on a 32 × 20.4 cm part-sheet (torn along the top), folded in half, of blue wove paper. Melville inscribed the first three pages, in ink.

LOCATION: MHS-D.

PUBLICATION: Harrison Hayford, "Two New Letters of Herman Melville," *ELH* 2 (March 1944), 76–77. Davis-Gilman 66.

TEXTUAL NOTES: hear of his] s *written over* m • shall read] shall *inserted above caret before* reads (*vestigial* s) • I do not] *before canceled* attempt to • bless] e *added* • nursery tale] *inserted with caret above canceled* work

TO EVERT A. DUYCKINCK
10 OCTOBER 1849 · NEW YORK

Originally scheduled to depart on 8 October, Melville's London packet was kept in port by violent storms. Melville boarded on 10 October, but returned home again for the night, evidently promising Duyckinck to visit him that evening. The ship finally sailed the next day. Although he expected that Duyckinck and perhaps others would accompany him aboard to the Narrows, then return on the tug with the pilot, as was often done, rainy weather prevented anyone from doing so. Among the last "familiar faces" Melville recorded seeing on the wharf was George Duyckinck's, but not Evert's (*Journals*, p. 3).

Wednesday Evening

My Dear Duyckinck

Having taken so dramatic a farewell of my kindred this morning, and finding myself among them again this evening, I feel almost as if I had indeed accomplished the tour of Europe, & been absent a twelvemonth; — so that I must spend my first evening of arrival at my own fireside. Release me from my promise then, and

save what you were going to tell me till tomorrow when we glide
down the bay.

Herman Melville.

ALS on a 24.9 × 20 cm part-sheet (torn along the top) of white wove paper, faintly embossed
with the manufacturer's circular stamp on the second leaf of the folded sheet. Melville in-
scribed the first page, in ink, and addressed the fourth page "Evert A Duyckinck Esq |
Clinton Square." Duyckinck noted in pencil below Melville's signature on the first page "Oct
10. 1849", underscored with a flourish.

LOCATION: NYPL-D.

PUBLICATION: *Log*, I, 317. Davis-Gilman 67.

TEXTUAL NOTE: first] s *added*

TO ELIZABETH SHAW MELVILLE
11 OCTOBER–4 NOVEMBER 1849 · ATLANTIC OCEAN

Unlocated. At the close of the journal Melville kept aboard ship on his voyage to
England, he wrote in his entry for 4 November: "For the last time I lay aside my
'*log*,' to add a line or two to Lizzie's letter — the last I shall write on board" (*Jour-
nals*, p. 12). One or more letters to his wife can be inferred from this entry. Allan
Melville later reported in a letter to Evert Duyckinck, dated only "Friday": "Mrs
Herman Melville, with Master Malcolm, has returned to town, from Boston & is
impatient for the return of the 'Able seaman' & has no objection to the East wind.
By the way Mrs Herman has read to me parts of a letter written on the passage out
by which it appears that the author was homesick from the start!" (NYPL-D).
Davis-Gilman Unlocated 310.

TO RICHARD BENTLEY
[8?] NOVEMBER 1849 · LONDON

Unlocated. Melville recorded in his London journal that on 8 November 1849—his
second day in London—he went to Bentley's office in New Burlington Street, only
to find that the publisher was in Brighton. Probably that day Melville sent a note to
him there saying he had arrived and requesting a meeting, since he received a reply
on 10 November (see the entry just below and *Journals*, p. 14). Davis-Gilman Unlocated 311.

TO RICHARD BENTLEY
10 NOVEMBER 1849 · LONDON

Unlocated. In his journal entry for 10 November 1849, Melville reported: "At
breakfast received a note from Mr Bentley in reply to mine, saying he would come

up from Brighton at any time convenient to me. Wrote him, 'Monday noon, in New Burlington St:' " (*Journals*, pp. 14–15). For Bentley's reply and their subsequent meeting, see LETTERS RECEIVED, p. 598, and *Journals*, pp. 16–17. Davis-Gilman Unlocated 312.

TO ELIZABETH SHAW MELVILLE AND FAMILY
13 NOVEMBER 1849 · LONDON

Unlocated. After witnessing the widely publicized hanging of the Manning couple (who had been found jointly guilty of murder) as well as visiting the Zoological Gardens and Regent's Park on 13 November 1849, Melville wrote a letter "home" that evening during a boring conversation with a shipboard acquaintance, as he recorded in his journal (*Journals*, p. 17). Davis-Gilman Unlocated 313.

TO JOHN MURRAY
16 NOVEMBER 1849 · LONDON

Headed only "Friday," this letter, written at the office of Melville's first British publisher, John Murray, can be dated 16 November 1849 on the basis of Melville's journal entry for that Friday in 1849, which states: "After breakfast at the old place in the Strand, went to the British Museum — big arm & foot — Rosetta stone — Ninevah sculptures — &c. From thence to Albemarle Street — Mr Murray was not in. Home, & wrote to Allan by the 'Canada'. Walked thro' Seven Dials to Oxford Street & so to Murray's again. Found him in — was very polite, but 'would not be in his line to publish my book'. Offered to give me some of his 'Hand Books' as I was going on the Continant" (*Journals*, p. 19).

Friday 1. P.M.

Dear Sir
    I am sorry not to find you in. They tell me you will here about 4. P.M. to day. I will call at that hour, and as I much desire to see you concerning some final arrangement concerning the book I left, I trust to find you in, then.

Very Truly
H Melville

John Murray Esq.

ALS on a 22.7 × 18.4 cm sheet, folded in half, of white wove paper, embossed with the manufacturer's small circular stamp enclosing a crown and the name "SUPERFINE LONDON SATIN". Melville inscribed the first page, in ink, and addressed the fourth "John Murray Esq. | Present."; another hand noted at the bottom of the letter "Herman Melville | author of Typee".

LOCATION: Collection of David Shneidman. *Provenance*: Sotheby's, London, 19–20 May 1975, lot 370; H. Holdsworth Rawnsley ("Melville for Sale," *Melville Society Extracts* 26 [June 1976], 18–19); Walter Benjamin Autographs, catalogue 916 (1986); Robert F. Batchelder Autographs 1988.

TEXTUAL NOTE: will here] *intervening word lacking (presumably "be")*

TO ALLAN MELVILLE
16 NOVEMBER 1849 · LONDON

Unlocated. On Friday, 16 November, having visited the British Museum and then having failed to find John Murray at his office, Melville returned to his lodgings "& wrote to Allan by the 'Canada' "—one of the Cunard steamers, which usually left Liverpool on Saturdays (*Journals*, p. 19; quoted more fully in the headnote just above). Melville's journal entry gives no indication of the letter's contents. Davis-Gilman Unlocated 314.

TO ELIZABETH SHAW MELVILLE
18 NOVEMBER 1849 · LONDON

Unlocated. Still unsuccessful in obtaining his asking price for *White-Jacket* from any of the publishers to whom he had offered it, Melville had to give up the plans he had made to visit Rome. He "wrote Lizzie" on 18 November 1849, a rainy Sunday, probably informing her of this. The next day, he reports sending this letter off by a ship named the *Herman* (*Journals*, pp. 21, 22). Davis-Gilman Unlocated 315.

TO LORD JOHN MANNERS
19 NOVEMBER 1849 · LONDON

Two unlocated letters. Lord John James Robert Manners (1818–1906), younger son of the duke of Rutland, left a "very kind" note for Melville at Bentley's office on 19 November, probably at the instance of Melville's acquaintance N. P. Willis (see the entry for Melville's 14 December 1849 letter to Willis, below, and *Journals*, pp. 21 and 305). Melville's journal records: "Went home & answered Manners' note, saying I would call tomorrow. Having no one to send it by took it myself to the Albany, & handing it to the beadle to be delivered was told that Lord J. M. had that morning left town. Wrote him therefore at Belvoir Castle" (*Journals*, p. 22). Despite efforts by both of them, as well as by the duke of Rutland, no meeting could be arranged (see the entry for Melville's unlocated letter to the duke of Rutland on 17 December 1849, below). Davis-Gilman Unlocated 316.

TO JOHN MURRAY
BETWEEN 19 AND 22 NOVEMBER 1849 · LONDON

Unlocated. On 19 November 1849, Melville received an invitation (now unlocated) from John Murray to dinner on Friday, 23 November (*Journals*, p. 22). Melville's journal does not record a visit to Murray's office between receiving the invitation and declining, on 22 November, another invitation for the same evening (*Journals*, p. 24); thus, a letter of acceptance to Murray can be inferred. For Melville's description of his evening at Murray's, see *Journals*, pp. 25–26.

TO JOSHUA BATES
21 NOVEMBER 1849 · LONDON

Unlocated. Joshua Bates (1788–1864), an American partner in the large banking house of Baring Brothers, was a man of influence, acquainted with the royal family, the future Napoleon III, and the late poet Coleridge, among others. Earlier in 1849 he had visited America, including Boston, where he may have met Chief Justice Shaw. Melville left his card and a letter of introduction (possibly from Lemuel Shaw) at Bates's residence in Portman Place on 20 November. Upon receiving on 21 November an invitation to dinner at Bates's country home in East Sheen, Surrey, Melville wrote a letter of acceptance (*Journals*, pp. 23–24; see also pp. 26–27 for Melville's description of the dinner in East Sheen and p. 311 for more on Bates). Davis-Gilman Unlocated 317.

TO ABBOTT LAWRENCE AND
KATHERINE BIGELOW LAWRENCE
22 NOVEMBER 1849 · LONDON

Unlocated. Abbott Lawrence (1792–1855), American minister to the Court of St. James's, recently appointed by Zachary Taylor, had received Melville on his first visit to the legation on 20 November (*Journals*, p. 22). Two days later, Lawrence and his wife sent Melville a dinner invitation, which Melville had to decline since he had already engaged to dine with John Murray (*Journals*, p. 24). Davis-Gilman Unlocated 318.

TO ELIZABETH SHAW MELVILLE
23 NOVEMBER 1849 · LONDON

Unlocated. After yet another unsuccessful attempt to interest a British publisher in *White-Jacket*, in this case David Bogue, Melville recorded in his journal that he came "home with a fit of the Blues" on 23 November 1849. He concluded his entry with the note: "Wrote Lizzie & Allan by the Steamer which goes to Boston this time" (*Journals*, p. 25). Davis-Gilman Unlocated 319.

TO ALLAN MELVILLE
23 NOVEMBER 1849 · LONDON

Unlocated. A letter to Allan was sent with the one to Elizabeth Melville, also written on 23 November (see the entry just above; *Journals*, p. 25). Davis-Gilman Unlocated 320.

TO ALLAN MELVILLE
26 NOVEMBER 1849 · LONDON

Unlocated. On 26 November, Melville cashed Richard Bentley's hundred-pound advance for *Redburn* at a discount, then deposited forty pounds at the London branch of the express agency of Livingston & Wells for Allan to draw upon from their New York head office. A letter written to Allan that evening from the Blue Posts tavern (cited in *Journals*, pp. 29–30) presumably reported these transactions. Davis-Gilman Unlocated 321.

TO GEORGE J. ADLER
29 NOVEMBER 1849 · PARIS

Two unlocated letters. George J. Adler (1821–68), a friend of the Duyckincks and a German-language scholar with an appointment at New York University, had published *A Dictionary of the German and English Language* in 1849 but had damaged his health in the severe labor of its compilation. To recuperate, he sailed on the *Southampton*, where he met Melville, who "talked metaphysics" with him during the voyage to England (*Journals*, pp. 8ff. and 251). In London they continued to meet until Adler left London for Paris a week before Melville. Arriving in Paris on 28 November 1849, Melville immediately took a cab to Adler's lodging but failed to find him. Trying again the next day, 29 November, Melville wrote Adler "two letters" (presumably similar in content if not identical), probably sending one to his lodging and the other to Galignani's Reading Room—the meeting place of Englishmen in Paris (*Journals*, p. 30). At least one reached Adler, since he sent Melville a reply the next day (*Journals*, p. 31). Davis-Gilman Unlocated 322 and 323.

TO EVERT A. DUYCKINCK
2 AND 14 DECEMBER 1849 · PARIS AND LONDON

This two-part letter to Duyckinck from Paris and London (responding, belatedly, to a now unlocated letter from Duyckinck) was presumably among a group of letters that Allan Melville found at his office on 2 January 1850. Allan's letter to Duyckinck on that morning states: "I found letters from my brother on coming here this morning, which by mistake had not been sent to the house as I had directed. Enclosed is one for yourself which I hasten to put into your hands" (NYPL–D).

Apart from Rachel (Élisa-Rachel Félix), the celebrated French tragedienne, whom Melville attempted to see in *Phèdre* on 1 December 1849 (see *Journals*, p. 32), the people Melville mentions in this letter were ones Duyckinck and his brother George knew and had apparently advised Melville to call on. The "book dealer in the Strand" was Edward C. Stibbs, whose store Melville visited several times while in London (*Journals*, pp. 18, 20, 40, and 44). David Davidson (d. 1863), the London agent of Wiley & Putnam, helped Melville cash his notes from Bentley for *Redburn* at a discount (*Journals*, pp. 25, 29). Before leaving for Paris,

Melville invited Davidson to dine with him at the Mitre tavern in Fleet Street, afterwards accompanying him to the Blue Posts tavern in Cork Street for punch (*Journals*, p. 30). On 22 December, Melville again invited Davidson to dine with him (*Journals*, p. 46). (See *Journals*, pp. 329 and 373, for Davidson's letter to George Duyckinck describing his "brace" of evenings with Melville.) Thomas Delf, to whom Evert Duyckinck had written a letter of introduction for Melville, was an export bookdealer in Little Britain, London. When Melville called he was out and Melville apparently made no further effort to meet him (*Journals*, p. 21). Mrs. George Daniel was the mother of the Mrs. Welford whom Melville also mentions, wife of the bookseller Charles Daniel Welford (1815?–85), a partner at this time in the New York firm of Bartlett & Welford, whose Astor House shop was a popular meeting place for New York book collectors and literary men in the 1840's. Melville called on Mrs. Daniel and her two daughters, sisters of Mrs. Welford, on 14 December and again on 15 December for an evening of "coffee, music, dancing" (*Journals*, pp. 40–41).

At the date of this letter, Melville was still without a publisher for *White-Jacket*, partly because of the current copyright situation (see, above, the headnote to Melville's letter of 20 July 1849, and *Journals*, pp. 175–78). Bentley was himself irritated by the state of the copyright, but three days after the second part of this letter was written, he concluded an agreement for *White-Jacket* with Melville on 17 December, and gave Melville his note for £200 (*Journals*, pp. 42, 176–77). The poor reviews of *Mardi* in England had contributed to Melville's difficulties in reaching this agreement. Melville's allusion here to Iago's phrase "Put money in thy purse" (*Othello*, 1.3.345) refers to the *Boston Post* 18 April 1849 review of *Mardi*, which stated: "In his preface, Mr Melville intimates that having previously written truth which was believed to be fiction, he has now attempted a romance 'to see whether it might not possibly be received as a verity.' We think he need be under no apprehension that the present volumes will be received as gospel—they certainly lack all show of truth or naturalness. He had better stick to his 'fact' which is received as 'fiction,' but which puts money in his purse and wreathes laurels round his head, than fly to 'fiction' which is not received at all, as we opine will be the case with 'Mardi,' in a very short time." To some degree, Melville took this advice to heart in writing *Redburn*, which received far more favorable reviews. That in the *Literary World* on 17 November 1849, which Melville mentions with regret at having been unable to see, praised the book for its "strong relishing style" and "fidelity to nature." (On 30 November in Galignani's Reading Room in Paris, Melville had seen the 10 November *Literary World*, which reprinted chapters 14 and 48 from the book and in a brief introduction dubbed Melville "the De Foe of the Ocean.")

The "critical" review that Melville regrets writing was of Francis Parkman's *The California and Oregon Trail*, published in the *Literary World* (31 March 1849); it had complained that the title was misleading, the book having nothing to do with California or Oregon, and that in depicting the Indians as brutes Parkman had wrongfully treated them with "disdain and contempt" (see the NN *Piazza Tales* volume, pp. 230–34).

Paris Dec 2ᵈ 1849

My Dear Mʳ Duyckinck,

I could almost whip myself that after receiving your most kind
& friendly letter, I should suffer so long an interval to go by without
answering it. But what can you expect of me? I have served persons
the nearest to me in like manner. Traveling takes the ink out of
one's pen as well as the cash out of one's purse. — Thank you for
the papers you sent me.

— The other evening I went to see Rachel — & having taken my
place in the "*que*" (how the devel do you spell it?) or tail — & having waited there for full an hour — upon at last arriving at the
ticket-box — the woman there closed her little wicket in my
face — & so the "tail" was cut off.

— Now my travelling "tail" has been cut off in like manner, by the
confounded state of the Copyright question in England. It has prevented me from receiving an inundative supply of cash — I am going home within three weeks or so. — But I have not failed to enjoy
myself & learn somewhat, notwithstanding.

Give my best remembrances to your brother. Tell him I stum-
bled upon an acquaintance of his — a book dealer in the Strand. Tell
him that Davidson proved a good fellow, & that we took some
punch together at the Blue Posts. — Mʳ Delf I was not so happy as
to see when I called there.

But I may see him on my return.

My compliments to Mrs Duyckinck & all your pleasant family,
& Beleive me Sincerely yours

H Melville.

London, Dec 14, 49.

My Dear Duyckinck — I meant to send this to you by a Havre
packet — but learning more about her — did not. So I have kept the
note by me, & send it to you now with a supplement, a sequel, &
my "last corrections", which as an author, you will duly
value. —— I sail hence on the 21ˢᵗ Inst: — and am only detained now
by reason of some business. Yesterday being at Mʳ Bentley's I enquired for his copies of the last "Literary Worlds" — but they had
been sent on to Brighton — so I did not see your say about the book
Redburn, which to my surprise (somewhat) seems to have been favorably received. I am glad of it — for it puts money into an empty

purse. But I hope I shall never write such a book again — Tho' when a poor devel writes with duns all round him, & looking over the back of his chair — & perching on his pen & diving in his ink-stand — like the devels about St: Anthony — what can you expect of that poor devel? — What but a beggarly "Redburn!" And when he attempts anything higher — God help him & save him! for it is not with a hollow purse as with a hollow balloon — for a hollow purse makes the poet *sink* — witness "Mardi" But we that write & print have all our books predestinated — & for me, I shall write such things as the Great Publisher of Mankind ordained ages before he published "The World" — this planet, I mean — not the Literary Globe. — What a madness & anguish it is, that an author can never — under no conceivable circumstances — be at all frank with his readers. — Could I, for one, be frank with them — how would they cease their railing — those at least who have railed. —— In a little notice of "The Oregon Trail" I once said something "critical" about another man's book — I shall never do it again. Hereafter I shall no more stab at a book (in print, I mean) than I would stab at a man. — I am but a poor mortal, & I admit that I learn by experience & not by divine intuitions. Had I not written & printed "Mardi", in all likelihood, I would not be as wise as I am now, or may be. For that thing was stabbed *at* (I do not say *through*) — & therefore, I am the wiser for it. — But a bit of note paper is not large enough for this sort of writing — so no more of it. Pardon it, & know me to be yours,

H Melville.

I this morning did myself the pleasure of calling on Mrs: Daniel for the first. I saw her, & also two very attractive young ladies. Had you seen those young ladies, you would have never told Mrs: Duyckinck of it. You must on no account tell Mrs Welford of this; for those nymphs were her sisters.

H. M.

ALS on a 26.5 × 20.4 cm sheet, folded in half, of white wove paper. Melville inscribed the Paris, 2 December 1849, section of the letter on the first two pages, with the concluding sentence on the third; he added the London, 14 December 1849, section in a much closer, even cramped, hand on the remaining two pages, using the same ink throughout.

LOCATION: NYPL-D.

PUBLICATION: (partial) Minnigerode, pp. 40–41, 51–52. Thorp, pp. 375–77. Davis-Gilman 68–69.

TEXTUAL NOTES: inundative] *conjectural reading* • me] e *written over* y • London] *after wiped* I meant *on preceding line* • (somewhat)] *before canceled* has • balloon — for] *before canceled* any • witness "Mardi"] "Mardi" *written below* witness *with a connecting line* • another] *miswritten* another's • never] *rewritten*

TO ELIZABETH SHAW MELVILLE
13–14 DECEMBER 1849 · LONDON

Unlocated. Returning to London on 13 December 1849 from his excursion on the Continent, Melville found letters from his wife and his brother Allan waiting for him. His journal for that day reports: "Most welcome but gave me the blues most terribly — Felt like chartering a small-boat & starting down the Thames instanter for New York. Dined at the 'Blue Posts' & took some punch to cheer me. Came home, had a fire made, & wrote Lizzie & Allan — While so employed the girl knocked & brought me a package of letters. They were from the Legation, & were from Lizzie & Allan — a week later than those I got in the morning. I read them, & felt raised at once" (*Journals*, p. 39). The following day after making some calls, Melville returned to his room "& wrote further to Lizzie & Allan & put up the 'Times' for Judge Shaw" (*Journals*, p. 40). Davis-Gilman Unlocated 324.

TO ALLAN MELVILLE
13–14 DECEMBER 1849 · LONDON

Unlocated. A letter to his brother Allan is cited in Melville's journal for 13 and 14 November (*Journals*, pp. 39–40, quoted in the entry just above). Davis-Gilman Unlocated 325.

TO N. P. WILLIS
14 DECEMBER 1849 · LONDON

Unlocated. Nathaniel Parker Willis (1806–67), the popular New York literary man, was at this time coeditor of the *Home Journal*, where his notices of Melville had been generous (for Melville's acquaintance with Willis, see the headnote to Melville's 2 September 1846 letter to John Murray, above). On 8 November 1849 the *Home Journal* carried an unsigned article, presumably by Willis, about Melville's trip to England: "With his genius, the popularity of his books in England, and the extraordinary charm of his narrative powers in conversation, we predict for him an 'open sesame' through the most difficult portals of English society." Willis himself had had extraordinary success in gaining entrance to upper-class English circles on his visits to England. On 19 November 1849 in London, Melville received from Willis letters of introduction to two Englishmen—Lord John Manners and

Martin Farquhar Tupper (*Journals*, p. 22; for Melville's subsequent efforts to reach Manners, see the entry above for Melville's unlocated letters of 19 November 1849; Melville's journal mentions no attempt to use his introduction to Tupper).

From London, Melville wrote to Willis on 14 December 1849, according to his journal entry for that day (*Journals*, p. 40). The contents of the letter are known only in an extract that appeared in the *Home Journal* on 12 January 1850 in a column by Willis entitled "Light Touchings." Melville apparently explained in the letter the difficulty that the lack of an international copyright was causing him in his efforts to find a publisher for *White-Jacket*. After denouncing the copyright situation, Willis stated that Melville "writes us that he has abandoned his more extended plans, with this disappointment, and will return sooner than he expected," and then went on to quote the passage from Melville's letter because, he explained, it was "so characteristic, that we cannot forbear giving it to the admirers of Typee and Omoo": "I very much doubt whether Gabriel enters the portals of Heaven without a fee to Peter the porter—so impossible is it to travel without money. Some people (999 in 1000) are very unaccountably shy about confessing to a want of money, as the reason why they do not do this or that; but, for my part, I think it such a capital clincher of a reason for not doing a thing, that I out with it, at once—for, who can gainsay it? And, what more satisfactory or unanswerable reason can a body give, I should like to know? Besides—though there are numbers of fine fellows, and hearts of blood, in the world, whom Providence hath blessed with purses furlongs in length—yet the class of wealthy people are, in the aggregate, such a mob of gilded dunces, that, not to be wealthy carries with it a certain distinction and nobility." Publication of the extract had the unintended consequence of involving Melville's name in a literary dispute then raging in New York (see the NN *Moby-Dick*, p. 608). Davis-Gilman 70.

TO LEMUEL SHAW
14 DECEMBER 1849 · LONDON

Unlocated. In his journal entry for 14 December 1849, Melville notes that he "put up the 'Times' for Judge Shaw" and that he wrote "the Judge" after finishing his letters to his wife, his brother Allan, N. P. Willis, and Evert A. Duyckinck (*Journals*, p. 40). Davis-Gilman Unlocated 326.

TO THE DUKE OF RUTLAND
17 DECEMBER 1849 · LONDON

Unlocated. Among the letters waiting for Melville upon his return from the Continent on 13 December 1849 was a note from the duke of Rutland (1778–1857), Lord John Manners's father, inviting Melville to visit Belvoir Castle in January. As his journal entry for 16 December 1849 records, the invitation was a very tempting one, even though it would have meant postponing his departure for home: "I am in a very painful state of uncertainty. I am all eagerness to get home — I ought to be home — my absence occasions uneasiness in a quarter where I must beseech heaven to grant repose. Yet here I have before me an open prospect to get some curious ideas of a style of life, which in all probability I shall never have again. I should much like to know what the highest English aristocracy really & practically is. And the Duke of Rutland's cordial invitation to visit him at his Castle furnishes me with just the thing I want. If I do not go, I am confident that hereafter I shall upbraid myself for neglecting such an opportunity of procuring '*material.*' And Allan & others will account me a ninny. — I would not debate the matter a moment, were it not that at least three whole weeks must elapse ere I start for Belvoir Castle — three weeks! If I could but get over *them!*" (*Journals*, pp. 41–42). In the end, Melville decided he could not postpone his departure. His journal entry for 17 December includes the brief comment "took a letter for a Duke to the Post of-fice"—presumably his letter declining the invitation (*Journals*, p. 43). Davis-Gilman Unlocated 327.

TO ELIZABETH SHAW MELVILLE [AND FAMILY?]
ON OR AFTER 17 DECEMBER 1849 · LONDON

Unlocated. Having decided to decline the duke of Rutland's invitation (see the en-try just above), Melville booked his passage home aboard the *Independence* on 17 December 1849 (*Journals*, p. 42). Three days later on 20 December he received a letter from home and noted with delight: "In a few days now my letter will be received announcing my sailing" (*Journals*, p. 45). Evidently Melville had written home shortly after booking his passage.

TO SAMUEL ROGERS
18 DECEMBER 1849 · LONDON

Unlocated. Melville left his card and Edward Everett's letter of introduction (see the headnote to Melville's 10 September 1849 letter to Lemuel Shaw) at the home of the poet and banker Samuel Rogers (1763–1855) on 20 November 1849. After Mel-ville's return from the Continent, Rogers sent him on 18 December an invitation to breakfast on 20 December, which Melville accepted the same afternoon by note. Rogers's literary breakfasts were famous, and Melville must have made an agree-able impression, since upon leaving he was invited to return to breakfast again on the following Sunday, 23 December (*Journals*, pp. 43, 44, and 46). Davis-Gilman Unlocated 328.

TO JOHN FORSTER
21 DECEMBER 1849 · LONDON

Unlocated. On 14 December 1849 Melville left his card and a letter of introduction at the lodgings of John Forster (1812–76), drama critic for the *Examiner*, the close friend and future biographer of Charles Dickens. Forster responded on 21 Decem-ber with an invitation to breakfast on 23 December—the same date that Melville had already agreed to breakfast for the second time with Samuel Rogers. Thus Melville in his reply on 21 December had to decline (*Journals*, p. 46). Davis-Gilman Unlocated 329.

1850

TO EVERT A. DUYCKINCK
2 FEBRUARY 1850 · NEW YORK

On 1 February 1850 Melville arrived home in New York from his trip to England and the Continent. The six gifts sent to Duyckinck with this letter all were acquired during that trip. The first, Duyckinck's presentation copy of the three-volume English edition of *Mardi*, is probably one of the three sets Melville got from Bentley on 20 December 1849 (it was "preserved" and is now in NYPL–Collections of the Rare Book Room, with its leaves no longer "uncut" but trimmed when it was rebound). His journal entry for that day notes: "Thence went to Bentley's — saw him — got some books out of him" (*Journals*, p. 44; see also p. 144 for his list of "Books Obtained in London"). The second gift, the copy of Samuel Butler's *Hudibras* (NYPL-D; Sealts 104), came from Stibbs's bookstore in London (*Journals*, pp. 20, 144). The book had been inscribed: "L. Duval R. Miles 1765". Below this Melville wrote: "Evert A Duyckinck from H. M. Feb 2^d 1850. 85 years after that Miles the old Englishman, in silk small clothes, bought the work at some stall — *you* own it now — who will own it next?" The imprint on the book's title page, to which Melville refers in this letter, reads: "Printed for John Baker, at the Black-Boy in Paternoster-Row. 1710". (Melville's speculations about the " 'Black Boy' " lead him to suggest facetiously that Baker must have specialized in black letter, an old gothic form of type. This copy of *Hudibras* was not printed in it, but such medieval works as those mentioned by Melville, the poetry of Thomas the Rhymer and John Lydgate or the Battle Abbey Roll, might have been. Later, in *Moby-Dick*, Melville used "black letter" several times to characterize older works [see the NN edition, pp. 10, 142, 858]; and in his [16 April?] 1851 letter to Hawthorne, below, he uses the term in discussing *The House of the Seven Gables*.)

Item "No: 3," a bronze medal, Melville bought in Paris, possibly on 5 December 1849, the same day that he "Descended into the vaults of the old Roman palace of Thermis" (*Journals*, pp. 33 and 345). It was probably one of the two medals on his list of " 'Curios' " bought in Paris (*Journals*, p. 146). He most likely bought the medals for young Evert and Henry Duyckinck ("Numbers 4 & 5") when visiting the Thames Tunnel, but he made no record of their purchase (*Journals*, p. 15). The last gift for Evert Duyckinck, item "No: 6," was presumably one of the porcelain stoppers Melville recorded on the list of " 'Curios' " he bought in Cologne (*Journals*, p. 146).

From the partial titles Melville gives in his postscript, three of the " 'outfit' of guide-books" he borrowed from George Duyckinck for his trip can be identified: George F. Cruchley's *Cruchley's Picture of London*, John Murray's *Handbook for Travellers in Central Italy*, and Murray's *Handbook for Travellers in Northern Italy*

(Sealts 166, 375, and 377; see also *Journals*, pp. 173–74). The two other unspecified guidebooks have not been identified (Sealts 77 and 78).

Saturday Evening, Feb 2^d

My Dear Duyckinck — Tho' somewhat unusual for a donor, I must beg to apologize for making you the accompanying present of "Mardi." But no one who knows your library can doubt, that such a choice conservatory of exotics & other rare things in literature, after being long enjoyed by yourself, must, to a late posterity, be preserved intact by your descendants. How natural then — tho' vain — in your friend to desire a place in it for a plant, which tho' now unblown (emblematicaly, the leaves, you perceive, are uncut) may possibly — by some miracle, that is — flower like the aloe, a hundred years hence — or not flower at all, which is more likely by far, for some aloes never flower.

Again: (as the divines say) political republics should be the asylum for the persecuted of all nations; so, if Mardi be admitted to your shelves, your bibliographical Republic of Letters may find some contentment in the thought, that it has afforded refuge to a work, which almost everywhere else has been driven forth like a wild, mystic Mormon into shelterless exile.

— The leaves, I repeat, are uncut — let them remain so — and let me supplementaryly hint, that a bit of old parchment (from some old Arabic M.S.S. on Astrology) tied round each volume, & sealed on the back with a Sphynx, & never to be broken till the aloe flowers — would not be an unsuitable device for the bookbinders of "Mardi." — That book is a sort of dose, if you please — (tho', in the present case, charitably administered in three parts, instead of two) and by way of killing the flavor of it, I hurry to follow it up with a fine old spicy duodecimo mouthful in the shape of "Hudibras" which I got particularly for yourself at Stribbs's in the Strand — & a little marvel that your brother George overlooked so enticing a little volume during his rummagings in the same shop. — Pray, glance at the title page, & tell me, if you can, what "Black Boy" that was in Paternoster Row. My curiosity is excited, and indeed aggravated & exacerbated about that young negro. Did the late Mr Baker have a small *live* Nubian standing at his shop door, like the moccasined Indian of our Bowery tobacconists? I readily see the propriety of the Indian — but in that "Black Boy" I perceive no possible affinity to books — unless, by the way, Mʳ Baker dealt altogether in black-letter, — Thomas the Rhymer, Lydgate, & Battle Abbey Directories. — Are they not delicious, & full flavored with suggestiveness, these old fashioned London imprints?

So much for No: 1 & No: 2. — No: 3 is a bronze medal which I mean for your brother George, if he will gratify me by accepting such a trifling token of my sense of his kindness in giving me an "outfit" of guide-books. It comes from a mountainous defile of a narrow street in the Latin Quarter of Paris, where I disinterred it from an old antiquary's cellar, which I doubt not connected, somehow, with the Catacombs & the palace of Thermes.

Numbers 4 & 5 are two medals (warranted *not* silver) which I wish little Evert & George ✗ to keep by way of rememberances that I remembered them, even while thirty feet under water. They come from the Thames Tunnel.

✗ Erratum: for "George" read "Henry".

No: 6 (which brings up the rear of this valuable collection) is a bottle-stopper from Cologne, for yourself. Do not despise it — there is a sermon in it. Shut yourself up in a closet, insert the stopper into a bottle of Sour Claret, & then study that face.

Wishing you a merry Saturday night, & a serene Sunday morrow, I am, My Dear Duyckinck

Truly Yours
H Melville.

I return, with my best thanks, to your brother, *three* of the books he loaned me. I can not account for "Cruchley" 's accident in the back — The Guide books for Northern & Central Italy are neither stolen, lost, sold, or mislaid. I will, I think, satisfactorily account for them when I see your brother. They are safe.

ALS on a 34.4 × 21.8 cm sheet, folded in half, of white wove paper with gilt edges, embossed with the manufacturer's oval stamp enclosing the name "BATH" (upside down at the bottom of both leaves). Melville inscribed all four pages, in ink. Duyckinck added in ink the year "1850" after Melville's partial date in the heading.

LOCATION: NYPL-D.

PUBLICATION: (partial) Minnigerode, pp. 41–43. Thorp, pp. 377–79. Davis-Gilman 71.

TEXTUAL NOTES: conservatory] *after canceled* coll • Republic] R *written over* r • forth] *before canceled* till • title] *miswritten* tittle • standing at] at *written over* in • these old] these *possibly* those • Latin] *miswritten* Latic • Erratum: for "George" read "Henry".] *written as a marginal correction; placed here editorially* • Sour] S *written over* s • Claret] C *written over* c • Duyckinck] *written over* Sir

TO HOPE SAVAGE SHAW
[3?] FEBRUARY 1850 · NEW YORK

Hope Savage Shaw (1793–1879), daughter of Samuel Savage of Barnstable, Massachusetts, married Lemuel Shaw in 1827, five years after the death of his first wife, Elizabeth Knapp Shaw, Elizabeth Melville's mother. In addition to the children from his first marriage, Elizabeth and her older brother John (1820–1902), Shaw had two sons from his second marriage: Lemuel Shaw, Jr. (1828–84), and Samuel Savage Shaw (1833–1915), at this time a freshman at Harvard.

On 15 December 1849 Melville noted in his journal that he had seen "many pretty things for presents — but could not afford to buy. Bought a bread trencher & bread knife near Charing Cross. 'The University bread trencher' used of old at Commons, now restored. Very generally used here. A fine thing, & English — Saxon." On the day before Christmas, his last day in London, he bought another "bread trencher & knife for Mrs Shaw, (£3.10.)." Presumably he gave her both the knife and the trencher, or wooden platter (*Journals*, pp. 40, 47). The medal for Lemuel from the cathedral at Cologne he bought during one of his two brief stays in the city (*Journals*, pp. 35–36, 38) on his travels through the Rhine country; since he refers to it in his postscript as "not silver," it may have been among the purchases described in his entry for his second stay in Cologne: "Stopped in a shop on my way home & made some purchases for presents, & was insidiously cheated in the matter of a breast-pin, as I found out after getting to London, & not before" (p. 38).

This letter, headed only "Sunday Afternoon," can be dated early in February 1850 by association with Melville's return from England (1 February 1850) and his presentation of gifts to members of his family and others, including a copy of *Mardi* to his brother Allan and another copy of *Mardi* and Butler's *Hudibras* to Evert Duyckinck (see the letter just above), on Saturday, 2 February. It has tentatively been assigned to Sunday, 3 February, on the assumption that Samuel Shaw, who carried the letter to his mother, returned to Boston on that date. On 23 January 1850 during his first vacation from college, he had escorted Elizabeth Melville back to New York from Boston where she had been staying in her husband's absence. Since he had already been in New York a week and a half when Melville arrived on 1 February, it is likely that he left soon afterwards. On 4 February Lemuel Shaw, Jr., in Boston, was able to append to a letter begun on 15 December 1849 to his cousin Samuel Savage the news that "Herman has arrived in New York" (MHS–Samuel H. Savage papers). Presumably he learned this from his brother Samuel.

Sunday Afternoon

My Dear Mrs: Shaw

I am sure you will not refuse to gratify me, by accepting a little present which Samuel brings with him. I thought of you while away, and hope you will receive it as a token of my having remembered you. — It is called a "University Bread Trencher" and has recently been generally introduced among English families. Some three or four centuries ago this article was used in the University Dining Halls. So that the present fashion is only the revival of a very ancient one; I shall feel myself very much flattered if you will occasionally use it — (if it be only once a year.)

Samuel will instruct you more particularly touching the mode of using it.

That interesting young Collegian has given us all great pleasure from his visit, which I hope he will often renew. Lizzie joins with me and the family in begging to be remembered to all under your roof.

Sincerely Yours
H Melville

I send Lemuel a little medal (not silver) which I bought in the famous cathedral of Cologne.

ALS on a 25 × 19.9 cm sheet, folded in half, of blue wove paper. Melville inscribed the first two pages, in ink. Hope Savage Shaw noted in pencil on the fourth page "Melvilles Note — ".

LOCATION: HCL-M.

PUBLICATION: Metcalf, p. 74. Davis-Gilman 72.

TO AUGUSTUS K. GARDNER
[4?] FEBRUARY 1850 · NEW YORK

Although Melville misspelled the surname, this letter was to Augustus Kinsley Gardner (1821–76), a New York physician. He was the son of Samuel Jackson Gardner (1788–1864), a New Jersey editor of the *Newark Advertiser* and contributor ("Decius") to Duyckinck's *Literary World*. After graduating from Harvard, Augustus Gardner spent three years studying medicine in Paris (1844–47), specializing in obstetrics, and then returned to become Professor of Diseases of Women and Children and Clinical Midwifery at the New York Medical College. A man of varied interests, he published several books in the general field of obstetrics and gynecology, imported English sparrows to kill off insect larvae, and wrote *Old Wine in New Bottles: or, Spare Hours of a Student in Paris* (New York: Francis, 1848; Sealts 222).

Melville met Gardner in the Duyckinck circle in 1847. Gardner gave him a copy of *Old Wine*, presumably before his 1849 trip abroad, and apparently recommended that he stay at Madame Capelle's in Paris (*Journals*, p. 29). Later Gardner may have been the Melville family physician, for he was called in at Malcolm Melville's death in 1867. The copy of *Redburn* Melville sent with this letter was presumably one of the three sets of the English edition (in two volumes) he got from Bentley while in London (*Journals*, pp. 44 and 144).

This letter is headed only "Monday Morning" but, like the letter to Hope Savage Shaw, just above, it can be placed in early February of 1850 by its association with the other gifts Melville distributed after his return from England on 1 February. The following Monday, 11 February, is also possible, and is the date Leyda tentatively assigned it in the *Log*.

Monday Morning

Dear Gardiner — Will you do me the favor to accept the accompanying set of "Redburn" as a slight token of my having remembered you while away. — I lodged with Madame Capelle in Paris & will tell you what I saw in that gay city, when I am so happy as to see you again

Sincerely Yours
H Melville.

ALS on a 19.9 × 15.8 cm sheet, folded in half, of white wove paper, embossed with the manufacturer's small circular stamp enclosing a crown with feathers above the name "DOBBS". Melville inscribed the first page, in ink. Another hand noted in pencil on the third page "Dr Augustus K Gardiner. | Gardner". The letter is now mounted on a larger sheet.

LOCATION: Essex Institute, Salem, Massachusetts.

PUBLICATION: *Log*, I, 366. Davis-Gilman 73.

TO EVERT A. DUYCKINCK
7 MARCH 1850 · NEW YORK

Melville had taken a green jacket to England with him in 1849, but even before he left the *Southampton* to go to London someone dropped him a "mysterious hint" about it. Two days later, as he walked along London streets, the "green coat attracted attention." Though he called on the publisher John Murray in the "*green jacket*," he later found it expedient to buy "a Paletot in the Strand, so as to look

decent — for I find my green coat plays the devel with my respectability here"
(*Journals*, pp. 12, 13, 18, and 39–40), a story Melville had probably told Evert
Duyckinck after returning to New York. In mentioning his green jacket in this
letter, Melville also alludes obliquely to *White-Jacket*. Allan Melville had supplied a
batch of proofs for this book to Duyckinck on 6 March with a note stating that
"when you have placed the accompanying sheets with those you got at Harpers
yesterday you will have a complete copy of 'White-jacket' " (NYPL-D). The note
in which Duyckinck evidently offered the concert tickets is now unlocated.

Thursday Morning

My Dear Duyckinck

   I hasten to return you the tickets which you were so good as to
send last evening. I should have gone — as I love music — were it
not that having been shut up all day, I could not stand being shut up
all the evening — so I mounted my *green* jacket & strolled down to
the Battery to study the stars.

Yours
H Melville

ALS on an 11.3 × 16.5 cm sheet of white wove paper. Melville inscribed only one side of the
leaf, in ink; it was mounted for insertion in Duyckinck's extra-illustrated copy of his
Cyclopædia of American Literature (New York: Scribner's, 1856; NYPL-D) and placed after an
engraving of the Gilbert Stuart portrait of General Peter Gansevoort (before p. 673) at the
beginning of the article on Melville (II, 672–76). (For more about the Stuart engraving, see
Melville's 12 June 1870 letter to his uncle Peter Gansevoort.) Duyckinck noted on it in pencil
"March 7. 1850 | Herman Melville" just below Melville's "Thursday Morning".

LOCATION: NYPL-D.

PUBLICATION: Thorp, p. 379. Davis-Gilman 74.

TO R. H. DANA, JR.
1 MAY 1850 · NEW YORK

Melville's earlier 6 October 1849 letter to Dana was written not long before starting
on his 1849–50 journey to London and the Continent. As that letter states, Dana
had furnished Melville with a letter of introduction to Dana's British publisher,
Edward Moxon. Now, with his journey behind him, Melville reports on his encounter with Moxon, a description which elaborates on his journal notation at the
time that he found Moxon "at first very stiff, cold, clammy, & clumsy" but that he
"managed to bring him to, tho', by clever speeches" (*Journals*, p. 23). The books
Moxon gave Melville were *The Works of Charles Lamb* (London, 1848; Sealts 316),
as well as Thomas N. Talfourd's *Final Memorials of Charles Lamb* (London, 1848;

Sealts 317). Moxon's acquaintance "Mr Rogers, the old Nestor," was the poet Samuel Rogers, with whom Melville had twice breakfasted in London (see the entry for Melville's unlocated letter of 18 December 1849 to Rogers, above).

Dana's now unlocated letter, to which Melville is replying, had evidently expressed enthusiasm for *White-Jacket* and possibly for *Redburn*. For a discussion of the reality of " 'the jacket,' " which Dana was evidently curious about, see Howard P. Vincent, *The Tailoring of Melville's WHITE-JACKET* (Evanston: Northwestern University Press, 1970), pp. 12–13, and for the ship's crew, also of interest to Dana, see the NN edition, pp. 410–17. Dana's letter must also have suggested Melville's writing about his " 'whaling voyage' " (as he had previously suggested one about Melville's man-of-war experience; see the 6 October 1849 letter, above); Melville's paragraph here about his new endeavor is his first surviving mention of the composition of *Moby-Dick*, which he worked on through 1850 and into the summer of 1851.

New York May 1st 1850

My Dear Dana — I thank you very heartily for your friendly letter; and am more pleased than I can well tell, to think that any thing I have written about the sea has at all responded to your own impressions of it. Were I inclined to undue vanity, this one fact would be far more to me than acres & square miles of the superficial shallow praise of the publishing critics. And I am specially delighted at the thought, that those strange, congenial feelings, with which after my first voyage, I for the first time read "Two Years Before the Mast", and while so engaged was, as it were, tied & welded to you by a sort of Siamese link of affectionate sympathy —— that these feelings should be reciprocated by you, in your turn, and be called out by any White Jackets or Redburns of mine — this is indeed delightful to me. In fact, My Dear Dana, did I not write these books of mine almost entirely for "lucre" — by the job, as a woodsawyer saws wood — I almost think, I should hereafter — in the case of a sea book — get my M.S.S. neatly & legibly copied by a scrivener — send you that one copy — & deem such a procedure the best publication.

You ask me about "the jacket". I answer it was a veritable garment — which I suppose is now somewhere at the bottom of Charles river. I was a great fool, or I should have brought such a remarkable fabric (as it really was, to behold) home with me. Will you excuse me from telling you — or rathar from putting on pen-&-ink record over my name, the real names of the individuals who officered the frigate. I am very loath to do so, because I have never indulged in any ill-will or disrespect for them, personally; & shrink from any thing that approaches to a personal identification of them with characters that were only intended to furnish samples of a tribe — characters, also, which possess some not wholly complimentary traits. If you think it worth knowing, — I will tell you all, when I next have the pleasure of seeing you face to face.

Let me mention to you now my adventure with the letter you furnished me to Mr Moxon. Upon this, as upon some other similar occasions, I chose to waive cerimoney; and so arranged it, that I saw Mr Moxon, immediately after his reception of the letter. — I was ushered into one of those jealous, guarded sanctums, in which these London publishers retreat from the vulgar gaze. It was a small, dim, religious looking room — a very chapel to enter. Upon the coldest day you would have taken off your hat in that room, tho' there were no fire, no occupant, & you a Quaker. — You have heard, I dare say, of that Greenland whaler discovered near the Pole, adrift & silent in a calm, with the frozen form of a man seated at a desk in the cabin before an ink-stand of icy ink. Just so sat Mr Moxon in that tranced cabin of his. I bowed to the spectre, & received such a galvanic return, that I thought something of running out for some officer of the Humane Society, & getting a supply of hot water & blankets to resuscitate this melancholy corpse. But knowing the nature of these foggy English, & that they are not altogether impenetrable, I began a sociable talk, and happening to make mention of Charles Lamb, and alluding to the warmth of feeling with which that charming punster is regarded in America, Mr Moxon brightened up — grew cordial — hearty; — & going into the heart of the matter — told me that he (Lamb) was the best fellow in the world to "get drunk with" (I use his own words) & that he had many a time put him to bed. He concluded by offering to send me a copy of his works (not Moxon's poetry, but Lambs prose) which I have by me, now. It so happened, that on the passage over, I had found a copy of Lamb in the ship's library — & not having previously read him much, I dived into him, & was delighted — as every one must be with such a rare humorist & excellent hearted man. So I was very sincere with Moxon, being fresh from Lamb. He enquired particularly concerning *you* — earnestly spoke in admiration of "Two Years Before the Mast" — & told me of the particular gratification it

?d particular persons of his acquaintance — including M^r
old Nestor, who poetically appreciated the scenic sea
, describing ice, storms, Cape Horn, & all that.

About the "whaling voyage" — I am half way in the work, &
am very glad that your suggestion so jumps with mine. It will be a
strange sort of a book, tho', I fear; blubber is blubber you know;
tho' you may get oil out of it, the poetry runs as hard as sap from a
frozen maple tree; — & to cook the thing up, one must needs throw
in a little fancy, which from the nature of the thing, must be ungain-
ly as the gambols of the whales themselves. Yet I mean to give the
truth of the thing, spite of this.

Give my compliments to Mrs Dana, and remember me to your
father.

Sincerely Yours
H Melville

ALS on a 34.2 × 21.7 cm sheet, folded in half, of white wove paper with gilt edges, embossed
with the manufacturer's oval stamp enclosing the name "BATH". Melville inscribed all four
pages, in ink.

LOCATION: MHS-D.

PUBLICATION: Harrison Hayford, "Two New Letters of Herman Melville," *ELH* 2 (March
1944), 77–79. Davis-Gilman 75.

TEXTUAL NOTES: well] *mended* · while so] so *written over* to · tribe — characters] characters
miswritten character · regarded] *after canceled* regarged · many] *before canceled* time · excellent]
miswritten excellented · particularly] *miswritten* particulary · afforded] *miswritten* afford

TO RICHARD BENTLEY
27 JUNE 1850 · NEW YORK

Although Melville expected to "have ready" by the autumn of 1850 the "romance
of adventure" proposed in this letter, proofs of the American edition were not sent
to Bentley until the next autumn—on 10 September 1851. Bentley published it with
Melville's original title, *The Whale,* in October of 1851. The book made use of
Melville's whaling experiences of "two years & more" (about twenty-six months)
aboard three different whaleships—the *Acushnet,* the *Lucy Ann,* and the *Charles and
Henry*—only on the last of which, for six months, was he possibly rated as a harpooneer (boatsteerer).

Since Melville reports here on his passage back from England during January
1850, this is probably the first letter he wrote to his British publisher after returning
to New York. He had clearly won his publisher's favor, as Bentley's 22 February

1850 letter to the Albany poet Alfred Billings Street indicates: "Mr Melville left us the day before Christmas, & I have just heard has arrived out after a voyage of 36 days! Isn't that a long voyage? He is a fine fellow, & made a most agreeable impression here. He will make a great name, if he is only careful; some of his opinions are too boldly put out to please the sober people — I speak of some passages in Mardi, or in Redburn & White Jacket. If he only be careful not to rub too violently against general opinion in religious matters, he cannot fail to be very popular. There is such vigour, & that air of truth about his writing and such a richness of inspiration that he must take a foremost place" (UV-Barrett). (For more about Street, see the headnote to Melville's 12 October 1876 letter to Catherine Lansing.)

In London Melville had met the two men to whom he sends greetings at the end of this letter—Robert Bell (1800–67) and Alfred Henry Forrester or "Alfred Crowquill" (1804–72)—among the guests at a dinner Bentley held on 19 December 1849. Bell was a journalist, whom Melville described in his journal as "connected with Literature in some way or other." He later edited an eight-volume edition of Chaucer in 1854–56 that Melville purchased (Sealts 138 and 139; see also Melville's letter to Catherine Gansevoort Lansing on 12 October 1876, below). Alfred Forrester wrote comic pieces, caricatures, and children's stories under the "Crowquill" pseudonym. Melville had found him a "good fellow — free and easy — and no damned nonsense, as there is about so many of these English." On Forrester's invitation he went to see "the Pantomime rehearsal at the Surrey Theater" on 20 December but arrived there too late to do anything but wander around "behind the scenes" (*Journals*, pp. 43–45). Although Melville asks that Bentley "at once write me," no record of a reply has been located in the Bentley letterbooks (British Library).

New York June 27th 1850

My Dear Sir, — In the latter part of the coming autumn I shall have ready a new work; and I write you now to propose its publication in England.

The book is a romance of adventure, founded upon certain wild legends in the Southern Sperm Whale Fisheries, and illustrated by the author's own personal experience, of two years & more, as a harpooneer.

Should you be inclined to undertake the book, I think that it will be worth to you £200. Could you be positively put in possession of the copyright, it might be worth to you a larger sum — considering its great novelty; for I do not know that the subject treated of has ever been worked up by a romancer; or, indeed, by any writer, in any adequate manner. But as things are, I say £200, because that sum was given for "White-Jacket"; and it does not appear, as yet, that you have been interfeared with in your publication of that book; & therefore there seems reason to conclude, that, at £200, "White Jacket" must have been, in some degree, profitable to you.

In case of an arrangement, I shall, of course, put you in early & certain possession of the proof sheets, as in previous cases.

Being desirous of early arranging this matter in London, — so as to lose no time, when the book has passed thro' the Harpers' press here — I beg, Mr Bentley, that you at once write me as to your views concerning it.

Circumstances make it indispensable, that if the book suits you at the sum above-named, that on the day of sale, you give your note for that sum — at four months say — to whomever I depute to ratify the arrangement with you.

Will you be so good as to tell me when you write, what has been the sale of "White Jacket" thus far? — And also will you immediately send me four copies of that book & one copy of Redburn, — addressed to Harper & Brothers, New York (for me); and the parcel can be left at Sampson Low's N° 169 Fleet Street, who is the Harpers' agent, & who will forward it to them.

So much for business. — I had a prosperous passage across the water last winter; & embarking from Portsmouth on Christmas morning, carried the savor of the plumb-puddings & roast turkey all the way across the Atlantic. But tho' we had a good passage, yet, the little mail of letters with which you supplied me (& by reading the superscriptions of which, I whiled away part of the voyage) hardly arrived in time to beat Her Majesty's Mail by the Cunard Steamer.

I have not forgotten the very agreeable evening I spent in New-Burlington Street last winter. Pray, remember me to Mr Bell & Alfred Crowquill when you see them.

With compliments to Mrs Bentley & Miss Bentley, Beleive Me
Very Truly Yours
H Melville

Richard Bentley Esq
London.

ALS on a 39.2 × 25 cm sheet, folded in half, of blue wove paper. Melville inscribed all four pages, in ink.

Location: at present unknown. *Provenance*: Hodgson & Co., sale 13, 27–28 April 1939, lot 563; Scribner's Book Store; H. Bradley Martin sale, Sotheby's, New York, sale

5971, 30–31 January 1990, in item 2167; 19th Century Shop in partnership with other book dealers.

PUBLICATION: Birss, "A Mere Sale to Effect," pp. 249–51. Davis-Gilman 76.

TEXTUAL NOTES: adventure] *after canceled* of · must have] *before canceled* proved · lose] s *rewritten* · sale,] *before canceled* of the

TO THE MELVILLE FAMILY
17 JULY 1850 · PITTSFIELD

Unlocated. By 10 July 1850 Melville, along with his wife and sister-in-law Sophia, had gone to stay with Robert Melvill in Pittsfield. Remaining at home on Fourth Avenue in New York, Augusta Melville wrote to Evert Duyckinck on 20 July 1850: "We received a letter from Herman yesterday he was, at the date of writing the 17th upon the eve of starting with a friend upon some rambling expedition, which may in the telling prove — perhaps — as interesting as the West Point excursion. He was to be absent a week, so we can hardly look for him before Tuesday or Wednesday" (NYPL-D). The "rambling expedition" must have been the agricultural inspection tour of south-central Berkshire County that Melville's cousin Robert made by wagon in July 1850. Melville accompanied his cousin for at least three days (18–20 July; see his account in *Journals*, pp. 589–98). He returned to New York, as Augusta anticipates here, but by 2 August he was back in the Berkshires with members of his family, entertaining guests (see his letter of 16 August 1850, just below). Augusta's reference to the trip to West Point is the only evidence now located of this earlier excursion. Davis-Gilman Unlocated 330.

TO EVERT A. DUYCKINCK
16 AUGUST 1850 · PITTSFIELD

Between 2 and 12 August 1850 Evert Duyckinck and Cornelius Mathews (see the next entry) visited Melville and his wife in Pittsfield at the old mansion of Melville's "Uncle the Major"—Thomas Melvill, Jr.—then being run as a select summer boardinghouse by his son Robert, though it had already been sold to the Morewoods, who later named it Broadhall (see the headnote to Melville's [17?] November 1851 letter to Hawthorne; see also the illustration on p. 550 below). Melville compares the house to a banyan tree, which sends out roots from the central trunk that in turn grow into more trees (cf. chap. 115 of *Mardi*). Duyckinck wrote his brother George later that Melville had insisted on treating him and Mathews as guests, refusing to let them pay (13 August 1850, NYPL-D). The day after he returned to New York, Duyckinck sent Melville the thank-you letter mentioned here (now unlocated), and spent nineteen dollars for a bread-and-butter present of a dozen quarts of Heidseck champagne in a basket ("Twelve . . . beautiful babies") and some cigars (receipted bill, NYPL-D). (The biblical phrase "thrones & dominations [i.e., dominions]" of cigars alludes to orders of angels in *Paradise Lost* [see

3.320; 5.601, 772, 840; 10.86–87 and 460; also Henry F. Pommer, *Milton and Melville* (Pittsburgh: University of Pittsburgh Press, 1950), pp. 34–35]; the reference to the "Six Nations," also used in relation to the cigars, alludes to the confederation of North American Indians formed in 1715.) These gifts Duyckinck sent by express to Melville along with "parcels" for Hawthorne (since Pittsfield was the nearest express station) that included copies of *Redburn*, *White-Jacket*, and *Mardi*—hence Melville's promise at the end of this letter to deliver the parcels (presumably without knowing what they contained) to Hawthorne (see Duyckinck's 13 August 1850 letter to his brother George describing the gift and Hawthorne's praise of the books in his 29 August 1850 acknowledgment of them [NYPL-D]).

During Duyckinck's visit, Melville had first met Hawthorne—then living with his family in a red cottage outside nearby Lenox—at a literary outing in Stockbridge organized by David D. Field on 5 August 1850 that also included Duyckinck, Mathews, Holmes, Hawthorne's publisher James T. Fields and his bride, and for the latter portion of the day, the historian J. T. Headley. The copy of the *Literary World* that Melville acknowledged in this letter carried the first of the two installments of his essay "Hawthorne and His Mosses" (17 and 24 August 1850); as he later told Sophia Hawthorne, he did not receive or correct proofs of either installment (see the NN *Piazza Tales* volume, pp. 654–55).

"Saddleback," "*Trans-Taconic*," and "Leabanon" are all references to the area surrounding Pittsfield. Saddleback (Mt. Greylock) was the name used in the early settlement period for the highest Massachusetts mountain, which stands just north of Pittsfield (both names—Saddleback and Greylock—were used in the nineteenth century). The Taconic mountain range runs north and south to the west of Pittsfield. The town of Lebanon, New York, a few miles west of Pittsfield, had a Shaker settlement well known to Melville.

In his humorous epithet "My Beloved" for Duyckinck, Melville alludes to the Song of Solomon. His jokes about street paving involve Clinton Place (where Duyckinck lived at No. 20), just west of Broadway, six blocks below Union Square (at Fourteenth Street) and a mile and a half north of the Astor House and City Hall. "Dipping your head in plaster at Fowler's" refers to Orson S. Fowler and his brother Lorenzo, who were immensely successful phrenologists, doing business at 131 Nassau Street in New York. Like other phrenologists, they took plaster casts of the heads of customers, which they used for comparative study and lectures. Melville may have known about the Fowlers as early as 1835, when Lorenzo lectured in Albany and one of their students, a Dr. Smith, practiced in Lansingburgh. The brothers had examined the heads of such dignitaries as William Cullen Bryant, N. P. Willis, and Walt Whitman (as well as that of John C. Hoadley—who became Melville's brother-in-law in 1853; Hoadley's analysis, signed by Lorenzo, is in NYPL-GL). See Orson S. and Lorenzo N. Fowler, *Phrenology Proved, Illustrated, and Applied*, 9th ed. (New York: Fowler, 1840), pp. 261, 266.

Finally, Melville's reference to "the Flitch of Bacon" is to the famous English tradition in Dunmow, Essex, where a side of pork was given annually to any couple who could prove they had lived in conjugal harmony for a year and a day. Following the elaborate ceremony of presentation, the couple (or the husband alone) were carried triumphantly through the town with the flitch before them. The custom had lapsed after 1751 but was revived nearly a century later; see W. Carew Hazlitt, *Faiths and Folklore* (London: Reeves & Turner, 1905), I, 198–99, and Charles Pavey, *Dunmow Flitch of Bacon* (1855; Dunmow: Robus, 1923).

Banian Hall Aug 16th 1850

I call it Banian Hall, My Dear Duyckinck because it seems the old original Hall of all this neighborhood — besides, it is a wide-spreading house, and the various outhouses seem shoots from it, that have taken root all round. — I write you this from the *garret-way*, seated at that little embrasure of a window (you must remember it) which commands so noble a view of Saddleback. — My desk is an odd one — an old thing of my Uncle the Major's, which for twelve years back has been packed away in the corn-loft over the carriage house. Upon dragging it out to day light, I found that it was covered with the marks of fowls — quite white with them — eggs had been laid in it — think of that! — Is it not typical of those other eggs that authors may be said to lay in their desks, — especially those with pigeon-holes?

Day before yesterday — Wednesday — I received your letter of the 13th, also Mathews', and was delighted & softened by both. But I could not avoid a real feeling of grief, to think of you, once more in those dreary regions which are *Trans-Taconic* to me. — What are you doing there, My Beloved, among the bricks & cobble-stone *boulders*? Are you making mortar? Surely, My Beloved, you are not carrying a hod? — That were a quizzical sight, to see any godly man, with a pen behind his ear, and a hod on his shoulder. —— I have a horrible presentiment that you are even now hanging round the City-Hall, trying to get a contract from the Corporation to pave Broadway between Clinton Place & Union-Square. For heaven's sake, come out from among those Hittites & Hodites — give up mortar forever. — There is one thing certain, that, chemically speaking, mortar was the *precipitate* of the Fall; & with a brickbat, or a cobble-stone *boulder*, Cain killed Abel. — Do you drink Lime-water in the morning by way of a stomachic? Do you use brick-bats for paper-weights in the office? Do you & Mathews pitch paving-stones, & play ball that way in the cool of the evening, opposite the Astor-House? —— How do they sell mortar by the quart now? Cheaper than ice-cream, I suppose. — A horrible something in me tells me that you are about dipping your head in plaster at Fowler's for your bust. —— But enough — the visions come too thick for me to master them.

Twelve more beautiful babies than you sent me in that wicker cradle by Express, I have never seen. Uncommon intelligence was in their aspect, and they seem full of animation & hilarity. I have no doubt, if they were let alone awhile, they would all grow to be demijohns. In a word, My Dear Fellow, they were but too well thought of you, — because so much more than I deserved.

—— Let me now tell you how that precious basket was carried in state to the farm — something like the Flitch of Bacon. —— A gentleman & a lady arrived here as boarders yesterday morning. In the afternoon in four carriages a party of us went to Leabanon. Returning, we stopped at the Express office in the village; and then, with the basket borne before me at my feet, I drove off full speed followed by the whole galloping procession. To day, at dinner, we cracked the Champaigne, & our first glass (all round the table) was Mr Duyckinck & Mr Mathews.

But the cigars! — The Oriental looking box! and the Antilles smell of them! And the four different thrones & dominations of bundles, all harmonizing together like the Iroquois. Had there been two more bundles, I should have called them the Six Nations.

I received the "Literary World". Under the circumstances the printing is far more correct, than I expected; but there are one or two ugly errors. However, no one sees them, I suppose, but myself. — Send me the other proof, if you can; but dont, if it will be the least inconvenience. If it is a fair day, I shall drive to Hawthorne's to morrow, & deliver his parcels. — Mrs H. Melville & others too numerous to enumerate send their best remembrances to you. — When you write, tell me that you are coming on for a second visit. Dont' forget it. — Good bye

H Melville

ALS on a 37.4 × 23.4 cm sheet, folded in half, of white laid paper, embossed with the manufacturer's oval stamp enclosing the name "SUPERFINE SATIN" (upside down at the bottom of both leaves). Melville inscribed all four pages, in ink.

LOCATION: NYPL-D.

PUBLICATION: (partial) Minnigerode, pp. 66–68. Thorp, pp. 379–81. Davis-Gilman 77.

TEXTUAL NOTES: seem] m *rewritten* • making mortar] *blotted* • trying] y *written over* i • There] T *written over* t • the Fall] the *miswritten* thae • ice-cream] ice-|cream • about] *before canceled* getting a · master] m *blotted* · would] *after wiped* a · of you] *intervening word lacking (presumably "by")* · Bacon] B *blotted* · in the village] *inserted above caret with connecting line* · I drove] *before canceled* to · than] *miswritten* that · to morrow] *inserted above caret*

TO CORNELIUS MATHEWS
[16?] AUGUST 1850 · PITTSFIELD

Unlocated. Melville in his 16 August 1850 letter to Evert Duyckinck, just above, mentions receiving two letters both dated 13 August—the first from Duyckinck, to whom he was replying, and the other from Cornelius Mathews (1817–89), who like Duyckinck had sent what was probably a letter of thanks for his stay in the Berkshires (now unlocated; the draft of a 15 August 1850 thank-you letter from Mathews to Elizabeth Melville survives; see LETTERS RECEIVED, p. 603). Mathews was a member of the Duyckinck circle in New York and from July 1847 until its discontinuation in October 1847 had been editor of *Yankee Doodle*, in which Melville published "Authentic Anecdotes of 'Old Zack' " (see the NN *Piazza Tales* volume, p. 637). Presumably Melville wrote a reply to Mathews as well as to Duyckinck, and presumably there was other correspondence between the two men; however, none of it has been located. Only a brief marginal note in one of Augusta Melville's letters, dated 6 January 1851, provides further evidence: "Mr Mathews sent Herman a copy of his new book — 'The Peabody Family' " (NYPL-GL). The full title of this book was *Chanticleer: A Thanksgiving Story of the Peabody Family* (Sealts 351a). Davis-Gilman Unlocated 331.

TO AUGUSTA MELVILLE
ON OR BEFORE 3 SEPTEMBER 1850 · PITTSFIELD

Unlocated. Augusta Melville's record of correspondence (NYPL-GL) lists a letter from her brother among those she received in September 1850. (It is listed with ditto marks below a letter received from Mrs. Ives in Lansingburgh, dated 3 September by Augusta. Both are out of chronological order, between 6 and 7 September on her list.) It is not clear whether Augusta was recording the dates on the letters themselves or the dates on which she received the letters in the mail. If Melville wrote this letter on 3 September, he wrote it on the same day that he paid a visit to Hawthorne in Lenox. According to Augusta's record, she replied to her brother on 6 September and again on 14 September. Their correspondence may have concerned his decision to move his family to Pittsfield (see the headnote to Melville's 6 October 1850 letter, just below).

TO EVERT A. DUYCKINCK
6 OCTOBER 1850 · PITTSFIELD

On 14 September 1850 Melville bought a farm adjoining the old Melvill estate in Pittsfield, which he named Arrowhead. As this letter indicates, he had just moved his family—including his mother and three of his sisters—from New York to their new home. Writing to Duyckinck in New York, Melville characterizes his rural remoteness with Shakespearean allusions ("Jacquesizing" in the woods [*As You Like It*] and taking "my ease on mine mountain" [*1 Henry IV*, 3.3.77]) and describes the Berkshire autumn with hyperbole (imagining "Charles' Wain," the Big Dipper, "heaped high as Saddle-Back" Mountain with leaves; for "Saddle-Back" see the headnote to his 16 August 1850 letter to Duyckinck).

Duyckinck remained one of Melville's chief correspondents and kept him abreast of events taking place beyond Pittsfield. Apparently he had recently sent Melville a newspaper (along with a now unlocated letter) with the news that flogging in the United States Navy had been abolished by an act of Congress on 28 September 1850 (see Charles Roberts Anderson, *Melville in the South Seas* [New York: Columbia University Press, 1939], p. 431). Melville's interest stemmed, of course, from his own observations as a sailor on the *United States* and from his vigorous attacks on flogging in *White-Jacket*.

Melville's greeting to "Adler" at the letter's close is to George Adler, whom Duyckinck first introduced to Melville when both were boarding the *Southampton* in 1849 (*Journals*, p. 4; see the entry for Melville's unlocated letters to Adler in Paris on 29 November 1849, above). Melville continued to send greetings to Adler in later letters to Duyckinck, but no letters written directly to Adler have been located. Against his will, Adler was committed to the Bloomingdale Asylum in 1853, where he remained until his death. Melville and Duyckinck were among the few friends who attended his funeral on 25 August 1868.

Headed only "Sunday Evening 1850," Melville's letter can be dated by its 7 October postmark. Thus, it was written on Sunday, 6 October, and mailed the following day.

Sunday Evening 1850.

My Dear Duyckinck — I hardly thought that I should find time or even *table* to write you this long while. But it is Sunday at last, and after a day chiefly spent in *Jacquesizing* in the woods, I sit down to do what with me is an almost unexampled thing — inditing a letter at night. It has been a most glowing & Byzantine day — the heavens reflecting the tints of the October apples in the orchard — nay, the heavens themselves looking so ripe & ruddy, that it must be harvest-home with the angels, & Charles' Wain be heaped high as Saddle-Back with Autumn's sheaves. — You should see the maples — you should see the young perennial pines — the red blazings of the one contrasting with the painted green of the others, and the wide flushings of the autumn air harmonizing both. I tell you that sunrises & sunsets grow side by side in these woods, & momentarily moult in the falling leaves. —— A hammer! yes a hammer is before me — the very one that so cruelly bruised the very finger that guides my pen. I can sentimentalise it no more.

Until to day I have been as busy as man could be. Every thing to be done, & scarcely any one to help me do it. But I trust that before a great while we shall be all "to rights," and I shall take my ease on mine mountain. For a month to come, tho', I expect to be in the open air all day, except when assisting in lifting a bedstead or a bureau.

Thank you for your letter with the paper the other day. I am offering up devout jubilations for the abolition of the flogging law.

My love to Adler, & tell him I hope to have him behind a cigar one of these days & talk over old times. Remember me to your brother — & take this meagre letter for lack of a longer & a better one — and beleive me to be what I am

Truly Yours
H Melville.

ALS on a 39.4 × 31.1 cm sheet, folded in half, of blue wove paper with lines, embossed with the manufacturer's ornate shield-like stamp enclosing the initials "P & S". Melville inscribed the first two pages, in ink, and addressed the fourth page "Evert A Duyckinck Esq | New York.", with the abbreviation "*Pvt. Doc.*," possibly for "Private Document." It was postmarked in Pittsfield on 7 October.

LOCATION: NYPL-D.

PUBLICATION: (partial) Minnigerode, pp. 68–69. Davis-Gilman 78.

TEXTUAL NOTES: while] w *written over* tim · apples] l *written over* e · flushings of] of *written over* in · jubilations for] for *written over* over · flogging] o *mended*

TO LOUIS A. GODEY
BEFORE DECEMBER 1850 · [PITTSFIELD?]

Unlocated. A letter replying to an invitation from Louis Antoine Godey (1804–78) to contribute to *Godey's Lady's Book* can be inferred from the advertisement at the back of the December 1850 and January 1851 issues of his *Lady's Book* that listed Melville, along with Hawthorne, Alfred B. Street, Kate Berry, and a number of others, as a promised contributor. For more on Godey's now unlocated invitation, see LETTERS RECEIVED, p. 603.

TO EVERT A. DUYCKINCK
13 DECEMBER 1850 · PITTSFIELD

Melville's circle of friends in Pittsfield was augmented by the new owners of the old Melvill estate—John Rowland Morewood (1821–1903), a New York commercial merchant, and his wife, Sarah Huyler Morewood (1824–63). Sarah Morewood was a remarkably vivacious woman, constantly organizing parties and outings. Cornelius Mathews wrote about one such outing of 10 August 1850 in a piece entitled "Several Days in the Berkshires," published in the *Literary World* on 24 August 1850. In it he described Gulf Road, which Melville mentions in this letter, as "a woody defile, wild, strange, and primeval," about twelve miles west of Pittsfield, along which Melville, Duyckinck, Mathews, and others had driven on 10 August.

Sarah Morewood's horse "Black Quake," whose accident Melville describes at length here, did not survive. In a 21 December 1850 letter to their sister Helen, Augusta Melville reported that "poor Black Quake is dead. — All the farmers could not save him." "Mr Doolittle," indirectly the cause of the accident, was, according to Hershel Parker, Melville's cousin Robert Melvill—who had remained in the area after selling the Melvill estate to the Morewoods. Augusta was apparently the " 'sad' young lady" mentioned at the close of this letter and the " 'Sad One' " of Melville's 12 February 1851 letter to Duyckinck. She and Duyckinck had an intermittent but familiar correspondence, and it is thus likely that she would be sending him greetings. She was copying his whaling book at this time and would have been one of the sisters (the other being Frances Priscilla) Melville regularly drove to the village. Elizabeth and Malcolm were in Boston from 25 November 1850 to 1 January 1851, but contrary to some earlier assumptions Melville did not visit Boston during this holiday season (see the NN *Moby-Dick*, pp. 625–26).

For George Adler, to whose newest work Melville refers, see the headnote to the 6 October 1850 letter to Duyckinck. Adler's "German translation" was of Goethe's *Iphigenia in Tauris* (New York: Appleton, 1850), the announcement for which Melville probably saw in the *Literary World*. Melville received a presentation copy of it on 8 January 1851 (Sealts 229).

The date of Melville's letter is 13 December despite Duyckinck's bracketed "Dec 12. 1850" on the first page, since "Friday" fell on 13 December. Whatever previous letters from Duyckinck Melville had "fail[ed] to answer" are unlocated.

Friday Evening
Pittsfield.

My Dear Duyckinck, If you overhaul your old diaries you will see that a long period ago you were acquainted with one Herman Melvill; that he then resided in New York; but removing after a time into a remote region called Berkshire, and failing to answer what letters you sent him, you but reasonably supposed him dead; at any rate did not hear anything of him again, & so by degrees you thought no more about him.

I now write to inform you that this man has turned up — in short, My Dear Fellow in spite of my incivility I am alive & well, & would fain be remembered.

Before I go further let me say here that I am writing this by candle light — an uncommon thing with me — & therefore my writing wont be very legible, because I am keeping one eye shut & wink at the paper with the other.

If you expect a letter from a man who lives in the country you must make up your mind to receive an egotistical one — for he has no gossip nor news of any kind, unless his neighbor's cow has calved or the hen has laid a silver egg. — By the way, this reminds me that one of my neighbors has really met with a bad accident in the loss of a fine young colt. That neighbor is our friend Mrs Morewood. Mr Doolittle — my cousin — was crossing the R.R. track yesterday (where it runs thro the wooded part of the farm.) in his slay — *sleigh* I mean — and was followed by all three of Mrs Morewood's horses (they running at large for the sake of the air & exercise). Well: just as Doolittle got on the track with his vehicle, along comes the Locomotive — whereupon Doolittle whips up like mad & steers clear; but the frightened horses following him, they scamper off full before the engine, which hitting them right & left, tumbles one into a ditch, pitches another into a snow-bank, & chases the luckless third so hard as to come into direct contact with him, & break his leg clean into two peices. — With his leg "in splints" that is done up by the surgeon, the poor colt now lies in his straw, & the prayers of all good Christians are earnestly solicited in his behalf. Certainly, considering the bounding spirit and full-blooded life in that colt — how it might for many a summer have sported in pastures of red clover & gone cantering merrily along the "Gulf Road" with a sprightly Mrs Morewood on his back, patting his neck & lovingly talking to him —— considering all this, I say, I really think that a broken leg for him is not one jot less bad than it would be for me — tho' I grant you, even as it is with him, he has one more leg than I have now.

I have a sort of sea-feeling here in the country, now that the ground is all covered with snow. I look out of my window in the morning when I rise as I would out of a port-hole of a ship in the Atlantic. My room seems a ship's cabin; & at nights when I wake up & hear the wind shrieking, I almost fancy there is too much sail on the house, & I had better go on the roof & rig in the chimney.

Do you want to know how I pass my time? — I rise at eight — thereabouts — & go to my barn — say good-morning to the horse, & give him his breakfast. (It goes to my heart to give him a cold one, but it can't be helped) Then, pay a visit to my cow — cut up a pumpkin or two for her, & stand by to see her eat it — for it's a pleasant sight to see a cow move her jaws — she does it so mildly & with such a sanctity. —— My own breakfast over, I go to my work-room & light my fire — then spread my M.S.S on the table — take one business squint at it, & fall to with a will. At 2½ P.M. I hear a preconcerted knock at my door, which (by request) continues till I rise & go to the door, which serves to wean me effectively from my writing, however interested I may be. My friends the horse & cow now demand their dinner — & I go & give it them. My own dinner over, I rig my sleigh & with my mother or sisters start off for the village — & if it be a Literary World day, great is the satisfaction thereof. — My evenings I spend in a sort of mesmeric state in my room — not being able to read — only now & then skimming over some large-printed book. — Can you send me about fifty fast-writing youths, with an easy style & not averse to polishing their labors? If you can, I wish you would, because since I have been here I have planned about that number of future works & cant find enough time to think about them separately. — But I dont know but a book in a man's brain is better off than a book bound in calf — at any rate it is safer from criticism. And taking a book off the brain, is akin to the ticklish & dangerous business of taking an old painting off a panel — you have to scrape off the whole brain in order to get at it with due safety — & even then, the painting may not be worth the trouble. —— I meant to have left more room for something else besides my own concerns. But I cant help it. — I see Adler is at work — or has already achieved a German translation. I am glad to hear it. Remember me to him.

— In the country here, I begin to appreciate the Literary World. I read it as a sort of private letter from you to me.

Remember me to your brother. My respects to Mrs Duyckinck & all your family. The "sad" young lady desires her regards.

H Melville.

Mrs Melville with Malcolm is in Boston — or that lady would send her particular regards.

ALS on a 39.6 × 25 cm sheet, folded in half, of blue wove paper, faintly embossed with the manufacturer's shield-like stamp (upside down at the bottom of both leaves). Melville inscribed all four pages, in ink. Duyckinck incorrectly noted in ink on the first page "[Dec 12. 1850]" after Melville's "Friday Evening".

LOCATION: NYPL-D.

PUBLICATION: (partial) Minnigerode, pp. 69–71. Thorp, pp. 381–84. Davis-Gilman 79.

TEXTUAL NOTES: news of] o *added* • neighbors has] *miswritten* neighbors has | has • chases] as *mended* • have sported] have *miswritten* has • merrily] *blotted* • ship in] in *possibly* on • workroom] work-|room • till I] *before canceled* ackn • whole brain] *before canceled* before you come • achieved] *conjectural reading* • Mrs Melville . . . regards.] *added in margin; placed here editorially*

1851

TO NATHANIEL HAWTHORNE
[29 JANUARY?] 1851 · PITTSFIELD

This is the first known letter from Melville to Nathaniel Hawthorne (1804–64). Melville had initially extended the invitation it concerns when he visited the Hawthornes at their home on 22 January. Two days later Augusta Melville reported in a letter to her sister Helen, who was visiting in Lansingburgh, that their brother had not returned from the Hawthornes' "until eleven. Had a very delightful visit he said, the warmest of welcomes, '& a cold chicken.' Mrs Hawthorne sent Malcolm a beautiful book, 'The Grandfather's Chair', a collection of holiday stories written by her husband, & Mr Hawthorne presented Herman with a copy of his 'Twice Told Tales' in two volumes. This was gladly received as an accession to his library. Herman has invited Mr & Mrs Hawthorne with their two beautiful little children to make a visit. They are coming week after next, on Monday or Tuesday & will return the next day. We are all looking forward to this visit with great pleasure. Herman says that they are the loveliest family he ever met with, or any one can possibly imagine. We are all delighted to hear that you will be home before they come. Herman said last evening, when your letter came, 'I am glad Helen is coming home, it will make it so much pleasanter for the Hawthorne's.' Now mind that you return to us with all your powers of entertainment in the happiest condition" (NYPL-GL). Sophia Hawthorne's diary (NYPL-B) also records Melville's visit along with her now unlocated letter—or "side-blow"—to him written on Sunday, 26 January, apparently promising only to "*spend the day,*" possibly because Hawthorne was then completing *The House of the Seven Gables* but also possibly because she was well into her pregnancy with her third child, Rose (born 20 May 1851).

Headed only "Wednesday," Melville's letter can be tentatively dated 29 January, the first Wednesday following Sophia Hawthorne's letter. In his now unlocated 3 February 1851 letter (see p. 606 below), Hawthorne apparently declined the repeated invitation. He and his six-year-old first child, Una (born 3 March 1844 and named for Spenser's heroine in his favorite *The Faerie Queene*), finally did make the

proposed visit the following month, as a 14 March letter from Hawthorne at Ar-
rowhead to Evert Duyckinck attests (see *Letters, 1843–1853*, ed. Thomas Woodson,
L. Neal Smith, and Norman Holmes Pearson [Columbus: Ohio State University
Press, 1985], p. 404).

                                                 Pittsfield, Wednesday.
That side-blow thro' Mrs Hawthorne will not do. I am not to be
charmed out of my promised pleasure by any of that lady's
syrenisims. *You*, Sir, I hold accountable, & the visit (in all its original integrity) must be made. —— What! *spend the day*, only with
us? — A Greenlander might as well talk of spending the day with a
friend, when the day is only half an inch long.

    As I said before, my best travelling chariot on runners, will be at
your door, & provision made not only for the accommodation of all
your family, but also for any quantity of *baggage*.

    Fear not that you will cause the slightest trouble to us. Your bed
is already made, & the wood marked for your fire. But a moment
ago, I looked into the eyes of two fowls, whose tail feathers have
been notched, as destined victims for the table. I keep the word
"Welcome" all the time in my mouth, so as to be ready on the instant when you cross the threshold.

    (By the way the old Romans you know had a *Salve* carved in
their thresholds)

    Another thing, Mʳ Hawthorne —— Do not think you are com-
ing to any prim nonsensical house — that is nonsensical in the ordinary way. You wont be much bored with punctilios. You may do
what you please — say or say *not* what you please. And if you feel
any inclination for that sort of thing — you may spend the period of
your visit *in bed*, if you like — every hour of your visit.

    Hark — There is some excellent Montado Sherry awaiting you
& some most potent Port. We will have mulled wine with wisdom,
& buttered toast with story-telling & crack jokes & bottles from
morning till night.

    Come — no nonsence. If you dont — I will send Constables
after you.

    On *Wednesday* then — weather & slieghing permitting I will be
down for you about eleven o'clock A.M.

    By the way — should Mrs Hawthorne for any reason conclude

To Nathaniel Hawthorne, 29 January 1851, p. 1 (reduced). Courtesy of the Harry Ransom Humanities Research Center, The University of Texas at Austin.

that *she*, for one, can not stay overnight with us — then *You* must — & the children, if you please.

H Melville.

ALS on a 24.7 × 20.1 cm part-sheet (torn along the top), folded in half, of blue wove paper, embossed with the manufacturer's rectangular stamp enclosing the name "CARSON'S DALTON MS" (in the upper right corner of the second leaf). Melville inscribed all four pages, in ink.

LOCATION: Harry Ransom Humanities Research Center, The University of Texas at Austin. *Provenance*: Stephen Wakeman sale, American Art Association, 28 April 1924, laid into Hawthorne's copy of *Redburn* (New York: Harper, 1850), lot 410; Miller-Beyer Autographs; Everett DeGolyer.

PUBLICATION: Davis-Gilman 80.

TEXTUAL NOTES: out] *inserted above caret* · provision] si *written over* sn *and on* added · carved] *before canceled* into · will be] *before canceled* aft

TO EVERT A. DUYCKINCK
12 FEBRUARY 1851 · PITTSFIELD

This letter responds to Duyckinck's now unlocated letter requesting a contribution (possibly a sea piece—a " 'dash of salt spray' ") and a daguerreotype for publication in *Holden's Dollar Magazine* (see LETTERS RECEIVED, pp. 605–6). It is written on paper with the embossed stamp of "CARSON'S DALTON MS," which was, as Melville's opening comment indicates, the trademark of a local paper manufacturer. (A 14 January 1851 letter from Augusta to Helen Melville relates that "Herman took Mamma Lizzie & Fanny" on an expedition to the Dalton paper factory on 11 January 1851 [NYPL-GL].) On the basis of Duyckinck's endorsement, the "Wednesday" of this letter can be dated 12 February 1851.

Evert and George Duyckinck were scheduled to become editors of *Holden's* beginning with the April issue, succeeding Henry Fowler and William H. Dietz (see the announcement in the March issue). As one of their notebooks for this magazine (NYPL-D) indicates, they were planning to do a series of articles on contemporary authors, with portraits. They promised for the first issue under their editorship "An Original Portrait and Biography of a Distinguished American in Public Life." Though the April number had no such article, it did have a sketch of George Borrow, and the May issue contained "Our Portrait Gallery—William H. Prescott, the Historian. With an Original Portrait by Charles Martin." About this time Rufus W. Griswold, editor of the *International Monthly Magazine*, promised his readers portraits and biographical sketches of Melville and other contemporary authors (2 [December–March 1850–51], preface). Though Hawthorne, Cooper, Simms, and Halleck were "written up" in this fashion—complete with portraits—in Griswold's publication, Melville never was. Similarly, Melville's portrait never appeared in *Holden's*, much to his mother's dismay (see her 12 March 1851 letter in the HISTORICAL NOTE, p. 785). For Melville's literary use of Duyckinck's request, see *Pierre*, bk. 17, sect. iii (pp. 252–56). Melville's objections to *Holden's*, as Fowler and Dietz had conducted it, were reflected in the Duyckincks' editorial in the April number. They swore not to "humbug" their readers with the conventional devices—"over-puffery, extravagant promises, parading before them absurd lists of contributors, dazzling their eyes with fashion plates, sheafs of bad engravings, and various other cheap delusions." The magazine would be popular but not cheap, and would cultivate a garden "on American soil, in American air." In spite of this new, literary nationalist editorial policy, Melville is not known to have published in the magazine.

Both of Melville's addenda to this letter of refusal shed light on his reading at this time. He had earlier borrowed *Twice-Told Tales* (Boston: American Stationers, 1837) from Duyckinck on or after 20 July 1849 (Sealts 258), but on 22 January 1851 Hawthorne presented Melville with the unmatched set in two volumes that Melville mentions here as having "recently read" (First Series, Boston: Munroe, 1845, and vol. II, Boston: Munroe, 1842; Sealts 259 and 260 [the inscription in both volumes is by Hawthorne, not Melville]). "Leigh Hunt's magazine" was *Leigh Hunt's Journal; A Miscellany for the Cultivation of the Memorable, the Progressive, and the Beautiful*, published in seventeen numbers from 7 December 1850 to 29 March 1851 (Sealts 325). Melville refers to a parody of Carlyle published in the first issue under the title "Two Hundred and Fifty Years Ago. [*From a Waste-Paper Bag of T. Carlyle's.*] Introductory." In a duel with Gervase Markham, a "loose-living" "squire-of-dames to the Dowager of Shrewsbury," John Holles "pierced and spitted him, through the lower abdominal regions, in very important quarters of the body, 'coming out at the small of the back!'. . . The doctor declared that Markham would live; but that—but that—Here, we will suppose, the Doctor tragi-comically shook his head, pleading the imperfections of language! Markham did live long after; breaking several of the commandments, but keeping one of them, it is charitably believed." The passage may be related to Ahab's vaguely described bodily impairment; see the NN *Moby-Dick*, pp. 894–95, the discussion at 437.26.

The enclosed "note from the 'Sad One,'" Augusta Melville (see the headnote to Melville's 13 December 1850 letter, above), is unlocated, but it was probably the one-page "note" to "Mr Duyckinck" that she entered in her record of correspondence on 11 February 1851 (NYPL-GL).

— about 5 miles from here, North East. I went there & got a sleigh-load of this paper. A great neighborhood for authors, you see, is Pittsfield.

Pittsfield, Wednesday, 1851.

My Dear Duyckinck,

"A dash of salt spray"! — where am I to get salt spray here in inland Pittsfield? I shall have to import it from foreign parts. All I now have to do with salt, is when I salt my horse & cow — not *salt them down* — I dont mean that (tho' indeed I have before now dined on "salt-horse") but when I give them their weekly salt, by way of seasoning all their week's meals in one prospective lump.

How shall a man go about refusing a man? — Best be round-about, or plumb on the mark? —— I can not write the thing you want. I am in the humor to lend a hand to a friend, if I can; — but I am not in the humor to write the kind of thing you need — and I am not in the humor to write for Holden's Magazine. If I were to go on to give you all my reasons — you would pronounce me a bore, so I will not do that. You must be content to beleive that I *have* reasons, or else I would not refuse so small a thing. — As for the Daguerreo-type (I spell the word right from your sheet) that's what I can not send you, because I have none. And if I had, I would not send it for such a purpose, even to you. — Pshaw! you cry — & so cry I. — "This is intensified vanity, not true modesty or anything of that sort!" — Again, I say so too. But if it be so, how can I help it. The fact is, almost everybody is having his "mug" engraved nowadays; so that this test of distinction is getting to be reversed; and therefore, to see one's "mug" in a magazine, is presumptive evidence that he's a nobody. So being as vain a man as ever lived; & beleiving that my illustrious name is famous throughout the world — I respectfully decline being *oblivionated* by a Daguerretype (what a devel of an un-spellable word!)

We are all queer customers, Mr Duyckinck, you, I, & every body else in the world. So if I here seem queer to you, be sure, I am not alone in my queerness, tho' it present itself at a different port, perhaps, from other people, since every one has his own distinct peculiarity. But I trust you take me aright. If you dont' I shall be sorry — that's all.

After a long procrastination, I drove down to see Mr Hawthorne a couple of weeks ago. I found him, of course, buried in snow; & the delightful scenery about him, all wrapped up & tucked away under a napkin, as it were. He was to have made me a day's visit, & I had promised myself much pleasure in getting him up in my snug room here, & discussing the Universe with a bottle of brandy & cigars. But he has not been able to come, owing to sickness in his family. — or else, he's up to the lips in the *Universe* again.

By the way, I have recently read his "Twice Told Tales" (I had not read but a few of them before) I think they far exceed the "Mosses" — they are, I fancy, an earlier vintage from his vine. Some of those sketches are wonderfully subtle. Their deeper meanings are worthy of a Brahmin. Still there is something lacking — a good deal lacking — to the plump sphericity of the man. What is that? — He does'nt patronise the butcher — he needs roast-beef, done rare. — Nevertheless, for one, I regard Hawthorne (in his books) as evincing a quality of genius, immensely loftier, & more profound, too, than any other American has shown hitherto in the printed form. Irving is a grasshopper to him — putting the *souls* of the two men together, I mean. — But I must close. Enclosed is a note from the "Sad One".

With remembrances to your brother, I am
Truly Yours
H Melville.

5. PM. Wednesday.

I am just on the point of starting a'foot for the village, and have glanced over the previous letter, before sealing. —— I thought there seemed an unkindness in it — & that had I, under the circumstances, rec'd such a letter from you, in reply to such a letter as yours to me — I would deem it not well of you. — Still, I can't help it — and I may yet be of some better service to you than merely jotting a paragraph for Holden's. ——

My respects to Mrs Duyckinck. Jog Adler's memory about me now & then. — The society here is very much pleased with Leigh Hunt's magazine. — What a quizzical thing that is of the Duel — the man who was wounded in certain *important* parts.

Adieu again.
H. M.

ALS on a 39.8 × 24.8 cm sheet, folded in half, of blue wove paper with lines, embossed with the manufacturer's rectangular stamp enclosing the name "CARSON'S DALTON MS". Melville inscribed all four pages, in ink. Duyckinck later noted in ink at the top of the first page "*Rcd Feb 14. 1851*".

LOCATION: NYPL-D.

PUBLICATION: (partial) Minnigerode, pp. 55–56, 72–73. Thorp, pp. 384–86. Davis-Gilman 81.

TO T. D. STEWART
BETWEEN 17 AND 22 MARCH 1851 · PITTSFIELD

Unlocated. In a 28 March 1851 letter to Melville, Maria Melville wrote from New York that "M͏r Stewart" had paid her a visit and said "he had a letter from you last week, & he hope'd to call in upon you soon, that he was soon going to Lansing-burgh" (for the full text of Maria Melville's letter, see LETTERS RECEIVED, pp. 609–12). "M͏r Stewart" was Tertullus D. Stewart (1804–57), whom the Melvilles had known in Lansingburgh. T. D. Stewart, as he is generally referred to in the Mel-villes' correspondence, moved to New York sometime around 1850, when he is first listed in the New York directories at Mary Vandervoort's boarding house at 7 Fifth Avenue. He apparently became involved in the sugar trade, probably import-ing it, since he is so listed in 1852–53, with a business address at 108 Front Street. The 1853–54 directory reveals that he had moved from Fifth Avenue to a house in Astoria, which is where he died only a few years later. Maria Melville's 28 March 1851 letter to her son seems to indicate that Stewart was married and had a son, John Dickinson Stewart. Melville in his 12 May 1856 letter to Lemuel Shaw (be-low) recalled declining a loan that Stewart offered to make him at the time he moved to Pittsfield. On 1 May 1851, however, Melville did borrow $2,050 for five years at nine percent after the Harpers turned down his request for an advance on 30 April 1851 (see LETTERS RECEIVED, pp. 612–13). Whether Melville's letter to Stewart was one declining Stewart's offer or one expressing renewed interest in the offer is unclear.

TO EVERT A. DUYCKINCK
26 MARCH 1851 · PITTSFIELD

The "old friend" on whose behalf Melville was subscribing to *Holden's Dollar Mag-azine* in this letter to Duyckinck was Eli James Murdock Fly, whom Melville had known since his youth (see the headnote to Melville's 10 November 1838 letter to his brother Allan, above). Recently Melville had probably accompanied him as far as Springfield, Massachusetts, where Fly presumably then took a train to Brat-tleboro, Vermont, possibly to seek treatment at Dr. Wesselhoeft's water cure (see Charles T. Morrissey, *Vermont* [New York: Norton, 1981], p. 119).

Fly died in Boston in January 1854, leaving a widow, Hannah Sturgis Hinkley Fly of Hingham, Massachusetts. A 4–5 March 1854 letter from Maria Melville in

Boston to her daughter Augusta recounts her meeting a woman at the Shaws' who had known Fly in Hingham: "The next morning Miss Titmarsh called to see your mother. Lizzie, the judge & I were alone, in the room, & Mrs Shaw very much engaged. So we had all her conversation. The subject happened to be about Hingham. In one of the pauses, I enquired if she knew Mr Fly[.] oh yes the most interesting man she had ever seen. She did not wonder, that not withstanding his bad health Miss Hinkley had married him[.] I then enquired about his death. Mr Fly had left a message to Herman said Mrs Titmarsh looking at the Judge & something about a Cloake, Sir, I believe which Mr Melville had given him. A post mortem examination had taken place. one lung was entirely gone of the other but half remained. The widow was inconsolable. No man is a prophet in his own country. I wish I could remember more. His sister was at the funeral. He died in Boston where they were passing the winter" (NYPL-GL).

On the basis of its 27 March postmark, this letter can be dated Wednesday, 26 March.

Pittsfield, Wednesday. 1851

My Dear Duyckinck — I have just returned from Springfield, having accompanied an old friend of mine, Mr J. M. Fly, so far on his way to Brattleboro': He has long been a confirmed invalid, & in some small things I act a little as his agent. He subscribed, thro' me, to the "Literary World" & paid something in advance. He will remain in Brattleboro' through the summer. Will you have his paper sent to him there instead of Greenbush. And also will you send him the Dollar Magazine. And when I get to New York, the subscription to both will be duly paid. Send him the March Number of the "Dollar"

The Spring begins to open upon Pittsfield, but slowly. I only wish that I had more day-time to spend out *in the day*; but like an owl I steal abroad by twilight, owing to the twilight of my eyes.

Remember me kindly to your Brother & to Adler.

H Melville

ALS on a 39.8 × 24.8 cm sheet, folded in half, of blue wove paper with lines, embossed with the manufacturer's rectangular stamp enclosing the name "CARSON'S DALTON MS". Melville inscribed the first page, in ink, and addressed the fourth page "Evert A Duyckinck Esq | New York"; it was postmarked in Pittsfield on 27 March.

LOCATION: NYPL-D.

PUBLICATION: (partial transcription with full reproduction between pp. 42–43) Minnigerode, p. 73. Metcalf, p. 102. Davis-Gilman 82.

TEXTUAL NOTE: there] *miswritten* theres

TO ALLAN MELVILLE
BEFORE 27 MARCH 1851 · PITTSFIELD

Unlocated. Writing on 28 March 1851 from New York, Maria Melville concluded her letter to Melville with the message: "Allan is waiting to hear from you your letter reach'd him yesterday but he wants the paper" (see LETTERS RECEIVED, pp. 609–12). This brief memorandum may imply that a second letter from Melville followed. As to what "the paper" was or the contents of the letter Allan had already received, no indication is given.

TO NATHANIEL HAWTHORNE
[16 APRIL?] 1851 · PITTSFIELD

On 27 March 1851 Nathaniel and Sophia Hawthorne wrote Melville asking him to find them a clock in Pittsfield and to oversee the work on a bedstead they were having made there (see LETTERS RECEIVED, pp. 606–9). Sophia Hawthorne's diary (NYPL-B) records that on 11 April Melville arrived at their cottage bringing the clock and bedstead with him. During this visit Hawthorne gave him a copy of his newly published (9 April) *The House of the Seven Gables*, which Hawthorne inscribed: "Herman Melville from Nath¹ Hawthorne," and which Mrs. Hawthorne dated "April 11ᵗʰ 1851 Friday evening" (HCL-M; Sealts 246 [inscription by Hawthorne, not Melville]). Presumably during this same visit Melville's further assistance was enlisted in finding a pair of shoes for Julian, the Hawthornes' second child, born 22 June 1846.

Melville's letter can be tentatively dated 16 April 1851, since the copy of *The House of the Seven Gables* must have occasioned the comments on it for "the 'Pittsfield Secret Review' " in this letter. If Melville read the book soon after his visit, as is most likely, the letter could then have been written on the following "Wednesday morning," 16 April. It was certainly written before 7 May 1851, when Sophia Hawthorne wrote to her sister Elizabeth enclosing a copy (now unlocated) of a portion of this letter, commenting: "I enclose a very remarkable quotation from a private letter to Mr Hawthorne about the House of S.G. but as it is wholly confidential *do not show it*. The fresh, sincere, glowing mind that utters it is in a state of 'fluid consciousness,' & to Mr Hawthorne speaks his innermost about GOD, the Devil & Life if so be he can get at the Truth — for he is a boy in opinion — having settled nothing as yet — informe — ingens — & it would betray him to make public his confessions & efforts to grasp — because they would be considered perhaps impious, if one did not take in the whole scope of the case. Nothing pleases me better than to sit & hear this growing man dash his tumultuous waves of thought up against Mr Hawthorne's great, genial, comprehending silences — out of the profound of which a wonderful smile, or one powerful word sends back the foam & fury into a peaceful booming, calm — or perchance, not into a calm — but a murmuring expostulation — for there is never a 'mush of concession' in him — Yet such a love & reverence & admiration for Mr Hawthorne as is really beautiful to witness" (NYPL-B).

This is the first of six of Melville's letters to Hawthorne that were printed (often unreliably transcribed, as the differences recorded in the textual notes suggest) by members of the Hawthorne family, but whose originals are now missing despite numerous searches by modern scholars. For the phrase "visable truth" see Harrison Hayford, "Melville's *Usable* or *Visible Truth*," *Modern Language Notes* 74 (December 1959), 702–5.

Pittsfield, Wednesday morning.

My dear Hawthorne, — Concerning the young gentleman's shoes, I desire to say that a pair to fit him, of the desired pattern, cannot be had in all Pittsfield, — a fact which sadly impairs that metropolitan pride I formerly took in the capital of Berkshire. Henceforth Pittsfield must hide its head. However, if a pair of *bootees* will at all answer, Pittsfield will be very happy to provide them. Pray mention all this to Mrs. Hawthorne, and command me.

"The House of the Seven Gables: A Romance. By Nathaniel Hawthorne. One vol. 16mo, pp. 344." The contents of this book do not belie its rich, clustering, romantic title. With great enjoyment we spent almost an hour in each separate gable. This book is like a fine old chamber, abundantly, but still judiciously, furnished with precisely that sort of furniture best fitted to furnish it. There are rich hangings, wherein are braided scenes from tragedies! There is old china with rare devices, set out on the carved buffet; there are long and indolent lounges to throw yourself upon; there is an admirable sideboard, plentifully stored with good viands; there is a smell as of old wine in the pantry; and finally, in one corner, there is a dark little black-letter volume in golden clasps, entitled "Hawthorne: A Problem." It has delighted us; it has piqued a re-perusal; it has robbed us of a day, and made us a present of a whole year of thoughtfulness; it has bred great exhilaration and exultation with the remembrance that the architect of the Gables resides only six miles off, and not three thousand miles away, in England, say. We think the book, for pleasantness of running interest, surpasses the other works of the author. The curtains are more drawn; the sun comes in more; genialities peep out more. Were we to particularize what has most struck us in the deeper passages, we would point out the scene where Clifford, for a moment, would fain throw himself forth from the window to join the procession; or the scene where the Judge is left seated in his ancestral chair. Clifford is full of an awful truth throughout. He is conceived in the finest, truest spirit. He is no caricature. He is Clifford. And here we would say that, did circumstances permit, we should like nothing better than to devote an elaborate and careful paper to the full consideration and analysis of the purport and significance of what so strongly characterizes all of this author's writings. There is a certain tragic phase of humanity which, in our opinion, was never more powerfully embodied than by Hawthorne. We mean the tragicalness of human thought in its own unbiassed, native, and profounder workings. We think that into no recorded mind has the intense feeling of the visable truth ever entered more deeply than into this man's. By visable truth, we mean the apprehension of the absolute condition of present things as they strike the eye of the man who fears them not, though they do their worst to him, — the man who, like Russia or the British Empire, declares himself a sovereign nature (in himself) amid the powers of heaven, hell, and earth. He may perish; but so long as he exists he insists upon treating with all Powers upon an equal basis. If any of those other Powers choose to withhold certain secrets, let them; that does not impair my sovereignty in myself; that does not make me tributary. And perhaps, after all, there is *no* secret. We incline to think that the Problem of the Universe is like the Freemason's mighty secret, so terrible to all children. It turns out, at last, to consist in a triangle, a mallet, and an apron, — nothing more! We incline to think that God cannot explain His own secrets, and that He would like a little information upon certain points Himself. We mortals astonish Him as much as He us. But it is this *Being* of the matter; there lies the knot with which we choke ourselves. As soon as you say *Me*, a *God*, a *Nature*, so soon you jump off from your stool and hang from the beam. Yes, that word is the hangman. Take God out of the dictionary, and you would have Him in the street.

There is the grand truth about Nathaniel Hawthorne. He says NO! in thunder; but the Devil himself cannot make him say *yes*. For all men who say *yes*, lie; and all men who say *no*, — why, they are in the happy condition of judicious, unincumbered travellers in Europe; they cross the frontiers into Eternity with nothing but a carpet-bag, — that is to say, the Ego. Whereas those *yes*-gentry, they travel with heaps of baggage, and, damn them! they will never get through the Custom House. What's the reason, Mr. Hawthorne, that in the last stages of metaphysics a fellow always falls to *swearing* so? I could rip an hour. You see, I began with a little criticism extracted for your benefit from the "Pittsfield Secret Review," and here I have landed in Africa.

Walk down one of these mornings and see me. No nonsense; come. Remember me to Mrs. Hawthorne and the children.

H. Melville.

P.S. The marriage of Phoebe with the daguerreotypist is a fine stroke, because of his turning out to be a *Maule*. If you pass Hepzibah's cent-shop, buy me a Jim Crow (fresh) and send it to me by Ned Higgins.

Original document not located. Text from first full publication (JH), emended by NN (with three emendations coming from the first partial publication [GL]). Variants in the partial publication (GL) are also listed in the textual notes.

PUBLICATION: (partial) George Parsons Lathrop (GL), *A Study of Hawthorne* (Boston: Osgood, 1876), pp. 230–31. Julian Hawthorne (JH), *Nathaniel Hawthorne and His Wife* (2 vols., Boston: Osgood, 1884), I, 385–89. Davis-Gilman 83.

TEXTUAL NOTES (for symbols used, see p. 840): Pittsfield . . . 344."] JH; *[not present]* GL • Henceforth] Hence-|forth • rich,] JH; *[not present]* GL • clustering,] JH; ~∧ GL • abundantly,] JH; ~∧ GL • judiciously,] JH; ~∧ GL • wherein] JH; whereon GL • tragedies!] JH; ~. GL • out] JH; about GL • buffet] JH; beaufet GL • as] JH; *[not present]* GL • "Hawthorne: A Problem."] JH; ∧ Hawthorne: A Problem. . . . . ∧ *(italicized)* GL • It has . . . say.] JH; *[not present]* GL • We think] JH; *[after paragraph break]* GL • book,] JH; ~∧ GL • interest,] JH; ~∧ GL • works] JH; work GL • more drawn] JH; now drawn GL • has most] GL; most JH • we would] JH; we should GL • moment] JH; minute GL • forth] JH; *[not present]* GL • window∧] JH; ~, GL • Judge] GL; judge JH • Clifford] JH; *[after paragraph break]* GL • say∧ that,] JH; ~, ~∧ GL • circumstances] JH; the circumstances GL • purport] JH; purpose GL • writings] JH; writing GL • humanity∧] JH; ~, GL • Hawthorne. We] JH; Hawthorne: we GL • tragicalness] GL; tragedies JH • unbiassed] JH; unbiased GL • profounder] JH; profound GL • visable] NN *(see Hayford, cited above)*; usable JH; whole GL • visable] NN *(see Hayford, cited above)*; usable JH; whole GL • him,] JH; ~. GL • — the man . . . Higgins.] JH; *[not present]* GL • of the matter] *Davis and Gilman conjectured that matters or that maddens (but adopted neither) speculating that Julian Hawthorne read M's that as of the and that he did not recognize M's final s both of which are possible and understandable mistranscriptions of M's hand* • hangman] hang-|man • daguerreotypist] daguerreo-|typist

TO FLETCHER HARPER
25 APRIL 1851 · PITTSFIELD

Unlocated. On 30 April 1851 Harper & Brothers replied to Melville's now unlocated letter of 25 April. Their reply shows that Melville had requested, in his letter "addressed to our Mr F. Harper," an advance on his account, which they declined to make (see LETTERS RECEIVED, pp. 612–13). He had already drawn $695.65 on his Harpers' account, and his protracted work on the book that became *Moby-Dick* had left him without income during the winter of 1850–51. On 1 May 1851 Melville borrowed $2,050 from T. D. Stewart (see the entry for Melville's unlocated March 1851 letter to Stewart, above). Davis–Gilman Unlocated 332.

TO NATHANIEL HAWTHORNE
[1 JUNE?] 1851 · PITTSFIELD

This letter—the second of the now-missing known letters to Hawthorne (see the headnote to Melville's [16 April?] 1851 letter, above)—carries no date in Julian Hawthorne's published transcription, but it can be placed in late May or early June 1851. It was written during spring planting time, but after the publication of the May 1851 issue of *Holden's Dollar Magazine* (Sealts 189) in which Hawthorne's "Ethan Brand" was reprinted and after the announcements of Hawthorne's new works (*The House of the Seven Gables* and *A Wonder-Book*). One notice appeared in the *Literary World* on 10 May: the "Publishers' Circular," an editor's column, noted that "Ticknor, Reed & Fields, Boston, have in Press . . . [a] New volume of Stories by Nathaniel Hawthorne" and "a new volume by Hawthorne." Also between 17 May and 9 August, a publisher's advertisement for the books appeared nearly continuously in the *Literary World*. At the other extreme, this letter was written before Melville's extended trip to New York to see his whaling book (not yet titled *Moby-Dick*) through the press, as indicated by his comment anticipating the "malicious" printer's devil "forever grinning in upon me" waiting for the completed book. The only known documentation of this trip is his 14 June return of the volumes of Scoresby borrowed from the New York Society Library (Sealts 450, 451) and Augusta Melville's memorandum of a 17 June letter sent to him while there (see LETTERS RECEIVED, p. 613). If Melville followed his plan to go to New York in "a week or so" to "work and slave" on his book, as he states in the letter, then he probably wrote to Hawthorne during the first week of June, which would also allow for "three weeks" to have passed in May during which he "left" his book in order to plant corn and potatoes and complete his spring work "out of doors," as he also states in the letter. The date 1 June can be assigned only tentatively, however.

Since it is unclear which portrait of Hawthorne Melville may have seen during his brief "four-and-twenty"-hour visit to New York, or even where he saw it, this incident adds no clue to the dating of the letter. Rita K. Gollin in *Portraits of Nathaniel Hawthorne* (DeKalb: Northern Illinois University Press, 1983), p. 38n., speculates that Melville may have seen the 1850 Cephas Thompson portrait in the office of the Duyckincks, since Hawthorne had agreed to let them prepare their own engraving for the *Dollar Magazine*; the Duyckincks ceased publication of that magazine before using Hawthorne's portrait, but the fact that Hawthorne was willing for them to do so had furnished Maria Melville with a strong argument in her efforts to get her son to consent to the Duyckincks' request for his portrait (see the HISTORICAL NOTE, p. 785). However, Melville may have seen any one of a number of Hawthorne portraits, including the unauthorized engraving of the Thompson portrait that appeared in the 1 May 1851 issue of Griswold's *International Monthly Magazine* or the Thomas Phillbrown steel engraving used as the frontispiece of the revised edition of *Twice-Told Tales*, which had been issued by Ticknor & Fields in March and which Melville also mentions in his letter.

In his discussion of the "aristocracy of the brain," Melville seems to have had in mind the quality pointed out in Wolfgang Menzel's criticism of Schiller, as quoted by Longfellow in *The Poets and Poetry of Europe* (Philadelphia: Carey & Hart, 1845), p. 308: "We turn now to the second secret of the beauty belonging to Schiller's ideal characters. This is their nobleness,—their honorableness. His heroes and heroines never discredit the pride and dignity which announce a loftier nature; and all their outward acts bear the stamp of magnanimity and inborn nobleness. Its perfect opposite is the vulgar character, and that conventional spirit which serves for a bridle and leading-strings to the vulgar nature." (A letter from Augusta Melville to her friend Mary Blatchford in January 1851 mentions that Schiller's *Ghost-Seer*—which Melville had brought home from London—was one of the books being read aloud during the long winter evenings at Arrowhead, but not whether Melville participated in these readings [NYPL-GL; Sealts 438a].) Among English families, the Howards, whom Melville mentions, had long held the first place, its head being the duke of Norfolk (see also *Moby-Dick*, chap. 87, p. 384).

Although Julian Hawthorne printed "revere the test of my Lord Shaftesbury," Melville's word must have been "reverse," since Shaftesbury maintained that one test of truth was its power to surmount the test of ridicule, not invite it. His piece "An Essay on the Freedom of Wit and Humour" declares, "Truth 'tis supposed, may bear *all* Lights: and *one* of those principal Lights or natural Mediums, by which Things are to be view'd, in order to a thorow Recognition, is *Ridicule* it-self, or that Manner of Proof by which we discern whatever is liable to just Raillery in any Subject" (*Characteristicks of Men, Manners, Opinions, Times* [1727], I, 161).

Melville's remark, in the latter part of the letter, about reading Solomon is parallel to a passage in *Moby-Dick*: "The truest of all men was the Man of Sorrows, and the truest of all books is Solomon's, and Ecclesiastes is the fine hammered steel of woe. 'All is vanity.' ALL. This wilful world hath not got hold of unchristian Solomon's wisdom yet" (chap. 96, p. 424).

The immediate source for Melville's discussion of Goethe in his final paragraph remains to be discovered. The idea is general in Goethe; the particular thought is presumably a translation of a phrase in stanza four of "Generalbeichte":

> Willst du Absolution
> Deinen Treuen geben,
> Wollen wir nach deinem Wink
> Unablässlich streben,
> Uns von Halben zu entwohnen
> Und im Ganzen, Guten, Schönen
> Resolut zu leben.

Carlyle paraphrased these lines at the conclusion of his essay "Death of Goethe" when he admonished, "To live, as he counselled and commanded, not commodiously in the Reputable, the Plausible, the Half, but resolutely in the Whole, the Good, the True" (*Critical and Miscellaneous Essays* [Boston: Munroe, 1839], III,

205). John S. Dwight translated them "We all half-life will forswear, | In the Whole, the Good, the Fair, | Resolutely living; — " (see George Ripley, ed., *Specimens of Foreign Standard Literature*, vol. 3: *Select Minor Poems Translated from the German of Goethe and Schiller* [Boston: Hilliard, Gray, 1839], p. 48). One of Ripley's notes on Goethe may have helped give currency to the idea Melville was deriding: "Total occupation of himself, heart and soul, in the object nearest him,—living *in* it, and identifying himself with it for the time,—left no room for sick yearnings, made each little sphere a world, each moment an eternity. This is evidently what he meant by 'Living in the Whole,' by finding 'All in One, and One in All' " (p. 365).

The final postscript to this letter is a reference to the relatively new practice of prepaid postage. Formerly all mail was paid for by the recipient. On 1 July 1847 the United States Post Office, following the new practice in England, first issued printed stamps (see the headnote to Melville's 1 July 1852 letter, below).

My dear Hawthorne, — I should have been rumbling down to you in my pine-board chariot a long time ago, were it not that for some weeks past I have been more busy than you can well imagine, — out of doors, — building and patching and tinkering away in all directions. Besides, I had my crops to get in, — corn and potatoes (I hope to show you some famous ones by and by), — and many other things to attend to, all accumulating upon this one particular season. I work myself; and at night my bodily sensations are akin to those I have so often felt before, when a hired man, doing my day's work from sun to sun. But I mean to continue visiting you until you tell me that my visits are both supererogatory and superfluous. With no son of man do I stand upon any etiquette or ceremony, except the Christian ones of charity and honesty. I am told, my fellow-man, that there is an aristocracy of the brain. Some men have boldly advocated and asserted it. Schiller seems to have done so, though I don't know much about him. At any rate, it is true that there have been those who, while earnest in behalf of political equality, still accept the intellectual estates. And I can well perceive, I think, how a man of superior mind can, by its intense cultivation, bring himself, as it were, into a certain spontaneous aristocracy of feeling, — exceedingly nice and fastidious, — similar to that which, in an English Howard, conveys a torpedo-fish thrill at the slightest contact with a social plebeian. So, when you see or hear of my ruthless democracy on all sides, you may possibly feel a touch of a shrink, or something of that sort. It is but nature to be shy of a mortal who boldly declares that a thief in jail is as honorable a per-

sonage as Gen. George Washington. This is ludicrous. Bu[
the silliest thing under the sun. Try to get a living
Truth — and go to the Soup Societies. Heavens! Let any cl[
try to preach the Truth from its very stronghold, the pul[
they would ride him out of his church on his own pulpit ba[
It can hardly be doubted that all Reformers are bottomed upon the
truth, more or less; and to the world at large are not reformers almost universally laughing-stocks? Why so? Truth is ridiculous to
men. Thus easily in my room here do I, conceited and garrulous,
reverse the test of my Lord Shaftesbury.

It seems an inconsistency to assert unconditional democracy in
all things, and yet confess a dislike to all mankind — in the mass.
But not so. — But it's an endless sermon, — no more of it. I began
by saying that the reason I have not been to Lenox is this, — in the
evening I feel completely done up, as the phrase is, and incapable of
the long jolting to get to your house and back. In a week or so, I go
to New York, to bury myself in a third-story room, and work and
slave on my "Whale" while it is driving through the press. *That* is
the only way I can finish it now, — I am so pulled hither and thither
by circumstances. The calm, the coolness, the silent grass-growing
mood in which a man *ought* always to compose, — that, I fear, can
seldom be mine. Dollars damn me; and the malicious Devil is forever grinning in upon me, holding the door ajar. My dear Sir, a presentiment is on me, — I shall at last be worn out and perish, like an
old nutmeg-grater, grated to pieces by the constant attrition of the
wood, that is, the nutmeg. What I feel most moved to write, that is
banned, — it will not pay. Yet, altogether, write the *other* way I
cannot. So the product is a final hash, and all my books are botches.
I'm rather sore, perhaps, in this letter; but see my hand! — four
blisters on this palm, made by hoes and hammers within the last few
days. It is a rainy morning; so I am indoors, and all work suspended. I feel cheerfully disposed, and therefore I write a little bluely.
Would the Gin were here! If ever, my dear Hawthorne, in the eternal times that are to come, you and I shall sit down in Paradise, in
some little shady corner by ourselves; and if we shall by any means
be able to smuggle a basket of champagne there (I won't believe in a
Temperance Heaven), and if we shall then cross our celestial legs in
the celestial grass that is forever tropical, and strike our glasses and
our heads together, till both musically ring in concert, — then, O

my dear fellow-mortal, how shall we pleasantly discourse of all the
things manifold which now so distress us, — when all the earth shall
be but a reminiscence, yea, its final dissolution an antiquity. Then
shall songs be composed as when wars are over; humorous, comic
songs, — "Oh, when I lived in that queer little hole called the
world," or, "Oh, when I toiled and sweated below," or, "Oh,
when I knocked and was knocked in the fight" — yes, let us look
forward to such things. Let us swear that, though now we sweat,
yet it is because of the dry heat which is indispensable to the nourishment of the vine which is to bear the grapes that are to give us the
champagne hereafter.

But I was talking about the "Whale." As the fishermen say,
"he's in his flurry" when I left him some three weeks ago. I'm going
to take him by his jaw, however, before long, and finish him up in
some fashion or other. What's the use of elaborating what, in its
very essence, is so short-lived as a modern book? Though I wrote
the Gospels in this century, I should die in the gutter. — I talk all
about myself, and this is selfishness and egotism. Granted. But how
help it? I am writing to you; I know little about you, but something
about myself. So I write about myself, — at least, to you. Don't
trouble yourself, though, about writing; and don't trouble yourself
about visiting; and when you *do* visit, don't trouble yourself about
talking. I will do all the writing and visiting and talking myself. — By the way, in the last "Dollar Magazine" I read "The Unpardonable Sin." He was a sad fellow, that Ethan Brand. I have no
doubt you are by this time responsible for many a shake and tremor
of the tribe of "general readers." It is a frightful poetical creed that
the cultivation of the brain eats out the heart. But it's my *prose* opinion that in most cases, in those men who have fine brains and work
them well, the heart extends down to hams. And though you smoke
them with the fire of tribulation, yet, like veritable hams, the head
only gives the richer and the better flavor. I stand for the heart. To
the dogs with the head! I had rather be a fool with a heart, than
Jupiter Olympus with his head. The reason the mass of men fear
God, and *at bottom dislike* Him, is because they rather distrust His
heart, and fancy Him all brain like a watch. (You perceive I employ
a capital initial in the pronoun referring to the Deity; don't you
think there is a slight dash of flunkeyism in that usage?) Another
thing. I was in New York for four-and-twenty hours the other day,

and saw a portrait of N. H. And I have seen and heard many flattering (in a publisher's point of view) allusions to the "Seven Gables." And I have seen "Tales," and "A New Volume" announced, by N. H. So upon the whole, I say to myself, this N. H. is in the ascendant. My dear Sir, they begin to patronize. All Fame is patronage. Let me be infamous: there is no patronage in *that*. What "reputation" H. M. has is horrible. Think of it! To go down to posterity is bad enough, any way; but to go down as a "man who lived among the cannibals"! When I speak of posterity, in reference to myself, I only mean the babies who will probably be born in the moment immediately ensuing upon my giving up the ghost. I shall go down to some of them, in all likelihood. "Typee" will be given to them, perhaps, with their gingerbread. I have come to regard this matter of Fame as the most transparent of all vanities. I read Solomon more and more, and every time see deeper and deeper and unspeakable meanings in him. I did not think of Fame, a year ago, as I do now. My development has been all within a few years past. I am like one of those seeds taken out of the Egyptian Pyramids, which, after being three thousand years a seed and nothing but a seed, being planted in English soil, it developed itself, grew to greenness, and then fell to mould. So I. Until I was twenty-five, I had no development at all. From my twenty-fifth year I date my life. Three weeks have scarcely passed, at any time between then and now, that I have not unfolded within myself. But I feel that I am now come to the inmost leaf of the bulb, and that shortly the flower must fall to the mould. It seems to me now that Solomon was the truest man who ever spoke, and yet that he a little *managed* the truth with a view to popular conservatism; or else there have been many corruptions and interpolations of the text — In reading some of Goethe's sayings, so worshipped by his votaries, I came across this, *"Live in the all."* That is to say, your separate identity is but a wretched one, — good; but get out of yourself, spread and expand yourself, and bring to yourself the tinglings of life that are felt in the flowers and the woods, that are felt in the planets Saturn and Venus, and the Fixed Stars. What nonsense! Here is a fellow with a raging toothache. "My dear boy," Goethe says to him, "you are sorely afflicted with that tooth; but you must *live in the all,* and then you will be happy!" As with all great genius, there is an immense deal of flummery in

Goethe, and in proportion to my own contact with him, a monstrous deal of it in me.

H. Melville.

P.S. "Amen!" saith Hawthorne.

N.B. This "all" feeling, though, there is some truth in. You must often have felt it, lying on the grass on a warm summer's day. Your legs seem to send out shoots into the earth. Your hair feels like leaves upon your head. This is the *all* feeling. But what plays the mischief with the truth is that men will insist upon the universal application of a temporary feeling or opinion.

P.S. You must not fail to admire my discretion in paying the postage on this letter.

Original document not located. Text from first publication, emended by NN.

PUBLICATION: Julian Hawthorne, *Nathaniel Hawthorne and His Wife* (2 vols., Boston: Osgood, 1884), I, 400–407. Davis-Gilman 84.

TEXTUAL NOTES: or something] or some-|thing · stronghold] strong-|hold · reverse] NN *(see the headnote)*; revere

TO NATHANIEL HAWTHORNE
29 JUNE 1851 · PITTSFIELD

This is the last of the known letters written to Hawthorne during the composition of *Moby-Dick* in 1851 and the third of those whose originals are now missing. Melville probably dated it only "June 29th," even though Julian Hawthorne also wrote the partial year "185 " after the month and day in his notebook transcription of the letter. This partial year most likely reflected his speculative knowledge that the letter belonged to the 1850's. His published version gave the full year "1851" (see the textual notes, below).

As Melville writes, he had been busy since Hawthorne had last paid him a visit with his daughter Una on 13–14 March 1851 (see the headnote to Melville's [29 January?] 1851 letter for more about that visit). While getting his whaling book into shape, he had also been building some sheds, probably at the back of the Arrowhead farmhouse, two activities that had become allied in his mind. He had also been doing his spring planting. Julian Hawthorne in his notebook transcribed Melville's description of his activities as "plowing and sowing and raising and fainting and printing and praying." In his printed text of the letter (see below), Julian omitted the words "and fainting," but given his unreliability as a copyist, it seems likely that Melville did list six activities, even if he did not write "fainting" as the fourth. NN follows Leyda in *Portable Melville*, p. 434, in emending "fainting" to "painting"; however, it is also possible that Melville wrote "pointing [i.e., punctuating, in nineteenth-century usage] and printing and proofing [*not* praying]" to describe the stages of a single process as he does in the first half of his list. NN also emends Julian Hawthorne's "feeble" as an error for "febrile"—a modifier for "temperament" more consonant with Melville's ascribing his "crazy letter" to the "intoxicating effects" of midsummer operating on that temperament.

Melville's demonic baptismal formula at the end of this letter appears in fuller form in *Moby-Dick*, chap. 113, when Captain Ahab uses the blood of the pagan harpooneers to baptize the harpoon with which he plans to kill the white whale, declaring: "Ego non baptizo te in nomine patris, sed in nomine diaboli!" (p. 489). It also appears in even more detail among the notes that Melville jotted in the back of the seventh volume of his set of Shakespeare (HCL-M; see his description, presumably of this set, in his 24 February 1849 letter to Duyckinck, above, and see the NN *Moby-Dick*, pp. 955–70, for a discussion and transcription of these notes).

Pittsfield — June 29th

My dear Hawthorne — The clear air and open window invite me to write to you. For some time past I have been so busy with a thousand things that I have almost forgotten when I wrote you last, and whether I received an answer. This most persuasive season has now for weeks recalled me from certain crotchetty and over doleful chimaeras, the like of which men like you and me and some others, forming a chain of God's posts round the world, must be content to encounter now and then, and fight them the best way we can. But come they will, — for, in the boundless, trackless, but still glorious wild wilderness through which these outposts run, the Indians do sorely abound, as well as the insignificant but still stinging mosquitoes. Since you have been here, I have been building some shanties of houses (connected with the old one) and likewise some shanties of chapters and essays. I have been plowing and sowing and raising and painting and printing and praying, — and now begin to come out upon a less bustling time, and to enjoy the calm prospect of things from a fair piazza at the north of the old farm house here.

Not entirely yet, though, am I without something to be urgent with. The "Whale" is only half through the press; for, wearied with the long delay of the printers, and disgusted with the heat and dust of the babylonish brick-kiln of New York, I came back to the country to feel the grass — and end the book reclining on it, if I may. — I am sure you will pardon this speaking all about myself, — for if I

say so much on that head, be sure all the rest of the world are thinking about themselves ten times as much. Let us speak, though we
show all our faults and weaknesses, — for it is a sign of strength to
be weak, to know it, and out with it, — not in set way and ostenta-
tiously, though, but incidentally and without premeditation. — But
I am falling into my old foible — preaching. I am busy, but shall not
be very long. Come and spend a day here, if you can and want to; if
not, stay in Lenox, and God give you long life. When I am quite free
of my present engagements, I am going to treat myself to a ride and
a visit to you. Have ready a bottle of brandy, because I always feel
like drinking that heroic drink when we talk ontological heroics together. This is rather a crazy letter in some respects, I apprehend. If
so, ascribe it to the intoxicating effects of the latter end of June operating upon a very susceptible and peradventure febrile temperament.

Shall I send you a fin of the *Whale* by way of a specimen mouthful? The tail is not yet cooked — though the hell-fire in which the
whole book is broiled might not unreasonably have cooked it all ere
this. This is the book's motto (the secret one), — Ego non baptiso te
in nomine — but make out the rest yourself.

H. M.

Original document not located. Text from Julian Hawthorne's transcription (pp. 10–11, head-
ed "*Herman Melville to N. H.*") in his notebook (N) labeled by him "Memorandum of Letters
Received & Written. Julian Hawthorne". NN emendations and variants in the first publication
(JH) are listed in the textual notes, below.

LOCATION (of notebook): The Pierpont Morgan Library, New York. MA 1375.

PUBLICATION: Julian Hawthorne (JH), *Nathaniel Hawthorne and His Wife* (2 vols., Boston: Osgood, 1884), I, 398–400. Davis-Gilman 85.

TEXTUAL NOTES (for symbols used, see p. 840): Pittsfield —] N; PITTSFIELD, JH • June 29ᵗʰ]
NN; June 29ᵗʰ 185 N; June 29, 1851 JH • My dear Hawthorne —] N; [*paragraph indentation*]
MY DEAR HAWTHORNE, — JH • The] JH; the N • crotchetty] N; crotchety JH • over doleful]
N; over-doleful JH • chimaeras] NN; chimearas N; chimeras JH • meₐ and] N; ~, ~
JH • for,] N; ~ₐ JH • of houses] f *written over* r • plowing] N; ploughing JH • and painting]
NN (*see the headnote*); and fainting N; [*not present*] JH • praying, —] N; ~, ₐ JH • bustling] N;
bristling JH • farm house] N; farmhouse JH • delay] N; delays JH • babylonish] N; Babylo-
nish JH • grassₐ —] N; ~, ₐ JH • may. —] N; ~. ₐ JH • myself, —] N; ~; ₐ JH • the
world] the *inserted above caret* • it, —] N; ~; ₐ JH • premeditation. —] N; ~. ₐ
JH • foibleₐ —] N; ~, — JH • always feel] *before canceled* the • febrile] NN; feeble N;
JH • Shall] N; [*no paragraph break*] JH • Whale] N; "Whale" JH • all] N; [*not present*]
JH • one), —] N; ~), ₐ JH • Ego . . . nomine] N; [*italicized*] JH

TO RICHARD BENTLEY
BEFORE 3 JULY 1851 · [NEW YORK?]

Unlocated. Melville's 20 July 1851 letter to Bentley, below, indicates that he had written to his British publisher about his whaling book for the second time in the late spring or early summer of 1851, possibly while he was in New York dealing with the typesetting of the American edition. Whether he repeated or lowered his price of two hundred pounds that he had asked in his initial letter of 27 June 1850 about the book is not known. This unlocated letter is presumably the one cited in the Bentley contract for *The Whale*: "an original work written by the said Herman Melville, descriptive of an American Whaling Voyage with its accompanying Adventures, more particularly described in a letter of the said Herman Melville to the said Richard Bentley" (HCL-M). For Bentley's 3 July reply to this unlocated letter, see LETTERS RECEIVED, pp. 613–14. Davis-Gilman Unlocated 333.

TO RICHARD BENTLEY
20 JULY 1851 · PITTSFIELD

As Bentley's 1849–54 letterbook indicates, he replied with a brief message on 3 July 1851 to Melville's earlier, now unlocated, letter proposing for the second time his new whaling book. Bentley offered Melville an advance of £150 on account of half-profits for the book, adding, with obvious misgivings, "as we shall be in the same boat, this mode of publication is the most suitable to meet all the contingencies of the case" (see LETTERS RECEIVED, p. 614). These terms were essentially the same as those under which Bentley had published *Mardi* and *Redburn* (but not *White-Jacket*; see *Journals*, pp. 176–77), although he had given larger advances for each of those books (£210 and £200). This letter is Melville's reply to Bentley's offer.

Pittsfield, Berkshire County, Mass:
July 20th 1851.

My Dear Sir — I promptly received your note of the 3^d Inst: in reply to mine concerning the publication of my new book.

I accept your offer for the work; but not without strong hope that before long, we shall be able to treat upon a firmer basis than now, & heretofore; & that with the more assurance you will be disposed to make overtures for American books. And here let me say to you, — since you are peculiarly interested in the matter — that in all reasonable probability no International Copyright will ever be obtained — in our time, at least — if you Englishmen wait at all for the first step to be taken in this country. Who have any motive in this country to bestir themselves in this thing? Only the authors. — Who are the authors? — A handful. And what influence have they to bring to bear upon any question whose settlement must necessarily assume a political form? — They can bring scarcely any influence whatever. This country & nearly all its affairs are governed by sturdy backwoodsmen — noble fellows enough, but not at all literary, & who care not a fig for any authors except those who write those most saleable of all books nowadays — ie — the newspapers, & magazines. And tho' the number of cultivated, catholic men, who may be supposed to feel an interest in a national literature, is large & every day growing larger; yet they are nothing in comparison with the overwhelming majority who care nothing about it. This country is at present engaged in furnishing material for future authors; not in encouraging its living ones.

Nevertheless, if this matter by any means comes to be made nationally conspicuous; and if you in England come out magnanimously, & protect a foriegn author; then there is that sort of stuff in the people here, which will be sure to make them all eagerness in reciprocating. For, be assured, that my countrymen will never be outdone in generosity. — Therefore, if you desire an International Copyright — hoist your flag on your side of the water, & the signal will be answered; but look for no flag on this side till then.

I am now passing thro' the press, the closing sheets of my new work; so that I shall be able to forward it to you in the course of two or three weeks — perhaps a little longer. I shall forward it to you thro' the Office of the Legation. And upon your receipt of it, I suppose you will immediately proceed to printing; as, of course, publication will not take place here, till you have made yourself safe. — You say you will give me your notes at three & six months; I infer that this means from the time of receiving the book.

Very Truly Yours
H Melville.

ALS on a 39.7 × 24.9 cm sheet, folded in half, of blue laid (line pattern) paper. Melville inscribed the first three pages, in ink, and addressed the fourth page *"For the Steamer.* | Richard Bentley Esq | New Burlington Street | London."; it was postmarked in Pittsfield on 29 July and canceled "Paid xc 11 Au 11 1851".

LOCATION: at present unknown. *Provenance*: Bentley sale, Hodgson & Co., sale 19, 8 July 1938, lot 250; Carroll A. Wilson; H. Bradley Martin sale, Sotheby's, New York, sale 5971, 30–31 January 1990, in item 2167; 19th Century Shop, catalogue 20 (April 1991), item 1, and catalogue 26 (October 1992), item 120.

PUBLICATION: Birss, "A Mere Sale to Effect," pp. 251–52. Davis-Gilman 86.

TEXTUAL NOTES: probability] *miswritten* probabilty • — A] *dash blotted* • any question] any *rewritten* • necessarily] *miswritten* necessarly • backwoodsmen] *miswritten* backswoodsmen • not at all] at *inserted above caret* • will be sure] will *added* • two] *this word visible on the portion of the leaf that adhered to the wax seal when the letter was opened* • immediately] *miswritten* immedily

TO NATHANIEL HAWTHORNE
22 JULY 1851 · PITTSFIELD

This is the fourth of Melville's known but now-missing letters to Hawthorne. Hawthorne's "easy-flowing long letter (received yesterday)" that occasioned this reply is also unlocated. In her first publication of Melville's letter, Rose Hawthorne Lathrop reported that her father endorsed it "Recd July 24th, 1851"; it can thus be dated Tuesday, 22 July. Like Melville's earlier [1 June?] 1851 letter in which he addressed Hawthorne as "my dear fellow-mortal" and spoke of writing "a little bluely," this note addresses Hawthorne as "my dear fellow-being" and speaks of burying "all the Blue Devils" (i.e., despondency). The letter probably had a further passage at the end where the ellipsis points occur in Rose Lathrop's two publications (cited below). Possibly the omission was made because Melville's handwriting was unclear. Rose Lathrop stated that Melville's handwriting required "second-sight to decipher, . . . being, apparently, 'writ in water' " (*Memories*, p. 155). However, the use of such ellipsis points throughout the other letters quoted in her *Century* article suggests that what she omitted was inconsequential domestic and personal details. For further commentary on her publication of these letters, see the HISTORICAL NOTE, p. 802.

Tuesday afternoon.

My dear Hawthorne:

This is not a letter, or even a note — but only a passing word said to you over your garden gate. I thank you for your easy-flowing long letter (received yesterday) which flowed through me, and refreshed all my meadows, as the Housatonic — opposite me — does in reality. I am now busy with various things — not incessantly though; but enough to require my frequent tinkerings; and this is the height of the haying season, and my nag is dragging me home his winter's dinners all the time. And so, one way and another, I am not yet a disengaged man; but shall be, very soon. Meantime, the earliest good chance I get, I shall roll down to you. ¶My dear fellow-being, we — that is, you and I — must hit upon some little bit of vagabondism, before Autumn comes. Gray-lock — we must go and vagabondize there. But ere we start we

must dig a deep hole and bury all the Blue Devils, there to abide till
the Last Day. . . .

Goodbye,

his X mark.

Original document not located. Text from typescript (T) in HCL-M, headed "Herman Melville to Nathaniel Hawthorne. (Upon which the latter writes: 'Rec'd July 24th, 1851.')", on an
off-white 20.1 × 26.7 cm leaf, watermarked "REGENT LINEN W.C. & CO", emended by NN
and from the first publication by Rose Hawthorne Lathrop (L). Though there is no record of
when or by whom it was made, T was evidently, like L, based on a transcription from the
original manuscript and seems clearly to have the better readings for one major passage ("My
dear fellow-being") and for two separate words ("dragging *me* home" and "all *the* Blue Devils"), as well as for several accidentals (such as the lowercase "afternoon", which is typical of
Melville's rendering of that word in his headings, and the spelling of "Goodbye" with an "e",
also typical of Melville's letters). Whatever the reason, T lacks the terminal ellipsis points
given in L, from which they are adopted here. That the transcription for T was made with L
in view—and hence meant to be a correction of it—is shown by its heading, which is identical
word-for-word with that of L as quoted in the headnote above. Although the second publication, also by Rose Hawthorne Lathrop (L2), appears to lack independent authority, since it
was evidently based on L without recourse to the original and since its minor variant readings
are attributable to the republication proccess, these variants are listed in the textual notes to
complete the textual record.

PUBLICATION: Rose Hawthorne Lathrop (L), "The Hawthornes in Lenox. Told in Letters by
Nathaniel and Mrs. Hawthorne," *Century Magazine* 49 [N.S. 27] (November 1894), 89. Rose
Hawthorne Lathrop (L2), *Memories of Hawthorne* (Boston: Houghton Mifflin, 1897), p. 156.
Davis-Gilman 87.

TEXTUAL NOTES (for symbols used, see p. 840): Tuesday] NN; L2; "~T; ~, L · afternoon] T;
L2; Afternoon L · My] T; [*indented*] L; L2 · Hawthorne:] T; L; ~, — L2 · This] T; [*no new
paragraph*] L; L2 · note —] T; L; ~, L2 · yesterday)∧] T; ~), L; L2 · in reality] L; L2; it really
T · things —] T; L; ~, L2 · dragging me] T; dragging L; L2 · yet] T; L; [*not present*]
L2 · man;] T; L; ~, L2 · be,] T; ~∧ L; L2 · you.] T; ~, L; L2 · ¶My] NN;))My T; ∧ my L;
L2 · dear] T; L; good L2 · fellow-being,] T; fellow, being, L; fellow, seeing
L2 · vagabondism,] T; ~∧ L; L2 · Autumn] T; autumn L; L2 · start∧] T;~, L; L2 · hole∧] T;
L; ~, L2 · all the] T; all L; L2 · Day. . . .] L; L2; ~. T · Goodbye,] T; Good-by. L; [*no new
line*] Good-by. L2 · his] T; [*no new line*] his L; HIS L2

TO EVERT A. DUYCKINCK
28 JULY 1851 · PITTSFIELD

In response to the invitation here, Evert and George Duyckinck arrived in Pittsfield
on Wednesday, 6 August 1851, the day Melville suggested, and remained until 14
August. They enjoyed an eventful week of picnics, along with a visit to Hawthorne
in Lenox and the Shaker settlement at Lebanon, and an excursion up Saddleback
Mountain (Mt. Greylock), as Evert Duyckinck reported in a series of long letters to

his wife (NYPL-D; see also Mansfield, "Glimpses," cited under publication, below).

Although Melville did not specify the year in his heading, Duyckinck added it at the top of the first page, a date that is confirmed by the reference in the letter to "next Tuesday (week from tomorrow)"—which indicates that Melville was writing on a Monday, the day on which 28 July fell in 1851.

Pittsfield July 28th

Dear Duyckinck

I do not know what little plans you & your brother may have made concerning the rest of the summer — but if it will not interfere with your other arrangements, — then our entire household will be sincerely happy to see you two here any time after next Tuesday (week from tomorrow) and the sooner after that time the better — say Wednesday. Come, and give yourself a week's holyday on the hay-mow. "In fact," Come.

If you will advise me of the day of your starting, I shall have our waggon at the Depot in time for you — as we are three miles from there. Mention whether you take the morning or afternoon train I recommend, by all means, the *morning* train By no means let George stay behind. If he does, I shall write to Chief of Police Matsell, to *send* him on.

Thine
H Melville

ALS on a 24.8 × 20 cm part-sheet (torn along the bottom), folded in half, of blue wove paper. Melville inscribed the first three pages, in ink. Duyckinck later noted in ink at the top of the first page "1851."

LOCATION: NYPL-D.

PUBLICATION: Luther S. Mansfield, "Glimpses of Herman Melville's Life in Pittsfield, 1850–1851," *American Literature* 9 (March 1937), 37–38. Davis-Gilman 88.

TEXTUAL NOTE: interfere] *miswritten* interefere

TO SAMUEL H. SAVAGE
24 AUGUST 1851 · PITTSFIELD

Samuel Hay Savage (1827–1901), the nephew of Hope Savage Shaw, Elizabeth Melville's stepmother, had, like Melville, lost his father as a child and gone to work at an early age. He had lived in the Shaw household after his father's death in 1839, with Lemuel Shaw providing for his high school education. Afterwards he served as a clerk at the firm of Atkins & Freeman in Boston, before deciding to go west to seek his fortune. In a 30 April 1847 letter to Hope Savage Shaw describing his visit to New York before going west, he mentions visiting his "friend" Allan Melville. He adds that he "found Herman there also," and that Herman inquired "a little more than particularly abo my Coz Eliz" (for this letter, and more on Savage, see the article cited under publication, below). After working for a summer on a farm in Illinois, he spent a few years working on his half-brother Henry Savage's hacienda in Guatemala, but feeling dissatisfied with his prospects returned to Boston in 1851. Elizabeth Melville's 3 August 1851 letter to Hope Savage Shaw records that he arrived unannounced at Arrowhead on 29 July 1851 to stay for several days, and that he went on at least one "ramble" with Melville in the Berkshires (HCL-M). As Melville's letter indicates, they also enjoyed smoking cigars and drinking " 'London Dock' " wine together (for "London Dock" cf. *White-Jacket*, chap. 37, p. 52). Samuel Savage then left for Red Hook, New York, to visit his stepmother, and probably from there wrote the bread-and-butter letter (now unlocated) that Melville answered with this sympathetic response. (Melville's questioned "Aug: 24th" was correct since it fell on Sunday in 1851.) Addressing what must have been Savage's complaint that he felt like a "*foot-ball*," Melville first cites Hamlet's speech about the "slings and arrows of outrageous fortune" (3.1.58), and then goes on to echo his own "Loomings" and "Hyena" chapters (1, 49) in his recently finished book (*Moby-Dick*, pp. 6, 226–28).

Samuel Savage must have acted on Melville's invitation in this letter to return for a second visit to Arrowhead, after making other visits in New York through 9 September. Evidence of his return is his signature, along with J. Rowland Morewood's, on the undated British contract for *The Whale*, which Bentley had sent from London after signing it there on 13 August.

Pittsfield. Sunday Morning

Aug: 24th (?)

My Dear Sam: — I thank you for your letter, which by its pleasant mood — its allusions to "jolly Gods' nectar" "cigars" "London Dock" "rambles" "discussions" &c awaked in me hearty desires that you would come back to us for a few days & live over again those same "rambles" & tap anew the cask of "London Dock." As — I suppose — you will before long be returning to Boston, & as Pittsfield lies in your route, why will you not stop here a few days? By all means, do so, & most welcome. You can not take us by surprise. There is no one with us now: nor do we anticipate any visitors at present — but yourself.

Concerning the *foot-ball* part of the business, why, we are all foot-balls, more or less — & it is lucky that we are, on some accounts. It is important, however, that our balls be covered with a leather, good & tough, that will stand banging & all "the slings & arrows of outrageous fortune". — It is — or seems to be — a wise sort of thing, to realise that all that happens to a man in this life is only by way of joke, especially his misfortunes, if he have them. And it is also worth bearing in mind, that the joke is passed round pretty liberally & impartially, so that not very many are entitled to fancy that they in particular are getting the worst of it. — In this way, I doubt not, the three old gossips comforted their unfortunate friend Job. But do you, Samuel, be as patient as he.

All the house desire to be remembered to you, & hope to see you before a great while.

Really Thine
H Melville

ALS on a 39.5 × 24.5 cm sheet, folded in half, of blue wove paper, faintly embossed with the manufacturer's stamp. Melville inscribed the first three pages, in ink.

LOCATION: Collection of John B. Edmunds, Jr. *Provenance*: Helen Savage Edmunds.

PUBLICATION: Joyce Deveau Kennedy and Frederick J. Kennedy, "Herman Melville and Samuel Hay Savage, 1847–1851," *Melville Society Extracts* 35 (September 1978), 1–10 (with reproduction).

TEXTUAL NOTES: over] *possibly* oer · realise] *after canceled* rela

TO EVERT A. DUYCKINCK
29 AUGUST 1851 · PITTSFIELD

Since Duyckinck is known to have visited Melville at Arrowhead only once—the period of 6–14 August 1851—this letter can be assigned to that year. Melville apparently wrote the letter on "Friday," 29 August, and mailed it the next day, since it is postmarked 30 August. For more on Duyckinck's visit see the headnote to Melville's 28 July 1851 invitation, above.

Whether Duyckinck returned to visit the Melvilles a second time, with his friend James W. Beekman (1815–77), the wealthy owner of the historic Beekman Mansion and other family property on the East River in New York, is not known. At this time Beekman was a New York state senator. His fortune had enabled him to forgo the legal profession, for which he had been trained, and to travel extensively on the Continent, where he studied various forms of government. He had known Hawthorne since the summer of 1838, when, as Hawthorne later recalled in a 9 April 1853 letter to him, Beekman had been one of the first "who ever thought it worth while" to visit him "as a literary man" (New-York Historical Society; see

Letters, 1843–1853, ed. Thomas Woodson, L. Neal Smith, and Norman Holmes Pearson [Columbus: Ohio State University Press, 1985], p. 671). In all likelihood the proposed visit did not occur. Duyckinck had suggested to Beekman in a 9 July 1851 letter that they "travel about" as "gentlemen in search of a country seat," adding, "it is a very happy avocation, full of hope & excitement & brings out the beauties everywhere. Like the ladies shopping, you need not buy" (New-York Historical Society). But no other evidence in the Hawthorne, Beekman, or Duyckinck papers indicates that they ever took this trip.

The brief reference on behalf of Augusta Melville to the "Household Words" at the close of the letter is to the magazine edited by Charles Dickens from 1850 to 1859.

Pittsfield. Friday.

Dear Duyckinck ——

Your letter to me announcing your happy arrival home; and your very acceptable present of a thermometer (which, if you will make haste to come & see it here before October, will show you that the temperature of this house's welcome has not fallen very much) both arrived here safely. The letter is in the file & the thermometer on the wall. ——

We shall glad to see yourself & Mr Beekman here, as soon as you please. You can stay here overnight & go to see Mr Hawthorne the next morning & come back here to a 4 or five o'clock dinner, & then be your own masters after that — for this house belongs to travellers, & we occupants but stewards.

Remember me to all.
H Melville

If you will foretell me the day & *train* of your coming, I shall see that you are provided with a conveyance to bring you here.

Augusta tells me to say that she has received your letter together with the Household Words, and is very much indebted to you.

ALS on a 26.5 × 20.2 cm sheet, folded in half, of white wove paper. Melville inscribed the first three pages, in ink, and addressed the envelope "Evert A Duyckinck Esq | New York."; it was postmarked in Pittsfield on 30 August. Another hand added the penciled query on the envelope "*Aug. 30?*".

LOCATION: NYPL-D.

PUBLICATION: (partial) *Log*, I, 426. Metcalf, pp. 123–24. Davis-Gilman 89.

TEXTUAL NOTE: shall glad] *intervening word lacking (presumably "be")*

TO RICHARD BENTLEY
5 SEPTEMBER 1851 · [NEW YORK?]

Unlocated. A letter of this date is cited in Richard Bentley's 25 September 1851 reply (see LETTERS RECEIVED, pp. 615–16), which also acknowledged receipt of a "packet" Melville had evidently promised him in the letter—proof sheets of the American edition of *The Whale*, forwarded by Allan Melville on 10 September. Shortly thereafter Allan ("in the absence of my brother from the city") wrote an undated letter to Bentley informing him of the decision to change the title of the new book to *Moby-Dick* and enclosing a proof sheet of the dedication. On 12 September, Allan signed a contract with Harper & Brothers for *Moby-Dick* (draft, HCL-M). Davis-Gilman Unlocated 334.

TO SARAH HUYLER MOREWOOD
[12 OR 19?] SEPTEMBER 1851 · PITTSFIELD

Melville dated this letter only "Pittsfield, Friday Morning," but the statement that the forthcoming book (*Moby-Dick*) "is off my hands, but must cross the sea before publication here" places it in September 1851, probably after Melville's final letter to Bentley on 5 September concerning the book and perhaps also after the final arrangements with Harper & Brothers had been made on 12 September for American publication. (The Friday following this would have been 19 September.)

This letter with its wordplay and arch references is typical of Melville's correspondence with his neighbor Sarah Morewood. His reference to "my Paradise in store," for instance, seems to involve a motif possibly connected with her (see p. 855 below). "Sweet-Briars" (European roses or eglantines) probably refers to the women who revolved socially around Mrs. Morewood, such as the two to whom Melville sends his regards at the close—Mrs. Pollock, an Englishwoman, and Miss Henderson, from Cincinnati—who had been members of two of Mrs. Morewood's picnic and mountain-climbing parties organized during the Duyckincks' stay at Arrowhead in mid-August of 1851, in which Melville had joined.

Sarah Morewood's husband, Rowland, had installed a fine library at Broadhall, from which the books mentioned in this letter may have come. *The Hour and the Man* by Harriet Martineau (1841; Sealts 350) was a historical romance, as was *Zanoni* by Bulwer-Lytton (1842; Sealts 334). The *Zanoni* in "fine print" was probably the 1842 two-volume Harper edition, set in much smaller type than the 1842 London three-volume edition published by Saunders & Otley.

Pittsfield, Friday Morning

If to receive some thoughtful kindness from one, upon whom self-delusion whispers we have some claims, — if this be so agreeable to us; then how far more delightful, to be the recipient of amiable offices from one who has claims upon ourselves, not we upon them. This indeed is to sow the true seed of Christianity among all the asperities of mankind; this converts infidels, & gives misanthropy no foot to stand on.

Most considerate of all the delicate roses that diffuse their blessed perfume among men, is Mrs: Morewood; (I say it not in "bitterness" — I appeal to all the Sweet-Briars, if I do;) for the little box contained nourishment for both body & soul; and the two flasks of Cologne — why, I have not done smelling of them yet.

The "Hour & the Man" is exceedingly acceptable to me. "Zanoni" is a very fine book in very fine print — but I shall endeavor to surmount that difficulty. At present, however, the Fates have plunged me into certain silly thoughts and wayward speculations, which will prevent me, for a time, from falling into the reveries of these books — for a fine book is a sort of revery to us — is it not? — So I shall regard them as my Paradise in store, & Mrs Morewood the goddess from whom it comes.

Concerning my own forthcoming book — it is off my hands, but must cross the sea before publication here. Dont you buy it — dont you read it, when it does come out, because it is by no means the sort of book for you. It is not a peice of fine feminine Spitalfields silk — but is of the horrible texture of a fabric that should be woven of ships' cables & hausers. A Polar wind blows through it, & birds of prey hover over it. Warn all gentle fastidious people from so much as peeping into the book — on risk of a lumbago & sciatics.

My best rememberances and sympathy to Mrs Pollock, who, I trust, is convalescent now. Fail not to remind Miss Henderson also, that I desire she will not entirely forget me; and present my regards to Mr: Morewood.

H Melville

To
Mrs: Morewood.

Augusta tells me to remember her to you.

ALS on a 26.5 × 20.2 cm sheet, folded in half, of white wove paper. Melville inscribed the first three pages, in ink.

LOCATION: Berkshire Athenaeum, Pittsfield, Massachusetts. *Provenance*: Agnes Morewood; Henry A. Murray.

PUBLICATION: (partial) *Log*, I, 427 (dated early September?). Davis-Gilman 90.

TEXTUAL NOTES: self-delusion] self-|delusion • agreeable] *after canceled* to • woven] *before canceled* from • Augusta tells . . . you.] *written vertically on the fourth page, which served as the outside of the letter; placed here editorially*

TO MARIA GANSEVOORT MELVILLE
BEFORE 25 SEPTEMBER 1851 · PITTSFIELD

Unlocated. Maria Melville's letter of 25 September 1851 from Lansingburgh, where she was visiting her cousin Maria Peebles, to her daughter Augusta in Pittsfield, reports: "I receiv'd . . . Hermans note — & its *delicate* enclosure, it is altogether inadequate — but I hope for better times" (NYPL-GL). With the publication of *Moby-Dick* arranged Melville evidently could now afford to send his mother some money, although as his 22 May 1856 letter to Lemuel Shaw indicates, his financial situation remained unimproved over the next several years.

TO LEMUEL SHAW
22 OCTOBER 1851 · PITTSFIELD

The Melvilles' second child, Stanwix (1851–86), was born in Pittsfield four days after the publication of *The Whale* in England. The errors in his official Pittsfield birth record (which gave the wrong birthdate, misspelled his name "Stanwicks," and listed Maria Melville as the mother) were not Melville's (see Harrison Hayford, "Melville's Freudian Slip," *American Literature* 30 [November 1958], 366–68). As Melville's letter of 7 November (just below) indicates, Stanwix was named so as to associate the boy with the triumph of Melville's maternal grandfather, General Peter Gansevoort, who successfully defended Fort Stanwix in upstate New York during the revolutionary war against the siege of the British colonel Barry St. Leger from 3 to 22 August 1777.

Wednesday 3. P.M.

My Dear Sir

Your daughter is the mother of another little boy — a fine fellow — born between 1 & 2 o'clock P.M. to day. Mother & child are doing very well.

Truly Yours
H Melville

ALS on a 15 × 17.4 cm part-sheet (cut at a slight angle along the left edge and also cut along the top and bottom) of blue wove paper with lines. Melville inscribed only one side of the leaf, in ink. At the top, written above and below Melville's date of "Wednesday 3. P.M." in another hand, is the date "May 1843 — ", which also appears as a blotting at the bottom—the result of the sheet's being folded in the middle. That date was already on the paper when Melville wrote on it, since the "Yours" of Melville's close is clearly written over the "1843". In pencil the "4" was later canceled and a "5" written above.

LOCATION: HCL-M.

PUBLICATION: *Log*, I, 430. Davis-Gilman 91.

TO EVERT A. DUYCKINCK
7 NOVEMBER 1851 · PITTSFIELD

Duyckinck dated this letter "Nov 7. 1851," thus confirming the date in the heading—changed by Melville from "Thursday" to "Friday"—the day of the week on which 7 November fell in 1851. Duyckinck, writing from New York, where he continued to edit the *Literary World* and to hold frequent convivial gatherings at his home for his circle of friends (here called "the Knights of the Round Table" by Melville), had enclosed in a previous, now unlocated letter to Melville a newspaper clipping that described the sinking of the *Ann Alexander* by a whale on 20 August in the Pacific. Originally printed in the Panama *Herald* of 16 October, the story was reprinted in the *New-York Daily Tribune* (2 November), and in other papers. One of the *Ann Alexander*'s boats had harpooned a whale, which turned and crushed the boat in its huge jaws into fragments the size of a chair. When another boat joined the chase it turned and crushed that one as well. The ship rescued the survivors, and the captain continued the pursuit. The ship avoided one attack, but as the captain stood in the bow ready to harpoon the whale he suddenly discovered it approaching at the rate of fifteen knots. "*In an instant,*" the story reads, "*the monster struck the ship with tremendous violence, shaking her from stem to stern.*" She sank quickly, barely giving the men a chance to flee into the remaining boats. Unlike the doomed crew of the *Pequod*, however, the sailors of the *Ann Alexander* lived to tell the story.

Although Melville refers here to the "sad fate of the Pequod" as occurring "about fourteen years ago" (i.e., about 1837), no ship by that name appears in the records of the American whaling industry. Nor has Melville transferred the name of his fictional ship to a real one, for the only other vessels known to have undergone the *Ann Alexander*'s fate were the *Essex* in 1820 and the *Parker Cook* in 1850 (cf. Alexander Starbuck, "History of the American Whale Fishery," in *Report of the Commissioner* [of Fish and Fisheries], *Part IV, 1875–76*, Washington, 1878).

The disasters Melville alludes to had all occurred recently. The *New-York Daily Tribune* of 18 October reported that the whole northern whale fleet, in attempting to make its spring passage through the Bering Strait, had gotten caught in the ice, with loss of or damage to nearly seventy ships. The same issue and others described a gale near Prince Edward Island which sank many vessels and piled up nearly a hundred on the shore (no such disaster off Newfoundland was reported in the New York papers in October or early November). On 23 October a succession of hard gales on Lake Erie did much damage to shipping.

Duyckinck's second enclosure, the "inestimable item of 'Herman [*possibly Norman*] de Wardt,'" is unidentified. Leyda conjectured an allusion to Wynkyn de

Worde's *The Boke of Keruynge* (*Log*, I, 431), a 1508 book on carving which includes a brief instruction about whalemeat, which would fit with Melville's comment that he wanted to "cut into" it (de Worde's book was not reprinted until 1867, however). Whatever the inestimable item was, it clearly contained some more of the sort of "random allusions to whales" gathered from the books found in the "long Vaticans and street-stalls of the earth" that Melville had brought together in the "Extracts" section prefacing *Moby-Dick* (p. xvii).

The reference to "*Stone's Life of Brandt*" is to William L. Stone's *Life of Joseph Brant–Thayendanegea: Including the Border Wars of the American Revolution and Sketches of the Indian Campaigns of Generals Harmar, St. Clair, and Wayne* (2 vols., New York: Dearborn, 1838; Sealts 491a). Years earlier Gansevoort Melville, in his *Index Rerum* begun in 1837 (see *New Log*), had noted from Stone's book this same story of Colonel Gansevoort's "gallant defence of Fort Stanwix."

Pittsfield. Friday Afternoon.

Dear Duyckinck —— Your letter received last night had a sort of stunning effect on me. For some days past being engaged in the woods with axe, wedge, & beetle, the Whale had almost completely slipped me for the time (& I was the merrier for it) when Crash! comes Moby Dick himself (as you justly say) & reminds me of what I have been about for part of the last year or two. It is really & truly a surprising coincidence — to say the least. I make no doubt it is Moby Dick himself, for there is no account of his capture after the sad fate of the Pequod about fourteen years ago. — Ye Gods! What a Commentator is this Ann Alexander whale. What he has to say is short & pithy & very much to the point. I wonder if my evil art has raised this monster.

The Behrings Straits Disaster, too, & the cording along the New Foundland coast of those scores & scores of fishermen, and the inland gales on the Lakes. Verily the pot boileth inside & out. And woe unto us, we but live in the days that have been. Yet even then they found time to be jolly.

Why did'nt you send me that inestimable item of "Herman de Wardt" before? Oh had I but had that pie to cut into! But that & many other fine things doubtless are omitted. All one can do is to pick up what chips he can buy round him. They have no Vatican (as you have) in Pittsfield here.

The boy you enquire about is well. His name will probably be "Stanwix" for some account of which, Vide *Stone's Life of Brandt*, where mention is made of how this lad's great grandfather spent his summers in the Revolutionary War before Saratoga came into being — I mean Saratoga Springs & Pavilions.

And now what is the news with you? I suppose the Knights of the Round Table still assemble over their cigars & punch, & I know that once every week the "Literary World" revolves upon its axis. I should like to hear again the old tinkle of glasses in your basement, & may do so, before many months.

For us here, Winter is coming. The hills & the noses begin to look blue, & the trees have stripped themselves for the December tussle. I have had my dressing-gown patched up, & got some wood in the wood-house, & — by the way, — have in full blast our great dining-room fire-place, which swallows down cords of wood as a whale does boats.

Remember me to all our friends
My compliments to Mrs Duyckinck & your family
& Beleive me Thine
H Melville

ALS on a 39.8 × 24.8 cm sheet, folded in half, of blue wove paper with lines, embossed with the manufacturer's rectangular stamp enclosing the name "CARSON'S DALTON MS". Melville inscribed the first three pages, in ink. Duyckinck later noted in ink at the top of the first page "Nov 7. 1851." An envelope in the Duyckinck collection postmarked [8?] November, addressed by Melville "Evert A Duyckinck Esq | New York.", and endorsed in pencil by David Davidson "opened by D D | in a hurry | *but not looked at*", may possibly belong with this letter.

LOCATION: NYPL-D.

PUBLICATION: (partial) Minnigerode, pp. 74–75. Leyda, *Portable Melville*, pp. 450–52. Davis-Gilman 92.

TEXTUAL NOTES: Friday] *inserted above canceled* Thursday • pithy &] *ampersand written over* but • Herman] *possibly* Norman • buy] *conjectural reading* • once] *inserted above caret* • fire-place] *after canceled* chim • whale] *inserted with caret above canceled* wale

TO NATHANIEL HAWTHORNE
[17?] NOVEMBER 1851 · PITTSFIELD

Melville headed his letter only "Monday afternoon," but stated that he had received Hawthorne's now unlocated letter about *Moby-Dick* (published on 1 November) the night before, on his way to the Morewoods'. Since a letter from Sarah Morewood to George Duyckinck, dated Friday, 21 November (NYPL-D), mentions Melville's presence at a recent evening party (during which Melville's sister Catherine be-

stowed the name Broadhall on the Morewood estate, and Melville himself bestowed the names Molly, Polly, and Dolly on the Morewood cows), Melville's
letter can be tentatively dated Monday, 17 November 1851. It is the last of the
letters to Hawthorne whose contents are known only from transcripts made by
members of the Hawthorne family, in this case Rose Hawthorne Lathrop.

Melville's statement that "Your letter was handed me last night on the road
going to Mr. Morewood's, and I read it there" is ambiguous; "there" could mean
either on the road or at the Morewoods'. In any case he could not write the spontaneous and ecstatic reply he felt moved to send. Nevertheless, his next day's answer
still contained "such gibberish" that he defends it with his biblical reference to Festus: "And as he thus spake for himself, Festus said with a loud voice, Paul, thou art
beside thyself; much learning doth make thee mad. But he said, I am not mad, most
noble Festus: but speak forth the words of truth and soberness" (Acts 26.24–25).

The implication of "Don't write a word about the book" is that Hawthorne
had offered to review *Moby-Dick*—just as Melville had written on *Mosses from an
Old Manse* in the *Literary World* on 17 and 24 August 1850. In accord with Melville's
directive, Hawthorne did not—although he later wrote to Duyckinck on 1 December 1851: "What a book Melville has written! It gives me an idea of much greater
power than his preceding ones. It hardly seemed to me that the review of it, in the
Literary World [15 and 22 November], did justice to its best points" (*Letters, 1843–
1853*, ed. Thomas Woodson, L. Neal Smith, and Norman Holmes Pearson [Co-
lumbus: Ohio State University Press, 1985], p. 508).

The mention of "Krakens" toward the close of this letter may be, as Perry
Miller suggests, an allusion to a passage in the book Melville had refused to review
several years earlier—Joseph C. Hart's *Romance of Yachting* (see Melville's 14
November 1848 letter to Duyckinck, above). Hart wrote: "Oh Shakespeare—Immortal bard—Mighty genius—Swan of Avon—thou Unapproachable!
Are there no more fish, no more krakens in that wondrous sea from which thou
wert taken? Shall there be no more cakes and ale?" (p. 209; see Miller's *The Raven
and the Whale* [New York: Harcourt, Brace & World, 1956], pp. 241–42). Melville
had made a passing reference to "the great Kraken" in *Moby-Dick* (chap. 59, p. 277;
see also Luther S. Mansfield and Howard P. Vincent's edition of *Moby-Dick* [New
York: Hendricks House, 1952], p. 753).

If Rose Hawthorne Lathrop's transcription is to be relied upon, this is the only
occasion in his extant letters, except to members of his family, when Melville
signed his first name only. Melville bids "Farewell" near the close of this long letter
possibly because Hawthorne and his family were about to move from Lenox to
West Newton, Massachusetts. Melville's first postscript is parallel to the opening of
his 1 May 1850 letter to Dana (see above), where he imagined writing only for him
and spoke of feeling "welded" to him by a "Siamese link of affectionate
sympathy."

Pittsfield, Monday afternoon.

My dear Hawthorne: People think that if a man has undergone
any hardship, he should have a reward; but for my part, if I have

done the hardest possible day's work, and then come to sit down in a corner and eat my supper comfortably — why, then I don't think I deserve any reward for my hard day's work — for am I not now at peace? Is not my supper good? My peace and my supper are my reward, my dear Hawthorne. So your joy-giving and exultation-breeding letter is not my reward for my ditcher's work with that book, but is the good goddess's bonus over and above what was stipulated for — for not one man in five cycles, who is wise, will expect appreciative recognition from his fellows, or any one of them. Appreciation! Recognition! Is Jove appreciated? Why, ever since Adam, who has got to the meaning of his great allegory — the world? Then we pigmies must be content to have our paper allegories but ill comprehended. I say your appreciation is my glorious gratuity. In my proud, humble way, — a shepherd-king, — I was lord of a little vale in the solitary Crimea; but you have now given me the crown of India. But on trying it on my head, I found it fell down on my ears, notwithstanding their asinine length — for it 's only such ears that sustain such crowns.

Your letter was handed me last night on the road going to Mr. Morewood's, and I read it there. Had I been at home, I would have sat down at once and answered it. In me divine magnanimities are spontaneous and instantaneous — catch them while you can. The world goes round, and the other side comes up. So now I can't write what I felt. But I felt pantheistic then — your heart beat in my ribs and mine in yours, and both in God's. A sense of unspeakable security is in me this moment, on account of your having understood the book. I have written a wicked book, and feel spotless as the lamb. Ineffable socialities are in me. I would sit down and dine with you and all the gods in old Rome's Pantheon. It is a strange feeling — no hopefulness is in it, no despair. Content — that is it; and irresponsibility; but without licentious inclination. I speak now of my profoundest sense of being, not of an incidental feeling.

Whence come you, Hawthorne? By what right do you drink from my flagon of life? And when I put it to my lips — lo, they are yours and not mine. I feel that the Godhead is broken up like the bread at the Supper, and that we are the pieces. Hence this infinite fraternity of feeling. Now, sympathizing with the paper, my angel turns over another page. You did not care a penny for the book. But, now and then as you read, you understood the pervading thought that impelled the book — and that you praised. Was it not so? You were archangel enough to despise the imperfect body, and embrace the soul. Once you hugged the ugly Socrates because you saw the flame in the mouth, and heard the rushing of the demon, — the familiar, — and recognized the sound; for you have heard it in your own solitudes.

My dear Hawthorne, the atmospheric skepticisms steal into me now, and make me doubtful of my sanity in writing you thus. But, believe me, I am not mad, most noble Festus! But truth is ever incoherent, and when the big hearts strike together, the concussion is a little stunning. Farewell. Don't write a word about the book. That would be robbing me of my miserly delight. I am heartily sorry I ever wrote anything about you — it was paltry. Lord, when shall we be done growing? As long as we have anything more to do, we have done nothing. So, now, let us add Moby Dick to our blessing, and step from that. Leviathan is not the biggest fish; — I have heard of Krakens.

This is a long letter, but you are not at all bound to answer it. Possibly, if you do answer it, and direct it to Herman Melville, you will missend it — for the very fingers that now guide this pen are not precisely the same that just took it up and put it on this paper. Lord, when shall we be done changing? Ah! it 's a long stage, and no inn in sight, and night coming, and the body cold. But with you for a passenger, I am content and can be happy. I shall leave the world, I feel, with more satisfaction for having come to know you. Knowing you persuades me more than the Bible of our immortality.

What a pity, that, for your plain, bluff letter, you should get such gibberish! Mention me to Mrs. Hawthorne and to the children, and so, good-by to you, with my blessing.

Herman.

I can't stop yet. If the world was entirely made up of Magians, I 'll tell you what I should do. I should have a paper-mill established at one end of the house, and so have an endless riband of foolscap rolling in upon my desk; and upon that endless riband I should write a thousand — a million — billion thoughts, all under the form of a letter to you. The divine magnet is in you, and my magnet responds. Which is the biggest? A foolish question — they are *One*.   H.

Don't think that by writing me a letter, you shall always be bored with an immediate reply to it — and so keep both of us delving over a writing-desk eternally. No such thing! I sha'n't always answer your letters, and you may do just as you please.

Original document not located. Text from first publication (L), emended by NN. Variants in the second publication (L2) are listed in the textual notes, below.

PUBLICATION: Rose Hawthorne Lathrop (L), "The Hawthornes in Lenox. Told in Letters by Nathaniel and Mrs. Hawthorne," *Century Magazine* 49 [N.S. 27] (November 1894), 90. Rose Hawthorne Lathrop (L2), *Memories of Hawthorne* (Boston: Houghton Mifflin, 1897), pp. 156–60. Davis-Gilman 93.

TEXTUAL NOTES (for symbols used, see p. 840 below): Hawthorne:] L; ~, — L2 • exultation-breeding] exultation-|breeding • Jove] NN; love *(in his 1945 Yale dissertation, Harrison Hayford suggested emending either* love to Jove *[which would look the same in Melville's hand—see "Rhyme by Jove" in the illustration on p. 125 above] or* his great *to* this great *[pp. 248–49]; the second alternative was adopted by Metcalf, p. 128, and by Davis-Gilman)* • pigmies] L; pygmies L2 • magnet is in you] magnet is on you *(see the NN* Pierre, *p. 157)* • I can't] L; P.S. I can't L2 • Don't think] L; P.P.S. Don't think L2

TO AUGUSTA MELVILLE
[4 DECEMBER?] 1851 · PITTSFIELD

Melville may have enclosed this brief letter dated only "Thursday Afternoon" to his sister Augusta (who was then visiting their brother Allan and his wife Sophia in New York) with another longer letter, now unlocated, that their sister Helen sent to Augusta from Pittsfield. The record of correspondence kept by Augusta in 1851 lists under the date 4 December 1851 (a Thursday) the receipt of a letter ("4" pages) from "Herman and Helen" (NYPL-GL). If so, Augusta was recording the date on the letter, not the date she received it. While the 4 December date must remain tentative, the reference here to cold weather makes it certain that this letter was written during the winter of 1851–52, since that is the only winter Augusta spent in New York during Melville's years at Pittsfield.

Melville's edition of Machiavelli's *The Florentine Histories* has not been found; Sealts (340a) conjectures that it may have been a two-volume translation by C. Edwards Lester (New York: Paine & Burgess, 1845).

Thursday Afternoon

My Dear Augusta:

I want you not to forget — if you please — to bring with you from Allan's when you return, Machiavelli's Florentine history which Allan borrowed from me. Dont forget.

I hope you have enjoyed yourself in New York. The weather here has been cold as ever. Other than the weather I know not what to write about from Pittsfield. My love to Sophia & the children & to yourself: in which all join.

Herman

ALS on an 11.5 × 18.3 cm part-sheet (torn along the left edge) of white laid paper, watermarked with the number "50" (incomplete). Melville inscribed only one side of the leaf, in ink.

LOCATION: NYPL-GL. *Provenance*: Lyrical Ballad Bookstore.

TEXTUAL NOTE: has] h *written over another letter*

TO RUFUS W. GRISWOLD
19 DECEMBER 1851 · PITTSFIELD

Rufus Wilmot Griswold (1815–57), the anthologist and treacherous editor of Poe, was a formidable and controversial figure on the New York literary scene. His *Poets and Poetry of America* (1842), *The Prose Writers of America* (1847), and *The Female Poets of America* (1848) gave him the reputation as the leading advocate of "Americanism" in literature. Despite this, he also compiled a large number of gift books largely made up of uncopyrighted English poetry—all the while advocating an international copyright (see the headnote to Melville's August 1849 letter to the secretary of legation, above). He later attacked the Duyckincks in his abusive review of their *Cyclopædia* (*New York Herald*, 13 February 1856). In December 1850 he was editor of the *International Monthly Magazine* (see the headnote to Melville's 12 February 1851 letter to Duyckinck, above).

Shortly after James Fenimore Cooper's death on 14 September a committee headed by Washington Irving, Griswold, and Fitz-Green Halleck planned a commemorative ceremony. Postponed from the originally planned date of 24 December because of the overwhelming public interest in the arrival in New York of Louis Kossuth, the Hungarian revolutionary leader, it was held on 25 February. Melville's letter was read to the gathering, along with those of Emerson, Longfellow, Hawthorne, William H. Prescott, Charles Sumner, Samuel F. B. Morse, William Gilmore Simms, John Pendleton Kennedy, and others. See the report of the meeting in the 26 February 1851 *New-York Daily Times* and *Memorial of James Fenimore Cooper* (New York: Putnam, 1852; Melville's letter [misdated 20 February 1852] is printed on p. 30). Also for a discussion of the "paltry accidents" that clouded Cooper's "latter years," see Ethel R. Outland, *The "Effingham" Libels on Cooper* (Madison: University of Wisconsin Press, 1929).

The "other reasons" Melville may have had for not attending the demonstration probably included his engagement for Christmas Day at the Morewoods' as well as concentrated labor on his new book, *Pierre*.

Pittsfield Dec: 19th 1851.

Rufus W Griswold Esq:

Sir, — I have been honored by receiving an official invitation to attend the Cooper Demonstration to be held in New York on the 24th of this month. — My very considerable distance from the city, connected with other reasons, will prevent my compliance. But I rejoice that there will not be wanting many better, tho' not more zealous, men than myself, to unite on that occasion, in doing honor to a memory so very dear, not only to American Literature, but to the American Nation.

I never had the honor of knowing, or even seeing, Mr Cooper personally; so that, through my past ignorance of his person, the man, though dead, is still as living to me as ever. And this is very much; for his works are among the earliest I remember, as in my boyhood producing a vivid, and awakning power upon my mind.

It always much pained me, that for any reason, in his latter years, his fame at home should have apparently received a slight, temporary clouding, from some very paltry accidents, incident, more or less, to the general career of letters. But whatever possible things in Mr Cooper may have seemed, to have, in some degree, provoked the occasional treatment he received, it is certain, that he possessed no slightest weaknesses, but those, which are only noticeable as the almost infallible indices of pervading greatness. He was a great, robust-souled man, all whose merits are not even yet fully appreciated. But a grateful Posterity will take the best of Care of Fennimore Cooper.

Assured that your Demonstration can not but prove a noble one, equally worthy of its illustrious object, & the numerous living celebrities who will partake in it, —

I am, Very Respectfully,
Yours, —
Herman Melville

ALS on a 39.8 × 24.8 cm sheet, folded in half, of blue wove paper with lines, embossed with the manufacturer's rectangular stamp enclosing the name "CARSON'S DALTON MS". Melville inscribed the first two pages, in ink. Another hand, probably a librarian's, later noted on the fourth page in pencil "Herman Melville | 1819 — | Poet and novelist. | See Drake, & Appleton".

LOCATION: Gratz Collection, Historical Society of Pennsylvania, Philadelphia. *Provenance*: Simon Gratz.

PUBLICATION: *Memorial of James Fenimore Cooper* (New York: Putnam, 1852), p. 30. Davis-Gilman 94.

TEXTUAL NOTES: official] *inserted above caret* • dear] r *mended* • had] *after canceled* hard • pained] e *inserted above caret* • fame] *after canceled* general • things] *before canceled* may • slightest] *inserted with caret above canceled* shadow of • noticeable] *miswritten* noticable • Demonstration] D *written over* d

1852

TO EVERT A. DUYCKINCK
JANUARY 1852 · PLACE UNKNOWN

Unlocated. Davis and Gilman cite an envelope postmarked January 1852 (NYPL-D) as the evidence for an unlocated letter; however, the envelope is at present unlocated. Davis-Gilman Unlocated 335.

TO EVERT A. DUYCKINCK
[2?] JANUARY 1852 · NEW YORK

Headed only with the address of Allan Melville's law office and "Friday Afternoon," this letter was endorsed by Duyckinck "Jan 1852." Lacking any documentation about the day trip Melville refers to here, and with limited documentation about the visit Melville made to New York in January 1852, the date assigned to this letter is necessarily provisional. Melville appears to have gone to New York sometime after a Christmas dinner at the Morewoods' and before 5 January when Sarah Morewood wrote from Pittsfield to George Duyckinck in New York: "Were you not surprised to see Herman Melville in Town? he has missed some of the most beautiful winter changes I ever saw — " (NYPL-D). He was in New York at least through 8 January—for he wrote Sophia Hawthorne from there on that day (see below). By Wednesday, 21 January, he had presumably left New York for Pittsfield, since Allan Melville wrote to the Harpers then on his behalf in regard to *Pierre* (HCL-M). On the basis of this evidence, Melville's letter could belong to one of the first three Fridays in January of 1852. However, because Melville thanks Duyckinck for a present of nutcrackers (probably a New Year's gift), his letter has been tentatively assigned to the first Friday—2 January 1852. (For a further argument for this dating based on the probable events leading to Melville's break with Duyckinck as indicated in his letter of 14 February 1852, see the NN *Moby-Dick*, p. 695.)

Friday Afternoon
14 Wall Street

Dear Duyckinck

    I am engaged to go out of town tomorrow to be gone all day. So I wont' be able to see you at 11 o'clock as you propose. I will be glad to call though at some other time — not very remote in the future, either. The nut-crackers are very curious and duly valued.

Yours

H Melvill

ALS on a 24.3 × 18.6 cm sheet, folded in half, of blue wove paper. Melville inscribed the first page, in ink, and addressed the unstamped envelope, which was probably hand delivered, "Evert A. Duyckinck Esq. | 20 Clinton Place". Duyckinck later noted in ink on the first page of the letter "Jan 1852".

LOCATION: NYPL-D.

PUBLICATION: *Log*, I, 444 (dated January 9?). Davis-Gilman 96.

TO SOPHIA PEABODY HAWTHORNE
8 JANUARY 1852 · NEW YORK

Sophia Hawthorne's "highly flattering" letter of 29 December 1851 elicited this appreciative response from Melville in New York. Like her husband's earlier letter praising *Moby-Dick* (see Melville's [17?] November 1851 reply, above), Sophia Hawthorne's letter, with its comments on the allegorical implications of "The Spirit-Spout" (chap. 51), is now unlocated. Melville's response (on gilt-edged paper, as he proudly announces, embossed with the Bath stationer's mark) is notable for his remarks on *Moby-Dick*; it is also notable for one of his first references to *Pierre*—the "rural bowl of milk" he commends to Sophia Hawthorne in contrast to the "salt water" of *Moby-Dick* (cf. chap. 36). Melville had been hard at work on his seventh book during December 1851 (see the NN *Moby-Dick*, pp. 689–93).

The Hawthornes' recent move to West Newton, Massachusetts, occasioned Melville's inquiries about the Hawthornes' older children, "Miss" Una (nearly eight years old) and "Master" Julian (five and a half). It also occasioned the questions about Hawthorne's social rounds, an ironic comment on Hawthorne's reclusive habits. The other "Wonder-(-full) Book" referred to was Hawthorne's most recent publication, *A Wonder-Book* (1852), made up of tales for children, adapted from Greek myths. On 7 November 1851 Hawthorne had given Melville's son Malcolm a copy of the book, as Melville noted in the front of that copy (Sealts 261). Melville's quotation " 'We can't help ourselves' " is possibly a paraphrase of the prayer "Almighty God, who seest that we have no power of ourselves to help ourselves . . ." (Book of Common Prayer, Collect for the Second Sunday in Lent).

New York Jan: 8th 1852

My Dear Mrs Hawthorne

I have hunted up the finest Bath I could find, gilt-edged and stamped, whereon to inscribe my humble acknowledgment of your highly flattering letter of the 29th Dec: —— It really amazed me that you should find any satisfaction in that book. It is true that some *men* have said they were pleased with it, but you are the only *woman* — for as a general thing, women have small taste for the sea. But, then, since you, with your spiritualizing nature, see more things than other people, and by the same process, refine all you see, so that they are not the same things that other people see, but things which while you think you but humbly discover them, you do in fact create them for yourself —— therefore, upon the whole, I do not so much marvel at your expressions concerning Moby Dick. At any rate, your allusion for example to the "Spirit Spout first showed to me that there was a subtile significance in that thing — but I did not, in that case, *mean* it. I had some vague idea while writing it, that the whole book was susceptible of an allegoric construction, & also that *parts* of it were — but the speciality of many of the particular subordinate allegories, were first revealed to me, after reading Mr Hawthorne's letter, which, without citing any particular examples, yet intimated the part-&-parcel allegoricalness of the whole. —— But, My Dear Lady, I shall not again send you a bowl of salt water. The next chalice I shall commend, will be a rural bowl of milk.

And now, how are you in West Newton? Are all domestic affairs regulated? Is Miss Una content? And Master Julian satisfied with the landscape in general? And does Mr Hawthorne continue his series of calls upon all his neighbors within a radius of ten miles? Shall I send him ten packs of visiting cards? And a box of kid gloves? and the latest style of Parisian handkerchief? — He goes into society too much altogether — seven evenings out, a week, should content any reasonable man.

Now, Madam, had you not said anything about Moby Dick, & had Mr Hawthorne been equally silent, then had I said perhaps, something to both of you about another Wonder-(-full) Book. But as it is, I must be silent. How is it, that while all of us human beings are so entirely disembarrased in censuring a person; that so soon as we would praise, then we begin to feel awkward? I never blush after denouncing a man; but I grow scarlet, after eulogizing him. And yet this is all wrong; and yet we can't help it; and so we see how true was that musical sentence of the poet when he sang —

"We can't help ourselves"

For tho' we know what we ought to be; & what it would be very sweet & beautiful to be; yet we can't be it. That is most sad,

too. Life is a long Dardenelles, My Dear Madam, the shores whereof are bright with flowers, which we want to pluck, but the bank is
too high; & so we float on & on, hoping to come to a landing-place
at last — but swoop! we launch into the great sea! Yet the geogra-
phers say, even then we must not despair, because across the great
sea, however desolate & vacant it may look, lie all Persia & the delicious lands roundabout Damascus.

So wishing you a pleasant voyage at last to that sweet & far
countree —

Beleive Me
Earnestly Thine —
Herman Melville

I forgot to say, that your letter was sent to me from Pittsfield —
which delayed it.

My sister Augusta begs me to send her sincerest regards both to
you & Mr Hawthorne.

ALS on a 34.7 × 21.7 cm sheet, folded in half, of white paper, gilt-edged and embossed with
the manufacturer's small oval stamp enclosing the name "BATH". Melville inscribed all four
pages, in ink. Sophia Hawthorne interlined the text in pencil with a correct word-by-word
transcription except the word "commend" and the second paragraph, neither of which is
transcribed. She also noted in ink at the top of the fourth page "Mr Melville".

LOCATION: at present unknown. *Provenance*: Descendants of Nathaniel and Sophia Hawthorne;
American Art Association, Anderson Galleries, sale 3911, 29 April 1931, lot 27; J. W. Bent-
ley; Cortlandt F. Bishop sale, American Art Association, Anderson Galleries, sale 4385, 5–8
April 1938, lot 1489 (with reproduction); H. Bradley Martin sale, Sotheby's, New York, sale
5971, 30–31 January 1990, lot 2168 (with reproductions); Joseph M. Maddalena, Profiles in
History [Autographs].

PUBLICATION: (partial) Clifford Smyth, "A Letter from Herman Melville," *The Literary Digest
International Book Review* 3 (December 1924), 22. Davis-Gilman 95.

TEXTUAL NOTES: "Spirit Spout] *closing double quotation mark lacking* • to me,] *before canceled
when* • without] *after canceled* tho' • Are] *written over* All • scarlet] *originally* scarelet *then the first
e marked out* • see] *inserted above caret* • help] lp *rewritten* • I forgot . . . Hawthorne.] *added above
the salutation on the first page; placed here editorially*

TO RICHARD BENTLEY
BEFORE 21 JANUARY 1852 · [PITTSFIELD?]

Unlocated. By the first week of January 1852 Melville had offered the manuscript
of his seventh book, *Pierre*, then expected to amount to about 360 pages, to his
American publishers, Harper & Brothers. The contract was probably drafted at this

time, but it was not formally signed by Allan Melville until 20 February 1852 (for a discussion of the terms of this contract and its possible implications, see the NN *Pierre*, pp. 378–79, the NN *Confidence-Man*, p. 270, n. 14, and Hershel Parker, "Contract: *Pierre*, by Herman Melville," *Proof: The Yearbook of American Bibliographical and Textual Studies* 5 [1977], 27–44). On 21 January 1852 Allan Melville notified the Harpers that the finished book would exceed the 360-page estimate (HCL-M). In all likelihood Melville's unlocated letter offering *Pierre* to his English publisher, Richard Bentley, was written before 21 January, since it apparently contained Melville's initial smaller page-estimate that he had to correct in his subsequent 16 April 1852 letter to Bentley, noting that nearly 150 pages had been added to the book since he had last written (see below). The unlocated letter is also cited in Bentley's 4 March 1852 reply (see LETTERS RECEIVED, pp. 618–19). While thanking Melville for the offer of his "new Work," Bentley was willing to publish it only on joint account, paying Melville half-profits but with no advance. Davis-Gilman Unlocated 336.

TO JULIAN HAWTHORNE
[9?] FEBRUARY 1852 · PITTSFIELD

Julian Hawthorne, almost six years old, had known Melville since August 1850, when Melville first became acquainted with Hawthorne and his family in the Berkshires (for his later published reminiscences about Melville, see the headnote to Melville's 10 August 1883 letter to him, below). His "printed note," to which Melville is responding, is unlocated. After a day's excursion in August 1851 Julian was so taken by Melville that he later declared, as Hawthorne noted in his journal, "he loved Mr. Melville as well as me, and as mama, and as Una" (*American Notebooks*, ed. Claude M. Simpson [Columbus: Ohio State University Press, 1972], p. 468). Melville's reference to "a Snow Image" (partially obscured by a burn mark in the manuscript) is to "The Snow-Image," the title piece of Hawthorne's *The Snow-Image, and Other Twice-Told Tales*, published shortly before Christmas in December 1851 (Melville's surviving marked copy was bought in 1871; Sealts 255). Although Melville dated his letter Monday, 8 February, Monday fell on 9 February in 1852.

Pittsfield, Monday,
February 8th 1852.

My Dear Master Julian
    I was equally surprised and delighted by the sight of your printed note. (At first I thought it was a circular (your father will tell you what *that* is)). I am very happy that I have a place in the heart of so fine a little fellow as you.
    You tell me that the snow in Newton is very deep. Well, it is still dee*p*er here, I fancy. I went into the woods the other day, and

got so deep into the drifts among the big hemlocks & maples that I thought I should stick fast there till Spring came, a Snow Image.

Remember me kindly to your good father, Master Julian, and Good Bye, and may Heaven always bless you, & may you be a good boy and become a great good man.

Herman Melville

Master Julian Hawthorne.

ALS on an 8.8 × 13.4 cm sheet of white wove paper, embossed with the manufacturer's small circular stamp enclosing a crown underneath the name "DOBBS". Melville inscribed both sides of the leaf, in ink. It was later burned in spots (see the textual notes, below).

LOCATION: NYPL-B. *Provenance*: Imogen Hawthorne Van Duzee.

PUBLICATION: *Log*, I, 447. Davis-Gilman 97.

TEXTUAL NOTES: Dear Master Julian] ian *effaced by burn mark* • fast] *partially effaced by burn mark* • a Snow] *partially effaced by burn mark*

TO THE EDITORS OF THE *LITERARY WORLD*
14 FEBRUARY 1852 · PITTSFIELD

This brusque letter, impersonally addressed to the "Editors of Literary World," marks an open rupture in Melville's friendship with Evert and George Duyckinck, the immediate cause of which can only be conjectured. It may have been related to the partly unfavorable review of *Moby-Dick* that appeared in the *Literary World* on 15 and 22 November 1851 (see the NN *Moby-Dick*, pp. 694–96 and 720–23). Most likely it followed some encounter Melville had with Evert Duyckinck in New York (for Melville's unflattering portrayal of a "joint editor" of a literary magazine, see *Pierre*, bk. 17; see also the NN *Moby-Dick*, pp. 693–98). In any case Melville was angered enough to cancel both his own subscription to the *Literary World* and the one he was maintaining for his old friend Eli James Murdock Fly (see Melville's 26 March 1851 letter to Duyckinck requesting this additional subscription). For some reason Melville's subscription continued, and he reiterated his cancellation notice two months later, on 16 April (see below).

Pittsfield

Feb: 14th 1852.

Editors of Literary World:

You will please discontinue the two copies of your paper sent to J. M. Fly at Brattleboro' (or Greenbush), and to H Melville at Pittsfield.

Whatever charges there may be outstanding for either or both copies, please send them to me, & they will receive attention.

Herman Melville

ALS on a 24.8 × 20 cm part-sheet (torn along the bottom), folded in half, of blue wove paper with lines on one side, embossed with the manufacturer's rectangular stamp enclosing the name "CARSON'S DALTON MS" (in the lower left corner of the first leaf). Melville inscribed the unlined first page, in ink. At the bottom of that page, a clerical hand noted with flourishes "Entered Stop [*undeciphered word*] Book"—possibly for "Stop Accounts Book."

LOCATION: NYPL-D.

PUBLICATION: *Log*, I, 447. Davis-Gilman 98.

TEXTUAL NOTE: will please] *final* e *written over* d

TO JOHN MURRAY
5 APRIL 1852 · NEW YORK

Chief Justice Shaw's second son and namesake and Elizabeth Shaw Melville's half-brother, Lemuel Shaw, Jr., left for Europe in April 1852, where he visited England before traveling throughout the Continent. Returning to England in 1853, he was joined in the summer by his father, with whom he traveled again on the Continent before they both returned to Boston in September 1853. Although the younger Shaw does not specifically record presenting Melville's letter of introduction to his first publisher, Shaw evidently used it, since four years later, in 1856, he wrote a letter of introduction to John Murray on behalf of his brother Samuel, in which he recalled attending the Annual Literary Fund dinner with Murray in July 1852 (Murray). He also wrote in a letter of 16 June 1853 to his mother, Hope Savage Shaw, that the next day he was "to dine with Mr. John Murray at Wimbledon" (MHS-S).

New York, April 5th '52

John Murray Esq —

Sir: — This will introduce to you my brother-in-law, Mr Lemuel Shaw of Massachusetts — a son of Chief Justice Shaw — who purposes passing some part of the coming summer in England.

If it shall lie in your power to extend his views of life in your metropolis, & add to the number of the agreeable acquaintances he will be sure to make there, I shall duly value such attentions.

You will find Mr Shaw — as a New-Englander and Boston-
ian — peculiarly ready to appreciate & admire all that you can show
him of what is admirable and enjoyable in England.

Very Truly Yours
Herman Melville

ALS on a 10 × 15.9 cm part-sheet (torn along the left edge) of white wove paper, embossed
with the manufacturer's rectangular stamp enclosing the word "PARIS". Melville inscribed
both sides of the leaf, in ink. The letter was once tipped to another sheet along the left edge.

LOCATION: UV-Barrett. *Provenance*: Times Bookshop, London (?); Seven Gables Bookshop,
1965.

PUBLICATION: *The American Writer in England: An Exhibition Arranged in Honor of the Sesquicen-
tennial of the University of Virginia* (Charlottesville: University Press of Virginia, 1969), p. 52.

TEXTUAL NOTE: brother-in-law] brother-|in-law

TO RICHARD BENTLEY
[5?] APRIL 1852 · NEW YORK

Unlocated. In his 16 April 1852 letter to Bentley (below), Melville wrote in a postscript that he had furnished his brother-in-law Lemuel Shaw, Jr., with a letter of
introduction to him. Presumably Melville wrote the letter at the same time and
along the same lines as the one he wrote to John Murray on behalf of his brother-
in-law, just above. In a 9 May 1852 letter to his parents, Lemuel reported leaving
the letter at Bentley's: "I did not see him. I saw his assistant & had some conversation about Herman's books & was sorry to hear that Mr. Bentley is unwilling to
take Herman's new work on the terms Herman wishes. I was told what I knew
before that he is losing the prestige of his name which he gained by his first books,
by writing so many books that nobody can read. I wish very much he could be
persuaded to leave off writing books for a few years & that is what his friends here
say" (MHS-S).

TO THE EDITORS OF THE *LITERARY WORLD*
16 APRIL 1852 · PITTSFIELD

This letter is placed in 1852 because it repeats Melville's earlier 14 February 1852
order to cancel his subscription to the *Literary World*. At some point a line was
drawn through his name in the *Literary World* subscription book (NYPL-D). Evert
and George Duyckinck continued to edit the *Literary World* until its discontinuation
on 31 December 1853. No record of any renewed direct contact between them and
Melville has been found before 1 October 1856, when Evert without further comment recorded in his diary: "Herman Melville passed the evening with me — fresh

from his mountain charged to the muzzle with his sailor metaphysics and jargon of things unknowable. But a good stirring evening — ploughing deep and bringing to the surface some rich fruits of thought and experience — " (NYPL-D).

Since Melville clearly dated this Pittsfield letter and the New York letter to Bentley just below as the "16ᵗʰ," it would appear that he went from one place to the other on that day—unless either date is an error or he deliberately misreported the place of writing the letter.

Pittsfield
April 16ᵗʰ

Editors
of the
Literary World: —
   You will please to discontinue the copy of your paper sent to me at Pittsfield.

Herman Melville

ALS on a 24.8 × 19.9 cm part-sheet (torn along the top), folded in half, of blue wove paper with lines, faintly embossed with the manufacturer's rectangular stamp (in the upper right corner of the second leaf). Melville inscribed the first page, in ink. David Davidson, who was in charge of subscriptions at the *Literary World*, noted in ink at the bottom: "Author of Typee: Omoo: Mardi: Whitejacket: Redburn: The Whale:".

LOCATION: Collection of David Shneidman. *Provenance*: Pepper & Stern, catalogue 20 (1984), item 789; Paul Richards Autographs, 1985.

PUBLICATION: (reproduction only) "A New Melville Letter," *Melville Society Extracts* 64 (November 1985), 11.

TO RICHARD BENTLEY
16 APRIL 1852 · NEW YORK

Melville postponed his reply to Bentley's 4 March 1852 offer of half-profits with no advance for *Pierre*, and Bentley's "statement touching [Melville's] previous books" included with that letter (see LETTERS RECEIVED, pp. 618–19), until he had the American proofs, which he sent with this letter. To Melville's counter-proposal that Bentley buy the English rights for one hundred pounds in advance (as he had bought *White-Jacket* for two hundred pounds), Bentley replied on 5 May 1852 asking Melville to agree to the half-profits arrangement instead and also to let Bentley "make or have made by a judicious literary friend such alterations as are absolutely necessary to 'Pierre' being properly appreciated here" (see LETTERS RECEIVED, pp. 619–21). Melville did not accept these conditions, and there is no known further correspondence between them apart from Melville's [5?] April 1852 letter of introduction, which Lemuel Shaw, Jr., presented in May 1852, and Melville's note to Bentley in November 1856 to forward his mail to Liverpool (cited in his November 1856 letter to Allan Melville, below). Harper & Brothers delayed bringing out *Pierre* in the United States by two weeks—until the end of July 1852—conceivably because Melville may have been trying to find another British publisher. In the end, only the American sheets of *Pierre* were issued in England in November 1852 by the Harpers' London agent, Sampson, Low, Son, & Company.

New York April 16ᵗʰ 1852.

My Dear Sir: — I have deferred my reply to your last note till I could send you the book concerning which we are negotiating: that so you might be better enabled to come to a satisfactory decision upon the amended terms I am about to submit. —— In the first place, however, let me say that though your statement touching my previous books do not, certainly, look very favorably for the profit side of your account; yet, would it be altogether inadmissible to suppose that by subsequent sales the balance-sheet may yet be made to wear a different aspect? — Certainly, — without reference to the possible future increased saleableness of at least some of those books, on their own independant grounds — the success, (in a business point of view) of any subsequent work of mine, published by you, would tend to react upon those previous books. And, of course, to your advantage. — I do not think that this view of the matter is unreasonable. Now, with these and other considerations in my mind, I can not possibly bring myself to accede to the overtures contained in your last note: —— overtures, based upon arguments, which, as above shown, do not seem absolutely conclusive to me. And more especially am I impelled to decline those overtures upon the ground that my new book possessing unquestionable novelty, as regards my former ones, — treating of utterly new scenes & characters; — and, as I beleive, very much more calculated for popularity than anything you have yet published of mine — being a regular romance, with a mysterious plot to it, & stirring passions at work, and withall, representing a new & elevated aspect of American life —— all these considerations warrant me strongly in not closing with terms greatly inferior to those upon which our previous negotiations have proceeded. ——— Besides, — if you please, Mʳ Bentley — let bygones be bygones; let those previous books, for the present, take care of themselves. For here now we have a *new book*, and what shall we say about *this?* If nothing has been made on the old books, may not something be made out of the new? — At any rate, herewith you have it. Look at it and see whether it will suit you to purchase it at the terms I shall state below. It is a larger book, by 150 pages & more, than I thought it would be, at the date of my first writing you about it. Other things being equal, this circumstance, — in your mode of publication — must of course augment its value to you.

—— I can not but beleive, that as the overtures you made me in your last note were based upon an almost entire ignorance as to the character of the new book (because, you could have no means of knowing what it was going to be) *now* that you see it before you, you will, upon a reconsideration, be induced not to decline the ultimate terms which I here submit, as follows: —— £100 (you buying the book — for England — out-&-out) to be drawn for by me at thirty days' sight, immediately upon my being apprised of your acquiescence. — I trust that our connection will thus be made to continue, and that on the new feild of productions, upon which I embark in the present work, you & I shall hereafter participate in many not unprofitable business adventures.

Very Truly Yours
Herman Melville.

P.S. If, Mʳ Bentley, you accede to the before-mentioned terms, you might then go on and publish without further hearing from me. For the book will reach you, I think, in the prime of the season. *At all events*, I shall suspend the publication at the Harpers' till I have concluded some satisfactory negotiation in London. So you may be sure that if you undertake the book, your publication will not be anticipated here by the Harpers. I send you the proofs from the type instead of the plates, for which I should have to wait some few days.

I presume that ere this sheet comes to your hand, Mʳ Lemuel Shaw will have arrived in London. I furnished him with a letter to you. And would here again invoke for him any attention you may be able to bestow. — H. M.

One more P.S. — I have thought that, on several accounts, (one of which is, the rapid succession in which my works have lately

been published) it might not prove unadvisable to publish this present book anonymously, or under an assumed name: — *"By a
Vermonter" say. I beg you to consider the propriety of this suggestion, but defer the final decision to your own better experience in
such matters, since I am prompted in throwing out the idea, merely
in regard to your advantage as publisher.

H. M.

*or "By Guy Winthrop.

ALS on a 39.4 × 26 cm sheet, folded in half, of white wove paper, embossed with the manufacturer's stamp of a ship. Melville inscribed the first three pages, in ink.

LOCATION: at present unknown. Provenance: Hodgson & Co., sale 13, 27–28 April 1939, lot
566; Scribner's Book Store; H. Bradley Martin sale, Sotheby's, New York, sale 5971, 30–31
January 1990, in lot 2167; 19th Century Shop in partnership with other book dealers.

PUBLICATION: Birss, "A Mere Sale to Effect," pp. 254–55. Davis-Gilman 99.

TEXTUAL NOTES: grounds —] dash largely torn off • popularity] before canceled that • elevated]
before canceled word-start • productions] miswritten productiones • before-mentioned] before-
|mentioned • One more P.S. . . . Winthrop.] added in slightly lighter ink • "By Guy Winthrop.]
closing double quotation mark lacking

TO LEMUEL SHAW
BEFORE 7 JUNE 1852 • [PITTSFIELD?]

Unlocated. On 7 June 1852 Chief Justice Shaw wrote to his son Lemuel Shaw, Jr.,
stating: "I am expecting to hold court at Nantucket, & Herman has promised to go
with me. I wish him to see some of the gents at New Bedford & Nantucket connected with whaling. If he goes, I propose after getting through with the business
of the court, to visit Martha's Vineyard & then Elizabeth Islands[.] I think we can
make it a pleasant excursion for July" (MHS-S). Melville's "promise" was presumably by letter. Davis-Gilman Unlocated 337.

TO WILLIAM H. SWEETSER
1 JULY 1852 • PITTSFIELD

In this letter Melville humorously thanks William Sweetser, an autograph collector
who lived in Charlestown, Massachusetts, for enclosing (as return postage) a stamp
with the head of George Washington on it. Stamps had been introduced in the
United States on 1 July 1847. Benjamin Franklin and Washington (on 2 July 1847)
were the two figures shown on the first five and ten cent stamps, respectively.

July 1st 1852.

The small head of Washington, which you were good enough to send me for inspection, is very well done. I return it (on the outside) with many thanks.

Yours
H Melville

Wm H Sweetser

ALS on a 12 × 18.3 cm sheet of blue wove paper. Melville inscribed only one side of the leaf, in ink. The letter is mounted in an extra-illustrated copy of the 1866 edition of John W. Francis's *Old New York; or, Reminiscences of the Past Sixty Years* (New York: Widdleton) made by S. Whitney Phoenix. It is in volume VI on p. 1694, which is placed just before p. 363 from Francis's book, where Melville is mentioned in the text. (For more on Francis, see his letter to Melville, LETTERS RECEIVED, pp. 628–29.)

LOCATION: Redwood Library and Athenaeum, Newport, Rhode Island.

PUBLICATION: Stanford Apseloff, "Queries and Answers," *Melville Society Extracts* 44 (November 1980), 13.

TO NATHANIEL HAWTHORNE
17 JULY 1852 · PITTSFIELD

Dated only 17 July, this letter can be placed in 1852 by its association both with Melville's 6–14 July 1852 "tour" of Nantucket accompanying Lemuel Shaw and with the publication of Hawthorne's *The Blithedale Romance* on 14 July 1852. Melville's sightings of Hawthorne's book can be pinpointed fairly certainly. He visited Naushon, the largest of the Elizabeth Islands, with Shaw during their trip, and the clergyman there on the "stately piazza" was almost certainly Ephraim Peabody (1807–56), born in New Bedford, minister of the Unitarian Church in New Bedford (1838–46) and of King's Chapel, Boston (1846–56), whom Shaw recorded meeting on Naushon in his 20 July 1852 letter to his son Lemuel Shaw, Jr. (MHS-S). The "gentleman in Brooklyne" was probably George Griggs (1814 or 1815–88), a lawyer from Brookline, Massachusetts, who married Melville's oldest sister Helen in January 1854. He was probably still residing in the household of Andrew H. Newell, a merchant—the family with whom Griggs's name was listed in the 1850 census. Melville may have visited Griggs with Shaw, since according to Maria Melville, "Judge Shaw has known him many years. About eight years earlier Helen had become acquainted with him at Judge Shaw's house" (see Maria Melville to her brother Peter Gansevoort, 23 September 1853 [NYPL-GL]). The "lively boy" on the train was presumably hawking the book. The copy that Melville received in the mail was the one Hawthorne requested Ticknor & Fields to send to him, in a letter of 7 July 1852 (Sealts 245; *Letters, 1843–1853*, ed. Thomas Woodson, L. Neal Smith, and Norman Holmes Pearson [Columbus: Ohio State University Press, 1985],

p. 564). As a compliment on his success with the book, Melville offered Hawthorne the manufacturer's embossed crown on the paper (see the manuscript description, below) and "embellished" it with a "plume" (reproduced here).

Addressed to Concord, Massachusetts, where the Hawthornes had moved in early June 1852, Melville's letter was written in response to a now unlocated invitation from Hawthorne for Melville to visit him at his new home. In it, Hawthorne had apparently referred to his hillside grounds as a "sand-hill," from which Melville here requests a "specimen." Melville's excuse that he had been "an utter idler and a savage" for the last three months probably refers to the excursions he had been taking with members of his family in the Pittsfield area (see Merton M. Sealts, Jr., " 'An utter idler and a savage': Melville in the Spring of 1852," *Melville Society Extracts* 79 [November 1989], 1–3). Melville's added " 'compliments' " to the " 'Rose-Bud' " at the close of this letter refers to the Hawthornes' one-year-old third child, Rose, and perhaps also to Melville's tale of the aromatic ship of that name in Chapter 91 of *Moby-Dick*, which may have been named for her as a private allusion meant for the Hawthornes (see the NN *Moby-Dick*, p. 891). Hawthorne later gave this letter to his British friend Henry A. Bright, an autograph collector who often asked him for letters in his possession (for more about Bright, see Melville's 18 November 1856 letter to him, below).

By the way, here's a crown. Significant this. Pray, allow me to place it on your head in victorious token of your "Blithedale" success. Tho' not in strict keeping, I have embellished it with a plume.

Pittsfield, July 17th

My Dear Hawthorne: — This name of *"Hawthorne"* seems to be ubiquitous. I have been on something of a tour lately, and it has saluted me vocally & typographically in all sorts of places & in all sorts of ways. — I was at the solitary Crusoeish island of Naushon (one of the Elizabeth group) and there, on a stately piazza, I saw it gilded on the back of a very new book, and in the hands of a clergyman. — I went to visit a gentleman in Brooklyne, and as we were sitting at our wine, in came the lady of the house, holding a beaming volume in her hand, from the city — "My Dear," to her husband, "I have brought you *Hawthorne's* new book." I entered the cars at Boston for this place. In came a lively boy *"Hawthorne's* new book!" — In good time I arrived home. Said my lady-wife "there is Mr *Hawthorne's* new book, come by mail" And this morning, lo! on my table a little note, subscribed *Hawthorne* again. — Well, the Hawthorne is a sweet flower; may it flourish in every hedge.

I am sorry, but I can not at present come to see you at Concord as you propose. — I am but just returned from a two weeks' absence; and for the last three months & more I have been an utter idler and a savage — out of doors all the time. So, the hour has come for me to sit down again.

Do send me a specimen of your sand-hill, and a sunbeam from the countenance of Mrs: Hawthorne, and a vine from the curly arbor of Master Julian.

As I am only just home, I have not yet got far into the book but enough to see that you have most admirably employed materials which are richer than I had fancied them. Especially at this day, the volume is welcome, as an antidote to the mooniness of some dreamers — who are merely dreamers ——— Yet who the devel aint a dreamer?

H Melville

My rememberances to Miss Una & Master Julian — & the "compliments" & perfumes of the season to the "Rose-Bud."

ALS on a 34.2 × 22 cm sheet, folded in half, of white wove paper, embossed with the manufacturer's circular stamp enclosing a crown and the name "BATH" over two branches. Melville inscribed the first two pages, in ink, and addressed the fourth page "Nathaniel Hawthorne | Concord | Mass:" adding "Melville" vertically to the left of the address. It was postmarked in Pittsfield on 20 July. Another hand later noted in pencil across the folded edges of the fourth page "Herman Melville | Author of Typee, | Omoo, Mardi, | Pierre, Redburn, | White Jacket | Moby Dick &c".

LOCATION: Beinecke Library, Yale University. *Provenance*: Henry A. Bright; Norman Holmes Pearson.

PUBLICATION: (partial) *Log*, I, 454. Leyda, *Portable Melville*, pp. 458–59. Davis-Gilman 100.

TEXTUAL NOTES: visit a] *possibly* meet a *or* wait on · brought] *possibly* bought · a sunbeam] *first* a *written over another letter* · at] t *written over* s · antidote] *miswritten* antidtote

TO NATHANIEL HAWTHORNE
13 AUGUST 1852 · PITTSFIELD

Though its salutation was later torn off and it was apparently unsigned, this letter was to Nathaniel Hawthorne, as Elizabeth Shaw Melville's notation at its top indicates. As the letter relates, Melville first heard the "story of Agatha" during his July trip to Nantucket with Chief Justice Shaw. The discreetly unnamed New Bedford lawyer who told it was evidently John H. Clifford (1809–76), who had been practicing in New Bedford since 1830 and was district attorney for the Southern District of Massachusetts in 1842 at the time of the legal case upon which the story is based. When Melville met Clifford, he was Attorney General of Massachusetts, and within a few months he was to become the successful Whig candidate for governor. In a 20 July 1852 letter to his son Lemuel Shaw, Jr., Shaw reported that he and Melville were joined by Clifford in New Bedford and that "after riding about the town a little, visiting Mr Arnolds beautiful garden, we dined with Mr. Clifford" (MHS-S). Clifford also accompanied them on the boat trip to Nantucket. Both Shaw (as judge) and Clifford (as prosecutor) had been involved in the sensational 1850 trial of Professor John W. Webster of Harvard, who was convicted and hanged for the murder of his creditor, Dr. George Parkman.

Clifford's accompanying letter, "the gentleman's note" to which Melville refers, is now unlocated. It was clearly a separate item from Clifford's account of the legal case, which Melville also enclosed with this letter and which Hawthorne subsequently returned to him (see LETTERS RECEIVED, pp. 621–25). The similarity of "Robinson" ("Robertson" in Clifford's account) to the title character Wakefield, the *"London husband"* in *Twice-Told Tales*, who also deserts his wife, was evidently only one of a number of reasons that prompted Melville to send the "story of Agatha" to Hawthorne along with this letter written, as he explains, "in a great hurry" (note the number of miswritten words listed in the textual notes, below, and the fact that in his hurry he left the letter unsigned—unless an additional signed page is now missing). Melville's suggestion that the father of Agatha "must be an old widower — a man of the sea, but early driven away from it by repeated disasters" was inspired by Melville's encounter on Nantucket in July 1852 with Captain George Pollard, who, as Melville had already recorded in Chapter 45 of *Moby-Dick*, suffered two shipwrecks before "forswearing the sea" (p. 206; for Melville's memoranda on Pollard in his copy of Owen Chase's *Narrative of the Most Extraordinary and Distressing Shipwreck of the Whale-Ship Essex*, see the NN *Moby-Dick*, pp. 975–95; see also the NN *Clarel*, pp. 755–56). As Elizabeth Melville's subsequent notation indicates (see the manuscript description, below), Hawthorne did not use the story and returned it to Melville. The various pencilings reported in the textual notes are of uncertain origin, but may have been made by Melville when he took up the story himself (for that decision, see his December 1852 letter to Hawthorne, below).

Pittsfield Aug: 13th 1852.
— While visiting Nantucket some four weeks ago, I made the acquaintance of a gentleman from New Bedford, a lawyer, who gave me considerable information upon several matters concerning which I was curious. — One night we were talking, I think, of the great patience, & endurance, & resignedness of the women of the island in submitting so uncomplainingly to the long, long abscences of their sailor husbands, when, by way of anecdote, this lawyer gave me a leaf from his professional experience. Altho'

Pittsfield . Aug: 13ᵗʰ 1852,

—— While visiting Nantucket some few weeks ago, I made the acquaintance of a gentleman from New Bedford, a Lawyer, who gave me considerable information upon several matters concerning which I was curious. —— One night we were talking, I think, of the great patience, & endurance, & resignedness of the women of the island in submitting so uncomplainingly to the long, long absences of their sailor husbands, when, by way of anecdote, this Lawyer gave me a leaf from his professional experience. Altho' his memory was a little confused with regard to some of the items of the story, yet he _told_ me enough to awaken the most lively interest in me; and I begged him to be sure and send me a more full account so soon as he arrived home —— he having previously told me that at the time of the affair he had made a record in his books. —— I heard nothing more, till a few days after arriving here at Pittsfield I received thro' the Post Office the enclosed document. —— You will perceive by the gentleman's note to me that he assumed that I purposed making literary use of the story; but I had not hinted anything of the kind to him, & my first spontaneous interest in it arose from very different considerations. I confess, however, that since then I have a little turned the subject over in my mind with a view to a regular story to be founded on these striking incidents. But, thinking again, it has occured to me that this thing lies very much in a vein, with which you are peculiarly familiar. To be plump, I think that, in this matter you would make a better hand at it than I would. —— Besides the thing seems naturally

his memory was a little confused with regard to some of the items
of the story, yet he told me enough to awaken the most lively interest in me; and I begged him to be sure and send me a more full
account so soon as he arrived home —— he having previously told
me that at the time of the affair he had made a record in his
books. —— I heard nothing more, till a few days after arriving here
at Pittsfield I received thro' the Post Office the enclosed document. —— You will perceive by the gentleman's note to me that he
assumed that I purposed making literary use of the story; but I had
not hinted anything of the kind to him, & my first spontaneous interest in it arose from very different considerations. I confess, however, that since then I have a little turned the subject over in my
mind with a view to a regular story to be founded on these striking
incidents. But, thinking again, it has occurred to me that this thing
lies very much in a vein, with which you are peculiarly familiar. To
be plump, I think that in this matter you would make a better hand
at it than I would. — Besides the thing seems naturally to gravitate
towards you (to speak . . . should of right belong to you. I could
. . . the Steward to deliver it to you. —

The very great interest I felt in this story while narrating to me,
was heightened by the emotion of the gentleman who told it, who
evinced the most unaffected sympathy in it, tho' now a matter of his
past. — But perhaps this great interest of mine may have been largely helped by some accidental circumstances or other; so that, possibly, to you the story may not seem to possess so much of pathos, &
so much of depth. But you will see how it is. ——————————

In estimating the character of Robinson charity should be allowed a liberal play. I take exception to that passage from the Diary which says that "*he must have received a portion of his punishment
in this life*" — thus hinting of a future supplemental castiga-
tion. — I do not at all suppose that his desertion of his wife was a
premeditated thing. If it had been so, he would have changed his
name, probably, after quitting her. — No: he was a weak man, &
his temptations (tho' we know little of them) were strong. The
whole sin stole upon him insensibly — so that it would perhaps
have been hard for him to settle upon the exact day when he could
say to himself, "*Now* I have deserted my wife; unless, indeed upon

the day he wedded the Alexandran lady. — And here I am reminded of your *London husband*; tho' the cases so widely contrast. — Many more things might be mentioned; but I forbear;
you will find out the suggestiveness for yourself; & all the better
perhaps, for my not intermeddling. ————————————————

If you should be sufficiently interested, to engage upon a regular
story founded on this narration; then I consider you but fairly entitled
to the following tributary items, collected by me, by chance, during
my strolls thro the islands; & which — as you will perceive — seem
legitimately to belong to the story, in its rounded & beautified &
thoroughly developed state; — but of all this you must of course be
your own judge — I but submit matter to you — I dont decide.

Supposing the story to open with the wreck — then there must
be a storm; & it were well if some faint shadow of the preceding
calm were thrown forth to lead the whole. — Now imagine a high
cliff overhanging the sea & crowned with a pasture for sheep; a little
way off — higher up, — a light-house, where resides the father of
the future Mrs Robinson the First. The afternoon is mild & warm.
The sea with an air of solemn deliberation, with an elaborate deliberation, ceremoniously rolls upon the beach. The air is suppressedly
charged with the sound of long lines of surf. There is no land over
against this cliff short of Europe & the West Indies. Young Agatha
(but you must give her some other name) comes wandering along
the cliff. She marks how the continual assaults of the sea have undermined it; so that the fences fall over, & have need of many shiftings
inland. The sea has encroached also upon that part where their
dwelling-house stands near the light-house. — Filled with medita-
tions, she reclines along the edge of the cliff & gazes out seaward.
She marks a handful of cloud on the horizon, presaging a storm
thro' all this quietude. (Of a maratime family & always dwelling on
the coast, she is learned in these matters) This again gives food for
thought. Suddenly she catches the long shadow of the cliff cast upon
the beach 100 feet beneath her; and now she notes a shadow moving
along the shadow. It is cast by a sheep from the pasture. It has advanced to the very edge of the cliff, & is sending a mild innocent
glance far out upon the water. There, in strange & beautiful contrast, we have the innocence of the land placidly eyeing the maligni-

ty of the sea. (All this having poetic reference to Agatha & her sea-lover, who is coming in the storm: the storm carries her lover to her; she catches a dim distant glimpse of his ship ere quitting the cliff.) —— P.S. It were well, if from her knowledge of the deep miseries produced to wives by marrying seafaring men, Agatha should have formed a young determination never to marry a sailor; which resolve in her, however, is afterwards overborne by the omnipotence of Love. — P.S. No 2. Agatha should be active during the wreck, & should, in some way, be made the saviour of young Robinson. He should be the only survivor. He should be ministered to by Agatha at the house during the illness ensuing upon his injuries from the wreck. —— Now this wrecked ship has driven over the shoals, & driven upon the beach where she goes to peices, all but her stem-part. This in course of time becomes embedded in the sand — after the lapse of some years showing nothing but the sturdy stem (or, prow-bone) projecting some two feet at low water. All the rest is filled & packed down with the sand. — So that after her husband has disappeared the sad Agatha every day sees this melancoly monument, with all its remindings. ————————————

After a sufficient lapse of time — when Agatha has become alarmed about the protracted abscence of her young husband & is feverishly expecting a letter from him — then we must introduce the mail-post — no, that phrase wont' do, but here is the *thing*. — Owing to the remoteness of the lighthouse from any settled place no regular mail reaches it. But some mile or so distant there is a road leading between two post-towns. And at the junction of what we shall call the Light-House road with this Post Rode, there stands a post surmounted with a little rude wood box with a lid to it & a leather hinge. Into this box the Post boy drops all letters for the people of the light house & that vicinity of fishermen. To this *post* they must come for their letters. And, of course, daily young Agatha goes — for seventeen years she goes thither daily As her hopes gradually decay in her, so does the post itself & the little box decay. The post rots in the ground at last. Owing to its being little used — hardly used at all — grass grows rankly about it. At last a little bird nests in it. At last the post falls.

The father of Agatha must be an old widower — a man of the sea, but early driven away from it by repeated disasters. Hence, is he subdued & quiet & wise in his life. And now he tends a light house, to warn people from those very perils, from which he himself has suffered.

Some few other items occur to me — but nothing material — and I fear to weary you, if not, make you smile at my strange impertinent officiousness. — And it would be so, were it not that these things do, in my mind, seem legitimately to belong to the story; for they were visably suggested to me by scenes I actually beheld while on the very coast where the story of Agatha occurred. — I do not therefore, My Dear Hawthorne, at all imagine that you will think that I am so silly as to flatter myself I am giving you anything of my own. I am but restoring to you your own property — which you would quickly enough have identified for yourself — had you but been on the spot as I happened to be.

Let me conclude by saying that it seems to me that with your great power in these things, you can construct a story of remarkable interest out of this material furnished by the New Bedford lawyer. — You have a skeleton of actual reality to build about with fulness & veins & beauty. And if I thought I could do it as well as you, why, I should not let you have it. —— The narrative from the Diary is instinct with significance. — Consider the mention of the *shawls* — & the inference derived from it. Ponder the conduct of this Robinson throughout. — Mark his trepidation & suspicion when any one called upon him. — But why prate so — you will mark it all & mark it deeper than I would, perhaps.

I have written all this in a great hurry; so you must spell it out the best way you may.

[Enclosure: the lawyer's account; see LETTERS RECEIVED, pp. 621–25]

AL on two sheets of green wove paper with lines. The first sheet, 42.2 × 26.5 cm, was folded in half to make two leaves (the upper left corner of the first leaf was later torn off); the second sheet, 21.1 × 26.5 cm, was left unfolded. Melville inscribed all six pages, in ink. The remainder of a down stroke next to the torn-off area on the first leaf indicates that the letter did have a salutation. Sometime after 1884 Elizabeth Shaw Melville placed Melville's letter and Clifford's account within a twice-folded sheet of white lined paper (lacking one quarter-segment), and on the two outside surfaces she wrote separate notations in pencil: " 'Agatha's Story' | Herman's letter to Mr Hawthorne" and "The story enclosed herewith is one of actual facts — told at Nantucket to Herman by a New Bedford lawyer — He offered it to Mr Hawthorne to elaborate — with a letter (here enclosed) of suggestions for the work — but after a while Mr. H. returned it — not desiring to undertake it — See letter concerning it in 'N. Hawthorne and his Wife' by Julian H. page 475 — Vol 1 — " (Melville's December 1852 letter to Hawthorne, below). Also in pencil at the top of the first page of Melville's letter, Elizabeth Melville wrote: "To Nathaniel Hawthorne" (not visible in reproduction).

Location: HCL-M.

Publication: Samuel Eliot Morison, "Melville's 'Agatha' Letter to Hawthorne," *New England Quarterly* 2 (April 1929), 296–307. Davis-Gilman 101 (with partial reproduction).

Textual Notes: experience] *miswritten* experence · literary] *miswritten* literrary · speak . . .] k *and the following half line removed by a tear in the sheet* · could . . .] ld *and the following half line removed by a tear in the sheet* · liberal] *miswritten* liberral · settle] *before canceled* the · *"Now* . . . deserted my wife] *closing double quotation mark lacking* · things might] *after canceled* thngs · perceive] *miswritten* peceive · legitimately] *miswritten* legititmaly · decide] ide *written over* ree · forth] *before canceled* for · a little] *after canceled* in the · suppressedly] *underlined in pencil and marked by a penciled x in the right margin* · Young] *added in margin* · (but you must give her some other name)] *deleted in pencil* · she reclines] she *miswritten* shee *and* nes *added* · There] *possibly* Here · contrast] *as* rewritten · placidly] *after canceled* & the · having] *inserted with caret above canceled* having · to wives] to *written over* by · afterwards overborne] afterwards *inserted above caret* · saviour] *inserted with caret above canceled* saviour · survivor] *after canceled* survivor · ministered to] *before canceled* thro · the illness] *after canceled* his · prow-bone] *underlined in pencil and marked by an x in the left margin* · packed down] *underlined in pencil and marked by an x in the left margin* · mail] *after canceled* male · The father . . . suffered.] *beside this paragraph M penciled the notation:* Seagull Paradise · & wise] *inserted above caret*

TO G. P. PUTNAM & CO.
AFTER 1 OCTOBER 1852 · PITTSFIELD

Unlocated. George Palmer Putnam (1814–72), a cousin of Sophia Hawthorne, first worked for the publishers Wiley & Long, then entered a partnership with John Wiley in 1840 to form the firm of Wiley & Putnam (dissolved in 1848). Settled in London, he also conducted an agency for selling American books in England and in 1846 arranged (apparently at the instigation of Washington Irving) with Gansevoort Melville for the publication of the American edition of *Typee*. After his return to New York, he founded *Putnam's Monthly Magazine of American Literature, Science, and Art* (first issue, 3 January 1853). On 1 October 1852, Putnam sent a form letter to more than seventy established American authors, describing the proposed magazine and soliciting articles and stories (see George H. Putnam, *A Memoir of George Palmer Putnam* [New York and London: Putnam, 1903], I, 286–87; and Parke Godwin, *George William Curtis: A Commemorative Address* [New York: Harper, 1893], pp. 16–17). No such letter to Melville has been discovered, but Parke Godwin

(1816–1904), involved in the editorship of the magazine at its inception, in his commemorative address on Curtis listed Melville "among our promised contributors—the most of whom complied with their promises" (p. 17; see also LETTERS RECEIVED, pp. 626–28). From this comment a letter by Melville expressing his interest can be inferred. Melville's first piece published in *Putnam's* was "Bartleby, the Scrivener. A Story of Wall-Street," which appeared in the issues of November and December 1853.

TO NATHANIEL HAWTHORNE
25 OCTOBER 1852 · PITTSFIELD

Although written over two months after his 13 August letter proposing the "story of Agatha" to Hawthorne, this 25 October letter is in part an addendum to that letter, showing that Melville had continued to turn aspects of the story over in his mind, as he here advises Hawthorne to do. The guidebook he mentions in closing, *Taghconic; or, Letters and Legends about Our Summer Home* (Boston: Reading, 1852; Sealts 478), was by his Pittsfield neighbor J. E. A. Smith, who published it under the pseudonym "Godfrey Greylock." The book included several chapters by Smith's friends, one of whom, "Mr. Buckham of Lenox" (Matthew Buckham [1832–1910], later president of the University of Vermont), wrote six pages on Hawthorne, laying stress upon his "secluded life" and the "unsympathising, morbid spirit" of his work. "Perhaps all his better sympathies," conjectured Buckham, "were chilled in those speculations with his dreamy brethren of the Brook Farm Community; perhaps he and Emerson, enraptured with the mystic perfection of their own fantasies, abjured all communion with this our gross humanity; he certainly could not have had his feelings frozen into hate by contact with the genial and sympathizing intellect of Ellery Channing, or at the warm hearthstone of Longfellow" (p. 103). At the bottom of Buckham's "abuse" was his resentment of Hawthorne's treatment of the Puritans and Calvinism, which he sought to redress (p. 104). Other contributors to *Taghconic* were Sarah Morewood and John C. Hoadley, who married Melville's sister Catherine in 1853; but "Herman," as his mother wrote in a 6 October 1852 letter accompanying a present of the book to her brother Peter Gansevoort, "has not contributed one line, tho often requested to do so" (NYPL-GL). Melville did figure in Smith's own chapters, however, which included two brief, flattering notices (pp. 13 and 16; see also Sealts, *Early Lives*, pp. 194–95). Smith revised and enlarged the book in 1879, adding further references to Melville (see Sealts, *Early Lives*, pp. 196–98).

Monday Morning
25th Oct: 1852.

My Dear Hawthorne —

If you thought it worth while to write the story of Agatha, and should you be engaged upon it; then I have a little idea touching it, which however trifling, may not be entirely out of place. Perhaps, tho', the idea has occurred to yourself. — The probable facility with which Robinson first leaves his wife & then takes another, may, possibly, be ascribed to the peculiarly latitudinarian notions, which most sailors have of all tender obligations of that sort. In his previous sailor life Robinson had found a wife (for a night) in every port. The sense of the obligation of the marriage-vow to Agatha had little weight with him at first. *It* was only when some years of life ashore had passed that his moral sense on that point became develloped. And hence his subsequent conduct — Remorse &c. Turn this over in your mind & see if it is right. If not — make it so yourself.

If you come across a little book called "Taughconic" — look into it and divert yourself with it. Among others, you figure in it, & I also. But you are the most honored, being the most abused, and having the greatest space allotted you. — It is a "Guide Book" to Berkshire.

I dont know when I shall see you. I shall lay eyes on you one of these days however. Keep some Champagne or Gin for me.

My respects and best rememberances to Mrs: Hawthorne & a reminder to the children.

H Melville

If you find any *sand* in this letter, regard it as so many sands of my life, which run out as I was writing it.

ALS on a 25.4 × 20 cm sheet, folded in half, of white laid paper, embossed with the manufacturer's small oblong stamp of flourishes connected at four points, enclosing the name "CARSON'S". Melville inscribed the first three pages, in ink, with the postscript in ink on the fourth page, and addressed the envelope "Nathaniel Hawthorne | Concord | Mass:"; it was postmarked in Pittsfield on 25 October. In the otherwise blank portion of the third page another hand added in pencil "TAGHCONIC", identifying Melville's misspelling on the facing page.

LOCATION: NYPL-B.

PUBLICATION: Harrison Hayford, "The Significance of Melville's 'Agatha' Letters," *ELH* 13 (December 1946), 311. Davis-Gilman 102.

TEXTUAL NOTES: port] *inserted with caret above canceled* port • Among others,] *inserted above caret before* You *(vestigial capital)* • Champagne] *miswritten* Champange • rememberances] *extraneous ink line under* ce • If . . . writing it.] *added sideways in ink on the otherwise blank fourth page; placed here editorially* • regard] *before canceled* them

TO NATHANIEL HAWTHORNE
BETWEEN 3 AND 13 DECEMBER 1852 · BOSTON

The original manuscript of this letter is unlocated, and Julian Hawthorne's published transcription, reprinted here, is undated. This letter can be placed in 1852, however, through its connection with the "story of Agatha." The visit Melville mentions in it took place on 2 December 1852: a note by Una Hawthorne the next day states that Melville had come to visit her father "yesterday" (see the entry under this date in the *New Log*). Thus the letter, from Boston where the Melvilles had been visiting the Shaws since Thanksgiving, was written between 3 and 13 December, when Melville returned to Pittsfield with Malcolm.

The Isles of Shoals (not "Isle" as both Hawthorne and Melville colloquially write) are a group of eight barren and rocky islands some ten miles southeast of Portsmouth, New Hampshire, inhabited largely by fishermen, though popular at the time as summer resorts. From 3 to 16 September 1852 Hawthorne vacationed there, keeping a journal, possibly with the "story of Agatha" in mind, as Melville's new working title used for it in this letter suggests (see *The American Notebooks*, ed. Claude M. Simpson [Columbus: Ohio State University Press, 1972], pp. 511–43). Clearly Hawthorne and Melville had discussed that setting in Concord on 2 December. Melville's statement that, having decided to write the story himself, he intends to "introduce the old Nantucket seaman" into the story is another indication that he saw Captain Pollard's story as thematically linked with the "story of Agatha" (see the headnote to his 13 August 1852 letter to Hawthorne). Hawthorne complied with Melville's request in this letter and returned Clifford's account to him (see LETTERS RECEIVED, pp. 621–25).

Two surviving letters in a correspondence between Augusta Melville and her cousin Priscilla Melvill indicate that Melville did indeed "endeavor to do justice" to the story, and completed it under the title of *The Isle of the Cross*. From the second of these, Priscilla's reply to her cousin's now unlocated 30 May 1853 letter, it can be inferred that Augusta must have announced that Melville had completed this story on or about the day his daughter Elizabeth (Bessie) was born: 22 May 1853. In her 12 June 1853 reply Priscilla remarked that "the 'Isle of the Cross' " was "almost a twin sister" of the new baby at Arrowhead (NYPL-GL). In his 24 November 1853 letter to Harper & Brothers, below, Melville refers to a work in his possession that he was "prevented from printing" the previous spring. *The Isle of the Cross* apparently remained unpublished; there is no known further reference to it. For the original suggestion that Melville wrote the "story of Agatha," and a discussion of its direction, see Harrison Hayford, "The Significance of Melville's 'Agatha' Letters," *ELH* 13 (December 1946), 299–310; for its title and all now known about it, see Hershel Parker, "Herman Melville's *The Isle of the Cross*: A Survey and a Chronology," *American Literature* 62 (March 1990), 1–16.

A related piece that Melville later published, "The Encantadas, or Enchanted Isles" (1854), did, significantly, attract the attention of Celia Laighton Thaxter (1835–94), one of the residents of Appledore Island, among the Isles of Shoals, whom Hawthorne met while there in 1852 (*American Notebooks*, pp. 515–17). In her book *Among the Isles of Shoals* (Boston: Osgood), published over two decades later in 1873, she wrote in her opening paragraph of finding in Melville's description of the "Encantadas" an apt comparison for the Isles of Shoals: "In a series of papers published not many years ago, Herman Melville made the world acquainted with the 'Encantadas,' or Enchanted Islands, which he described as lying directly under the equator, off the coast of South America, and of which he says: 'It is to be doubted whether any spot of earth can, in desolateness, furnish a parallel to this group.' But their dark volcanic crags and melancholy beaches can hardly seem more desolate than do the low bleached rocks of the Isles of Shoals to eyes that behold them for the first time. Very sad they look, stern, bleak, and unpromising, yet are they enchanted islands in a better sense of the word than are the Great Gallipagos of which Mr. Melville discourses so delightfully" (p. 7).

Boston.

My dear Hawthorne, — The other day, at Concord, you expressed uncertainty concerning your undertaking the story of Agatha, and, in the end, you urged *me* to write it. I have decided to do so, and shall begin it immediately upon reaching home; and so far as in me lies, I shall endeavor to do justice to so interesting a story of reality. Will you therefore enclose the whole affair to me; and if anything of your own has occurred to you in your random thinking, won't you note it down for me on the same page with my memorandum? I wish I had come to this determination at Concord, for then we might have more fully and closely talked over the story, and so struck out new light. Make amends for this, though, as much as you conveniently can. With your permission I shall make use of the "Isle of Shoals," as far as the name goes at least. I shall also introduce the old Nantucket seaman, in the way I spoke to you about. I invoke your blessing upon my endeavors; and breathe a fair wind upon me. I greatly enjoyed my visit to you, and hope that you reaped some corresponding pleasure.

H. Melville.

Julian, Una, and Rose, — my salutations to them.

Original document not located. Text from first publication. A transcription by Elizabeth Shaw Melville of the first publication is in HCL-M.

PUBLICATION: Julian Hawthorne, *Nathaniel Hawthorne and His Wife* (2 vols., Boston: Osgood, 1884), I, 475. Davis-Gilman 103.

1853

TO ELIZABETH DOW
10 JANUARY 1853 · PITTSFIELD

Elizabeth Dow of Milton, Massachusetts, was Elizabeth Shaw Melville's first cousin—their mothers, Elizabeth Knapp Shaw (1784–1822) and Dorothy Knapp Dow
(1788–1868), were sisters. In response to the invitation in this letter, Elizabeth Dow
briefly visited the Melvilles in Pittsfield the following summer, traveling from Boston with Samuel Shaw, as Elizabeth Melville reported in a 10 August 1853 letter to
her father (HCL-M). At the time of this January letter, Elizabeth Melville had just
returned from a visit with her family in Boston, evidently bringing with her for
Melville a now unlocated and unidentified picture executed by her cousin.

Pittsfield Jan 10th 1853.

Miss Lizzie Dow:

I was very much pleased when your namesake brought home
the picture of the "old gentleman". You have succeeded much better than I had thought it possible. And I take this mode of putting
my thankful obligations to you on epistolary record.

If you will come & see us next summer, you shall see how we
have disposed of the picture. Consider this note as another renewal
of the original invitation — only still more urgent.

Truly Yours,
H Melville

ALS on a 17.5 × 13.4 cm sheet, folded in half, of white wove paper, embossed with the
manufacturer's small circular stamp enclosing a crown underneath the name "DOBBS". Melville inscribed the first page, in ink, and addressed the fourth page "Miss Lizzie Dow." A
bookseller's code number, with the price "235⁰⁰" and the query "Picture of Justice Shaw?" is
also penciled on that page.

LOCATION: UV-Barrett. *Provenance*: Timothy F. McGillicuddy; Charles Hamilton
Autographs.

PUBLICATION: Davis-Gilman 104.

TO J. ROWLAND MOREWOOD
BEFORE 21 MARCH 1853 · PITTSFIELD

Unlocated. A letter by Melville is cited in Maria Melville's 21 March 1853 letter to
her daughter Catherine, describing a visit that she and her youngest daughter Frances Priscilla paid to the Morewoods, who were staying in New York at the time.

She reports, in passing, that "Mr Morewood had received Herman's letter, but had given up at present all thoughts of going to see the farm" (NYPL-GL). Apparently Melville was keeping Rowland Morewood apprised of developments at Broadhall in his absence.

TO LEMUEL SHAW AND HOPE SAVAGE SHAW
22 MAY 1853 · PITTSFIELD

Unlocated. A letter from Melville is cited in Lemuel Shaw's 24 May 1853 letter to his son Lemuel Shaw, Jr., who was traveling on the Continent (MHS-S). The judge proudly announced to his son "the gratifying intelligence of the birth of a granddaughter"—the Melvilles' third child and first daughter, Elizabeth or "Bessie" (1853–1908): "We received a letter last evening from Herman, informing us, that Elizabeth gave birth to a daughter yesterday & is very well, that is, very well compared with her situation on the last similar occasion." Since the judge received Melville's letter on the evening of 23 May, Melville probably wrote it on the day of the birth, 22 May. Davis-Gilman Unlocated 338.

TO THE PITTSFIELD FOURTH OF JULY COMMITTEE
23 MAY 1853 · PITTSFIELD

Having received a (now unlocated) invitation from the Pittsfield Fourth of July Committee, Melville in this reply declined the honor of delivering an oration. It was received by Julius Rockwell (1805–86), who was to serve as "President of the Day" at the 1853 celebration. A prominent citizen, Rockwell had been a lawyer in Pittsfield since 1830. From 1843 to 1851, he had held a seat in the U.S. Congress and in 1854 was appointed to fill Edward Everett's unexpired senatorial term. He later served as a judge in the Superior Court of Massachusetts from 1859 until his death. In his unlocated reply, he evidently asked Melville at least to attend the celebration—an invitation which Melville accepted on 2 July 1853 (see below).

Pittsfield, May 23^d 1853

Gentlemen — By your note of this day's date you officially invite me to deliver the next Fourth of July oration before our fellow-citizens of Pittsfield. You also express a personal desire that I should comply.

Were I in the habit of doing anything of this sort — did it lie within the scope of my ability, I can hardly think of any Celebration in which I would more willingly take part in an active way, than the one to which I am in so friendly and flattering a manner invited. As it is, I must respectfully beg to decline.

Sincerely, Your Friend & Fellow-citizen
H Melville

To,
The Committee.

ALS on a 25.4 × 20 cm sheet, folded in half, of white laid paper, embossed with the manufacturer's small oblong stamp of flourishes connected at four points. Melville inscribed the first page, in ink. Another hand, presumably Rockwell's, noted in ink on the fourth page "H. Melville | May 23. 1853". A third hand, presumably a librarian's, noted on the third page in pencil "Oct. 20, 1958".

LOCATION: New-York Historical Society.

PUBLICATION: Hennig Cohen, "New Melville Letters," *American Literature* 38 (January 1967), 556–59.

TO ROBERT F. COOKE
BEFORE 11 JUNE 1853 · [NEW YORK?]

Unlocated. Robert Francis Cooke (1816–91) was cousin and partner of the publisher John Murray, and Melville first met him in 1849 at a dinner at Murray's (*Journals*, p. 25). Although after this dinner Melville dismissed Cooke in his journal entry simply as Murray's "factotum," he later dined with him and his brother in their rooms in Elm Court, Temple—an occasion that served as the basis for Part I of "The Paradise of Bachelors and the Tartarus of Maids" (*Journals*, p. 44; NN *Piazza Tales* volume, pp. 316–35). Melville probably wrote a letter of introduction to Cooke for his uncle Peter Gansevoort shortly before the latter sailed with Judge Amasa J. Parker, also of Albany, for England on 11 June 1853. Melville was in New York at this time, staying with his brother Allan, and saw his uncle off at the dock. In London, Peter Gansevoort called on Cooke when he was out and left the letter, which Cooke acknowledged on 28 June ("I regret being out when you called upon me & left your card & a letter from my friend Herman Melville" [NYPL-GL]). The following day, after receiving Peter Gansevoort's reply—regretting that he and his party could not join Cooke for a dinner—Cooke urgently wrote back, asking, "What will Typee say, if we dont put our legs under the same Mahogany together?!!!" (NYPL-GL). Shortly afterwards, a dinner including the Cooke brothers, Gansevoort, Parker, and Judge Shaw and Lemuel Shaw, Jr., who were also in London, was held on 4 July, as Peter Gansevoort later related in a 9 October 1856 letter to Melville written just before Melville's return trip to England in 1856 (see LETTERS RECEIVED, pp. 649–51). Davis-Gilman Unlocated 339.

TO JULIUS ROCKWELL
2 JULY 1853 · PITTSFIELD

On 7 July 1853, the *Pittsfield Sun* reported that "a townsman, Mr. Herman Melvill" attended the Fourth of July celebration (as he promised in this letter) and that Julius Rockwell, as "President of the Day" for the Pittsfield Fourth of July Committee (see the letter of 23 May 1853), had made some "appropriate remarks," including the fact that "the ancestor of Mr. Melvill was one of the celebrated party who threw overboard the tea into Boston harbor; and to the other fact, well known to the present generation, that the grandson had drawn from the sea rich and various materials for the entertainment and instruction of the world." Although Melville dated his letter 1852, it clearly belongs to 1853, as shown by the endorsement ("July 2, 1853.") and by the fact that Rockwell was "President of the Day" in 1853 but not in 1852.

Pittsfield July 2^d 1852

My Dear Sir — I honestly thank you for the compliment of your friendly invitation to join in the celebration of the approaching festival. I comply with the greatest pleasure.

Sincerely Your friend

H Melville

Hon: Julius Rockwell
President of the Day.

ALS on a 34.4 × 20.7 cm sheet, folded in half, of white wove paper, embossed with the manufacturer's circular stamp flanked by a lion and a unicorn, surmounted by a crown, and underlined with a banner. Melville inscribed the first page, in ink. Another hand, presumably Rockwell's, noted on the fourth page "Mr Melville. | July 2. 1853." Still another hand, probably a librarian's, noted on the third page in pencil "Oct. 20, 1958".

LOCATION: New-York Historical Society.

PUBLICATION: Hennig Cohen, "New Melville Letters," *American Literature* 38 (January 1967), 556–59.

TO LEMUEL SHAW
BEFORE 10 AUGUST 1853 · PITTSFIELD

Unlocated. While her father was abroad in the summer of 1853, Elizabeth Shaw Melville, on 10 August, wrote him a long letter, describing among other things the preparations for the marriage of Melville's sister Catherine to John Hoadley: "she is to be married in church in about four weeks or so — the 15th September. Herman told you about Mr. Hoadley I believe — His first wife was a daughter of your classmate Mr. Kimball, and they were married the *same day* that Herman & myself were, and Mary Nourse officiated as bridesmaid on the occasion — It is rather odd that with such a conjunction of associations, he should accidentally connect himself with our family — I wish you to be here as usual this year to be at the wedding — " (HCL-M). Since there is no evidence that Melville had seen Shaw since December 1852, it can be inferred that he had told the judge about John Chipman Hoadley (1818–86) in a letter. As Jay Leyda wrote in his note on Hoadley in the *Log*, "family tradition tells that M[elville] was at first opposed to Hoadley as a suitor of his sister" (I, xxvii); however, as the only complete letter now located from their correspondence—Melville's 31 March 1877 letter to Hoadley, below—attests, Melville came to value him as a friend and sympathetic reader self-schooled in the classics (see the NN *Clarel*, pp. 662–65, for a discussion of Hoadley's careful reading of that work, and LETTERS RECEIVED, pp. 715–18, for two of Hoadley's own efforts as an amateur poet). In August 1847 Hoadley, a manufacturer and engineering designer, had married Charlotte Sophia Kimball, who died less than a year later in June 1848. He first met the Melvilles in Pittsfield, where he was associated with Gordon McKay in the manufacture of locomotives and textile machinery. He married Melville's sister Catherine in 1853 and settled in Lawrence, Massachusetts, as superintendent of a machine shop. His invention of the Hoadley portable engine and his manufacturing enterprises made him wealthy, but later reverses required his return to his engineering profession. Catherine Hoadley sold his extensive library at auction after his death; see the 13–14 January 1887 auction catalogue published by Charles F. Libbie & Co. of Boston. Davis-Gilman Unlocated 340.

TO HARPER & BROTHERS
13 AUGUST [1853?] · PITTSFIELD

Although Melville does not give the year, this letter, because it accompanied a relatively large submission (three articles), can tentatively be dated 13 August 1853 (not 1854 as Davis and Gilman thought, or 1855, when Melville was both still in Pittsfield in August and still offering articles to *Harper's New Monthly Magazine*). As Merton M. Sealts, Jr., indicates in the Historical Note to the NN *Piazza Tales* volume, Melville sent fewer of his magazine pieces to *Harper's* than to *Putnam's Monthly Magazine* after *Harper's* proved slow in publishing them. After August 1854 only two of his pieces—"Jimmy Rose" (November 1855) and "The 'Gees" (March 1856)—were bought and published in *Harper's* and neither was ready for submission until September 1854. The letter that accompanied them was probably that of 18 September 1854, below. (A third piece, "The Paradise of Bachelors and the Tartarus of Maids," was not published until April 1855, but it was paid for in May 1854.) While Melville may have submitted pieces in 1854 and 1855 that were rejected by the Harpers (as with "The Apple-Tree Table"; see the headnote to Melville's 10 December 1855 letter to them), it seems unlikely that all three of those sent with this letter would have been refused. Furthermore, this letter is written on white paper rather than the blue paper of the other letters to the Harpers in 1854 and 1855.

Noting the formal wording of its first sentence, Sealts conjectures that this letter was Melville's earliest offering of items specifically for *Harper's*. (Negotiations with the Harpers for magazine pieces had clearly been going on earlier in the summer of 1853, since Melville's mother-in-law reported in a 27 July letter to her nephew Samuel Savage that "the Harpers have persuaded Herman to write for him [them]; and he is admirably paid"—see Frederick J. Kennedy and Joyce Deveau Kennedy, "Additions to *The Melville Log*," *Melville Society Extracts* 31 [September 1977], 8.) If so, one of the three items, Sealts suggests, would have been "Cock-A-Doodle-Doo!" (published December 1853). The other two, he argues, were probably "The Happy Failure" (published July 1854) and "The Fiddler" (published September 1854). See the NN *Piazza Tales* volume, pp. 486–94. Sealts assumes that Harpers did not pay for the two stories published later until the following spring (see Melville's 25 May 1854 letter, below).

Pittsfield Aug 13th

Gentlemen: —

Herewith are three articles which perhaps may be found suitable for your Magazine. Be so good as to give them your early attention, and apprise me of the result, and oblige

Yours Very Truly
H Melville

Harper & Brothers,
New York.

ALS on a 26.8 × 20.1 cm sheet, folded in half, of white laid paper with lines, embossed with the manufacturer's shield-like stamp enclosing an armed figure beneath the name "CARSON'S CONGRESS". Melville inscribed the first page, in ink. Another hand, presumably a clerk's, noted in ink on the fourth page "H. Melville", underlining it with a flourish.

LOCATION: The Pierpont Morgan Library, New York. MA 1950, the Harper Collection.

PUBLICATION: Davis-Gilman 115.

TO HARPER & BROTHERS
BEFORE 20 SEPTEMBER [1853?] · PITTSFIELD

Unlocated. In a letter dated only 20 September, Charles F. Briggs, an editor at *Putnam's Monthly Magazine*, wrote to Harper & Brothers forwarding a "Ms. and note" from Melville intended for the Harpers but "directed to *Putnam's Monthly*" (The Pierpont Morgan Library, New York: MA 1950, the Harper Collection). Merton M. Sealts, Jr., conjectures that this mix-up occurred in 1853 and that the enclosed manuscript was either "a fourth contribution for *Harper's* or a revision of one of the three manuscripts submitted in August" (see the letter just above and the NN *Piazza Tales* volume, pp. 486–87).

TO GEORGE P. PUTNAM
BEFORE 20 SEPTEMBER [1853?] · PITTSFIELD

Unlocated. In his 20 September [1853?] letter (see the entry just above), Charles Briggs also inquired of the Harpers whether, "as something was Expected from Mr Melville perhaps he may have misdirected it to you" (The Pierpont Morgan Library, New York: MA 1950, the Harper Collection). At least one, and perhaps two, letters can be inferred from this inquiry. Melville had apparently sent *Putnam's* a note informing them that a manuscript was on its way (see Melville's 7 June 1854, 16 August [1854?], and 9 November [1854?] letters for other examples of his practice of notifying George P. Putnam when a manuscript was being sent). A second letter may have accompanied the manuscript as well. Merton M. Sealts, Jr., proposes that the manuscript was that of "Bartleby, the Scrivener," which was published in the November and December issues of *Putnam's* (see the NN *Piazza Tales* volume, pp. 486–87).

TO HARPER & BROTHERS
24 NOVEMBER 1853 · PITTSFIELD

Neither of the proposed works discussed here was published by Harper & Brothers. The first, Melville's rendering of the "story of Agatha," whose title at the time it was completed was *The Isle of the Cross*, was finished on or about 22 May 1853 (see Melville's December 1852 letter to Hawthorne and its headnote, above). The *Springfield Republican* of 11 June 1853 under "Pittsfield Items" reported that "Herman Melville has gone to New York to superintend the issue of a new work." However, as this letter indicates, he was "prevented from printing" his now unlocated manuscript "at that time." See Hershel Parker, "Herman Melville's *The Isle of the Cross*: A Survey and a Chronology," *American Literature* 62 (March 1990), 1–16.

The second manuscript of "300 pages" probably included the sketches that were ultimately published as "The Encantadas," which begin with two sections chiefly on tortoises and include among its other sketches several that could be generally labeled "nautical adventure." However, these sketches were published not by Harper & Brothers, but by *Putnam's Monthly Magazine* in March, April, and May 1854 under the pseudonym "Salvator R. Tarnmoor." (See the headnote to Melville's [20?] February 1854 letter to Harper & Brothers for a possible explanation of this change of publishers.) Whether his 1853 book manuscript included these and other sketches, or was something quite different, is impossible to say, but the sketches as published in *Putnam's* would have amounted to only a fraction of "300 pages" in manuscript and an even smaller proportion in print. Although Melville writes that he was "pretty well on towards completion" of this work, his subsequent letters of [20?] February 1854 and 22 June 1854 to Harper & Brothers, below, indicate that it was still incomplete several months later.

Despite the fact that the Harpers published neither *The Isle of the Cross* nor the "Tortoise-Hunters" manuscript (and that "Declined" was later penciled at the top of this letter), Melville did receive from them the three-hundred-dollar advance he sought (see his 6 December 1853 acknowledgment, just below). Also penciled in the margin of this letter was "Col Harper"—the in-house nickname for John

Harper, who acted as business manager for the firm. Later, when Fletcher Harper was considering the letter, a separate sheet summarizing Melville's sales record with them was inserted in it. To Fletcher Harper's inquiry at the top of the sheet, "How many copies have been sold of Melville's three last works?" William Demarest, the Harper bookkeeper, wrote:

Typee	1779
Omoo	6328
Mardi	2544
Redburn	4316
White Jacket	4145
Moby Dick	2771
Pierre	1916

Pittsfield Nov 24th 1853

Gentlemen: — In addition to the work which I took to New York last Spring, but which I was prevented from printing at that time; I have now in hand, and pretty well on towards completion, another book — 300 pages, say — partly of nautical adventure, and part- ly — or, rather, chiefly, of Tortoise Hunting Adventure. It will be ready for press some time in the coming January. Meanwhile, it would be convenient, to have advanced to me upon it $300. — My acct: with you, at present, can not be very far from square. For the abovenamed advance — if remitted me now — you will have securi- ty in my former works, as well as security prospective, in the one to come, (The Tortoise-Hunters) because if you accede to the aforesaid request, this letter shall be your voucher, that I am willing your house should publish it, on the old basis — half-profits.

Reply immediately, if you please,

And Beleive Me, Yours

Herman Melville

ALS on a 33.8 × 21.8 cm sheet, folded in half, of white wove paper, embossed with the manufacturer's circular stamp enclosing a crown. Melville inscribed the first page, in ink. Across the top of that page, another hand noted in pencil "*Declined*" and added in the margin "Col Harper" half-encircled with a line. A third hand noted in ink on the fourth page "Her- man Melville | Nov. 24th 1853". Subsequently attached to this letter for filing, as shown by matching pin marks and the duplication of folds in both, was a 10.4 × 20 cm part-sheet of blue laid paper with Demarest's listing of the sales figures of Melville's works up to this time.

LOCATION: The Pierpont Morgan Library, New York. MA 1950, the Harper Collection.

PUBLICATION: Davis-Gilman 105.

TEXTUAL NOTE: pretty] y *rewritten*

TO HARPER & BROTHERS
6 DECEMBER 1853 · PITTSFIELD

With this letter, Melville acknowledged the three-hundred-dollar cash advance that he had requested in his 24 November 1853 letter, just above. If Melville's repeated date 6 December in this letter is the correct one for both the Harpers' transmittal letter (now unlocated) and this reply, their letter was both mailed from New York and received and acknowledged by Melville in Pittsfield on that same day—a notably but not impossibly swift transaction. Melville's Harper account was debited $300 cash as of 7 December, the next day, according to the Harpers' tenth account (HCL-M), which has entries through 6 October 1854 and was docketed by Allan Melville with that date.

Pittsfield Dec: 6th

1853

Gentlemen:

I acknowledge, with pleasure, yours of the 6th, enclosing $300. as an advance upon my new book (Tortoise Hunting.)

Very Truly

Yours

Herman Melville

Harper & Brothers,

Franklin Square.

ALS on an 11.3 × 18.5 cm part-sheet (torn along the left edge) of blue wove paper, embossed with the manufacturer's circular stamp enclosing a crown and the name "SUPERFINE SATIN". Melville inscribed only one side of the leaf, in ink. Another hand, presumably a clerk's, noted on the verso in ink "Herman Melville | Dec. 6, 1853."

LOCATION: The Pierpont Morgan Library, New York. MA 1950, the Harper Collection.

PUBLICATION: Davis-Gilman 106.

TEXTUAL NOTE: acknowledge] *underlined later in pencil*

TO [EDWARD LIVINGSTON WELLS?]
14 DECEMBER 1853 · PITTSFIELD

This letter to an unidentified autograph collector appears to have been written in haste, with the first "Melville" and the addressee's name unclearly spelled. The donor of the letter to Dartmouth College gave Edward Livingston Wells as the addressee's name, but did not indicate the source of this information. Wells was probably the Episcopalian minister of that name (1834–80), who later served in St. Stephen's church in Pittsfield from 1866 to 1870 and would have been nineteen at the time of this exchange (see Kate M. Scutt, *The First Century of St. Stephen's Parish, 1830–1930* [Pittsfield: St. Stephen's, 1930], pp. 36–37).

> Pittsfield Dec 14th
>
> 1853
>
> M[r] Melville takes pleasure in exchanging autographs with M[r] E L Welles
>
> Herman Melville

ALS on an 11.5 × 18.5 cm part-sheet (torn along the left edge) of blue wove paper, embossed with the manufacturer's circular stamp enclosing a crown and the name "SUPERFINE SATIN". Melville inscribed only one side of the leaf, in ink. The notation "Original autograph letter by Herman Melville" was later typed at the bottom of the letter, presumably by an autograph dealer. It is now tipped in following the front free endpaper of a first American edition of *Moby-Dick*.

LOCATION: Dartmouth College Library. *Provenance*: George Matthew Adams.

PUBLICATION: Davis-Gilman 107.

TEXTUAL NOTE: Welles] *second* e *written over an earlier* s

TO SARAH HUYLER MOREWOOD
[20 DECEMBER?] 1853 · PITTSFIELD

Melville addressed this letter "For, The Honorable & Beautiful Lady, The Countess of Hahn-Hahn. — Now at her Castle of Southmount. — " It can be identified as a letter to Sarah Morewood not only by its arch references but by two penciled endorsements. It can be dated on a "Tuesday Evening" after 10 November 1853, the birth date of Anne Rachel Morewood (the "infant Countess Hahn-Hahn" of the letter; see also p. 855 below), and before Christmas of that year. It is here tentatively assigned to the Tuesday (20 December) nearest Christmas.

The original Countess Ida von Hahn-Hahn (1805–80), whose name Melville plays upon in this letter, was a writer of romances, sometimes called the German George Sand. Early divorced from a unfaithful husband, she wrote a series of novels in which the heroine is usually separated from her husband and moves through high society, colliding with artificial conventions and romantically pursuing but never attaining an ideal happiness. The only one of her novels available in English at this time was *Countess Faustina* (London, 1844 and 1845), which was true to this formula and which had been reviewed by Margaret Fuller in the *New-York*

Daily Tribune (12 March 1845), but two volumes of travels had been translated and also a polemical apologia, *From Babylon to Jerusalem* (London, 1851). In 1850 she became a Roman Catholic and shortly thereafter founded a convent in Mainz (without, however, giving up her literary efforts); she was associated with the convent until her death. Her collected works occupy forty-five volumes. Perhaps Sarah Morewood had lent Melville one of the countess's books.

The Lady Brittain to whom Melville sends his regards was Ellen Brittain (1814–97), Sarah Morewood's sister. The "Lady Drew" is unidentified.

(Particularly Private and Exclusively Confidential)

The Hill. Tuesday Evening.

My Lady Countess: — Some months ago a rumor was rife of a Christmas Dinner to be given by your Ladyship at your princely seat of Southmount in the heart of the Hemlock Land. Later there came report of a grand Christmas Eve to be celebrated at the same hospitable castle. Latest of all came report that both a Christmas Day Dinner and a Christmas Eve Supper were to be given by your Ladyship of Southmount.

Bewildered by these various rumors I now presume — but only upon the strength of that not disdainful feeling wherewith you have condescended to honor me — I now presume to set before your Ladyship the following considerations as respects myself, concerning these festivities rumored to be coming at your castle; not — beleive me — flattering myself that they will weigh with you to alter aught, but simply to preinform you of what may be anticipated from this loyal knight.

There are, your Ladyship, three hypotheses:

First: The Christmas Dinner.

Second: The Christmas Eve Supper

Third: The Christmas Day Dinner & the Christmas Eve Supper.

If the first, I shall be delighted to attend.

If the second, I shall deeply regret my inability to do so.

If the third, I shall be delighted to attend the Day-Dinner; but deeply regret my inability to attend the night Supper.

All of which is respectfully submitted to your Ladyship of Southmount by the humble Knight on the Hill.

My most Knightly compliments to your lovely guest the Lady Drew and the charming Lady Brittian, and that sweet heiress of your noble name, the infant Countess Hahn-Hahn.

These are, your Ladyship, three Hypotheses:

First: The Christmas Dinner.

Secon: The Christmas Eve Supper

Third: The Christmas Day Dinner & the Christmas Eve Supper.

Of the first, I shall be delighted to allow.

Of the secon, I shall deeply regret my inability to do so.

Of the third, I shall be delighted to allow the Day-Dinner; but deeply regret my inability to allow the night Supper.

All of which is respectfully submitted to your Ladyship of Southmount by the humble Knight on the Hill.

My most knightly compliments to ~~the~~ your lovely guest the Lady Drew and the charming Lady Brittain, and that sweet heiress of your noble name, the infant Countess Hahn-Hahn.

With due obeisance, & three times kissing of your Ladyship's hand, & salutes to all your Ladyship's household, I am

Dear Lady of Southmount

Your Ladyship's

Knight of the Hill

To Sarah Huyler Morewood, [20 December?] 1853, p. 3 (reduced).
Courtesy of the Berkshire Athenaeum, Pittsfield, Massachusetts.

With due obesiance, & three times kissing of your Ladyships
hands, & salutes to all your Ladyship's household, I am

Dear Lady of Southmount

Your Ladyship's

Knight of the Hill.

ALS, "Knight of the Hill", on a 39.8 × 24.9 cm sheet, folded in half, of white laid paper,
watermarked with the name "MOINIER'S 1849" and embossed with the manufacturer's circular
stamp enclosing the words "UNITED STATES SENATE" and an eagle. Melville inscribed the first
and third pages, in ink. Another hand noted in pencil on the fourth page "H. M. to Mrs J. R.
M" (Mrs. John Rowland Morewood). Melville addressed the unstamped envelope, which
was probably hand-delivered, "For, | The Honorable & Beautiful Lady, | The Countess of
Hahn-Hahn. | — Now at her Castle of Southmount. — "; on it the other hand repeats in
pencil "H. M. to Mrs J. R. M."

LOCATION: Berkshire Athenaeum, Pittsfield, Massachusetts. *Provenance*: Agnes Morewood.

PUBLICATION: Davis-Gilman 108.

TEXTUAL NOTES: Day Dinner &] Day *inserted above caret* · Day-Dinner] Day-|Dinner · com-
pliments to] *before canceled* the · household] *miswritten* houshold

1854

TO GEORGE P. PUTNAM
6 FEBRUARY 1854 · PITTSFIELD

In all likelihood this letter accompanied the submission of "The Encantadas" (probably recast from the "Tortoise Hunting" manuscript). The pieces must have been
quickly accepted, because on 14 February in the *New-York Evening Post* "The Encantadas" was announced as forthcoming; the pieces appeared in the March, April,
and May 1854 issues of *Putnam's* (see the headnote to Melville's letter of 24 November 1853, above, and the NN *Piazza Tales* volume, pp. 492–93). G. P. Putnam &
Co. later donated this letter, along with other letters from their contributors, to an
autograph auction held in Cincinnati in 1864 for the benefit of the Civil War Sanitary Commission. In this auction, where many of the letters sold for less than a dollar, it brought twenty cents and was bought by "R. Clarke" (see the headnote to
the 15 December 1863 letter to George McLaughlin, and also Charles Boynton,
History of the Great Sanitary Western Fair [Cincinnati: Vent, 1864], p. 438).

Pittsfield Feb 6th 1854

George P Putnam Esq:

Herewith I send you 75. pages adapted for a magazine. Should they suit your's, please write me how much in present cash you will give for them.

Very truly Yours
H Melville.

ALS on a 12 × 11 cm part-sheet (cut somewhat unevenly on all but the left edge) of white laid paper with lines. Melville inscribed only one side of the leaf, in ink. Below Melville's letter, another hand (or hands) added the numbers "231", in pencil, and "1214", in ink. Davis-Gilman Unlocated 340a.

LOCATION: Crosby N. Boyd Collection, Library of Congress. *Provenance*: Great Western Sanitary Fair Auction, 15 March 1864, lot 352; Robert Clarke & Co.

TO THOMAS MELVILLE
BETWEEN 14 AND 19 FEBRUARY 1854 · [NEW YORK?]

Unlocated. Melville's youngest brother, Thomas, was by this time a well-traveled officer in the merchant service. In early 1854, he was ashore for a brief period, and Melville inscribed a 1746 edition of *Seneca's Morals* (Sealts 458) to him on 26 January at Pittsfield. By mid-February he was in Boston, staying with their sister Helen in the suburb of Longwood, preparing for another voyage. In a 15 February letter to their sister Augusta at Pittsfield, Tom reported that he had written "yesterday" to "Herman, Allan, and Sophia" (see LETTERS RECEIVED, p. 633). Melville apparently answered Tom's letter, for on 19 February, before sailing, Tom wrote again to Augusta at Pittsfield, asking her to "Give my Best love to Herman and Lizzy thank them for their kind letters and that I am sorry that I shall not be able to answer them" (NYPL-GL). The ship Tom sailed on at this time was the *Meteor*, the ship on which in 1860 Melville would join him—by then promoted to captain—and sail to San Francisco (see Melville's September 1860 letters to his children Malcolm and Elizabeth, below).

TO HARPER & BROTHERS
[20?] FEBRUARY 1854 · PITTSFIELD

Possibly because of the fire of 10 December 1853 at the Harpers' Cliff Street establishment (which destroyed, among other things, 2,300 bound and unbound copies—but not the plates—of Melville's books), the firm did not pressure Melville for a final manuscript of his "Tortoise" book nor did they require him to repay their advance on it. Perhaps thinking that in the wake of the fire the Harper firm would be unable or slow to publish his projected book, Melville had apparently already reshaped some of his "Tortoise" material into "The Encantadas" for *Putnam's Monthly Magazine* (see the headnote to his 6 February 1854 letter to Putnam, above). As a result, he was preparing these sketches for publication in *Putnam's* at the time he wrote this letter to the Harpers. However, his subsequent letters of 25 May and 22 June to them attest that he still planned to supply a "Book" on tortoise-hunting if the firm was willing to accept it.

With the original manuscript of this letter now unlocated, its date remains uncertain. Jay Leyda transcribed the letter with the date 20 February 1854 (*Log*, I, 485), but Eleanor Metcalf dated it 29 February (pp. 152–53). Since there was not a twenty-ninth day in February 1854 and since Metcalf may not have seen the original document, Leyda's date is tentatively adopted here.

Feb: 20th 1854

Harper & Brothers
Gentlemen: —
　　When I procured the advance of $300 from you upon the "Tortoises" or "Tortoise Hunting", I intimated that the work would be ready for press some time in January. I have now to express my concern, that, owing to a variety of causes, the work, unavoidably, was not ready in that month, & still requires additional work to it, ere completion. But in no sense can you loose by the delay.

　　I shall be in New York in the course of a few weeks; when I shall call upon you, & inform you when these proverbially slow "Tortoises" will be ready to crawl into market.

Very truly yours
H. Melville

Original document not located. Text from Jay Leyda's 1948 typed transcription (in Davis-Gilman file) from the ALS, then in the collection of Dr. A. S. W. Rosenbach of Philadelphia (Davis and Gilman were already unable to locate it in this collection in 1959).

LOCATION: at present unknown. *Provenance*: James F. Drake, catalogue 76 (1944), item 187; Dr. A. S. W. Rosenbach.

PUBLICATION: *Log*, I, 482, 485, 486. Davis-Gilman 109.

TO SARAH HUYLER MOREWOOD
[10?] MARCH 1854 · PITTSFIELD

This incompletely dated letter thanks Sarah Morewood for Edward Bulwer-Lytton's *The Pilgrims of the Rhine* (London: Tilt, 1840). Either her gift or Melville's letter seems to have been some two months delayed, since she inscribed the book

"Herman Melville From his Friend S. H. Morewood Jan. 1st 1854" (NYPL-GL; Sealts 333). Leather-bound and elaborately embossed with a gilt design, the book contained twenty-seven engraved illustrations, many of places Melville had seen on his 1849 trip to the Rhine, including Drachenfels, Ehrenbreitstein, and the Tomb of the Three Kings (see *Journals*, pp. 36–38).

Melville's dating "Day of Ill Luck — Friday. March &c" is now unclear. Since the tradition of Friday the thirteenth was apparently not established until later (see Iona Opie and Moira Tatem, *A Dictionary of Superstitions* [Oxford: Oxford University Press, 1989], which cites 1908 as the earliest printed reference to it), and since the thirteenth did not fall on Friday in March 1854, Melville's reference was probably to the superstition that held all Fridays unlucky, which was well established by then (see E. Cobham Brewer, *Dictionary of Phrase and Fable* [New York: Cassel, 1892]; see also Melville's [29 August 1856?] letter to Sarah Morewood). Conceivably his vague "March &c" refers to 10 March, the Friday in 1854 within the seven-day period before 15 March broadly known as the notoriously unlucky Ides of March.

Melville's comment on his handwriting is facetious; no improvement is discernible in the letter.

Day of Ill Luck — Friday. March &c

Dear Mrs Morewood

(See how my hand improves as the name is traced — compare, I say the writing of the second line with the first)

Madam: —

The Pilgrims come, not as of old with staff and scrip, but splendidly gilt like kings. A superstitious, a fanciful mind might almost, by anticipation, distrust the wisdom taught by a book so bound. But ——

The engravings are beautiful, & I have enjoyed them much. No doubt too, pictures equally fine will be found in the text when I come to read it — which will not be long from now.

H Melville

ALS on a 12.6 × 19.1 cm part-sheet (torn along the left edge) of blue laid paper with lines, embossed with the manufacturer's small oblong stamp of flourishes connected at four points. Melville inscribed both sides of the leaf, in ink.

LOCATION: Berkshire Athenaeum, Pittsfield, Massachusetts. *Provenance*: Agnes Morewood.

PUBLICATION: Davis-Gilman 110.

TO ALLAN MELVILLE
BEFORE 17 MARCH 1854 · PITTSFIELD

Unlocated. In his [20?] February 1854 letter to Harper & Brothers, Melville indicated that he would be in New York "in the course of a few weeks." On 17 March
1854 Augusta Melville at Pittsfield wrote to her sister Frances Priscilla, who was
visiting in Lawrence, reporting that Melville was "making preparations to go down
to New York, that is he is getting his M.S. ready (not *the book*, for the Harpers
owing to the two fires, are not in a situation to publish it now) but Magazine articles &c; & has written Allan that he will probably leave here within a fortnight"
(NYPL-GL). For more about "*the book*" and the first fire on 10 December 1853 at
Harpers, see the headnote to Melville's [20?] February 1854 letter, above; the second
fire occurred on 5 March 1854 at a printer's on Spruce Street, where the Harpers
had sent some of their work after the December fire (see Eugene Exman, *The Brothers Harper* [New York: Harper & Row, 1965], pp. 353–62).

TO SOPHIA THURSTON MELVILLE
BEFORE 26 MARCH 1854 · PITTSFIELD

Unlocated. Melville's trip to New York (see the entry just above) was evidently
delayed by bad weather. On 27 March Melville's cousin Priscilla Melvill, who was
visiting at Arrowhead, wrote to Lemuel Shaw: "*We — that is —* Lizzie, Augusta,
Herman, the little folks, & myself are driven to the necessity of being *very* amiable,
and *obliged* to play the agreeable for mutual entertainment — *within* doors — for the
weather continues very severe, gales, and snow storms prevail" (MHS-S). Melville
had apparently written to Allan's wife, Sophia, arranging to stay with them in New
York at the end of March, for on 26 March Sophia wrote to Augusta at Pittsfield
inquiring, "What has become of Herman we have been expecting for several days.
His room is ready for him. I received a comical letter from him, advising me of his
proposed visit." She went on jokingly, "I suppose he did not expect any answer,
for it would never do to have the 'Argus eyes' of *that Lizzie* scanning the contents,
for of course I should write in the same affectionate strain, and I should fear the
indignation of the 'Lamb' " (NYPL-GL). As the 9 April 1854 letter to Richard
Lathers (just below) indicates, Melville was in New York by early April.

TO RICHARD LATHERS
9 APRIL 1854 · NEW YORK

Dated only "Sunday April 9th," this letter, which extends an invitation to visit the
Melville home in Pittsfield, can be placed in 1854, since that is the only year in
which Sunday fell on the ninth of April while Melville lived in the Berkshires.
Clearly, however, Melville wrote it while visiting his brother Allan in New York.
   Richard Lathers (1820–1903) was closely linked with the Melvilles through his
marriage in 1846 to Abby Pitman Thurston (1821–1904), the oldest sister of Allan
Melville's first wife, Sophia Thurston Melville. A Southerner by birth, he was a

wealthy New York insurance executive with a large library at his estate (Winyah) outside New Rochelle, where Melville often visited (a 19 June 1853 letter from Allan's wife Sophia to Augusta Melville [NYPL-GL] reports, for example, that Melville had recently been to Winyah twice, staying three days the second time). Lathers's posthumously published autobiography, *Reminiscences of Richard Lathers* (New York: Grafton Press, 1907), mentions his encounters with Melville at Evert Duyckinck's in New York and later at Pittsfield, where he and his wife often visited before buying several farms near Arrowhead and Broadhall, on which they built a house named Abby Lodge, to which they moved in 1869. See also p. 855 below.

The first of the volumes Melville names of those he had borrowed from Lathers's library was evidently an edition of Coleridge's *The Friend: A Series of Essays*, originally published in 1818 (Sealts 154a). The second volume he names—"the Essays of Combe &c."—Sealts has conjectured to be George Combe's *Essays on Phrenology* (Philadelphia: Carey & Lea, 1822?; Sealts 156b); this volume also contained translations of essays by Gall and Spurzheim, which may explain Melville's "&c." (A work by the eighteenth-century satirist William Combe [1741-1823] is another possible explanation of Melville's reference.)

Sunday April 9th

My Dear Fellow: —

I purposed inviting myself out to Winyah for a day or so — but have been prevented. Tomorrow I go home. So I can not, in person, return the books I borrowed from your library. Allan has them, & upon his next trip to Winyah will take them along.

By the way — did I get *two* or *three* volumes? I made a Mem: at the time, but have mislaid it. I return "The Friend" & the Essays of Combe &c. When I get home I will look particularly among my books, and see if my impression is correct about having had *three* volumes.

I hope we shall see you in Pittsfield this summer. Come & *stay with us* a few days. You & Mrs: Lathers. We shall all be delighted to see you. No fudge — but bona fide.

My best remembrances to the household of Winyah.

Thine
H Melville

Colonel Richard Lathers
Lord of Winyah.

ALS on a 25.6 × 19.8 cm sheet, folded in half, of white laid paper, embossed with the manufacturer's small oblong stamp of flourishes connected at four points. Melville inscribed the first and third pages, in ink. Another hand noted on the fourth page "*h. Melville*".

LOCATION: Rare and Manuscript Collections, Cornell University Library.

PUBLICATION: Lynn Horth, "Letters Lost / Letters Found: A Progress Report on Melville's *Correspondence*," *Melville Society Extracts* 81 (May 1990), 1–8 (with reproduction on p. 6).

TEXTUAL NOTES: trip to Winyah] W *rewritten* · "The] T *written over* t

TO CHARLES F. BRIGGS
BETWEEN 12 AND 16 MAY 1854 · PITTSFIELD

Unlocated. In his 16 May 1854 letter to George P. Putnam (just below), Melville stated that he had already written to *Putnam's* editor Charles F. Briggs, replying to a 12 May 1854 letter from Briggs rejecting "The Two Temples." See LETTERS RECEIVED, pp. 636–39, and the headnote to the letter just below, for more about the correspondence surrounding Melville's controversial piece.

TO GEORGE P. PUTNAM
16 MAY 1854 · PITTSFIELD

This letter to George Putnam was prompted by two letters Melville had received—the first a 12 May 1854 letter from *Putnam's* editor Charles F. Briggs, rejecting "The Two Temples" because of what he called its "pungent satire" of Grace Church, and the second a 13 May letter from George P. Putnam himself apologizing for the rejection and tactfully asking Melville for a daguerreotype for use in a current series of portraits in the magazine (for both letters, see LETTERS RECEIVED, pp. 636–39). Neither an engraving from a daguerreotype of Melville (see his earlier 12 February 1851 letter refusing to furnish one to Duyckinck) nor "The Two Temples" was published in *Putnam's*. For this unpublished piece, see the NN *Piazza Tales* volume, pp. 303–15 and 700–709.

Pittsfield May 16th 1854

Dear Sir —

I have your note about the "Two Temples". And in reply to a line from Mr Briggs have written him concerning the Article. — About the Dagguerreotype, I dont know a good artist in this rural neighborhood. — Ere long I will send down some other things, to which, I think, no objections will be made on the score of tender consciences of the public.

Truly yours
H Melville

George P Putnam Esq
New York.

ALS on a 25.3 × 19.9 cm sheet, folded in half, of white laid paper, embossed with the manufacturer's small oblong stamp of flourishes connected at four points. Melville inscribed the
first page, in ink, and there is a random ink stroke on the fourth page.

LOCATION: Collection of William Reese. *Provenance*: Goodspeed's Bookstore; Paul C. Richards, catalogue 68 (1970), item 1 (with reproduction); Seven Gables Bookshop; William
Stockhausen sale, Sotheby Parke Bernet, sale 3694, 19–20 November 1974, lot 345; Seven
Gables Bookshop; H. Bradley Martin sale, Sotheby's, New York, sale 5971, 30–31 January
1990, lot 2169.

PUBLICATION: Lynn Horth, "Letters Lost / Letters Found: A Progress Report on Melville's
Correspondence," *Melville Society Extracts* 81 (May 1990), 1–8 (with reproduction on p. 3).

TEXTUAL NOTE: George] ge *rewritten*

TO CATHERINE MELVILLE HOADLEY
BEFORE 25 MAY 1854 · PITTSFIELD

Unlocated. A 25 May 1854 letter from Catherine Hoadley to Augusta Melville in
Pittsfield includes an oblique reference to a joke Melville had played by apparently
switching two letters he had written to his sisters Catherine and Helen: "What possessed Herman to send my letter to Helen, & hers to me, how we did laugh over it.
I received such a comical letter from George [Griggs], enclosing mine. He did it for
a joke I know. I told John [Hoadley] that I knew he had written to both of us, &
enclosed them so on purpose" (NYPL-GL). (Helen had married George Griggs on
5 January 1854; for Griggs, see the headnote to Melville's 17 July 1852 letter to
Hawthorne.) Since both of these letters remain unlocated the exact nature of the
joke remains unexplained.

TO HELEN MELVILLE GRIGGS
BEFORE 25 MAY 1854 · PITTSFIELD

Unlocated. As the preceding entry indicates, Melville also wrote a humorous letter
to his sister Helen (who had recently moved to a new home in Longwood, Massachusetts) and then mailed it to their sister Catherine. This is probably the letter that
prompted Helen's 29 May reply (see LETTERS RECEIVED, pp. 639–41). From that
reply, it is possible to infer several of the topics touched upon in Melville's letter.
Helen quickly rejects with good humor what was apparently Melville's recommendation that she read " 'Plutarch on the Cessation of the Oracles' " ("Why the Oracles Cease to Give Answers"; Sealts 404.2). She then comments on what must have
been Melville's wry descriptions of the spring housecleaning at Arrowhead. And
she reports, at Melville's request, on her husband's recovering health at that time.
Oddly enough, Helen's reply makes no mention of Melville's joke of switching his
two letters, but it does make plain that she had neither received a letter from her
brother nor written to him in quite some time. So it seems unlikely that the joke
involved a separate, but recent, second letter.

Melville's letter is also probably the same one Helen later referred to when writing to her sister Augusta at Pittsfield. Complaining that she had had no letters from home, she briefly stated, "it is more than three weeks since Herman's letter reached me" (NYPL-GL). Although Helen's letter to Augusta is dated only "Tuesday evening," it probably belongs to Tuesday, 13 June, since Helen comments that she wrote it the very day she received a letter from Augusta. According to Augusta's notation on Helen's 29 May letter to Melville, Augusta had answered Helen's enclosure with the 29 May letter (addressed to "Gus, Fan, and Lizzie") on Monday, 12 June (next-day mail delivery would not have been unusual at this time, particularly since George Griggs brought the letter home from the city). Clearly Helen's letter was written not long before the appearance in *Putnam's* of *Israel Potter: . . . A Fourth of July Story*, for she writes to Augusta: "I shall be quite wild to make the acquaintance of 'Israel Potter,' and to have the Fourth of July come. I shall make George procure me *my* Independence namely — a new novel & a paper of candy. I wish I could help you with your copying, dear, but I can sympathise in your state of entire employment" (NYPL-GL). The serialization of *Israel Potter* began in *Putnam's* in July 1854 (the book form was not published until March 1855). Whether Melville himself had written Helen about *Israel Potter* in his letter is not indicated.

TO HARPER & BROTHERS
25 MAY 1854 · PITTSFIELD

The one hundred dollars Melville acknowledged in this letter must, according to Merton M. Sealts, Jr. (NN *Piazza Tales* volume, pp. 485–86), have been a payment not only for "The Paradise of Bachelors and the Tartarus of Maids" (April 1855) but also for the entire group of contributions (possibly designated here by his "&c.") that began to appear in *Harper's* in the spring and summer of 1854. These pieces were "Poor Man's Pudding and Rich Man's Crumbs" (June 1854), "The Happy Failure" (July 1854), and "The Fiddler" (September 1854). Sealts speculates that since these pieces were probably not set in type far in advance of publication, the payment of one hundred dollars was made on the basis of total wordage. In any case, their final printed total length came to nineteen and a half pages, which would have yielded nearly one hundred dollars at five dollars per printed page—the rate he later requested and received for *Israel Potter* from *Putnam's* (see his 7 June 1854 letter, below).

Melville's reference to his " 'Tortoises' extract" here, taken with his subsequent reference to it in his 22 June letter, indicates that he had sent the Harpers, sometime before this 25 May letter, an extract from his manuscript material (see his 24 November 1853 letter first proposing this unpublished book). Neither the contents of the extract nor a letter that may have accompanied it has been located. Melville's inquiry about publishing a "Serial" suggests that he contemplated also offering them *Israel Potter*, but there is no known further correspondence on the matter. The Harpers may have rejected the idea of a serial, or rejected the book itself, or failed to respond quickly enough (they did not immediately reply to him about his " 'Tortoises' extract" since Melville was still urging them to do so a

month later in his 22 June letter). At any rate, *Putnam's*, not *Harper's*, published
Israel Potter serially, beginning in July 1854.

Pittsfield May 25ᵗʰ 1854

Harper & Brothers: —
Gentlemen —
    I have received your letter enclosing $100 on acct: of the "Para-
dise of Batchelors &c."
    When you write me concerning the "Tortoises" extract, you
may, if you choose, inform me at about what time you would be
prepared to commence the publication of another Serial in your
Magazine — supposing you had one, in prospect, that suited you.
                                                Yours Very Truly
                                                H Melville

By writing soon, on the latter subject, you will greatly oblige me.

ALS on a 12.5 × 19.1 cm part-sheet (torn along the left edge) of blue laid paper with lines,
embossed with the manufacturer's small oblong stamp of flourishes connected at four points.
Melville inscribed only one side of the leaf, in ink. Another hand, presumably a clerk's, noted
on the verso in ink "H. Melville, | May 25ᵗʰ, 1854."

LOCATION: The Pierpont Morgan Library, New York. MA 1950, the Harper Collection.

PUBLICATION: Davis-Gilman 111.

TEXTUAL NOTE: Magazine] *miswritten* Magainze

TO GEORGE P. PUTNAM
7 JUNE 1854 · PITTSFIELD

The original manuscript of this letter offering *Israel Potter* to *Putnam's* is now unlocated, but it was published by George Haven Putnam in the 1903 privately printed
memoir of his father (see under publication, below). The date "July 7, 1854" given
in that publication is incorrect, because *Israel Potter* had already begun serialization
in the magazine's July number. That date has been emended here to 7 June—before
Putnam's 10 June reply, now unlocated, which is cited in Melville's following 12
June letter assenting to Putnam's counter-offer for *Israel Potter*. The discovery of
Melville's 12 June letter obviates the speculations about this 7 June letter in the NN
edition of that work, pp. 181–84. As Melville's 12 June letter also indicates, Putnam
did not comply with all of Melville's terms proposed here. The work was published
in *Putnam's* in nine installments, July 1854 through March 1855, and ran to 82¼
pages; five were less than 10 pages.

Pittsfield, June 7, 1854

George P. Putnam, Esq.

Dear Sir: I send you prepaid by Express, to-day, some sixty and odd pages of MSS. The manuscript is part of a story called "Israel Potter," concerning which a more particular understanding need be had. . . .

This story when finished will embrace some 300 or more MS. pages. I propose to publish it in your Magazine at the rate of five dollars per printed page, the copyright to be retained by me. Upon the acceptation of this proposition (if accepted) $100. to be remitted to me as an advance. After that advance shall have been cancelled in the course of publication of the numbers, the price of the subsequent numbers to be remitted to me upon each issue of the Magazine as long as the story lasts. Not less than the amount of ten printed pages (but as much more as may be usually convenient) to be published in one number.

On my side, I guarantee to provide you with matter for at least ten printed pages in ample time for each issue. I engage that the story shall contain nothing of any sort to shock the fastidious. There will be very little reflective writing in it; nothing weighty. It is adventure. As for its interest, I shall try to sustain that as well as I can. . . .

Very truly yours,
Herman Melville.

Original document not located. Text from first publication (P), emended by NN.

PUBLICATION: George H. Putnam (P), *A Memoir of George Palmer Putnam* (2 vols., New York and London: Putnam [privately printed], 1903), I, 319. Davis-Gilman 112.

TEXTUAL NOTES: June] NN *(see the headnote)*; July • to-day] to- | day • had. . . .] *ellipses are in* P • can. . . .] *ellipses are in* P

TO GEORGE P. PUTNAM
12 JUNE 1854 • PITTSFIELD

Although Putnam did not agree in his now unlocated 10 June letter to grant Melville the advance for *Israel Potter* requested in Melville's 7 June letter, he did make him monthly payments at five dollars a printed page, normally *Putnam's* highest rate to authors (for Melville's drawing on *Putnam's* for an installment of *Israel Potter* see his 25 November 1854 letter). Melville's full return for the magazine publication of the work was $421.50 (see the NN *Israel Potter*, pp. 206–7). Putnam later availed himself of the "privilege" of publishing the work in book form, but evidently chose not to change the terms of payment from twelve and one-half percent to half-profits (see the headnote to Melville's 21 August 1855 letter to Putnam).

Melville's abbreviation "L.R. Man" (miswritten with an extra "R.") refers to "The Lightning-Rod Man," which was published with the second installment of *Israel Potter* in the August number of *Putnam's*. Although a Putnam's ledger (now unlocated) showed Melville receiving a payment of eighteen dollars for the three-page piece in August (see the NN *Piazza Tales* volume, p. 598), it must have been that payment which was advanced to him in June, perhaps in an effort to offset the Putnam decision not to advance Melville one hundred dollars for *Israel Potter*.

Pittsfield, Monday, 12th June

Dear Sir: — Yours of the 10th is received. Tho' I should have preferred receiving the $100 at once, yet I am willing to consider the arrangement as closed, conceding to you the refusal of the privilege of subsequent publication of the thing in book form. For 12½% however, I should prefer half-profits. There may be no difference; but, 12½% does not seem much.

I acknowledge the receipt of the cash for the L.R. Man.

Very Truly Yours

H Melville

G. P. Putnam Esq
New York.

ALS on a 25 × 19.1 cm sheet, folded in half, of blue laid paper, embossed with the manufacturer's small oblong stamp of flourishes connected at four points. Melville inscribed the first page, in ink.

LOCATION: Collection of Bruce Lisman. *Provenance:* Samuel T. Freeman, 19 February 1941, lot 247; Pierre S. duPont III sale, Christie's, 8 October 1991, lot 174.

TEXTUAL NOTE: L.R.] *miswritten* L.R.R.

TO HARPER & BROTHERS
22 JUNE 1854 · PITTSFIELD

This letter contains Melville's last known inquiry about the prospects for publishing extracts from his projected book, here titled *Tortoise Hunters*. For Melville's earlier correspondence with Harper & Brothers about the matter, see his letters of 24 November 1853, [20?] February 1854, and 25 May 1854, above. See also the 25 July [1854?] letter to the Harpers, below.

Pittsfield June 22ᵈ 1854

Gentlemen: — You have not as yet favored me with your views as to the Extract from the *Tortoise Hunters* I sent you.

I am desirous to learn your views with regard to that Extract, so as to know whether it be worth while to prepare further Extracts for you, at present.

Though it would be difficult, if not impossible, for me to get the entire Tortoise Book ready for publication before Spring, yet I can pick out & finish parts, here & there, for prior use. But even this is not unattended with labor; which labor, of course, I do not care to undergo while remaining in doubt as to its recompence.

Be so good therefore by an early reply to releive my uncertainty.

Very Truly Yours
H. Melville.

Harper & Brothers
New York.

ALS on a 25 × 19.1 cm sheet, folded in half, of blue laid paper with lines, embossed with the manufacturer's small oblong stamp of flourishes connected at four points. Melville inscribed the first and third pages, in ink. Another hand, presumably a clerk's, noted in ink on the fourth page *"H. Melville"*.

LOCATION: The Pierpont Morgan Library, New York. MA 1950, the Harper Collection.

PUBLICATION: Davis-Gilman 113.

TEXTUAL NOTES: care to] *before* (over) *in bottom margin* · doubt] *altered from* dout

TO HARPER & BROTHERS
25 JULY [1854?] · PITTSFIELD

Although Melville did not give its year, this brief letter can be tentatively dated 1854 by its association with the sequence of letters of 25 May, 22 June, and 18 September of that year. All were written in black ink on blue, lined paper (see the manuscript descriptions). On the basis of this assumption, Merton M. Sealts, Jr., speculates that the "M.S.S." in this letter must have been "parts, here & there" of Melville's projected tortoise-hunting book (see Melville's 22 June 1854 letter, just above) rather than new magazine pieces, since Melville's final contributions to *Harper's*—"Jimmy Rose" (November 1855) and "The 'Gees" (March 1856)—were not ready for submission until September 1854 (NN *Piazza Tales* volume, p. 490).

Pittsfield July 25th

Harper & Brothers: —

Gentlemen —

Tomorrow there will leave here a parcel from me containing M.S.S. for you — by Express.

Yours Truly

H. Melville

ALS on a 25 × 19.1 cm sheet, folded in half, of blue laid paper with lines, embossed with the manufacturer's small oblong stamp of flourishes connected at four points. Melville inscribed the first page, in ink.

LOCATION: The Pierpont Morgan Library, New York. MA 1950, the Harper Collection.

PUBLICATION: Davis-Gilman 114.

TEXTUAL NOTE: 25th] *above canceled* 24th

TO GEORGE P. PUTNAM
16 AUGUST [1854?] · PITTSFIELD

This brief letter, lacking the year in its heading, presumably refers to a work that was already expected by Putnam. The most likely such item would have been a further installment in Melville's serial publication of *Israel Potter*, which had begun in *Putnam's* in the July 1854 issue. However, it may refer to an installment of "Bartleby," which appeared in the November and December 1853 issues (see the NN *Piazza Tales* volume, p. 492); therefore its dating must remain tentative.

Pittsfield Aug 16th

Dear Sir:

By Express there will leave here tomorrow a parcel of M.S. for you.

Yours Truly

H Melville

G. P. Putnam Esq

ALS on a 12.6 × 16.3 cm part-sheet (torn along the left edge and trimmed along the remaining three edges) of blue laid paper with lines, embossed with the manufacturer's small oblong stamp of flourishes connected at four points. Melville inscribed only one side of the leaf, in ink. The penciled word "autograph" has been partially cut off at the bottom of the verso, which was pasted at four points to another sheet at one time, but has now been detached.

LOCATION: NYPL–Miscellaneous Papers. *Provenance*: Gordon Lester Ford; J. P. Morgan.

PUBLICATION: Lynn Horth, "Letters Lost / Letters Found: A Progress Report on Melville's *Correspondence*," *Melville Society Extracts* 81 (May 1990), 1–8.

TEXTUAL NOTE: 16] *above canceled* 14

TO HARPER & BROTHERS
18 SEPTEMBER 1854 · PITTSFIELD

This letter can be placed in 1854 by the notation, in another hand, on the verso. Merton M. Sealts, Jr., conjectures that Melville's two final contributions to *Harper's*—"Jimmy Rose" (November 1855) and "The 'Gees" (March 1856)—may have been the "brace of fowl" that Melville submitted to Harper & Brothers with this letter (see the NN *Piazza Tales* volume, p. 486).

Pittsfield
Sept: 18th

Gentlemen:
  I send you by Express a brace of fowl — wild fowl.
  Hope you will like the flavor.

Yours Truly
H. Melville

Harper & Brothers.

ALS on a 12.5 × 19.1 cm part-sheet (torn along the left edge) of blue laid paper with lines, embossed with the manufacturer's small oblong stamp of flourishes connected at four points. Melville inscribed only one side of the leaf, in ink. Another hand, presumably a clerk's, noted on the verso in ink "H. Melville | Sept. 18, 1854 — ".

LOCATION: The Pierpont Morgan Library, New York. MA 1950, the Harper Collection.

PUBLICATION: Davis-Gilman 116.

TO GEORGE P. PUTNAM
31 OCTOBER 1854 · PITTSFIELD

In his subsequent 3 November 1854 letter to Putnam, Melville refers to a letter written the "Day before yesterday" (1 November 1854) notifying Putnam to expect twenty-five more pages of *Israel Potter* manuscript. Even though this letter is dated 31 October and anticipates "about thirty more pages of M.S.," it is almost certainly the one referred to in his 3 November letter. Putnam's unlocated letter of 22 October had apparently requested a page estimate.

The discovery of this 31 October letter and the 9 November letters to Putnam (below) confirms the speculation in the NN edition (p. 206) that Melville was finishing the story at this time. Despite his statement at this point (i.e., after the first four installments, through chap. 13) about there being no errors in the magazine printing "worth correcting," there were some forty-five corrections in the book edition (seven in the first thirteen chapters). This statement on Melville's part lends some support to the suggestion in the NN edition (pp. 245–47) that a careful reader at Putnam's could have made the corrections, and that Melville did little, if any, revising in the book edition, apart from changes in the "title-page, preface &c."

Pittsfield Oct: 31st

Dear Sir: — Yours of the 22^d was received, and should have been answered before, had I been earlier able to give an explicit reply.

The story of 'Potter' will be completed in about thirty more pages of M.S. which I shall send you in a week or so.

You are correct with respect to the understanding you speak of about the terms in case of publication in book form.

Whenever you shall have actually put the book to press, if you will have the kindness to write me to that effect, I will supply you with title-page, preface &c

There seem no errors of the press (in the Magazine) worth correcting.

Truly Yours
H Melville

G. P. Putnam Esq
New York

ALS on a 24.9 × 13 cm sheet, folded in half, of blue laid paper with lines. Melville inscribed the first and third pages, in ink. The top right corner is faded from water damage. The letter is mounted in an album with shaken green cloth binding, one of seven albums of Putnam letters probably put together at some later date. The album in which Melville's letters were placed (see also his 9 November [1854?] and 25 November 1854 letters, below) contains primarily letters from minor writers, many of them requesting the return of rejected manuscripts. His letters were not included in the three extra-illustrated Putnam albums that contain letters from Cooper, Irving, Hawthorne, Emerson, Longfellow, Duyckinck, Mrs. Sigourney, and other "prominent" figures of the period. Davis-Gilman Unlocated 341 (dated 1 November 1854).

LOCATION: Firestone Library, Princeton University. *Provenance*: Swann Galleries, sale 1555, 14 March 1991, in lot 16.

TEXTUAL NOTES: should] sh *rewritten* • form.] *before* (over) *in bottom margin*

TO GEORGE P. PUTNAM
3 NOVEMBER 1854 · PITTSFIELD

Melville's reference in this letter to a "returned M.S." remains problematic. It may have been an early draft of a proposed work that had been accepted—in which case it had been returned for completion. On the other hand, it may have been either an early draft or a completed manuscript that had been rejected (e.g., Melville's "Two Temples" manuscript; see his 16 May 1854 letter to Putnam, above). It was probably not a manuscript of an already published work returned as a souvenir, since there is no evidence of *Putnam's* returning Melville's manuscripts in any other case after publication (see, however, Melville's later 22 May 1860 instructions to his brother Allan, which specify that the manuscript of his poetry be returned by whatever publisher Allan engaged).

Pittsfield, Nov: 3ᵈ 1854

Dear Sir: The returned M.S. is received; also the note accompanying it, in which you allude to I. Potter. — Day before yesterday I wrote you on that subject. But there was an error in my note; which I now rectify, that it may not cause you future trouble.

I said in my note that there would be some 25 more pages of M.S. — It should have been forty five — 45.

I will send it all down in a few days.

Truly Yours
H Melville

G. P. Putnam Esq.
New York.

ALS on a 12.5 × 19.1 cm part-sheet (torn along the left edge) of blue laid paper, faintly embossed with the manufacturer's small oblong stamp of flourishes connected at four points. Melville inscribed only one side of the leaf, in ink.

LOCATION: Butler-Gunsaulus Collection, Regenstein Library, University of Chicago. *Provenance*: Adrian H. Joline sale, Anderson Galleries, sale 1132, 23–24 February 1915, in lot 348; Edward B. Butler.

PUBLICATION: Davis-Gilman 117.

TO GEORGE P. PUTNAM
9 NOVEMBER [1854?] · PITTSFIELD

In preparing to send Putnam the final chapters of *Israel Potter*, Melville may have mailed this letter separately to announce the imminent arrival of the parcel (as in his 16 August [1854?] letter to Putnam, above). Although this letter states that the parcel will leave "tomorrow," 10 November, Melville's letter accompanying the final chapters is also dated 9 November (just below). While this letter announcing a "parcel" could conceivably belong to November 1853 when Melville may have been sending some other piece, it was written, like the second 9 November letter, which clearly belongs to 1854, on the same lined, white Carson's paper.

Pittsfield
9th Nov:

Dear Sir —
I send you a parcel by Express leaving here tomorrow

Yours Truly
H Melville

G. P. Putnam Esq.

ALS on a 12.9 × 20.1 cm part-sheet (torn along the left edge) of white laid paper with lines, embossed with the manufacturer's small oblong stamp of flourishes connected at four points, enclosing the name "CARSON'S". Melville inscribed only one side of the leaf, in ink. It is mounted in the same album as Melville's 31 October 1854 letter (for that album, see the manuscript description of that letter). Between the two letters, there are five intervening album pages with letters by other individuals with surnames that also begin with "M."

LOCATION: Firestone Library, Princeton University. *Provenance*: Swann Galleries, sale 1555, 14 March 1991, in lot 16.

TO GEORGE P. PUTNAM
9 NOVEMBER 1854 · PITTSFIELD

Although Melville did not give its year, this letter can be placed in 1854, when his only serial work with "chapters" published by Putnam, *Israel Potter*, was being completed. Putnam's earlier "request" of 7 November 1854 is unlocated. Possibly the publisher needed the completed work in connection with production of the book; the last installment of *Israel Potter* did not appear in the magazine until March 1855, but Putnam's issued it in book form that same month (see the letter just above for a possible announcement that this parcel of manuscript chapters was about to be shipped).

Pittsfield, Nov: 9th

Dear Sir: —
I hasten to comply with the request in yours of the 7th received last evening. I am sorry there should have been need of it.
Herewith you have the affair to the Finis.

Having forgotten the number of the last chapter sent you, I leave the numbering of the following ones to the printer.

Truly Yours
H Melville

G. P. Putnam Esq.
New York.

ALS on a 25.8 × 20.1 cm sheet, folded in half, of white laid paper with lines, embossed with the manufacturer's small oblong stamp of flourishes connected at four points, enclosing the name "CARSON'S". Melville inscribed the first page, in ink.

LOCATION: Cincinnati Historical Society. *Provenance*: Albert W. Whelpley.

TO GEORGE P. PUTNAM
25 NOVEMBER 1854 · PITTSFIELD

Anticipating the payment he would receive for the December segment of *Israel Potter*, Melville apparently drew sixty dollars on his Putnam's account. The Putnam ledger recorded that Melville's actual payment for that segment was fifty dollars (see the NN *Israel Potter*, p. 207).

Pittsfield
Nov. 25th 1854

Gentlemen:
I have taken the liberty to draw on you to day at this day's sight for Sixty Dollars ($60) about which sum will probably be due in Dec: No. of Israel Potter.

Truly yours
H Melville

G. P. Putnam & Co.
New York

Original document not located. Text from an offset that appears vertically on half of the album page now facing Melville's 9 November [1854?] letter (see above). Two intervening album pages are missing from the quire in which the 9 November letter is mounted. Possibly one or more preceding quires are missing as well. The letter was written in ink and the offset paper size of this letter appears to measure 13.2 × 12.1 cm.

LOCATION (of album): Firestone Library, Princeton University. *Provenance*: Swann Galleries, sale 1555, 14 March 1991, in lot 16.

1855

TO HELEN MELVILLE GRIGGS
BEFORE 14 JANUARY 1855 · PITTSFIELD

Unlocated. This unlocated letter was apparently remarkable not only for its humorous passages, but for its illustrations as well, which few of Melville's surviving letters include (see pp. 353 and 549 for examples of his artwork). Helen Melville Griggs cites it in a 14 January 1855 letter from Longwood to her sister Augusta at Pittsfield: "Herman's letter with the spirited etching as a vignette at the close, afforded us much amusement, George is well acquainted with the unfortunate individual left in the Cimmerian darkness of the dèpot, but until Herman's letter arrived, had no idea that his more happy brother, about to leave it for the opening realms of day, had condescended to bid adieu to the last sojourner in the confines of gloom. He fully reciprocates the love, or respects, whichever sentiment he intended for him, and looking upon him (Herman) as a glorious leader, has followed his illustrious footsteps even to the counter of the Ship-Bread-Baker, where he purchased a half-barrel of the self same flinty abomination; three times a day, he essays to bite, break, soak, or otherwise subdue its innate hardness of nature, and crunches, and munches, the vile concentrated essence of bread-stuff, with so much apparent gusto, that my teeth stand on edge, and my throat feels dry and husky, in pure sympathy with what I imagine to be the state of his chewing & swallowing apparatus. In mercy to his elbows (the *cloth* ones, I mean) and his hands, please get from Herman a full, true, minute, and succinct account of the process of breaking these adamantine biscuits. George proposes that I shall say masticating instead of *chewing* — deglutinating instead of *swallowing* — take your choice" (NYPL-GL). The incidents at the depot may have occurred during November 1854 when Melville and his family were spending Thanksgiving with the Shaws—a time when Melville would have had an opportunity to take the train out from Boston to see his sister and brother-in-law George in Longwood. Helen's letter, however, assumes that these incidents, whenever they occurred, were already well known to her sister (along with the reason both Melville and his brother-in-law were chewing sea biscuits three times a day).

TO DIX & EDWARDS
7 AUGUST 1855 · PITTSFIELD

In March 1855, George P. Putnam, in debt, sold his magazine to Joshua A. Dix and Arthur T. Edwards. They offered full editorship to G. W. Curtis, who declined but agreed to stay on as literary adviser to the new firm (for more on Curtis, see the headnote to Melville's 15 September 1857 letter to him, below). The "article" discussed here was "The Bell-Tower," which Curtis in a 19 June 1855 letter had advised Dix to publish (calling it "too good to lose") and which appeared in the August 1855 issue of *Putnam's* (see the NN *Piazza Tales* volume, pp. 617–18). As the notation on Melville's letter indicates, Dix answered it, but his reply is now unlocated. Presumably he explained the financial arrangements being introduced by the new management of the magazine.

Pittsfield Aug 7th

Gentlemen: — Returning home after a few days abscence I find your letter of Aug 1st enclosing check for $37.50 in payment for article in Aug: No: of Putnam's Magazine. Having previously drawn upon you, and supposing that you have honored the draught, I reenclose your check, regretting that you should have been twice troubled about one affair.

Truly Yours
H Melville

Dix & Edwards
Publishers Putnam's Monthly
N° 10 Park Place. New York.

ALS on a 12.4 × 19 cm part-sheet (cut along the left edge) of blue laid paper with lines, embossed with the manufacturer's small oblong stamp of flourishes connected at four points. Melville inscribed only one side of the leaf, in ink. Dix noted in ink at the top of the letter "I have answered him | Dix"; also another hand added the penciled year "1855" after Melville's partial date in the heading. On the verso another hand, presumably a clerk's, noted in ink "An | H. Melville | Aug 7/55". The letter is now mounted along its left edge to a larger sheet, which bears a notation in pencil "The Bell Tower | Put. Aug. 18".

LOCATION: Rosenbach Museum & Library, Philadelphia. *Provenance*: James Lorimer Graham sale, Parke-Bernet Galleries, sale 1825, 29–30 April 1958, lot 268.

PUBLICATION: Clara Louise Dentler, *A Privately Owned Collection of Letters, Autographs, and Manuscripts with Many Association Items* [Graham Family Collection] (Florence: Spinelli, 1947), partially reproduced in illus. leaf V, verso (but incorrectly identified as Melville's 19 January 1856 letter in the catalogue listing). Davis-Gilman 119.

TO DIX & EDWARDS
10 AUGUST 1855 · PITTSFIELD

This letter responds to the now unlocated letter Joshua A. Dix had written in reply to Melville's 7 August letter (just above) concerning the payment for "The Bell-Tower." The "expences" Melville had paid may have been those for postage. Melville continued to publish articles in *Putnam's Monthly Magazine*, including "Benito Cereno" (October, November, and December 1855); "I and My Chimney" (March 1856); and "The Apple-Tree Table" (May 1856).

Pittsfield Aug 10th 1855.

Gentlemen:

I have just received yours of the 8th. — The explanation explains all. The expences are inconsiderable. I have paid them. I was not aware of your arrangement as to sending your check regularly to contributors on the 1st of the month.

Very Truly Yours

H. Melville

Dix & Edwards
Publisher
N° 10 Park Place
New York.

ALS on a 20 × 24.8 cm part-sheet (torn along the left edge) of white laid paper with lines, embossed with the manufacturer's shield-like stamp, enclosing a figure beneath the name "CARSON'S CONGRESS". Melville inscribed only one side of the leaf, in ink. Another hand later penciled the letter "M" above Melville's salutation. This letter was later mounted along the left edge on a larger sheet with a printed listing of the letter by Walter Benjamin Autographs stapled to it.

LOCATION: NYPL-GL. *Provenance*: Walter Benjamin Autographs, catalogue 621 (December 1942), item 4910.

PUBLICATION: *Log*, II, 505. Davis-Gilman 120.

TO G. P. PUTNAM & CO.
21 AUGUST 1855 · PITTSFIELD

Since the agreement to publish *Israel Potter* in book form has not been located, it is not known what schedule of payments was agreed upon for the work; however, the Putnam account for *Israel Potter*, dated "July 1/55" but not drawn up in full until 8 October, suggests that this letter is requesting what was to be the first payment. The account records that three "editions" of the book had been printed, totaling 3,700 copies, of which 2,577 had been sold at 75 cents each by 1 July. Melville's share was initially figured at 10 percent of the total, or $193.27; but figures added to the original account by an unknown hand make his share $241.58, or 12½ percent, so that $48.31 was still due him (account in HCL-M; for Melville's percentage of 12½, see his 12 June 1854 letter to Putnam, above, and 7 January 1856 letter to Dix & Edwards, below; for a second letter requesting payment for this book, see his letter of 18 February 1856).

Pittsfield Aug 21ˢᵗ
1855.

Gentlemen:

By reference to our Agreement about *Israel Potter*, I see there is to be a payment (by note) during the present month.

Could you conveniently send me the acct: & note by the beginning of next week, and oblige

Yours Faithfully
H Melville

G. P. Putnam & Co
New York

ALS on a 25.2 × 19.1 cm sheet, folded in half, of blue laid paper with lines, embossed with the manufacturer's small oblong stamp of flourishes connected at four points. Melville inscribed the first page, in ink. That page was subsequently used as a practice sheet for penmanship: "Y Yours | Yours Most respectfully | Most | Yours Most | Yours most | respectfully | Yours"; also a flourishing line was drawn through the text of the letter. Another hand, probably a librarian's, later wrote at the bottom in pencil "Herman Melville | author & traveller".

LOCATION: Dreer Collection, Historical Society of Pennsylvania, Philadelphia. *Provenance*: Ferdinand J. Dreer.

PUBLICATION: *Log*, II, 505. Davis-Gilman 121.

TEXTUAL NOTE: oblige] *miswritten* obliges

TO OSMOND TIFFANY
26 AUGUST [1855?] · PITTSFIELD

Osmond Tiffany (1823–95) was at this time a Baltimore merchant with literary aspirations. A contributor to periodicals such as the *Knickerbocker Magazine* and the *Atlantic Monthly*, he published three books, *The Canton Chinese; or, The American's Sojourn in the Celestial Empire* (Boston: Munroe, 1849), *Brandon; or, A Hundred Years Ago. A Tale of the American Colonies* (New York: Stanford & Delisser, 1858), and *Sacred Biography and History; or, Illustrations of the Holy Scriptures* (Springfield: Bill, 1860, and many other printings). Probably Tiffany had written to Melville requesting assistance in finding a publisher for *Brandon*. His preface to the book stated that he had finished the novel three years earlier but had been unable to find anyone to publish it. Washington Irving also answered what was apparently such a request from Tiffany on 15 December 1855 (*Letters* [Boston: Twayne, 1982], IV, 566–67; cf. p. 470). (Both Melville's publisher and Irving's was Putnam.) Tiffany later sent Irving a copy of *Brandon*; whether he sent Melville one is not known. On the basis of Irving's letter, this letter has been tentatively assigned to 1855.

Pittsfield Aug 26

Osmond Tiffany Esq.

My Dear Sir,

 With pleasure I comply with your request, but hardly think that any letter will further your object; still, if the accompanying one can be made of the least service, I shall be happy.

 Wishing you all success in your affair, I am

Very Truly Yours

H Melville

ALS on a 12.6 × 19.2 cm part-sheet (torn along the left edge) of blue laid paper with lines, embossed with the manufacturer's small oblong stamp of flourishes connected at four points. Melville inscribed only one side of the leaf, in ink. Another hand later noted on the back in pencil "Herman Melville | Author of 'Typee' 'Omoo' &c &c | War poetry &c". The letter is now attached at the top to a larger sheet along with a clipping of Grant Overton's article on Melville, "America's Ancient Mariner," from the 15 April 1927 New York *Mentor* (pp. 14–15).

LOCATION: at present unknown. *Provenance*: Charles Goddard Slack; Dawes Memorial Library, Marietta College; Sotheby's, 16 December 1992, item 91 (with reproduction).

PUBLICATION: Gloria Young, "Queries and Answers," *Melville Society Extracts* 47 (September 1981), 10 (with reproduction).

TEXTUAL NOTE: be made] b *written over* m

TO UNKNOWN
26 AUGUST [1855?] · PITTSFIELD

Unlocated. An accompanying letter of recommendation or introduction, probably to a publisher, is cited in Melville's 26 August letter to Osmond Tiffany, just above.

TO GEORGE P. PUTNAM
7 SEPTEMBER 1855 · PITTSFIELD

On 31 August 1855 George P. Putnam, secretary of the New York Book Publishers' Association, began sending some 230 invitations to authors and editors across the country requesting them to attend the "Complimentary Fruit & Flower Festival" (*American Publishers' Circular and Literary Gazette*, I [29 September 1855], 75). To be held at the close of the New York Publishers' Trade Sale, the "Entertainment," as Melville calls it in this noncommittal acknowledgment of the (now unlocated) invitation, was a lavish supper intended to foster good relations between publishers and authors. On 27 September over six hundred guests—including, among others, Irving, Bryant, Seba Smith, the Cary sisters, and Melville's friends the Duyckincks and Dr. Augustus K. Gardner—assembled at the Crystal Palace on Forty-second Street to dine on cold boned turkey, ham, and chicken, and various "ornamental dishes" and pastries designed as a "Monument of Literature," a "Temple of America," and "Serpents destroying Bird's Nest." There were long speeches and numerous toasts but no alcoholic drinks. Melville's name appeared among a list of guests, including Emerson, Dana, and Longfellow, who had sent letters of regret (*American Publishers' Circular*, cited above, p. 75); see the entry for Melville's unlocated letter of regret written before 27 September, below.

Pittsfield Sep: 7th 1855

Dear Sir: I have been honored by an invitation to an Entertainment to be given by the N.Y. Book-Publishers' Association on the 27th Inst: —

If in my power I shall be most happy to be present at so attractive a festival.

Respectfully Yours
H. Melville

G. P. Putnam Esq.
Secretary

ALS on a 25 × 19.1 cm sheet, folded in half, of blue laid paper with lines, embossed with the manufacturer's small oblong stamp of flourishes connected at four points. Melville inscribed the first page, in ink.

LOCATION: NYPL–Book Publishers' Association Collection.

PUBLICATION: (partial) *Log*, II, 507. Davis-Gilman 122.

TO ELIZABETH SHAW MELVILLE
15 SEPTEMBER 1855 · GANSEVOORT

Unlocated. A letter from Melville to his wife written on a Saturday afternoon is cited in the letter Maria Melville wrote to her daughter Augusta the next morning, Sunday, 16 September 1855, and which was enclosed with Melville's letter when it was mailed Monday morning. As Maria Melville's letter records, she and Melville were traveling in upstate New York, visiting various relatives (see the headnote to the letter just below). She remarks that "Herman heard from Lizzie yesterday morning answered it in the afternoon, & shall enclose this, there being no mail until tomorrow morning." Melville's letter may have included some allusion to his desire to return home, since his mother in her letter wrote: "Herman is getting homesick & with his usual restlessness would not have staid so long at Lansingburgh if I had not been with him" (NYPL-GL).

TO PETER GANSEVOORT AND
SUSAN LANSING GANSEVOORT
18 SEPTEMBER 1855 · ALBANY

In mid-September 1855 Melville and his mother took "a few days jaunt," as he writes here, traveling to Lansingburgh, Gansevoort, and Albany. Maria Melville's 16 September 1855 letter (see the entry just above) from Gansevoort indicates that they had originally planned to spend the night in Albany and return to Pittsfield on Wednesday, 19 September, but as her hurried postscript to that letter—written at six A.M. on Monday, 17 September—states, Melville, feeling homesick, "changed his mind," announcing that they would stop in Albany at the home of his uncle Peter and aunt Susan Gansevoort only to dine on Tuesday, 18 September, and take the afternoon train to Pittsfield to arrive home a day early. These plans changed two more times, however, as this penciled letter Melville left at the home of his aunt and uncle indicates.

To
Uncle Peter & Aunt Susan

Mama & I, on our return towards home from a few days jaunt, arrived at the depot here this morning, intending to greet you and dine with you, and then take the afternoon train for Pittsfield. But as it proved very stormy, we thought that, unless it cleared off, we might stay overnight. At any rate, up *here* we came — you were gone — for which, need we say, we felt much regret. However your people have kindly cared for the travelers, so after a pleasant lunch we are off in the afternoon train, spite of the storm.

Affectionately Yours
H. Melvill

Tuesday 18ᵗʰ Sep.
2½ P.M.

ALS on a 24.6 × 19.8 cm part-sheet (torn along the bottom) of white wove paper with lines, embossed with the manufacturer's rectangular stamp enclosing the name "E. H. BEND-ER | ALBANY". The sheet was folded to make two leaves with vertical lines and the manufactur-er's stamp in the lower right corner of the first leaf; Melville inscribed the first page, in pencil, writing across the lines. He addressed the fourth page "Gen. Peter Gansevoort". Peter Gansevoort later noted in ink on that page "1855. Sept — 18 | Note left at our | House by Herman | Melville in our | absence." Another hand noted in pencil on the first page "Sept. 18, 1855".

LOCATION: NYPL-GL.

PUBLICATION: Paltsits, pp. 11–12. Davis-Gilman 123.

TO GEORGE P. PUTNAM
BEFORE 27 SEPTEMBER 1855 · PITTSFIELD

Unlocated. In a 31 September 1855 letter from Longwood, Massachusetts, where she was visiting her daughter Helen Melville Griggs, Maria Melville wrote to her daughter Augusta at Pittsfield, inquiring briefly at the conclusion of her letter: "Did Herman write an apology to the publishers. — 'Fruit Festival[']'" (NYPL-GL). The reference is to the "Complimentary Fruit & Flower Festival," the publishers' dinner to which Melville had been invited (see his 7 September 1855 letter, above, acknowledging the invitation). Since Melville's name appeared on a list of those who had sent letters of regret (*American Publishers' Circular and Literary Gazette*, I [29 September 1855], 75), he evidently did write.

TO HARPER & BROTHERS
8 OCTOBER [1855?] · PITTSFIELD

Lacking any clear indication as to which "article" accompanied this letter, it can be dated only tentatively. It may belong to any of the years between 1853 and 1855 when Melville was submitting short pieces to *Harper's New Monthly Magazine*, but most likely it belongs after March 1854 when Melville is known to have been using the type of blue laid paper on which it is written. Because of the emphasis on receiving a prompt payment, it possibly belongs to 1855 when Melville's financial problems were becoming increasingly serious (see the headnote to his 12 May 1856 letter to Lemuel Shaw, below). If this is true, it may have accompanied "The Apple-Tree Table," which was rejected by the Harpers later that winter (see Melville's 10 December 1855 letter, just below).

Pittsfield Oct: 8th

Gentlemen: — Herewith is an article, which, if it suit, will you, according to what you have said to me, send me the money for, without further trouble to yourselves or me.

Very Truly Yours
H Melville

Harper & Brothers
New York.

ALS on a 25 × 19 cm sheet, folded in half, of blue laid paper with lines, embossed with the manufacturer's small oblong stamp of flourishes connected at four points. Melville inscribed the first page, in ink. Another hand, presumably a clerk's, noted on the fourth page "H. Melville".

LOCATION: Collection of William Reese. *Provenance*: Alfred L. Rose; William Rose II.

TEXTUAL NOTES: Oct:] ct *written over word-start, possibly Au* • money for,] *before canceled* me at

TO HARPER & BROTHERS
10 DECEMBER 1855 · PITTSFIELD

The Harpers apparently responded to this letter of inquiry with a rejection, since "The Apple-Tree Table" was published by *Putnam's* in May 1856. This piece, submitted "Some time ago," may have been sent two months earlier with Melville's 8 October [1855?] letter to the Harpers (just above).

Pittsfield Dec: 10th 1855

Gentlemen:

Some time ago I sent you an Article called the "Apple Tree Table", from which I have not yet heard.

Will you be good enough to enlighten me on this point, and oblige

Yours
Very Truly
H Melville

Harper & Brothers
New York

ALS on a 12.4 × 14.3 cm part-sheet (torn along the left edge and cut at the top and bottom) of blue laid paper with lines. Melville inscribed only one side of the leaf, in ink. The letter is mounted in volume II, p. 86, of the Albert Lee Butler autograph collection.

LOCATION: Butler Collection, Connecticut Historical Society, Hartford. *Provenance*: Albert Lee Butler.

1856

TO UNKNOWN
1856 · PLACE UNKNOWN

Unlocated. Charles De F. Burns's December 1878 *Catalogue of Autographs* (157 Mercer Street, New York) listed as item 304: "MELVILLE, HERMAN. Author of 'Typee,' etc. A.L.S. 1 p. 8 vo. 1856." The price, common for other items in the catalogue, was seventy-five cents. This letter may have been one of the single-page 1856 letters below, or possibly a now unlocated letter.

TO DIX & EDWARDS
7 JANUARY 1856 · PITTSFIELD

This is the first of four known letters dealing with the publication of the book ultimately titled *The Piazza Tales*. Five of the pieces included in that book Melville had earlier published in *Putnam's Monthly Magazine*. Whether Melville had proposed the book in person (perhaps through his brother Allan) or by letter is unknown, but he had made the proposal before 2 January 1856, when G. W. Curtis wrote Joshua A. Dix (HCL-D) that the proposed book would probably not sell well, Melville having lost "his prestige." Nevertheless Curtis advised that Melville would be "a good name on your list" and that Dix probably would not lose much in publishing the book (for more on Curtis, see the headnote to Melville's 15 September 1857 letter to him). Dix accordingly wrote the now unlocated 3 January letter Melville is answering. For the written agreement Melville requests, see the headnote to his 24 March 1856 letter, below; the earlier agreement for *Israel Potter* is unlocated. The numbers of *Putnam's* that Melville lacked were those containing the second of the two installments of "Bartleby" and the second of the three installments of "The Encantadas."

Pittsfield, Jan 7th
1856

Gentlemen: — Yours of 3^d Inst. is received. Since you are disposed to undertake the book, were it not well to have a written Agreement? Such, if you please, you may prepare & send me for signature. I am ready to sign one of the same sort made concerning "I. Potter" with Mr Putnam.

In your note you state *12 per cent* as the terms I mentioned. But I meant to say *12 & ½ per cent;* that is, the same terms as I had for "I Potter"; which was *12 & ½* as I now find *by reference to the Agreement.* Pray, understand me so now.

Upon looking over my set of the Magazine, I find two Nos., that I want, gone: — Dec. N° 1853, & Ap. N° 1854. Will you be kind enough to send those two Nos. to me by mail, so that I can do my share of the work without delay.

Very Respectfully Yours
H. Melville

Dix & Edwards
N° 10 Park Place
New York

ALS on a 23.2 × 18.1 cm sheet, folded in half, of white wove paper watermarked with the script letters "F T". Melville inscribed the first and third pages, in ink. Another hand placed the numeral "16." at the top of the first page in pencil.

LOCATION: HCL-D.

PUBLICATION: Egbert S. Oliver, ed., *The Piazza Tales* (New York: Hendricks House; Farrar Straus, 1948), p. 225. Davis-Gilman 124.

TEXTUAL NOTE: now.] *before* (Over) *in bottom margin*

TO DIX & EDWARDS
19 JANUARY 1856 · PITTSFIELD

After receiving the requested numbers of *Putnam's* (see his 7 January letter, just above) and talking with Joshua A. Dix probably at some point between 7 and 19 January, Melville prepared copy for the printer and returned it with this letter. (For a discussion of some of the "improvements" Melville made in preparing it, see the NN *Piazza Tales* volume, p. 556; see also p. 581 in that volume as well as his 16 February letter, just below, for his later excision of one of the "desirable" notes added to "Benito Cereno" at this time.) Along with this letter he enclosed a sheet bearing his suggested book title, "Benito Cereno & Other Sketches," and a table of contents. For the "Memorandum of Agreement" drawn up by Dix & Edwards for the book, see Melville's 16 February and 24 March letters to them.

Pittsfield Jan 19th 1856.

Gentlemen: Agreeably to our understanding, I have prepared for republication the Articles agreed upon, — which herewith you have.

Aside from ordinary corrections, some few other improvements have been made, and a desirable note or two added.

During my talk with Mr Dix I volunteered something about supplying some sort of prefatory matter, with a new title to the Collection; but upon less immature consideration, judge that both those steps are not only unnecessary, but might prove unsuitable

Enclosed is the Title and Table of Contents.

I have numbered the magazine pages, so as to correspond with the order of the Table of Contents.

About having the author's name on the title-page, you may do as you deem best; but any appending of titles of former works is hardly worth while.

I have not yet received the Agreement to be signed.

Very Truly Yours
H Melville

Dix & Edwards
New York

[Enclosure:]

/ Title /

Benito Cereno
&
Other Sketches

/ Table of Contents /

Benito Cereno
Bartleby
Bell-Tower
Encantadas
Lightning-Rod Man.

ALS on a 23.2 × 17.9 cm sheet, folded in half, of white wove paper. Melville inscribed the first and third pages, in ink. Another hand noted in ink on the fourth page "Author | H. Melville". The enclosure is on an 11.6 × 17.9 cm part-sheet (torn along the left edge) of white wove paper, watermarked with the script letters "F T". Melville inscribed only one side of the leaf, in ink. Both the letter and the enclosure are now mounted along the left edges to one larger sheet.

LOCATION: Rosenbach Museum & Library, Philadelphia. *Provenance*: James Lorimer Graham sale, Parke-Bernet Galleries, sale 1825, 29–30 April 1958, lot 267 (with reproduction).

PUBLICATION: (listed by date only) Clara Louise Dentler, *A Privately Owned Collection of Letters, Autographs, and Manuscripts with Many Association Items* [Graham Family Collection] (Florence: Spinelli, 1947), in item 280. Davis-Gilman 125.

TEXTUAL NOTE: numbered the] *before* (over) *in bottom margin*

TO DIX & EDWARDS
16 FEBRUARY 1856 · PITTSFIELD

At some point after his earlier 19 January letter, Melville again changed his mind about the title and "prefatory matter" for his collection of *Putnam's* pieces and wrote "The Piazza." Possibly this change was prompted by what was either an intervening letter from his publishers or a conversation with them in New York that can be inferred from Melville's comment here about changing the placement of "Bartleby" from its assigned order in the enclosure to his 19 January letter. The six pieces appeared in *The Piazza Tales* in the order Melville listed them here. By this point, Melville may already have received proofs of the five other pieces, since he here asks only for proofs of "The Piazza" (for the now unlocated note appended to the title of "Benito Cereno," see the NN *Piazza Tales* volume, p. 581, and his

earlier 19 January letter). Dix & Edwards drew up the "Memorandum of Agreement," by which they agreed to publish *The Piazza Tales*, allowing Melville the
12½ percent he asked for, and stipulating that he was to have "the manuscript book
... ready for publication by February 20ᵗʰ 1856" (HCL-M). Melville signed one
copy (now unlocated) on 17 March and returned it on 24 March (see his letter of
that date, below); his own copy (now in HCL-M) was endorsed in ink by Allan
Melville with the date "March 7, 1856"—apparently his misreading of "March 17"
in the document.

Pittsfield Feb. 16. 1856

Gentlemen: —

The new title selected for the proposed volume is "*The Piazza
Tales*" and the accompanying piece ("*The Piazza*") as giving that
name to the book, is intended to come first in order. I think, with
you, that "*Bartleby*" had best come next. So that, as amended, the
order will be

> The Piazza
> Bartleby
> Benito Cereno
> Lightning-Rod Man
> Encantadas
> Bell Tower.

In the corrected magazine sheets I sent you, a M.S. note is *appended
to the title* of 'Benito Cereno'; but as the book is now to be published
as a collection of '*Tales*', that note is unsuitable & had better be
omitted.

I should like to have a proof sent to me of '*The Piazza*'. Please
send by *mail*.

The blank agreements I have not received.

It was understood that the copyright was to stand in my name.
You can take it out, & charge the cost to me.

With much respect
Truly Yours
H Melville

Dix & Edwards
Publishers
N.Y.

ALS on a 25 × 19.1 cm sheet, folded in half, of blue laid paper with lines, embossed with the
manufacturer's small oblong stamp of flourishes connected at four points. Melville inscribed

the first and third pages, in ink. Another hand, presumably a clerk's, noted on the fourth page in ink "H. Melville | Feby 16 / 56".

LOCATION: Beinecke Library, Yale University. *Provenance*: Owen Franklin Aldis (tipped into a first edition of *The Piazza Tales*).

PUBLICATION: Merton M. Sealts, Jr., "The Publication of Melville's *Piazza Tales*," *Modern Language Notes* 59 (January 1944), 56. Davis-Gilman 126.

TEXTUAL NOTES: 1856] 6 *written over* 5 • Bell Tower.] *before* (Over) *in bottom margin* • The Piazza] T *and* P *written over* t *and* p • Please send by *mail.*] *added* • Melville] *miswritten* Melvillee

TO G. P. PUTNAM & CO.
18 FEBRUARY 1856 · PITTSFIELD

Like Melville's letter of 21 August 1855, this letter discussing "the next acct: of 'Israel Potter' " must refer to a semiannual payment for the book rather than for the magazine publication of *Israel Potter*, since Putnam's had paid Melville on a regular monthly basis for the magazine serialization (see the NN *Israel Potter*, pp. 206–7, 211–12).

Pittsfield Feb: 18th 1856

Gentlemen: The present month is the time fixed upon for rendering the next acct: of 'Israel Potter' — Will you have the kindness to make it up, and send it to me here, before the expiration of the month.

Very Truly Yours
H Melvill

G. P. Putnam & Co.
New York

ALS on a 12.2 × 15.4 cm part-sheet (now framed, and apparently trimmed on all four edges) of blue wove paper. Melville inscribed only one side of the leaf, in ink.

LOCATION: Collection of Kate Whitney. *Provenance*: Rulon-Miller Books, catalogue 71 (1983), item 78 (misdated 1854); Paul Richards Autographs, catalogue 197 (June 1985), item 5.

TO DIX & EDWARDS
24 MARCH 1856 · PITTSFIELD

It is not clear in this March letter whether Melville was returning the "proofs" for other pieces in *The Piazza Tales* or only those for "The Piazza" (requested in his earlier 16 February letter) along with the "Copy of Agreement." In either case,

however, his remark about the "profusion of commas" is also applicable to the
magazine pieces reprinted in the book, as the three collations made by the editors of
the NN *Piazza Tales* volume attest. Their findings confirmed the suggestion made
by Davis and Gilman that not only was nothing done about giving a "final hand"
to the punctuation but Melville's own deletions were ignored; see the NN *Piazza
Tales* volume, pp. 539–40. The title page of *The Piazza Tales* was entered for copyright on 20 May 1856, and the book appeared for sale during the week of 24–31
May (see the NN *Piazza Tales* volume, pp. 498–99).

Pittsfield, March 24th

Gentlemen: — Enclosed is Copy of Agreement, with proofs. —
    There seems to have been a surprising profusion of commas in
these proofs. I have struck them out pretty much; but hope that
some one who understands punctuation better than I do, will give
the final hand to it.

Yours Truly
H Melville.

Dix & Edwards
New York.

ALS on a 12.8 × 14.5 cm part-sheet (torn along the left edge and probably cut along the top
and bottom) of white laid paper with lines, embossed with the manufacturer's small oblong
stamp of flourishes connected at four points. Melville inscribed only one side of the leaf, in
ink. Another hand, presumably a clerk's, noted on the verso in ink "H Melville | Mch 24/56".
It is attached at the left edge to a larger sheet bearing the penciled notation "Herman Mel-
ville | Amer Novelist".

LOCATION: NYPL-GL.

PUBLICATION: Paltsits, p. 12. Davis-Gilman 127.

TEXTUAL NOTE: these] *final* e *written over another letter*

TO DIX & EDWARDS
1 APRIL 1856 · PITTSFIELD

Melville dated this letter 1855, but it is here reassigned to 1856 on the basis of Alma
A. MacDougall's research in "The Chronology of *The Confidence-Man* and 'Benito
Cereno': Redating Two 1855 Curtis and Melville Letters," *Melville Society Extracts*
53 (February 1983), 3–6. As MacDougall points out, Melville did not have anything
in press with Dix & Edwards in the spring of 1855 that would have been ready to
make "up in page form." The "proof" in this letter could not be that of "The Bell-
Tower," as Davis and Gilman suggested, because Curtis did not approve the man-

uscript until mid-June 1855; nor could it be that, as Sealts in his "Chronology of Melville's Short Fiction, 1853–1856," *Harvard Library Bulletin* 28 (October 1980), 401, suggested, of "Benito Cereno," which was not approved until 19 April 1855 (see the NN *Piazza Tales* volume, pp. 495, for Sealts's later correction). These facts along with the original endorsement on the back of the letter show that Melville misdated it (as he had originally misdated his 16 February 1856 letter; see the textual note, above) and that "the whole" he requested in "page form" was proofs of *The Piazza Tales*, which was in press at just this time.

Pittsfield
April 1ˢᵗ 1855

Gentlemen: — Enclosed is the proof last sent.
It may be well to send the whole as made up in page form.

Truly Yours
H Melville

Dix & Edwards

ALS on a 12 × 11.9 cm part-sheet (probably cut along the left and bottom edges) of blue laid paper with lines, embossed with the manufacturer's small oblong stamp of flourishes connected at four points. Melville inscribed only one side of the leaf, in ink. Another hand, presumably a clerk's, noted in ink on the verso "H. Melville | April 1/56", with the last digit later changed to "5" (see the article cited in the headnote). Written sideways on the verso in pencil are the numerals "15. 49." and "14, 8, 6" totaled to "28".

LOCATION: Rosenbach Museum & Library, Philadelphia. *Provenance*: James Lorimer Graham sale, Parke-Bernet Galleries, sale 1825, 29–30 April 1958, lot 269.

PUBLICATION: (listed by date only) Clara Louise Dentler, *A Privately Owned Collection of Letters, Autographs, and Manuscripts with Many Association Items* [Graham Family Collection] (Florence: Spinelli, 1947), in item 280. Davis-Gilman 118.

TO JOSEPH M. LANGFORD
5 APRIL 1856 · PITTSFIELD

Melville had met Joseph Munt Langford (1809–84) in London in 1849 through a letter of introduction furnished to Melville by the wife of a New York bookseller. Langford had given him a "very civil reception" and taken him to see Macready in *Othello* at the Haymarket Theatre, where they "went into the critics' boxes" (*Journals*, pp. 21–22). A few days later he invited Melville to supper at his lodgings and introduced him to Albert Richard Smith, the humorist, "Tom Taylor the Punch man & Punch poet," and five or six congenial "young fellows." It was a "plain supper — no stiffness," with lots of porter, gin, brandy, whiskey, cigars, and funny stories (*Journals*, p. 24). Langford was head of the London branch of William Blackwood & Sons from 1845 to 1881 and for many years drama critic for the

London *Observer*. As a bookman he knew Thackeray, Dickens, George Eliot, Charles Reade, and many other literary figures. He also dabbled in playwriting; only four days after Melville wrote this letter, *Like and Unlike*, which Langford and W. J. Sorrell translated and adapted from a French play, was presented at the Adelphi Theatre in London (see the *Athenæum*, 6 September 1884). Since this letter of introduction was among the family papers given to Harvard by Melville's granddaughter Eleanor Melville Metcalf, presumably Elizabeth Melville's half-brother Samuel Shaw never used it while in London.

Dear Sir: — Allow me to introduce to you Mr Samuel Shaw of Boston, Massachusetts, — son of Chief Justice Shaw of that state — who, being on a European tour, proposes to spend some time in London.

He is of that temper and those tastes, which, I am sure, will not prove uncongenial to you and your friends; while from your acquaintance, he could not fail to reap, as a traveller, both pleasure and profit.

Whatever you may be able to do for him, in the way of directing his attention to interesting objects or persons in London, will be gratefully remembered by,

His brother-in-law
Yours Very Truly
Herman Melville

Mr. Langford,
Furnival's Inn.

Pittsfield, Mass. April 5th 1856

ALS on a 32.8 × 20 cm sheet, folded in half, of white wove paper, embossed with the manufacturer's stamp enclosing the name "PARIS PAPER" in a shield-like design below a crown. Melville inscribed the first page, in ink.

LOCATION: HCL-M.

PUBLICATION: Metcalf, p. 155. Davis-Gilman 128.

TO LEMUEL SHAW
12 MAY 1856 · PITTSFIELD

This letter to Chief Justice Shaw provides a summary of Melville's tenuous finances during his residence at Pittsfield. Shaw had initially contributed two thousand dollars to help Melville and his brother Allan buy a house in New York shortly after their marriages. When Melville moved his family to Pittsfield, Shaw loaned him three thousand dollars more to help buy the farm Melville later named "Arrowhead" from Dr. John M. Brewster. This loan, as Melville states in his letter, was not formally drawn up, but a formal mortgage to Dr. Brewster was undertaken at that time (Berkshire Athenaeum). Melville's subsequent "loan" from T. D. Stewart (see the entry for his unlocated March 1851 letter to Stewart, above) was not secured by a mortgage, so it gave Stewart no formal claim to the farm at Pittsfield; however, as Melville explains in this letter, by 1856 Stewart was pressing for payment "in such a way" as to endanger the farm. (Melville had begun to default on the Stewart loan on 1 May 1852 and had recently defaulted for the first time on his payments to Brewster on 14 September 1855 [New Log].) It was for this reason that Allan drew up a second mortgage on the farm to Lemuel Shaw, dated 9 May 1856 (which Shaw saved in the same packet as this letter), giving Shaw precedence after Brewster to any claims made on the farm. The extreme measure of having to move into the village would have involved only Melville and his wife and children (his mother and two unmarried sisters, Augusta and Frances Priscilla, were now in Gansevoort, New York, assisting Herman Gansevoort; see the headnote to Melville's 14 September 1857 letter to his brother Allan, below). After advertising the wooded eighty acres of the farm in the *Pittsfield Sun*, Melville was able to sell the land to a neighbor, George S. Willis, by the end of June 1856 and was able with an additional loan of five thousand dollars from Judge Shaw to remain on the farm and presumably to pay Stewart. For a discussion of Melville's possible literary use of his dealings with T. D. Stewart in *The Confidence-Man*, see Hershel Parker, " 'The Story of China Aster': A Tentative Explication," *The Confidence-Man* (New York: Norton, 1971), pp. 353–56 (written before the publication of this letter).

Pittsfield, May 12ᵗʰ 1856

My Dear Sir: — To the extent of the amount you advanced towards the purchase of this farm, I have always considered the farm to that extent, but nominally mine, (my real ownership at present being in its enhanced value) and my notes, given you at the time, as representing, less an ordinary debt, than a sort of trust, or both together. Agreeably to this, my view of the matter from the beginning, I have executed to you a mortgage for the sum. —— The reason why I secure you at the present time is this: When I first removed to this place Mʳ T. D. Stewart volunteered to loan me any sum I might need, which offer, though declined at the time, I was, some months after, induced to accept, to the amount of two thousand dollars, which money was expended in building the new kitchen, woodhouse, piazza, making alterations, painting, — and, in short, all those improvements made upon these premises during the first year of occupancy; and likewise a part went towards making up the deficiency in the sum received from the sale of the New York house, which sum fell short of the amount expected to have been realized and paid over to Dr. Brewster as part of the purchase-money for the farm; and the residue went for current expences. ——— For the money received from Mr Stewart I gave him my note at five years, not without hopes of being able to pay him, by that time, from my earnings. — The first six months' interest I paid; but, after that, could not pay more. The note is now matured, and Mr Stewart presses the whole payment; and, in such a way, as to raise the notion, that possibly he may yet take such measures, as, without precaution on my part, might involve, with the sacrifice of this farm, not only injustice to a prior & larger claim, but (as it seems to me) what would look like the forced settlement of a personal debt with property virtually held in trust — at any rate, not, truly, mine. — If this view of the matter seems right to you, you will accept the mortgage. If not, you will do what is best.

During a visit of mine to New York from which day before yesterday I returned, Allan prepared the document. It secures you but for the principal sum. I judged you would be satisfied with that, and under the circumstances I felt that I could not with proprity do more. No public record has been made of the mortgage. Is it necessary? About Lizzie's "dower" &c, Allan tells me, that can be attended to at any time. If you accept the mortgage, I will, to make it perfect, do whatever you suggest.

Lizzie & I have concluded that it may be best for us to remove into some suitable house in the village, that is, if the whole farm can be advantageously sold. I have accordingly advertised it in New York, & placed it in the hands of a broker there, and have also advertised the wooded part in the village paper I hope, either by the sale of the whole farm to realise, through its enhanced value, a sum sufficient to pay off Dr Brewster's mortgage, and the accompanying one, and also, in whole or in part, Mr Stewart; or else, by the sale of the wooded part (reserving two or three acres of wood) to obtain such a sum as that Mr Stewart can, in whole or in part, be paid out of it, and yet leave a balance, which, added to the value of the remaining portion of the farm, will nearly equal the original price of the whole.

In reading over the foregoing from the beginning, I am anew made sensible of a certain difficulty in my position, which makes it not so very clear what, all things considered, is right to be done. And, therefore, the views I have presented, I hold subject to the revision of less embarrased judgements.

I am sorry to trouble you with so long a letter, and one which can not be pleasing to you, — but I deemed it unavoidable.

With much respect

H. Melville

It is my purpose, upon your acceptance of the mortgage, to inform Mr Stewart that there is such a mortgage, and give him my reasons for executing it, and showing him that the act has its original basis in the circumstances under which the property was purchased.

ALS on a 39 × 24.9 cm sheet, folded in half, of blue wove paper with lines (on the first three pages), faintly embossed with the manufacturer's square stamp enclosing some initials. Melville inscribed the first, third, and fourth pages, in ink.

LOCATION: Social Law Library, Boston.

PUBLICATION: Patricia Barber, "Two New Melville Letters," *American Literature* 49 (November 1977), 418–20.

TEXTUAL NOTES: (my real . . . value)] *inserted above caret* • those] *altered from* the • have been realized] e been *written over wiped* real • what would look] wh *written over wiped* W • forced] *altered from* enforced • through its enhanced value,] *inserted above caret* • equal] *inserted above caret* • the views] *after canceled* for • circumstances] *inserted above canceled* conditions

TO LEMUEL SHAW
22 MAY 1856 · PITTSFIELD

Lemuel Shaw's intervening reply of 14 May to Melville's earlier letter of 12 May, just above, is unlocated. In effect an addendum to that 12 May letter, this one supplies a fuller picture of Melville's current financial troubles in 1856. The mortgage payment he owed was to the holder of his first mortgage, Dr. Brewster (see the headnote to his 12 May letter). Although Melville was already nearly three hundred dollars in debt to the Harpers before the fire that occurred on 10 December 1853 in their Cliff Street building in New York (according to the 21 March 1853 account he had received from them), the fire prolonged his debt. It destroyed all of their sheet stock and bound copies, including nearly 2,300 bound and unbound copies of his books. Fortunately the plates for them were not destroyed. However, since the majority of his book contracts with the Harpers called for half-profits, any expense the Harpers incurred reprinting the destroyed books necessarily lessened any eventual profits to be divided with Melville.

In listing his resources, Melville includes the "book to be published this week"—*The Piazza Tales* (which appeared on 20 May 1856)—and the book of "about a year ago"—*Israel Potter* (1855). The "certain books in hand" included *The Confidence-Man*, which he was working on during the period between early May 1855 and October 1856, and possibly *The Isle of the Cross* (see the headnote to his 24 November 1853 letter to Harper & Brothers, above). Since the last magazine article Melville is known to have published was "The Apple-Tree Table" in May 1856, Melville's statement that his "immediate resources" consisted of what he could get for "articles sent to magazines" may support the inference that he intended *The Confidence-Man* for serialization by *Putnam's* (see the NN *Confidence-Man*, pp. 277–79).

Although Melville ends this letter by again raising the possibility of moving into a rented house in Pittsfield, he and his family remained on the farm for nearly six more years. Melville did enter into a contract in 1857 to buy a house in Brooklyn, but with the assistance of his brother Allan and brother-in-law George Griggs obtained release from it (see Patricia Barber, "Melville's House in Brooklyn," *American Literature* 45 [November 1973], 433–34). Only in 1862 did Melville rent a house in Pittsfield for a year before moving back to New York City.

Pittsfield, May 22ᵈ 1856

My Dear Sir: The assurances, in your letter of the 14ᵗʰ, concerning my indebtedness to you, are received as they should be, and as you would wish them to be.

You say that in regard to the mortgage, you have doubts whether it would be expedient to put it on record &c. For the present therefore I shall not inform Mʳ Stewart about it.

You desire to know particularly what claims there are against me, and what are my resources. — Omitting Mʳ Stewart's claim there is nothing payable by me except $90 being last year's interest on the $1500 mortgage, and perhaps $50 on inconsiderable bills. I know not whether I ought to include (as a present indebtedness) a balance of some $400 against me in the last Acct: from the Harpers; a balance which would not have been against me but for my loss of about $1000 in their fire, and the extra charges against me, consequent upon the fire, in making new impressions, ahead of the immediate demand, of the books. The acct: will gradually be squared (as the original balance has already been lessened) by sales. Before the fire, the books (not including any new publication) were a nominal resource to me of some two or three hundred dollars a year; though less was realised, owing to my obtaining, from time to time, considerable advances, upon which interest had to be paid. After the present acct: is squared, the books will very likely be a moderate resource to me again. I have certain books in hand which may or may not fetch in money. My immediate resources are what I can get for articles sent to magazines.

I beleive I have given all the information you desired, and can only feel sorry that it is not of a more satisfactory nature.

With much respect
H. Melville.

I should have mentioned above a book to be published this week, from which some returns will ere long be had. Likewise some further returns, not much, may be looked for from a book published about a year ago by Mr Putnam. — The articles in Harpers Magazine are paid for without respect to my book acct: with them.

You enquire whether I have settled upon any house — or have one in my mind, which would be suitable for us, should we remove from the farm. — I have learned (without more special inquiry) that a suitable house might be had for about $150 a year.

ALS on a 25 × 19.1 cm sheet, folded in half, of blue laid paper with lines, embossed with the manufacturer's small oblong stamp of flourishes connected at four points, enclosing the name "CARSON'S". Melville inscribed all four pages, in ink.

LOCATION: Social Law Library, Boston.

PUBLICATION: Patricia Barber, "Two New Melville Letters," *American Literature* 49 (November 1977), 420–21.

TEXTUAL NOTE: acct: with them.] *before* (over) *in bottom margin*

TO RICHARD T. GREENE
AFTER 16 JUNE 1856 · PITTSFIELD

Unlocated. At the conclusion of his 16 June 1856 letter to Melville praising *The Piazza Tales*, Richard Tobias (Toby) Greene requested: "Will you spare time to drop me á line or two? it will prove my identity, for I still am proud of the immortality with which you have invested me" (see LETTERS RECEIVED, pp. 644–46). Presumably Melville did so, since their correspondence continued. Davis-Gilman Unlocated 342.

TO HENRY G. WEBBER
AFTER 12 JULY [1856?] · PITTSFIELD

Unlocated. Henry G. Webber, an artist, wrote Melville on 12 July [1856?] offering
for sale illustrations he had made for "The Bell-Tower" (see LETTERS RECEIVED, pp.
646–48). Probably Melville replied quickly, since Webber stated he was about to
move. Davis-Gilman Unlocated 343.

TO LEMUEL SHAW
BEFORE 15 JULY 1856 · [PITTSFIELD?]

Unlocated. A letter from Melville is cited in a 15 July 1856 letter from Lemuel
Shaw, Jr., to his brother Samuel, then in Europe: "Herman writes that he has sold
the western half of his farm at Pittsfield — upon pretty good terms — I believe is
now preparing another book for the press of which Augusta is making a fair copy
for the printer & which will be published before long. I know nothing about it; but
I have no great confidence in the success of his productions — " (MHS-S). Melville's letter was probably written to Chief Justice Shaw, who had helped him buy
the farm at Pittsfield and was currently assisting him with his financial difficulties
(see Melville's letters of 12 and 22 May 1856, above). He had sold the western half
of his farm to his Pittsfield neighbor George S. Willis. Evidently some other member of the family had written the Shaws including the news about Melville's new
book, *The Confidence-Man*, published 1 April 1857 (see the NN edition, pp. 277ff.).

TO DIX & EDWARDS
25 AUGUST 1856 · PITTSFIELD

Unlocated. Melville's 25 August 1856 request to Dix & Edwards for a statement of
the sales of *The Piazza Tales* is cited in their 30 August reply (see LETTERS RE-
CEIVED, pp. 648–49). Davis-Gilman Unlocated 344.

TO SARAH HUYLER MOREWOOD
[29 AUGUST 1856?] · PITTSFIELD

This undated letter, headed "Friday Morning," is written on Carson's white laid
paper, which Melville used at least from 1852 through 1860 (see, for example, his
letters of 25 October 1852, 9 November 1854, 3 October 1857, and 22 May 1860).
Melville's reference to "this day" (Friday) as a "fortunate one, instead of a luckless"
offers no assistance in dating the letter, since in the nineteenth century any Friday
was considered an unlucky day (see the headnote to his earlier [10?] March 1854
letter also to Sarah Morewood). Davis and Gilman tentatively assigned this letter
the date Friday, 29 August 1856, before the second of Sarah Morewood's fancy
dress picnics, on 3 September, which Elizabeth Melville, Augusta, and three-year-
old Bessie attended, but which Melville is known to have missed. There undoubtedly were, however, other invitations from Sarah Morewood which Melville de-

clined, between October 1850, when the Morewoods moved into Broadhall, and 16 October 1863, when she died. Thus this date can be assigned only tentatively. For a possible explanation of the sobriquet "Lady of Paradise," see p. 855 below.

Friday Morning

My Dear Lady Broadhall: —
　　Forever hereafter be this day thought a fortunate one, instead of a luckless. For has it not brought me some share of a kind invitation from the ever-excellent & beautiful Lady of Paradise — — slip of the pen — of Broadhall, I mean? —
　　But then, unfortunately, I am absolutely compelled to decline my part of the merry summons. It gives me great grief; — but I shall be with you in sympathy.

So Adieu to Thee
Thou Lady of All Delight;
even Thou, The peerless Lady
of Broadhall.
H. M.

ALS on a 12.8 × 20.1 cm part-sheet (torn along the left edge) of white laid paper with lines, faintly embossed with the manufacturer's small oblong stamp of flourishes connected at four points. Melville inscribed only one side of the leaf, in ink.

LOCATION: Berkshire Athenaeum, Pittsfield, Massachusetts. *Provenance*: Agnes Morewood.

PUBLICATION: Davis-Gilman 264.

TEXTUAL NOTES: fortunate] fo *rewritten* • a kind] a *written over* an

TO PETER GANSEVOORT
7 OCTOBER 1856 · NEW YORK

Long before the autumn of 1856 the combined strains of authorship and financial burdens had worn Melville down. On 1 September 1856, Lemuel Shaw explained the situation to his son Samuel Shaw, then in Berlin: "I suppose you have been informed by some of the family, how very ill, Herman has been. It is manifest to me from Elizabeth's letters, that she has felt great anxiety about him. When he is deeply engaged in one of his literary works, he confines him to hard study many hours in the day, with little or no exercise, & this specially in winter for a great many days together. He probably thus overworks himself & brings on severe nervous affections. He has been advised strongly to break off this labor for some time & take a voyage or a journey & endeavor to recuperate" (MHS-S). Shaw advanced

the funds necessary for the trip (see LETTERS RECEIVED, p. 674), and after visiting his
mother and uncle Herman at Gansevoort, Melville went to New York on 29 September for two weeks of preparations. He wrote this farewell letter to his uncle
Peter during that time. His uncle replied on 9 October (see LETTERS RECEIVED, pp.
649–51), just two days before Melville sailed for Glasgow aboard the steamer *Glasgow* on Saturday, 11 October. (The title "General" refers to his uncle's service as
Judge Advocate General on the military staff of Governor DeWitt Clinton from
1819 to 1821. See Cuyler Reynolds, *Genealogical and Family History of Southern New
York and the Hudson River Valley* [New York: Lewis Historical Publishing Co.,
1913], I, 69.)

New York, Oct. 7ᵗʰ 1856

My Dear Uncle — I think of sailing for the other side of the ocean
on Saturday next, to be gone an uncertain time. Ten days ago I went
to Gansevoort to bid Mama good bye, and in returning from thence
would have stopped to bid *you* also good bye & Aunt Susan, had not
engagements forbid. Pray, make my adieus to Aunt Susan & to Kate
& Henry, and beleive me, affectionately

Yours
H. Melville

Gen. Peter Gansevoort.

ALS on an 18.1 × 22.5 cm part-sheet (torn along the left edge) of blue wove paper with lines,
embossed with the manufacturer's ornate oval stamp and five vertical watermarked lines.
Melville inscribed only one side of the leaf, in ink. He addressed an envelope that was proba-
bly used for this letter "Gen. Peter Gansevoort | Albany | N.Y."; it was postmarked in New
York on 8 October. (The folds in the paper do not match the outline of the folds on the
envelope, but the two probably go together.)

LOCATION: NYPL-GL.

PUBLICATION: *Log*, II, 523. Davis-Gilman 129.

TEXTUAL NOTE: affectionately . . . Melville] *smeared*

TO ELIZABETH SHAW MELVILLE
BETWEEN 26 AND 29 OCTOBER 1856 · GLASGOW

Unlocated. In his November 1856 letter to his brother Allan, below, Melville
writes: "By the way . . . send this letter on to Lizzie, as it may contain items omitted in my letters to her." This statement implies that he had written more than one
letter to his wife, but possibly it anticipates the letter he was planning to write to
her from Liverpool, also mentioned in his letter to his brother. In any case, only

one letter had reached Elizabeth Melville in Boston on 23 November when Lemuel Shaw wrote to his son Samuel in Berlin: "Elizabeth has received but one letter from her husband, written soon after his arrival at Glasgow. He expected after a few days in Scotland to proceed to Liverpool & thence to London, where he would inquire for you at Baring Bro. Co. & thus probably be enabled to put himself in communication with you. I hope you will meet him, and so make your arrangements, as to travel together" (MHS-S). Melville had probably been given instructions by the family to write to Samuel Shaw, but on 2 November Samuel wrote from Berlin to his brother Lemuel, "As yet I have heard nothing of Herman, but expect a letter every day" (MHS-S), and three weeks later, in a 23 November letter to his brother, Samuel reported that he still had not heard anything (MHS-S). In all likelihood Melville did not write. On 29 December Lemuel Shaw, Jr., wrote from Boston that "we have heard nothing from Herman since I last wrote you, when he was on the point of leaving Liverpool for Constantinople [probably Melville's unlocated 18 November letter to his wife, below] — we do not know whether he will go from there to Trieste & Venice or Naples or Ancona & cannot put you in the way of meeting him, when we do hear from him we will let you know" (HCL-M). Melville did not meet Samuel Shaw until they were both in Rome (see the entry for Melville's unlocated 21 March 1857 letter to him, below). Davis-Gilman Unlocated 346.

TO MARIA GANSEVOORT MELVILLE
BETWEEN 29 OCTOBER AND 10 NOVEMBER
1856 · EDINBURGH AND LIVERPOOL

Unlocated. In the 10 November section of his Liverpool letter to his brother Allan, below, Melville wrote that he had "written Mama." Upon receiving the letter on 25 November, Maria Melville in turn wrote to her brother Peter Gansevoort, stating, "I receive'd the enclosed letter from Herman this morning, knowing you feel an interest in all that concerns him, I thought you would like to read this letter the first I have had from him — " (NYPL-GL). On 27 November 1856 Peter Gansevoort replied to Maria: "I thank you my dear Sister for enclosing a letter from Herman at Edinburgh & Liverpool, which I have read with very great pleasure, & am happy to learn his health is improving & that he is aware of the necessity of cessation from writing — & is convinced that by travelling he is renovating his system. I am glad that he has gone to the Mediterranean, & hope he will remain absent until his health is reestablished. I now return his letter & after reading the Glasgow paper will return it also — " (draft letter, NYPL-GL). (Melville must have sent a Glasgow paper to his mother or another family member.) The next day Maria Melville wrote back acknowledging the return of the letter and adding that she hoped "Herman will feel content to remain away for six months at least for he has sadly overworked his strength — & requires recreation, freedom from care; from writing, & the little petty cares, & annoyances, of the farm which are ever recurring & are so distasteful to him — " (NYPL-GL). Since Melville arrived in Edinburgh on 29 October, this letter must have been written in intervals between that date and

10 November when he referred to having "written Mama" in his letter to Allan. Davis-Gilman Unlocated 345.

TO JOHN MURRAY
BETWEEN 8 AND 10 NOVEMBER 1856 · LIVERPOOL

Unlocated. A note to his former publisher John Murray in London, asking him to forward to Liverpool any letters sent to Melville in his care, is cited in the 10 November section of Melville's letter to his brother Allan, below. Davis-Gilman Unlocated 347.

TO RICHARD BENTLEY
BETWEEN 8 AND 10 NOVEMBER 1856 · LIVERPOOL

Unlocated. A note to his former publisher Richard Bentley in London, asking him to forward to Liverpool any letters sent to Melville in his care, is cited in the 10 November section of Melville's letter to his brother Allan, below. Davis-Gilman Unlocated 348.

TO ALLAN MELVILLE
10, 13, AND 14 NOVEMBER 1856 · LIVERPOOL

Since Melville's 1856–57 journal contains no account of his voyage from New York to Glasgow, or of his travels in Scotland and England between 26 October and 8 November, this letter covering that period is a crucial supplement to it. On the Atlantic voyage, Melville's "philosopher" companion was George Campbell Rankin (1801–80), who is mentioned three times in the journal notebooks (see *Journals*, pp. 141 ["the Colonel"], 148–49, 159, and 533–34). Rankin had served as the surgeon of the Twenty-fifth Regiment of Native Infantry, which arrived at its station of Hajeepore in December 1849, and was the author of *What Is Truth? or, Revelation Its Own Nemesis* (London: Chapman, 1854), an indictment of Christianity.

The parish of Scoonie, which Melville inquired about aboard ship and in Scotland, was the ancestral home of the Melville family, where Melville's great-great-grandfather had been minister for many years and where Melville's father had visited in 1818 (Allan Melvill to Thomas Melvill, Sr., 31 May 1818 [NYPL-GL]; see Gilman, p. 12). It was in the district of Leven, Fifeshire. (The family arms of the earls of Melville were quartered with those of the earls of Leven; see the NN *Clarel*, pp. 839–40.)

Melville's subsequent and less satisfactory traveling companion in Scotland and England was Henry Willard, born in Troy, New York, in 1830. He graduated from Dartmouth in 1851, studied medicine a year, taught in a country grammar school another year, and then took two years of theological study at Andover Theological Seminary before transferring to Princeton Theological Seminary, from which he had graduated only a few months before Melville met him. Following this journey he studied two more years at Andover and after ordination in the Congregational church held positions in a number of Presbyterian and Congregational churches in Ohio, Minnesota, and Illinois. From 1885 to his death in 1904 he lived in Chicago. See Charles H. Pope, ed., *Willard Genealogy* (Boston, 1915), pp. 322, 488; and the *Necrological Report Presented to the Alumni Association of Princeton Theological Seminary* (Princeton: Princeton University Press, 1906), pp. 414–15.

Although Melville, in the 10 November portion of this letter, only briefly mentions his intention to call upon "Mʳ Hawthorne," then serving as consul to Liverpool, and, in the later sections of the letter, only alludes indirectly several times to Hawthorne, he in fact spent four full days conversing and sightseeing with him after calling at the consulate on 10 November. As Hawthorne's account in his English notebooks reveals, Melville stayed with Hawthorne and his family at the seaside town of Southport from Tuesday, 11 November, to Thursday, 13 November. (It was on the journey to Southport that Melville learned of George Duyckinck's accident; see also the headnote to Melville's earliest known letter to him of 6 November 1858, below.) Melville then returned to Liverpool with Hawthorne, who introduced him the next day to Henry Bright (see Melville's 18 November letter to Bright, below). On Saturday, 15 November, Melville and Hawthorne toured Chester. Hawthorne returned to Southport that evening, but saw Melville once more on the following Monday in Liverpool. For both Hawthorne's notebook account of his visits and conversations with Melville and the edited version that was printed during Melville's lifetime, see *Journals*, pp. 624, 627–33.

1856

Liverpool — Nov 10ᵗʰ

Monday evening.

My Dear Allan — I have been ashore about two weeks, and as my plans of further travel are now beginning to mature, I proceed to write you. But first let me speak of my movements thus far. — As for the voyage over, it was upon the whole not disagreeable, though the passengers were not all of a desirable sort. There was, I think, but one American beside myself. The rest were mostly Scotch with a sprinkling of English. Among others there were some six or seven "commercial travellers", a hard set who did little but drink and gamble the whole way over. With these fellows of course I had precious little to do. But there was one man, who interested me considerably, one who had been an officer of the native troops in India, and besides was a good deal of a philosopher and had been all over the world. With him I had many long talks, and we so managed to kill time. The weather was pretty good with the exception of a gale which lasted about 36 hours, which obliged us to "lay to" about 18. — I staid in Glasgow three or four days. It is a very fine commercial city, with a great commerce, noble streets, and an interesting old cathedral. I went to Dumbarton Castle, some twenty miles distant and to Loch Lomond near by. From Glasgow I went to Edinburgh, remaining there five days, I think. I was much pleased there. I went to Abbottsford & Melrose. And I went to Perth & Stirling. — Of some Scotchmen on board the steamer, I enquired about "Scoonie" (How is it spelt?) and learned there was such a place, and that was all. I endeavored to find out more about it; but though I consulted the books containing lists of all the clergy in Scotland, I could find no clergyman or parish called "Scoonie." But even if I had learned more, I do not know as I would have sought out the place to make a personal call upon any one; because, unfortunately, the evening we arrived at Greenock I received an ugly hurt upon the bridge of my nose, which by no means improved my appearance. A sailor was lowering a boat by one of the tackles; the rope got foul; I jumped to clear it for him, when suddenly the tackle started, and a coil of the rope (new Manilla) flew up in my face with great violence, and for the moment, I thought my nose was ruined for life. But the wound has now healed, and I hope that in a few days little or no scar will remain. — But for the week succeeding the accident I presented the aspect of one who had been in a bar-room fight.

—— From Edinburgh I finally went to York, by way of Berwick & Newcastle, on the east coast, and after a day's stay in York to view the minster, I came here. — I have, with one small exception, travelled entirely in the "Parliamentary" trains, that is, the cheapest ones. Travelling any distance by the first class or even the second, is exceedingly dear. And yet it is not easy to travel in the "Parliamentary," because only one such train runs a day on any road, & generally starts before day-light in the morning; and the Parliamentary trains on different roads do not connect. — I propose calling to see Mr Hawthorne here.

— About my further travel, at present I think that, if no obstacle interpose, I shall take a steamer to Constantinople from this port. I can go for $100; which is cheaper than the transatlantic steamers. The steamers hence for Constantinople touch at Gibralter & Malta. If I go by this route to Constantinople, I shall save money. The only difficulty is about getting my passport in order for the various places afterwards. From Constantinople I should go to Alexandia by

steamer, & so to Cairo, & from thence by steamer to Trieste, Venice, and bring up at Rome for a considerable stay. I may be mistaken, but I think that what funds I have, will enable me to accomplish this, though my abscence from home will not probably be prolonged beyond March at the furthest. So at least I think now. — I have been ashore now two weeks, and spent in all about thirty five dollars. But this has been by the strictest economy, both in R.R. lodging, & eating. — Concerning my enjoyment of the thing, it is rather solitary business, poking about the world without a companion. Still, my health is benefited. My hip & back are better, & also my head. But I find that in walking I have pretty often to rest. —— All this is about myself. How are you? And Sophia? and the small ones? I hope all goes well. I have written Mama.
— About the trunk, it is as I told you — I am going to store it here at Liverpool till I return from the continent. I shall take nothing but the carpet-bag. — Part of my tour in Scotland I had with me a Mr Willard of Troy (you remember the name at the steamer office) a theological student, very uninteresting, but better than nobody. He left me for London at York. I am now alone, & expect to be for some time.
— I shall write to Lizzie the day I leave here for good, (which will probably be in about a week, as no suitable steamer for the Mediterranean sails previous to then) and in that letter to her, I will endeavor to state, where letters from home will reach me; though I doubt whether I shall be in the way of getting any letters after quitting England. — Thinking that letters might have been sent for me to the care of Murray or Bentley at London, I have written to them to forward such letters to me at this place.

Thursday Nov 13th
Evening.

Ere you get this you will have been pained to hear of the serious accident to George Duyckinck on one of the rail roads near London. I only heard of it day before yesterday from Mr Hawthorne in the cars as we were going out to his place. My first feeling was to go on at once to London to see Mr Duyckinck, thinking that possibly he might have no acquaintance near him; but Mr Hawthorne told me that upon reading an acct of the affair in the paper (containing G. Duyckinck's name among others) he had at once written to a friend

To Allan Melville, 10, 13, 14 November 1856, p. 8 (reduced).
Formerly in the collection of Agnes Morewood.

in London to interest himself in Mr Duyckinck's behalf; and had obtained a reply to the effect that no one was allowed to see him where he lay at St. Thomas' Hospital, I think. But this morning Mr H. received another letter saying, that Mr D. was getting on well, and had friends about him; which I was the more rejoiced to hear, since as matters have turned out, I could not have gone to London without the utmost disarrangement of my plans. Nevertheless, did I suppose that my prescence would be particularly welcome to Mr Duyckinck, or give him ease, I would go on to see him as it is. But the extent of my acquaintance with him hardly justifies me in supposing that such would be the case. There are probably those about him now; whom he would rathar have than me. May God grant him a speedy recovery. I have not written to him, thinking of course that letters he does not read. —

I have now as good as determined upon sailing hence in the screw-steamer "Egyptian" for Constantinople, on Monday next. I have been on board the ship. I think this voyage is the best thing I can do — it is certainly the cheapest way in which I can spend the coming 26 days — for such will be the length of the voyage, including stoppages. I shall miss much however in going at this season of the year — June is so much better. But that can't be helped.

By the way, you had better (after reading it) send this letter on to Lizzie, as it may contain items omitted in my letters to her. And Lizzie can send it to Helen &c, if it be worth while.

Liverpool
Friday evening, 14th Nov.

The "Persia" sails tomorrow early. This will go in her. I am going to take the Meditterranean tour — will start on Monday early. You will not probably hear from me again in some time. But I will write when I can. God bless you,

My love to Sophia & kisses for children.

Affectionately Your Brother
Herman.

Saw Mr Hawthorne this morning — but heard nothing further of Mr G. Duyckinck. It is not improbable, I suppose, that ere this reach you his brother may have crossed the seas to him.

H M.

Original document not located. Text from photocopy (in Davis-Gilman file). The Davis-Gilman typed transcription was made from the ALS, then in the possession of Agnes Morewood; it differs from NN only in a few accidentals and in the reading "reaches" for NN "reach". From the Davis-Gilman notes the letter can be described as on two 24.5 × 20.2 cm sheets, folded in half, of white paper, embossed with the manufacturer's oval stamp enclosing the name "PARIS". Melville inscribed all eight pages, in ink.

LOCATION: at present unknown (see p. 806 below). *Provenance*: Agnes Morewood.

PUBLICATION: Davis-Gilman 130.

TEXTUAL NOTES: considerably] *miswritten* considearly • generally] *possibly* usually • I shall save] *miswritten* I | I shall save • considerable] *miswritten* consideale • day before] *inserted above caret* • Thomas'] Th *rewritten* • justifies] *miswritten* justicies • Liverpool] ver *covered by sealing wax* • I am] *miswritten* I amy

TO ELIZABETH SHAW MELVILLE
18 NOVEMBER 1856 · LIVERPOOL

Unlocated. A letter can be inferred from the 10 November section of Melville's letter, just above, to his brother Allan, in which he states, "I shall write to Lizzie the day I leave here for good, (which will probably be in about a week, as no suitable steamer for the Mediterranean sails previous to then) and in that letter to her, I will endeavor to state, where letters from home will reach me; though I doubt whether I shall be in the way of getting any letters after quitting England." This would be the last news Elizabeth Melville had of her husband for quite some time. In a 25–27 December letter to her son Samuel in Europe, Hope Savage Shaw wrote in a postscript that "Elizabeth has not heard one word from Herman since her Husband left Liverpool, for Constantinople" (HCL-M). Davis-Gilman Unlocated 349.

TO HENRY A. BRIGHT
18 NOVEMBER 1856 · LIVERPOOL

Melville met Henry Arthur Bright (1830–84) through Hawthorne on 14 November and spent the day with him seeing "whatever was worth seeing" in Liverpool, as Hawthorne recorded in his notebook (see *Journals*, p. 629). This undated letter of thanks can be assigned to Tuesday, 18 November 1856, the Tuesday after their 14 November meeting and the same day Melville left Liverpool aboard the "Egyptian" (one day later than anticipated in the 14 November section of his letter to Allan, above). Bright had been a warm friend of Hawthorne's since 1852, when Longfellow introduced them in Concord. He was later to become an editor, a writer for Unitarian magazines, a literary critic, and the center of the literary circles in Liverpool. Melville's journal indicates that Bright gave him lunch at his club and took him to a Unitarian church (presumably the one on Renshaw Street of which Bright was a member), the Free Library, and a cemetery—probably nearby St. James's (see *Journals*, pp. 51, 388). In the small graveyard adjacent to the Renshaw Street church, which Melville probably saw, Joseph Blanco White (1775–1841) was buried. A Catholic priest, turned skeptic, later a member of the Anglican church, and finally a somewhat uncertain Unitarian, whose continual oscillations between faith and doubt contributed to chronic physical illness, White would have aroused deep interest in Melville, particularly in the wake of his conversations with George Rankin on "fixed fate &c." during his transatlantic crossing (for Rankin, see *Journals*, pp. 141, 533–34, and the headnote to Melville's 10, 13, and 14 November letter to his brother Allan, above). Among White's many books, largely anti-Catholic, were *Second Travels of an Irish Gentleman in Search of Religion* (1833) and *Observations on Heresy and Orthodoxy* (1835). If Bright's unexplained "kind perseverance" had to do with procuring a book on Blanco White for Melville, the book may have been *The Life of the Reverend Joseph Blanco White Written by Himself*, ed. John H. Thom (3 vols., London: Chapman, 1845), or possibly *Extracts from Blanco White's Journal and Letters*, printed for the American Unitarian Association (Boston: Crosby & Nichols, 1847); see Sealts 556.1a.

Tuesday Morning

I am sure I am much obliged to you for your kind perseverance concerning "Blanco White."

Not forgetful of your civilities and hoping to meet you again upon my return. Believe Me

Very Truly Yours
Herman Melville

Henry A. Bright Esq
Liverpool

Original document not located. Text from Jay Leyda's 1951 handwritten transcription (in Davis-Gilman file) from the ALS, then at Parke-Bernet Galleries.

LOCATION: at present unknown (not in Barrett as queried by Davis-Gilman). *Provenance*: Parke-Bernet Galleries, sale 1249, 1 May 1951, lot 505.

PUBLICATION: Davis-Gilman 131.

1857

TO [MARIA GANSEVOORT MELVILLE AND DAUGHTERS?]
[3 JANUARY?] 1857 · [ALEXANDRIA?]

Two or more unlocated letters. When his steamer was detained and Melville was forced to spend two days waiting for it in Alexandria before continuing on to Jaffa and the Holy Land, he used the second day to "jot down" in his journal his impressions of Cairo, including the pyramids (*Journals*, pp. 73–78). It is likely that Melville also wrote at this time the letters, probably to his mother and unmarried sisters, that were later reported in the 21 February issue of the *Albany Atlas*: "The friends of Herman Melville, who sailed for Europe in October to recruit his health, will be glad to learn that by letters from Egypt, received by the last steamer, he speaks of being so much restored in health and strength that he 'climbed Cheops the other day, an enterprise of prodigious exertion[.]' He was to go to Jerusalem, and expected to be in Rome in the course of a few days." Davis-Gilman Unlocated 350 and 351.

TO [ELIZABETH SHAW MELVILLE? AND OTHERS]
BETWEEN 7 AND 18 JANUARY 1857 · JERUSALEM

Two or more unlocated letters. A small envelope labeled in pencil "Personal" by Elizabeth Shaw Melville (HCL-M) contains, among other clippings concerning Melville's 1856–57 and 1860 voyages, an unidentified newspaper clipping which reports on letters sent by Melville from Jerusalem in January 1857: "Private letters from Herman Melvill report him at last accounts at Jerusalem, about to turn his face homeward, with his old robust health and spirits fully restored. He is expected home in Pittsfield about the middle of May. The Berkshire County Eagle says: 'Mr. Melvill's hosts of friends the country over will be glad to learn of that renewed strength which gives promise of many future contributions from his pen to that literature which he has much enriched' " (the clipping is misdated "1860." on the verso in pencil, possibly by Elizabeth Shaw Melville). Presumably at least one of these letters was to his wife. For more on his visit to Jerusalem, see *Journals*, pp. 79–94.

TO [ELIZABETH SHAW MELVILLE? AND OTHERS]
19 FEBRUARY 1857 · NAPLES

Two or more unlocated letters. In his journal entry for 20 February in Naples, Melville recorded that first thing in the morning he "Walked to Post Office with letters"—presumably written the night before (*Journals*, p. 102). Hope Savage Shaw read one of these letters, probably addressed to Elizabeth Melville, who was staying with the Shaws in Boston, since Mrs. Shaw wrote to her son Samuel, who was also in Europe, on 20 March 1857: "I am afraid that you will miss Herman as his last date was the 19 of Feby in Naples, — from there he was going to Rome — he did not say how long he would be in Rome, but from there he intended going to England and then after arriving in Liverpool to America. His health is improving much, — if he could only be absent one whole year, I think it would restore his health" (MHS-S). A second of these Naples letters was probably sent to his mother and sisters at Gansevoort; see the entry for his unlocated letter of 27 February 1857, below. Davis-Gilman Unlocated 352.

TO ELIZABETH SHAW MELVILLE
BETWEEN 25 FEBRUARY AND 21 MARCH 1857 · ROME

Unlocated. In a 17 April 1857 letter to his son Samuel in Italy, Judge Shaw wrote, "We are strongly in hope that you will meet Herman in Rome. It appears by letters received from him, that he was in Rome, about the same time that you were at Genoa" (MHS-S). Melville had arrived at Rome on 25 February and stayed until 21 March when he met Samuel Shaw there. The "letters received" from Melville included at least one letter to Elizabeth Melville at the Shaws' since both Judge Shaw in his 17 April letter and Lemuel Shaw, Jr., in a 21 April letter to Samuel Shaw, reported that Elizabeth now expected her husband to return in May and had gone to Pittsfield to put the house in order (MHS-S). (Both of these letters also commented on the recent publication of *The Confidence-Man* [1 April].) The news of Melville's imminent return was probably passed along to Melville's cousin Priscilla Melvill, then in Pittsfield, in a letter accompanying the semiannual remittance Judge Shaw sent (for Shaw's connection with this branch of the Melville family, see the headnote to Melville's 19 March 1846 letter to him). Shortly afterwards on 6 April the nearby *Springfield Republican* included a notice that "Private letters from Herman Melville, who has been travelling in Egypt for some time past for his health, state that he is about to return to his home in Pittsfield, with renewed health." A similar notice appeared in the *New-York Daily Tribune* on 7 April and in the *Pittsfield Sun* on 9 April. For Samuel Shaw's brief meeting with Melville in Rome, see the entry for Melville's 21 March letter to him, below. Davis-Gilman Unlocated 354.

TO MARIA GANSEVOORT MELVILLE AND DAUGHTERS
27 FEBRUARY 1857 · ROME

Unlocated. One of the letters Melville recorded in his journal as mailed on 20 February in Naples (see the entry for 19 February 1857, above) probably went to his mother and sisters at Gansevoort, New York. A second letter from Italy to them is cited in Augusta Melville's 7 April 1857 letter to Peter Gansevoort, which begins: "Another letter received from Herman dated Rome Feby 27th, announcing his return home next month, leads me to write you upon the subject of which we were speaking the day before I left Albany. We all feel that it is of the utmost importance that something should be done to prevent the necessity of Herman's writing as he has been obliged to for several years past." She goes on to request help in securing him a post in the Custom House (NYPL-GL). Davis-Gilman Unlocated 353.

TO SAMUEL S. SHAW
21 MARCH 1857 · ROME

Unlocated. A brief note from Melville written the day he left Rome (21 March) is cited in Samuel Shaw's 24–25 March 1857 letter to his father, Judge Shaw. Samuel Shaw wrote: "I have seen Herman. When I arrived I learned he was at the Hotel de Minerve, and the first thing I did was to call there, but he was out. Returning to my own hotel in the course of the forenoon I found that he had been there and left a note for me stating that all his arrangements were made to leave for Florence in the afternoon and that I must see him between 3 and 4 or not at all. Accordingly I went and saw him off. He has been almost entirely alone but has found travelling companions, who are of service to him — Although his general health is much improved, yet at Rome, the climate and the dampness have affected him somewhat. He is considerably sunburnt and is stout as usual. It was a very great disappointment that things should have happened as they have both for him and for me. He expects to sail for America by the 1st of May, and doubtless you have heard his plans from himself before this" (MHS-S). For the dates of Shaw's unlocated letters to Melville in Europe, see LETTERS RECEIVED, p. 651, and for Melville's account of their 21 March meeting, see *Journals*, p. 113.

TO PHILLIPS, SAMPSON, & CO.
19 AUGUST 1857 · PITTSFIELD

In the spring of 1857 the editor Francis H. Underwood (1825–94), then working for the Boston publishers Phillips, Sampson, & Co., revived the proposal he had made to the firm four years earlier—to start the magazine that was ultimately called the *Atlantic Monthly*. Letters inviting contributions went out to major writers, largely in New England, and Underwood was sent abroad to attract English contributors. When he returned in midsummer, the panic of 1857 raised such doubts about the success of the magazine that Underwood, who had expected to be editor, voluntarily proposed the more prominent literary figure James Russell Lowell for the post. Underwood continued to solicit contributions, and Melville here answered what must have been a form letter from the publishers. His name was included in a list of "literary persons interested in [the publishers'] enterprise," which was printed on the back cover of the first two issues. Authors of articles were not identified until the issue of November 1862, but it does not appear that Melville, in fact, ever published in this "laudable enterprise." Underwood did, however, include entries on Melville and an excerpt from *Typee* in two books he compiled on American authors (see the headnote to Melville's 13 February 1890 letter to the publishing firm of Lee & Shepard).

                                                    Pittsfield Aug 19ᵗʰ 1857.
Gentlemen — Your note inviting my contributions to your proposed Magazine was received yesterday.
    I shall be very happy to contribute, though I can not now name the day when I shall have any article ready.
    Wishing you the best success in your laudable enterprise, I am
                                                    Very Truly Yours
                                                    H Melville

Phillips Sampson & Co.
Boston

ALS on a 12.5 × 19.1 cm part-sheet (torn along the left edge) of blue laid paper with lines, embossed with the manufacturer's small oblong stamp of flourishes connected at four points. Melville inscribed only one side of the leaf, in ink. It was later tipped along the left edge to another sheet with the penciled notation, probably by an autograph dealer: "In answer to Francis Underwood's | Invitation to contribute an article to | the projected 'Atlantic Monthly. | Was article ever sent? | see Melville Log p 581".

LOCATION: UV-Barrett. *Provenance*: George S. Babbitt; Seven Gables Bookshop.

PUBLICATION: Bliss Perry, "The Editor Who Was Never the Editor," *Atlantic Monthly* 100 (November 1907), 667. Davis-Gilman 132.

TO G. W. CURTIS
[8 OR 9] SEPTEMBER 1857 · PITTSFIELD

Unlocated. When Dix & Edwards dissolved on 27 April 1857, only shortly after their publication of *The Confidence-Man* on 1 April, their plates of that book and of *The Piazza Tales* were acquired by Miller & Co. (Miller & Curtis after 1 June), who took over the old firm's advertisements, featuring *The Confidence-Man*, and continued to bring out new books. But the new firm failed, apparently in August, and decided to sell all its books and plates at the annual auction sale conducted by the New York Book Publishers' Association. Since Melville's contract (HCL-M) for *The Confidence-Man* gave him joint ownership and the right, if the firm failed, to purchase the plates at twenty-five percent of their first cost, G. W. Curtis notified Allan Melville of the plan to sell the plates in a 4 September 1857 letter. Allan then apparently wrote to Melville, who in turn replied with an unlocated letter to Curtis, cited in Curtis's 10 September reply: "I had also a note from [Melville] yesterday. He thinks well of lecturing, and wants to be hung for the whole sheep, and go the entire swine. His animal tastes can easily be gratified, I presume." (Both letters from Curtis to Allan Melville were formerly in the possession of Agnes Morewood, but are at present unlocated; see *Log*, II, 582.) Melville's 15 September letter to Curtis (below) also refers to this unlocated letter written "the other day," in which he stated that he "would soon tell" Curtis of his decision about buying the plates of his two books. For his later negative decision, see his 26 September 1857 letter, below. Davis-Gilman Unlocated 355.

TO ALLAN MELVILLE
BEFORE 10 SEPTEMBER 1857 · PITTSFIELD

Unlocated. When his brother Allan notified him of the imminent sale of the plates of his books (see the entry just above), Melville apparently replied with a letter to Allan as well as one to G. W. Curtis. Allan then forwarded this letter to Curtis, as Curtis's 10 September letter returning it to Allan indicates ("I enclose your note from your brother, and await further events" [formerly in the possession of Agnes Morewood, but at present unlocated; see *Log*, II, 582]). Davis-Gilman Unlocated 356.

TO ALLAN MELVILLE
14 SEPTEMBER 1857 · LENOX

This letter was pinned with a series of family documents and letters concerning the title and mortgage of the Gansevoort mansion in Gansevoort, Saratoga County, New York (Berkshire Athenaeum). In 1783 that property, confiscated from "Hugh Munro, Tory," had been given to Melville's grandfather, General Peter Gansevoort, for his part in the American revolutionary war. It passed into the hands of Melville's uncle Herman Gansevoort, but on 10 November 1847 was transferred to Melville's uncle Peter Gansevoort in a legal maneuver designed to protect Herman Gansevoort's property from claimants at that time. A year later on 1 December 1848 Peter Gansevoort transferred the title of the property in trust to Herman and Allan Melville and their wives. Herman Gansevoort continued to live in the mansion, and after the death of his wife Catherine on 29 October 1855, was joined by Melville's mother and youngest sister, Frances Priscilla. This became their home, as well as that of Augusta Melville, who like Frances Priscilla never married. For a fuller discussion of the legal maneuvering surrounding this property, see Alice P. Kenney, *The Gansevoorts of Albany* (Syracuse: Syracuse University Press, 1969), pp. 208–10, and for an illustration, see p. 550 below.

In September 1857 Allan was arranging a mortgage on the property to the Citizens Insurance Co., for which a title search had to be made (the mortgage was signed on 25 September [Berkshire Athenaeum]). This was probably the "business" Melville saw his uncle about in Albany on 9 September that is mentioned in a draft letter of that date from Peter Gansevoort to his son Henry (NYPL-GL); the mortgage was probably also the reason for this 14 September letter from Melville to Allan. Since Allan's letter to his brother instructing him to find a "Commissioner" (probably a government officer) is unlocated, the specific reason for this errand is not known. Adopting the course of action recommended by Melville's Pittsfield neighbor Julius Rockwell must have involved going to nearby Lenox, Massachusetts, where this letter was written (for more on Rockwell, see the headnotes to Melville's 23 May and 2 July 1853 letters).

After Herman Gansevoort's death in 1862 the title to the mansion house was transferred on 16 April to Augusta Melville (who died in 1876) and Frances Priscilla Melville (who died in 1885). For the final disposal of the mansion, see Melville's March 1889 correspondence with Abraham Lansing, the executor of Frances Priscilla's estate.

Sep 14th
Lenox

My Dear Allan —

There is no Commissioner in Pittsfield, and Mr Rockwell tells me that there is none within 25 miles of Pittsfield.

I have therefore adopted the course he reccommended, & which he says he has known followed in many cases, and without difficulty.

Yours
Herman

ALS on a 25.4 × 20.4 cm sheet, folded in half, of white wove paper with lines, embossed with the manufacturer's stamp enclosing a figure above the initials "P & S" and surmounted by an arm wielding a sword. Melville inscribed the first page, in ink.

LOCATION: Berkshire Athenaeum, Pittsfield, Massachusetts. *Provenance*: Agnes Morewood.

TEXTUAL NOTE: Commissioner] *conjectural reading*

TO G. W. CURTIS
15 SEPTEMBER 1857 · PITTSFIELD

Although George William Curtis (1824–92) is not named in its salutation, this letter was certainly written to him, as the partner at Miller & Curtis who had notified Allan Melville about the possible sale of the plates of *The Confidence-Man* and *The Piazza Tales* (see the entry for Melville's unlocated letter of [8 or 9] September to Curtis, above). Curtis, a writer and editor, had spent time at Brook Farm and later Concord, where he became a good friend of Hawthorne. He went on to travel in the Middle East as a correspondent for the *New-York Tribune*, and published on his return in 1851 his *Nile Notes of a Howadji*, which included a tribute to Melville (as did some of his later writings). As a magazine writer, Curtis was most closely associated with the Harper periodicals. For nearly forty years, beginning in 1853, he wrote the essays for "The Editor's Easy Chair" column in *Harper's New Monthly Magazine* and was one of the main writers for *Harper's Weekly Magazine* after it was established in 1857. As an editor, he was most closely associated with *Putnam's*, having initially proposed a magazine publishing only pieces by American writers to Charles F. Briggs, who with him interested George P. Putnam in the idea. Curtis remained with the magazine after it was sold to Dix & Edwards, and advised them on Melville's pieces published after 1855 as well as on the publication of *The Piazza Tales* (see the headnotes to Melville's 7 August 1855 and 7 January 1856 letters to Dix & Edwards, above).

Curtis was also instrumental in helping Melville launch his lecturing career, as Melville's 26 September 1857 letter to him indicates. Curtis's own lectures were on serious matters of contemporary concern—such as the antislavery movement, women's rights, and civil service reform; he may have advised Melville at some point to choose a "good, earnest" subject, prompting Melville's ironic title for one on progress as seen in the history of Fifth Avenue and Five Points, the first a very wealthy area of New York City and the second a notorious slum on the city's lower east side. (The comparison was not new; Dickens in his chapter on New York in his *American Notes* [1850] contrasted Broadway [an avenue running close to Fifth] and Five Points.)

Pittsfield Sep 15th 1857

My Dear Sir — I said the other day in my note that I would soon tell you about the plates. Well, I have now to say that I can not at present conveniently make arrangements with regard to them.

It strikes me, though, that under the circumstances (copyright &c) they can bring but little at the Trade Sale, or any other sale. Whereas, if held on to for a while, they might be transferred to me to the common advantage of all concerned. But I do not wish to suggest anything in the way of a prompt settling up of the affairs of the late firm. Do with the plates whatever is thought best.

— I have been trying to scratch my brains for a Lecture. What is a good, earnest subject? *"Daily progress of man towards a state of intellectual & moral perfection, as evidenced in history of 5th Avenue & 5 Points"*

Yours Truly
H Melvill

ALS on a 26.5 × 20.3 cm sheet, folded in half, of white laid paper with lines. Melville inscribed the first page, in ink. Another hand, probably an autograph dealer's, noted at the top of the first page "Herman Melville" and on the fourth page "plates of 'Israel Potter' | Leyda says (Confidence Man?)" followed by what was probably the dealer's code "275 — | mtfxr | 849".

LOCATION: UV-Barrett. *Provenance*: Carroll A. Wilson (inserted in a first edition of *Israel Potter*); Timothy F. McGillicuddy.

PUBLICATION: (partial) Carroll A. Wilson, *Thirteen Author Collections of the Nineteenth Century and Five Centuries of Familiar Quotations* (New York: Privately Printed for Charles Scribner's Sons, 1950), I, 311–12. *Log*, II, 582. Davis-Gilman 133.

TO THE YOUNG MEN'S INSTITUTE, NEW HAVEN
[BEFORE 26 SEPTEMBER 1857?] · PITTSFIELD

Unlocated. A reply to a now unlocated invitation to lecture at the Young Men's Institute in New Haven, Connecticut, was probably one of the "two or three" responses to lecture invitations cited as already sent in Melville's 26 September 1857 letter to G. W. Curtis (see the headnote to that letter, below). On 30 December 1857 at New Haven, Melville delivered his lecture "Statues in Rome," for which he was paid fifty dollars. See the NN *Piazza Tales* volume, pp. 803 and 806.

TO THE YOUNG MEN'S ASSOCIATION, AUBURN
[BEFORE 26 SEPTEMBER 1857?] · PITTSFIELD

Unlocated. A reply to a now unlocated invitation to lecture for the Young Men's Association, Auburn, New York, was probably one of the "two or three" responses to lecture invitations cited as already sent in Melville's 26 September 1857 letter to G. W. Curtis (see the headnote to that letter, below). On 5 January 1858 at Auburn, Melville delivered his lecture "Statues in Rome," for which he was paid forty dollars. See the NN *Piazza Tales* volume, pp. 802 and 806.

TO THE CLEVELAND LIBRARY ASSOCIATION
[BEFORE 26 SEPTEMBER 1857?] · PITTSFIELD

Unlocated. A reply to a now unlocated invitation to lecture for the Cleveland Library Association, Cleveland, Ohio, was probably one of the "two or three" responses to lecture invitations cited as already sent in Melville's 26 September 1857 letter to G. W. Curtis (see the headnote to that letter, below). On 11 January 1858 in Cleveland, Melville delivered his lecture "Statues in Rome," for which he was paid fifty dollars. See the NN *Piazza Tales* volume, pp. 802 and 806. Richard Tobias (Toby) Greene's wife, Mary J. Greene, in a 14 November 1892 letter to Elizabeth Melville, recalled hearing this lecture in Cleveland where she was visiting at the time (HCL-M; see also LETTERS RECEIVED, pp. 660–61).

TO G. W. CURTIS
26 SEPTEMBER 1857 · PITTSFIELD

This letter is Melville's final response to G. W. Curtis about his option to buy the stereotype plates of *The Confidence-Man* and *The Piazza Tales* (see Melville's two earlier letters to Curtis: his unlocated letter of [8 or 9] September 1857 and his 15 September letter, above). Because Melville, as he indicates here, still could not afford to buy the plates, they were put up for sale on 19 September 1857 and then withdrawn (the only ones to receive this treatment) at the annual auction conducted by the New York Book Publishers' Association. Although some plates went at very low prices—fifteen dollars for works of Parke Godwin and J. W. DeForest—no one would risk a dollar on Melville (*American Publishers' Circular and Literary Gazette* 3 [22 August, 19 and 26 September 1857]). The ultimate disposal of the plates is unknown.

As Melville's two earlier letters also indicate, Curtis was advising him about his plans to lecture and apparently solicited several lecture invitations for him. Sealts, in *Melville as Lecturer*, p. 6, speculates that these were from New Haven, Connecticut; Auburn, New York; and Cleveland, Ohio—where both men lectured on different dates during the 1857–58 season.

Pittsfield Sep. 26th

My Dear Sir — I will try and do something about the plates as soon as I can. Meantime if they bother you, sell them without remorse. To pot with them, & melt them down.

I have received two or three invitations to lecture, — invitations prompted by you — and have promptly accepted. I am ready for as many more as may come on.

Sincerely Yours
H Melville

George W[m] Curtis Esq.

ALS on a 25 × 19.1 cm sheet, folded in half, of blue laid paper with lines, embossed with the manufacturer's small oblong stamp of flourishes connected at four points. Melville inscribed the first page, in ink.

LOCATION: HCL–Autograph File. *Provenance*: Dr. Bernard J. Cipes.

PUBLICATION: Davis-Gilman 134.

TEXTUAL NOTE: George] *smeared*

TO WILLIAM P. S. CADWELL
3 OCTOBER 1857 · PITTSFIELD

According to Melville's 26 September 1857 letter to G. W. Curtis, just above, he began to get lecture invitations at the end of September 1857. The now unlocated invitation from William P. S. Cadwell, to which this letter replies, was not among the first, since Melville told Curtis he had already answered those promptly. Although his reply does not say where he had been invited to lecture, the New Bedford Lyceum can be inferred from the fact that Cadwell was listed from 1838 through 1879–80 as an apothecary in New Bedford directories (see G. Thomas Tanselle, "Melville Writes to the New Bedford Lyceum," *American Literature* 39 [November 1967], 391–92). Despite his request for an early date, Melville lectured there on 23 February 1858, his last engagement during the 1857–58 season, and was paid fifty dollars. For the later correspondence that can be inferred from this letter, see the next entry.

Pittsfield Oct 3[d] 1857.

Dear Sir — I accept with pleasure your invitation to lecture before your Lyceum, and shall await the receipt of the list of evenings not yet taken. — A somewhat early part of the season would probably be most convenient to me, if equally so to you.

Very Truly Yours
H Melville

Wᵐ P. S. Cadwell Esq.

ALS on a 25.6 × 20 cm sheet, folded in half, of white laid paper with lines, embossed with the manufacturer's small oblong stamp of flourishes connected at four points, enclosing the name "CARSON's". Melville inscribed the first page, in ink. Another hand noted in pencil in the middle of the fourth page "Anonymous|Jan. 28, 1953", and a third hand noted in pencil at the top of that page "Melville". It is now mounted on a larger sheet.

LOCATION: Boston Public Library. *Provenance*: Virginia and Richard Ehrlich.

TO [WILLIAM P. S. CADWELL?]
AFTER 3 OCTOBER 1857 · PITTSFIELD

Two unlocated letters. At least two further letters from Melville to William Cadwell or another representative of the New Bedford Lyceum can be inferred from Melville's 3 October reply to Cadwell, above, and from Melville's lecture engagement notebook (HCL-M). After receiving Cadwell's first letter, Melville listed New Bedford in his notebook followed by the notation: "List of days to be sent." Below this notation, Elizabeth Melville listed the dates 4 December and 16 February with the notation "*Fixed*" after the second date, presumably after receiving a reply from New Bedford. A further exchange of letters, however, must have occurred, since Elizabeth Melville canceled all of her earlier notations and inserted to the side the date when Melville actually lectured in New Bedford, 23 February, followed by a new notation "Fixed". For a reproduction of this page from Melville's lecture engagement notebook, see the NN *Piazza Tales* volume, p. 803.

TO W. O. VANCE
20 OCTOBER 1857 · [PITTSFIELD?]

W. O. Vance was one of five members of the Clarksville, Tennessee, Literary Association who invited Melville in a letter dated 12 October 1857 to address the association during the fall or winter of the 1857–58 lecture season (Melville was instructed in that invitation to "Direct reply to W. O. Vance"; see LETTERS RECEIVED, pp. 656–57). Melville's letter in reply, possibly in his wife's hand, is unlocated; this text is that of her summary of the letter (or possibly a draft for the letter) written below the signatures on the invitation. According to Melville's lecture engagement notebook, he delivered his lecture "Statues in Rome" there on 22 January 1858, for a fee of seventy-five dollars. (For a reproduction of this page from the notebook, see the NN *Piazza Tales* volume, p. 806.)

Octr 20th

Accepted — cannot name precise day but it will probably be some time in the latter part of January — $50 is considered average sum — will write again — as soon as arrangements are completed

H. M.

Original document not located. Text from summary of letter, in ink, in the hand of Elizabeth Shaw Melville, inscribed below the signatures on p. 2 of the Clarksville Literary Association's 12 October 1857 letter to Melville. On the outside of the invitation she wrote "Lecture *No. 1* | Clarksville. Tenn. | Octr 12th 1857."

LOCATION (of letter to Melville): HCL-M.

PUBLICATION: *Log*, II, 583. Davis-Gilman 135. (Both misattribute the handwriting to Melville.)

TEXTUAL NOTE: H. M.] *added in pencil by Elizabeth Shaw Melville*

TO THE YOUNG MEN'S SOCIETY, DETROIT
BEFORE 16 NOVEMBER 1857 · PITTSFIELD

Unlocated. A letter replying to a now unlocated invitation to lecture for the Young Men's Society, Detroit, Michigan, can be inferred from Melville's statement in his 16 November letter (below) that "I am engaged at Detroit on the 12th Jan." The date is also recorded in his lecture engagement notebook (see the NN *Piazza Tales* volume, pp. 802 and 806). On 12 January 1858 at Detroit, Melville delivered his lecture "Statues in Rome," for which he was paid fifty dollars.

TO [LOUIS W. BURNHAM?]
BEFORE 16 NOVEMBER 1857 · PITTSFIELD

Unlocated. As his 16 November 1857 letter, just below, indicates, Melville had already been in correspondence with a representative of either the Rockford, Illinois, Young Men's Association or of "Burnham's Commercial Institute," probably to acknowledge a lecture invitation.

TO [LOUIS W. BURNHAM?]
16 NOVEMBER 1857 · PITTSFIELD

This letter regarding a possible lecture engagement at Rockford, Illinois, was probably written to Louis Woodworth Burnham (1831–93), the corresponding secretary in 1857–58 of the Rockford Young Men's Association. Burnham was the principal of a business school called "Burnham's Commercial Institute," which also sponsored a series of lectures in Rockford. (His name is suggested by the penciled notation on the back of the letter made by one of the letter's owners; however, this notation could refer to Burnham's Antique Book Store in Boston.) Melville wrote the letter only a few days before he left for Boston, where he stayed with the Shaws before delivering his first lecture, at Lawrence, Massachusetts, on 23 November. His proposed lecture in Rockford was not given during the 1857–58 season, but he lectured there during the following season through the agency of James Grant Wilson, secretary of the Chicago Young Men's Association in 1858–59 (see the letter of 8 December 1858, below). (Thus the 1857–58 Chicago secretary, Charles A. Dupee, may have been the recipient of this letter, but the lack of any mention of Chicago discounts this possibility.) Presumably Melville received a reply to this letter, but whether his correspondent, or he in a second letter, canceled the proposed lecture engagement is not known.

Pittsfield Nov. 16th 1857

Dear Sir — As my arrangements are about maturing, it is necessary for me to know of my positive engagements. And would therefore like to fix upon the time for lecturing in your part of the country, at one place or more, as you may have already arranged, or as may be hereafter arranged. ——
I am engaged at Detroit on the 12th Jan. and would like to go on to you as speedily as may be from there. Would 15th, or 16th Jan. at Rockford answer? Or as you know the routes &c better than I, perhaps you could name the earliest day after the 12th which would best accommodate me. Please write at once, addressing me at *Boston, Mass. care of Chief Justice Shaw*.

Yours Truly
H Melville

ALS on a 12.4 × 16.9 cm sheet of white laid paper with lines. Melville inscribed only one side of the leaf, in ink. The penciled notation on the back of this letter, ".50¢ | Bought of | Burnham | Jan 1885", is attributed by Frederick James Kennedy to the Reverend E. F. Strickland of Benton Harbor, Michigan (who wrote to famous people in the 1880's asking for their autographs, but also occasionally bought letters).

LOCATION: Collection of Frederick James Kennedy and Joyce Deveau Kennedy. *Provenance*: [E. F. Strickland?]; Hamilton Auction, sale 39, 29 January 1970, lot 241 (with reproduction).

PUBLICATION: (reproduction only) Kenneth Walter Cameron, "A Melville Letter and Stray Books from His Library," *ESQ* 63 (Spring 1971), 48.

TEXTUAL NOTE: *Mass.*] *inserted above caret*

TO LEMUEL SHAW
BEFORE 19 NOVEMBER 1857 · [PITTSFIELD?]

Unlocated. A letter from Melville to Lemuel Shaw may be inferred from Shaw's 19 November 1857 letter to Peter Gansevoort, stating: "We expect Herman & his wife on Saturday evening. He is to make his first essay at lecturing at Lawrence on Wednesday next" (NYPL-GL; cited by Leyda in the *Log*, II, 584, but at present unlocated). Davis-Gilman Unlocated 357.

TO THE PROVIDENT SOCIETY, LAWRENCE
BEFORE 23 NOVEMBER 1857 · [PITTSFIELD?]

Unlocated. A letter replying to a now unlocated invitation to lecture for the Provident Society of Lawrence, Massachusetts, can be inferred from Melville's lecture engagement notebook (see the NN *Piazza Tales* volume, pp. 803 and 806). Merton M. Sealts, Jr., suggests that Melville's brother-in-law John Hoadley, then living in Lawrence, arranged for him to deliver his lecture "Statues in Rome" on 23 November, a benefit engagement and his first on the season's lecture circuit (*Melville as Lecturer*, p. 21). Possibly Melville's correspondence was with Hoadley.

TO THE PENNACOOK LYCEUM, CONCORD
BEFORE 24 NOVEMBER 1857 · [PITTSFIELD?]

Unlocated. A letter replying to a now unlocated invitation to lecture for the Pennacook Lyceum, Concord, New Hampshire, can be inferred from Melville's lecture engagement notebook (see the NN *Piazza Tales* volume, pp. 803 and 806). On 24 November 1857, Melville delivered at Concord his lecture "Statues in Rome," for which he was paid thirty dollars.

TO [A. D. LAMSON?]
27 NOVEMBER 1857 · BOSTON

Leyda (*Log*, II, 584) suggested that this letter written from Judge Shaw's home in Boston where the Melvilles were spending Thanksgiving was addressed to A. D. Lamson of Malden, Massachusetts. The last of Melville's entries for 1857 in his lecture engagement notebook reads: "Malden Dec 28th? | Call on A. D. Lamson — 70 State st. | after 1st Jan — see note"; later he canceled the date (for a reproduction of this page, see the NN *Piazza Tales* volume, p. 803). This is Melville's only lecture cancellation recorded in his notebook for December 1857 (his cancellations for Wilmington and Rockford both had tentative January dates; his third cancellation, for Syracuse, is not followed by a date in his notebook). Melville's expense sheets, included in his notebook, show that he spent Christmas with his uncle Herman, his mother, and his sister Augusta at Gansevoort, which he left on 28 December for a brief visit home in Pittsfield before lecturing in New Haven on

30 December—possibly the reason he declined a 28 December engagement to lecture.

Melville's final comment in this letter refers to Charles Mackay (1814–89), Scottish poet, journalist, and songwriter, who came to the United States for an eight-month lecture tour in 1857. Although Melville's comment seems to be suggesting Mackay as a substitute, Mackay's published account of his lecture tour, *Life and Liberty in America* (London: Smith, Elder, 1859), shows that he was in Philadelphia and Washington between 19 December 1857 and 11 January 1858 and that he did not lecture in Malden.

Boston Nov. 27th 1857.

Dear Sir — Yours of the 23^d has been handed to me. — I am sorry that it will be quite impossible for me to be with you in Dec. and must therefore regret that our negotiation must, for this season at least, fall through.

Mr Mackay's lectures have, I hear, given very great pleasure.

Truly Yours
H Melville

ALS on a 12.3 × 18.5 cm part-sheet (torn along the left edge) of white laid paper. Melville inscribed only one side of the leaf, in ink. It is now mounted in a British Library manuscript book.

LOCATION: British Library. *Provenance*: American Art Association, Anderson Galleries, sale 4180, 8 and 9 May 1935, item 250; T. O. Mabbott.

PUBLICATION: T. O. Mabbott, *Notes & Queries* 176 (28 January 1939), 60. Davis-Gilman 136.

TEXTUAL NOTE: handed] *inserted above canceled* forwarded

TO THE MERCANTILE LIBRARY ASSOCIATION, BOSTON
BEFORE 2 DECEMBER 1857 · [PITTSFIELD?]

Unlocated. A letter replying to a now unlocated invitation to lecture for the Mercantile Library Association, Boston, Massachusetts, can be inferred from Melville's lecture engagement notebook (see the NN *Piazza Tales* volume, pp. 803 and 806). On 2 December 1857 at Tremont Temple in Boston, Melville delivered his lecture "Statues in Rome," for which he was paid forty dollars. In the audience was his cousin Henry Gansevoort, who described the lecture in a 9 December letter to his father Peter Gansevoort, paraphrasing the account in the *Boston Daily Courier* (NYPL-GL; see the NN *Piazza Tales* volume, pp. 727–51).

TO UNKNOWN
4 DECEMBER 1857 · BOSTON

This brief letter was presumably written in response to an autograph collector.

Boston

Dec. 4th 1857

Dear Sir. Your note is received and in accordance with your request, I am

Very Truly Yours

H Melville

Original document not located. Text from catalogue reproduction.

LOCATION: at present unknown. *Provenance*: Kenneth Rendell, catalogue 67 (November 1971), item 150 (with reproduction).

TO THE MERCANTILE LIBRARY ASSOCIATION, MONTREAL
BEFORE 11 DECEMBER 1857 · [PITTSFIELD?]

Unlocated. A letter replying to a now unlocated invitation to lecture for the Mercantile Library Association in Montreal can be inferred from Melville's lecture engagement notebook. Melville delivered his lecture "Statues in Rome" at Montreal on 11 December, not 10 December as recorded in his notebook, and was paid fifty dollars (see the NN *Piazza Tales* volume, pp. 800, 803, and 806). Possibly there was an additional exchange of letters concerning this shift.

TO THE SARATOGA SPRINGS LECTURE COMMITTEE
BEFORE 21 DECEMBER 1857 · [PITTSFIELD?]

Unlocated. A letter replying to a now unlocated invitation to lecture at St. Nicholas Hall in Saratoga Springs, New York, can be inferred from Melville's lecture engagement notebook. Melville delivered his lecture "Statues in Rome" on 21 December, not 30 December as recorded in his notebook (see the NN *Piazza Tales* volume, pp. 800 and 806). Possibly there was an additional exchange of letters concerning this shift.

1858

TO UNKNOWN
1858 · PLACE UNKNOWN

Unlocated. Charles De F. Burns's September 1881 *Catalogue of Autographs* (157 Mercer Street, New York) listed as item 709: "MELVILLE, HERMAN. Author of

Omoo, etc. A.L.S. 1 p. 8 vo. 1858." The price, common for other items in the catalogue, was fifty cents. Since all of the single-page letters extant for 1858 either do not bear that date in their heading or remained among the Duyckinck papers, this letter was probably not one of them, and it is now unlocated. Davis–Gilman Unlocated 362.

TO THE ITHACA LECTURE COMMITTEE
BEFORE 7 JANUARY 1858 · [PITTSFIELD?]

Unlocated. A letter replying to a now unlocated invitation to lecture at Ithaca, New York, can be inferred from Melville's lecture engagement notebook (see the NN *Piazza Tales* volume, pp. 802 and 806). On 7 January 1858 at Ithaca, Melville delivered his lecture "Statues in Rome," for which he was paid fifty dollars. His entry for the Ithaca lecture was inserted in his lecture engagement notebook above the canceled earlier entry of "Syracuse"—possibly an indication that he had had correspondence with the lecture committee of that town, but that the arrangement had fallen through (see Sealts, *Melville as Lecturer*, p. 27n.).

TO RICHARD T. GREENE
AFTER 9 JANUARY 1858 · [CLEVELAND?]

Unlocated. Learning of his engagement to lecture in Cleveland on 11 January 1858, Melville's old shipmate Richard Tobias (Toby) Greene, then living in Sandusky, Ohio, wrote to him on 9 January inviting him to visit (see LETTERS RECEIVED, pp. 660–61). Presumably Melville replied. Davis–Gilman Unlocated 358.

TO THE CLARKSVILLE LITERARY ASSOCIATION
BEFORE 22 JANUARY 1858 · [PITTSFIELD?]

Unlocated. Melville had promised in his 20 October 1857 letter (above) to W. O. Vance, a member of the Clarksville Literary Association, to "write again — as soon as arrangements are completed." This unlocated letter presumably specified the date of 22 January 1858 for his lecture there. Davis–Gilman Unlocated 359.

TO THE WILMINGTON LECTURE COMMITTEE
BEFORE 25 JANUARY 1858 · [PITTSFIELD?]

Unlocated. A letter replying to a now unlocated invitation to lecture at Wilmington, Delaware, can be inferred from Melville's lecture engagement notebook (see the NN *Piazza Tales* volume, p. 802). This lecture was tentatively planned for the last week of January or the first week of February 1858; however, as Elizabeth Melville's notation below the entry indicates, this engagement fell through for some reason and was "*given up*." Therefore there may have been a further exchange of letters.

TO THE MERCANTILE LIBRARY ASSOCIATION, CINCINNATI
BEFORE 2 FEBRUARY 1858 · [PITTSFIELD?]

Unlocated. A letter replying to a now unlocated invitation to lecture for the Mercantile Library Association, Cincinnati, Ohio, can be inferred from Melville's lecture given there on 2 February 1858, for which he was paid fifty dollars (see the NN *Piazza Tales* volume, p. 806). However, Cincinnati was not listed among the tentative engagements in Melville's lecture notebook.

TO THE GYMNASIUM AND LIBRARY ASSOCIATION, CHILLICOTHE
BEFORE 3 FEBRUARY 1858 · [PITTSFIELD?]

Unlocated. A letter replying to a now unlocated invitation to lecture for the Gymnasium and Library Association, Chillicothe, Ohio, can be inferred from Melville's lecture given there on 3 February 1858, for which he was paid forty dollars (see the NN *Piazza Tales* volume, p. 806). However, Chillicothe was not listed among the tentative engagements in Melville's lecture notebook.

TO THE MISHAWUM LITERARY ASSOCIATION, CHARLESTOWN
BEFORE 10 FEBRUARY 1858 · [PITTSFIELD?]

Unlocated. A letter replying to a now unlocated invitation to lecture for the Mishawum Literary Association, Charlestown, Massachusetts, can be inferred from Melville's lecture engagement notebook (see the NN *Piazza Tales* volume, pp. 803 and 806). On 10 February 1858 at Charlestown, Melville delivered his lecture "Statues in Rome," for which he was paid twenty dollars.

TO NATHANIEL PAINE
13 FEBRUARY [1858?] · BOSTON

Nathaniel Paine (1832–1917) was an autograph collector and local antiquarian of Worcester, Massachusetts. This letter can tentatively be placed in 1858, since that year Melville was in Boston between his lectures in Charlestown, Massachusetts, on 10 February and Rochester, New York, on 18 February, after a "prolonged absence" from home (since 23 November 1857) on the lecture circuit. It appears to have been written on the same paper as the 13 February 1858 letter Melville wrote to another autograph collector, L. J. Cist (just below).

Boston, Feb. 13th

Dear Sir — Yours of Dec. 26 has only just come to hand owing to my prolonged absence.

Truly Yours
H Melville

Nath. Paine Esq.
Worcester

ALS on an 11.3 × 11.8 cm part-sheet (torn along the left edge and cut along the top) of white laid paper. Melville inscribed only side of the leaf, in ink. Another hand later printed in red ink at the bottom of the page "Herman Melville | Author". The letter remains mounted on p. 94 of Edward Leland Spalding's autograph album.

LOCATION: American Antiquarian Society, Worcester, Massachusetts. *Provenance*: Edward Leland Spalding; Herbert Edwin Lombard.

PUBLICATION: Davis-Gilman 267.

TO L. J. CIST
13 FEBRUARY 1858 · BOSTON

Lewis Jacob Cist (1816–85) was a St. Louis banker who collected autographs and published a volume of poetry, *Trifles of Verse* (Cincinnati: Robinson & Jones, 1845). Although another hand, possibly Cist's, dated the letter "1857," this was an obvious mistake for 1858, when Melville was in Boston on that date. On 13 February 1857 he had been off the coasts of Calabria and Sicily on his Mediterranean trip. He returned on 20 May 1857, as the clipping that was later pasted to the bottom of this letter states (see the manuscript description, below). Only one letter by Melville, dated 1863, is listed among the autographs from Cist's collection auctioned by Bangs & Co. of New York at four different sales held in 1886 and 1887 (see under provenance, below). Possibly that letter was a second one that Cist later collected or possibly it was a misdating of this letter.

Boston Feb 13th

Dear Sir — Yours of the 1st Inst, is received, and I beg leave to subscribe myself

Very Truly Yours
H Melville

L J. Cist Esq
St. Louis

ALS on a 22.6 × 17.7 cm sheet, folded in half, of white laid paper, partially watermarked with the name "JOHNSON" and the date 1857 and embossed with the manufacturer's small shield-like stamp enclosing the name which appears to read "DELARUP & CO | LONDON". Melville inscribed the first page, in ink. Another hand, possibly Cist's, added the date "1857" in ink after Melville's "Feb 13ᵗʰ", rewriting the "18". Later pasted on the bottom of the letter was a newspaper clipping: "Herman Melville returned on the 20ᵗʰ instant [20 May 1857], in the steamer City of Manchester, from Liverpool, after a seven months' absence abroad."

LOCATION: UV-Barrett. *Provenance*: [possibly the Melville letter listed in the Bangs & Co., Cist Autograph Sale, part 4, 16–19 May 1887, lot 10–55 (dated, however, 1863)]; Charles Hamilton Autographs, 28 November 1953; Scribner's Book Store, April 1954.

PUBLICATION: Davis-Gilman 137.

TO THE ATHENAEUM AND MECHANICS' ASSOCIATION, ROCHESTER
BEFORE 18 FEBRUARY 1858 · [PITTSFIELD?]

Unlocated. A letter replying to a now unlocated invitation to lecture for the Athenaeum and Mechanics' Association, Rochester, New York, can be inferred from Melville's lecture engagement notebook. The lecture—"Statues in Rome," for which he was paid fifty dollars—took place on 18 February 1858, not on 23 February as recorded in the second entry in his lecture engagement notebook (see the NN *Piazza Tales* volume, pp. 802 and 806). Possibly there was an additional exchange of letters concerning this change of date.

TO GEORGE L. DUYCKINCK
6 NOVEMBER 1858 · PITTSFIELD

George Long Duyckinck (1823–63), editor and biographer, was the younger brother of Evert Duyckinck, with whom he edited the *Literary World* (1848–53) and the *Cyclopædia of American Literature* (1855). He also prepared an edition of Shakespeare in eight volumes (New York: Redfield, 1853) and was at this time preparing biographies, as an officer in the General Protestant Episcopal Sunday School Union and Church Book Society (four of these, on George Herbert, Thomas Ken, Jeremy Taylor, and Hugh Latimer, were published before his death). Only slightly acquainted with Melville when *Typee* was published (he doubted its "sober verity"), Duyckinck was touring Europe with William A. Butler in 1847 and 1848 when Melville lived in New York (for Butler see the headnote to Melville's 24 February 1849 letter to Evert Duyckinck). He was in the party that climbed Saddleback Mountain with Melville in 1851 and shared his interest in bookstores, but as late as 1856 Melville did not feel that the "extent" of his "acquaintance" with George Duyckinck justified an interruption of travel plans to visit him in a London hospital as long as other friends were there (see Melville's November 1856 letter to his brother Allan, above). Although several of Melville's letters to Evert Duyckinck contain greetings or messages for George, who also lived at 20 Clinton Place (see, for example, his letters of 24 February 1849, 2 and 14 December 1849, and 2 February 1850, above), this is the earliest known letter Melville wrote him.

On 12 September 1858 George Duyckinck, who was staying with his brother in the Berkshires, joined Melville on a two-day trip in the mountains near Pittsfield. After returning to New York, he sent Melville a five-volume set of Chapman's translation of Homer's *Iliad, Odyssey,* and related pieces (HCL-M: Sealts 276, 277, and 278). Although Melville's letter is dated only 6 November, it can be assigned to 1858 on the basis of the inscriptions he made in all five of the volumes, which read: "H. Melville from George Duyckinck Nov. 1858" (with "Pittsfield" added before the date in the first volume of *Iliad*). Evidently he was suffering again from chronic eye-trouble, and it was probably some time before he compared Pope and Chapman, and heard, as he suggests in this letter, Apollo's "hollow shriek" ("On the Morning of Christ's Nativity"; see Henry F. Pommer, *Milton and Melville* [Pittsburgh: University of Pittsburgh Press, 1850], pp. 25–26). Melville took these volumes of Chapman's Homer on his 1860 trip around Cape Horn, as his notations in them show (see *Journals*, p. 200).

Pittsfield Nov. 6th

My Dear Duyckinck —

Indisposition has prevented me from writing you ere now. Your gift is very acceptable — could not have been more so. I am glad to have a copy of Chapman's Homer. As for Pope's version (of which I have a copy) I expect it, — when I shall put Chapman beside it — to go off shrieking, like the bankrupt deities in Milton's hymn.
— Thus far I have been mostly engaged in cutting the leaves by way of pastime — as it wont do to read at present. Remember me to your brother & household. Mrs. M. joins

H Melville

ALS on a 24.5 × 19.7 cm part-sheet (torn along the top) of white wove paper, embossed with the manufacturer's rectangular stamp enclosing a three-domed capitol surrounded by the name "CONGRESS | PLATNER SMITH". The sheet was folded in half to form two leaves (with the manufacturer's stamp on its side in the top outside corner of the second leaf); Melville inscribed the first page, in ink, and addressed the envelope "George L. Duyckinck Esq. | N° 20 Clinton Place | New York"; it was postmarked in Pittsfield on 8 November. Another hand noted on the first page "[Nov. 6, 1858]".

LOCATION: NYPL-D.

PUBLICATION: (partial) *Log*, II, 596. Metcalf, p. 171. Davis-Gilman 138.

TEXTUAL NOTE: go] *written over* see

TO LEMUEL SHAW
AFTER 8 NOVEMBER 1858 · PITTSFIELD

Unlocated. On 8 November 1858 Judge Shaw wrote Melville, enclosing a check for
one hundred dollars toward "supplies for the approaching winter," which Melville
presumably acknowledged (see LETTERS RECEIVED, pp. 662–63). Davis-Gilman Unlocated 360.

TO JAMES GRANT WILSON
BEFORE 1 DECEMBER 1858 · [PITTSFIELD?]

Unlocated. A "former note," evidently responding to a now unlocated invitation
to lecture for the Young Men's Association in Chicago, is cited in Melville's 8 December 1858 letter to James Grant Wilson, the representative of their lecture committee (see below). This may have been the unidentified one-page letter by Melville
that was listed under item 384 in Part II of the Merwin-Clayton catalogue of the
James Grant Wilson autograph collection, auctioned in part on 16–17 May 1905.
That letter was sold with an 1893 ALS of the poet Will Carleton. Davis-Gilman
Unlocated 361.

TO THE YONKERS LIBRARY ASSOCIATION
BEFORE 6 DECEMBER 1858 · [PITTSFIELD?]

Unlocated. A letter replying to a now unlocated invitation to lecture for the Yonkers Library Association, Yonkers, New York, can be inferred from Melville's lecture engagement notebook (see the NN *Piazza Tales* volume, p. 807). Melville
delivered his second lecture "The South Seas" for the first time at Yonkers on 6
December 1858, for which he was paid thirty dollars.

TO JAMES GRANT WILSON
8 DECEMBER 1858 · NEW YORK

James Grant Wilson (1832–1914), best known as coeditor of *Appletons' Cyclopædia
of American Biography* (1887–89), was at this time editor and proprietor of the
Church Record (later the *Chicago Record*) and a member of the lecture committee of
the Chicago Young Men's Association. Besides Melville, his committee had invited
Horace Greeley, Oliver Wendell Holmes, and James Russell Lowell to lecture in the
1858–59 season (see the *Church Record* 2 [1 November 1858], 121). According to his
lecture engagement notebook, Melville delivered his lecture "The South Seas" on
24 February 1859, for a fee of fifty dollars. His following lectures in Milwaukee,
Wisconsin, and in Rockford and Quincy, Illinois, were also apparently solicited by
Wilson for Melville (see the next entry). Melville was in New York at this time
after having delivered his first lecture for the 1858–59 season at Yonkers. His "former note" is unlocated, as are Wilson's original invitation and his 1 December letter
cited here.

New York Dec 8th

Dear Sir: Yours of the 1st Inst. has just been forwarded to me.

I am willing to come for the amount which the other lecturers you name receive — $50; hoping, that, as you suggest, you will be able to make additional appointments for me in your quarter; for which I shall be much obliged to you.

Of the two vacant evenings you name, I select that of Feb. 24th. I am not sure whether in my former note I named my subject.

It is *The South Seas*.

Yours Very Truly
H Melville

James G. Wilson Esq.
Chicago.

ALS on a 26.9 × 20.3 cm sheet, folded in half, of white laid paper with lines, embossed with the manufacturer's circular stamp enclosing a hand with a pen. Melville inscribed the first and third pages, in ink. Another hand noted in pencil at the top of the first page "Herman Melville | ALS [1858?]" and at the bottom "very rare". The fourth page was labeled in pencil "(51M61)", presumably by a dealer.

LOCATION: NYPL-GL. *Provenance*: possibly the unidentified Melville ALS in lot 384 of the James Grant Wilson sale, Merwin-Clayton, 16–17 May 1905 (however, this item is listed as a single-page letter); Goodspeed's Bookstore; Jay Leyda (1947); Zeitlin & Ver Brugge Booksellers (1951).

PUBLICATION: (partial) *Log*, II, 597. Davis-Gilman 139.

TEXTUAL NOTE: Feb. 24th.] *before* (over) *in bottom margin*

TO JAMES GRANT WILSON
AFTER 8 DECEMBER 1858 · [PITTSFIELD?]

Unlocated. A reply to a third letter, now unlocated, from James Grant Wilson, listing "additional appointments" for Melville in towns near Chicago, can be inferred from Melville's 8 December letter to Wilson, asking Wilson to make lecture appointments for him in nearby cities. Melville delivered his lecture "The South Seas" at three additional "western" associations: the Young Men's Association in Milwaukee, Wisconsin, on 25 February 1859, the Young Men's Association in Rockford, Illinois, on 28 February 1859, and the Lyceum in Quincy, Illinois, on 2 March 1859 (see the NN *Piazza Tales* volume, p. 807). See the entry for Wilson's unlocated third letter to Melville, written after 8 December 1858 (LETTERS RECEIVED, p. 664), for the reasons it is likely that Melville corresponded with only Wilson as the representative of these associations rather than with the individual lecture committees.

TO GEORGE L. DUYCKINCK
13 DECEMBER 1858 · PITTSFIELD

Although dated only 13 December, this letter's association with Melville's lecture engagements places it in 1858. While in New York during the second week of December 1858, Melville had evidently called at the Duyckinck house in Clinton Place and discussed with George Duyckinck plans for a lecture before the New-York Historical Society. Duyckinck's now unlocated note which had greeted Melville on his return to Pittsfield evidently mentioned no date for the lecture, but his subsequent note (also unlocated) specified the date 7 February 1859. See Melville's 20 December 1858 letter to Duyckinck for his acknowledgment of this arrangement. Melville's call to see the Duyckincks' friend David Davidson was also an effort to arrange a lecture engagement at Jersey City, which did not, however, materialize. Melville knew Davidson, formerly the London agent of Wiley & Putnam, from his 1849–50 stay in London (see *Journals*, pp. 21, 30, 46, 302–3, 329, 373).

Pittsfield Dec. 13th

My Dear Duyckinck —

Would it make too much trouble if for the two days in February I named to you (to choose from) for my lecture before your Society, I should substitute the 10th & 17th of January? either of which, would, as I now see, be more convenient to me. —

But if such change would involve troublesome change in other quarters — of course I would not think of it. In that case, consider the above unwritten.

I called to see Mr Davidson the day I saw you in Clinton Place, but he was out. After waiting for him awhile, I went away. If by chance you should meet him, wont' you mention that I called?

I should like to procure an engagement through Mr Davidson, especially if it could be made to fall about the time of my lecture before The Historical Society.

Upon getting home, I was greeted by your note. — My regards to your brother, and Beleive me

Truly Yours
H Melville

ALS on a 25 × 20.3 cm sheet, folded in half, of white laid paper with lines, embossed with the manufacturer's oval stamp enclosing a shield bearing the word "LONDON" and encircled by the name "ALBION MILLS". Melville inscribed the first and third pages, i ink, and addressed the envelope "George L. Duyckinck Esq. | 20 Clinton Place | New York ; it was postmarked in Pittsfield on 13 December.

LOCATION: NYPL-D.

PUBLICATION: (partial) *Log*, II, 597. Davis-Gilman 140.

TEXTUAL NOTES: Dec. 13ᵗʰ] 3 *written over 2* • January?] *question mark wr ten over a comma*

TO THE PITTSFIELD LECTURE COM ITTEE
BEFORE 14 DECEMBER 1858 · [PITTS ELD?]

Unlocated. Although Melville's engagement to lecture in hi own village may have been simply arranged in person, a letter possibly may be i ferred from his lecture engagement notebook (see the NN *Piazza Tales* volume p. 807). Melville delivered his lecture "The South Seas" in Pittsfield on 14 D   mber 1858.

TO THE MERCANTILE LIBRARY, BALTIMORE
BEFORE 20 DECEMBER 1858 · [PI TSFIELD?]

Unlocated. A letter replying to a now unlocated invitation to lecture for the Mercantile Library, Baltimore, can be inferred from Melville's lecture engagement notebook (see the NN *Piazza Tales* volume, p. 807) and from his 20 December 1858 letter to George Duyckinck, just below, in which he mentions that his engagement for Baltimore had been set. Melville delivered his lecture "The South Seas" at the Universalist Church in Baltimore on 8 February 1859.

TO GEORGE L. DUYCKINCK
20 DECEMBER 1858 · PITTSFIELD

This letter was written in response to a now unlocated note from George Duyckinck, answering Melville's 13 December 1858 letter requesting a different date for his New York lecture. Despite the close timing, Melville did lecture at the New-York Historical Society on 7 February 1859 and at the Universalist Church in Baltimore on 8 February. According to his lecture engagement notebook he received fifty-five dollars for his New York lecture and one hundred for his Baltimore lecture (see the NN *Piazza Tales* volume, p. 807). Both received favorable reviews. The New York one was attended by Peter Gansevoort's son, Melville's cousin Henry, who wrote on 8 February to his sister Catherine praising the lecture "The South Seas": "It was in Cousin Hermans true vein. He was emphatically himself, and the lecture was to me like a quantity tied together — of his vivid and colloquial sketches (always too short) told under the inspiration of Madeira after dinner or drawn forth by some proper association elsewhere" (NYPL-GL). The possible engagement at Jersey City to be arranged by Duyckinck's friend David Davidson never came about (for more on Davidson, see the headnote to Melville's earlier 13 December 1858 letter to Duyckinck, above).

Pittsfield Dec. 20th — Monday.
My Dear Duyckinck — Your note (received on Saturday) is unaccountably among the missing. — Some one must have pilfered it for the autograph. I can't otherwise account for its mysterious disappearance.

But, as I remember, you have named *Feb. 7th* for my day, and deprecate any change. — Well & good. Let that be the day — only, is it certain that I can get to Baltimore the day following in time to immortalise myself there also? But I suppose I can.

Touching Mr Davidson & Jersey City, I am sure I am most obliged to you for your good offices in speaking to him. I don't know that I can do anything about it at present, further at least than to let the matter alone, and dispose myself according to the event. — I should be glad to lecture there — or anywhere. If they will pay expences, & give a reasonable fee, I am ready to lecture in Labrador or on the Isle of Desolation off Patagonia.

Bear with mine infirmity of jocularity (which, I am aware, should hardly intrude into a semi-business letter like this) and Beleive me

Sincerely Yours
H Melville

George Duyckinck Esq.
New York.

ALS on a 24.9 × 20.3 cm sheet, folded in half, of white laid paper with lines, embossed with the manufacturer's oval stamp enclosing a shield bearing the word "LONDON" and encircled by the name "ALBION MILLS". Melville inscribed the first and third pages, in ink, and addressed the envelope "George Duyckinck Esq. | — 20 Clinton Place — | New York"; it was postmarked in Pittsfield on 21 December.

LOCATION: NYPL-D.

PUBLICATION: Thorp, pp. 396–97. Davis-Gilman 141.

TEXTUAL NOTE: disappearance] *miswritten* disappearce

1859

TO THE MECHANIC APPRENTICES' LIBRARY ASSOCIATION,
BOSTON
BEFORE 31 JANUARY 1859 · [PITTSFIELD?]

Unlocated. A letter replying to a now unlocated invitation to lecture for the Mechanic Apprentices' Library Association, Boston, Massachusetts, can be inferred from Melville's lecture engagement notebook (see the NN *Piazza Tales* volume, p. 807). Melville delivered his lecture "The South Seas" there on 31 January 1859. For a 1 February letter from one of his listeners, Norman W. Stearns, see LETTERS RECEIVED, pp. 666–67, and the entry for Melville's now unlocated response to Stearns (written after 1 February 1859), below.

TO UNKNOWN
31 JANUARY [1859?] · [BOSTON?]

This brief note dated only 31 January was probably written on the day of Melville's lecture for the Mechanic Apprentices' Library Association in Boston. That is the only lecture he is known to have delivered on the last day in January during his three-year career as a lecturer.

Please admit the bearer.

Herman Melville

31st Jan.

Original document not located. Text from catalogue reproduction.

LOCATION: at present unknown. *Provenance*: Kenneth Rendell catalogue, November 1988 (with reproduction).

TO NORMAN W. STEARNS
AFTER 1 FEBRUARY 1859 · [PITTSFIELD?]

Unlocated. After hearing Melville give his lecture "The South Seas" to the Boston Mechanic Apprentices' Library Association, Norman W. Stearns, a draughtsman in Boston, wrote Melville a letter about his own experiences in Polynesia (see LETTERS RECEIVED, pp. 666–67). Stearns enclosed his address for Melville's reply, and presumably Melville acknowledged the letter. Davis-Gilman Unlocated 363.

TO OLIVER RUSS
AFTER 4 FEBRUARY 1859 · [PITTSFIELD?]

Unlocated. On 4 February 1859 Oliver Russ, an old shipmate on the U.S.S. *United States* in 1844, wrote Melville an account of his life since their shipboard days and entreated him to write back (see LETTERS RECEIVED, pp. 667–68). Apparently Melville did so not long afterwards and then again on 18 December 1860 (see below), as Russ acknowledged in a 24 December 1860 letter (see LETTERS RECEIVED, pp. 675–77). Davis-Gilman Unlocated 364.

TO WILLIAM H. BARRY
12 FEBRUARY 1859 · PITTSFIELD

William H. Barry, listed in the 1860 Lynn, Massachusetts, directory as a shoe manufacturer, was a member of the Lynn Young Men's Debating Society from 1852 to 1854 (see David N. Johnson, *Sketches of Lynn* [Lynn: Nichols, 1880], pp. 239–40, 252). Barry's notes of 2 and 8 February extending the invitation to Melville are now unlocated, as are the reply Melville asks Barry to write immediately and the letter by which Melville presumably arranged the "exact day" to lecture. On 16 March 1859 Melville gave his lecture "The South Seas" at Sagamore Hall in Lynn; no record of when he delivered his second lecture, "Statues in Rome," there has been found (Sealts, *Melville as Lecturer*, pp. 91–92).

Pittsfield, Feb. 12th 1859

Dear Sir: Absence from home has prevented an earlier reply to your notes of the 2d and 8th Inst. — I should be happy to lecture at Lynn, if we can agree upon the time &c.

The latter part of next week I leave for the West, to be gone two weeks, more or less. Upon my return I shall be able to name an exact day (of course, a near one) to be with you.

I have two lectures:

The South Seas

Statues in Rome

If, as you intimate, you should like me to deliver both, well and good.

My terms, of course, I find it necessary to adapt to the means of various Societies. I should think that, in the present case, thirty dollars for each lecture would not be too much.

If two lectures are delivered I should like them to be on successive nights, or at least upon nights as near together as possible.

If the above meets with your views, be kind enough to reply immediately, that I may get your letter before leaving home again.

Very Truly Yours
H. Melville

W. H. Barry Esq.
Lynn.

ALS on a 24.9 × 20.3 cm sheet, folded in half, of white laid paper with lines, embossed with the manufacturer's oval stamp enclosing a shield bearing the word "LONDON" and encircled by the name "ALBION MILLS". Melville inscribed the first and third pages, in ink.

LOCATION: Collection of William Reese. *Provenance*: Carroll A. Wilson (inserted in an American first edition of *Moby-Dick*); Dr. Joseph E. Fields; Charles E. Feinberg sale, Parke-Bernet Galleries, sale 2676, 2–3 April 1968, lot 481 (with reproduction); H. Bradley Martin sale, Sotheby's, New York, sale 5971, 30–31 January 1990, lot 2170 (with reproduction).

PUBLICATION: (partial) Carroll A. Wilson, *Thirteen Author Collections of the Nineteenth Century and Five Centuries of Familiar Quotations* (New York: Privately Printed for Charles Scribner's Sons, 1950), I, 313. Davis-Gilman 142 (partial).

TO WILLIAM H. BARRY
LATE FEBRUARY 1859 · PITTSFIELD

Unlocated. In his 12 February 1859 letter to William H. Barry (just above), Melville promised that upon his return from a two-week trip to the West he would "name an exact day . . . to be with you." Presumably he arranged by letter in late February the 16 March date of his lecture in Lynn.

TO GIOVANNI SPAGGIARI
AFTER 9 APRIL 1859 · [PITTSFIELD?]

Unlocated. Giovanni Spaggiari, an Italian anthologist, wrote to Melville on 9 April 1859 requesting him to acknowledge whether he had indeed written an "apostrophe to America" that had been attributed to him in a Turin magazine (see LETTERS RECEIVED, pp. 669–71). Presumably Melville answered this query in the negative, since Spaggiari did not attribute this item to Melville when he published a translation of it in his 1861 *Latin-English-Italian Anthology*, but did include and attribute to Melville the poem from *Mardi* from which the apostrophe had been loosely derived. See the headnote to Spaggiari's letter for a fuller discussion of this matter. Davis-Gilman Unlocated 365.

TO [HARPER & BROTHERS?]
18 MAY 1859 · PITTSFIELD

The "two Pieces" that accompanied this letter remain unidentified and could have been either prose or poetry, since Melville used the term "piece" to refer to both. It is also uncertain which publisher Melville was addressing. Davis and Gilman report that David Randall of Scribner's Book Store thought he recalled obtaining the letter from the library of one of the Harper associates. However, no pieces by Melville are known to have appeared in *Harper's* after 18 May 1859 until seven years later in 1866, when five of his Civil War poems (later among those collected in *Battle-Pieces*) were published. Although Melville dated the letter simply 18 May, it can be placed with some certainty in 1859, since it is endorsed with this date in ink. (Because the letter until recently was pasted to another sheet, this endorsement went unnoticed by Davis and Gilman. Their study of its paper showed it to have the same manufacturer's stamp of Albion Mills, London, which Melville used for his letters to George Duyckinck on 13 and 20 December 1858 and all of his surviving located letters from 1859—thus placing it in the same time-period.)

Pittsfield May 18th

Gentlemen:

Here are two Pieces, which, if you find them suited to your Magazine I should be happy to see them appear there. — In case of publication, you may, if you please, send me what you think they are worth.

Very Truly Yours
H Melville.

ALS on a 12.5 × 20.3 cm part-sheet (torn along the left edge) of white laid paper, faintly embossed with the manufacturer's oval stamp enclosing a shield bearing the word "LONDON" and encircled by the name "ALBION MILLS". Melville inscribed only one side of the leaf, in ink. Another hand, presumably a clerk's, noted in ink on the verso "H. Melville | May 18 1859". A third hand penciled "[1859]" after Melville's date. It was formerly pasted to a sheet with the notation "Purchased from Ben Bloomfield, Dec. 12, 1940 | Gansevoort-Lansing Collection Fund."

LOCATION: NYPL-GL. *Provenance*: Scribner's Book Store; Bodley Head Book Shop (September 1939); Ben Bloomfield Autographs.

PUBLICATION: *Log*, II, 606. Davis-Gilman 143.

TO DANIEL SHEPHERD
6 JULY 1859 · PITTSFIELD

Daniel Shepherd (d. 1870), lawyer and author, was Allan Melville's law partner for a number of years. The first indication of his connection with Melville is his 1850 witnessing with Allan of the indenture assigning the copyright of *Typee* and *Omoo* to John Murray (HCL-M). A 7 August 1856 notation in Melville's uncle Herman Gansevoort's remembrancer indicates that Shepherd was more than just a business associate: "Herman & Allan gone to Lake George, expected to meet D Shepherd in the Carrs to join them on an excursion of pleasure" (NYPL-GL). In 1856 Shepherd published, anonymously, *Saratoga: A Story of 1787* (Philadelphia: Peterson). Allan sent the book, a historical romance very much in the style of Cooper, to Duyckinck on 8 October, along with a note introducing Shepherd as a "friend of Hermans" (NYPL-D). Duyckinck noted in his diary that he joined a gathering the following evening at Shepherd's apartment, along with "Herman & Allan Melville," and commented, "Good talk — Herman warming like an old sailor over the supper" (NYPL-D).

This letter in verse is the only known correspondence between Melville and Shepherd, and this fair copy (with only the word "withhold" misspelled) may in fact not have been sent, since it was among the papers inherited by Allan Melville's granddaughter Agnes Morewood. It is not known whether Shepherd ever visited Arrowhead as Melville encourages him to do here, despite Melville's lack of claret and otard (for another disquisition on otard, see *Israel Potter*, chap. 9, pp. 50–52). Clearly in part an exercise, Melville's verse-letter contains numerous "poetic" allusions to the pastoral tradition. In the second stanza, Melville's reference is to the Italian resistance against Austria, masterminded by Count Camillo Benso di Cavour, which had recently broken out into warfare (see also Melville's unpublished poem "Naples in the Time of Bomba," in *Collected Poems*, ed. Howard P. Vincent [Hendricks House: Chicago, 1947], pp. 339–68, and in the NN volume *Billy Budd, Sailor and Other Late Manuscripts*).

To Daniel Shepherd:

Come, Shepherd, come and visit me:
Come, we'll make it Arcady;
Come, if but for charity.
Sure, with such a pastoral name,
Thee the city should not claim.
Come, then, Shepherd, come away,
Thy sheep in bordering pastures stray.

Come, Daniel, come and visit me:
I'm lost in many a quandary:
I've dreamed, like Bab'lon's Majesty:
Prophet, come expound for me.
— I dreamed I saw a laurel grove,
Claimed for his by the bird of Jove,

Who, elate with such dominion,
Oft cuffed the boughs with haughty pinion.
Indignantly the trees complain,
Accusing his afflictive reign.
Their plaints the chivalry excite
Of chanticleers, a plucky host:
They battle with the bird of light.
Beaten, he wings his Northward flight,
No more his laurel realm to boast,
Where now, to crow, the cocks alight,
And — break down all the branches quite!
Such a weight of friendship pure
The grateful trees could not endure.
This dream, it still disturbeth me:
Seer, foreshows it Italy?

But other visions stir my head;
No poet-problems, fancy-fed —
Domestic prose of board and bed.
I marvel oft how guest *unwined*
Will to this farm-house be resigned.
Not a pint of ruby claret
    Cooleth in our cellar-bin;
And, ripening in our sultry garret,
    Otard glows no flask within.
[Claret and Otard here I name
Because each is your fav'rite flame:
Placed 'tween the two decanters, you,
Like Alexander, your dear charmers view,
And both so fair you find, you neither can eschew: —
— That's what they call an Alexandrine;
Do'nt you think it very damn'd fine?]
— Brackets serve to fence this prattle,
Pound for episodic cattle. —

I said that me the Fates do cripple
In matter of a wholesome "tipple."
Now, is it for oft cursing gold,
    For lucre vile,

The Hags do thus from me withold
   Sweet Bacchus' smile?
Smile, that like other smiles as mellow,
Not often greets Truth's simple fellow: —
For why? Not his the magic Dollar?
You should know, you Wall-Street scholar!
— Of Bourbon that is rather new
I brag a fat black bottle or two, —
Shepherd, is this such Mountain-Dew
As one might fitly offer you?
Yet if cold water will content ye
My word, of that ye shall have plenty.
Thanks to late floods, our spring, it brims, —
Will't mind o'ermuch of goblet-rims?

— I've told some doubts that sadly pose me:
Come thou now, and straight resolve me.
Come, these matters sagely read,
Daniel, of the prophet breed.

Daniel Shepherd, come and rove —
   Freely rove two faery dells;
The one the Housatonic clove,
   And that where genial Friendship dwells.

Pittsfield July 6th 1859.

AL on a 24.8 × 20.1 cm sheet, folded in half, of white laid paper, embossed with the manufacturer's oval stamp enclosing a shield bearing the word "LONDON" and encircled by the name "ALBION MILLS". Melville inscribed all four pages, in ink.

LOCATION: Berkshire Athenaeum, Pittsfield, Massachusetts. *Provenance*: Agnes Morewood; Henry A. Murray; Eleanor Melville Metcalf.

PUBLICATION: Thorp, pp. 346–48. Davis-Gilman 144.

TEXTUAL NOTES: stray.] *written over wiped word-start* • the cocks] the *written over wiped word-start* • This dream . . . Italy?] *added between stanzas* • But] *after bracket added in margin to indicate new stanza, when original space above was filled in by two added lines* • And that] *inserted with caret above canceled* And that *written over* The one

TO THE YOUNG MEN'S ASSOCIATION, FLUSHING
BEFORE 7 NOVEMBER 1859 · [PITTSFIELD?]

Unlocated. A letter replying to a now unlocated invitation to lecture for the Young Men's Association, Flushing, Long Island, can be inferred from Melville's lecture engagement notebook (see the NN *Piazza Tales* volume, p. 807). Melville delivered his lecture "Traveling" at Flushing on 7 November 1859.

TO GEORGE L. DUYCKINCK
14 DECEMBER 1859 · PITTSFIELD

This brief December letter—with its Shakespearean allusion to "winter & rough weather" (*As You Like It*, 2.5.47)—is Melville's reply to a now unlocated inquiry from George Duyckinck concerning George Herbert's *The Temple* (Philadelphia: Hazard, 1857; Sealts 270), which conforms to Melville's bibliographical description. Duyckinck's interest in this book probably stemmed from his 1858 biography, *The Life of George Herbert*, the first in the series for the General Protestant Episcopal Sunday School Union and Church Book Society (see the headnote to Melville's 6 November 1858 letter to Duyckinck, above).

Pittsfield Dec. 14, 1859

My Dear Duyckinck:

Certainly: — Pages, 384: Price, 25 cts (at least that's all I gave for it) Publisher, Willis P. Hazard, Phil. — Date, 1857.

As to the size — there you have me. But by *rule*, it is 5½ In. by 4¼, and 1 In. thick. I am a sorry arithmetician; but, seems to me, if you figure this up by cord-measure and compound reduction, the result will be the size of the book, technically expressed.

My regards to your brother, and Beleive Me

"In spite of winter & rough weather"

Yours Truly
H Melville

George Duyckinck Esq.

ALS on a 24.9 × 20.3 cm sheet, folded in half, of white laid paper with lines, embossed with the manufacturer's oval stamp enclosing a shield bearing the word "LONDON" and encircled by the name "ALBION MILLS". Melville inscribed the first page, in ink, and addressed the envelope "George L. Duyckinck Esq. | 20 Clinton Place | New York"; it was postmarked in Pittsfield on [15?] December.

LOCATION: NYPL-D.

PUBLICATION: (partial) *Log*, II, 609–10. Davis-Gilman 145.

TEXTUAL NOTES: by 4¼] by *written over wiped* an • size of the book] *after canceled* techn

1860

TO THE PEABODY INSTITUTE, SOUTH DANVERS
BEFORE 14 FEBRUARY 1860 • [PITTSFIELD?]

Unlocated. A letter replying to a now unlocated invitation to lecture for the Peabody Institute in South Danvers, Massachusetts, can be inferred from Melville's lecture engagement notebook (see the NN *Piazza Tales* volume, p. 807). Melville delivered his lecture "Traveling" for the institute on 14 February 1860.

TO THE DOWSE INSTITUTE, CAMBRIDGEPORT
BEFORE 21 FEBRUARY 1860 • [PITTSFIELD?]

Unlocated. A letter replying to a now unlocated invitation to lecture for the Dowse Institute in Cambridgeport, Massachusetts, can be inferred from Melville's lecture engagement notebook (see the NN *Piazza Tales* volume, p. 807). Melville delivered his lecture "Traveling" for the institute on 21 February 1860.

TO LEMUEL SHAW
BEFORE 15 MAY 1860 • [PITTSFIELD?]

Unlocated. A letter from Melville is cited in Judge Shaw's reply, dated 15 May 1860 (see LETTERS RECEIVED, pp. 672–75). Melville had apparently written to his father-in-law about his decision to join his youngest brother, Thomas, now a ship's captain, on his next voyage. (For more background on this trip and Melville's journal of it, see *Journals*, pp. 131–35, 194–207.) Davis-Gilman Unlocated 366.

TO EVERT A. DUYCKINCK
21 MAY 1860 • PITTSFIELD

This is the first of three letters concerning the volume of poems Melville put together for publication before leaving with his brother Captain Thomas Melville on their 1860 *Meteor* voyage around Cape Horn. With the manuscript still being copied by his wife on the eve of his departure, Melville enlisted the expertise of his "old acquaintance" Evert Duyckinck to assist her efforts and those of his brother Allan in seeking a publisher and seeing the volume through the press. Despite all this preparation, however, the volume was not published. Neither Charles Scribner nor Rudd & Carleton was willing to take the book. Evidently, however, Duyckinck praised the poems to Elizabeth Melville, as indicated by a 23 June letter she wrote to him after the Scribner rejection: "I think infinitely more of yours and your brother's opinion of it, and feel more confidence in its worth, since it has been looked at by persons of judgment and taste, than ever before — it has been such a profound secret between Herman and myself for so long, that I rejoice to have my own prejudice in its favor confirmed by some one in whose appreciation we can feel confidence — for I do not believe you would speak favorably of it, unless you could do so sincerely" (NYPL-D). She went on to suggest that Duyckinck submit the book to Derby & Jackson, "the first named being a brother-in-law of 'Toby' of Typee memory" (see LETTERS RECEIVED, p. 644 below). For discussions of the possible contents of Melville's unpublished volume, see Leon Howard, *Herman Melville: A Biography* (Berkeley: University of California Press, 1951), pp. 264–65; William H. Shurr, *The Mystery of Iniquity* (Lexington: University of Kentucky Press, 1972), p. 4; and the Historical Note to the NN *Published Poems* volume.

Pittsfield, May 21st. 1860

Dear Duyckinck: If you have met Allan lately he has perhaps informed you that in a few days I go with my brother Tom a voyage round Cape Horn. It was only determined upon a short time since; and I am at present busy, as you may imagine in getting ready for a somewhat long absence, and likewise in prepareing for type certain M.S.S.

Now may I with propriety ask of you, conditionally, a favor? Will you, upon the arrival of the M.S.S. in New York — that is, in the course of two weeks, or less — look over them and if they seem of a sort that you care to be any way concerned with, advice with Allan as to a publisher, and form of volume, &c. And, since I can hardly summon the impudence to ask you in the midst of better avocations, to go over the proof-sheets; and there appears to be no one, in fact, to attend to that matter but the printer — will you at least see that the printer's proof-reader is a careful and competent hand? — In short, may I, without seeming too confident, ask you, as a veteran & expert in these matters, and as an old acquaintance, to lend something of an overseeing eye to the launching of this craft — the committing of it to the elements?

Remember me with kindest regards to your brother; and answer me as soon as you can; and whether you say yea or nay, Beleive me

Sincerely Yours,
H. Melville.

Evert Duyckinck
New York.

ALS on a 37.2 × 22.9 cm sheet of white laid paper, watermarked with a large ornate design including a crown, a shield-like shape, and the initials "A C & L". The sheet was folded in half to make two leaves, which have now separated along the fold. Melville inscribed the first and third pages, in ink. A photocopy of the envelope, which Melville addressed "Evert Duyckinck Esq. | N° 20. Clinton Place | New York", and which was postmarked in Pittsfield on 2[1?] May, is in the Davis-Gilman files, but the original is at present unlocated at NYPL.

LOCATION: NYPL-D.

PUBLICATION: Minnigerode, pp. 78-79. Davis-Gilman 146.

TEXTUAL NOTES: over them] them *written over it*, · if they] they *written over it*

TO ALLAN MELVILLE
22 MAY 1860 · PITTSFIELD

The day after writing to Duyckinck (see the letter just above), Melville sent his brother Allan these instructions concerning the publication of his manuscript volume of poetry. Allan apparently then gave them to Duyckinck since they were preserved among his papers. These "memoranda" (including the signature at the end) are in the hand of Elizabeth Melville, either taken down by dictation or recopied by her. For a surmise as to why Melville directed Allan not to offer his volume to the Harpers for publication, see the NN *Published Poems*. The Harpers did bring out Melville's first published book of poems, *Battle-Pieces*, in 1866.

Memoranda for Allan
concerning the publication of my verses.

1 — Don't stand on terms much with the publisher — half-profits after expenses are paid will content me — — not that I expect much "profits" — but that will be a fair nominal arrangement — They should also give me 1 doz. copies of the book —

2 — Don't have the Harpers. — I should like the Appletons or Scribner — But Duyckinck's advice will be good here.

3 — The sooner the thing is printed and published, the better — The "season" will make little or no difference, I fancy, in this case.

4 — After printing, dont let the book hang back — but publish & have done.

5 — For God's sake don't have *By the author of "Typee" "Piddledee"* &c on the title-page.

6 — Let the title-page be simply,

Poems

by

Herman Melville.

7 — Dont have any clap-trap announcements and "sensation" puffs — nor any extracts published previous to publication of book — Have a decent publisher, in short.

8 — Don't take any measures, or make inquiries as to expediency of an English edition simultaneous with the American — as in case of "Confidence-Man".

9 — In the M.S.S. each piece is on a page by itself, however small the piece. This was done merely for convenience in the final classification; and should be no guide for the printer — Of course in printing two or more pieces will sometimes appear on the same page — according to length of pieces &c. You understand —

10 — The poems are divided into books as you will see; but the divisions are not *called* books — they are only numbered — Thus it is in the M.S.S., and should be the same in print. There should be a page with the number between every division.

11 — Anything not perfectly plain in the M.S.S. can be referred to Lizzie — also have the M.S.S. returned to her after printing.

12 — Lizzie should by all means see the printed sheets *before* being bound, in order to detect any gross errors consequent upon misconstruing the M.S.S. —

These are the thoughts which hurriedly occur to me at this moment. Pardon the abruptness of their expression, but time is precious. —
— Of all human events, perhaps, the publication of a first volume of verses is the most insignificant; but though a matter of no moment to the world, it is still of some concern to the author, — as these

Mem. show — Pray therefore, don't laugh at my *Mem.* but give heed to them, and so oblige

Your brother
Herman —

May 22^d
1860

LS on a 25.5 × 20.1 cm sheet, folded in half, of white laid paper with lines, embossed with the manufacturer's small oblong stamp of flourishes connected at four points, enclosing the name "CARSON'S". Elizabeth Melville inscribed all four pages, in ink. This non-holograph source for the letter is emended by NN at one point (see below).

LOCATION: NYPL-D.

PUBLICATION: Minnigerode, pp. 82–84. Davis-Gilman 147.

TEXTUAL NOTES: Duyckinck's] NN; Duycinck's • *Piddledee*] dd *rewritten* • their expression] *originally* these expressions

TO EVERT A. DUYCKINCK
28 MAY 1860 • BOSTON

The postmark of 28 May on its envelope corrects Melville's questioned date of 29 May in the heading of this letter. In an intervening, now unlocated, reply to Melville's letter of 21 May, Duyckinck had evidently agreed to oversee publication of Melville's book of poetry in his absence (see the headnote to Melville's 21 May letter for more about that unpublished volume). Melville finally left Boston Harbor aboard the *Meteor* on 30 May, planning to "round the world" with his brother. More than a dozen of the "good lot" of books he took with him are known to survive (see *Journals*, p. 200, and Sealts, *Melville's Reading*, pp. 108–10).

Boston, May 29th (?) 1860
On board ship "Meteor"

My Dear Duyckinck: I am glad that the postponement of the ship's day of sailing gives me a chance to answer your letter, received, in reply to mine, on the eve of my leaving Pittsfield. It was a very welcome one — quite a wind from the feilds of old times.

My wife will send you the parcel in the course of a week or so — there remaining something to be finished in copying the M.S.S.

As my wife has interested herself a good deal in this matter, and in fact seems to know more about it than I do — at least about the *merits* of the performance — I must therefore refer you to her in case of any exigency requiring information further than you are now in possession of.

If your brother George is not better employed, I hope he will associate himself with you in looking over my scribblings.

That is enough in the egotistic way. Now for something else.

I anticipate as much pleasure as, at the age of fourty, one temperately can, in the voyage I am going. I go under very happy auspices so far as ship & Captain is concerned. A noble ship and a nobler Captain — & he my brother. We have the breadth of both tropics before us, to sail over twice; & shall round the world. Our first port is San Francisco, which we shall probably make in 110 days from Boston. Thence we go to Manilla — & thence, I hardly know where, — I wish devoutly you were going along. I think it would agree with you. The prime requisite for enjoyment in sea voyages, for passengers, is 1st health — 2^{d} good-nature. Both first-rate things, but not universally to be found. — At sea a fellow comes out. Salt water is like wine, in that respect.

I have a good lot of books with me — such as they are; — plenty of old periodicals — lazy reading for lazy latitudes. —

Here I am called away, & must close.

Good bye to you
& God bless you
H Melville

ALS on a 23.4 × 18.3 cm part-sheet (torn along the bottom) of white laid paper with lines, faintly embossed with the manufacturer's stamp. The sheet was folded in half to make two leaves, with the lines vertical and the stamp at the bottom of the first leaf. Melville inscribed the first three pages, in ink, writing across the lines, and addressed the envelope "Evert A. Duyckinck Esq. | New York | N° 20 Clinton Place."; it was postmarked in Boston on 28 May.

LOCATION: NYPL-D.

PUBLICATION: Minnigerode, pp. 79–81. Davis-Gilman 148.

TEXTUAL NOTES: eve] *rewritten* • quite] *rewritten* • finished] *second* i *added* • copying the] the *written over an earlier word-start* • I must therefore refer] *blotted* • as, at] *miswritten* as at, at • both] *written over* the • in sea] in *possibly* on

TO MALCOLM MELVILLE
1 AND 16 SEPTEMBER 1860 · PACIFIC OCEAN

When Melville left on his voyage aboard the *Meteor*, his oldest child, Malcolm, to whom this letter is addressed, was eleven years old. His three other children—Stanwix, Elizabeth (Bessie), and Frances (Fanny)—mentioned at its close, were nine, seven, and five (see *Journals*, p. 637, for a photograph of the Melville children from this period). Two events described in the letter's eight pages—the *Meteor* rounding Cape Horn and the death of one of the ship's crew—are also recorded in his 1860 journal (*Journals*, pp. 131–35; see also p. 549 below for a drawing of Arrowhead Melville made during the voyage).

Pacific Ocean
(Off the coast of South America
On the Tropic of Capricorn)
Saturday September 1st 1860

My Dear Malcolm: It is now three months exactly since the ship "Meteor" sailed from Boston — a quarter of a year. During this long period, she has been continually moving, and has only seen land on two days. I suppose you have followed out on the map (or my *globe* were better — so you get Mama to clean it off for you) the route from Boston to San Francisco. The distance, by the straight track, is about 16000 miles; but the ship will have sailed before she gets there nearer 18 or 20000 miles. So you see it is further than from the apple-tree to the big rock. When we crossed the Line in the Atlantic Ocean it was very warm; & we had warm weather for some weeks; but as we kept getting to the Southward it began to grow less warm, and then coolish, and cold and colder, till at last it was winter. I wore two flannel shirts, and big mittens & overcoat, and a great Russia cap, a very thick leather cap, so called by sailors. At last we came in sight of land all covered with snow — uninhabited land, where no one ever lived, and no one ever will live — it is so barren, cold and desolate. This was Staten Land — an island. Near it, is the big island of Terra del Fuego. We passed through between these islands, and had a good view of both. There are some "wild people" living on Terra del Fuego; but it being the depth of winter there, I suppose they kept in their caves. At any rate we saw none of them. The next day we were off Cape Horn, the Southernmost point of all America. Now it was very bad weather, and was dark at about three o'clock in the afternoon. The wind blew terribly. We had hail-storms, and snow and sleet, and often the spray froze as it touched the deck. The ship rolled, and sometimes took in so much water on the deck as to wash people off their legs. Several sailors were washed along the deck this way, and came near getting washed overboard. And this reminds me of a very sad thing that happened the very morning we were off the Cape — I mean the very *pitch* of the Cape. — It was just about day-light; it was blowing a gale of wind; and Uncle Tom ordered the topsails (big sails) to be furled. Whilst the sailors were aloft on one of the yards, the ship rolled and plunged terribly; and it blew with sleet and hail, and was very cold & biting. Well, all at once, Uncle Tom saw something falling through the air, and then heard a thump, and then, — looking before him, saw a poor sailor lying dead on the deck. He had fallen from the yard, and was killed instantly. — His shipmates picked him up, and carried him under cover. By and by, when time could be spared, the sailmaker sewed up the body in a peice of sail-cloth, putting some iron balls — cannon balls — at the foot of it. And, when all was ready, the body was put on a plank, and carried to the ship's side in the prescence of all hands. Then Uncle Tom, as Captain, read a prayer out of the prayer-book, and at a given word, the sailors who held the plank tipped it up, and immediately the body slipped into the stormy ocean, and we saw it no more. — Such is the way a poor sailor is buried at sea. This sailor's name was Ray. He had a friend among the crew; and they were both going to California, and thought of living there; but you see what happened.

We were in this stormy weather about forty or fifty days, dating from the beginning. But now at last we are in fine weather again, and the sun shines warm.

Pacific Ocean
On the Line, Sept. 16th 1860

My Dear Malcolm: Since coming to the end of the fourth page, we have been sailing in fine weather, and it has continued quite warm. — The other day we saw a whale-ship; and I got into a boat and sailed over the ocean in it to the whale-ship, and stayed there about an hour. They had eight or ten of the "wild people" aboard. The Captain of the whale-ship had hired them at one of the islands called Roratonga. He wanted them to help pull in the whale-boat when they hunt the whale. — Uncle Tom's crew are now very busy making the ship look smart for San Francisco. They are tarring the rigging, and are going to paint the ship, & the masts and yards. She looks very rusty now, oweing to so much bad weather that we have been in. — When we get to San-Francisco, I shall put this letter in the post office there, and you will get it in about 25 days afterwards. It will go in a steamer to a place called Panama, on the Isthmus of Darien (get out your map, & find it) then it will cross the Isthmus by rail road to Aspinwall or Chagres on the Gulf of Mexico; there, another steamer will take it, which steamer, after touching at Havanna in Cuba for coals, will go direct to New York; and there, it will go to the Post Office, and so, get to Pittsfield.

I hope that, when it arrives, it will find you well, and all the family. And I hope that you have called to mind what I said to you about your behaviour previous to my going away. I hope that you have been obedient to your mother, and helped her all you could, & saved her trouble. Now is the time to show what you are — whether you are a good, honorable boy, or a good-for-nothing one. Any boy, of your age, who disobeys his mother, or worries her, or is disrespectful to her — such a boy is a poor shabby fellow; and if you know any such boys, you ought to cut their acquaintance.

Now, my Dear Malcolm, I must finish my letter to you. I think of you, and Stanwix & Bessie and Fanny very often; and often long to be with you. But it can not be, at present. The picture which I have of you & the rest, I look at sometimes, till the faces almost seem real. — Now, my Dear Boy, good bye, & God bless you

Your affectionate father
H Melville

I enclose a little baby flying-fish's wing for Fanny

[Enclosure: "wing"]

ALS, with the first four pages on a 26.8 × 20.6 cm folded sheet of white laid paper; pp. 5 and 6 on each side of a 13.4 × 20.6 cm part-sheet of the same white laid paper torn along the left edge; and pp. 7 and 8 on a part-sheet of blue laid paper torn unevenly on all but the bottom edge to roughly 13 × 13.5 cm. Melville inscribed the letter in ink and numbered all but the fourth and eighth pages to make the sequence clear. This letter and the 2 September 1860 letter to his daughter Elizabeth were probably both enclosed in the envelope addressed by Melville "Mrs. Herman Melville | Pittsfield | Berkshire Co. | Mass."; it was postmarked "San Francisco

Oct 1[9]" and marked "Overland." It was readdressed "Care Justice Shaw," and "Pittsfield Berkshire Co." was crossed out. Elizabeth Melville noted on the back "On the Meteor | Sept 1–& 16th | 1860 | To the | Children." Accompanying this letter is also her notation on a separate sheet enclosing a fish's "wing," which states: "Wing of a baby flying-fish | sent to 'little Fanny' by her | father from the Pacific | Ocean in a letter dated | Sept. 22d 1860 — ".

LOCATION: HCL-M.

PUBLICATION: Thorp, pp. 397–400. Davis-Gilman 149 (with partial reproduction).

TEXTUAL NOTES: has only] a *written over another letter* • Line] L *written over* l • The wind] The *blotted* • often] f *written over another letter* • heard] *inserted above caret* • warm.] *before* (see page 5th) • San-Francisco] San-|Francisco • get it in] it *originally* in • Post] P *written over* p • boys, you] you *written over wiped* I • acquaintance.] *written in bottom margin and connected by a line* • Now, my Dear Malcolm] *after* [Continued from 6th page.] • Dear Boy] D *written over* d • I enclose . . . Fanny] *on the unnumbered verso of p. 7; placed here editorially*

TO ELIZABETH MELVILLE
2 SEPTEMBER 1860 · PACIFIC OCEAN

Melville's letter to his son Malcolm, just above, and this one to his daughter Elizabeth (Bessie) are the only other known letters from his time at sea in 1860 (for the unlocated letter to his wife that was possibly enclosed with these, see the next entry, and for a fragment of a letter possibly written to his second son Stanwix at this time, see Undated Letters, p. 537). He wrote this letter partly in large printed letters and partly in his normal script, probably so that Bessie could read the printing herself while her mother would read the script to her. The speckled birds Melville describes in this letter were probably the speckled haglets he noted in his journal on 21 July 1860 (*Journals*, p. 133).

Pacific Ocean

Sep. 2d 1860

My Dear Bessie: I thought I would send you a letter, that you could read yourself — at least a part of it. But here and there I propose to write in the usual manner, as I find the printing style comes rather awkwardly in a rolling ship. Mamma will read these parts to you. We have seen a good many sea-birds. Many have followed the ship day after day. I used to feed them with crumbs. But now it has got to be warm weather, the birds have left us. They were about as big as chickens — they were all over speckled — and they would sometimes, during a calm, keep behind the ship, fluttering about in the water, with a mighty cackling, and whenever anything was thrown overboard they would hurry to get it. But they never would light on the ship — they kept all the time flying or else resting themselves

Pacific Ocean
Sep. 2ᵈ 1860

My Dear Bessie: I thought
I would send you a letter, that
you could read yourself—at
least a part of it. But here and
there I purpose to write in the usual
manner, as I find the printing style
comes rather awkwardly in a rolling ship.
Mamma will read these parts to you. We
have seen a good many
sea-birds. Many have follow-
-wed the ship day after day.
I used to feed them with
crumbs. But now it has got
to be warm weather, the birds
have left us. They were about
as big as chickens — They were,
all over speckled — and they would

To Elizabeth (Bessie) Melville, 2 September 1860, p. 1 (reduced). Courtesy
of the Houghton Library, Harvard University (Melville Collection).

sometimes, during a calm, keep behind
the ship, fluttering along in the water,
with a mighty cackling, and whenever
anything was thrown overboard they would
hurry to get it. But they never would
light on the ship — they kept all the
time flying or else resting themselves
by floating on the water like ducks
in a pond. These birds have no
home, unless it is some wild rocks
in the middle of the ocean. They never
see any orchards, and have a taste of
the apples & cherries, like your gay little
friend in Pittsfield, Robin Red Breast Esq.
—— I could tell you a good
many nice things about the sea, but I
I think defer the rest till I get home.
I hope you are a
good girl; and give Mama
no trouble. Do you help
Mama keep house?

To Elizabeth (Bessie) Melville, 2 September 1860, p. 2 (reduced). Courtesy of the Houghton Library, Harvard University (Melville Collection).

That little bag you
made for me, I use very
often, and think of you
every time.

I suppose you have had
a good many walks on the hill, and
picked the strawberries.

I hope you take
good care of little

F A N N Y

and that when you go on
the hill, you go this way:

That is to say, hand in hand.

By-by
Papa.

To Elizabeth (Bessie) Melville, 2 September 1860, p. 3 (reduced). Courtesy of the Houghton Library, Harvard University (Melville Collection).

by floating on the water like ducks in a pond. These birds have no home, unless it is some wild rocks in the middle of the ocean. They never see any orchards, and have a taste of the apples & cherries, like your gay little friend in Pittsfield Robin Red Breast Esq.

—— I could tell you a good many more things about the sea, but I must defer the rest till I get home.

I hope you are a good girl; and give Mama no trouble. Do you help Mama keep house? That little bag you made for me, I use very often, and think of you every time.

I suppose you have had a good many walks on the hill, and picked the strawberries.

I hope you take good care of little

FANNY

and that when you go on the hill, you go this way:

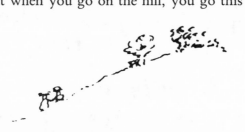

that is to say, hand in hand.

By-by
Papa.

ALS, "Papa", on a 26.8 × 20.6 cm sheet, folded in half, of white laid paper. Melville inscribed the first three pages, in ink, and addressed the letter "Bessie" on the fourth page. The letter was probably enclosed in the same envelope with the 1 September letter to Malcolm.

LOCATION: HCL-M.

PUBLICATION: Eleanor Melville Metcalf, "A Pilgrim by Land and Sea," *The Horn Book* 3 (February 1927), 8–10 (with partial reproduction). Davis-Gilman 150.

TEXTUAL NOTES: Pacific] *second* i *inserted above caret* · Pacific Ocean . . . part of it.] *hand-printed* · But here . . . parts to you.] *script* · find] *before canceled* it · We have seen . . . speckled] *hand-printed* · They were] were *miswritten* we · and they would . . . I get home.] *script* · I hope . . . every time.] *hand-printed* · I suppose . . . strawberries.] *script* · I hope you take . . . way:] *hand-printed* · that is . . . Papa.] *script*

TO ELIZABETH SHAW MELVILLE
[22 SEPTEMBER?] 1860 · PACIFIC OCEAN

Unlocated. A letter to his wife probably accompanied Melville's September letters to his children Malcolm and Elizabeth (Bessie), which came in an envelope addressed to "Mrs. Herman Melville" sent "Overland" from San Francisco on 19 October (see pp. 349–50 above and *Journals*, p. 203n.). The separate sheet she later enclosed with those letters—with the notation "Wing of a baby flying-fish sent to 'little Fanny' by her father from the Pacific Ocean in a letter dated Sept. 22ᵈ 1860"—may indicate the date of her letter since neither Malcolm's nor Bessie's was written on 22 September. This letter and the following one are cited in Davis-Gilman as Unlocated 368.

TO ELIZABETH SHAW MELVILLE
BETWEEN 12 AND 20 OCTOBER 1860 · SAN FRANCISCO

Unlocated. During Melville's brief stay in San Francisco from 12 to 20 October 1860 (see *Journals*, pp. 201–3), he wrote a letter to his wife and sent it not "Overland" (see the entry just above) but by the swifter Pony Express to let her know he was not continuing his voyage aboard the *Meteor* with his brother. It is cited without a date in Maria Gansevoort Melville's 5 November 1860 letter to Peter Gansevoort: "I am sorry to say that our dear Herman will return home from Liverpool. By Pony Express, Lizzie had a letter saying he was not at all benefitted by the Voyage — I feel so much disappointed. I had fondly hoped that a Voyage to India under kind Tom's care would have quite brought Herman back to health. He had written us to come by Steamer — Lizzie writes" (NYPL-GL). "Liverpool" here must be a slip for "San Francisco." Davis and Gilman report this and the [22 September?] letter as one: Unlocated 368.

TO LEMUEL SHAW
[16?] OCTOBER 1860 · SAN FRANCISCO

Unlocated. A letter to Judge Shaw is cited in Melville's 16 October 1860 letter to Shaw's son Samuel that accompanied it, just below. Presumably Melville told of his decision to return home (see *Journals*, pp. 201–3). Davis-Gilman Unlocated 367.

TO SAMUEL S. SHAW
16 OCTOBER 1860 · SAN FRANCISCO

After returning from Europe in 1857, where he crossed paths with Melville in Rome (see the entry for Melville's 21 March 1857 unlocated letter to him there), Elizabeth Melville's half-brother Samuel Shaw took up residence once again at his parents' home at 49 Mount Vernon Street in Boston and entered into the practice of law. Why he wrote to Melville in San Francisco or why his letter merited a "more communicative" reply remains unknown since it is unlocated.

San Francisco
Oct. 16th 1860

My Dear Sam: In a few days I shall be at sea again, and as I want to see what I can while here, you may imagine I have not much idle time. I have just written to your father, and slip this little note in, just to say that your letter received here was very interesting to me, and merits a longer & more communicative reply than I shall be able to make. Indeed, as I write by night (rather unusual for me) and my eyes feel tired, all I can add here is, that I hope you are a good enough Christian in this matter of correspondence to be willing cheerfully to give much and receive little.

Thine
H Melville

ALS on an 11.5 × 17.8 cm part-sheet (torn along the top and left edges) of blue laid paper with lines on one side. Melville inscribed the unlined side of the leaf, in ink. Another hand noted in pencil on the verso "Samuel Shaw", and still another hand wrote in ink "d'Halbach."

LOCATION: HCL-M.

PUBLICATION: *Log*, II, 628. Davis-Gilman 151.

TEXTUAL NOTE: tired] *miswritten* tried

TO SARAH HUYLER MOREWOOD
2 DECEMBER 1860 · BOSTON

Returning from San Francisco, Melville arrived in New York on 13 November and went directly to Boston, where his family had been staying in his absence. This letter sent from Boston is the last known letter he wrote to his Pittsfield neighbor Sarah Morewood, who died of tuberculosis three years later at the age of thirty-nine. After her death, her sister Ellen Brittain, mentioned at the close of this letter, took charge of Broadhall, where the family remained and where Melville's niece Maria Melville (Allan's daughter) eventually lived after marrying Sarah's son William (see the headnote to Melville's 22 October 1867 letter to her).

Melville's letter was probably written in reply to a now unlocated invitation from Sarah Morewood addressed to either Melville or his wife for them to stay at her house while they got their own in order. At the end of Melville's letter, Elizabeth Melville appended a comment about the changed plans: "Dear Mrs. Morewood, You see the order of things is completely reversed, since Herman is going on to Pittsfield to get the house ready for me — that is, to get Mr Clark to put the stoves up, and get it *warm* for me to go to work in — A new proverb should be added 'Wives propose — husbands dispose' — don't you think so? — I send you a scrap from a late paper which — or rather the spirit of which, I would recommend to the deliberate consideration of the united parishes of Christ Church & St Stephens — We know Mr Baury (pronounce *Boree*) and now I like him better than ever — Good bye — I shall see you soon — with much love E. S. M." (In September 1860 the two Episcopal churches in Pittsfield had united after having been divided only a year earlier; see Kate M. Scutt, *The First Century of St. Stephen's Parish, 1830–1930* [Pittsfield: St. Stephen's, 1930]. The enclosed clipping was probably by the Reverend Alfred Louis Baury, an Episcopal clergyman of French descent, who resided in Boston and was rector of St. Paul's Church, Hopkinton.)

Sunday Evening Dec. 2^d 1860

My Dear Mrs. Morewood:

Lizzie has written you, I beleive, that we purposed leaving for home on Monday (tomorrow) — but we have changed our plans. Lizzie and the children will remain here till Thursday; and I — in advance, — will go to Pittsfield on *Tuesday*, to get matters in readiness for them — putting up the stoves, airing the bedding — warming the house, and getting up a grand domestic banquet. I shall leave here in *the morning train on Tuesday*; and will be very happy to accept, for myself, your kind & neighborly invitation for a day or two.

Let me take this opportunity of saying that Tom charged me with his best rememberances to you. I think he wrote to Mrs Brittain, thereby sending his rememberances to that lady by his own hand. And to you I, in the same manner, send mine; &, through you, to Mrs Brittian. —

Very Truly & Sincerely
Your Friend & Neighbor
H Melville

— P.S. Very scratchy pen.

ALS on a 32.8 × 20.1 cm sheet, folded in half, of white laid paper. Melville inscribed the first page, in ink, and Elizabeth Melville added her note, also in ink, on the third page (see above).

LOCATION: Berkshire Athenaeum, Pittsfield, Massachusetts. *Provenance*: Agnes Morewood.

PUBLICATION: Davis-Gilman 152.

TEXTUAL NOTE: charged me] me *inserted above caret*

TO OLIVER RUSS
18 DECEMBER 1860 · [PITTSFIELD?]

Unlocated. A letter, apparently Melville's second to Oliver Russ, his former ship-mate aboard the U.S.S. *United States*, is cited in Russ's 24 December 1860 reply (see LETTERS RECEIVED, pp. 675–77). Melville's letter evidently mentioned his 1860 trip around Cape Horn and inquired about arrangements for sending the "keepsake" Russ had requested for his son named Herman Melville Russ. Davis-Gilman Unlocated 369.

TO RICHARD T. GREENE
LATE DECEMBER 1860 · [PITTSFIELD?]

Unlocated. A letter from Melville is cited in Richard T. Greene's 4 January 1861 reply (see LETTERS RECEIVED, pp. 678–80). Since Melville did not know that Greene had moved to Chicago some eighteen months earlier, this seems to be their first communication since their letters in January 1858 (see LETTERS RECEIVED, pp. 660–61). Here Melville must have proposed sending engraved spoons to his name-sakes—Greene's son and nephew. He probably got the idea from Oliver Russ's letters of 4 February 1859 and 24 December 1860, both of which had requested that Melville send his son, also named after Melville, a "keepsake" (see LETTERS RE-CEIVED, pp. 667–68, 675–77). Davis-Gilman Unlocated 370.

1861

TO RICHARD T. GREENE
10 JANUARY 1861 · [PITTSFIELD?]

Unlocated. A letter from Melville, presumably in reply to Greene's 4 January 1861 letter, is cited in Greene's 16 January 1861 reply (see LETTERS RECEIVED, pp. 681–82). Melville had asked for the full names and addresses of his namesakes, Richard Melville Hair (Greene's nephew) and Herman Melville Greene (Greene's son), in order to arrange for the engraved spoons he was sending them. (For Richard T. Greene's and Richard Melville Hair's acknowledgments, see LETTERS RECEIVED, pp. 682 and 685–86.) Davis-Gilman Unlocated 371.

TO OLIVER RUSS
BEFORE 14 JANUARY 1861 · [PITTSFIELD?]

Unlocated. A letter announcing the present Melville sent Herman Melville Russ is cited in Oliver Russ's 14 January 1861 letter acknowledging the gift (see LETTERS RECEIVED, pp. 680–81). Melville may also have sent at this time the ambrotype Russ requested in his 24 December 1860 letter. As the postscript to Russ's 14 January 1861 reply indicates, Melville in this letter reciprocally asked for one of Russ. Davis-Gilman Unlocated 372.

TO MARIA GANSEVOORT MELVILLE
BEFORE 12 MARCH 1861 · [PITTSFIELD?]

Unlocated. A letter from Melville is cited in a 12 March 1861 letter from Maria
Melville in Gansevoort, New York, conveying various bits of family news, to her
niece Catherine Gansevoort (Peter Gansevoort's daughter, the "Kitty" Melville refers to in his 15 and 20 March letters to her father, just below), at home with her
family in Albany. Maria Melville ends her letter, saying: "The enclosed part of a
letter from Herman & the printed paper you will please give to your Father for his
amusement & when you write please send it back to me" (NYPL-GL). Left unclear
is what was in Melville's letter and whether it, as well as the paper, was for the
"amusement" of Melville's uncle Peter; possibly the letter discussed Melville's decision to seek, yet again, a consular post (see the letter just below). Davis-Gilman
Unlocated 373.

TO PETER GANSEVOORT
15 MARCH 1861 · PITTSFIELD

By February of 1861 Melville's family was once again considering a possible consulship for him. In a letter to Lemuel Shaw, Allan Melville discussed the consulship
in Florence, which was "worth only about $500 per year" but was for that reason
less sought after by other office-seekers with stronger political connections (NYPL-
GL). Florence also offered the advantages of fewer duties, less expensive living, and
cultural surroundings, as Shaw later mentioned in a 21 March 1861 letter enlisting
the support of Charles Sumner (National Archives). Melville himself had resolved
by March to seek the post, as this letter to his uncle Peter Gansevoort shows. Not
among the Free-Soil Democrats who had turned Republican, Peter Gansevoort had
no direct political influence with the new Lincoln administration, but he did have
influence with Thurlow Weed of Albany, who was in turn closely connected with
William H. Seward (1801–72), the former governor of New York (1838–42) and
Lincoln's new secretary of state (see Melville's subsequent 20 March letter to his
uncle and his letter to Weed of the same date, below). Thus as in all of the earlier
attempts to obtain government jobs for Melville—the 1839 effort to get him a position in the engineering department of the state canal system, the 1847 attempt to
obtain one of the Treasury department jobs created by the New Loan Bill of that
year, the 1853 bid for a consulship, and the effort to obtain a customs post after his
1856–57 trip—the support of his uncle Peter was enlisted. For more on Melville's
efforts at this time, see his later March 1861 letters and Hayford-Davis, pp. 380–86.

Pittsfield March 15th 1861

My Dear Uncle: It has been suggested to me that I might procure
some foreign appointment under the new Administration — the
consulship at Florence, for example. In many respects such an appointment would be desirable for me, altho' the emoluments are not

very considerable. At all events, it is my purpose to apply. And I
write for the purpose of enlisting your kind offices, which I know,
you will cheerfully render; — and also to say, that early next week
(perhaps on Monday) I shall leave here for New York, and have
thought it advisable to take Albany in my way, for the purpose of
seeing & consulting with you, touching my design. — I write in
much haste, in order to get this into the mail. I have only time to
send love to Aunt Susan & Kitty, and to say that as ever, I am Sincerely & Affectionately Yours

Herman Melville

ALS on a 16.5 × 20.1 cm part-sheet (torn along the left edge) of white laid paper with lines,
embossed with the manufacturer's oval stamp enclosing the name "BATH". Melville inscribed
only one side of the leaf, in ink. He addressed the envelope "Hon. Peter Gan-
sevoort | Albany | N.Y."; it was postmarked in Pittsfield on 15 March.

LOCATION: NYPL-GL.

PUBLICATION: Paltsits, pp. 16–17. Davis-Gilman 153.

TO PETER GANSEVOORT
20 MARCH 1861 · NEW YORK

Arriving in New York on 19 March after staying overnight at his uncle Peter Gansevoort's in Albany, Melville began his most recent campaign as office-seeker.
While in Albany, he had apparently called on Thurlow Weed, formerly the editor
of the *Albany Evening Journal* (see Melville's 15 August 1846 letter to him, above)
and now a powerful New York Republican politician, only to learn that Weed was
in New York. Missing him again at the Astor House in New York on 20 March,
Melville wrote this letter to his uncle Peter, enclosing one to Weed (just below). For
Peter Gansevoort's 23 March reply, see LETTERS RECEIVED, pp. 683–84.

New York March 20th 1861

My Dear Uncle: Upon inquiring for Mr Weed at the Astor this
morning, I find the bird flown back to its perch — Albany.

I have thought it advisable, under the circumstances, to address
to him a note, which I here enclose to you. Were you as well now,
as you will be ere long, I should beg you to deliver the note to him,
& urge my suit to him, in person. But as it is, may I ask you to
write him a note, enclosing mine? I think you can thus greatly aid
me. *But it ought to be done immediately.* A very brief note will answer,

so it be *strong & urgent*. I leave here tomorrow for Washington; and letters will reach me there any time during the next ten days.

    With love to Aunt Susan and Kitty, I am, always

Truly & affectionately Yours
H Melville

ALS on a 13.2 × 20.7 cm part-sheet (torn along the left edge) of white laid paper, faintly embossed with the manufacturer's shield-like stamp. Melville inscribed only one side of the leaf, in ink, and addressed the envelope "Hon. Peter Gansevoort | Albany | N.Y."; it was postmarked in New York on 20 March. Peter Gansevoort noted in ink on the envelope "1861. Mar. 20 | Letter from Herman | Melville at New York | Rec^d & ans^d | 23^d Mar '61". Another hand marked the name "Mr Weed" with a penciled check and placed a corresponding check mark before the penciled notation "Mr. Weed" at the bottom of the page.

LOCATION: NYPL-GL.

PUBLICATION: Paltsits, p. 17. Davis-Gilman 156.

TEXTUAL NOTES: find] i *written over another letter* • Were] We *written over* Wa

TO THURLOW WEED
20 MARCH 1861 · NEW YORK

This appeal to Thurlow Weed, enclosed with the letter of the same date to Melville's uncle Peter, failed to reach Albany before Weed had left for Washington, as Peter Gansevoort reported in his 23 March letter (see LETTERS RECEIVED, pp. 683–84). Following his uncle's advice, Melville may have met with Weed in Washington and sought his help there. A letter dated only March 1861 was sent on Melville's behalf from New York with the signatures of men known to Weed and his close political ally, Secretary of State William Henry Seward, former governor of New York. There is no evidence of any further efforts by Weed to help the nephew of Peter Gansevoort (see Hayford-Davis, pp. 381–82, 385). For Senator Charles Sumner's efforts on his behalf, see the headnote to Melville's 28 March letter to the senator, below.

New York March 20th 1861

Dear Sir: I have thought that you might remember me sufficiently to justify my asking your friendly aid. — I desire to obtain the appointment of Consul at Florence.

    I have taken steps to secure strong letters to Senator Sumner of Massachusetts — the state of my present residence. But, above all, an earnest letter from yourself to Gov. Seward would further my design

I am aware, of course, that in your position you must be harassed by similar applications, but yet I am not without hope of your assistance.

Without trespassing upon you further, I will only add — in case you should interest yourself in the matter — that letters will reach me at Washington any time during the next ten days.

Very Truly Yours
H. Melville

Hon. Thurlow Weed
Albany

ALS on a 26.5 × 20.7 cm sheet, folded in half, of white laid paper, embossed with the manufacturer's shield-like stamp enclosing the name "R. C. ROOT | ANTHONY & CO. | NEW-YORK". Melville inscribed the first and third pages, in ink. Another hand, presumably Weed's, noted in ink on the fourth page "Herman Melville | N.Y. March 20. 1861". Still another hand, probably a librarian's, noted in pencil on the first page "Weed March 20, 1861" and on the third page below the signature "H[erman] Melville".

LOCATION: Rush Rhees Library, University of Rochester.

PUBLICATION: Hayford-Davis, p. 381. Davis-Gilman 155.

TEXTUAL NOTE: similar] *before* (over) *in bottom margin*

TO R. H. DANA, JR.
20 MARCH 1861 · NEW YORK

Besides his letters to his uncle and Thurlow Weed, above, Melville also wrote on 20 March to R. H. Dana, Jr. Earlier, in May 1853 at Lemuel Shaw's request, Dana had written a letter in aid of Melville's bid for a consular post then. Replying to Shaw on 10 May 1853, Dana declared, "I am very glad to do what I can in favor of my friend & sincerely hope he will prevail" (MHS-S). By 1861 Dana had made it a rule not to make such recommendations, but agreed to write on Melville's behalf in his regular correspondence with the newly designated chairman of the Foreign Relations Committee, Charles Sumner of Massachusetts (see LETTERS RECEIVED, p. 683).

New York March 20th 1861
Dear Sir: I beleive you are apprized of my design as to obtaining, if possible, the consulship at Florence.

I am persuaded, from all I hear, that if Senator Sumner could be earnestly enlisted in the cause, I should, in all likelihood, succeed. May I therefore ask your good services in that quarter? I should be greatly obliged to you for a strong letter from yourself, and for procuring for me other strong letters from suitable persons in Boston. It is important that the business should be pressed at once. I leave here for Washington tomorrow, and letters will reach me there any time for the next eight or ten days.

> Very Truly & Sincerely Yours
> H Melville

Richard H. Dana Jr. Esq.

ALS on a 13.2 × 20.8 cm part-sheet (torn along the left edge) of white laid paper, faintly embossed with the manufacturer's shield-like stamp. Melville inscribed only one side of the leaf, in ink. Another hand noted at the top of it in pencil "Melville".

LOCATION: MHS-D.

PUBLICATION: James D. Hart, "Melville and Dana," *American Literature* 9 (March 1937), 53–54. Davis-Gilman 154.

TO JULIUS ROCKWELL
20 MARCH 1861 · NEW YORK

To bolster his case with Senator Sumner (see the 20 March letters just above), Melville also wrote on 20 March to his Pittsfield neighbor Julius Rockwell (see Melville's letters of 23 May and 2 July 1853). Both a former congressional representative and senator and now a justice of the Superior Court of Massachusetts, Rockwell was a prominent state Republican. He had already signed on 14 March a letter of recommendation sent on Melville's behalf from Pittsfield (National Archives). Apparently prompted by this letter from Melville as well as a now unlocated one from Melville's brother-in-law John Hoadley, a former resident of Pittsfield, Rockwell wrote to Charles Sumner on 25 March (see LETTERS RECEIVED, pp. 684–85, and Melville's later 27 March letter thanking Rockwell).

> New York March 20th 1861

Dear Sir: Mr Hoadley, probably, apprised you of my design as to obtaining a consulship. May I beg of you your efforts — earnest efforts — in my behalf.

Any letter or letters you could procure to be written, in urgent terms, from suitable persons, to Senator Sumner would be very desirable. A letter from yourself I should much like. A brief, but urgent note from you to the Congressman from our District, enlisting his interest with Mr Sumner — this would be well.

In short, whatever you can do for me, do, and receive, before-hand, my thanks. I am obliged to write in haste, as I leave for Washington tomorrow, to remain there a week or so.

Very Sincerely Yours
H Melville

Hon. Julius Rockwell
Pittsfield

Letters will reach me at Washington any time during the ensuing ten days.

ALS on a 13.4 × 20.7 cm part-sheet (torn along the left edge) of white wove paper. Melville inscribed both sides of the leaf, in ink. Another hand, presumably Rockwell's, noted in ink on the second page "Herman Melville | March 20. 1861." A third hand noted on that page in pencil "Oct. 20, 1958".

LOCATION: New-York Historical Society.

PUBLICATION: Hennig Cohen, "New Melville Letters," *American Literature* 38 (January 1967), 556–59.

TEXTUAL NOTES: apprised] *possibly* apprized • or so.] *before* (Over) *on same line* • Hon.] *written over* Julius

TO ELIZABETH SHAW MELVILLE
[22?] MARCH 1861 · WASHINGTON, D.C.

Unlocated. A note, probably written on the day Melville arrived in Washington, 22 March, is cited in his 24 and 25 March letter, just below, to his wife. Davis-Gilman Unlocated 374.

TO ELIZABETH SHAW MELVILLE
24 AND 25 MARCH 1861 · WASHINGTON, D.C.

Of the many letters Melville wrote to his wife, this is the only one known to survive (see the HISTORICAL NOTE, pp. 786–88). Headed only "Sunday Afternoon" and "Monday Morning," it can be dated 24 and 25 March, the only Sunday and Monday Melville spent in Washington in 1861. There with Melville, also apparently seeking an appointment from the new administration, was Dr. Amos Nourse (1794–1877), the second husband of Melville's aunt Lucy (see the headnote to Melville's 1828 letter to her, above). Nourse had graduated from Harvard with a medical degree in 1817 and had had a varied career, as an obstetrician, professor at Bowdoin College, and politician. He served in a number of government posts, including postmaster of Hallowell, Maine, Collector of Customs at Bath, Maine,

and briefly U.S. senator from Maine. A converted Republican, he was a close political ally of Lincoln's vice president, Hannibal Hamlin (1809–91), former governor
of Maine.

 Melville's sightseeing in Washington—while waiting for letters of introduction
and recommendation—included Lafayette Park opposite the White House, the new
extensions to the House of Representatives and Senate on the wings of the Capitol
building—completed in 1857 and 1859—and the Washington Monument, which
was only partially completed at this time, work on it having been suspended in
1855 (and not resumed until 1877).

My Dearest Lizzie:

Sunday Afternoon

Washington

 I wrote you the other day from here, and now for another note.
In the first place I must say that as yet I have been able to accomplish
nothing in the matter of the consulship — have not in fact been able
as yet so much as even to *see* any one on the subject. I called last
night at Senator Sumner's, but he was at a dinner somewhere. I shall
call again tomorrow. After leaving Sumner's I went with Dr Nourse
to a little sort of a party given by the wife of a man connected with
one of the Departments. Had quite a pleasant evening. Several Senators were there with wives, daughters &c. The Vice President also &
wife. Mrs Hamlin is in appearance something like you — so she
struck me at least. I need not add that she was very pleasing in her
manners. — The night previous to this I was at the second levee at
the White House. There was a great crowd, & a brilliant scene. Ladies in full dress by the hundred. A steady stream of two-&-two's
wound thro' the apartments shaking hands with "Old Abe" and immediately passing on. This continued without cessation for an hour
& a half. Of course I was one of the shakers. Old Abe is much better
looking than I expected & younger looking. He shook hands like a
good fellow — working hard at it like a man sawing wood at so
much per cord. Mrs Lincoln is rather good-looking I thought. The
scene was very fine altogether. Supurb furniture — flood of
light — magnificent flowers — full band of music &c.

 I have attended the Senate twice; but nothing very interesting.
The new wings of the Capitol are noble buildings, by far the richest
in marble of any on the continent. I allude more particularly to the
marble of the interior — staircases &c. They are in short palatial.
The whole structure taken together is truly immense. It would

(179)

My Dearest Lizzie :

Sunday afternoon 1861

Washington

I wrote you the other day from here and now for another note. In the first place I must say that as yet I have been able to accomplish nothing in the matter of the consulship — have not in fact been able as yet so much as even to see any one on the subject. I called last night at Senator Sumner's but he was at a dinner somewhere. I shall call again tomorrow. After leaving Sumner's I went up Dr Nurse to a little sort of a party given by the wife of a man connected with one of the Departments. Had quite a pleasant evening. Several Senators were there with wives, daughters &c; The Vice President also & wife. Mrs Hamlin is in appearance something like you — so she struck me at least, I need not add that she was very pleasing in her manners. — The night previous to this I was at the second levee at the White House. There was a great crowd, & a brilliant scene. Ladies in full.

To Elizabeth Shaw Melville, 24–25 March 1861, p. 1 (reduced). Courtesy of the Houghton Library, Harvard University (Melville Collection).

astonish you to get lost among the labyrinths of halls, passages & splendid corridors.

This morning I spent in the park opposite the White House, sunning myself on a seat. The grass is bright & beautiful, & the shrubbery beginning to bud. It is just cool enough to make an overcoat comfortable sitting out of doors. The wind is high however, & except in the parks, all is dust. I am boarding in a plain home — plain fare plain people — in fact all plain but the road to Florence. But if nothing else comes of it, I will at least derive good from the trip at this season. Though, to tell the truth, I feel home-sick at times, strange as it may seem. How long I shall remain is uncertain. I am expecting letters every day, & can do little or nothing till they arrive.

This afternoon I visited the Washington Monument. Huge tower some 160 feet high of white marble. Could not get inside. Nothing been done to it for long time.

Dr Nourse is as facetious as ever. I went with him to the White House at the levee. But he is the greater part of the time engaged prosecuting his application for office. I venture to say he will not succeed, & he begins to think so himself, I judge, from what he tells me of his experiences thus far. He leaves here probably on Tuesday.

Monday Morning.

Dearest Lizzie: Feel rather overdone this morning — overwalked yesterday. But the trip will do me good. Kisses to the children. Hope to get a letter from you today

Thine, My Dearest Lizzie
Herman

ALS on a 25.2 × 20 cm sheet, folded in half, of white wove paper with lines. Melville inscribed all four pages, in pencil, writing across the vertical lines. Elizabeth Melville added the year "1861" in pencil after "Sunday Afternoon" in Melville's heading.

LOCATION: HCL-M.

PUBLICATION: Thorp, pp. 400–401. Davis-Gilman 157.

TEXTUAL NOTES: Senator Sumner's] *miswritten* Senator's Sumner's • tomorrow] to- | morrow • There] *written over* On • Abe is] Abe *miswritten* Able • looking than] *miswritten* looking that • shall] *possibly* still

TO JULIUS ROCKWELL
27 MARCH 1861 · WASHINGTON, D.C.

In accord with Melville's 20 March request, above, Julius Rockwell wrote Senator Charles Sumner on 25 March a fervent appeal on Melville's behalf, which he apparently enclosed with a now unlocated letter of 25 March to Melville (see LETTERS RECEIVED, pp. 684–85, for the "eloquent" enclosure).

Melville's reference to the "Petition" in this letter thanking Rockwell is to a 14 March letter from Pittsfield residents on his behalf. One of the signers, James D. Colt, Rockwell's former law-partner and a selectman of Pittsfield, had evidently organized the writing and signing of it and had sent it to Melville.

Washington March 27th

My Dear Sir: I have just taken from the office yours of the 25th, enclosing the eloquent note to Mr Sumner; and can not refrain from instantly acknowledging so strong an instance of kindness.

Not so much for the compliments to me expressed in what you say to Mr Sumner, but for the exceeding and unforseen warmth of benevolence evinced — for *this* permit me respectfully, and gratefully, and promptly, to thank you with all my heart.

Tell Mr Colt, if you please, that I duly received the Petition he mailed me here, and him my best thanks. He knows how hurried and flurried a novice of an office-seeker like me must be at Washington, and will, I am sure, excuse a letter in reply from me, just at present.

My suitable acknowledgments also, to all the gentlemen who signed the Petition.

This is a crumpled and shabby sheet, but the best at hand, and (as I said above) I wished *promptly* to thank you.

Truly and Sincerely
And Respectfully
Yours
H. Melvill

Hon. Julius Rockwell
Pittsfield
Mass.

ALS on a 23.4 × 19.5 cm sheet, folded in half, of white laid paper with lines, embossed with the manufacturer's circular stamp enclosing a crown. Melville inscribed the first three pages, in ink. Another hand, presumably Rockwell's, noted in ink on the fourth page "Mr Herman Melville | March 27. 1861". A third hand noted in pencil on the third page "Oct. 20, 1958".

LOCATION: New-York Historical Society.

PUBLICATION: Hennig Cohen, "New Melville Letters," *American Literature* 38 (January 1967), 556–59.

TEXTUAL NOTES: Mr Colt] M *written over* m • and him] *intervening word lacking (such as* "*give*") • Pittsfield] *miswritten* Pittsfiled

TO CHARLES SUMNER
28 MARCH 1861 · WASHINGTON, D.C.

Melville finally gained an appointment with Senator Charles Sumner (1811–74) of Massachusetts on 28 March, the day after the Florence consulship had been awarded to T. Bigelow Lawrence, the son of Abbott Lawrence, who had been minister to the Court of St. James's when Melville was in London in 1849–50 (*Journals*, pp. 22, 308–9). Along with Julius Rockwell and R. H. Dana, Jr. (see the headnotes to Melville's letters to them, above), Melville's brothers-in-law John Hoadley and George Griggs, and father-in-law, Lemuel Shaw, had all written Sumner on Melville's behalf. Receiving him cordially, Sumner advised Melville to apply for the posts at Glasgow, Geneva, or Manchester (Hayford-Davis, p. 453). However, despite Sumner's endorsement, Melville's application for the Glasgow post was unsuccessful. Melville left Washington on 29 March, after receiving the letter mentioned here—probably from his wife advising him of her father's serious illness. Judge Shaw died shortly afterwards on 30 March 1861 in Boston.

Washington March 28th

Hon. Charles Sumner:

Dear Sir:

A letter received since my seeing you this morning necessitates my leaving town early tomorrow; and I fear I shall not be able to return verry soon.

I have tried to find you this afternoon and evening without success, and learn that you will not be at your rooms again untill it is too late for me to renew my call.

Permit me to thank you very much for your friendliness, and to hope that you may yet efficaciously exert it in my behalf.

I desire to be considered as an applicant for the consulship at Glasgow.

My affair has thus far been pretty much entirely in your hands, and with you I must now leave it.

With much respect
I am very truly yours
H. Melville

ALS on a 23.4 × 19.5 cm sheet, folded in half, of white laid paper with lines, embossed with the manufacturer's small circular stamp enclosing a crown. Melville inscribed the first and third pages, in ink. Another hand, presumably a clerk's, noted in ink on the fourth page "Consul — Glasgow | Herman Melville's | letter"; Sumner added the comment "I call attention | to this letter from | Herman Melville. | Charles Sumner". It was preserved among the "Letters of Application and Recommendation for Public Office During the Administrations of Abraham Lincoln and Andrew Johnson 1861–1869" and numbered in red ink "N° 11" in the eleven-item file concerning Melville's application for an appointment.

LOCATION: National Archives.

PUBLICATION: Hayford-Davis, p. 384. Davis-Gilman 158.

TEXTUAL NOTES: shall not be] not *written over* be • to thank] to *written over* th

TO AUGUSTA MELVILLE
BEFORE 11 JULY 1861 · PITTSFIELD

Unlocated. A letter to Augusta Melville is cited in Stanwix Melville's 11 July 1861 letter to his step-grandmother, Hope Savage Shaw. Stanwix was staying at Gansevoort, New York, with Melville's mother, sisters Augusta and Frances Priscilla, and uncle Herman Gansevoort. In his six-page letter describing all of his adventures, he mentions that "Aunt Augusta had a letter from papa, and he sent me a stamp with Benjamin Franklin head on it. . . . I was very glad to hear that Papa, and Mamma are coming in the buggy to Gansevoort, I hope they will find some way to bring Mackey [Malcolm Melville] along" (HCL-M). Adding a note to the end of Stanwix's letter, Augusta Melville wrote, "We are expecting a visit from Herman & Lizzie very soon. . . . Mamma is quite well, but uncle's strength has been failing for some time past." As Melville's 10 August letter (just below) written from Gansevoort indicates, his uncle Herman remained weak; he lived until March 1862. Davis-Gilman Unlocated 375.

TO PETER GANSEVOORT
10 AUGUST 1861 · GANSEVOORT

Although Stanwix had expected his parents to come to Gansevoort "in the buggy" (see the entry for the unlocated early July letter, just above), Melville and his wife apparently decided to go by train instead. They remained in Gansevoort, visiting Melville's ailing uncle Herman, for several more days before returning to Pittsfield via Albany on Wednesday, 14 August. As Melville's subsequent letter of 15 August indicates, his proposed visit with his uncle Peter, aunt Susan, and cousin Catherine (here "Kitty") while between trains in Albany did not take place, because the Gansevoort family left Albany for a vacation on Long Island. Peter Gansevoort's intervening 12 August reply (see the endorsement) informing Melville of their plans and inviting Melville and his wife for a later visit in Albany is unlocated.

Gansevoort Aug. 10th 1861

My Dear Uncle: Lizzie and I have been making a visit here for a few days, and we propose returning home on Wednesday next, taking the early morning train from this place, which reaches Albany about nine o'clock. The interval between that hour and the departure of the afternoon train East, we propose to spend at your house — that is to say, if you and Aunt Susan will let us.

I am glad to say, that Uncle Herman, although feeble, and almost entirely confined to his sofa during the day, is yet, for the most part, free from pain, has a pretty good appetite, and sleeps well. — With love to Aunt Susan and Kitty, Beleive me

Truly and Affectionately Yours

H. Melville

ALS on a 33.2 × 20.1 cm sheet, folded in half, of white laid paper with lines, embossed with the manufacturer's oval stamp enclosing the name "BATH". Melville inscribed the first and third pages, in ink, and addressed the envelope "Hon. Peter Gansevoort | Albany | N.Y."; it was postmarked in Gansevoort on 10 August. Peter Gansevoort later noted in pencil on the envelope "Herman Melville | Rec^d & Ans^d | 12. Augt 1861 — ".

LOCATION: NYPL-GL.

PUBLICATION: Paltsits, pp. 17–18. Davis-Gilman 159.

TO PETER GANSEVOORT
15 AUGUST 1861 · PITTSFIELD

In his earlier 12 August letter (now unlocated), Peter Gansevoort, replying to Melville's 10 August letter, invited him and his wife to come for a visit of several days at Albany. Melville sent this reply to Rockaway, Long Island, "At the 'Pavilion,' " where his uncle, aunt, and cousin Catherine (Kitty) were vacationing.

Pittsfield, Aug. 15th 1861

My Dear Uncle:

After thinking over it a day or two, I fear that I will not be able, at present, to fix upon a time for a visit to Albany, with Lizzie, as you kindly propose. We were sorry that it so happened, that we necessarily missed seeing you yesterday, in passing through the city.

I write this in some haste to secure the mail. I hope, My Dear Uncle, that you will find good weather, good company, and good wine, where you are. Tell Aunt Susan & Kitty that I wish them a continuation of clear cheeks and sparkling eyes, & that the best way to insure it, is to roll night and morning in the surf at Rockaway. Owing to this sort of exercise, the porpoises, they say, have very fine skins, & enjoy admirable health.

Truly and Affectionately
Thine
H Melville

Peter Gansevoort Esq.

ALS on a 12.6 × 20.4 cm part-sheet (torn along the left edge) of blue laid paper, embossed with the manufacturer's shield-like stamp enclosing the name "CARSON'S CONGRESS". Melville inscribed only one side of the leaf, in ink, and addressed the envelope "Hon. Peter Gansevoort | Rockaway | Long Island | At the 'Pavilion.' ''; it was postmarked in Pittsfield on 16 August.

LOCATION: NYPL-GL.

PUBLICATION: Paltsits, p. 18. Davis-Gilman 160.

1862

TO EVERT A. DUYCKINCK
[1?] FEBRUARY 1862 · NEW YORK

This letter, undated by Melville, clearly belongs to February 1862 when he and his family were wintering in New York, presumably at the address in the heading of the letter. Since Evert Duyckinck's endorsement at the top of the first page can be read as either "[Febr. 1862]" or "[Feb 1. 1862]," the specific Saturday—"come round tomorrow (Sunday) evening"—when Melville wrote this letter remains uncertain.

The "volumes of the Elizabethan dramatists" Melville requested from Duyckinck's library are identified by Sealts (188) as the third edition of a set originally edited by Robert Dodsley: *A Select Collection of Old Plays*, newly edited by John Payne Collier (London: Prowett, 1825–27). From this set, Duyckinck probably sent Melville volumes three and six. Volume three contained both parts of Thomas Dekker's *The Honest Whore*, and volume six included John Webster's *The White Devil*, as well as *The Roaring Girle*, which Dekker had written with Thomas Middleton. The Marlowe that Melville had already read was probably the volume of "Marlowe's Plays" he bought in London in 1849 (Sealts 348). The "bearer" for the books was very possibly Melville's ten-year-old son, Stanwix (his older son Malcolm was in boarding school in 1862).

150 E. 18th St.

My Dear Duyckinck:

For the past week I have been lying here rheumatism-bound, or I should have been to see you to tell you where we are to be found.

I want you to loan me some of those volumes of the Elizabethan dramatists. Is Deckar among the set? And Webster? If so, please put them up and let the bearer have them. — Send me any except Marlowe, whom I have read.

Mrs. Melville and I will be glad to see you & your brother any evening. If you have nothing better to do, come round tomorrow (Sunday) evening, and we will brew some whiskey punch and settle the affairs of the universe over it — which affairs sadly need it, some say.

Thine
H Melville

P.S. Dont fear that the books will get wet, as the bearer travels under cover by rail, all but the unavoidable corners.

ALS on a 24.5 × 20.2 cm sheet, folded in half, of white wove paper, embossed with the manufacturer's oval stamp enclosing the name "PARIS". Melville inscribed the first and third pages, in ink. Duyckinck later noted in ink at the top of the first page either "[Febr. 1862]" or "[Feb 1. 1862]".

LOCATION: NYPL-D.

PUBLICATION: (partial) *Log*, II, 644–45. Metcalf, pp. 196–97. Davis-Gilman 161.

TEXTUAL NOTES: volumes of] of *blotted* • up] *before canceled* among

TO AUGUSTA MELVILLE
2 MAY 1862 · PITTSFIELD

At the end of April 1862 Melville, his wife, and younger son Stanwix had recently returned from a visit at Gansevoort, New York. On 30 April Stanwix wrote a letter to his aunt Augusta at Gansevoort, and before it was mailed, Melville added his brief message on Friday, 2 May. As Stanwix's letter describes it, the household at Pittsfield was in confusion because Elizabeth Melville was sick. Stanwix wrote: "We arrived home safely. Mamma was taking sick on Monday but she is better to-day. I have a good deal to do, to bring in wood, and water; and help papa, and

To Augusta Melville, 2 May 1862 (reduced). Courtesy of the Rare Books and Manuscripts Division, The New York Public Library, Astor, Lenox and Tilden Foundations (Gansevoort-Lansing Collection).

Mamma, and a host of other things, so I could not write to you before. Papa has a new horse on trial, from Mr Nash, the horse will go as fast as Jehu. It is worth a $145. Mackey [Malcolm] is coming home today. Papa is well. My time is so taking up that I have not had my lessons. My things are in my trunk. Everything in the house is upside down, topsy turvy. I can-not write much[.] love to Grandmamma, and all." (The reference to Jehu is probably an echo of a comparison by Melville of his new horse to the biblical king that "driveth furiously," 2 Kings 9.20.) In a post-script Stanwix added: "Mrs Chapman came and stayed all day and night with us. . . . Mamma is sick in bed since Monday morning and that is the reason that she could not write to you." To find some permanent household help, Melville placed an advertisement which ran in the 1 and 8 May issues of the *Berkshire County Eagle* promising the "highest" wages for a "competent" person. Augusta Melville's 5 May reply to this letter (see her endorsement) is unlocated.

Friday Morning.

My Dear Augusta, — Stannie wrote this note two days since. It is my fault it has not gone ere now.

We have been in a state of great commotion since arriving here. Lizzie has overexerted herself & been confined to her bed. But is now better. We have managed to procure assistance from the neighbors & in a day or two hope to get permanent "help".

I write in great hurry
Herman

Macky is here.

P.S. Dont write to Helen or Fanny or Kate about our affairs here.

ALS on a 23.7 × 19.2 cm sheet, folded in half, of white laid paper. On the upper left corner of the first page is a blue and red printed eagle and star with the words "NOT A STAFF MUST FALL". Stanwix inscribed the first two pages, in ink; Melville added his message in pencil on the third page. Augusta Melville noted in ink on the fourth page "*No 1* | Ans^d | May 5th | 1862 | to Stanwix | & | Herman". At the top of the first page is a word-start in Stanwix's hand: "Ga".

LOCATION: NYPL-GL. *Provenance*: Lyrical Ballad Bookstore.

TEXTUAL NOTES: Lizzie] *after canceled* No help. • P.S. . . . here.] *added in top margin; placed here editorially*

TO THOMAS MELVILLE
25 MAY 1862 · PITTSFIELD

Thomas Melville, Melville's youngest brother, was at this time captain of the *Bengal* (owned by Curtis & Peabody), sailing for Hong Kong. The "long and very entertaining" letter he had written to their mother is now unlocated. Melville's jocular response, accusing Tom of having taken to writing sonnets on his "mistress' eyebrow" (*As You Like It*, 2.7) and on her " 'tournure' " (a bustle), is the only letter to his youngest brother now located. Its reminiscence of the "romantic moonlight night" on their 1860 trip to California adds an episode to Melville's brief 1860 journal (*Journals*, pp. 131–35), and its wry advice about corporal punishment sounds a recurring and ambivalent strain in Melville's writing. He humorously attributes to the Bible his slight adaptation of Byron's passage from *Don Juan*: "Oh ye! who teach the ingenuous youth of nations | Holland, France, England, Germany or Spain, | I pray ye flog them upon all occasions, | It mends their morals,—never mind the pain" (2.11.1–4), which plays on Samuel Butler's "spare the rod and spoil the child" (*Hudibras*, 2.1.844), itself adapted from Proverbs 13.24. Although Melville advocates corporal punishment here, he did not always agree with it (see *Journals*, pp. 602–3n., for a further discussion of this theme). His hyperbole about selling off his poetry to a trunk-maker for linings, as Stanton Garner has pointed out, was long used by various writers (but while sheets of unsold books were actually used for trunk-linings, there is no record of manuscripts being used as such; see Garner's "Herman Melville and the Trunkmaker," *Notes & Queries* 224 [August 1979], 307–8). Though Melville implies here that "the whole stock" was destroyed, it is usually assumed that versions of some of his unpublished poems of 1860 (see his letters of May of that year) appeared as "Fruit of Travel Long Ago" in *Timoleon* (1891).

Melville's shorthand description of recent Civil War events, with its allusion to Macbeth's cry of " 'Enough!' " (5.8.34), is to the Peninsular Campaign of the Army of the Potomac under Major General George Brinton McClellan. At this time Peter Gansevoort's son Henry was a second lieutenant of the U.S. Artillery in that army. Melville's other cousin in the war was Guert Gansevoort (1812–68), the son of Melville's uncle Leonard Gansevoort (see also LETTERS RECEIVED, p. 566). When not commanding a ship, Guert Gansevoort served during the Civil War as Ordnance Officer at the New York Naval Shipyard at Brooklyn. At this time his recent appointment was as commanding officer of the U.S. Steam Sloop *Adirondack*, which had been built at the Brooklyn yard. He commanded this vessel in the South Atlantic Blockading Squadron until it ran onto a reef on the northeast point of Little Bahama Bank, Man of War Cay, on 23 August 1862 and was lost. In 1863 he was given command of the U.S. Steam Frigate *Roanoke*, involved in maneuvers off Hampton Roads, Virginia. He returned to the Brooklyn naval yard in the fall of 1864.

Pittsfield May 25th 1862

My Dear Boy: (or, if that appear disrespectful)

My Dear Captain: Yesterday I received from Gansevoort your long and very entertaining letter to Mamma from Pernambuco.

Yes, it was very entertaining. Particularly the account of that interesting young gentleman whom you so uncivilly stigmatize for a
jackass, simply because he improves his opportunities in the way of
sleeping, eating & other commendable customs. That's the sort of
fellow, seems to me, to get along with. For my part I love sleepy
fellows, and the more ignorant the better. Damn your wide-awake
and knowing chaps. As for sleepiness, it is one of the noblest qualities of humanity. There is something sociable about it, too. Think
of those sensible & sociable millions of good fellows all taking a
good long friendly snooze together, under the sod — no quarrels,
no imaginary grievances, no envies, heart-burnings, & thinking
how much better that other chap is off — none of this: but all equally free-&-easy, they sleep away & reel off their nine knots an hour,
in perfect amity. If you see your sleepy ignorant jackass-friend again
give him my compliments, and say that however others may think
of him, I honor and esteem him. — As for your treatment of those
young ones, there I entirely commend you. Strap them, I beseech
you. You remember what the Bible says: —
   "Oh ye who teach the children of the nations,
       Holland, France, England, Germany or Spain,
    I pray ye *strap* them upon all occasions,
       It mends their morals — never mind the pain"
In another place the Bible says, you know, something about spare-
ing the strap & spoiling the child. — Since I have quoted poetry
above, it puts me in mind of my own doggerel. You will be pleased
to learn that I have disposed of a lot of it at a great bargain. In fact, a
trunk-maker took the whole stock off my hands at ten cents the
pound. So, when you buy a new trunk again, just peep at the lining
& perhaps you may be rewarded by some glorious stanza stareing
you in the face & claiming admiration. If you were not such a devel
of a ways off, I would send you a trunk, by way of presentation-
copy. I cant help thinking what a luckless chap you were that voyage you had a poetaster with you. You remember the romantic
moonlight night, when the conceited donkey repeated to you about
three cables' length of his verses. But you bore it like a hero. I cant
in fact recall so much as a single *wince*. To be sure, you went to bed
immediately upon the conclusion of the entertainment; but this
much I am sure of, whatever were your sufferings, you never gave
them utterance. Tom, my boy, I admire you. I say again, you are a

hero. — By the way, I hope in God's name, that rumor which reached your owners (C & P.) a few weeks since — that dreadful rumor is not true. They heard that you had begun to take to —— drink? — Oh no, but worse —— to sonnet-writing. That off Cape Horn instead of being on deck about your business, you devoted your time to writing a sonnet on your mistress' eyebrow, & another upon her "tournure". — "I'll be damned" says Curtis (he was very profane) "if I'll have a sonneteer among my Captains." — "Well, if he has taken to poetizing," says Peabody — God help the ship!" — I have written them contradicting the rumor in your name. What villian & secret enemy of yours set this cursed report afloat, I cant imagine. —— Do you want to hear about the war? — The war goes bravely on. McClellan is now within fifteen miles of the rebel capital, Richmond. New Orleans is taken &c &c &c. You will see all no doubt in the papers at your Agents. But when the *end* — the wind-up — the grand pacification is coming, who knows. We beat the rascals in almost every feild, & take all their ports &c, but they dont cry "Enough!" — It looks like a long lane, with the turning quite out of sight. — Guert has recently been appointed to the command of a fine new sloop of war. I am rejoiced to hear it. It will do him good in more ways than one. He is brave as a lion, a good seaman, a natural-born officer, & I hope he will yet turn out the hero of a brilliant victory. — I dont write you, My Dear Boy, about family matters, because I know that the girls keep you posted there. But I will just say that of late Lizzie has not been very well, tho' she is now getting better. The children are all well. Macky is studying Latin — "Hic-heac-hoc" — "horum, harum, horum", he goes it every night. — And now, my boy, if you knew how much laziness I overcame in writing you this letter, you would think me, what I am

Always your affectionate brother
Herman.

ALS on a 33.2 × 20.1 cm sheet, folded in half, of white laid paper, embossed with the manufacturer's oval stamp enclosing the name "BATH". Melville inscribed all four pages, in ink. A transcription (in The Newberry Library) by John H. Birss of an accompanying envelope (HCL-M; at present unlocated) reports that Melville addressed it "Captain Thomas Melville | Ship 'Bengal' | — Care, Augustine Heard & Co. | Hong-Kong | China." and noted in the upper left-hand corner "*For the Steamer* | ^c/o Southampton"; it was postmarked in Pittsfield on 30 May, in New York on 31 May, and in Hong Kong on 7 August 1862. Another hand noted on the back of the envelope in pencil "Herman 1862."

LOCATION: HCL-M.

PUBLICATION: (partial) Weaver, pp. 359–60. Leyda, *Portable Melville*, pp. 602–5. Davis-Gilman 162 (with partial reproduction).

TEXTUAL NOTES: teach] *inserted above caret* · night] g *added* · bore it] it *inserted above caret* · whatever] *miswritten* whateve · God . . . ship!"] *opening double quotation mark lacking* · Agents] A *written over* a · they] *inserted above* · not been] *miswritten* not being · heac] a *written over* i · my boy] my *written over* you *and an undeciphered word*

TO PETER GANSEVOORT
AFTER 8 AUGUST 1862 · PITTSFIELD

Unlocated. A letter can be inferred from Peter Gansevoort's 8 August 1862 letter to Melville, informing him that his uncle Wessel Gansevoort (1781–1862; his mother's second oldest brother) of Danby, Vermont, had died on 7 August and that the funeral would be held at the Gansevoort house in Albany (see LETTERS RECEIVED, pp. 686–87). Presumably Melville sent a reply. Davis-Gilman Unlocated 376.

TO GORHAM D. GILMAN
29 NOVEMBER [1862?] · PITTSFIELD

In her forthcoming article "Melville and Hawaii: An Unpublished Letter," Ruth Blair identifies the recipient of this letter as Gorham D. Gilman (1822–1909), a prominent Boston businessman and politician who had begun his business career in Hawaii between 1841 and 1861. The "Journal" that Melville returned to Gilman with this letter had included at least one and possibly all of the manuscripts Gilman later donated to the Hawaiian Historical Society. The one which Melville certainly read and was particularly charmed by records the tale of Umi as narrated to Gilman by King Kamehameha III (24 pp.), a traditional Hawaiian legend about an illegitimate royal son who eventually becomes king. The other manuscripts include Gilman's intermittent journal at Honolulu from 4 July to 10 August 1843 (16 pp.), which covers the political events that Melville also described in the Appendix to *Typee*, and one largely made up of Gilman's account of a tour he made of the island of Hawaii from 19 November to 9 December 1844 (129 pp.). All of the journals indicate that Gilman was closely associated with the Hawaiian missionaries and familiar with members of the Hawaiian royal family.

It is not known how Melville first became acquainted with Gilman, although possibly it was in New York, where they may have enjoyed a good dinner at the Metropolitan Hotel at Broadway and Prince streets. Melville dated the letter only 29 November; it has been tentatively assigned to 1862 on the basis of the penciled year 1862, which was added after Melville's date by another hand, possibly Gilman's. Melville had possibly, however, read Gilman's manuscript before preparing his South Seas lecture first given on 6 December 1858, which includes what may be an allusion to it (see the NN *Piazza Tales* volume, pp. 418–19, 776).

Pittsfield Nov. 29th

Dear Sir:

I desire to thank you most heartily for the loan — such a long loan too — of the manuscripts, which I now return to you agreeably to your request received yesterday.

Your Journal was interesting to me, — the tale of Umi exceedingly so. I was charmed with it. It is graceful & Greekish. Some time ago I tried my hand at elaborating it, but found I bungled, and gave it up. You ought to do something with it — Show it to people.

Wishing you every happiness upon your return, and wishing you good company and good dinners at the Metropolitan, I am

Very Truly Yours
H Melville

ALS on a 13 × 20.5 cm part-sheet (torn along the left edge) of blue laid paper, embossed with the manufacturer's shield-like stamp. Melville inscribed only one side of the leaf, in ink. Another hand, possibly Gilman's, later added the year 1862 in pencil after Melville's partial date. The letter was folded widthwise and mounted sideways on the front free endpaper of Gilman's copy of a first American edition of *Typee*.

LOCATION: Punahou School, Honolulu, Hawaii.

PUBLICATION: Ruth Blair, "Melville and Hawaii: An Unpublished Letter," forthcoming.

TEXTUAL NOTE: Metropolitan] *written over another word*

TO SAMUEL S. SHAW
10 DECEMBER 1862 · PITTSFIELD

Melville wrote this letter to his brother-in-law Samuel Shaw while recuperating from his serious accident on 31 October 1862 on the road outside Pittsfield. According to the 7 November report in the *Berkshire County Eagle*, Melville's horse bolted and threw him from his wagon, breaking or dislocating one of his shoulder blades and injuring several ribs. This occurred shortly after the move from Arrowhead to "the square old-fashioned house on South street in the rear of Backus block" in the town of Pittsfield, where Melville and his family remained until the fall of 1863 (thus his comment on the household not "being quite in order yet"; see J. E. A. Smith, "Herman Melville," in Sealts, *Early Lives*, p. 135). The epithet "spoony," which Melville uses to refer to himself, means "fool" or "silly person."

Pittsfield Dec. 10th 1862

My Dear Sam: I remember that some days after my mishap, when I was able to give the necessary attention, Lizzie read to me the letter you wrote her on that occasion. — I can not help telling you how sensible I am of the kindness you showed, and write you this that you may have the ocular evidence of my recovery. To be sure, I still carry my arm (the left one, happily) in a sling, and the neuralgia gives me a love-pinch in the cheek now and then. But upon the whole I am now in a fair way of being completely restored to what I was before the accident. —

This recovery is flattering to my vanity. I begin to indulge in the pleasing idea that my life must needs be of some value. Probably I consume a certain amount of oxygen, which unconsumed might create some subtle disturbance in Nature. Be that as it may, I am going to try and stick to the conviction named above. For I have observed that such an idea, once well bedded in a man, is a wonderful conservator of health and almost a prophecy of long life. I once, like other spoonies, cherished a loose sort of notion that I did not care to live very long. But I will frankly own that I have now no serious, no insuperable objections to a respectable longevity. I dont like the idea of being left out night after night in a cold churchyard. — In warm and genial countries, death is much less of a bugbear than in our frozen latitudes. A native of Hindostan takes easily and kindly to his latter end. It is but as a stepping round the corner to him. He knows he will sleep warm. — Pretty topics these (🕱✂) for a friendly note, you say. (By the way, Death, in my skull, seems to tip a knowing sort of wink out of his left eye. What does that mean, I wonder?)

But my page is more than half gone, so I must stop this trifling.

Lizzie is quite well, though a little jaded by her manifold cares, we not yet being quite in order yet. The children are flourishing as usual. Tomorrow we expect the gratification of a visit from my mother, whom we hope to be able to keep some time with us. — My best rememberances to your mother, Lemuel, and the rest of the family.

Adieu
H. M.

ALS on a 25.2 × 20.4 cm sheet, folded in half, of blue laid paper, faintly embossed with the manufacturer's shield-like stamp. Melville inscribed the first three pages, in ink.

LOCATION: HCL-M.

PUBLICATION: Thorp, pp. 402–3. Davis-Gilman 163.

TEXTUAL NOTES: my recovery] *second* e *added* • other] h *written over another letter*

TO T. APOLEON CHENEY
19 DECEMBER 1862 • [PITTSFIELD?]

Unlocated. T. Apoleon Cheney's 7 December 1869 letter cites a 19 December 1862 letter received from Melville (see LETTERS RECEIVED, pp. 701–4). According to Cheney, Melville had agreed in it to send the Georgic Society and Library in Watkins, New York, a copy of one of his works. He apparently had never sent the book, since Cheney once again requested one in his 1869 letter. Davis-Gilman Unlocated 377.

1863

TO MARIA GANSEVOORT MELVILLE AND DAUGHTERS
BEFORE 10 FEBRUARY 1863 • NEW YORK

Unlocated. A letter from Melville is cited in Maria Melville's 13 February 1863 letter from Glens Falls, New York, where she was visiting relatives, to her daughters Augusta and Frances Priscilla at Gansevoort. Melville was in New York at this time and had written to his mother and sisters at Gansevoort. Maria Melville, commenting on his letter that Augusta and Frances had forwarded to her, remarked: "Hermans letter was quite amusing. I hope he continues well & that New York will continue to amuse him & that he went to Grace Church to witness the queer couple that were so splendidly attended, & so peculiar in all respects" (NYPL-GL). The "queer couple" were Tom Thumb and his bride Lavinia Warren, who were married at Grace Church on 10 February 1863. Melville had probably commented on some of the newspaper accounts of the lavish wedding preparations. It is not known whether he joined the large crowd that witnessed the event. For Melville's portrayal of Grace Church in 1853–54, see his piece "The Two Temples," NN *Piazza Tales* volume, pp. 303–15.

TO ELIZABETH SHAW MELVILLE
BEFORE 11 FEBRUARY 1863 • NEW YORK

Unlocated. A letter from Melville to his wife during his stay in New York (see the entry just above) can be inferred from an 11 February 1863 letter that Elizabeth Melville wrote to her sister-in-law Augusta at Gansevoort. Reporting on Melville's recovery since his accident of 31 October 1862, she noted: "Herman has been steadily improving, & when he found that he could dress himself without assistance, he began to think of going to New York for a visit — He has been there now about ten days and is enjoying it very much — his health has been better this winter I think, and he has

walked a good deal . . . & in N.Y. he has walked from Trinity Church to 35th St."
(NYPL-GL). Although Elizabeth Melville does not specifically state that she had received a letter from her husband, she clearly had had news of his stay, and it is most
likely that Melville himself, rather than his brother Allan, conveyed this news.

TO CATHERINE GANSEVOORT
17 FEBRUARY 1863 · PITTSFIELD

The photographs of Melville's maternal grandparents—General Peter Gansevoort and
Catherine Van Schaick Gansevoort—for which he thanks his cousin Catherine (Kate) in
this letter were probably of portraits by Gilbert Stuart (see p. 544 for a reproduction of
an engraving of General Gansevoort taken from the Stuart painting; for more about his
grandfather's victory at Fort Stanwix, see Melville's letter of 7 November 1851, above).
Kate's "note enclosing the pictures" is now unlocated.

Lieutenant Henry Gansevoort, Kate's older brother, whom Melville had visited in New York on 7 February, was at this time temporarily assigned to Fort Hamilton, in New York Harbor, while recovering from a fever he caught while fighting
at the second battle of Bull Run and at Antietam. He never returned to his battery
during the war, but accepted the rank of lieutenant colonel of volunteers in the
Thirteenth New York Volunteer Cavalry (see John C. Hoadley, ed., *Memorial of
Henry Sanford Gansevoort* [Boston: Rand & Avery, 1875], pp. 77–78).

My Dear Cousin Kate:

Upon returning from New York I was made happy by finding
your note enclosing the pictures. The one of our grandmother is
clear and admirable. But alas for the Hero of Fort Stanwix! Photographically rendered, he seems under a sort of eclipse, emblematic
perhaps of the gloom which his spirit may feel in looking down
upon this dishonorable epoch. — But dont let us become too earnest. A very bad habit.

The other day, be it known unto you, Incomparable Kate, I went
with Allan and his wife to Fort Hamilton, where we saw Lieutenant
Henry Gansevoort of the U.S. Artillery. He politely led us to the ramparts, pointing out all objects of interest. He looked well and war-like,
cheerfully embarked in the career of immortality. I saw him upon two
other occasions, and dined with him at Allan's one Sunday.

With best rememberances to your mother and father, in which
Lizzie joins,

> Beleive me Incomparable Kate
> Affectionately Your Cousin
> Herman

Pittsfield Feb. 17th 1863

ALS on a 25.3 × 20.4 cm sheet, folded in half, of blue laid paper, embossed with the manufacturer's shield-like stamp enclosing the name "CARSON'S CONGRESS". Melville inscribed the
first and third pages, in ink, and addressed the envelope "Miss Catherine Gansevoort
| — Care of Hon. Peter Gansevoort — | Albany | N.Y."; it was postmarked in Pittsfield on 17
February. Another hand noted on the envelope "2–17–1863" and "1863" in pencil.

LOCATION: NYPL-GL.

PUBLICATION: Paltsits, pp. 18–19. Davis-Gilman 164.

TEXTUAL NOTES: eclipse] *miswritten* eclipsse • the gloom] *after canceled* what • embarked in] in
possibly on • career] *miswritten* carreer • Pittsfield . . . 1863] *at the bottom of the otherwise blank*
second page; placed here editorially • Feb.] F *written over wiped* J

TO ELIZABETH SHAW MELVILLE
BEFORE [27?] MARCH 1863 · PITTSFIELD

Unlocated. A brief letter from her husband is cited in a hurried [27?] March 1863
letter that Elizabeth Melville wrote to her sister-in-law Augusta, who was staying
with the family in Pittsfield while Elizabeth visited her stepmother in Boston. At
the close, she added, "My love to Herman and Macky and thank Herman for his
note" (NYPL-GL).

TO MARIA GANSEVOORT MELVILLE
BEFORE 7 MAY 1863 · PITTSFIELD

Unlocated. A letter from Melville is cited in Maria Melville's 11 May 1863 letter to
her daughter Augusta, who was visiting Catherine and John Hoadley, at this time
living in New Bedford, Massachusetts. Along with other family news, Maria Melville reports, "I had a letter from Herman[.] They go to New York in October.
Allan has taken the Pittsfield Farm in part payment. Sam Shaw was the agent &
made the legal transfer of the 26 St House to Lizzie. Herman seems to be much
pleased with the prospect. He has always liked New York, & is not the first man
who has been beguiled into the country, & found out by experience that it was not
the place for him" (NYPL-GL). Melville's letter is probably the same one cited in
Elizabeth Melville's 7 May 1863 letter to Frances Priscilla Melville at Gansevoort, in
which she briefly states, "Herman has written to Mama about our plans, so no
matter about them at present" (NYPL-GL). The New York house, like the farm at
Pittsfield, was placed in Elizabeth Melville's name, since her father had bequeathed
his mortgage on the farm to her in his will (see the headnote to Melville's 22 May
1856 letter to Judge Shaw, above).

TO PETER GANSEVOORT
AFTER 12 JUNE 1863 · PITTSFIELD

Unlocated. On 12 June 1863 Peter Gansevoort wrote to Melville inviting him to
attend the semicentennial celebration of the Albany Academy, where Melville had

gone to school in 1830–31 and 1836–37 (see LETTERS RECEIVED, pp. 689–92). Since he was present at the celebration on 26 June (see the entry for his unlocated 27 or 28 June letter to his wife, below), he presumably answered his uncle and accepted the invitation to stay with him. Davis-Gilman Unlocated 378.

TO THOMAS MELVILLE
AFTER 15 JUNE 1863 · PITTSFIELD

Unlocated. A letter to Melville's brother Thomas, then bound for San Francisco from the Orient, can be inferred from Frances Priscilla (Fanny) Melville's 15 June 1863 letter to their sister Augusta, in which she states that having received a letter from Tom she is writing to "Herman about Tom's direction, so he & Lizzie can write" (NYPL-GL). Fanny's letter to Melville is unlocated, but her insistence in her 15 June letter that Augusta as well as their sister and brother-in-law, Catherine and John Hoadley, with whom Augusta was visiting, "write *at once*" was probably repeated in her letter to Melville, and presumably heeded.

TO FRANCES PRISCILLA MELVILLE
[18?] JUNE 1863 · PITTSFIELD

Unlocated. A letter to Melville's sister Frances Priscilla (Fanny) is cited in her 22 June 1863 letter to their sister Augusta, who was still visiting in New Bedford with their sister Catherine Hoadley. Along with the recent news from Gansevoort, Fanny wrote, "I send you a letter from Lizzie received last week. Saturday I had a note from Herman, but I believe I will enclose it it is so funny, mind & send it back. I wrote to him this morning saying how glad we were that he was coming & that he must bring one or two of the children with him" (NYPL-GL). After attending the semicentennial celebration at the Albany Academy (see LETTERS RECEIVED, p. 689), Melville was planning to visit his mother and sister Fanny in Gansevoort.

TO ELIZABETH SHAW MELVILLE
[27 OR 28] JUNE 1863 · GANSEVOORT

Unlocated. Melville wrote to his wife from Gansevoort, New York, after attending the semicentennial celebration of the Albany Academy on Friday, 26 June (see LETTERS RECEIVED, p. 689). In a 29 June 1863 letter from Pittsfield, Elizabeth Melville summarized his letter for Augusta Melville in New Bedford: "On Friday Herman went to Albany to join in the Semi Cen. Cel. of the Alumni of the Albany Academy — , his name was on the Committee, and Uncle Peter urged him strongly to unite with them. Herman writes that they had interesting exercises at 'Tweddle Hall' (to which he marched in the procession) and a supper in the eveg of which he did *not* partake, though he was present. He staid at Uncle Peters alone with him (as the family are at Saratoga) and had a good time. On Saturday he went to Gansevoort to stay a few days — None of the children could accompany him, as the vacations have not begun yet — " (NYPL-GL).

TO RICHARD T. GREENE
BEFORE 20 OCTOBER 1863 · NEW YORK

Unlocated. Melville's Harper account on 11 August 1863 lists the charge "3 Typee to R
T Green" (HCL-M). Greene, then with the Union army at Vicksburg, acknowledged
receiving the books in a 20 October 1863 letter (see LETTERS RECEIVED, pp. 693–94).
The account suggests that the Harpers sent the books directly from their store, but
Greene's reply also acknowledges a letter from Melville, which probably advised him
that the books had been ordered. Davis-Gilman Unlocated 379.

TO SOPHIA VAN MATRE
10 DECEMBER 1863 · NEW YORK

In November of 1863 Melville and his family moved to 60 East Twenty-sixth
Street (renumbered 104 shortly thereafter) in New York, where he lived for the rest
of his life. As a result of the move, Sophia Van Matre's now unlocated letter, soliciting from him any autograph letters in his possession that could be sold at the
December 1863 Great Western Sanitary Fair in Cincinnati, was delayed in reaching
him. (For a similar letter from George McLaughlin and more about the sanitary
fair, see the headnote to the letter just below.)

Sophia Van Matre, listed in the 1860 census as twenty-five years old, was the
oldest daughter of Daniel Van Matre, a Cincinnati lawyer, and Maria Van Matre, a
member at this time of the Fruits and Flowers Committee of the Horticultural and
Pomological Department for the Cincinnati sanitary fair (see Charles Boynton, *History
of the Great Western Sanitary Fair* [Cincinnati: Vent, 1864], p. 63). Sophia Van Matre had
apparently attended a number of Berkshire picnics, probably as a guest of Sarah Morewood, who had other friends in Cincinnati (see the headnote to Melville's letter of [12
or 19?] September 1851, above). Although Melville did not supply her with any "autographs from old letters," she placed his letter in an album with some sixty other letters
from figures such as Washington Irving, General Grant, and Henry Ward Beecher,
which she had collected for the sanitary fair auction, where two of Melville's other
letters were also sold separately (see the headnotes to his 6 February 1854 letter to
George P. Putnam and his 15 December 1863 letter to McLaughlin). According to
Charles Boynton, cited above, Miss Van Matre's "magnificent" album was sold to
"M. Addy"—possibly Matthew Addy, a prominent Cincinnati businessman at the
time—for $21.75. But according to the annotated auction catalogue now at The New-
berry Library, it was sold for the same price to "Adae"—possibly Carl F. Adae, head of
the German Savings Institute in Cincinnati.

New York Dec. 10th 1863

My Dear Miss Van Matre:

Owing to my recent return to this, my native town, after a
twelve years' visit in Berkshire, your note was delayed in reaching
me.

Though involved in the thousand and one botherations incident to a removal of one's household a hundred & sixty miles, the fitting up & furnishing of a house &c &c, I yet hasten to respond.

I should be very happy indeed to comply with your request to furnish you with autographs from old letters, were it not that it is a vile habit of mine to destroy nearly all my letters. Such as I have by me would hardly be to your purpose.

With lively rememberance of our pick-nicks, & the warmest wishes for the success of your Fair, Beleive me

Very Sincerely Yours
Herman Melville

Miss Van Matre,
Cincinnati.

ALS on a 25.3 × 20.4 cm sheet, folded in half, of blue laid paper, embossed with the manufacturer's shield-like stamp enclosing the name "CARSON'S CONGRESS". Melville inscribed the first and third pages, in ink.

LOCATION: Rosenbach Museum & Library, Philadelphia. *Provenance*: Great Western Sanitary Fair Auction, 15 March 1864, in lot 572; "M. Addy" or "Adae"; the album was then broken up and the letters sold separately at the Hawaiian Book Exchange; Frank L. Pleadwell sale, Parke-Bernet Galleries, sale 1840, 7–8 October 1958, lot 349.

PUBLICATION: *Log*, II, 664. Davis-Gilman 165.

TEXTUAL NOTE: visit in] in *written over* to

TO GEORGE McLAUGHLIN
15 DECEMBER 1863 · NEW YORK

George McLaughlin was on the Committee for Coins and Autographs of the Great Western Sanitary Fair in Cincinnati (see Boynton, cited under publication, below, p. 62). Established to raise money for the medical care of wounded Northern soldiers, the sanitary fairs were held in many Northern cities. Unlike Sophia Van Matre (see the letter just above), McLaughlin apparently had written to Melville asking only for a reply that could be sold at the fair. According to Boynton, Melville's reply sold for fifty cents at the sanitary fair auction, where many of the single letters sold for less than a dollar. It was bought by "R. Clarke," who also purchased Melville's 6 February 1854 letter to George P. Putnam for twenty cents (see the headnote to that letter). Robert Clarke was the founder of the Cincinnati publishing firm Robert Clarke & Co., which published the catalogue by S. G. Hubbard for the sale. The actual purchaser at the sale, however, was, according to an annotated copy of the catalogue (in The Newberry Library), a Mr. Barney—presumably

Roderick Barney, listed as an employee of Clarke's in the 1864 Cincinnati directory. Since Clarke had advertised on the inside cover of the Hubbard catalogue that his company would purchase items "*without charge*, for those who can not personally attend the sale," Clarke may have bought both letters on behalf of another collector.

New York, Dec. 15, 1863

Dear Sir:

Owing to my change of residence, back to this, my native place, your letter was delayed in reaching me.

The Sanitary Fairs to be held in several of the large cities, will do an immense service to our soldiers. God prosper them, and those who work for them, and the great Cause which they are intended to subserve

With much respect
Yours Truly
Herman Melville

Geo. M. Laughlin Esq.
Cincinnati

ALS on a 25.1 × 20.4 cm sheet, folded in half, of blue laid paper, embossed with the manufacturer's shield-like stamp enclosing the name "CARSON'S CONGRESS". Melville inscribed the first page, in ink. It was later glued on the fourth page to another sheet, but has since been removed. A penciled dealer's mark "osek | 265⁰⁰" is on the fourth page.

LOCATION: UV-Barrett. *Provenance*: Great Western Sanitary Fair Auction, 15 March 1864, lot 353; Robert Clarke & Co.; Charles Hamilton catalogue 9 (28 November 1956), item 208.

PUBLICATION: Charles Boynton, *History of the Great Western Sanitary Fair* (Cincinnati: Vent, 1864), pp. 187–88. Davis-Gilman 166.

TO EVERT A. DUYCKINCK
31 DECEMBER 1863 · NEW YORK

The book Melville returned with this letter to his old friend Evert Duyckinck is unidentified. No longer directly associated with a literary journal since the *Literary World* ceased publication in 1853, Duyckinck had nonetheless remained active in literary circles and probably recommended that Melville write a review for one of the New York magazines.

Two notable absences from Melville's list in this letter of guests at his New Year's gathering were Duyckinck's brother George, who had died in March, and Ellen Brittain's sister Sarah Morewood, who had died in October.

Last Day of 1863

Dear Duyckinck:

I return the book, thinking you may want it. I have read it with great interest. As for scribbling anything about it, tho' I would like to please you, I have not spirit enough.

We are going to have Allan & his family here to night, with Mrs Britton from Pittsfield, & one or two other friends, who will come early, stay sociably & go early. If convenient, pray, join us.

Thine

H. M.

ALS on a 25.2 × 20.4 cm sheet, folded in half, of blue laid paper, embossed with the manufacturer's shield-like stamp enclosing the name "CARSON'S CONGRESS". Melville inscribed the first page, in pencil, and addressed the unstamped fourth page "Evert A. Duyckinck Esq. | 20 Clinton Place"; it was apparently delivered by hand. Duyckinck later noted on the fourth page in pencil "Herman Melville".

LOCATION: NYPL-D.

PUBLICATION: *Log*, II, 665. Davis-Gilman 167.

1864

TO ALEXANDER BLISS
BEFORE 22 MARCH 1864 · NEW YORK

Unlocated. A letter answering a now unlocated request from Lieutenant Colonel Alexander Bliss that Melville contribute to the collection *Autograph Leaves of Our Country's Authors* is cited in Melville's 22 March 1864 letter, just below. Enclosed with this letter was the manuscript poem reproduced in that volume, "Inscription For the Slain At Fredericksburgh," the original of which is now in the Harry Ransom Humanities Research Center at the University of Texas at Austin, in a bound volume of manuscripts related to *Autograph Leaves*, including most of the holograph originals of items that appeared in that book. Davis-Gilman Unlocated 380.

TO ALEXANDER BLISS
22 MARCH 1864 · NEW YORK

Alexander Bliss (1827–96), a lieutenant colonel in the quartermaster corps, compiled with John Pendleton Kennedy the collection *Autograph Leaves of Our Country's Authors* (Baltimore: Cushings & Bailey, 1864), made up of facsimiles of manuscript pieces by well-known American writers prepared for the benefit of the Sanitary Commission. As Melville's letter explains, the first version of the poem he sent with his initial reply was an "uncorrected draught." Bliss, however, evidently got Melville's letter too late to "*suppress*" the first version and insert the second. The poem was reproduced in facsimile as "Inscription For the Slain At Fredericksburgh" with other variations from the "*right*" version Melville sent with this letter (see the textual notes, below), but Bliss apparently did draw upon the second version for the collection's table of contents, where the title is "Inscription to the dead at Fredericksburg." This poem was not included in Melville's collection of Civil War poems, *Battle-Pieces* (1866). See the Northwestern-Newberry *Published Poems* volume, p. 321.

Please acknowledge the receipt of this.

New York, March 22ᵈ 1864

Dear Sir: In the hurry of despatching my Contribution the other day, I now find that I enclosed to you an uncorrected draught — in fact, the *wrong sheet.* Herewith you have the *right one*, which I trust you will substitute. Or, if that be too late, may I beg of you, by all means, to *suppress* the one you have. — I sincerely regret that my carelessness should be the cause of trouble.

With much Respect
Your Obt. Svt.
Herman Melville

Lt. Col. Alexander Bliss.
Baltimore Md.

[Enclosure:]

Inscription
—— ‖ ——
For the Dead
At Fredericksburgh.
—————— ‖ ——————

A dreadful glory lights an earnest end;
In jubilee the patriot ghosts ascend;
Transfigured at the rapturous height
    Of their passionate feat of arms,
Death to the brave's a starry night, —
    Strewn their vale of death with palms.

Herman Melville

ALS on a 25.3 × 20.4 cm sheet, folded in half, of blue laid paper, embossed with the manu-facturer's shield-like stamp enclosing the name "CARSON'S CONGRESS". Melville inscribed the first page, in ink. The enclosure is on a 19.9 × 24.5 cm part-sheet (torn along the left edge) of white wove paper, embossed with the manufacturer's stamp of a three-domed capitol under the name "CONGRESS". Melville inscribed only one side of the leaf, in ink. Another hand noted in pencil at the top of the page "Herman Melville".

LOCATION: Bancroft-Bliss Collection, Library of Congress.

PUBLICATION: Davis-Gilman 168.

TEXTUAL NOTES (variations in the facsimile; for symbols used, see p. 840): Dead] Slain • dreadful] *[not present]* • ascend;] ~. • Of their] *[no indentation]* • Strewn] Strown *and no indentation*

TO HENRY S. GANSEVOORT
10 MAY 1864 · NEW YORK

On 16 April 1864 Melville and his brother Allan arrived in Vienna, Virginia, at Henry Gansevoort's camp—that of the Cavalry Brigade, Tyler's Division, Washington Defenses. Their cousin Henry, now a lieutenant colonel and commander of the Thirteenth New York Volunteer Cavalry, was away at the time, but returned on 19 April while Melville was on a scout into "Mosby's Confederacy" led by Colonel Charles Russell Lowell (1835–64), a nephew of James Russell Lowell. Although Allan left for Washington on 17 or 18 April, Melville stayed and visited with their cousin on 20 and 21 April—the visit he mentions at the opening of this letter. As this letter also indicates, Melville became acquainted with a number of other men in the camp: Benjamin Rush Taylor (b. 1820), the regimental surgeon, "the Dr" whom Melville unsuccessfully looked for at the Willard hotel in Washington (see the article by Stanton Garner cited below, pt. 1, p. 13); Brigadier General Robert Ogden Tyler (1831–74), Henry Gansevoort's division commander (for more on Tyler and the copies of Johann Richter's *Titan* and Terence's *Comedies* that he gave Melville, see the headnote to Melville's 21 July 1864 letter to him, below); Captain George Henry Brewster (1834–1903), Henry Gansevoort's former law-partner and Allan Melville's current partner (thus Melville's reference to "Coke on Lyttleton, and Strap on the Shoulder"), who accompanied the Melville brothers from New York to Washington on his way to join Henry Gansevoort's regiment (and apparently loaned Melville his horse and some warm clothes for the scout); Edwin Yates Lansing (1841–1937), nephew of Henry Gansevoort's stepmother, Susan Lansing Gansevoort; and Dr. Oscar C. DeWolf (1835–95), brigade surgeon and graduate (in 1857) of the Berkshire Medical Institute in Pittsfield. For a full account of Melville's visit in his cousin's camp and its bearing on his narrative poem "The Scout toward Aldie," see Stanton Garner's "Melville's Scout toward Aldie" (*Melville Society Extracts* 51 [September 1982], 5–16, and 52 [November 1982], 1–14); see also Garner's *The Civil War World of Herman Melville* (Lawrence: University of Kansas Press, 1993).

This is the only letter from Melville that Henry Gansevoort preserved in his letter albums (covering the years 1855–68), which he kept meticulously. In a memorandum (NYPL-GL) about the albums, he explained that after losing his "letters received up to" March 1855 in a fire, which consumed the building where he roomed at Princeton, he had taken special care to preserve the subsequent letters he received—a fact which suggests that there were few if any other letters from Melville to his cousin.

New York May 10th 1864

My Dear Henry: I embrace the earliest opportunity afforded by my recovery from an acute attack of neuralgia in the eyes, to thank you for your hospitality at the camp, and make known the fact that I have not forgotten you. I enjoyed my visit very much, & would not have missed it on any account, and can only regret that you happened to be away when we arrived. But as when the sun reappears after being hidden; so — &c &c &c. Your imagination and modesty will supply the rest. I missed seeing the Dr at Washington, although I sought him at Willard's. I trust he has got rid of his temporary disfigurement. When in your tent you introduced him to Gen. Tyler, you should have said: — General, let me make you acquainted with my friend here. Dont be frightened. This is not his face, but a masque. A horrible one, I know, but for God's sake dont take it to be the man. General, that horrible masque, my word for it, hides a noble and manly countenance. &c &c &c Your wit & invention render further strumming on this string idle. — How is Captain Brewster? Coke on Lyttleton, and Strap on the Shoulder. My friendly regards & best wishes to the Captain & say to him that I hear the neigh of his war-horse in my dreams, Likewise that I have a flannel shirt of his in my keeping; which I hope one day to exhibit as the identical shirt worn by that renowned soldier shortly after his entrance into the army. — Edwin Lansing — remember me to him. Tell him I frequently think of him & his tent & there is pleasure in the thought. Tell him to tell Dr Wolf (savage name, but sweet man) that my prayers ascend for him.

And Gen Tyler, too. Pray, give my respects to him, & say that I agree with him about "Titan." The worst thing I can say about it is, that it is a little better than "Mardi" The Terence I highly value; indeed both works, as memorials of the hospitalities of an accomplished General & jolly Christian.

And now, Col. Gansevoort of the 13th N.Y. Cavalry, conceive me to be standing some paces from you, in an erect attitude and with manly bearing, giving you the military salute. Farewell. May two small but choice constellations of stars alight on your shoulders. May your sword be a terror to the despicable foe, & your name in after ages be used by Southern matrons to frighten their children by. And after death (which God long avert, & bring about after great battles, quietly, in a comfortable bed, with wife & children around) may that same name be transferred to heaven — bestowed upon some new planet or cluster of stars of the first magnitude. Farewell, my hero

& God bless you
Herman Melville

Col. Gansevoort.

Lizzie wishes to be remembered to you.

ALS on a 25.3 × 20.4 cm sheet, folded in half, of blue laid paper, embossed with the manufacturer's shield-like stamp enclosing the name "CARSON'S CONGRESS". Melville inscribed all four pages, in ink. On the left folded edge of this letter are remnants of the adhesive binding Henry Gansevoort used to paste this letter into his album of letters, from which it was removed at NYPL.

LOCATION: NYPL-GL.

PUBLICATION: Jay Leyda, "The Army of the Potomac Entertains a Poet," *Twice a Year, Art and Action* (New York: Twice a Year Press, 1948), pp. 269–70. Davis-Gilman 169.

TEXTUAL NOTES: General &] General *miswritten* Genearl *and* & *written over comma* · small] sm *written over* ch · Lizzie . . . you.] *written sideways in the top margin of the first page; placed here editorially*

TO MARIA GANSEVOORT MELVILLE
BEFORE 19 MAY 1864 · [NEW YORK?]

Unlocated. Maria Melville enclosed a letter from Melville in her 24 May 1864 letter to her brother Peter Gansevoort. Apparently Melville had sent it to Albany for his uncle Peter to forward to his mother, for she wrote, "I enclose to you Herman's letter thinking you would like to read it. It is the one you forwarded to me" (NYPL-GL; cited by Leyda in the *Log*, II, 669, but at present unlocated). Since her letter also refers to a later letter from Elizabeth Melville reporting that Melville was "shocked" at the news of Hawthorne's death, it can be inferred that his letter was written before 19 May, when Hawthorne died. Davis-Gilman Unlocated 381.

TO ROBERT O. TYLER
21 JULY 1864 · GANSEVOORT

As Melville's letter of 10 May 1864 (above) indicates, he became acquainted with Brigadier General Tyler during his visit to the Union camp of his cousin Henry Gansevoort. The evening of 20 April 1864, after returning that day from the scout he had accompanied, Melville went with his cousin to Tyler's headquarters at Fairfax Court House. Tyler, a West Point graduate with an interest in literature, probably presented Melville at this time the copies of Johann Richter's *Titan* and Terence's *Comedies* (Sealts 425 and 509) mentioned in Melville's 10 May letter. (That letter also indicates another meeting with Tyler in Henry Gansevoort's tent, but it is unclear when the meeting took place.) Later Tyler was wounded at the battle of Cold Harbor on 1 June, while in command of a brigade in the Second Army Corps, Army of the Potomac, and, despite the information Melville had received, never fully recovered.

Although Melville closes by giving his New York address, this letter was written from Gansevoort, New York, where his mother and sisters Augusta and Frances Priscilla were living.

Gansevoort, Saratoga Co. N.Y.
July 21st 1864

Dear General:

When I read of you at Cold-Harbor, I recalled your hospitality at Fairfax, and the agreeable evening I spent with you there, in company with my cousin, Col. Gansevoort, and would have written you, had I known how to address the note.

Though I hope I *am* patriotic — enthusiastically so — yet I will not congratulate you, General, upon your wound, but will reserve that for the scar, which will be equally glorious and not quite so irksome. — I am glad it is no worse with you, and rejoice to learn that you are in a promising way. I trust that you are in a condition to enjoy your book and your cigar, also (but this should have gone before) the sweet eyes of the sympathetic ladies, who, you know, have a natural weakness for heroes. How they must hover over you — the angels! — and how must your dreams be mingled of love and glory. I dont know but that I ought to congratulate you at once, after all.

But methinks I hear somebody say, Dont bore him with too long a yarn.

Of course I shall not look for any reply to this note, or that you will trouble yourself any further about it than to receive it as an expression of respect and good-feeling.

Very faithfully and Sincerely Yours
Herman Melville

Brig. Gen. Robert O. Tyler
Philadelphia.

Should you at any future time desire to know my address, I give it: — 60 E 26th St. New York.

ALS on a 26.8 × 20.3 cm sheet, folded in half, of white laid paper. Melville inscribed the first three pages, in ink.

LOCATION: NYPL-B. *Provenance*: W. T. H. Howe.

PUBLICATION: Jay Leyda, "The Army of the Potomac Entertains a Poet," *Twice a Year, Art and Action* (New York: Twice a Year Press, 1948), p. 270. Davis-Gilman 170.

TEXTUAL NOTES: book and] and *written over* & · yourself] *before canceled* in

1865

TO BAYARD TAYLOR
AFTER 24 FEBRUARY 1865 · [NEW YORK?]

Unlocated. On 24 February 1865 Bayard Taylor wrote to Melville inviting him to the Travellers' Club (see LETTERS RECEIVED, pp. 695–96). Presumably Melville replied to Taylor's invitation. Davis-Gilman Unlocated 383.

TO PETERSON & BROTHERS
[AFTER 11 MARCH 1865?] · [NEW YORK?]

Unlocated. A letter concerning T. B. Peterson & Brothers' publication of *Israel Potter* under the title *The Refugee* is cited in Melville's 7 April 1888 letter to James Billson. Explaining that he had not authorized the title change, Melville told Billson: "A letter to the publisher arrested the publication." Since Peterson & Brothers advertised the book as early as 11 March 1865 and deposited it for copyright a month later, presumably Melville's letter was written shortly thereafter. Possibly, however, Melville did not write it immediately, since the Philadelphia publishers continued to list the book for some time. For more on *The Refugee* and Melville's objections to it, see the NN *Israel Potter*, pp. 224–26, the headnote to Melville's 7 April 1888 letter, and his undated letter to the *World*, p. 538 below.

TO MARIA GANSEVOORT MELVILLE AND DAUGHTERS
BEFORE 7 OCTOBER 1865 · NEW YORK

Unlocated. A letter from Melville can be inferred from Augusta Melville's 7 October 1865 letter written from Gansevoort to their cousin Catherine Gansevoort in Albany. Augusta writes, "We have just heard from Herman & Lizzie. He has been unusually well ever since his visit here" (NYPL-GL). Melville, joined later by his wife and children, had visited at Gansevoort between 17 August and 9 September 1865. Possibly this letter was written by Elizabeth Melville, since she was the primary correspondent with the women at Gansevoort, but Augusta's wording suggests that both Melville and his wife had written.

A few days later, on 12 October 1865, Maria Melville wrote a letter from Gansevoort to Catherine Gansevoort, reporting on a proposed visit to New York, and adding that "Herman & Tom are urgent that we should come at once" (NYPL-GL). Again this invitation may have been written by Melville (possibly in the same letter), but could have just as easily been by his youngest brother Thomas or by another family member. Davis-Gilman Unlocated 384.

TO UNKNOWN
9 OCTOBER 1865 · NEW YORK

This brief note was evidently in reply to a request from an unidentified autograph collector. The catalogue description supplies the 9 October 1865 date.

Dear Sir:
    You are quite welcome.

Truly yours
Herman Melville

Original document not located. Text from catalogue transcription.

LOCATION: at present unknown. *Provenance*: Charles E. Feinberg sale, Parke-Bernet Galleries, 2–3 April 1968, lot 482.

1866

TO AUGUSTA MELVILLE
20 MARCH 1866 · NEW YORK

Unlocated. A letter from Melville is cited in Augusta Melville's 23 March 1866 letter written from New York to her cousin Catherine Gansevoort in Albany, explaining why she had suddenly left Albany, where she had been visiting the Van Rensselaer family: "On Tuesday afternoon I received a few lines from Herman saying that Mamma had been quite sick for three days, & although she was then able to sit up, he thought I had better come down as soon as possible. So I packed up at once & took the morning train on Wednesday. Found Lizzie & Stannie waiting for me at the dèpôt who told me that my dear Mother had improved much since Herman had written me" (NYPL-GL). Davis-Gilman Unlocated 385.

TO RICHARD LATHERS
[6?] DECEMBER 1866 · NEW YORK

In late 1866 Melville became a customs inspector in New York, a position he held until his retirement in 1885. It is not known how he obtained the post (an earlier effort on the part of his family to secure such a post for him in 1857 had failed; see Hayford-Davis, pp. 377–80). One benefactor may have been Henry A. Smythe, the customs collector in New York whom Melville had met in Switzerland (see Hayford-Davis, pp. 386–88, and *Journals*, pp. 125, 126, 519). However, this undated note to Richard Lathers indicates that Lathers was also instrumental in procuring the job for Melville (for Melville's long-standing friendship with Lathers, see the headnote to his 9 April 1854 letter to Lathers, above). An 1880 register of the New York Custom House employees lists Melville as employed on 5 December 1866 (Bayonne, New Jersey, regional archives), and Melville's oaths of loyalty and of office as Inspector Number 188 of Customs at New York—probably the warrant referred to in this letter—are dated 5 December 1866 (National Archives). Assuming that Melville signed the warrant and took his oath on the day before he actually started working, this letter can be dated 6 December 1866. For more on Melville's tenure as a customs inspector, see Stanton Garner, "Surviving the Gilded Age: Herman Melville in the Customs Service," *Essays in Arts and Sciences* 15 (June 1986), 1–13.

60 E. 26th

My Dear Sir: I called to see you yesterday, but was too early for you.

Accept my sincere thanks for your friendly and successful effort on my behalf.

I received my warrant yesterday, and go at it to day

Very Truly Yours
H Melville

Richard Lathers Esq.

ALS on a 12.6 × 20.4 cm part-sheet (torn along the left edge) of blue laid paper, embossed with the manufacturer's shield-like stamp enclosing the name "CARSON'S CONGRESS". Melville inscribed the first page, in ink. The letter was later placed in an envelope labeled "Herman Melville — | Letter | to Richard Lathers. | 60 E 26th." Included in the envelope is a letter dated 23 August 1940 from Frank L. Pleadwell to an unidentified addressee, consisting of a typed quotation from Weaver, pp. 308–9, about Lathers and a penciled note below: "Reading this book recently (I received a copy from Francis Edwards) I came across the above reference to the recipient of your Melville letter, so send it on to you." All three items—Melville's 1866 letter, the envelope, and Pleadwell's 1940 letter—have been wormholed.

LOCATION: The Lilly Library, University of Indiana. *Provenance*: unidentified private collector, known to Frank L. Pleadwell, as indicated by a letter, lacking a salutation, from Pleadwell, dated 23 August 1940; John Howell Books.

PUBLICATION: Lynn Horth, "Letters Lost / Letters Found: A Progress Report on Melville's *Correspondence*," *Melville Society Extracts* 81 (May 1990), 1–8 (with reproduction on p. 7).

TEXTUAL NOTE: sincere] cer *destroyed by wormholing*

1867

TO CHARLES W. STODDARD
20 JANUARY 1867 · NEW YORK

Charles Warren Stoddard (1843–1909) grew up in San Francisco and was a friend of Bret Harte, Mark Twain, and other western writers. To improve his health he traveled to Hawaii in 1864, and returned twice before writing *South-Sea Idylls* (Boston: Osgood, 1873), with a preface referring several times to Melville. After serving as Mark Twain's secretary in London and living three years in Hawaii, he settled down as a teacher of English literature, first at Notre Dame and then at the Catholic University of America. (For more on Stoddard, see Carl G. Stroven, "A Life of Charles Warren Stoddard" [Ph.D. dissertation, Duke University, 1939], and Roger Austen, *Genteel Pagan: The Double Life of Charles Warren Stoddard,* ed. John W. Crowley [Amherst: University of Massachusetts Press, 1991].) For Melville's brief sojourn in Hawaii, of which Stoddard found "no traces," see Charles Roberts Anderson, *Melville in the South Seas* (New York: Columbia University Press, 1949), pp. 324–45. The "printed Verses" that Stoddard sent to Melville with a now unlocated letter were entitled *Poems* (San Francisco: Roman, 1867; Sealts 490b). This was his first book, edited by Bret Harte. The "little effusion" singled out for comment by Melville in this thank-you note appeared on p. 73:

Cherries and Grapes

Not the cherries' nerveless flesh,
However fair, however fresh,
May ever hope my love to win
For Ethiop blood and satin skin.

Their luster rich and deep their dye;
Yet under all their splendors lie—
That which I cannot tribute grant—
Their hateful hearts of adamant.

I love the amber globes that hold
That dead-delicious wine of gold;
A thousand torrid suns distill
Such liquors as these flagons fill.

Yet tropic gales with souls of musk
Should steep my grapes in steams of dusk:
And orient Eden nothing lacks
To spice their purple silken sacks.

New York. Jan. 20th 1867

Dear Sir: I have read with much pleasure the printed Verses you sent me, and, among others, was quite struck with the little effusion entitled "Cherries & Grapes".

I do not wonder that you found no traces of me at the Hawaiian Islands

Yours Very Truly

H. Melville

Charles Warren Stoddard Esq.
San Francisco

ALS on a 12.7 × 19.8 cm part-sheet (torn along the left edge and cut along the top) of blue laid paper, embossed with the manufacturer's shield-like stamp enclosing the name "CARSON'S CONGRESS". Melville inscribed only one side of the leaf, in ink. Another hand noted in pencil on the verso "To Charles Warren Stoddard". The letter was glued to another sheet at one time, but has since been removed.

LOCATION: UV-Barrett. *Provenance*: Goodspeed Catalogue 150 (March–April 1923), item 2013; Goodspeed Catalogue 387 (June 1945), item 127A; Timothy F. McGillicuddy; Charles Hamilton Catalogue 9 (28 November 1956), item 208a.

PUBLICATION: *Log*, II, 693 (dated only 1867). Davis-Gilman 171.

TO JOHN C. HOADLEY
BETWEEN 14 AND 18 SEPTEMBER 1867 · NEW YORK

Unlocated. A brief extract from a letter to Melville's brother-in-law John C. Hoadley is quoted in a clipping of a letter to the editor (NYPL-GL) from an unidentified Boston newspaper that was signed "J. C. H." This lengthy communication from Hoadley addressed the issues surrounding the death of Melville's older son, Malcolm (Mackie), who died on 11 September 1867 of a pistol shot to the head—first ruled to be suicide by the coroner's jury, but soon changed to a verdict of accidental death. Malcolm, eighteen years old, had been employed as a clerk by Richard Lathers at his firm, the Atlantic & Great Western Insurance Co. (For further discussion of this tragedy, see Metcalf, pp. 207–15, and Edwin S. Shneidman, "Some Psychological Reflections on the Death of Malcolm Melville," *Suicide and Life-Threatening Behavior* 6 [1976], 231–42.)

Hoadley's effort was to speak to the "shocking" telegraphic report that "the son of Herman Melville and the grandson of the late Chief Justice Shaw" had "committed suicide during an attack of temporary insanity," to counter the "imputation of such a crime as suicide or of such a fearful scourge as insanity." Hoadley argued that the death was in fact accidental, stating that to the boy's mother his memory "needs no vindication," and to "his father who writes,—'I wish you could have seen him as he lay in his last attitude, the ease of a gentle nature. Mackie never gave me a disrespectful word in his life, nor in any way ever failed in filialness,'—to this father he needs no vindication."

Melville's letter can be approximately dated by the evidence in the clipping. Following Hoadley's letter is a reprinted article from the *New-York Evening Post*, dated 16 September 1867; the clipping can thus be dated 17 or 18 September, allowing time for the *Evening Post* article to be reprinted. If Melville's phrase "last attitude" alludes to Malcolm at his funeral, as it appears to, the letter can then be placed between the date of the funeral on 14 September and that of the clipping on 17 or 18 September. Davis-Gilman 172.

TO MARIA MELVILLE
22 OCTOBER 1867 · NEW YORK

In this letter to his niece Maria (Milie) Gansevoort Melville (1849–1935), the oldest daughter of Allan Melville and namesake of Maria Melville, Melville was responding to her now unlocated letter written shortly after the death of her cousin Malcolm (Mackie). Her letter probably carried added poignancy because she was just two days younger than Malcolm (see Melville's 20 February 1849 letter to Allan written shortly after their births). Her sisters, whom Melville mentions, were Florence (Flossy) Melville (1850–1919) and Katherine (Kitty) Gansevoort Melville (1852–1939). Later, in 1874, Milie married William B. Morewood, son of Rowland and Sarah Morewood.

New York Oct. 22^{d} 1867

My Dear Milie: I was much gratified by your note, and was touched at the way in which you speak of Mackie. That to you, and your sisters, he was — to use your own words — always obliging and affectionate, this was but of a piece with his whole nature and conduct. And no one can sincerely appreciate these qualities in Mackie without shareing them.

We have been getting some photographs made from two tintypes — one representing him in his ordinary dress, and the other in the regimental one. They have been reproduced (on a somewhat enlarged scale) much better than we could have anticipated. We have reserved one for you, and also one of the original tintypes which we learn he had taken for you.

Uncle Tom is about leaving for New Haven on business. Mrs. Shaw and Sam got here from Baltimore last evening. They went as far as Washington — Mrs. Shaw's first visit to the Capitol

Tell your father I have his two notes, and have made inquiry (yesterday afternoon) at the 42^d St Depot for the piano, potatoes, & apples. They had not yet arrived — not *there*. This morning I shall inquire at the Centre St. Depot. I will look out for them. Give him my thanks for his present.

Flossy & Kitty are well. They dined with us Sunday. I saw them yesterday. — I dont know whether this will be in time to reach you at Pittsfield.

Remember me kindly to your father & mother

And Beleive me Affectionately Yours

H. Melville

ALS on a 25.5 × 20.2 cm sheet, folded in half, of white laid paper. Melville inscribed the first two pages, in ink. He addressed the envelope "Miss. Maria Melville | Care Allan Melville Esq. | Pittsfield | Berkshire Co. | Mass."; it was postmarked in New York on 22 October.

LOCATION: Berkshire Athenaeum, Pittsfield, Massachusetts. *Provenance*: Agnes Morewood.

PUBLICATION: Davis-Gilman 173.

TEXTUAL NOTE: 22^d] *written over* 21st

TO [THE COLLECTOR OF CUSTOMS?]
31 OCTOBER 1867 · NEW YORK

One of Melville's colleagues in the Custom House was Henry Langdon Potter (1828–1907), a native of the Berkshires, who had served bravely (sustaining many wounds) as lieutenant colonel and colonel of the Seventy-first New York Volunteer Infantry, Excelsior Brigade, until 1864, when he was accused of corruption. After being cleared, he entered the Customs Service and became Melville's first partner in district number four along the North (i.e., Hudson) River waterfront (see Stanton Garner, "Surviving the Gilded Age: Herman Melville in the Customs Service," *Essays in Arts and Sciences* 15 [June 1986], 5). Shortly thereafter, Melville gave him on 19 December 1866 a copy of *Battle-Pieces* (UV-Barrett), which had been published in August. Just what financial or practical arrangement this 31 October letter represented is not known.

District Office, No 4 N.R.

Oct 31. 1867

Mr. Henry L. Potter, my associate, is authorised to draw the money on my Pay Roll for the present month.

H. Melville

Dist. Inspector

ALS on a 15.5 × 11.2 cm part-sheet (cut along the bottom at a slight angle) of white laid paper with lines. Melville inscribed only one side of the leaf, in ink. On the verso are remnants of glue spots.

LOCATION: Beinecke Library, Yale University. *Provenance*: Owen Franklin Aldis (tipped into a first edition of *Battle-Pieces*).

PUBLICATION: *Log*, II, 692. Davis-Gilman 174.

TO THE EDITORS OF *PUTNAM'S MAGAZINE*
[DECEMBER?] 1867 · [NEW YORK?]

Unlocated. Only an excerpt from Melville's reply to an invitation to contribute to the new *Putnam's Magazine* was printed along with excerpts from the replies of many other authors in an undated seven-page prospectus (copy in The Newberry Library) entitled "To Contributors" (p. 5), evidently issued before the first number of the magazine appeared in January 1868. The prospectus quotes Melville (identified as "author of '*Typee*'") as saying, "I feel much complimented. . . . You may include me in the list of probable contributors." The original *Putnam's Monthly Magazine* had lasted nearly four years before merging with *Emerson's United States Magazine* in October 1857. The new *Putnam's Magazine: Original Papers on Literature, Science, Art, and National Interests* was organized by Charles F. Briggs and George P. Putnam in 1867, with Edmund C. Stedman as associate editor and book reviewer. Contributions were solicited from such writers and public figures as George Henry Boker, Phoebe Cary, G. W. Curtis, Robert Dale Owen, Charles W. Elliott, Francis Parkman, and Edwin M. Stanton. Articles on "home topics"—i.e., life and society in America—were to receive the bulk of the space, but there was to be a fiction section in each issue. The new *Putnam's* lasted until November 1870, when the magazine merged with *Scribner's* (see Frank L. Mott, *A History of American Magazines* [Cambridge: Harvard University Press, 1938], II, 428–30). Despite his willingness to be included among the "probable contributors" to the new *Putnam's*, Melville is not known to have contributed. The opening article of its first number ("The Old and the New") inquired, "And where, let us ask, is Herman Melville? Has that copious and imaginative author, who contributed so many brilliant articles to the MONTHLY, let fall his pen just where its use might have been so remunerative to himself, and so satisfactory to the public?" (p. 3). Davis-Gilman 175.

TO T. APOLEON CHENEY
4 DECEMBER [1867?] · [NEW YORK?]

Unlocated. A letter enclosing a carte de visite is cited in Professor T. Apoleon Cheney's 7 December 1869 reply to Melville (see LETTERS RECEIVED, pp. 701–4). Leyda read Cheney's date for Melville's letter as 4 December 1869 (*Log*, II, 706). However, Cheney's apology for allowing such a "long delay" to occur before acknowledging Melville's "kind favor" would have been unnecessary if Melville's letter had been sent only three days earlier. (For the other unlocated letter from Melville cited in Cheney's letter, see the entry for 19 December 1862, above.) Davis-Gilman Unlocated 392.

1868

TO GEORGE P. PUTNAM AND
VICTORINE HAVEN PUTNAM
15 JANUARY [1868?] · NEW YORK

Melville wrote this letter on a type of Carson's Congress stationery that he often used in the 1860's (see the manuscript description, below). This was not when Putnam was his publisher (in 1846 and between the fall of 1853 and March of 1855); however, as the excerpt of Melville's letter printed in a prospectus for *Putnam's Magazine* indicates, he remained on good terms with his former publisher and was invited to contribute to Putnam's newly revived magazine in 1868 (see the headnote to that letter probably written in December 1867, above). Consequently this partially dated letter accepting an invitation from Putnam and his wife has been tentatively placed in 1868.

M^r. H. Melville is much obliged to Mr and Mrs George P Putnam for their friendly invitation, and accepts it with pleasure.

N.Y. Jan 15th

ALS, third person, "M^r. H. Melville", on a 25.3 × 20.4 cm sheet, folded in half, of blue laid paper, faintly embossed with the manufacturer's shield-like stamp. Melville inscribed the first page, in ink. Another hand later noted in pencil on the top of that page "H. Melville | author of '*Typee.*' " and at the bottom "42" and "ndt". A different hand noted in pencil on the fourth page "Walter Benjamin 9 Dec 1942 | 42M102". For Melville's use of the same paper in the 1860's, see, for example, his 10 December 1862 letter to Samuel Shaw, his 17 February 1863 letter to Catherine Gansevoort, his 10 May 1864 letter to Henry Gansevoort, his [6?] December 1866 letter to Richard Lathers, and his 20 January 1867 letter to Charles Stoddard.

LOCATION: NYPL-GL. *Provenance*: Walter Benjamin Autographs, catalogue 616 (June 1942), item 4016.

PUBLICATION: Davis-Gilman 266.

TO MARIA GANSEVOORT MELVILLE
BEFORE 6 MAY 1868 · NEW YORK

Unlocated. A letter from Melville to his mother can be inferred from her 6 May 1868 letter, written from Gansevoort, to her niece Catherine Gansevoort in Albany.

Catherine had just agreed to be a bridesmaid at Thomas Melville's wedding, and Maria Melville's 6 May letter to her is full of plans for the coming event (see also Melville's 29 May 1868 letter, just below). She writes, "I shall go to New York & take Hermans advice, to come on at least one week before the '4ᵗʰ.['] Why cannot you join me at Albany & spend a week in the City at your cousin Hermans, or Allans" (NYPL-GL). Presumably "Hermans advice" had been by letter. Davis-Gilman Unlocated 390.

TO CATHERINE GANSEVOORT
29 MAY 1868 · NEW YORK

On 6 June 1868 the wedding of Thomas Melville and Catherine Bogart (1842–1928) took place in New York City. Staying at the Melville house on Twenty-sixth Street for the event were, among others, Maria Melville, Catherine Hoadley and her children, and Catherine (Kate) Gansevoort, who served as a bridesmaid. Although dated only 29 May, this letter with its reference to such "occasions" as the wedding, for which Melville's mother arrived on the Hudson River Railroad, belongs to 1868.

104 E. 26ᵗʰ St.
May 29ᵗʰ, 4 P.M.

My Dear Kate:

"Cousin Herman and Cousin Lizzie" will be very glad indeed to have you stay with them so long as you please. We shall be a little crowded, but, on these occasions, the more the merrier, you know.

I have just brought Mama over from the H.R.R.R Depot. She told me about your plans for coming down &c, so I hasten to despatch this note.

My affectionate rememberances to Uncle Peter & Aunt Susan.

We shall count on having you with us.

Cousin Herman.

ALS on a 12.8 × 20.2 cm part-sheet (torn along the left edge) of white laid paper. Melville inscribed only one side of the leaf, in ink. Two penciled dates, "[1870?]" and "[1868?]", were added at the top of the first page. Davis and Gilman speculated that the first was perhaps written by Catherine Gansevoort; the second was evidently added later since they did not note it.

LOCATION: NYPL-GL.

PUBLICATION: Paltsits, p. 23 (misdated 1870). Davis-Gilman 176.

TEXTUAL NOTE: with us.] *added leaving vestigial period after* you

TO PETER GANSEVOORT AND FAMILY
BEFORE 14 AUGUST 1868 · [NEW YORK?]

Unlocated. On his two-week vacation from the Custom House in 1868, Melville first went to Gansevoort, where he visited his mother and sisters, then to Albany, where he stayed at the home of his uncle Peter Gansevoort, and finally to Pittsfield, where he joined his family at Arrowhead (see his 18 August letter, just below). Since Catherine Gansevoort wrote to her brother Henry on 14 August that they expected "Cousin Herman Melville" to arrive the following day, it can be inferred that he had written ahead as usual to make arrangements for his stay in Albany (NYPL-GL). Davis-Gilman Unlocated 391.

TO CATHERINE GANSEVOORT
18 AUGUST 1868 · PITTSFIELD

According to Catherine Gansevoort's diary, Melville spent three days of his 1868 vacation at Albany before leaving for Pittsfield on 17 August to join his wife and children (NYPL-GL). His brother Allan in 1863 had taken Arrowhead in partial payment for Melville's house in New York, and the farm had become Allan's summer home, often visited by members of the family. The "Kate" presiding at Arrowhead was probably Allan's daughter Katherine, who was sixteen at the time. For a rhapsody by Melville on "all the Kates," see his early letter of 20 January 1845 to his sister Catherine (Kate).

Arrowhead, Aug 18th
1868

My Dear Cousin Kate:

Unhappy that I am, I went off without bidding you good-bye. But my bundles and my baggage, and the catching of the car, with my desire to be "on time" too much engrossed me. However, here-in — if you have the faith to perceive — you will find enclosed a cousinly salute, which I entreat you to appropriate.

I had a very pleasant ride over to Pittsfield, and at the house I found Lizzie and the children, who had arrived a few hours before me, and were well and frisky. Allan's family are all absent for a few days, leaving only Kate to preside. But Kate, like all the Kates, inherits the good old Dutch talent for housekeeping, and takes good care of us.

I hope Uncle Peter enjoyed his afternoon ride yesterday, and was the better for it. My respectful and affectionate rememberances to him, and also to Aunt Susan; and say to both that I shall not soon forget my most agreeable visit to Albany, full of diversified pleasure.

The country hereabouts is looking as fresh as — yourself. I was going to say a rose, but chose the more appropriate comparison. However, I must cease this strain, for Lizzie just sat down by me and may catch me at it, and consider that I slightly, it may be, exceed the due limits of cousinly compliment. So here is the end of the page, and of my note.

Adieu

H. Melville

Lizzie sends her love to all, with thanks for the kind invitation.

ALS on a 25.6 × 20.2 cm sheet, folded in half, of white laid paper. Melville inscribed the first and third pages, in ink, and addressed the envelope "Miss Kate Gansevoort | — Care of Gen. Peter Gansevoort — | Albany, | N.Y."; it was postmarked in Pittsfield on 18 August. Peter Gansevoort noted on the front of the envelope "Rec'd Aug 19ᵗʰ | 1868.", and Catherine Gansevoort endorsed the back "Cousin Herman | & | Lizzie Shaw Melville | 1868".

LOCATION: NYPL-GL.

PUBLICATION: Paltsits, pp. 19–20. Davis-Gilman 177.

TEXTUAL NOTES: over] *miswritten* overe • Lizzie . . . invitation.] *added sideways on the otherwise blank fourth page; placed here editorially*

TO CATHERINE GANSEVOORT
9 SEPTEMBER 1868 · NEW YORK

Since both Catherine (Kate) Gansevoort's earlier letter and the photograph that arrived shortly after it are now unlocated, Melville's reference here to the "imposing mass of masonry" remains unidentified. This top-heavy structure which Melville humorously describes as contrary to the principles of the Roman architect and engineer Vitruvius was probably one of the monuments in the Albany Rural Cemetery, where Kate Gansevoort was busily involved in refurbishing the family plots at this time. During his three-day visit to Albany in August (see the headnote to the letter just above), Melville accompanied her to that cemetery on Saturday, 15 August. In a letter to her brother Henry, Kate recounted: "Made a long tour & found all of interest stopped at the Dudley monum't & that of Prince John Van Buren. A cross — entwined with Ivy — The Dudley Freestone shaft contains a history of the Dudley's & Bleecker's from the birth/of Charles E. D. to Blandina Bleeker including *Anneke Jantz* of Trinity church history [in Albany] — We this time found the Lot of Uncle Herman Gansevoort & the Melvilles — It looks nicely but not to my fancy too crowded" (NYPL-GL). (Only a year earlier in October 1867, Melville's sister Augusta and brother Thomas had arranged for the remains of their father and their brother Gansevoort to be removed from their original graves in Albany and

buried in this plot; in that same month, for Malcom's interment, Herman and Elizabeth Melville had purchased two sections of Lot 656 in Woodlawn Cemetery in
the Bronx.) Davis and Gilman suggested that the "imposing mass" was a reference
to the monument at the grave of Guert Gansevoort, who had died on 15 July 1868.
He was not, however, buried in the Albany Rural Cemetery, and it seems unlikely
that Melville would be humorously criticizing, particularly in a letter to his cousin
Kate, the monument of their cousin who had died so recently. Almost certainly,
however, Melville's reference to the "newspaper account of Cousin Guert" is to an
obituary. For more about this cousin, see Melville's 25 May 1862 letter to his
brother Thomas, above, and LETTERS RECEIVED, p. 566.

The reference to "Stanny" is to Melville's son Stanwix, now seventeen.
"Lizzy-Ann" (also "Lizzie-Ann") must be Melville's wife, Elizabeth Knapp Shaw,
though no other reference to this middle name is known.

New York Sep^t 9th

Inimitable Kate: Thank you for your note. Following it came the
photograph. What an imposing mass of masonry. But a critic must
needs be fastidious. There appears on the central pediment a sort of
dilated sentry-box, which seems to be without due foundation.
Look for yourself, and if you agree with me, drop a polite note to
the architect, and quote Vitruvius the great classic authority,
— though old as our Era, — in architecture, you know.

About the newspaper account of Cousin Guert, I have diligently
searched my room, but in vain. During my two weeks' absence, the
apartment underwent a horrible cleaning & setting-to-rights, which
means putting things where one can't find 'em. I will look again, &
if successful, you will hear of it.

Concerning Stanny — tell Uncle Peter that the main reason why
he did not stop at Albany was a violent cold, from which he still
suffers in a measure. He sends his love to all. As for Lizzy-Ann and
the young ladies, I enjoined upon them not to omit that visit. But
Lizzie-Ann is wilful, and I can't make her mind. However, she may
obey in this present instance. Best love to Uncle Peter & Aunt Susan. Forget not to remember me kindly to the Lansings.

And so farewell for the time,

Inimitable Katherine

H. Melville

ALS on a 25.4 × 20.2 cm sheet, folded in half, of white laid paper. Melville inscribed the first
and third pages, in ink. Catherine Gansevoort added the year "1868" in pencil after Melville's
partial date.

LOCATION: NYPL-GL.

PUBLICATION: Paltsits, pp. 20–21. Davis-Gilman 178.

TEXTUAL NOTES: sort of] of *inserted above caret* • architect] *miswritten* archictect • things where] where *written over* out

1869

TO MISS H. I. TRUE
FEBRUARY 1869 · NEW YORK

Miss True, evidently an autograph collector, is unidentified, and her request with its questions for Melville is unlocated. The catalogue description gives the date of this reply as February 1869.

I am happy to comply with your request.

Truly yours,
H. Melville.

Miss H. I. True.

It would give me pleasure to answer your questions, but regretfully I lost the requisite information.

Original document not located. Text from catalogue transcription.

LOCATION: at present unknown. *Provenance*: Harry J. Sonneborn sale, Sotheby Parke Bernet, sale 3655, 11 June 1974, lot 476.

TO UNKNOWN
3 FEBRUARY 1869 · NEW YORK

This brief letter is apparently to an autograph collector. It follows the same formula as Melville's response to Miss H. I. True, just above.

New York, Feb. 3, 1869

Dear Sir:
I am happy to comply with your request.

Herman Melville

Original document not located. Text from William Gilman's January 1954 handwritten transcription (in Davis-Gilman file) from the ALS, then in the collection of Timothy F. McGillicuddy of Worcester, Massachusetts. The one-page letter can be described from Gilman's notes as on a 20.5 × 12.7 cm sheet of laid paper with lines, embossed with the manufacturer's stamp of several bunches of grapes hanging from a branch.

LOCATION: at present unknown. *Provenance*: Carnegie Bookshop catalogue 223 (August 1958), item 430; Timothy F. McGillicuddy.

PUBLICATION: Davis-Gilman 179.

TO ELIAS DEXTER
13 MAY 1869 · NEW YORK

Elias Dexter was a picture-framer who also sold engravings and had a shop at 564 Broadway. The mezzotint Melville had left for him to frame was probably from the painting by Nicolas Poussin of Christ healing the blind men of Jericho, painted in 1651, now in the Louvre.

Down Town — May 13. '69

Mr. E. Dexter:

Dear Sir — That mezzotint, The Healing of the Blind, which I left at your place — pray, be good enough to cause the Lettering at bottom, when cut off, to be glued upon the back of the frame. — I am glad, by the way, that my chance opinion of that picture receives the confirmation of such a judge as yourself. — Let me thank you for the little print after Murillo.

Respectfully Yours,
Herman Melville

ALS on a 19 × 24.4 cm sheet of white wove paper. Melville inscribed only one side of the leaf, in ink. It was later mounted for framing.

LOCATION: Berkshire Athenaeum. Pittsfield, Massachusetts. *Provenance*. James F. Drake, catalogue 94 (1916), item 147; James F. Drake, Catalogue of Autograph Letters (1922), item 193; Henry A. Murray.

PUBLICATION: *Log*, II, 701. Davis-Gilman 180.

TO PETER GANSEVOORT
9 JUNE 1869 · NEW YORK

Only two days after this letter was sent to the Gansevoort house at 115 Washington Avenue in Albany, Catherine Gansevoort, according to her diary, arrived in New

York and went directly to 104 East Twenty-sixth Street, where she received a
"hearty welcome from Cousin Herman & Lizzie" (NYPL-GL).

Melville's report on "His Excellency the Governor of the S.S.H." refers to his
brother Thomas, who had become governor of Sailors' Snug Harbor, at New
Brighton, on Staten Island, on 19 November 1867, shortly before his marriage to
Catherine Bogart, the daughter of Dr. S. V. R. Bogart, the Resident Physician
there (see the headnote to Melville's 29 May 1868 letter to Catherine Gansevoort).
Incorporated in 1806, the institution was formally opened in 1833 for "aged, de-
crepit and worn-out seamen." By 1876 it listed five hundred "inmates" and assets
of three hundred acres of land, several buildings, and property-income of $200,000
a year. (See Louis Bagger, "The Sailors' Snug Harbor," *Harper's New Monthly Magazine* 46 [January 1873], 188–97, and *Copy of the Last Will and Testament of the Late
Robert Richard Randall, Esq., of the Act of Incorporation, and of the Other Acts of the
Legislature of the State of New-York Respecting the Sailors' Snug Harbor* [New York:
Slote & Janes, 1876], pp. 15–16 and 18–19.) Thomas Melville remained governor
until his death in 1884 at the age of fifty-four.

New York June 9th '69

My Dear Uncle: Hearing that Kate thinks of visiting New York, I
desire to say, that Lizzie and I will be extremely happy to welcome
her in 26th St. We have a vacant room at her service, and expect her
to occupy it ere long. All she has to do, is to notify us a day or two
beforehand.

By letter from Gansevoort we heard how much Mama enjoyed
her visit on Washington Avenue. — The weather here is cool and
pleasant, though we have had some sultry and unseasonable days.

My love and Lizzie's to Kate, and tell her to hasten her preparations, and come down before the Dog Star rageth.

His Excellency the Governor of the S.S.H. is, I am happy to
state, well and happy. So is his wife.

With kindest rememberances to Aunt Susan, Beleive me
Affectionately
H. Melville

ALS on a 25.7 × 20.2 cm sheet, folded in half, of white laid paper. Melville inscribed the first
and third pages, in ink.

LOCATION: NYPL-GL.

PUBLICATION: *Log*, II, 702. Davis-Gilman 181.

TEXTUAL NOTES: letter] *possibly* letters · unseasonable] *the first* a *added* · tell] *after canceled*
th · hasten] *miswritten* hastern

1870

TO MARIA GANSEVOORT MELVILLE AND DAUGHTERS
BEFORE 27 JANUARY 1870 · NEW YORK

Unlocated. A letter from Melville and his wife is cited in Augusta Melville's 27 January 1870 letter from Gansevoort to their cousin Catherine Gansevoort at Albany. She reports that among other letters that had arrived from New York that morning, "Herman & Lizzie write that they are all well there. They want us to come down next month, but the winter is so mild, Mamma sometimes thinks she will not leave home" (NYPL-GL). Davis-Gilman Unlocated 393.

TO MARIA GANSEVOORT MELVILLE
BEFORE 2 MAY 1870 · NEW YORK

Unlocated. Melville wrote in his 5 May 1870 letter, just below, to his mother, that he was complying with her wish in her letter of 2 May to hear from him "again" before she left Albany, where she was visiting her brother Peter Gansevoort and his family. Thus the implication is that he had written her an earlier letter. Davis-Gilman Unlocated 394.

TO MARIA GANSEVOORT MELVILLE
5 MAY 1870 · NEW YORK

This letter (surviving only in a copy made by John Hoadley) is the only one of Melville's letters to his mother, Maria Gansevoort Melville, now located (although at least twenty-two can be inferred). It discusses a long-standing issue between them—Melville's portrait. She had been extremely disappointed when Melville refused to have a daguerreotype taken for an engraved portrait to be published in *Holden's Dollar Magazine* (see the headnote to Melville's 12 February 1851 letter to Evert Duyckinck, above). In 1870 John Hoadley, as a present for Melville's mother, made arrangements for Melville's portrait to be painted by Joseph Oriel Eaton (1829–75)—perhaps the reason Hoadley was shown, and copied, this letter. The portrait was completed by 3 June, and now hangs in the Houghton Library, Harvard University (see Sealts, *Early Lives*, pp. 19–20, 175). For an engraved reproduction, see p. 772.

Melville's report on the lack of letters from his son Stanwix echoes similar reports in family letters during his own 1841–44 sea voyage (see, for example, Gansevoort Melville's comment on his brother's now unlocated March 1841 letter from Rio de Janeiro, above). In 1869 Stanwix had convinced his parents to let him go to sea. Through Thomas Melville, arrangements were made for him to ship on the *Yokohama*, commanded by a Captain Paul, whom, according to a [1?] April 1869 letter that Augusta Melville wrote their cousin Catherine Gansevoort, Melville had known "for years" (NYPL-GL). The *Yokohama* sailed on 4 April for Canton, went on to Shanghai, and eventually to London (for the one earlier reference to a letter from Stanwix prior to the London letter mentioned here, see LETTERS RECEIVED, pp. 700–701). After he returned from his first voyage, Stanwix's travels took him to Kansas (twice), Nicaragua, California, back home to New York, and finally to San Francisco, where he died in 1886. (For more about Stanwix's great-grandfather, General Peter Gansevoort, the "hero of Fort Stanwix," see Melville's letters of 22 October 1851 to Lemuel Shaw and 7 November 1851 to Evert Duyckinck, above. The street [now called Little West Twelfth Street] where the New York hotel named after General Gansevoort stood was very close to Melville's customs post at this time, probably at the Gansevoort Docks at the foot of Gansevoort Street.)

New York, May 5. '70.

My Dear Mamma:

As you express a wish in your last letter dated the 2nd, inst. to hear from me again before you leave Albany, I accordingly write this; and that you may be satisfied that I have not been dilatory about the portrait, I will say that I have already had two sittings, and it is getting on.

We have not heard from Stanwix since receiving his London letter in February, but are daily in expectation of one, tho' boy-like he may not think how anxiously we await it.

The other day I visited out of curiosity the Gansevoort Hotel, corner of "Little twelfth Street" and West Street. I bought a paper of tobacco by way of introducing myself: Then I said to the person who served me: "Can you tell me what this word 'Gansevoort' means? is it the name of a man? and if so, who was this Gansevoort?" Thereupon a solemn gentleman at a remote table spoke up: "Sir," said he, putting down his newspaper, "This hotel and the "street of the same name are called after a very rich family who in "old times owned a great deal of property hereabouts." The dense ignorance of this solemn gentleman, — his knowing nothing of the hero of Fort Stanwix, aroused such an indignation in my breast, that, disdaining to enlighten his benighted soul, I left the place without further colloquy. Repairing to the philosophic privacy of the District Office, I then moralized upon the instability of human glory and the evanescence of —— many other things.

Lizzie and the girls are well, and for some time past have devoted themselves to the shrine of Fashion, engaged in getting up the unaccountable phenomena and wonderful circumferential illusions which in these extraordinary days invest the figure of lovely woman.

— I am called away and must close.

My remembrances to Uncle Peter, Aunt Susan, the Superb Kate and the benignant Lansing; and believe me,

Affectionately Your Son,
Herman.

Original document not located. Text from manuscript copy made by John C. Hoadley on the rectos of two 20.5 × 27.2 cm sheets. It is headed "/Copy./" and is concluded opposite the signature: "(Signed.) | /Herman Melville./ | /Copied by J. C. Hoadley, Lawrence, May 15. 1870./" This alternative source for the letter is emended by NN at three points (see below). Hoadley enclosed it in an envelope with the notation "Copy of a Letter from | Herman Melville to | his Mother, Madame | Maria Gansevoort Melville. | May 5. 1870".

LOCATION (of copy): NYPL-GL.

PUBLICATION: Paltsits, pp. 22–23. Davis-Gilman 182.

TEXTUAL NOTES (for symbols used, see p. 840): daily] i *written over* y • Gansevoort Hotel] *hand-printed rather than script* • introducing] ing *written over* ion • means?] NN; ~?" • instability] NN; instability | instability • many other] many *written over* things • phenomena] NN; phenomina • extraordinary] extra- | ordinary

TO PETER GANSEVOORT
12 JUNE 1870 · NEW YORK

At Peter Gansevoort's request as a gift for Melville, Thomas Melville evidently had an engraving of their uncle's father (their grandfather), General Peter Gansevoort, the "Hero of Fort Stanwix," framed. The engraving was probably the one later reproduced in John C. Hoadley's *Memorial of Henry Sanford Gansevoort* (Boston: Rand, Avery, 1875), facing p. 72; see also the illustration on p. 544 below.

The "proposed visit" to Sailors' Snug Harbor, of which Thomas Melville was governor, was to include Melville's youngest sister, Frances Priscilla, and Peter Gansevoort's daughter, Catherine.

New York, June 12, '70

My Dear Uncle: On a visit to the Harbor the other day, Tom handed me a handsomely framed engraving of the Hero of Fort Stanwix, saying that he was acting upon your request & that I was to regard it as a gift from Uncle Peter. — I write this to offer my acknowledgments for your kindness, and to say how much I prize it.

Tom and his wife are both well, and their place is looking beautifully at this season.

He told me of the proposed visit of Fanny and Cousin Kate. When do they come? I trust that Tom will not wholly imprison them in his Paradise, but will permit the people of 26th St to have a share of their company.

My kindest rememberances to Aunt Susan & Kate, and best regards to the Lansings,

And Beleive me
Sincerely Yours
H. Melville

ALS on a 25.4 × 20.2 cm sheet, folded in half, of white laid paper. Melville inscribed the first and third pages, in ink, and addressed the envelope "Gen. Peter Gansevoort | Albany | N.Y."; it was postmarked in New York on 13 June. Peter Gansevoort noted the date "1870" in ink on the envelope.

LOCATION: NYPL-GL.

PUBLICATION: Paltsits, p. 24. Davis-Gilman 183.

TEXTUAL NOTES: Harbor] H *written over* h • have] *inserted above caret*

TO ELLEN MARETT GIFFORD
DECEMBER 1870 · NEW YORK

Unlocated. When he learned that his cousin Henry Gansevoort would be spending the winter in Nassau for his health, as Elizabeth Melville's cousin Ellen Marett Gifford was also doing, Melville wrote a letter for Henry to present when he called on Mrs. Gifford. This letter of introduction is cited in Melville's 15 January 1871 letter to his aunt Susan Gansevoort (Henry's stepmother), just below. For more about Ellen Marett Gifford, see Melville's 5 October 1885 and 6 November 1888 letters to her, below. Davis-Gilman Unlocated 395.

1871

TO SUSAN LANSING GANSEVOORT
15 JANUARY 1871 · NEW YORK

Henry Gansevoort, Peter Gansevoort's son and Susan Gansevoort's stepson, had throughout his life suffered from various illnesses and infections. This weakness was exacerbated by the unhealthy climates and living conditions that he experienced while in the army during and after the Civil War, until in 1870 he became very ill (see the headnote to Melville's 17 February 1863 letter to Henry's sister, Catherine). In December of that year he sailed for Nassau to recuperate (see the entry for Melville's unlocated letter of introduction for him to Elizabeth's cousin

Ellen Gifford, just above). Ellen Gifford's now unlocated letter that was enclosed with this one apparently reported on Henry's health favorably. The intermediary, Abraham Lansing, who told Allan Melville of the "favorable tidings of Henry," was the man Catherine Gansevoort later married (see the headnote to Melville's 29 October 1874 letter to him, below).

New York Jan 15, '71.

My Dear Aunt Susan:

When Henry left here I gave him a note of introduction to Mrs. Gifford, a cousin of Lizzie's now spending the winter at Nassau for her health. She has very kindly written me in reply.

I enclose the letter to you. I felt some reluctance in so doing until Allan happened to inform me this evening of Abraham Lansing's leaving here for Havana, and that you had heard so favorable tidings of Henry from some passenger in the last steamer from Nassau. — I write in much haste to secure the delivery of this at the general Post office to night.

With my best rememberances to Uncle Peter in which Lizzie & the rest unite,

Beleive me
Sincerely
H. Melville

ALS on a 25.5 × 20.5 cm sheet, folded in half, of white wove paper with lines. Melville inscribed the first and third pages, in ink, and addressed the envelope "Mrs. Peter Gansevoort | Albany | N.Y. | [1]15 Washington Av."; it was postmarked in New York on 16 January.

LOCATION: NYPL-GL.

PUBLICATION: Paltsits, pp. 24–25. Davis-Gilman 184.

TO CATHERINE GANSEVOORT
13 NOVEMBER 1871 · NEW YORK

Despite the efforts of his sister Catherine (Kate), who went to Nassau to care for him, Henry Gansevoort died on 12 April 1871 aboard a Hudson River steamboat en route to Albany (see the headnote to Melville's 15 January letter, just above). Melville had visited him only four days before, while he was in New York. In memory of her brother, Kate Gansevoort sent Melville a ring, at the request of the dying Henry, who, as she explained in her accompanying letter, "desired that all his blood Cousins should be given rings in his memory" (see LETTERS RECEIVED, pp. 706–7). For Kate Gansevoort's description of her brother's final days, see John C. Hoadley, *Memorial of Henry Sanford Gansevoort* (Boston: Rand, Avery, 1875), pp. 309–11. See also Melville's earlier comments to his cousin about death in his 10 May 1864 letter to him, above.

New York, Nov 13, '71

My Dear Cousin Kate:

This afternoon I received the Intaglio with your accompanying note.

Be assured that I shall sacredly preserve the ring, esteeming it as if it had been given me by the living hand — *his* who now lies so honorably at rest.

Lizzie & the children unite with me in best remembrances to your Mother, Uncle Peter, and yourself.

Affectionately Your Cousin
H. Melville

Promptitude must ⎫
atone for brevity ⎭

ALS on a 24.2 × 18.4 cm sheet, folded in half, of white laid paper. Melville inscribed the first page, in ink, and addressed the envelope "Miss Kate Gansevoort | — Care Gen. Peter Gansevoort — | Albany | N.Y."; it was postmarked in New York on 13 November. Both the letter and envelope were pasted into a Gansevoort family album containing other letters relating to the death of Henry Gansevoort. A manuscript copy of Catherine Gansevoort's letter presenting the ring (see LETTERS RECEIVED, pp. 706–7) is pasted into the middle fold of the letter, between the blank second and third pages.

LOCATION: NYPL-GL.

PUBLICATION: (partial) *Log*, II, 721. Davis-Gilman 185.

TO PETER GANSEVOORT
26 DECEMBER 1871 · NEW YORK

This Christmas letter to Peter Gansevoort, written at Melville's customs office, reads like a Melville family census. At the dinner that Melville describes, all but his brother Allan's family were present. The "two Kates" were Melville's sister Catherine Hoadley and his sister-in-law Catherine Bogart Melville. Minnie, Lottie, and Frankie were the Hoadley children: Maria Gansevoort (1855–1904), Charlotte Elizabeth (1859–1946), and Francis Washburn (1865–1930). The two names "Fanny" (Frances) in the list refer to Melville's younger daughter and his youngest sister. Peter Gansevoort's son Henry, remembered in a toast at the dinner, had died in April. (In explaining why he had not been to see his uncle, Melville responds that he had spent his most recent vacation in the White Mountains of New Hampshire instead of making his usual annual visit to his mother and sisters Augusta and Fanny in "Northumberland"—the township in which Gansevoort, New York, is located.)

The following Christmas, Elizabeth Melville would write on 29 December quite differently to uncle Peter's daughter, Catherine Gansevoort: "Our Christmas time has been a very quiet and sad one — The losses in our family circle come home forcibly to our hearts at these anniversary times" (NYPL-GL). During 1872 both Allan Melville, on 9 February, and Maria Melville, on 1 April, had died.

New York,
470 West St.
Day after Christmas, 1871.

My Dear Uncle:

I write this at my office, so you must excuse the paper; it is the best I happen to have at hand here.

Augusta tells me that during her late visit in Washington Avenue you kindly enquired after me, asked why I did not come to see you, and also expressed a desire that I should write you.

About not coming to see you. — I am only allowed two weeks' vacation. This I take in the summer; and last summer I spent it, for a change, at North Conway, with Lizzie. Had I gone to Northumberland as usual, I should not have failed seeing you on the way, going or returning. During the coming season I hope to have the pleasure of re-visiting Albany.

Yesterday (Christmas) we all dined on Staten Island at Tom's, who gave us a bountiful and luxurious banquet. It was a big table, belted round by big appetites and bigger hearts, but the biggest of all the hearts was at the head of the table — being big with satisfaction at seeing us enjoying ourselves. Mama looked uncommonly well; and Helen, Augusta, Kate (two Kates) Fanny, Minnie, Lottie, Frankie, Bessie, Fanny, Stanny, Mr Hoadley, Mr Griggs, not excluding the present modest writer — we all looked very well indeed.

Among the toasts Uncle Peter was remembered, Aunt Susan & Cousin Kate; nor was Henry forgotten. Tom offered that toast to his memory.

Stanny and I were obliged to leave at an early — or rather early hour, in order to take the last boat for New York. We left them still enjoying themselves in the parlors.

With much love to Aunt Susan & sympathy for her illness, and love to Kate, Beleive me

> With much respect
> Affectionately
> Herman Melville

ALS on a 25 × 19.6 cm sheet, folded in half, of white wove paper with lines, embossed with the manufacturer's stamp of a shield surmounted by a helmet. Melville inscribed the first three pages, in ink.

LOCATION: NYPL-GL.

PUBLICATION: Paltsits, pp. 25–26. Davis-Gilman 186.

TEXTUAL NOTES: re-visiting] re- *added in left margin* • early —] *before canceled* early —

1872

TO MISS COFFIN
13 JANUARY 1872 · NEW YORK

The only member of the large Nantucket Coffin family with whom Melville is known to have been acquainted was Robert Barry Coffin (1826–86), a novelist who worked in the New York Custom House as an auditor's clerk during the years 1863–69 and from 1875 until shortly before his death. Coffin inscribed to Melville four of his novels (Sealts 150–53), and had a daughter, Mary Ellen, who would have been only fourteen when this letter was written. More likely the 9 January inquiry (now unlocated) by the unidentified Miss Coffin, which prompted this response, came from a member of the Coffin family unknown to Melville, and possibly concerned the reference to the Coffin family in his "Spouter-Inn" chapter (3) of *Moby-Dick* (pp. 12–24).

> New York Jan 13, '72

Miss Coffin:

So long a time has elapsed that I can not recall where I got the facts alluded to in your note of the 9th Inst. Neither — I am sorry to say — can I direct you where to get information additional to what you may now possess.

> With much respect
> H. Melville

ALS on a 12.6 × 20.4 cm sheet of blue laid paper, faintly embossed with the manufacturer's shield-like stamp enclosing a garland-like design. Melville inscribed only one side of the leaf, in ink.

LOCATION: at present unknown. *Provenance*: The Rendells, catalogue 137 (September 1978), item 19; Biblioctopus Books, Bibliamerica catalogue (1981), item 18; Richard Manney sale, Sotheby's, sale 6218, 11 October 1991, lot 227 (with reproduction); 19th Century Shop; Historicana, catalogue 1 (1992), item 60.

TEXTUAL NOTES: additional] *miswritten* addititional • what] *inserted above caret*

TO ELIZABETH SHAW MELVILLE
BEFORE 22 APRIL 1872 · [NEW BRIGHTON?]

Unlocated. Maria Gansevoort Melville had died on 1 April 1872 at New Brighton, on Staten Island, where she had been staying with her youngest son, Thomas. After her death, Augusta Melville remained for several weeks at New Brighton, answering letters of condolence. In such a letter of 22 April 1872 to Hope Savage Shaw, Augusta reported on Herman and Stanwix, who were staying at New Brighton while Elizabeth Melville and their daughters were staying with the Shaws in Boston: "We hope that she [Lizzie] may soon be able to join Herman here. He & Stannie left us with Tom for New York after our seven O'clock breakfast. He is quite like his old natural self, & seems to take an interest in every thing; & it is very pleasant having him here" (HCL-M). Writing of Stanwix, Augusta added at the close of her letter: "He is full of the idea of going West again. Herman, I believe, has written Lizzie about it." (Since Melville was commuting to the city, he may have written his letter while there instead of at New Brighton.) Davis-Gilman Unlocated 396.

TO SAMUEL A. DRAKE
30 APRIL 1872 · NEW YORK

In writing his now unlocated inquiry, to which Melville responds here, Samuel Adams Drake (1833–1905), the eminent Boston antiquarian, was apparently collecting information for the centennial of the Boston Tea Party, held in Faneuil Hall in 1873. In the same year he published *Old Landmarks and Historic Personages of Boston* (Boston: Osgood); the "historic personages" included Melville's paternal grandfather, Thomas Melvill (1751–1832), who had been a leader in the Boston Tea Party and served as a major in the Revolution. In three paragraphs Drake sketched Melvill's ancestry, education, and career; he also mentioned that "Herman Melville, the well-known author, is his grandson" (p. 372). As Drake's endorsement shows, he wrote to Lucy Nourse, Major Melvill's only surviving child, at Melville's later suggestion (see the entry just below) and may also have written to one or more of Lemuel Shaw's three sons, John, Lemuel, Jr., and Samuel—as Melville recommends here.

New York Ap. 30, '72.

Dear Sir: I am sorry that the little that is peculiar in the information I possess with regard to my grandfather, the late Major Melville of Boston is but of that familiar sort hardly adapted to historical use.

Concerning the more interesting event — his connection with the "Tea Party", I think I know nothing that has not already received local mention

Permit me to suggest that it might be well for you to mention the subject to the sons of the late Chief Justice Shaw. Their honored father was well acquainted with Major Melville.

I renew my regret at being forced to send you so barren a responce

With great respect

H. Melville

Samuel A. Drake Esq.
Boston.

Original document not located. Text from photocopy (in Davis-Gilman file). Jay Leyda made an undated handwritten transcription (in Davis-Gilman file) of the ALS, then in the collection of J. C. Pearson of Cleveland, Ohio. William Gilman checked Leyda's transcription against the original in February 1954; the resulting transcription (in Davis-Gilman file) is identical to NN. From Gilman's notes, the two-page letter can be described as on a 25.1 × 20.1 cm sheet, folded in half, of white laid (graph-pattern) paper. Samuel A. Drake later noted in ink on the letter, "He afterwards wrote me to address Mrs Lucy M. Nourse, Bath Me only surviving dau. of Major Melville — & w of Dr Amos Nourse. At my request the lady received an invitation to be present at the Centennial of the Tea Party in Faneuil Hall."

PUBLICATION: (partial) *Log*, II, 725. Davis-Gilman 187.

TEXTUAL NOTE: Shaw.] *before* (over) *in bottom margin*

TO SAMUEL A. DRAKE
AFTER 30 APRIL 1872 · NEW YORK

Unlocated. A second letter to Samuel Drake is cited in Drake's notation on Melville's 30 April 1872 letter, just above. It states that Melville suggested Drake write his aunt Lucy Nourse, in Bath, Maine, by that time the only surviving child of Major Melvill. As a result, Drake invited her to attend the centennial of the Boston Tea Party in Faneuil Hall. (For more on this aunt, see the headnotes to Melville's letters to her—his early one of 1828 and his much later one written shortly after the death of her second husband, Amos Nourse, on 7 April 1877.)

TO STANWIX MELVILLE
[JULY?] 1872 · [NEW YORK?]

Unlocated. A fragment of manuscript in the Berkshire Athenaeum bears the cut-out closing "Your affectionate father | H. Melvill" and, on the verso, four partial lines of text: "rejoiced that you have g | of going to New Orleans | can not but think tha | to Ellis on the farm". The fragment is inscribed in ink on white wove paper with lines and cut unevenly on all four edges to roughly 7.3 × 3.2 cm. It, along with another such fragment (undated; see p. 537 below), is all that is known to remain of Melville's correspondence with his second son. Presumably a member of the family destroyed the body of these letters. Eleanor Melville Metcalf labeled, in pencil, the envelope in which both fragments, written on similar paper, were later kept: "Signatures of letters to Stanwix".

The letter from which this fragment was cut can be placed in the summer of 1872, when Stanwix went west to Kansas for a second time, from a 17 July 1872 letter Elizabeth Melville wrote to Catherine Gansevoort, mentioning that "Stanny is still in Sedgwick, Harvey Co Kansas — where he went first, & he expects to remain there for the present — " (NYPL-GL). According to a 23 February 1873 letter Stanwix wrote to his step-grandmother, Hope Savage Shaw, recounting his travels, he stayed this time only a few weeks in Kansas, then, thinking he "could do better South," went through the Indian Territory and Arkansas to New Orleans, and traveled down the Central American coast to Nicaragua before returning to New York (HCL-M). "Ellis on the farm"—possibly a farmhand at Arrowhead or Gansevoort—is unidentified.

Melville may have written his letter from New York, or possibly from the home of his brother Thomas, at Sailors' Snug Harbor in New Brighton on Staten Island, where Melville's family often went to escape the heat of the city. (Elizabeth Shaw Melville's 17 July letter cited above was written from New Brighton.) Davis-Gilman 188.

TO RICHARD H. STODDARD
5 JULY 1872 · NEW YORK

Richard Henry Stoddard (1825–1903)—husband of the novelist Elizabeth Stoddard—was a poet who knew Melville as a fellow customs inspector in New York, where he had held a position—obtained with Hawthorne's help—since 1853. After leaving the Custom House in 1870, Stoddard went on to become a prominent figure in New York literary life. His autobiography, *Recollections Personal and Literary* (New York: A. S. Barnes, 1903), recalls his having met Melville "some twenty-five years before" encountering him in the Customs Service when Melville began his career there, and states that Melville "was one of our great unrecognised poets, as he manifested in his version of 'Sheridan's Ride' " (p. 143)—a reference to Melville's "Sheridan at Cedar Creek," one of the seven poems by Melville that Stoddard included in his 1873 revision of Rufus W. Griswold's *Poets and Poetry of America* (1842).

The "Sheet" Melville thanks Stoddard for in this letter was an offprint (now in HCL-M [MS Am 188, in clippings box]) of the two pages (pp. 630–31) on which Melville's poems appear in the revised anthology. The otherwise blank verso of the offprint is inscribed in ink, presumably by Stoddard: "New Edition of Griswold's 'Poets of America'; | With additions by R. H Stoddard, | Who begs to be remembered to | Herman Melville". The letter with which Stoddard apparently enclosed the offprint is now unlocated. The six other poems from *Battle-Pieces*, Melville's only published book of poetry at this time, that Stoddard included in the anthology were "Battle of Stone River, Tennessee," "An Uninscribed Monument on One of the Battle-Fields of the Wilderness," "The Victor of Antietam," "The Mound by the Lake," "The Returned Volunteer to His Rifle," and "Shiloh." Melville later inscribed a copy of his second book of poems, *John Marr and Other Sailors*, to Stoddard in November 1888 (now in the Beinecke Library, Yale University).

After Melville's death, Stoddard wrote to Elizabeth Melville on 28 October 1892 thanking her for the copy of *Timoleon* she had sent to him. In his letter he recalled that he had known her husband "somewhat more than twenty years ago, when we both sat at the receipt of customs, I at the cold stone building in Wall Street, and he on the river front, but I did not know him as well as I could have wished, for we only met casually and officially, and he was as reserved as a man of genius had a right to be. That I respected him as much as I admired him I need not say, for no one who knew him, however slightly, could do otherwise" (HCL-M). For a discussion of several essays about Melville that have been attributed to Stoddard, see Merton M. Sealts, Jr., "Melville and Richard Henry Stoddard," *American Literature* 43 (November 1971), 359–70.

New York

July 5. '72

My Dear Sir:

I thank you for the Sheet you enclose me, — received today.

I appreciate the generosity which prompts you to include me in your forthcoming Volume.

Happiness attend you up to the gate of Paradise.

H. Melville

Richard H. Stoddard.

ALS on a 24 × 18.4 cm sheet, folded in half, of white laid (graph-pattern) paper. Melville inscribed the first page, in ink. Another hand, either a librarian's or autograph dealer's, noted in pencil on the second page "4500 — Mad — 18 Je 35 — 1142" and on the fourth page "m–2 kmty | 164".

LOCATION: Abernethy Collection of American Literature, Egbert Starr Library, Middlebury College. *Provenance*: Thomas F. Madigan Autographs (Winter 1934), item 66.

PUBLICATION: Davis-Gilman 189.

TO SUSAN LANSING GANSEVOORT
30 NOVEMBER 1872 · NEW YORK

Unlocated. Two surviving passages of a letter to Melville's uncle Peter's second wife were probably preserved for the autograph signature, when the body of the letter was apparently destroyed. Dated "New York | Nov. 30, '72", the letter began with "My Dear Aunt Susan:" and closed with "And now with affection-ate | remembrances to Uncle Peter, | Believe me, My Dear Aunt Susan, | Sincerely Yours | Herman Melville | Bessie & Fanny | unite in love." (NYPL-GL). The passages, inscribed in ink, appear on two fragments (roughly 12.5 × 5.4 and 12.5 × 8 cm) cut from the same white laid (graph-pattern) paper. Melville addressed the accompanying envelope "Mrs. Gansevoort | — Care Gen. Peter Gansevoort — | Al-bany N.Y."; it was postmarked in New York on 10 November.

The letter was most likely written in reply to Susan Gansevoort's now unlocat-ed letter to Melville which is cited in Elizabeth Melville's 4 December 1872 letter to Melville's aunt (see the entry just below and LETTERS RECEIVED, pp. 708–9). Like his wife's letter, Melville's also presumably expressed gratitude for the five-hundred-dollar gift Peter Gansevoort sent them in order to mitigate the loss of income they were facing from the destruction of Elizabeth Melville's property in Boston in the November 1872 fire. Davis-Gilman 190.

TO ELIZABETH SHAW MELVILLE
[2?] DECEMBER 1872 · NEW YORK

Unlocated. On 4 December 1872 Elizabeth Melville, who was in Boston inspecting the losses that her property incurred in the recent fire (see the entry just above), wrote to Susan Gansevoort: "Herman has sent me your kind note addressed to him from Albany" (NYPL-GL; see LETTERS RECEIVED, p. 709, for more of Elizabeth's letter). Presumably Melville enclosed a letter of his own with his aunt Susan's "kind note," which was probably the now unlocated letter from her which he answered with his 30 November reply (just above).

TO ELIZABETH SHAW MELVILLE
[8?] DECEMBER 1872 · NEW YORK

Unlocated. A letter from her husband is cited in a 10 December 1872 letter to Cath-erine (Kate) Gansevoort from Elizabeth Melville, who was still in Boston (see the entry just above). Her letter states that "Herman wrote" her about "the beautiful ladle that you presented us with" as an anniversary present (see Melville's 9 Decem-ber letter, just below, thanking Kate) and goes on to reiterate her thanks for the five hundred dollars sent by Kate's father, Peter Gansevoort, in the wake of the No-vember 1872 Boston fire. Speaking more frankly to Kate than she had in her 4

December letter to Kate's stepmother (see LETTERS RECEIVED, pp. 708–9), Elizabeth wrote that the money removed "the necessity of renting our house, or part of it, which I feared" and allowed her to "bear my loss with equanimity — I say *I*, because Herman from his studious habits and tastes being unfitted for practical matters, all the *financial* management falls upon me — and one cannot make bricks with straw — you know — " (NYPL-GL). Davis-Gilman Unlocated 397.

TO CATHERINE GANSEVOORT
9 DECEMBER 1872 · NEW YORK

The Melvilles' twenty-fifth wedding anniversary occurred on 4 August 1872, but Catherine Gansevoort probably did not give them the silver soup ladle acknowledged in this letter until early December. (On 24 November 1872, while visiting in New York, she also wrote to her stepmother Susan Gansevoort, with a message to her father, urging him "to send them a check for their Silver Wedding," adding "I know it would be very acceptable & appreciated by Cousin Herman" [NYPL-GL; cited by Leyda in revisions of the *Log*, but at present unlocated]). Because Melville was quite ill and his wife was in Boston at the time (see the entry for his unlocated letter to her, just above), their daughter Elizabeth first acknowledged the soup ladle in a letter dated 7 December: "Papa wanted me to write a few lines to thank you for the soup ladle — he would write himself but he has a very bad attack of influenza which keeps him in the house today — He was very much pleased with it, thought it was beautiful" (NYPL-GL). In another letter to Catherine Gansevoort apparently written the next day, but also dated 7 December, she again explained that her father's illness was preventing him from writing ("he can not use his eyes at all"; NYPL-GL). On 10 December Melville's wife added a fourth letter of thanks (see the entry just above).

   As to the "Natural History of Angels," compare Melville's reference in *Clarel* to guardian angels of St. Cecilia leaving the "perfumed spell | Of Paradise-flowers invisible" (1.29.24–26; see p. 743 of the NN edition).

104 E. 26 St.
Dec. 9, '72

My Dear Cousin Kate: Do you know much about the Natural History of Angels? Well, there is one variety known by this: in the place where they may have tarried for a time, they leave behind them a fragrance as of violets. Another sort, besides bequeathing the fragrance, leave along with it — what do ye think? — Silver soup ladle. — But I must alter my tone. It is a serious business receiving presents, and calls for serious acknowledgments. Well then: cordial thanks to you for your memorial of the

Silver Wedding.

Lizzie and I will ever think of you at our soup; and I shall always pour out a libation from the tureen to the angelic donor, before helping a mere vulgar broth-bibbing mortal like myself

And now so far as this is an acknowledgment of your valued gift, it is the earliest I could make with my own hand and eyes. You know I would not be guilty of the Hottentotishness (word just imported by the Cambria) of a causeless delay. — With affectionate remembrances to my Sister Fanny, Aunt Susan & Uncle Peter, Beleive me

Thy loving cousin
Herman

ALS on a 25.7 × 20.4 cm sheet, folded in half, of white laid (line-pattern) paper, watermarked with the name "A PIRIE & SONS". Melville inscribed the first and third pages, in ink, and addressed the envelope "Miss Kate Gansevoort | — Care Gen. Peter Gansevoort — | Albany | N.Y."; it was postmarked in New York on 10 December. Catherine Gansevoort noted in ink on the envelope "Herman Melville | Dec. 1872" and probably also penciled the note "*17 West 38th*" on its verso.

LOCATION: NYPL-GL.

PUBLICATION: Paltsits, pp. 27–28. Davis-Gilman 191.

TEXTUAL NOTE: for your] your *miswritten* yourn

1873

TO [M. LAIRD SIMONS?]
8 SEPTEMBER 1873 · NEW YORK

Leyda conjectured that this letter was written to Richard H. Stoddard (*Log*, II, 735). However, Rufus W. Griswold's *Poets and Poetry of America*, which Stoddard was revising (see the headnote to Melville's 5 July 1872 letter to him, above), was published in 1873 and advertised as early as 25 October 1873 in *Publishers' Weekly*. Griswold had not included Melville in his original edition, so Stoddard, in including him in the revision, was not "adding to or omitting or amending" anything that was already written. It seems more likely, as Davis and Gilman decided, that the recipient was M. Laird Simons, who was preparing a new edition (published in 1875), of the Duyckincks' *Cyclopædia of American Literature* (1855, rev. ed. 1866). When published, his edition included a paragraph added at the end of the article on Melville that contained two errors (see Sealts, *Early Lives*, p. 91).

New York
Sep. 8, '73.

Dear Sir: The delay in responding to your note was not intentional. — As to the Article in question I dont remember anything in it
which it would be worth your while to be at the trouble of adding
to or omitting or amending.

With much respect
H. Melville

ALS on an 11.4 × 17.3 cm part-sheet (torn along the left edge) of white wove paper. Melville
inscribed only one side of the leaf, in ink. Another hand later noted in pencil near the signature
"Herman Melville".

LOCATION: Beinecke Library, Yale University. *Provenance*: Owen Franklin Aldis (tipped into a
first American edition of *Moby-Dick*).

PUBLICATION: Davis-Gilman 192.

1874

TO AUGUSTA MELVILLE AND
FRANCES PRISCILLA MELVILLE
BEFORE 12 AUGUST 1874 · WHITE MOUNTAINS

Unlocated. In a 12 August letter to their aunt Susan Gansevoort in Albany, Augusta and Frances Priscilla Melville reported that they "were much disappointed that
Herman could not pass a part of his two weeks' vacation with us, but he wrote us,
that he could not tear himself away from the White Mountains" (NYPL-GL; cited
by Leyda in revisions of the *Log*, but at present unlocated).

TO SUSAN LANSING GANSEVOORT
BEFORE 2 OCTOBER 1874 · NEW YORK

Unlocated. After returning from his vacation in the White Mountains of New
Hampshire, Melville wrote to his aunt Susan Gansevoort, as the letter quoted in the
next entry indicates.

TO AUGUSTA MELVILLE
BEFORE 2 OCTOBER 1874 · NEW YORK

Unlocated. Replying to a letter from her aunt Susan Gansevoort, Augusta Melville
wrote on 2 October 1874: "I have a letter too from Herman. He has been very well

since his return from the White Mts" (NYPL-GL; cited by Leyda in revisions of the *Log*, but at present unlocated).

TO PETER GANSEVOORT
29 OCTOBER 1874 · NEW YORK

This letter, dated only 29 October, can be placed in 1874 by its association with the death of Peter Gansevoort's second wife, Susan, on 28 October 1874. It was preserved in a Gansevoort family album containing other letters of condolence.

New York, Oct. 29.
My Dear Uncle: I write this note to assure you of my own and Lizzie's true sympathies, and how we share in feelings which on such an occasion it is hardly for words to express. — May God keep you, and console you.

H. Melville

ALS on a 13.5 × 19.6 cm part-sheet (torn along the left edge and cut along the top) of white laid (graph-pattern) paper, embossed with the letter "M". Melville inscribed only one side of the leaf, in ink, and addressed the envelope "Gen. Peter Gansevoort | Albany | N.Y. | 115 Washington Av."; it was postmarked in New York on 29 October. Both the letter and the envelope were pasted into a Gansevoort family album, grouped with other letters of condolence written at the time of Susan Gansevoort's death.

LOCATION: NYPL-GL.

PUBLICATION: *Log*, II, 739. Davis-Gilman 193.

TO ABRAHAM LANSING
29 OCTOBER 1874 · NEW YORK

Abraham Lansing (1835–99), nephew of Susan Lansing Gansevoort, married her stepdaughter, Melville's first cousin Catherine Gansevoort, on 25 November 1873 after a long and tumultuous engagement (broken off several times) that had begun in 1862. The namesake of a number of Abrahams in the Lansing family (one of whom, Abraham J. Lansing [1720?–91], had founded Lansingburgh), he was the son of Christopher Yates Lansing (1796–1872), a leading Albany lawyer. He was educated at the Albany Academy, Williams College, and the Albany Law School.

He went on to hold a number of public offices, including city attorney of Albany, supreme court reporter, acting state treasurer, and Democratic state senator. This letter concerning Susan Gansevoort's death is written on the same paper as Melville's letter of the same date to Peter Gansevoort (above) and was preserved in the same album.

New York, Oct 29

My Dear Sir: All of us here — Lizzie and I particularly — sympathise and mourn with you. My recollections of Aunt Susan are of a kind to make me keenly alive to the loss which has befallen Uncle Peter as well as all others united by blood or socially to so true a woman.

Lizzie writes to Kate — to whom give my kindest cousinly rememberances.

Sincerely
H. Melville

ALS on a 27 × 20 cm sheet, folded in half, of white laid (graph-pattern) paper, embossed with the letter "M". Melville inscribed the first and third pages, in ink, and addressed the envelope "Abraham Lansing Esq. | Albany | N.Y. | 115 Washington Av."; it was postmarked in New York on 29 October. Both the letter and the envelope were pasted into a Gansevoort family album, grouped with other letters of condolence written at the time of Susan Gansevoort's death.

LOCATION: NYPL-GL.

PUBLICATION: (partial) *Log*, II, 739. Metcalf, p. 230. Davis-Gilman 194.

TEXTUAL NOTES: My recollections] y *rewritten* • my] *inserted above caret* • rememberances] n *rewritten*

1875

TO [FRANCES PRISCILLA MELVILLE?]
BEFORE 30 JULY 1875 · NEW YORK

Unlocated. A letter from Melville is cited in a 30 July 1875 letter from his sister Frances Priscilla to their cousin Catherine Gansevoort Lansing. As Frances's letter indicates, Melville had written to either her or Augusta (or both) at Gansevoort, telling of his plans to go to Albany on his way to Gansevoort, where he intended to spend his two-week vacation: "Herman writes, that he will be in Albany next Saturday, & will stop to see Uncle & You & Abe" (NYPL-GL). For Melville's letters to Catherine and Abraham Lansing, informing them of his plans, see the next two entries. Davis-Gilman Unlocated 398.

TO CATHERINE GANSEVOORT LANSING
BEFORE 5 AUGUST 1875 · NEW YORK

Unlocated. A letter to Catherine Lansing announcing his plan to visit Albany is cited in Melville's 5 August letter to her husband, just below. Davis-Gilman Unlocated 399.

TO ABRAHAM LANSING
5 AUGUST 1875 · NEW YORK

According to the plan outlined in this reply to Lansing's now unlocated "note of yesterday," Melville left New York for his vacation on the evening of Saturday, 7 August, aboard a night boat, which arrived in Albany on Sunday morning. He stayed overnight with the Lansings and left for Gansevoort by train the following evening, 9 August (see also the two entries just above for Melville's earlier letters arranging his vacation plans).

New York, Aug 5, '75

My Dear Mr Lansing: I have just received your note of yesterday. I thank you for the prospective welcome. But as for meeting me on the wharf — dont mention it. When the Shah of Persia or the Great Khan of Tartary comes to Albany by the night-boat — *him* meet on the wharf and with salvoes of artillery — but not a Custom House Inspector.

I should have mentioned in my note to Kate that I should not appear upon the scene till some time after breakfast — since on Sunday morning my appetite will be clamorous at an hour too early for any rational household to satisfy. As for my plunder or impedimenta, I shall carry nothing but what I take in my hand.

Looking forward with pleasure to meeting you all

I remain
Truly yours
H. Melville

ALS on a 25.2 × 20.4 cm sheet, folded in half, of white wove paper with lines, embossed with the manufacturer's stamp of the head of a goddess. Melville inscribed the first, third, and fourth pages, in ink.

LOCATION: NYPL-GL.

PUBLICATION: Paltsits, p. 34. Davis-Gilman 195.

TEXTUAL NOTES: comes] *blotted* · breakfast] *after canceled* the · will] *blotted* · remain] *blotted*

TO CATHERINE GANSEVOORT LANSING
BETWEEN 9 AND 23 AUGUST 1875 · GANSEVOORT

At some point during his 1875 vacation at Gansevoort with his sisters Frances Priscilla and Augusta (see the three entries just above), Melville wrote this letter to his cousin Catherine Lansing concerning the book being prepared by John C. Hoadley about her brother Henry. When published, the 335-page volume—*Memorial of Henry Sanford Gansevoort* (Boston: Rand, Avery, 1875; Sealts 273)—contained two portraits of Henry. The first, the frontispiece, was a three-quarter-length portrait in officer's dress uniform, engraved by A. H. Ritchie from a photograph by Mathew Brady. This was possibly the photograph recommended here by Melville. The second (opposite p. 182) was from a photograph that showed a troubled face, staring eyes, puckered brows, and unkempt hair. This portrait, also engraved by A. H. Ritchie, contrasts with the more flattering frontispiece portrait. For another portrait, similar to the second one, see p. 545 below.

Gansevoort, Aug. — '75

Cousin Kate: Lounging on the sofa after dinner just now in the parlor which was my mother's, my eye chanced to fall on a photograph of Henry in a gilt frame hanging under my mother's portrait. I took it down & brought it to the window, & looked at it. —

Now let me say, that the engraving you showed me of Henry, meant for the book, is detestable. Also, I have seen other pictures, claiming to be he, which do not look like him, and are a caricature of him. The picture for the book is the one that I referred to at the outset. It is he, and is not bad-looking, and it has character. —

Michael, the angel of truth, inspired me to write this to you on the instant. — Take it for what its worth, and so good bye.

H Melville

— P.S. Since writing the foregoing Fanny tells me that Mr Hoadley much dislikes the engraving. There's confirmation. — Stop tinkering, and do the right thing, I pray you, and impute to the right motive my outspokenness.

H. M.

ALS on a 25.1 × 19.9 cm sheet, folded in half, of white wove paper. Melville inscribed the first, third, and fourth pages, in pencil.

LOCATION: NYPL-GL.

PUBLICATION: Paltsits, p. 33. Davis-Gilman 196.

TEXTUAL NOTES: brought] h *added* · me of] *after canceled* of · and are] and *written over* are · caricature] i *written over* e · referred to] *after canceled* referred to

TO AUGUSTA MELVILLE AND
FRANCES PRISCILLA MELVILLE
[24?] AUGUST 1875 · NEW YORK

Unlocated. A letter from Melville is cited in a 26 August 1875 letter written by Augusta Melville, signed also by her sister Frances Priscilla, thanking Abraham Lansing for sending two baskets of peaches to Gansevoort from Albany and for a letter enclosing fifty dollars. She goes on to report: "With your kind letter came one from Herman, saying how much he enjoyed his little visit in Albany. I do not know any one he thinks more highly of than he does of you" (NYPL-GL). This same letter from Melville is also cited in a 26 August 1875 letter from Augusta Melville to Catherine Lansing. Listing recent letters, Augusta writes, "With your package & Abe's letter this morning came letters from Tom, & Jenny Townsend, besides one from Herman I wrote Abe about" (NYPL-GL). Misdating this second citation as an 1878 letter, Davis and Gilman reported this single letter as two: Unlocated 400 and 406.

TO PETER GANSEVOORT
26 AUGUST 1875 · NEW YORK

While Melville was in Albany on 8 and 9 August 1875, his uncle Peter Gansevoort offered to finance the publication of Melville's long poem *Clarel*, having learned of its manuscript from some member of the family. The poem, which drew on Melville's 1857 visit to the Holy Land, was not, however, published by G. P. Putnam's Sons until 3 June 1876—six months after Peter Gansevoort's death on 4 January 1876, at the age of eighty-seven. For Melville's dedication of the book to his uncle, see the headnote to his 4 January 1876 letter of condolence to Abraham Lansing, below. See also the NN *Clarel*, pp. 536–39, with a reproduction of this letter.

New York, Aug. 26, '75

My Dear Uncle Peter:

Last evening I received through a note from Mr. Lansing a check for $1200, which he says you requested him to send me. — I shall at once deposite the money in a Savings Bank, there to remain till needed for the purpose designed.

And now, My Dear Uncle, in receiving this generous gift from you, so much enhanced by the circumstances, I feel the same sentiments which I expressed to you in person at Albany when you so kindly made known your intention. I will not repeat them here; but only pray God to bless you, and have you in His keeping.

With respect and true affection,

Your Nephew
Herman Melville

ALS on a 22.8 × 17.9 cm sheet, folded in half, of white wove paper, watermarked with the initials "S M C". Melville inscribed the first and third pages, in ink, and addressed the unstamped envelope "Gen. Peter Gansevoort, | Albany." He enclosed this letter with the letter of the same date to Abraham Lansing (below). Catherine Gansevoort noted in ink on the envelope "Cousin Herman | Melville acknowledging | *rect. of check* | Aug. 26th 1875 — ".

LOCATION: NYPL-GL.

PUBLICATION: Thorp, p. 403. Davis-Gilman 197.

TO ABRAHAM LANSING
26 AUGUST 1875 · NEW YORK

This letter accompanied the one of the same date, just above, addressed to Melville's uncle Peter Gansevoort, eighty-six years old and physically dependent on his daughter and son-in-law, Catherine and Abraham Lansing. It acknowledges Abraham Lansing's note (now unlocated) enclosing the $1200 check for *Clarel*, which Melville received shortly after returning from his vacation in Albany and Gansevoort (see the headnote to the letter just above).

New York, Aug. 26, '75

My Dear Mr. Lansing:

I received your note last night, enclosing the draft. — Herewith is a note for my Uncle, which you — or Cousin Kate — will be kind enough to read to him; or seal and deliver; you know best.

Thanking you again — — and, through you, Cousin Kate — for your great hospitality and kindness to me during my Albany visit, Beleive Me

Sincerely Yours
H Melville

ALS on a 22.8 × 17.9 cm sheet, folded in half, of white wove paper, watermarked with the initials "S M C". Melville inscribed the first and third pages, in ink.

LOCATION: NYPL-GL.

PUBLICATION: Paltsits, p. 34. Davis-Gilman 198.

TEXTUAL NOTE: during] g *added*

TO CATHERINE GANSEVOORT LANSING
8 OCTOBER 1875 · NEW YORK

The "book of the sainted queen" referred to in this letter is *The Life of Saint Elizabeth of Hungary* by the Comte de Montalembert, translated by Mary Hackett (New York: Sadlier, 1870; Sealts 368). Melville inscribed the gift: "Kate Gansevoort Lansing. from Cousin Herman." and dated it in pencil "Oct 4th 1875." (NYPL-GL).

104 E. 26.
Oct. 8. '75.

Cousin Kate: — By all means. Send it down at once. — I am glad you were pleased with that book of the sainted queen.
— My best love to my sister Kate, and Fanny, and say that they both must come down & see us before leaving for the East. —
My affectionate regards to your father and Abraham.
Lizzie is writing you, I think; so she will send rememberances for herself.

Thy Cousin
Herman

ALS on a 22.8 × 17.9 cm sheet, folded in half, of white wove paper, watermarked with the initials "S M C". Melville inscribed the first and third pages, in ink. At some point this letter was tipped to the rear pastedown of Catherine Lansing's copy of *The Life of Saint Elizabeth of Hungary*, where it remains.

LOCATION: NYPL-GL.

PUBLICATION: Paltsits, p. 35. Davis-Gilman 199.

TO AUGUSTA MELVILLE
BEFORE 9 OCTOBER 1875 · NEW YORK

Unlocated. A letter from Melville is cited in Augusta Melville's 9 October 1875 letter to Hope Savage Shaw, in which she writes that "we had a charming visit from Herman in August. I dont know when I have seen him better. I had a letter from him this week, & from Lizzie too" (HCL-M). The "charming visit" refers to Melville's 1875 vacation, which he spent in Gansevoort with his two sisters (see the entry for his unlocated letter to his sister Frances Priscilla written at the end of July 1875, above). Possibly this letter was in part a thank-you note for his visit.

1876

TO EVERT A. DUYCKINCK
[1876?] · NEW YORK

While this apparently hand-delivered letter (like the five other undated letters to Duyckinck; see pp. 532–36 below) could have been written at any time when Melville was in New York during their long acquaintance, it was probably written after he had moved back from Pittsfield to New York in 1863. The lined paper on which it is written matches that of three letters to Catherine Gansevoort Lansing all belonging to 1876 (see his letters of 5 June, 2 August, and 8 September). The work that it accompanied, "D.D.," remains unidentified.

Monday P.M.

Dear Duyckinck:

I return with my thanks D.D. which you were so kind as to procure for me.

I can not stop in this evening, but will be happy to do so ere long.

By-the-bye —, you should read, or at least look over D.D. It is well worth any one's reading. It is the last leaf out of the *Omnium Gatherum* of miscellaneous opinion touching the indeterminate Ethics of our time.

With which Johnsonian sentence, I conclude.

H. M.

ALS on a 22.8 × 17.8 cm sheet, folded in half, of white wove paper with lines, embossed with the manufacturer's stamp of a three-domed capitol above the name "CONGRESS". Melville inscribed the first and third pages, in pencil, and addressed the fourth page "Evert A. Duyckinck Esq."

LOCATION: NYPL-GL.

PUBLICATION: Hershel Parker, "Melville to Duyckinck: A New Letter," *Melville Society Extracts* 81 (June 1990), 9 (with reproduction).

TEXTUAL NOTE: I conclude] I *mended*

TO ABRAHAM LANSING
4 JANUARY 1876 · NEW YORK

Melville's uncle Peter Gansevoort died on the Tuesday this letter was written; it was also, as the letter explains, the day Melville had arranged for the publication of *Clarel* (for his uncle Peter's financial assistance with this book, see Melville's earlier 26 August 1875 letter to him). Melville later dedicated the poem to his uncle: "By a spontaneous act, not very long ago, my kinsman, the late Peter Gansevoort of Albany, N. Y., in a personal interview provided for the publication of this poem, known to him by report, as existing in manuscript. Justly and affectionately the printed book is inscribed with his name."

104 E. 26, N.Y.
Jan. 4, '76.
6 P.M.

My Dear Mr. Lansing:

I received the despatch not long since. A letter from Augusta received this morning had prepared me for it. Uncle is released from his suffering. — *In pace.* — The event happens at a time which brings it home to me most sensibly, since, as it happens, only to-day I made arrangements for that publication which he (inspired by the spirit of Aunt Susan) enabled me to effect.

Express my truest sympathies to Cousin Kate — my love to Augusta and Fanny; and for yourself — beleive that no one holds you in more sincere esteem than

H. Melville

Abraham Lansing Esq.

I will be up on Saturday, and will have to return that evening.

ALS on a 25.2 × 20.5 cm sheet, folded in half, of white wove paper with lines, embossed with the manufacturer's rectangular stamp enclosing a three-domed capitol. Melville inscribed the first and third pages, in ink, and addressed the envelope "Abraham Lansing Esq. | Albany | N.[Y.] | 115 *Washington Av.*"; it was postmarked in New York on 4 January. Both letter and envelope were pasted in a Gansevoort family album, grouped with other letters of condolence received after the death of Peter Gansevoort.

LOCATION: NYPL-GL.

PUBLICATION: (partial) *Log*, II, 746. Davis-Gilman 200.

TEXTUAL NOTE: Abraham Lansing Esq.] *on the otherwise blank second page; placed here editorially*

TO GEORGE PARSONS LATHROP
BEFORE JUNE 1876 · NEW YORK

Unlocated. Before completing his book *A Study of Hawthorne* (Boston: Osgood), which was issued in June 1876, George Parsons Lathrop, husband of Nathaniel Hawthorne's daughter Rose, wrote a now unlocated letter to Melville, requesting permission to publish letters Melville had written to Hawthorne. In reply, Melville gave his consent (Lathrop in fact used only Melville's [16 April?] 1851 letter in his *Study*, pp. 230–31). Lathrop later characterized Melville's letter of consent as having "a sort of gloomy reluctance" (see LETTERS RECEIVED, p. 711, for more of Lathrop's recollection and the controversy his book caused within the Hawthorne family).

TO CATHERINE GANSEVOORT LANSING
5 JUNE 1876 · NEW YORK

On 4 April 1876 Melville's sister Augusta died at the home of their brother Thomas on Staten Island at the age of fifty-four. Melville and his cousin Catherine Lansing must have had the conversation mentioned in this letter after the funeral. As his letter of 25 July, just below, indicates, her "special object" in that conversation and in her now unlocated note was to provide him with an additional sum to cover various remaining costs of *Clarel* after its publication, which had occurred on 3 June, two days before this letter. Catherine must have been sensitive to Melville's intense concern about the book, having received a 2 February 1876 letter from Elizabeth Melville that described it as having undermined Melville's mental health and "all our happiness" (NYPL-GL).

104 E. 26th St.
June 5, '76.

Aside from your special object in writing it, you do not know how deeply I felt the sincere tone of your note to me, Cousin Kate.

You repeat, and with added emphasis, what you verbally said to me at the depot here last April, as to carrying out your father's intentions: I appreciate your fidelity, my cousin. — But though the matter is not yet developed into a clear statement rendered; I think now, as before, that nothing more is necessary. —

— When are we to see you here next? Come down before the heat fairly begins. — Tom & Kate dined with us yesterday. Lizzie & the girls are well, and unite in love to you and Abe. Me too remember to him, and warmly. — And now — with my heart upbraiding me for writing so cold a response to so cousinly a note as yours — I hasten to end the sheet — and let it be with a benediction: —

God bless you!
H. Melville

ALS on a 22.8 × 17.8 cm sheet, folded in half, of white wove paper with lines, embossed with the manufacturer's stamp of a three-domed capitol above the name "CONGRESS". Melville inscribed the first, third, and fourth pages, in ink.

LOCATION: NYPL-GL.

PUBLICATION: Paltsits, p. 37. Davis-Gilman 201.

TO CATHERINE GANSEVOORT LANSING
25 JULY 1876 · NEW YORK

After receiving this estimate of the remaining expenses for the publication of *Clarel*, Catherine Lansing on 31 July sent Melville a check (with a now unlocated letter) for the full one hundred dollars, as she noted on his letter. The matter did not end quite so simply, however; five more letters of Melville's in his correspondence with his cousin—those of 2 August 1876, 13 September 1876, 26 September 1876, 4 January 1877, and 7 March 1877—all discuss her gift and his final disposition of it.

The overturned yacht to which Melville alludes near the close of this letter was the *Mohawk*, which capsized off Staten Island on 20 July, with the loss of three passengers and three crewmen.

104 E. 26 St.
July 25, '76

Cousin Kate:

You have made such earnest assurances to me in reference to that book of mine, and in connection with what, you tell me, were your father's expressed wishes, that I can not doubt your sincerity. And so I make the following statement to you:

As it turned out, the 1200 covered the printing expenses, with a fraction to spare. But the supplementary charges — not long ago brought to my attention — against the account of the book — advertizing &c, and customary copies distributed for advertising purposes — will make a difference with me in any receipts to come, of about one hundred dollars.

Whether this comes within the scope of Uncle Peter's design or not, I do not venture to determine. But enough. ——

Lizzie got your note yesterday. I thank you again for your repeated invitation to come up & spend some Sunday with you. I should be most happy so to do if practicable.

Lizzie & Fanny (Fanny the Little) are busily completing their arrangements for the White Mountain campaign. — Lizzie and I went to see Tom at the island the other day (starting in 5 P.M boat, &

returning on 9 P.M Quarantine) Found Tom & Kate well. — How tragical a thing that oversetting of the yacht. We passed the wreck in the boat — the two masts projecting from the water. — My kindest remembrances to Abraham. — O, Fanny is with you — my love to her, & say I hope to see her yet ere she leaves you. — And now, accept this note in testimony that as regards your cousinly interest in me I am neither insensible nor incredulous.

                                                                    Herman.

P.S. Lizzie thanks you for your note; and says she will attend to your commissions and write you after getting to the mountains.

ALS on a 25.2 × 20.2 cm sheet, folded in half, of white wove paper with lines, embossed with the manufacturer's stamp of a three-domed capitol above the name "CONGRESS". Melville inscribed all four pages, in ink. Catherine Lansing noted in ink at the top of the first page "Ans'd | July 31ˢᵗ 1876 | enclosing | check for $100.ᵒᵒ".

LOCATION: NYPL-GL.

PUBLICATION: Paltsits, pp. 38–39. Davis-Gilman 202.

TEXTUAL NOTES: expenses] *first* s *written over* c • returning on] on *possibly* in • P.S. . . . mountains.] *written sideways on the fourth page; placed here editorially* • for your] y *written over* h

TO CATHERINE GANSEVOORT LANSING
2 AUGUST 1876 · NEW YORK

The address at the head of this brief letter is that of Melville's customs office at this time. He was replying to his cousin's now unlocated 31 July, letter, which had enclosed her check for the remaining expenses for *Clarel*. See Melville's letter of 25 July, just above, for the background of this gift.

                                                        Aug. 2, '76
                                                        507 West St.
Cousin Kate: The postman has just handed me yours of July 31, enclosing check for the $100; and, while the first impulse stirs me, I square round to my desk to tell you — however briefly — how deeply I feel the frank and affectionate spirit which penetrates it. I wont say anything more — only this: that I heartily reciprocate your wish that we may always be true and sincere friends. Amen!

My best love to my sister Fanny, and kindest remembrances to Abraham.

> And Beleive me,
> My Dear Cousin Kate,
> Always faithful
> H. Melville

ALS on a 22.8 × 17.8 cm sheet, folded in half, of white wove paper with lines, embossed with the manufacturer's stamp of a three-domed capitol above the name "CONGRESS". Melville inscribed the first and third pages, in ink.

LOCATION: NYPL-GL.

PUBLICATION: Paltsits, p. 40. Davis-Gilman 203.

TO CATHERINE GANSEVOORT LANSING AND ABRAHAM LANSING
27 AUGUST 1876 · NEW YORK

After her father's death, Catherine Gansevoort Lansing and her husband Abraham moved into Peter Gansevoort's home at 115 Washington Avenue in Albany, the address to which Melville sent the used set of Chaucer he had found for Abraham Lansing's collection. The set is unidentified (Sealts 140), but clearly was not the one edited by Robert Bell that Melville later found for Lansing (see his letters of 26 September 1876, 12 October 1876, and 5 September 1877, below). Melville's reference to Chaucer as "the old poet who did'nt know how to spell" alludes to the humorous sketch "At the Tomb of Shakespeare" by Charles Farrar Browne (1834–67) that appeared in the 29 September 1866 issue of *Punch* under Browne's pseudonym Artemus Ward (later collected in *Artemus Ward in London* [New York: Carleton, 1867]). Like much of Browne's humor, this sketch is filled with comic misspellings: "Some kind person has sent me Chawcer's *poems*. Mr. C. had talent, but he couldn't spel. No man has a right to be a lit'rary man onless he knows how to spel."

Although dated only 27 August, this letter can be placed in 1876 through its mention of the Lansings' new address and Melville's 1876 vacation in the White Mountains (see his 25 July letter, above, describing the preparations of his wife and daughter Frances for their summer "campaign"). Although other vacations were spent in the White Mountains, this is the only time Melville is known to have visited his sister and brother-in-law, Helen and George Griggs, at their home outside Boston, on his return from the mountains.

Melville's postscript to Abraham Lansing concerns Stanwix Hall, in Albany, which had been built in 1833 by Peter and Herman Gansevoort as a hotel and office building, and was now the property of Catherine and Abraham Lansing. It was the same building where the debating club, the Philo Logos Society, to which Melville belonged during his Albany years, had held their meetings (see the headnote to his 24 February 1838 letter to the *Albany Microscope*). His interest in the building and its name was also, of course, tied to his interest in his grandfather's victory at Fort Stanwix during the American Revolution (see also his 5 May 1870 letter, above). Despite Melville's suggestion, the name Stanwix Hall was kept when it reopened in January 1878 (see Melville's 26 January 1878 letter to his cousin).

104 E. 26
Aug. 27. — P.M.

Dear Cousin Kate:

It was you that charged me with that commission touching the venerable Chaucer; it is to you therefore that I now address this note.

Passing thro' Nassau St. to-day I chanced upon a good set of the poet, at a very moderate price — ($4.) and, as these things are fugitive, I snapped it up immediately, and ordered it to be sent by Express to 115 Wash. Ave. Albany. — What with his other volumes Chaucerian, Abraham will now have quite a variorum library of the old poet who did'nt know how to spell, as Artemus Ward said.

I arrived in N.Y. this morning by Fall River Route from Boston on my way from White Mountains. Lizzie & the girls are jolly. Helen, whom I saw — & also Mr Griggs — at Brookline, are well & jovial. I myself am ever hilarious, & pray sincerely that you & your Abraham may likewise ever be so.

Your affectionate cousin
Herman.

To Abraham. I have been thinking of what you said about changing the name of the Hotel. — I think that "*The Fort Stanwix Hotel*" is the right thing. You need a change. Besides, "Stanwix Hall" is indefinite — it may (in the opinion of strangers) mean anything or nothing; but the prefix "*Fort*" fixes it, and provokes a question; and the answer is at hand. Then the late celebrations of the Centennial Year are auspicious, and make the new title appropriate and popular. — See if Kate dont agree with me.

Final P.S. — "*Fort Stanwix Hotel*." That is genuine, historic, natural, and purely American. It avoids the snobbish imitation of English names to our N.Y. Hotels. It sets a good example. It *is the thing*.

ALS on a 26.5 × 21 cm sheet, folded in half, of white laid paper, partially watermarked with the name "CAREW CO". Melville wrote his letter to Catherine Lansing in ink on the first and third pages and added his note in ink to her husband on the second and fourth, writing sideways across those two pages. He placed a circled page number at the top of each of the four pages to make the sequence clear. Another hand, probably Catherine Lansing's, dated the letter in pencil "[1876]" above Melville's incomplete date on the first page.

LOCATION: NYPL-GL.

PUBLICATION: Paltsits, pp. 40–41. Davis-Gilman 204.

TEXTUAL NOTES: price —] dash blotted · immediately] blotted · ordered it to] miswritten ordered it to | to · whom] blotted · Mʳ Griggs —] blotted · am] blotted · affectionate cousin] blotted · To Abraham . . . thing.] written sideways on the second and fourth pages; placed here editorially · Fort Stanwix] i added · to our N.Y. Hotels] inserted above caret

TO CATHERINE GANSEVOORT LANSING
8 SEPTEMBER 1876 · NEW YORK

As both this penciled letter from his customs office and his earlier 27 August letter to the Lansings indicate, Melville enjoyed haunting the secondhand bookstores of New York, many of them on Nassau Street, looking for books well under the price for which they were sold in stores such as Scribner, Welford & Armstrong (probably the most prominent bookstore in New York, it specialized in importing both new and out-of-print British books). For a discussion of Melville's book-buying habits in his later years, as well as various book dealers' reminiscences of him, see Sealts, *Melville's Reading*, p. 127, and the NN *Moby-Dick*, pp. 1032–33. The "Chaucer" which Catherine Lansing had requested Melville to find for her husband's collection in her now unlocated letter was probably the eight-volume set edited by Robert Bell discussed in Melville's letters to her of 26 September 1876, 12 October 1876, and 5 September 1877, below. Dated only 8 September, this letter can be placed in 1876 through its association with this book-search.

N.Y. 507 West St.

Sep. 8

Cousin Kate: Your note reached me yesterday in the midst of a jumping tooth-ache, which, spite remedies, still clings, tho' now with merciful intimations of letting me off ere long. Nevertheless with one hand to my "jole", with the other I indite this note. — About the Chaucer: I infer that Abraham does not wish to pay the "Scribner" price for the book. Well then, I will keep a look out for a fair copy at the Nassau St prices, & secure it, if I find it. How much it will be, depends upon the seller &c. Should I not succeed in lighting on a copy such as I speak of, before your visit to us in October — then we three — yourself, Abraham & your humble servant — will take council together touching the matter, and doubtless hit upon some wise decision. —

About the pears. Many thanks for your kind intimation. Should your purpose hold, and your pear-harvest admit of the gift without robbery to yourself — you had better defer sending them till Lizzie's return which will be — tho' no day is determined on — some time about the latter part of the month. — Lizzie & the girls have been greatly benefited by the mountain air — entirely escaping the annual cold, &c.

— I am glad you chanced to mention incidentally the present whereabouts of Fanny & Helen, as I purpose a letter to Fanny & hardly knew where precisely she was. — And so, Cousin Kate, I remain always

Affectionately
Herman

ALS on a 22.9 × 17.8 cm sheet, folded in half, of white wove paper with lines, embossed with the manufacturer's stamp of a three-domed capitol above the name "CONGRESS". Melville inscribed all four pages, in pencil. Another hand dated the first page of the letter "[1876]" in pencil.

LOCATION: NYPL-GL.

PUBLICATION: Paltsits, p. 41. Davis-Gilman 205.

TEXTUAL NOTES: will be] *after canceled word-start* • your purpose] r *added to* your • some time] *inserted above caret* • greatly] *altered from* greaty

TO FRANCES PRISCILLA MELVILLE
AFTER 8 SEPTEMBER 1876 · NEW YORK

Unlocated. After Augusta Melville's death in April 1876, Melville's youngest sister Frances Priscilla, who had never married, was left alone. As his letters of 25 July and 2 August 1876 to Catherine Lansing indicate, she first went to stay with Catherine Lansing in Albany after the funeral. By early September she had returned to Gansevoort, accompanied by their sister Helen Melville Griggs. In his 8 September 1876 letter to Catherine Lansing (just above), Melville stated his intention to write to his sister, which he presumably did. Davis-Gilman Unlocated 401.

TO CATHERINE GANSEVOORT LANSING
13 SEPTEMBER 1876 · NEW YORK

As Melville's 27 August 1876 letter reports, he once again spent his two-week vacation in the White Mountains of New Hampshire with his wife and daughters, who stayed on after he returned to New York by way of Boston. In his family's absence, he apparently took his meals at the house of the Misses Hartnett on Twenty-fifth Street, near the Melville house on Twenty-sixth Street. His guests there on 12 September were Edwin Yates Lansing, Abraham Lansing's younger brother, who had served during the Civil War with Henry Gansevoort (see Melville's 10 May 1864 letter, above), and probably Charles Brewster (1837–1904), Edwin Lansing's business partner in a Kansas City land agency (he was also the brother of George Brewster, former law-partner of Henry Gansevoort and Allan Melville). Both men, according to a 17 May 1871 letter from Elizabeth Melville to Catherine Gansevoort (NYPL-GL), had assisted Melville's son Stanwix when he was in Kansas.

The now unlocated "slip" enclosed with this letter was a receipt from the New-York Society for the Relief of the Ruptured and Crippled. As he explains, Melville had donated to the society the one hundred dollars Catherine Lansing had sent him on 31 July, which she had intended to cover the additional expenses of publishing *Clarel* (see LETTERS RECEIVED, p. 711, and Melville's 25 July 1876 letter to his cousin, above). For a draft version of his cousin's 17 September reply, see LETTERS RECEIVED, p. 712. This donation would have equaled roughly one month's salary for Melville, who received four dollars a day for his six-day-a-week job as customs inspector. The enclosed report of the society is also now unlocated. The centennial Catherine and Abraham Lansing planned to visit later in the fall was the exposition in Philadelphia (see Melville's letter of 12 October 1876 for his opinion of it).

New York, Sep. 13, '76

My Dear Cousin Kate:

Your kind note of the 10th announcing the plums, was received on Monday. Last night (Tuesday) the fruit arrived all right in 25th St, giving great pleasure to the Misses Hartnett, and furnishing to me an added example of your cousinly good feeling. Edwin, with Mr Brewster dined with us (at the Misses Hartnett's) last evening, and spent the remainder of it with me in my room at 26th St. I was well pleased to see him again, & looking so well. — About the enclosed slip. You perceive that you have become a contributor, and, in some degree, a priveleged one, to an excellent Charity. — You pause, methinks, and say — "Pray, explain yourself." — Well then — and for sweet charity's sake dont take offence — I have upon consideration determined that as touching the provision for the publication of "Clarel," it is best to restrict myself to what Uncle Peter

so kindly presented me with, in person, as I may say. By your subsequent supplemental act you faithfully carried out what, as you
averred, was your father's directions or wishes: you are irreproacha-
ble there; and anything that I can do or have now done, does not and
can not revoke that affectionate act of yours, while yet *my* action
operates in a way favorable to the unembarrassed freedom of mutual
good will. (Rather *"tall writing"*, that last clause.) — Well; but you
take nothing back — you receive nothing back — but are <u>forced</u> to
acquiese in the step I have taken. The result of all is — the benefit of
suffering humanity. Let us therefore, My Dear Cousin, congratulate
ourselves all round — you, me, and the poor cripples, and say no
more about it. ——

Lizzie & the girls are coming home next Monday. We confidently expect you to visit us on your way to the Centennial — you and
Abraham. Dont forget it. Arms of welcome will be extended to
you. — And now, beleive me always faithfully & affectionately, and
devoutly

Your Cousin Herman

P.S. I send by same mail the last report of the Society, which, I
know, will be interesting to you.

ALS on a 26.7 × 21 cm sheet, folded in half, of white laid paper, partially watermarked with
the name "CAREW CO". Melville inscribed all four pages, in ink.

LOCATION: NYPL-GL.

PUBLICATION: Paltsits, p. 42. Davis-Gilman 206.

TEXTUAL NOTES: contributor,] *before canceled* to an • irreproachable] *blotted* • does not] *after canceled* can • mutual] *after canceled word-start* • all round] *after canceled* all • cripples,] *comma blotted* • P.S. . . . you.] *written sideways on the fourth page; placed here editorially*

TO CATHERINE GANSEVOORT LANSING
26 SEPTEMBER 1876 · NEW YORK

This letter touches on the two recurring topics in Melville's 1876–77 correspondence with his cousin and her husband—the matter of the additional one hundred
dollars for the post-publication expenses of *Clarel* and the set of Chaucer for Abraham Lansing's collection. In reply to Melville's 13 September 1876 letter reporting

his donation of the money to charity, Catherine Lansing had on 17 September thanked Melville for "giving me, the credit for your own 'sweet charity['] to the destitute & suffering" (see LETTERS RECEIVED, p. 712). His cousin's 1 October reply to this letter is unlocated. The eight-volume set of Chaucer's *Poetical Works* that Melville found for six dollars was edited, with a memoir, by Robert Bell (London: Parker, 1854–56; Sealts 138 and 139).

New York
104 E. 26 St.
Sep. 26. '76

Cousin Kate:

I was glad to get your note of the 17th, and was much gratified with the tone of it. By the way — your rainy Sunday was also experienced by me, alone here as it chanced, to chew the cud of sweet and bitter fancies. I doubt not there was no lack of others — a plentiful sprinkling of them all over the world. — We are all well pleased to know that you and Abe are going to shed your benign presence on us, and Fanny also (from whom we got a letter to day, & likewise from Helen) on your way to the Centennial. —

A man in Nassau St. tells me that he can procure me a copy of Chaucer — Bell's edition, and new — for six dollars. What say you? If yea, I will invest. I think Abe will hardly do better. —

We relish your pears much — good thing at breakfast — and remember you thereby.

With friendliest regards to Abraham

Beleive me, Affectionately
Herman

P.S. We rely & count upon that visit — you & Abe & Fanny; and only regret that my sister Helen is not also one of the party. I write her to day at Gansevoort.

ALS on a 26.6 × 21 cm sheet, folded in half, of white laid paper, watermarked with the name "CAREW CO". Melville inscribed the first, third, and fourth pages, in ink. Catherine Gansevoort noted in ink on the first page "Ans'd | Sunday | Oct. 1st 1876."

LOCATION: NYPL-GL.

PUBLICATION: Paltsits, pp. 43–44. Davis-Gilman 207.

TEXTUAL NOTE: We rely] We *miswritten* W

TO HELEN MELVILLE GRIGGS
26 SEPTEMBER 1876 · NEW YORK

Unlocated. A letter is cited in Melville's 26 September 1876 letter to his cousin Catherine Lansing, just above. Regretting that his sister Helen (who had been staying in Gansevoort with their youngest sister Frances Priscilla) was not coming with Catherine and Abraham Lansing and Frances to visit on the way to the centennial exposition at Philadelphia, he added, "I write her to day at Gansevoort"—perhaps in an effort to convince her to come, but she evidently did not change her mind. Davis-Gilman Unlocated 402.

TO CATHERINE GANSEVOORT LANSING
12 OCTOBER 1876 · NEW YORK

Catherine Lansing's now unlocated letter of 1 October 1876 apparently asked for further information about the Chaucer set described in Melville's earlier 26 September letter. Melville already owned a copy of the set, as he indicates here, perhaps bought because he met Robert Bell in London in 1849 (see *Journals*, pp. 44 and 365). Why a delay occurred is unclear, but it appears that Melville did not send his cousins a set of this edition until nearly a year after they attended the centennial exposition ("a sort of tremendous Vanity Fair," in Melville's opinion) in Philadelphia in November 1876 (see his letter of 5 September 1877 to Catherine Lansing, below).

The poem Catherine Lansing had either sent or recommended to Melville is unidentified, but its author, Alfred Billings Street (1811–81), was well known at the time. A New York lawyer and librarian, he moved in 1839 to Albany, where he edited the *Northern Light* (1843–44), was director of the New York State Library from 1848 to 1862, and published several volumes of sentimental nature poetry. Melville heard him read at the Pittsfield Young Ladies' Institute on 30 September 1852, although, according to his uncle Peter in a letter to Maria Melville, he failed to favor Street "with a Call or the least attention" on this occasion (NYPL-GL). They shared the same British publisher, Richard Bentley, who included a number of Street's poems in his *Miscellany* and who published Street's "metrical romance" *Frontenac* in 1849 (for Bentley's comments about Melville in one of his letters to Street, see the headnote to Melville's 27 June 1850 letter to Bentley, above). Street is also mentioned in Melville's 14 August 1877 letter to the Lansings, below.

Oct. 12 '76.
104 E. 26 St.

Dear Cousin Kate:

In responce to yours of the 1st: The Chaucer is in eight vols. — good print — same edition as mine — Bell's — but it is perfect. — However, as I understand, the Nassau St. man will procure it for me at the price named ($6, I think) at any time I may desire it, it will be better to let it rest until your visit to us ere long, on your return from the Centennial.

By the way, I was there yesterday — went & returned same day; you will be much impressed with it; it is immense — a sort of tremendous Vanity Fair.

I was very much pleased with Mr Street's little poem. It is admirable in its fidelity to nature and happy ensemble.

With kind regards to Abraham

Affectionately
Herman

ALS on a 26.6 × 21 cm sheet, folded in half, of white laid paper, partially watermarked with the name "CAREW CO". Melville inscribed the first and third pages, in ink. He addressed the envelope "Mrs. Abraham Lansing | Albany | N.Y. | *115 Washington Ave.*"; it was postmarked in New York on 12 October. Catherine Gansevoort noted on the envelope in ink "Cousin Herman | Melville & | Cousin Lizzie | 1876".

LOCATION: NYPL-GL.

PUBLICATION: Paltsits, p. 44. Davis-Gilman 208.

TEXTUAL NOTE: With] h *added*

1877

TO ABRAHAM LANSING
2 JANUARY 1877 · NEW YORK

Only one of the three works mentioned in this New Year's letter replying to Abraham Lansing's now unlocated letter can be positively identified. Melville's present to him, *The Songs of Béranger, in English*, by Pierre Jean de Béranger (Philadelphia: Carey & Hart, 1844), one of the books Melville took with him on his 1860 voyage round Cape Horn, has the inscriptions: "H. Melville Pacific Ocean Sep 4th 1860 19° S.L." and "Abraham Lansing Xmas, 1876" (NYPL-GL; Sealts 58). The "Christmas Story" Lansing gave Melville has not been identified. The almanac he gave him was probably the 1877 *Webster's Calendar; or, The Albany Almanac*, established in 1784 by Charles R. and George Webster (Sealts 553); and the Boston almanac Melville refers to was probably *The (Old) Farmer's Almanack*, established in 1793 by Robert B. Thomas (Sealts 388). Melville's postscript about Catherine Lansing's "commission" may also have referred to a book—possibly the Chaucer set Melville was procuring for Abraham at Catherine's request (see his 26 September 1876 letter to her, above); however, as his 4 January 1877 letter to her, just below, illustrates, he often performed various services in New York for his Albany cousin.

104 E 26, N.Y.
Jan. 2, 1877

My Dear Abraham:

I was glad to get your note, and to know that you were so
pleased with Beranger — *the volume*: a shabby looking little cask it
is, but then, the contents! —

I liked that Christmas Story you sent me, especially in the opening portion — the good old Dutch saint's lamentation over these
"degenerate days" which we account such an "advance."

Tell *Catherine* that her New Year Cake came along all right, and
that we duly appreciated her Christmas kindliness. By *we* I mean
Lizzie and myself, the special donees, and also Bessie & Fanny, assistant *eatees*. — By the way, — the Almanac — I should have been
sorry to have forgotten it — that venerable Almanac, which bears
witness to the old times when some imagination yet lingered in this
sort of publication. I relish looking over it mightily. It has set me to
getting from Boston a similar almanac which still continues to be
published there. — Lizzie sends love to Kate and begs her to accept
thro' me her acknowledgments for her share of the Christmas ham-
per. My best remembrances also. Bessy & Fanny join.

Sincerely Yours
H Melville

Oh — A happy New Year to you — you & Kate

Tell Kate I have not forgotten her commission.

ALS on a 26.5 × 21 cm sheet, folded in half, of white laid paper, partially watermarked with
the name "CAREW CO". Melville inscribed the first three pages, in ink, and addressed the enve-
lope "Abraham Lansing Esq. | Albany | N.Y. | *115 Washington Ave.*"; it was postmarked in
New York on 2 January.

LOCATION: NYPL-GL.

PUBLICATION: Paltsits, pp. 44–45. Davis-Gilman 209.

TEXTUAL NOTES: all] *before (over) in bottom margin* • we] *after canceled (underlined)* we • special]
inserted above caret with guideline • Oh . . . Kate] *at the bottom of the second page, in ink; placed here
editorially* • Tell . . . commission.] *added vertically in the middle of the second page, in pencil; placed
here editorially*

TO CATHERINE GANSEVOORT LANSING
4 JANUARY 1877 · NEW YORK

In her undated "note" cited here, Catherine Lansing had enclosed a check for one hundred dollars, which she felt determined to send Melville after he gave her first check to charity (see LETTERS RECEIVED, pp. 713–14, and Melville's earlier letter of 13 September 1876, above). For the final resolution of this matter, see his letter of 7 March 1877, just below.

New York Jan. 4, '77

Cousin Kate: After some delay hardly avoidable, let me acknowledge your note, with enclosure. — What shall I say? — Well, so be it. Yes, in the repetition, how can I otherwise than accept it in the spirit in which it is proffered, and as coming thro' you from Uncle Peter in the carrying out of his kindly purpose.

— About the picture: It is in the framer's hands, and doubtless you will receive it in a day or two. In the absence of your Mr. Joiner I communicated with another person who seemed not unacquainted with your artistic affairs &c. He was very polite, so much so indeed that, fearing, were the matter left entirely to his discretion, he might enshrine the print too sumptuously, I felt forced to make some humble suggestions. But I hope the result will be satisfactory.

Lizzie sends love. So do Bessie & Fanny. — We all daily munch our New Year Cake; — which reminds me to wish you and Abraham a happy time for the next twelve months.

Sincerely & affectionately
H. Melville

ALS on a 26.6 × 21 cm sheet, folded in half, of white laid paper, watermarked with the name "CAREW CO". Melville inscribed the first and third pages, in ink, and addressed the envelope "Mrs. Abraham Lansing | Albany | N.Y. | *115 Washington Av.*"; it was postmarked in New York on 4 January. Catherine Lansing noted on the envelope in ink "Herman Melville | Cousin Lizzie S. M | 1877 — " on one side of the address and repeated the date "1877" on the other.

LOCATION: NYPL-GL.

PUBLICATION: Paltsits, p. 45. Davis-Gilman 210.

TO CATHERINE GANSEVOORT LANSING
7 MARCH 1877 · NEW YORK

This letter is the seventh and last about the money Catherine Lansing had first offered Melville in April 1876 (see his 5 June 1876 letter to her, above). As with her earlier gift, he felt unable to accept the money (see his letter of 13 September 1876, above). According to Catherine Lansing's endorsement on this letter, Melville returned the money on 23 June 1877 while she was in New York. Her letter acknowledging this, also noted in her endorsement, is now unlocated.

Melville wrote this letter just two days after Rutherford B. Hayes (1822–93) took the oath of office as president of the United States on 5 March 1877. He had been awarded the presidency on 2 March 1877, after the disputed election was settled by a senatorial agreement of Republicans with Southern Democrats that was labeled "the bargain." He received 185 electoral votes, and Samuel J. Tilden, governor of New York and the Democratic candidate, received 184. The *Albany Argus* on 5 March 1877 printed a front-page article announcing this decision, which was headed in part "Usurper Hayes Takes the Oath."

My Dear Cousin Kate:

I was disappointed by your not dropping in upon us during your last trip to town — and, chiefly, because I have had something to say to you which I did not want formally to annoy you about in a letter, but meant to say to you then. — However, I will now no longer delay it. —

It was this: You should have let that matter of the $100 rest where it was left for a finality last summer. Your subsequent letter — not very long ago — re-inclosing the money, made such an appeal to me, and placed the matter on such grounds as to make declination difficult without an appearance of obstinacy and rudeness. But I repented my assent. — And I revoke it. Be prepared therefore, sooner or later, I beg you, to receive the money back without comment. Should you return it, some Charity shall receive it, and down goes your name again for the Lady Bountiful of Albany. —

Now, my dear Kin, my cousinly disposition towards you may not be worth much to you; still, if you desire me to retain it unimpaired, you must uncomplainingly indulge me in my whims, for such you may call it, if you like. Indeed, you are welcome to almost any opinion, except that I am prompted by the remotest thought of wounding you, or any absurd idea of setting up for myself a spurious dignity. —

P. How about President Hayes? I chanced to turn over a file of your Albany Argus yesterday, and was all but blown off the stool by the tremendous fulminations of that indignant sheet. — But what's the use? life is short, and Hayes' term is four years, each of 365 days.

Lizzie, the girls, & I anticipate yours & Fanny's visit with pleasure.

With the sincerest regards to Abe, Beleive me

Truly and affectionately
Herman

March 7th '77.

— Dont concern yourself, I implore, as to replying to this note. Simply acknowledge its receipt, if you will, by a newspaper. —

ALS on a 26.6 × 21 cm sheet, folded in half, of white laid paper, partially watermarked with the name "CAREW CO". Melville inscribed all four pages, in ink. Catherine Lansing noted in ink at the top of the first page "Saturday | *June 23ᵈ 1877* | Cousin Herman | gave me the | 100= Dollars | which he in | this note said | he would refund | to me, | given to me | at his house | 104. E. 26ᵗʰ St | N.Y. City | & ack by me | by mail a few | days afterwards | K. G. L."

LOCATION: NYPL-GL.

PUBLICATION: Paltsits, pp. 46–47. Davis-Gilman 211.

TEXTUAL NOTES: on such grounds] *after canceled* and placed the thing · sooner or later,] *inserted above caret* · receive it,] *before* again, *inserted above caret, then canceled* · How about] How *possibly* Now · fulminations] *inserted with caret above canceled* indignation of

TO JOHN C. HOADLEY
31 MARCH 1877 · NEW YORK

This letter can be dated Saturday, 31 March, which was the "Saturday in Easter Week" in 1877. It is the only manuscript letter now located from Melville to his brother-in-law John Hoadley. Hoadley (a year older than Melville) and his wife—Melville's sister Catherine—by this time had three children (the oldest two of whom were daughters—the "two Princesses of India"). Hoadley was currently serving on the Massachusetts State Board of Health, Lunacy and Charity, a position he held from 1873 to 1882 (to which Melville's postscript may refer; see also RELATED DOCUMENTS, pp. 857–60). Hoadley's letter of 25 February is unlocated, but his poems that were apparently enclosed with it exist in various manuscript copies (see LETTERS RECEIVED, pp. 715–18). The first poem cited by Melville, based on a legend told by Marco Polo, was entitled "Foundation Stones," and the second, a paraphrase of the *Aeneid*, 5.485–540, was entitled "He Wins Who Highest Aims." Melville's question about this poem ("whose translation is that?") suggests that he didn't know it was Hoadley's.

Hoadley, like Melville, had broad reading habits, which was probably the reason Melville recommended two quite different books to him in the course of the letter—first the book he had given Catherine Lansing in 1875 (see his 8 October 1875 letter to her), the Comte de Montalembert's *The Life of Saint Elizabeth of Hungary* (Sealts 368), and second Gibbon's *Decline and Fall of the Roman Empire* (Sealts 223b), to which Melville's enclosed poem (later published in *Timoleon* [1891]) was linked. Moreover, Hoadley, with his reading in the classics, would have shared Melville's interest in the ship from Girgenti, the ancient Agrigentum, on the south coast of Sicily. It was probably the Italian brig *Carolus*, from Catania on the eastern coast of Sicily, which arrived in New York on 24 March carrying sulfur.

Saturday in Easter Week
1877

My Dear Fellow:

I propose buying a hair-shirt and a scourge, and putting them to use for a week or so, as a penalty for my remissness in allowing your most friendly note of the 25 ult. to remain unanswered so long. — And yet I might say something in palliation of my incivility. You are young; but I am verging upon three-score, and at times a certain lassitude steals over one — in fact, a disinclination for doing anything except the indispensable. At such moments the problem of the universe seems a humbug, and epistolary obligations mere moonshine, and the — well, nepenthe seems all-in-all.

Your legend from Marco Polo I had never previously met with. How full of significance it is! And beauty too. These legends of the Old Faith are really wonderful both from their multiplicity and their poetry. They far surpass the stories in the Greek mythologies. Dont you think so? See, for example, the life of St. Elizabeth of Hungary.

— "He wins who highest aims": — whose translation is that? Tell me. Thank you for sending me so beautiful a thing engrossed by your deft & dexterous digits. (The alliteration there was irresistable)

In return for your M.S. favors I send you something I found the other day — came across it — in a lot of papers. I remember that the lines were suggested by a passage in Gibbon (Decline & Fall) Have you a copy? Turn to *"Antonine"* &c in index. What the deuce the thing means I dont know; but here it is.

— By the way I have a ship on my District from Girgente. — Where's that? Why, in Sicily — the ancient Agrigentum. Ships arrive from there in this port, bringing sulphur; but this is the first one

I have happened to have officially to do with. I have not succeeded in seeing the captain yet — have only seen the Mate — but hear that he has in possession some stones from those magnificent Grecian ruins, and I am going to try to get a fragment, however small, if possible, which I will divide with you.

Best love to Kate & your two Princesses of India.

H Melville

Lizzie and the girls are well, and if they knew of my writing would send their affectionate rememberances to all.

[Enclosure:]

The Age of the Antonines.

I.

While hope awaits Millenial years,
    Though dim of late the signs,
Back to the past a glance be cast —
    The Age of the Antonines!
Oh, summit of fate and zenith of time,
    When a pagan gentleman reigned,
And the olive was nailed to the inn of the world,
    Nor the peace of the just was feigned.
        A halcyon age — afar it shines
        The imperial age of the Antonines!

2.

Hymns to the nation's federate gods
    Went up from friendly shrines;
No demagogue beat the pulpit-drum
    In the age of the Antonines!
Ere the sting was dreamed to be taken from death —
    Ere the saving of scamps was taught,
They reasoned of fate at the flowing feast
    Nor stifled the fluent thought:
        We sham, we shuffle, while faith declines:
        They were *frank* in the age of the Antonines!

3.

Orders and grades and due degree —
　　None felt how the leveller pines;
Yea, men were better than blatantly free
　　In the age of the Antonines!
Under Law, made Will, the world reposed,
　　And the Ruler's right confessed,
For the Gods elected the Emperor then —
　　The foremost of men the best!
　　　Ah, might we read in the Future's signs
　　　The Past revived in the Antonines!

——— ‖ ———

P.S. to the Note.

Just looked over the accompanying letter which I wrote this morning. It is a queer sort of an absurd scribble, but if it evidences good-fellowship and good feeling, it serves the purpose. You are young (as I said before) but I aint; and at my years, and with my disposition, or rather, constitution, one gets to care less and less for everything except downright good feeling. Life is so short, and so ridiculous and irrational (from a certain point of view) that one knows not what to make of it, unless — well, finish the sentence for yourself.

Thine
In these inexplicable fleshly bonds
H. M.

N.B. *I aint crazy.*

ALS, with the body of the letter on a 26.4 × 21 cm sheet, folded in half, of white laid paper, watermarked with the name "CAREW CO". Melville inscribed all four pages, in ink, with the opening of his letter on the second page and the closing on the first page. It has now become cleanly separated at the fold. The poem is on the rectos of three part-sheets of yellow laid paper, one stanza per part-sheet. The first part-sheet is 17.8 × 14.3 cm, torn along the left and bottom edges; the other two are 17.8 × 14.4 cm, torn along all edges except the top. Melville inscribed the poem (and made the revisions listed in the textual notes) in ink; he also made and then erased various tentative revisions in pencil (for a full report, see the NN *Published Poems* volume). The postscript, in ink, begins on the verso of the third part-sheet and is concluded on the verso of the second.

LOCATION: NYPL-GL.

PUBLICATION: Paltsits, pp. 47–50. Davis-Gilman 212.

TEXTUAL NOTES: putting] ting *added* · lassitude] *after canceled* intellectual · Elizabeth] za *rewritten* · digits] *after* fi *changed to* di *then canceled* · irresistable] *miswritten* irresisable · Ships] *altered from* ships *after canceled* Plenty of · Lizzie . . . to all.] *in the right margin of the third page; placed here editorially* · of late] *inserted with caret over canceled* be now · We sham, we shuffle,] *originally* We shuffle, we sham, *then* we sham, *canceled and* sham, we *inserted with caret before* shuffle · accompanying] *miswritten* accompaning

TO LUCY MELVILL NOURSE
AFTER 7 APRIL 1877 · NEW YORK

Nearly fifty years stand between this letter from Melville to his aunt Lucy and his childhood letter to her in 1828. In the intervening period Melville's aunt had married Justin Wright Clark, who died in 1833, and later Dr. Amos Nourse (see the headnote to Melville's letter to his wife of 24 and 25 March 1861). This brief note survives on the verso of an undated fragment of a letter from Melville's wife to his aunt Lucy, apparently about the death of Dr. Nourse, and can thus be dated soon after that day, 7 April 1877. Melville's aunt died the following October, leaving him $150 and his wife $100. The Lemuel Shaw papers (MHS-S) indicate the friendly relationship between the Nourses and the Shaws as well as the affectionate interest of the Nourses in both Melville and his wife. (Elizabeth had remained a favorite of the Nourses after spending the summer with them in 1839.)

My Dear Aunt Lucy:

    Lizzie has written you above; and I hardly know what I can add unless it be to assure you, with my own hand, of my sincerest sympathy and affectionate rememberance,

H. Melville

ALS on a 13.3 × 9.9 cm part-sheet (torn along the top and the right edge) of white laid paper. Melville apparently added this note at the close of his wife's letter. Only a portion of her letter now remains on the opposite side of Melville's note. Both were inscribed in ink.

LOCATION: HCL-M.

PUBLICATION: *Log*, II, 761. Davis-Gilman 213.

TEXTUAL NOTE: rememberance] *blotted*

TO EVERT A. DUYCKINCK
13 APRIL 1877 · NEW YORK

This letter to Duyckinck, written on the back of a New York Custom House form for the discharging of vessels, is dated only 13 April. It is associated, however, with an overnight visit Melville made to his brother Thomas's home and a letter Thomas

subsequently wrote to Duyckinck, dated 13 April 1877, thanking him for his gift to
Sailors' Snug Harbor of pictures portraying Nelson's victory of the Nile and adding, "Hearing from Herman that they are ready for delivery, I will send the Express
men for them on Tuesday the 18ᵗʰ" (NYPL-D). This last date appears to be in error
by one day, since 17 April and not 18 April was a Tuesday in 1877. On that Tuesday Thomas sent with the expressmen a note to Duyckinck, correctly dated "April
17ᵗʰ 1877," which stated, in part, "Please deliver to bearer four Pictures" (NYPL-
D).

In 1877 a new "building for the accommodation of inmates" and a kitchen had
recently been added at Sailors' Snug Harbor (*Copy of the Last Will and Testament of
the Late Robert Richard Randall, Esq., of the Act of Incorporation, and of the Other Acts of
the Legislature of the State of New-York Respecting the Sailors' Snug Harbor* [New York:
Slote & Janes, 1876], p. 16). This addition is probably what Melville calls the "new
wing" where the pictures were to be hung. Duyckinck may have had such a gift in
mind for some years, since after a visit to Snug Harbor, where his relative Ben
Conklin was living, he had entered in his diary under 3 November 1847 that it was
"very well conducted but with no resources for the *imagination* to allay the oppres-
sive uniformity and routine. The library with few books was dull and theological — no Smolletts or Fieldings — no paintings or statues" (Donald Yannella and
Kathleen Malone Yannella, "Evert A. Duyckinck's 'Diary: May 29–November 8,
1847,'" *Studies in the American Renaissance* 2 [1978], 247).

This is the last known letter from Melville to his old friend Duyckinck, who
died on 13 August 1878.

Corner Jane & West
Ap. 13, noon

My Dear Duyckinck:

Last evening I went down to the Island and anchored for the
night in the

"Snug Harbor,"

getting back this morning in an early boat.

Tom was greatly pleased with your proposed gift to the Institution, and charged me to express to you as much — and more. I
understood him to say that, pursuant to your suggestion as to time,
he will send a proper person for the pictures next Tuesday. —

We visited the new wing, and selected a good place for the
Prints, where the old Salts can look up at them from off their domi-
noes — a favorite game with them. — All you have now to do, is to
provide for an annual Lecture, to be delivered before the old veter-
ans in the big hall of the Institution, on the Battle of the Nile, the
pictures serving to illustrate the matter.

With Friendliest Regards
H Melville

[not abounding in note-paper in this shanty of an office, I write on the best substitute at hand.]

ALS on a New York Custom House form for the discharging of vessels (a 25.4 × 20.3 cm sheet, folded in half, of white wove paper) turned upside down so that the form is on the fourth page of Melville's letter. He inscribed the first and third pages, in ink. The envelope Melville used was a business one with the printed firm name "Chapman Slate Co., | 505 & 507 West St., N.Y." crossed out in pencil. He addressed it "Evert A. Duyckinck Esq. | No. 20 Clinton Place | *City*"; it was postmarked in New York on 13 April.

LOCATION: NYPL-D.

PUBLICATION: *Log*, II, 761. Davis-Gilman 214.

TEXTUAL NOTES: proposed] r *added* • send] *inserted with caret above canceled* sent • [not . . . hand.]] *at the bottom of the otherwise blank second page; placed here editorially*

TO ABRAHAM LANSING
4 JUNE 1877 · NEW YORK

On 1 June 1877, Abraham Lansing, as executor, sent Melville his legacy of five hundred dollars from his uncle Peter Gansevoort's estate (Lansing's accompanying note is now unlocated). The day after this acknowledgment by Melville, Elizabeth Melville also acknowledged receipt of the money in a letter to Catherine Lansing: "Today probably Cousin Abe has acknowledgment from Herman of his missive rec^d yesterday — I need not say that the kindly remembrance from your dear father gave him great pleasure — and I hope it will make him really happier to have something to call his own — poor fellow he has so much mental suffering to undergo (and oh how *all* unnecessary) I am rejoiced when anything comes into his life to give him even a moment's relief — " (NYPL-GL). Melville's letter was preserved in the same album as the letters of condolence received at the death of Susan Gansevoort and then that of Peter Gansevoort (see also Melville's letters of 29 October 1874 and 4 January 1876).

New York, June 4, '77

My Dear Mr. Lansing:

I immediately acknowledge the receipt of your note of the 1st Inst.; and, agreeably with your request, sign and return the accompanying paper.

With kindest rememberences to Kate, in which Lizzie & the girls join, Beleive Me

Sincerely Yours
H. Melville

ALS on a 15.2 × 20.4 cm part-sheet (cut along the left edge to the left of a fold line) of white laid paper with lines, embossed with the manufacturer's stamp of a shield surmounted by an arm wielding a sword. Melville inscribed only one side of the leaf, in ink. The letter was later pasted into a Gansevoort family album, grouped with other letters concerning Peter Gansevoort's bequests.

LOCATION: NYPL-GL.

PUBLICATION: Davis-Gilman 215.

TO CATHERINE GANSEVOORT LANSING
12 JULY 1877 · NEW YORK

In mid-June 1877 Catherine Lansing stayed with the Melvilles while visiting in New York. It was at this time that Melville returned to her one hundred dollars, an amount that she had twice tried to press upon him for the remaining expenses on *Clarel* (see Melville's 7 March 1877 letter, refusing the gift). In a now unlocated letter she acknowledged the return of the money "a few days afterwards" upon her return to Albany (according to her endorsement on his 7 March letter). She also sent Melville at this time a set of engraved silver sleeve-buttons as part of one of her large-scale gift-giving campaigns in memory of her brother Henry. John Hoadley, for example, also received a set of silver buttons and George Griggs a gold set.

104 E 26
July 12, '77

Dear Cousin Kate:

I heartily thank you for the sleeve-buttons which — it is all but needless to say — I shall always preserve as a lasting memorial of one whom I have more than one reason to remember with love.

— I am glad to note that you have caused the inscription upon them to be made full and complete. — In themselves they are very handsome, and — as a minor matter, I will add — much to my taste. —

Altho' Lizzie acknowledged for me, with my thanks, the receipt of your note to me on your last return home; let me here re-acknowledge it, and also express the pleasure it gave me — only, as regards all that dreadful trouble you lament you give on your travels, I really know nothing about it; and, in fact, have only to say *anent* it, what indeed you are already aware of — namely — that your visits, long or short, are always welcome to all of us. If I, for one, have any fault to find it is that

Abraham

dont come along with you.
    Kindest regards to him;
And with love to yourself
    in which Lizzie & all join, Beleive me
                                    Your affectionate Cousin
                                                    Herman

P.S. — By Lizzie's commands I open my note to say that she thanks
you for your letter
— Bessie will write you about the box.

ALS on a 25.2 × 20.4 cm sheet, folded in half, of white laid paper with lines, faintly embossed with the manufacturer's stamp of a shield surmounted by an arm wielding a sword.
Melville inscribed the first, third, and fourth pages, in ink. The letter was later pasted into a
Gansevoort family album, grouped with other letters acknowledging Catherine Lansing's
1877 gifts in memory of her brother Henry.

LOCATION: NYPL-GL.

PUBLICATION: (partial) *Log*, II, 763. Davis-Gilman 216.

TEXTUAL NOTES: find] *before canceled* it • which] i *added*

TO CATHERINE GANSEVOORT LANSING
BEFORE 9 AUGUST 1877 · NEW YORK

Unlocated. A letter of "a few days before" 9 August, referring to the Lansings as
"people of leisure," is cited in Melville's 5 September 1877 letter to his cousin Catherine, below. Davis-Gilman Unlocated 403.

TO CATHERINE GANSEVOORT LANSING AND
ABRAHAM LANSING
14 AUGUST 1877 · GANSEVOORT

On his annual two-week vacation that began in 1877 on 10 August, Melville
stopped first in Albany with the Lansings. He called with them on Judge Elisha P.
Hurlbut and his wife, Melville's second cousin Catherine Van Vechten Hurlbut (see
the headnote to Melville's 20 January 1845 letter to his sister Catherine, above, and
the postscript to his 5 September 1877 letter, just below). The "Miss Lansing and
Miss Anna" he failed to call on while there were probably Abraham Lansing's oldest sister, Anna Lansing, and another member of the Lansing family. From Albany,
Melville went on to Saratoga Springs for three hours, then on to Gansevoort,
where his three surviving sisters were summering: Frances Priscilla, Catherine

Hoadley, and Helen Griggs (who arrived later), along with the Hoadley children—Minnie, Lottie, and Frankie. From there Melville joined his wife and daughters in the White Mountains.

Although this letter is dated only 14 August, it can be placed in 1877 by Melville's "*Final P.S.*," which states that he had been reading a poem by Alfred Street
(see the headnote to his 12 October 1876 letter, above), entitled "The Old Garden."
The poem appeared in the 18 August 1877 issue of *Frank Leslie's Illustrated
Newspaper*:

THE OLD GARDEN.

A garden, a lovely old garden, I see,
    As I shut my tired eyes in the night;
With alleys and walks and green groupings of trees!
    As a picture it shines to my sight.
Not the picture it shone, but neglected and rude,
    Its borders all ragged with moss;
Its beds tracts of weeds, and its blossoms run wild,
    As if ruin had driven across.

There stood the old pear—a pagoda of green—
    With fruitage like bells covered o'er;
The whole Summer sunshine, its dews and its scents,
    Mellowed in from the peel to the core.
And there stood the cherry-tree's rich coral gems,
    Where the cherry-thieves pecked might and main;
With the boy in the harvest moon, robbing the boughs,
    And the mastiff up-leaping in vain.

And the peach, with its rich, luscious, velvety globes,
    That sensitive child of the sun!
The red down cleft open to show the gold flesh;
    And the mounds where the cucumbers run.
The nectarine's smooth sheeny fruit by their side;
    The apricot's pin-speckled rust;
The damson's bright blue; the large, oval egg-plum!
    And the grape's silver, delicate dust.

Yes, the old fruitful garden-plot shone a bouquet,
    The richest and rarest of bloom!
When the jewel-eyed May came in youthful array
    And shed round her gladsome perfume.
In the hot Summer nights, the dull beetle began,
    With its bagpipe, to skim o'er the ground,
Sip the nectar of flowers and honey-dewed plants,
    The fire-fly lighting him round.

Then the glow-worm her green-and gold lanterns held forth
  Where the gooseberry sprawled by the wall;
And the fox-fire's pale silver shone out of the black;
  The lilac stretched wide like a pall.
And the bat—the winged mouse—left his beam in the barn,
  And wheeled in his pathway askance;
While the cricket its shrill, hollow violin scraped
  For the fairies to come to the dance.

When the sun, to draw water, his ladder let down,
  The garden expanded its breast;
And soon the bright pellets glanced rich on the rose,
  And danced on the hollyhock's crest.
The bumblebee's jacket was spangled with drops,
  As he tumbled inside the cupped flower,
And the butterfly's fans found their velvet wet through
  In the warm, balmy bliss of the shower.

The old crooked quince in a nook of the fence
  Its silver-gold product displayed;
And the currant hung out its red tassels of fruit
  Where the sunflower kindled the shade.
What wealth of rich health the syringa poured out
  When Spring shone again on the scene!
What world of sweet violets, blue, gold and white,
  Awoke in their tuftings of green!

The old garden spot has now vanished away;
  A dwelling stands forth in its place;
And a street, hard and stony, runs straight by the fence,
  Where the roses no longer I trace.
Those pictures of bygones! how lovely they look
  In the desert and glare of to-day!
They glow like the mirage with blossoms and streams
  That in Eden but flourish and play.

Since Leslie's paper was often published a number of days earlier than the date on its masthead, that date does not indicate that Melville remained in Gansevoort after 15 August, the departure date he gives in this letter (see Budd Leslie Gambee, Jr., *Frank Leslie and His Illustrated Newspaper, 1855–1860* [Ann Arbor: University of Michigan Press, 1964], p. 62). If Melville's sister Frances did append a message to this letter, it is now unlocated.

Gansevoort
Aug. 14

My Dear Cousin Kate
&
My Dear Fellow, Abraham:

Let me repeat to you my acknowledgments for your genial hospitality and great kindliness during my brief visit in Albany. I enjoyed it right well. And was glad to have seen Judge Hurlburt's
place and spent so agreeable an evening there.

I staid over about three hours or so at the Springs. I lunched at a
neat little restaurant I found there, and visited the hotels, presenting
no doubt a distinguished appearance in my duster, and finally took
up a commanding position on the piazza of the Grand Union, and
surveyed at my leisure the moving spectacle of fashion and — in
some instances — folly. A New York paper also of the day helped
to occupy the time.

I found Kate and Fanny and Frankie here — all well and warm in
welcome.

To-day is faultless weather, and I shall dedicate it to leisure and
the piazza.

To morrow I must break away — as I did from you — and start
for the mountains. Kate & Fanny send abundance of love. Accept as
much from me, and Helen, always

& sincerely Yours
H. Melville

P.S. — I go off visiting so seldom, that, really, I omit to do some
things I ought to do, and would take pleasure in doing: they, simply, do not occur to me at the time, but reproachfully molest me
afterwards in the omission. — Well, I did not call to pay my respects
to Miss Lansing and Miss Anna. But apologies are awkward, and
incredulity is but natural in some circumstances. Pray, Abraham, do
the fitting thing for me, and redeem me in the good opinion of the
ladies.
N.B. I will subject myself to any penance the ladies may be pleased
to assign.

Final P.S. — Having, at Fanny's request, left this letter open, so
that she might add something or enclose, I am tempted to say one

word more — namely: I have just been reading in a copy of Frank Leslie's Illustrated paper *"The Old Garden"* by Mr Street. How beautiful, and poetically true to nature it is! It is like a flower-and-fruit piece by some mellow old Fleming. —— There, I wont bore you any more. — H M:

ALS on a 27 × 21 cm sheet, folded in half, of white laid (graph-pattern) paper. Melville inscribed all four pages, in ink.

LOCATION: NYPL-GL.

PUBLICATION: Paltsits, pp. 50–51. Davis-Gilman 217.

TEXTUAL NOTES: surveyed] r *added* · occupy] oc *written over* en · penance] *blotted; marked by an x with dots in the interstices matching a similar mark within parentheses at the bottom of the page next to* penance · Fanny's] 's *added* · Illustrated] *second* l *added* · H M] *digraph*

TO CATHERINE GANSEVOORT LANSING
5 SEPTEMBER 1877 · NEW YORK

This letter, written from Melville's custom-house office, was in reply to Catherine Lansing's now unlocated 9 August 1877 letter and to two subsequent notes from her (also unlocated). It brings to a close the correspondence between Melville and his cousin concerning the set of Bell's Chaucer that she had commissioned him to procure for her husband, Abraham Lansing (see Melville's letters to her of 8 September 1876, 26 September 1876, and 12 October 1876, above). Evidently Melville had sent the set shortly after returning from his vacation (see his 14 August letter, just above). The reference to "Bessie" (i.e., his daughter Elizabeth) may be a slip for "Lizzie" or another name he used for his wife (though nowhere else does he use this shortened form of Elizabeth). For the Hartnetts, see also his 13 September 1876 letter to his cousin.

Jane & West Sts.
Sep. 5. '77.

Dear Cousin Kate:

Your note of the 2ᵈ acknowledging the receipt of the set of Chaucer; and also your note of the 3ᵈ enclosing the price of the set — Thank you for both of them.

You mention having spent a peaceful Sunday at Gansevoort, enjoying it much, with Abraham. I should have liked it well to have been of the company. I was so sorry that, purposing my main visit among the mountains, I was not able to devote more time to Gansevoort. Helen, Kate, Fanny, & Minnie must be having a pleasant time there together. —— Oh, I have to acknowledge the receipt of a note from you of Aug. 9 in responce to mine of a few days before. This note did not come to my hands until after my arrival home from the mountains, it, probably, arriving here the afternoon of the day I left, and was kept for me. — I have just looked over the note again. — So it appears that I used in my letter to you the expression *"people of leisure"*. If I did, it was a faulty expression — as applied in that case. I doubtless meant people the disposition of whose time is not subject to another. But it amused me — your disclaiming the thing, as if there was any merit in *not* being a person of leisure. Whoever is not in the possession of leisure can hardly be said to possess independence. They talk of the *dignity of work*. Bosh. True work is the *necessity* of poor humanity's earthly condition. The dignity is in leisure. Besides, 99 hundreths of all the *work* done in the world is either foolish and unnecessary, or harmful and wicked. But bless my heart! I am scribbling here at a pretty rate. I will stop at once; and promise never to do so again.

Bessie & the girls are doing well at the White Mountains, and will remain there yet for a time. Their absence makes it decidedly lonely often in the house. But I take my meals at the Hartnetts', who are all that one can wish as hostesses. There are some agreeable people there too whom I meet.

My kindest regards to Abraham. Tell him not to be rash now, and sit up all night reading Chaucer, and comparing his variorum editions &c.

Always affectionately
Yours
Cousin Herman.

— My kindest regards to Cousin Kate Hurlburt and the Judge, and family, when you see them. I enjoyed my visit to them very much — &, let me add — my entire visit at Albany. —

ALS on a 25.2 × 20.4 cm sheet, folded in half, of white laid paper with lines, embossed with the manufacturer's stamp of a shield surmounted by an arm wielding a sword. Melville inscribed all four pages, in ink.

LOCATION: NYPL-GL.

PUBLICATION: Paltsits, pp. 51–52. Davis-Gilman 218.

TEXTUAL NOTES: whose] *written over* whom • possession] *first* s *added* • True] *inserted above caret before* Work *(vestigial capital)*

1878

TO CATHERINE GANSEVOORT LANSING
26 JANUARY 1878 · NEW YORK

This letter acknowledges the receipt of the *Memorial of Henry Sanford Gansevoort*, edited by John C. Hoadley (Boston: Rand, Avery, 1875). The Melville copy is inscribed: "Mr & Mrs Herman Melville. with the love of Catherine Gansevoort Lansing. Albany N.Y. Dec. 1877." (HCL-M; Sealts 273). For Melville's earlier advice to his cousin about the frontispiece to this volume, see the letter he wrote between 9 and 23 August 1875, above. Although the title page of the book is dated 1875, in a preface dated 12 April 1882, which was added when a second printing of the memorial was issued, Catherine Lansing recalled that the book had not yet been bound at the time of her father's death on 4 January 1876. Since the book was not deposited for copyright, it is difficult to determine when it was actually completed. Whatever the book's actual publication date, Catherine Lansing first distributed it in January of 1878—as indicated by more than a dozen other letters like Melville's received during the last two weeks of that month and preserved with his.

The reopening of Stanwix Hall, to which Melville also alludes, was announced in front-page advertisements that ran in the January *Daily Argus* in Albany. They stated that "Stanwix Hall" had been "newly furnished throughout with all the modern improvements" and was available to guests at the rate of three dollars a day. Evidently Melville's suggestion in his 27 August 1876 letter for changing the name to the "Fort Stanwix Hotel" had not prevailed.

New York
Jan 26, '78.

Kate:

The box has arrived in good order. — The Volume in its finally completed state makes a truly beautiful memorial.

Though, of course, neither Lizzie nor I have as yet had opportunity and time to give the book a thorough and deliberate examination; yet, from glimpses here and there, added to previous acquaintance with portions of the sheets, I can not but again praise the taste which it evinces, and also the literary skill and good judgement of Mr Hoadley the editor.

Lizzie desires me to express her acknowledgments for her share of the gift, and will write you herself ere long.

We all congratulate you and Abraham upon the re-opening of Stanwix Hall.

We are all well, and write in affectionate rememberances to Fanny, yourself, and Abraham.

H. Melville

ALS on a 25.2 × 20.4 cm sheet, folded in half, of white laid paper with lines, embossed with the manufacturer's stamp of a shield surmounted by an arm wielding a sword. Melville inscribed the first and third pages, in ink. The letter was later pasted into a Gansevoort family album, grouped with other letters acknowledging the receipt of the *Memorial* volume from Catherine Lansing.

LOCATION: NYPL-GL.

PUBLICATION: (partial) *Log*, II, 766–67. Metcalf, pp. 253–54. Davis-Gilman 219.

TO JOHN C. HOADLEY
BEFORE 25 MAY 1878 · NEW YORK

Unlocated. A letter from Melville is cited in Frances Priscilla Melville's letter of 28 May 1878 to Catherine Lansing, in which she reports that "Last week Mr Hoadley had a short note from Herman, much to my relief, for it proved that he could again use his right hand. His left is improving" (NYPL-GL). It is not known what accident or illness had affected Melville's hands, but the affliction still persisted several weeks later, according to Frances's letter of 15 June 1878 to their cousin in Albany (see the entry just below). Davis-Gilman Unlocated 404.

TO FRANCES PRISCILLA MELVILLE
[13?] JUNE 1878 · NEW YORK

Unlocated. A letter from Melville is both cited and partially quoted in Frances Priscilla Melville's letter of 15 June 1878 to Catherine Lansing. Commenting on the recent impairment of Melville's hands (see the entry just above), she writes: "I heard from Herman yesterday, his left hand has not yet, he tells me, entirely recovered" (NYPL-GL). Since she received her brother's letter "yesterday," 14 June, it was probably written the day before. The passage that she quotes from Melville's letter concerns the death of Charles M. Thurston, a brother of Allan Melville's first wife. It is the only known passage from the letters Melville wrote his youngest sister. "Speaking of Mr Charles Thurston's sudden death," she writes, "he says, 'whose end by the way may hardly be thought unhappy — the manner of it I mean — since he died in summer and suddenly, and in the open air, and in a garden.'" Davis-Gilman 220.

TO CATHERINE GANSEVOORT LANSING
1 AUGUST 1878 · NEW YORK

Founded in 1870, the library established by James Lenox opened to the public in 1877 at Fifth Avenue between Seventieth and Seventy-first streets. It later combined with the Astor Library to form the nucleus of the New York Public Library. Catherine Lansing's letter requesting Melville's aid in presenting the Lenox Library with a copy of John Hoadley's *Memorial of Henry Sanford Gansevoort* is now unlocated. Catherine Lansing advised him that the book had been shipped in a 4 August letter (also now unlocated), and according to his promise, Melville delivered the volume on 6 August (see his letter of that date, below). Catherine Lansing inscribed the copy: "Presented to the 'Lenox Library'. New York City. by Mrs Abraham Lansing of Albany N.Y. July 1878." It was, in 1992, still in the general collection of the New York Public Library. For the "travellers," see LETTERS RECEIVED, p. 719.

104 E 26
Aug 1, '78

Dear Cousin Kate:

Of course — as I said when you broached the matter to me here — I should be very happy to be your agent in presenting to the Lenox Library a copy of Henry's Memorial.

Send it down by Adams Express, to be left and called for there, at their office in 23^d St. near 5th Ave. Advise me by mail at the time of sending, and it will be all right.

You refer to the travellers. They were to have left Boston — as Lizzie said in her note received Wednesday — yesterday for the mountains.

Copious showers we have been having here of late, but cooler weather.

Hoping you are well, and with kind regards to Abraham, Beleive me

Sincerely
Your Cousin

ALS, "Your Cousin", on a 22.7 × 17.7 cm sheet, folded in half, of white wove paper. Melville inscribed the first and third pages, in ink.

LOCATION: NYPL-GL.

PUBLICATION: Paltsits, p. 54. Davis-Gilman 221.

TEXTUAL NOTE: Ave.] *before* (over) *in bottom margin*

TO FRANCES PRISCILLA MELVILLE
BETWEEN 4 AND 9 AUGUST 1878 · NEW YORK

Unlocated. A letter from Melville is briefly cited by Frances Priscilla Melville in a 10 August 1878 letter to Catherine Lansing, which states that she had "Heard from Herman this week. He & Mr Thomas were at Tom's last Sunday" (NYPL-GL). In his wife and daughters' absence (see the letter just above), Melville apparently took Henry B. Thomas, fiancé of his younger daughter Frances (see the headnote to Melville's 12 August 1878 letter, below), out to visit his brother Thomas on Staten Island on Sunday, 4 August 1878. Since Melville went to stay with the Lansings from 9 to 11 August (see his 6 August letter, below), this letter to his youngest sister, then visiting the Hoadleys in Lawrence, Massachusetts, was probably written before his departure. Davis-Gilman Unlocated 405.

TO GEORGE HENRY MOORE
5 AUGUST 1878 · NEW YORK

Unlocated. A "brief note" to the superintendent of the Lenox Library is cited in Melville's 6 August 1878 letter to his cousin Catherine, just below.

TO CATHERINE GANSEVOORT LANSING
6 AUGUST 1878 · NEW YORK

Catherine Lansing's 4 August letter, now unlocated, had apparently advised Melville of the mailing of a copy of her brother's memorial biography for him to deposit at the Lenox Library (see the 1 August letter, above). Since Melville's Custom House post was now "up-town"—probably at Seventy-sixth Street and the East River—the library, on Fifth Avenue between Seventieth and Seventy-first streets, was on his way to work (see Stanton Garner, "Surviving the Gilded Age: Herman Melville in the Customs Service," *Essays in Arts and Sciences* 15 [June 1986], 9). George Henry Moore (1823–92), whom Melville knew at the library, had formerly been assistant librarian of the New-York Historical Society, before becoming librarian of the Lenox in 1849, and then in 1872 its superintendent and trustee.

104 E 26
Aug 6. '78

Dear Cousin Kate: I got yours of the 4th last night, and this morning on my way to my far up-town "District", I took the Memorial Volume to the Lenox Library, hoping to see there Mr Moore the librarian, whom I have met two or three times. Unfortunately he was not there; and the library it seems, is closed for the season. I got in, however, and left the Book with the janitor in perfect security, leaving a brief note for Mr Moore, in which I said I should take an early opportunity to call again & say something to him especially about the gift. — By the way, it is a beautiful copy; and upon my first opening the parcel in the janitor's prescence, he exclaimed admiringly at the binding.

About the invitation to stay over with you Saturday & Sunday next — thank you for your kindness. Yes, I will come with pleasure. I will leave here Friday night in the boat, & will probably be at 115 Wash. Ave. at breakfast time — if convenient to you.

With kind regards to Abraham

Sincerely
Your Cousin

ALS, "Your Cousin", on a 25.3 × 20.3 cm sheet, folded in half, of white laid paper with lines, embossed with the manufacturer's stamp of a shield surmounted by an arm wielding a sword. Melville inscribed the first, third, and fourth pages, in ink, and addressed the envelope "Mrs. Abraham Lansing | Albany | N.Y. | 115 *Washington Av.*"; it was postmarked in New York on 6 August.

LOCATION: NYPL-GL.

PUBLICATION: Paltsits, pp. 54–55. Davis-Gilman 222.

TEXTUAL NOTE: prescence] *miswritten* prescen

TO CATHERINE GANSEVOORT LANSING
12 AUGUST 1878 · NEW YORK

According to their daughter Eleanor Melville Thomas Metcalf (*Herman Melville: Cycle and Epicycle*, p. 251), the "gentleman by the name of Thomas," Henry Besson Thomas (1855–1935), fell in love with Melville's daughter Frances (Fanny) in 1877 when he saw her sitting on the railing of the Plaisted House piazza in the White Mountains in Jefferson Hill, New Hampshire. They were married three years later on 5 April 1880.

This letter mentioning Henry Thomas, but dated only 12 August, has been placed in 1878 from the evidence of the writing paper (the same as Melville used for his letter of 6 August 1878, just above) and from its reference to a just completed visit to Albany, no doubt the one agreed to in that letter.

New York
104 E. 26
Aug 12
P.M.

Dear Cousin Kate:

After two prodigious bumpers of coffee at the depot (from the effect of which I have hardly yet recovered) off we started for New

York where we arrived about ½ past 10. Upon unlocking the front door — two letters awaited me (thanks to the "letter-slip") one from Lizzie & one from a young gentleman by the name of Thomas. The latter dated his note from Jeffers Hill. Curious coincidence — Fanny is there. —

I enjoyed myself very much while with you — in fact, so much, that upon returning to this solitary house the lonliness is enhanced. I dont know that I shall visit you & Abraham again, if the eventual result is but an augmentation of the blues. — Howsomedever, every one manages to rub along; and so, Cousin Kate, with love to yourself and friendliest remembrances to him whom you only a thousandeth part appreciate

I remain
Your Cousin

ALS, "Your Cousin", on a 25.2 × 20.4 cm sheet, folded in half, of white laid paper with lines, embossed with the manufacturer's stamp of a shield surmounted by an arm wielding a sword. Melville inscribed the first, third, and fourth pages, in ink.

LOCATION: NYPL-GL.

PUBLICATION: Paltsits, p. 55. Davis-Gilman 223.

TO FRANCES PRISCILLA MELVILLE AND
HELEN MELVILLE GRIGGS
BEFORE 16 OCTOBER 1878 · NEW YORK

Unlocated. A letter to Melville's sisters Frances Priscilla Melville and Helen Melville Griggs, both then at Gansevoort, is listed among others received from various family members in a 16 October 1878 letter that Frances Priscilla wrote to Catherine Lansing: "We have had letters from Fannie, Lizzie, Tom Katie Lottie & Herman, within a day or two" (NYPL-GL). Davis-Gilman Unlocated 407.

TO CATHERINE GANSEVOORT LANSING
26 NOVEMBER 1878 · NEW YORK

Catherine Lansing's date of 1878 after Melville's "Nov. 26" is confirmed by this letter's references to: (1) " 'the young man' " Henry B. Thomas, recently engaged (April 1878) to Melville's daughter Frances; (2) Catherine Lansing's expected visit with the Melvilles, confirmed by her diary entry of 5 December 1878 (NYPL-GL); and (3) Elizabeth Shaw Melville's departure for a visit in Boston, confirmed by a 19 December 1878 letter from Melville's daughter Frances to Catherine Lansing

(NYPL-GL). Both Catherine Lansing's "note of yesterday" and the one from Melville's sister Frances Priscilla, visiting the Lansings in Albany, are now unlocated.

104 E. 26
Nov. 26

Dear Cousin Kate:

Your note of yesterday with Fanny's were received this A.M. And I write forthwith as to your kind invitation, regretting for myself, Bessie & Fanny, that we shall not be able to accept it, seeing that it is arranged already that we are to have a little Thanksgiving affair here, of which "the young man" will of course be the central figure

But we are well pleased to learn both from you and Aunt Fanny that next Monday you will be on your way hitherward, and that the next day we shall welcome you at 104. — 104 reminds me of your trunk. By all means let the Expressman bring it at once to the house.

My kind regards to Abraham, with hopes that he may soon be all right again

Best love to Fanny, who will, I know, overlook my not writing her in especial, seeing that this note is substantially addressed to you together.

Affectionately
Herman

Lizzie is in the midst of her preparations for tomorrow's departure for Boston; and so, I fancy, will hardly have time to write. She is not at hand just now, or would send love.

ALS on a 25.4 × 20.3 cm sheet, folded in half, of white wove paper. Melville inscribed the first and third pages, in ink. Catherine Lansing added the year "1878" in ink near Melville's partial date.

LOCATION: NYPL-GL.

PUBLICATION: Paltsits, pp. 56–57. Davis-Gilman 224.

TEXTUAL NOTES: overlook my] my *miswritten* by • writing her] her *miswritten* here • Lizzie . . . love.] *in the middle of the otherwise blank second page; placed here editorially*

1879

TO G. P. PUTNAM'S SONS
27 MARCH 1879 · NEW YORK

Melville must have written this letter at the office of G. P. Putnam's Sons at 182 Fifth Avenue in New York, since it is on the company letterhead. Beneath Melville's brief instruction to "dispose of cases 2 & 3" of *Clarel*, the following notation was made, presumably by a clerk:

Sent to Paper Mill   April 18 / 79
    108   in case 3 Books
    112   "   "   2 Books
    220 Sets
    110 Pounds of covers
    305   "   of Clarel

Perhaps with this wholesale destruction of his book still in mind, Melville later wrote in his 10 October 1884 letter to James Billson that *Clarel* was "a metrical affair, a pilgrimage or what not, of several thousand lines, eminently adapted for unpopularity." For a reproduction and further discussion of this 1879 letter, see the NN *Clarel*, pp. 638 and 659.

March 27 1879

Please dispose of cases 2 & 3 ("Clarel") containing two hundred and twenty four copies, on my account, to paper mill.

H. Melville

Original document not located. Text from Quaritch reproduction (in NN file). The one-page letter was inscribed on the publisher's stationery with the printed heading "G. P. PUTNAM'S SONS, | Publishers, Booksellers, and Importing Stationers, | 182 FIFTH AVENUE, (Near 23D ST.) | New York, . . . 187 ".

LOCATION: at present unknown. *Provenance*: Swann Galleries, sale 1400, 17 April 1986, lot 122 (with reproduction); Bernard Quaritch, catalogue 1066 (Winter 1986), item 116, and catalogue 1083 (February 1988), item 30 (with reproduction); Glen Horowitz, New York; 19th Century Shop, catalogue 20 (April 1991), in item 172.

PUBLICATION: "Collecting Melville et al.," *Melville Society Extracts* 66 (May 1986), 14 (with reproduction).

TEXTUAL NOTE: 187] *part of the printed letterhead (see above)*

TO FRANCES PRISCILLA MELVILLE
BEFORE 13 AUGUST 1879 · NEW YORK

Unlocated. A letter from Melville is cited in Frances Priscilla Melville's 13 August 1879 letter to Catherine Lansing, reporting: "Herman writes me that Lizzie & the girls are enjoying themselves very much at the 'Overlook' Catskill, & that he will soon join them there" (NYPL-GL). According to a 30 August 1879 letter Frances wrote to Abraham Lansing, Melville was supposed to leave for the "Overlook Mountain House" in Woodstock, New York, on 29 August (NYPL-GL). Davis-Gilman Unlocated 408.

TO ABRAHAM LANSING
17 NOVEMBER 1879 · NEW YORK

Catherine Lansing noted in her diary (NYPL-GL) on 15 November 1879 that an invitation (now unlocated) for Christmas dinner was sent to Melville and his family, including Henry Thomas. As with most of his correspondence with the Lansings, Melville's reply was prompt.

New York Nov 17, '79

My Dear Mr Lansing:

We are all very much obliged to you for your Christmas invitation, but upon consideration, hardly think we shall be able to accept it. The truth is Lizzie is not very robust, and the journey northward at midwinter — why, she rather dreads it. — However, we all wish you & Cousin Kate a Merry Christmas (in advance) wherever you or we may happen to be at the time.

With love to Cousin Kate Beleive me

Sincerely Yours
H. Melvill.

ALS on a 25.5 × 20.5 cm sheet, folded in half, of white wove paper. Melville inscribed the first page, in ink, and addressed the envelope "Abraham Lansing Esq. | Albany | New York. | 115 Wash. Ave."; it was postmarked in New York on 17 November.

LOCATION: NYPL-GL.

PUBLICATION: Paltsits, p. 58. Davis-Gilman 225.

1880

TO HARPER & BROTHERS
BEFORE 28 FEBRUARY 1880 · NEW YORK

Unlocated. The 28 February 1880 letter from Harper & Brothers enclosing Melville's account states that it was sent at Melville's request (see LETTERS RECEIVED, p. 722). Although Melville may have made the request in person, most likely he did so by letter.

TO CATHERINE GANSEVOORT LANSING
15 APRIL 1880 · NEW YORK

This letter of condolence concerns John Thomas Lansing (1833–80), Abraham Lansing's oldest brother. Most of his adult life had been spent in foreign business and later as a consul in Peru, with the result that he spoke English with an accent. He died on 14 April 1880; Catherine Lansing's note announcing his death is now unlocated.

The reason Melville found it "hardly possible" to attend the funeral was his strict schedule as a customs officer. The "occasion of the 5th" on which he was not even entirely free was the wedding of his daughter Frances to Henry B. Thomas.

April 15, '80
104 E. 26

My Dear Cousin Kate:

Your note announcing the decease of Mr John Lansing is just received. — How sudden the event. Express to Abraham the true sympathies of all of us.

—— Though I met M^r. John Lansing but two or three times, yet each time I was most agreeably impressed with his inteligence and social disposition. —

I am sorry that my being at the funeral is hardly possible. Even on the occasion of the 5th I was not at perfect liberty for the day.

Lizzie & the girls and myself unite in love to Abraham and you.

Always sincerely
Herman

ALS on a 22.7 × 17.2 cm sheet, folded in half, of white wove paper with lines. Melville inscribed the first and third pages, in ink. Catherine Lansing later noted in ink at the top of the first page "Ack through | Cousin Lizzie | April 22. 1880."

LOCATION: NYPL-GL.

PUBLICATION: Paltsits, p. 59. Davis-Gilman 226.

TEXTUAL NOTES: April 15, '80] *added slantwise at the top of the page with* A *written over* a · you] *after canceled* yourself

TO ABRAHAM LANSING
8 DECEMBER 1880 · NEW YORK

Named after the fort that Dutch traders, soldiers, and farmers established in the Hudson river valley in 1624, the Fort Orange Club in Albany was founded in 1880 by descendants of the valley's Dutch settlers. One of the founding members of the club, which was headquartered at 110 Washington Avenue, was Abraham Lansing, who lived directly across the street in the Gansevoort home at 115 Washington Avenue. Lansing's "polite invitation" is now unlocated.

> 104 E 26
> Dec. 8, '80

Dear Mr Lansing:

Many thanks for your polite invitation to the Reception at the Fort Orange Club — thanks in behalf of the family, I mean, myself included. But Lizzie is in Boston & Bessie is keeping house, and I am an — old fogy; so none of us can comply, much as we regret it.

With kind remembrances to Kate — — and, by the way, acknowledgments for the paper, — I am, very truly yours

H. Melville

ALS on a 12.6 × 20.4 cm part-sheet (cut along the left edge) of white wove paper with lines, embossed with the manufacturer's wave-like stamp bearing the name "OCEAN MILLS". Melville inscribed only one side of the leaf, in ink.

LOCATION: NYPL-GL.

PUBLICATION: Paltsits, p. 59. Davis-Gilman 227.

TEXTUAL NOTE: Reception at] at *written over* by

1881

TO CATHERINE MELVILLE HOADLEY
28 DECEMBER 1881 · NEW YORK

This letter from Melville to his sister Catherine Hoadley is the second of only three letters now located that he wrote her (see his letters of 20 January 1845 and 12 April

104 E 26th

3d day after Xmas

1881

My dear Kate:

Dont be alarmed by
more beautiful flourishes
of mine; I have been
recently improving my
penmanship by lessons

To Catherine Melville Hoadley, 28 December 1881, p. 1. Courtesy of the Rare Books and Manuscripts Division, The New York Public Library, Astor, Lenox and Tilden Foundations (Gansevoort-Lansing Collection).

1882). According to Stanton Garner, the penmanship exercises jokingly referred to in this one were a serious consideration for the promotion examinations in the Custom House (see "Melville in the Customhouse, 1881–1882," *Melville Society Extracts* 35 [September 1978], 14).

104 E 26th

3^d day after Xmas

1881

My Dear Kate:

Dont be alarmed by these beautiful flourishes of mine; I have been recently improving my penmanship by lessons from a High Dutch professor who teaches all the stylish flourishes imaginable. —

But my object in dropping you this line is to thank you, My Dear Kate, for your little vase. It is now on my mantle, and contributes much to the embellishment thereof, and I value it as your gift.

We are all as usuel — that is to say, jolly; and trusting that you too are in the same happy case, — with kind regards to John & love to the girls, Beleive me

Affectionately

Herman

ALS on a 22.8 × 17.8 cm sheet, folded in half, of white laid paper, watermarked with the name "OLD BERKSHIRE MILLS". Melville inscribed the first, third, and fourth pages, in ink.

LOCATION: NYPL-GL.

PUBLICATION: Paltsits, p. 60. Davis-Gilman 228 (with partial reproduction).

1882

TO CATHERINE MELVILLE HOADLEY
12 APRIL 1882 · NEW YORK

No longer showing off his "penmanship" (see the letter just above), this letter to Melville's sister Catherine concerns various family matters. Neither of the letters mentioned in it has been located: the first from his niece, Catherine Hoadley's oldest daughter, Maria (Minnie) Gansevoort Hoadley (who later married William H. Mackintosh of Boston in 1887); and the second from his sisters Helen Griggs and Frances Priscilla Melville, both presumably at Gansevoort.

The "babby" referred to in this letter was Melville's first grandchild, Eleanor Melville Thomas, born 24 February 1882 in Orange, New Jersey. In April 1913 she married Henry K. Metcalf; the poet Paul Metcalf (b. 1917) is their son. She became the gracious unofficial family representative to Melville scholars, beginning with Raymond Weaver, who acknowledged her generosity and "keen sympathy" in the 1 October 1921 preface to his biography *Herman Melville: Mariner and Mystic*. In 1948 she published Melville's *Journal of a Visit to London and the Continent* (Cambridge: Harvard University Press) and in 1953 *Herman Melville: Cycle and Epicycle* (Cambridge: Harvard University Press). She died in 1964 and is buried, with her husband, near Herman and Elizabeth Melville in Woodlawn Cemetery, in the Bronx. See also *Enter Isabel: The Herman Melville Correspondence of Clare Spark and Paul Metcalf,* ed. Paul Metcalf (Albuquerque: University of New Mexico Press, 1991).

The "Lieutenant," who accompanied Melville's daughter Elizabeth (Bessie) to the zoo and to meet the impresario P. T. Barnum, was Catherine Hoadley's sixteen-year-old son, Francis (Frankie).

104 E. 26
April 12 '82

Dear Kate:

Just received a note from Minnie, — for the which, pray, give her my affectionate acknowledgments — Wherein, among other interesting matters, she says — what we previously had heard distant rumors of — or did we read it under the head of *"Personal"* in the newspaper? — I say, she says that you and John propose a visit to these parts some time next week. Well: I write at once to say that, altho', I suppose, you will spend some days with Tom, you must not fail — you & John — to spend a portion of the time with us. We should be most happy to greet you. Lizzie — who at present is at Orange helping Fanny to break in the "babby" to going without its nurse — — would cheerfully unite with me in this invitation, were she here. Indeed, she was talking with me about making the invitation some days ago.

Lizzie & I recd letters from Helen & Fanny (jointly to & from) which I acknowledged by paper; & will ere long be happy to reciprocate by letter. With love to them and yourself & all, I remain — *No, I don't,* for I forgot to say we had a pleasant visit from the Lieutenant, who went with Bessie to the Zoo & shook hands with Mr Barnum. — How he has grown! Now then, I *remain* — at 104 E. 26 St. as usual, and am

Affectionately
Herman.

ALS on a 22.7 × 17.8 cm sheet, folded in half, of white laid paper, partially watermarked with the name "OLD BERKSHIRE MILLS". Melville inscribed the first, third, and fourth pages, in ink.

LOCATION: NYPL-GL.

PUBLICATION: Paltsits, pp. 60–61. Davis-Gilman 229.

TEXTUAL NOTE: previously had] had *inserted above caret*

TO HELEN MELVILLE GRIGGS AND
FRANCES PRISCILLA MELVILLE
AFTER 12 APRIL 1882 · NEW YORK

Unlocated. In his 12 April 1882 letter, just above, Melville wrote that he replied to a letter from his sisters Helen and Frances by sending them a paper and intended "ere long" to "reciprocate by letter." Presumably he did so before the [26?] August letter cited in the entry just below. Davis-Gilman Unlocated 409.

TO HELEN MELVILLE GRIGGS AND
FRANCES PRISCILLA MELVILLE
[26?] AUGUST 1882 · NEW YORK

Unlocated. A letter from Melville is cited in a joint letter of 28 August 1882 from Melville's sisters Helen and Frances in Gansevoort to their cousin Catherine Gansevoort Lansing in Albany, reporting: "Helen has just brought the mail, letters from Tom, Lottie & Herman, with *Albany paper* from K. G. L. Herman writes, that he hopes to get away for a weeks vacation soon, to join Lizzie at the Overlook. — " (NYPL-GL). Elizabeth Melville was staying at the Overlook Mountain House in Woodstock, New York, where the Melvilles had also summered in 1879. Davis-Gilman Unlocated 410.

TO ELIZABETH SHAW MELVILLE
BEFORE 8 SEPTEMBER 1882 · NEW YORK

Unlocated. In an 8 September 1882 letter written from the Overlook Mountain House in Woodstock, New York, Elizabeth Melville explained to Catherine Lansing why she had not spent more time with some friends of Catherine who were also staying at the Overlook: "I did not see as much of them as I should had I not gone down to New York for a few days. Herman sent me word that he was not well. — He had one of the attacks of 'crick in the back' " (NYPL-GL).

TO THE FOUNDERS OF THE AUTHORS CLUB
[OCTOBER?] 1882 · NEW YORK

Two unlocated letters. Both letters, the first accepting and the second declining an invitation from the founding committee of the Authors Club in New York, are cited in Charles De Kay's unpublished reminiscences of the club: "Rather to my surprise Herman Melville the elusive accepted the original invitation, but as he soon wrote, he had become too much of a hermit, saying his nerves could no longer stand large gatherings and begged to rescind his acceptance" (*Log*, II, 781). The club was formed at the end of 1882 and limited to one hundred and fifty members; many of those who joined, including G. W. Curtis, Richard H. Stoddard, Julian Hawthorne, and Edmund C. Stedman, would have been known to Melville (see George Parsons Lathrop, "The Literary Movement of New York," *Harper's New Monthly Magazine* 73 [November 1886], 830–31).

TO UNKNOWN
13 NOVEMBER 1882 · ALBANY

Unlocated. The only known evidence for a letter of this date is a fragment of manuscript bearing the dateline "13 November 1882 | Albany" inscribed by Melville, in ink (NYPL-GL). Measuring roughly 12.5 × 4.8 cm, the fragment was cut from the upper right corner of the recto of a leaf of white wove paper. The verso of the fragment is covered with ink offset spots, suggesting that the letter had at least two leaves, with writing, in ink, on at least the first and third pages.

1883

TO JULIAN HAWTHORNE
10 AUGUST 1883 · NEW YORK

In the interim between Julian Hawthorne's childhood acquaintance with Melville (see Melville's [9?] February 1852 letter to him at the age of five), he had gone on to pursue a literary career of his own, publishing by 1883 several works including two popular novels, *Bressant* (1873) and *Garth* (1877). His letter to Melville in which he probably asked about material for his book *Nathaniel Hawthorne and His Wife* (2 vols., Boston: Osgood, 1884) is now unlocated. He later remembered his subsequent visit with Melville as one in which he inquired for Hawthorne's letters to Melville but was told that they had been long since destroyed (see "When Herman Melville was 'Mr. Omoo'," *Literary Digest International Book Review* 4 [August 1926], 562). He also later described the visit in an essay entitled "Herman Melville and His Dog" (*Dearborn Independent* 27 [24 September 1927], 26): "During the incoherent talk between us on that occasion he let fall several hints as to his interpretation of the source of Hawthorne's insight into the human soul. It was a sad interview; he seemed partly to shrink from the idea that obsessed him, and partly to reach out for companionship in the dark region into which his mind was sinking. I was writing a biography of my father and my mother at that time, and had applied to him for any letters that Hawthorne might have written to him in reply to several of his own during the 1850's. But he said, with agitation, that he had kept nothing; if any such letters had existed, he had scrupulously destroyed them." For other recollections of Melville by Julian Hawthorne, see *Nathaniel Hawthorne and His Wife* (cited above); "Hawthorne at Lenox," *Booklover's Weekly* 10 (30 December 1901), 225–31; and *Hawthorne and His Circle* (New York: Harper, 1903). As Harrison Hayford pointed out in his dissertation (Yale, 1945), these accounts are contradictory and often unreliable.

Dear Mr. Hawthorne:

I am sorry that circumstances have prevented my answering your note earlier. — It gave me pleasure to receive it, and this for reasons you can readily imagine.

As to the information you seek — little enough, I think, it will prove, at least for the purpose you name — it can be more conveniently conveyed personally than by note. So if you will be kind enough to come & see me, as you propose, I shall be happy to greet you.

My wife & daughter being absent in the country, for the present I am alone at the house 104 E. 26 St.

I am obliged to be away good part of the day, nor, during these summer nights am I much at home except when in bed. — That I may be sure to be in when you call, let me name day & hour — Wednesday next the 15th about 7½ P.M. Should this be inconvenient for you, name your own time — so it be in the evening.

Very Truly Yours

H. Melville

Aug. 10, 83

Mr. Julian Hawthorne

Original document not located. Text from photocopy (in Davis-Gilman file). Amy Puett checked the Davis-Gilman text against the ALS (3 pp.), then in the collection of Roger Barrett of Winnetka, Illinois. Her 12 February 1970 report (in NN file) noted no discrepancies except to correct their description of the placement of the last line (see the textual note), resulting in its inclusion in the NN text.

LOCATION: at present unknown. *Provenance*: Charles Hamilton Autographs, 11 December 1953; Scribner's Book Store, December 1953; Carnegie Bookshop; Roger Barrett; traded to H. Bradley Martin for a Paul Klee painting, but not included in the H. Bradley Martin sale at Sotheby's on 30–31 January 1990.

PUBLICATION: Davis-Gilman 230.

TEXTUAL NOTE: Mr. Julian Hawthorne] *on the otherwise blank second page; placed here editorially*

TO HELEN MELVILLE GRIGGS AND
FRANCES PRISCILLA MELVILLE
BEFORE 14 SEPTEMBER 1883 · RICHFIELD SPRINGS

Unlocated. According to Melville's 10 August 1883 letter to Julian Hawthorne, above, his wife and unmarried daughter were "absent in the country." A letter to his sisters, cited in Helen and Frances's 14 September 1883 letter from Gansevoort to Catherine Lansing in Albany, reveals that the country spot was Richfield Springs, New York, where Melville later joined them: "We are expecting Herman to-morrow, coming to spend Sunday with us, on his way home from Richfield Springs. He writes that he has enjoyed the beauty of the country all about exceedingly, has passed his vacation very pleasantly. Lizzie & Bessie are to stay on, so their coming to Gansevoort will be later" (NYPL-GL). Davis-Gilman Unlocated 411.

1884

TO JAMES BILLSON
10 OCTOBER 1884 · NEW YORK

Charles James Billson (1858–1932) was just three years out of Oxford when he began corresponding with Melville. A student of the classics, in which he had taken honors (later translating the *Aeneid* [1906] and Pindar [1931]), he became a solicitor in his father's firm in Leicester, where for many years he also taught classes in Latin and Greek at the Working Men's College. His interest in Melville's books was probably first spurred by J. W. Barrs, also of Leicester, who had been introduced to them by the poet James Thomson (1834–82). For Barrs's 13 January 1890 letter to Melville, see LETTERS RECEIVED, pp. 759–62, and for more on Thomson, see the headnote to Melville's 1 December 1884 letter to Billson.

In his initial letter of 21 August 1884 to Melville (the only one of his letters in their correspondence now located), Billson thanked Melville for the "immense deal of good" he had received from reading *Typee, Omoo, Mardi, Redburn, Moby-Dick, Pierre, Israel Potter, The Piazza Tales*, and *The Confidence-Man*, regretting only that Melville's books were so hard to find (see LETTERS RECEIVED, pp. 724–25). Billson later copied this reply and the eight subsequent letters he is known to have received from Melville on his own stationery (with the printed heading "98. Regent Road, Leicester.") for Melville's daughter Elizabeth. The copies, which contain various inaccuracies, are now in the Melville Collection of the Houghton Library, Harvard University; for a reproduction of part of Melville's original letter, see the NN *Clarel*, p. 541. For a listing of Billson and Melville's known correspondence, see the "Calendar of Melville's Correspondence," pp. 861–88 below.

104 E. 26th St. New York
Oct 10, '84

My Dear Sir: After considerable delay — on this side, I suppose — your note of Aug. 21 reached me but the other day. — I can
not but thank you for the kind expressions in it, and really wish that
the books you have so patiently disinterred better merited what you
say of them. — You ask me to give you the names of any *other*
books of mine, with the names of the publishers. The following occur to me: —

"White Jacket" published in London by Bentley.

"Battle Pieces," in verse, published in New York by Harper &
Brothers.

"Clarel", published by George P. Putnam's Sons, New
York — a metrical affair, a pilgrimage or what not, of several thousand lines, eminently adapted for unpopularity. — The notification
to you here is ambidexter, as it were: it may intimidate or allure.

Again thanking you for your friendly note, and with best wishes
to yourself and your circle, I am

Very truly yours
Herman Melville

ALS on a 22.8 × 17.8 cm sheet, folded in half, of white laid paper, partially watermarked
with the name "OLD BERKSHIRE MILLS". Melville inscribed the first and third pages, in ink.
Billson numbered the letter at the top of the first page "(1)" in ink.

LOCATION: at present unknown. *Provenance*: C. A. Stonehill, Ltd., catalogue 137 (1938), in
item 91 (with reproduction); Frank J. Hogan sale, Parke-Bernet Galleries, 23–24 January 1945,
in lot 438; H. Bradley Martin sale, Sotheby's, New York, sale 5971, 30–31 January 1990, in
lot 2170A; 19th Century Shop, catalogue 17 (September 1990), item 152.

PUBLICATION: *The Nation and the Athenæum* 29 (13 August 1921), 712. Davis-Gilman 231.

TEXTUAL NOTES: London by] by *after canceled* By • in verse,] *written above and circled with a line
attached to a caret*

TO JAMES BILLSON
1 DECEMBER 1884 · NEW YORK

In this letter Melville acknowledges Billson's 28 October letter (a now unlocated
reply to Melville's previous 10 October letter) and receipt of a "volume of poems":
James Thomson's *Vane's Story, Weddah and Om-el-Bonain, and Other Poems* (London:
Reeves & Turner, 1881; Sealts 521, now unlocated). It included the autobiographi-

cal poem "Vane's Story" and was the first of five volumes of Thomson's works that Billson eventually sent Melville—whose Thomson collection was also augmented by two other British admirers of Melville: J. W. Barrs (see Melville's 2 April 1886 letter to Billson mentioning this gift) and H. S. Salt (see Melville's 25 February 1890 letter acknowledging Salt's biography of Thomson). These gifts were in part prompted by the fact that all of these men directly or indirectly owed their knowledge of Melville to Thomson. In a 21 August 1935 letter to Willard Thorp, Billson wrote, "Thomson was a great friend of Mr Barrs & talked to us abundantly & consequently through this talk we heard about Melville" (The Newberry Library). For a brief account of these young men and their circle, see Hershel Parker in the Historical Note to the NN *Moby-Dick*, pp. 737–40; see also H. S. Salt, *Company I Have Kept* (London: Allen & Unwin, 1930), pp. 108–9; Bertram Dobell, *The Laureate of Pessimism* (London: Dobell, 1910), pp. 48–49; Stephen Winsten, *Salt and His Circle* (London: Hutchinson, 1951), pp. 82–83 and *passim*; and George Hendrick, *Henry Salt* (Urbana: University of Illinois Press, 1977), pp. 163–64 and *passim*.

Although Melville had no photograph to send Billson at this time, he did eventually send one a year later (see his 20 December 1885 letter, below).

New York
Dec 1st '84

Dear Sir:

I thank you for yours of Oct. 28th, and its kindly expressions. I would have acknowledged it ere now but for reasons which it suffices to say — since you will beleive it — are adequate.

I owe you sincere thanks also for the volume of poems you were so good as to mail me. The "Weddah and Om-el-Bonain" gave me more pleasure than anything of modern poetry that I have seen in a long while. The fable and the verse are alike supremely beautiful. It is exactly that kind of a *gem* which some of Keats' pieces are; and what can one say more? — You should be happy to think that you personally knew the author of such a poem. —

You say something about my photograph. I should be happy to oblige you, but really, there is none that at present I can lay hold of. However, should I have one taken again, I will take pleasure in causing one to be mailed to you. —

With much respect and kindly wishes, I am

Very Truly Yours
H. Melville

James Billson Esq.

ALS on a 22.8 × 17.8 cm sheet, folded in half, of white laid paper, partially watermarked with the name "OLD BERKSHIRE MILLS". Melville inscribed the first, third, and fourth pages, in ink. Billson numbered the letter at the top of the first page "(II)" in ink.

LOCATION: at present unknown. *Provenance*: C. A. Stonehill, Ltd., catalogue 137 (1938), in item 91; Frank J. Hogan sale, Parke-Bernet Galleries, 23–24 January 1945, in lot 438; H. Bradley Martin sale, Sotheby's, New York, sale 5971, 30–31 January 1990, in lot 2170A; 19th Century Shop, Occasional List 24 (1991), and catalogue 26 (October 1992), item 126.

PUBLICATION: *The Nation and the Athenæum* 29 (13 August 1921), 712. Davis-Gilman 232.

TEXTUAL NOTES: modern] *after canceled* a · James Billson Esq.] *on the otherwise blank second page; placed here editorially*

1885

TO JAMES BILLSON
22 JANUARY 1885 · NEW YORK

The copy of James Thomson's *The City of Dreadful Night, and Other Poems* (London: Reeves & Turner, 1880; Sealts 517 and Bercaw 704) that Melville acknowledges in this letter is now in the Melville Collection of the Houghton Library of Harvard University. Among the other poems included in this volume is the light-hearted love poem "Sunday up the River"—standing in sharp contrast, as Melville points out, to the pessimism of the title poem of the book, "The City of Dreadful Night," which became Thomson's best-known piece.

Billson's "last note" (probably a reply to Melville's 1 December 1884 letter) is now unlocated. His other "former note" in which Billson regretted not being able to unearth *Clarel* probably refers to Billson's unlocated one of 28 October 1884 (see LETTERS RECEIVED, p. 725). The copy of *Clarel* (now unlocated) enclosed with this letter was not the "sole presentation-copy" of the book; the best known one contains Melville's inscription (dated 6 June 1876) to his wife: "This copy is specially presented to my wife, without whose assistance in manifold ways I hardly know how I could have got the book (under the circumstances) into shape, and finally through the press" (HCL-M; see the NN *Clarel*, pp. 864–66, with a reproduction). Strangely, however, there is no record of a copy having been presented to either Catherine Lansing or John Hoadley (Hoadley's annotated copy bears no presentation inscription; see the NN *Clarel*, pp. 662–65).

104 East 26th St.
N.Y.

Dear Sir:

I am grateful for the last volume you kindly sent me, received yesterday. — "*Sunday up the River*," contrasting with the "*City of Dreadful Night*", is like a Cuban humming-bird, beautiful in faery

tints, flying against the tropic thunder-cloud. Your friend was a
sterling poet, if ever one sang. As to his pessimism, altho' neither
pessimist nor optomist myself, nevertheless I relish it in the verse if
for nothing else than as a counterpoise to the exorbitant hopefulness,
juvenile and shallow, that makes such a bluster in these days — at
least, in some quarters.

——— In a former note you mentioned that altho' you had un-
earthed several of my buried books, yet there was one
— "Clarel" — that your spade had not succeeded in getting at.
Fearing that you never will get at it by yourself, I have disinterred a
copy for you of which I ask your acceptance and mail it with this
note.

It is the sole presentation-copy of the issue.

Repeating my thanks for both the rare volumes you have been
good enough to send me, and thanking you also for your last note, I
am

Very Truly Yours
Herman Melville

M^r. James Billson
Jan. 22^d '85.

ALS on a 22.8 × 17.8 cm sheet, folded in half, of white laid paper, partially watermarked
with the name "OLD BERKSHIRE MILLS". Melville inscribed the first three pages, in ink. Billson
numbered the letter at the top of the first page "(3)" in ink and also noted "*recved 1885*".

LOCATION: at present unknown. *Provenance*: C. A. Stonehill, Ltd., catalogue 137 (1938), in
item 91; Frank J. Hogan sale, Parke-Bernet Galleries, 23–24 January 1945, in lot 438; H. Bradley Martin sale, Sotheby's, New York, sale 5971, 30–31 January 1990, in lot 2170A; 19th
Century Shop in partnership with other book dealers.

PUBLICATION: *The Nation and the Athenæum* 29 (13 August 1921), 712. Davis-Gilman 233.

TEXTUAL NOTES: faery] *possibly* fairy • sterling] ter *blotted* • spade] s *rewritten* • Jan. 22^d '85.]
written at the bottom of the page; placed here editorially

TO LAURA M. WACHSCHLAGER
12 JULY 1885 · NEW YORK

Clearly Melville's reply to a now unlocated piece of fan mail, this letter to Laura M.
Wachschlager, who remains unidentified, recommends the works of the British author W. Clark Russell, with whom Melville later corresponded (see what may be

the draft of his first letter to Russell, written between 7 April and 21 July 1886, below).

New York
July 12, '85

Miss Laura M. Wachschlager:

You tell me you like my sea-tales. I am glad to know it.

But have you read something yet better — the sea-tales of *W. Clark Russell*, the author of the *"Wreck of the Grosvenor"*? Since you like sea-tales, read these by all means.

Herman Melville

ALS on a 22.8 × 17.9 cm sheet, folded in half, of white laid paper with lines, watermarked with the name "OLD BERKSHIRE MILLS". Melville inscribed the first page, in ink.

LOCATION: Betsy Beinecke Shirley Collection of American Children's Literature, Beinecke Library, Yale University. *Provenance*: Rev. Cornelius Greenway sale, Parke-Bernet Galleries, sale 3103, 29 October 1970, lot 182 (with reproduction); H. Bradley Martin sale, Sotheby's, New York, sale 5971, 30–31 January 1990, lot 2171; Justin Schiller, Ltd.

PUBLICATION: Lynn Horth, "Letters Lost / Letters Found: A Progress Report on Melville's *Correspondence*," *Melville Society Extracts* 81 (May 1990), 1–8 (with reproduction on p. 2).

TEXTUAL NOTES: like my] l *written over word-start* · like sea-tales] sea *rewritten*

TO ABRAHAM LANSING
[29?] JULY 1885 · NEW YORK

Unlocated. Melville's youngest sister, Frances Priscilla (Fanny) Melville, died at their sister Helen Griggs's home in Longwood, Massachusetts, on 9 July 1885 at the age of fifty-seven. Abraham Lansing, as the executor of Fanny's estate, wrote Melville on 27 July asking for permission to probate her will (see LETTERS RECEIVED, p. 726). Presumably Melville responded promptly, as he did after receiving Abraham Lansing's letter of 19 August enclosing the will (see the letter just below).

TO ABRAHAM LANSING
21 AUGUST 1885 · NEW YORK

Although he did not record writing to Melville in his letterbook, Abraham Lansing evidently sent Melville a copy of his sister Frances Priscilla Melville's will on 19 August 1885. This formal letter is Melville's reply. For the initial settlement of Melville's legacy from her, see the entry for his unlocated letter of 12 October 1886 to Abraham Lansing.

New York

Aug. 21ˢᵗ '85

My Dear Mr. Lansing

I received yours of the 19ᵗʰ yesterday, inclosing the will and the "waiver"; and herewith you have the latter duly signed and acknowledged.

Yours Truly

H. Melville

ALS on a 12 × 19.8 cm part-sheet (torn along the left edge) of white laid paper with lines, embossed with the manufacturer's stamp of a three-domed capitol above the name "CONGRESS". Melville inscribed only one side of the leaf, in ink.

LOCATION: NYPL-GL.

PUBLICATION: Paltsits, p. 61. Davis-Gilman 234.

TEXTUAL NOTE: acknowledged] *miswritten* acknowleged

TO JAMES BILLSON
5 SEPTEMBER 1885 · NEW YORK

As this letter acknowledges, James Billson continued to send Melville items to read. His own article, "James Thomson: Poet, Essayist, and Critic," appeared in the *Liverpool Daily Post* on 10 February 1885. The second article was probably an unsigned one that appeared in the London *Daily Telegraph* on 16 January 1885, mentioning the "lovely imaginations" of *Typee* and *Omoo*. (Since Billson's next letter, of 7 October 1885, like his earlier letter of 18 February acknowledged here, is unlocated, his answer—if he made one—to Melville's query about the article's authorship is lost.)

The final "Piece" cited in this letter was Robert Buchanan's poem "Socrates in Camden, with a Look Round (Written after First Meeting the American Poet, Walt Whitman, at Camden, New Jersey)." It appeared in the *Academy* on 15 August 1885 (pp. 102–3). The "incidental allusion" to Melville in it praised him as the "sea-compelling man, | Before whose wand Leviathan | Rose hoary white upon the Deep, | With awful sounds that stirred its sleep"; it also complained that Melville "Sits all forgotten or ignored, | While haberdashers are adored!" In a footnote Buchanan added that in New York "No one seemed to know anything of the one great imaginative writer fit to stand shoulder to shoulder with Whitman on that continent." (For a rebuttal of Buchanan's claim, see Sealts, *Early Lives*, pp. 23–24, and for an indication of Melville's interest in Whitman, see Edmund C. Stedman's 1 February 1888 letter in LETTERS RECEIVED, pp. 740–41.)

New York
Sept. 5, '85

Dear Sir:

I have to thank you for two papers received some months ago, one containing an article by your hand on the poet Thomson, the other referring to the South Sea Islands (and was this too written by yourself?) both interesting to me: the first because my interest in the author of The "City of Dreadful Night" was measurably gratified by it.

Moreover, I must thank you for your note of Feb. 18th Beleive me, its friendly proffer of good offices, should occasion occur, this I was, and remain, grateful for.

But yet further to bring up arrears, my acknowledgments are due for a copy of "The Academy" received the other day containing a poem by Robert Buchanan — "Socrates in Camden". For more than one reason, this Piece could not but give me pleasure. Aside from its poetic quality, there is implyed in it the fact, that the writer has intuitively penetrated beneath the surface of certain matters here. It is the insight of genius and the fresh mind. The tribute to Walt Whitman has the ring of strong sincerity. As to the incidental allusion to my humble self, it is overpraise, to be sure; but I can't help that, tho' I am alive to the spirit that dictated it.

But a letter on almost any theme, is but an inadequate vehicle, so I will say no more.

With good wishes for you

Very Truly
Herman Melville

M[r] James Billson

ALS on a 22.8 × 17.9 cm sheet, folded in half, of white wove paper. Melville inscribed the first, third, and fourth pages, in ink. Billson numbered the letter at the top of the first page "(4)" in ink.

LOCATION: at present unknown. *Provenance*: C. A. Stonehill, Ltd., catalogue 137 (1938), in item 91; Frank J. Hogan sale, Parke-Bernet Galleries, 23–24 January 1945, in lot 438; H. Bradley Martin sale, Sotheby's, New York, sale 5971, 30–31 January 1990, in lot 2170A; 19th Century Shop in partnership with other book dealers.

PUBLICATION: *The Nation and the Athenæum* 29 (13 August 1921), 712. Davis-Gilman 235.

TEXTUAL NOTES: any] *rewritten* • for you] for *written over* to

TO ELLEN MARETT GIFFORD
5 OCTOBER 1885 · NEW YORK

Ellen Marett Gifford (d. 1889), the daughter of Philip Marett and Martha Bird Knapp Marett (1796–1878), was a niece of Lemuel Shaw through his first wife, Elizabeth Knapp Shaw, and a first cousin of Elizabeth Melville. She was a semi-invalid most of her life. Her father was president of the New England Bank until 1847, when he resigned under scandalous circumstances (*Log*, I, 245). During the Melvilles' early married years in New York, the Maretts lived in Brooklyn, and both then and after her marriage to Arthur N. Gifford, a broker on the New York Exchange, Ellen and the Melvilles seem to have maintained a close relationship. As his familiar tone intimates, Melville wrote her many letters, which were returned to him by her lawyer after her death, and with the exception of this letter and a 6 November 1888 letter (below) are now unlocated (*Log*, I, xxvi; see also the entry for the unlocated letter of introduction he wrote to her in December 1870 on behalf of his cousin Henry Gansevoort). Both of Melville's letters suggest that he shared his writing with her. The "little rhyme of his about a Kitten" mentioned in this letter probably refers to his unpublished poem "Montaigne and His Kitten" (in *Collected Poems*, ed. Howard P. Vincent [Chicago: Hendricks House, 1947], pp. 381–82, and in the NN volume *BILLY BUDD, SAILOR and Other Late Manuscripts*).

The photograph that accompanied this letter (also in the Beinecke Library of Yale University) was the one taken by George G. Rockwood in October 1885 (see Nos. 12.1–12.5 in Morris Star's "A Checklist of Portraits of Herman Melville," *Bulletin of the New York Public Library* 71 [September 1967], 472, although this particular print is not listed). Elizabeth Melville labeled the back "Herman Melville Esq". The rose leaves (unlocated) that Melville evidently also enclosed were from his garden, which had become one of his major pastimes.

N.Y.
104 E. 26 St.
Oct. 5, '85

Dear Mrs. Gifford: It is now quite a time since you first asked me for my photo: — Well, here it is at last, the veritable face (at least, so says the Sun that never lied in his life) of your now venerable friend — venerable in years. — What the deuse makes him look so serious, I wonder. I thought he was of a gay and frolicsome nature, judgeing from a little rhyme of his about a Kitten, which you once showed me. But is this the same man? Pray, explain the inconsistency, or I shall begin to suspect your venerable friend of being a two-faced old fellow and not to be trusted.

~~≈≈≈≈≈~~ *That* is to signify an abrupt change in the text. — Bessie returned home from her vacation Saturday last, and Lizzie would also have come, but was detained in Boston by an ailment which temporarily keeps her there. But I look for her tomorrow or next

day. Trusting that you are at present exempt from your mo[st]
ous pain, I mean the neuralgia; and begging you not to exer[t your]
self, out of courtesy, in the unnecessary matter of answer[ing my]
note, I am always, in one respect at least, like yourself —

Friendly to the friendly
H. Melville

P.S.

You see the rose-leaves have not yet given out. I shall always try
and have a rose-leaf reserved for you, be the season what it may.

ALS on a 24.7 × 15 cm sheet, folded in half, of pink laid paper with lines. Melville began his
letter on the first page, continued it on the third, then turned to the fourth, and concluded it
on the second; with the exception of the postscript added in pencil, he inscribed the letter in
ink. Page numbers in blue pencil appear at the top of each page, added, presumably by Melville, to make the sequence clear.

LOCATION: Beinecke Library, Yale University.

PUBLICATION: (partial) *Log*, II, 793–94. Leyda, *Portable Melville*, pp. 622–23. Davis-Gilman
236.

TEXTUAL NOTES: Sun] S *written over* s • in one respect at least,] *inserted above caret* • P.S. . . .
may.] *in pencil*

TO JAMES BILLSON
20 DECEMBER 1885 · NEW YORK

On 7 October 1885 James Billson had sent Melville a now unlocated "friendly
note" and two collections of James Thomson's prose pieces: *Essays and Phantasies*
(London: Reeves & Turner, 1881; Sealts 518; HCL-M) and *Satires and Profanities*
(London: Progressive Publishing Co., 1884; Sealts 519, unlocated). The specific essays from these volumes that Melville refers to in this letter are "Bumble, Bum-
bledom, and Bumbleism," an elaboration on Matthew Arnold's essay on philistin-
ism; "Indolence: A Moral Essay," a cavil against Carlyle's cry of "Work!"; "Per
Contra: The Poet, High Art, Genius," an essay on the overvaluation of genius; and
"The Devil in the Church of England," a discussion of the diminishing role of the
devil in church doctrine.

Melville's comments on fame, prompted by Thomson's discussion of the
"house of Fame" in "Per Contra," were specifically aimed at the "House of Harper," as Harper & Brothers were often called. An 1845 edition of Moses Yale Beach's
Wealthy Citizens described the Harpers' power to generate "fame" for their authors:
"They have in different parts of America, from twelve to fifteen hundred booksellers acting as their agents, besides a large number of travelling clergymen and other
itinerants. So extensive is their business connexion that should they dispose of but

one or two copies to each agency, they would be sure to pay the expenses of publication, and no matter what work they may publish, (and they have published several of the worst and most stupid books ever issued) they are sure to dispose of an average more than two copies to each house with which they deal" (cited in Eugene Exman, *The Brothers Harper* [New York: Harper & Row, 1965], p. 232).

The photograph Melville enclosed with this letter is now unlocated but was presumably one of those taken by Rockwood in October 1885, like that enclosed with his letter of 5 October 1885 to his wife's cousin Ellen Gifford, above. As Melville requests here, Billson reciprocated with one of his own (now unlocated) in his now unlocated response of 31 January 1886 (see LETTERS RECEIVED, p. 730, and Melville's 2 April 1886 letter to Billson, below).

New York
Dec. 20, '85

Dear Sir: Do not think me indifferent or ungrateful if your last friendly note and gift remain unacknowledged till now. — There are natures that after receiving a certain impression as to another, that *other* need thenceforth hardly ever enter into intricate explanations, happen what may. — This may perhaps be a little obscure to some, but you will understand.

For the two books I thank you much. It is long since I have been so interested in a volume as in that of the "Essays & Phantasies". — "Bumble" — "Indolence" — "The Poet" &c, each is so admirably honest and original and informed throughout with the spirit of the noblest natures, that it would have been wonderful indeed had they hit the popular taste. They would have to be painstakingly diluted for that — diluted with that prudential worldly element, wherewithall Mr Arnold has conciliated the conventionalists while at the same time showing the absurdity of Bumble. But for your admirable friend this would have been too much like trimming — if trimming in fact it be. The motions of his mind in the best of the Essays are utterly untrameled and independent, and yet falling naturally into grace and poetry. It is good for me to think of such a mind — to know that such a brave intelligence has been — and may yet be, for aught anyone can *demonstrate* to the contrary. — As to his not acheiving "fame" — what of that? He is not the less, but so much the more. And it must have occurred to you as it has to me, that the further our civilization advances upon its present lines so much the cheaper sort of thing does "fame" become, especially of the literary sort. This species of "fame" a waggish acquaintance says can be manufactured to order, and sometimes is so manufactured thro the agency of a certain house that has a correspondent in every one of the almost innumerable journals that enlighten our millions from the Lakes to the Gulf & from the Atlantic to the Pacific. — But this "vanity of vanities" has been inimitably touched upon by your friend in one of his Essays. — "Satires & Profanities" are of course written for another plane than that to which the "Essays" are levelled. But many touches are diverting enough. "The Devel in the Church of England", for instance. But I must close. — You asked me for my photograph, but I had none to send you. Now that I *have*, I forward it to you, conditional however upon your reciprocating with your own, and this, permit me to insist on.

Very Truly Yours
H. Melville

ALS on a 22.8 × 17.9 cm sheet, folded in half, of white wove paper. Melville inscribed all four pages, in ink, beginning on the first page, continuing on the third, then turning to the fourth, and concluding on the second. Billson numbered the letter at the top of the first page "(5)" in ink. Page numbers in blue pencil appear at the top of each page, added, presumably by Melville, to make his sequence clear.

LOCATION: at present unknown. *Provenance*: C. A. Stonehill, Ltd., catalogue 137 (1938), in item 91; Frank J. Hogan sale, Parke-Bernet Galleries, 23–24 January 1945, in lot 438; H. Bradley Martin sale, Sotheby's, New York, sale 5971, 30–31 January 1990, in lot 2170A; 19th Century Shop in partnership with other book dealers.

PUBLICATION: *The Nation and the Athenæum* 29 (13 August 1921), 712–13. Davis-Gilman 237.

TEXTUAL NOTES: into intricate] *inserted with caret above canceled* intricate • to some] *rewritten* • anyone] *blotted* • a correspondent] *after canceled* a c • journals that] that *written over* of • plane than] than *altered from* that • You] *before canceled* have

1886

TO J. W. HENRY CANOLL
AFTER 23 JANUARY 1886 · NEW YORK

According to the 18 January 1886 New York *Commercial Advertiser*, J. W. Henry Canoll (1827–91) gave a talk on Melville at the "New York College of Archaeology and Aesthetics" on 15 January. His biographical sketch of Melville had appeared in the *Commercial Advertiser* on 14 January and his "Verse"—entitled "Melville"—appeared in that paper on 18 January (see LETTERS RECEIVED, pp. 728–29).

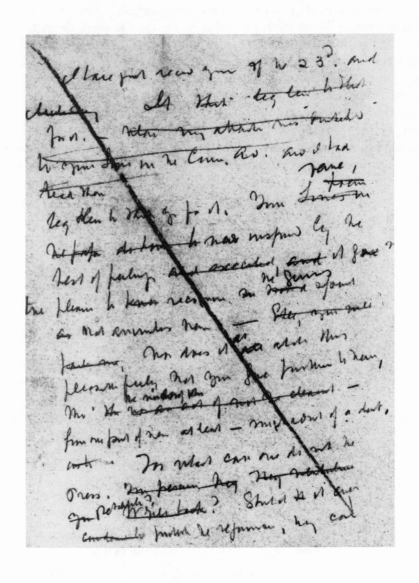

Draft of letter to J. W. Henry Canoll, after 23 January 1886 (reduced).
Courtesy of the Houghton Library, Harvard University (Melville
Collection).

This draft of Melville's letter to Canoll commenting on the printing of the poem in the *Commercial Advertiser* (see the textual notes, below, for Melville's canceled reference to the "Comm. Ad.") survives on the verso of the sixth page of the "Orme" manuscript (HCL-M). It can be dated shortly after 23 January 1886, since Melville mentions receiving a letter "of the 23ᵈ" from Canoll (now unlocated).

According to the obituaries on 14 October 1891 in the *New-York Times* and in the *New York Herald*, Canoll, a native of Albany, began his career as a Unitarian minister, but found church doctrine too literal-minded. New York city directories indicate that he settled there around 1879, when he listed himself as a "keramic artist." Two years later he was listed as a "consulting editor." In 1883 he was a "dean of college of archaeology," and in 1884 "consulting editor and dean." These directories list the same address (120 E. 105 Street) for both Canoll's home and the "New York College of Archaeology and Aesthetics." The obituaries also state that Canoll was a translator of Sanskrit and Aryan languages as well as the author of several books on Theosophical topics, although none are listed in the *National Union Catalog*. In poor health and suffering from depression, he committed suicide on 13 October 1891.

I have just received yours of the 23ᵈ and beg leave to thank you for it. Your Verse, was inspired by the best of feelings, it gives me true pleasure to recognize the generous spirit that animates them. — Nor does it abate this pleasurable feeling that you gave publication to them, tho' the wisdom of this — from one point of view at least — might admit of a doubt,

For what can one do with the Press. Retaliate? Should it ever publish the rejoinder, they can

Final document not located. Text from draft letter (unsigned), on a 14.2 × 17.8 cm part-sheet (torn along the top and right edges) of white laid paper. Melville inscribed the draft on only one side of the leaf, in pencil; he later canceled the page with a single orange crayon line and used the verso as the sixth page (final leaf 6) of the "Orme" manuscript.

Location (of draft): HCL-M.

Publication: *Melville's BILLY BUDD,* ed. F. Barron Freeman (Cambridge: Harvard University Press, 1948), p. 369. Davis-Gilman 238.

Textual Notes: beg] *after successively canceled* [*undeciphered word*] || It || thank || beg leave to thank for it. — || When my attention was directed to your Lines in the Comm. Ad. and I had read them • leave] *conjectural reading* • Verse,] *inserted above canceled* poem *inserted above canceled* Lines in • was] *altered from* were *after successively canceled* the paper || do honor to • feelings] *before successively canceled* and executed, || and • gives] *altered from* gave *without adding* s *which has been editorially supplied* • me] *added in right margin* • true] *added in left margin* • recognize] *after canceled* know • the generous] *inserted above canceled* in such a • spirit] *before canceled* as • Nor] *after canceled* Still, you will pardon me, • abate] *after at* inserted *without caret before* all *then* all *canceled leaving vestigial* at • the wisdom of this] *added above canceled* this was an act of not the

clearest • doubt,] *before canceled* as to • Press.] *before successively canceled* You per-
ceive || they || they ?venture || you • Retaliate?] *conjectural reading; inserted before canceled* Write
back? • Should] *before canceled* th • publish] *after canceled* condescend to

TO STANWIX MELVILLE
BEFORE 14 FEBRUARY 1886 · NEW YORK

Unlocated. A letter must have accompanied this power of attorney written in Melville's hand. It appointed Melville to collect his son Stanwix's legacy from the estate
of Melville's youngest sister, Frances Priscilla. Stanwix added "14th" to the date and
signed the document in San Francisco, then apparently returned it with a now unlocated letter. (This was evidently the "memorandum" Melville forwarded to Abraham Lansing, executor of the estate, on 12 October 1886; see Lansing's 15 October
acknowledgment, p. 736 below.) The manuscript fragment of Melville's signature
identified as having come from a letter Melville wrote to Stanwix (see Undated
Letters, p. 537) possibly may have belonged to Melville's accompanying letter.
Only nine days after signing this document, Stanwix Melville died at the German
Hospital in San Francisco. Davis–Gilman Unlocated 412.

[Enclosure:]

San Francisco California
I authorise my Father Herman Melville to receive for me, from the
Executor or Administrator of my Aunt Fanny Melvilles "will" the
sum of one hundred "$100.^{00}" therein bequeathed to me — and to
give his receipt for the same as if paid to me personally
Feby   1886

Manuscript enclosure, on a 19.8 × 12.6 cm sheet of white laid paper, watermarked with a
crown-like design and the name "CROWN LINEN". Melville inscribed only one side of the leaf,
in ink. Stanwix Melville, in a slightly lighter ink, later signed the document and added "14th"
between the month and the year in the last line.

LOCATION (of enclosure): NYPL-GL.

TO JAMES BILLSON
2 APRIL 1886 · NEW YORK

Like many of Melville's letters to Billson, this one acknowledges a number of gifts
received. According to Elizabeth Melville's memorandum, Billson's present of a
"semi-manuscript" copy of *The Rubáiyát of Omar Khayyám* and J. W. Barrs's pres-

ent of James Thomson's *A Voice from the Nile, and Other Poems* were both sent on 15 February 1886 in the wake of Billson's 31 January letter (now unlocated) describing his friend J. W. Barrs. (For more on Barrs, see the headnote to Melville's 10 October 1884 letter to Billson, above, and for Elizabeth Melville's memorandum, see p. 730 below.) Melville already owned the 1878 first American edition of Fitzgerald's *Rubáiyát* (HCL-M; Sealts 391), but what Billson sent, as he explained in a 21 August 1935 letter to Willard Thorp (The Newberry Library), was one of a number of hand-copied transcriptions that had been made by a "Book seller" at the Secular Hall in Leicester. Billson had provided the bookseller with a hand-copied transcription he had made from one Thomson earlier had made from an unidentified source, since, as Billson wrote, there were no "correct" printed copies of the poem available in England at the time (Sealts 393). This item is now unlocated, as is the photograph of Billson that was also enclosed. But *A Voice from the Nile*, which included a memoir of Thomson by Bertram Dobell and was inscribed by Barrs ("to Herman Melville from J. W. Barrs as a small tribute of admiration to Typee & Omoo. Feb 15/86") is now in the Firestone Library at Princeton University (Sealts 522).

   The article in the *Pall Mall Budget* that Melville also mentions could have come with either the letter or the books. It was probably the article entitled "The Best Hundred Books. By the Best Hundred Judges" that appeared in the issue of 21 January 1886. However, three continuations of the article were published, in the issues for 28 January, and 4 and 11 February; and various related articles on the subject also appeared, including one by John Ruskin, "The Best Hundred Books," in the issue for 25 February.

New York, Ap. 2, '86

Dear Sir: — If I am late in acknowledging your last kind note and the receipt of the welcome gifts it announced, it is from any cause but indifference. —— I am pleased that you have observed the condition imposed on you, and that, accordingly, you have put me in possession of the photograph of so friendly a correspondent

   For the semi-manuscript "Omar" — the text, coming in that unique form to me, imparted yet added significance to that sublime old infidel. —

—— The discussion about the 100 best books in the Pall Mall is perhaps more curious and diverting than profoundly instructive.

—— For the "Voice from the Nile" containing the added poems of Thomson the memoir and the portrait, pray, give my best thanks to Mr. Barrs. The Pieces having a peculiar interest for that gentleman are extremely pleasing — especially two of them. And yet, if one consider the poet's career, one could heave a big sigh for the fatality investing so genial a spirit. But perhaps the gods may make it all up

to him wherever he now may sojourn. If they do not, the shabby
fellows ought to be ashamed of themselves.

—— It pleases me to learn from you that Thomson was interested in
Wm Blake. — But I must end.

Very Truly Yours
H. Melville

Mr. James Billson

ALS on a 22.8 × 17.9 cm sheet, folded in half, of white wove paper. Melville inscribed the
first three pages using two different inks: brown, at first; black, beginning with "big sigh". In
rereading the letter Melville used black ink to dot the "i"s in "semi-manuscript," "discussion," and "memoir". Billson numbered the letter at the top of the first page "(6)" in ink.

LOCATION: at present unknown. *Provenance*: C. A. Stonehill, Ltd., catalogue 137 (1938), in
item 91; Frank J. Hogan sale, Parke-Bernet Galleries, 23–24 January 1945, in lot 438; H. Bradley Martin sale, Sotheby's, New York, sale 5971, 30–31 January 1990, in lot 2170A; 19th
Century Shop in partnership with other book dealers.

PUBLICATION: *The Nation and the Athenæum* 29 (13 August 1921), 713. Davis-Gilman 239.

TEXTUAL NOTES: coming] *after canceled* conveying · investing] *possibly* inverting · interested]
miswritten intrested

TO [W. CLARK RUSSELL?]
[BETWEEN 7 APRIL AND 21 JULY 1886?] · NEW YORK

This draft is all that has been located of what may have been Melville's first letter to
William Clark Russell (1844–1911), the English maritime writer, best known, as
Melville pointed out in his 12 July 1885 letter to Laura Wachschlager, for his novel
The Wreck of the Grosvenor (1877). Russell probably came to Melville's attention
through this book; and certainly he did so again through the article entitled "Sea
Stories" that Russell published in the *Contemporary Review* (September 1884), praising Melville, R. H. Dana, Jr., Michael Scott, and Captain Cupples as "the poets of
the deep," and ranking Melville the highest. This is perhaps the article Melville is
referring to in his discussion of Dana—"R H Dn, Jun"—in this draft. Melville in
his later "Inscription Epistolary to W. C. R." in *John Marr and Other Sailors, with
Some Sea-Pieces* (New York: De Vinne, 1888), p. 5, compared Russell with "our
own admirable" Dana as one who "knows the sea, and the blue water of it; the
sailor and the heart of him; the ship, too, and the sailing and handling of a ship."
Since there is no date on this draft, there is no way of determining absolutely
whether it was a draft for Melville's first letter to Russell or a discarded draft for his
paragraph discussing praise in his "Inscription Epistolary"—as Robert C. Ryan argues in the NN *Published Poems* volume. The unlocated letter that Melville did
send, as Russell's 21 July reply indicates (see LETTERS RECEIVED, pp. 731–32), was
delivered by the artist Peter Toft (1825–1901) sometime after 7 April 1886, when

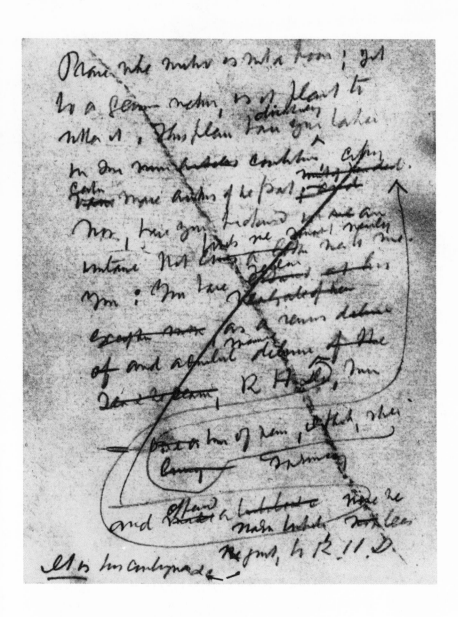

[Draft of letter to W. Clark Russell?], between 7 April and 21 July 1886 (reduced). Courtesy of the Houghton Library, Harvard University (Melville Collection).

Toft gave Melville two watercolors before he left for England. Russell's reply also confirms that Dana was a subject of Melville's letter.

Praise when merited is not a boon: yet to a generous nature, is it pleasant to utter it. This pleasure have you doubtlessly taken in some various contributions, citing certain marine authors of the past — two of them, I think, still surviving. Now, have you bestowed in an instance that touches me somewhat nearly. You: You have rendered as a serious and admirable marine delineator R H Dn, Jun and offered a warm tribute, none the less just, to R. H. D
It is his countrymen &c

Final document not located. Text from draft (unsigned), on a 14.2 × 17.8 cm part-sheet (torn along the bottom and right edges) of white laid paper. Melville inscribed the draft on only one side of the leaf, in pencil; he later canceled the page with a large X in orange crayon and used the verso as the seventh page (final leaf 7) of the "Orme" manuscript.

LOCATION (of draft): HCL-M.

PUBLICATION: *Melville's* BILLY BUDD, ed. F. Barron Freeman (Harvard University Press, 1948), pp. 369–70. Davis-Gilman 242.

TEXTUAL NOTES: doubtlessly] *conjectural reading; inserted above caret* • various] *conjectural reading* • contributions] *after canceled* articles • certain] *above canceled* various • marine] *conjectural reading* • — two . . . surviving.] *originally* ; — *and canceled, then* most of them dead. *inserted above, then canceled and* nearly all of them *added farther down on the page without guideline, then canceled and* — one or two of them, I think, still living *added further below, with a guideline and arrow; then* one or *canceled and* surviving *inserted after canceled* living • an instance] *after canceled* one • touches . . . nearly.] *inserted above incompletely canceled* comes a little near to me. • rendered] *conjectural reading; inserted above canceled* ?exclaimed *or possibly* ?esteemed • as a] *after successively canceled* at his || ?exceptional work • serious] *before canceled* ?delineation of • marine] *inserted above* • delineator] *conjectural reading; before canceled* of the sea & the seaman, • and offered . . . to R. H. D] *added below, with guideline to caret misplaced after* ?delineator (*placed after* Jun *editorially*) • offered] *inserted above canceled* made • warm tribute] *added below canceled* tribute &c • none the less] *originally* not less than *then* none the *inserted above canceled* not *and* than *canceled* • It . . . &c] *added below*

TO HELEN MELVILLE GRIGGS
BEFORE 7 JUNE 1886 · NEW YORK

Unlocated. A letter from Melville is cited in a 7 June 1886 letter from his sister Helen Griggs to their cousin Catherine Lansing in Albany. From her home in Longwood, Massachusetts, Helen was arranging for the dispersal of the furniture in their late uncle Herman's house at Gansevoort, New York, where their sister Frances Priscilla Melville had last lived. Reporting on Melville's interest in a sideboard for his own house and a clock for his daughter, Frances Thomas, in Orange, New Jersey, Helen states: "Herman writes me — , that if the side board can be accommodated, in the back parlor of their house, he would be very thankful to recieve it under his roof. And the old clock, (which Uncle Herman gave him) is to go to Fanny's at Orange, and will be sent to some *horologist* in New York, on its way to her" (NYPL-GL). Davis-Gilman Unlocated 413.

TO LEONARD G. SANFORD
22 JUNE 1886 · NEW YORK

Leonard G. Sanford, to whose now unlocated note Melville replies here, was identified by Jay Leyda through Sanford's granddaughter, Mrs. Robert T. Tankersley of Cornwall, Connecticut. She wrote Leyda on 18 August 1947 that she did not "know why Leonard G. Sanford wrote to Melville in 1886 except to ask him some question or make some comment on a whaling episode in one of Melville's stories" (UCLA-Leyda). She then still had her grandfather's 1856–57 diary, kept while at sea aboard the whaleship *Lancer*. Sanford, the son of a congressman, went to sea at sixteen, jumped ship at Paita, Peru, and later became the U.S. consul in Tumbez, Peru (both places Melville mentioned in his works), before returning home in 1862. Charles Boardman Hawes used the diary as the basis for his chapter "A Boy Who Went Whaling" in his book *Whaling* (Garden City: Doubleday, 1924).

Sanford's mistaken notion that Melville took a voyage round the world in 1863—prompting Melville's wry comment on the relatively recent 1870 proclamation of Papal Infallibility—may have come from the 1875 revised edition of the Duyckincks' *Cyclopædia of American Literature*. Edited by M. Laird Simons, it stated: "In 1860 Mr. Melville made another whaling voyage around the world"—an error probably arising from his 1860 *Meteor* voyage to San Francisco, originally planned to take him "round the world" (see Sealts, *Early Lives*, p. 91, and *Journals*, p. 197).

104 E. 26th St. N.Y.
June 22, '86

Dear Sir: Your note has met with delay, having been forwarded by the P.M. from Pittsfield. —— No, I did not go a voyage round the world in 1863. — The Cyclopedias are not infallible, no more than the Pope.

I am glad to know that you like some of the books.

I beg leave to congratulate you upon the honor of having been a whale-hunter in your time

Yours very truly
Herman Melville

Leonard G. Sandford Esq.

ALS on a 12.4 × 15 cm part-sheet (torn along the left edge) of pink laid paper with lines. Melville inscribed only one side of the leaf, in ink. When sold to C. A. Stonehill by Sanford's family it was pasted in the front of a copy of *Moby-Dick*.

LOCATION: Beinecke Library, Yale University. *Provenance*: C. A. Stonehill, Ltd.; Charles Scribner's autograph catalogue, 1945, item 146; Bennett Book Studio; Seven Gables Bookshop.

PUBLICATION: (partial) *Log*, II, 800. Leyda, *Portable Melville*, pp. 622–23. Davis-Gilman 240.

TEXTUAL NOTE: beg] b *written over* r

TO HELEN MELVILLE GRIGGS
BEFORE 15 JULY 1886 · NEW YORK

Unlocated. A quotation from a letter Melville wrote to his sister Helen survives in her 15 July 1886 letter to their cousin Catherine Lansing. Continuing her negotiations about the disposal of the furniture at Gansevoort (see the entry for Melville's unlocated letter to his sister written sometime before 7 June 1886, above), Helen explains that "Herman wrote me, when I asked how *his* furniture should be forwarded, 'that the packers could proportion what each person's charge of material & time should be, and the account should be [should be *inserted above caret*] sent to each'" (NYPL-GL). She adds that she had accordingly sent the apportioned accounts "To *Herman; Milie; Florence;* and *Fannie*." Melville's letter is probably also the one mentioned in an earlier, undated letter from Helen to their cousin Catherine Lansing: "Herman wrote directions about his packing, and I shall send his things off first" (NYPL-GL; cited by Leyda in *Log*, II, 800, but at present unlocated). Davis-Gilman 241.

TO JOSEPH BARTON
AFTER 1 AUGUST 1886 · NEW YORK

Unlocated. On 1 August 1886 Joseph Barton's daughter wrote to Melville on his behalf, inquiring whether he was "the same Herman Melville" with whom Barton had sailed aboard the *United States* (see LETTERS RECEIVED, pp. 732–33). Although Melville's reply is unlocated, the fact that he preserved the daughter's letter suggests that he probably answered it.

TO ABRAHAM LANSING
12 OCTOBER 1886 · NEW YORK

Unlocated. A letter, the third concerning the settlement of the will of Melville's sister Frances Priscilla, is cited in Abraham Lansing's 15 October 1886 reply (see LETTERS RECEIVED, pp. 736–37). According to that reply, Melville had enclosed signed receipts for his wife's and his daughter Elizabeth's legacies as well as a "memorandum" about Stanwix Melville's legacy (evidently the document Stanwix had signed on 14 February 1886; see the entry on p. 496 above). (With the death of Stanwix Melville on 23 February 1886, Melville had become the beneficiary of his son.) For the final settlement of the estate, see Melville's 16 March 1889 letter to Abraham Lansing.

1887

TO ROSSITER JOHNSON
11 DECEMBER [1887?] · NEW YORK

The long career of Edwin Rossiter Johnson (1840–1931) as a prolific editor of encyclopedias, dictionaries, abridged classics, and anthologies (including Melville's piece "The Bell-Tower" in the third volume, "Tragedy" [1875], of his *Little Classics*, 1874–81 [Sealts 299]), together with implications in this letter, make it likely that Melville was replying to a 9 December invitation (now unlocated) to write something for such a work. Although this letter cannot be dated exactly, Davis and Gilman reported that it was written on the same paper as that of Melville's 29 January 1888 letter to Edmund C. Stedman. If so, this letter probably refers either to *Appletons' Cyclopædia of American Biography*, for which Johnson was managing editor under James Grant Wilson and John Fiske between 1886 and 1889 (see Melville's letter of 6 January 1888 to Johnson, just below) or *Appletons' Annual Cyclopædia*, of which Johnson was sole editor between 1883 and 1902.

Dec. 11th
104 E. 26th St.

My Dear Sir:

Yours of the 9th is received. — Your friendly proposition I must decline. And this — in part at least — from a sense of incompetence. For I am unpractised in a kind of writing that exacts so much of heedfulness — heedfulness, I mean, of a sort not demanded in some other departments.

With best wishes
H. Melville

Rossiter Johnson Esq.

Original document not located. Text from Christie's catalogue reproduction. Jay Leyda made an undated, typed transcription (in Davis-Gilman file) from the ALS, then in the Estelle Doheny Collection of the Edward Laurence Doheny Memorial Library, St. John's Seminary, Camarillo, California. Merrell R. Davis corrected Leyda's transcription from the original document in March 1954, and the resulting Davis-Gilman text is identical to NN. From Davis's notes the one-page letter can be described as in ink, with "Dec. 11th" added later by Melville in a lighter ink, on a 24 × 20.5 cm sheet, folded in half, of white laid paper, watermarked with an ornate shield-like design.

LOCATION: at present unknown. *Provenance*: Estelle Doheny; St. John's Seminary; Doheny sale, Christie's, 1–2 February 1988, lot 818 (with reproduction); Profiles in History Catalogue 4 (September 1988), item 201 (with reproduction).

PUBLICATION: *Log*, II, 766. Davis-Gilman 269.

1888

TO ROSSITER JOHNSON
6 JANUARY 1888 · NEW YORK

Melville's reference here to supplying dates and a name probably concerns the entry on Melville in *Appletons' Cyclopædia of American Biography* (1888, IV, 293–94), of which Rossiter Johnson was managing editor (see also Melville's 11 December [1887?] letter to him, just above).

    The date assigned to this letter is from the date that was placed by another hand, probably Johnson's, just below Melville's address.

104 E. 26th St.

My Dear Sir:

    Herewith you have the proof. I have supplied the dates & name wanted, and see nothing else to do

    With thanks for your courtesy,

Very Truly Yours

H. Melville

Rossiter Johnson Esq.

Original document not located. Text from photocopy (in NN file) of the ALS (1 p.). Another hand, probably Johnson's, noted in ink "Jan. 6, 1888" just below the address in the heading; a second hand noted in pencil in the top margin "Herman Melville | Author of 'Typee.' "

LOCATION: at present unknown. *Provenance*: Christie's, sale 5152, 11 June 1982, lot 35 (with reproduction); The Current Co., Miscellany 14, August 1982, item 46; Gallery of History, Inc.

TEXTUAL NOTE: you have] have *rewritten*

TO THE EDITORS OF
"A LIBRARY OF AMERICAN LITERATURE"
27 JANUARY 1888 · NEW YORK

Edmund Clarence Stedman (1833–1908) began his literary career editing newspapers, publishing poems, and reporting the Civil War. He then became a broker but used his means and social position to promote literature and assist authors. He was one of the founders of the Authors Club (1882) and president of the National Institute of Arts and Letters (1904–7). Besides writing several volumes of poetry and two critical works—*Victorian Poets* (1875) and *Poets of America* (1885)—he edited *A Library of American Literature* (1889–90), *A Victorian Anthology* (1895), and *An American Anthology* (1900).

For the first of these anthologies, he and his coeditor, Ellen Mackay Hutchinson (1851–1933), sent a form letter on 24 January to Melville, asking permission to include extracts from his work published by Harpers and inquiring about his date and place of birth (see LETTERS RECEIVED, pp. 738–40). This letter is Melville's response. When the ten-volume *Library* appeared, it included "The Bell-Tower" from *The Piazza Tales*, and "The Stone Fleet," "Sheridan at Cedar Creek," and "In the Prison Pen" from *Battle-Pieces*. It also included the first reproduction of the 1870 Eaton portrait of Melville (see p. 772 below), secured by Stedman's son Arthur (1859–1908), who later became Melville's literary executor (see Sealts, *Early Lives*, p. ii). Stedman's one-volume *American Anthology* also included four other poems from *Battle-Pieces* and two previously unpublished poems.

104 E. 26 St
Jan, 27, 1888

To
The Editors &c —
Of course you are at liberty to make the extracts.
Wishing you success
Respectfully Yours
H. Melville

[H M. was born in New York City Aug 1, 1819.]

ALS on a 22.6 × 17.4 cm sheet, folded in half, of beige wove paper with a white border. Melville inscribed the first page, in ink.

LOCATION: Beinecke Library, Yale University. *Provenance*: probably the ALS in either lot 1966 or 1968 of the Edmund C. Stedman sale, Anderson Galleries, sale 885, 19–20 January 1911 (neither ALS is adequately described); Arthur W. Butler.

PUBLICATION: (partial) *Log*, II, 805. Davis-Gilman 243.

TEXTUAL NOTE: H M] *digraph*

TO EDMUND C. STEDMAN
29 JANUARY 1888 · NEW YORK

On 20 January 1888 Stedman wrote Melville asking for an autograph copy of one of Melville's "best known" shorter poems, to be used in "illustrating and 'extending' " his own copy of his *Poets of America* (Melville received passing mention in the second chapter; see LETTERS RECEIVED, pp. 737–38). The poem Melville sent Stedman with this reply—"Ditty of Aristippus"—was far from the best known of his poems; it had been published only once, in *Clarel* (1876), where in the fourth canto of Part 3, the Cypriote sings it as a "hymn of Aristippus." (For a further discussion of this poem and a reproduction of Melville's autograph copy enclosed with this letter [now in the American Antiquarian Society] see the NN *Clarel*, pp. 867–70.) Among the several items associated with this letter in the Beinecke Library at Yale University is one of the 1885 photographs by Rockwood (see Morris Star's "A Checklist of Portraits of Herman Melville," *Bulletin of the New York Public Library* 71 [September 1967], Nos. 12.1–12.5, although this particular print is not listed). Melville apparently sent it since no engravings of his portrait had, as he explains here, ever been published (see the headnote to Melville's 12 February 1851 letter to Evert Duyckinck). Stedman's autograph collection, including all associated items, was sold by Anderson Galleries in 1911.

104 E 26 St
Jan 29

Mr Edmund C Stedman
Dear Sir:

I accede with pleasure to your request. Accordingly you will find enclosed a short Piece

As to the engraving, none have been published — to my knowledge

Hoping you may fully realize your pleasant fancy you speak of, I am

Very Truly Yours
H. Melville

[Enclosure:]

Ditty of Aristippus

Noble gods at the board
Where lord unto lord
Light pushes the care-killing wine:
Urbane in their pleasure,
Superb in their leisure —
Lax ease —
Lax ease after labor divine!

Golden ages eternal,
Autumnal, supernal,
Deep mellow their temper serene:
The rose by their gate
Shall it yield unto fate?
They are gods —
They are gods and their garlands keep green.

Ever blandly adore them;
But spare to implore them:
They rest, they discharge them from time;
Yet beleive, light believe
They would succor, reprieve —
Nay, retrieve —
Might but revellers pause in the prime.

Herman Melville

ALS on a 12 × 20.5 cm part-sheet (torn along the left edge) of white laid paper, watermarked with an ornate shield-like design. Melville inscribed only one side of the leaf, in ink, and addressed the envelope "Edmund C. Stedman Esq. | 44 E. 26th St. | City"; it was postmarked in New York on 29 January. Another hand noted on the envelope in blue pencil "H. Melville". The other items in Anderson Galleries lot 1969—"a cut autograph, a pencilled autograph on a card, a newspaper sketch, and a cabinet photograph" along with two additional newspaper items—all now remain with this letter in the bound blank-volume labeled "Manuscript | Melville" in which they are mounted. The text of the poem enclosed by Melville with his letter is from the original manuscript (2 pp.) in the American Antiquarian Society, Worcester, Massachusetts, on a full sheet of the same paper as the letter (see the NN *Clarel*, pp. 867–70, for a description and reproduction of the manuscript). According to a notation at the American Antiquarian Society the poem manuscript was apparently bought by P. K. Foley for C. H. Taylor with a different letter from Melville to Stedman (inaccurately described in the sale catalogue only as the "ALS accompanying" the poem) as lot 1968 at the Anderson auction (see the provenance for Melville's 27 January 1888 and 20 February 1888 letters to Stedman). Another hand later penciled two arrows pointing at the words "Superb" and "into" on the first page of the poem manuscript.

LOCATION (of letter): Beinecke Library, Yale University. *Provenance*: Edmund C. Stedman sale, Anderson Galleries, sale 885, 19–20 January 1911, lot 1969; Owen Franklin Aldis.

PUBLICATION: (partial) *Log*, II, 805. Davis-Gilman 244.

TO UNKNOWN
31 JANUARY 1888 · NEW YORK

This letter signed with "much respect" was written in reply to a now unlocated letter from an unknown correspondent, quite possibly the author of the unsigned article on the historical Israel Potter in *Appletons' Cyclopædia of American Biography*. A proof copy (presumably Melville's) of the article is in the Melville Collection of the Houghton Library of Harvard University. That article repeated as fact two of Melville's fictions about Israel Potter and his narrative (see the NN *Israel Potter*, pp. 280–81)—an error Melville may have encouraged with this letter. He answers here what must have been an inquiry about the "authenticity" of his portrayal of the historic Israel Potter by citing his opening dedication to the Bunker Hill Monument in *Israel Potter*, which states disingenuously that his account "with the exception of some expansions, and additions of historic and personal details, and one or two shiftings of scene" was drawn from Henry Trumbull's *Life and Remarkable Adventures of Israel R. Potter* (Providence: Trumbull, 1824) and "may, perhaps, be not unfitly regarded something in the light of a dilapidated old tombstone retouched" (p. vii). For a more accurate account of the relation of his book to its several sources, including Trumbull's book, see the NN *Israel Potter*, pp. 277ff., which reproduces the *Life* and gives further details of Potter's life with a contemporary picture of him. See also Hennig Cohen, "The Real Israel Potter," *Melville Society Extracts* 53 (February 1983), 7–10; and Cohen's annotated edition (New York: Fordham University Press, 1991), pp. 303–18.

104 E. 26th St.

Jan 31 1888

Dear Sir: — Israel Potter was born Aug. 1st 1744 at Cranston, R.I. So says the Narrative written by himself. — The date of his death I do not know, nor do I think it ascertainable.

In what light the book entitled *I. P. or 50 Years of Exile* is to be regarded, may be clearly inferred from what is said in the Dedication.

With much respect

H. Melville

ALS on a 22.8 × 17.5 cm sheet, folded in half, of white wove paper. Melville inscribed the first page, in ink. Another hand, probably the recipient's, noted in ink at the top of the first page "Rec'd feb 1. '88".

LOCATION: Lehigh University Library.

TEXTUAL NOTE: nor] *written over another word or word-start*

TO EDMUND C. STEDMAN
20 FEBRUARY 1888 · NEW YORK

On 1 February 1888, Stedman sent Melville a letter along with two books and also a "chapter" of his own (see LETTERS RECEIVED, pp. 740–41). The first book was a volume of Richard Henry Horne's works and the second a work by George Walter Thornbury (see the headnote to Stedman's 1 February letter for a complete discussion of these books). Stedman's own "chapter," which Melville calls a "book," was on Whitman—probably the one in his *Poets of America*. These are most likely the "books" Melville was returning with this letter of 20 February, which also suggests that it was an evening's conversation at Melville's home that first had led Stedman to send them to him (Stedman and Melville lived within a short distance of each other on Twenty-sixth Street).

104 E. 26th St.
Feb. 20th '88

Dear Sir:

I return the books you so kindly sent me.

I have been interested in all of them. And your own book in many of its views has proved either corroborative or suggestive to me. — I have not by any means so many external demands upon my evenings as you probably have. I am the one most likely to be at home in the evening. Pray, remember this, and give me the pleasure of dropping in again here when you feel like it.

With much respect,
H. Melville

ALS on a 22.8 × 17.5 cm sheet, folded in half, of white wove paper. Melville inscribed the first page, in ink, and addressed the unstamped envelope (that was probably hand-delivered) in ink "Mr. Stedman | 44 E. 26th St. | Personal", noting on it in pencil "With Books". Another hand added in blue pencil "Melville". A typewritten transcript made by Stedman, misdated 20 October 1888, in the Columbia University Library, was the only copy of this letter Davis and Gilman and Leyda were able to obtain (hence their misdating; see under publication, below).

LOCATION: at present unknown. *Provenance*: probably the ALS in either lot 1966 or 1968 in the Edmund C. Stedman sale, Anderson Galleries, sale 885, 19–20 January 1911 (neither ALS is adequately described); H. Bradley Martin sale, Sotheby's, New York, sale 5971, 30–31 January 1990, lot 2172 (with reproduction); Bauman Books.

PUBLICATION: (partial) *Log*, II, 810 (misdated 20 October 1888). Davis-Gilman 247 (misdated 20 October 1888).

TEXTUAL NOTES: its] *mended* · corroborative] rro *mended* · here] *inserted above caret*

TO W. CLARK RUSSELL
BETWEEN 26 MARCH AND 10 APRIL 1888 · [NEW YORK?]

Unlocated. A letter asking W. Clark Russell's permission to dedicate *John Marr and Other Sailors* to him is cited in Russell's affirmative reply of 10 April 1888 (see LETTERS RECEIVED, pp. 742–43). In his letter Melville apparently mentioned his trip to Bermuda from 8 to 26 March 1888. Davis-Gilman Unlocated 414.

TO JAMES BILLSON
29 MARCH 1888 · NEW YORK

The "paper" Melville acknowledges in this letter is unidentified, but according to a penciled note made later by Billson in its top margin, the "volume" he also acknowledges was Marcus Andrew Hislop Clarke's *For the Term of His Natural Life* (Sealts 146). It was first published in Melbourne, Australia, in 1874, and later in London. Sealts speculates that the copy Billson sent Melville (now unlocated) was the 1885 London edition published by Bentley. Clarke's narrative concerned life aboard a prison-ship, and his opening chapter was a melodramatic account of the circumstances that unjustly placed his hero aboard that ship as a prisoner. Clarke was an admirer of Melville; his "Noah's Ark" Dialogues published in the 18 May 1872 Melbourne *Australasian* characterized *Moby-Dick* as "a glorious book," in which "one breathes brine, and hungers for the freedom of the sea." Melville's next letter to Billson, 7 April 1888, acknowledges Billson's delayed letter (now unlocated) that was intended to arrive with Clarke's book.

March 29, 1888
New York
104 E. 26th St.

Dear Sir: Some time ago I received a paper from you containing matter interesting to me; and now thro' the post I get a volume which I must needs think comes from the same kind quarter. I promise myself much pleasure in its perusal, since it opens in a manner to arrest one's attention.

   Trusting that you are in health & happiness I am

Very Truly Yours
H. Melville

To
James Billson

ALS on a 22.8 × 17.5 cm sheet, folded in half, of white wove paper. Melville inscribed the first page, in ink. Billson added a penciled note on the top margin identifying the "volume" mentioned in Melville's letter as "referring | Marcus Clark's | 'For the Term of His Natural Life.' " and numbered the letter at the top of the first page "(7)" in ink.

LOCATION: at present unknown. *Provenance*: C. A. Stonehill, Ltd., catalogue 137 (1938), in item 91; Frank J. Hogan sale, Parke-Bernet Galleries, 23–24 January 1945, in lot 438; H. Bradley Martin sale, Sotheby's, New York, sale 5971, 30–31 January 1990, in lot 2170A; 19th Century Shop, catalogue 20 (April 1991), item 170.

PUBLICATION: Davis-Gilman 245.

TEXTUAL NOTE: I get] *inserted above caret*

TO JAMES BILLSON
7 APRIL 1888 · NEW YORK

This letter answering Billson's now unlocated inquiry concerns the reprinting in 1865 by T. B. Peterson & Brothers of *Israel Potter* (originally published by Putnam's in 1855) under the title *The Refugee*. A Philadelphia firm, Peterson & Brothers had purchased the plates of the book, which was then out of print, from Putnam in September 1857. They advertised *The Refugee* as "by Herman Melville, Author of 'Typee', 'Omoo', 'The Two Captains,' 'The Man of the World,' etc. etc." as early as 11 March 1865 (and so described it on the title page, as Melville notes here). The firm continued to list it at least into 1876, apparently despite Melville's remonstrance about their using his name in connection with that title (see the entry for his unlocated letter probably written in March 1865, p. 395 above, and his undated letter to the *World*, p. 538 below).

As Melville's comments suggest, Billson had recently moved to a new home, " 'Birds Nest Farm' " (also mentioned in Melville's 31 December 1888 letter to Billson). For the letter and book mentioned at the opening of this letter, see the headnote to Melville's 29 March letter to Billson, just above.

April 7, 1888.
New York
104 E. 26th St.

My Dear Sir: — I acknowledged — to your previous address — the receipt of the parcel you so kindly sent me; and now, something in the rear, your note turns up which, I suppose, should have accompanied the book. —

Time, just now, hardly admits of my responding to your inquiries as fully as I should like. But let me say that you have all my published books except the "Piazza Tales" now out of print. As for the "Two Captains and "Man of the World" they are books of the air — I know of none such. The *names* appear, tho', on the title-page

of a book of mine — "Israel Potter" which was republished by a
Philadelphia house some time ago under the unwarrantably altered
title of "The Refugee". A letter to the publisher arrested the
publication.

I thank you for the very friendly tone of your note, and appreciate it; and I hope that some egg in the "Birds Nest Farm" may hatch
the Bird of Paradise for you — — happiness.

Sincerely Yours
H. Melville

Mr. James Billson

ALS on a 22.8 × 17.5 cm sheet, folded in half, of white wove paper. Melville inscribed the
first, third, and fourth pages, in ink. Billson numbered the letter at the top of the first page
"(8)" in ink.

LOCATION: at present unknown. *Provenance*: C. A. Stonehill, Ltd., catalogue 137 (1938), in
item 91; Frank J. Hogan sale, Parke-Bernet Galleries, 23–24 January 1945, in lot 438; H. Bradley Martin sale, Sotheby's, New York, sale 5971, 30–31 January 1990, in lot 2170A; 19th
Century Shop in partnership with other book dealers.

PUBLICATION: *The Nation and the Athenæum* 29 (13 August 1921), 713. Davis-Gilman 246.

TEXTUAL NOTES: admits] *after canceled* permits • "Two Captains] *closing double quotation mark
lacking* • such. The] The *altered from* They • names] *inserted above caret* • on the title-page] *after
canceled word-start* • arrested] *after canceled* stopped

TO PETER [PAST? TOFT?]
5 NOVEMBER 1888 · NEW YORK

Unlocated. Walter Benjamin Autographs listed a letter by Melville to "Peter Past"
as item P-544 in their 1982 catalogue (number 885). Their entry indicates that the
brief letter concerned a small package and that Melville was unsure of his correspondent's address; it quotes Melville as writing: "should this reach you, pray, instruct me." The small package was probably a copy of Melville's *John Marr and
Other Sailors*, which he was distributing at this time (see the letter just below). Although the catalogue entry gave only the year 1888 for the letter, the 5 November
date was noted in an article ("Boston's Sixth International Fair," *AB Bookman's
Weekly* 70 [8 November 1982], 3147) about the 1982 Boston Book Fair, where the
Benjamin company exhibited the letter. "Peter Past" has not been identified, and is
possibly a mistranscription for Melville's artist friend Peter Toft, a likely recipient
of *John Marr* (see pp. 498–500 above).

TO ELLEN MARETT GIFFORD
6 NOVEMBER 1888 · NEW YORK

The "small volume"—now unlocated—that accompanied this letter to Elizabeth Melville's cousin was Melville's *John Marr and Other Sailors*; his presentation copy to his wife is dated just the day before—5 November 1888 (NYPL–Osborne Collection). Less than a year later Ellen Gifford died, on 7 September 1889. Her mother, who died in 1878, had willed twenty thousand dollars to Elizabeth Melville and her children, and in November 1879 Ellen Gifford herself willed ten thousand dollars to Elizabeth and eight thousand to Herman, later adding five thousand to the former bequest. Thus, after her death in 1889 the family benefited heavily from her generosity. See above, Melville's 5 October 1885 letter to her—the only other letter from their extensive correspondence now known to survive.

104 E. 26th St.
Nov. 6th 1888

My Dear Mrs Gifford:

By mail I send you a small volume, some portions of which, I hope, may prove more or less interesting to you. — Lizzie tells me she is about writing you, so I leave her to tell you whatever news there may be.

Your Friend
H. Melville

ALS on an 11.3 × 17.5 cm sheet of white wove paper. Melville inscribed only one side of the leaf, in ink.

LOCATION: Collection of Hennig Cohen. *Provenance*: Baldwin family descendants (see p. 517); Whitlock Farm Booksellers, 1974.

PUBLICATION: Hennig Cohen, "Melville to Mrs. Gifford, 1888," *College Literature* 2 (Fall 1985), 229.

TO MARIA HOADLEY MACKINTOSH
13 DECEMBER 1888 · NEW YORK

Unlocated. Only the postmarked envelope of a letter to Melville's niece Maria, the oldest daughter of his sister Catherine Hoadley, is cited by Davis and Gilman (Berkshire Athenaeum; at present unlocated). She had married William H. Mackintosh of Boston in 1887. According to a transcription in Jay Leyda's hand in the Davis-Gilman file, Melville addressed the envelope: "Mrs. William H. Mackintosh | Roxbury | Mass. | *The Warren*."; it was postmarked in New York on 13 December 1888. Davis-Gilman Unlocated 415.

TO JAMES BILLSON
31 DECEMBER 1888 · NEW YORK

This is Melville's last known letter to James Billson, and like many of his earlier ones it is an extended letter of thanks. On 4 December Billson had sent him James Thomson's *Shelley, A Poem: With Other Writings Relating to Shelley by the Late James Thomson, to Which Is Added an Essay on the Poems of William Blake, by the Same Author* (London: Whittingham, 1884; Sealts 520), according to Elizabeth Melville's memorandum (1861–1902; Sealts, *Early Lives*, p. 172). Billson's [4?] December letter concerning the gift is unlocated. Possibly Billson sent Melville this book because Melville had written in his 2 April 1886 letter that he was glad to learn of Thomson's interest in Blake. In the essay that Melville read, Thomson praised the "truth and depth" of Blake's "genius" (p. 127).

Melville's reference to "those lines on Patti" is to the last section of "He Heard Her Sing"—one of the last poems Thomson wrote, which was published posthumously in *A Voice from the Nile* (London: Reeves & Turner, 1884). In it Thomson described the power and beauty of an unnamed singer's voice, evidently that of Adelina Patti (1843–1919), the famous soprano of the later nineteenth century—an identification Billson may have passed on to Melville in one of his now unlocated letters.

It is not known how Billson got two copies of *John Marr*, if not from Melville, who controlled all the twenty-five copies printed; perhaps Melville had sent him both with instructions to give the second one to another of his British admirers. In any case, J.W. Barrs was an obvious candidate for the "superfluous copy." He had sent Melville a copy of Thomson's *A Voice from the Nile*, which Melville acknowledged in his 2 April 1886 letter to Billson. The clipping about Thomson, mentioned at the close of this letter as supplied by Elizabeth Melville, is unidentified.

104 E 26th St. N.Y.
The last day of 1888.

My Dear Sir: I have your letter, and thank you for it, and not less for the book accompanying it. You could hardly have sent me anything more welcome. All the contents are highly interesting; but I agree with you in thinking the Essay on Blake the most so. I learned much from it. — But "The City of Dreadful Night", one can hardly overestimate it, massive and mighty as it is, — its gloom is its sublimity. The confronting Sphinx and Angel, where shall we go to match them? —— Thomson's criticisms in general are very refreshing in their total ignoring of the conventional in criticism. — But I must rein up. My eyes have been annoying me for some days past; and I know of hardly anything more disconcerting. But let me think of those lines on Patti, and forget that.

You did well in giving your superfluous volume of "John Marr" to Mr Barrs, to whom I am indebted for "A Voice from the Nile"

&c — an appreciated gift. — May the Powers long keep snug your *Birds Nest!*

Most Truly Yours
Herman Melville

I enclose a slip that will interest you & other appreciators of Thomson, something my wife came across in her newspaper reading.

H. M.

To Mr. James Billson

ALS on a 22.8 × 17.5 cm sheet, folded in half, of white wove paper. Melville inscribed the first, third, and fourth pages, in ink. Billson numbered the letter at the top of the first page "(9)" in ink.

LOCATION: at present unknown. *Provenance*: C. A. Stonehill, Ltd., catalogue 137 (1938), in item 91; Frank J. Hogan sale, Parke-Bernet Galleries, 23–24 January 1945, in lot 438; H. Bradley Martin sale, Sotheby's, New York, sale 5971, 30–31 January 1990, in lot 2170A; 19th Century Shop in partnership with other book dealers.

PUBLICATION: *The Nation and the Athenæum* 29 (13 August 1921), 713. Davis-Gilman 248.

TEXTUAL NOTES: enclose] *initial* e *written over* i • something] *after canceled* a sh • To Mr. James Billson] *on the otherwise blank second page; placed here editorially*

1889

TO ABRAHAM LANSING
16 MARCH 1889 · NEW YORK

On 14 March Abraham Lansing, as administrator, had sent Melville a check for $1216.89—Melville's share in his sister Frances Priscilla's estate, which was probated on 11 March 1889. Discovering that a mistake had been made, Lansing then telegraphed Melville and sent him a substitute check for $1123.79 (see LETTERS RECEIVED, pp. 747–48). With this formal reply Melville enclosed the earlier check and two prepared typewritten receipts, on which Lansing had filled in the revised amount of the inheritance. Presumably Lansing filed the first of these receipts with the surrogate records. The second, which he marked "Duplicate" at the top and which Melville signed and dated, remains with the letter (see Paltsits, p. 64).

N.Y. March 16

Dear Mr Lansing:

I have your first note, and the telegram following it, and also your second note.

Enclosed herewith you have the duplicate receipts and the first cheque.

Truly Yours
H. Melville

The first receipt ⎱
I have destroyed. ⎰

ALS on an 11.4 × 17.5 cm part-sheet (torn along the left edge) of white wove paper. Melville inscribed only one side of the leaf, in ink. Another hand later noted in pencil "[1889]" at the top of that page.

LOCATION: NYPL-GL.

PUBLICATION: Paltsits, p. 63. Davis-Gilman 249.

TO JOHN W. PALMER
23 MARCH 1889 · NEW YORK

The "friendly note" John Williamson Palmer (1825–1906) wrote to Melville is un-located, as are the copies he sent of two of his books, the travel account *The Golden Dagon; or, Up and Down the Irrawaddi* (New York: Dix & Edwards, 1856; Sealts 396.2), and the novel *After His Kind* (New York: Holt, 1886; Sealts 396.1), published under the pseudonym John Coventry. It appears Melville waited at least several days to write this note, since Palmer's account of his adventures in the Burman Empire was about three hundred pages, a length which would have taken Elizabeth Melville many more than one or two evenings to read aloud. Nothing is known of any acquaintance Palmer may have had with Melville. He worked as a doctor in San Francisco during the gold rush of 1849, traveled to Hawaii and India, and then settled in New York as a writer, translator, and editor. As a correspondent for the *New-York Tribune* he reported the Civil War from the South. Besides the two works he sent Melville he wrote other travel sketches, a comedy, two books on engraving and art, and a number of poems.

104 E 26ᵗʰ St.
March 23ᵈ, '89.

Dear Dʳ Palmer:

Let me thank you for your friendly note and the gift accompanying it. — To night my wife will conclude the reading to me of "*Up & Down the Irrawaddy*." Those stirring adventures in scenes so orientally novel make the book unique to me, and have interested me more than any volume I have read for a long time. As to that "exuberance" you allege against the work, it is the exuberance of that prime staple — vitality.

"*After his Kind*" (a significant title) I have as yet, of course, been able but to dip into; but the flavor so obtained bespeaks the ripe wine

Sincerely yours

H. Melville

ALS on a 22.6 × 17.5 cm sheet, folded in half, of white wove paper. Melville inscribed the first and third pages, in ink. The letter was at one time attached on the fourth page to another sheet, but has since been removed.

LOCATION: UV–Barrett.

PUBLICATION: Davis–Gilman 250.

TEXTUAL NOTES: volume] *after canceled* pages • you allege] you *altered from* your

TO HARPER & BROTHERS
BEFORE 19 JUNE 1889 · NEW YORK

Unlocated. On 18 March 1889 Harper & Brothers, who were preparing their *Fifth Reader* (Sealts 239), wrote Melville asking permission to include in it an extract from Chapter 61 of *Moby-Dick* (see LETTERS RECEIVED, pp. 749–50). Melville's letter granting permission was received "several weeks ago" according to the Harpers' 19 June reply (see LETTERS RECEIVED, p. 750) and must therefore have been written in late May or early June. See the NN *Moby-Dick*, pp. 774–75, for a discussion of the published extract. Davis–Gilman Unlocated 416.

TO SIMEON E. BALDWIN
17 NOVEMBER 1889 · NEW YORK

In addition to the eight thousand dollars that Elizabeth Melville's cousin Ellen Gifford willed Melville (see the headnote to his 6 November 1888 letter to her), she left him her "share or right in the New York Society Library — without assessments on the share — should he desire it — " (MHS-S). Simeon Baldwin, the executor of her will, apparently wrote to Melville about this on 15 November in a now unlocated letter. Melville's new membership, free from all annual payments, was issued by the library on 20 November. (For more about the settlement of Ellen Gifford's estate, see LETTERS RECEIVED, p. 763.)

Simeon E. Baldwin, Esq.
Dear Sir:
    In reply to yours of the 15th Inst. — Herewith you have a paper which, if you sign &c, as executor, and re-mail to

W. S. Butler, Librarian,
Society Library,
University Place
New-York
N.Y.

he will thereupon issue a new certificate in my name and send it to
me.

Yours Truly
H. Melville

New York ⎱
Nov. 17 '89 ⎰

ALS on white paper framed in an 11 × 17 cm mat. Melville inscribed the page, in ink.

Location: Collection of David Shneidman. *Provenance*: Baldwin family descendants; Whitlock Farm Booksellers, 1974.

Publication: (reproduction only) *Melville Society Extracts* 58 (May 1984), 7.

TO ARCHIBALD MacMECHAN
5 DECEMBER 1889 · NEW YORK

When Archibald MacMechan (1862–1933) wrote to Melville in 1889 he had recently
received a Ph.D. from Johns Hopkins and been appointed Munro Professor of English at Dalhousie University, Halifax, Nova Scotia. Later he lectured at Harvard,
Columbia, and the University of Chicago, edited works by Carlyle and Tennyson,
and published a number of histories and anthologies of Canadian literature. In his
letter of 21 November 1889 (which Melville mistakenly refers to as a 12 November
letter), MacMechan had asked for particulars of Melville's life and "*literary methods*"
to use in an article he planned to write about him (see Letters Received, pp. 752–
53). His essay on *Moby-Dick*, "The Best Sea-Story Ever Written," was published in
Queen's Quarterly 7 (October 1899), 120–30, and in Henry Salt's *Humane Review* 7
(October 1901), 242–52, at the suggestion of one of Melville's early admirers, Dr.
Samuel A. Jones. (For Jones's 17 January 1900 letter to MacMechan with this sug-
gestion and a reminiscence of Melville as a frequenter of New York bookstores, see
Frederick J. Kennedy, "Dr. Samuel Arthur Jones and Herman Melville," *Melville
Society Extracts* 32 [November 1977], 3–7.)

On 23 December 1889 MacMechan replied to this letter and proposed calling
on Melville "in the spring months" (see Letters Received, pp. 753–54).

104 E. 26 St.
N.Y.

Dear Sir: I beg you to overlook my delay in acknowledging yours of the 12th ult. It was unavoidable.

Your note gave me pleasure, as how should it not, written in such a spirit.

But you do not know, perhaps, that I have entered my eighth decade. After twenty years nearly, as an outdoor Custom House officer, I have latterly come into possession of unobstructed leisure, but only just as, in the course of nature, my vigor sensibly declines. What little of it is left I husband for certain matters as yet incomplete, and which indeed may never be completed.

I appreciate, quite as much as you would have me, your friendly good will, and shrink from any appearance to the contrary.

Trusting that you will take all this, and what it implies, in the same spirit that prompts it, I am Very Truly Yours

Herman Melville

To Professor MacMechan
Dec. 5, '89

ALS on a 22.7 × 17.5 cm sheet, folded in half, of white wove paper. Melville inscribed the first and third pages, in ink.

LOCATION: Dalhousie University. *Provenance*: Mrs. C. R. E. Willets, Halifax, Nova Scotia.

PUBLICATION: Weaver, pp. 380–81. Davis-Gilman 251.

TEXTUAL NOTES: would have] *before canceled word-start* • To Professor . . . '89] *on the otherwise blank second page; placed here editorially*

TO BEN W. AUSTIN
5 DECEMBER 1889 · NEW YORK

Ben W. Austin, of Sioux City, Iowa, started collecting autographs as early as 1875. In 1884–85 he formed a fictitious society, "The Northwestern Literary and Historical Society," with a fictitious president and with himself as secretary. His practice was to write to well-known individuals informing them of their election as honorary members of the society. If he received a reply, he then wrote back, generally asking for the correspondent's photograph and for any letters from men of note they might possess (see Simon Gratz, *A Book about Autographs* [Philadelphia: Campbell, 1920], pp. 35–38). This method of collecting might suggest that Austin had been in earlier correspondence with Melville; however, no earlier letters from Melville were listed in the sale catalogue for Austin's collection (see under provenance, below). Austin's 26 November letter to Melville is unlocated; it apparently mentioned Judge Shaw and the names of some other relatives but did not include a request for a photograph. According to Gratz, very few "honorary members" complied with Austin's requests for the autographs of other well-known individuals, as Melville does here.

Ben. W. Austin Esq.
Dear Sir:
    In reply to yours of the 26th Inst. —
    I inclose you an autograph of Judge Shaw.
    For the others, I have none; but refer you to a grand daughter of Gen. Gansevoort of Fort Stanwix — Mrs Abraham Lansing, 119 Washington Avenue, Albany, N.Y.

Yours &c
H. Melville

N.Y. Dec 5th '89

ALS on an 11.4 × 17.5 cm part-sheet (torn along the left edge) of white wove paper. Melville inscribed only one side of the leaf, in ink. It was later mounted on another sheet with a clipping of Melville's listing in *Appletons' Cyclopædia* and a reproduction of a drawing by Francis Day made of Melville from the 1861 Dewey photograph.

LOCATION: American Antiquarian Society, Worcester, Massachusetts. *Provenance*: Austin sale, C. F. Libbie & Co., 10–11 April 1900, in lot 1035.

PUBLICATION: Davis-Gilman 252.

TEXTUAL NOTE: Lansing] *after* L *added in ink in margin; then both* L *and* Lansing *canceled and* Lansing *written below and inserted with line and caret, all in pencil*

1890

TO RICHARD GARNETT
[1890?] · [NEW YORK?]

Unlocated. An exchange with the man-of-letters Richard Garnett (1835–1906), first assistant keeper (1875–84) and later keeper (1890–99) of printed books at the British Museum, is cited at the beginning of an article entitled "Moby-Dick and Mocha-Dick," by Garnett's son, Robert Singleton Garnett (1866–1932), which appeared in *Blackwood's Magazine* 226 (December 1929), 841–58. Although primarily concerned with the similarities between Melville's *Moby-Dick* and J. N. Reynolds's "Mocha Dick" (*Knickerbocker Magazine*, May 1839), Garnett's essay opened with a reminiscence of his father's writing to Melville and receiving a reply: "Next, I think, my recollection is of the postman at our door with a letter written on a piece of yellowish paper from Herman Melville. Its exact language I cannot recall, but its tenor was: 'Your suggestion comes too late, and it astonishes me, for I had thought my books long forgotten. All the same, I thank you for asking me to write my life and adventures.' " Richard Garnett, who had published numerous biographical monographs, may have wanted the details of Melville's life for such an article, or possibly he had solicited such an autobiographical piece for a publication of which he was editor. No such article, however, has been located. Although his son gives no date for this letter, he recalled that "not long" after receiving Melville's reply "there followed the news of the death of the author of 'Moby-Dick,' on 28th September 1891."

TO H. S. SALT
12 JANUARY 1890 · NEW YORK

After taking a first in the Classical Tripos at Cambridge in 1875, Henry Stephens Salt (1851–1939), a Fabian Socialist, taught nine years at Eton and then wrote biographies of James Thomson (referred to in this letter by Thomson's adopted pseudonymous initials, "B. V.") and Thoreau, critical studies of Shelley and Tennyson, and several other works. He had learned of Melville through the bookseller and publisher Bertram Dobell, a friend of Thomson. His 1889 letter to Melville proposing the republication of *Typee* is now unlocated, but Melville's letter on his behalf to the publisher John Murray written on the same day as this one does survive (see just below).

As Melville's postscript shows, Salt's earlier letter had also mentioned his article in the November 1889 *Scottish Art Review*, entitled "Herman Melville," which surveyed Melville's works with the general aim of increasing public appreciation. Salt's friend J. W. Barrs sent this article to Melville and then wrote on 13 January 1890, expressing his disappointment that Salt had not done justice to *Mardi, Moby-Dick, Pierre,* or *Israel Potter*, and adding appreciative comments of his own on these works and on *John Marr* (see LETTERS RECEIVED, pp. 759–62).

In his 1930 reminiscences, *Company I Have Kept* (London: Allen & Unwin), Salt later quoted Melville's sentence from this letter about *The City of Dreadful Night* (see LETTERS RECEIVED, pp. 762–63, for this passage). For Salt's continuing interest in Melville's works, see the headnote to Melville's 25 February letter to him, below.

104 E. 26th St.
New York
Jan 12, 1890

Dear Sir: Illness has prevented an earlier reply to your note. — The proposition to reprint "Typee" somewhat embarrasses me, since the circumstances are such, that I can not feel myself at liberty to entertain it without first seeking light from Mr. Murray.

I shall write that gentleman by the same mail that conveys this and upon receiving his reply, will forthwith communicate with you

again. — Yes, "B. V." interests me much. I shall try and procure
here that "Life" which you have written. The *"City of Dreadful
Night"* is the modern Book of Job, under an original poem duskily
looming with the same aboriginal verities. Much more might be
said; but enough

Yours truly

H. Melville

Mr. H. S. Salt

   I have not yet received the "Scottish Art Review" containing
your critique, which you say Mr. Barrs was kind enough to mail
me. —

Original document not located. Text from Jay Leyda's 1948 typed transcription (in Davis-
Gilman file) from the ALS (1 p.?), then in the collection of Dr. A. S. W. Rosenbach of Phila-
delphia (Davis and Gilman were already unable to locate it in this collection in 1959). Melville
addressed the envelope "Mr. H. S. Salt | 38 Gloucester Road | Regent's Park | London |
Eng."

PUBLICATION: (partial) *Log*, II, 821. Davis-Gilman 253.

TO JOHN MURRAY
12 JANUARY 1890 · NEW YORK

As indicated by both Melville's 25 February 1890 letter to H. S. Salt (below) and Arthur Stedman's 24 October 1892 letter to the United States Book Co. (Yale University
Library), John Murray answered this letter with a refusal to allow *Typee* (and *Omoo*) to
be published in the Camelot Series (for more on this now unlocated reply, see LETTERS
RECEIVED, p. 759). The series was published by the Walter Scott company of London
and included Hazlitt's *Essays*, edited by Frank Carr; Saadi's *Gulistan*, translated by
James Ross; and Walter Savage Landor's *The Pentameron*, edited by Havelock Ellis. It
was later assimilated into "The Scott Library: The World's Literary Masterpieces,"
which sold for a shilling and included in 1889, among American writers, Thoreau,
Lowell, Longfellow, Whitman, Emerson, and Holmes.

104 E. 26th St.

New York

Jan. 12, 1890

Dear Sir:

   I have received a note from a gentleman writing for the Editor
of the *Camelot Series*, asking me whether I would have any objection

to the reprinting of "*Typee*" in that Series. To which note I have written to the effect, that I do not feel myself at liberty to entertain such a proposition without first communicating with you.

I have no exact knowledge as to the bearing at this present time of the Copyright Law in the matter. But even if that set the book free, I should, under the circumstances, still feel myself bound to write you this note, and say that my consent to the proposition in question must be contingent upon yours.

Be good enough to advise me, at your convenience.

Very truly Yours
H. Melville

Mr. John Murray.

ALS on a 22.8 × 17.5 cm sheet, folded in half, of white wove paper. Melville inscribed the first and third pages, in ink. Another hand, presumably a clerk's, noted in ink on the fourth page "1890. January 12 | Melville H".

LOCATION: Murray.

PUBLICATION: (partial) *Log*, II, 820–21. Davis, p. 218. Davis-Gilman 254.

TEXTUAL NOTES: Law in] in *possibly* on • must] *after canceled* can • contingent] en *written over* n • at your] *after canceled* when • Mr. John Murray.] *on the otherwise blank second page; placed here editorially*

TO W. CLARK RUSSELL
9 FEBRUARY 1890 · NEW YORK

After Melville dedicated *John Marr* to him (see LETTERS RECEIVED, pp. 742–43), Russell, in turn, dedicated his three-volume novel *An Ocean Tragedy* (London: Chatto & Windus, 1890) to Melville. He wrote Melville on 5 January 1890 announcing that he had asked his English publishers to send Melville an advance copy of the book and lamenting the fact that the Harpers' American edition did not include the dedication (see LETTERS RECEIVED, pp. 754–56). Four days later Russell sent along a proof-copy of the dedication (see LETTERS RECEIVED, pp. 756–59). Both the volumes and the proof-copy dedication are now in the Melville Collection of the Houghton Library of Harvard University (Sealts 433). The volumes apparently took several weeks to arrive, since Melville did not acknowledge them until this letter of 9 February.

Although this is the only letter by Melville apart from a possible draft now located from Melville's correspondence with Russell, there were certainly others (see, for example, the inferred one apparently written between 26 March and 10 April 1888). Russell's son, Herbert Russell, who served as secretary for his rheuma-

tism-bound father, later reminisced that Melville and Russell "maintained an intimate friendship for many years, altho, curiously enough, the two never met. But
they were drawn together, not only by the freemasonry of the sea, but by a mutual
generosity of recognition which was profound in its sincerity. I remember Melville
writing to him: 'Where do you get your wonderful wealth of description?' and his
answering: 'From the same place that you get yours'" ("When the Sea Came into
Literature," *Literary Digest International Book Review* 3 [May 1925], 373).

104 E. 26 St.
New York
Feb. 9th '90

My Dear Mr Russell:

Your three handsome volumes have arrived. — Now shall I
have the satisfaction of reading a book of yours in fair type, tho' yet,
on account of my eyes, it must be by piecemeal.

For the Dedication, nothing in the way of mere literary commendation ever gave me a tithe of the pleasure. And how highly do
I estimate that kindly magnanimity which has led you, in one point
at least, so much to overrate me.

God bless you.
Herman Melville

ALS on a 22.8 × 17.5 cm sheet, folded in half, of white wove paper. Melville inscribed the
first and third pages, in ink.

LOCATION: at present unknown. *Provenance*: Jolly & Son, 18 July 1969, lot 216; Seven Gables
Bookshop; H. Bradley Martin sale, Sotheby's, New York, sale 5971, 30–31 January 1990, lot
2173; Ximenes Books.

PUBLICATION: Lynn Horth, "Letters Lost / Letters Found: A Progress Report on Melville's
Correspondence," *Melville Society Extracts* 81 (May 1990), 1–8 (with reproduction on p. 4).

TEXTUAL NOTES: Russell] *crossed out later in black ink by another hand* • piecemeal] ec *mended*

TO LEE & SHEPARD
13 FEBRUARY 1890 · NEW YORK

Lee & Shepard was a publishing firm at 10 Milk Street in Boston. Their inquiry of
10 February is now unlocated, but it concerned their forthcoming book *The Builders of American Literature: Biographical Sketches of American Authors Born Previous to
1826* (1893) by Francis H. Underwood. The entry on Melville (pp. 233–34) was an
updating of Underwood's earlier biographical sketch that preceded an excerpt from
Typee in his *Handbook of English Literature* (vol. 2, 1873; pp. 458–60), also published

by Lee & Shepard. Melville's inexact citation of the title *Clarel: A Poem and Pilgrimage in the Holy Land* was copied by Underwood in his entry. (For more about Underwood, see the headnote to Melville's 19 August 1857 letter to the publishers Phillips, Sampson, & Co.)

To Lee & Shephard.

New York
Feb. 13, '90

Gentlemen:

In reply to yours of the 10th. —

My present address is 104 E. 26th St. New York.

No book of mine has been published since the date you name (1870) but *"Clarel, A Pilgrimage and Poem,"* New York, 1876.

Yours &c
H. Melville

ALS on an 11.3 × 16.2 cm part-sheet (torn along the left edge) of white wove paper. Melville inscribed only one side of the leaf, in ink. Another hand (or hands) noted in pencil at the top of the letter "Clarel" and below wrote "h —".

LOCATION: Beinecke Library, Yale University. *Provenance*: Owen Franklin Aldis (tipped into a first edition of *Clarel*).

PUBLICATION: Davis-Gilman 255.

TO H. S. SALT

25 FEBRUARY 1890 · NEW YORK

In Melville's 12 January 1890 letter to H. S. Salt, he wrote that he would try to get "that 'Life' which you have written"—*The Life of James Thomson ("B. V.") With a Selection from His Letters and a Study of His Writings* (London: Reeves & Turner, 1889). Melville did buy a copy, now unlocated, which his wife later gave to Arthur Stedman (Sealts 435a; cited in Stedman's 4 May 1892 letter to Salt [The Newberry Library]). On 2 February 1890, according to Elizabeth Melville's memorandum, Salt also sent Melville the presentation copy acknowledged here (HCL-M; Sealts 435; Sealts, *Early Lives*, p. 172), along with his now unlocated 2 February note.

When Salt revised this biography in 1898 for the publishers A. & H. B. Bonner, he included (pp. 51, 139–40) two of Melville's brief comments praising Thomson's poetry in his letters of 1 December 1884 and 22 January 1885 to Salt's friend James Billson. Salt's final revision of the book in 1914, published by Watts, included both of these quotations as well as an additional one from Melville's 22 January 1885 letter to Billson (pp. 45, 117, and 151). (Salt had first quoted from Melville's letters to Billson [those of 10 October 1884 and 22 January 1885] in his earlier article " 'Marquesan Melville,' " which appeared in the *Gentleman's Magazine* 272 [March 1892], 248–57.)

This 1890 letter conveying John Murray's unwillingness to sanction the publication of Melville's early books in the Camelot Series closes what is now known of Melville's brief correspondence with H. S. Salt. At the invitation of John Murray IV (1851–1928; the son of Melville's publisher, who died in 1892), Salt did later write an essay entitled "Memoir of Herman Melville" that served as preface for the 1893 reprintings of both *Typee* and *Omoo* that the Murray firm brought out (Salt accepted the invitation in a 15 March 1893 letter; Murray). Later in a 20 July 1910 letter, Salt proposed a biography of Melville to Murray, and after receiving a now unlocated reply, Salt wrote back on 28 July 1910 that he "had better get into touch with the family, and see whether they would like me to have the use of such material as they possess. I understand they have letters, diaries, and even unpublished stories" (Murray). Just how far Salt proceeded with his research is not known, but he later turned over all his material to John Freeman, who published his *Herman Melville* (London: Macmillan) in 1926 (see Stephen Winsten, *Salt and His Circle* [London: Hutchinson, 1951], p. 14).

104 E. 26th St.
New York
Feb. 25, '90

Dear Sir:

Thanks for your note of the 2^d Inst. — with added thanks for the book.

I have read it with the greatest interest, and can sincerely say that I feel under obligations to you as the author of so excellent a biography of a very remarkable poet and man. —

Concerning "Typee." — As I engaged to do, I wrote to Mr. Murray. The information contained in the reply is such, and the manner of conveying it is such, that I consider myself bound, by considerations both of right and courtesy, not to sanction any English issue of the book — (during my lifetime) other than that of the original purchaser and publisher. —

Were matters otherwise, I should be glad to accede to your proposition, especially as it would put me into such good company as that embraced in the Camelot Series. — Feeling that you will appreciate the spirit in which I write this, I am

With much respect
Yours very truly
H. Melville.

To
Mr. H. S. Salt
London

ALS on a 22.4 × 17.5 cm sheet, folded in half, of white wove paper. Melville inscribed the first and third pages, in ink, and addressed the envelope "Mr. H. S. Salt | 38 Gloucester Road | Regent's Park | London | England"; it was postmarked in New York on 28 February and in London on 10 March.

LOCATION: at present unknown. *Provenance*: H. Bradley Martin sale, Sotheby's, New York, sale 5971, 30–31 January 1990, lot 2174; Biblioctopus Books.

PUBLICATION: (partial) *Log*, II, 822–23. Davis-Gilman 256.

TEXTUAL NOTES: the reply] the *written over* this · embraced] *after canceled of* · To . . . London] *on the otherwise blank second page; placed here editorially*

TO CATHERINE GANSEVOORT LANSING
23 MAY 1890 · NEW YORK

A Post Office money order for $134, the subject of this letter, was sent to cover Melville's share in the expense of the family burial plot in the Albany Rural Cemetery, at the request of Melville's sister Catherine (Kate) Hoadley and of her daughter Charlotte (Lottie) Hoadley (whose note "received the other day" is now unlocated). Catherine Lansing's 27 May acknowledgment (see her endorsement) is also unlocated.

New York
May 23, '90

Dear Kate:

Agreeably to Lottie's request, in note received the other day, I send you in form of a P.O. order my apportioned quota toward defraying certain expences.

For the interest you have shown in overseeing the work — an interest whereof Kate (my sister) and Lottie (at present both here in N.Y.) have told me, I, for one, am by no means unappreciative.

With kind regards to Abraham I am, affectionately,

H. Melville

ALS on a 22.7 × 17.6 cm sheet, folded in half, of white wove paper. Melville inscribed the first page, in ink. Catherine Lansing wrote diagonally in ink in the left top corner "ack^d & | sent recpt. — | May 27, 1890."

LOCATION: Berkshire Athenaeum, Pittsfield, Massachusetts. *Provenance*: Agnes Morewood.

PUBLICATION: *Log*, II, 824–25. Davis-Gilman 257.

TO HAVELOCK ELLIS
10 AUGUST 1890 · NEW YORK

In 1889 Havelock Ellis (1859–1939) was already pursuing his numerous sociological and psychological studies, with which he combined an interest in literature and the creative process. While editing Cesare Lombroso's *Men of Genius* (1891) he came to oppose Lombroso's idea that the genius and the criminal were "complementary forms of degeneration." Convinced that objective, statistical methods would demonstrate his view, he began collecting data on "the ancestry of distinguished English & American poets and imaginative writers." He knew a number of Melville's British admirers such as H. S. Salt (see Melville's 25 February 1890 letter to Salt, above), and was a close friend in particular of Edward Carpenter (see the NN *Moby-Dick*, p. 742, and Phyllis Grosskurth, *Havelock Ellis* [New York: Knopf, 1980], pp. 69, 107–109, and *passim*). On 19 July he wrote to ask Melville about his ancestry (see LETTERS RECEIVED, pp. 764–65). His researches led, among other writings, to "The Ancestry of Genius," *Atlantic Monthly* 7 (March 1893), but there he dealt only with English and French writers and did not use the information in Melville's letter (see Houston Peterson, *Havelock Ellis, Philosopher of Love* [Boston: Houghton Mifflin, 1928], pp. 187–88). In reply to a 5 August 1933 inquiry from John H. Birss, Ellis wrote that there was "nothing to add regarding my so slight contact with Herman Melville. I was (& am) interested in the ancestry of genius, & I wrote to H. M. & a few other writers I admired to ask if they would tell me something about their ancestry. Nothing further happened" (UV-Barrett).

Melville's genealogical report to Ellis is correct in purport if not in detail. His paternal great-grandfather was Allan Melvill (1727–61), a native of Scoonie parish, Fifeshire, Scotland, who emigrated in 1748. His maternal great-grandfather was Harme Gansevoort (1712–1801), who was born in Albany, not, as Melville states, in Holland. It was his great-great-great-grandfather Harme Van Ganzvort (d. 1710) who was in fact born in Holland before emigrating in 1660. Melville's paternal grandmother was Priscilla Scollay (1755–1833), of Scottish—not Irish—descent. However, his great-great-grandmother, Mary Cargill, who raised Melville's grandfather, Thomas Melvill, after both of his parents had died, was of Irish descent (see Merton M. Sealts, Jr., "The Melvill Heritage," *Harvard Library Bulletin* 34 [Fall 1986], 337–61, and Cuyler Reynolds, *Genealogical and Family History of Southern New York and the Hudson River Valley* [New York: Lewis Historical Publishing Co., 1913], I, 61–63 and 65–66).

104 E. 26th St. N.Y.

Aug 10, '90

Dear Sir: I have been away from town, a wanderer hardly reachable for a time, so that your letter was long in coming to hand.

And now in responce thereto.

My great grandfather on the paternal side was a native of Scotland. On the maternal side, and in the same remove, my progenitor was a native of Holland; and, on that side, the wives were all of like ancestry.

As to any strain of other blood, I am ignorant, except that my paternal grandfather's wife was of Irish Protestant stock.

Very Truly yours
Herman Melville

To
Mr. Havelock Ellis

ALS on a 22.4 × 17.6 cm sheet, folded in half, of white laid paper. Melville inscribed the first and third pages, in ink, and addressed the envelope "Mr. Havelock Ellis | Earlsbrook Road | Redhill, Surrey | England"; it was postmarked in New York on 12 August 1890. An autograph copy of this letter made by Havelock Ellis is in the Huntington Library, San Marino, California.

LOCATION: UV-Barrett. *Provenance*: Carroll A. Wilson (inserted in a first edition of *Clarel*).

PUBLICATION: Carroll A. Wilson, *Thirteen Author Collections of the Nineteenth Century and Five Centuries of Familiar Quotations* (New York: Privately Printed for Charles Scribner's Sons, 1950), I, 315. Davis-Gilman 258.

TEXTUAL NOTES: on the paternal side] *inserted above, circled, and connected to caret* • wife] *before canceled word-start* • To . . . Ellis] *on the otherwise blank second page; placed here editorially*

TO T. FISHER UNWIN
10 AUGUST 1890 · NEW YORK

Unlocated. A one-and-a-half-page letter to T. Fisher Unwin (1848–1935), the British publisher, was listed as lot 309 in the catalogue for the sale held at Sotheby's in London on 16–17 December 1974 (reportedly bought for £850 by the dealer Charles W. Sachs). The catalogue description of the letter states that the heading included Melville's 104 E. Twenty-sixth Street address in New York and the date 10 August 1890. It goes on to report that Melville explains briefly in the letter why he is "unwilling to act on Unwin's 'friendly proposition' that he should revise his early novel *Redburn* for a new edition."

TO WILLIAM J. BOK
24 NOVEMBER 1890 · NEW YORK

Born in Holland in 1861, William John Bok was brought to America by his parents in 1870, where with his more illustrious brother Edward he achieved early success in newspaper work. The two brothers founded the Bok Syndicate Press in 1886 and sold their syndicated columns to some one hundred papers around the country. Edward had included Seba Smith and Melville among others in two of his "Literary

104 E. 26 St.

nov. 24, '90

Dear Sir,

Thank you for the "literary letter" you sent me, which was quite interesting, especially the reference to *John Smith.*

Yours very truly

[signature]

William J. Bok

To William J. Bok, 24 November 1890. Courtesy of the Rare and Manuscript Collections, Cornell University Library.

Leaves" columns (25 October and 7 November 1890). As a devoted autograph collector William evidently sent the " 'literary letters' " to Melville, hoping for a reply.
Both columns lamented the vicissitudes of literary fame that had left Smith in a
forgotten grave and Melville in a condition so obscure that Edward thought there
were more people who believed "Herman Melville dead than there are those who
know he is living." The 7 November column included, along with passages on
Horatio Alger and J. T. Headley, a paragraph on Melville, stating that "if one
choose to walk along East Eighteenth street, New York city, any morning about 9
o'clock, he would see the famous writer of sea stories—stories which have never
been equaled, perhaps, in their special line. Mr. Melville is now an old man, but
still vigorous. He is an employe of the Customs Revenue Service, and thus still
lingers around the atmosphere which permeated his books. Forty-four years ago,
when his most famous tale, 'Typee,' appeared, there was not a better known author
than he, and he commanded his own prices. Publishers sought him, and editors
considered themselves fortunate to secure his name as a literary star. And to-day?
Busy New York has no idea he is even alive, and one of the best informed literary
men in this country laughed recently at my statement that Herman Melville was his
neighbor by only two city blocks. 'Nonsense,' said he, 'Why, Melville is dead these
many years!' Talk about literary fame? There's a sample of it!'" The information in
the column was outdated, however; Melville had resigned his position as customs
inspector at the end of 1885 (and had last served at the foot of Seventy-ninth Street
on the East River).

104 E. 26 St.
Nov. 24, '90

Dear Sir,
    Thank you for the "literary letters" you sent me, which was
quite interesting, especially the reference to Seba Smith.

Yours Very Truly
Herman Melville

William J. Bock

ALS on a 22.8 × 17.5 cm sheet, folded in half, of white wove paper. Melville inscribed the
first page, in ink. The letter was later glued on the fourth page to another sheet, but has since
been removed.

LOCATION: Rare and Manuscript Collections, Cornell University Library. *Provenance*: Robert
H. Elias, Ithaca, New York.

PUBLICATION: Davis-Gilman 259.

TEXTUAL NOTES: interesting] *miswritten* intresting · especially] *miswritten* especally

Undated Letters

TO UNKNOWN
25 JUNE [1845–47?] · LANSINGBURGH

Unlocated. The Samuel T. Freeman auction catalogue for a sale held on 20 September 1933, lot 317, listed an ALS, 8vo., one-and-a-half-page letter by Melville, described only as an "interesting friendly letter" and dated only 25 June. Two years later an American Art Association, Anderson Galleries auction catalogue, for a sale held on 13–14 November 1935, listed an ALS, 8vo., two-page letter by Melville written from Lansingburgh and dated only 25 June in lot 254 along with a whaling log book (begun on 23 May 1844) that had been kept by David Carrick aboard the ship *Hope II* of New Bedford. This log, into which Melville's letter had been laid, contained a record of a gam with the *Acushnet* in December 1846. Possibly Melville wrote two letters dated only 25 June; but the identical date and size, and the inscription on two pages, suggest that these two items were the same letter.

TO EVERT A. DUYCKINCK
BETWEEN 1847 AND 1850 · NEW YORK

This letter, apparently delivered by hand to Duyckinck, cannot be dated exactly, but it was written on a part-sheet of "Superfine Satin" paper which Melville used throughout his residence in New York from late September 1847 to late September 1850.

There are several possible candidates for the "Mʳ Ward" mentioned here. He may be Samuel Ward (1814–84), the banker-poet of New York, brother of Julia Ward Howe and uncle of the author F. Marion Crawford. His first wife was a daughter of William B. Astor and he was himself associated in New York with his own father's banking firm of Prime, Ward, & King, both connections that could have brought him to Duyckinck's attention. His appointment as a trustee of the Astor Library is mentioned in Evert Duyckinck's 4 April 1848 letter to his brother George (NYPL-D). A second candidate is Thomas Wren Ward (1786–1858), son of a Salem merchant and from 1830 to 1853 resident American agent of Baring Brothers (for Melville's connection with Baring Brothers, see *Journals*, pp. 27, 46, 310–11, and 374). He was reading *Typee* in 1847 and, as a friend of Judge Shaw in Boston, dined with Melville in 1853, but there is no evidence that he knew Evert Duyckinck (*Log*, I, 245, 476). A third possibility is Thomas Ward (1807–73), poet, playwright, musician, contributor to the *Knickerbocker Magazine*, and author of *Passaic: A Group of Poems Touching that River* (New York: Wiley & Putnam, 1842). He may have known Duyckinck in New York literary circles, for he is called a "kindly" man in the Duyckincks' *Cyclopædia of American Literature* (1855 ed., II, 455). Finally, there was Henry Dana Ward (1797–1884), an Episcopal clergyman and educator, who with his wife, a linguist, opened a successful private school for girls in New York in 1847. Duyckinck's Episcopal affiliation could have introduced him to Ward.

Monday Afternoon

Dear Duyckinck — I am verry sorry, but a confounded head-ache — something that altogether upsets me socially — will prevent me from coming round this evening. You will excuse me, I know. I am sorry not to meet Mr Ward.

Sincerely Yours

H Melville

ALS on a 23.3 × 18.6 cm part-sheet (torn along the bottom), folded in half, of white laid paper. (Although this part-sheet does not include the manufacturer's embossed stamp, it clearly was from a sheet of Superfine Satin paper.) Melville inscribed the first page, in ink, and addressed the unstamped fourth page "Evert A Duyckinck Esq | Clinton Place."; it was presumably hand-delivered.

LOCATION: NYPL-D.

PUBLICATION: Davis-Gilman 260.

TO EVERT A. DUYCKINCK
BETWEEN 1847 AND 1850 · NEW YORK

No exact dating of this letter seems possible, although it was evidently written during Melville's residence in New York from late September 1847 to late September 1850 and was probably associated with one or another of the reviews that he prepared for Evert Duyckinck, editor of the *Literary World*. It cannot refer to his first review of 6 March 1847 ("Etchings of a Whaling Cruise"), since Melville "procured" that book himself (see his 2 February 1847 letter to Duyckinck). It may refer to any one of his other reviews: "Mr. Parkman's Tour" of *The California and Oregon Trail* (31 March 1849), "Cooper's New Novel" of *The Sea Lions* (28 April 1849), or "A Thought on Book-Binding" of Cooper's *The Red Rover* (16 March 1850). In addition, Melville received Joseph C. Hart's *Romance of Yachting* from Duyckinck for review and wrote him a refusal on 14 November 1848. Leyda associates this note with that refusal and dates it, therefore, "November 13?" 1848 (*Log*, I, 282), but there is no conclusive evidence to link the two letters. The letter could also refer to some other book Melville ultimately declined to review. Melville's misspelling of Duyckinck's name, however, suggests that it belongs to an early period in their acquaintance (see Melville's letters of 3 July 1846, [30?] July 1846, and 14 November 1848 to Duyckinck).

Dear Duyckincke

I have just received your package. I will look over the book with pleasure. And will contrive to write something about it, but being much engaged just now, wont' be able to say a very great deal. — I will see you before long.

Sincerely Yours

H Melville

Monday Evening

ALS on a 25 × 19.7 cm part-sheet (torn along the bottom), folded in half, of blue wove paper. Melville inscribed the first page, in ink, and addressed the unstamped fourth page "Evert A Duyckincke Esq | Clinton Place"; it was presumably hand-delivered. Duyckinck noted on the first page in pencil "Herman Melville".

LOCATION: NYPL-D.

PUBLICATION: (partial) *Log*, I, 282. Davis-Gilman 263 (labeled 261 in error).

TEXTUAL NOTES: received] *possibly* rcvd • contrive] r *added* • you] *inserted above caret*

TO EVERT A. DUYCKINCK
BETWEEN 1847 AND 1850 · NEW YORK

This letter was written after late September 1847 when Melville and his brother Allan, both newly married, set up housekeeping at this Fourth Avenue address in New York and probably before September 1850 when Melville and his family moved to Pittsfield. Although the house remained in his possession until early 1851 when Allan bought it from him, there is no evidence that Melville returned to New York in the intervening period or that Allan—with whom Melville usually stayed when visiting New York—ever lived in the Fourth Avenue house again (in the meantime Allan had moved to East Thirty-first Street near Lexington Avenue and then to 47 East Twenty-fourth Street).

103 4th Avenue

My Dear Duyckinck

I sincerely regret that I shall not be able to be with you this evening — as I have something to attend to that I can not see about at any other time

Yours truly

Herman Melville

Saturday morning

Original document not located. Text from Frank Pleadwell's undated typed transcription (in Davis-Gilman file) from the ALS (1 p.), then in his own collection.

LOCATION: at present unknown. *Provenance*: Adrian Hoffman Joline [but not in Joline sale catalogue]; Frank L. Pleadwell sale, Parke-Bernet Galleries, sale 1840, 8 October 1958, lot 350.

PUBLICATION: Davis-Gilman 262.

TO EVERT A. DUYCKINCK
BETWEEN 1848 AND 1850 · NEW YORK

This reply to an invitation for Melville and his brother Allan to picnic with "Mrs Cooper" (perhaps Sarah W. Cooper, one of Duyckinck's friends) was "carried" by Evert Duyckinck, Jr. (1841–57), who would have been seven and a half years old in the summer of 1848 and able then, but scarcely so a year earlier, to perform such a service. Since it was written while Melville was sharing a house in New York with his brother Allan, it can be placed in the period between the summer of 1848 and late September 1850. No documentation of Sarah Cooper's activities provides any further evidence for the letter's date. Leyda placed it as "early August?" 1848 (*Log*, I, 279), apparently associating it with Melville's picnic with Duyckinck at Fort Lee in late July of that year. But it could have been written at any time when the weather was warm enough for picnics.

The "two ladies" may have been any of the women in Melville's family, including his wife, his sister-in-law Sophia, his mother, or his sisters—all of whom were in and out of the New York household.

My Dear Sir, I should be very happy to comply with Mrs Cooper's friendly invitation, were it not that here are two ladies by my side *already* half shawled for a little excursion in a quite contrary direction, & I am the elected escort.

So give my rememberances to Mrs Cooper, & take my prayers for a happy Pic-nic.

H. M.

I opened your note without observing the superscription — & have this moment discovered that it has a joint address. But Allan is not well to day — & will therefore be forced to decline.

ALS on a 23.3 × 18.5 cm part-sheet (torn along the top), folded in half, of white laid paper, faintly embossed with the manufacturer's oval stamp in the right corner of the first leaf. Melville inscribed the first and second pages, in ink, and addressed the fourth page "Evert A Duyckinck Esq | carried [c *written over* F] by | Evert Duyckinck Jr Esq." Melville used this Superfine Satin paper throughout the period when this letter could have been written.

LOCATION: NYPL-D.

PUBLICATION: *Log*, I, 279. Davis-Gilman 261.

TEXTUAL NOTES: Cooper's] *miswritten* Cooper · Pic-nic] P *written over* p · H. M.] *before* (over) *in bottom margin* · has] h *written over* w

TO EVERT A. DUYCKINCK
BETWEEN 1847 AND 1878 · NEW YORK

This undated letter was apparently addressed to Evert Duyckinck on the outside of the folded sheet. It could have been written during either of Melville's periods of New York residence (1847–50 and after 1863) or during one of his visits from Pittsfield to New York but of course not after 1878, when Duyckinck died. Its formal language, however, suggests that it was early in their acquaintance. Since the original manuscript is now unlocated, no evidence can be adduced from the paper.

My Dear Sir

In compliance with your friendly invitation I will be very happy to call this evening about eight o'clock. Do not let me detain you home however if otherwise engaged.

Yours Very Truly
Herman Melvill

Wednesday Morning.

Original document not located. Text from Gimelson catalogue reproduction. According to two catalogue descriptions this is a one-page letter with an integral address leaf. Another hand later noted on it, "Herman Melville | Author of | Life in Typee".

LOCATION: at present unknown. *Provenance*: Paul C. Richards, catalogue 19 (March 1966), item 328; Walter Shatszki; Eleventh Cooperative Catalogue of the Middle Atlantic Chapter of the Antiquarian Booksellers Association of America (May 1967), item 363; Bruce Gimelson catalogue, June 1968, item 1037 (with reproduction); Charles Hamilton Galleries, sale 34, 8 May 1969, lot 252 (with reproduction); Paul C. Richards, catalogue 57 (October 1970), item 47 (with reproduction); Rendells, catalogue 124 (March 1977), item 88.

PUBLICATION: Kenneth Walter Cameron, "Scattered Melville Manuscripts," *American Transcendental Quarterly* 1 (First Quarter 1969), 63 (with reproduction).

TO UNKNOWN
AFTER 1849 · PLACE UNKNOWN

Unlocated. A manuscript fragment of one of Melville's letters, roughly 9.1 × 3.2 cm, which was cut along the top and left edges to leave only the closing "And oblige Yours &c | Herman Melville", inscribed in ink, now remains in the Gansevoort-Lansing Collection of the New York Public Library (box 310, folder 10). It is written on blue laid paper similar to paper of the type that Melville used intermittently after 1849 for his letters (see his 20 February 1849 letter to his brother Allan for his earliest known use of such paper).

TO SARAH HUYLER MOREWOOD
BETWEEN 1850 AND 1863 · [PITTSFIELD?]

This apparently hand-delivered letter, dated only "Friday Morning," could have been written at any time during Sarah Morewood's reign at Broadhall from 1850 to 1863.

Mr H. Melville and friends accept, with the most boisterous pleasure Mrs: Morewood's invitation for to night.

Friday Morning.

ALS, third person, "Mr H. Melville", on a 21.2 × 17.2 cm sheet, folded in half, of white wove paper, embossed with the manufacturer's stamp of two tulips. Melville inscribed the first page, in ink, and addressed the fourth page "Mrs: Morewood." Another hand later noted in ink on that page "Mr H. Melville".

LOCATION: Firestone Library, Princeton University. *Provenance*: Robert H. Taylor.

TO STANWIX MELVILLE
BETWEEN [1860?] AND 1886 · [NEW YORK?]

Unlocated. A fragment of manuscript in the Berkshire Athenaeum bears the closing "Good bye, & God bless you | Your affectionate Father | H. Melville." cut from a letter to preserve the signature (presumably the rest was destroyed). It was inscribed, in ink, on a piece of lined white wove paper cut on all but (possibly) the right edge to 9.8 × 3.3 cm; the verso is unlined and blank. It was placed in an envelope labeled by Eleanor Melville Metcalf "Signatures of letters to Stanwix" (the other fragment in the envelope is from a letter to Stanwix tentatively dated July 1872, above).

Leyda assigned this fragment to the unlocated letter Melville must have sent to Stanwix in 1886 with a manuscript power of attorney (*Log*, II, 797–98; see also the entry for that unlocated letter written before 14 February 1886). No final evidence for Leyda's assignment has been found, but possibly this fragment of Melville's letter was preserved because it was returned with the power of attorney or was among Stanwix's effects after his death on 23 February 1886. Many other assignments are equally possible, however. Possibly it belongs as early as Melville's 1860 trip to San Francisco, during which he wrote letters to his two other older children (the lined paper on which it is written, however, does not match the paper of those letters). Davis-Gilman 268.

TO THE EDITOR OF THE *WORLD*
BETWEEN 1865 AND 1888 · NEW YORK

As Melville's 7 April 1888 letter to James Billson indicates, he was outraged by T.
B. Peterson & Brothers' republication of his book *Israel Potter* under the title of *The
Refugee* in 1865 (see both the headnote to that letter and the NN *Israel Potter*, pp.
224–26, for more about this matter). An advertised list of Peterson publications
which included *The Refugee* apparently prompted Melville to write this letter to the
editor. Most likely it was addressed to and published in one of the several publications of the *New York World*, which included daily, semi-weekly, and weekly issues. Neither the original manuscript letter nor the date of the newspaper that
printed it, however, has been located; only a clipping preserved by a member of the
Lansing family is known. Leyda dated it "March? 1865" (*Log*, II, 672) on the basis
of the advertisement by T. B. Peterson & Brothers in the *New-York Times* (11
March 1865), announcing *The Refugee*. (It was deposited for copyright, as if it were
a new work, on 11 April 1865.) This letter, however, emphasizes that Melville
"conveyed" a "remonstrance" to Peterson & Brothers "long ago," which would
seem to place it some time after 1865. Years later, when Melville wrote James Billson (7 April 1888) that "A letter to the publisher arrested the publication" of *The
Refugee*, he was either not aware that Peterson continued to publish the book after
1865 or did not write his "remonstrance" until a much later date, because *The Refugee* was still listed (both in hard and paper cover) in *The American Catalogue . . . of
Books in Print and For Sale . . . July 1, 1876* (New York: Armstrong, 1880). Consequently, this letter can only be placed between 11 March 1865 and 7 April 1888.

To the Editor of the World.
    Sir: Permit me through your columns to make a disavowal.
T. B. Peterson & Brothers, of Philadelphia, include in a late list of
their publications "The Refugee; by Herman Melville."
    I have never written any work by that title. In connection with
that title Peterson Brothers employ my name without authority,
and notwithstanding a remonstrance conveyed to them long ago.
                                  Herman Melville.

Original document not located. Text from an undated clipping pasted on the verso of the title
page of a copy of *The Refugee* (Philadelphia, [1865]), inscribed with Susan Gansevoort's name
and the date 17 March 1865 on both the recto of the front free endpaper and the first page of
text. The clipping includes the heading: "A PROTEST FROM HERMAN MELVILLE." Davis-Gilman
265.

LOCATION (of clipping): NYPL-GL.

TO UNKNOWN
[1870's?] · PLACE UNKNOWN

Unlocated. Davis and Gilman (p. xviii, n.2) report a fragment of manuscript inscribed by Melville, in ink, "Sincerely and Affectionately | H. Melville" (NYPL-GL; at present unlocated). According to their description, the paper matches the white laid (graph-pattern) stationery Melville (and his wife) used in the 1870's; see the entries for 30 April 1872, 30 November 1872, 5 July 1872, and 14 August 1877, above.

TO ELIZABETH SHAW MELVILLE
UNDATED · FLORIDA

Unlocated. A letter that Melville sent to his wife from Florida can be inferred from a clipped autograph tipped into a rebound copy of *John Marr* (now in the Parkman D. Howe Library at the University of Florida). The autograph was clipped from an envelope addressed to "Mrs. Herman Melville," since the clipping bears part of a circular postmark, with "FLA." clearly visible at the bottom. Knowledge of Melville's travels has so far provided no clue to the dating of this unlocated letter. While he is known to have gone to Savannah, Georgia, in 1889 (and could have traveled on to Florida), the only previous evidence of any visit to Florida on his part is Leyda's entry (*Log*, II, 806) citing a memorandum by Eleanor Melville Metcalf (at present unlocated) that he had a rough passage home from St. Augustine; Leyda places this episode "before March 29" 1888, during Melville's trip to Bermuda. Although a few other such clippings with Melville's autograph bear remnants of postmarks (see p. 787, footnotes 20 and 21, below), this is the only one that gives some clue as to the place of mailing, if not the date, of a letter by Melville. For a reproduction, see G. Thomas Tanselle, *The Parkman Dexter Howe Library, Part VI: The Nathaniel Hawthorne Collection, The Herman Melville Collection* (Gainesville: University of Florida, 1989), p. [34] (of the Melville section).

TO UNKNOWN
25 NOVEMBER [18??] · BOSTON

Since Melville was with his family in Boston on this date for Thanksgiving in 1847, 1852, and 1857, this brief letter dated only 25 November to an unknown correspondent—presumably responding to an autograph request—probably belongs to one of these years, although other Thanksgivings in Boston that went unrecorded are also possible.

Boston Nov. 25th

Dear Sir — Your note is received, and I comply with your request.

Truly Yours

H Melville

Original document not located. Text from catalogue reproduction.

LOCATION: at present unknown. *Provenance*: Diana J. Rendell, catalogue 5 (1985), item 38 (with reproduction).

TO UNKNOWN
UNDATED · [NEW YORK?]

This brief undated letter to an unknown addressee was probably written while Melville was living or staying in New York. Since the original manuscript is now unlocated, no evidence as to its date can be adduced from the paper.

I shall be very happy to call upon you at ½ past seven.

Very truly,
H. Melville

Original document not located. Text from Davis-Gilman's typed copy (in Davis-Gilman file) of Jay Leyda's transcription (it is unknown whether from the original or from the catalogue transcription). The catalogue notes that Melville inscribed the letter in ink.

LOCATION: at present unknown. *Provenance*: Swann Catalogue, sale 2, 3 April 1942, lot 242.

PUBLICATION: Davis-Gilman 270.

TO UNKNOWN
UNDATED · PLACE UNKNOWN

Although this manuscript has neither an addressee nor a date, it is written on letterpaper and is possibly from a letter to an autograph seeker. Its close parallel to a passage in Melville's late poem "To Major John Gentian" in the Burgundy Club pieces, where his narrator quotes this same stanza (with one small variant) from Charles Fenno Hoffman's poem "Monterey," suggests that it may belong in the late 1880's (see Robert Allen Sandberg, "Melville's Unfinished *Burgundy Club* Book: A Reading Edition Edited from the Manuscripts with Introduction and Notes," Ph.D. dissertation, Northwestern University, 1989, p. 102).

Melville had known Charles Fenno Hoffman in the late 1840's (see Melville's 5 April 1849 letter to Duyckinck in which he regrets Hoffman's mental breakdown in January 1849). Hoffman first published "Monterey" anonymously in the 13 November 1846 *New York Evening Gazette* (see Homer F. Barnes, *Charles Fenno Hoffman* [New York: Columbia University Press, 1930], p. 166). When Hoffman's nephew collected and edited his poetry in 1873, he acknowledged that "Monterey" was one of the poems that had "kept alive" his uncle's reputation (*The Poems of Charles Fenno Hoffman*, ed. Edward Fenno Hoffman [Philadelphia: Porter & Coates,

1873], p. 8). Melville's quotation of the fourth stanza follows the indentation and punctuation of that edition exactly (pp. 181–82):

MONTEREY.

"Pends toi Brave Crillon! Nous avons combattu, et tu n' y etois pas."
—*Lettre de Henri IV. a Crillon.*

We were not many—we who stood
  Before the iron sleet that day—
Yet many a gallant spirit would
Give half his years if he then could
  Have been with us at Monterey.

Now here, now there, the shot, it hailed
  In deadly drifts of fiery spray,
Yet not a single soldier quailed
When wounded comrades round them wailed
  Their dying shout at Monterey.

And on—still on our column kept
  Through walls of flame its withering way;
Where fell the dead, the living stept,
Still charging on the guns which swept
  The slippery streets of Monterey.

The foe himself recoiled aghast,
  When, striking where he strongest lay,
We swooped his flanking batteries past,
And braving full their murderous blast,
  Stormed home the towers of Monterey.

Our banners on those turrets wave,
  And there our evening bugles play;
Where orange boughs above their grave
Keep green the memory of the brave
  Who fought and fell at Monterey.

We are not many—we who press'd
  Beside the brave who fell that day;
But who of us has not confess'd
He'd rather share their warrior rest,
  Than not have been at Monterey?

Do you remember Charles Fenno Hoffman's "Monterey"? How fine it is — for example: —

"The foe himself recoiled aghast,
  When, striking where he strongest lay,
We swooped his flanking batteries past,
And braving full their murderous blast,
  Stormed home the towers of Monterey."

Herman Melville

ALS on a 28.7 × 16.8 cm sheet, folded in half, of white laid paper, watermarked with an ornate design of a crown and a shield above a set of flourishes. Melville inscribed the first page, in ink. The manuscript was once tipped along the left edge to another sheet, but has since been removed. Hinges were also placed at one time along the top edge.

LOCATION: UV-Barrett. *Provenance*: Charles Hamilton Autographs, 11 December 1953; Scribner's Book Store, April 1954.

PUBLICATION: Davis-Gilman 271.

Melvill[e]

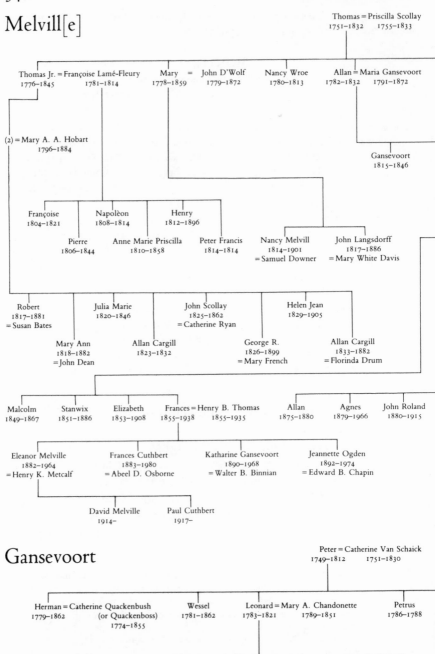

Gansevoort

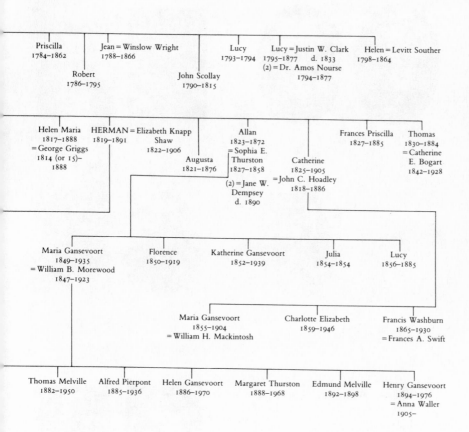

Priscilla
1784–1862

Jean = Winslow Wright
1788–1866

Lucy
1793–1794

Lucy = Justin W. Clark
1795–1877   d. 1833
(2) = Dr. Amos Nourse
1794–1877

Helen = Levitt Souther
1798–1864

Robert
1786–1795

John Scollay
1790–1815

Helen Maria
1817–1888
= George Griggs
1814 (or 15)–
1888

HERMAN = Elizabeth Knapp
1819–1891   Shaw
1822–1906

Augusta
1821–1876

Allan
1823–1872
= Sophia E.
Thurston
1827–1858
(2) = Jane W.
Dempsey
d. 1890

Catherine
1825–1905
= John C. Hoadley
1818–1886

Frances Priscilla
1827–1885

Thomas
1830–1884
= Catherine
E. Bogart
1842–1928

Maria Gansevoort
1849–1935
= William B. Morewood
1847–1923

Florence
1850–1919

Katherine Gansevoort
1852–1939

Julia
1854–1854

Lucy
1856–1885

Maria Gansevoort
1855–1904
= William H. Mackintosh

Charlotte Elizabeth
1859–1946

Francis Washburn
1865–1930
= Frances A. Swift

Thomas Melville
1882–1950

Alfred Pierpont
1885–1936

Helen Gansevoort
1886–1970

Margaret Thurston
1888–1968

Edmund Melville
1892–1898

Henry Gansevoort
1894–1976
= Anna Waller
1905–

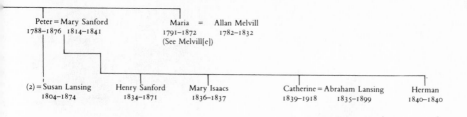

Peter = Mary Sanford
1788–1876   1814–1841

Maria   =   Allan Melvill
1791–1872   1782–1832
(See Melvill[e])

(2) = Susan Lansing
1804–1874

Henry Sanford
1834–1871

Mary Isaacs
1836–1837

Catherine = Abraham Lansing
1839–1918   1835–1899

Herman
1840–1840

Top row, left to right: Major Thomas Melvill and Priscilla Scollay Melvill, Herman's grandparents; Maria Gansevoort Melvill and Allan Melvill, Herman's parents; George Griggs, Helen Melville Griggs, Catherine Melville Hoadley, John C. Hoadley. Second row: Frances Priscilla Melville, Thomas Melville, Allan Melville, Herman Melville, Gansevoort Melville, Augusta Melville.

Third row: General Peter Gansevoort and Catherine Van Schaick Gansevoort, Herman's grandparents; Susan Lansing Gansevoort and Peter Gansevoort, Herman's aunt and uncle. Bottom row: Abraham Lansing, Catherine Gansevoort Lansing, Henry Sanford Gansevoort.

The Melvill[e] and Gansevoort Families

Lemuel Shaw

Hope Savage Shaw

Elizabeth Shaw Melville

The Melville children: Malcolm,
Elizabeth, Frances, and Stanwix

Richard T. Greene ("Toby")

Nathaniel Hawthorne

Sarah Huyler Morewood

Richard Henry Dana, Jr.

W. Clark Russell

Edmund C. Stedman

Evert A. Duyckinck   Richard Bentley   John Murray III

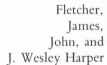

George L. Duyckinck

Fletcher,
James,
John, and
J. Wesley Harper

Charles F. Briggs   George William Curtis   George P. Putnam

Arrowhead

Melville's 1860 drawing of Arrowhead

The Gansevoort family mansion

Broadhall in the 1870's

Letters Received

1832

FROM HELEN MARIA MELVILLE
BEFORE 8 AUGUST 1832 · PITTSFIELD

Two or more unlocated letters. While Melville worked in Albany during the cholera epidemic of the summer of 1832 (see pp. 5–6 above, for his unlocated letters to his mother written at that time), his sister Helen wrote him from Pittsfield, where the rest of the family had retreated. In an 8 August letter to their uncle Peter Gansevoort, Helen complained: "I am sorry that my brother Herman cannot find time to answer my last, but tell him I am expecting a letter every day and shall be sadly disappointed if I return to Albany before he writes" (NYPL-GL).

1837

FROM "R."
PUBLISHED 15 APRIL 1837 · ALBANY

At some point during his term in the Latin section of the Albany Academy between September 1836 and March 1837, Melville joined the Ciceronian Debating Society and, when that failed, the Philo Logos Society. This letter signed "R." and published in the local entertainment paper, the *Albany Microscope*, was probably written in jest, and there is no evidence that Melville wrote or published a reply. It is a sample of the type of vituperative letters that appeared in the *Albany Microscope* the following year, after Melville was elected president of the Philo Logos Society in February 1838. For more about that society and Melville's part in it, see the head-note to his 24 February 1838 letter.

Mr. Editor: — Your paper abundantly testifies to the fact, that there is in all associations, pestiferous animals of a two–legged kind; who have crept in unawares, and scattered the seeds of dissolution in the once fair and flourishing institutions. I think your paper the proper place to show them forth to the execration and contempt of the good of our community. It serves the purpose of ancient punishment, termed the *whipping post,* or the modern *tar and feathers* — *riding the rail* — or the still more modern *cowhide* manner of getting redress for grievances, without violating the spirit of the law in the last mentioned cases. Such an animal is the P***o L***s Society cursed with. He is there known by the title of Ciceronian Baboon; and his personal appearance fully establishes the correctness of the title. He is also known as *dignitatus* melvum; but it would be needless to multiply instances — let the two above suffice. To show this perturbator in his true light, it will be necessary to give a hasty sketch of the above mentioned institution, which I think will be somewhat interesting to the general reader, as its fame has spread both far and near. The society was formed for the purpose of improvement in composition, elocution and debate. It has met with unprecedented success; having "astonished the natives" of this fair city with two very spirited public debates. And it continued to flourish and spread its branches like a green bay tree, until the bohun upus melvum was transplanted into its fertile soil, from the Ciceronian Debating Society, of which he was the principle destroyer. — Then commenced the reverse of that tranquil, strait forward course of doing business; a continual scene of confusion has, and is like to continue till the society shall be annihilated. The reason why we cannot get rid of him is common to all associations. He, like a wary pettifogger, never considers "this side right, and that stark naught," or in other words, has no fixed principles, but can bear as the wind blows without gripings of conscience. This he considers a masterly display of his political powers; but, by-the-by, such politicians can only flourish in a corrupt country; for an honest man would never give a two faced man his vote. I hope the mirror is sufficiently polished to set forth this two faced gentleman in such a light, as to make associations careful how they receive such a character; or if they have an animal of this pestiferous class, to get rid of him as soon as possible. I think truth has been made sufficiently plain, and I shall hear that the young man has reformed, or proved incorrigible and been dismissed from the society. If so, I hope other associations will follow their example.

R.

Original document not located. Text from first publication, emended by NN.

PUBLICATION: *Albany Microscope*, 15 April 1837. (Partial) Gilman, pp. 74–75.

TEXTUAL NOTES (for symbols used, see p. 840): without] NN; with[ ]|out · necessary] NN; neces[ ]|sary · bear] NN; hear · by-the-by] by-the-|by · incorrigible] NN; in[ ]|corrigible

FROM MARIA GANSEVOORT MELVILLE
25 SEPTEMBER 1837 · ALBANY

Unlocated. A letter is cited in Maria Melville's 25 September 1837 letter to her daughter Augusta: "I have just written Herman a few lines, his conduct delights me, he has shown himself to possess an independant spirit not deficiant in enterprise and willing to exert himself when necessary. I shall be delighted to see him once more, before we leave Albany" (NYPL-GL). Melville's earlier work on his uncle Thomas's farm all summer and his new job as a teacher in the Sikes district near Pittsfield were most likely the source of his mother's delight.

1838

FROM "SANDLE WOOD"
PUBLISHED 17 FEBRUARY 1838 · ALBANY

This letter signed "Sandle Wood" was the first of eight letters during February through April of 1838 in the *Albany Microscope* debating Melville's election to the presidency of the Philo Logos Society. Although not directly addressed to Melville, it prompted his published reply of 24 February 1838. Melville identified "Sandle Wood" as Charles Van Loon—an identification Van Loon denied in his 10 March 1838 letter in the *Microscope* (just below). For more about the Philo Logos controversy, see the headnote to Melville's 24 February letter.

Mr. Editor: — I noticed the other day an advertisement in the columns of the Evening Journal, containing a report of the election for officers of the Philo Logos Society of this city, purporting to have been held in the room of the Association in Stanwix Hall.

Now, Sir, to my certain knowledge no such room is rented, owned, or in any manner used by that Society; and as to the election, it is a mere farce, indeed the whole concern is essentially a hoax.

In a word the institution alluded to, having been always of a consumate habit, after languishing in obscurity and neglect for the few last months, some few weeks since expired in the arms of oblivion.

Hoping that you will by giving publicity to the above expose this paltry hoax.

I remain,

Very respectfully,

Your Ob't Serv't, Sandle Wood.

Original document not located. Text from first publication, emended by NN.

PUBLICATION: *Albany Microscope*, 17 February 1838. *Log*, I, 75.

TEXTUAL NOTES: advertisement] NN; advestisement · paltry] NN; palfry · Wood.] NN; WOOD,

FROM "EX-PRESIDENT" CHARLES VAN LOON
PUBLISHED 10 MARCH 1838 · ALBANY

Responding to Melville's letter of 24 February 1838 with its personal attacks on "that silly and brainless *loon*," Charles Van Loon published this counter-attack on the "Ciceronian baboon," a title that had first appeared in print in the 15 April 1837 *Albany Microscope* letter signed "R." (above). Van Loon's letter was published, under the heading "PHILOLOGOS SOCIETY," in the 10 March issue of the *Microscope*. In turn, Melville then published his extended and inflammatory letter that appeared in the 17 and 24 March issues of the *Microscope* (see pp. 12–18 above).

Mr. Editor: — The basest villification does not unfrequently find a transitory lodgment in the public breast; the most fragile mesh of sophistry does not fail to ensnare for a moment the public mind; but, it is for the hand of truth and reason to raise the veil of black hypocrisy, to brush away the cobweb net, and expose the coward slanderer in all the shameful nakedness of vice, and unseemly deformity of guilt.

Regard for the welfare of society, and a sense of what is due to myself as an individual, impel me to hold up to the scorn and execration of the good and virtuous, the author of a foul, dastardly attack upon my character, in your paper of the 24th inst. As the name of this individual does not admit of an ingenious analytical introduction into the columns of the Microscope, I will inform the members of the Philologos Society, that it is none other than he, whose "fantastic tricks" have earned for him the richly merited title "*Ciceronian baboon;*" but I shall lead him up before the public under the more romantic appellation of Hermanus Mel*villian*. Hermanus Melvillian, a moral Ethiopian, whose conscience qualms not in view of the most atrocious guilt; whose brazen cheek never tingles with the blush of shame, whose moral principles, and sensibilities, have been destroyed by the corruption of his own black and bloodless heart. With regard to his billingsgate effusion in the Microscope, I as heartily repel its infamous allegations, as I despise the character, and detest the principles of its infamous author. Reserving a more explicit statement of particular transactions (if it be demanded) for another number, I shall now proceed to state a few facts, and leave the public to judge who is destitute of truth and veracity, and "who the author of infamous falsehoods." At a time when the Philologos Society, watered by the refreshing showers of public admiration, and cheered by the cordial "God speed" of private friendship, was fast rising to the elevation of her elder sisters, and bid fair to fulfil a career of honorable usefulness; Hermanus Melvillian entered her happy domain, and with a ruthless hand severed the ties of friendship, wantonly injured the feelings of her most estimable members, incessantly disturbed the equanimity of her proceedings, abused her unsuspecting confidence; and forever destroyed her well earned reputation. The society forbore with long suffering; reproving, exhorting and beseeching, until "forbearance ceased to be a virtue," and then did she declare in a voice of thunder, that "*the conduct of Hermanus Melvillian was disgraceful to himself, discreditable to the society, and insulting to the chair.*" In the course of time Mr. Melvillian left the city; but not until the Society, whose infant bloom and youthful vigor, gave promise of a long and useful existence, enervated by the repeated "stabs" of the assassin's poignard, dipped in the venom of his own heart, stood with her wasted form and haggard visage tottering over the grave of oblivion. — Repeated attempts were made by the few whom repeated insult, and vile defamation had not provoked to recede in disgust, to revive the dying flame, and restore the society to its wonted strength, and pristine glory. — But that untiring perseverance, that generous devotion which once characterized these individuals, was no longer exercised; and their laudable, though imbecile efforts, proved worse than in vain. The Society lingered on between life and death, when the prodigal Melvillian returned, with the face of a saint and the heart of a devil, to grieve over the ruins of the Society, and to water his victim with the tears of a human crocidile. But to "weep is vain," so thought Melvillian, and set about applying the remedy — persevering exertion. The little dispirited remnant of members were got together; a committee appointed to draft a new constitution; and it was resolved that at the next meeting the society should go into a new election. The then President having signified his intention of resigning; the devoted, penitent, leisureful Melvillian was nominated by a committee of two (himself being one) to fill the chair. Authorized by the President, Mr. M. was to have called a meeting on a specified Tuesday; but took the liberty of calling the meeting at a different time from that specified, without the consent and without notifying the President. At this unauthorized and unconstitutional meeting, Mr. M. was DULY elected President. Justice, to myself and the Society called upon me to expose this base treachery, and ungown this fawning hypocrite; which I did in the presence of the Society; detecting in his contemptable, abortive defence, the most absurd contradictions and abominable falsehoods. For the present I have done with Hermanus Melvillian. His abusive language in the last Microscope, is but the raving of an unmasked hypocrite, the "wincing, of a gall'd jade." I am not accountable for the "inelegancies" or "fabrications" of "Sandle Wood;" for myself I will say, I do not want "the ability" to defend myself against the dastardly attacks, of Hermanus Melvillian, (*alias* Philologean,) or the moral courage to expose vice, and "lash a rascal naked through the world."

Ex-President.

Original document not located. Text from first publication, emended by NN.

PUBLICATION: *Albany Microscope*, 10 March 1838. Gilman, pp. 253–54.

TEXTUAL NOTES (for symbols used, see p. 840): villification] NN; villifacation • fragile] NN; fragrile • Melvillian, a moral] NN; Melvilian, a moral • atrocious] NN; attrocious • black] NN; blace • falsehoods] NN; falshoods • perseverance] NN; perseverence • committee appointed] NN; committe appointed • absurd] NN; absurb • "lash] NN; ∧~

FROM "EX-PRESIDENT" CHARLES VAN LOON
PUBLISHED 31 MARCH AND 7 APRIL 1838 · ALBANY

This letter by "Ex-President" Van Loon, replying to Melville's letter of 17 and 24 March, appeared in the 31 March and 7 April issues of the *Albany Microscope*, under the heading "THE EXTINGUISHER." That same 31 March issue contained Melville's final published Philo Logos letter, which was not an attack on Van Loon in any way. Indeed Melville is not known to have written a reply to this letter by Van Loon, despite all its acrimony, including the assertion that Melville was a "child of the devil . . ." (Acts 13.10).

Lotus Niles, identified here as the secretary of the society at the time Melville was censured, was elected to the vice presidency at the controversial meeting over which these correspondents were quarreling. In the *Albany Microscope* printing of Van Loon's letter, his name was misplaced at the beginning of the second installment (and misspelled "Sotus"). As Van Loon pointed out in his next letter (14 April) to the *Microscope*, "Mr. N's name should have been attached to the certificate which closed the preceding part of the article" (and it is so placed here).

Mr. Editor: — Had not the late malicious attacks of Herman Melville upon my honor and integrity, extended beyond the pales of the Philologos Society or the circle of my acquaintance; I should have treated them with the silent contempt they so richly deserve; but having been perused by those, with whom the author and myself have yet to become acquainted; such silence though abundantly justified by the falsity and illiberality, might be construed into a tacit admission of their truth. This is my apology for again soliciting the favor of your columns. To Herman Melville — Sir, — the sensible Hudibras has well observed, that, there is no kind of argument like matter of fact; now, in my own opinion, he, who after announcing his intention of giving a general survey of particular transactions; indulges at the expense of an entire sheet, in contemptible criticisms, displaying all the stiffness and swelling bombast of Johnson, to the entire exclusion of his irresistable reasoning and beautiful thoughts; is not only guilty of an unpardonable sacrifice of valuable stationary, but evinces a miserable destitution of that substantial matter, which should constitute the broad basis of every discussion. A reflection or two on your dastardly attempt at a retreat beneath the shadow of my principles and professions, and I shall proceed to deliver a round unvarnished tale of your whole course of — hypocrisy. — As in the society when the unprovoked thunderbolt hurled by your own reckless hand, has recoiled, and wasted its fury upon your own head; so in this public contest, beaten with the rod of indignant truth, you have attempted a retreat to the old quarters, (my principles) and will assuredly meet with the same gracious reception. The charge, that in defending myself against your libellous reflections upon my character; and in using severe and pointed language in pourtraying yours, I have done violence to the meek and charitable spirit of the gospel I hold in the most "*frigid contempt.*" Sir, in the principles avowed by me I glory: but, if those principles, demand the sacrifice of my dearest right, the right of free discussion; if those principles involve the necessity of surrendering my character to the "tender mercies" of an unprincipled foe; if those principles demand that — I should suffer hypocrisy to hold her masked sway unreproved; or finally, if those principles demand that I should call "bitter sweet, and sweet bitter," then sir, by me those principles shall be disavowed, "henceforth and forevermore." But, sir, I have yet to learn that when I intend to speak of the wily serpent or the ravening wolf, I am out of respect to my principles and professions, to style him the harmless dove, or the gentle lamb. If, however, (for we are fallible mortals) in denouncing you as a "moral Ethiopean, whose conscience qualms not in view of the most atrocious guilt, whose brazen cheek never tingles with the blush of shame," I have done violence to the spirit of the gospel, most cordially do I recall the objectionable language, and in the meek and charitable spirit of Peter the Apostle, honestly and conscientiously pronounce you Herman Melville, a "child of the devil, full of all subtility and all mischief." So much, sir, for my inconsistency and want of charity. Having thus cursorily noticed your introduction (constituting two thirds of your article) I shall proceed to prove, beyond a question of doubt, not that you have given an exaggerated review of the late proceedings of the society, but that you have wilfully perpetrated the most abominable falsehoods. — In denying the charge made by me, that you forever destroyed the well earned reputation of the society, you aver, that "*when called from town for a few months, you left the society in an apparently healthy and prosperous condition.*" The following extract of a letter received from you during that absence and now in my possession will stamp false upon the declaration, "*but I have been digressing from the beginning of my letter my object is to know the existing situation of the society; whether it is on the rapid decline I left it in, or whether like the Phoenix it hath risen from its ashes, &c., &c.*" In your communication to the Microscope, you deny with unparalleled effrontery, that in consequence of your gross misconduct and incessant violation of its wholesome laws, the society was obliged to pass upon your *riotous* proceedings the severest censure. Sir, among the barefaced falsehoods perpetrated, the secretary's accompanying certificate will abundantly prove, that this the paragon stands in bold relief: — *I do hereby certify that a resolution was adopted in the Philologos Society pronouncing the conduct of H. Melville "disgraceful to himself, discreditable to the society, and insulting to the chair," and that, the resolution stands in full force at this date. Lotus Niles.*

Ex-President.

Sir — Having thus convicted you of two absolute falsehoods, and these forming the pillar of your defence, and the only *points* in your communication, I shall now give a faithful sketch of the memorable altercation which ensued between us at the "debut" of the society in Stanwix Hall; now, sir, you know, that, so far from "sallying with all the dignity of offended pride into the midst of the assemblage" when "the meeting progressed with the utmost harmony and good feeling," I entered the Hall before the deliberations of the society had commenced; that (the secretary being absent) at your request I read the minutes, and that on miscellaneous business being called for, I arose with calm dispassion, and proposed the following interrogatory to the chair: Mr. Chairman — "will you be so good as to inform me, by what authority a meeting of this society was called, and an election holden, on Friday evening last?" To which you replied, after some hesitation, "extraordinary circumstances demand extraordinary action; the members of the society being together, and some of the officers being present, it was thought expedient to go into a new election; and beside this, those of the society, who had absented themselves twice successively, were by virtue of the constitution expelled." To which I rejoined, "Sir, out of your own mouth shall I condemn you; you have intimated that I, the president being no longer a member of the society, had no longer the authority to call a meeting, and hence the fact that I did not authorise the meeting holden on Friday evening, did not effect its constitutionality; but, sir, my name has just been called from your roll, and I am now officiating in the capacity of Secretary." And here I divulged the fact; that you have been authorised by me to call a meeting of the society on *Monday* evening, but, that from motives not understood by me, you have taken the liberty of calling a meeting on Friday evening, without my knowledge or consent. After this unpleasant *expose* you remarked, that, "you understood me to invest you with authority to call a meeting upon any evening of the week deemed most suitable by yourself." To this I replied; Sir, in answer to my first interrogatory, you intimated very clearly, that I was no longer a member of the society; and not a syllable did you utter in relation to the power vested in you by the President; but, now, would you make it appear, that I, who by virtue of the constitution am expelled; authorised the call of that unlawful meeting. — Sir, "there is something rotten about Denmark." At about this point as the last resource in your perilous plight, I was called to order. Appealing from the decision of the chair, it was sustained by the bare majority of one. I must here do my fellow members of the society the justice to remark; that the decision of the chair was sustained, as I have since been assured, not from disrespect to me whom they have for two years sustained in the Presidency, and who but for *positively* declining would have still occupied the chair; but, because the affair was at first considered of a somewhat personal character, and because they were not willing to postpone the discussion of "the question" then before the society. Sir, notwithstanding, your imbecile efforts to avoid another harsh encounter; at the close of the regular debate it was unanimously resolved, that I should be at liberty to pursue the scorching enquiry, and "bring to light the hidden things of darkness." I have observed that when called to order, I left you in an unhappy predicament, and at the close of the protracted discussion which ensued on the passage of the resolution referred to, you remained, sir, in *"statu quo"*. Since, that dreadful night you have stood almost alone in your glory; some half dozen solitary individuals have occasionally congregated in "that dismal place," not "as to a grand military review," but "as to the chamber of a dying friend;" not to engage in those spirited debates, so admirably combining *"utile cum dulces,"* but *again to censure your disgraceful conduct.* Sir, if the nature of your steel heart does not forbid shame, and repentance let your head be a fountain of tears, and let your body be clothed in sackcloth and ashes. I have been obliged to speak the unwelcome truth, I have vindicated my own character, and you have been convicted of falsehood and hypocrisy.

Sir, I will not glory vainly in your downfall. It dont become me to hate the man, though I detest his principles. Had your ability been equal to your zeal, I should weep over the ruins of an unsullied reputation; and yet cordially do I forgive the injustice committed; and earnestly do I entreat you to devote the talents thus basely prostituted in the service of satan; to higher, nobler, and more honorable purposes.

I am Sir,
Your friend,
Ex-President.

P.S. I deny the most distant relationship to "Sandle Wood." If I was the author of an article over that signature the Editor of the Microscope is at liberty to publish the fact.

E. P.

Original document not located. Text from first publication, emended by NN.

PUBLICATION: *Albany Microscope*, 31 March and 7 April 1838. Gilman, pp. 258–62.

TEXTUAL NOTES (for symbols used, see p. 840): criticisms] NN; critiscisms • the sacrifice] NN; the sacrafice • fallible] NN; falible • atrocious] NN; attrocious • *condition."*] NN; ~.∧ • *&c."*] NN; ~.∧ • wholesome] whole-|some • *Lotus Niles.* Ex-President.] NN *(see the headnote)*; EX-PRESIDENT. Sotus Niles, *this name italicized, and with intervening italicized editor's notes:* [Concluded next week.] *and* (Concluded.) • you understood] you under-|stood • regular] NN; r[ ]gular • friend;"] NN; ~;∧ • falsehood] false-|hood • hypocrisy] NN; hypocricy

FROM "AMERICUS"
PUBLISHED 7 APRIL 1838 · ALBANY

In the same issue of the *Albany Microscope*, 7 April 1838, as the conclusion of Charles Van Loon's long second reply to Melville, an unidentified correspondent, also a member of the Philo Logos Society, placed this letter to the editor (meant for the eyes of both Melville and Van Loon) calling for a reconciliation.

Mr. Editor: — A member of the Philologos Society and a friend to Messrs. Van Loon and Melville, I have not *cum multis alliis* regarded their recent controversy with an incurious or an indifferent eye.

That two individuals of their attainments and character, who hitherto, I am confident, reciprocated the kindly feelings of a generous friendship — who mutually labored in building up and preserving an institution, whose highest honors they have respectively enjoyed; should at length so far forget the dignity of their station, the intimacy of their former acquaintance, and the well being of the common object of their care and solicitude, as to fall into a newspaper discussion; is highly reprehensible, and has been a source of deep and sincere regret to those whose good opinion neither of these "lords appellent" would be willing to forego.

Whatever provocation either of the parties may have originally, I am sure, a private interview, wherein they might have stated their mutual grievances, would have been accompanied by a retraction of all obnoxious expressions, a redress of injuries, and a renewal of their former amity, and have been infinitely preferable to the wrangling altercation, with which they have disturbed the harmony of the society, marred the equanimity of its proceedings, and filled your columns with a string of recrimination and abuse, whose venom and asperity argues a disordered state of moral sentiment, and a lack of discretion which I should hardly have expected from either of the parties concerned.

Sorry am I that these hasty steps cannot be retraced, but still, with the exercise of a little moderating forbearance, they can for the future refrain from gratifying an animosity, which as it derived its origin from an incident the most trivial, can be terminated with little trouble and to great advantage.

I do earnestly hope therefore, they will incontinently abandon the further prosecution of their warfare, and seek if possible to bury their enmity so deep in forgetfulness, that its memory may henceforth never be recalled to cast a shade on their future lives, and disturb the tranquil flow of that prosperity, which I hope, may be their's forever.

Americus.

Original document not located. Text from first publication, emended by NN.

PUBLICATION: *Albany Microscope*, 7 April 1838. (Partial) *Log*, I, 78.

TEXTUAL NOTES (for symbols used, see p. 840 below): Mr.] NN; ~, · attainments] NN; attainmnnts · marred] NN; mared

FROM "EX-PRESIDENT" CHARLES VAN LOON
PUBLISHED 14 APRIL 1838 · ALBANY

Because of the error in the placement of Lotus Niles's name in his 31 March and 7 April letter to the *Microscope*, Charles Van Loon placed this "CORRECTION" in the next issue (14 April) of the paper. Taking his cue from the 7 April letter by "Americus" (just above), Van Loon also calls for an end to the quarrel, quoting in the process both Shakespeare (*Othello*, 1.3) and (loosely) the Reverend Charles Caleb Colton's *Lacon* (London: Longman, Hurst, Rees, Orme, & Brown, 1820), aphorism 35. Whether Melville ever "brought forth 'fruits for repentance' " to allow such a reconciliation is not known, but since no further evidence of the controversy has been found, the public discussion apparently came to an end with this "correction" by Van Loon.

In consequence of a typographical error my communication in the last Microscope was apparently addressed to my esteemed friend Mr. Lotus Niles. Mr. N's name should have been attached to the certificate which closed the preceding part of that article. It was applicable only to Mr. Herman Melville. The discussion between this last named individual and myself being now at an end, I invite those who have felt any solicitude or curiosity as to the issue, to examine all that has been said by either party and then determine who has evinced a want of *true* veracity, and who has been convicted of infamous falsehood. The suggestions of "Americus" in the last Microscope, deserve a passing notice. This controversy, sir, was entirely unsought on my part. — Mr. M. took the liberty of making a public attack upon my character in the Microscope; justice to myself demanded a refutation, and regard for the welfare of society an expose. I have answered both these demands to my own satisfaction at least; and, although silly prejudice may condemn me for publishing in the Microscope, I shall enjoy my "exceeding great reward." I might indeed have trusted in the virtue of my own character for defence, but I am unwilling to learn by experience as I have by observation, that vigilant falsehood is an over match for slumbering truth. "The head and front of my offending hath this extent no more." I will cordially meet Mr. Melville on terms of friendship, when he shall have brought forth "fruits for repentance." In the mean time I shall cherish no enmity; in the language of the Rev. Colton, "I will *forgive* an injury, that I owe to my enemy, but, I will *remember it,* and *that* I owe to myself."

I took up my pen simply to correct an error, and will not therefore indulge myself in further comments. The courtesy, and manly regard to truth, evinced by Mr. Niles in furnishing me with a certificate to be used thus publicly, shall be held in grateful remembrance.

Ex-President.

Original document not located. Text from first publication, emended by NN.

Publication: *Albany Microscope*, 14 April 1838. (Partial) *Log*, II, 907.

Textual Notes (for symbols used, see p. 840): falsehood is] false-|hood is • *forgive*] *for-|give* • injury,] NN; ~∧ • myself."] NN; ~.∧ • remembrance] NN; remembradce

1839

FROM WILLIAM J. LAMB
PUBLISHED 20 APRIL 1839 · ALBANY

This notice meant for Melville was inserted in the 20 April 1839 *Democratic Press, and Lansingburgh Advertiser* by its editor, William J. Lamb. Melville's "communication" may have been a cover letter enclosed with his two "Fragments from a Writing Desk," which were published on 4 and 18 May 1839 in the *Democratic Press* under the initials "L. A. V." See the NN *Piazza Tales* volume, pp. 191–204, 622–25.

To Correspondents. The communication of "L. A. V." is received. An interview with the writer is requested.

Publication: *Democratic Press, and Lansingburgh Advertiser*, 20 April 1839. Gilman, p. 108.

1840

FROM GANSEVOORT MELVILLE
AFTER 21 JANUARY 1840 · NEW YORK

Unlocated. A letter is promised in Gansevoort Melville's 21 January 1840 letter to their brother Allan: "Give my best love to Herman — I sometimes send him papers — Does he ever call at the Greenbush Post Office? — Tell him, to enquire at the aforesaid place on or before the 1st prox, as I hereby promise him a letter. I know no other reason for his remissness but laziness — not general laziness by any means — but that laziness which consists in an unwillingness to exert oneself in doing at a particular time, that which ought then to be done — or to illustrate [*after canceled* to speak more plainly] — that disinclination to perform the special duty of the hour which so constantly beset one of the most industrious men of the age — Sir Walter Scott — " (Berkshire Athenaeum). In closing Gansevoort asked Allan to write soon, telling him "about yourself, Herman & particularly the *present condition* of the family"—which suggests that he did not expect to hear from his brother Herman soon. On 3 April, Gansevoort complained in another letter to Allan, "Herman has not yet written me" (Berkshire Athenaeum).

1844

FROM [THE MELVILLE FAMILY?]
[FEBRUARY?] 1844 · NEW YORK

Two or more unlocated letters. The missionary paper *The Friend of Temperance and Seamen*, published for Honolulu, Oahu, and the Sandwich Islands, printed in its 4 September 1844 issue under the heading "To Whom It May Concern" the announcement: "If Mr. Herman Melville, formerly officer on board Am. W. S. Acushnet, is in this part of the world, and will call upon the seamen's chaplain, he may find several letters directed to his address" (p. 84). These letters may have been those Allan Melville refers to in his 17 October 1844 letter to his brother, just below, when he writes, "In Feby we sent you a number of letters." Melville presumably never received the letters, since he had left the Hawaiian Islands in August of 1843 as an ordinary seaman on the U.S. frigate *United States* (contrary to the notice in *The Friend*, Melville had been only an ordinary seaman on the whaling ship *Acushnet* as well). The 1 April 1845 issue of *The Friend* (p. 51) listed three letters as being held for Herman Melville—presumably the same ones.

FROM ALLAN MELVILLE
17 OCTOBER 1844 · NEW YORK

This ebullient reply to Melville's now unlocated 13 October letter announcing his arrival in Boston aboard the U.S.S. *United States* is a summary by Melville's younger brother Allan of many of the events in the family during Melville's four years' absence from home.

In the immediate family, Allan recounts the fortunes of only the Melville brothers. The oldest, Gansevoort, had through his political connections gained an appointment as Examiner in Chancery in New York. Then he embarked on a political career, which included a three-month stump-speaking tour of the West at the close of the 1844 presidential election. Melville had already "seen an a/c" of Gansevoort's tour—which he apparently mentioned in his 13 October letter—and he probably did see the "bushell" of newspapers containing notices of their brother that Allan mentions, since in his "Appendix" to *Typee* he alludes to reading newspaper accounts that appeared in his absence (p. 254). (For more on the background of Gansevoort's political career, see Hershel Parker, "Gansevoort Melville's Role in the Campaign of 1844," *New-York Historical Society Quarterly* 49 [April 1965], 143–73.) Allan himself, four years younger than Melville, had succeeded Gansevoort as Examiner in Chancery, and Thomas, the youngest, who had been only ten years old when Melville left, was now in the Lansingburgh Academy, where Melville had been enrolled in 1838.

Much of the other news in this letter concerns their uncle Peter Gansevoort's family. His first wife, Mary Sanford Gansevoort, had died in February 1841. (It was her brother Edward Sanford [1805–76] whom Allan mentions as having been recently nominated as a New York state senator in 1843.) After nearly three years, Peter Gansevoort remarried in December 1843. His second wife, Susan Lansing, was a sister of a leading Albany lawyer, Christopher Yates Lansing. Although she never had children, she became a virtual mother to Peter Gansevoort's surviving son and daughter, Henry Sanford and Catherine, Melville's cousins.

Allan also reports on the family of their aunt Mary Chandonette Gansevoort—the second "Aunt Mary" he mentions. Her husband Leonard Gansevoort had died in 1821, leaving her with six children to raise. The oldest son to survive, Guert—Melville's cousin—had entered the navy as a midshipman in 1823, been promoted to lieutenant in 1837, and served in that rank aboard the *Somers* during the famous "mutiny" of 1842. (For more on this mutiny and Guert Gansevoort's role in it, see Harrison Hayford, *The Somers Mutiny Affair* [Englewood Cliffs: Prentice-Hall, 1959].) Leonard and Mary's oldest daughter, Catherine ("Kate," 1814–87) had married George Curtis in 1836—both of whom Allan mentions.

The one other relative mentioned in this letter, "Old Mr Peebles," was Gerrit Peebles (1769–1841), the husband of Melville's mother's cousin, Maria Van Schaick Peebles (Peebles's second wife). Since the Peebles family was primarily located in Lansingburgh, the Melvilles had seen much of them after moving there in May 1838 (see also Melville's 7 December 1839 letter to Allan).

In addition to all of the family news, Allan takes care to report on Gansevoort's friend Alexander Bradford (called "Alley" here), and Melville's friend Eli James Murdock Fly. For more about each of these acquaintances, see the headnotes to Melville's 23 May 1846 letter to Bradford and his 10 November 1838 letter to his brother Allan.

Whether Allan went to Boston to greet his brother, as he proposes in this letter, or whether Melville made his own way to New York or directly to Lansingburgh is not known; nor is the nature or the amount of Melville's "bill to Mrs Garaham"; but as the tone of this letter makes clear, Melville's homecoming was a momentous occasion for his family. Allan's excitement at his brother's safe arrival probably caused his slight confusion about the postmark on Melville's letter. While Allan dates his own letter Thursday, 17 October 1844 (the weekday on which 17 October fell in 1844), he clearly gives the date "18th" for the postmark on Melville's letter, which he says arrived "yesterday." In fact, "yesterday" would have been 16 October—probably the date Melville's 13 October letter was actually postmarked.

For the "circumstances" that detained Melville in Boston, see the entry for Melville's unlocated 13 October letter.

> New York Oct 17. 1844
> Thursday Evg. 8 P.M.
> office 1. Nassau St

Beloved Brother:

I need not express to you my feelings when I opened your letter dated at Boston on the 13 inst & postmarked the 18.th inst (yesterday) this morning. You can imagine that they overcame me. I was indeed unprepared for such good fortune and trembled while perusing your epistle — a prayer of gratitude played upon my lips — & I thanked the Giver of all good for your safe return. Herman! we are once more all together & I pray God that we may never be seperated more — Let these hasty lines be the forerunner of the hearty & true welcome you will receive when we can take you by the hand, look upon you, and embrace you. Oh! hasten your departure that my words may be soon confirmed. — But I will not keep you in suspence as to the situation of affairs at home. The family are still at Lansingburgh where you left them. All well. & when I was there and saw them all, some two weeks since our kind mother spoke of her far distant son & expressed a hope that before many months she should see him But how little does she expect to be so soon comforted with your presence! — Tom has grown to be quite a man & is at the Academy in L.—. G— was admitted in Dec. 1841 & practiced with some considerable success until May 1843 when he rec^d an appointment of Examiner in Chancery who's duty consists in taking the testimony of witnesses in writing when attended by counsel in suits in Chancery — a very fair office and one which pays quite well. This appointment is conferred by the Governor of the State & G— continued to perform the duties under his appointment until May last (1844) when he resigned & succeeded in obtaining my appointment in his place just ten days before I was myself admitted as an Attorney of the Supreme Court & a solicitor in Chancery. I having passed my examination & obtained my sheepskins on the 17. of the same month. So brother mine when you next see me you see a "member of the bar" having his suit of offices at No 1. Nassau

From Allan Melville, 17 October 1844, p. 4 (reduced).
Courtesy of Nina Murray.

street opposite the Custom House. I must say that so far I have been favored. — Now for G. About two years since he made his first attempt at a political speach before a meeting of the Democrats of one of our wards & from that time to the present his course has been singularly triumphant. Never probably in the political annals of our country has so young a man in so short a time earned for himself so prominant a position before the public. In March last he delivered an address on the occasion of Genl. Jacksons birth day to some 5000 persons assembled in the Tabernacle in Broadway (including a large number of ladies) A fine report of his effort appeared in the city papers & was universally copied by the Democratic press of the Country. His first appearance since the nomination of Mr Polk was at the ratification meeting to which you refer as having seen an ^{a}/$_c$. In the latter part of July he left this city to attend the great Nashvill (Tenn.) Convention which was held on the 15 Aug. Here he followed Genl Cass who was the first Speaker. Since then he has stumped it through Tennessee, Kentucky & Ohio & he is now passing through this State on his return. Tomorrow the 18. he speaks at Troy, his last appointment. To day he was to have spoken at Schenectady as I presume he did. I now expect him in New York about the 23.rd He was advertised at all the principal points from Buffalo down. I wish you were here. I would show you a bushell of news papers containing notices of him such as the "orator of the human race" the "eloquent Melville" "the great New York orator" "the Champion of the New York Democracy" for to him belongs the honor of christening Polk "Young Hickory" He made a visit of some days at Mr Polks residence Columbia Tenn. & also with the "old man of the Hermitage" under his own roof. The opposition have of course made their attacks upon him & some of them are very severe. Prentiss the witty editor of the Louisville Journal was right down upon him. In Ohio they dubbed him Col! that is the Democratic papers. To change the subject. —— . —— Aunt Mary Uncle Peters wife is dead. She died in Feby 1841. after a long illness. I regretted her loss very much as I was a favorite of hers. Last December Uncle married Susan Lansing a sister of Christopher Y. Lansing of Albany an exceedingly fine woman & no doubt they are a very happy couple. Old Mr Peebles also has been gathered to his fathers. Aunt Mary before her death lost another child, a boy. — Two children are still living Henry & a beautiful little

Girl — Kate. Mr Curtis & Cousin Kate and Aunt Mary are all well. Guert you will find at the Charlestown Navy Yard near Boston on the ship Ohio. Do you know that an attempt was made to procure a bill of indictment for Murder against him & Com McKenzie & after an argument of some four days before the United States Court here it was denied The excitement here at the time was very great. Edward Sanford uncles brother in law has been nominated for Senator from this District Alley Bradford published a book in 1841 called "American Antiquity & the History of the Red Race" which took very well. In Feby we sent you a number of letters.

Now Herman as for yourself. On reading your letter a second time I was under the apprehension that "the circumstances connected with the ship" which you use to excuse your immediate presence among us may mean something more serious than I at first supposed & involve something of importance to yourself = the word 'circumstances' indeed admits of a wide meaning — I trust there is nothing in it, but really you might have been explicit. Do write immediately what it is. Dont delay a moment. On receipt of your letter this mg. my first impulse was to make immediate arrangements to go to you but on reflection I found that to gratify my anxious desire to see you I should be obliged to break several appointments for tomorrow which might prove injurious to my business. So I made up my mind to write to you at once. I may possibly leave here tomorrow afternoon & be with you on Saturday mg. i.e. if I can fix things accordingly

Write immediately at any rate God Bless you   Allan

Come here before you go to L. that we may rig you out with clothes. Your not stating where you were to be found will give me trouble in finding you if I go to Boston.

Your bill to Mrs Garaham has been paid.

Be at the Tremont House at 9 oclock on Saturday mg. You will probably see me. if not you will find a letter in the P.O.

I find I have not said a word about Fly. he was in Gansevoort's office about a year. last April he went up to Rhinebach Dutches Co in this State & formed a law connection with a Mr. Armstrong. He is doing quite well according to his letters.

Your letters written in June 1843 were rec^d as also a package once before that

I have not yet written home yet but will wait for a reply from you before doing so ie if I don't see you at Boston

In case I am prevented from going tomorrow afternoon and you should come on immediately you will find me either at the house No. 7. Greenwich St near the Battery or at the office No 1. Nassau st — Good by —

ALS on a 42.4 × 27.2 cm sheet, folded in half, of blue wove paper. Allan Melville inscribed all four pages, in ink, and addressed the fourth page "Mr. Herman Melville | Boston | Mail Single." and postmarked "New York | Oct 18".

LOCATION: at present unknown. *Provenance*: Agnes Morewood[?]; Henry A. Murray; David L. O'Neal, Antiquarian Bookseller.

TEXTUAL NOTES: Beloved] *originally written* Bl *with* l *canceled* · Giver] *altered from* giver · expressed a] *inserted above caret* · hope] *altered from* hoped · triumphant] *after canceled* triumphant · earned] *after canceled* obtained · birth] *miswritten* brith · ladies) A] *ies and* A *rewritten* · the city] city *miswritten* cit · the Democratic] *after canceled* all · press] *written over* papers · Hermitage"] ge" *torn off by the seal* · roof] *after canceled* roff · course] se *torn off by the seal* · are very] ry *torn off by the seal* · Louisville] *possibly before a word now torn off where the seal was opened* · In Feby] *after wiped* H · than . . . supposed] *inserted above caret* · Come here . . . Boston.] *in the lower left margin of p. 1; placed here editorially* · Your bill . . . paid.] *in the upper left margin of p. 1; placed here editorially* · Be at . . . P.O.] *written above the salutation on p. 1; placed here editorially* · I find . . . letters.] *in the left margin of p. 2; placed here editorially* · Your letters . . . that] *in the bottom, center margin of pp. 2 and 3 and marked by a bracket; placed here editorially* · 1843] *inserted above canceled* last · I have . . . Boston] *in the center margin of pp. 2 and 3; placed here editorially* · In case . . . by —] *added on the fourth page, above the seal; placed here editorially*

1845

FROM AUGUSTA MELVILLE
BEFORE 20 JANUARY 1845 · LANSINGBURGH

Unlocated. A "long & delightful" letter from his sister Augusta is cited in Melville's 20 January 1845 letter to their sister Catherine.

FROM GANSEVOORT MELVILLE
15 SEPTEMBER 1845 · LONDON

Unlocated. Gansevoort Melville's 16 September 1845 letter to his mother reports:
"In a letter to Herman under date of yesterday I spoke at some length on the subject
of my personal expenses here and refer you to that letter for information on that
point & also as to 'Typee' " (NYPL-GL; see Parker, *Gansevoort Melville's London
Journal and Letters*, pp. 62–63).

FROM GANSEVOORT MELVILLE
26 SEPTEMBER 1845 · LONDON

Unlocated. A letter for Melville accompanied Gansevoort Melville's 26 September
1845 letter to their mother, which states: "The Times, Spectator, & Punch accompany this, as also a letter to Herman" (NYPL-GL; see Parker, *Gansevoort Melville's
London Journal and Letters*, pp. 63–64).

FROM GANSEVOORT MELVILLE
[3?] NOVEMBER 1845 · LONDON

Unlocated. Gansevoort Melville's 3 November 1845 letter to his mother cites a
recent letter to his brother: "I have written Herman a long letter about his Mss, I
entertain good hopes of its success — If it succeeds it will pave the way for anything
he may do in that line hereafter — 'Ce n'est que le premier pas qui conte' " (NYPL-
GL; see Parker, *Gansevoort Melville's London Journal and Letters*, p. 65).

FROM GANSEVOORT MELVILLE
AFTER 18 NOVEMBER 1845 · LONDON

Unlocated. A letter for Melville is promised in Gansevoort Melville's 18 November
1845 letter to their brother Allan: "I shall write Herman a note as to 'Typee', in
regard to which I am estopped from making any movement until I hear from him
again & receive the additional Mss chapters" (NYPL-GL; see Parker, *Gansevoort
Melville's London Journal and Letters*, p. 67).

FROM GANSEVOORT MELVILLE
BEFORE 3 DECEMBER 1845 · LONDON

Unlocated. A letter to Melville from his brother Gansevoort is referred to in Gansevoort's 3 December 1845 letter to their mother: "As you will perceive by my
letter to Herman which I snatched time to write while half a dozen persons were
talking to me 'Typee' is going to have a fair chance for favor in the literary world"
(NYPL-GL; see Parker, *Gansevoort Melville's London Journal and Letters*, p. 67).

FROM GANSEVOORT MELVILLE
AFTER 4 DECEMBER 1845 · LONDON

Unlocated. A letter to Melville from his brother Gansevoort can be inferred from Gansevoort's 4 December 1845 letter to John Murray: "At a late hour last eve^g (having been at the Legation all day) I received your note too late to communicate its contents to the author of the Mss, by the steamer of to-day, which tho' desirable, is the less important because I have a recent letter from him giving me carte blanche in the premises. Owing to the absence of Mr McLane the American Minister in Paris, I am more than usually occupied, and on that score beg leave to crave your indulgence for the very few days which I propose to take to consider your proposition" (Murray). Although Gansevoort could not write his brother by the 4 December steamer, he most likely did write him not long thereafter about Murray's offer of a hundred pounds for *Typee*.

1846

FROM GANSEVOORT MELVILLE
3 JANUARY 1846 · LONDON

Unlocated. Gansevoort Melville's diary includes in the list of his letters written 3 January 1846: "1 to Herman covering £5 & informing him of Murray's having purchased his Mss" (NYPL-GL; see Parker, *Gansevoort Melville's London Journal and Letters*, p. 19). Davis and Gilman misreport this as a letter from Melville to his brother (Davis-Gilman Unlocated 284).

FROM GANSEVOORT MELVILLE
17 JANUARY 1846 · LONDON

Unlocated. Along with four other letters that Gansevoort Melville wrote between 11 A.M. and 5 P.M. on 17 January 1846, one to Melville is listed in his diary entry for that day (NYPL-GL; see Parker, *Gansevoort Melville's London Journal and Letters*, p. 25).

FROM GANSEVOORT MELVILLE
3 FEBRUARY 1846 · LONDON

Unlocated. "After finishing the Despatches &c" on 3 February 1846, Gansevoort Melville "found time to write Herman a long letter" (along with eleven other letters, including one to Charles Fenno Hoffman about *Typee*), according to his diary entry for that day (NYPL-GL; see Parker, *Gansevoort Melville's London Journal and Letters*, p. 33). Probably this is the same letter referred to in Maria Melville's 28 February 1846 letter, quoted in the entry just below. In his 28 February reply (now unlocated) to this letter, Melville apparently referred to its contents as "gratifying enough" (see pp. 32–33 above).

FROM ALLAN MELVILLE
BEFORE 23 FEBRUARY 1846 · NEW YORK

Unlocated. A letter to Melville from Allan Melville concerning the uncertain state of the American publication of *Typee* is cited in Maria Melville's 28 February 1846 letter from Lansingburgh to her daughter Augusta in Albany: "Herman left us last Monday Evening [23 February] for Troy on his way to New York by the early cars — he receiv'd a letter from Allan in the morning regarding his book which none of us understood, so contradictory in its information, Herman was very desirous of having it come out in Wiley & Putnams 'Library of Choice Reading,' and from Allan's letter, the thing was not determined, and indeed the arrival of the Book — itself by the Cambria by the reading of Allan's letter was more than uncertain.

"If the book was not got out by the first of March he would lose the Copy right in America, so Gansevoort wrote. Herman had no Idea of that you may suppose, to have the copy right was all to Herman — so he concluded to go to New York, altho Gansevoort particularly requested him to remain here — but too much was at stake and he went down — to assure himself that all was safe.

"Gansevoort wrote Helen by the Cambria, he also wrote Herman that he believed that book would have brilliant success, and do you believe Augusta — he even went so far — *was so very kind* as to offer him some advice about not being too much elated — with his success — and the numerous advances, complimentary &c — that would be made to him" (NYPL-GL). The letter from Gansevoort referred to in this account is probably his unlocated letter of 3 February 1846, just above.

FROM GANSEVOORT MELVILLE
2 MARCH 1846 · LONDON

Unlocated. On 2 March 1846 Gansevoort Melville recorded in his diary that having felt unwell and taken a nap in the late afternoon, he arose and "wrote letters, long ones for the steamer to Cramer, Herman &c." He also sent his brother six newspapers, probably containing reviews of *Typee* (NYPL-GL; see Parker, *Gansevoort Melville's London Journal and Letters*, p. 46).

FROM AUGUSTA MELVILLE
5 MARCH 1846 · ALBANY

Unlocated. In her 28 February 1846 letter, cited in the entry above, Maria Melville advised her daughter Augusta: "You had better write Herman on Thursday [5 March] at New York" (NYPL-GL). Being a dutiful daughter, Augusta Melville probably did so. The reason for Augusta's letter may have been to inquire when her brother intended to return to Lansingburgh, so that she could return from Albany at the same time—a plan mentioned earlier in Maria Melville's letter.

FROM GANSEVOORT MELVILLE
3 APRIL 1846 · LONDON

Although Gansevoort Melville's diary and other letters record some ten letters to his brother from London, only this one was among the family papers given by Melville's granddaughter Eleanor Melville Metcalf to Harvard, and it remains the only letter from Gansevoort to his brother now located. It was probably saved because it was the last letter that Melville received from Gansevoort, who was already seriously ill, as its quotation from *Hamlet* (2.2.316) relates, and who died on 12 May 1846. As Melville's 6 June 1846 letter to James Buchanan stated, Gansevoort's death left the family in " 'exceedingly embarrassed circumstances,' " with some of Gansevoort's debts from the failure of his fur and hat business still unpaid—the debts referred to in this letter. The documents Gansevoort enclosed with this letter had to do with Wiley & Putnam's acceptance of *Typee* through Gansevoort's connections in London; see the headnote to Melville's 7 May 1846 letter to that firm. Gansevoort recorded sending this letter in his diary entry for 4 April 1846 (NYPL-GL; see Parker, *Gansevoort Melville's London Journal and Letters*, p. 60). The 28 February letter Gansevoort had received "a few days ago" is unlocated.

Both Weaver (p. 255) and Leyda (*Log*, I, 209; with reproduction) stated that a manuscript in Gansevoort's hand titled "Death" (HCL-M), quoting Claudio's speech about the fear of death in *Measure for Measure*, 3.1, was enclosed with this letter, but the quotation is written on different paper and there is no physical evidence to connect the two items. Nor is there any explicit mention of the quotation in Gansevoort's letter. Thus it has not been included in this edition as an enclosure, on the assumption that Gansevoort, who had early made it a practice to copy out quotations (see the reference to his *Index Rerum*, p. 209 above), may have inscribed the quotation at a different time, but not have enclosed it with this letter.

London April 3rd 1846.

My dear Herman,

Herewith you have copy of the arrangement with Wiley & Putnam for the publication in the US of your work on the Marquesas. The letter of W & P under date of Jan 13th is the result of a previous understanding between Mr Putnam & myself. As the correspondence speaks for itself, it is quite unnecessary to add any comment. By the steamer of tomorrow I send to yr address several newspapers contg critiques on your book. The one in the "Sun" was written by a gentleman who is very friendly to myself, and who may possibly from that reason have made it unusually eulogistic —
Yours of Feb 28 was recd a few days ago by the sailing packet Joshua Bates. I am happy to learn by it that the previous intelligence transmitted by me was "gratifying enough." I am glad that you continue busy, and in my next or the one after that will venture to make

some suggestions about your next book. In a former letter you informed me that Allan had sent $100, home the fruit of my collections (I refer to the money sent at yr request). It appears that this was not so, for Allan informs me that the $100 — was part of the £90 & 10 — making £100, which I sent out by the Jany steamer. Allan seems to find it entirely too much trouble to send me the monthly accounts of receipts & disbursements, I have rec^d no accounts from him later than up to Nov 30th and consequently am in a state of almost entire ignorance as to what is transpiring at No 10 Wall St. This is very unthinking in him for my thoughts are so much at home that much of my time is spent in disquieting apprehensions as to matters & things there. I continue to live within my income, but to do so, am forced to live a life of daily self denial. I do not find my health improved by the sedentary life I have to lead here. The climate is too damp & moist for me. I sometimes fear that I am gradually breaking up. If it be so — let it be — God's will be done. I have already seen about as much of London society as I care to see. It is becoming a toil to me to make the exertion necessary to dress to go out, and I am now leading a life nearly as quiet as your own at Lansingburgh — I think I am growing phlegmatic & cold. Man stirs me not, nor woman either. My circulation is languid. My brain is dull. I neither seek to win pleasure or avoid pain. A degree of insensibility has been long stealing over me, & now seems permanently established, which, to my understanding is more akin to death than life. Selfishly speaking I never valued life much — it were impossible to value it less than I do now. The only personal desire that I now have is to be out of debt. That desire waxes stronger within me, as others fade. In consideration of the little egotism which my previous letters to you and the family have contained, I hope that Mother, brothers & sisters will pardon this babbling about myself.

As to Fanny — when I receive the accounts I will write fully. Tom's matter has not been forgotten. You say there is a subject &c &c "on which I intended to write but will defer it" — What do you allude to. I am careful to procure all the critical notices of 'Typee' which appear & transmit them to you. The steamer which left Boston on the 1st inst will bring me tidings from the US as to the success of Typee there. I am, with love & kisses to all, Affectionately, Your brother,

Gansevoort Melville

ALS on a 37 × 22.6 cm sheet, folded in half, of blue laid paper, watermarked with the name "J WHATMAN". Gansevoort Melville inscribed all four pages, in ink. Elizabeth Shaw Melville noted in pencil at the bottom of the last page "Died in London May 12–1846".

LOCATION: HCL-M.

PUBLICATION: Weaver, pp. 253–55.

TEXTUAL NOTE: allude to] *miswritten* allude too

FROM McHENRY BOYD
BEFORE 12 MAY 1846 · LONDON

Unlocated. Two letters from McHenry Boyd at the American legation in London, reporting on Gansevoort Melville's illness prior to his death on 12 May 1846, are cited in Melville's 29 May 1846 letter to his (already dead) brother Gansevoort.

FROM MARIANNE GRAY BRADFORD
BEFORE 23 MAY 1846 · ALBANY

Unlocated. In his 23 May 1846 letter to Marianne Gray Bradford's husband, Alexander W. Bradford, Melville asked him to "Present my renewed complements to Mrs Bradford for the honor of her letter"—but gave no indication as to its contents. For more on the Bradfords, see the headnote to that letter.

FROM LOUIS McLANE
BEFORE 6 JUNE 1846 · LONDON

Unlocated. A "most friendly letter to the family of the deceased" from Louis McLane, the United States minister to the Court of St. James's, is cited in Melville's 6 June letter to James Buchanan and in Melville's 6 June letter to William L. Marcy (which included extracts, now unlocated, from McLane's letter). It was probably addressed to Melville, who was now the acting head of the family.

FROM JAMES BUCHANAN
9 JUNE 1846 · WASHINGTON, D.C.

As requested in letters from Louis McLane, the United States minister to the Court of St. James's (dated 18 May), Edwin Croswell (dated 5 June), and Melville (dated 6 June), James Buchanan, secretary of state under President Polk, agreed to allow fifty pounds to cover the expenses entailed by Gansevoort Melville's sickness and death. See the headnote to Melville's 6 June letter to Buchanan for more about the financial straits in which Gansevoort's death left his family.

Department of State, Washington, June 9, 1846.
Herman Melville, Esq
Lansingburg, Renssalear co. N.Y.

Sir: I have just received your letter of the 6th instant, referring to certain pecuniary claims connected with the sudden death of Mr. Gansevoort Melville, late Secretary of the Legation of the United States at London; and have to state, in reply, that Mr. McLane has been authorized to charge the sum of fifty pounds in his account of the contingent expenses of the Legation for the funeral expenses of Mr. Melville. The funds left by the deceased having been applied to defray these expenses, to the exclusion of those attendant upon his sickness, the sum now allowed will be applicable to the payment of the latter.

Very sincerely condoling with yourself and the other members of Mr. M^s family at this sudden bereavement, I am, &c

James Buchanan

Original document not located. Text from Buchanan's letterbook (presumably inscribed by a clerk), p. 26 (one-third page).

LOCATION (of letterbook): National Archives.

PUBLICATION: (partial) *Log*, I, 218.

TEXTUAL NOTES: Sir] *paragraph indicated by large space after* N.Y. • Very] *after slash indicating new paragraph*

FROM RICHARD T. GREENE
PUBLISHED 1 JULY 1846 · BUFFALO

After seeing a notice (in the 9 April *New York Evangelist*) of *Typee*, in which he himself figured as "Toby," Richard T. Greene decided to publish this communication that appeared in the *Buffalo Commercial Advertiser* on 1 July 1846 and was later reprinted in Albany and New York papers. Aimed to catch Melville's eye, it concludes with Greene's request for Melville's address and the comment "*Mortarkee* was the word I used when I heard of his being alive." (In *Typee*, chap. 3, pp. 69, 71, "Mortarkee" is given as the equivalent to the word "good.") The letter was printed under the heading "How strangely things turn up!" with an introductory paragraph discussing *Typee* and identifying Greene as "now living in this city, following the business of a house and sign painter. His father is a respectable farmer in the town of Darien, Genesee Co." Melville's 3 July 1846 letter to Evert Duyckinck indicates that, as Greene had hoped, this communication did catch Melville's eye. Melville's reply is now, however, like all of his letters to Greene, unlocated. For more on their friendship, see pp. 48–49 above.

To the Editor of the Buffalo Com. Adv.:

In the *New York Evangelist* I chanced to see a notice of a new publication in two parts, called "*Typee, a residence in the Marquesas,*" by Herman Melville. In the book he speaks of his comrade in misfortune, "Toby," who left him so mysteriously, and whom he supposed had been killed by the Happar natives. The *Evangelist* speaks rather disparagingly of the book as being too romantic to be true, and as being too severe on the missionaries. But to my object: I am the true and veritable "Toby," yet living, and I am happy to testify to the entire accuracy of the work so long as I was with Melville, who makes me figure so largely in it. I have not heard of Melville or "Tommo," since I left him on the Island, and likewise supposed him to be dead; and not knowing where a letter would find him, and being anxious to know where he is, and to tell him my "yarn" and compare "log" books, I have concluded to ask you to insert this notice, and inform him of my yet being alive, and to ask you to request New York, Albany and Boston papers to publish this notice, so that it may reach him. My true name is Richard Greene, and I have the scar on my head which I received from the Happar spear and which came near killing me. I left Melville and fell in with an Irishman, who had resided on the Island for some time, and who assisted me in returning to ship, and who faithfully promised me to go and bring Melville to our ship next day, which he never did, his only object being money. I gave him five dollars to get me on board, but could not return to Melville. I sailed to New Zealand and thence home; and I request Melville to send me his address if this should chance to meet his eye. *Mortarkee* was the word I used when I heard of his being alive.

"Toby."

Original document not located. Text from first publication, emended by NN.

PUBLICATION: *Buffalo Commercial Advertiser*, 1 July 1846. Minnigerode, pp. 17–19.

TEXTUAL NOTES: Greene] NN; GREEN · Irishman] Irish-|man

FROM RICHARD T. GREENE
BETWEEN 7 AND 11 JULY 1846 · BUFFALO

In his 15 July 1846 letter to his British publisher John Murray, Melville referred to this letter by Richard Tobias (Toby) Greene (first published in the *Buffalo Commercial Advertiser* on 11 July) as having been sent to him by Greene as a "draught" of a letter. Responding to Melville's momentary accusation in *Typee* that Toby "perfidiously" deserted him (chap. 14, p. 108), the letter recounts the events that forced Greene to leave his friend behind on the island of the Typees. With that "draught" sent to Melville now unlocated, its first publication is reprinted here. It was prefaced by an introductory paragraph, headed "Typee. TOBY'S OWN STORY," which called attention to the revised edition of Melville's first book: "It [this letter] is a mere sketch, however, and in a new edition of *Typee*, which we see has been called for, will be doubtless given with all necessary details." Newspapers that reprinted this letter included the *Albany Evening Journal* (13 July) and the *Albany Argus* (16 July). The earlier paragraph in the *Argus* cited by Greene at the close of this letter was probably the brief synopsis printed on 7 July of Melville's 4 July letter to the editor, Edwin Croswell. It commented on Greene's reappearance and offered "to account for what may seem to be inexplicable in 'Toby's' statement, viz: the five dollars paid the Irishman," Jimmy Fitch (see the headnote to Melville's 4 July letter for the full text of this paragraph).

Friend "Tommo," If you were rejoiced at hearing that "Toby" was still in the land of the living, imagine to yourself my feelings on hearing that my companion "Tommo" was still alive. I am indeed happy to be able to clear myself from what you call "perfidious." Was it possible you could for a moment harbor the thought that I would endeavor to make my escape from the island, and leave you at the mercy of the Typees? No, far from it. I would have sacrificed my life first, as you well know I came near losing it once for you, and would willingly have undertaken the same journey again if necessary.

But to my escape. The morning I left you, it was with a buoyant hope that I would soon have you with myself on board a ship, or somewhere in safety, that you might be attended to till you recovered from your lameness.

As soon as we arrived on the beach, I discovered a white man standing there, surrounded by a number of natives. This man had just arrived from Nukeheva. You probably recollect him. He came on board of the *Dolly* shortly after our arrival in port. He had a great deal of tattooing about his person. He was an Irishman, called Jimmy Fitch. On his perceiving me, he welcomed me to the beach, asked me if I wished to leave the bay and get a ship. I told him I did, but that I had a shipmate up in the valley, who, on account of lameness, could not come down; that I would go up to him and get some assistance to carry him to the beach. To this he assented, but reminded me, at the same time, that he tho't it doubtful whether I could get to the place where my shipmate then was. I started to go up the valley, and had not proceeded a "ship's length" when I felt two or three hands laid heavily upon my shoulders. Imagine to yourself my surprise and horror on learning that I could go no farther, as the natives had just discovered that I wished to leave the bay. One of them that laid hold of me was "*Marheyo*." The Irishman then came to me and then told me that in all probability if I should force my way up where Melville was, we would never come down. He then made me a faithful promise that he would have my companion away the next day, as he was coming over from Nukeheva the following morning with a ship's boats for the purpose of trading, for you must understand no boats arrived in Typee that day. The Irishman had been there that day for the purpose of engaging fruit, pigs, &c., for the ships then lying at Nukeheva. He came across by land through Happar. I then told Jimmy I would never leave the valley until I was convinced he could get you away. To this he assured me he was a tabooed man, that he could go any where through the island, and take with him who and what he pleased; and to prove this he would take a Typee native to Nukeheva with us, to carry a small hog, a present from one of the natives. — As incredible as this may seem, it is nevertheless true. It is strange you never saw this fellow after his return to Typee. You must certainly recollect us speaking to a native at one time, who told us he had often been in Nukeheva, and we doubted his statement.

But to my story. Said Jimmy, if I bring you and a Typee native safe through the valley of the Happars, can I not as easily bring your shipmate? This seemed plausible enough, but he added it is impossible for you to stay here tonight, now the natives know your intentions. So come, it is getting late, we have a long journey before us, the sooner we start the better, and be assured you will have your companion with you tomorrow evening. With a heavy heart and a long look up the valley, I started forward, the natives looking daggers at me, but dared not advance towards me, as I was tabooed. We ascended the mountain in a much easier manner than you and I had done a few weeks before, and in about two hours found ourselves in the valley of the Happars. We got something to eat there, and while resting ourselves I could not help noticing how savage the natives looked at our Typee friend, who kept close to the tabooed man. Had he been alone, poor fellow, I fear his time would have been short. — It was then I acknowledged the superiority of Jimmy Fitch and the power of the taboo. While sitting in the Happar's house, Jimmy made me promise I would give him five dollars on my arrival on board a ship for his trouble. This, I told him, he should have, and my shipmate would do the same, and better than that, if he wished.

We arrived in Nukeheva about dark the same day, and I was immediately hurried on board the *London Packet*, as the Captain wanted me — badly; but my sorry appearance after the loss of much blood boded no good in my favor. The Captain was loth to ship me, as he thought I was sick. — However I entered my name on the ship's articles. I told him I had a companion in Typee, and asked for a boat and crew armed that we might go and release him. But the Captain had no such idea. No, he was not going to trust his men amongst the bloody cannibals, though I must say the crew were eager for the enterprise. He told me Jimmy would have my friend on board the next evening.

The next evening came, and found me on the beach waiting to welcome my shipmate. I could descry his form seated in the stern sheets as the boats approached the shore. But alas! he was not there. My brain grew dizzy, the savage villains have killed him, but I will be revenged on the scoundrel that took me from the valley. So soon as Jimmy struck the beach I seized him, shouting in a voice that startled him, where is Melville? He assured me he was not able to come down to the beach that day, though he knew the boats were in Typee bay, but that he had engaged a native to carry him to the boat the next day, as he was going around there again. This partly satisfied me, but I had some doubts as to the truth of his statement. I bade him good night, telling him that if Melville was not forthcoming the next evening he might consider himself in a dangerous situation.

I went on board my ship, filled with gloomy thoughts. The next morning I saw the boats depart with Jimmy. Now, thought I, I soon shall have the pleasure of seeing him and explain all; but how was I mistaken. At twelve o'clock that day, the Captain came forward and gave orders to "man the windlass." If I should here attempt to relate to you the anguish I felt at leaving you, it would appear like affectation, I will not attempt it. When I recovered from my feelings the good ship was ploughing the billows like a thing of life, while the mountains of Marquesas were "hull down" in the distance.

You recollect that I started a little after sunrise out of the valley, and with me went, Fayaway, Marheyo, Mow Mow with the one eye, and the two young Typees, living in our house, and some one hundred and fifty besides, carrying hogs, cocoa nuts, banana &c., to trade, expecting boats in the bay. We arrived on the beach in about three hours and found no one there but the Irish Jimmy, who had escaped from an English Man of War, and who I have since learned was captured by the English after this event. Here ensued the above conversation. You will recollect that on the Typee beach there is a tabooed house, against which Jimmy made me sit. After I took my place there all the natives formed a circle around me, looking savage, and talking and discussing the subject of my intentions, and how they should prevent my departure. But no one dared to approach me, but an old woman, who was a King's wife in the other Typee bay, for you will recollect there were two Typees, who asked me *"Typee Mortarkee?"* I answered *"Mortarkee,"* and then by signs asked me if I was going to Nukeheva? I answered by nodding, yes, and then she left. I sat there half an hour before we started when Jimmy called the Typee, and me, and then the fair Fayaway, your Typee dulcinea, came up to me and shook hands with me and said "how you do," in English, as you recollect we taught her a few words of English, such as "good bye" and "how do you do," and she mistook the words and said for good bye *"how you do,"* and then the Typee shouldered his hog, and we started off, the natives still looking, talking, and leaving their fruit on the beach, left for the valley before we were out of sight. This is all I recollect of my escape. We weighed anchor and set sail the second day after I got on board, and sailed on a cruise among the Islands for four months, when our ship sprung a leak, and we shifted our course for New Zealand, where we arrived in about four months after I left Nukeheva. There I left the *London Packet,* and shipped on the English brig *Harlequin*, on board of which I was three months, trading on the coast of New Zealand, when I again left her for the *Nimrod,* on board of which I was about one month. Left her and took the *London Packet* again, in which latter vessel I left Nukeheva, and left for home after five months. So that it was one year after I left Typee before I arrived home — landing at Fairhaven, Mass.

I have seen in the *Argus* a paragraph doubting the truth of my statement in regard to the five dollars I gave Jimmy the Irishman; but you know when we shipped at New Bedford, the ship's owners advanced some $84, on the strength of our future services and earnings, and on this principle when I got on board the *London Packet* I told her captain I had promised Jimmy $5, who said I had better not give it to him, but he would pay it if I desired. I told him I had a comrade ashore, whom he might not bring if I cheated him, and the captain advanced the money.

In regard to the cognomen, "Toby," my name is Richard Tobias Greene, under which name I shipped, and the crew getting hold of Tobias, corrupted it into *Toby*, by which name I was called after — this I think will sufficiently explain the doubts.

"Toby."

Original document not located. Text from first publication, emended by NN.

PUBLICATION: *Buffalo Commercial Advertiser*, 11 July 1846. (Partial) *Log*, I, 221. Gordon Roper, "Before Moby Dick," *University of Chicago Magazine* 48 (October 1955), 7–9.

TEXTUAL NOTES (for symbols used, see p. 840): from Nukeheva.] NN; ~ ~[ ] • *Marheyo*] NN; *Mareho* • the better] NN; the the better • resting ourselves] resting our-|selves • sunrise] sun-|rise • Marheyo] NN; Markeyo • *Mortarkee?"*] NN; ~?∧ • a leak] NN; aleak • for New Zealand] NN; for New Zeeland • coast] NN; cost

FROM JOHN MURRAY
3 AUGUST 1846 · LONDON

Unlocated. The March 1846–April 1858 letterbook of the John Murray publishing house contains the following record of a 3 August 1846 reply to Melville's 15 July letter: "Mr Murray wrote to Mr Hermann Melville & offered to give him an additional £50 at the end of the year for his *corrections* & his *Sequel* — giving an account of Toby, — to the 'Narrative of his Residence in the Marquesas Islands' " (p. 9; Murray). Melville's 2 September 1846 reply—which characterizes the letter as "friendly and welcome"—indicates that Murray also asked for "documentary evidences" of Melville's stay in the Marquesas.

FROM THE YOUNG MEN'S ASSOCIATION
BEFORE 28 NOVEMBER 1846 · TROY

Unlocated. In an announcement dated 28 November 1846 in the *Troy Budget* the Young Men's Association of Troy, New York, listed "Herman Melville, Esq., of

Lansingburgh" among lecturers for the coming season. Presumably Melville was invited to lecture in a letter to which he responded with "a conditional promise" (according to his 19 January 1847 letter to Hooper Van Vorst about another lecture invitation; see also the entry for his unlocated reply to the Troy group, p. 67 above).

FROM THE YOUNG MEN'S ASSOCIATION
BEFORE 25 DECEMBER 1846 · SCHENECTADY

Unlocated. A letter to Melville is cited in Helen Melville's 25 December 1846 letter to their sister Augusta, which reports that along with other letters that morning came "a letter from Schenectada for Herman, which Mama took the liberty of opening, as it had a very *unconfidential* exterior. It proved to be an invitation from the Young Men's Association to lecture before them sometime in March" (NYPL-GL). Melville's 19 January 1847 letter to Hooper C. Van Vorst indicates that he declined this offer.

FROM JOHN MURRAY
BEFORE 30 DECEMBER 1846 · LONDON

Unlocated. In his letter of 15 July 1846 Melville proposed his second book, *Omoo*, to his British publisher John Murray, requesting his "views about this proposed publication." Although Murray's letterbooks record nothing concerning the proposal, both Melville's 29 January 1847 letter to Murray and his earlier 30 December 1846 letter to John Brodhead refer to a letter from Murray that promised a "liberal" offer for the book.

1847

FROM HOOPER C. VAN VORST
14 JANUARY 1847 · ALBANY

Unlocated. A letter extending an invitation to lecture in Albany (and apparently mentioning invitations for Melville to lecture in Troy and Schenectady) is cited in Melville's 19 January 1847 reply.

FROM JOHN R. BRODHEAD
14 JANUARY 1847 · LONDON

Unlocated. John Brodhead noted above the dateline on Melville's 30 December 1846 letter requesting him to act as Melville's London agent: "Recd & ansd | *14 Jany 1847.*" Since Brodhead went on to serve as Melville's agent, this letter must have stated his willingness to do so. According to Brodhead's diary (Alexander Library, Rutgers University), he sent a letter—presumably this same one—to "H. Mel." by

the *Sarah Sands* on 19 January 1847. This is probably also the letter referred to in
Maria Melville's 19 February 1847 letter to her daughter Augusta, which simply
states that Melville had "received letters from Messrs Murray & Broadhead"
(NYPL-GL).

FROM PETER GANSEVOORT
6 FEBRUARY 1847 · ALBANY

At present only the draft of this letter has been located. In it Peter Gansevoort was
replying to Melville's 3 February 1847 request for a letter of introduction to Senator
John Adams Dix. The draft of Peter Gansevoort's letter to Melville is written below a draft of his letter to Dix dated 6 February. Presumably he enclosed the letter
to Dix with the letter to Melville and directed the packet, as instructed, to Melville's address in Washington, D.C. For more about Melville's office-seeking efforts at this time—in aid of which all of these letters were written—see the headnote
to Melville's initial 3 February 1847 letter to his uncle.

My Dear Herman
I rec'd your letter while engaged in Court & have availed myself
of the earliest moment to write to Gen'l Dix as you desired — When
you are introduced to Mrs Dix, please present my respects to her &
as she is an excellent sensible & a charming woman you must make
yourself very agreeable to her, which will greatly aid you in carrying out your views at Washington —
Be particular at your first interview with Genl Dix, not to say a
word about your business — He will invite you to his House — & at
a proper time, you can explain yourself fully —
When you call on Genl Marcy, present my respects to him —

[Enclosure:]

Albany Feb 6. 1847
My dear General
I have great pleasure in presenting to you my Nephew Herman
Melville who desires the honor of an introduction.
You doubtless have some knowledge of him as the author of
Typee & am satisfied a personal acquaintance will increase any
favorable judgement you had formed of him in its perusal
He shall at a proper time explain to you the object of his visit to
Washington — Any advice or assistance you may be pleased to ex-

tend to him, in the furtherance of his visit, will be fully appreciated by him and most thankfully considered by

Your sincere friend
P. G.

Final documents not located. Texts from draft letters, on a 20.4 × 31.3 cm sheet of blue wove paper with lines. Peter Gansevoort inscribed the unsigned draft of his letter to Melville on the bottom half of one side of the leaf, with the draft of his letter to Dix on the top half of the leaf, in ink, and noted on the verso "1847 | Feb. 6. | Herman | Melville" along with a memorandum about a real estate transaction.

LOCATION (of drafts): NYPL-GL.

PUBLICATION: (partial) *Log*, I, 235.

TEXTUAL NOTES: When] *inserted above canceled* If · an excellent sensible &] *inserted above* · aid] *added after canceled* assist · carrying] *after canceled* your · Be particular] *after* Be particular not to state at your first interview with Gen¹ Dix, the object of your visit to W. *with the object . . .* W. *canceled and* not to say a word on business. *inserted above and also canceled* then Be . . . Dix, *canceled* · interview] inter-|view · at] *inserted above caret* · you can] *after successively canceled* open || then · When . . . him —] *in the left margin; placed here editorially* · 6] *written over* 5 · I have] *after canceled* I have · presenting] *inserted above canceled* introducing · desires] *inserted above canceled* merits · the honor] *after canceled* will do himself · an] *inserted above before canceled* calling upon you at Washington — · introduction] *after canceled* being *and before canceled* to you · have] *inserted with caret above canceled* are · knowledge] *inserted with caret above canceled* acquaintance with · of him] *inserted above caret* · am] *after canceled* I · a personal] *after canceled* you will be much pleased with *with* much *inserted above caret* · will increase . . . perusal] *added, after canceled* with · favorable judgement] *conjectural reading* · had] ad *written over* ave · at a proper time] *inserted above caret* · the object] *after canceled* his intention & · Any] *after successively canceled* Any attention you find || Your · advice or] *inserted above caret* · to him] *inserted above caret*

FROM UNKNOWN
14 FEBRUARY 1847 · LANSINGBURGH

Unlocated. A valentine for Melville from an unknown admirer is cited in Helen Melville's 15 February 1847 letter to their sister Augusta: "We opened one directed to Herman, quite a pretty one, from some fair lady in the village" (NYPL-GL).

FROM RICHARD T. GREENE
BEFORE 19 FEBRUARY 1847 · BUFFALO

Unlocated. Melville's old shipmate Richard Tobias (Toby) Greene referred to his letter demanding a share of the profits of *Typee* as a "cursed" one in his subsequent letter apologizing for it. See the entry for the second and also unlocated letter from Greene, just below.

FROM RICHARD T. GREENE
BEFORE 19 FEBRUARY 1847 · BUFFALO

Unlocated. A letter of apology from Richard Tobias (Toby) Greene is cited in Helen Melville's 19 February 1847 letter to her sister Augusta: "By to-days mail we received a letter from 'Toby' dated Buffalo. To Herman of course; but we recognized the handwriting and opened it. It is really a beautiful letter, begging pardon for that 'cursed letter, which he *copied*, but never composed', and saying that he was put up to it by people who professed to be his friends, and who were continually pestering him with entreaties to apply to Herman for his share of the profits, in the immense sales of Typee; and — goes on to say — 'I find on consideration that I have no right to any such thing. You must my dear friend forgive and forget all, as an old ship-mate and friend, you must remember human nature is liable to err. I am heartily sorry, that I ever penned that infernal scrawl.'

"He says he wants to know all about Herman, says he has been the means of selling a great many copies of Typee — feels highly flattered with the mention of him in the second edition — hears he is writing again, and wishes him good success. —— I shall write Herman tomorrow and enclose Toby's letter. Are you not glad? I could not bear that a cloud should come between such old and tried friends. Herman's reply to his letter, so beautifully gentle & noble, without any spice or anger of contempt for his unworthy conduct, has brought him to his senses, and the result really rejoices me" (NYPL-GL).

FROM JOHN MURRAY
BEFORE 19 FEBRUARY 1847 · LONDON

Unlocated. A letter with the promised payment for the revised edition of *Typee* is cited in Maria Melville's 19 February 1847 letter to her daughter Augusta, which reports that Melville "recieved letters from Messrs Murray & Broadhead, the former with the £50, enclosure" (NYPL-GL). (For the letter from Brodhead cited here, see the entry for his now unlocated 14 January 1847 letter to Melville.)

FROM HELEN MARIA MELVILLE
20 FEBRUARY 1847 · LANSINGBURGH

Unlocated. According to Helen Melville's 19 February 1847 letter to her sister Augusta, she planned to enclose Richard Tobias (Toby) Greene's letter of apology to her brother in one of her own to him on the next day (see the entry for the second letter Greene wrote before 19 February 1847, above).

FROM JOHN R. BRODHEAD
3 MARCH 1847 · LONDON

Unlocated. A letter about the contract arrangements for *Omoo* is cited both in Melville's letter of the same date to John Murray and in his 31 March 1847 reply to

Brodhead. See the headnotes to those letters for the arrangements which this letter communicated. This is the same letter that Brodhead's diary entry for 3 March 1847 lists as a letter sent to "Har Mel." by the *Hibernia* (Alexander Library, Rutgers University).

FROM JOHN R. BRODHEAD
3 APRIL 1847 · LONDON

Unlocated. Brodhead's diary entry for 3 April 1847 simply lists "H. Mel." as among the correspondents to whom he sent letters by the *Cambria*. This letter probably conveyed the matters Brodhead recorded in his diary entry for 30 March 1847: "Melville's book published to day — & Murray gave me his check of £144.3.4 which I gave to Miller to deposit with Barrings to meet Mr Melville's draft on me by the steamer of 1st April — " (Alexander Library, Rutgers University). For more on these financial arrangements made through Baring Brothers, see Melville's 31 March 1847 letter to Brodhead.

FROM JOHN R. BRODHEAD
19 APRIL 1847 · LONDON

Unlocated. Brodhead recorded in his diary on 19 April 1847 that "To day received & accepted Melville's Bill for £140. at one days sight" (see the preceding entry for more about this financial agreement). Brodhead also listed in his diary on 19 April "H. Mel." as among the correspondents to whom he sent letters by the *Caledonia* that day (Alexander Library, Rutgers University). He wrote this letter in reply to Melville's 31 March 1847 letter, as indicated by his endorsement of it: "Ansd 19 Apl."

FROM RICHARD BENTLEY
17 MAY [1847?] · LONDON

Unlocated. An initial letter to Melville from the publisher Richard Bentley is cited in Melville's reply dated 19 June, here tentatively assigned to 1847. None of the Bentley letterbooks in the British Library covers this year.

FROM AUGUSTUS P. VAN SCHAICK
6 JULY 1847 · RIO DE JANEIRO

Unlocated. On 26 April 1847 Melville wrote a letter to his second cousin Augustus Van Schaick, who was staying in Rio de Janeiro for his health, and who, according to his endorsement on it, received and immediately answered the letter on 6 July. For more on this cousin, see the headnote to Melville's letter.

FROM EVERT A. DUYCKINCK
[8 OR 29?] JULY 1847 · NEW YORK

Unlocated. A letter from Duyckinck enclosing a favorable review of *Omoo* is cited as having been received the "Day before yesterday" in Melville's undated reply, here tentatively assigned to 10 or 31 July 1847.

FROM JOHN MURRAY
3 DECEMBER 1847 · LONDON

John Murray wrote this friendly but firm reply to Melville's letter of 29 October that questioned Murray's financial dealings with him, particularly in not offering more for *Omoo* (see that letter and its headnote). John Brodhead (the "friend" Murray refers to here), who had negotiated the sale of *Omoo*, had also apparently criticized Murray's offer in his now unlocated 3 March 1847 letter, as Melville's 31 March reply to Brodhead suggests.

As before, Murray complains in this letter of the public's perception of a lack of authenticity in Melville's books. The offer he makes here for Melville's next book proved to be "not altogether satisfactory," according to Melville's 1 January 1848 reply.

Albemarle St Decr 3rd

Dear Sir

I thank you very much for your friendly letter of Octr 29. — for as friendly I regard it even tho it expresses dissatisfaction with the remuneration which you have received from me for your 2 Books — Omoo, & Typee — These Works have been greatly admired in this Country and I appreciate them highly myself. Yet you must not altogether estimate their popularity here by their Success in your own Country I myself have been disappointed I confess at the result. Of Typee I printed 5000 Copies and have sold *4104*. Of Omoo, 4000 and have sold *2512* — Thus I have gained by the former 51 — 2. 3. & by the latter am a loser of 57 — 16 — 10 — I do not willingly enter into such details but this is bona fide the state of the Case. I sho^d not have entered into such details with an Author but that it is evident from your Manner of Writing that you and your friend suppose me to be reaping immense advantages in which you ought to be participating — understand I pray that I do not eventually expect to be a loser but *I cannot anticipate* from what has occurred that I shall be any great gainer except in credit as the publisher of these two Books

You may fairly suggest that it is my fault in Choosing so cheap a form of publication but of other Numbers of my Colonial Library I have sold 6000, 10,000 & 15,000 even of some. I am willing however nay desirous to continue your publisher and will next time if opportunity is offered me print in a different form and trust to higher remuneration from smaller sale — If you will send me over the Sheets of your next Work and allow me to read them and to decide that the work is one which I can undertake with Advantage to you as well as to myself I would propose this arrangement I will at once on the publicat^n advance you 100 g^s. and when the Sale of the Work shall have repaid all expence of outlay I will pay you one half of the profits of every Edition — I wish some means could be taken to convince the English Public that your Books are not fictions imitations of Robinson Crusoe — T'is this Feeling of being tricked which impedes their Circulat^n here, hoping you will favor me with a Letter in answer at your Convenience I remain dear Sir Yours very faithfully

(signed) John Murray

Herman Melville Esq
New York

Original document not located. Text from Murray's March 1846–April 1858 letterbook (presumably inscribed by a clerk), pp. 50–52.

LOCATION (of letterbook): Murray.

PUBLICATION: (partial) *Log*, I, 265–66. Davis, pp. 60–61.

TEXTUAL NOTES: 15,000] *originally* 150000 *then final digit canceled and comma added* · some] o *written over* a · print in] in *rewritten* · expence] *originally* expences *then* s *canceled*

1848

FROM JOHN MURRAY
17 JANUARY 1848 · LONDON

Unlocated. A letter, possibly answering Melville's 1 January letter and again asking for "documentary evidence" of Melville's adventures, is cited in Melville's 25 March 1848 reply to his British publisher, John Murray. According to Melville's reply, Murray's letter had also expressed, in its "closing sentence," a desire to "test the corporeality" of Melville "by clapping eyes upon him in London."

FROM A BERLIN PUBLISHER
BEFORE 4 FEBRUARY 1848 · BERLIN

Unlocated. On 4 February 1848 Elizabeth Shaw Melville reported in a letter to her
stepmother, Hope Savage Shaw, a "communication" Melville had received "from
Berlin to translate from the first sheets into German" his third book, *Mardi* (HCL-
M). See also the entry, pp. 102–3 above, for Melville's unlocated letters to the
publisher.

FROM HENRY WILLCOX
BEFORE 1 MAY 1848 · WESTPORT POINT

Unlocated. A letter from the owner of the *Theophilus Chase*, the whaleship aboard
which Melville's youngest brother, Thomas, had sailed from Westport Point, Massachusetts, in 1846, is reported by Elizabeth Shaw Melville in a letter to her stepmother, Hope Savage Shaw, dated 5 May 1848: "We are looking out for Tom to
return every day his ship has been reported in the papers several times lately as
homeward bound and Herman wrote to the owner at Westport and received answer that he looked for the ship the first of May. that has already past and we are
daily expecting a letter to announce her actual arrival. Then Herman will have to go
over to Westport for Tom and see that he is regularly discharged and paid, and
bring him home" (HCL-M). For Melville's unlocated letter to Willcox inquiring
about the progress of the ship, see p. 108 above.

FROM HENRY WILLCOX
ON OR AFTER 4 MAY 1848 · WESTPORT POINT

Unlocated. Presumably Henry Willcox wrote to Melville as he had promised (see
the preceding entry) when his whaleship, the *Theophilus Chase*, arrived in Westport
Point, Massachusetts, on 4 May 1848.

FROM JOHN MURRAY
20 MAY 1848 · LONDON

Unlocated. A letter from Murray replying to Melville's 25 March proposal of a
" 'Romance of Polynisian Adventure' " is cited in Melville's subsequent 19 June
1848 reply. In it Melville characterized Murray's letter as having an "Antarctic
tenor."

FROM JOHN R. BRODHEAD
7 JULY 1848 · LONDON

Unlocated. Brodhead's diary entry for 7 July 1848 lists "Har. Mel." as one of the
correspondents to whom he wrote that day (Alexander Library, Rutgers University). No indication of the contents of the letter is given.

FROM HARPER & BROTHERS
11 NOVEMBER 1848 · NEW YORK

This incomplete draft of a letter from the Harpers (with the last paragraph added by Melville on the third page) outlines the terms of the contract for *Mardi*, which Melville signed on 15 November 1848. For some reason the letter ends without a complimentary close or signature. The final eight-clause contract (HCL-M) included the points made in all three of the letter's numbered clauses, but not Melville's unnumbered fourth clause (possibly because the book was, in the event, published without illustrations). For more on the financial arrangements with the Harpers for Melville's third book, see the headnotes to his 28 January 1849 letter to John Murray and his 26 March 1849 letter to the Harpers.

New York Nov. 11th 1848 —

Dear Sir —

We propose publishing your new Work upon the following terms:

1. We will publish the work from stereotype Plates in such form and at such price as may be mutually agreed upon and pay you one half of the profits arising from its sale.

2. If, after the Plates, &c are paid for you wish a certain sum per copy, we will make such an arrangement, and agree that it shall be equal to one-half of the profits.

3. We will make you an advance of Five hundred dollars, on the day of publication, if you desire it.

In case it is hereafter agreed between us, that it would be profitable to illustrate the book, Mess Harper will defray the expences of the engravings, without charging any portion thereof to the account of H. M. But H. M. shall receive half the profits as before.

No final document located. Text from incomplete draft, on a 41 × 25.4 cm sheet, folded in half, of green wove paper. Presumably a Harper employee inscribed the first page, in ink; the last paragraph was added on the third page in Melville's own hand. The employee noted on the fourth page in ink "$500 on" and Elizabeth Melville noted on that page in pencil "Mem. | Harpers | Nov 11. 1848".

Location: HCL-M.

Publication: (partial) *Log*, I, 281.

1849

FROM ALLAN MELVILLE
19 FEBRUARY 1849 · NEW YORK

Unlocated. Allan Melville's 19 February 1849 letter about the birth of his first child, Maria Gansevoort Melville, is cited in Melville's 20 February reply.

FROM JOHN R. BRODHEAD
23 FEBRUARY 1849 · LONDON

Unlocated. Brodhead's diary entry for 23 February 1849 lists "*H. Melville*" as one of the correspondents to whom he sent letters by the *America* (Alexander Library, Rutgers University). In his letter, Brodhead probably reported on the safe arrival of the proof sheets for *Mardi*, and possibly on Murray's rejection of the book (Brodhead recorded that rejection in a 24 February entry in his diary, but did not specify on which day Murray had told him of it).

FROM EVERT A. DUYCKINCK
BETWEEN 24 FEBRUARY AND 3 MARCH 1849 · NEW YORK

Unlocated. Although a letter is not specifically cited, Melville's 3 March 1849 letter to Duyckinck was evidently written in reply to one that accused Melville of "oscillat[ing] in Emerson's rainbow" and of irreverence in his earlier 24 February letter.

FROM JOHN R. BRODHEAD
BETWEEN 1 MARCH AND 3 APRIL 1849 · LONDON

Unlocated. A letter from John Brodhead is cited in Melville's 3 April 1849 letter to Richard Bentley. Brodhead, who settled the publication of *Mardi* with Bentley on 1 March 1849, evidently wrote to Melville not long afterwards, perhaps enclosing the 5 March letter that he received from Bentley, which stated Bentley's decision to issue the book in three volumes instead of two (HCL-M). This letter is not, however, recorded in Brodhead's London diary for this period (Alexander Library, Rutgers University).

FROM RICHARD BENTLEY
5 MARCH 1849 · LONDON

Unlocated. The "frank & friendly" letter from Bentley concerning *Mardi*, cited without a date in Melville's 3 April 1849 reply, is probably the same letter as the 5 March one from Bentley cited in Melville's 26 March 1849 letter to the Harpers. Although a 5 March 1849 letter to John R. Brodhead concerning *Mardi* was recorded in the Bentley 1849–54 letterbook (British Library), this letter to Melville was not. For its possible contents, see Lynn Horth, "Richard Bentley's Place in Melville's Literary Career," *Studies in the American Renaissance 1992*, pp. 229–45.

FROM EVERT A. DUYCKINCK
BEFORE 5 APRIL 1849 · NEW YORK

Unlocated. Duyckinck's "note," followed shortly by a copy of the 31 March 1849 *Literary World*, is cited in Melville's 5 April reply.

FROM JOHN R. BRODHEAD
1 JUNE 1849 · LONDON

Unlocated. Brodhead's diary entry for 1 June 1849 lists "H. M." as one of the correspondents to whom he sent letters by the *Cambria* that day (Alexander Library, Rutgers University). No indication of the contents of the letter is given.

FROM RICHARD BENTLEY
20 JUNE 1849 · LONDON

Responding in this letter to Melville's 5 June 1849 letter, which commented on the "broadside" English reviewers had fired into *Mardi*, Bentley offered his analysis of the book's failure. He also responded to Melville's proposal of a "plain, straightforward, amusing narrative," the book he would publish as *Redburn* (1849). For more on both of these books, as well as on Bentley's promise in this letter to expedite Melville's copies of *Mardi*, see the headnote to Melville's 5 June letter.

Writing only shortly after the 5 June 1849 ruling by Sir Frederick Pollock in the case of *Boosey v. Purday* that precluded foreigners from gaining a copyright in Great Britain by priority of publication (making American books even more susceptible to piracy and even less desirable to British publishers), Bentley was careful to assure Melville of his continued commitment to publishing American writers. On the same day, he wrote a similar letter to James Fenimore Cooper, stating that the "decision of our sapient Sir F. Pollock declaring that no foreigner had a copyright here . . . shall not interfere with my course of business, for I rely upon the common sense of the matter and the principle of justice" (Robert E. Spiller and Philip C. Blackburn, *A Descriptive Bibliography of James Fenimore Cooper* [New York: Bowker, 1934], p. 244). See Melville's 20 July reply to Bentley for his comment on the copyright situation.

The bottom of the second letterbook page on which this copy was written was later used for Melville's signed acceptance of one hundred pounds in partial payment for *Redburn* when Melville visited Bentley in his London office on 12 November 1849 (see the manuscript description, below, and see *Journals*, p. 16, for Melville's record of this visit and payment).

Herman Melville Esq

8 New Burlington S^t
June 20. 1849

Dear Sir

I beg to acknowledge the receipt of your letter of the fifth instant. As you observe the English critics generally have fired quite a broadside into "Mardi." This I cannot help thinking, has arisen in a great measure from the nature of the work: the first volume was eagerly devoured, the second was read — but the third was not perhaps altogether adapted to the class of readers whom "Omoo" and "Typee", and the First Volume of "Mardi" gratified. The effect somehow or other has been decidedly to check, nay I may almost say, to stop the sale of the book. In the first instance in consequence of the popularity of your two former books, the booksellers thought well of it and took liberally — since the first issue a few — a very few copies have been sold, so as to leave me without profit at any rate. To complicate matters still further, our sapient Sir Fred^k Pollock with Justices Platt & Rolfe have decided that a foreigner has *no copyright*. This drivelling absurdity can scarcely be suffered to remain, I trust, but in the mean time this decision will expose publishers like myself, who am so largely engaged in this department of publishing to the risk of attack from any unprincipled persons who may choose to turn Pirate. This decision must be reversed in the end; but the slow and tumble down machinery of our precious laws may defer the decision to the Greek Kalends. I am determined, however, notwithstanding this decision, to go on, relying firmly that I shall not be permitted to suffer for this folly. Well, then, with regard to your new book, I cannot help coming to the conclusion that it will not receive any additional welcome from "Mardi," of which I have not sold sufficient to cover my expenses. The new work will I presume make two light volumes like "Mardi" and that will be decidedly the only way to publish it with any advantage. I am willing to give you £100 secured to you on account of half profits. More than this, surrounded as I am with the want of success of Mardi and the stupid decision, at present with regard to copyright, it will not be in my power to give. With this promise that I shall be enabled to publish here a few days before the appearance of the work in the States. Why do not you a people, with the grand literature the United States now has, why not at once with dignity come into the International copyright Act. Surely your literary men have power to accom-

plish this, and now is the time to do it & shame, our miserable, paltry, shabby lawgivers, & settle the matter beyond question
Note Not finding Mr Brodhead at home yesterday when I called (for
he had gone to Oxford to join Mr Bancroft), I have thought it best
not to delay sending you copies of Mardi so I have adopted your
direction to send them by Harnden's Express

> I Remain, Dear Sir
> Yours faithfully
> (signed) R. Bentley

Original document not located. Text from Bentley's 1849–54 letterbook (presumably inscribed by a clerk), pp. 36–37, emended by NN at two points (see below). When in London,
Melville signed, in ink, the bottom of the second page of the copy next to the letter's close:
"Received Mr R Bentleys | promissory Note at 3 months date | for £100 [at *canceled*] Nov 12
1849 Herman Melville".

LOCATION (of letterbook): British Library.

PUBLICATION: Bernard R. Jerman, " 'With Real Admiration': More Correspondence between
Melville and Bentley," *American Literature* 25 (November 1953), 308–10.

TEXTUAL NOTES (for symbols used, see p. 840): this department] NN; the department • Act.]
after canceled with dignity • Bancroft)] NN; ~∧

FROM MR. BALDWIN
BEFORE 6 OCTOBER 1849 · PLACE UNKNOWN

Unlocated. In his 6 October 1849 letter to Judge Shaw, Melville reported that he
had received a "few days ago" a letter of introduction "(thro' the post) from Mr
Baldwin to his son in Paris." Although Davis and Gilman speculated that Melville
may have solicited this letter from the unidentified Mr. Baldwin (Davis-Gilman
Unlocated 309), it seems most likely that Shaw had done so. See the headnote to
Melville's 6 October letter to Shaw for a discussion of Baldwin's possible identity.

FROM R. H. DANA, JR.
BEFORE 6 OCTOBER 1849 · BOSTON

Unlocated. Dana's letter enclosing a letter of introduction to the publisher Edward
Moxon is cited in Melville's 6 October 1849 reply.

FROM RICHARD BENTLEY
[9?] NOVEMBER 1849 · LONDON

Unlocated. Arriving in London on 6 November 1849, Melville called at Bentley's
office on 8 November only to find that the publisher was in Brighton. He left a
note for him, and on 10 November, as he recorded in his London journal, he re-

ceived "at breakfast" a "note from Mr Bentley in reply to mine, saying he would
come up from Brighton at any time convenient to me" (*Journals*, p. 14).

FROM RICHARD BENTLEY
[11?] NOVEMBER 1849 · LONDON

Unlocated. In reply to Bentley's earlier [9?] November letter (see the entry just
above), Melville wrote suggesting they meet in London the following Monday, 12
November. That day Melville recorded in his London journal that he received "another note from Mr Bentley saying he would be in town this morning, according to
my suggestion, at 12. A.M." (*Journals*, p. 16).

FROM HENRY COLBOURN
17 NOVEMBER 1849 · LONDON

Unlocated. On Friday, 16 November, Melville went to the offices of Henry Colbourn
to offer him *White-Jacket*. The following day, Melville noted in his journal that
Colbourn declined the offer by letter, "on the ground, principally, of the cursed state of
the copyright matter." This news was a blow to Melville, since it meant he would not
have the funds to travel to Rome as he had planned (*Journals*, p. 20).

FROM ROBERT H. GRISWOLD
BETWEEN 17 AND 19 NOVEMBER 1849 · LONDON

Unlocated. Melville helped take up a collection from his fellow passengers aboard
the *Southampton* to buy a present, a book (Melville does not give its title in his
journal), for Captain Griswold, as was traditional when a captain was well liked.
Melville delivered the volume to Griswold on 17 November 1849 (*Journals*, p. 20)
and then found a note at his lodgings from Griswold "acknowledging" the volume
on the evening of 19 November (*Journals*, p. 22).

FROM N. P. WILLIS
BEFORE 19 NOVEMBER 1849 · NEW YORK

Unlocated. On 19 November 1849 Melville went to Richard Bentley's office "to
see if there should be any letters" and received "two budgets" or packets of letters
from "home." One was a letter from N. P. Willis enclosing letters of introduction,
to Lord John Manners, written by Manners's sister in New York, and to Martin
Farquhar Tupper, presumably written by Willis himself (*Journals*, pp. 22, 306).

FROM ELIZABETH SHAW MELVILLE AND FAMILY
BEFORE 19 NOVEMBER 1849 · NEW YORK

Two or more unlocated letters. The second packet of letters that Melville received
on 19 November 1849 (see the entry just above) was from his family. After reading

them, he noted in his journal: "All well thank God — & Barney a bouncer." Although he does not specify who wrote the letters, at least one, describing his son Malcolm (called "Barney" as a baby), was most likely from his wife (*Journals*, p. 21).

FROM LORD JOHN MANNERS
ON OR BEFORE 19 NOVEMBER 1849 · LONDON

Unlocated. Lord John Manners, probably at the instance of N. P. Willis, left a "very kind" note for Melville at Bentley's office on 19 November 1849 (*Journals*, p. 21). Melville received his note at the same time that he received a letter from N. P. Willis (see the entry above) enclosing a letter of introduction to Manners. For more on Manners and Melville's unsuccessful efforts to meet him, see the entry for Melville's two unlocated 19 November replies to this letter and *Journals*, p. 305.

FROM JOHN MURRAY
19 NOVEMBER 1849 · LONDON

Unlocated. Returning home from the theater on the evening of 19 November 1849, Melville found "a note from Murray inviting me to dine & meet Lockhart on Friday" (*Journals*, p. 22). Melville's response is now unlocated. For his description of his evening at Murray's and of the guests he encountered there, including John Gibson Lockhart, the editor of the *Edinburgh Review*, see *Journals*, pp. 25–26.

FROM WILLIAM LONGMAN
19 NOVEMBER 1849 · LONDON

Unlocated. On 19 November 1849 Melville visited the offices of the Longman firm, probably seeing William Longman and offering him *White-Jacket*. Melville recorded in his journal finding "a note on top of my blackened boots" the following morning, saying the firm "abided by their original terms"—which most likely meant that while they would accept the book, they were not willing to give him an advance for it (*Journals*, pp. 22 and 304).

FROM JOSHUA BATES
21 NOVEMBER 1849 · LONDON

Unlocated. On 20 November 1849 Melville had left his card and a letter of introduction at the residence of Joshua Bates, an American partner in the banking house of Baring Brothers. The following day Melville received an invitation to dinner at Bates's country home in East Sheen, Surrey, which he accepted in a now unlocated letter (*Journals*, pp. 23–24; see also pp. 26–27 for Melville's description of the dinner and p. 311 for more on Bates).

FROM ABBOTT LAWRENCE AND
KATHERINE BIGELOW LAWRENCE
22 NOVEMBER 1849 · LONDON

Unlocated. Abbott Lawrence, the American minister to the Court of St. James's, received Melville on his first visit to the legation (*Journals*, p. 22). Two days later, on 22 November 1849, Lawrence and his wife sent Melville a dinner invitation, which Melville had to decline (in a now unlocated letter) since he was already engaged to dine at John Murray's (*Journals*, p. 24).

FROM DAVID BOGUE
23 NOVEMBER 1849 · LONDON

Unlocated. On 23 November 1849, Melville went to the offices of David Bogue to offer him *White-Jacket*. Melville noted in his journal that "B. was all ears" and promised to send his decision about the book by letter that evening (*Journals*, p. 25). Returning from dinner at John Murray's, Melville found the letter and wrote in his journal: "I knew its contents at once — there seemed little use in opening it. — He declined; alleging among other reasons, the state of the copyright question. — So we go" (*Journals*, p. 26).

FROM EVERT A. DUYCKINCK
BEFORE 27 NOVEMBER 1849 · NEW YORK

Unlocated. Melville probably received Duyckinck's "most kind & friendly letter" before leaving London on 27 November 1849 for Paris, where on 2 December he began his reply, with apologies for his delay (finishing it on 14 December).

FROM GEORGE J. ADLER
30 NOVEMBER 1849 · PARIS

Unlocated. In reply to one of Melville's two letters to him of 29 November—written shortly after arriving in Paris—George Adler, Melville's shipboard friend, left Melville a brief letter the following day, arranging to meet him that evening (*Journals*, p. 31). For more about Adler, see the entry for Melville's two unlocated letters to him, p. 146 above.

FROM THE DUKE OF RUTLAND
BEFORE 13 DECEMBER 1849 · [LONDON?]

Unlocated. Returning to London from the Continent on 13 December, Melville found a letter from the duke of Rutland, inviting him to visit Belvoir Castle in January. As his entry for 16 December 1849 records, the invitation was a very tempting one—but nonetheless he decided to turn it down (*Journals*, p. 39). For more about the duke of Rutland and Melville's decision to return home rather than accept this invitation, see the entry for Melville's unlocated reply of 17 December.

FROM ELIZABETH SHAW MELVILLE
BEFORE 13 DECEMBER 1849 · NEW YORK

Unlocated. At the offices of Richard Bentley, Melville found on his return to London from the Continent two letters from home—one of them from his wife. His journal entry comments: "Most welcome but gave me the blues terribly — Felt like chartering a small-boat & starting down the Thames instanter for New York" (*Journals*, p. 39).

FROM ALLAN MELVILLE
BEFORE 13 DECEMBER 1849 · NEW YORK

Unlocated. The other letter from home waiting for Melville on his return to London—see the entry just above—was from his brother Allan (*Journals*, p. 39).

FROM ELIZABETH SHAW MELVILLE
BEFORE 13 DECEMBER 1849 · NEW YORK

Unlocated. During his first evening back in London, while answering the letters from his wife and brother retrieved from Bentley's earlier in the day (see the two entries just above), Melville received a delivery from the American legation containing two letters, one of them from his wife, written a week later than the earlier ones. Melville commented in his journal: "I read them, & felt raised at once" (*Journals*, p. 39).

FROM ALLAN MELVILLE
BEFORE 13 DECEMBER 1849 · NEW YORK

Unlocated. The other letter from home delivered to Melville's room on 13 December 1849—see the entry just above—was from his brother Allan.

FROM SAMUEL ROGERS
18 DECEMBER 1849 · LONDON

Unlocated. Returning to his lodgings on 18 December, Melville found an invitation to breakfast from the poet and banker Samuel Rogers (*Journals*, p. 43). For more about Rogers and their breakfast, see the entry for Melville's unlocated acceptance of the same date.

FROM [ELIZABETH SHAW MELVILLE?]
BEFORE 20 DECEMBER 1849 · NEW YORK

Unlocated. At his lodgings on the evening of 20 December 1849, Melville found a
letter "from home"—presumably from his wife since it commented on their son
Malcolm ("Barney"). He noted in his journal: "All well & Barney more bouncing
than ever, thank heaven" (*Journals*, p. 45).

FROM JOHN FORSTER
21 DECEMBER 1849 · LONDON

Unlocated. Having received Melville's card and letter of introduction, John Forster,
the drama critic and friend of Dickens, responded on 21 December 1849 with an
invitation to breakfast on 23 December—the same date that Melville had already
agreed to breakfast for the second time with Samuel Rogers (*Journals*, p. 46). For
more about Forster, see the entry for Melville's unlocated reply of the same date
and *Journals*, p. 357.

FROM ROBERT F. COOKE
22 DECEMBER 1849 · LONDON

Unlocated. Robert F. Cooke, John Murray's cousin and partner, with whom Melville had dined earlier in the week, sent Melville on 22 December 1849 a brief letter
enclosing a pass to the Reform Club, which Melville used two days later (*Journals*,
p. 46). For more about Cooke, see *Journals*, p. 321, and the entry for Melville's
unlocated letter to him written before 11 June 1853.

1850

FROM EVERT A. DUYCKINCK
6 MARCH 1850 · NEW YORK

Unlocated. A brief letter from Duyckinck accompanying a gift of some concert
tickets can be inferred from Melville's 7 March 1850 letter acknowledging the gift.

FROM R. H. DANA, JR.
BEFORE 1 MAY 1850 · BOSTON

Unlocated. A letter from Dana praising Melville's *Redburn* and *White-Jacket* and
suggesting that he write a book about a "whaling voyage" is cited in Melville's 1
May 1850 reply.

FROM LOUIS A. GODEY
AFTER 10 AUGUST 1850 · PHILADELPHIA

Unlocated. A letter to Melville can be inferred from the 10 August 1850 inquiry Lemuel Shaw received from Louis Antoine Godey (1804–78), asking briefly: "Can you favor me with the address of Mr Herman Melville?" (MHS-S). Presumably Shaw sent the address, and Godey wrote to Melville, inviting him to contribute to *Godey's Lady's Book*, since he was later listed as a promised contributor in an advertisement that appeared at the back of the December 1850 and January 1851 issues.

FROM EVERT A. DUYCKINCK
13 AUGUST 1850 · NEW YORK

Unlocated. Having visited Melville and his wife in Pittsfield, with Cornelius Mathews, at the old Melvill family home (later named Broadhall) between 2 and 12 August 1850, Evert Duyckinck, on returning to New York, sent on 13 August a present of cigars and a dozen quarts of Heidseck champagne in a basket along with a letter of thanks, according to Melville's 16 August reply. For more about Duyckinck's visit, see the headnote to that reply.

FROM CORNELIUS MATHEWS
13 AUGUST 1850 · NEW YORK

Unlocated. A note of thanks from Cornelius Mathews for the visit he and Evert Duyckinck had enjoyed with Melville in the Berkshires (see the entry just above) is cited in Melville's 16 August letter to Duyckinck (see the headnote to that letter and the entry for Melville's unlocated [16?] August reply to this letter, for more about Mathews and his visit). In a thank-you letter to Elizabeth Shaw Melville, dated 15 August, Mathews wrote: "Mr. Cornelius Mathews presents his respects to Mrs. Herman Melville & begs her acceptance of the enclosed autograph of Mrs. Browning's Poem 'The Cry of the Human:' also a couple of little books for the boy popularly known as Barney — " (HCL-M; the manuscript poem by Elizabeth Barrett Browning is also in HCL-M). The "boy popularly known as Barney" was the Melvilles' first child, Malcolm.

FROM AUGUSTA MELVILLE
6 SEPTEMBER 1850 · NEW YORK

Unlocated. A two-page letter "To Herman" at Pittsfield, probably in reply to his unlocated letter written on or before 3 September 1850, is listed in Augusta Melville's record of correspondence (NYPL-GL).

FROM AUGUSTA MELVILLE
14 SEPTEMBER 1850 · NEW YORK

Unlocated. A four-page letter "To Herman" at Pittsfield is listed in Augusta Melville's record of correspondence (NYPL-GL).

FROM JOHN TROY
BEFORE 23 SEPTEMBER 1850 · CALIFORNIA

Unlocated. A letter from John Troy, one of Melville's shipmates aboard the *Lucy Ann*, is cited in a 23 September 1850 letter from George Duyckinck to Joann Miller (1817–52), who was one of Duyckinck's regular correspondents. Whether she actually met Melville is not known, but her letters to Duyckinck show that she was clearly an admirer of Melville's writing. For his part George Duyckinck sometimes included news of Melville in his letters to her, as he did in his 23 September one: "Herman Melville has taken us by surprize by buying a farm of 160 acres in Berkshire County. It is mostly woodland which he intends to preserve and have a road through, making it more of an ornamental place than a farm. Part of it is on a hill commanding a view of twenty miles where he intends eventually to build. He removes at once with his mother and sisters to our great sorrow as the house was one of the pleasantest to visit at I ever came across and we are much attached to them all. Do you remember 'Long Ghost' in one of his books? He had a letter from him the other day dated from California — that mesh net of humanity" (NYPL-D).

The "book" in which John Troy had figured as Doctor Long Ghost was *Omoo*. After remaining in Tahiti for some time, he went to California during the gold rush and later shipped out in October 1852 aboard the trader *Chatham* under the name "Dr. R——" (see Harrison Hayford, in *Omoo*, ed. Harrison Hayford and Walter Blair [New York: Hendricks House, 1969], pp. 349–52 and 436–37).

FROM EVERT A. DUYCKINCK
BEFORE 6 OCTOBER 1850 · NEW YORK

Unlocated. Duyckinck's letter, enclosing a newspaper article on the law abolishing flogging in the navy, is cited in Melville's 6 October 1850 reply.

FROM EVERT A. DUYCKINCK
BETWEEN 6 OCTOBER AND 13 DECEMBER 1850 · NEW YORK

Two or more unlocated letters. Letters from Duyckinck can be inferred from Melville's apology in his 13 December 1850 letter for "failing to answer what letters" Duyckinck had sent him since "removing" to "a remote region called Berkshire." (Melville's last known reply was written on 6 October shortly after his move.)

FROM ELIZABETH SHAW MELVILLE
BEFORE 21 DECEMBER 1850 · BOSTON

Unlocated. Before Thanksgiving on 25 November 1850 Elizabeth (Lizzie) Shaw Melville and Malcolm left for Boston to spend the holidays with her family while Melville remained in Pittsfield working on his new whaling book. On 21 December 1850 Augusta Melville, also in Pittsfield, wrote to her sister Helen in Lansingburgh, noting, "We hear from Lizzie quite frequently. She is not to return until after the holidays, so thoroughly is she enjoying her visit. Malcolm continues to excite the admiring gaze of all visitors, & has lost his shrinking shyness" (NYPL-GL). Presumably at least one of the frequent letters to Pittsfield from Elizabeth Melville was to her husband.

FROM ELI JAMES MURDOCK FLY
BEFORE 21 DECEMBER 1850 · PLACE UNKNOWN

Unlocated. A letter from Melville's boyhood friend is cited in Augusta Melville's 21 December 1850 letter to their sister Helen: "Herman had a letter from Mr Fly acknowledging the receipt of the guava" (NYPL-GL). An earlier letter of 5 December 1850 also from Augusta to Helen, who was visiting in Lansingburgh, had included the query: "Has the package been sent to Mr Fly? & did you write him by the mail?" Apparently Helen Melville had been commissioned to send some guava—probably jellied—from Lansingburgh to Melville's friend. For more on Fly, see the headnote to Melville's 10 November 1838 letter to his brother Allan.

FROM ELIZABETH SHAW MELVILLE
BEFORE 31 DECEMBER 1850 · BOSTON

Unlocated. A letter from Melville's wife, still in Boston with their son Malcolm (see the entry for her letter written before 21 December 1850, above), is cited in Augusta Melville's 31 December 1850 letter from Arrowhead to her sister Helen: "Herman begins to be quite impatient for Lizzie's return — & last evening when he was reading a letter from her, he told us that she would be home tomorrow. But that is New Year's day — & I dont believe she's coming — For he laughed. As for Malcolm — I almost tremble for him — Herman will fairly devour him" (NYPL-GL).

1851

FROM EVERT A. DUYCKINCK
BEFORE 14 JANUARY 1851 · NEW YORK

Unlocated. Augusta Melville's 14 January 1851 letter from Arrowhead to her sister Helen in Lansingburgh cites a letter: "Mr Duyckink wrote Herman a most amusing letter the other day. He calls him a Blue-Beard, who has hidden away five agreeable ladies in an icy glen, & conjures him when next he takes the key from his girdle to carry them food, to say to them, the 'sad one' particularly that New York pines for their presence" (NYPL-GL). This is probably the letter that Melville answered on 12 February 1851, since his reply enclosed a now unlocated note from the " 'Sad One' "—Augusta. Her record of correspondence shows that she wrote a one-page note on 11 February 1851 "To Mr Duyckinck" (NYPL-GL).

FROM SOPHIA PEABODY HAWTHORNE
26 JANUARY 1851 · LENOX

Unlocated. A letter, or "side-blow," from Sophia Hawthorne, declining Melville's invitation for the Hawthorne family to spend the day and to stay the night at Arrowhead, is cited in his [29 January?] 1851 letter to Nathaniel Hawthorne and in Sophia Hawthorne's diary: "Mild day. I read all over to myself 'The House of the Seven Gables' in manuscript. In evening wrote a note to Mr. Melville" (NYPL-B).

FROM NATHANIEL HAWTHORNE
3 FEBRUARY 1851 · LENOX

Unlocated. Sophia Hawthorne recorded in her diary that on 3 February her husband went at noon "to the Postoffice, with notes to Mr Melville and Mr Dana" (NYPL-B). Probably the note for Melville declined Melville's [29 January?] invitation for Hawthorne and his family to come to Arrowhead on Wednesday, 5 February 1851 (Melville's 12 February 1851 letter to Evert Duyckinck reported that Hawthorne "was to have made me a day's visit . . . . But he has not been able to come, owing to sickness in his family. — or else, he's up to the lips in the *Universe* again").

FROM NATHANIEL HAWTHORNE AND
SOPHIA PEABODY HAWTHORNE
27 MARCH 1851 · LENOX

This joint letter from Nathaniel and Sophia Hawthorne is the only one from either to Melville now located. It is in part a letter of thanks for Hawthorne's 13–14 March visit to Arrowhead with their daughter Una. It primarily concerns, however, a series of errands of the sort that Melville, living near the comparatively urban Pittsfield, was commissioned to perform for the Hawthornes (see Melville's [16 April?] 1851 letter to Hawthorne for a similar request to find some shoes for Hawthorne's son Julian, which he was unable to obtain). On 11 April Sophia Hawthorne's diary records that Melville arrived at their cottage near Lenox bringing the requested clock and bedstead with him (NYPL-B). The fate of the box, containing, among other things, inexpensive clothes for Hawthorne, is not recorded (for the contents of the box and the identity of the expressman, "Mr Steele," see the Cente-

From Nathaniel Hawthorne and Sophia Peabody Hawthorne, 27 March
1851, p. 1 (reduced). Courtesy of the Rare Books and Manuscripts Division, The New York Public Library, Astor, Lenox and Tilden Foundations
(Gansevoort-Lansing Collection).

nary Edition of Hawthorne's *Letters, 1843–1853*, cited under publication, below, pp. 408–9 and 412–13).

Lenox, March 27th, 1851

Dear Melville,

The next time you go to Pittsfield (and I believe you to go every day) will you be kind enough to inquire at the railroad depôt, or express-office, for a large box, directed to me? We have been expecting one for some days past; and knowing that it has left Boston, cannot otherwise account for its non-arrival than by supposing it to be delayed in Pittsfield.

We want a kitchen-clock. There are wooden ones, of Connecticut manufacture, and excellent time-keepers, at $1.50. If such are to be found in Pittsfield, I wish you would buy us one

Una has very delightful reminiscenses of our visit to Melville Castle. So have I. With my regards to Mrs Melville and your sisters

Truly yours
Nathl Hawthorne

P.S. Dear Sir,

Will you direct the box that we are sure is at the Pittsfield depôt — to the Post office, Lenox. I believe a certain Mr Steele is the Express man. It was to arrive at Pittsfield on Monday & now it is Thursday eve.

I doubt whether you can find a clock for less than $2.00 in your good town. If that cabinet-maker intends to make a bedstead which cannot be taken down & put up with ease, on account of the sacking bottom which he is going to nail on, I think it will not be worth having — & I wish he would not do any thing about it. Will you tell him so? & for your manifold kind offices receive our cordial thanks. With my love to Mrs Melville   yrs truly

S. A. Hawthorne

P.S. 2^d The clock might come with the bedstead.

N H

ALS on a 24.7 × 19.1 cm part-sheet (torn along the top) of blue wove paper. Hawthorne inscribed the first page, in ink, Sophia Hawthorne added her postscript on the second and third pages, in ink, and Hawthorne added the second postscript on the third page, in ink.

LOCATION: NYPL-GL. *Provenance*: Lyrical Ballad Bookstore.

PUBLICATION: Centenary Edition of *The Works of Nathaniel Hawthorne*, vol. 16, *The Letters, 1843–1853*, ed. Thomas Woodson, L. Neal Smith, and Norman Holmes Pearson (Columbus: Ohio State University Press, 1985), pp. 412–13.

TEXTUAL NOTES: railroad] rail-|road *with* road *rewritten* • reminiscenses] *altered from* remaniscences • our visit] our *written over* of • for your manifold] for *written over* buy

FROM MARIA GANSEVOORT MELVILLE
28 MARCH 1851 · NEW YORK

While visiting her son Allan, his family, and her daughter Catherine in New York, Maria Melville wrote this hasty letter to Herman, the only full letter now located that she wrote to him. Their direct correspondence was in any case apparently not frequent, as suggested by her request that he answer her "through Augusta, or Helen" and by her acerbic remark, "I should be pleased to hear you reply to me yourself." (She also wrote to him "through" his sisters, as indicated by her 10 February 1854 letter to Augusta with its "message to Herman" [see pp. 631–33 below].)

Whether Melville replied directly to his mother on this occasion or answered her through his sisters is not known; no letter by any of them has been located that issues instructions on the matters of asparagus roots, oak paper, sugar, brandy, and a new hired hand. Later correspondence among the Melville women does suggest, however, that oak paper (i.e., paper with a wood-grain design) was settled on for the back parlor and that asparagus was planted in the garden at Pittsfield. The various individuals mentioned in this letter—Martin Farquhar Tupper, T. D. Stewart, and the Duyckincks—were all well known to Melville, though in quite different respects. Tupper (1810–89) was an Englishman whose *Proverbial Philosophy*, published between 1838 and 1842, was a popular success. Melville's acquaintance N. P. Willis.published extracts from Tupper's writings in his *Home Journal* and sent Melville a letter of introduction to Tupper when Melville was in London in 1849 (*Journals*, p. 22). Although Melville noted Tupper's country address on the last page of one of his journal notebooks, there is no indication that he went there or met Tupper while in England. When Tupper arrived in New York on 14 March 1851, William Cullen Bryant, editor of the *New-York Evening Post*, published an announcement, reporting what was probably Tupper's remark that he had had a "passage as Horace wished for Virgil, when he called on the tutelary goddess of Cyprus and the twin stars, brothers of Helen, and the father of the winds, to send favorable breezes and restrain all others, until his friend should have landed on the shore of Attica." Bryant also printed three of Tupper's poems, two written on the voyage over and one written on his arrival, dated 14 March. None, however, included the lines about the "dust of England upon his Boots and the dews of America upon his shoulders" that Maria Melville mentions in this letter.

Evert Duyckinck and his wife were old acquaintances of Melville's. One topic of conversation at Maria Melville's tea with them may have been her son's adamant—and to her mind, obstinate—refusal to have a daguerreotype made for Duyckinck's *Dollar Magazine*. Earlier in her visit to New York, Maria Melville had discussed this matter with them, as her 12 March 1851 letter to her daughter Augusta recounts (see the HISTORICAL NOTE, p. 785, and Melville's 12 February 1851 letter of refusal).

T. D. Stewart was known to the Melvilles from their time in Lansingburgh; the infant Maria Melville discusses was his son (for more on Stewart and the loan he later made to Melville, see the entry for Melville's unlocated March 1851 letter to him, p. 182 above, and the headnote to Melville's 12 May 1856 letter to Lemuel Shaw). The event to which Stewart took Catherine Melville was the second series of Sattler's Cosmoramas, a collection of twenty-six views of Europe, Asia, and the Middle East by the Viennese landscape artist Hubert Sattler (1817–1904), at the corner of Broadway and Thirteenth Street (see the *New-York Tribune*, 17 March 1851).

Maria Melville's parting instruction—"tell Aunt Mary she must not go away before I come back"—refers to Mary Hobart Melvill (1796–1884), the second wife of Melville's uncle Thomas Melvill, Jr., who had come to Pittsfield during the War of 1812 with his first wife, Françoise Lamé-Fleury Melvill (1781–1814). He married Mary Hobart in 1815 and bought the estate on Lenox Road (later owned by the Morewoods) in 1816, where they lived until 1837 when he decided to resettle in Galena, Illinois (members of his family remained in Pittsfield, however, into 1851). For Melville's summer spent with this branch of the Melvill family, see the headnote to his 30 December 1837 letter to Peter Gansevoort.

New York March 28th
past ten P.M. 1851.

My dear Herman,

Rocborn advertises asparagus roots remarkably fine put up in 100, roots in bundles at 75. each. I would advise you to authorise me to purchase five bundles at least, it would be a good investment. give you a healthy vegetable for the table, & as the roots extend year after year, the beds will increase in number, and in a few years we will have a superabundance it is our earliest vegetable & one of the best & healthyest.

The cost would be $3.75. Had I not better get the seeds for our garden here say $5 for asparagus, seeds, & a few good cuttings &c — . I should like to know as nearly as possible how many peices of *Oak paper* will be wanted, I can find none under 3/ a peice. & how many peices will be required for the parlour. I think six peices for each. The peices of paper contain nine yards, so that you can calculate carefully allowing for matching. Also covering for the Sofa's & chairs which are badly soiled by misuse.

You also spoke of white & brown sugar, & a demijohn of brandy —

Now whatever is wanted, had I not better bring up with me, when I return.

Kate, Allan, & I, took tea at the Duyckincks last wednesday Evg.

I heard that Martin Farquar Tupper went almost direct after landing to the Editor of the Evg Post and repeated four lines of poetry I cannot remember the lines, but that he had arrive'd on our shore with the dust of England upon his Boots and the dews of America upon his shoulders

I asked why he went there so promptly I was answer'd because he wished to be reported. He also address'd a missionary meeting at St Bartholomews church last sunday evg — in Poetry.

I can get nice Parlour paper for 2/. but Oak paper the cheepest is 3/. will you please to answer me through Augusta, or Helen promptly what I am to get. I should be pleased to hear you reply to me yourself.

Now is it about a man, you cannot do without & this is the place to procure one, Marys brother is expected daily. if his appearance, that is of capability is favorable would it not be best to engage him. Marys sister told me he intended to go out to see her when he came, will you wait till he comes or shall I see a few so as to have a selection — There are so many emigrants in the City that you can get a man to answer our purpose at low wages — & he would at the same time do better than to stay here at high wages & uncertain work — Allan has promised to enquire what wages are given to ordinary men, by the year or month.

I shall remain here until I hear from you on the above subjects. when I shall appoint & write you the day of our leaving here. This morning is bright suny & beautiful, the walking fine. Kate & I are going to Brooklyn for the last visit. Mr Stewart was here a few Evn'^g since took Kate to the Cosmorama on his return gave us four tickets saying we must go & see it all of us — He said he had a letter from you last week, & he hope'd to call in upon you soon, that he was soon going to Lansingburgh.

When I call'd to see the infant "John Dickinson Stewart" he had gone out but I saw his mother & expect a call from the young Gen^t soon. his papa promised to send him up some pleasant day.

My love to Lizzie, Helen, Augusta, Fanny & a sweet affectionate kiss to dear Malcolm whom I hope soon to see.

My love to all at the farm. tell Aunt Mary she must not go away before I come back —

Affectionately your

devoted friend

&

Mother

Maria G Melville

Allan is waiting to hear from you your letter reach'd him yesterday but he wants the paper —

ALS on a 33.5 × 21.8 cm sheet, folded in half, of white wove paper, embossed with the manufacturer's oval stamp enclosing the name "BATH" (upside down on both leaves). Maria Melville inscribed all four pages, in ink.

LOCATION: NYPL-GL. *Provenance*: Lyrical Ballad Bookstore.

TEXTUAL NOTES: Rocborn] *conjectural reading* · in bundles] in *added* · and in a] a *written over wiped* few · & one of the] of the *written over* occur · be $3.75] be *inserted above* · Duyckincks] *miswritten* Dyyckincks *with second* y *wiped and rewritten* · shoulders] hou *rewritten* · nice] *inserted above caret* · Now is it] Now *possibly* How · do without] *before canceled* one · City that you] you *written over rubbed out* that · do better than] *inserted above caret* · Affectionately your] your *altered from* yours · &] *before canceled* affectionate

FROM HARPER & BROTHERS
30 APRIL 1851 · NEW YORK

Immediately after receiving this letter from the Harpers turning down the request for an advance he had made on 25 April (now unlocated), Melville borrowed $2,050 on 1 May 1851 from T. D. Stewart. Maria Melville's 28 March 1851 letter to her son (just above) indicates that Melville had recently corresponded with Stewart (see the entry for Melville's unlocated March 1851 letter to Stewart, p. 182 above) and that Stewart had "hope'd" to call on Melville at Pittsfield "soon." The fact that Melville was able to procure a loan from Stewart the day after the Harpers wrote suggests that Stewart was in fact in Pittsfield when Melville received this refusal from the Harpers. For more on Melville's financial situation, see the headnote to his 12 May 1856 letter to Lemuel Shaw.

New York, April 30, 1851.

H. Melville, Esq., ⎫
Pittsfield, 　　　⎬
Mass. 　　　　　⎭
Dear Sir,

Your favor of the 25th inst., addressed to our Mr F. Harper, was duly received.

The requirements of our business have compelled us to make an extensive and expensive addition to our establishment: one which will demand all our resources. We feel unable, therefore, to make the advance desired, especially as, on making up your account, a copy of which we send you, we find there is a balance due us of nearly seven hundred dollars.

Regretting that circumstances forbid our compliance with your request, we are

Yours truly,
Harper & Brothers

ALS on a 39.2 × 24.8 cm sheet, folded in half, of blue wove paper with lines. Only the first page was inscribed, in ink. Allan Melville noted on the fourth page, "Harper & Brothers | April 30th 1851. | *Letter*"; three sets of penciled calculations are also on that page.

LOCATION: HCL-M.

PUBLICATION: (partial) *Log*, I, 410.

FROM AUGUSTA MELVILLE
17 JUNE 1851 · PITTSFIELD

Unlocated. A one-page letter "To Herman" in New York is listed in Augusta Melville's record of correspondence (NYPL-GL). For Melville's description of his stay at this time in New York, where he had gone to work on his "Whale" (later titled *Moby-Dick*), see his 29 June 1851 letter to Hawthorne.

FROM RICHARD BENTLEY
3 JULY 1851 · LONDON

Only the letterbook copy is known to survive of this reply from Richard Bentley to Melville's now unlocated letter written in the late spring or early summer of 1851 (see p. 197 above). In his letter Melville had offered Bentley his whaling book for the second time. The actual reply that Melville received probably included some

personal remarks and pleasantries from Bentley that were not recorded in the letterbook (see, for example, Bentley's 25 September 1851 letter, below). For Melville's acceptance of the terms outlined in this letter, see his 20 July 1851 reply.

Herman Melville Esq
    New York

                                                    New Burlington St
                                                    July 3. 1851
My dear Sir
    — I am ready to give you £150 on account of half profits for
your new work in my notes at three & six months; and think that, as
we shall be in the same boat, this mode of publication is the most
suitable to meet all the contingencies of the case.
                                                    Yours sincerely
                                                    Signed   R. B.

Original document not located. Text from Bentley's 1849–54 letterbook (presumably inscribed by a clerk), p. 261. A notation in ink identifying the book referred to in this letter "(x
The Whale)" was added in the same clerk's hand opposite the signature, with a corresponding
"x" placed after "Sir" in the salutation.

LOCATION (of letterbook): British Library.

PUBLICATION: Bernard R. Jerman, " 'With Real Admiration': More Correspondence between
Melville and Bentley," *American Literature* 25 (November 1953), 310.

FROM NATHANIEL HAWTHORNE
ON OR BEFORE 21 JULY 1851 · LENOX

Unlocated. Melville's 22 July 1851 letter to Hawthorne cites an "easy-flowing long
letter" from his friend that arrived from nearby Lenox "yesterday"—21 July—possibly the date Hawthorne wrote it.

FROM SAMUEL H. SAVAGE
BEFORE 24 AUGUST 1851 · [RED HOOK?]

Unlocated. A letter from Samuel Savage, probably visiting his stepmother in Red
Hook, New York, is cited in Melville's 24 August 1851 reply.

FROM EVERT A. DUYCKINCK
BEFORE 29 AUGUST 1851 · NEW YORK

Unlocated. A letter from Duyckinck, accompanied by a present of a thermometer in gratitude for his stay at Arrowhead earlier in the month, is cited in Melville's 29 August 1851 reply.

FROM RICHARD BENTLEY
25 SEPTEMBER 1851 · LONDON

Melville's letter of 5 September 1851, which this letter acknowledges, is now unlocated, but it probably announced that the American proof sheets of *The Whale*—the "packet," which this letter also acknowledges—were soon to be sent to Bentley via the American legation in London. See the entry for Melville's unlocated letter for more about these arrangements. And for more on Melville's visits with Bentley in London, see *Journals*, pp. 16, 43–44, and *passim*.

New Burlington Street
Sept 25 1851

My dear Sir

   Your letter of the 5th inst. safely reached me on the 22nd & your packet yesterday from the Secretary of Legation. Your notes in payment of the "Whale" drawn on me will be of course just the same to me, and are no doubt more available to you for discounting them

   It will give me great pleasure to place to your order Six copies of the Whale as well as the other books. A certain number of copies are always presented to the Author by his publisher

   I shall take care to make your recollection of my friends known to them. From my own family I am charged with kind regards to you, and a hope that you may be induced to pay us another and more prolonged visit

Yours very faithfully
Richard Bentley

Herman Melville Esq

ALS on a 22.7 × 18.2 cm sheet, folded in half, of white laid paper, watermarked with a crown and embossed with the manufacturer's circular stamp enclosing a lion and the words "FIDE ET FIDUCIA" against a blue background. Bentley inscribed the first three pages, in ink. Elizabeth Shaw Melville noted in ink on the fourth page "R. Bently | London Sept 25th 1851"; two sets of penciled calculations are also on the fourth page. Bentley's 1849-54 letterbook copy (pp. 299–300) of this letter (without the last paragraph), presumably inscribed by a clerk, is in the British Library; the letterbook indicates that it was addressed to "Herman Melville Esq | Pittsfield — Berkshire County | Massachusetts".

LOCATION: HCL-M.

PUBLICATION: (partial) *Log*, I, 428.

TEXTUAL NOTES: Street] *miswritten* Stree • you for] for *written over* in • induced to] to *altered from* a

FROM EVERT A. DUYCKINCK
BETWEEN 2 AND 7 NOVEMBER 1851 · NEW YORK

Unlocated. A letter from Duyckinck, enclosing an unidentified newspaper clipping that probably appeared on 2 November reporting the sinking of the *Ann Alexander* by a whale, is cited in Melville's 7 November 1851 reply.

FROM NATHANIEL HAWTHORNE
ON OR BEFORE [16?] NOVEMBER 1851 · LENOX

Unlocated. Hawthorne's "plain, bluff letter" about *Moby-Dick* is cited in Melville's [17?] November 1851 rapturous reply, written after receiving Hawthorne's letter "last night." In it Hawthorne apparently offered to review the book, an offer Melville declined in his reply. Melville later mentioned this letter again in his 8 January 1852 letter to Hawthorne's wife, Sophia, in which he described it as intimating "the part-&-parcel allegoricalness of the whole" of *Moby-Dick*.

FROM RUFUS W. GRISWOLD
BEFORE 19 DECEMBER 1851 · NEW YORK

Unlocated. An invitation to attend a memorial for James Fenimore Cooper, originally planned for 24 December, is cited in Melville's 19 December 1851 reply declining it.

FROM AUGUSTA MELVILLE
28 DECEMBER 1851 · NEW YORK

Unlocated. A two-page letter "To Herman" at Arrowhead is listed in Augusta Melville's record of correspondence (NYPL-GL).

FROM ELIZABETH SHAW MELVILLE
BEFORE 29 DECEMBER 1851 · BOSTON

Unlocated. A letter from Melville's wife, who had gone to Boston with their two-month-old child, Stanwix, is cited in Maria Melville's 29–30 December 1851 letter to her daughter Augusta. In the section dated 30 December, Maria Melville wrote that "from a letter received by Herman last Evg," they learned that Elizabeth (Lizzie) Melville was suffering "a good deal of pain" and had "been compell'd to wean her infant, she suffered so much when nursing that Dr Heyward said the child must be weaned, Lizzie's right breast gather'd & broke five weeks since previous to which she dried the milk. When she went to Boston her left breast rather under the arm had a large lump, which kept increasing in size. This lump did not interfere at all with the milk vessels, so that the Doc^t desired her to continue nursing, but she suffered a great deal of pain when nursing him which kept increasing. Doc^t Heyward commenced poulticing this after Lizzie's arrival at Boston, but the pain when nursing increased to such a degree that it seems she has been urged by it to do that which from the begining I told her would have to be the final result but to which she was very averse, that was, to wean Stanwix" (NYPL-GL).

FROM SOPHIA PEABODY HAWTHORNE
29 DECEMBER 1851 · WEST NEWTON

Unlocated. A "highly flattering" letter from Sophia Hawthorne in West Newton, Massachusetts, commenting on *Moby-Dick*, is cited in Melville's 8 January 1852 reply.

1852

FROM EVERT A. DUYCKINCK
ON OR BEFORE [2?] JANUARY 1852 · NEW YORK

Unlocated. A letter from Duyckinck proposing an eleven o'clock meeting can be inferred from Melville's [2?] January 1852 letter expressing his regret at not being free to meet with his friend on the following day.

FROM JULIAN HAWTHORNE
BEFORE [9?] FEBRUARY 1852 · WEST NEWTON

Unlocated. A "printed note" from five-year-old Julian Hawthorne in West Newton, Massachusetts, is cited in Melville's [9?] February 1852 reply.

FROM RICHARD BENTLEY
3 MARCH 1852 · LONDON

Unlocated. According to Bentley's 4 March 1852 letter (just below), a half-finished version of that letter was mistakenly sent off to Melville the previous day. Bentley may have left the letter unfinished while waiting for the profit/loss memorandum dated 4 March 1852 (see Birss, "A Mere Sale to Effect," pp. 252-53), which provided him with the figures cited in the finished letter. No record of his earlier partial letter appears in the 1849–54 letterbook of the Bentley firm (British Library), which does contain the 4 March letter.

FROM RICHARD BENTLEY
4 MARCH 1852 · LONDON

Only the letterbook copy survives of this letter replying to Melville's now unlocated letter—written before 21 January 1852—offering *Pierre* to Bentley. For Melville's reply to this unencouraging response by Bentley to the prospect of another book by Melville, see his letter of 16 April 1852. And for the "half finished Epistle" mentioned at the opening of this letter, see the entry for that unlocated item, just above.

U.S.A.
Herman Melville Esqr
Pittsfield.

March 4. 1852.

My Dear Sir,

By a most ridiculous Blunder, my half finished Epistle was dispatched yesterday to you. However, this comes close on its heels to repair the folly.

Many thanks for the offer of your new Work. Of course if I could see my way, as the phrase is, in acquiring the copyright, I should be glad. Since the receipt of your Note I have had the accounts of all your Works published by me brought under my attention.

By Mardi, I have lost	£68.7.6
By Redburn Do	£76.7.6
By White Jacket	£173.9.6
By The Whale ——	£135.".''
	£453.4.6

This may be lessened in the end by £100: leaving me a loss of 350£! Your books, I fear, are produced in too rapid succession. It was not long ago since The Whale was published — not time sufficient has yet been given to it, before another is ready! Under the circumstances, I put the matter to you whether your new book should not be put into my hands to publish on our joint account; I yielding to you half the profits as they arise. For my sake I shall do the best for it — in fact, no publisher can do more for it than I can.

Thanks for your kind recollections to all around me, who respond to it in best regards to yourself.

Yours faithfully
(Signed) R. B.

Original document not located. Text from Bentley's 1849–54 letterbook (presumably inscribed by a clerk), pp. 389–90, emended by NN at two points (see below).

LOCATION (of letterbook): British Library.

PUBLICATION: Bernard R. Jerman, " 'With Real Admiration': More Correspondence between Melville and Bentley," *American Literature* 25 (November 1953), 311–12.

TEXTUAL NOTES: repair] NN; repain *with* p *written over* fr · offer] *originally* offers *then* s *canceled* · Jacket] NN; Jackets

FROM ALLAN MELVILLE
BEFORE 6 MARCH 1852 · NEW YORK

Unlocated. A letter from Melville's brother Allan is cited in their mother's 6 March 1852 letter to their sister Augusta, who had been visiting with friends in New York. In her letter, Maria Melville simply remarks that "Allan wrote to Herman" conveying the news that Augusta expected to leave New York the next day (NYPL-GL).

FROM RICHARD BENTLEY
5 MAY 1852 · LONDON

This reply to Melville's 16 April 1852 letter, which accompanied the American proof sheets of *Pierre*, repeats Bentley's earlier 4 March offer of half-profits without an advance for that book (see the headnote to Melville's 16 April letter for the final outcome of these negotiations). This letter is significant for Bentley's statement that "it would have been impossible for any publisher with any prudent regard to his own interests to have put out your books here without revisal, & occasional omission"—tantamount to an avowal that such "revisal" and "omission" were performed on *The Whale*, as the textual differences between that book and the American *Moby-Dick* reveal. For a further discussion of the changes made in it by Bentley's reader, see the NN *Moby-Dick*, pp. 680–83.

Bentley is not known to have written to Melville again. Richard B. Kimball, the lawyer and novelist (1816–92), mentioned Melville in a 1 February 1853 letter advising Bentley about which American authors would be interested in publishing pieces in *Bentley's Miscellany*, but it is not known whether Bentley actually invited Melville to contribute (as Leyda inferred in the *Log*, I, 465, 467).

May 5. 1852

Herman Melville Esq.

I have to acknowledge the receipt of your letter of the 16th Ult. together with the early sheets of "Pierre." Having now been long connected with you in literary ventures, I should naturally feel desirious of continuing that connection if it would be done with any adequate returns. I cannot consent to ignore all my experience of your previous works — in England they have all with the exception of Omoo & Typee proved failures. Will you allow in all frankness, and certainly not intended by me to be said in any other than the most friendly spirit, to say, that I conceive if you had revised your work "Mardi", to the latest, the "Whale", and restrained your imagination somewhat, and had written in a style to be understood by the great mass of readers — nay if you had not sometimes offended the feelings of many sensitive readers you would have succeeded in England. Everybody must admit the genius displayed in your writings; but it would have been impossible for any publisher with any prudent regard to his own interests to have put out your books here without revisal, & occasional omission. Therefore it is, that without being much altered your previous, the popularity which any subsequent work might have could have small influence on the earlier works.

If you will give me permission to make or have made by a judicious literary friend such alterations as are absolutely necessary to "Pierre" being properly appreciated here, I would undertake this; and I will add that I think that you would have no reason to regret this course. Perhaps somebody ignorant of the absolute failure of your former works might be tempted to make a trifling advance on the chance of success; but I learn this in consequence of the reception by the English public of your later works, any new book would have an uphill fight of it and would require a considerable outlay of advertisements to make it pay, much more to yield a profit. I have ventured to speak with great frankness, because I know you will appreciate it. Rely upon it, that if I could reconcile it with prudence, I should not hesitate a moment; but I cannot. I have only to repeat my offer, to publish the New Work if I may be allowed to make such alterations as are actually necessary, not to charge you commission but account for the books at the prices I obtain for them, and to yield you one half of all the net profits.

Beleive, to be my dear Sir with all truth, with real admiration of
your genius and entertaining a sincere value for your friendship

Your very faithful
(Signed) R. B.

Original document not located. Text from Bentley's 1849–54 letterbook (presumably inscribed by a clerk), pp. 404–6, emended by NN at two points (see below).

LOCATION (of letterbook): British Library.

PUBLICATION: Bernard R. Jerman, " 'With Real Admiration': More Correspondence between
Melville and Bentley," *American Literature* 25 (November 1953), 312–13.

TEXTUAL NOTES: sheets] NN; sheet • adequate] *after canceled* adeqa • offended] en *rewritten* • the feelings] NN; the the feelings • Therefore . . . works.] *incoherent sentence, possibly lacking a word or words* • know] *after canceled* have • that if] if *inserted above caret*

FROM NATHANIEL HAWTHORNE
BETWEEN 5 JUNE AND 17 JULY 1852 · CONCORD

Unlocated. In his 17 July 1852 letter to Hawthorne, Melville expressed regret to his
friend: "I am sorry, but I can not at present come to see you at Concord as you
propose"—implying that Hawthorne had earlier written to Melville inviting him to
visit the Hawthornes at their new home in Concord, Massachusetts, where they
had moved, after some delay, on 5 June.

FROM WILLIAM H. SWEETSER
BEFORE 1 JULY 1852 · CHARLESTOWN

Unlocated. A letter from Sweetser, a Charlestown, Massachusetts, autograph collector, is cited in Melville's 1 July 1852 reply.

FROM JOHN H. CLIFFORD
14 JULY 1852 · NEW BEDFORD

Unlocated. Only the enclosure, a clerk's transcription of the New Bedford lawyer
John H. Clifford's account written at the time of the James Robertson case, has
been located from the 14 July letter sent to Melville by Clifford. (The postscript is
presumably in Clifford's own hand.) The letter is cited (without identifying Clifford) in Melville's 13 August 1852 letter to Hawthorne, which enclosed both it and
the transcription: "You will perceive by the gentleman's note to me that he assumed that I purposed making literary use of the story." The brief canceled note,
evidently dictated by Clifford to his clerk, that appears just before the postscript, is
not the "gentleman's note" that Melville enclosed, since it does not mention the

possible literary use of the story, as Melville indicates Clifford's letter had done. It is included here in lieu of the unlocated one. Hawthorne later returned the transcription, as Elizabeth Melville later recorded (see the manuscript description of Melville's 13 August letter, and for more on Clifford and the "story of Agatha," which the Robertson case inspired, see the headnote to that letter).

[Enclosure:]

May 28ᵗʰ 1842 Saturday. I have just returned from a visit to Falmouth with a Mʳ Janney of Mᵒ on one of the most interesting and romantic cases I ever expect to be engaged in. — The gentleman from Missouri Mʳ Janney came to my house last Sunday Evening and related to myself and partner that he had married the daughter of a Mʳˢ Irvin formerly of Pittsburgh Pa. and that Mʳˢ Irvin had married a second husband by the name of Robertson. The latter deceased about two years since He was appointed Admʳ to his Estate which amounted to $20 000 — about 15 months afterwards Mʳˢ Robertson also died and in the meantime the Admʳ had been engaged in looking up heirs to the Estate — He learned that Robertson was an Englishman whose original name was Shinn — that he resided at Alexandria D.C. where he had two nephews — He also wrote to England and had ascertained the history and genealogy of the family with much accuracy, when on going to the Post Office one day he found a letter directed to James Robertson the deceased, post marked Falmouth Massᵗᵗˢ On opening it he found it from a person signing herself Rebecca A. Gifford and addressing him as "Father." The existence of this girl had been known before by Mʳˢ Robertson and her husband had pronounced her to be illegitimate The Admʳ then addressed a letter to Mʳˢ Gifford informing her of the decease of her father. He was surprized soon after by the appearance in Sᵗ Louis of a shrewd Quaker from Falmouth named Dillingham with full powers and fortified by letters and affidavits shewing the existence of a wife in Falmouth whom Robertson married in 1807 at Pembroke Mss & the legitimacy of the daughter who had married a Mʳ Gifford and laying strong claims to the entire property.

The Admʳ and heirs having strong doubts arising from the declarations of Robertson during his lifetime & the peculiar expressions contained in the letters exhibited, as to the validity of the marriage & the claim based upon it, determined to resist and legal proceedings were at once commenced. The object of the visit of Mr Janney was to attend the taking of depositions, upon a notice from the claimants — The Minister Town Clerk and Witnesses present at the ceremony established the fact of a legal marriage and the birth of a child in wedlock, beyond all cavil or controversy all of the witnesses were of the highest respectability and the widow and daughter interested me very much.

It appeared that Robertson was wrecked on the coast of Pembroke where this girl, then Miss Agatha Hatch was living — that he was hospitably entertained and cared for, and that within a year after, he married her, in due form of law — that he went two short voyages to sea. About two years after the marriage, leaving his wife *enciente* he started off in search of employment and from that time until *Seventeen* years afterwards she never heard from him in any way whatsoever, directly or indirectly, not even a word. Being poor she went out nursing for her daily bread and yet contrived out of her small earnings to give her daughter a first rate education. Having become connected with the Society of Friends she sent her to their most celebrated boarding school and when I saw her I found she had profited by all her advantages beyond most females. In the meantime Robertson had gone to Alexandria D.C. where he had entered into a successful and profitable business and married a second wife. At the expiration of this long period of 17 years which for the poor forsaken wife, had glided wearily away, while she was engaged away from home, her Father rode up in a gig and informed her that her husband had returned and wished to see her and her child — but if she would not see him, to see her child at all events — They all returned together and encountered him on the way coming to meet them about half a mile from her father's house. This meeting was described to me by the mother and daughter — Every incident seemed branded upon the memories of both. He excused himself as well as he could for his long absence and silence, appeared very affectionate refused to tell where he was living and persuaded them not to make any inquiries, gave them a handsome sum of money, promised to return for good and left the next day — He appeared again in about a year, just on the eve of his daughter's marriage & gave her a bridal present. It was not long after this that his wife in Alexandria died — He then wrote to his son-in-law to come there — He did so — remained 2 days and brought back a gold watch and three handsome shawls which had been previously worn by some person — They all admitted that they had suspicions then & from this circumstance that he had been a second time married.

Soon after this he visited Falmouth again & as it proved for the last time — He announced his intention of removing to Missouri & urged the whole family to go with him, promising money land and other assistance to his son-in-law. The offer was not accepted He shed tears when he bade them farewell — From the time of his return to Missouri till the time of his death a constant correspondence was kept up money was remitted by him annually and he announced to them his marriage with Mrs Irvin — He had no children by either of his last two wives.

Mr Janney was entirely disappointed in the character of the evidence and the character of the claimants. He considered them, when he first came, as parties to the imposition practised upon Mrs Irvin & her children. But I was satisfied and I think he was, that their motives in keeping silence were high and pure, creditable in every way to the true Mrs Robertson.

She stated the causes with a simplicity & pathos which carried that conviction irresistibly to my mind. The only good(?) it could have done to expose him would have been to drive Robertson away and forever disgrace him & it would certainly have made Mrs Irvin & her children wretched for the rest of their days — "I had no wish" said the wife "to make either of them unhappy, notwithstanding all I had suffered on his account" — It was to me a most striking instance of long continued & uncomplaining submission to wrong and anguish on the part of a wife, wch made her in my eyes a heroine.

Janney informed me that R. and his last wife did not live very happily together and particularly that he seemed to be a very jealous suspicious man — That when a person called at his house he would never enter the room till he knew who it was & "all about him. He must have recieved a portion of his punishment in this life. The fact came out in the course of examination that they had agreed to give Dillingham one half of what he might obtain deducting the expenses from his half — After the strength of the evidence became known Mr Janney commenced the making of serious efforts to effect a compromise of the claim What the result will be time will shew — This is, I suspect, the end of my connexion with the case —

New Bedford July 14th 1852

Herman Melville
Dr Sir
   Above I send you the little story I promised you —
                                        Respectfully Yours.

P.S. The business was settled in a few weeks afterwards, in a most amicable & honorable manner, by a division of the property. I think Mrs. Robinson & her family refused to claim or recieve anything that really belonged to Mrs. Irwin, or which Robinson had derived through her. —

Manuscript enclosure on two sheets of blue wove paper. The first sheet, 39.6 × 24.9 cm, was folded in half to make four pages; the second sheet, 19.8 × 24.9 cm, not so folded, made two more pages. Clifford's clerk inscribed the story on the first five pages (with one line on the sixth), in ink, and the unsigned canceled note to Melville, in ink, on the sixth page. Another hand, presumably Clifford's own, added the postscript, in ink, on the last page. The first five pages are numbered (1–5) in pencil at the top.

LOCATION (of enclosure): HCL-M.

PUBLICATION: Samuel Eliot Morison, "Melville's 'Agatha' Letter to Hawthorne," *New England Quarterly* 2 (April 1929), 296–307. Davis-Gilman 101 (enclosure).

TEXTUAL NOTES: of Robertson] *after canceled* of · notice from] from *altered from original* of · witnesses] *before canceled* estab · forsaken wife] wife *above canceled* widow · their days] their *altered from* her · notwithstanding] not-|withstanding · "all about him.] *closing double quotation mark lacking* · New Bedford . . . Yours.] *canceled in same ink*

FROM G. P. R. JAMES
28 JULY 1852 · STOCKBRIDGE

George Payne Rainsford James (1799–1860), the English author, was best known for his historical romances such as *Richelieu* (1829) and *Philip Augustus* (1831). (Sealts reports that Augusta Melville owned a copy of the 1845 Tauchnitz edition of James's *The Smuggler* [294].) James had brought his family from England to New York, where they arrived on 4 July 1850; they then moved to Stockbridge in the Berkshires in 1851, where they stayed until later in 1852. In a 5 November 1851 letter to her daughter Augusta, Maria Melville described a tea at the home of the Sedgwick family in Stockbridge where she and her family, especially Herman, were invited specifically to meet the Jameses. Herman, Maria Melville remarked, had "seem'd pleased" at the prospect. Upon arriving, however, they found only Mrs. James, who explained that her husband " 'commenced a new book to day,' & could not break out on any account" (NYPL-GL). This letter, written nearly six months after that first attempt, indicates that James and Melville had still not met. Although there is no record of their ever meeting, Melville's abortive efforts and James's clear expression here of his desire to do so suggest that they probably eventually did. For more on James, see Stewart Marsh Ellis, *The Solitary Horseman; or, The Life and Adventures of G. P. R. James* (Kensington: The Cayme Press, 1927).

Stockbridge Mass
28 July 1852

My Dear Mr Melville

Few things could have vexed me more than to find, on my return from a little open air dinner at my farm, that you had been at my house and gone away again. Why did not my people send you over? it is but a mile across. I will come to see you as soon as I can; but pray do not let me pass you if we ever meet on the road. I should not know you of course by sight; nor you me. But I will tell you how you can recognize me: by a great rough pair of nearly white mustachoes very like those of a wiry haired terrier dog. There is not such a pair in the county as those of

Yours ever
G. P. R James

ALS on a 39.8 × 24.9 cm sheet, folded in half, of white laid paper, watermarked with the name "MOINIER'S 1851". James inscribed the first page, in ink, and addressed the envelope "Paid | Box 22 | Herman Melville Esq | Near Pittsfield | Mass | G. P. R J"; it was postmarked on 28 July in Stockbridge.

LOCATION: HCL-M.

PUBLICATION: *Log*, I, 455.

FROM G. P. PUTNAM & CO.
1 OCTOBER 1852 · NEW YORK

On 1 October 1852, G. P. Putnam & Co. sent this form letter to more than seventy established American authors, describing their proposed magazine, mentioning their "eminent" advisers, including Irving, Bryant, and the distinguished Episcopal clergyman and historian Francis Lister Hawks (1798–1866), and soliciting articles and stories (see George H. Putnam, *A Memoir of George Palmer Putnam* [cited under publication, below], pp. 286–87; and Parke Godwin, *George William Curtis: A Commemorative Address* [New York: Harper, 1893], pp. 16–17). It is apparent that Melville received the form letter and sent a reply (now unlocated), since Parke Godwin, associated with Curtis and Charles Briggs in the editorship of the magazine at its inception, listed Melville as "among our promised contributors" (p. 17); Melville did, of course, contribute many articles, the first published of which was "Bartleby" in November and December 1853. Although no copy of this letter is now among Melville's papers (HCL-M), there are two in the Duyckinck papers (NYPL-D).

(*Private*)

10 Park Place. New York
October 1st 1852.

Sir

We take the liberty of informing you of our intention to publish an original periodical of a character different from any now in existence, and, as it is our wish to have the best talent of the country to aid us in the undertaking, to solicit your assistance as a contributor.

We propose to publish *monthly* a work which shall combine the popular character of a Magazine, with the higher & graver aims of a Quarterly Review, but to preserve in all its departments an independent & elevated tone; and to make it as essentially an organ of American thought as possible.

The want of such a publication, we believe, has long been felt in this Country, and it is only after mature consideration, and on the advice of some of the most eminent literary & scientific men of the Union who have offered us their aid that we have determined on the attempt to supply this want. We believe that the facilities connected with an established publishing business will enable us to place the work at once on a high footing, and beyond ordinary contingencies.

The work will be wholly original, and, as we are well aware that gratuitous contributions ought not to be relied on, even though they could be, we expect to pay as liberally as the nature of the work will allow for all articles that we may accept.

The first number of the work will be issued on the first of next January; it will contain about 144 pages, occasionally illustrated, printed in the best manner, and sold at $3. a year.

As it is desirable that we should know the extent of our literary resources, we shall be greatly obliged by as early an answer as may suit your convenience, whether or not you will be able to furnish us an occasional article, and if you will be willing that your name should be announced as a probable contributor. Business considerations making it important that no publicity should be given to our design before all our arrangements have been completed, you will oblige us by regarding this as a confidential communication until we make our public announcement.

We are Sir

Yours very resp^y

G. P. Putnam & Co

We are authorized to say that we shall have the special & active co-operation & advice of Washington Irving, Mr Bryant, Rev Dr Hawks and other eminent men.

Melville's copy not located. Text from one manuscript copy of the letter, presumably inscribed by a clerk. The other manuscript copy varies at one point (listed below).

LOCATION (of copies): NYPL-D.

PUBLICATION: (from G. P. Putnam's draft, with slight variations) George H. Putnam, *A Memoir of George Palmer Putnam* (New York and London: Putnam [privately printed], 1903), I, 286–87.

TEXTUAL NOTES: The want] *after large space, indicating new paragraph* • G. . . . Co] *underlined with a flourish* • We . . . men.] *added in left margin after three x marks; placed here editorially* • special &] *other copy reads* special and

FROM J. W. FRANCIS
3 NOVEMBER 1852 · NEW YORK

Dr. John Wakefield Francis (1789–1861), the eminent obstetrician and public figure who helped found the New York Academy of Medicine in 1846, was a friend of Dr. Augustus K. Gardner and the Duyckincks and was among the guests at Allan Melville's wedding in 1847 (this letter is addressed to Melville at Allan's home). Thus he would have known Melville through a number of different connections. In a 16 January 1852 address before the Typographical Society of New York, Francis had extended praise to a number of writers including "Melville, for *Typee*" ("Reminiscences of Printers, Authors, and Booksellers," printed in the New York *International Magazine* 5 [February 1852], 265; see *Log*, I, 445).

Francis had a broad range of interests outside of medicine, including history and typography. The book Melville had given him was an edition of Alexis Marie de Rochon's *Voyage to Madagascar and the East Indies* published in French in 1791. The first English translation appeared a year later (London: Robinson, 1792) and a second the following year (London: Jeffrey, 1793). Melville may have given Francis either of these two early translations, or he may have given him, as Sealts speculates, *An Abridgement of a Voyage to Madagascar* (London: Westley, 1821; Sealts 428.1). What apparently interested Francis in this book were the two accounts included in it of the "Quimos" (or "Kimos")—said to be a fair-skinned pygmy population living in the interior of Madagascar (pp. 163–82 in the 1792 edition; see also pp. 129–44 in the 1793 edition and pp. 44–53 in the 1821 abridgement, both of which, however, give the spelling "Quimosses" [or "Kimosses"]; all three editions consistently prefer the alternative spellings beginning with "K"). Neither this book nor any books or letters by Melville were included in the three auctions of Francis's books and papers held after his death (Bangs, Merwin, & Co., 9 June 1862; Anderson Auction, 19 October 1908; Scott & O'Shaughnessy, 21 November 1917). A number of the books and letters of other American writers, such as Hawthorne, were, however, included.

N.Y. Nov. 3^d 1852

Dear Sir,

I thank you most fully, for the curious volume Rochon's Voyage to Madagascar. Casually for forty years past I have looked out for something touching those *Quimos*. Perhaps I shall be able to make something of an account of that curious race by it with what I allready possess. Had I seen the whole world as you have, and possessed your graphic powers I hardly think I could fail of my design. Again I renew my thanks for the useful volume and am

Dear sir
yours sincerely
J. W. Francis

H. Melville Esq.

ALS on a 20.2 × 16 cm part-sheet (torn along the top and the edge of the second leaf), folded in half, of white wove paper. Francis inscribed the first and second pages, in ink, and addressed the unstamped envelope "Herman Melville Esq | 24th St. | N York", underlined with a flourish.

LOCATION: NYPL-GL. *Provenance:* Lyrical Ballad Bookstore.

TEXTUAL NOTES: allready] all-|ready • J. W. Francis] *underlined with a flourish*

FROM NATHANIEL HAWTHORNE
AFTER [5?] DECEMBER 1852 · CONCORD

Unlocated. In his letter written sometime between 3 and 13 December 1852, after having seen Hawthorne in Concord, Massachusetts, on 2 December, Melville requested Hawthorne to "enclose the whole affair" of the "story of Agatha" to him along with any suggestions Hawthorne might have for the development of the story. Hawthorne returned to Melville both Melville's long 13 August memorandum and the account that was enclosed with it of the legal case on which the story was based (see pp. 231–38 and 621–25 above), and they are now among the papers given to Harvard by Melville's granddaughter. Whether Hawthorne's presumable cover letter included his thoughts about the story is not known. Melville had instructed him to note any such "random" thoughts "on the same page with my memorandum"; however, that memorandum contains no notes by Hawthorne.

1853

FROM THE PITTSFIELD FOURTH OF JULY COMMITTEE
23 MAY 1853 · PITTSFIELD

Unlocated. A letter inviting Melville to deliver the Pittsfield Fourth of July oration is cited in Melville's 23 May 1853 reply.

FROM AUGUSTA MELVILLE
10 JUNE 1853 · PITTSFIELD

Unlocated. A one-page letter "To Herman" in New York is listed in Augusta Melville's record of correspondence (NYPL-GL). This is probably the same letter that is cited in Sophia Melville's [20?] June 1853 letter to Augusta. Asking why she had not received further instructions to purchase items for Catherine Melville's forthcoming wedding to John Hoadley, Sophia wrote, "Why did you not send another list in Herman's letter" (NYPL-GL).

FROM JULIUS ROCKWELL
BEFORE 2 JULY 1853 · PITTSFIELD

Unlocated. A letter, probably an acknowledgment of Melville's 23 May 1853 letter declining an invitation to deliver the oration at the Pittsfield Fourth of July celebration (see the entry for that 23 May invitation, above), is cited in Melville's 2 July 1853 reply. In his letter Rockwell apparently extended an invitation for Melville to attend the celebration in any case, since Melville's reply thanks Rockwell for his invitation.

FROM HARPER & BROTHERS
6 DECEMBER 1853 · NEW YORK

Unlocated. A letter from the Harpers enclosing a three-hundred-dollar advance in response to Melville's 24 November request is cited in Melville's 6 December 1853 acknowledgment.

FROM [EDWARD LIVINGSTON WELLS?]
BEFORE 14 DECEMBER 1853 · PLACE UNKNOWN

Unlocated. A letter from an autograph collector can be inferred from Melville's 14 December 1853 letter (for his identity see the headnote to that reply).

1854

FROM MARIA GANSEVOORT MELVILLE
10 FEBRUARY 1854 · LONGWOOD

In closing her 10 February 1854 letter to her daughter Augusta at Pittsfield, Maria Melville, who was visiting with her daughter Helen in Longwood, Massachusetts, appended this "message to Herman." Although she begins by addressing him through Augusta, she concludes by writing directly to "my dear darling Herman." Her theme—evidently an old one—was the desirability of his going on the lecture circuit. She had clearly been looking into the matter in nearby Lawrence, where Melville ultimately did lecture in 1857. To convince her recalcitrant son, she triumphantly lists the eminent men who had been willing to lecture there for a mere twenty-five dollars: John Godfrey Saxe (1816–87), the lawyer and journalist best known as a writer of humorous verse; Robert Winthrop (1809–94), descendant of the Massachusetts Bay Winthrops and a politician who had served both in the House of Representatives (1840–50) and in the Senate (1850–51); Dr. Oliver Wendell Holmes (1809–94), Melville's literary neighbor in Pittsfield; Josiah Quincy (1772–1864), the statesman and former president of Harvard (1829–45); and Henry Giles (1809–82), the Unitarian clergyman and abolitionist.

Now, with love to Lizzie & yourself kisses innumerable to the three darlings, & this message to Herman —

That *one Lecture* prepared by himself can be repeated seventy times with success. That Mr Saxe has done so that all the lecturers *now* prepare one lecture & travel the rounds with this one for the whole season, are feasted made much of, & seldom less than fifty dollars are given to the lecturer. Many places double that, at Lawrence $25. are given Robert Winthrop, Oliver W Holmes, Mr Giles are not too big to receive even this comparatively small sum. Josiah Quincy lectured last week, & Mr Giles this week at Lawrence. This is the present style of enlightening the many who have no time to devote to reading & research —

& now my dear darling Herman all your friends, relatives & admirers, say that you are the very man to carry an audience, to create a sensation. to do wonders. to close this subject I will only request

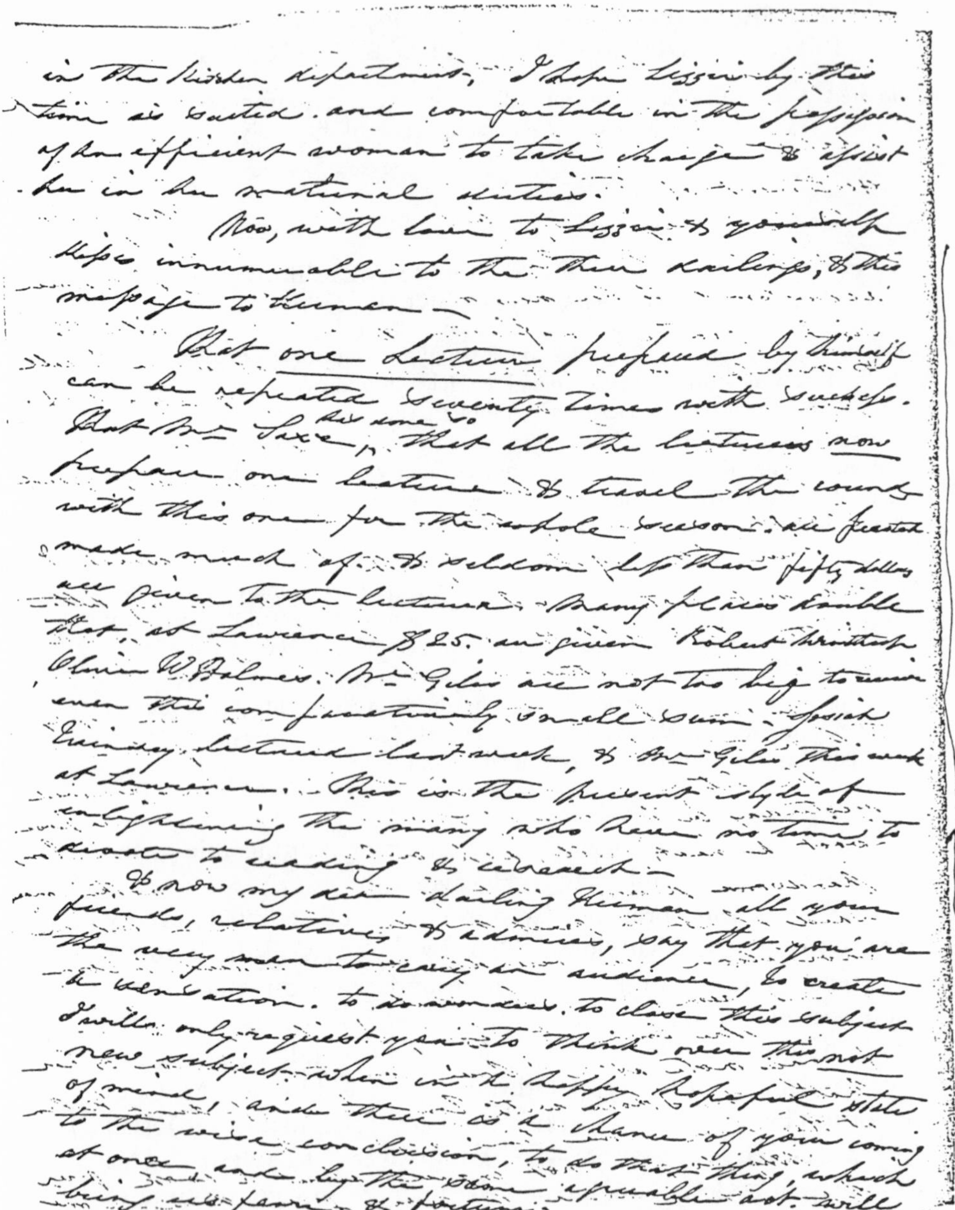

in the kitchen department, I hope Lizzie by this time is suited and comfortable in the possession of an efficient woman to take charge & assist her in her maternal duties.

Now, with love to Lizzie & yourself kisses innumerable to the three darlings, & this message to Herman —

That one Lecture prepared by himself can be repeated seventy times with success. That Mr Saxe has done so, that all the lecturers now prepare one lecture & travel the country with this one for the whole season. are feasted made much of. & seldom less than fifty dollars are given to the lecturer. Many places double that, at Lawrence $25. are given Robert Winthrop, Oliver W. Holmes. Mr Giles are not too big to receive even this comparatively small sum. Josiah Quincy lectured last week, & Mr Giles this week at Lawrence. This is the present style of enlightening the many who have no time to devote to reading & research —

& now my dear darling Herman all your friends, relatives & admirers, say that you are the very man to carry an audience, to create a sensation. to do wonders. to close this subject I will only request you to think over this new subject when in the happy hopeful state of mind, and there is a chance of your coming to the wise conclusion, to do that thing, which at once and by the same agreeable act. will bring all fame & fortune.

From Maria Gansevoort Melville, 10 February 1854 (reduced). Courtesy of the Rare Books and Manuscripts Division, The New York Public Library, Astor, Lenox and Tilden Foundations (Gansevoort-Lansing Collection).

you to think over this *not* new subject when in a happy hopeful state of mind, and there is a chance of your coming to the wise conclusion, to do that thing, which at once, and by the same agreeable act, will bring us fame & fortune.

ALS, "your loving Mother," on a 39.6 × 24.9 cm sheet, folded in half, of white wove paper, faintly embossed with the manufacturer's stamp. Maria Melville inscribed all four pages, in ink, with her "message to Herman" on the fourth page and the closing and signature of the letter at the top of the first page.

LOCATION: NYPL-GL. *Provenance:* Lyrical Ballad Bookstore.

PUBLICATION: Hershel Parker, in the Historical Supplement to the NN *Clarel*, pp. 644–45.

TEXTUAL NOTE: has done so] *inserted above caret*

FROM THOMAS MELVILLE
14 FEBRUARY 1854 · LONGWOOD

Unlocated. A letter to his brother is cited in Thomas Melville's 15 February 1854 letter written from Longwood, Massachusetts, to their sister Augusta in Pittsfield. In it he reports: "Yesterday I wrote Herman, Allan, and Sophia telling them of the change in my plans" (NYPL-GL). See also the entry, p. 256 above, for Melville's unlocated reply to this letter.

FROM CATHERINE MELVILLE HOADLEY
BEFORE 30 MARCH 1854 · LONGWOOD

Unlocated. On 30 March 1854 Augusta Melville wrote a letter to her sister Frances Priscilla, who (along with their mother) had been staying in the Boston area with their married sisters Catherine Hoadley and Helen Griggs. In her letter, Augusta mentioned invitations—one of which was probably from Catherine—for Melville to come for a visit. It probably was addressed directly to Melville, although it may have been sent indirectly through other family letters, the way his reply was included in Augusta's 30 March letter: "Herman desires many acknowledgments for the kind invitations received, but thinks his visit East cannot take place until June, as he must needs return home from New York" (NYPL-GL). For Melville's trip to New York, see the entries, p. 259 above, for his unlocated March 1854 letters to his brother Allan and sister-in-law Sophia.

FROM HELEN MELVILLE GRIGGS
BEFORE 30 MARCH 1854 · LAWRENCE

Unlocated. Probably a second of the invitations Melville received from Boston (see the entry just above) was from his sister Helen in nearby Lawrence.

FROM HELEN MELVILLE GRIGGS
AFTER 11 APRIL 1854 · LONGWOOD

Unlocated. In a letter dated 11 April 1854 to her sister Augusta outlining the plans
of their mother and youngest sister Frances Priscilla to return to Pittsfield from
Boston (see the entries just above), Helen wrote: "I propose writing a letter to
Herman, to know 'whether upon the whole I had better stay with George, or go
back to Arrowhead. I feel so lonesome' " (NYPL-GL). Whether Helen actually
went to Arrowhead is uncertain; her 29 May 1854 letter to her brother, below,
mentions only the proposed family gathering for August and gives no indication
that she had recently been to Arrowhead.

FROM CHARLES SCRIBNER
MAY 1854 · NEW YORK

Charles Scribner, the publisher of Evert and George Duyckinck's *Cyclopædia of
American Literature* (1855), sent a form letter to the authors who were to be featured
in that work. Although the printed letter contained no date, a printed copy in the
Duyckinck papers is dated "May, 1854" in Evert Duyckinck's hand. Melville's
copy is unlocated, but he most likely received one of these letters since he was one
of the authors included in the encyclopedia. See Sealts, *Early Lives*, pp. 191–93, for
a reproduction of a manuscript (NYPL-D), written partially in Allan Melville's
hand and partially in another unidentified hand, which may have been drawn up in
response to the queries in this form letter.

145 Nassau Street, New York.
As it is my intention to publish the coming season a work, entitled *AN ENCYCLOPÆDIA OF AMERICAN LITERATURE*,
*embracing Personal and Critical Notices of Authors, with passages from
their Writings, from the earliest period to the present day, with Portraits,
Autographs, and other illustrations*, I have adopted the method of addressing to you a Circular letter, as the best means of rendering the
book as complete in regard to points in which you may be interested, as possible, and as faithful as may be to the memories and claims
of the families and personages whose literary interests will be represented in it. The plan of the work is to furnish to the public, at one
view, notices of the Lives and Writings of all American authors of
importance. As it is quite probable you may have in your possession
material or information which you would like the opportunity of
seeing noticed in such a publication, you will serve the objects of the
work by a reply to this circular, in such answers to the following
suggestions as may appear desirable or convenient to you.

1. Dates of birth, parentage, education, residence, with such biographical information and anecdote, as you may think proper to be employed in such a publication.

2. Names and dates of Books published, references to articles in Reviews, Magazines, &c., of which you may be the author.

3. Family notices and sources of information touching American authors no longer living, of whom you may be the representative.

Dates, facts, and precise information, in reference to points which have not been noticed in collections of this kind, or which may have been misstated, are desirable. Your own judgment will be the best guide as to the material of this nature which should be employed in a work which it is intended shall be of general interest and of a NATIONAL character. It will represent the whole country, its only aim being to exhibit to the readers a full, fair, and entertaining account of the literary products thus far of AMERICA.

It is trusted that the plan of the work will engage your sympathy and concurrence, and that you will find in it a sufficient motive for a reply to this Circular. The materials which you may communicate will be employed, so far as is consistent with the limits and necessary literary unity of the work, for the preparation of which I have engaged EVERT A. and GEORGE L. DUYCKINCK, who have been prominently before the public for several years in a similar connection, as Editors of the "LITERARY WORLD."

Yours, respectfully,
CHARLES SCRIBNER.

N.B. All Communications upon this subject should be addressed, "CHARLES SCRIBNER, Publisher, 145 Nassau Street, New York."

Melville's copy not located. Text from printed copy.

LOCATION (of copy): NYPL-D.

FROM CHARLES F. BRIGGS
12 MAY 1854 · NEW YORK

The magazine piece, "The Two Temples," rejected in this letter by *Putnam's* editor
Charles F. Briggs (1804–77) was not published in Melville's lifetime. Melville's
barely disguised description of Isaac Brown, sexton of Grace Church (the most
fashionable church in New York), as a "fat-paunched, beadle-faced" man, in the
first section of the piece, was one of the worrisome points that deterred the *Putnam's*
editors from accepting it. For more about Brown and his influential position within
New York society, see Charles R. Horner, "Isaac Brown: Melville's 'Beadle-Faced
Man,' " *Melville Society Extracts* 26 (June 1976), 11–13; see also the NN *Piazza
Tales* volume, pp. 700–709. The "slight alteration" that Briggs apologizes for making in Melville's "Encantadas" was probably undertaken for the same reason that
"The Two Temples" was rejected—deference to the "religious sensibilities" of *Putnam's* readers. Although Melville's manuscript of "The Encantadas" does not survive, the alteration was probably of a reference to Christ on the cross, as a similar
description in *Clarel,* 2.1.199–207, suggests. For a further discussion of this alteration, see the NN *Piazza Tales* volume, pp. 605–6. Melville's reply to Briggs's letter, cited in his 16 May 1854 letter to George P. Putnam, is unlocated.

May 12 1854.

Dear Sir,

I am very loth to reject the Two Temples as the article contains
some exquisitely fine description, and some pungent satire, but my
editorial experience compels me to be very cautious in offending the
religious sensibilities of the public, and the moral of the Two Temples would array against us the whole power of the pulpit, to say
nothing of Brown, and the congregation of Grace Church.

I will take this opportunity to apologise to you for making a
slight alteration in the Encantadas, in the last paragraph of the
Choula Widow, which I thought would be improved by the omission of a few words. That I did not injure the idea, or mutilate the
touching figure you introduced, by the slight excision I made, I receive good evidence of, in a letter from James R Lowell, who said
that the figure of the cross in the ass' neck, brought tears into his
eyes, and he thought it the finest touch of genius he had seen in
prose. The only complaint that I have heard about the Encantadas
was that it might have been longer.

Very truly
Your Obd^t
Chas. F. Briggs.

H. Melville Esq.

ALS on a 26.6 × 21 cm sheet, folded in half, of white laid paper, embossed with the manufacturer's crown-like stamp and printed with the letterhead: "Office of 'Putnam's Monthly,' | 10 *Park Place, New-York,* ..... 185" (which Briggs did not fill in). Briggs inscribed the first three pages, in ink. Elizabeth Melville noted in pencil on the fourth page, "Chas. F. Briggs | 'Putnams Monthly' | 'Two Temples' | & | 'Encantadas' | May 12, 1854".

LOCATION: HCL-M.

PUBLICATION: *Log,* I, 487–88.

FROM GEORGE P. PUTNAM
13 MAY 1854 · NEW YORK

Although signed "G P Putnam & Co," this letter is in the hand of George P. Putnam himself. It followed fast on the heels of Charles Briggs's 12 May letter rejecting "The Two Temples" (just above). Its apologetic tone and its request for a daguerreotype suggest that Putnam regarded Melville as a valued writer. For Melville's reply, see his letter of 16 May 1854.

May 13, 1854

Herman Melville Esq
Pittsfield
Mass

Dear Sir,
    There seems to be some reason to fear that some of our Church readers might be disturbed by the *point* of your sketch. I regret this very much, as we sh^d have been glad to have had it in this number. — Do you think this could be avoided? —
    We wish very much to have your *head* as one of our series of portraits. Curtis will be in the July N°. Have you not some drawing or daguerreotype that you can lend us? — Or can you oblige us by having a daguerreotype taken in Pittsfield & let us know the cost, which will be remitted at once?
    We hope you will give us some more of your good things
    In haste, Truly yours

G P *Putnam* & Co

ALS on a 28 × 22 cm sheet, folded in half, of blue laid paper, with the printed letterhead "GEO. P. PUTNAM & CO., American and Foreign Booksellers and Publishers, Purchasing Agents for the Trade and for Public Institutions. | [GEORGE P. PUTNAM. JOHN W. LESLIE.] [Office of Putnam's Monthly. | 10 Park Place, New York, 185 ". Putnam inscribed the

From George P. Putnam, 13 May 1854 (reduced). Courtesy of the Houghton Library, Harvard University (Melville Collection).

first page, in ink. Elizabeth Melville noted in pencil on the fourth page "Putnam & Co — | asking for likeness | May 13 – 1854".

LOCATION: HCL-M.

PUBLICATION: *Log*, I, 488.

TEXTUAL NOTES: 185] *part of printed letterhead (see above)* • oblige us] us *written over word-start*

FROM HARPER & BROTHERS
BEFORE 25 MAY 1854 · NEW YORK

Unlocated. A letter from the Harpers enclosing one hundred dollars for Melville's "The Paradise of Bachelors and the Tartarus of Maids" is cited in his 25 May 1854 acknowledgment of the payment.

FROM HELEN MELVILLE GRIGGS
29 MAY 1854 · LONGWOOD

This letter—enclosed with another addressed to "Gus, Fan, and Lizzie" (Melville's sisters Augusta and Frances Priscilla and his wife)—is the only full letter now located from Helen Melville Griggs to her brother. It was in reply to a now unlocated letter from Melville, probably the joking one he sent before 25 May (see pp. 262–63 above). Like their mother's 28 March 1851 letter (see pp. 609–12 above), this one from Helen also indicates that Melville's letters to family members were infrequent—though very welcome.

Apart from her brief reference to " 'Plutarch on the Cessation of the Oracles' " ("Why the Oracles Cease to Give Answers"; Sealts 404.2), Helen's letter is wholly concerned with family news. Indeed everyone in Melville's immediate family is mentioned at some point—Catherine and John Hoadley in Lawrence, Sophia and Allan Melville in New York, Melville's two unmarried sisters Augusta and Frances Priscilla in Pittsfield, and of course Helen herself and her husband George Griggs (much improved in appearance after a long illness) in Longwood, which Helen refers to as "this nice quiet corner of the Commonwealth" of Massachusetts.

The August gathering of the family that Helen mentions had been planned for several months. In a 17 March letter to their sister Frances Priscilla, Augusta Melville had commented: "I am so glad Helen & Kate are to make their visit in August. How delightful it will be to have them home again, & we four be together once more. Herman says, he is going to devote himself to excursions then" (NYPL-GL). The destination Helen mentions for at least one of these excursions—the "Bash-Pish" (i.e., Bash Bish, either miswritten or, less probably, a family joke) Falls near Egremont in western Massachusetts—was a place Melville and his wife later visited again in an August 1863 excursion by buggy.

Although the envelope for this letter was endorsed "Ansᵈ June 12ᵗʰ 54" by Augusta Melville, the notation probably refers to Augusta's reply to the letter to "Gus, Fan, and Lizzie" enclosed with Melville's, not to a reply by him.

Longwood May 29th 1854.

My dear Herman,

I should have sent one of my numerous epistles to your particular address ere now, if I had not been so well acquainted with your usual mode of treating such documents — "Any letters? Herman?" cries Gus, or Lizzie, or Fanny, as you are reining up old Charlie in gallant style at the pump-room door. "Y – e – s – s" — "one from Helen I guess — for some of you — here 'tis." "Why Herman, it's directed to you!" — "Is it? let me see — why so it is! Well, take it along, I'll be in presently, and then some of you can read it to me."

Now I feel particularly flattered & pleased with the acquisition of a letter from you, and shall prize it highly. "Plutarch on the Cessation of the Oracles" must be a work of deep interest, but I'll take your word for it, having no ambition to peruse the same.

Why did you not come and stay with me while they were suffering under the house-cleaning dispensation? I could have made you very comfortable, and you need not have been driven to such a strait as sleeping in a barrel. I hope the children were not crowded, but had a *keg* apeice to themselves. Bessie might have occupied the *mortar*, if the pestle were taken out.

I will answer your repeated inquiries concerning M[r] Griggs' health at once; pardon me for not allaying your obvious anxiety on the subject before. He is apparently very well at present, has a tolerable appetite for plain food; rests well at night, and *too* well in the morning, when I am sorry to say, he seems to be slightly lethargic, his faculties benumbed, and inactive, so much so, that it is at times very difficult, to make him understand the obvious necessity of arousing himself from this alarming state of stupor. With this exception, I should pronounce him in perfect health; although, when once awakened from this daily trance, he exhibits a restless desire for action, and continued exertion, so much on the *other* extreme, that I almost fear a tendency to febrile irritation; but perhaps this is entirely unfounded, for no one else seems to observe any indications of disordered health. And indeed to look at him, you would not suspect that even these premonitory symptoms could ever be obvious enough, to alarm the most anxious & devoted wife. For in deference to my superior taste, he has allowed the lower part of his face, to be clothed upon with a full and abundant continuation of whisker, which change is becoming in the extreme. He does not look as much like Uncle Peter, since he has thus amplified and extended the hirsute territory of his chin, but the alteration for the better, (as Dickens says) "the imagination can scarcely depictur."

We are quite longing for August to come that we may be all gathered once more under one roof-tree. That excursion to Bash-Pish is just the thing for a family party, and if George's health continues to be progressive & his morning attacks of lethargy wear off, he will no doubt be well enough to join us in our excursions, and bear the consequent fatigue as well as any of the party.

I wish you would come and see us next month, dear Herman; George would be delighted to have you, and you could be as happy as a king in this nice quiet corner of the Commonwealth, with the privilege of visiting the noisy, busy, bustling, & now excited and tumultuous city as often as you please.

Kate and John were here yesterday, they came in on Saturday morning. I met them at George's office, & Kate & I did a power of shopping; while John, between the pressure of his business engagements, ran down to the New York dèpot to see if Allan & Sophia had arrived, for if Allan were well enough they were to be at Lawrence on that day. If they came, Kate was to go back; but they did not. You know, I suppose, that Allan has been quite sick, & they accepted Kate's invitation at once, as change of air was thought to be a good thing for poor Ally. When they have finished their visit there, they are to come here, I dont know whether they are to bring any of the olive branches or not. My best love to Mama & Lizzie, & a thousand kisses to the little ones, and hoping to see you soon, & to hear from you sooner, I am dear Herman your

loving sister
Helen.

George desires his most kind remembrance.

ALS on a 34.5 × 20.8 sheet of white laid paper, embossed with the manufacturer's stamp of a circular device surmounted by a crown, flanked on either side by a lion and a unicorn above a scroll. Helen Melville inscribed all four pages, in ink, and addressed the envelope "Herman Melville. | *Pittsfield.* | Massachusetts."; it was postmarked in Boston on 31 May, and bears computations in pencil on both sides. Augusta Melville endorsed it "Ans^d | June 12th | 54". The postscript is at the top of an enclosed 17.2 × 20.8 part-sheet (torn along the left edge) of the same white laid paper, addressed by Helen to "Gus, Fan, and Lizzie", and inscribed on both sides in the same ink.

LOCATION: NYPL-GL. *Provenance:* Lyrical Ballad Bookstore.

TEXTUAL NOTES: Oracles] *partially rewritten* • repeated] *inserted above with caret* • lethargic,] *before* canceled and • the party] the *written over* us. • Commonwealth] C *altered from* c

FROM GEORGE P. PUTNAM
10 JUNE 1854 · NEW YORK

Unlocated. A 10 June 1854 reply to Melville's 7 June letter about the financial agreement for *Israel Potter* is cited in Melville's subsequent 12 June 1854 reply. Putnam's letter also apparently enclosed an advance payment for Melville's "The Lightning-Rod Man," which appeared in the August 1854 number of his magazine.

FROM GEORGE P. PUTNAM
22 OCTOBER 1854 · NEW YORK

Unlocated. Putnam's letter requesting a page estimate for the remaining segment of *Israel Potter* is cited in Melville's reply of 31 October.

FROM GEORGE P. PUTNAM
BETWEEN 22 OCTOBER AND 3 NOVEMBER 1854 · NEW YORK

Unlocated. A letter from Putnam discussing *Israel Potter* and accompanying an unidentified "M.S." that *Putnam's* was returning to Melville is cited in his 3 November 1854 reply.

FROM GEORGE P. PUTNAM
7 NOVEMBER 1854 · NEW YORK

Unlocated. A letter from Putnam making an undetermined request is cited in Melville's 9 November 1854 reply, apparently the second of two letters Melville wrote to Putnam that day.

1855

FROM DIX & EDWARDS
1 AUGUST 1855 · NEW YORK

Unlocated. A letter from Dix & Edwards, new owners of *Putnam's Monthly Magazine*, enclosing a payment of $37.50 for "The Bell-Tower," is cited in Melville's 7 August 1855 acknowledgment.

FROM DIX & EDWARDS
8 AUGUST 1855 · NEW YORK

Unlocated. A reply by Joshua A. Dix to Melville's 7 August 1855 letter is both recorded in Dix's notation on that letter and cited in Melville's 10 August 1855 reply to it.

FROM OSMOND TIFFANY
BEFORE 26 AUGUST [1855?] · BALTIMORE

Unlocated. A letter from the Baltimore merchant and author Osmond Tiffany can be inferred from Melville's 26 August [1855?] reply.

FROM GEORGE P. PUTNAM
BETWEEN 31 AUGUST AND 7 SEPTEMBER 1855 · NEW YORK

Unlocated. A letter inviting Melville to the "Complimentary Fruit & Flower Festival" sponsored by the New York Book Publishers' Association, of which Putnam was secretary, is cited in Melville's 7 September 1855 reply.

FROM ELIZABETH SHAW MELVILLE
[13?] SEPTEMBER 1855 · PITTSFIELD

Unlocated. A letter from Elizabeth Melville to her husband, who was visiting relatives with his mother at Gansevoort, New York, is cited in Maria Melville's 16 September 1855 letter to her daughter Augusta (NYPL-GL). For more about the circumstances surrounding his wife's letter, see the entry for Melville's unlocated 15 September reply.

FROM HARPER & BROTHERS
AFTER 10 DECEMBER 1855 · NEW YORK

Unlocated. In a 10 December 1855 letter, Melville requested Harper & Brothers to let him know whether they intended to publish "The Apple-Tree Table." Since that piece was ultimately published by *Putnam's* in May 1856, the Harpers must have declined it.

1856

FROM DIX & EDWARDS
3 JANUARY 1856 · NEW YORK

Unlocated. A letter accepting Melville's proposal to publish a collection of his pieces that had appeared in *Putnam's Monthly Magazine* is cited in his 7 January 1856 reply.

FROM DIX & EDWARDS
BEFORE 16 FEBRUARY 1856 · NEW YORK

Unlocated. Melville's 16 February 1856 letter to Dix & Edwards, discussing the arrangement and table of contents for his *Piazza Tales* pieces, contains a statement from which a letter can be inferred. Commenting on which piece should follow "The Piazza," Melville wrote, "I think, with you, that '*Bartleby*' had best come next." The changes discussed in his 16 February letter were possibly prompted by a conversation with the publishers in New York, but more likely by a letter from them, evidently in reply to Melville's 19 January letter.

FROM LEMUEL SHAW
14 MAY 1856 · BOSTON

Unlocated. A 14 May 1856 reply from Judge Shaw to Melville's 12 May letter apparently reassured Melville of his willingness to support his son-in-law financial-ly and inquired further as to the precarious state of Melville's finances at this time. Melville's 22 May letter to Shaw is a response to those queries.

FROM RICHARD T. GREENE
16 JUNE 1856 · SANDUSKY

This is the first letter Melville is known to have received from his old shipboard friend Richard Tobias (Toby) Greene since Greene's now unlocated February 1847 letters (see pp. 587–88 above). Evidently Greene had not been able to "keep the *run*" of Melville well enough to know that he no longer lived in New York. And in the meantime Greene himself had moved from Buffalo, New York, to Sandusky, Ohio, where he was apparently working for his brother-in-law Chauncey L. Der-by's publishing and bookselling firm. (Derby himself had moved to New York to become the director of the Cosmopolitan Art Association in 1855; see Walter Sut-ton, "The Derby Brothers: 19th Century Bookmen," *University of Rochester Library Bulletin* 3 [Winter 1948], 21–29.)

Melville's reply—assuming he complied with Greene's request at the close of this letter and answered his numerous questions—is unlocated. For Melville's own memorandum about the steward of the *Acushnet*, Henry Hayner, see the NN *Moby-Dick*, pp. 1000, 1002–3; for more on the 10 December 1853 Harpers' fire in New York, see the headnote to Melville's 22 May 1856 letter to Lemuel Shaw; and for Melville's later gift of three copies of *Typee* to Greene, see Greene's 20 October 1863 letter acknowledging the books, below. See also the headnote to Greene's 20 October 1863 letter for more about his son, Herman Melville Greene.

Sandusky O
June 16th /56

Dear Melville:

I have just been reading the "Piazza Tales", which my brother-in-law, Derby, presented me. The "Encantadas" called up reminis-cences of days gone bye — the *Acushnet* — the "turpin" &c. The

Sandusky O
June 16th /56

Dear Melville:

I have just been reading
the "Piazza Tale", which my brother-in-
law, Herby, presented me. The
"Encantadas" called up reminiscences of
days gone bye — the Aeushnet & the
"turpin". &c, The tales are charming.
I read them with delight; but when I
say so, no doubt I reiterate the
sayings of thousands of your readers.
By the way do you remember
Haynor, the Steward? Well I found
him in New Orleans last winter
keeping a Hotel! He wished to be
remembered to you; should I
write you.
What has become of "Typee"? Were
the plates burned in Harpers' big
fire? It is out of the question to

From Richard T. Greene, 16 June 1856, p. 1 (reduced). Courtesy of the
Houghton Library, Harvard University (Melville Collection).

tales are charming. I read them with delight, but when I say so, no doubt I reiterate the sayings of thousands of your readers.

By the way do you remember Haynor, the Steward? Well I found him in New Orleans last winter keeping a Hotel! He wished to be remembered to you, should I write you.

What has become of "Typee"? Were the plates burned in Harpers' big fire? It is out of the question to procure a copy. I am asked for it every day. Do you still retain the copy right?

I am determined to keep you in remembrance. So you would think if you could see my little son, two years old, who glories in the name of "Herman Melville" — I have been promising myself the pleasure of a peep at you among the hills this long time, and shall do so one of these days. I was in New York last summer but was told that you were off some where on a visit.

I am engaged with C. L. Derby in the Cosmopolitan Art Association and from his connection with the different publishers I am enabled to keep the *run* of you.

Will you spare time to drop me a line or two? it will prove my identity, for I still am proud of the immortality with which you have invested me.

Yours truly
R. T. Greene.

ALS on a 26 × 20.1 cm sheet, folded in half, of white laid paper with lines, embossed with the manufacturer's oval stamp enclosing a shield and the name "DURAND & CO LONDON". Greene inscribed the first three pages, in ink.

LOCATION: HCL-M.

PUBLICATION: (partial) *Log*, II, 516.

TEXTUAL NOTES: brother-in-law] brother-in-|law • So you] S *altered from* s *after* remembrance, (*vestigial comma*)

FROM HENRY G. WEBBER
12 JULY [1856?] · CHARLESTOWN

Dated only 12 July, this letter has been tentatively assigned to 1856, after the August 1855 printing of "The Bell-Tower" in *Putnam's*. The illustrations discussed in this letter remain a mystery. No illustrations accompanied Melville's piece either in the magazine or in *The Piazza Tales*, in which "The Bell-Tower" was reprinted in the spring of 1856. Nor is there any record of Melville's having bought illustrations. On 8 August 1856 the *Berkshire County Eagle*, however, reprinted part of an article on Cooper, Dana, and Melville entitled "A Trio of American Sailor-Authors," which had first appeared in the January 1856 issue of the *Dublin University Magazine*. To this the *Eagle* added a postscript about Melville's more recent publications, including "The Bell-Tower," which was "a picturesque and arabesque tale well fitted to inspire an artist, as it did one in New York who has made four striking sketches from it, which we trust will be engraved." The New York artist may have been Henry G. Webber (though the address Webber gives is Charlestown, New Hampshire), but no artist by this name has been found in listings for the period (including the Princeton University data-base for the *Index to Nineteenth Century American Art Periodicals*).

Herman Melville Esq.

Charlestown, July 12th

Sir

I have heard once or twice from Mr Geo P. Putnam of N. York that you wished to possess some illustrations of your tale of the Bell Tower, drawn by me, which were at Mr Putnam's last fall; But, as I understood, you did not feel like paying such a price as you supposed would be asked. The drawings are in pretty good preservation now, but are of no particular use to me, and I shall be glad to have you take them, if you wish, at any price that you may set. I expect to *move* in a week or ten days, and if you will write to me at once, if you would like the drawings, I will send them, & you can pay your own price for them. I had rather you should have them than any one else

I authorized Mr Wells (of the firm of G. P. P. & C°) to tell you this when he first spoke to me on the matter, but he told me this spring he had not seen you since.

Very Respectfully
Yours &c
Henry G. Webber

Address
H. G. Webber
Charlestown
New Hampshire

ALS on a 12.8 × 20.5 cm sheet of blue laid paper, embossed with the manufacturer's rectangular stamp enclosing the initials "O & V". Webber inscribed both sides of the leaf, in ink. Melville wrote, in ink, at the bottom of the second page, the word "Decline" (or possibly the name "Dellins").

LOCATION: HCL-M.

PUBLICATION: (partial) *Log*, II, 517.

FROM DIX & EDWARDS
30 AUGUST 1856 · NEW YORK

Melville's 25 August 1856 request for a statement from his publishers on the sales of *The Piazza Tales* is now unlocated. Given his strained financial situation at this time (see the headnotes to his 12 and 22 May 1856 letters to his father-in-law, Lemuel Shaw), he was presumably anxious to know whether his latest book would be profitable. It was not, however, as this report dated 28 August and included with the publishers' 30 August reply states. Melville's contract stipulated that he would receive a return from the book only after its expenses had been paid—and consequently he received none at this time (see the NN *Piazza Tales* volume, p. 499).

New York August 30th 1856

Herman Melville Esqr
Dear Sir:

In reply to your favor of 25th inst. we beg to enclose a statement of sales of Piazza Tales to this date, by which you will see that it has not yet paid expenses.

We published late in May, and business has been dull since that time, but is reviving with the opening of fall trade, and we feel the good influence upon sales of all our books.

The statement of Cost does not include any advertising or incidental expenses — We hope our next statement will show a handsome return.

Yours Respectfully
Dix, Edwards & Co

Copyright,
      Piazza Tales,
           For ª/c of Herman Melville Esqr
                    By Dix Edwards & Co

Composition & Stereotyping	260.98
Press Work	83.60
Paper	401.54
Binding	302.50
	$1.048.62

Published May
N° Copies bound   2.500.
On hand August 28/56 = 1.193.
Editors Copies given Away 260. = 1.453.
                    1.047. Copies sold @ 60¢
                           $6.28.20

New York August 28th 1856
E. & O. E.   Dix, Edwards & Co

ALS on a 40.2 × 25.3 cm sheet, folded in half, of white laid paper, watermarked with a design including a crown and the letter "M" and embossed with the manufacturer's oval stamp enclosing a shield-like design. A clerk inscribed the report in black ink on the first page and the letter in black ink on the third. Allan Melville noted in ink on the fourth page "*Piazza Tales* | Dix Edwards & Co | ª/c | Aug 28 *1856*", and another hand added in pencil "New York".

LOCATION: HCL-M.

PUBLICATION: *Log*, II, 520–21.

TEXTUAL NOTES: Dix, Edwards & Co] *underlined with a flourish* • Copyright . . . Esqʳ] *underlining in red ink* • By . . . & Co] *underlining in red ink* • Dix, Edwards & Co] *underlined with a flourish*

FROM PETER GANSEVOORT
9 OCTOBER 1856 · ALBANY

Before leaving on his 1856–57 voyage to Europe and the Levant, Melville visited his mother and his uncle Herman at Gansevoort (abbreviated G. here); but he did not have time to visit his uncle Peter and family in Albany before going to New York on 29 September for two weeks of preparations. (Apparently Melville and his family had also failed to visit his uncle Peter during the gala tenth meeting of the American Association for the Advancement of Science held at the capitol in Albany from 20 to 28 August 1856.) On 7 October, however, he did write his uncle a farewell letter (see the headnote to that letter for more about Melville's trip). Peter Gansevoort wrote his reply just two days before Melville sailed for Glasgow aboard the steamer *Glasgow* on Saturday, 11 October. For Robert F. Cooke and Judge Amasa J. Parker, both mentioned by Peter Gansevoort, see the entry for Melville's unlocated letter to Cooke written before 11 June 1853; for Cooke see also *Journals*, pp. 321 and 366.

Alb^y 9 Oct 56

My dear Herman

I thank you for your letter rec'd last evening advising of your intention to sail for the other side of the ocean on Saturday next —

I regret that y^r engagements prevented you stopping with us on y^r return from G. It would have not only gratified us but have removed the edge of the disappt. during the Scientific Convention when we reserved the whole house for you, Lizzie & the Children —

Let me say now, what I had not an opportunity before — that your letter of introduction (the only letter I delivered while abroad), made us acquainted with the three brothers Cooke in London; & that we dined with Robt Fr. Cooke, & his brothers in Co, with Chief J. Shaw & Lemuel S. on 4 July 1853 at 38 Nottingham Place New road & had a delightful party — If you see them, please present my best regards & also that of Judge Parker & say that if either of them visit the U.S. I shall be most happy to see them —

Your mother arrived yesterday we hope for a long visit. We will endeavor restore her to perfect health before her return to G. She required a change

She unites with Susan, Kate & myself in best wishes & sincere prayers for a pleasant & safe voyage & the restoration of y^r health on your return to your family & friends —

Y^{rs} Truly & most affection

Final document not located. Text from draft letter (unsigned), on a 20 × 31.6 cm part-sheet of blue laid paper with lines, faintly embossed with the manufacturer's circular stamp. Peter Gansevoort inscribed both sides of the leaf, in ink, and noted in ink on the second page "1856. Octr. 9. | Dft letter to Herman | Melville in answer | to his letter advising | of his sailing for | Europe".

LOCATION (of draft): NYPL-GL.

PUBLICATION: (partial) *Log*, II, 524–25.

TEXTUAL NOTES: the other] the *mended* • regret] *after canceled* seriously • It would have] *after canceled* It would have gratified y^r Aunt Susan & *with* y^r *inserted above* • not only] *inserted above caret* • us] *added before canceled* not only • when] *after canceled* here • house] *inserted above caret* • had not] had *altered from* have • before] *after canceled* of doing • I] *inserted above canceled* we • in London] in *inserted above canceled* of • delightful] *inserted above canceled* most charming • & say] *after canceled* to them • either of] *inserted above* • most] *inserted above caret* • we hope] *after canceled ampersand* • visit.] visit, *(vestigial comma) before successively canceled* when || is well || & will be || have no doubt she will be • We will endeavor restore . . . health] *inserted*

above, with the exception of restore *altered from* restored *without adding "to"* · her return] her
written over the · pleasant &] *inserted above caret* · the restoration] the *inserted above caret*

FROM SAMUEL S. SHAW
BEFORE 19 OCTOBER 1856 · BERLIN

Unlocated. Soon after receiving the news from his brother Lemuel Shaw, Jr., that
Melville was also going to be in Europe, Samuel Shaw directed a letter to the port
of Havre in order to try to get in touch with him upon his arrival. This letter is
cited in his 19 October 1856 letter to his mother, Hope Savage Shaw: "I was anxious to hear if Herman had sailed on the 4th as Lem intimated he might do. However I suppose that if he comes he will communicate with me through the Barings,
if he does not get the letter which I have sent to Havre in time to meet him" (HCL-
M). It is doubtful that Melville received this letter since he did not land at Havre,
but at Glasgow. In a 23 November 1856 letter Judge Shaw informed his son of this,
adding that Melville "expected after a few days in Scotland to proceed to Liverpool
& thence to London, where he would inquire for you at Baring Bro. & Co. & thus
probably be enabled to put himself in communication with you. I hope you will
meet him, and so make your arrangements, as to travel together" (MHS-S). Melville, however, did not go to London, but instead sailed directly for Constantinople
from Liverpool. For Shaw's subsequent effort to meet his brother-in-law, see the
entry just below.

FROM SAMUEL S. SHAW
BEFORE 7 DECEMBER 1856 · BERLIN

Unlocated. A letter is cited in Samuel Shaw's 7 December 1856 letter to his mother,
Hope Savage Shaw: "I received your letter week before last, and one from Elizabeth this last week, in which she gives me Herman's direction — I have a letter
ready for him & hope to get some news from him" (HCL-M). Melville had sent
his wife his "direction" in his now unlocated 18 November 1856 letter from Liverpool. There is no evidence to indicate where Shaw decided to send this letter to his
brother-in-law or whether Melville received it. Melville did finally cross paths with
Shaw in Rome on 21 March 1857 and noted briefly in his journal that Shaw had
with him a "letter," probably Elizabeth's, "from home to 20th Feb. All
well"(*Journals*, p. 113).

1857

FROM [MARIA GANSEVOORT MELVILLE AND DAUGHTERS?]
BEFORE 25 FEBRUARY 1857 · GANSEVOORT

Unlocated. In his journal entry for his first day in Rome, Melville recorded that he
found his "first letter from home" waiting for him when he arrived at 10 A.M. on
25 February (*Journals*, p. 105). This may have been a letter from his wife; however,

since Augusta Melville reported that she and her sisters and mother in Gansevoort received a letter from Melville dated 27 February (see the entry for that unlocated letter, p. 309 above), he may have been writing in reply to a letter from them.

FROM [ELIZABETH SHAW MELVILLE? AND FAMILY?]
BEFORE 4 MAY 1857 · [BOSTON? AND GANSEVOORT?]

Two or more unlocated letters. Melville's 4 May 1857 entry in his 1856–57 journal notes that he "got letters from Brown, Shipley & Co."—the American mercantile firm that served as agent in Liverpool for the New-York and Liverpool United States Mail Steamers (*Journals*, p. 129). This packet of mail probably was comprised of letters from Melville's immediate family—presumably at least one from his wife, who knew he could next be reached in Liverpool after Rome, and perhaps one or more others from his mother and sisters in Gansevoort, New York.

FROM ELIZA GORDON
13 MAY 1857 · ARBROATH, SCOTLAND

In preserving this letter, Elizabeth Melville characterized it as "very odd" (see the manuscript description, below). Little is known about Miss Eliza Gordon, who apparently lived in the Scottish port of Arbroath (between Dundee and Montrose in Forfarshire [later Angus]), her friends the Weeds (possibly Anson and Rachel Weed, who according to the 1860 census lived on a farm in the town of Malta, in Saratoga County, New York), or her cousin "Alexd Miller" in Lewiston, Niagara County, New York (probably Alexander Miller, a farmer born in Dundee, Scotland, who is listed in the 1860 census as being sixty-five years old with a wife and eight children). But reading between the lines, it appears that she had become infatuated with Melville—at least with her image of him shaped by "the Master peice of all Gods works," Jack Chase (see *White-Jacket*, chap. 4 and *passim*). And this prompted her to relate the story of the troubadour Jaufre Rudel's love-lorn voyage and to quote from Pope's "Eloisa to Abelard" (lines 51–52) at the close. Although she was also apparently acquainted with works by Captain Frederick Marryat, Washington Irving, Harriet Beecher Stowe, Edgar Allan Poe, and the unidentified "Late James Abbott" (possibly a garbled reference to Jacob Abbott [1803–79], author of the popular "Rollo" series), both her spelling and her hand suggest that she had received little formal schooling. As a result, some of her references, such as "Omidi," remain obscure. In the first paragraph she loosely quotes from three excerpts of reviews of *Mardi* and *Redburn* that were included by Harper & Brothers in a full-page advertisement bound into the first two printings of *White-Jacket* (the advertisement also appeared in *Moby-Dick*; see Hershel Parker, *The Recognition of Herman Melville* [Ann Arbor: University of Michigan Press, 1967], pp. 20–22). The phrase "rich in wisdom and briliant with beauty" comes from the excerpt from the *Chronotype*'s review of *Mardi*; the next passage (from "ships and the sea" through "delightful book") comes from the first two excerpts included for *Redburn*—from the *New York Albion* and from the *Courier*.

Nº 2 Guthree Port Arbroath   13 May 1857 —
Herman Melvile Esquire

Author of the white Jacket Mardi and others" Honour'd Sir
Let it not displease you to be addressed by a stranger to your person not so to your merits, I have read the white Jacket with much
pleasure and delight "I found it rich in wisdom and briliant with
beauty, ships and the sea and those who plow it with their belong-
ings on shore — those subjects are idintified with Herman Melvils
name for he has most unquestionably made them his own" No
writer not even Marryt himself has observed them more closely or
pictured them more impressively, a delightful book it is. I long
exceedingly to read Mardi, but how or where to obtain it is the
task?

I have just now received an invitation to cross the Atalantic from
a Mr. and Mrs Weed, Malta between Balston springs and saratoga
Countie, as also from Mr Alexd Miller my own Cousin, Rose bank
Louistown

I have for this many a day been wishing to see you "to hear you
speak to breathe the same air in which you dwell" Are you the picture of him you so powerfully represent as the Master peice of all
Gods works Jack Chase? —

write me dear sir and say where Omidi s'to be gote. ——— I do
much admire the American Authors, Washington Irven Mrs Stow
Alan Edgar Po the Late James Abbott — And Last tho' not least
your good self —

Did you ever read the history of Jeffery Rudel. he was a young
Nobleman of Provence and reconed one of the handsomest and
polite persons of the age he lived in the time of Richard the first sir
named cour de Lion who invited Jeffery to his Court and it was
there he first heard of the beauty wit, learning and virtue of the
Countess of Tripoly by which he became so enamoured that he
resolved upon seeing her purchased a vesel and in opesition to the
King and the luxury of a Court set sail for Tripoly the Object of
his affection reached his most sanguine expectations. —

were you to cross the Atalantic you should receive a cordial reception from Mr George Gordon my beloved & only Brother and
I'd bid you welcome to Old S't Thomas a Becket famed for kindness to strangers. ——

permite me Dear Sir to subskribe myself your friend although
unseen and at a Distance.   Eliza Gordon

Heaven first sent letters,
For some wretches aid,
Some banished Lover,
Or some Captive maid.
                                                                    Pope

ALS on a 43 × 25.9 cm sheet, folded in half, of white laid paper. Eliza Gordon inscribed the
first two pages, in ink. Elizabeth Melville placed the letter in a folded sheet of lined paper,
with her penciled note on the front: "A very odd letter | from a stranger Eliza
Gordon | Scotland | May 1857".

LOCATION: HCL-M.

PUBLICATION: Weaver, pp. 240–41.

TEXTUAL NOTES: Author . . . others"] *opening double quotation mark lacking, and closing double
quotation mark is subscript* • his own"] *subscript closing double quotation mark* • I have just] *after two
or more canceled words* • Po] *after canceled* a

FROM PHILLIPS, SAMPSON, & CO.
[17?] AUGUST 1857 · BOSTON

Unlocated. A letter "received yesterday" from the publishers of the *Atlantic Monthly* is cited in Melville's 19 August 1857 reply.

FROM ALLAN MELVILLE
BETWEEN 5 AND 8 SEPTEMBER 1857 · NEW YORK

Unlocated. On 4 September 1857, G. W. Curtis notified Allan Melville of the possible sale of the plates for *The Piazza Tales* and *The Confidence-Man* after the failure
of the firm of Miller & Curtis, which had tried to resurrect the publishing firm of
Dix & Edwards. Apparently Allan wrote to his brother soon afterwards, since a
reply from Melville to Allan on this matter is cited in a 10 September letter from
Curtis to Allan. For more on these negotiations, see the entry for the unlocated
letter Melville wrote to Curtis on [8 or 9] September 1857.

FROM ALLAN MELVILLE
BEFORE 14 SEPTEMBER 1857 · NEW YORK

Unlocated. Melville's 14 September letter reporting that he could not find a "Commissioner" in Pittsfield was probably written in reply to a letter from his brother

Allan. For more about this correspondence concerning the Gansevoort mansion, see the headnote to Melville's letter.

FROM THE YOUNG MEN'S INSTITUTE
[BEFORE 26 SEPTEMBER 1857?] · NEW HAVEN

Unlocated. An invitation to lecture for the Young Men's Institute in New Haven, Connecticut, was probably among the "two or three" invitations cited as already received in Melville's 26 September 1857 letter to G. W. Curtis. Melville delivered his lecture "Statues in Rome" at New Haven on 30 December 1857. See the NN *Piazza Tales* volume, pp. 803, 806, and Sealts, *Melville as Lecturer*, p. 6.

FROM THE YOUNG MEN'S ASSOCIATION
[BEFORE 26 SEPTEMBER 1857?] · AUBURN

Unlocated. An invitation to lecture for the Young Men's Association in Auburn, New York, was probably among the "two or three" invitations cited as already received in Melville's 26 September 1857 letter to G. W. Curtis. Melville delivered his lecture "Statues in Rome" at Auburn on 5 January 1858. See the NN *Piazza Tales* volume, pp. 802, 806, and Sealts, *Melville as Lecturer*, p. 6.

FROM THE CLEVELAND LIBRARY ASSOCIATION
[BEFORE 26 SEPTEMBER 1857?] · CLEVELAND

Unlocated. An invitation to lecture for the Library Association in Cleveland was probably among the "two or three" invitations cited as already received in Melville's 26 September 1857 letter to G. W. Curtis. Melville delivered his lecture "Statues in Rome" at Cleveland on 11 January 1858. See the NN *Piazza Tales* volume, pp. 802, 806, and Sealts, *Melville as Lecturer*, p. 6.

FROM WILLIAM P. S. CADWELL
BEFORE 3 OCTOBER 1857 · NEW BEDFORD

Unlocated. An invitation to lecture for the New Bedford Lyceum is cited in Melville's 3 October 1857 reply to their representative, William P. S. Cadwell.

FROM [WILLIAM P. S. CADWELL?]
AFTER 3 OCTOBER 1857 · NEW BEDFORD

Three or four unlocated letters. A series of further letters from William Cadwell or another representative of the New Bedford Lyceum can be inferred from Melville's lecture engagement notebook (see the NN *Piazza Tales* volume, p. 803). An initial letter replying to Melville's 3 October letter contained a list of possible dates, a second presumably acknowledged Melville's first choice of 16 February, and a third and possibly a fourth concerned the subsequent change of the date to 23 February. See the entry for Melville's unlocated replies to these letters, p. 317 above, for more about these arrangements.

FROM THE CLARKSVILLE LITERARY ASSOCIATION
12 OCTOBER 1857 · CLARKSVILLE

According to his lecture engagement notebook, Melville delivered the lecture "Statues in Rome" in Clarksville, Tennessee, on 22 January 1858, for a fee of seventy-five dollars (see the NN *Piazza Tales* volume, p. 806). He did not, however, lecture in either Louisville or Nashville as proposed in this invitation. For the draft or summary of a reply written in pencil below the signatures on the invitation in Elizabeth Melville's hand, see the entry for Melville's letter to W. O. Vance dated 20 October 1857.

Clarksville, Tenn. Oct 12th/57

Herman Melville esq
Dear Sir
    Having seen your name announced in the N.Y. Tribune amongst the list of forthcoming Lecturers, We, as corresponding committee of the Clarksville Literary Association, are instructed to tender you the earnest invitation of our Society to address them at whatever time during the coming Fall or Winter as may best suit your convenience. We are aware that it is the impression with our Northern Brethren that Literary men meet with poor appreciation in the South, but we can assure you, there are many amongst us who have delightedly perused your productions, and who are eager to render personal, that charming acquaintance they have formed with you through the medium of your genial pen. Presuming that your Steps have never wandered this far West, we indulge the hope, that this opportunity of seeing our portion of the Union and our forms of society will induce you to accept the invitation. The facilities for reaching our city are both pleasant and expeditious either by way of Nashville, which is but 3 days distant from Boston, or via Louisville. You could Lecture at both these places, did you desire to make the trip more remunerative. If it is possible for you to accept, please inform us what time it would suit you to come — and also

what amt you would require as compensation. Hoping you will respond in accordance with our wishes, we have the honor to be

With cordial admiration
Yr very obt Svts

Direct reply to W. O. Vance

G C Breed
W O Vance
G G Poyndexter
E B Haskins
Hon G A Henry

ALS on a 40 × 25.1 cm sheet, folded in half, of white laid paper with lines, embossed with
the manufacturer's stamp, a shield-like design beneath a bird-like figure. W. O. Vance, presumably secretary of the Clarksville Literary Association, inscribed the first two pages of the
letter, in ink, and addressed it on the fourth page "Herman Melville | Pittsfield | Mass". Eliza-
beth Melville noted in pencil on that page "*Lecture No 1* | Clarksville, Tenn | Oct 12ᵗʰ 1857",
and on the second page below the signatures, she wrote the summary (or draft) of Melville's
reply reported on pp. 317–18 above.

LOCATION: HCL-M.

PUBLICATION: (partial) *Log*, II, 583.

TEXTUAL NOTES: Fall or] or *inserted above canceled* and · Steps] *written over* fe · accept the] the
written over our · days] *written over* miles

FROM THE YOUNG MEN'S SOCIETY
BEFORE 16 NOVEMBER 1857 · DETROIT

Unlocated. A letter inviting Melville to lecture for the Young Men's Society in
Detroit can be inferred from his lecture engagement notebook (see the NN *Piazza
Tales* volume, pp. 802, 806). Melville delivered his lecture "Statues in Rome" at
Detroit on 12 January 1858; the engagement had been settled by 16 November
1857, as indicated in Melville's letter of that date, probably to Louis W. Burnham.

FROM [LOUIS W. BURNHAM?]
BEFORE 16 NOVEMBER 1857 · ROCKFORD

Unlocated. A letter inviting Melville to lecture either for the Young Men's Association or for the Commercial Institute in Rockford, Illinois, can be inferred from
Melville's 16 November 1857 letter, probably addressed to Louis W. Burnham,
secretary of the association and principal of the institute.

FROM [LOUIS W. BURNHAM?]
AFTER 16 NOVEMBER 1857 · ROCKFORD

Unlocated. Melville requested a reply in his 16 November 1857 letter probably addressed to Louis W. Burnham, secretary of the Young Men's Association and principal of the Commercial Institute in Rockford, Illinois. For its possible contents, see the headnote to Melville's letter.

FROM THE PROVIDENT SOCIETY
BEFORE 19 NOVEMBER 1857 · LAWRENCE

Unlocated. A letter inviting Melville to lecture for the Provident Society of Lawrence, Massachusetts, can be inferred from his lecture engagement notebook (see the NN *Piazza Tales* volume, pp. 803 and 806). Sealts suggests that Melville's brother-in-law John Hoadley, then living in Lawrence, arranged for this 23 November engagement, the first that Melville had as a lecturer (*Melville as Lecturer*, p. 21). Possibly Melville's correspondence was with Hoadley; in any event it must have been arranged by 19 November (see the entry for Melville's unlocated letter of that date to Lemuel Shaw).

FROM [A. D. LAMSON?]
23 NOVEMBER 1857 · MALDEN

Unlocated. A letter is cited in Melville's 27 November 1857 reply to "Dear Sir," probably addressed to A. D. Lamson of Malden, Massachusetts (see the headnote to that letter).

FROM THE PENNACOOK LYCEUM
BEFORE 24 NOVEMBER 1857 · CONCORD

Unlocated. A letter inviting Melville to lecture for the Pennacook Lyceum, Concord, New Hampshire, can be inferred from his lecture engagement notebook (see the NN *Piazza Tales* volume, pp. 803 and 806). Melville delivered his lecture "Statues in Rome" at Concord on 24 November 1857.

FROM NATHANIEL HAWTHORNE
[DECEMBER 1857?] · LIVERPOOL

Unlocated. In 1947 Agnes Morewood, Melville's grandniece (the daughter of Allan's daughter Maria and William B. Morewood, son of Sarah and Rowland Morewood) remembered seeing a Christmas card, by then "mislaid and . . . perhaps permanently lost," which Melville received from Hawthorne, with a comment on the back about *The Confidence-Man* (see *Melville Society Extracts* 2 [10 November 1947], 2). She recalled no date for this card, but presumably it was written in

1857—the year the book appeared. Leyda did not include this Christmas card in the *Log*, but perhaps having heard a slightly different version of the same family story, he stated in his entry for "May?" 1857 that Hawthorne wrote to Melville about *The Confidence-Man*.

FROM THE MERCANTILE LIBRARY ASSOCIATION
BEFORE 2 DECEMBER 1857 · BOSTON

Unlocated. A letter inviting Melville to lecture for the Mercantile Library Association of Boston can be inferred from his lecture engagement notebook (see the NN *Piazza Tales* volume, pp. 803 and 806). Melville delivered his lecture "Statues in Rome" at Tremont Temple in Boston on 2 December 1857.

FROM UNKNOWN
BEFORE 4 DECEMBER 1857 · PLACE UNKNOWN

Unlocated. A letter, evidently from an unidentified autograph collector, is cited in Melville's 4 December 1857 reply.

FROM THE MERCANTILE LIBRARY ASSOCIATION
BEFORE 11 DECEMBER 1857 · MONTREAL

Unlocated. A letter inviting Melville to lecture for the Mercantile Library Association in Montreal can be inferred from his lecture engagement notebook. Melville delivered his lecture "Statues in Rome" at Montreal on 11 December, not 10 December as recorded in his notebook (see the NN *Piazza Tales* volume, pp. 800, 803, and 806). Possibly there was an additional exchange of letters concerning this change.

FROM THE SARATOGA SPRINGS LECTURE COMMITTEE
BEFORE 21 DECEMBER 1857 · SARATOGA SPRINGS

Unlocated. A letter inviting Melville to lecture at St. Nicholas Hall in Saratoga Springs, New York, can be inferred from his lecture engagement notebook. Melville delivered his lecture "Statues in Rome" at Saratoga on 21 December, not 30 December, as recorded in his notebook (see the NN *Piazza Tales* volume, pp. 800 and 806). Possibly there was an additional exchange of letters concerning this change.

FROM NATHANIEL PAINE
26 DECEMBER [1857?] · WORCESTER

Unlocated. An autograph request is cited in Melville's 13 February [1858?] reply.

1858

FROM THE ITHACA LECTURE COMMITTEE
BEFORE 7 JANUARY 1858 · ITHACA

Unlocated. A letter inviting Melville to lecture at Ithaca, New York, can be inferred from his lecture engagement notebook (see the NN *Piazza Tales* volume, pp. 802 and 806). Melville delivered his lecture "Statues in Rome" at Ithaca on 7 January 1858. His entry for the Ithaca lecture was inserted in his lecture engagement notebook above his canceled earlier entry of "Syracuse"—possibly an indication that he had corresponded with the lecture committee of that town, but that the arrangement had fallen through (see Sealts, *Melville as Lecturer*, p. 27n.).

FROM RICHARD T. GREENE
9 JANUARY 1858 · SANDUSKY

Melville's old shipmate Richard Tobias (Toby) Greene, then living in Sandusky, Ohio, wrote this letter just two days before Melville was engaged to lecture in nearby Cleveland on 11 January 1858. Greene's first sentence implies that perhaps his wife delivered the letter by hand (since she was present at the lecture; see below); but no envelope indicating how it was sent is now known to survive, nor is a reply from Melville (though presumably he did answer). Melville's expense records from his first lecture tour do not show a train or "buss" ride from Cleveland to Sandusky; however, Elizabeth Melville had recorded "Toby's address" in his lecture engagement notebook (see the NN *Piazza Tales* volume, pp. 804; possibly she added the address later, but this seems less likely). Later, Greene's wife, Mary J. Greene, in a 14 November 1892 letter to Elizabeth Melville, recalled attending this lecture in Cleveland (HCL-M). Greene himself had been on the lecture circuit in 1855, presenting a lecture entitled "Typee; or Life in the South Pacific" in towns in Ohio and New York.

Sandusky Jan 9th 1858

Dear Old Shipmate:

Hearing that you were to be in Cleveland and my wife being there on a visit, I wished her to see you. Were it at all possible I would go down myself for I would like much to see you. Cant you take this place in your route? You would be warmly recieved. As the young men's Association has broken up here we have a scarcity of lecturers. If you will come I will give good notice here and 'tend door for you if necessary. Your being at Cleveland is noticed in our daily papers. There are a number of Pittsfield folks here, who know you by reputation. How I would like a *yarn* from you about the East Will you come up here?

Yours truly
"Toby"

ALS, " 'Toby' ", on a 16.7 × 21.3 cm part-sheet (torn along the left edge) of white laid paper with lines, embossed with the manufacturer's square stamp enclosing a shield above two branches. Greene inscribed the first page, in ink.

LOCATION: HCL-M.

PUBLICATION: (partial) *Log*, II, 588–89.

FROM THE WILMINGTON LECTURE COMMITTEE
BEFORE 25 JANUARY 1858 · WILMINGTON

Unlocated. A letter inviting Melville to lecture at Wilmington, Delaware, can be inferred from his lecture engagement notebook (see the NN *Piazza Tales* volume, pp. 802). This lecture was tentatively planned for the last week of January or the first week of February 1858; however, as Elizabeth Melville's notation below the entry indicates, this engagement was *"given up."* Possibly a further exchange of letters took place.

FROM L. J. CIST
1 FEBRUARY 1858 · ST. LOUIS

Unlocated. A letter requesting an autograph is cited in Melville's 13 February 1858 reply.

FROM THE MERCANTILE LIBRARY ASSOCIATION
BEFORE 2 FEBRUARY 1858 · CINCINNATI

Unlocated. A letter inviting Melville to lecture for the Mercantile Library Association in Cincinnati can be inferred from his lecture given there on 2 February 1858. However, Cincinnati was not listed among the tentative engagements in his lecture notebook.

FROM THE GYMNASIUM AND LIBRARY ASSOCIATION
BEFORE 3 FEBRUARY 1858 · CHILLICOTHE

Unlocated. A letter inviting Melville to lecture for the Gymnasium and Library Association in Chillicothe, Ohio, can be inferred from his lecture given there on 3

February 1858. Chillicothe was not listed among the tentative engagements in Melville's lecture notebook.

FROM THE MISHAWUM LITERARY ASSOCIATION
BEFORE 10 FEBRUARY 1858 · CHARLESTOWN

Unlocated. A letter inviting Melville to lecture for the Mishawum Literary Association in Charlestown, Massachusetts, can be inferred from his lecture engagement notebook (see the NN *Piazza Tales* volume, pp. 803 and 806). Melville delivered his lecture "Statues in Rome" at Charlestown on 10 February 1858.

FROM THE ATHENAEUM AND MECHANICS' ASSOCIATION
BEFORE 18 FEBRUARY 1858 · ROCHESTER

Unlocated. A letter inviting Melville to lecture for the Athenaeum and Mechanics' Association in Rochester, New York, can be inferred from his lecture engagement notebook. The lecture—"Statues in Rome"—was given in Rochester on 18 February 1858, not on 23 February as recorded in his lecture engagement notebook (see the NN *Piazza Tales* volume, pp. 802 and 806). Possibly there was an additional exchange of letters concerning this change.

FROM GEORGE L. DUYCKINCK
BEFORE 6 NOVEMBER 1858 · NEW YORK

Unlocated. A letter from George Duyckinck (accompanying his gift to Melville of Chapman's Homer [Sealts 276–78]) can be inferred from Melville's 6 November 1858 letter acknowledging the gift.

FROM LEMUEL SHAW
8 NOVEMBER 1858 · BOSTON

From the outset of Melville's marriage to Elizabeth Shaw, his father-in-law, Judge Lemuel Shaw, had come to his aid repeatedly with financial assistance, helping to buy their first house at 103 Fourth Avenue in New York and later to buy Arrowhead. Shaw advanced the funds necessary for Melville's 1856–57 trip to Europe and the Levant (see his 15 May 1860 letter to Melville, below) and came to Melville's aid that same year when T. D. Stewart was pressuring him for the repayment of a loan and the interest on it (see Melville's 12 and 22 May 1856 letters to Shaw). This unsigned copy of Shaw's letter issuing one hundred dollars, half of it designated for Elizabeth Melville's use, is a further example of his assistance and also a further indication of Melville's difficult financial situation.

New England Bank
$100 Boston 8 Nov 1858
Pay to Herman Melville Esq. or order
one hundred dollars.
Lemuel Shaw
— To the Cashier. —

Boston 8 Nov 1858

My Dear Herman,

Believing that in providing your family supplies for the approaching winter, some pecuniary assistance will be convenient to you I enclose you above my check, on the New England Bank above for $100 one hundred dollars, for which I have no doubt, the Bank in your town will give you the money. To avoid danger of loss or miscarriage, I have made it payable to your order. I will thank you to hand half of it, to Elizabeth for her use, though it will all come to the same use in the end.

We shall sadly miss your visit with that of Elizabeth & your children as Thanksgiving approaches. Our family circle will show a large vacancy. We expect a visit from you however, whether Elizabeth can accompany you or not, as I perceive you have an engagement to deliver a lecture here; though if she could make arrangements for the care of the family/

Original document not located. Text from unfinished manuscript copy (unsigned) on a 20 × 24.9 cm sheet of white wove paper with lines, embossed with the manufacturer's oval stamp enclosing a train above the initials "P & R". Shaw inscribed both sides of the leaf, in ink, and noted on the second page "copy of letter to Herman".

LOCATION (of copy): HCL-M.

PUBLICATION: (partial) *Log*, II, 596.

TEXTUAL NOTES: New England . . . cashier. —] *later crossed through in ink, with* 100 *and* Pay . . . Shaw *also lined through in ink* • will be convenient to you] *interlined* • Thanksgiving] Thanks- | giving

FROM JAMES GRANT WILSON
BEFORE 1 DECEMBER 1858 · CHICAGO

Unlocated. A letter inviting Melville to lecture for the Chicago Young Men's Association can be inferred from his second letter, of 8 December 1858, to the representative of the lecture committee, James Grant Wilson. For more on Wilson, see the headnote to Melville's 8 December letter.

FROM JAMES GRANT WILSON
1 DECEMBER 1858 · CHICAGO

Unlocated. A second letter from James Grant Wilson, listing the other lecturers engaged to speak in Chicago, their fees, and the possible dates for Melville's engagement, is cited in his 8 December 1858 reply to Wilson.

FROM THE YONKERS LIBRARY ASSOCIATION
BEFORE 6 DECEMBER 1858 · YONKERS

Unlocated. A letter inviting Melville to lecture for the Library Association in Yonkers, New York, can be inferred from his lecture engagement notebook (see the NN *Piazza Tales* volume, p. 807). Melville delivered there, for the first time, his second lecture, "The South Seas," on 6 December 1858.

FROM JAMES GRANT WILSON
AFTER 8 DECEMBER 1858 · CHICAGO

Unlocated. A third letter from James Grant Wilson listing "additional appointments" for Melville in towns near Chicago can be inferred from Melville's 8 December 1858 letter to Wilson. The 14 March 1856 minutes of the Young Men's Association of Milwaukee record that Milwaukee had joined with Chicago, Rockford, and Madison in an agreement that "the several Associations should unite in obtaining lecturers for the winter" in order to "induce acceptance on the spot of desirable men who would refuse a single call," and apparently that cooperation was still in effect (Area Research Center, Golda Meir Library, University of Wisconsin–Milwaukee). Thus it seems likely that Wilson arranged Melville's lectures for the Young Men's Association in Milwaukee, Wisconsin, on 25 February 1859, the Young Men's Association in Rockford, Illinois, on 28 February 1859, and the Lyceum in Quincy, Illinois, on 2 March 1859.

FROM GEORGE L. DUYCKINCK
BEFORE 13 DECEMBER 1858 · NEW YORK

Unlocated. A note, possibly about arrangements for Melville's lecture for the New-York Historical Society, is cited in his 13 December 1858 letter to George Duyckinck.

FROM THE PITTSFIELD LECTURE COMMITTEE
BEFORE 14 DECEMBER 1858 · PITTSFIELD

Unlocated. Although Melville's engagement to lecture in his own town may simply have been arranged in person, a written invitation can be inferred from his lecture engagement notebook (see the NN *Piazza Tales* volume, p. 807). Melville delivered his lecture "The South Seas" at Pittsfield on 14 December 1858.

FROM GEORGE L. DUYCKINCK
[17?] DECEMBER 1858 · NEW YORK

Unlocated. A brief letter from George Duyckinck declining Melville's 13 December 1858 request to change his date to lecture for the New-York Historical Society was immediately misplaced, as Melville humorously explained in his 20 December reply: "Your note (received on Saturday) is unaccountably among the missing. — Some one must have pilfered it for the autograph."

FROM THE MERCANTILE LIBRARY
BEFORE 20 DECEMBER 1858 · BALTIMORE

Unlocated. A letter inviting Melville to lecture for the Mercantile Library in Baltimore can be inferred from his lecture engagement notebook (see the NN *Piazza Tales* volume, p. 807) and from his 20 December 1858 letter to George Duyckinck, worrying whether he could get to Baltimore the day after lecturing in New York. In the event, Melville was able to deliver his lecture "The South Seas" at Baltimore on 8 February 1859.

1859

FROM GEORGE L. DUYCKINCK
BEFORE 30 JANUARY 1859 · NEW YORK

Unlocated. A letter from George Duyckinck about Melville's forthcoming 7 February lecture for the New-York Historical Society is cited in Elizabeth Melville's 30 January 1859 response on her husband's behalf: "Mr Melville is absent in Boston, and in reply to your letter (which I open in accordance with his instructions) I am happy to give you the desired information. The title of his lecture is 'The South Seas,' and may be so advertised" (NYPL-D).

FROM THE MECHANIC APPRENTICES' LIBRARY ASSOCIATION
BEFORE 31 JANUARY 1859 · BOSTON

Unlocated. A letter inviting Melville to lecture for the Mechanic Apprentices' Library Association in Boston can be inferred from his lecture engagement notebook (see the NN *Piazza Tales* volume, p. 807). Melville delivered his lecture "The South Seas" there on 31 January 1859. For a response from one of his listeners, see the letter just below.

FROM NORMAN W. STEARNS
1 FEBRUARY 1859 · BOSTON

Norman Whitney Stearns (b. 1831) is listed in the 1860 Adams-Sampson Boston directory as a draughtsman who worked at 3 State Street and lived in Jamaica Plain. In 1864 he became listed as a patent-lawyer. Nothing more has been located about Stearns's earlier residence in the Samoan Islands, nor does the *National Union Catalog* list a grammar or vocabulary of the Polynesian language by Stearns. Whether Melville answered him is not known, although it seems likely that he did so, since he saved Stearns's letter. The card Stearns enclosed with his address is now unlocated.

Boston, Feb. 1, 1859.

Herman Melville Esq,

Last evening I was present at your lecture on the South Seas, before the Mechanics Apprentices Library Association, and as I have recently returned from Polynesia where I lived in various localities for nearly six years, I feel assured I am in possession of valuable information relating to the languages manners and customs of some of the groups in the vicinity of the equator, more particularly of the Samoan or Navigator's Isl's, where I resided for 20 months, (8 months of which time) I was domiciled with the natives. As I was not a "Beach Comer" I had every facility for obtaining a correct and thorough knowledge of their peculiarities and have just finished a vocabulary of their tongue, comprising a grammar and a dictionary of about 3000 words.

There has never been any printed language of the Samoans nor yet any manuscript of the same. I am quite positive in saying that my vocabulary is accurate and complete. I am satisfied if you intend to enlarge on your favorite theme I can furnish you with abundant material for an interesting yarn. I will warrant that what I may have to furnish you respecting the Samoans shall be true narritives of my own experience and will comprise many pleasant anecdotes of this intelligent race.

Should you choose to notice this, direct as per card enclosed.

Respectfully,
Norman W. Stearns.

ALS on a 20 × 31.3 cm part-sheet (torn along the left edge) of white wove paper with lines, embossed with the manufacturer's shield-like stamp enclosing the name "CARSON BROS. & CO." Stearns inscribed both sides of the leaf, in ink.

LOCATION: HCL-M.

PUBLICATION: (partial) *Log*, II, 599.

TEXTUAL NOTE: manuscript] m *written over* of

FROM WILLIAM H. BARRY
2 FEBRUARY 1859 · LYNN

Unlocated. A letter inviting Melville to lecture at Lynn, Massachusetts, is cited in his 12 February 1859 reply. Barry sent a second letter on 8 February (see below).

FROM OLIVER RUSS
4 FEBRUARY 1859 · CORFU

Perhaps prompted by a newspaper report of one of Melville's lectures, Oliver Russ, an old shipmate from the U.S.S. *United States*, now living in Corfu, New York, wrote Melville this account of his life since their shipboard days. Melville apparently answered shortly afterwards and then wrote again on 18 December 1860, as Russ acknowledged in his 24 December 1860 letter, below. Neither of Melville's letters has been located. See the NN *White-Jacket*, p. 416, for a discussion of Russ as the prototype for White Jacket's intelligent and well-read friend Nord (cf. Melville's description of him in chap. 13).

Dear Sir I write you a few lines agreeable to a promis long since made to my wife and son but first of all I will let you know who I am you probably have not forgoen all of the crew of the Old Frigate United States and more especialy our visit to the city of Lima. my name is Oliver Russ although I went by another name when at sea to conceal from my friends the unwise step I had taken and that name was Edward Norton I assumed my right name on coming home. Now what I wish to say is that I in the course of the next year after our return from sea I took to wife one of the fair daughters of the state of Maine and in two years from that day a son was born to us a substancial token of our mutual love and to manifest the high regard in which I have ever held yourself I named him Herman Melville Russ at that time I did not expect ever to hear of you again or that you would be numbered among the literary writers of the day. I say this to let you know that it was not the almost universal desire to name after great men that led me to do it, but a regard for those qualities which an acquaintance of eighteen month with you led me so much to admire. Now there is nothing that would give me more pleasure than to see you or even to have you write to me yet I do not expect it would afford you any pleasure; but as I have often promised my boy that I would write to you and that you would probably send him some present as a keepsake I now proseed to keep my promis

I am doing all my means (which are quite limited) will allow in educating my son as he is an only child and has a great affinity for books If you will answer this I will write more particular if desired

I remain your humble servt

Oliver Russ

To Herman Melville

Corfu Feb 4th 1859
> Direct to Oliver Russ
> > Corfu Genesee Co
> > N.Y.

P.S. I live near Mr Green the Father of Toby, although Richard has been home several times I have not seen him

---

ALS on a 23.4 × 19.4 cm sheet, folded in half, of white laid paper, faintly embossed with the manufacturer's oval stamp. Russ inscribed the first three pages, in ink. Elizabeth Melville noted in pencil on the fourth page "Oliver Russ | old shipmate | Feb 4–1859". The envelope is addressed "Herman Melville Esq | Pittsfield Mass"; its stamp was later torn off.

LOCATION: HCL-M.

PUBLICATION: (partial) *Log*, II, 599–600.

TEXTUAL NOTES: regard in] *before* over *in bottom margin* • promis] *before* over *in bottom margin*

FROM WILLIAM H. BARRY
8 FEBRUARY 1859 · LYNN

Unlocated. A second letter in addition to Barry's 2 February letter (above), inviting Melville to lecture at Lynn, Massachusetts, is cited in Melville's 12 February 1859 reply. See also the entry just below.

FROM WILLIAM H. BARRY
AFTER 12 FEBRUARY 1859 · LYNN

Unlocated. In his 12 February 1859 reply (above) to William H. Barry's 2 and 8 February invitations to lecture in Lynn, Massachusetts, Melville asked Barry to be "kind enough to reply immediately, that I may get your letter before leaving home again." Presumably Barry complied with Melville's request, and upon his return

Melville made specific arrangements with Barry in a now unlocated letter. On 16 March 1859 Melville gave his lecture "The South Seas" at Sagamore Hall in Lynn; no record of when he delivered his second lecture, "Statues in Rome," has been found, but he was paid for two lectures (Sealts, *Melville as Lecturer*, pp. 91–92).

FROM GIOVANNI SPAGGIARI
9 APRIL 1859 · NEW YORK

Giovanni Spaggiari was a translator of Latin and Italian who had been in New York since at least November 1858 (the date on one of his translations published in New York). As he indicates in his letter, the editor of the *New-York Evening Post*, William Cullen Bryant, published at least two samples of his work. The 4 January 1859 issue included his Latin and Italian versions of Bryant's "The Death of the Flowers" along with the English original, and the 24 March issue included his Latin and Italian versions of John MacMullen's "The Jasmine" along with the English original. (Trow's New York directory lists MacMullen as a teacher who lived at the 900 Broadway address Spaggiari gives for his own mail in this letter.) The enclosed "Apostrophe to America" (in the form of both a printed clipping and Spaggiari's handwritten translation of it) was in fact a quite literal Italian translation from the very free French translation by Philarète Chasles of Yoomy's song in Chapter 154 of *Mardi* (see the NN edition, pp. 501-2 and 670). Chasles's translation appeared in the *Revue des deux mondes* 2 (15 May 1849), 566-67; reprinted in his *Études sur la littérature et les moeurs des Anglo-Américains au XIXe siècle* (Paris: Amyot, 1851), p. 229. The source of the printed clipping is not known: the *Mondo Illustrato* cited by Spaggiari ceased publication from before *Mardi* appeared until after this letter was written. Spaggiari's proposed *Latin-English-Italian Anthology* described in this letter was issued in fascicles during 1861 and 1862 (London: Trübner; Rome: Spithoever; New York: Wiley). Next to each other on the same wide unnumbered page was Yoomy's song from *Mardi*, credited to Melville, and Spaggiari's further Latin translation of the apostrophe, with the initials J. S. The fact that Spaggiari did not attribute the apostrophe to Melville or designate Yoomy's song (or Chasles's translation) as its source suggests that Melville did reply to his letter, disavowing his authorship of the apostrophe as worded but pointing out its source in Yoomy's song. Whether or not Melville was aware of the French translation as the direct source is not known: it was not included in the portion of Chasles's article printed, in English translation, in the *Literary World* (4 and 11 August 1849), nor in the article as translated in his *Anglo-American Literature and Manners* (New York: Scribner's, 1852), where instead Melville's own text of Yoomy's song was given (p. 136; Melville's wife owned a copy of this book, Sealts 135).

Herman Melville, Esq.

Dear Sir,
I take the liberty of addressing this letter to you, desirous as I am of knowing whether the enclosed apostrophe to America, which I

found a few years ago in the "Mondo Illustrato," a magazine of Turin, as a translation from the English of "Ermanno Meiville" is really yours; and if it is so, would you be so kind as to let me know (in a note to be addressed to me, 900 Broadway, — politeness of Mr. J. MacMullen) where I can find the English original? I should be greatly obliged to you for such a favour; and then I could avail myself of it for the Latin-English-Italian translated Anthology which I am preparing: a specimen of which I had the honour to show to your brother, Allan Melville, Esq., and a sample of this publication is to be found in the Evening Post of the 4th of January (the Death of the Flowers by W. C. Bryant, translated into Latin and Italian verses) and another in the number of the 24th of March —

I have the honour to be, with the highest sentiments of respect and esteem,

New-York, April 9th 1859

Your Obediant Servant,
Giovanni Spaggiari
from Ca'-del-Bosco-di-Sopra (Reggio-in-Lombardy)

[Enclosure: manuscript retranslation from printed Italian version (also enclosed)]

My free America, I salute thee! Land of Spring! Spring, Spring, is better than autumn; It has the whole year before it. Behold the new Land, the Land of Spring — Behold the race which knows no past, which knows no ruins, which does not march in lugubrious triumph beneath old crumbling and falling arches. The wild rose and sweet scented fir form its triumphal arch. It loves the pleasant valleys but does not hide itself in the dark cave of the hermit. Hail to the race of Spring! It is a new Land, in the dawn of its life; It is a giant "neonato" which smiles in its own strength. New World; world of joy! Cradled in the ocean, the morning dew covers its brow. The verdure which hangs around its youthful temples is perfumed. for it, all is freshness, hope, future, joy, enterprise and novelty. The slender fawn gambols around it. The young flowers are still in bud. The Redbreast tries its wings and its morning songs — The Giant extends its arms and tries their strength. Hail to the young bold giant! — Hail to the race of Spring and of the future.

[Enclosure: printed clipping]

«Ti saluto! mia libera America! terra della primavera! La prima-
«vera, la primavera è meglio dell' autunno; essa ha tutto l' anno din-
«nanzi a sè. Ecco la terra nuova, la terra della primavera! Ecco la
«razza che non conosce passato, che non conosce ruine, che non
«marcia in lugubre trionfo sotto vecchi archi che crollano e cadono!
«Il rosajo selvatico e l' abete odoroso sono il suo arco trionfale. Essa
«ama il fondo delle amene valli; non si chiude sotto la cupa grotta
«del romito. Viva la razza della primavera! È una terra nuova nell'
«alba della sua vita; è un gigante neonato che sorride nella sua forza.
«Mondo nuovo, mondo di gioja! l' oceano lo culla, la rugiada del
«mattino copre la sua fronte; la verzura che accarezza le sue giovani
«tempie è profumata. Tutto per lui è freschezza, speranza, avvenire,
«gioja, intrapresa e novità. Lo svelto cerbiatto saltella intorno a lui; i
«giovani fiori sono già in bottone; il pettirosso prova le sue ali ed i
«suoi canti mattutini. Il gigante stende le sue braccia e prova le sue
«forze! Viva il giovane e ardito gigante! Viva la razza della primave-
«ra e dell' avvenire!»

ALS on a 12.7 × 19.9 cm sheet of white wove paper. Spaggiari inscribed only one side of the
leaf, in ink. He inscribed the manuscript enclosure, in ink, on the first two pages of a 22.6 ×
17.9 cm sheet, folded in half, of white laid paper, embossed with the manufacturer's stamp, a
crown, a shield, and two branches (upside down at the bottom of both leaves).

LOCATION: HCL-M.

PUBLICATION: (partial) *Log*, II, 614 (dated 9 April 1860).

TEXTUAL NOTES: Ermanno Meiville] *cut from a printed source (apparently same source as clipping)
and pasted to the letter* • sweet scented] *inserted with caret above canceled* odorous

FROM THE YOUNG MEN'S ASSOCIATION
BEFORE 7 NOVEMBER 1859 · FLUSHING

Unlocated. A letter inviting Melville to lecture for the Young Men's Association,
Flushing, Long Island, can be inferred from his lecture engagement notebook (see
the NN *Piazza Tales* volume, p. 807). Melville delivered his lecture "Traveling" at
Flushing on 7 November 1859.

FROM GEORGE L. DUYCKINCK
BEFORE 14 DECEMBER 1859 · NEW YORK

Unlocated. A letter concerning George Herbert's *The Temple* (Philadelphia: Hazard, 1857; Sealts 270) is cited in Melville's 14 December 1859 reply.

1860

FROM THE PEABODY INSTITUTE
BEFORE 14 FEBRUARY 1860 · SOUTH DANVERS

Unlocated. An invitation from the Peabody Institute in South Danvers, Massachusetts, can be inferred from Melville's lecture engagement notebook (see the NN *Piazza Tales* volume, p. 807). Melville delivered "Traveling" there on 14 February 1860.

FROM THE DOWSE INSTITUTE
BEFORE 21 FEBRUARY 1860 · CAMBRIDGEPORT

Unlocated. An invitation from the Dowse Institute in Cambridgeport, Massachusetts, can be inferred from Melville's lecture engagement notebook (see the NN *Piazza Tales* volume, p. 807). Melville delivered "Traveling" there on 21 February 1860.

FROM LEMUEL SHAW
15 MAY 1860 · BOSTON

In a now unlocated letter, to which this letter is a reply, Melville had apparently written to his father-in-law about his decision to join his youngest brother, Thomas, now a ship's captain, on his next voyage. (For more on this trip and Melville's journal of it, see *Journals*, pp. 131–35, 194–207.) As with all of Shaw's now known letters to Melville, the larger part of this letter deals with financial arrangements. In recounting Shaw's various loans and advances to his son-in-law, it serves as a summary of their financial dealings. As Shaw states at the conclusion, the "effect" of this letter was to cancel all of Melville's debts to him, leaving Elizabeth Melville as the sole owner of the Pittsfield property (15 May 1860 conveyance [MHS-S]). Shaw's attorney in Pittsfield, James D. Colt, to whom Shaw refers Melville for further legal advice, later organized a petition supporting Melville's search for a consulship (see Melville's 27 March 1861 letter to Julius Rockwell).

Boston 15 May 1860.

My dear Herman
    I am very glad to learn from your letter that you intend to accept

Thomas' invitation to go on his next voyage. I think it affords a fair prospect of being of permanent benefit to your health, and it will afford me the greatest pleasure to do anything in my power to aid your preparation, and make the voyage most agreeable and beneficial to you.

The prospect of your early departure renders it proper and necessary to bring to a definite conclusion the subject we have had a considerable time under consideration, a settlement of the matter of the Pittsfield estate, with a view to which you handed me your deeds, when I was in Pittsfield last autumn.

You will recollect that when you proposed to purchase a house in N. York I advanced to you $2000. and afterwards, when you purchased the Brewster place, I again advanced you $3000. For these sums, as well as for another loan of $500, afterwards, I took your notes. This I did, not because I had then any fixed determination to treat the advances as debts, to be certainly repaid, but I was in doubt at the time in reference to other claims upon me, and how my affairs would be ultimately arranged, what I should be able to do by way of provision for my daughter, and I put these advances upon the footing of loans until some future adjustment.

I always supposed that you considered the two first of the abovenamed advances as having substantially gone into the purchase of the Brewster farm, and that I had some equitable claim upon it as security. I presume it was upon that ground that you once sent me a mortgage of the estate prepared by your brother Allan. I never put that mortgage on record nor made any use of it; and if the conveyances are made, which I now propose, that mortgage will become superseded and utterly nugatory.

What I now propose is to give up to you the above mentioned notes in full consideration of your conveyance to me of your present homestead, being all the Brewster purchase except what you sold to Mr. Willis. This being done and the estate vested in me, I propose to execute a deed conveying the same in fee to Elizabeth. This will vest the fee as an estate of inheritance in her, subject of course to your rights as her husband during your life. If you wish to know more particularly what will be the legal effect and operation of these conveyances Mr. Colt will explain it to you fully. I have written to him and enclosed him a draft of a deed for you to execute to me and my deed executed, to be delivered to you and your notes to be surren-

dered. I have explained the whole matter to Mr. Colt and I have full
confidence in his prudence and fidelity. I do not see any advantage in
giving the business any more notoriety than will arise from putting
the deeds on record.

Elizabeth now writes me that you wish the note for $600., given
by the town and coming from the sale of the Brewster place, that
part of it not sold to Mr. Willis, so placed that it may be applied as
you have heretofore, in your own mind, appropriated it, for building a new barn.

I propose to treat this as I did the estate itself; first purchase it of
you for a full consideration and then apply it to Elizabeth's use. In
looking for a consideration for this purchase there is the interest of
the above notes not computed in the consideration for the deed and
now amounting to several thousand dollars.

But there is another consideration, respecting which I have
never had any direct communication I believe, but I can see no
reason why it should not be now clearly understood. When you
went to Europe in the fall of 1856 I advanced the money necessary
for your outfit and the expenses of your tour. This was done
through your brother Allan and amounted to about fourteen or
fifteen hundred dollars. In my own mind, though I took no note
or obligation for it, I treated it like the other advances, to be regarded as advance by way of loan or a gift according to some future arrangement. I propose now to consider that sum as a set off
against the note of $600. and, as to all beyond that, to consider it
cancelled and discharged. This will make the note mine. At the
same time I propose to appropriate it to its original use, to build a
barn, in which case it will go to increase the value of the estate
already Elizabeth's, or should anything occur to prevent such use
of the money I shall appropriate it in some other way to her use.
The effect of this arrangement will be to cancel and discharge all
debt and pecuniary obligations of every description from you to
myself. You will then leave home with the conscious satisfaction
of knowing that you are free from debt; that if by a Providential
dispensation you should be prevented from ever returning to your
beloved family some provision will have been made at least for a
home, for your wife and children.

Affectionately and ever faithfully
your sincere friend

Original document not located. Text from manuscript copy (unsigned) on a 39.8 × 24.8 cm sheet, folded in half, of white laid paper with lines, embossed with the manufacturer's oval stamp with the name "HOPPER, LEWIS & CO" surrounding a shield with "BOSTON" printed across it. Samuel S. Shaw inscribed all four pages, in ink. This alternative source for the letter is emended by NN at one point (see below). Eleanor Melville Metcalf noted in pencil below the closing, "*Copy*, made by Samuel S. Shaw, of a letter of Judge Shaw's."

LOCATION (of copy): HCL-M.

PUBLICATION: Weaver, pp. 366–69.

TEXTUAL NOTES (for symbols used, see p. 840): homestead] home- | stead · Elizabeth.] NN; ~∧

FROM EVERT A. DUYCKINCK
BETWEEN 22 AND 26 MAY 1860 · NEW YORK

Unlocated. A letter responding to Melville's 21 May 1860 request that Duyckinck supervise the publication of a volume of his poetry is cited in Melville's subsequent 28 May reply. Melville's reply states that he received Duyckinck's letter "on the eve of my leaving Pittsfield" (sometime between 22 and 26 May).

FROM SAMUEL S. SHAW
BEFORE 16 OCTOBER 1860 · BOSTON

Unlocated. A "very interesting" letter from his brother-in-law is cited in Melville's 16 October 1860 reply.

FROM SARAH HUYLER MOREWOOD
BEFORE 2 DECEMBER 1860 · PITTSFIELD

Unlocated. After returning from San Francisco in November of 1860, Melville apparently went to Boston, where his wife and children had been staying with the Shaws. A letter from Sarah Morewood to either Melville or his wife, inviting them to stay with her in Pittsfield while they got their own house warmed up and in order, can be inferred from Melville's 2 December 1860 reply.

FROM OLIVER RUSS
24 DECEMBER 1860 · PEMBROKE

This second known letter from Oliver Russ (see his earlier letter dated 4 February 1859, above) replied to a now unlocated 18 December letter from Melville, written not long after his 1860 voyage to San Francisco via Cape Horn (see *Journals*, pp. 131–35, 194–207). In the meantime Russ had experienced some bad luck and had moved to Pembroke, New York. Since Melville had originally planned to go around the world, the notice that Oliver Russ saw in print may have been correct in reporting that Melville was embarking on a trip that included Europe. The fact that Russ construed Melville's single trip as two trips, however, shows what an exalted notion he had of Melville's life as a famous writer. Melville had evidently tried to explain the "rather primitive stile" in which he actually lived in Pittsfield, but his willingness to send Russ's son the requested keepsake, despite the meager state of his finances at this time, presumably further fueled Russ's fanciful image of his old shipmate's life (see Russ's 14 January 1861 acknowledgment of this gift, below).

Pembroke Dec 24th 1860

Friend Melville Dear Sir I recd your kind favour of the 18' inst in due time and its perusal gave me the greatest pleasure posable its reception was altogather unexpected but not unwelcomed. my neglect to answer your last favour was owing to the fact that I delayed it from time to time untill I saw a notice in some public print that you was about going to Europe. If I understand your letter aright you have been enjoying another trip around Cape Horn to the ever delightful Pacific did its scenes appear to you as they did when we were there has sixteen years wrought no change there. if not I fear it has with you and me. although the years are recording their exit on my furrowed brow and whitened for locks I should like to revisit those scenes once more You ask me to write what I am doing out here. I will tell you with the greatest pleasure I have been farming on a small scale for a few years but last summer I had my dwelling house burned and sustained considerable loss and finally sold out and I have bought a pleasent situation in a small vilage called Richville in the town of Pembroke Genesee Co. N.Y. I keep a boot & shoe store and shop for making and repairing I intend to start a small grocery in the spring that and the Post Office and boots & shoes will comprise my whole business for the present. by this you may infer that I live like yourself in rather primitive stile only a little more so, but if you will but pay me a visit I will convince you that we can welcome you as warmly as if I were a Prince and that we enjoy some of the comforts of life in our humble way *Say will you Come* You ask if there is any Express that reaches us I can say yes any package directed to me would come direct by Express.   Mark   Oliver Russ,

Pembroke Genesee C^o
N.Y.
By Express to Richville Station
New York Central RR

In regard to your sending something as a keepsake to my boy I would say that you would gratify a long cherished desire to possess something of the kind I always told him from his infancy up that sometime I would write to you on the subject and I thought you would send him something to remember you by I did not expect nor do I desire that it should be a valuable present I think your selection a good one and I have only one request more to make and that is with your approbation I should like to have your *Ambrotype*, and that of your *family* I live but a short distance from Mr Green the father of Toby I often see the old gentleman but have never seen Richard (Toby) but learn that he is now in Mishagan, and that he is not a very desirable patern for a husband and father but perfection is not to be found in man

Receive our respects and best wishes for your self and family. From your old friend and

Shipmate
Oliver Russ

To Herman Melville

Write soon and often.
Direct to Oliver Russ
   Pembroke N.Y.

ALS on a 38.6 × 24.4 cm sheet, folded in half, of white laid paper, faintly embossed with the manufacturer's circular stamp. Russ inscribed the first three pages, in ink. Elizabeth Melville noted in pencil on the fourth page "Oliver Russ | Old Shipmate | Dec 24 – 1860".

LOCATION: HCL-M.

PUBLICATION: (partial) *Log*, II, 630.

TEXTUAL NOTES: town of] *before* over *in bottom margin* · little] *written over* great · sending something] thing *inserted above caret* · remember you] you *added before canceled* him

1861

FROM CHARLES SCRIBNER
1861 · NEW YORK

In preparation for a revised edition (published in 1866) of the Duyckincks' *Cyclopædia of American Literature* (1855), the publisher, Charles Scribner, sent a form letter to all the writers included in the work (see Scribner's earlier May 1854 form letter, pp. 634–35 above, for more about the first edition). Although Melville's copy of the printed letter is unlocated, it was presumably the same as the copy preserved in the Duyckinck papers. No reply either from Melville or his brother Allan (see the headnote to Scribner's May 1854 form letter, p. 634 above) is known to survive among the Duyckinck papers, and no entry on Melville was included in their 1866 *Supplement to the Cyclopædia of American Literature*.

New York,   1861

To

IT is our intention to prepare for the coming season, a new revised and enlarged edition of the CYCLOPÆDIA OF AMERICAN LITERATURE, by Messrs. EVERT A. and GEORGE L. DUYCKINCK. A Supplement will be added, bringing the work down to the present year. Will you oblige us by such information in reference to yourself and your writings as may supply us with the necessary authentic material for *A Biographical and Literary Notice* according to the plan of the work already executed. Please communicate the full and exact titles of your books and other publications, with their dates and such explanatory statements of their scope and object as may aid us in placing an adequate, though brief, chronicle of them before the public. Any information you may send will be used with care, following the well known method of the book, which hitherto, it is believed, has proved useful alike to authors and the public. The work will be edited as heretofore in the several editions, by the Messrs. DUYCKINCK. An early reply will oblige

Yours respectfully,
CHARLES SCRIBNER.

Address, CHARLES SCRIBNER,
Publisher Cyclopædia American Literature,
124 Grand Street, N.Y.

Melville's copy not located. Text from printed copy (with blank spaces for the addressee and date).

LOCATION (of copy): NYPL-D.

FROM RICHARD T. GREENE
4 JANUARY 1861 · CHICAGO

Although Melville's old friend Richard Tobias (Toby) Greene dated this letter 4 January 1860, his remarks on " 'Old Abe' " taking "the oath of office on the Capitol Steps in spite of all fire eating braggadocios" indicates that it was written on 4 January 1861, a year later, after Lincoln's election and prior to his inauguration on 4 March 1861. As Melville did not know that Greene had moved to Chicago some eighteen months earlier, this seems to be their first communication since their letters in January 1858 (see above). In his recent letter cited here, Melville must have proposed sending engraved spoons to his namesakes—Herman Melville Greene (Greene's son) and Richard Melville Hair (Greene's nephew). He was probably prompted to do so by Oliver Russ's 4 February 1859 and 24 December 1860 letters, both of which had expressed the wish that Melville send his son, Herman Melville Russ, a "keepsake." The correspondence about this matter continued with Melville's now unlocated 10 January letter to Greene asking for his namesakes' addresses and with Greene's 16 January reply to that inquiry.

Just exactly why Greene wrote, quoting Gray's *Elegy*, that he was " 'wasting [his] sweetness on the desert air' of this fast country" is not entirely clear. He was listed in 1859 and 1860 Chicago directories as well as the 1860 census as a "physician" in partnership with James W. Flower, a relative, with whom he had offices first at 189 Lake Street and then at 202 State Street. In the 1861 Chicago directory, however, he was listed with only a home address—at the corner of Warren and Robey avenues—and with no professional title, even though Flower continued to be listed as a physician at the State Street address.

Chicago Jany. 4th 1860

My dear Old Shipmate; —

Your kind favour only received yesterday. I removed from Sandusky about eighteen months since, and your letter, after some delay, was forwarded to me here.

For your kind remembrance of me, accept my warmest thanks. We are all up in this Prairie country, and if you will send the "spoons" by Express to me at *202 State St. Chicago*, I will see that the boys get them

Hope you enjoy good health, and can yet stow away your "five shares of duff"! I would be delighted to see you and "freshen the nip" while you would be spinning a yarn as long as the Main top bowline. I shall most certainly avail myself of your kind invitation if ever I travel that way, which may not be far distant

For myself I am doing nothing, except "wasting my sweetness on the desert air" of this fast country. I often have the pleasure of seeing our future President. "Old Abe" looks all right, and its my opinion, he will take the oath of office on the Capitol Steps in spite of all fire eating braggadocios.

I think I will go to New York soon and see if I can get into business there I have been very unfortunate up here, and would like, at least, to get a situation, if I cannot retrieve whats lost

Mrs Greene & Herman Melville(!) join me in kind remembrances to you

Truly yours
"Toby"

ALS, " 'Toby' ", on a 16.3 × 20.3 cm part-sheet (torn along the left edge) of white laid paper with lines, embossed with the manufacturer's stamp of St. George killing the dragon. Greene inscribed both sides of the leaf, in ink.

LOCATION: HCL-M.

PUBLICATION: (partial) *Log*, II, 632.

TEXTUAL NOTE: braggadocios] *first* g *written over* a

FROM OLIVER RUSS
14 JANUARY 1861 · PEMBROKE

This letter acknowledging Melville's gift—presumably of an engraved spoon—to Russ's son and Melville's namesake, Herman Melville Russ, is the last known letter from Melville's former shipmate. Melville's earlier letter, which evidently announced the gift and asked for an ambrotype, is unlocated.

Friend Melville Dear Sir Your letter and present arrived in due time all safe and were received with the greatest satisfaction and delight by us all, and after a thourough inspection by all the house hold were consigned to a secluded corner of a drawer there to be kept for years to come, but its occasional appearance will ever revive those kindly feelings which we have ever cherished for the giver, it brings to mind anew all those circumstances which made us acquainted and all the incedents which hapened while we were togather.

How is your health now did your voyage around the cape improve it how do you enjoy your self living in the country all these things and many more I should like to know write soon as conveniant for it will be greatfully received by your old friend

Oliver Russ

To Herman Melville

Pembroke Jan 14th 1861

PS I will send that ambrotype as soon as I can obtain a good one O. R

ALS on a 19.4 × 24.5 cm sheet of white laid paper, faintly embossed with the manufacturer's circular stamp. Russ inscribed only one side of the leaf, in ink. Elizabeth Melville noted in pencil on the verso "Oliver Russ | Old Shipmate | Jan 14 – 1861".

LOCATION: HCL-M.

PUBLICATION: (partial) *Log*, II, 632.

TEXTUAL NOTE: How] *paragraph indicated by large space on same line*

FROM RICHARD T. GREENE
16 JANUARY 1861 · CHICAGO

In his 10 January 1861 letter, now unlocated, Melville apparently asked Greene for the full names and addresses of his nephew, Richard Melville Hair, and son, Herman Melville Greene, in order to arrange for the engraved spoons he was sending them (see Greene's earlier letter of 4 January 1861 and his subsequent 8 April 1861 letter acknowledging the spoons).

Chicago Jany 16/61

Dear Melville

In reply to your note of the 10th

The name of my Nephew is "*Richard Melville Hair*" His mother's name and address is *Mrs Mary Anne Hair* Corfu*, Genesee Co N.Y. There is an Express office there, it is on the NY Central RR.

My Son's name is Herman Melville Greene, Residence 202 *State St, Chicago*

*The name given this place on the RR is *Pembroke* Genesee Co. but the P.O. is Corfu. A line to Richard At Corfu will reach him so he will get the Spoon

Sincerely Yours
Toby

ALS, "Toby", on a 12.4 × 20.2 cm part-sheet (torn along the left edge) of white laid paper with lines, embossed with the manufacturer's stamp of a lion atop a crown. Greene inscribed both sides of the leaf, in ink, and addressed the envelope "Herman Melville Esq | Pittsfield | Mass"; it was postmarked in Chicago on 18 January. Elizabeth Melville noted in pencil on the envelope "Toby".

LOCATION: HCL-M.

PUBLICATION: (very partial) *Log*, II, 632.

TEXTUAL NOTE: him] *before wiped period*

FROM R. M. HAIR
13 FEBRUARY 1861 · BUFFALO

As directed in Richard Tobias (Toby) Greene's 16 January letter (just above), Melville sent his gift for Richard Melville Hair to Corfu, New York, in care of Hair's mother (Greene's sister). Little is known of Hair, but this letter indicates that he was old enough to be living away from home by this time (and two years later he was a lieutenant in General Nathaniel P. Banks's Louisiana campaign to open the Mississippi River; see Greene's 20 October 1863 letter, below). The "appropriate present" was presumably an engraved spoon (see Greene's letter of 4 January 1861 to Melville, above).

Buffalo Feby, 13ᴵᴵ 1861.

Herman Melville Esq. ⎫
Pittsfield, Mass.   ⎭ Dear Sir

The Package containing your really nice and appropriate present was duly received at Corfu. But as I now am and have been for some time residing in Buffalo, Some delay was occasioned in my receiveing it; but at the earliest possible moment I beg leave to offer you my Sincere thanks for your Kind rememberance of myself.

Respecty. Yours
R M. Hair

ALS on a 19.8 × 25.1 cm part-sheet (torn along the left edge) of white laid paper with lines, embossed with the manufacturer's stamp of a domed building. The letter is inscribed on only one side of the leaf, in ink. Elizabeth Shaw Melville noted in pencil below the signature "Toby's nephew".

LOCATION: HCL-M.

FROM R. H. DANA, JR.
21 MARCH 1861 · [BOSTON?]

Unlocated. Responding promptly to the request in Melville's 20 March 1861 letter from New York, Dana wrote to Charles Sumner in Melville's behalf on 21 March. Dana's letter to Sumner also states that he had sent a letter to Melville explaining his policy toward making political recommendations: "I have told Melville that my rule prevents my giving him a letter or paper; but does not prevent my naming him favorably in my regular correspondence, & that I should do in my letters to you. I like the notion of such consulships going to men of letters, — of note in the Republic of letters; & Melville is a capital good fellow, good manners & feelings. Duty requires me to suggest a doubt whether his health is sufficient. Of that I know nothing, & you can judge, on seeing him" (HCL–Sumner Collection). Since Melville had explained that he was leaving for Washington, Dana probably directed his letter there.

FROM PETER GANSEVOORT
23 MARCH 1861 · ALBANY

This letter replies to Melville's 20 March 1861 request that Peter Gansevoort forward to Washington a letter from Melville to his uncle's acquaintance Thurlow Weed (see p. 361 above), in aid of Melville's office-seeking efforts. See the headnote to Melville's 20 March request and his earlier letter of 15 March 1861 to his uncle for a full discussion of those efforts.

Saturday
Albany 23 March 1861

My dear Herman

Your letter of 20ᵗʰ insᵗ enclosing one to Mʳ Weed did not reach me until this evening — I immediately sent your note to Mʳ Weed — My waiter left it at his house — & was informed that Mʳ Weed had yesterday gone to Washington — You of course will see him there & thus have the best opportunity to so avail yourself of his kind services & powerful influence

He will no doubt, advise you frankly as to your prospects & if the Post at Florence is engaged, suggest some other position — With my earnest wishes for your success & welfare I remain

Yours truly & affectionately

Final document not located. Text from draft letter (unsigned) on a 19.9 × 14.7 cm part-sheet (torn along the right and bottom edges) of blue wove paper with lines. Peter Gansevoort inscribed only one side of the leaf, in pencil.

LOCATION (of draft): NYPL-GL.

PUBLICATION: (very partial) *Log*, II, 637.

TEXTUAL NOTES: enclosing . . . Weed] *inserted above caret* • your] *inserted above canceled* it • My waiter] *inserted above successively canceled* it | | but | | It was *and before successively canceled* who | | left • left it] it *inserted above caret and before canceled* the le • & was] *inserted above caret* • that Mʳ] *below* yesterday *inserted in pencil; later canceled in ink* • yesterday] *inserted above in ink* • gone to] *inserted above canceled* left for • Washington] *before canceled* on the yesterday • You] *added before* Of *(vestigial capital)* • course] *before canceled* you • thus] *inserted above* • opportunity to] to *written over of* • avail] *altered from* availing of *without deleting of (vestigial)* • kind] *after canceled* influence & • & powerful influence] *added* • advise] *after canceled* word-start • & welfare] *inserted above* • I] *rewritten*

FROM JULIUS ROCKWELL
25 MARCH 1861 · PITTSFIELD

Unlocated. A letter from Julius Rockwell, enclosing a letter of recommendation to Senator Charles Sumner on Melville's behalf, is cited in Melville's 27 March 1861 reply. Melville presented the letter of recommendation to Sumner on 28 March; it survives in the archives of the Lincoln administration.

[Enclosure:]

Pittsfield (Mass)
March 25. 1861.

Honorable Charles Sumner
My Dear Sir
    Give me credit to say I have not troubled you before for your love & patronage But my neighbor & friend *Herman Melville*, author of Omoo — Typee — and many, many, other things which are "joys forever," does want an office. I trust he may have a Consulship. I hope you will aid him in it. Let his genius — his imperfect health — his "res augusti domi" — his noble wife, and his four children — plead, with trumpet tongues for him; and add to them my poor, but earnest, persistent will & wishes. I cannot say more — I will not say less; and if it can be of any use, please say to the President as much as you can in my name, which I trust he may remember with some kindness —

Truly your friend
Julius Rockwell

Manuscript enclosure, preserved among the "Letters of Application and Recommendation for Public Office During the Administrations of Abraham Lincoln and Andrew Johnson 1861-1869" in the eleven-item file concerning Melville's application for an appointment.

LOCATION: National Archives.

TEXTUAL NOTES: "res] e *rewritten* · if] f *written over* t

FROM [ELIZABETH SHAW MELVILLE?]
BEFORE 28 MARCH 1861 · [BOSTON?]

Unlocated. A letter probably from Melville's wife advising him of her father's illness is cited in Melville's 28 March 1861 letter to Charles Sumner. (Lemuel Shaw died two days later on 30 March 1861 in Boston.) Melville may have received an earlier letter from his wife as well, since his 24–25 March 1861 letter to her ends with his comment that he hopes for a letter from her "today"—25 March.

FROM RICHARD T. GREENE
8 APRIL 1861 · CHICAGO

Written shortly after the death of Lemuel Shaw (see the entry just above), this letter acknowledges the receipt of the engraved spoons Melville sent to Greene's son and nephew. Although Greene in his 16 January 1861 letter had directed Melville to send his son's spoon to his Chicago address, Melville evidently sent both of the spoons to Greene's sister Mary Anne Hair, at Corfu, New York, where Greene's father also lived. For more about Greene's son, Herman Melville Greene, see Greene's 20 October 1863 letter to Melville, below, and for more about his nephew, Richard Melville Hair, see Hair's 13 February 1861 letter, above.

Chicago April 8th 1861

Dear Friend:

I should have written you before this, but having learned through the papers of the death of your honoured father-in-law I thought I would not intrude on your sad hours.

Permit me to sympathise with you, and your excellent wife in your recent afflication I too, lost my father-in-law a few weeks since. He died in Ohio at the age of 73, in the blessed hope of a home beyond the grave.

My Sister Mrs Hair recieved the Spoons. I have not got mine yet. It is at my fathers. I shall get it soon.

In the name of your namesake I thank you sincerely for this pledge of kind remembrance, and hope that the kind feelings which exist between us may never be darkened by a shadow. My mind often reverts to the many pleasant moonlight watches we passed together on the deck of the "Acushnet" as we whiled away the hours with yarn and song till "eight bells" I long to meet you once more and should I ever have the opportunity, I shall certainly go and see you

    Mrs Greene joins me in kind remembrance to you

Your Old Shipmate
Toby

ALS, "Toby", on a 12.5 × 20.3 cm part-sheet (torn along the left edge) of white laid paper with lines, faintly embossed with the manufacturer's oval stamp. Greene inscribed both sides of the leaf, in ink.

LOCATION: HCL-M.

PUBLICATION: (partial) *Log*, II, 639–40.

TEXTUAL NOTES: namesake] name-| sake · Toby] *followed by a flourish*

FROM PETER GANSEVOORT
12 AUGUST 1861 · ROCKAWAY

Unlocated. In a letter written while vacationing on Long Island, Peter Gansevoort replied to Melville's 10 August 1861 letter, apparently explaining that he and his family would not be home on "Wednesday next" (14 August), when Melville and his wife hoped to stop in on their way home from Gansevoort, but inviting them to spend a few days at some later time. Peter Gansevoort's letter is cited in his endorsement of Melville's 10 August letter and in Melville's 15 August reply.

1862

FROM AUGUSTA MELVILLE
5 MAY 1862 · [GANSEVOORT?]

Unlocated. Augusta Melville recorded a reply to "Stanwix & Herman" on the fourth page of the 30 April 1862 letter she had received from Stanwix Melville, to which Melville had appended a note on 2 May.

FROM PETER GANSEVOORT
8 AUGUST 1862 · ALBANY

A letter to "Herman at Pittsfield. — " is cited in Peter Gansevoort's memorandum at the bottom of the leaf with his draft letters to Maria Melville and Allan Melville, notifying them of the death of his and Maria's brother (Herman and Allan's uncle),

Wessel Gansevoort, on 7 August 1862. Presumably the letter to Melville was similar to this one drafted to Allan; the reply Melville presumably wrote is unlocated.

                                        Albany 8 Aug^t — 6. P.M.

Dear Allan

    Your Uncle Wessel Gansevoort died at Danby, Vermont, yesterday morning the remains will be brought to my House & the funeral take place at 4 P.M on Saturday. —

                                        Yours very truly —

Original document (of letter to Melville) not located. Text from draft letter (unsigned) to Allan Melville, on a 19.8 × 26 cm part-sheet (torn along the left edge) of blue laid paper with lines. Peter Gansevoort inscribed only one side of the leaf (as described above), in ink.

LOCATION (of draft): NYPL-GL.

TEXTUAL NOTES: Aug^t] *written over wiped* July · Allan] *before canceled* Melville Esq · Danby] D *written over wiped* G · very] v *written over wiped* t

FROM GORHAM D. GILMAN
BEFORE 28 NOVEMBER [1862?] · [NEW YORK?]

Unlocated. A letter from Gilman requesting that Melville return his manuscript "Journal" is cited in Melville's 29 November [1862?] reply. Gilman apparently wrote to Melville while away from his home in Boston, possibly while in New York at the Metropolitan Hotel.

FROM T. APOLEON CHENEY
BEFORE 19 DECEMBER 1862 · WATKINS

Unlocated. A letter requesting a copy of one of Melville's works for the Georgic Library in Watkins, New York, can be inferred from T. Apoleon Cheney's 7 December 1869 letter, below. According to Cheney's letter, Melville answered this request (in a now unlocated letter) on 19 December 1862.

1863

FROM CATHERINE GANSEVOORT
BEFORE 17 FEBRUARY 1863 · ALBANY

Unlocated. A "note enclosing the pictures" of Melville's and Catherine Gansevoort's grandparents is acknowledged in Melville's 17 February 1863 reply to his cousin.

FROM ELIZABETH SHAW MELVILLE
BEFORE 21 MARCH 1863 · BOSTON

Unlocated. A letter from Elizabeth Melville in Boston to her husband in Pittsfield is cited in her 21 March 1863 letter to Augusta Melville, who was also in Pittsfield at this time. She states briefly, "Herman will tell you what I wrote him about Mr Storrow — poor man, he is a great sufferer — " (NYPL-GL). "Mr Storrow" may have been Charles S. Storrow (1809–1904), an eminent Boston engineer, who signed John Hoadley's 19 March 1861 petition to Abraham Lincoln on behalf of Melville's effort to obtain a consulship in 1861.

FROM PETER GANSEVOORT
ON OR AFTER 4 APRIL 1863 · ALBANY

Unlocated. Melville's uncle Peter, as President of the Board of Trustees of the Albany Academy, which Melville had attended in 1830–31 and 1836–37, apparently wrote to his nephew after Melville was appointed to the "committee to make arrangements" for the academy's semicentennial celebration. He did so on or after 4 April, the date on the printed circular which he enclosed. Whether Melville attended the committee meeting on 8 April is not known; he did attend the celebration (see the headnote to the letter just below).

[Enclosure:]

ALBANY ACADEMY ⎱
Dear Sir: *Albany, April 4, 1863* ⎰
    The Albany Academy during the present year completes half a century of its history. The board of trustees have thought that perhaps this event might not be without interest to the thousands who during that time have been educated within its walls. They have therefore resolved that the semi-centennial anniversary of this institution shall in some suitable way be celebrated, and for this purpose they ask that you, as one of its Alumni, should serve as a member of a committee to make arrangements for the occasion.
    This committee is requested to meet for organization and business, on Wednesday evening, April 8th, 1863, at the library of the Academy.

PETER GANSEVOORT,
President of Board of Trustees.

DAVID MURRAY,
Clerk.

Original printed enclosure not located. Text from first publication.

PUBLICATION: *Celebration of the Semi-Centennial Anniversary of the Albany Academy* (Albany: J. Munsell, 1863), p. 4.

FROM PETER GANSEVOORT
12 JUNE 1863 · ALBANY

With the semicentennial celebration of the Albany Academy drawing near (see the entry just above), Melville's uncle Peter enclosed with this letter a circular dated 26 June (Melville's copy of the circular is now unlocated). As the circular indicates, Alexander W. Bradford, a long-time friend of the Melville family (see Melville's 23 May 1846 letter to him), was to give an oration, and an evening meeting was to be held in the chapel, "at which addresses [were to] be made by various distinguished speakers," one of whom, Peter Gansevoort evidently hoped, would be Melville. Other members of the "committee of alumni" included Abraham Lansing, who later married Peter Gansevoort's daughter Catherine, and William B. Sprague, Jr., son of the Reverend William B. Sprague, who had asked for Melville's autograph soon after the publication of *Typee* (see Melville's 24 July 1846 reply).

Melville's reply to this invitation is also unlocated, but he did attend the celebration on 26 June and stayed with his uncle (see the entry, p. 385 above, for his unlocated letter to his wife about the visit). The memorial volume of the celebration (cited under publication, below) does not mention whether Melville gave "an expression of [his] feeling" during the evening meeting in the chapel, but it did single him out as accompanying his uncle: "The meeting was presided over by the Honorable PETER GANSEVOORT, . . . and by his side were his associates and the guests of the festival, among whom was warmly welcomed HERMAN MELVILLE, whose reputation as an author has honored the Academy, world-wide" (p. 11).

Albany 12 June 1863

My dear Herman

I have much pleasure in sending to you the Circular of the Com. app^d for the celebration of the semi centennial anniversary of the Albany Academy —

You are a member of the Committee; Permit me to indulge the hope, that you will shew your gratitude to the Academy & your appreciation of the services it has rendered the cause of Science by uniting in the celebration & favoring us with an expression of your feeling, during the Evening Meeting in the Chapel of the Academy

I expect to go to Saratoga Sp. next week with yr Aunt Susan & Kate, to remain until about 4 July —

However I shall be in Albany on 26ᵗʰ insᵗ & if you come you will find my house open

Yours very affectionately

P. G.

Herman Melville Esq
Pittsfield Mass

[Enclosure:]

ALBANY ACADEMY, ⎱
June 26th, 1863. ⎰

Dear Sir:

The Albany Academy has completed the fiftieth year of its existence. It was chartered, by the Regents of the university of the state of New York, March 4th, 1813. During this period over five thousand students have been received and educated within its walls. It has been thought that perhaps such of the former students and officers of this institution as still survive, might deem it a privilege to unite in celebrating this occasion in some suitable way.

To this end, the undersigned, who have been appointed by the board of trustees as a committee of arrangements, earnestly solicit your attendance at Albany, Friday, June 26th, 1863, at the following

CELEBRATION

OF THE

SEMI-CENTENNIAL ANNIVERSARY

OF THE

ALBANY ACADEMY.

At 3 p. m. a public meeting of the Alumni of the Academy will be held at Tweddle hall.

Honorable ALEXANDER W. BRADFORD, LL. D., of New York, will pronounce a Commemorative Oration.

ORLANDO MEADS, LL. D., will read a History of the Institution.

At 8½ o'clock in the evening a reünion of the Alumni and Officers of the Academy will be held in the chapel and rooms of the Academy building. Refreshments will be provided.

Music has been kindly proffered by vocalists and artists of the Alumni.

During the evening a meeting will be organized in the chapel, at which addresses will be made by various distinguished speakers.

It is proposed to publish as the result of this celebration a memorial volume, which shall contain besides proceedings of the meetings, a complete catalogue of the students of the Academy from its commencement.

From those not residing in the city of Albany, an answer to this communication is respectfully solicited, and may be addressed to David Murray, Esq., Principal of Albany Academy.

The committee have endeavored by every means in their power to obtain the addresses of the former students of the Academy, and to send invitations to them; but there is no doubt that with all the diligence they have employed that many will have been omitted.

They will, therefore, be under great obligations if any gentleman to whom these invitations may be sent, will extend the same invitation to others.

N. B. The Alumni and officers are requested to assemble at the Academy building at two o'clock, in order to proceed to the Hall in a body.

COMMITTEE OF ALUMNI.

Hon. JOHN V. L. PRUYN, LL. D., Albany.
Hon. JOHN VAN BUREN, New York.
JOSEPH HENRY, LL. D., Washington.
Hon. ALEXANDER W. BRADFORD, LL. D., New York.
Rev. J. TRUMBULL BACKUS, D. D., Schenectady.
Hon. GEORGE W. CLINTON, Buffalo.
HERMAN MELVILLE, Pittsfield.
WILLIAM H. BOGART, Aurora.
Prof. ISAAC W. JACKSON, LL. D., Schenectady.

PETER CAGGER,	Albany.
JOHN TAYLER HALL,	do.
FRANKLIN TOWNSEND,	do.
GEORGE W. CARPENTER,	do.
DAVID I. BOYD,	do.
ROBERT H. WATERMAN,	do.
JAMES CRUIKSHANK, LL. D.,	do.
WILLIAM B. SPRAGUE, Jr.,	do.
CHARLES H. STRONG,	do.
JOHN T. McKNIGHT,	do.
ABRAHAM LANSING,	do.
FREDERIC P. OLCOTT,	do.

Final document (of letter) not located. Text from draft letter on a 28.6 × 23 cm part-sheet (torn along the top), folded in half, of white wove paper. Peter Gansevoort inscribed the draft to Melville on the second page, in ink, and drafted a similar letter to "Hon. G. W. Clinton" on the third page. Melville's copy of printed enclosure not located; text from first publication.

LOCATION (of draft): NYPL-GL.

PUBLICATION (letter): (partial) *Log*, II, 659; (enclosure): *Celebration of the Semi-Centennial Anniversary of the Albany Academy* (Albany: J. Munsell, 1863), pp. 6–8.

TEXTUAL NOTES: much] *inserted above caret* · I expect] *below canceled* Aunt Susan · go] *inserted above canceled* take · to Saratoga] *after canceled* yͬ Aunt Susan & Kate · about] *inserted above caret* · However] H *written over word-start* · I shall] *inserted above caret over canceled* will · open] *before canceled* for you

FROM FRANCES PRISCILLA MELVILLE
AFTER 15 JUNE 1863 · GANSEVOORT

Unlocated. A letter from Melville's youngest sister is cited in her 15 June 1863 letter to their sister Augusta in New Bedford, which reports that their brother Thomas was "on his way to San Francisco, where he hopes to receive many long letters from us all." She added, "I shall write Herman about Tom's direction, so he & Lizzie can write" (NYPL-GL). Presumably Melville acted upon his sister's letter and wrote to their brother (see the entry for Melville's unlocated letter, p. 385 above).

FROM FRANCES PRISCILLA MELVILLE
22 JUNE 1863 · GANSEVOORT

Unlocated. Frances Priscilla Melville's letter written in reply to a "funny" but now unlocated "note from Herman" that she received on 20 June 1863 is cited in her 22 June 1863 letter to their sister Augusta (see the entry on p. 385 above for Melville's "note," probably written on 18 June). After praising the humor of it, she continues, "I wrote to him this morning saying how glad we were that he was coming & that he must bring one or two of the children with him" (NYPL-GL). Melville did visit his mother and sister in Gansevoort, after attending the celebration at the Albany Academy, but could not bring his children, who were still in school (see the entry, p. 385 above, for his unlocated letter to his wife from Gansevoort).

FROM MARIA GANSEVOORT MELVILLE
BEFORE 31 JULY 1863 · GANSEVOORT

Unlocated. Maria Melville's letter to her son is cited in Helen Griggs's 31 July 1863 letter to Augusta Melville. Probably because Melville had been unable to bring any of his children with him on his visit to Gansevoort in late June, a July visit had been proposed for two of his children—Malcolm and Elizabeth (Bessie)—as well as for Allan's daughter Maria (Milie), to be accompanied by their aunt Augusta. Apparently all was not going according to plan, however. Helen wrote Augusta, "Mama wrote to Herman a week ago urging the coming on of the children: Malcolm Bessie & *Milie* alone, as your coming on had been put off so long, but we have had no reply of any kind" (NYPL-GL).

FROM RICHARD T. GREENE
20 OCTOBER 1863 · MEMPHIS

Melville's 6 October 1863 statement from the Harpers shows that on 11 August 1863 he ordered "3 Typee" to be sent to "R T Green" (HCL-M). Greene's acknowledgment of those books is the last known letter that he wrote to Melville. Since May 1861 he had served in the Union army, first as a surgeon's orderly in the Sixth Missouri Volunteer Infantry Regiment, then, after deserting briefly, as a private in Company K, Eleventh Illinois, and finally after another brief desertion, in the Sixth Missouri again, as a clerk on General Grant's staff (Grant had on 4 July 1863 taken Vicksburg, Mississippi, where Melville's unlocated letter announcing the books was apparently sent or forwarded). Shortly thereafter in the summer of 1863 Greene was sent home on sick leave and had just returned on 16 October. He found a clerical position in General Sherman's Fifteenth Army Corps, then doing a "clean job" in Mississippi in the operations leading to the surrender of Vicksburg that summer. In September he was sent to Memphis to help General William S. Rosecrans in the defense of Chattanooga (Rosecrans, however, had been relieved of command the day before Greene wrote this letter). Greene stayed with the corps as a clerk until his enlistment expired on 24 June 1864 at Big Shanty, Georgia. He returned to Chicago—only to reenlist with the First Illinois Volunteer Light Artillery—and served until 3 July 1865 in Battery A, then on garrison duty. Whether he made the visit he proposes at the close of this letter is not known.

The 1880 census shows Richard T. Greene, a "chemist," living with his wife and son, a "physician," and several relatives, in Fulton, Illinois. His death in Chicago eleven months after Melville's, in 1892, was reported in prominent obituaries, such as the extended one in the 25 August 1892 Chicago *News Record*, because of his fame as the "Toby" of *Typee* (the *News Record* referred to him as "the hero" of that book). Nine of his obituaries were preserved by Elizabeth Melville (HCL-M). Greene's son (b. 1853), Melville's namesake, remained in Chicago after his father's death and married Myrtle Means in 1894. City directories give his profession as a weigher after 1904 and as a clerk from 1911 to 1912. He died 19 April 1914, and was buried with his parents in Rosehill Cemetery in Chicago. For Greene's nephew,

Richard Melville Hair, on whom Greene also reports here, see Hair's 13 February 1861 letter to Melville.

Memphis Tenn
Oct. 20th 1863

Dear Melville

I was home on leave of absence when your letter reached Vicksburg.

The "Typees" came in good order; they are very nice copies too. I thank you a thousand times. I wanted a copy for your namesake. I found him and Mother well when I met them. I had been absent 27 months Herman has grown a fine tall boy, and Richd Melville Hair is a Lieutenant in Gen Bank's Army, at New Orleans.

We are removing the Headqts to some other field, perhaps Nashville cant say though. We have done a clean job on the Mississippi, and I think we are going to help Rosecrans in this State When I get out of this Army which will be in June next, I shall certainly make you a visit

Yours truly
"Toby"

ALS, " 'Toby' ", on a 12.8 × 20.5 cm part-sheet (torn along the left edge) of white laid paper. Greene inscribed both sides of the leaf, in ink.

LOCATION: HCL-M.

PUBLICATION: (partial) *Log*, II, 663.

FROM SOPHIA VAN MATRE
BEFORE 10 DECEMBER 1863 · CINCINNATI

Unlocated. Sophia Van Matre's letter requesting "autographs from old letters" to be auctioned at the Great Western Sanitary Fair in Cincinnati is cited in Melville's 10 December 1863 reply.

FROM GEORGE McLAUGHLIN
BEFORE 15 DECEMBER 1863 · CINCINNATI

Unlocated. George McLaughlin's letter requesting Melville's support of the Great Western Sanitary Fair in Cincinnati is cited in Melville's 15 December 1863 reply.

1864

FROM ALEXANDER BLISS
BEFORE 22 MARCH 1864 · BALTIMORE

Unlocated. Alexander Bliss's request for an autograph poem, to be included in a book being published to benefit the Sanitary Commission, is cited in Melville's 22 March 1864 reply.

FROM ALEXANDER BLISS
AFTER 22 MARCH 1864 · BALTIMORE

Unlocated. Presumably Alexander Bliss complied with Melville's request in his 22 March 1864 letter to "*acknowledge the receipt*" of Melville's letter and enclosed poem.

FROM HENRY S. GANSEVOORT
BEFORE 3 NOVEMBER 1864 · FALLS CHURCH

Unlocated. Henry Gansevoort's letter written from his Union encampment in Falls Church, Virginia, is cited in his 3 November 1864 letter to Allan Melville: "How is Cousin Herman? My love to him & Cousin Lizzie; I hope to hear from him in answer to my last" (NYPL-GL; cited by Leyda in the *Log*, II, 671, but at present unlocated). No reply from Melville has been located. Davis and Gilman assumed that Melville did reply (Davis-Gilman Unlocated 382), but given the care with which Gansevoort saved his letters (see the headnote to Melville's 10 May 1864 letter to him), this seems unlikely.

1865

FROM BAYARD TAYLOR
24 FEBRUARY 1865 · NEW YORK

By 1865 Bayard Taylor (1825–78), the popular travel writer, had long been known to Melville. They had met by February of 1848 when Taylor was "obliged to write" and then read aloud several Valentine poems, one of them addressed to Melville, at a literary party given by Anne Lynch (*Log*, I, 270 and 272). Melville had bought in December 1846 Taylor's first book, *Views A-Foot* (New York: Wiley & Putnam, 1846; Sealts 495), and Taylor belonged to the Duyckinck circle in New York, writing briefly for the *Literary World*, but there is nothing to indicate that Melville sought Taylor's company out, as he did that of Taylor's cousin, Dr. Franklin Taylor, aboard ship in 1849 (see *Journals*, pp. 4, 6–12, 14–18, and 251–52). Melville mentioned Taylor's name—which had become more celebrated as his own became more obscure—in a remark that Evert Duyckinck recorded in his diary on 2 October 1856: "as some augur predicted the misfortunes of Charles I from the infelicity of his countenance so Taylor's prosperity 'borne up by the Gods' was written in his face" (NYPL-D).

It is not known whether Melville accepted this invitation to the Travellers' Club in New York (officially incorporated on 11 April 1865); the invitation is significant, however, in that it suggests Melville's wide circle of acquaintance. The illustrator Felix Darley (1822–88) and the painters Frederick Church (1826–1900) and Albert Bierstadt (1830–1902) were all well-known artists by this time. "Gottschalk" was Louis Moreau Gottschalk (1829–69), the pianist and composer. Cyrus Field (1819–92) was a financier and Townsend Harris (1804–78) an American diplomat. "Bellows" was Albert F. Bellows (1829–83), the landscape painter, and "Hunt" refers to one of the Hunt brothers, either Richard Morris (1827–95), the architect, or William Morris (1824–79), the painter.

Taylor also probably invited, among others, the publisher and man-of-letters George William Curtis (well known to Melville; see the headnote to Melville's 15 September 1857 letter) and the author Donald Grant Mitchell (1822–1908) to this same Monday gathering. In the February 1865 section of the *Life and Letters of Bayard Taylor*, ed. Marie Hansen-Taylor and Horace E. Scudder (2 vols., Boston: Houghton, Mifflin, 1884) a letter from Taylor to Mitchell (for which no date is given) states: "If you intend coming to the city soon, pray come next Monday. A 'close corporation,' called the *Travellers*, meets here on that evening, and I, as host, have the right of invitation. . . . We simply talk, smoke, and take frugal refreshments, but the evenings so far have been very pleasant. I shall also ask Curtis and Herman Melville" (I, 428).

No. 139 East 8th St.
(Between B'way & 4th Avenue)
Feb. 24, 1865.

My dear Sir:

On Monday evening next, the 27th, "The Travellers" meet here, and it will give me great pleasure to see you among the guests of the Club. Many of the members are no doubt old friends of yours — Darley, Church, Bierstadt, Gottschalk, Cyrus Field, Hunt, Bellows and Townsend Harris. We simply meet to talk, winding up our evenings with a cigar and frugal refreshments.

Very truly yours,
Bayard Taylor.

ALS on a 26 × 18.5 cm sheet, folded in half, of white laid paper, watermarked with a crown-like design. Taylor inscribed the first page, in ink. Elizabeth Melville noted in pencil on the fourth page " 'Travellers Club' — | Bayard Taylor".

LOCATION: HCL-M.

PUBLICATION: *Log*, II, 672.

FROM [EVERT A. DUYCKINCK?]
SEPTEMBER 1865 · NEW YORK

Unlocated. According to Leyda (*Log*, II, 676), Evert Duyckinck sent a form letter at this time to writers included in his *Cyclopædia* (1855), concerning the anticipated 1866 revised edition and requesting corrections and additions for it. No copy of this letter has been found, and Leyda may mistakenly have been referring to the 1861 form letter Charles Scribner sent on Duyckinck's behalf, dated 1861, when the revision was first undertaken (see pp. 677–78 above). If Duyckinck did send such a letter in September 1865, Melville probably received one.

1866

FROM ALFRED H. GUERNSEY
[31 MAY?] 1866 · NEW YORK

The five poems listed in this undated memorandum appeared in *Harper's New Monthly Magazine* in advance of the August 1866 publication of Melville's volume of Civil War poetry, *Battle-Pieces*, by the Harpers. Since only the last poem is listed as having not yet appeared in the magazine, this memorandum to the Harpers from "A. H. G." (Alfred H. Guernsey), who had become the magazine's editor in 1856 (Eugene Exman, *The Brothers Harper* [New York: Harper & Row, 1965], pp. 316–17) has been tentatively assigned to 31 May 1866, the postmarked date on the envelope in which it was apparently sent.

Although this memorandum was not addressed to Melville, it was evidently transmitted to him, and Melville made notations on it and on the envelope to the effect that he was never paid for the magazine appearance of his poems (see below; no record of payment appears in the Harper account statements sent to him now in HCL-M). Elizabeth Melville later annotated the first four titles listed—"The March to the Sea," "The Cumberland," "Philip" (published as "Sheridan at Cedar Creek" in *Battle-Pieces*), and "Chattanooga"—with the dates of the issues in which they appeared in *Harper's*.

From Mr. Melville's Volume, besides "The March to the Sea," settled for, have been used in the Magazine.
  "The Cumberland"
  "Philip"
  "Chattanooga"
  "Gettysburg" (to appear in the July No.)
I think you ought to agree with Mr Melville what should be paid for these poems for this use in the Magazine, apart from their use in the volume.

They will make, one with another, a half page each of the Magazine.

A. H. G.

Autograph memorandum on a 17.1 × 20.9 cm part-sheet (torn along the left edge) of white wove paper. Guernsey inscribed only one side of the leaf, in ink. Melville wrote "June 1866" in pencil opposite the signature and below that notation wrote in blue pencil "I never got." after the canceled letters "I b". Elizabeth Melville noted in pencil on the verso "Feb – | 1866 | A. H. G. | Note to Harpers | Poems in | Mag. not paid | for" and she supplied dates, in pencil, to the right of the first four titles listed: "Feb. 1866 | March 1866 | April 1866 | June 1866". The envelope is addressed in a clerk's hand to "Herman Melville, Esq. | 104 East 26ᵗʰ st. | City"; it was postmarked on 31 May in New York. Melville wrote on the front of the envelope in green pencil "Containing | memoranda | of things not paid for — "; he noted in pencil on the back "*Harper Accounts.*"

LOCATION: HCL-M.

PUBLICATION: (partial) *Log*, II, 680 (dated late June?).

FROM WILLIAM H. DEMAREST
7 DECEMBER 1866 · NEW YORK

According to the later Harper account of the initial sales of Melville's *Battle-Pieces*, which was sent to Melville on 13 February 1868, the projection in this letter by the Harpers' long-time bookkeeper, William Demarest, proved fairly accurate. The actual sales through February 1868 came to 486. An additional 263 copies were given to newspaper and magazine editors for review. Thereafter most statements reported a few copies as sold, but by 4 March 1887 the Harpers still had 155 sets of sheets and 365 bound copies on hand.

New York, Dec 7, 1866.

Dear Sir,

According to promise I beg to report that there were printed of the "Battle Pieces," 1260 copies: there have been given to Editors, say in round numbers, 300: there were on hand yesterday 409. So there were sold or in hands of booksellers on sale, up to yesterday, say 551 copies.

Yours, respectfully,
Wᵐ H. Demarest.

Herman Melville, Esq.

ALS on a 26.6 × 20.9 cm sheet, folded in half, of white laid paper with lines, embossed with the manufacturer's oval stamp enclosing the name "CAREW". Demarest inscribed the first page, in ink. Elizabeth Melville noted in pencil on the fourth page "Harpers | 'Battle Pieces' | Dec. 7 – 1866".

LOCATION: HCL-M.

PUBLICATION: *Log*, II, 684.

TEXTUAL NOTE: Wᵐ H. Demarest.] *underlined with a flourish*

1867

FROM CHARLES W. STODDARD
BEFORE 20 JANUARY 1867 · SAN FRANCISCO

Unlocated. A letter from Charles Stoddard (accompanying his gift to Melville of his first book, *Poems*) can be inferred from Melville's 20 January 1867 letter acknowledging the gift.

FROM MARIA MELVILLE
BETWEEN 11 SEPTEMBER AND 22 OCTOBER 1867 · PITTSFIELD

Unlocated. A letter of condolence from Allan Melville's daughter Maria Gansevoort Melville, written after Malcolm Melville's death on 11 September 1867, is cited in Melville's 22 October 1867 reply to his niece. In it Maria (Milie) apparently remembered her cousin as "always obliging and affectionate."

FROM ALLAN MELVILLE
BEFORE 22 OCTOBER 1867 · PITTSFIELD

Two unlocated letters. Allan's "notes," one of which requested Melville to make inquiry at the New York depots at Forty-second Street and at Centre Street for a "piano, potatoes, & apples," and the other of which may have accompanied a "present," are cited in Melville's 22 October 1867 letter to Allan's daughter Maria.

FROM THE EDITORS OF *PUTNAM'S MAGAZINE*
BEFORE [DECEMBER?] 1867 · NEW YORK

Unlocated. An invitation to contribute to the newly revived *Putnam's Magazine* can be inferred from the undated excerpt of Melville's reply printed in the [December?] 1867 prospectus for the magazine (see the entry on p. 402 above).

1868

FROM GEORGE P. PUTNAM
AND VICTORINE HAVEN PUTNAM
ON OR BEFORE 15 JANUARY [1868?] · NEW YORK

Unlocated. A "friendly invitation" from the Putnams is cited in Melville's 15 January [1868?] formal letter of acceptance.

FROM CATHERINE GANSEVOORT
BEFORE 9 SEPTEMBER 1868 · ALBANY

Unlocated. Catherine Gansevoort's "note," probably concerning their recent visit to the Albany Rural Cemetery, is cited in Melville's 9 September 1868 reply.

1869

FROM MISS H. I. TRUE
[FEBRUARY?] 1869 · PLACE UNKNOWN

Unlocated. An autograph request, with some questions Melville could not answer, is cited in his February 1869 reply.

FROM UNKNOWN
BEFORE 3 FEBRUARY 1869 · PLACE UNKNOWN

Unlocated. An autograph request is cited in Melville's 3 February 1869 reply.

FROM MARIA GANSEVOORT MELVILLE
BEFORE 9 JUNE 1869 · GANSEVOORT

Unlocated. In his 9 June 1869 letter to his uncle Peter Gansevoort, Melville remarked, "By letter from Gansevoort we heard how much Mama enjoyed her visit" with Peter Gansevoort's family in Albany. Her letter reporting on this visit was probably addressed to both Melville and his wife.

FROM STANWIX MELVILLE
BEFORE 28 SEPTEMBER 1869 · SHANGHAI

Unlocated. According to a 29 September 1869 letter from Augusta Melville to Peter Gansevoort, Melville and his family had received their first "letters" from their son Stanwix "yesterday"—28 September (NYPL-GL). Presumably at least one of these shipboard letters was addressed in part to Melville. Maria Gansevoort Melville later reported in an 8 October 1869 letter to her niece Catherine Gansevoort that Stanwix had written that "his deafness has nearly left him" and that he "liked the Sea even better than he had thought he would" (NYPL-GL). For more about Stanwix's voyage, see the headnote to Melville's 5 May 1870 letter to his mother.

FROM ELIZABETH SHAW MELVILLE
BEFORE 29 SEPTEMBER 1869 · BOSTON

Unlocated. In her 29 September 1869 letter to Peter Gansevoort (see the entry just above), Augusta Melville also mentioned a letter from Elizabeth Shaw Melville, then in Boston recuperating from an illness while Augusta took care of the family in New York. Augusta reported that Elizabeth's "last letter speaks of her gaining strength daily, so we may look for her return next week" (NYPL-GL). Presumably this letter was addressed to her husband.

FROM T. APOLEON CHENEY
7 DECEMBER 1869 · WATKINS

Theseus Apoleon Cheney (1830–78) had by this time written two books on New York state history—*Ancient Monuments in Western New York* (Albany: University of the State of New York, 1860) and *Historical Sketch of the Chemung Valley* (Watkins, N.Y., 1868). The 11 September 1868 *New-York Evening Post* review of his second book stated that "Dr. Cheney has shown great research in gathering materials for his work, and has collected a mass of information which has enabled him to construct a narrative more capable of fixing the attention of the general reader than such local histories commonly are." Cheney had attended the Oberlin Preparatory School in 1849 and 1850, but no record has been found of his college or university career. His obituary, published in the 8 August 1878 *Watkins Express*, referred to him as an LL.D. as well as "one of the most eccentric of men." It went on to state that he "was a member of the Royal Historical Society of England, also a member of the Historical Society of this State, and, an author of some note; but his natural talents were always beclouded by poverty and ill health, and apparently by ill fate, all of which combined prevented his achieving the fame and distinction to which he ardently aspired; and at last, with hopes unrealized and ambition ungratified, he has gone to his final rest."

Cheney wrote to Melville and evidently other well-known figures such as the poet and editor William Cullen Bryant and the military man and politician John Adams Dix, on the letterhead of the Georgic Society and Library, which he had founded, but which may have progressed no further than his requests for autographs and other "souvenirs." No record or local memory of it seems to have survived in Watkins. Cheney's hand is anything but plain, so that the year of the 4 December letter from Melville that he cites must remain tentative (see the entries for both of Melville's unlocated letters to Cheney, pp. 382 and 402–3 above), but it is clear that he had managed to persuade Melville to reply to his requests and to send him an autograph and carte de visite (probably the "new 'carte'" Elizabeth Melville wrote to Augusta Melville about in letters of 16 and 28 October 1863

From T. Apoleon Cheney, 7 December 1869, p. 1 (reduced). Courtesy of the Houghton Library, Harvard University (Melville Collection).

[NYPL-GL], unmistakably pleased with her husband's new picture). Whether Melville sent him an inscribed copy of one of his books is not known, nor is it known whether Cheney, in turn, sent Melville a copy of his *Historical Sketch of the Chemung Valley*.

December 7th 1869.

My dear Sir,

I had the great pleasure to be in receipt of your kind favor of Dec. 4th, '67 — and I will ask that you excuse this long delay in acknowledging my sincere thanks for it, together with the complimentary enclosure of your carte-de-visite, in pursuance with wish which I had expressed. The picture of one of the most gifted, most truly distinguished novelists among those whose names honor the Literature of our country, indeed forms a deeply prized and valued contribution to *this* Souvenir. — The Library continues to meet with best success; within several weeks past, in instances, has rec'd from authors residing in or near your city, W. C. Bryant, Hon. J. A. Dix, Etc., contributions of the series of their respective Works. — The principal Authors in our own Country, & several in Europe, since first organization of Library have contributed entire series of their respective works; this deriving its interest & value, not more from the character of the volumes sent than from their *presentation* by such distinguished authors — forming prized mementoes in our collection.

I will beg to suggest — in accordance with mention made in your note of Dec. 19, '62 — that if you may now have it at your *convenience* to present our Library with any part of your works, or any one of your works (as Mardi, or Omoo, or Typee, etc.) as a representative production of your gifted pen, the generous favor would be gratefully appreciated. And, if you can thus send any specimen work, I would too beg that you allow the honor of writing an Inscription, or Presentation, in the work — which would indeed give these memento vol^s of your genius, and of your kindness, a double value. — (You can forward any p'ck'ge, for Express, directed 'Prof. T. Apoleon Cheney — Georgic Library — *Watkins*, Schuyler County, N.Y.' — I will indulge hope that it may be at your convenience to contribute some memento work, some characteristic publication of yours to our collections — which will take its place with series of works presented by other eminent & illustrious authors, in our Library. —— I have been assaying, for Library, a choice Autograph Souvenir — already embracing autographs of large numbers of prominent Authors, Artists, Etc; I will be gratified if you may allow honour of enclosing, *for* souvenir, your brief autograph — a line or two, or sentence, with date etc., and your signature; — I too would be glad if you might be able to render favor of enclosing autographs of any eminent authors — as Irving, Morris, Poe, Willis, Etc. Etc. Etc. — and as they would be of inestimable value toward completing this Library souvenir, be assured I should gratefully appreciate your especial kindness. ——

The preliminary part of my "Historical Sketch of Chemung County, Etc." (of which you may have seen notice, by W. C. Bryant, in "Evening Post" of Sep. 11 '68.) was issued last season, — if you will inform me of your precise address, number, street, ec. — I will take pleasure to mail you a copy? — I will be extremely gratified in your allowing favour of writing me at your earliest convenience; will anticipate to hear from you soon. I remain, with great Regard, yours,

T. Apoleon Cheney.

H. Melville Esq. —

ALS on a 25.6 × 20.5 cm sheet, folded in half, of white wove paper, embossed with the manufacturer's shield-like stamp enclosing the name "EXTRA SUPER FINE". The first page bears the letterhead "GEORGIC LIBRARY. | WATKINS, SCHUYLER CO., N. YORK." Cheney inscribed all four pages, in ink, and addressed the envelope "Herman Melville, Esqr | (Author, Etc.) | New-York City. — " with the notation, later canceled in ink, below, "If Mr M. is not at New York, | P. Master, might please forward this to Pittsfield Mass." Later the "New-York City. — " portion of the address was canceled in pencil and next to it "Pittsfield | Mass" added in pencil by another hand. Above the address, another notation added in pencil, and later canceled in pencil, advised "Try Garrison *Ford*" and, in ink, the word "over" was written twice above this directive and also once below the address. On the verso of the envelope, another hand wrote in ink "[C]are of Allen Melville | 37 Pine St | New York". Since the envelope was later torn in the upper right corner, presumably to remove the stamp, only a portion of the postmark, stamped in Watkins, New York, remains. This tear also removed part of Elizabeth Melville's endorsement on the verso, which presumably read "T. Apoleon Che[ney] | Georgic Lib[rary] | Watkins N.[Y.] | Dec 7 – 18[69]."

LOCATION: HCL-M.

PUBLICATION: (partial) *Log*, II, 706.

1870

FROM STANWIX MELVILLE
ON OR AFTER [18 JANUARY?] 1870 · LONDON

Unlocated. Stanwix's letter from London, probably addressed to both of his parents, is cited in Melville's 5 May 1870 letter to his mother. On the basis of a clipping from an 18 January London newspaper marked "From Stanny" (now in HCL-M), Leyda speculated that the date of Stanwix's letter, which was received in "February," may have been 18 January (*Log*, II, 709).

FROM MARIA GANSEVOORT MELVILLE
2 MAY 1870 · ALBANY

Unlocated. A letter from Melville's mother in Albany, admonishing him not to be dilatory about sitting for the portrait that Joseph Eaton was then painting and requesting another letter from him before her departure from Albany, is cited in that requested letter, dated 5 May 1870.

1871

FROM ELLEN MARETT GIFFORD
BEFORE 15 JANUARY 1871 · NASSAU

Unlocated. Elizabeth Melville's cousin Ellen Marett Gifford, vacationing in the Bahamas, wrote a letter in reply to Melville's earlier letter of introduction on behalf of his cousin Henry Gansevoort. Ellen Gifford's letter is cited in Melville's 15 January 1871 letter to his aunt Susan Gansevoort, Henry's stepmother.

FROM PETER GANSEVOORT
[13?] APRIL 1871 · ALBANY

Unlocated. Melville's name is listed among those to whom telegrams were sent at the death on 13 April 1871 of Peter Gansevoort's son, Henry. Only four days earlier, in New York, Melville had seen his cousin, who died on the trip home to Albany (for more on Henry Gansevoort at this time, see the headnote to Melville's 15 January 1871 letter to Susan Lansing Gansevoort). Both this telegram and one to Allan Melville were sent to Allan's office at 37 Pine Street in New York. The list was preserved in an album containing items concerning Henry Gansevoort's death; although it contains many letters of condolence, none from Melville or his wife is included (NYPL-GL).

FROM STANWIX MELVILLE
BEFORE 17 MAY 1871 · [KANSAS?]

Two or more unlocated letters. At least two letters to Melville and his wife from their second son, Stanwix, are cited in Elizabeth Melville's 17 May 1871 letter to Catherine Gansevoort in Albany, where Melville's mother was staying after Henry Gansevoort's death. Stanwix had decided to travel west not long after his return in July 1870 from sailing around the world. Of his new travels, Elizabeth Melville wrote: "Please tell Mama (and I know that you will be interested to hear) that we had another letter from Stanny today, from the interior of Kansas — on the line of the Santa Fe R.R. whither he had gone by advice of Mr Lansing (or Brewster, or both) both of whom he found on his first arrival in Kansas City — They have been exceedingly kind to him, and it is a great relief to me that he has found such good friends" (NYPL-GL). These friends were Abraham Lansing's younger brother Edwin and Edwin's business partner Charles Brewster (for more about these men, see the headnote to Melville's 13 September 1876 letter and the entry just below).

FROM EDWIN LANSING
BEFORE 17 MAY 1871 · KANSAS CITY

Unlocated. A letter from Edwin Lansing (see the entry just above) reporting on Stanwix Melville's arrival in Kansas City is cited in Elizabeth Melville's 17 May 1871 letter to Catherine Gansevoort. Clearly relieved that her son had benefactors he could rely upon in the West, she reported, " — Mr Lansing was kind enough to write to Herman himself, the other day about him [Stanwix] — " (NYPL-GL).

FROM CATHERINE GANSEVOORT
BEFORE 13 NOVEMBER 1871 · ALBANY

A memorandum made by Catherine (Kate) Gansevoort shortly after the death of her brother Henry states, "*Henry* requested his sister Kate to send *gifts* to all *Blood Cousins* and their children and friends who I think will accept them as intended — " (NYPL-GL). This letter accompanied the ring that she sent to Melville in Henry's memory. (A partial bill seems to indicate that the rings and other gifts—such as sleeve buttons—were bought at Tiffany's [NYPL-GL].) For Melville's reply, see his 13 November 1871 letter to his cousin.

Albany. N.Y.

Dear Cousin Herman

I send you an intaglio ring which I have chosen for you at the request of my dear Brother Henry S. Gansevoort. He desired that all his blood Cousins should be given rings in his memory — as his gift. I hope you will wear this as a memorial of one who lived a pure & noble life, & was sincerely attached to you & your family.

Herman Melville
104 E. 26th St.
New York. NY

Original document not located. Text from manuscript copy (unsigned) on a 13.1 × 10.2 part-sheet (cut possibly on all four edges) of white laid paper. Catherine Gansevoort inscribed only one side of the leaf, in ink; it was later tipped into the inner fold of Melville's response of 13 November 1871, which was in turn tipped into a Gansevoort family album with other letters concerning Henry Gansevoort's death.

LOCATION (of copy): NYPL-GL.

PUBLICATION: *Log*, II, 721.

TEXTUAL NOTE: should] *above canceled* might

1872

FROM MISS COFFIN
9 JANUARY 1872 · [NANTUCKET?]

Unlocated. Miss Coffin's letter, requesting the source of "facts" given in one of Melville's published works, is cited in his 13 January 1872 reply.

FROM AUGUSTUS PEEBLES
[10?] FEBRUARY 1872 · [LANSINGBURGH?]

Unlocated. After Allan Melville's death on 9 February 1872, Helen Melville Griggs, staying at Thomas Melville's home on Staten Island, answered what must have been a letter of condolence sent to Melville from their cousin Augustus Peebles. In her 12 February 1872 reply, Helen wrote: "Your letter to Herman, Mamma asked me to answer; he sent it over to us to-day" (NYPL-GL; cited by Leyda in the *Log*, II, 723, but at present unlocated). Metcalf (p. 222) incorrectly identified Helen's correspondent as Augustus Van Schaick, who had died in 1847. For more about Peebles, see the headnote to Melville's 13 June 1846 letter.

FROM HELEN MELVILLE GRIGGS
[18?] FEBRUARY 1872 · NEW BRIGHTON

Unlocated. Other family members who stayed at Thomas Melville's home on Staten Island after Allan Melville's death (see the entry just above) included Catherine Gansevoort, who returned to Albany on 17 February, and Maria Melville, clearly devastated by her son's death. On 18 February, Melville's daughter Frances wrote to Catherine Gansevoort, relaying news her father had received from his sister Helen, also still at Tom's: "Papa had a note from Aunt Helen this afternoon, saying that Grandma was about the same. She passed rather a restless night last night and this morning took a sponge bath" (NYPL-GL). Maria Melville's condition did not improve; she died on 1 April 1872.

FROM SAMUEL A. DRAKE
BEFORE 30 APRIL 1872 · BOSTON

Unlocated. A letter requesting information about Melville's grandfather, Major Thomas Melvill of Boston Tea Party fame, can be inferred from Melville's 30 April 1872 reply.

FROM STANWIX MELVILLE
[JULY?] 1872 · SEDGWICK

Unlocated. A letter from Stanwix can be inferred from the small fragment that remains of a letter that Melville wrote to his son probably in July 1872 when he was in Sedgwick, Kansas, for a second time. Since two partial lines on that fragment read "rejoiced that you have" and "of going to New Orleans," it seems likely that Melville was replying to an earlier letter from Stanwix announcing his plans for going to New Orleans, as he soon did.

FROM RICHARD H. STODDARD
BEFORE 5 JULY 1872 · NEW YORK

Unlocated. A letter enclosing an offprint from Stoddard's revision of Griswold's anthology *Poets and Poetry of America* (1842) is cited in Melville's 5 July 1872 reply. For the enclosure, see the headnote to Melville's reply.

FROM AUGUSTA MELVILLE AND
FRANCES PRISCILLA MELVILLE
[20?] NOVEMBER 1872 · GANSEVOORT

Unlocated. On 1 April 1872 Maria Gansevoort Melville died at Thomas Melville's home on Staten Island. She was buried next to her husband in the Albany Rural Cemetery. In November 1872, arranging for the inscription on the headstone, Augusta and Frances Priscilla Melville enclosed a letter to their brother with one dated 20 November to their cousin Catherine Gansevoort, who was about to go to New York, asking her "to hand the enclosed note to Herman. He will tell you if he thinks with us, & approves [of the inscription]. I spoke to Tom, but Herman will enclose his note if he does not see him" (NYPL-GL; cited by Leyda in the *Log*, II, 728, but at present unlocated).

FROM SUSAN LANSING GANSEVOORT
BEFORE 30 NOVEMBER 1872 · ALBANY

Unlocated. On 4 December 1872 Elizabeth Melville, in Boston inspecting the losses that the property inherited from her father had incurred in the large fire of the previous month, wrote to Melville's aunt Susan Gansevoort (uncle Peter's wife) that "Herman has sent me your kind note addressed to him from Albany, and I hasten to express my grateful acknowledgments to Uncle for his kind and generous gift. It relieves me of a great weight of anxiety for the coming year, the resources of which had been so sadly crippled by the dreadful fire — " (NYPL-GL). The gift, probably in response to news of the fire, was for five hundred dollars, the amount of income that Elizabeth Melville's Boston properties had generated annually before the fire. Melville's 30 November 1872 letter to his aunt, most of which was later destroyed, was probably also written in response to her letter.

1873

FROM [M. LAIRD SIMONS?]
BEFORE 8 SEPTEMBER 1873 · [NEW YORK?]

Unlocated. A letter, probably from M. Laird Simons, who was preparing a second revision (published in 1875) of the Duyckincks' *Cyclopædia of American Literature* (1855, 1866), is cited in Melville's 8 September 1873 reply.

1874

FROM GEORGE A. NOURSE
BEFORE 14 MARCH 1874 · CALIFORNIA

Unlocated. A letter addressed to both Melville and his wife from George Augustus Nourse is cited in Elizabeth Melville's 14 March 1874 letter to Hope Savage Shaw. Nourse was a relative of Amos Nourse, the husband of Melville's aunt Lucy (see the headnote to Melville's 24–25 March 1861 letter to Elizabeth); he had, like Edwin Lansing and Charles Brewster in Kansas (see the entry for Stanwix's unlocated letters written before 17 May 1871, above) been enlisted to help Stanwix get established in California. From his letter, Elizabeth Melville was able to report to her stepmother: "We have better news from Stanny — He is on a sheep-ranch in California where George Nourse who has very kindly interested himself for him advised him to go — Today we have a letter from George enclosing one from his employer expressing satisfaction with him and promising to give him 25.00 a month from the time he commenced, as long as he has work for him — George wrote to Stanny encouraging him, and advising him to stick at it till he gets a chance of 'taking sheep to keep on shares, and gradually get up a flock of his own['] — He says that sheep raising is *now* the most profitable business in California — and if Stanny will only *perservere* he will come out all right —

    "Stanny's address is

Care of Smith & Chapman
Merced — Merced Co.
Chowchillon } Cal.

    "I wonder if Sam would not write to him, or send him a paper to let him feel that his friends are interested in him — I suppose it is very hard work, for Stanny, but *every* thing is hard work" (HCL-M). It is not known whether Samuel Shaw wrote to his nephew, but in any case Stanwix did not persevere in the sheep business, and eventually moved to San Francisco (see the entry for his unlocated letter written to his parents before 2 January 1877, below).

1875

FROM ABRAHAM LANSING
4 AUGUST 1875 · ALBANY

Unlocated. Abraham Lansing's letter, written in response to Melville's earlier letter (now unlocated) to Catherine Lansing announcing his plans to stop in Albany during his vacation, is cited in Melville's 5 August 1875 reply.

FROM ABRAHAM LANSING
BEFORE 26 AUGUST 1875 · ALBANY

Unlocated. At Peter Gansevoort's request, Abraham Lansing sent Melville a note enclosing a check for twelve hundred dollars intended to cover the expenses of publishing *Clarel*. It is cited in Melville's 26 August 1875 letter to his uncle Peter acknowledging the gift.

FROM CATHERINE GANSEVOORT LANSING
BEFORE 8 OCTOBER 1875 · ALBANY

Unlocated. Catherine Lansing's letter inquiring whether a package should be sent down to New York from Albany is cited in Melville's 8 October 1875 reply.

1876

FROM AUGUSTA MELVILLE
BEFORE 4 JANUARY 1876 · ALBANY

Unlocated. A letter from Melville's sister Augusta, conveying the news that their uncle Peter Gansevoort was close to death, is cited in Melville's 4 January 1876 letter to Peter Gansevoort's son-in-law, Abraham Lansing.

FROM ABRAHAM LANSING
4 JANUARY 1876 · ALBANY

Unlocated. A "despatch," probably a telegram, telling of Peter Gansevoort's death is cited in Melville's 4 January 1876 reply.

FROM GEORGE PARSONS LATHROP
BEFORE JUNE 1876 · [BOSTON?]

Unlocated. In a 20 October 1890 letter to Horace E. Scudder, George Parsons Lathrop, husband of Hawthorne's daughter Rose, recalled writing a letter to Melville: "when I was making my *Study of Hawthorne* I wrote to him for permission to use two or three letters, & received his consent given with a sort of gloomy reluctance" (HCL–Scudder Collection). When Lathrop's *A Study of Hawthorne* (Boston: Osgood) was published in June 1876, it included Melville's [16 April?] 1851 letter to Hawthorne. Julian Hawthorne in an 8 July 1876 letter in the *New-York Tribune* protested Lathrop's publication of private letters to his father (see the HISTORICAL NOTE, pp. 793–94, for more about this controversy). Lathrop responded in the *Tribune* on 15 July stating that he had obtained the consent of all the authors of the letters he had published.

FROM CATHERINE GANSEVOORT LANSING
BEFORE 5 JUNE 1876 · ALBANY

Unlocated. A letter from his cousin Catherine, repeating her offer to pay for the remaining expenses on *Clarel*, is cited in Melville's 5 June 1876 reply.

FROM CATHERINE GANSEVOORT LANSING
31 JULY 1876 · ALBANY

Unlocated. After receiving Melville's 25 July 1876 letter estimating the remaining expenses for the publication of *Clarel*, Catherine Lansing sent Melville a letter with a check for the full amount, noting on his letter "Ans'd July 31st 1876 enclosing check for $100.^{00}," thus beginning a long drawn out exchange of letters between the strong-willed cousins. Paltsits, p. 39, mistakenly identified a draft letter (in NYPL-GL) as her 31 July letter and Leyda followed this dating (*Log*, II, 752), but actually the draft letter must have been written after Melville had donated this first check to charity—a fact mentioned in that letter—and must therefore be the letter cited in Melville's 4 January 1877 letter to his cousin (see the headnote to the draft letter, pp. 713–14 below).

FROM CATHERINE GANSEVOORT LANSING
BEFORE 8 SEPTEMBER 1876 · ALBANY

Unlocated. A letter from his cousin Catherine Lansing, requesting Melville's assistance in finding a set of Chaucer for her husband, Abraham Lansing, is cited in Melville's 8 September 1876 reply.

FROM CATHERINE GANSEVOORT LANSING
10 SEPTEMBER 1876 · ALBANY

Unlocated. Catherine Lansing's letter, announcing a shipment of plums to be sent from Albany to Melville in New York, is acknowledged in his 13 September 1876 letter.

FROM CATHERINE GANSEVOORT LANSING
17 SEPTEMBER 1876 · ALBANY

In response to Melville's 13 September letter, announcing that he could not accept his cousin's money for the remaining expenses for *Clarel* and that he had donated her check to the New-York Society for the Relief of the Ruptured and Crippled, Catherine Lansing drafted this answer. Her finished letter, now unlocated, must have included some remark about how rainy a Sunday it was on 17 September in Albany, since Melville in his 26 September reply—after saying how "gratified" he was with the "tone" of her letter—mentions that the same "rainy Sunday" occurred in New York.

The financial matter did not end here, however. As her later draft letter written between 28 December 1876 and 3 January 1877 indicates (see pp. 713–14 below), Catherine Lansing attempted to insist once again that Melville accept her money.

Dear Cousin Herman

Your letter of 13th inst rec'd, as well as the enclosed reciept for the 100 Dollar Contribution to the N.Y. Society for the relief of the Ruptured & crippled. I should have been glad to have you allow Papa to pay the whole expense of "Clarel", but as you have thought best to assume part yourself I thank you for the gift you have bestowed on me, in giving me, the credit for your own "sweet charity to the destitute & suffering. May it do good & give comfort to those unfortunates for whose good it has been bestowed. &c &c

Sunday afternoon ⎱
Sept. 17th 1876   ⎰
Albany. N.Y

Final document not located. Text from draft letter (unsigned) on a 12.4 × 19.5 cm sheet of white wove paper. Catherine Lansing inscribed both sides of the leaf, in ink.

LOCATION: (of draft): NYPL-GL.

PUBLICATION: Paltsits, pp. 42–43.

TEXTUAL NOTE: "sweet charity] *closing double quotation mark lacking*

FROM HELEN MELVILLE GRIGGS
BEFORE 26 SEPTEMBER 1876 · GANSEVOORT

Unlocated. A letter from Melville's sister Helen, who was visiting their sister Frances Priscilla at Gansevoort, is cited in Melville's 26 September 1876 letter to Catherine Lansing.

FROM FRANCES PRISCILLA MELVILLE
BEFORE 26 SEPTEMBER 1876 · GANSEVOORT

Unlocated. A letter from Melville's sister Frances Priscilla, probably announcing her and the Lansings' plans to stop at the Melvilles' in New York on their way to the centennial exposition in Philadelphia, is cited in Melville's 26 September 1876 letter to Catherine Lansing.

FROM CATHERINE GANSEVOORT LANSING
1 OCTOBER 1876 · ALBANY

Unlocated. His cousin's letter asking for further information about the Chaucer set described in Melville's earlier 26 September letter was noted by her on the first page of that letter—"Ans'd Sunday Oct 1ˢᵗ 1876."—and cited in Melville's 12 October 1876 reply.

FROM CATHERINE GANSEVOORT LANSING
BETWEEN 28 DECEMBER 1876 AND 3 JANUARY 1877 · ALBANY

This draft letter is Catherine Lansing's second appeal that Melville accept one hundred dollars from her for the remaining expenses for *Clarel*, to which he replied on 4 January 1877 (he had donated her first check to the New-York Society for the Relief of the Ruptured and Crippled; for more on the matter of the one hundred dollars, see the headnote to Melville's 25 July 1876 letter, as well as Catherine Lansing's 17 September 1876 letter, above). Although the draft letter is undated, Catherine Lansing's brief reference to "Mʳ Otis D Swan" at its close dates it fairly precisely. Swan was a socially prominent stockbroker who misappropriated funds from private trusts and at least one organization with which he was connected—the Union League Club—in order to gamble on the market. On 28 December 1876 his misconduct was exposed, and he fled New York as a defaultor (*New-York Times*, 29 December 1876). Thus this letter must have been written after that date. Catherine Lansing's reference to Swan was probably ironic, since there is no evidence that he was connected with the New-York Society for the Relief of the Ruptured and Crippled, located at Forty-second Street and Lexington Avenue.

Cousin H.

Herewith I send you a check to meet the balance due for Clarel's publication.

I beg you to receive it, as a contribution of my fathers to that object. He desired it, & for that reason I am the more Earnest in having his wishes fulfilled.

The check which went to the society for Ruptured & Crippled stands in my name. I hope Mr Otis D Swan did not take it with him

Final document not located. Text from draft letter (unsigned) on a 14 × 22.5 cm sheet of white wove paper. Abraham Lansing inscribed only one side of the leaf, in green pencil, and Catherine Lansing revised it, in ink (see the textual notes). Victor Hugo Paltsits annotated the top of this letter, in pencil: "[Draft by Abraham Lansing for his wife's letter to Herman Melville]" and also incorrectly dated it: "[July 31, 1876]" (with "July 31" written over "August").

LOCATION (of draft): NYPL-GL.

PUBLICATION: Paltsits, p. 39.

TEXTUAL NOTES: Cousin H.] *below canceled* Dear • Clarel's] 's *added by Catherine Lansing in ink* • Ruptured] uptured *added by Catherine Lansing in ink* • Crippled] rippled *added by Catherine Lansing in ink before* infirm. I had & have *partially canceled by Catherine Lansing in ink leaving* have *(vestigial)* • stands] *after* the credit of on it *with* of *canceled first by Abraham Lansing in green pencil, then the entire phrase canceled by Catherine Lansing in ink and* for *added above in ink (vestigial)* • name.] *below* & is an admirable *added and then canceled by Catherine Lansing in ink* • Otis D] *inserted above caret* • him] *before* For was the Almoner of my *added and then canceled by Catherine Lansing in ink with* was *inserted above canceled* were

1877

FROM ABRAHAM LANSING
BEFORE 2 JANUARY 1877 · ALBANY

Unlocated. A "note" from Abraham Lansing thanking Melville for the Christmas present of *The Songs of [Pierre Jean de] Béranger*, in English (Philadelphia: Carey & Hart, 1844), is cited in Melville's 2 January 1877 reply.

FROM STANWIX MELVILLE
BEFORE 2 JANUARY 1877 · SAN FRANCISCO

Unlocated. A letter from Stanwix Melville to his parents is mentioned in Elizabeth Melville's 2 January 1877 letter to her stepbrother Lemuel Shaw, Jr.: "We have a letter from Stanny this morning — he is employed in an 'iron & steel firm' at present, engaged in settling matters previous to dissolving partnership — he has 2.50 a day, and a *prospect* of a steady engagement with the partner who goes on with the business — I earnestly hope he will be able to make it sure" (HCL-M).

FROM HELEN MELVILLE GRIGGS
31 JANUARY 1877 · LAWRENCE

Unlocated. In a 31 January 1877 letter to Abraham Lansing, Melville's sister Helen, visiting their sister Catherine Hoadley in Lawrence, Massachusetts, summarized the letter she had just written to Melville about the Hoadleys' two daughters, Maria and Charlotte. Of her nieces, Helen reported: "I have just been writing to Herman, and among other interesting items, 'wished he could have seen the blackbirds,' as he calls them, last evening, as they left us arrayed for conquest, with their two attendant cavaliers.

"They went to an assembly, and returned 'among the sma' hours', with their eyes as bright, and their cheeks as rosy, as when they started; all rapturous with having each 'danced *every* dance', and displaying their well filled tablets, to attest the truth of the statement.

"As I commented, to Herman — 'Ah me! what a thing it is to be young, to be sure!' To be able to enjoy such protracted weary fatigue, as we in our more sober years would think it, and come home, all agog for just such another delightful time, despite of tired feet, and the loss of a night's natural rest in sleep!" (NYPL-GL). (Melville apparently referred to his nieces as "blackbirds," but he also called them the "two Princesses of India" in his 31 March 1877 letter to John Hoadley.)

FROM JOHN C. HOADLEY
25 FEBRUARY 1877 · LAWRENCE

Unlocated. A letter of "the 25 ult." from his brother-in-law John Hoadley in Lawrence, Massachusetts, is cited in Melville's 31 March 1877 reply. Although Hoadley's letter itself is unlocated, the two poems he enclosed with it exist in various manuscript copies (all in NYPL-GL), none of which, however, is likely to have been one of the actual copies enclosed to Melville. For the first poem cited by Melville, based on a legend told by Marco Polo and entitled "Foundation Stones," there are two undated manuscripts, a fair copy (transcribed here), which was inscribed after 1883 (see the paper description, below), and a working one. For the second poem, a paraphrase of the *Aeneid*, 5.485–540, entitled "He Wins Who Highest Aims," two manuscript copies also survive. The earlier (transcribed here) is dated "Monday night Club, Lawrence, Jan. 22, 1877," and is an elaborately hand-printed copy. The second is signed "J. C. Hoadley — Boston, May 11, 1885" and concludes with the comment, "A condensed paraphrase from Virgil."

[Enclosures:]

Foundation Stones.

Marco of Venice, son of Nicolo,
Whose surname was Paul, from far Cathay
Returned, war-prisoner in Florence,
Told to the ready scribe, Rusticians,
This tale of Orient wonder.
                       Ciagatai,
Brother of Gengis Khan, lord of fair lands,
Ruler of Samarcand, in far Bokara
Ere Timour-the-lame, warrior and saint,
Had made of it his gorgeous capital,
Believed and was baptized.
                    Great joy thereat
Among the Christians, who, of gratitude
Reared a basilica named of St. John the Baptist.
Wide its walls, and high; and soaring still
And bending inward like the vaulted sky,
The roof was gathered in a central knot
Poised on a single column.
                    Tall was the shaft
As some gigantic monarch of the grove
In Californian or Australian glen
That prop the heavens.
                 Firm its base reposed
Upon a ponderous stone, owned by the Saracens.
These with anger saw their cherished stone
So desecrate, yet no redress might gain
While lived Ciagatai. He dead, they thought
By force to take their own; since ten to one
Their numbers to the Christians.
                  But their elders,
First, with imperious meekness asked the stone.
Most willingly the Christians would restore it
But that their church would fall: "Name, then, its price."
"Nor gold nor treasure seek we," said the Saracens;
"We ask our own." And the new lord, nephew of Gengis,
Ruler of Samarcand, decreed that in two days

The stone should be restored.
                              Help was there none
But from the Baptist. Him with tears they prayed
To save his shrine; And lo! a miracle!
The ponderous shaft with all the vaulted roof
Rose, by the power of our Lord, three palms,
And so remained, poised like the rolling spheres,
On empty air, by faith sustained no less
Than by the rock.
                        Science may ask the stone,
The corner stone of immortality,
May take no less; and Reason, time's new lord,
Decree the restitution.
                              Yet can faith
Uplift the pillared fane, the spheral roof,
And heaven is safe though earth dissolve, a house
Not built with hands, eternal in the skies.

He Wins Who Highest Aims.

Far off upon the sand a slender mast:
A-top, with flaxen tether bound, the mark
Of archers, sits a timid dove. Four chiefs
Contend, — the prizes three. Hippocoön
Cleaves the slender mast's fine tip. Mnestheus
Cuts the flaxen tie. Eurytion
Strikes the soaring dove, a speck in heaven;
She, falling, brings the arrow back to earth.
What mark for old Acestes now remains, —
What but Athena's shield? Drawing the shaft
Until its feathers touch his swelling breast,
Its barb his out-stretched hand, he aims
Full at the veiléd stars. Shrill twangs the string,
The singing arrow flies, a gleam of light
Athwart the blue, like a resurgent star
Restored to heaven where the Mantuan bard
Hath bid it shine for aye. The highest aim
Hath won the highest prize.
                              Aim high and do your best:

Then, though the mark be hid, the generous deed
Shall ever shine, — itself the noblest prize.

Original enclosures not located. Text of "Foundation Stones" from a fair copy, on three 21.3
× 27.8 cm sheets of white laid paper, partially watermarked with the name "A. PIRIE & SONS,
1883". Hoadley inscribed only one side of each leaf, with the poem in ink and horizontal lines
drawn in pencil. This alternative source is emended by NN at one point (see below). Text of
"He Wins Who Highest Aims" from a hand-printed copy (see above), on a 20.9 × 26.8 cm
sheet of white wove paper. Hoadley inscribed only one side of the leaf, in ink.

LOCATION (of poems): NYPL-GL.

TEXTUAL NOTE: meekness] NN; meeknes

FROM ABRAHAM LANSING
1 JUNE 1877 · ALBANY

Unlocated. As executor of Peter Gansevoort's estate, Abraham Lansing wrote to
Melville enclosing a check for five hundred dollars and a document for Melville to
sign; the letter is cited in Melville's 4 June 1877 acknowledgment of its receipt.

FROM CATHERINE GANSEVOORT LANSING
BETWEEN 23 AND 28 JUNE 1877 · ALBANY

Unlocated. According to Catherine Lansing's endorsement at the top of the first
page of Melville's 7 March 1877 letter to her, he returned the second check for one
hundred dollars that she had given him for the remaining expenses of *Clarel* on 23
June 1877 while she was in New York (see the headnote to his letter). She wrote:
"Saturday *June 23ᵈ 1877* Cousin Herman gave me the 100= Dollars which he in this
note said he would refund to me, given to me at his house 104. E. 26ᵗʰ St N.Y. City
& ack by me by mail a few days afterwards *K. G. L.*" Her acknowledgment of "a
few days afterwards" was in turn acknowledged by Elizabeth Melville on 28 June
1877: "Herman sends love and was much pleased with his letter" (NYPL-GL). Enclosed with Catherine Lansing's unlocated letter were probably the sleeve buttons
later acknowledged in Melville's 12 July 1877 letter to her.

FROM CATHERINE GANSEVOORT LANSING
9 AUGUST 1877 · ALBANY

Unlocated. His cousin's letter, disclaiming Melville's assertion in an earlier letter
(now unlocated) that the Lansings were "people of leisure," is cited in Melville's 5
September 1877 reply.

FROM CATHERINE GANSEVOORT LANSING
2 SEPTEMBER 1877 · ALBANY

Unlocated. A "note," acknowledging the receipt of the set of Chaucer that Melville had found for Abraham Lansing, is cited in Melville's 5 September 1877 reply.

FROM CATHERINE GANSEVOORT LANSING
3 SEPTEMBER 1877 · ALBANY

Unlocated. Catherine Lansing's letter of this date, enclosing a check for the Chaucer set, is also cited, like her letters of 9 August and 2 September (see the entries just above), in Melville's 5 September 1877 letter to his cousin.

1878

FROM FRANCES PRISCILLA MELVILLE
[28?] JULY 1878 · LAWRENCE

Unlocated. Writing to her cousin Catherine Lansing on 28 July 1878, Melville's sister Frances Priscilla, who was staying with the Hoadleys in Lawrence, Massachusetts, reported on the members of the Melville family: "Lizzie goes to Boston tomorrow with Fannie. Bessie was to leave Pittsfield yesterday & on the 1st they start for the Mountains — how rejoiced they will be to leave the hot city behind. Herman will spend his vacation there also. I have just been writing asking him to take Lawrence on his way, so we can see him — as Gansevoort is not open" (NYPL-GL). Although there is no evidence that Melville visited his sisters in Lawrence either before or after his visit with his cousin in Albany (see his 12 August 1878 letter) and his time in New Hampshire in August 1878, he may well have done so.

FROM ELIZABETH SHAW MELVILLE
BEFORE 31 JULY 1878 · [BOSTON?]

Unlocated. A letter from his wife, probably in Boston about to leave with their daughters for the White Mountains, is cited in Melville's 1 August 1878 letter to Catherine Lansing.

FROM CATHERINE GANSEVOORT LANSING
BEFORE 1 AUGUST 1878 · ALBANY

Unlocated. Catherine Lansing's request for Melville's aid in presenting the Lenox Library with a copy of the memorial biography of her brother Henry Gansevoort is cited in his 1 August 1878 reply.

FROM CATHERINE GANSEVOORT LANSING
4 AUGUST 1878 · ALBANY

Unlocated. A letter from Melville's cousin, saying she had mailed the copy of Henry Gansevoort's memorial biography intended for the Lenox Library, is cited in Melville's 6 August 1878 reply.

FROM ELIZABETH SHAW MELVILLE
BEFORE 12 AUGUST 1878 · JEFFERSON HILL

Unlocated. A letter from his wife, vacationing in the White Mountains of New Hampshire, is cited in Melville's 12 August 1878 letter to Catherine Lansing.

FROM HENRY B. THOMAS
BEFORE 12 AUGUST 1878 · JEFFERSON HILL

Unlocated. A letter from Henry Thomas, who married Melville's daughter Frances two years later, is cited in Melville's 12 August 1878 letter to Catherine Lansing. On 4 August Melville had taken Henry Thomas to visit his brother Thomas on Staten Island (see the entry for Melville's early August letter to his sister Frances Priscilla, p. 468 above). Henry Thomas's letter was from the White Mountains of New Hampshire; as Melville explained to his cousin, "Curious coincidence — Fanny is there."

FROM CATHERINE GANSEVOORT LANSING
25 NOVEMBER 1878 · ALBANY

Unlocated. An invitation from his cousin for Melville and his daughters to spend Thanksgiving in Albany is cited in his 26 November 1878 reply.

FROM FRANCES PRISCILLA MELVILLE
25 NOVEMBER 1878 · ALBANY

Unlocated. A letter from Melville's sister Frances, who was visiting in Albany with the Lansings, is cited in his 26 November 1878 letter to their cousin Catherine Lansing.

1879

FROM CATHERINE GANSEVOORT LANSING
14 APRIL 1879 · ALBANY

Unlocated. A letter to Melville was recorded, with no indication of its contents, by Catherine Lansing in the letter list she kept in the back of her diary (NYPL-GL).

FROM CATHERINE GANSEVOORT LANSING AND
ABRAHAM LANSING
BEFORE 25 JUNE 1879 · ALBANY

Unlocated. In response to an invitation from the Lansings for Melville to visit them in Albany, Melville's daughter Frances wrote on 25 June 1879 to Catherine Lansing: "Papa wants me to thank you for yours and Cousin Abe's invitation to spend next Sunday with you, but says he will not be able to come as he does not like to leave home when mamma is feeling so miserably" (NYPL-GL). (Elizabeth Shaw Melville was suffering as she often did from allergies, which Frances refers to as "her cold.")

FROM ABRAHAM LANSING
BEFORE 10 AUGUST 1879 · NEW YORK

Unlocated. In 1879 Abraham Lansing was sent as a delegate to a conference on international law in London (see Alice P. Kenney, *The Gansevoorts of Albany* [Syracuse: Syracuse University Press, 1969], p. 261). Lansing wrote Melville a note before leaving and arranged for his brother Edwin Yates Lansing to deliver it, as a 10 August letter from Edwin to Abraham in London indicates: "On leaving the wharf I went down town and while there called at the Custom house to endeavor to find Herman Melville as agreed upon, but ascertaining that I would have to go as far up town as 76th St. and East river to see him I concluded to leave your message of farewell to Mʳ Brewster, whom I afterwards met, who agreed to deliver it soon" (NYPL-GL). Somehow the message miscarried, however; Frances Priscilla Melville wrote Abraham Lansing on 30 August 1879 that "Herman met your brother Edwin in the street, & heard of Kate & you having gone abroad, from him — Too bad that your note turned up in London & not, at 104 East 26 Street" (NYPL-GL).

FROM ELIZABETH SHAW MELVILLE
BEFORE 13 AUGUST 1879 · WOODSTOCK

Unlocated. A letter from Melville's wife, who was summering with their daughters at the Overlook Mountain House in the Catskills, can be inferred from a letter Melville wrote to his sister Frances Priscilla, which is cited in her 13 August 1879 letter to Catherine Lansing (see p. 473 above).

FROM ABRAHAM LANSING
15 NOVEMBER 1879 · ALBANY

Unlocated. Catherine Lansing's letter list, in the back of her diary (NYPL-GL), noted that among those to whom her husband Abraham sent invitations for Christmas dinner were "Cousin Herman" and his family. The invitation is also cited in Melville's reply, declining, on 17 November 1879.

1880

FROM HARPER & BROTHERS
28 FEBRUARY 1880 · NEW YORK

Neither Melville's request asking for an account statement from the Harpers, nor his acknowledgment of it, if he made one, is now located. The account that was enclosed with this letter is now among the statements Melville received from them in the Melville Collection of the Houghton Library of Harvard University. As this letter states, it shows a balance due Melville of $68.62 after several book orders he had made, as well as a cash advance for $64.38 that he had received on 9 February 1878 (see G. Thomas Tanselle, "The Sales of Melville's Books," *Harvard Library Bulletin* 17 [1969], 205).

Feb'y 28th 1880

H. Melville, Esq.,   }
104 E. 26th. St., N.Y.   }
Dear Sir:

In accordance with your request we take pleasure in enclosing herewith a statement of your account from Dec'r 27/77 to Feb'y 19/80, and our check for $68⁶²⁄₁₀₀ to balance. Please acknowledge its receipt, and oblige,

Yours truly,
Harper & Brothers,
Muller.

ALS on a 12.8 × 20.5 cm part-sheet (torn along the left edge) of white wove paper with the Harpers' printed insignia in the upper left corner (an oval belt enclosing two hands, one passing a torch to the other, with the words "HARPER & BROTHERS, FRANKLIN SQUARE, NEW YORK . . . . 18 " on the oval belt). Muller, apparently a clerk, inscribed only one side of the leaf, in ink. Melville noted on the verso in blue pencil (with underlinings in red pencil) "Harper acct".

LOCATION: HCL-M.

TEXTUAL NOTE: 18] *part of the printed letterhead (see above)*

FROM CATHERINE GANSEVOORT LANSING
14 APRIL 1880 · ALBANY

Unlocated. A letter notifying Melville of the death of Abraham Lansing's brother John Thomas Lansing is recorded in Catherine Lansing's diary (NYPL-GL) and cited in Melville's 15 April 1880 reply (see the headnote to that letter for more about John Lansing).

FROM ABRAHAM LANSING
BEFORE 8 DECEMBER 1880 · ALBANY

Unlocated. An invitation from Abraham Lansing for Melville and his family to attend a reception at the Fort Orange Club in Albany is cited in Melville's 8 December 1880 letter declining the offer.

1882

FROM MARIA HOADLEY
BEFORE 12 APRIL 1882 · LAWRENCE

Unlocated. A letter from his niece Maria (Minnie) Hoadley is cited in Melville's 12 April 1882 letter to her mother, his sister Catherine Hoadley.

FROM HELEN MELVILLE GRIGGS AND
FRANCES PRISCILLA MELVILLE
BEFORE 12 APRIL 1882 · [GANSEVOORT?]

Unlocated. A letter to Melville and his wife from his sisters Helen and Frances Priscilla (Fanny), who were probably writing from Gansevoort, is cited in Melville's 12 April 1882 letter to their sister Catherine Hoadley.

FROM STANWIX MELVILLE
BEFORE 8 SEPTEMBER 1882 · SAN FRANCISCO

An indeterminate number of unlocated letters. In an 8 September 1882 letter to Catherine Lansing, Elizabeth Melville reported: "We hear constantly from Stanny. I wish I could say he is materially better — but he keeps about the same, & cannot yet get rid of his cough — I feel very anxious about him — that it holds on so long" (NYPL-GL). On 23 February 1886, Stanwix died at the German Hospital in San Francisco.

FROM THE FOUNDERS OF THE AUTHORS CLUB
[OCTOBER?] 1882 · NEW YORK

Unlocated. An invitation to Melville from the founding committee of the Authors Club in New York is cited in Charles De Kay's unpublished reminiscences of the club. For De Kay's account of Melville's two replies, probably written during October 1882, see the entry on p. 480 above.

1883

FROM JULIAN HAWTHORNE
BEFORE 10 AUGUST 1883 · NEW YORK

Unlocated. Julian Hawthorne's letter requesting information for his book *Nathaniel Hawthorne and His Wife* is cited in Melville's 10 August 1883 reply.

1884

FROM JAMES BILLSON
21 AUGUST 1884 · LEICESTER

Although James Billson, a young British solicitor and political and religious radical, is known to have written Melville at least eight letters, only this one, the first in the sequence, is now located. For more about Billson, see the headnote to Melville's 10 October 1884 reply to this letter.

> Tower St Leicester – England –
> Aug *21ˢᵗ* 1884

My Dear Sir: —

I have to thank you for an immense deal of good I have derived from reading your works & can assure you that here in Leicester your books are in great request. We have had a great deal of trouble in getting them in the first place on account of most of them having been published in America & again through being unable to secure a full list — as soon as one is discovered (for that is what it really is with us) it is eagerly read & passed round a rapidly increasing knot of "Melville readers." However I am writing not merely to tell you this since I suppose that monotonous to you long ago have been — I will not say flattering letters — but such expressions of appreciation as herein conveyed. My object in writing was a more practical one — to ask if you would kindly give me the names of any other works you may have written besides those I mention below — which are what we have succeeded in unearthing. "Mardi", "Typee", "Confidence Man", "Piazza Tales" "Omoo", "Redburn", "Moby Dick", Israel Potter" & "Pierre". If at the same time you would give me the names of the publishers I would esteem it a very great favour.

I have liked the Mardi best although not feeling quite sure I have perceived all the meaning of the allegory.

You will I hope pardon this letter & believe me if I may say so without impertinence that the delight you have given has been the means even of arousing feelings of affection to yourself emphasized as it is by the intimate acquaintance I have with you although hitherto you have done all the talking —

I am Dear Sir

Yours very Truly

James Billson

Mᴿ Herman Melville

ALS on a 22.6 × 17.4 cm sheet, folded in half, of white laid paper, watermarked with the name "JAPANESE NOTE PAPER J S & CO". Billson inscribed the first three pages, in ink, and addressed the envelope "Mʳ Herman Melville | 104 East 26ᵗʰ St., | New York City."; it was postmarked "F | 9–30 | 12M" and the stamp was later torn off. Elizabeth Melville endorsed the envelope in pencil "Aug 21 – 1884 | Mr Billson" and wrote on the recto "Mr. Billson".

Location: HCL-M.

Publication: (partial) *Log*, II, 785.

Textual Notes: Israel Potter"] *opening double quotation mark lacking* • Billson] *underlined with a flourish* • Mʳ Herman Melville] *underlined with a flourish*

FROM JAMES BILLSON
28 OCTOBER 1884 · LEICESTER

Unlocated. Billson's letter, which probably accompanied his gift of James Thomson's *Vane's Story, Weddah and Om-el-Bonain, and Other Poems,* is cited in Melville's 1 December 1884 reply (see the headnote to that letter for more about Thomson and his books). It was presumably a reply to Melville's 10 October 1884 letter and was probably also the one Melville refers to in his 22 January 1885 letter as "a former note" in which Billson mentioned the difficulty he had encountered in trying to find a copy of *Clarel.*

1885

FROM JAMES BILLSON
BEFORE 21 JANUARY 1885 · LEICESTER

Unlocated. A letter, presumably in reply to Melville's 1 December 1884 letter and probably announcing Billson's gift of James Thomson's *The City of Dreadful Night, and Other Poems,* is cited in Melville's 22 January 1885 reply.

FROM JAMES BILLSON
18 FEBRUARY 1885 · LEICESTER

Unlocated. A letter from Billson, presumably in reply to Melville's 22 January 1885 letter and containing a "friendly proffer of good offices," is cited in Melville's 5 September 1885 reply and in Elizabeth Shaw Melville's memorandum book (Berkshire Athenaeum; see Sealts, *Early Lives*, p. 171).

FROM LAURA M. WACHSCHLAGER
BEFORE 12 JULY 1885 · PLACE UNKNOWN

Unlocated. Miss Wachschlager's letter, apparently praising Melville's "sea-tales," is cited in his 12 July 1885 reply.

FROM ABRAHAM LANSING
27 JULY 1885 · ALBANY

Two weeks earlier, on 9 July, Melville's youngest sister, Frances Priscilla, had died at the age of fifty-seven. Presumably Melville answered this request from Abraham Lansing, the executor of her estate, to approve the probate of her will, but his reply is unlocated.

July 27   5.

My Dear Mr Melville:

Will it meet your approval, if steps shall be taken at once for the probate of Fanny's will. It has not yet been opened. Please let me know.

Kate & I send our kind regards to you & to Cousin Lizzie & to Bessie. We are both well.

Truly Yours,
Abraham Lansing

Herman Melville Esq.

Original document not located. Text from Abraham Lansing's 20 May 1880–September 1888 letterbook, p. 152 (one-half page).

LOCATION (of letterbook): NYPL-GL.

PUBLICATION: (partial) *Log*, II, 791.

TEXTUAL NOTE: Abraham Lansing] *underlined with a flourish*

FROM ABRAHAM LANSING
19 AUGUST 1885 · ALBANY

Unlocated. Abraham Lansing's 19 August letter to Melville, enclosing a copy of his sister Frances Priscilla's will and a waiver to sign, is cited in Melville's 21 August 1885 reply.

FROM ABRAHAM LANSING
9 SEPTEMBER 1885 · ALBANY

This third letter from Abraham Lansing continues the correspondence about Melville's sister Frances Priscilla's estate (see the two entries just above).

Sept. 9 5.

Dear Mr Melville:

The tenant of Fanneys farm writes for an extention of his lease, so as to sow with a prospect of being able to reap next harvest His ground has been ploughed.

It seems to be a good plan to extend the lease for a year. If you agree with it, will you please sign & return to me the enclosed power of attorney.

Only your signature is necessary

Yours truly
Abraham Lansing

Herman Melville Esq

Original document not located. Text from Abraham Lansing's 20 May 1880–6 September 1888 letterbook, p. 176 (one-half page).

LOCATION (of letterbook): NYPL-GL.

PUBLICATION: Paltsits, pp. 61–62.

FROM JAMES BILLSON
[7 OCTOBER?] 1885 · LEICESTER

Unlocated. A "friendly note" from James Billson (presumably in reply to Melville's 5 September letter), as well as his gift of two of James Thomson's books of prose pieces (*Essays and Phantasies* and *Satires and Profanities*), is cited in Melville's 20 December 1885 reply. Assuming Billson's note accompanied the books, it can be dated 7 October 1885—the date Billson inscribed in the copy of *Essays and Phantasies* (HCL-M; Sealts 518).

1886

FROM J. W. HENRY CANOLL
23 JANUARY 1886 · NEW YORK

Unlocated. Canoll's letter, cited in Melville's undated draft reply, was probably either accompanied by a copy of his poetic tribute to Melville that had been published in the *Commercial Advertiser* on 18 January 1886 or made reference to that tribute, since Melville mentions it in his draft. For more about Canoll, see the headnote to Melville's letter, presumably written shortly after 23 January, p. 493 above. Both that tribute and Canoll's sketch of Melville that appeared in the 14 January 1886 *Commercial Advertiser* are reprinted here. The sketch was part of his unsigned article entitled "Echoes of the Hour. Notes on Men, Women and Things" that also included sketches of Bartley Campbell, a playwright, Roger A. Pryor, a lawyer, and Cornelius Mathews, Melville's friend (see p. 169 above). The concluding mistaken assertion that Melville's last voyage was in 1860 around the world in a whaling vessel suggests that Canoll got at least some of his information from the 1875 revision of the Duyckincks' *Cyclopædia*.

Herman Melville exemplifies the transiency of literary reputation. Before the civil war he enjoyed wide fame, and his very clever books were much admired. To-day, his name would not be recognized by the rising generation. Still, he is not very old—sixty-five—and his rather heavy, thick-set figure and warm complexion betoken health and vigor. He is a native Manhattanese, who, in his teens had so idealized the life of a sailor that he shipped before the mast on a foreign voyage. Nor did his experience cure him of his love of the ocean. Four years later he sailed for the Pacific on a whaling expedition, but the captain of the vessel was so brutal that he deserted while lying at Nukahiva, one of the Marquesas. Having lost his way, he wandered off into the Typee Valley and fell into the hands of its savage inhabitants. Although fierce and martial, they did him no harm. On the contrary, they took a fancy to him and treated him with great kindness. After staying with them six months he was taken off by an Australian whaler bound for Tahiti. He passed a year on the Society and Sandwich Islands, and finally returned to his native land at the age of 25. Not long after he published "Typee," a record, half fanciful, of his adventures on Nukahiva—his account of the sentimental Fayaway delighted his feminine readers—and the book won renown, both in this country and Great Britain. "Omoo," describing his experiences in the South Seas, "Mardi," "Redburn," and other productions followed; but none of them was so much liked as his first. His latest books, especially "Pierre," and the "Confidence Man," were so queer and dull as to leave the impression that he was written out. He has lived at Boston, at Pittsfield, Massachusetts, and here, and of late years has done nothing in literature. For a long while he has been in the custom house as inspector, and is dependent on his salary. Although his early works are still popular, the author is generally supposed to be dead. He has, indeed, been buried in a government office. His wife is the daughter of Chief Justice Shaw, of Massachusetts. He is a genial pleasant fellow, who, after all his wanderings, loves to stay at home—his house is in

Twenty-sixth street—and indulge in reverie and reminiscence. His last voyage was in 1860 around the world on a whaling vessel.

MELVILLE.

He rests, whose feet have trod all continents;
Whose song has been of Nature's heart and Man's;
Who worded legends of mysterious isles,
Of Maori's paradise and opal skies,
Till pleasure's thrill gave pulse to Saxon veins—
Till bloom, and odorous mist, and vapored gems,
Seemed borne by mystic breeze and unkent cloud
From amber caskets floating southern seas.
The ocean monarch's friend and kindly scribe,
He loved each grain of earth, each drop of sea,
Where his keen microscope of mind discerned
Or home or tomb of Nature's sentient motes,
He rests, this gleaner of Judæan plains,
Who culled the fruit of Egypt's faith as well,
Beheld in Parsee's symbol guiding light
And learned the mystery of Grove and Palm.
Neptune he knew, Apollo, Venus, Jove,
Yet bowed, uncovered, in the courts of Brahm—
Revered as sire of Roman gods, and Greek.

He rests: though diverse climes beguiled, enthralled,
The western stars were sacred light and beacon,
That guided to the hallowed fires of home.
No cortege waited there, no coarse ovation;
His footsteps ever modest fell and peaceful
As blessed foot whose prints he traced at Saba.
In mart or park, at rest or bent by toil—
The nation's rights he ever toiling guarded—
He still was true—to every man a neighbor,
Though rude Presumption dare not grasp his hand.
His palm was friendly, kind his eye of blue
While rending mask of Vice of piercing Pride.

He rests, this seedsman of the Western Field,
Who scattered golden grain from either hand;
All golden will the era be when Time
Shall scatter germs of life like his—for bloom or balm.

FROM JAMES BILLSON
31 JANUARY 1886 · LEICESTER

Unlocated. Billson's "kind note" of 31 January, presumably in reply to Melville's 20 December 1885 letter and announcing a number of gifts that he sent not long thereafter on 15 February, is acknowledged in Melville's 2 April 1886 reply. Elizabeth Melville also noted this letter in her memorandum book, apparently quoting part of it: "In letter of Jan 31. 1886 Mr Billson writes of Mr. Barrs — a friend of Mr H. S. Salt who wrote notice in the Scottish Art Review 'Mr Barrs one of your readers desires to forward you "A Voice from the Nile" &c by James Thomson. Mr Barrs had Thomson for a visitor, and Mr Barr also figured in the poem "Belvoir" — Mr Barrs sister was the subject of the poem "The Sleeper" in the above named volume['] — sent Feb 15th 1886 — At same date Mr Billson sent a 'semi-manuscript' copy of a poem of 'Omar Khayam['] translated by Fitzgerald — " (Berkshire Athenaeum). For explanations of the individuals and works mentioned in her memorandum, see the headnotes to Melville's 2 April 1886 letter to Billson and his 12 January 1890 letter to H. S. Salt. For a complete transcription of Elizabeth Melville's memorandum book, see Sealts, *Early Lives*, pp. 167–77.

FROM STANWIX MELVILLE
14 FEBRUARY 1886 · SAN FRANCISCO

Unlocated. A letter can be inferred as accompanying the power of attorney that Stanwix signed and dated on 14 February 1886. See the entry for the unlocated letter that Melville presumably wrote when sending that document to Stanwix for his signature (p. 496 above).

FROM LEONARD G. SANFORD
BEFORE 22 JUNE 1886 · [CORNWALL?]

Unlocated. A letter from Leonard Sanford, possibly of Cornwall, Connecticut, who had also spent time aboard a whaler as a young man, is cited in Melville's 22 June 1886 reply.

FROM HELEN MELVILLE GRIGGS
BEFORE 15 JULY 1886 · GANSEVOORT

Unlocated. In his unlocated letter to his sister Helen Griggs, written sometime before 15 July 1886, Melville advised her to send separate apportioned accounts to all the family members receiving shipments from the breakup of the house at Gansevoort (see the entry for Melville's unlocated letter, p. 502 above). Explaining this plan in her 15 July letter to Catherine Lansing, Helen added that she had accordingly done so, listing Melville as one of the family members to whom she had sent an account.

FROM W. CLARK RUSSELL
21 JULY 1886 · ST. LAWRENCE ON SEA

W. Clark Russell, the British sea-author, then living in St. Lawrence on Sea, Kent, wrote this letter in response to Melville's earlier 1886 letter hand-delivered by their mutual friend, the artist Peter Toft, of which only a possible draft survives (see pp. 498–500 above). Both that draft and this reply indicate that R. H. Dana, Jr., was one subject of the letter Melville sent. Russell had already written an article linking Melville and Dana entitled "Sea Stories," published in the *Contemporary Review* 46 (September 1884), 343–63, and he later wrote an article on them entitled "A Claim for American Literature," published in the *North American Review* 154 (February 1892), 138–49.

July 21st 1886

My dear M[r] Herman Melville,

Your letter which M[r] Toft has been good enough to convey to me has given me a very great and singular pleasure. Your delightful books carry the imagination into a maritime period so remote that often as you have been in my mind I could never satisfy myself that you were still amongst the living. I am glad indeed to learn from M[r] Toft that you are still hale and hearty and I do most heartily wish you many years yet of health and vigour.

Your books I have in the American edition: they were kindly obtained for me by Mess[rs] Harper Bros. I have "Typee," "Omoo," "Redburn," and that noble piece "Moby Dick." These are all I have been able to obtain. There have been many editions of your works in this country particularly your lovely South Sea sketches; but the editions are not equal to those of the American publishers. Your reputation here is very great. It is hard to meet a man whose opinion as a reader is worth having who does not speak of your works in such terms as he might hesitate to employ, with all his patriotism, towards many renowned English writers.

Dana is indeed great. There is nothing in literature more remarkable than the impression produced by Dana's portrature of the homely inner life of a little brig's forecastle.

I beg that you will accept my thanks for the kindly spirit in which you have read my books. I wish it were in my power to cross the Atlantic, for you assuredly would be the first whom it would be my happiness to visit; but a wretched malady afflicts me. I am prostrated by rheumatism and its concurrent curse, nervous exhaustion.

I have just made the voyage to the Cape but without any result. The condition of my right hand obliges me to dictate this to my son; but painful as it is to me to hold a pen I cannot suffer this letter to reach the hands of a man of so admirable a genius as Herman Melville without begging him to believe me to be with my own hand his most respectful and hearty admirer

W. Clark Russell

LS on a 25 × 20 cm sheet, folded in half, of white wove paper with the letterhead "6, GRAN-VILLE GARDENS, | ST LAWRENCE ON SEA, | THANET." Russell's son, Herbert Russell, inscribed all four pages, in ink; Russell himself signed the letter. Herbert Russell addressed the envelope "Herman Melville Esq | 104 East Twenty-Sixth Street | New York | U.S.A.; it was postmarked in Ramsgate on 21 July and in New York on 31 July and again on 1 August. Elizabeth Melville noted on the envelope in pencil "July 21st | 1886 | W C | Russell" and Melville, also in pencil, wrote on it "Address | Office of the | Daily Telegraph | London"—later canceled in pencil. It was later stamped—probably for ownership purposes—with Melville's son-in-law's name and address, "H. B. Thomas | 60 Montrose Ave. | South Orange, N.J."

LOCATION: HCL-M.

PUBLICATION: (partial) Weaver, pp. 365–66.

TEXTUAL NOTES: towards] wards *added* • forecastle] fore-|castle

FROM ANNE BARTON
1 AUGUST 1886 · SYRACUSE

According to Elizabeth Melville's endorsement on this letter, Joseph Barton had been Melville's shipmate aboard the *United States.* The 1 July 1843 muster rolls for that ship list him as an ordinary seaman. According to the 1867–68 Syracuse directory, he ran a tobacco shop on Genesee Street after his return.

210 E. Genesee St.
Syracuse N.Y. Aug. 1–86.

Herman Melville: —
Dear Sir —

As my father, Joseph Barton, is at present out of town, he wished me to write to you and see if you were the same Herman Melville with whom, many years ago, he took a voyage around Cape Horn in the Frigate United States.

He has repeatedly tried to obtain your works but has so far not been successful.

If he is not mistaken he would like to hear from you and to learn where he may obtain your works.

Anne Barton.

ALS on a 22.7 × 17.9 cm sheet, folded in half, of white wove paper with lines, embossed with the manufacturer's oval stamp enclosing the name "RIALTO". Anne Barton inscribed the first and third pages, in ink, and addressed the envelope "Herman Melville | Fire Island | Suffolk Co., | N.Y.", the middle two lines of which were later canceled in pencil with "104 E. 26 St | New York" added in pencil; it was postmarked in Syracuse, New York, on 1 August, on Fire Island on 3 August, and in New York on 4 August. Elizabeth Melville endorsed the envelope in pencil "Ann Barton | Aug 1 – 1886 | for her | father | old shipmate".

LOCATION: HCL-M.

PUBLICATION: (partial) Log, II, 801.

FROM ELEANOR THOMAS AND FRANCES MELVILLE THOMAS 7 AUGUST 1886 · MENDHAM

While summering in Mendham, New Jersey, Melville's daughter Frances, by now the mother of two daughters of her own—Eleanor Melville Thomas (1882–1964) and her namesake Frances Cuthbert Thomas (1883–1980)—took this letter in dictation from four-year-old Eleanor, adding a note of her own at the end (now incomplete) about the bicycling tour her husband Henry ("Harry") was taking and her receipt of a clock from the breakup of the house in Gansevoort (for the arrangements concerning this clock, see the entry for Melville's unlocated letter written before 7 June 1886). For more about Eleanor Thomas, and the two books concerning her grandfather which she later published under her married name Metcalf, see the headnote to Melville's 12 April 1882 letter to his sister Catherine Hoadley, written only a few months after Eleanor's birth.

Aug 7 1886

My dear Grandpa,

Frances and I have got a new doll, my dolly's name is Dinah and Frances' dolly's name is Susie & you haven't seen them — When I was just getting into bed, I saw a 'ittle fly in the water, & I took him out with my hand & put him on the floor. We went out to take a walk with Mamma & we saw the biggest rooster he ever saw in his life — and we saw the pigs and they were going to sleep, and we gave them some grass to eat. And we saw a picture of a circus, and a horse was sitting up at a table with a bib on eating his dinner & two

waitress. And there was a horse going on a bicycle. And we are
having a very, very, nice time up here. and we got very nice picture
books up here. There is a 'ittle girl called Eloise, and she's got two
hammocks at her house. Frances & me got sick eating green apples,
but we are all well now. Mamma lets me have corn for dinner if I
eat my meat. We had 'ittle tiny kitties and they runned away — I
send a kiss to Grandpa — Goodbye

From Eleanor M. Thomas

Mendham
Aug. 7th
1886

My dear Papa,

I hope you will find this letter entertaining I wrote just what
Eleanor told me. They are having a good time here — The weather
is very cool, and it is raining hard to day — Harry left here yesterday on his bicycle, he expected to meet a friend in New York and
take a little trip through Berkshire Co. with him, returning the latter part of the week — He tells me the clock arrived in pretty good
order, some of the wood work had come apart — & when we get
settled at home again, we can have it put in order, it will be an
ornament to the hall, and I am delighted to have it — I am very
anxious

LS and AL (lacking final page with signature) on a 22.8 × 17.7 cm sheet, folded in half, of
white wove paper. Frances Melville Thomas inscribed the first three pages, in pencil, with her
daughter's letter, and inscribed the fourth page, in ink, with the beginning of her own letter.
The remainder of her letter is unlocated.

LOCATION: Berkshire Athenaeum, Pittsfield, Massachusetts. *Provenance*: Agnes Morewood.

PUBLICATION: (partial) *Log*, II, 801.

TEXTUAL NOTE: Aug. 7th | 1886] 1886 *added in pencil*

FROM ABRAHAM LANSING
19 AUGUST 1886 · ALBANY

In settling the estate of Melville's sister Frances Priscilla (see Lansing's 27 July 1885
letter, above), Abraham Lansing first distributed the legacies she had bequeathed in
her will (see the two letters just below for her legacies to Melville's wife and chil-

dren). The final settlement of the estate did not occur until the Gansevoort mansion she had inherited was sold (see Lansing's March 1889 letters, below).

Aug 19   6

My Dear Mr Melville:

I enclose herewith my check as administrator with the will arranged of Fannys Estate for $3019.⁵⁹⁄₁₀₀ = in payment of the legacy of $3000 = left you by the will, with interest thereon from July 10, 1886.

Will you please sign & return to me the enclosed receipt & duplicate & oblige

Yours very truly
Abraham Lansing
Admin &c

Herman Melville Esq
104 E 26th St N.Y.

Original document not located. Text from Abraham Lansing's 20 May 1880–6 September 1888 letterbook, p. 339.

LOCATION (of letterbook): NYPL-GL.

PUBLICATION: Paltsits, p. 62.

TEXTUAL NOTE: arranged] *possibly* annexed

FROM ABRAHAM LANSING
28 SEPTEMBER 1886 · ALBANY

As acknowledged in Abraham Lansing's 15 October 1886 letter, Melville replied to this 28 September letter on 12 October 1886, enclosing the signed receipts requested and, evidently, the power of attorney authorizing him to collect Stanwix Melville's legacy (see the entries on pp. 496 and 502–3 above). With his son's death on 23 February 1886, Melville had become his beneficiary.

Sep 28   6.

Dear Mr Melville:

I send herewith checks payable to the order of Mrs Melville & Bessie in payment of the legacies bequeathed to them by Fannys will less 5 per cent tax under the act of 1885, & with interest from July

10. 1886. Also a receipt & duplicate for their signatures, to be returned to me.

Stanwix had a legacy of $100= under the will. Is there any administration upon his estate?

Will you kindly deliver the checks & return me the receipt executed & oblige

Yours very truly
Abraham Lansing

Herman Melville Esq.

Original document not located. Text from Abraham Lansing's 20 May 1880–6 September 1888 letterbook, p. 368.

LOCATION (of letterbook): NYPL-GL.

PUBLICATION: Paltsits, p. 63.

TEXTUAL NOTE: Abraham Lansing] *underlined with a flourish*

FROM ABRAHAM LANSING
15 OCTOBER 1886 · ALBANY

This letter enclosing the check for Stanwix's legacy concludes the first exchange of correspondence about the settlement of Frances Priscilla Melville's will; however, the final settlement of the will did not occur until March 1889 (see Abraham Lansing's 14 and 15 March 1889 letters to Melville, below).

Oct 15   6

My Dear Sir:

I have yours of 12ᵗʰ inst with receipt & duplicate for legacies also a memorandum directing payt of Stanwix legacy to you.

I send herewith my check as admʳ &c for $96.⁴⁹⁄₁₀₀ in payment of the legacy to Stanwix less the legacy tax, & with interest.

In the absence of testamentary disposition & of claims of creditors you are entitled to the legacy as next of kin. I therefore make the payment to you assuming these facts without the form of administration.

Yours very truly
Abraham Lansing

Herman Melville Esq

Original document not located. Text from Abraham Lansing's 20 May 1880–6 September 1888 letterbook, p. 378 (one-half page).

LOCATION (of letterbook): NYPL-GL.

PUBLICATION: Paltsits, p. 63.

TEXTUAL NOTES: Abraham Lansing] *written only partially at the bottom of the page* • Herman Melville Esq] *added in pencil*

1887

FROM ROSSITER JOHNSON
9 DECEMBER [1887?] · [NEW YORK?]

Unlocated. Rossiter Johnson's letter, evidently inviting Melville to contribute to one of his encyclopedias, is cited in Melville's 11 December [1887?] reply.

1888

FROM EDMUND C. STEDMAN
20 JANUARY 1888 · NEW YORK

Edmund C. Stedman published *Poets of America* (Boston: Houghton, Mifflin) in 1885 and included a brief reference to Melville in the second chapter ("There is native fire in the lyrics of McMaster, Melville, O'Hara, Finch . . ." [p. 49]). In reply to this request from Stedman for a poem with which to extra-illustrate his own copy of that book, Melville wrote on 29 January enclosing an autograph copy of his "Ditty of Aristippus," from the fourth canto in the third part of *Clarel* (lines 1–21). He also included one of his 1885 photographs by Rockwood, probably in response to Stedman's canceled line in this letter asking for a photograph if a portrait in "steel or wood" was not available (see the textual notes, below). For more about Stedman and his literary activities, see the headnotes to Melville's 27 and 29 January 1888 letters.

44 East 26th St.,
New York, January 20th, 1888.

Mr. Herman Melville,
Dear Sir:
    Having borne my share of the trouble caused by autograph-hunters, I am somewhat disconcerted to find myself for once in their ranks. Yet I trust you will assist me in realizing a pleasant fancy.

I possess already many manuscripts and portraits of authors referred to in my book entitled POETS OF AMERICA, and am illustrating and "extending" my own large paper copy of this work by inserting these choice memorials and such others as I can procure. With some hesitation I venture to petition you for one of your best known shorter poems, in your own handwriting, (signed) to add further grace and value to my collection.

One thing more. Will you kindly tell me which is the best portrait in steel or wood of yourself, and where it may be found, in case it is not already in my possession? You see that I have a strong desire to make a beautiful and unique book — one that will be treasured in years to come — or I should not trespass thus on your indulgence.

With much respect,
Very sincerely yours,
Edmund C. Stedman

TLS on a 20.4 × 26.8 cm sheet of white laid paper, watermarked with the name "STS LINEN" and the image of a typewriter. The body of the letter is typed on only one side of the leaf; the insertions, complimentary close, and signature are handwritten.

LOCATION: HCL-M.

TEXTUAL NOTES: (signed)] *inserted by hand in ink* · possession?] *before canceled* If none exists, will you favor me with one of your photographs? · Edmund C. Stedman] *underlined with a flourish*

FROM THE EDITORS OF
"A LIBRARY OF AMERICAN LITERATURE"
24 JANUARY 1888 · NEW YORK

This printed form-letter with relevant blanks filled in by hand was sent to Melville by Edmund C. Stedman and his coeditor, Ellen Mackay Hutchinson, in connection with their ten-volume *A Library of American Literature* (1889–90). Melville agreed to their requests in a brief 27 January 1888 letter. For more on Stedman and the specific pieces by Melville included in the *Library*, see the headnote to that letter.

Jan. 24ᵗʰ 1888

Mr. Herman Melville,
DEAR Sir:

A section of the LIBRARY OF AMERICAN LITERATURE will be devoted to authors of a recent date. Many of them already have au-

A LIBRARY OF AMERICAN LITERATURE,

FROM THE EARLIEST SETTLEMENT TO THE PRESENT TIME.

COMPILED AND EDITED BY

EDMUND CLARENCE STEDMAN

AND

ELLEN MACKAY HUTCHINSON.

IN TEN OCTAVO VOLUMES.

NEW YORK CITY:

PUBLISHED BY CHARLES L. WEBSTER & CO.

"The initial volume of an extensive work will soon be given to the public. During the past year or two, Mr. E. C. Stedman and Miss Ellen M. Hutchinson, of THE TRIBUNE editorial staff, have been collecting material for 'A Library of American Literature,' of which they are the joint editors. Their projected work is a compendium, in ten octavo volumes, of specimens of American literature from the earliest settlement to the present time. The editors aim to give distinctive, readable examples, from authoritative texts, of the writings of every class and period; to form a collection that shall be to our literature what a 'National Gallery' is to national art. Longer extracts will be given than are usual in compilations of the kind. The work will be illustrated with portraits and sold by subscription only. The first two volumes, soon to appear, are rich in early and later Colonial Literature—embracing a more various summary than hitherto has been collected in handy form."—*N. Y. Tribune.*

CONTENTS.

Prospectus (1888) for "A Library of American Literature" (reduced). Courtesy of the Houghton Library, Harvard University (Melville Collection).

thorized us to include such specimens of their writings as will best represent them within the limits of our compilation.

We ask your kind permission to use, for the purpose of this work, some extracts from your prose romances, and selections from your poems.

The Messrs. Harper have given their consent.

We shall be greatly facilitated by an early reply. If our request is granted, you will place us under further obligations by a line stating the place and date of your birth.

Respectfully yours,
The Editors.

ALS, "The Editors" (Edmund C. Stedman and Ellen Mackay Hutchinson), and prospectus (see p. 739) on a 32 × 24.1 cm sheet, folded in half, of white wove paper. The letter is on the first page, with its blanks filled in, in ink (see the textual notes), and the prospectus is on the third page. The letter bears the printed heading " 'A LIBRARY OF AMERICAN LITERA-TURE.' " (centered), "*EDITORS:* | EDMUND C. STEDMAN, | ELLEN M. HUTCHINSON." (to the left), and "OFFICE OF CHARLES L. WEBSTER & CO., | 3 East 14th Street, | NEW YORK CITY,   188 " (to the right). Elizabeth Melville noted in pencil on the fourth page "E. C. Stedman | Jan 24 – 1888".

LOCATION: HCL-M.

PUBLICATION: (partial) *Log*, II, 805.

TEXTUAL NOTES: Jan. 24th] *inserted by hand, in ink (also final 8 in year, with* 188 *part of printed letterhead)* • Mr. Herman Melville,] *inserted by hand, in ink* • Sir:] *inserted by hand, in ink* • some extracts . . . their consent.] *inserted by hand, in ink* • The Editors.] *inserted by hand, in ink, under-lined with a flourish and followed by the printed instruction* [OVER]

FROM UNKNOWN
BEFORE 31 JANUARY 1888 · PLACE UNKNOWN

Unlocated. A letter inquiring about *Israel Potter* is cited in Melville's 31 January 1888 reply.

FROM EDMUND C. STEDMAN
1 FEBRUARY 1888 · NEW YORK

When Melville wrote Stedman on 20 February 1888 to thank him for the "books" he had "kindly sent," he was probably referring to the books and chapter that ac-companied this letter of Stedman's. That reply also suggests that it was an evening's conversation at Melville's home that had led Stedman to send the books and letter.

The "three vols. of our Old Orion's works" were by Richard Henry Horne (1803–84), who was best known as the author of the epic "Orion" (1843), published at a farthing "to mark the public contempt into which epic poetry had fallen." The 1911 Anderson Galleries sale catalogue of Stedman's books lists as lot 1435 a single volume including Horne's *Gregory VII, Prometheus the Fire Bringer,* and *The Death of Marlowe* (Sealts 285) that matches the description in this letter. The second book was probably either George Walter Thornbury's *Lays and Legends; or, Ballads of the New World* or his *Songs of the Cavaliers and Roundheads: Jacobite Ballads* (Sealts 525). Stedman's own "chapter," which Melville's letter calls a "book," on Whitman was probably the one in his *Poets of America* (1885). The petition and portrait Stedman alludes to in the second paragraph are unidentified.

44 East 26th St.
New York, Feb. 1st 88

Dear Mr. Melville,

Here are three vols. of our Old Orion's works — some of the Contents, including "The Death of Marlowe", possibly will be new to you. I had the "Tragedies" bound up together.

In one I insert the "Petition" of which I spoke, & also his portrait.

Do glance at Walter Thornbury's Ballads. The book is one which I doubt if you have seen, as I never have been able to procure another copy. The Cavalier Songs, (Browningesque, with a difference), are my perennial delight.

Moreover, as you said so much of Whitman, I will run the risk of showing you my chapter on him — not that it is of any great importance.

With much respect,
Yours very truly,
E. C. Stedman.

ALS on a 25.4 × 20.4 cm sheet, folded in half, of white wove paper. Stedman inscribed the first and fourth pages, in ink.

LOCATION: HCL-M.

PUBLICATION: *Log,* II, 805–6.

TEXTUAL NOTE: E. C. Stedman.] *underlined with a flourish*

FROM JAMES BILLSON
BEFORE 29 MARCH 1888 · LEICESTER

Unlocated. A delayed letter from Billson is cited in Melville's 7 April 1888 reply; it was apparently intended to arrive with the book by Marcus Andrew Hislop Clarke that Melville acknowledged in his earlier 29 March 1888 letter to Billson.

FROM W. CLARK RUSSELL
10 APRIL 1888 · ST. LAWRENCE ON SEA

Melville's earlier, unlocated letter, probably written after his return from Bermuda on 26 March 1888, had apparently asked William Clark Russell's permission to dedicate *John Marr and Other Sailors* to him. This gesture, prompted in part by Russell's tribute to Melville in an article published in the September 1884 *Contemporary Review*, was clearly appreciated by the British sea-writer. For more about that tribute and their mutual friend Peter Toft, mentioned at the close of this letter, see the headnote to Melville's possible draft letter to Russell written between 7 April and 21 July 1886, pp. 498–500 above.

April 10th 1888.

My dear Mr Melville,

Your letter gave me very much more pleasure than I am capable of expressing. I can fully sympathise with your dislike to letter writing more particularly when as I fear your general health is not as I should wish to know it to be. It gratifies me immensely to think that my humble testimony to your genius was expressed long before I had the honour of hearing from you; at a time indeed when I really did not know whether you were living or dead. Quite recently I have been reading your "Redburn" for the third or fourth time and have closed it more deeply impressed even than heretofore with the descriptive power that vitalises every page, especially with your marvellous creation of the man Jackson whose character I know to be absolutely true to forecastle life. Much indeed should I have enjoyed a visit to the Bermudas in your company. But I very much fear that the fell disease rheumatism has converted me into a sheer hulk for the rest of my days. We have had a hideously bitter winter here and the cold serves me as a ferocious skipper, claps me into the bilboes, slips on the hand-cuffs and throws me into the forepeak there to languish until the sun has power enough to deliver me. I believe I have to thank old ocean for this disorder. It is my one obligation to the Mother of All and I should be glad to be able to discharge it in kind.

I shall await your volume with real anxiety and expectation. The honour you propose to do me must always prove a memorable one in my professional career. But do not send the book to the "Daily Telegraph" office. The clerks are neglectful; besides they might regard it as a volume for review, send it upstairs and so procure its miscarriage. This address is sure to find me though in all probability I shall have left this house by June for the old smuggling town of Deal which is seven miles distant just across the Bay here within view of my windows; the Downs right opposite. I have my eye on a house with the wash of the sea within twenty feet of the garden railing. In truth I cannot exist away from the brine though I would rather live alongside of it than on it. Accept dear Mr Melville my warmest regards and believe me,

Always Sincerely yours
W. Clark Russell.

P.S. I have to dictate this to my son, my hand is so bad. Remember me to Peter Toft if you write to or see him. I owe him a letter but have mislaid his address. It is number two or three thousand somewhere!

LS on a 22.5 × 17.9 cm sheet, folded in half, of white wove paper with the letterhead "6, GRANVILLE GARDENS, | ST LAWRENCE ON SEA, | THANET." Russell's son, Herbert Russell, inscribed all four pages, in ink; Russell himself signed the letter and wrote the postscript, in ink. This non-holograph source for the body of letter is emended by NN at one point (see below). Herbert Russell addressed the envelope "Herman Melville Esq | 104 E. 26th Street | New York." with "U.S.A." in the upper left corner; it was postmarked in Ramsgate on 10 April and in New York on 21 April. Elizabeth Melville endorsed the envelope in pencil "April 10th 1888 | W. C. Russell" and wrote on the front "W. C. | Russell"; it was later stamped—probably for ownership purposes—with Melville's son-in-law's name and address, "H. B. Thomas | 60 Montrose Ave. | South Orange, N.J.".

LOCATION: HCL-M.

PUBLICATION: (partial) *Log*, II, 806–7.

TEXTUAL NOTES: hand-cuffs] hand-|cuffs · than on it] NN; then on it · P.S. . . . somewhere!] *written sideways in the upper left corner next to the letterhead; placed here editorially* · to Peter] *miswritten* t Peter

FROM W. CLARK RUSSELL
18 SEPTEMBER 1888 · DEAL

Melville's extended "Inscription Epistolary to W. C. R." at the opening of *John Marr and Other Sailors* (1888), for which Russell thanks Melville in this letter, had praised Russell's *The Wreck of the Grosvenor* (1877) and closed with the statement: "Thus far as to matters which may be put into type. For personal feeling—the printed page is hardly the place for reiterating that. So I close here as I began, wishing you from my heart the most precious things I know of in this world—Health and Content." For Russell, suffering from rheumatism, this wish clearly had special significance. Of the two copies of *John Marr* Melville inscribed to W. Clark Russell (HCL-M; Berkshire Athenaeum), the former seems more likely the one Melville sent to him with this letter.

Russell's father, mentioned here, was Henry Russell (1812–1900), a composer of numerous popular melodies, including one for George Pope Morris's poem "O Woodman, Spare That Tree," as well as complete songs, such as "Cheer, Boys, Cheer." "Charles Sᵗ Johnstone" is presumably Russell's garbled reference to Alfred St. Johnston (ca. 1858–91), author of a number of boys' books, including one with a setting in Polynesia entitled *Camping among Cannibals* (London: Macmillan, 1883). If Melville did hear from St. Johnston, the letter is now unlocated. For Russell's move to Deal, Kent, see his letter just above.

September 18ᵗʰ 1888

My dear Mʳ Melville,

I have received "John Marr" and have read the little volume with the liveliest interest and pleasure. How to thank you for the sentiments to which you give exquisite expression in your dedication I do not know. The closing sentences I read with emotion. Suffer me however to regret that your name is not upon the title page. I must confess that I should like the world to know that my books were thought worthy of commendation by the author of "Omoo," "Typee" and "Moby Dick." My father Mʳ Henry Russell happened to be with me when your little volume arrived. You will probably remember him as the composer of numerous popular songs such as "To the West," "A Life on the Ocean Wave" "Woodman Spare that Tree" and scores more. I read aloud to him the little poem "The Figure Head", the gem of the collection as I think, a brilliant, delicious fancy and of a class of thought peculiar to yourself. He exclaimed "If I were ten years younger I should put those words to music." But at the age of seventy five a man has little melody left in him. "Tom Deadlight" is profoundly good. The line: —

"The black scud a'flying; but, by God's blessing, dam'me"

Is profoundly maritime. I was infinitely amused last night on being asked by the author of several boys' books, a Mr Charles St Johnstone whether I had ever read the noblest sea book ever written called "Moby Dick". I smiled and handed him "John Marr". "Is Herman Melville alive?" he shouted. He took down your address and I expect you will hear from him. Once again best, sincerest, most cordial thanks. May we yet meet in this world! But I fear it — I fear it.

Believe me, my dear Mr Melville,
Yours most sincerely
W. Clark Russell

P.S. Rheumatism very bad & I am forced to dictate to my son whose spelling is still a bit shaky.

LS on a 26.2 × 20.3 cm sheet, folded in half, of white laid paper, watermarked with the initials "L J D L & C°" and bearing the letterhead "3, SANDOWN TERRACE, | DEAL." Russell's son, Herbert Russell, inscribed the first three pages, in ink; Russell himself signed the letter, made some corrections, and wrote the postscript, in ink. Herbert Russell addressed the envelope "Herman Melville Esq | 104 E 26th Street | New York | U.S.A"; it was postmarked in Deal on 18 September and in New York on 29 September. Elizabeth Melville wrote on the recto in pencil "W. C. | Russell | Sept 18 – 1888"; it was later stamped—probably for ownership purposes—with Melville's son-in-law's name and address, "H. B. Thomas | 60 Montrose Ave. | South Orange, N.J."

LOCATION: HCL-M.

PUBLICATION: (partial) Log, II, 809.

TEXTUAL NOTES: Moby] Mo *written over* Mow *by W. Clark Russell* • of a class] of *inserted above* caret • Moby] *originally* Mowby *with* w *canceled probably by W. Clark Russell*

FROM JAMES BILLSON
[4?] DECEMBER 1888 · LEICESTER

Unlocated. Billson's letter that accompanied a copy of James Thomson's *Shelley: A Poem* (Sealts 520) is cited in Melville's 31 December 1888 reply. According to Elizabeth Melville's memorandum, the book was sent on 4 December 1888 (see Sealts, *Early Lives*, p. 172). Billson's letter may have been sent with the book or under separate cover (as with his 31 January 1886 letter announcing a forthcoming shipment of books; see p. 730 above).

1889

FROM W. CLARK RUSSELL
10 FEBRUARY 1889 · DEAL

Less than a year after Melville's dedication to Russell of *John Marr and Other Sailors*, Russell in turn dedicated to Melville his novel *An Ocean Tragedy*, which he had apparently completed shortly before writing this February 1889 letter. Russell's statement that the book was first to appear "in the newspapers" implies that it was being syndicated by one of the "fiction bureaus" which had lately become popular—supplying even the smallest of provincial papers (see Graham Pollard, "Serial Fiction," in *New Paths in Book Collecting*, ed. John Carter [London: Constable, 1934], pp. 265–71). After this serial publication, the book was then published in the U.S. by the Harpers in 1889 and in England by Chatto & Windus in 1890. For Melville's acknowledgment a year later after receiving the published book, see his 9 February 1890 letter.

The article Russell mentions in this letter, "The Honour of the Flag," had appeared in *America: A Journal of To-Day* 1 (24 January 1889), 1–3. In it Russell discussed a number of sea-writers, including Dana, but he singled out Melville as the preeminent sea-writer, declaring "there is no name in American letters that deserves to stand higher for beauty of imagination, for accuracy of reproduction, for originality of conception, and for a quality of imagination."

10th February 1889

My dear Mr Melville,

I have done myself the honour to dedicate to you a novel I have recently completed entitled "An Ocean Tragedy." It will be published in the newspapers and then take volume form.

Did you happen to come across an article of mine entitled "The Honour of the Flag" published two or three weeks ago in a Chicago weekly called "America"? I should have liked to hear your opinion on that contribution. At all events the writing of it gratified me with an opportunity of publicly stating how amongst your warmest admirers is, my dear Mr Melville,

Yours always sincerely
W. Clark Russell
pr H. R.

P.S. You will grieve to hear that I have been in bed now continuously for hard upon four months thanks to a wild and ferocious attack of my old stubborn complaint. I shall have to leave this country for some land where the sun is to be seen. Would to heaven New

York were closer to Florida than it is, or at all events clear of the embrace of the Fiend of the Arctic circle. I would settle in your country forthwith. What do you think of the Marquesas as a residence for a man prostrate with rheumatism?

LS on a 26.2 × 20.3 cm sheet, folded in half, of white laid paper, watermarked with the initials "L J D L & C°" and bearing the letterhead "3, SANDOWN TERRACE, | DEAL." Russell's son, Herbert Russell, inscribed the first and fourth pages, in ink, and addressed the envelope "Herman Melville Esq | 104 E. 26ᵗʰ Street | New York." with "U.S.A." in the lower left corner; it was postmarked in Deal on 11 February and in New York on 24 February. Elizabeth Melville wrote on the recto in pencil "W. C. Russell | Feby 10 – 1889"; it was later stamped—probably for ownership purposes—with Melville's son-in-law's name and address, "H. B. Thomas | 60 Montrose Ave. | South Orange, N.J."

LOCATION: HCL-M.

PUBLICATION: (partial) *Log*, II, 813.

TEXTUAL NOTES: New York were] were *inserted above canceled* was *possibly by W. Clark Russell* · forthwith] forth-|with

FROM ABRAHAM LANSING
14 MARCH 1889 · ALBANY

In September 1888 the Gansevoort mansion, which Melville's sister Frances Priscilla had owned at her death, had been sold at auction for four thousand dollars. This letter was intended to conclude the settlement of her estate, but as Abraham Lansing's telegram and letter the next day announced, an error in his calculations required him to cancel the check that accompanied this letter and to issue a second one for the correct amount.

Mch 14   9

Dear Mʳ Melville:

I send herewith my cheque as admʳ &c of Fannys will, for $1216⁸⁹/₁₀₀ being for the share belonging to you on the distribution of her estate as per decree of Surrogate.

I enclose also a receipt for you to sign & return if you will.

With kind regards to Mʳˢ Melville, & to Bessie & to you

Yours truly
Abraham Lansing

Herman Melville Esq

Original document not located. Text from Abraham Lansing's 28 December 1888–20 July 1899 letterbook, p. 17 (one-half page).

LOCATION (of letterbook): NYPL-GL.

PUBLICATION: (partial) *Log*, II, 813.

TEXTUAL NOTE: Abraham Lansing] *underlined with a flourish*

FROM ABRAHAM LANSING
15 MARCH 1889 · ALBANY

Unlocated. A telegram, probably requesting Melville not to cash the check that Abraham Lansing had sent on 14 March, is cited in Melville's 16 March 1889 reply.

FROM ABRAHAM LANSING
15 MARCH 1889 · ALBANY

Discovering an error of $93.10 in his calculation of Melville's share in his sister Frances Priscilla's estate, Abraham Lansing sent him this letter, preceded by the telegram noted in the entry just above. Melville's 16 March reply concluded the correspondence concerning his sister's will.

Mch 15   9

Dear Mr Melville;
    The amount for distribution of the residuum of Fannys estate is 5309^{9}/_{100}$.
    Your interest, one fifth, being 1123^{79}/_{100}$
    The cheque sent to you yesterday was accidentally made for 1216^{89}/_{100}$ = will you please return it to me in Exchange for the Enclosed and also sign the Enclosed receipt & duplicate, as I need one receipt to keep & another to file with the surrogate.

Truly Yours
Abraham Lansing

Herman Melville Esq.

Original document not located. Text from Abraham Lansing's 28 December 1888–20 July 1899 letterbook, p. 18.

LOCATION (of letterbook): NYPL-GL.

FROM HARPER & BROTHERS
18 MARCH 1889 · NEW YORK

As the Harpers' letters of 19 June and 25 September reveal (see below), Melville agreed to their request in this letter to allow Chapter 61 of *Moby-Dick* ("Stubb Kills a Whale") to be published in their *Fifth Reader*, edited by "James Baldwin, Ph.D." Baldwin (1841-1925), who wrote this letter, was a former educator and now a member of the educational department at Harper & Brothers; he had already edited the four previous *Readers* published by the Harpers. When issued the following September, the *Fifth Reader*, "comprising one hundred articles by leading American authors" (p. [iii]), included in an endnote a brief biographical sketch of Melville, which focused on his early adventures at sea and listed *Typee, Omoo, Mardi, Redburn, Moby-Dick*, and *Battle-Pieces* as his most notable works (p. 474). For further publication details about this textbook, see the headnote to the Harpers' 25 September letter, below.

Mar. 18, 1889

Mr. Herman Melville,
104 E. 26th Street —
Dear Sir: —

We have in course of preparation a new *Fifth Reader* containing selections from the works of American authors, and should be pleased to include in the volume an extract of a few pages from *Moby-Dick* including the passage describing the capture of the whale. Not having a copy at hand, we cannot now give the exact page.

Before using the selection, however, in the manner designated, we should like to have your consent. Besides publishing your name in connection with the piece, we shall wish to include within the volume a brief biographical sketch of yourself with especial reference to your literary work. Trusting that this may meet your approval, we are

Sincerely Yr's &c
Harper & Brothers
per J. Baldwin.

ALS on a 12.7 × 20.3 cm sheet of white wove paper with the printed letterhead "HARPER & BROTHERS, | PUBLISHERS. | EDUCATIONAL DEPARTMENT." in the upper left corner and the address "FRANKLIN SQUARE, NEW YORK." printed just below to the left. James Baldwin inscribed only one side of the leaf, in ink. Elizabeth Melville noted in pencil on the verso "Harper & Bros | March 18 – 1889 | (5th Reader)".

LOCATION: HCL-M.

PUBLICATION: (partial) *Log*, II, 814.

FROM JOHN W. PALMER
BEFORE 23 MARCH 1889 · NEW YORK

Unlocated. Palmer's letter and his two books that accompanied it are cited in Melville's 23 March 1889 reply.

FROM HARPER & BROTHERS
19 JUNE 1889 · NEW YORK

Melville's reply to the Harpers' earlier letter of 18 March 1889 is now unlocated. However, as indicated in this letter by James Baldwin, editor of their *Fifth Reader* (see the headnote to the Harpers' 18 March 1889 letter), Melville had granted the permission they sought to publish an extract from *Moby-Dick* in that anthology.

June 19 1889.

Mr Herman Melville.
New York City,
Dear Sir:
    Allow us to thank you most sincerely for your favor, received several weeks ago, kindly granting us permission to use an extract from one of your books in our forthcoming Fifth Reader. We shall take pleasure in sending you a copy of the Reader as soon as it is published, and we trust that you will be pleased both with the general plan of the work and with our presentation of the selection from your works. Again thanking you, we are

Very truly Yours
Harper & Brothers
per J. Baldwin

ALS on a 12.7 × 20.3 cm sheet of white wove paper with the printed letterhead "HARPER & BROTHERS, | PUBLISHERS. | EDUCATIONAL DEPARTMENT." in the upper left corner and the address "FRANKLIN SQUARE, NEW YORK." printed just below to the left. James Baldwin inscribed only one side of the leaf, in ink, and addressed the envelope "Mr Herman Melville | 104 East 26th st. | New York City."; it was postmarked in New York on 19 June. Melville wrote just above the address in pencil "*Please preserve*". Elizabeth Melville endorsed the envelope in pencil "Harper & Bros. | June 19 – 1889 | '5th Reader' ".

LOCATION: HCL-M.

FROM HARPER & BROTHERS
25 SEPTEMBER 1889 · NEW YORK

As promised in their 19 June 1889 letter, the Harpers sent Melville a copy—now unlocated—of their *Fifth Reader* (New York: Harper, 1889; Sealts 239) with its re-printing of Chapter 61 from *Moby-Dick*. Edited for clarity, with the deletion of some passages presumably thought inappropriate for children (such as Stubb's cry to "start her like grim death and grinning devils"), it appeared under the title "Whale Fishing in the Indian Ocean" (pp. 99–104). For a further discussion of the changes made in this extract, see the NN *Moby-Dick*, pp. 774–75. Like the two earlier letters from the Harpers, this one was inscribed by their editor, James Baldwin.

Sep't 25th 1889.

Mr. Herman Melville,
New York City,
Dear Sir: —

We take pleasure in sending you a copy of our new Fifth Reader, published today, which we beg you will accept with our com-pliments.

Trusting that you will be pleased with its contents, and thanking you for the kind aid received from you in permitting the use of an extract from your works, we are

Very truly Yours,
Harper & Brothers.
J. Baldwin.

ALS on a 12.7 × 20.3 cm sheet of white wove paper with the printed letterhead "HARPER & BROTHERS, | PUBLISHERS. | EDUCATIONAL DEPARTMENT." in the upper left corner and the address "FRANKLIN SQUARE, NEW YORK." printed just below to the left. James Baldwin inscribed only one side of the leaf, in ink, and addressed the envelope "Mr Herman Melville | 104 E. 26th st. | New York City."; it was postmarked in New York on 25 September. Elizabeth Melville endorsed the envelope in pencil "Harper & Bros — | about 5th Reader | Sept 25 | 1889".

LOCATION: HCL-M.

TEXTUAL NOTE: Harper & Brothers.] *underlined with a flourish*

FROM SIMEON E. BALDWIN
15 NOVEMBER 1889 · [NEW HAVEN?]

Unlocated. A letter from the executor of the will of Elizabeth Melville's cousin Ellen Marett Gifford is cited in Melville's 17 November 1889 reply.

FROM ARCHIBALD MacMECHAN
21 NOVEMBER 1889 · HALIFAX

Professor Archibald MacMechan's research on Melville up to this point evidently consisted of reading Melville's books (although in addition to *Moby-Dick* he specifically cites only *Redburn* in his later 23 December letter to Melville) and encyclopedia articles on Melville, such as that in Evert and George Duyckinck's *Cyclopædia of American Literature* (New York: Scribner's, 1855; revised and enlarged, 1866; revised again, Philadelphia: Zell, 1875). Melville replied to this letter on 5 December 1889, apparently mistaking the "12" in MacMechan's address for the date of his letter. See the headnote to that reply for more about MacMechan and his other research interests.

> 12 Lucknow Terrace
> Halifax N.S.
> Nov. 21st 1889

Dear Sir:

Although a stranger, I take the liberty of addressing you on the ground of my ardent admiration for your works. For a number of years I have read and re-read "Moby-Dick" with increasing pleasure on every perusal: and with this study, the conviction has grown up that the unique merits of that book have never received due recognition. I have been a student for ten years and have dabbled in literature more or less myself. And now I find myself in a position which enables me to give myself to literature as a life-work. I am anxious to set the merits of your books before the public and to that end, I beg the honour of correspondence with you. It would be of great assistance to me, if I could gather some particulars of your life and *literary methods* from you, other than given in such books as Duyckinck's dictionary. In the matter of style, apart from the matter altogether, I consider, your books, especially the earlier ones, the most thoroughly New World product in all American literature.

Hoping that I am not asking too much, I remain

> Yours most respectfully
> Arch^d MacMechan Ph.D.

Munro Professor of English at Dalhousie University.

Herman Melville Esq.
104 East 26th st.
New York City

ALS on a 25.2 × 18.6 cm sheet, folded in half, of white laid paper, watermarked with an ornate pedestal-like design and the words "PARCHMENT | SILK | FIRST". MacMechan inscribed the first three pages, in ink, and addressed the envelope "Mr. Herman Melville | 104 East 26th st. | New York City."; it was postmarked in Halifax on 21 November and in New York on 24 November. Elizabeth Melville endorsed the envelope in pencil "Archibald MacMechan | Halifax Nov 21 – 1889".

LOCATION: HCL-M.

PUBLICATION: Weaver, p. 380.

TEXTUAL NOTES: to that end,] after canceled in · particulars] after canceled personal · consider,] after canceled consid

FROM BEN W. AUSTIN
26 NOVEMBER 1889 · SIOUX CITY

Unlocated. A letter from an autograph collector and founder of the fictitious Northwestern Literary and Historical Society, Ben W. Austin of Sioux City, Iowa, is cited in Melville's 5 December 1889 reply.

FROM ARCHIBALD MacMECHAN
23 DECEMBER 1889 · HALIFAX

MacMechan apparently never called on Melville in the spring of 1890 as he proposed in this reply to Melville's 5 December 1889 letter (C. L. Burnett, Head of the Department of English at Dalhousie University, reported in an 11 October 1947 letter to Jay Leyda [UCLA] that both he and MacMechan's widow were certain no such visit occurred). In attributing his image of Melville to the "portrait" in the Duyckincks' Cyclopædia (to which he had also referred in his earlier 21 November letter, above), MacMechan must have meant the verbal one, since no illustrated portrait was included with that article. Or perhaps he was thinking of either the one in Appletons' Cyclopædia of American Biography (1888), which was the first biographical sketch of Melville to be accompanied by a portrait—a line-drawing of his October 1885 photograph—or the one in Edmund C. Stedman's Library of American Literature (New York: Webster, 1889), VII, 464, based on the 1870 Eaton portrait.

12 Lucknow Terrace
Halifax N.S.
Dec. 23rd 1889

Dear Sir:

I was very much gratified to receive your cordial letter of the 5th. I was aware of your advanced age and should have been more thoughtful perhaps in making my vague proposals to you which at the same time would draw heavily upon your time. But from both your portrait in Duyckinck, and the style of your books and your letter to me, I think there cannot be much abatement of your mental or bodily vigour. It *is* too much to ask you to correspond but I hope to do myself the pleasure of calling on you in New York in the spring months, and making your acquaintance. I have enjoyed your books so much and, having had at least one adventure like "Redburn", I feel certain we should be at once on common ground.

Hoping then that you may complete what you are interested in, and be spared for many years to come, I remain

Very truly yours
Archibald MacMechan

ALS on two 12.8 × 20.4 cm sheets of white wove paper. MacMechan inscribed only one side of each leaf (numbering the second one at the top with a "2"), in ink, and addressed the envelope "Herman Melville Esq. | 104 East 26 st. | New York City."; it was postmarked in Halifax on 23 December. Elizabeth Melville noted on the front of the envelope, in pencil, "Archibald MacMechan | Halifax Dec 23ᵈ | 1889."

LOCATION: HCL-M.

PUBLICATION: (partial) *Log*, II, 819.

TEXTUAL NOTES: thoughtful] thought-|ful • from both] from *inserted above caret*

1890

FROM RICHARD GARNETT
[1890?] · LONDON

Unlocated. A letter received toward the end of Melville's life from the British man-of-letters Richard Garnett is cited in his son Robert Singleton Garnett's article, "Moby-Dick and Mocha-Dick," *Blackwood's Magazine* 226 (December 1929), 841–58. For more about Garnett and the full statement in the *Blackwood's* article about Garnett's exchange of letters with Melville, see the entry for Melville's unlocated reply, pp. 520–21 above.

FROM W. CLARK RUSSELL
5 JANUARY 1890 · DEAL

As Russell had announced in his earlier 10 February 1889 letter, his novel *An Ocean Tragedy*, first serialized in newspapers, was to be dedicated to Melville when published in book form. In an interview published in the *Pall Mall Gazette* in December

1889 (pp. 1–2), Russell had used the publicity surrounding the publication of his book to bring attention to Melville's works as well, producing a copy of *John Marr* during the interview and referring to Melville as "that magnificent American sea-novelist." Now with his book already published by the Harpers in the U.S. and about to be issued in three volumes by Chatto & Windus in England, Russell wrote Melville partly to announce that publication, but also to warn him that the American edition did not include the dedication. Melville's copy of the three-volume British edition that Russell later sent him is now in the Melville Collection of the Houghton Library of Harvard University (Sealts 433).

Russell's acquaintance, "Monsignor Seton of New Jersey City," was Robert Seton (1839–1927), the Roman Catholic prelate (and grandson of Mother Elizabeth Ann Seton) who was at this time pastor of St. Joseph's Church in Jersey City. It is not known whether he called on Melville at Russell's request.

5th January 1890.

My dear Mr Melville,

I have asked my English publishers to send you a copy of "An Ocean Tragedy". It is not yet issued, but I trust they may be able to muster an advance copy. Harper sent me their reprint. It is a villainous thing reprinted from the serial issue, full of illiterate blunders, and without the dedication. I have written to them about it. You are, I sincerely hope, well, and I trust that the New Year which has dawned may prove a happy and a healthy one for you and yours. I have lately had some correspondence with Peter Toft, and believe that he returns to America this month. I wish the beastly rheumatism would let me accompany him. I asked Monsignor Seton of New Jersey City to call upon you and give you a handshake from me if he happened to be in your city. I hope he has done so.

Adieu, my dear Mr Melville, and believe me always, your warm admirer and sincere well-wisher and friend

W. Clark Russell

P.S. My son has transcribed this from short-hand notes, so please forgive the corrections.

LS on a 25.2 × 20.3 cm sheet, folded in half, of white wove paper, with the letterhead "3, SANDOWN TERRACE, | DEAL." Russell's son, Herbert Russell, inscribed the first and fourth pages, in ink; Russell himself signed the letter, made the alterations, and wrote the postscript. Herbert Russell addressed the envelope "Herman Melville Esq | 104 E. 26th S^t | New York" and wrote "*U.S.A*" in the upper left corner; it was postmarked in Deal on 5 January and in New York on 20 January. Elizabeth Melville wrote on the recto in pencil "W. C. Russell | Jan

5 – 1890"; it was later stamped—probably for ownership purposes—with Melville's son-in-law's name and address, "H. B. Thomas | 60 Montrose Ave. | South Orange, N.J."

LOCATION: HCL-M.

PUBLICATION: (partial) *Log*, II, 820.

TEXTUAL NOTES: advance] *altered from* advanced • illiterate] *above canceled* literary • I trust] *inserted above caret*

FROM W. CLARK RUSSELL
9 JANUARY 1890 · DEAL

Following closely on the heels of Russell's earlier letter (just above), this note in his own hand enclosed an early "Proof" of the dedication in the English edition of *An Ocean Tragedy*. Although this is the last letter Russell is known to have written Melville, his interest in Melville's work continued. In an 11 December 1899 letter to the New York publisher Charles Scribner's Sons, he wrote, "I have tried for years past in this country to popularize the works of Herman Melville with whom I corresponded for some years before his death. But though 'Moby Dick' is a work of great genius and though all his other books are in my humble opinion out and away ahead of the best of the sea novels in our tongue, they uniformly possess this negative defect: they have no heroine" (Firestone Library, Princeton University). In 1899 Scribner's published an edition of *Moby-Dick*—the second illustrated edition—in their series "Famous Novels of the Sea" (see G. Thomas Tanselle, *A Checklist of Editions of MOBY-DICK, 1851–1976* [Evanston and Chicago: Northwestern University Press and The Newberry Library, 1976], pp. 9, 11).

Dear Mr Melville,
The printers have just sent me this at my request. The English edition will not be published, the publishers tell me, till *March*. God bless you,

Ever
W. Clark Russell
Jan 9. 1890

ALS on the verso of the printed dedication (see p. 757), which is on a 19.2 × 12.8 cm sheet of white wove paper. Russell himself inscribed the verso, in ink. Russell's son, Herbert Russell, addressed the envelope "Herman Melville Esq | 104 E. 26th Street | New York" with "*U.S.A.*" in the upper left corner; it was postmarked in Deal on 9 January and in New York on 22 January. Elizabeth Melville wrote on its recto in pencil "W. C. Russell | Jan 9–1890 | Dedication"; it was later stamped—probably for ownership purposes—with Melville's son-in-law's name and address, "H. B. Thomas | 60 Montrose Ave. | South Orange, N.J."

To *HERMAN MELVILLE, Esq.*

MY DEAR HERMAN MELVILLE,

      In words of beauty and of kindness you lately wished me health and content. Health, alas! you cannot give me; but content you have filled me with. My books have done more than ever I had dared dream, by winning for me the friendship and approval of the Author of 'Typee,' 'Omoo,' 'Moby-Dick,' 'Redburn,' and other productions which top the list of sea literature in the English tongue. I beg you to accept this dedication as a further public avowal of my hearty admiration of your genius.

      In all faithfulness yours,

         W. CLARK RUSSELL.

Dedication to Melville of W. Clark Russell's *An Ocean Tragedy* and (over) Russell's 9 January 1890 letter to Melville written on the verso of the dedication (both reduced). Courtesy of the Houghton Library, Harvard University (Melville Collection).

Dear Mr. Melville!

The printers have just sent me this at my request. The English edition will not be published till March. Doubtless you —

Ever

Mark Twain

Jan 9. 1890

LOCATION: HCL-M.

PUBLICATION: *Log*, II, 820.

FROM H. S. SALT
BEFORE 12 JANUARY 1890 · LONDON

Unlocated. Salt's letter, probably written in late 1889, proposing the republication of *Typee* in Walter Scott's Camelot Series, is cited in Melville's 12 January 1890 reply.

FROM JOHN MURRAY
AFTER 12 JANUARY 1890 · LONDON

Unlocated. In response to Melville's 12 January 1890 letter requesting permission for the publication of *Typee* in the Camelot Series, Murray apparently refused to give his consent, as Melville in his 25 February letter then informed H. S. Salt, who had first proposed to Melville the inclusion of the book in that series: "Concerning 'Typee.' — . . . I wrote to Mr. Murray. The information contained in the reply is such, and the manner of conveying it is such, that I consider myself bound . . . not to sanction any English issue of the book." Murray's reply is not recorded in his letterbook for this period, but it is also cited in Arthur Stedman's 24 October 1892 letter to the U.S. Book Co., which states: "Three or four years ago Mr. Walter Scott wished to bring out shilling editions of 'Typee' and 'Omoo' and Mr. Murray at that time wrote Mr. Melville that he would not permit them and Mr. Scott dropped the matter" (Beinecke Library, Yale University). Murray himself reprinted *Typee* in 1893 from his original 1846 plates, with added illustrations and an introduction by Salt.

FROM J. W. BARRS
13 JANUARY 1890 · LEICESTER

J. W. Barrs was a close friend of the poet James Thomson, who had first introduced him to Melville's works. Barrs had earlier sent Melville a copy of Thomson's *A Voice from the Nile*, which Melville acknowledged indirectly in a 2 April 1886 letter to their mutual friend James Billson. Melville later, in his 31 December 1888 letter to Billson, expressed his pleasure that Billson had given an extra copy of *John Marr* to Barrs and again acknowledged Barrs's earlier gift to him. Melville's only other known mention of Barrs is in his 12 January 1890 letter to H. S. Salt, expressing interest in Salt's article "Herman Melville" in the November 1889 issue of the *Scottish Art Review*, which Barrs sent to Melville on Salt's behalf, shortly before sending this letter.

Although no evidence of a reply from Melville has been found, he probably did send Barrs his thanks (perhaps indirectly again), since he was indebted to Barrs for Salt's article. Barrs's long letter clearly was written to elicit a reply, through its numerous queries about Melville's works and about Walt Whitman, and its comments on a wide array of literary contemporaries, mentioning, among others: W. Clark Russell, Melville's long-time correspondent (see the headnote to Russell's 5 January 1890 letter, above, for the *Pall Mall* interview cited in this letter); Philip Bourke Marston (1850–87), the blind British poet; Louise Chandler Moulton (1835–1908), the American poet, novelist, and children's writer; and Pierre Loti (1850–1923), the French novelist, whose Tahiti novel, first published in France in 1879, was issued in an English translation, *Rarahu; or, The Marriage of Loti*, by Clara Bell in November 1890 (London: Paul; Sealts 536).

Jany 13 90

Dear Sir

Some weeks ago I promised my friend M^r H S Salt that I w^d forward to you the Scottish Art Review. It was not until ten days or a fortnight after I wrote him telling him of my intention to forward the Review containing his paper on your books that I mailed it to you. I hope it has reached you ere now. I intended to write you by same mail but Poes Imp of the Perverse continually attacks me & most successfully when I have made a distinct promise to myself to do some certain thing. I have had almost nightly opportunities for writing but the aforesaid Imp prevailed until tonight when having set pen to paper I believe I have routed his forces, temporarily at least.

I was exceedingly pleased to find the SAR had accepted & printed Salts article Singularly enough almost directly afterwards, in reporting an interview with the author of the Wreck of the Grosvenor, the Pall Mall also contained more than the customary passing reference to yr books & quoted some lines from the John Marr. So you see notwithstanding the inadequacy of the recognition of your books, on this side, they are not without warm admirers.

What you may think of Salts contribution to the SAR of course I can only guess; but I confess I was somewhat disappointed with it & wish instead of slightly passing in review half a dozen volumes he had more or less exhaustively reviewed one say Mardi or Moby Dick but after all he may be the best judge of the kind of notice likely to reawaken interest in yr writings. Then again I have a very deeprooted fondness for Babbalanja & consequently resented the way Salt dealt with the 2nd & 3rd volume of Mardi, & much as I admire the first volume I'd rather have Babbalanja and Yoomy slight though the sketch of the latter may be thought to be I once read to Philip Bourke Marston the chapter Lombardo & his Costanza to his great delight and altho' Marston was perhaps not more than one of our best minor poets he was a true critic. He was so interested that he obtained for reading all yr books accessible to him & some time after an American writer of some magazine popularity, Mrs Chandler Moulton, and a great friend of Marstons, coming over to London he made enquiries of her concerning you but she only possessed the vaguest impressions of either yourself or yr books; a lack of patriotism & information which when Marston told me of it certainly did not prepossess me in Mrs Moultons favour from a literary point of view. "Pierre" I have always liked & dont think Salt does it anything like justice & Israel Potter ought not to have been passed over, though Salt may not have read it. Whilst writing of Israel Potter I am reminded of the John Marr you so kindly sent me through Mr Billson, & for which I take this chance of thanking you. The prose story reminds me of Israels latter days. Am I right in feeling a similarity? Ned Bunn, among the verse is my favorite, and I have written out the lines for Salt. They recall delightfully the atmosphere of Omoo & Typee. Pierre Loti a quite recent French writer & an officer in the French Navy has published a volume on a twelve months experience of his on one of the South Pacific Isles. I have seen a review of the book but cannot recall its title. The review however was very flattering & I hope shortly to get the volume when, if it interests me, I will post it to you. It may be his scene is laid in the Marquesas & if so it will doubtless be of additional interest to you as his book has only been out some two or three years & was — if I remember aright — written & published soon after his return from the Pacific to Paris & is therefore probably the most recent of attractive volumes on the South Sea Islands.

In Brownings death we lose our first poet although the popularity of his verse was almost a cipher compared with that of Tennysons or your Longfellow. The "public" like more sugar than Browning cared to put into his poems & hence, notwithstanding his power, he had — & will have — but a few readers. It w^d not be exaggerating to say that out of every hundred praising him as a poet not three have read a hundred lines of his verse. That comes of being buried in Westminster Abbey! Do you know Walt Whitman? One cannot write or speak of the Poet of Democracy as "Mister." Indeed I cannot recall to my mind ever having seen him written of as Mr Whitman. Do you not think he is your most characteristic poet? I know of no poet with whom one feels such a sense of *Camaraderie* or who has voiced the democratic Aspirations so nobly & yet with such calm confidence in their realisation & fearless recognition of the dangers to be met & overcome before the democratic idea is attained. I shall be glad to have a line from you whenever & if ever you feel moved to write, but do not trouble to acknowledge this just because I have troubled you to read it. With sincere wishes for your good health

Believe me
Yours Truly
J. W. Barrs

Herman Melville Esq
New York

P.S. It w^d interest me much to learn which among yr literary progeny is yr favorite child — excluding Omoo & Typee from the selection.

J. W. B.

ALS on two 22.7 × 17.8 cm sheets of white laid paper, watermarked with the name "SUPERFINE | TURKEY MILL | VELLUM". Both sheets were folded to make four pages each, with the printed letterhead at the top of both first pages, "Chantry House, | Leicester." to the right of the printed monogram "JWB". Barrs inscribed all eight pages, in ink. Elizabeth Shaw Melville annotated the signature, in pencil, "Barrs".

LOCATION: HCL-M.

PUBLICATION: (partial) *Log*, II, 821.

TEXTUAL NOTES: Singularly] S *altered from* s *after canceled ampersand* • reviewed] *after canceled* have • critic] *the first* i *inserted above caret* • thanking you] *before canceled* for • quite recent] *inserted above caret* • Longfellow] *terminal* s *canceled* • notwithstanding] *miswritten* nothwithstanding • every hundred] *after canceled* every • & if ever] *inserted above caret* • health] lth *rewritten* • J. W. Barrs] *underlined with a flourish* • New York] *underlined with a flourish* • P.S.] *underlined with a flourish* • J. W. B.] *underlined with a flourish*

FROM H. S. SALT
2 FEBRUARY 1890 · LONDON

Unlocated. Salt's letter accompanying a copy of his biography, *The Life of James Thomson ("B. V.")*, is cited in Melville's 25 February 1890 reply. Salt later recalled the matter in his reminiscences, *Company I Have Kept* (London: Allen & Unwin, 1930): "I was brought into touch with Herman Melville through my biography of the pessimist poet James Thomson. He was a great admirer of Melville; and Melville in his turn highly valued *The City of Dreadful Night*. Knowing this, I had sent him a copy of my book, and in consequence received from him two or three letters in one of which he very characteristically wrote that Thomson's poem is 'the modern Book of Job, under an original form, duskily looming with the same aboriginal verities'" (p. 108; the letter described is that dated 12 January 1890 to Salt).

FROM LEE & SHEPARD
10 FEBRUARY 1890 · BOSTON

Unlocated. A letter from Lee & Shepard about their forthcoming book *The Builders of American Literature: Biographical Sketches of American Authors Born Previous to 1826* (1893), by Francis H. Underwood, is cited in Melville's 13 February 1890 reply.

FROM SIMEON E. BALDWIN
BETWEEN 17 AND 21 FEBRUARY 1890 · NEW HAVEN

Unlocated. According to a 28 February 1890 letter from Simeon Baldwin announcing the probate of Ellen Marett Gifford's will (see the entry just below), a copy of that will was enclosed to the beneficiaries during the previous week.

FROM SIMEON E. BALDWIN
[28 FEBRUARY?] 1890 · NEW HAVEN

Unlocated. A formal letter to Melville as one of the beneficiaries of Ellen Marett Gifford's will can be inferred from a 28 February 1890 letter addressed to Miss Lucia Dow (another beneficiary) that is now in the Shaw family papers (MHS-S). Typed on stationery with the printed letterhead of the New Haven, Connecticut, law office of Simeon E. Baldwin, it states: "The decree of the Probate Court, in the matter of Mrs. Ellen M. Gifford's estate, of which a copy was sent you by the clerk, last week, was passed to-day, and we are ready to begin paying the legacies left by Mrs. Gifford, as settled by the decree. I enclose you a receipt for your legacy of $15000, and you can either sign and return it to me, in which case I will send you a check by mail for this amount, or you can draw on me, as executor of the Estate of Ellen M. Gifford, for the amount, payable at sight, pinning the receipt to the draft, when you give it to the Bank." Like Lucia Dow, Elizabeth Melville received fifteen thousand dollars from her cousin's bequest, and Melville received eight thousand dollars and her share in the New York Society Library (see Melville's 17 November 1889 letter to Baldwin concerning this bequest). It is not known whether Melville replied to Baldwin or drew directly on his account. For more about Ellen Gifford, see the headnotes to Melville's 5 October 1885 and 6 November 1888 letters to her.

FROM CHARLOTTE HOADLEY
BEFORE 23 MAY 1890 · NEW YORK

Unlocated. A request from his niece that Melville send his portion due for the up-keep of the family plot in the Albany Rural Cemetery is cited in his 23 May 1890 letter to Catherine Lansing.

FROM CATHERINE GANSEVOORT LANSING
27 MAY 1890 · ALBANY

Unlocated. In his 23 May 1890 letter to his cousin Melville had enclosed a money order for his share in the expenses of the family plot in Albany (see also the entry just above). At the top of Melville's letter, Catherine Gansevoort Lansing recorded sending him an acknowledgment of the money, along with a receipt.

FROM HAVELOCK ELLIS
19 JULY 1890 · REDHILL

Melville replied to this letter from the British psychologist Havelock Ellis on 10 August 1890 (see the headnote to that letter for more about Ellis and his specific researches at this time).

As the stationery on which Ellis's letter is written indicates, he was also on the staff of Walter Scott's publishing house and had been party to the recent unsuccessful attempt to bring out *Typee* in the Camelot Series (see Melville's 12 January 1890 letters to H. S. Salt and John Murray). Although Ellis dated his letter 20 July, its envelope was postmarked 19 July.

Earlsbrook Road,   Mr H. Melville
Redhill, Surrey   20 July/90

Dear Sir,

I am making some investigations into the ancestry of distin-guished English & American poets and imaginative writers, with reference to the question of race. Will you kindly tell me to what races you trace yourself back on fathers & on mother's side, & what (if any) recent strains of foreign blood you lay claim to?

I was very sorry to hear that the project of reprinting one of your works in the Camlot Series had fallen through. At present your books are, practically, not before the public at all in this coun-try, and a very large number of people are thus deprived of the delight which they would certainly derive from them, if they were accessible.

With kind regards, Very truly yours
Havelock Ellis

ALS on a 20.7 × 26.2 cm sheet of white wove paper, watermarked with the name "INDIANA MILL | FINE | RHENISH MAKE" and a flag and banner. The paper bears the printed letterhead "WALTER SCOTT, | PUBLISHER, | The Contemporary Science Series | General Editor: HAVELOCK ELLIS. | 24 WARWICK LANE, | PATERNOSTER ROW, | LONDON, E C." Each of the headings is written in a ruled box—Ellis's address is written under the printed statement "*From HAVELOCK ELLIS*," in one box, and Melville's name and the date are written on two dotted lines after the word "*To*" in the other box. Ellis inscribed both sides of the leaf, in ink, and addressed the envelope "Mr Herman Melville | 104 East 26th Street. | New York. | U.S.A."; it was postmarked on 19 July in Redhill, Surrey, and on 30 July in New York. Elizabeth Melville endorsed the envelope in pencil "Havelock Ellis | Surrey | July 19 | 1890".

LOCATION: HCL-M.

PUBLICATION: *Log*, II, 825.

TEXTUAL NOTES: recent] *inserted above caret* · Havelock Ellis] *underlined with a flourish*

FROM T. FISHER UNWIN
BEFORE 10 AUGUST 1890 · [LONDON?]

Unlocated. A letter from the British publisher T. Fisher Unwin proposing a new edition of *Redburn* can be inferred from the catalogue description of Melville's now unlocated 10 August 1890 reply.

FROM WILLIAM J. BOK
BEFORE 24 NOVEMBER 1890 · NEW YORK

Unlocated. A letter from William Bok including clippings of or extracts from two of his brother Edward Bok's literary columns is cited in Melville's 24 November 1890 reply. See the headnote to that letter for the pertinent segments from those columns cited by Melville in his reply.

Undated Letters

FROM EVERT A. DUYCKINCK
BETWEEN 1848 AND 1850 · NEW YORK

Unlocated. An invitation to a picnic, addressed jointly to Melville and his brother
Allan and delivered by Duyckinck's son Evert Duyckinck, Jr., is cited in Melville's
undated reply, written while Melville and his brother were sharing a house in New
York (see p. 535 above).

FROM J. LORIMER GRAHAM, SR.
BEFORE 1876 · NEW YORK

Unlocated. A letter to Melville from James Lorimer Graham, Sr. (1835–76), an
autograph collector, can be inferred from a letter dated only "Wednesday" from
Graham to Evert A. Duyckinck: "You will greatly oblige me by giving the bearer
the address of Mr Herman Melville, for me" (NYPL-D). Although it appears Graham wrote to Melville, there is no evidence that Melville replied. Both when the
Graham collection was catalogued by Clara Louise Dentler in 1947 (*A Privately
Owned Collection of Letters, Autographs, and Manuscripts with Many Association Items*
[Florence: Spinelli]) and when it was sold at Parke-Bernet Galleries on 29 and 30
April 1958, letters from Melville to his publishers Dix & Edwards were listed (see
those dated 7 August 1855, 19 January 1856, and 1 April 1856) but none from Mel-
ville to Graham himself.

FROM UNKNOWN
BEFORE 25 NOVEMBER [18??] · PLACE UNKNOWN

Unlocated. A note evidently requesting an autograph is cited in Melville's reply,
dated only 25 November (see p. 539 above).

Editorial Appendix

THE FIRST *of the three parts of this* APPENDIX *is a* HISTORICAL NOTE *contributed by the volume editor, Lynn Horth. The second part records textual information not already covered in the textual reports for individual letters. It consists of a* NOTE ON THE TEXT, *which sets out the editorial principles of this edition, followed by a list reproducing all conjectural and alternative readings and by a reprinting of Davis and Gilman's seminal discussion of Melville's hand. The third part presents related documents: a letter possibly by Melville and two Shaw family letters that vitally discuss Melville.*

To insure uniform textual policy in all volumes of the Northwestern-Newberry Edition, the same three editors, Harrison Hayford, Hershel Parker, and G. Thomas Tanselle, participate in the planning and establishment of textual policy for all volumes, except as otherwise noted; even when other editors are named, the final decisions still rest with one or more of these editors, here with the general editor. Final responsibility for all aspects of every volume is exercised by the general editor, Harrison Hayford.

Editorial work on the Northwestern-Newberry Correspondence volume was begun in 1965 under an initial grant from the U.S. Office of Education. For its subsequent history, see pp. 815–16 below. In 1988 Lynn Horth, under grants from the National Endowment for the Humanities and The Newberry Library, assumed full-time responsibility for editing the volume. In revising the Davis-Gilman Letters as the basis of this volume, she restructured its format, verified its texts from the manuscripts and other sources, and updated and corrected its footnote annotations for incorporation in her headnotes. Through research at over forty libraries and other collections, including The Newberry Library, the New York Public Library, and the Houghton Library of Harvard University, she assembled the new letters in this volume, establishing their texts and textual reports, gathered background information used in the headnotes and other entries, and wrote the HISTORICAL NOTE *and the first section of the* NOTE ON THE TEXT. *The following paragraphs are her statement of the assistance she received as editor of the volume.*

In the whole course of its preparation, Harrison Hayford worked closely on the volume with the original editor, William H. Gilman, with Amy Puett (later Emmers) and Robert A. Sandberg, and with Lynn Horth. He assisted Horth in verifying the texts from manuscripts and photocopies and in reviewing her headnotes, textual reports, and the editorial appendix at each successive stage. He deciphered some difficult words and took responsibility for some problematic readings. His unflagging work on the volume is a renewed testament to the reason Davis and Gilman dedicated their 1960 edition in part to him.

G. Thomas Tanselle, as bibliographical editor of the whole Edition, wrote the sections on textual policy and textual apparatus for the NOTE ON THE TEXT, *adapting materials from the Northwestern-Newberry Journals volume and following, where applicable, the basic pattern and wording set by the series editors in other volumes. For the editor, he generously wrote many letters, assisting her in communicating with dealers and private owners of Melville letters. He conferred with her repeatedly in New York, and with her as well as Alma A. MacDougall in numerous telephone conferences.*

As associate general editor, Hershel Parker criticized the style and content of three successive early printouts of the editorial headnotes and textual reports in this volume, supplying many biographical details and pointing the editor to many relevant documents. He also looked over the volume while it was in page proofs, providing several improvements and clarifications. Parker was able to assist so extensively because of his in-progress work not connected with the Northwestern-Newberry Edition: a narrative biography of Melville and The New Melville Log, of which he is co-editor with the late Jay Leyda. In 1988, after

Leyda's death, Parker put the 1951 Log and the 1969 Supplement on disk (in chronological order) and transcribed new documents into place, among them the papers of Melville's sister Augusta acquired by the New York Public Library in 1983. During 1989, 1990, and 1991 Parker generously welcomed the editor into his home for three extended research stays (totaling some six weeks) so that she could consult the "Oracle"—his on-screen working computer files of the constantly growing Log. Free access to Parker's transcriptions on-screen greatly facilitated the editor's study of his photocopies of the Augusta Melville papers and other documents and her subsequent study of the originals and her own photocopies of these documents, particularly since Parker had made first identifications of many people and events mentioned in them, had identified the occasions of some puzzling documents, and had corrected many of the New York Public Library datings. The editor expresses her gratitude for Parker's professional generosity and expresses as well her gratitude to Parker and his wife, Heddy Richter, for their repeated hospitality.

Alma A. MacDougall, as editorial coordinator of the Edition since 1981, contributed to every aspect of the volume. She supervised its production, provided copyediting and proofreading, raised numerous queries suggesting further research, worked closely with the editor, Hayford, and Tanselle in both shaping and implementing the textual policy and textual reports, compiled the "Calendar of Melville's Correspondence," planned and edited the index, and made a final thorough review of the proofs.

The editor was also given invaluable aid and counsel by the bibliographical associate, Richard Colles Johnson of The Newberry Library, who read and carefully criticized three of the successive printouts of this volume and tirelessly researched historical and bibliographical questions pertaining to it. Robert C. Ryan, manuscript associate, conferred repeatedly with the editor in Cambridge, Massachusetts, reexamined numerous textual readings in the manuscripts in the Houghton Library of Harvard University, and generously provided her with information concerning Melville's poetry from his own forthcoming Northwestern-Newberry volumes. Brian Higgins, editorial associate, read and advised on a late printout of the headnotes, letters, and textual reports. R. D. Madison, editorial associate, of the U.S. Naval Academy, consulted on nautical matters. Donald Yannella, editorial associate, consulted on the Duyckinck papers. Staff members of The Newberry Library provided essential assistance: Kenneth Cain in photographing illustrations and John Aubrey in locating books and articles. Jo Ann Casey collaborated meticulously in generating the index. Further close assistance on the volume was given by Theresa Biancheri, Ann Larson, Eugene Perchak, and Nancy Scheller.

Authorization to edit manuscripts and permission to publish material from their collections has been granted by the following institutions: the American Antiquarian Society, the Berkshire Athenaeum, the British Library, Boston Public Library, the Cincinnati Historical Society, the Connecticut Historical Society, Cornell University Library, Dalhousie University, Dartmouth College Library, the Essex Institute, the Houghton Library of Harvard University, the Historical Society of Pennsylvania, the Lilly Library at Indiana University, Lehigh University Library, Dawes Memorial Library at Marietta College, the Massachusetts Historical Society, Egbert Starr Library at Middlebury College, the Mitchell Library in Sydney, Australia, the Pierpont Morgan Library, John Murray, Ltd., the National Archives at the Library of Congress, the New-York Historical Society, the New York Public Library, Astor, Lenox and Tilden Foundations (Duyckinck Family Papers and Gansevoort-Lansing Collection, Rare Books and Manuscripts Division), The Newberry Library, Princeton University Libraries, Punahou School, Honolulu, Hawaii, Redwood Library and Athenaeum, The Rosenbach Museum & Library, the Social Law Library,

Cody Memorial Library at Southwestern University, the Regenstein Library at the University of Chicago, University of Illinois Library at Champaign-Urbana, Rush Rhees Library at the University of Rochester, the Harry Ransom Humanities Research Center at the University of Texas, the University of Virginia Library, and the Beinecke Library at Yale University. The following auction houses and private collectors also granted authorization to edit manuscripts (some no longer now in their possession) and permission to publish material from their holdings: Christie's, Hennig Cohen, John B. Edmunds, Jr., the Gallery of History, Inc., Frederick James Kennedy and Joyce Deveau Kennedy, Richard Manney, William Reese, William Rose II, Maurice Sendak, David Shneidman, Sotheby's, and Kate Whitney. Additional materials were found in the collections of the Berkshire Athenaeum, the British Library, the Rare Book and Manuscript Library at Columbia University, the Widener Library at Harvard University, the Huntington Library, the New Bedford Free Public Library, the general collections at the New York Public Library, the New York State Library, Northwestern University Library, the Philadelphia Free Library, Alexander Library at Rutgers University, the U.S. Naval Academy Museum, the University Research Library at the University of California at Los Angeles, and the Golda Meir Library at the University of Wisconsin–Milwaukee. The editor is indebted for information and assistance to Carolyn E. Banfield of the Friends of Arrowhead, Giuseppe Bisaccia of the Boston Public Library, Sally Brown of the British Library, Robert G. Carroon of the Diocese of Connecticut, James Corsaro of the New York State Library, Ruth T. Degenhardt of the Berkshire Athenaeum, Thomas L. Edsall of the 19th Century Shop, Stephen Ferguson of Princeton University, Arthur Freeman of Bernard Quaritch, Ltd., Helen Hansen of the Sandusky Historical Society, Kimball Higgs of the Grolier Club, Christopher C. Jaeckel of Walter Benjamin Autographs, Bill Kelly of the Watkins Review & Express, Thomas Knowles of the American Antiquarian Society, Leslie A. Morris, formerly of The Rosenbach Museum & Library, Howard S. Mott of Howard S. Mott, Inc., Virginia Murray of John Murray, Ltd., Robert E. Parks of the Pierpont Morgan Library, A. W. C. Phelps of the Rowfant Club, Michael Plunkett of the University of Virginia, Justin Schiller of Justin Schiller Books, John D. Stinson and Valerie Wingfield of the New York Public Library, Gerald Stodolski, formerly of Paul C. Richards Autographs, Kathleen M. Tivnan of the Lansingburgh Historical Society, and Patricia C. Willis of the Beinecke Library at Yale University. Expert help of various kinds was also rendered by these scholars, researchers, or collectors: Mrs. William Ambrose, Claire Badaracco, Ruth Blair, Hennig Cohen, John B. Edmunds, Jr., Jonathan Eller, Richard Garnett, Thomas F. Heffernan, T. Walter Herbert, Patricia G. Holland, Frederick James Kennedy and Joyce Deveau Kennedy, Joseph J. Moldenhauer, Bernard Mosher, Nina Murray, William Reese, Maurice Sendak, Doris R. Sheridan, David Shneidman, Heidi and Chris Snow, Robert Spradlin, David L. Vander Meulen, Robert K. Wallace, and Richard E. Winslow III. In addition Stanton Garner and Merton M. Sealts, Jr., deserve special thanks for their expert contributions.

In the course of editing this volume, Lynn Horth found one person to be simply indispensable: John Tarnow.

Deep gratitude is rendered here by all the editors and staff of The Writings of Herman Melville *to:*

Lawrence William Towner
(1921–1992)
Humane and imaginative scholar

As president of The Newberry Library, Bill Towner was the true friend and most constant supporter of the whole Northwestern-Newberry Melville Edition Project: he made the Library its joint sponsor, editorial second home, and co-publisher; he enabled the Melville Collection there; and through faltering times he sustained the Edition and its editors.

Herman Melville,
an engraving from the oil portrait by Joseph Oriel Eaton, 1870.

Historical Note

T HE LETTERS by and to Melville in this volume span the greater part of his lifetime, extending from letters he wrote at the age of nine in 1828 to ones he sent and received during the year before his death at seventy-two in 1891. The best of his own letters, some of them now anthology classics, are brilliantly revealing. These reflect the meteoric rise and excitement of his early literary career, from 1846 to 1851, as well as its equally precipitous subsequent fall; and the fullest and boldest of them, those to Evert A. Duyckinck, Richard Henry Dana, Jr., and especially Nathaniel Hawthorne, were written at the pinnacle of that brief career. Yet Melville's letters through the years, even with their sporadic flashings-forth, were mostly occasional, businesslike, and never gossipy, expansive, or voluminous. The paucity of his actual as well as of his preserved correspondence contrasts surprisingly with the gregarious rush of to-and-fro epistolary traffic engaged in by such American literary contemporaries as Emerson, Longfellow, Whitman, Simms, Hawthorne, and even the soul-selective Emily Dickinson, to say nothing of the great English and Continental men and women of letters in his time.

Presented here in one sequence are the 313 texts, newly edited, that are known to survive of letters by Melville, and for the first time, in a separate sequence, the 88 texts that are known to survive of letters to him. Taken together, however, these surviving texts provide only a spotty chronicle of Melville's outer, and intermittent revelations of his inner, life. They provide so little not only because by all indications he wrote relatively few, and mostly sparse, letters but also because so many of those he did write, and receive, have been lost or destroyed. He himself, as he declared, habitually destroyed letters he received, including those he had prized from Hawthorne; and his daughter or some other too-proper descendant in the twentieth century lamentably destroyed his numerous letters to his wife.[1] Consequently, to fill the gaps within the correspondence, 542 editorial entries are chronologically interspersed for letters both by and to Melville for which no full text has been located but for which some evidence survives. These entries, like the editorial headnotes for the known letters, flesh out the specific historical and biographical contexts for the unlocated letters. Both supply the editor's full annotations, placing circumstances, persons, and allusions, from a wide range of documentary and scholarly sources, and drawing upon family archives of both Melville and his wife, including the correspondence in the recently recovered portion, now in the New York Public Library, of a trove preserved by his sister Augusta.[2]

The three sections of this HISTORICAL NOTE discuss Melville's aloof role in the close-knit family letter-writing world of widowed mother, three brothers, four sisters, and numerous uncles, aunts, and cousins; his limited though at times full-hearted letter-writing engagement with his editors and congenial fellow writers in the professional literary world he entered in 1846 with the publication of his first book, *Typee,* and, briefly, the long delayed valuing and at last the scholarly editing and publishing of his letters.

I

Had Herman's father, Allan Melvill, not died in 1832 leaving his wife and eight children in near-poverty, letters need not have come

1.   See pp. 786–88 and 800 below for further discussion of these incidents.

2.   The first extensive biographical use of this material was made for purposes of the Northwestern-Newberry Edition, by Hershel Parker in the Historical Note to *Moby-Dick* (see pp. 586ff.). It will be more extensively excerpted by Parker in *The New Melville Log* and used in his forthcoming Melville biography.

to play so vital a role in the Melville family (as the name came to be spelled after Allan's death). But without him, Allan's widow, Maria Gansevoort Melville, and her children depended on letters as an emotional and economic lifeline. With their self-enclosed prosperous world shattered by his death, all three older sons, Gansevoort, Herman, and his namesake, Allan, were forced to spend long periods separated from the family, working for its common support. The first summer after his father's death, thirteen-year-old Herman had to leave the rural safety of Pittsfield, where the family had fled from a cholera epidemic in Albany, to return to his job as clerk in an Albany bank. When he did not answer a letter from his oldest sister, Helen, she included a strongly worded rebuke in a letter of 8 August 1832 to their uncle Peter Gansevoort, with whom Melville was staying: "I am sorry that my brother Herman cannot find time to answer my last, but tell him I am expecting a letter every day and shall be sadly disappointed if I return to Albany before he writes" (NYPL-GL).[3] The desired reply was not a matter of social pleasantry, but of family unity.[4]

Whether Melville answered his sister is not known, although very likely he did, given her insistent tone and the fact that she addressed her complaint to their uncle Peter, who was Herman's employer and guardian at the time. Yet the wider implication is that young Herman was less than a faithful correspondent during his early travels. Between 1832 and 1840, he journeyed to Pittsfield (where he ran his uncle Thomas's farm in the summer of 1837 and then taught school the following autumn), to Liverpool (to which he voyaged in 1839 aboard a merchant ship as a common sailor), to Greenbush, New York (where he taught school in the winter of

3. The section on "Sources" at the end of this NOTE explains its documentation; for a list of abbreviations and short titles used here, see pp. xi–xiii above. The frequent nonstandard spelling and punctuation in the ensuing quotations are those of their manuscript sources. Full texts and information about quotations from Melville's correspondence may be found in the chronologically dated entries above.

4. Helen herself later received while visiting in Lansingburgh a similar, although slightly more muted, rebuke from their sister Augusta in a letter of 21 December 1850 from Pittsfield: "It was high time, Miss Helen, I should think to write to us. Two weeks & not one line from you. I was really beginning to get alarmed, as evening after evening passed without a letter, & was upon the point of writing you again, thinking that you must actually be ill, when it happily arrived" (NYPL-GL).

1839–40), and to Galena, Illinois (where he visited his uncle Thomas and unsuccessfully looked for work), before embarking on 3 January 1841 as a common sailor aboard the *Acushnet*, bound for the South Pacific. Only nine letters from this eight-year period are known to survive, and few additional ones can be inferred. And of the known letters, two to his brother Allan are tongue-in-cheek notes rather than the earnest letters of a distant brother.

Early on, Melville's role in the family correspondence seems to have been more as a postman than as a regular participant. In 1840, his sister Helen portrayed him as such in her letter of 5 January from Lansingburgh to their sister Augusta, who was staying at their uncle Peter's home in Albany: "Herman leaves directly after church, and I must therefore write you a few lines now. . . . Mamma sends her best love to you, & says you must write a letter every Thursday, so that Allan can give it to our family post-man [Herman] on Friday" (NYPL-GL). As the family moved from place to place, Herman continued to carry letters between Lansingburgh and Albany, New York and Pittsfield, Boston and Pittsfield, and Albany and New York.[5]

By contrast Herman's older brother Gansevoort and younger brother Allan were devoted correspondents with their mother when away from home during the family's early struggles. (Gansevoort Melville, after the failure of his fur and cap store in Albany during the panic of 1837, left for New York to establish himself there as a lawyer and later embarked on a political career, which included a three-month stump-speaking tour in 1844 on behalf of the presidential candidacy of James K. Polk. Allan Melville remained in Albany as a clerk when the rest of the family moved to Lansingburgh in 1838, and later moved to New York to study law in Gansevoort's

---

5. Instances of Melville's role as family postman abound: Maria Gansevoort Melville, for example, reports in a letter of 21 June 1847 to her daughter Augusta, who was visiting in Boston, "Herman was in Albany last week, Kate, the Van Vechtens, Aunt Susan &c — all well — we expect an answer fully to our two letters"—which Melville had presumably carried to them (NYPL-GL). Similarly Hope Savage Shaw writing to Samuel H. Savage on 7 March 1849 reports, "Last Saturday I sent a letter by Herman who was returning as business called him & as I have mentioned before Elizabeth being blessed with a beautiful boy" (MHS–Samuel P. Savage papers).

office.) Did Herman write dutiful letters during these years to his mother like Gansevoort and Allan?[6] If so, they have left no trace.

Yet it is unlikely that Melville was oblivious to the role letters played in his family even if he was not always an active writer of them.[7] His letter of 13 October 1844 (now unlocated) announcing his return from the Pacific elicited an overwhelmed reply from his brother Allan on 17 October:

> I need not express to you my feelings when I opened your letter dated at Boston on the 13 inst . . . this morning. You can imagine that they overcame me. I was indeed unprepared for such good fortune and trembled while perusing your epistle — a prayer of gratitude played upon my lips — & I thanked the Giver of all good for your safe return. Herman! we are once more all together & I pray God that we may never be seperated more.

In fact, the family was still separated, with Gansevoort and Allan in New York and their mother and sisters in Lansingburgh; and shortly afterwards on 31 July 1845 Gansevoort left for his new diplomatic post in London—the fruit of all of his political stumping. Less than a year later the family was then separated irrevocably from him when he unexpectedly died there on 12 May 1846. His last letter to Herman, written on 3 April, reiterated the importance letters carried in the family. In it he complained of Allan's not keeping him adequately informed about the family's finances and so causing his thoughts to be "so much at home that much of my time is spent in disquieting apprehensions as to matters & things there." Such anguish is not unusual in nineteenth-century family letters. But had the Melville family somehow been able to remain intact in one place, that pain would have been reserved for its less immediate members. More typical would have been the concern Melville felt in 1847 at the news of the illness of Judge Lemuel Shaw, the father of his intended bride, Elizabeth Shaw—a concern which not he but his mother described in a letter of 15 June to her daughter Helen, who was staying with the Shaws in Boston: "M^r C.

6. Allan, for example, docketed his letter of 10 November 1838 from their mother "answered the same day" (Berkshire Athenaeum). For examples of Gansevoort's letters to their mother, see Parker, *Gansevoort Melville's London Journal and Letters from England,* pp. 61–67.

7. Significantly, his first known published piece took the form of a self-confident, highly stylized letter to a father-figure—the letter he actually might have written had his father lived. See the NN *Piazza Tales* volume, pp. 191–96 and 622–25.

P. sent us the Lowell paper containing a rather serious account of Judge Shaws illness. We waited anxiously for the mail which brought your letter, we were much reliev'd after reading it, and most sincerely hope that he is getting better. Poor Herman felt very bad — but your letter had the effect of recalling his spirits & he is again as he has been since his return from Boston, perfectly happy" (NYPL-GL). For Maria Melville and her family such anxiety was all too frequent, and sometimes their hope was defeated. When Melville wrote his last letter to his brother Gansevoort on 29 May, he began it optimistically, attempting to allay his brother's anxieties about the family:

> My Dear Gansevoort — I look forward to three weeks from now, & think I see you openning this letter in [one] of those pleasant hamlets roundabout London, of which we read in novels. At any rate I pray Heaven that such may be the case & that you are mending rapidly. Remember that composure of mind is every thing. You should give no thought to matters here, until you are well enough to think about them. As far as I know they are in good train.

What Melville did not know was that Gansevoort had died nearly three weeks earlier—news that had not yet had time to cross the Atlantic. Seven years later Melville would conclude his story "Bartleby," about a former clerk in the dead-letter office, with a lament, heavy with Victorian sentimentality, for such unreceived letters:

> Sometimes from out the folded paper the pale clerk takes a ring:—the finger it was meant for, perhaps, moulders in the grave; a bank-note sent in swiftest charity:—he whom it would relieve, nor eats nor hungers any more; pardon for those who died despairing; hope for those who died unhoping; good tidings for those who died stifled by unrelieved calamities. On errands of life, these letters speed to death. (NN *Piazza Tales* volume, p. 45)

After the success of *Typee* and *Omoo* and the consolidation in 1847 of the larger part of the Melville family in New York—in a household that included Maria Melville, the four Melville sisters, and Herman and Allan with their brides—the anxious letters become less frequent in what remains of the family correspondence.[8] Yet with one or more of the women frequently traveling to stay

8. The youngest brother, Thomas, remained the only distant traveler in the family. In 1846, at age sixteen, he sailed as a green hand aboard the whaleship *Theophilus Chase*. Melville's now unlocated 1848 letter to the ship's owner, Henry Will-

with relatives and friends, letters remained important—particularly among the women. After Melville and his wife, along with his mother and three of his sisters, moved to Pittsfield in the fall of 1850, Augusta Melville wrote a letter on 14 January 1851 to her friend Mary Blatchford in New York describing their new routine, clearly making letters the key item of importance on her list: "Then there are the letters to be read, of which we generally have two or three, & the New York papers — & when those fail — we take up some interesting book. We have just begun 'David Copperfield' " (NYPL-GL). And as Augusta had already written on 22 November 1850 to their sister Helen, the arrival of a letter—this one in Herman's overcoat pocket—could set the whole household in an uproar:

> The arrival of your letter created quite an excitement. Lizzie (who brought in Hermans over coat with her from the waggon in order to loose no time in placing it in our hands,) was quite frowned upon for having lighted upon the wrong pocket, at first, and had we not been restrained by the respect we invariably show matrons, Fanny & I would have possessed ourselves of the garment on the instant, so incensed were we at her awkwardness. At last the letter was produced. Expectations ran high — whose address did it bear? — Mama's — Now for the spectacles! — Another delay! — Patience — Patience. — Here they are, — & with heads bent forward, eyes fixed & ears intent we drank in the contents. A great event this. — The first arrival of the first letter of the first absentee of Arrowhead. (NYPL-GL)

Yet Melville seems always to stand on the periphery of this constant round of letters among the women. His letter of 25 May 1862 to his youngest brother Thomas concludes, "I dont write you, My Dear Boy, about family matters, because I know that the girls keep you posted there."9 And in fact very few details of daily life emerge in

---

cox, inquiring about its expected date of return, was probably prompted by the impatient concerns of his mother and sisters (see the entry for this letter, p. 108 above).

9. Often news of their brother Herman was solicited from other members of the family by his sisters or mother. For example, their cousin Julia Melvill in Pittsfield where Herman was working replied on 2 June 1837 to such a request from his sister Augusta: "You next desire that I will tell you how Herman comes on in his new line of life. firstly you wish to know if he behaves himself with propriety, next if he conducts himself with politeness. I answer you with pleasure he is very good very polite. You need not feel uneasy about him we will not try to make him quite a savage while he resides in the country as you fear we shall" (NYPL-GL).

Melville's letters; it is primarily through the women's letters, not Melville's, that we learn about Allan's new houses, Augusta's engagement (and its lapse), and all the comings and goings of various family members. His letters that do contain "information" were generally written while he was away from home—his 1856 letter from Liverpool to his brother Allan, his 1860 letter from the Pacific Ocean to his son Malcolm, and his 1861 letter from Washington, D.C., to his wife. Others have a specific purpose to accomplish—particularly those to his uncle Peter Gansevoort and father-in-law, Lemuel Shaw.[10] But most often when facing up to "epistolary obligations" Melville reached for hyperbolic "moonshine" rather than supplying mundane descriptions of daily events to "fill out" his sheet.[11] Thus, rather than a description of the actual family celebrations accompanying the birth of his first son Malcolm, his letter of 20 February 1849 to his brother Allan has all the bells in the city and all the ships in the harbor proclaiming the momentous event; rather than wishing his ill second cousin a speedy recovery, his letter of 26 April 1847 to Augustus Van Schaick desires him to send "a challenge across the water" to fight the British champion Bendigo; and rather than predicting Henry Gansevoort's success as a Union commander, his letter of 22 March 1864 anticipates "two small but choice constellations of stars" alighting on his cousin's shoulders and his name being used "by Southern matrons to frighten their children." Even his comments on small matters are couched in such fanciful terms. His letter of 5 August 1875 to Abraham Lansing con-

---

10.   In writing such a letter on 4 December 1851 to his sister Augusta, then in New York, to remind her to retrieve from Allan his copy of Machiavelli's *The Florentine Histories*, he concludes abruptly once having stated that purpose: "I hope you have enjoyed yourself in New York. The weather here has been cold as ever. Other than the weather I know not what to write about from Pittsfield. My love to Sophia & the children & to yourself: in which all join." One exception to this silence about daily life in his letters is perhaps his letter of 13 December 1850 to Evert Duyckinck, describing his routine of rising, feeding his horse and cow, and writing until midafternoon dinner time. The humorous tone he writes in, however, only emphasizes how ironically Melville viewed such epistolary accounts.

11.   See his 31 March 1877 letter to his brother-in-law John C. Hoadley, where he jocularly writes that, in certain moods, "epistolary obligations" seem "mere moonshine" to him. Similarly, his letter of 20 January 1845 counsels his younger sister Kate: "Now I want you to write me a long letter, dont' take pattern after mine & fill it with nonsense, but send me a sober sheet like a good girl."

cerning an upcoming trip to Albany proclaims: "When the Shah of Persia or the Great Khan of Tartary comes to Albany by the night-boat — *him* meet on the wharf with salvoes of artillery — but not a Custom House Inspector."

By all accounts Melville's letters to family members, though unorthodox, were highly prized among them. After receiving one, his sister Helen responded on 29 May 1854 that she felt "particularly flattered & pleased" to have a letter from him, and in apologizing for not having written him sooner she dramatized what must have been a noticeable disregard on his part for the women's interest in day-to-day newsy letters:

> I should have sent one of my numerous epistles to your particular address ere now, if I had not been so well acquainted with your usual mode of treating such documents — "Any letters? Herman?" cries Gus, or Lizzie, or Fanny, as you are reining up old Charlie in gallant style at the pump-room door. "Y – e – s – s" — "one from Helen I guess — for some of you — here 'tis." "Why Herman, it's directed to you!" — "Is it? let me see — why so it is! Well, take it along, I'll be in presently, and then some of you can read it to me."[12]

Given Melville's disregard for the family's correspondence, it is not surprising that his sister Augusta's record of correspondence for 1849–54 (NYPL-GL) indicates that his letters to her and probably other family members were relatively infrequent.[13] For example, while visiting in New York between Thanksgiving and the end of January in 1851–52, she recorded receiving one joint letter from

12. See also the entry for Melville's [18?] June 1863 letter to his sister Frances Priscilla. She was delighted with this letter, which she found to be "so funny" that she, in turn, enclosed it in a letter of 22 June 1863 to their sister Augusta, with strict instructions to return it.

13. Probably typical was Thomas Melville's complaint in a letter of 18 September 1852 from Boston to their sister Augusta in Pittsfield: "Why does not Herman write me" (NYPL-GL). And when Melville did write, his letter was often made to do double duty—sent by the recipient to other members of the family usually with instructions to return it (see, for example, the entry for the letter Melville wrote to his mother between 29 October and 10 November 1856 while abroad). That Melville was well aware of this practice is clear from his instructions at the close of the 13 November section of his extended 1856 letter from Liverpool to his brother Allan: "By the way, you had better (after reading it) send this letter on to Lizzie, as it may contain items omitted in my letters to her. And Lizzie can send it to Helen &c, if it be worth while."

Herman and their sister Helen on 4 December and sending one letter to Herman on 28 December. By contrast she herself wrote four letters to Helen during this period and received five letters from her in addition to the joint one with their brother. To their youngest sister Frances Priscilla she sent four letters and received eight, and to their mother she sent six and received two.[14]

Rather than contributing more fully to the constant flow of family letters with his own pen, Melville often requested his sisters or wife to add a message from him at the close of their letters. Most such messages are perfunctory, occasioned simply by his presence in the room. His sister Augusta, for example, explains in a letter of 6 April 1846 to their second cousin Catharine Van Schaick: "Herman just passed through the room. 'Who are you writing to Gus?' [']Kate Van Schaick.' [']Well, give her my very best love[']" (New York State Library).[15] Yet some of his messages were substantial enough that they may have prompted a letter from the recipient. His wife's letter of 2 July 1873 to his cousin Catherine Gansevoort, for example, states: "Herman sends his love, and wishes to know if you have

14. This same numerical contrast is readily apparent in the Gansevoort-Lansing papers in the New York Public Library when the bulging folders of letters from Elizabeth Shaw Melville to Herman's cousin Catherine Gansevoort Lansing are seen side by side with the slim folders of those from Melville to his cousin. According to Amy Puett (later Emmers), "A Calendar of Elizabeth Melville's Letters" (pp. 273–310 in "Melville's Wife: A Study of Elizabeth Shaw Melville," Ph.D. dissertation, Northwestern University, 1969), Elizabeth Melville wrote over sixty letters to Catherine Gansevoort Lansing, roughly twice as many as her husband. Moreover, Elizabeth Melville's letters were usually much longer than her husband's letters to his cousin. Since this cousin appears to have preserved letters carefully, the contrast is a significant one. Similarly, the fact that only one letter from Melville survives among those preserved by Catherine's brother Henry Gansevoort, also preserved carefully, is another strong indication of the relative infrequency of Melville's letters (see p. 392 above for more about Henry's letter-saving habits).

15. A similar scene is repeated in Maria Gansevoort Melville's letter of 17 May 1847 from Lansingburgh to Augusta in Boston: "Herman just left the room & sends his love to you" (NYPL-GL). No doubt some of the appended greetings were added by the women on their own initiative—messages such as that at the close of his wife's letter of 14 June 1863 from Pittsfield to Frances Priscilla at Gansevoort: "Much love to Mamma in which Herman joins" (NYPL-GL), and possibly even messages like that in her letter of 10 November 1868 to his cousin Catherine Gansevoort: "Herman wished me to say how sorry he was that he was not able to see [Uncle Peter] either of the times he called" (NYPL-GL).

succeeded in getting the book you wished — if not to let him know, and he will get it for you" (NYPL-GL). In addition to relaying such messages from Herman, both his wife and his brother Allan wrote full letters on his behalf from time to time.[16]

Perhaps nowhere is Melville's vicarious participation in the family's letter-writing more apparent than in Elizabeth Shaw Melville's correspondence with his cousin Catherine Gansevoort Lansing while he was getting *Clarel* through the press. On 2 February 1876 Elizabeth wrote politely to Catherine, explaining that they could not receive visitors with the book "going through the press, and every minute of Herman's time and mine is devoted to it"; she then wrote a second letter on a separate sheet, which she smuggled into the same envelope:

> Dear Kate,
> I have written you a note that Herman could see, as he wished, but want you to know how painful it is for me to write it, and also to have to give the real cause — The fact is, that Herman, poor fellow, is in such a frightfully nervous state, & particularly now with such an added strain on his mind, that I am actually *afraid* to have any one here for fear that he will be upset entirely, & not be able to go on with the printing — He was not willing to have even his own sisters here, and I had to write Augusta before she left Albany to that effect — that was the reason she changed her plan, and went to Tom's — If ever this dreadful *incubus* of a *book* (I call it so because it has undermined all our happiness) gets off Herman's shoulders I do hope he may be in better mental health. (NYPL-GL)

This second letter is revealing not only for the glimpse it gives of the tensions within the Melville household at this time but also for its indication that Melville saw much of the mail going out of the house as well as coming into it even when he was not an active correspon-

---

16. At Melville's request, for example, Allan wrote to Evert Duyckinck on 22 July 1846, conveying the news that Melville had met with his shipboard friend Richard T. Greene, the "Toby" of *Typee*. Since Melville merely requested that his brother write, but did not dictate or outline this letter, it is not entered as a part of the correspondence in this edition. Similarly, no entry is given for Elizabeth Melville's letter of 30 January 1859 to George Duyckinck, communicating the title of her husband's new lecture, "The South Seas," in his absence. This was probably one of a number of letters she wrote on his behalf while he was traveling on the lecture circuit, although no others have been located (see *Log*, II, 598).

dent. Later in the process of getting *Clarel* through the press, Elizabeth Melville wrote another letter to Melville's cousin Kate on 22 April 1876, this time including a message from him: "Congratulate us that the book is *at last*, in type. . . . Now, he wants me to tell you he is going to inscribe that book in your father's name, as seems most natural and fit" (NYPL-GL).

In the same way many messages were directed to Melville within the letters between his wife, sisters, and other relatives. Many of these messages are as perfunctory as his own. A typical one is from Melville's sister Frances Priscilla, concluding her letter of 20 March 1863 from the family home in Gansevoort, New York, to her sister Augusta in Pittsfield: "Mamma sends love to Herman & Malcolm" (NYPL-GL). But other messages are more purposeful. Several months after Melville's wagon-accident, Helen wrote on 6 March 1863 from her home in Brookline, Massachusetts, to Elizabeth in Pittsfield, adding, "Love best to Herman I am glad he is so much better" (NYPL-GL). Melville's brother-in-law John Hoadley even included strongly worded praise for the story "Cock-A-Doodle-Doo!" in a letter of 27 December 1853 to Augusta, rather than to Herman himself: "Tell Herman I thank him with all my heart for that noble, spirited lesson of hope, — enduring, triumphant, — never despairing, — in the 'Crowing of the noble Cock Beneventano' " (NYPL-GL). And in 1854 Augusta received a letter of 1 March from their brother Allan with a timely piece of advice concerning Melville's magazine pieces: "Say to Herman that he ought to reserve to himself the right to publish his magazine matter in book form. It might be desirable & could probably be secured by agreement made at the beginning. Tell him I regretted to hear of his '*Horrid Week*' of weak eyes & congratulate him on his recovery" (NYPL-GL). Of all the members of the family, the matriarch, Maria Melville, wielded this device of the indirect message most skillfully. Writing to Augusta on 10 March 1851 shortly after arriving in New York, she clearly intended the following "message" to reach her recalcitrant son: "Herman I hope returned home safe after dumping me & my trunks out so unceremoniously at the Depot — Altho we were there more than an hour before the time, he hurried off as if his life had depended upon his speed, a more ungallant man it would be difficult to find. I hope to hear from *Herman*" (NYPL-GL).[17] Not satis-

---

17. Maria Melville wrote the word "man" over the apparent word "son".

fied with this rebuke, she wrote two days later—once again to Augusta but also once again with a clear agenda for her son—this time concerning the issue of his having a daguerreotype taken so that his portrait could be published, something he had been stubbornly refusing:

> We met Mrs Duyckinck & sister in the street. In the Eve^g Mr Duyckinck came up & pass'd the Eve^g with us, both inquired very particularly about you
> Mr Bancroft has set for his portrait it will soon appear in the Dollar Magazine. Mr Duyckinck has Mr Hawthornes which will also appear in the same. Mr Duyckinck said Herman must sit to a first rate artist when he comes on — & also told me the International Magazine had advertized among the Portraits that of Herman Melvilles as forthcoming with other American Authors, Mr Prescott has also had his Portrait taken for Mr Duyckinck's magazine all at the expense of M^r D— & brother.
> So Herman with all those illustrious examples will have to do likewise or appear very strangely stiff. (NYPL-GL)[18]

A year later when Melville failed to call upon the Albany poet Alfred Street when he gave a reading in Pittsfield, Melville's uncle Peter Gansevoort in a letter of 9 October 1852 to his sister, Melville's mother, adopted the same device for chastising his nephew:

> Alas — Herman, thou art a sorry boy — Thou might have tipped thy beaver, kissed thy hand & last tho' not least dropped thy Card, but tho' Hat & Hand & Card were thine, all those were withheld by thee Typee from Alfreds anxious hopes — no, no the Poet sings, no, no — he took no friendly token from his quiver, and locked up "Arrowhead" . . . Herman, Herman, Herman truly thou art an "Ambiguity" — .(NYPL-GL)

The scarcity, in this volume, of Melville's letters to family members must be discounted by his habit of writing letters infre-

---

18. For yet another example of Maria Melville's practice of taking aim at her son in letters to her daughters, see pp. 631–33 above. See also Melville's letter of 12 February 1851 to Evert Duyckinck, for his refusal to have his "mug" published in the *Dollar Magazine*. His adamancy on this point clearly became a matter of comment within the family. In a letter of 23 December 1854, Allan Melville wrote to their mother, then in Pittsfield, ending with: "Ask Herman to write what he is doing. . . . Does he regret that his portrait does not appear with the 40 odd in Clarks book" (NYPL–GL; Allan refers to *The Knickerbocker Gallery* [New York: Hueston, 1855]). No reply from Melville is known.

quently and his practice of sending messages in the letters of other members of the family. Still, there is no doubt that he did write many letters to them that are missing. Although nearly a third of his letters printed in this volume (ninety-three letters) were written to relatives, most of them are not to his immediate family but to his cousin Catherine Gansevoort Lansing and other members of her family in his later years. These predominate now because they were preserved so carefully. This volume includes only one letter from Melville to his mother, fourteen letters to his seven brothers and sisters, and two letters to his own children. The full evidence, however, indicates that these are a small part of those he actually wrote to members of his family. There are only five letters to his sisters, two to Augusta and three to Kate, for example, although an additional twenty-eight letters to his sisters can be inferred. Only a single letter to his wife—that of 24 and 25 March 1861 from Washington—is now known to survive, yet a large number of his letters to her certainly survived into the twentieth century. In 1929 Frank Jewett Mather, Jr., recalled:

> About twenty-five years ago I sought Herman Melville's daughter, Elizabeth, who was living in the old Florence amid her father's books and pictures. She talked of him with constraint, but was interested in my quest, giving me two privately printed pamphlets of poems, which completed my first editions, and letting me read casually from that japanned tin cakebox which contained Melville's letters and unpublished manuscripts. Thus I took a few notes from the diaries of travels, sampled "Billy Budd," and the last poems. Miss Melville generously promised me the use of all the papers except Melville's letters to his wife. In high hopes I wrote to the American publishers [Houghton, Mifflin] whose list is heaviest with our classics, and proposed a modest biography in one volume. The answer was friendly but decisive: Herman Melville was a hopelessly bad risk, and one that no prudent publisher could undertake even to the extent of a few hundred dollars.[19]

Mather's recollection is the only published reference to Melville's letters to his wife. Raymond Weaver, Melville's first twentieth-century biographer, left no record of seeing them. The only sur-

19. "Herman Melville," *Saturday Review of Literature* 5 (27 April 1929), 945. Mather's visit of about "twenty-five years ago" can be more precisely dated by the 28 September 1906 letter of introduction that Edmund C. Stedman wrote to Bessie Melville on his behalf (see Metcalf, pp. 291–92).

viving tangible clues to their having existed are a number of "Herman Melville" autographs evidently clipped from "Mrs. Herman Melville" on their envelopes. Harrison Hayford recalls that in the late 1950's when he along with William Gilman and Merrell Davis visited Melville's granddaughter, Eleanor Melville Metcalf, she brought out a group of clipped Melville autographs, which she accounted for in that way, and generously allowed each of them to choose one. She also presented such clippings to a number of other scholars, including Luther Mansfield, Merton M. Sealts, Jr., and Stanley T. Williams.[20] Davis and Gilman in the introduction to their 1960 *Letters of Herman Melville* report that Mrs. Metcalf had "some forty-six" such clippings, some of them from "envelopes that Melville addressed to his wife, now cut down—apparently for the autograph signatures—from 'Mrs. Herman Melville' to 'Herman Melville.' By the use of paper evidence, one might establish that at least three of these were written sometime in 1860 or shortly thereafter . . . during Melville's trip around the Horn, and that another was written after 1882 (the date of the manufacturer's mark on the paper)" (p. xviii). Davis and Gilman concluded that these clippings represented "positive evidence" of letters from Melville to his wife that had been destroyed.[21] Since no family let-

---

20. Each of those given to Mansfield, Sealts, and Williams was affixed to a photograph of Melville. See Sealts to Horth, 13 September 1991, in the Melville Edition files, also Williams to Tyrus Hillway, n.d., and Arnold Bartini to Donald Yannella, 7 August 1978, in the Melville Society Papers (The Newberry Library). Still other clipped autographs (in effect signatures, if not always intended as such) survive tipped into copies of Melville's works (some given by family members as gifts after his death): see the entry on p. 539 above for one in a copy of *John Marr* which bears enough of a postmark to establish that he wrote to his wife from Florida; see also Sealts, *Early Lives*, p. 63, for reproduction of one in a copy of *Timoleon*. That some of the autographs came from letters to others, not just from envelopes addressed to his wife, is suggested by Henry K. Metcalf's letter of 2 January 1954 to Tyrus Hillway, which inquired: "Have you one of Melville's autographs which were cut out of letters and envelopes? If not, and if you would care to have one, Mrs. Metcalf wants me to say that she would be glad to send it to you" (Melville Society Papers, The Newberry Library).

21. Confirming their conclusion, Sealts (in the letter to Horth cited above) writes that the clipped autograph Mrs. Metcalf gave him appears to have been preceded by "Mrs."—that is, it was probably from an envelope addressed to "Mrs. Herman Melville." A similar collection of eight clipped Melville autographs is in NYPL-GL; they are of uncertain origin. Four of these clippings bear remnants of postmarks (but not enough to establish a place or date), showing that they came

ters lacking Melville's signature or envelopes lacking "Mrs. Herman Melville" in their address are known to have survived, the letters and envelopes from which these autographs were cut appear to have been destroyed (and from Mather's report, the destruction of those to his wife must have taken place after his visit to Melville's daughter Elizabeth in 1906).[22]

Just how many other family letters Melville wrote is hard to judge. Of letters to his five aunts on the paternal side of the family, only two, to his aunt Lucy, have been located. Yet his childhood visits to Boston, where Melville's grandparents Major Thomas Melvill and Priscilla Scollay Melvill lived and his aunts congregated, and to Bristol where his uncle John D'Wolf and aunt Mary Melvill D'Wolf lived, make it likely that he had subsequent correspondence with these close relatives. Similarly, no letters to his uncle Thomas Melvill, Jr., with whose family he lived in Pittsfield and later visited in Galena, Illinois, have been found, yet at least a few were probably written. And to his three Gansevoort uncles, his mother's brothers, only letters to his uncle Peter have been located, yet Melville dedicated his second book, *Omoo*, to his uncle Herman (for whom he was named) and probably wrote to him at that time as well as at others. In addition, at least ten further letters to members of Elizabeth Shaw Melville's family, including her father Lemuel Shaw, can be inferred, and apparently an extensive correspondence with his wife's cousin Ellen Marett Gifford has been lost.[23] Also a few other scattered letters, not part of extended series, such as those to his second cousin Augustus Van Schaick and his wife's half-cousin Samuel Savage, may survive unlocated.[24]

As for the letters Melville received from family members, texts for only twenty have been located. Jay Leyda speculated that Mel-

---

from addressed envelopes. A fifth bears a complimentary close (see the entry on p. 536 above), and three more have slight remnants of further writing at the edges. Davis and Gilman noted another with a complimentary close that is at present unlocated (see the entry on p. 539 above).

22.   For Jay Leyda's surmise as to which family members seem to have burned these and other Melville letters after his death, see *Log*, I, xiv–xv.

23.   See Melville's 5 October 1885 letter to her, p. 490 above.

24.   See Joyce D. and Frederick J. Kennedy, "In Pursuit of Manuscripts: True Yarns, or, Seek and Ye Shall Find," *Melville Society Extracts* 43 (September 1980), 8–11, for the unearthing of Melville's letter to Samuel Savage and other Savage family material. Another family connection with whom he may have corresponded was the nephew of his aunt Susan Lansing Gansevoort, Edwin Yates Lansing, to

ville destroyed some of his papers, including letters received, first before his move from New York to Arrowhead in the fall of 1850, and later before his move from Arrowhead into the village of Pittsfield during the summer of 1862.[25] Encouraging the speculation that Melville may already have burned family and other letters by the time he wrote *Pierre* in 1851–52 (or at least that such an act would be congenial to his own inclinations) is his highly dramatic description of such a bonfire in *Pierre*:

> ". . . Hitherto I have hoarded up mementoes and monuments of the past; been a worshiper of all heir-looms; a fond filer away of letters, locks of hair, bits of ribbon, flowers, and the thousand-and-one minutenesses which love and memory think they sanctify:—but it is forever over now! If to me any memory shall henceforth be dear, I will not mummy it in a visible memorial for every passing beggar's dust to gather on. Love's museum is vain and foolish as the Catacombs, where grinning apes and abject lizards are embalmed, as, forsooth, significant of some imagined charm. It speaks merely of decay and death, and nothing more; decay and death of endless innumerable generations; it makes of earth one mold. How can lifelessness be fit memorial of life?—So far, for mementoes of the sweetest. As for the rest—now I know this, that in commonest memorials, the twilight fact of death first discloses in some secret way, all the ambiguities of that departed thing or person; obliquely it casts hints, and insinuates surmises base, and eternally incapable of being cleared." . . .
>
> [Pierre] ran back to the chest, and seizing repeated packages of family letters, and all sorts of miscellaneous memorials in paper, he threw them one after the other upon the fire. (bk. 12, sect. iii, pp. 197–98)

Yet suggestive as Pierre's bonfire is as to the possible fate of some of Melville's own family letters (at whatever time or times), bonfires did not engulf them all, for family letters both by and to Melville have continued to surface. In 1977 Patricia Barber found Melville's important letters of 12 and 22 May 1856 to his father-in-law that had

---

whom Melville inscribed a copy of *Battle-Pieces*; however, no record of any correspondence was found in Lansing's August 1878–July 1892 letterbook (both the inscribed copy and the letterbook formerly in the collection of Richard Manney).

25. See *Log*, I, xiii. Leyda does not cite the following passage or refer specifically to family letters, but quotes only the passage from *Pierre* that is quoted below on p. 795, about Pierre's bonfire of "silly" letters from admirers of his writings.

gone previously unnoticed in the Shaw papers.[26] And in 1983 came
startling news of a trove of papers that had been in the possession of
Augusta Melville. There were over five hundred family letters,
mostly among Melville's mother and sisters, including three by
Melville and four to him.[27] Furthermore, Melville's childhood letter
of 11 October 1828 to his aunt Lucy surfaced as recently as 1985,
and the exuberant letter of 17 October 1844 that he received upon
his homecoming from the Pacific from his brother Allan was among
Henry A. Murray's papers in 1989. Therefore, we may reasonably
hope that further Melville family letters, some of them remarkable,
will continue to surface.

II

If it is difficult to determine how much more lost correspondence Melville had with family members, it is even more difficult to
tell how much more he had beyond his family. No one could have
anticipated the existence of such letters as those to Daniel Shepherd
and to Julius Rockwell, until they were brought to light. If the
Duyckinck brothers had not preserved Melville's letters to them,
would we have any way of guessing just how extensive that corre-

26. Patricia Barber, "Two New Melville Letters," *American Literature* 49
(November 1977), 418–21.

27. For reports, see the *New York Times*, 28 December 1983, and *The Chronicle of Higher Education*, 21 November 1984. The "Augusta papers" came from the
barn of an elderly woman near the town of Gansevoort, New York, where Augusta Melville last lived in the old family mansion. They were initially noticed by a
local historian, Francis E. Plumeau, who described them in a 10 February 1984
letter to Jay Leyda as being in "trunks" when he first saw and photographed them
(UCLA-Leyda). Apparently a portion, if not all, of them had been transferred to a
cardboard box when an antique dealer spotted them and contacted the DeMarcos of
the Lyrical Ballad Bookstore in Saratoga Springs, who arranged for their sale to the
New York Public Library. There they have been added in three manuscript containers to the extensive Gansevoort-Lansing Collection, which already included
some four hundred containers of manuscript materials. The find proved both rich
and disappointing—adding, as already noted, only a few actual letters to Melville's
correspondence, but containing other family letters citing thirty-six unlocated letters to or from him. Overall, the "Augusta papers" have served to give a fuller
picture of Melville's domestic circumstances and of what his wife, sisters, and
mother were like personally. Since 1983 a few further miscellaneous manuscript
items, none by Melville, were sold by the Lyrical Ballad Bookstore and are now in
the collection of William Reese.

spondence was? Even though Melville belonged to the Duyckinck circle, he was never enough a part of it—or any other circle—that his letters were frequently discussed in its members' own letters the way they were within those of his family.[28] And while it seems likely that Melville had some correspondence with other members of the Duyckinck circle—such as Cornelius Mathews, George J. Adler, David Davidson, and William Allen Butler, as well as other literary men around New York, such as Thomas Powell—there is little known evidence of any.[29]

Melville's reluctance to accept the public role of a man-of-letters for himself—evident early on in his unwillingness to accept the initial lecture invitations he received or to have his "mug" appear in literary journals[30] —is also reflected in his sometimes cavalier attitude toward letter-writing. As the "Calendar of Melville's Correspondence" compiled for this volume indicates, he rarely wrote without first being written to—and then usually only to accomplish a specific purpose.[31] When he did write first and without specific business, he wrote impulsively and polemically—in a way very different from the rambling, discursive letters from abroad that built the careers of such

28. Ironically, the one "Melville letter" mentioned in Evert Duyckinck's other correspondence was apparently a forgery. Duyckinck wrote to William Gilmore Simms on 1 June 1869: "The Melville letter must be a stupid joke of some possessor of the volume. It is not in M's hand writing and of course is not at all like him in any way. I will return it to you presently — though I do not see how I can throw any further light upon it. It is a curious affair even in the light of a stupid hoax" (Edmund Clarence Stedman Papers, Rare Book and Manuscript Library, Columbia University). Simms's preceding letter to Duyckinck enclosing the forgery is unlocated, and nothing more is known about the forgery.

29. Only one exchange of letters (now unlocated) between Melville and Mathews is known to have occurred—in August 1850—and only two notes to Adler (now unlocated) are recorded in Melville's 1849–50 journal. The only relic of whatever correspondence Melville may have had with Butler is a large manila envelope addressed "Herman Melville Esq. | Care of E A Duyckinck | 20 Clinton Place | With compliments of William Allen Butler" (NYPL-D). No known evidence points to any correspondence with Davidson or with Powell.

30. See above, p. 785, and also Maria Gansevoort Melville's 10 February 1854 letter, pp. 631–33 above.

31. Another contributing factor to Melville's relatively meager output of letters was his strained eyesight. As his letters of 6 October and 13 December 1850 to Evert Duyckinck and of 16 October 1860 to Sam Shaw all comment, he found it painful to read or write after nightfall; daylight hours, of course, had to be mostly reserved for the writing that was his livelihood, or later for his Custom House job.

contemporaries as Bayard Taylor and G. W. Curtis.[32] Typically, his one "published" letter from abroad—the excerpt that N. P. Willis printed in his weekly column in 1850 because it was "so characteristic, that we cannot forbear giving it to the admirers of Typee and Omoo"—was not a rambling descriptive letter but a diatribe against the indignity of traveling without enough money ("I very much doubt whether Gabriel enters the portals of Heaven without a fee to Peter the porter—so impossible is it to travel without money. . . . ").[33] So brash by nineteenth-century standards were his letters of 25 March 1848 to John Murray and of 24 February 1849 to Evert Duyckinck that both men evidently chided Melville in their replies.[34] In both cases Melville had been stirred by his awakening literary ambitions—the letter to Murray about *Mardi* as a work in progress defied the publisher's strictures against writing romances ("To be blunt: the work I shall next publish will in downright earnest [be] a 'Romance of Polynisian Adventure' "); and the letter to Duyckinck was written shortly after the completion of that romance, during Melville's first extended reading of Shakespeare. Similarly he wrote just as brash and impetuous letters to Dana (1 May 1850) and Hawthorne ([1 June?] 1851) when his ambitions for his "whaling book" were taking shape. Replies by Dana and Hawthorne to these letters are not known to survive, but the reactions of late-nineteenth-century readers to several of the subsequently published letters to Hawthorne give further proof of just how atypical Melville's heartfelt literary epistles were. When she read Melville's letter to her husband of [16 April?] 1851, Sophia Hawthorne was so pleased with its praise of *The House*

32. That Melville felt impatient with the niceties of formal letter-writing is apparent in various comments in his letters. In his [17?] November 1851 letter to Hawthorne, he warned: "Don't think that by writing me a letter, you shall always be bored with an immediate reply to it — and so keep both of us delving over a writing-desk eternally. No such thing! I sha'n't always answer your letters, and you may do just as you please." See also his letters of 19 January 1847, 19 August 1848, [10?] March 1854, 27 January 1888, 5 December 1889 (to Austin), and 13 February 1890 for his use of "&c" to abbreviate a formal opening or closing.

33. See pp. 150–51 above. Willis's papers have been lost, and this excerpt is the only remnant of Melville's correspondence with him now known; again, just how extensive it may have been is hard to tell.

34. Neither reply is located, but see Melville's subsequent letters of 19 June 1848 to Murray (referring to the "Antarctic tenor" of Murray's reply) and 3 March 1849 to Duyckinck (mentioning Duyckinck's charge of "irreverence").

of the Seven Gables that she copied out a passage to enclose with a letter to her sister—but with the firm warning *"do not show it"*:

> The fresh, sincere, glowing mind that utters it is in a state of "fluid consciousness," & to Mr Hawthorne speaks his innermost about GOD, the Devil & Life if so be he can get at the Truth — for he is a boy in opinion — having settled nothing as yet — informe — ingens — & it would betray him to make public his confessions & efforts to grasp — because they would be considered perhaps impious, if one did not take in the whole scope of the case.[35]

Ironically, over thirty years later when Hawthorne's son Julian did "show" this letter to the world along with three others from Melville in his *Nathaniel Hawthorne and His Wife* (2 vols., Boston: Osgood, 1884), two important reviews singled them out for criticism—not as "impious" but as uninteresting. In its 22 November 1884 review the London *Spectator* declared that Julian Hawthorne's book was "swollen-out with letters of little interest,—often very random letters,—from Hawthorne's friends. The letters of Mr. Bridge, for example, and of Mr. Melville, and of one or two other correspondents, are not unfrequently harum-scarum letters, which tell us hardly anything of Hawthorne, except that his friends were not afraid to write rattling nonsense to him." Similarly, Thomas Wentworth Higginson noted in the *Atlantic Monthly* of February 1885 that the letters of Hawthorne's American correspondents which had been included betrayed "habitually the tone of secondary minds, not of men meeting him [Hawthorne] on high ground," and added: "In some cases the letters are given so fully as to give an impression of 'padding,' as where we have nine consecutive pages of not very interesting epistles from Herman Melville."[36] Significant in

35. See the headnote to Melville's [16 April?] 1851 letter for a fuller quotation from Sophia Hawthorne's letter.

36. These reviews probably surprised Julian Hawthorne. In a long letter in the *New-York Daily Tribune* on 8 July 1876, he had protested George Parsons Lathrop's publication of several letters to Hawthorne (including portions of Melville's [16 April?] 1851 letter) on the grounds that they were "letters of a peculiarly private and delicate nature." Underlying this protest no doubt was Julian's outrage that Lathrop, his brother-in-law, had usurped his own plans for publishing these letters, but his public description of them as "private and delicate" is significant. Lathrop defended his book, *A Study of Hawthorne* (Boston: Osgood, 1876), from Julian's charges of impropriety in a rejoinder published in the *Tribune* on 15 July, stating that he had

these reviews is the fact that regardless of whether Melville's letters were considered impious or uninteresting, literary high priests like Higginson found them too undistinguished to be taken seriously.

Melville's own sense of alienation from the complacent world of men-of-letters he had entered as the young author of *Typee* culminated in his seventh published book—*Pierre*. This was the first of his books in which letters played a significant role. Indeed an "amazing" letter from Pierre's self-proclaimed illegitimate sister Isabel sets the whole narrative in motion:

> This letter, inscribed in a feminine, but irregular hand, and in some places almost illegible, plainly attesting the state of the mind which had dictated it;—stained, too, here and there, with spots of tears, which chemically acted upon by the ink, assumed a strange and reddish hue—as if blood and not tears had dropped upon the sheet;—and so completely torn in two by Pierre's own hand, that it indeed seemed the fit scroll of a torn, as well as bleeding heart;—this amazing letter, deprived Pierre for the time of all lucid and definite thought or feeling. (bk. 3, sect. ii, pp. 64–65)

Like Melville's own impulsive letters, this is a bold, truth-telling one, as are several others central to the narrative of *Pierre*.[37] Taken together, Melville's fictional letters reflect a hyperbolic assertion repeated in two of his actual letters (those of 1 May 1850 to Dana and of [17?] November 1851 to Hawthorne) that a single letter to a receptive correspondent far outweighed the value of a book sold to a wide audience of dull and uncomprehending readers. In both he wished all of his writing could simply be in the form of such letters.

---

printed no more than a half-dozen letters, which were not "of a confidential nature," and going on to explain that "they consist of letters from other persons to Nathaniel Hawthorne; and the consent of the writers was obtained in all cases." (See the entry for Lathrop's unlocated letter to Melville requesting that consent, p. 711 above, and Melville's 10 August 1883 letter to Julian prior to the publication of his book.) See also footnote 53 below, for the reaction of one member of Melville's family—his second cousin Mary Louise Peebles—who found the publication of his private letters in Julian Hawthorne's book "indiscreet"—probably the reaction Julian expected.

37. See bk. 15, sect. iii, pp. 227–28, for Pierre's letter to his cousin Glen, with its "words . . . placarded upon it in heavy though rapid lines, only six or eight to the page"—a description that could also describe Melville's own hand in a number of his letters, particularly those to his cousin Augustus Van Schaick (see the reproduction on p. 90 above). See also bk. 23, sect. ii, pp. 309–11, for Lucy's "artless, angelical letter."

To "My Dear Dana," he declared that "did I not write these books of mine almost entirely for 'lucre' — by the job, as a woodsawyer saws wood — I almost think, I should hereafter — in the case of a sea book — get my M.S.S. neatly & legibly copied by a scrivener — send you that one copy — & deem such a procedure the best publication." And to Hawthorne, in a postscript, he recast this scheme in larger, more fantastic terms:

> I can't stop yet. If the world was entirely made up of Magians, I'll tell you what I should do. I should have a paper-mill established at one end of the house, and so have an endless riband of foolscap rolling in upon my desk; and upon that endless riband I should write a thousand — a million — billion thoughts, all under the form of a letter to you. The divine magnet is in you, and my magnet responds. Which is the biggest? A foolish question — they are *One*.

In contrast with the "amazing" letters in *Pierre* are others, including those to Pierre from family members, literary acquaintances, lecture committees, autograph seekers, and admirers of his youthful literary efforts, letters which are repeatedly associated with all that is false and vain.[38] They are from correspondents who, unlike Dana and Hawthorne, are incapable of understanding the deeper truths embedded in his writing. As in the bonfire passage quoted above, these letters are treated with authorial contempt, and a second fire is devoted to all the literary correspondence Pierre has received:

> And it may well be believed, that after the wonderful vital world-revelation so suddenly made to Pierre at the Meadows—a revelation which, at moments, in some certain things, fairly Timonized him—he had not failed to clutch with peculiar nervous detestation and contempt that ample parcel, containing the letters of his Biographico and other silly correspondents, which, in a less ferocious hour, he had filed away as curiosities. It was with an almost infernal grin, that he saw that particular heap of rubbish eternally quenched in the fire, and felt that as it was consumed before his eyes, so in his soul was forever killed the last and minutest undeveloped microscopic

---

38. See bk. 12, sect. iii, pp. 197–98 (quoted on p. 789 above); bk. 17, sect. i, pp. 247–48; bk. 17, sect. ii, pp. 250–52; bk. 17, sect. iii, pp. 254–55.

germ of that most despicable vanity to which those absurd correspondents thought to appeal. (bk. 17, sect. iii, p. 255)[39]

Such passages in *Pierre* read almost like an irreverent inversion of a
letter that Melville's brother Gansevoort wrote from New York on
21 January 1840 to their younger brother Allan, then in Albany:

> My dear Allan — It gives me great pleasure to acknowledge the re-
> ceipt of your epistles of the 11th ult & 2nd inst — both of which I have
> preserved — It is a good habit to preserve the letters of those who are
> near & dear to us — They serve in after days as mementos of the
> past — kindling in our minds vivid recollections of former emotions
> & forgotten scenes, & serving to prove the falsehood of some & the
> faith of others — I would have you my dear brother form this hab-
> it — You will never regret its acquirement. (Berkshire Athenaeum)

Melville probably saw Gansevoort's letter, since he was living in nearby Greenbush and since it included a pointed message for him ("Give
my best love to Herman — I sometimes send him papers — Does he
ever call at the Greenbush Post Office? — Tell him . . . I hereby promise him a letter. I know no other reason for his remissness but laziness — not general laziness by any means — but that laziness which
consists in an unwillingness to exert oneself in doing at a particular
time, that which ought then to be done — or to illustrate — that disinclination to perform the special duty of the hour which so constantly
beset one of the most industrious men of the age — Sir Walter Scott").

39. Does this bonfire also point to an actual bonfire of Melville's literary letters that had already occurred by the time he wrote his romance? Certainly a number of such letters addressed to Melville do survive, but none dated before 1852,
when *Pierre* appeared. The only known remnants of Melville's early fan mail are the
letters from Mrs. Ellen Astor Oxenham, an Englishwoman living in New York.
Although these are addressed to Melville's sister Augusta, two contain comments
directed toward Melville. On 5 October 1846, for example, she blurted out:
"Typee, you dear creature; I want to see you so amazingly" (NYPL-GL). No
doubt other such letters were addressed directly to Melville after the popular success of *Typee* (see, for example, his 24 July 1846 reply to Dr. William Sprague's
now unlocated request for an autograph: "You remember some one woke one
morning and found himself famous — And here am I, just come in from hoeing in
the garden, writing autographs"). For another literary immolation, this time fueled
by his own manuscripts, see Melville's undated but late unpublished poem "Immo-
lated" (see Hennig Cohen, ed., *Selected Poems of Herman Melville* [Carbondale:
Southern Illinois University Press, 1964], p. 166; see also the forthcoming vol. 13
of the Northwestern-Newberry Edition).

That Melville had Gansevoort's letter specifically in mind when he wrote *Pierre* over a decade later may be doubtful, but that he sought to challenge the ideal of the writer as an august and dutiful public man-of-letters—a role Gansevoort had anticipated for himself at one time—goes without saying.[40]

Judging by what is now known of Melville's letters, his "amazing" and defiant letters all but ceased after 1852, the year he canceled his subscription to the Duyckincks' *Literary World* in two letters (bringing a hiatus in his correspondence with them) and failed to publish *Pierre* in England (ending summarily further correspondence with British publishers). After that year his correspondence consists primarily of short letters to his American publishers (George P. Putnam, Harper & Brothers, and later Dix & Edwards), a scattering of coy notes to his Pittsfield neighbor Sarah Morewood, to his sisters, and his cousin Catherine Gansevoort Lansing, and cursory replies to letters received (to his brother-in-law Samuel Savage he wrote such a brief reply on 16 October 1860, adding, "I hope you are a good enough Christian in this matter of correspondence to be willing cheerfully to give much and receive little"). His random comments on letter-writing were rarely enthusiastic and became less and less so. His letter of 5 September 1885 to James Billson closes with the weary comment: "But a letter on almost any theme, is but an inadequate vehicle, so I will say no more." And the British sea-novelist W. Clark Russell replied on 10 April 1888 to one of Melville's letters (now unlocated) with the remark: "I can fully sympathize with your dislike to letter writing." Whereas many of his letters around mid-century to Murray, Duyckinck, Dana, and Hawthorne were of the sort Bruce Redford has called "campaigns for intimacy"[41]—campaigns to confess his feeling of brotherhood in authorship and true ambitions as a

40. For Gansevoort Melville's preparations to become a man-of-letters, see the selections from his *Index Rerum*, begun in 1837, in the *New Log*.

41. Bruce Redford, *The Converse of the Pen* (Chicago: University of Chicago Press, 1986), p. 10. Notably, Melville's confessional letters are often signed differently from his usual "Sincerely" or "Truly yours, H. Melville." His 25 March 1848 pronouncement to Murray closes emphatically "In all sincerity Yours | Herman Melville"; however, his 6 October 1849 letter to Dana concludes "Yours — a sea-brother — | H Melville"; his 24 August 1851 letter to his wife's half-cousin Samuel Savage closes with "Really Thine" and similarly his 31 December 1863 letter to his old friend Evert Duyckinck closes with "Thine"; and perhaps most significantly his

writer—his later letters are nearly always restricted to the business at hand. This is apparent as early as the late 1840's in Melville's correspondence with his second British publisher, Richard Bentley—written in the wake of the stern rebuff over *Mardi* that he had received from John Murray. Despite Bentley's interest in Melville's "genius" and their immediate compatibility when they met in London in 1849, none of Melville's known letters to him is confessional. Instead they focus on selling book-publishing rights. His letters describing *Redburn*, *The Whale*, and *Pierre* all argue for the popular appeal of his books—an argument that became progressively more difficult to make as he tried to embed his ambitious literary purposes within the form of popular romances.[42] Bentley's letter of 5 May 1852, which insisted on revising and cutting portions of *Pierre* as a precondition for publishing it, was apparently greeted only by silence from Melville—one silence among many in his correspondence after 1852. And what letters he wrote were in many ways a campaign for non-intimacy. Often the only personal element in these later letters is what Melville called his "infirmity of jocularity" when writing George Duyckinck on 20 December 1858—an infirmity which, he acknowledged, "I am aware should hardly intrude into a semi-business letter like this." These sallies, however, gave some of his later letters a characteristic stamp they would not otherwise have had.[43] Still, his real concerns, the concerns which emerge within his late poetry, are not revealed in the letters of the latter part of his career.

Although this volume includes a number of letters to and from personal and literary friends, both early and late in Melville's life—men such as Alexander Bradford, Thurlow Weed, Edwin Croswell, Julius Rockwell, Daniel Shepherd, John W. Francis, Richard Lathers, Augustus Gardner, George Duyckinck, G. P. R. James,

[17?] November 1851 letter to Hawthorne is simply signed "Herman"—the one time he is known to have signed only his first name in a letter to anyone but a family member.

42. See Melville's 5 June 1849, 27 June 1850, and 16 April 1852 letters to Bentley. (There is no letter about *White-Jacket* since Melville proposed it to Bentley face to face in London in 1849.) See also Lynn Horth, "Richard Bentley's Place in Melville's Literary Career," *Studies in the American Renaissance 1992*, pp. 229–45, for a fuller discussion of Melville's letters to Bentley.

43. See, for example, his business letters of 18 September 1854 to the Harpers and of 15 September 1857 to G. W. Curtis.

General Robert Tyler, Richard H. Stoddard, and Edmund C. Stedman—there is nothing in them to suggest more than casual friendships he entertained but had no intention of cultivating further. Of course, unlike Melville's late correspondence with his British admirers James Billson, Henry Salt, and W. Clark Russell, which was confined to their cordial but relatively formal letters because of the ocean between them, Melville often had more personal association with many of his friends that went unrecorded in letters—particularly during the early part of his career while he was still in New York. Elizabeth Shaw Melville's letter of 23 December 1847 to her stepmother describes a constant round of calls on "Herman's and Allan's friends" ("no sooner do we do up a few, than they all come again, and so it has to be done over again"). Similarly, Melville's 1849–50 journal indicates that he became good friends with George Adler, talking with him of " 'Fixed Fate, Free-will, foreknowledge absolute' &c." (p. 4), but none of that talk is known to have made its way into letters. It also seems likely that after moving back to New York in 1863 Melville spoke with acquaintances such as Stoddard and Stedman more than he wrote to them.[44] Yet Melville's habits also suggest a reluctance on his part to mix socially as a literary man. Elizabeth Melville's letter of 23 December 1847 states that "excepting calls, I have scarcely visited at all. Herman is not fond of parties, and I don't care anything about them here." And at the other end of his career, when asked to join the Authors Club in New York, he ultimately declined on the grounds that "he had become too much of a hermit, saying his nerves could no longer stand large gatherings and begged to rescind his acceptance."[45] This reticence must also have carried over into his letter-writing habits, making him less likely to initiate or prolong correspondence with anyone with whom he was not already closely associated.

Certainly there is nothing at all to suggest that Melville ever thought of himself as maintaining a correspondence that would ultimately be published and read because of the role he had played as an author. Although he answered autograph requests, he usually did so hurriedly, probably sometimes letting two or three accu-

44. As a result, Melville's biographers have focused on his friendship with Hawthorne almost to the exclusion of others that went undocumented in letters.

45. *Log*, II, 781. See also the entry for Melville's two unlocated 1882 letters to the club, pp. 479–80 above.

mulate and then answering them all at once with similar wording (see, for example, his replies of February 1869). His replies to invitations for literary "events" of the day are polite but never enthusiastic. When he received an invitation to the "Complimentary Fruit & Flower Festival" sponsored by the New York Book Publishers' Association in 1855, his mother felt it necessary to write to his sister Augusta in Pittsfield to make sure that he had sent a letter of regret in reply to the invitation.[46] Moreover, a large number of his letters in this volume were only partially dated, and eleven were misdated—they were not the studied letters of a man writing for posterity but messages only for the individuals receiving them. Thus, when he headed a letter in 1854 to Sarah Morewood "Day of Ill Luck — Friday. March &c," he was writing only to a friend and neighbor who would understand his allusion—which now over a century later is obscure. Nor, of course, did Melville carefully save his letters from friends and associates for posterity, or keep any copies of his own letters in a letterbook. Although he does mention a "file" in his letter of 29 August 1851 to Evert Duyckinck ("The letter is in the file & the thermometer on the wall"), his letter of 10 December 1863 to Sophia Van Matre comments on that "vile habit of mine to destroy all my letters."[47] He repeated this assertion twenty years later when Julian Hawthorne asked him for letters from his father.[48] (It was very likely Elizabeth Shaw Melville who preserved the relatively few letters addressed to her husband that are now in the Houghton Library, many of

46.   See the entry for his unlocated letter of regret written before 27 September 1855.

47.   Nevertheless, destroying letters apparently was not a consistent or immediate practice; he goes on in his 10 December letter to Miss Van Matre to acknowledge having some letters in his possession ("Such as I have by me would hardly be to your purpose").

48.   See the headnote to Melville's 10 August 1883 letter to Julian. Some scholars have questioned whether Melville did in fact destroy his letters from Hawthorne. In a 25 January 1945 letter to Tyrus Hillway, Harrison Hayford argued, "I suspect that Hawthorne's letters might exist—the ones he wrote Melville, though Melville told Julian they were destroyed. Why should he destroy them, when he preserved the books so carefully and proudly?" (Melville Society Papers, The Newberry Library). Davis and Gilman, as well as Leyda, conducted hopeful but fruitless searches for them.

which belong in the category Pierre calls "silly" letters.)[49] In several cases he apparently thought enough of an occasion or correspondent to draft a letter first and then recopy it—as indicated by the two drafts now on verso pages of the "Orme" manuscript.[50] Other letters, such as his 19 December 1851 one to Rufus Griswold regarding the Cooper memorial, are so cleanly written as to suggest that he sometimes wrote formal letters in draft form first. (Melville probably knew that Griswold intended to publish that letter in his *Memorial of James Fenimore Cooper*.)[51] Yet Melville

49. All of these letters were docketed for filing in Elizabeth Shaw Melville's hand (see the manuscript descriptions). Some of the business letters were evidently preserved on Melville's instructions, such as the 19 June 1889 one from the Harpers on which he noted "Please preserve." Just how successful his wife was in preserving what remained of the letters her husband had received over the years is uncertain. In a letter of 2 November 1892 to Arthur Stedman, who advised her on publication matters after her husband's death, she wrote: "Before speaking of any business matters [with a Mr. Phelps], I should like to consult with you. The Bentley letters are at hand for you at your own convenience. I shall be glad to collect my scattered papers together once more — as soon as I have little more leisure I shall set them out in better regular order" (Edmund Clarence Stedman Papers, Rare Book and Manuscript Library, Columbia University). Only one letter from Richard Bentley to Melville—that of 5 March 1849—now survives among his papers at the Houghton Library, yet this 1892 letter to Stedman suggests that Elizabeth Melville once had a number of the Bentley letters (now known only from the letterbooks) in her possession. She had at least one—that of 20 June 1849—which Stedman had already examined by 24 October 1892. Writing to the United States Book Co. in a letter of that date, he mentioned the letter in an effort to convince the company that the reissue of Melville's works in England would not be hampered by earlier copyright agreements: "It will be interesting for you to know that, in 1852 (I think), Mr. Bentley, who had already published copyrighted editions of 'White Jacket' and 'Moby Dick', wrote Mr. Melville that a recent (act or) decision had left the matter of copyrighting American books in England in such a doubtful state that he could not make the same advantageous terms for a proposed new book by Mr. Melville as for the previous ones. . . . I have not consulted Mrs. Melville in this matter, for the reasons indicated above. As I have examined Mr. Melville's papers very thoroughly since his death, I really know more about these matters than she does" (Beinecke Library, Yale University). The fact that Stedman misdated the letter suggests that he probably also saw at least one of the 1852 letters Bentley wrote to Melville.

50. These drafts were to J. W. Henry Canoll and W. Clark Russell; see pp. 493–95 and 498–500.

51. Melville's business-related letters—such as those to his publishers and to his father-in-law, Judge Shaw—tend to be cleanly written (see the reproduction, p. 101 above, from his 1 January 1848 letter to Murray). Offhand notes to

clearly did not expect or desire the publication of his private letters. When George Parsons Lathrop, Hawthorne's son-in-law, requested permission to print "two or three" of Melville's letters to
Hawthorne in his *Study of Hawthorne* (1876), Melville's letter in
reply had "a sort of gloomy reluctance," so Lathrop later reported.[52] Apart from the six known letters Melville wrote specifically

---

family and friends tend to be more scrawled (see the reproduction, on p. 374
above, of his 2 May 1862 letter to his sister Augusta). Rose Hawthorne Lathrop
described Melville's handwriting in his letter of 22 July 1851 to her father as
"being, apparently, 'writ in water'" (*Memories of Hawthorne* [Boston: Houghton
Mifflin, 1897], p. 155), and Sophia Hawthorne found it necessary to interline
most of his 8 January 1852 letter to her with a penciled transcription, with one
word undeciphered.

52. See the entries for this unlocated correspondence, pp. 436 and 711. After
her husband's death, Elizabeth Shaw Melville also expressed reluctance to permit
the publication of some of the wording in two of Melville's letters, although probably for different, more personal reasons. In the Houghton Mifflin papers, now at
Harvard, is a letter of 30 May 1897 from Rose Hawthorne Lathrop soon after the
firm published her *Memories of Hawthorne*. She enclosed "two letters from Mrs.
Melville, which may lead you to have the words she objects to in her husband's
letters, in 'Memories of Hawthorne,' omitted. I have argued with her by letter as
well as I knew how, but this does not seem to have made her any happier than she
was before. If I can or should do anything about having the words erased, will you
let me know? Perhaps the opinion of some one else would, if favorable to my idea
of leaving a man of genius safely in care of his own expressions, have effect in
inducing Mrs. Melville to let the printed record stand as it is." Neither of these
letters from Elizabeth Shaw Melville has been located, so we do not know just what
words she wanted excised from her husband's letters of 22 July and [17?] November 1851. Rose Lathrop's biographer, Theodore Maynard, later conjectured,
wrongly, that the ellipsis points at the end of Melville's 22 July letter in both Mrs.
Lathrop's magazine and book publications of it were the result of Elizabeth Shaw
Melville's objections; see *A Fire Was Lighted: The Life of Rose Hawthorne Lathrop*
(Milwaukee: Bruce, 1948), pp. 306–9. However, both the date of Rose Lathrop's
letter to Houghton Mifflin and its content make clear that Elizabeth Melville's pro-
tests were not raised until after publication of the book. She had earlier consented
(perhaps without seeing them) to the publication of both by Rose Lathrop in the
November 1894 *Century Magazine*, where her "kind permission" is acknowledged.
A few years later Elizabeth Melville again attempted to censor her husband's writings, this time successfully when *Moby-Dick* was being reissued by Dana Estes &
Co. in the United States and G. P. Putnam's Sons in Great Britain. A letter of 28
April 1900 to her from the Publishers Plate Renting Co. states: "Replying to yours
of the 26th inst., we are very glad that you have given your consent to Mess. G. P.
Putnam's Sons publishing an edition of 'Moby Dick,' in Great Britain. . . . We
informed them of your wish that the foot-note on Pp 366 was to be left out" (HCL-

for publication (his 1838 *Microscope* letters, his communication printed in the 21 April 1846 *Albany Argus*, his letter to Rufus Griswold, cited just above, and his undated letter to the *World* [c. 1865–88]), only seven of his letters seem to have been published in his lifetime.[53]

From a literary point of view, Melville's not writing letters for the eyes of posterity is a disappointment—compounded by the failure of many recipients and later owners to preserve the letters he did write, such as those to his wife. Likewise, no trace now exists of some letters we suppose he would have written. For example, after Hawthorne's death on 19 May 1864, Elizabeth Shaw Melville wrote to Melville's mother reporting that Herman was "shocked" by the news of his friend's passing.[54] That Melville wrote no letter of condolence to Sophia Hawthorne would be strange, even though none has surfaced with those from other contemporary writers.[55] The explanation, in general, is of course that Melville's fame died so quickly within his own lifetime that his letters were not highly valued. Even such admirers as Henry Salt and W. Clark Russell, who corresponded with him late in his life, made little effort to keep his letters

M). The footnote in question elaborated on "Leviathan amours," describing, among other matters, a whale's "two teats, curiously situated, one on each side of the anus" (chap. 87, p. 388).

53. In addition to the extract published by Willis, mentioned above, p. 792, an extract from a [December 1837?] letter to Charles Van Loon was printed in the *Albany Microscope* exchange and a September 1867 letter was included by John Hoadley in his newspaper report about Malcolm Melville's death. George Parsons Lathrop ultimately printed only part of Melville's [16 April?] 1851 letter, which Julian Hawthorne later printed, apparently in full, along with three others in his *Nathaniel Hawthorne and His Wife* (1884). A comment about this book in an 1885 letter from Melville's second cousin Mary Louise Peebles to Abraham Lansing gives further evidence that Melville was reluctant to have his private letters published: "I have been reading Hawthornes life and find it very entertaining, principally because it is so indiscreet. It does not chloroform the poor little literary butterflies in its collection, but just sticks a pin through them, and calls you to look. I wonder if Herman Melville was consulted about the appearance of his name? I should think some of the allusions would be very trying to a person of his sensitive nature" (*Log*, II, 790).

54. *Log*, II, 669.

55. Emerson's letter of condolence, for example, is now in the Pierpont Morgan Library and Longfellow's in the Houghton Library of Harvard University.

to them.[56] Similarly, neither Melville nor his letters figure prominently in the reminiscences of the well-known men of his acquaintance.[57] And although letters by him appear in a number of early autograph catalogues, the prices assigned to them indicate that he was considered a minor writer valued primarily for rounding out a collection of American autographs.[58]

Melville's continued fame could not have saved some of his letters, such as those to his former shipmate Richard Greene, which

56. After the revival of Melville's reputation Henry Salt wrote to Willard Thorp on 1 September 1935 that "about what became of the originals I have no notion, unless I sold them! Alas, one often regrets these things, when too late." Herbert Russell (Russell's son) wrote to Thorp on 27 August 1935, "in reply to many requests I have made all possible efforts to ascertain whether any of these letters are still in existence but have failed to trace them and am pretty sure they have long since vanished. You see, in those days we did not regard private correspondence as likely to have a 'commercial value' and took less trouble to preserve it." James Billson wrote to Thorp on 16 February 1936: "I sold the letters together with some of Melville's 1st editions to an English bookseller & he no doubt sold them in his turn" (The Newberry Library). All of the letters Melville is known to have written to Billson (those Billson published in The Nation and the Athenæum and one other one) and probably all those he wrote to Salt have subsequently come on the market. One of Melville's letters to Russell has subsequently appeared, but at least two others can be inferred (see pp. 498–500, 510, and 523–24 above).

57. Nor do the published reminiscences of Richard Lathers and Richard H. Stoddard (see pp. 259–60 and 421–22)—who do mention knowing him—quote any of his letters.

58. At the auction held on behalf of the Cincinnati sanitary fair, for example, the two Melville letters offered separately (see pp. 386–88 above) sold for twenty and fifty cents, while two Hawthorne letters sold for $1.90 and $1.60 and a John Adams letter for $5.00. The William Evarts Benjamin Catalogue 2 (pre–1889) listed an unidentified Melville letter for $1.00 (where prices generally ranged between fifty cents and $2.00, with some exceptions—such as $6.00 for an Edmund C. Stedman manuscript poem). Benjamin's December 1896 catalogue included a large Melville signature for fifty cents. Goodspeed's September 1905 Catalogue 34 listed a half-page 1855 note for seventy-five cents (this could have been any one of the five short letters to publishers now known for 1855 or another unidentified letter). By 1914 the price of a Melville letter in a James F. Drake catalogue had risen to $3.50 for his 20 February 1854 letter, while the price of a letter by Francis Parkman was $5.00 and that of a Thomas Paine letter $100.00. Twenty of the letters published in this volume were originally included in early autograph collections assembled in the nineteenth century, including the collections of Albert Lee Butler, Ferdinand J. Dreer, Simon Gratz, Gordon Lester Ford, James Lorimer Graham, Adrian H. Joline, S. Whitney Phoenix, Albert W. Whelpley, and James Grant Wilson, as well as the unidentified collectors who purchased the three Melville letters sold at the Cincinnati sanitary fair.

probably were destroyed in the Chicago fire, or whatever letters he wrote to William Cramer, Gansevoort's friend, whose papers were also destroyed in a fire; but it is tempting to speculate that whatever letters he wrote to Eli James Murdock Fly, Oliver Russ, Robert Barry Coffin, Peter Toft, or Richard Garnett would have surfaced by now had they been more valuable earlier. Also, for that reason, possibly more of his letters about lecture engagements to the various presidents and secretaries of Young Men's Associations and civic organizations would have been preserved. Yet, on the other hand, despite the dramatically rising prices commanded by Melville letters during the twentieth century,[59] known letters have disappeared. For example, what became of the manuscripts of the four letters that Julian Hawthorne published remains a mystery. Charles Olson commented to Jay Leyda on their disappearance in a letter of 14 June 1950: "I was told [Julian] was irregular about property, so it is possible he sold, without the wife's knowledge, materials. (he knew their value, obviously.)"[60] A few months later Norman Holmes Pearson wrote to Leyda on 30 August, adding: "Julian . . . made a regular business of trucking H's papers, selling them, buying them back and re-selling or acting as agent"; yet if Julian did sell Melville's letters to a collector, they have remained hidden from scholars for over half a

59. After the rediscovery of Melville in the early 1920's, prices for his letters began to climb. Thomas F. Madigan listed Melville's 5 July 1872 letter to Richard H. Stoddard for $50 in 1934. By 1948 Howard S. Mott was asking $650 for two of Melville's letters to Augustus Van Schaick accompanied by one from Melville's sister Helen. And in 1966 Paul C. Richards listed a brief note dated only "Wednesday Morning" to Duyckinck for $1250. Quaritch's price of $10,000 for Melville's 27 March 1879 letter to G. P. Putnam's Sons set a new high in 1988, and with the H. Bradley Martin sale in 1990, which included twenty-four Melville letters, prices over $10,000 have become common. The 19th Century Shop in its October 1992 catalogue listed Melville's 20 July 1851 letter to Richard Bentley for $95,000.

60. UCLA-Leyda. Julian Hawthorne's notebook (Pierpont Morgan Library) reveals that in preparation for the volume he was meticulously listing the letters his father had saved, and included on his "Summary" page all four of the Melville letters he had listed earlier as "important letters." His notebook is also significant in that it records that one of Melville's 1851 letters was esteemed highly enough that it was kept in an autograph book. Julian Hawthorne would certainly have known their value after 1931 when the auction of Melville's 8 January 1852 letter to Sophia Hawthorne for $3,100 at Anderson Galleries was widely publicized; see, for example, the New York Times, 30 April 1931.

century since Julian's death in 1934.[61] Likewise, other Melville letters, long after their high value was well known, have fallen through the cracks. The fate of Melville's long intimate letter to his brother Allan from Liverpool in 1856 is the most perplexing. In publishing that letter Davis and Gilman reported it as in the Berkshire Athenaeum, in anticipation (as their files reveal) of its donation by Agnes Morewood; however, according to Robert Newman and Ruth Degenhardt of the Berkshire Athenaeum, that letter was never received there. This important letter may reappear, but the likelihood is that it was inadvertently destroyed (or, less likely, purchased and still undivulged) during the breakup of the Morewood estate.[62] Fortunately Davis and Gilman had secured an excellent photocopy, now in the Melville Edition files at The Newberry Library. This instance underscores how essential scholarly publications have been in helping to preserve the words, even if not the original manuscripts, of Melville's correspondence.[63]

III

Because Melville was not a canonized man-of-letters when he died in 1891, no effort to collect his letters for publication was made until the early twentieth century. Fifteen years later, in 1906, Frank Jewett Mather, Jr., hoping to write Melville's biography (see p. 786 above), was the first to take an active interest in seeing to the preservation of the letters that remained within the family. He had ob-

61. Julian's sister Rose Hawthorne Lathrop also is known to have sold some of the papers she inherited from their father. Her letter of 29 August 1887 to Houghton Mifflin discusses her plans to sell Hawthorne's "autographs" with the publisher's help. She also adds, "The letters I would sell for a hundred dollars, also" (HCL-Houghton Mifflin). These letters possibly included the two Melville letters she published; see pp. 199–200 and 210–14 above.

62. The same fate may also have befallen Melville's 30 April 1872 letter to Samuel Adams Drake in the 1963 breakup of the J. C. Pearson estate, and possibly Melville's 10 August 1883 letter to Julian Hawthorne in the 1988 breakup of the H. Bradley Martin estate.

63. See the NOTE ON THE TEXT, p. 817, footnote 10, below, for six other letters whose texts are now available only because of their publication in the Davis and Gilman edition.

tained a letter of introduction to Melville's widow Elizabeth from Edmund C. Stedman, but failed to meet her. After her death in 1906 he wrote to Stedman, urging him to ask Melville's daughter Elizabeth (Bessie) Melville "what biographical materials are extant, suggesting, if you see fit, that letters should be given to a public library or otherwise preserved?"[64] Mather later met with this daughter, who possibly because of his interest made an early effort to collect her father's letters. On 24 November 1906 the following notice on her behalf appeared in the "Literary Gossip" section of the London *Athenæum*: "The family of the late Herman Melville, author of 'Typee,' 'The Whale,' &c., are collecting materials for a memoir, and would be grateful if any persons having letters by him would send them to Miss Elizabeth Melville, 'The Florence,' Fourth Avenue and Eighteenth Street, New York. Such letters will be promptly copied and returned." At least two of Melville's British correspondents, James Billson and Henry Salt, sent her letters, evidently at Mather's request.[65] However, Miss Elizabeth Melville died only two years later, in 1908, without publishing such letters as she had collected. Not until 1921 in Raymond Weaver's *Herman Melville: Mari-*

64. Sealts, *Early Lives*, p. 59.

65. In a letter of 20 November 1906 Billson explained to Bessie Melville: "A letter has reached me from Mʳ Mather stating it is intended to write a memoir of Herman Melville & asking if I have any material that will help in its production. I am happy to be able to enclose copies of all the letters received from him & I hope they will be of use in carrying out your object. I have carefully checked the copies myself & can vouch for their correctness. But if for any reason you prefer to have the originals, I shall be glad to forward them if you will acquaint me with your wishes" (HCL-M). The copies Billson sent are now in HCL-M; however, those sent by Henry Salt are now unlocated. Only an undated note to Salt ("Miss Melville begs to acknowledge the receipt of copies of two letters from her father"), now in the Melville Collection of The Newberry Library, indicates their having been made and sent. This drive for letters in 1906 may also account for the typewritten transcript Edmund C. Stedman made of Melville's 20 February 1888 letter to him, now in the Stedman Papers of the Rare Book and Manuscript Library, Columbia University, and for the handwritten copy Havelock Ellis made of Melville's 10 August 1890 letter to him, now in the Huntington Library. There is no evidence, however, to support the following assertion made in the Bernard Quaritch Catalogue 1083, February 1988, under item 30: "Melville's letters are notoriously rare, the bulk of them having been arbitrarily destroyed by his family after soliciting the originals."

ner and Mystic (New York: Doran) were a number of Melville's letters brought together in a book about him. In addition to five of the
already published letters to Hawthorne, Weaver included for the
first time either full or partial texts of eight letters by Melville and
seven letters to him, all of which were then in the possession of
Melville's granddaughter Eleanor Melville Metcalf and which she
gave to the Harvard College Library in 1937.[66] Also in the 1920's, as
in Weaver's biography, most of the publications of Melville letters
consisted of clusters from single collections. James Billson published
in *The Nation and the Athenæum* (13 August 1921) all but one of the
nine letters Melville is known to have written to him. The following
year, Meade Minnigerode first published in *Some Personal Letters of
Herman Melville and a Bibliography* (New York: Brick Row Book
Shop, 1922) seventeen Melville letters (mostly partial texts) from the
Duyckinck papers in the New York Public Library. In 1929 Victor
H. Paltsits's *Family Correspondence of Herman Melville, 1830–1904* (New
York: New York Public Library) first published either full or partial
texts of forty-nine of Melville's letters, as well as six letters to him.[67]
In a 28 February 1945 letter to Tyrus Hillway, secretary of the Mel-
ville Society, Paltsits recalled: "Back in 1919 when I gave the Gan-
sevoort-Lansing Collection to The New York Public Library, including the Family Correspondence of Herman Melville which I edited
later, there was but little interest in him" (Melville Society Papers,
The Newberry Library).

Not until Willard Thorp's 1938 *Melville* volume in the American
Writers Series was there published a selection of Melville's letters
drawn from various manuscript collections. Thorp's little anthology
included twenty-one letters from Melville's correspondence with his
family and with Evert Duyckinck, Nathaniel Hawthorne, and James

---

66. For the donation, see the NN *Confidence-Man*, p. 402. In 1919, Mrs. Metcalf, clearly pleased that an interest was being taken in her grandfather's papers,
wrote to her mother (Melville's daughter Frances) on 28 September that "Mr.
Weaver arrived yesterday afternoon and fell upon the records with enthusiasm. He
is a keen, comprehending young man, eager about his subject" (HCL-M).

67. Beginning in 1907 various scholars published shorter sequences of letters
or single ones from individual collections, as recorded in the notes to the letters in
this volume.

Billson.[68] "Melville was born late to fame," Thorp wrote in his preface, but his landmark volume finally signaled Melville's canonization as an American man-of-letters. By that time Melville's secure place warranted a full calendar of his letters, which Thorp listed as undertaken by John H. Birss and Robert S. Forsythe. Birss, then of New York University, wrote to Tyrus Hillway on 10 February 1945 announcing that "the collection of M. letters grows—so that I have now three volumes (loose-leaf) of transcripts" and explaining that he had begun his edition while preparing a bibliography of Melville's works because the letters often gave publication details. On 28 April 1945 he reported to Hillway: "The Melville letters now number 181. Of these I lack texts for 17, and there are many original MSS. untraced. Minnigerode is untrustworthy in his printing of the letters, both in dating and transcription. His bib. is even worse. At any rate, texts or partial texts for 164 letters is not a bad haul—considering that back in 1921 Melville letters were considered *rarissimi*" (Melville Society Papers, The Newberry Library). Birss wrote to Jay Leyda on 3 May 1945 that he planned to include a "calendar of all possible correspondence as the structure of the whole volume" with "any letters *to* Melville which are pertinent" (UCLA-Leyda). The following February, in 1946, Howard P. Vincent wrote asking Birss to agree to publication of his edition of the letters as a volume in the Packard (later Hendricks House) Edition; however, Birss was evasive and never committed that volume to the Hendricks House series, nor was his edition ever published (Melville Society Papers, The Newberry Library).

As a stop-gap measure, for a summer class at the University of Chicago in 1949 Gordon Roper prepared a mechanically reproduced (holographed) "Collection of Published Melville Letters" (a copy is in The Newberry Library), containing 145 letters either by Melville, to him, or about him (over 40 of them either in extract or summary

---

68. Thorp also published for the first time Melville's only known letter to Daniel Shepherd (6 July 1859) in the poetry section of his volume—an event which exasperated Henry A. Murray, who had obtained it from Agnes Morewood, framed it, and given it to Mrs. Metcalf, by whose permission Thorp printed it (see Harrison Hayford's interview with Murray in *Melville Society Extracts*, forthcoming). Subsequently, along with Melville's canonization would come a continuing number of such contretemps among scholars, caused mostly by the scarcity of Melville-related manuscript materials.

form). As Roper stated in the preface, the letters were not transcribed from the original manuscripts but copied "with reasonable accuracy from the published texts."

Not until mid-century were extensive extracts from the known letters and some full texts brought together in book form, in Jay Leyda's *The Melville Log* (New York: Harcourt, Brace & Company, 1951), in his *The Portable Melville* (New York: Viking Press, 1952), and in Eleanor Melville Metcalf's *Herman Melville: Cycle and Epicycle* (Cambridge: Harvard University Press, 1953). Finally, with the publication of the Davis and Gilman volume by Yale University Press in 1960 (originally scheduled to be published in 1954), an edition of Melville's then-known letters carefully edited from the manuscripts became available.

Despite his own efforts to the contrary, Melville's "mug" now appears regularly in anthologies, and despite the present drive to revise the canon, no move has been made to displace his works from it, and there is little chance that they will return to relative obscurity. His present major status, coupled with the recent jump in prices for his letters, and soon to be stimulated by the specific listing in this volume of so many unlocated ones, virtually guarantees that more will be brought to light.[69] Most likely a number of these will be letters to his American publishers (thirteen of the fifty-two new letters found since the Davis-Gilman edition are to Putnam or Harper & Brothers). The fact that so many nineteenth-century autograph collections contained such letters suggests that the publishers were willing to give away or sell letters from their files. Another scattering will probably be perfunctory letters to collectors. But we may confidently hope that some of these new letters will also be the kind of delightful personal letters Melville sometimes wrote to his family and the boldly revealing ones to literary friends.

SOURCES

T HROUGHOUT THIS VOLUME, references to dates, events, and documents for which printed sources are not footnoted or

69. For the increasing value of his letters, see footnote 59 above. Even as this volume was going into final proofs, Ruth Blair of the University of Tasmania arrived at The Newberry Library and shared her discovery of Melville's 29 November [1862?] letter (see pp. 379–80 above).

otherwise indicated are based on the standard biographical and reference works listed with short titles on pp. xi–xiii above, as well as on other volumes of the Northwestern-Newberry Edition, published and forthcoming. Many documents and some factual information not covered by these printed sources have been located in the manuscript collections cited, by the volume editor and by other members of the editorial staff, notably by Hershel Parker in preparation of *The New Melville Log* and of his forthcoming biography; much of this material will be more fully included in those works. Unless otherwise indicated, however, transcriptions are based on the editor's own examination of the originals; thus, there may be variations between a document as transcribed in these printed and forthcoming sources and as printed here, as well as variations in dating. All quotations are *literatim* (except for editorial matter supplied in brackets). Unless otherwise specified, all quotations (and page references cited) from Melville's writings follow the Northwestern-Newberry Edition (e.g., vol. 15, *Journals*).

Imprint of the initials "A M", of Allan Melvill, Herman Melville's father, made by one of several different signets Allan used to press the hot wax with which he sealed his letters, in the way common before the introduction of envelopes with adhesive flaps. He used this initialed signet to seal his letter of 2 August 1819, in which he announced to his brother-in-law, Peter Gansevoort, the birth of his son Herman on the day before.

Herman Melville himself used various signets. He used this same initialed signet thirty years later, to seal his letter of 6 October 1849 to Lemuel Shaw about his forthcoming visit to London (see pp. 137–39 above). The signet itself is now unlocated. The photoreproduction above is enlarged from the 1.3 × 1 cm imprint it left on that letter, courtesy of the Massachusetts Historical Society (Shaw Collection).

Note on the Text

THIS VOLUME presents Melville's correspondence in two chronological sequences, a total of 943 annotated entries. The first sequence consists of 313 entries that print those of Melville's letters for which an apparently complete text is known, and 237 entries that present information about additional letters by him. The second sequence consists of 88 entries that print those letters received by Melville for which full texts are known, here edited together for the first time, and 305 entries for additional letters to him.[1] Included among the 401 complete letters by and to Melville are his few letters to editors, his parts of joint family letters, printed form-letters to him, published letters to editors not addressed to Melville but clearly written for his eyes, and letters for which only a

---

1. For a joint listing of the two sequences, see pp. 861–88 below. The largest number of extant manuscripts of letters by Melville (114) is in the collections of the New York Public Library; another 19 are in the Houghton Library of Harvard University. These two collections also contain all but 2 of the extant manuscripts of letters to Melville, 5 at the New York Public Library and 45 at Harvard. Other notable holdings of Melville's manuscript letters are in the Berkshire Athenaeum (13), the C. Waller Barrett Library at the University of Virginia Library (12), and the Beinecke Library at Yale University (12). At the time of preparation of this volume, the rest of the original Melville letters (108) were held by 31 libraries, 8 private collections, and 8 dealers.

draft version is known.[2] (In addition, one letter of possible attribution to Melville is printed and discussed below, pp. 853–56.)[3] Not included are legal documents that Melville signed, joint family letters that he signed but did not write, financial statements from his publishers, and clippings and newspapers that he sent or received without an accompanying letter, as well as his inscriptions in presentation copies of books or in autograph albums.[4] The 542 entries for additional letters by and to Melville report letters for which sufficient evidence survives but for which no full text has been located.

Whenever possible the copy-text of each letter by or to Melville in this edition is its original holograph manuscript as dispatched.[5] In fourteen instances a photographic or other reproduction of such a manuscript provided the text in the absence of the original document.[6] When a dispatched holograph (or its reproduction) was not available (66 letters), the text was drawn from one of five other sources: a draft, giving the text in an unfinished state (10 letters); a manuscript inscribed for the author in another hand (7 letters); a

2.   Also included are any texts that have survived of enclosures (even if no text for the accompanying letter is available), with the exception of financial statements or legal documents (e.g., the mortgage probably enclosed with Melville's 12 May 1856 letter to Lemuel Shaw) and long newspaper articles or books. Information about these longer enclosures is given in the headnotes.

3.   A 25 September 1842 letter Melville wrote for his shipmate George Lefevre, however, is included with Melville's other letters. As in most such letters written for an illiterate (one who in this case did not even sign his own name), the phrasing and vocabulary betray the fact that Melville supplied the wording to convey his shipmate's message.

4.   For Melville's inscriptions in books, see Merton M. Sealts, Jr., *Melville's Reading* (Columbia: University of South Carolina Press, 1988), and "A Supplementary Note to *Melville's Reading* (1988)," *Melville Society Extracts* 80 (February 1990), 5–10.

5.   In a few cases, a letter may not actually have been mailed—such as the communication William J. Lamb printed in his 20 April 1839 *Democratic Press, and Lansingburgh Advertiser* and possibly the 6 July 1859 verse letter that Melville wrote to his friend Daniel Shepherd but may not have sent (see the headnote to that letter, p. 337 above).

6.   The other forms of reproduction include the curious instance of Melville's 25 November 1854 letter, the text of which is from the legible offset of the now-missing original onto a once-facing album leaf, and two cases in which the original text is available from another copy of a machine-printed form-letter. For three of the photographic reproductions, the location of the original manuscripts was known, but it was not feasible to examine them (see footnote 14 below).

manuscript copy in the hand of the writer (10 letters); a subsequent
transcription made by a recipient or person other than the author (21
letters);[7] or the earliest known publication (18 letters). The volume
editor, Lynn Horth, examined all but eleven of the over three hundred available original letters, drafts, or other manuscript copy-
texts. Of those exceptions, eight were examined for her by John B.
Edmunds, Jr., Harrison Hayford, T. Walter Herbert, Mary S. Judd,
Frederick James Kennedy, Joseph J. Moldenhauer, and G. Thomas
Tanselle.[8]

The following pages discuss the relation of the Northwestern-
Newberry edition to the 1960 Davis-Gilman edition (cited below),
set forth its editorial policy, and describe its textual apparatus. While
its textual policy is stated primarily in terms of Melville's own letters, the same policy has also been followed for the letters to him.

THE TEXTS

T HE ONLY full edition of Melville's letters before the present
Northwestern-Newberry edition was *The Letters of Herman Melville* (New Haven: Yale University Press, 1960), edited by Merrell
R. Davis and William H. Gilman. These editors described their volume as "an attempt to collect all the available letters into one convenient edition with appropriate commentary and careful transcription
for each letter" (p. xvi). It contained texts for 271 letters by Melville, of which 10 were partial and 2 were drafts. Of these letters 43
were previously unpublished. The Davis-Gilman edition for the first
time established an editorial policy for treating the letters; it also
provided a detailed analysis of Melville's idiosyncratic and often difficult hand (reprinted below, pp. 847–51). Although both the policy
and the analysis differ somewhat from those of the present edition
(see p. 847 below), the Northwestern-Newberry edition from the
outset in 1964 was projected and prepared as a revision and augmen-

7. Six of these letters are drawn from transcriptions by earlier scholars or
owners (see footnote 10 below).

8. The numerous other manuscripts (not part of Melville's correspondence)
used in annotating the entries were transcribed by the editor from photocopies and
checked to the originals of all but fourteen, which were not available. This material
is quoted *literatim* in the entries except for the occasional insertion of bracketed
punctuation for the sake of clarity.

tation of their edition, including its annotations, to be edited by William H. Gilman (Merrell R. Davis died in 1961). The Davis-Gilman texts were to be newly collated to the manuscripts, misreadings corrected, footnotes verified and updated, and newly discovered letters added; consideration was also given, at first, to emending the texts to standard spellings, and progress was made by Gilman with the assistance of Amy Puett (later Emmers) in all of these directions. Subsequently, however, the present textual policy for manuscripts was adopted for all volumes of the *Writings*, Puett left the project in 1969, and Gilman died in 1976, bequeathing the complete Davis-Gilman working files for use in the Northwestern-Newberry editorial project. In 1981–82 Robert A. Sandberg of the Northwestern-Newberry editorial staff devoted an academic year to work on the volume. In 1988 its active preparation was resumed under the full-time editorship of Lynn Horth. The decision was then confirmed to include all surviving texts of letters to Melville and consequently to change the volume title from *Letters* to *Correspondence*. Further decisions were to present the letters by and those to Melville in two separate series;[9] to include entries within each series for additional letters for which no full texts have been located; and to supply an explanatory headnote and textual endnotes for each letter printed, thus subsuming or replacing the footnotes, textual notes, and other commentary of Davis and Gilman. As volume editor Lynn Horth executed all of these decisions, in constant consultation with the general editor, Harrison Hayford.

The Davis-Gilman files included photocopies of most of the then-known manuscript letters, relevant documentation, and their successive transcriptions with notes about the original manuscripts, if they had examined them. These files have subsequently been supplemented by Horth with further documentation and with manuscript reproductions which Davis and Gilman had been unable to obtain. New files have also been added by Horth, including both reproductions

9. The main reason for this decision, in a volume of Melville's *Writings*, was to set his own letters apart from those of other writers. In any case, there are no sustained back-and-forth sequences in his surviving correspondence; and in an interspersed arrangement in only 16 instances would one of the 88 letters to Melville stand just before or after his letter that evoked or answered it. For the interspersed back-and-forth sequence, see the "Calendar of Melville's Correspondence," pp. 861–88 below.

and documentation for (1) the letters by Melville for which full texts have been discovered since the Davis-Gilman edition, (2) the letters to Melville for which full texts have been located, and (3) the letters for which no full text has been located.[10] All of these files are now in the Melville Collection of The Newberry Library.

No complete new independent transcriptions of the 261 full Melville letters that were edited by Davis and Gilman were made from the manuscripts or other copy-texts for the Northwestern-Newberry texts, and therefore it is proper to refer to the newly edited texts of those letters in this edition as "revised."[11] Acknowledgment is thereby made that the Northwestern-Newberry texts of those letters were initially based, though they do not rely, upon the Davis-Gilman texts, which in most cases, as their files show (in conflict with their statement printed on p. 848 below), were transcribed first from photocopies and then checked against the manuscripts.[12] Apart from misreadings of some words, and deliberate emendations

10. Only ten of the letters by Melville whose manuscripts are known to have survived into the twentieth century are now without reproductions in the Northwestern-Newberry files. All ten of these are letters whose present location is unknown: Melville's letters to Harper & Brothers, [23 or 30?] January 1847 and [20?] February 1854; to Henry A. Bright, 18 November 1856; to unknown, 9 October 1865; to Miss True, February 1869; to unknown, 3 February 1869; to Peter [Past? Toft?], 5 November 1888; to H. S. Salt, 12 January 1890; to Evert Duyckinck, undated, p. 534 above, Davis-Gilman 262; and to unknown, undated, pp. 540–41 above, Davis-Gilman 270. Also lacking is a complete reproduction of Melville's 6 June 1846 letter to William Marcy (for which only a partial catalogue reproduction could be obtained). Nevertheless, for all but one of these letters, a text has been presented on the basis of transcriptions made before they disappeared—by Jay Leyda for four letters, by Frank Pleadwell for a fifth, and by Gilman for a sixth; all of these transcriptions were preserved by Davis and Gilman in their files. For three more letters, the text is drawn from a substantially complete catalogue transcription. The catalogue listing for the 5 November 1888 letter, however, gives only a brief quotation.

11. Original manuscripts have been located for the following letters Davis and Gilman published on the basis of sources other than the dispatched holograph: 24 July 1846 to William B. Sprague (Davis-Gilman 22); 2 April 1847 to Edwin Croswell (Davis-Gilman 38); 27 November 1857 to [A. D. Lamson?] (Davis-Gilman 136); 12 February 1859 to William H. Barry (Davis-Gilman 142—a partial text); 20 February 1888 to Edmund C. Stedman (Davis-Gilman 247); and 5 December 1889 to Archibald MacMechan (Davis-Gilman 251).

12. Of the 243 original manuscripts or drafts located by Davis and Gilman, they examined all but 25 of the original documents.

in spelling and punctuation, these texts were substantially accurate, as determined by repeated manuscript (and photocopy of manuscript) collations performed for the Northwestern-Newberry edition. A collation of the final Northwestern-Newberry texts of these 261 letters against the Davis-Gilman texts shows differences in wording at some forty-five points and numerous differences in spelling and punctuation in almost every letter.

In preparation of the Northwestern-Newberry texts of Melville's letters, the texts printed in Davis and Gilman's 1960 edition were scanned onto computer disk in 1989. The resulting printout was then proofread twice against the Davis-Gilman original to correct the many errors produced in the scanning process. Transcriptions by Horth (verified by Hayford) from the manuscripts or other copy-texts of the 52 texts that had surfaced since the Davis-Gilman edition were then key-processed onto the disk in their appropriate sequence along with her transcriptions of the texts of letters to Melville (also verified by Hayford) and the entries documenting the existence of the other letters by and to Melville for which no full texts have been located. Horth and Hayford initially each made one collation of the printout against the manuscript letters or other copy-texts in photocopy, then read her ensuing series of corrected printouts against the photocopies, progressively verifying the texts.[13] Horth also verified the texts against the original documents whenever possible.[14]

13. The final texts of all the letters, along with the editorial matter, were transmitted to the typesetter on computer disk, and the first resulting proofs were read twice, by Horth and by Hayford, against photocopies of the copy-texts. The second proofs were also read once thus by Hayford.

14. Whenever a manuscript description is given in the textual report, the original letter was examined. In eight cases, other scholars (listed above, p. 815) examined manuscript letters for Horth. For three letters, reproductions were obtained and added to the files, but the original manuscript could not later be examined—either because its present location is an undisclosed private collection (Melville's 27 March 1879 letter to G. P. Putnam's Sons), or because its present location made it unfeasible to examine (the 25 September 1842 letter Melville wrote for his shipmate Henry Smyth and Melville's 6 January 1888 letter to Rossiter Johnson); for these letters no manuscript description is given. However, many others whose present location is now unknown were examined in manuscript by Horth before they were last sold. In addition, Davis and/or Gilman examined four letters whose present location is now unknown: Melville's 10–14 November 1856 Liverpool letter to his brother Allan (formerly in the possession of Agnes Morewood); his 3

Because Melville's letters (like those to him) were written to be read by others, they present far fewer problems of transcription than his journals and draft manuscripts. All along, undeciphered and uncertain words were reexamined in the manuscripts by Horth and one or more of these Northwestern-Newberry editors and associates: Harrison Hayford, Hershel Parker, Robert C. Ryan, G. Thomas Tanselle, and Donald Yannella. Every word for which the editor, thus assisted, found no satisfactory reading is noted in the textual notes as either (1) "conjectural" or (2) having "possible" alternative readings (see pp. 843–46 below, for reproductions of these 48 words). The Northwestern-Newberry edition presents Melville's final wording for each letter in clear text with an editorial headnote before and a textual report after each letter (both in smaller type), whereas the Davis-Gilman edition interrupted the text with bracketed information, footnote numbers, and other symbols.

The present edition adds the texts of fifty-two letters by Melville to those printed by Davis and Gilman. Of these added letters, twenty-three have been published earlier by various scholars, as listed in the textual reports to the individual letters. The remaining twenty-nine are first published in this edition or in Horth's "Letters Lost/Letters Found" (*Melville Society Extracts* 81 [May 1990], 1–8), and were turned up in large part by Horth's 1989 census of the holdings of various libraries, by her letters to dealers, auction houses, and private owners in an attempt to trace the sales of individual letters, and by the calls and letters to her of librarians and owners reporting their discoveries or acquisitions. Some of the fifty-two post–Davis-Gilman letters come from additions to and discoveries in large, well-established Melville collections such as those of the New York Public Library and of H. Bradley Martin (now dispersed). More of them come from smaller deposits of letters in a wide variety of institutions, including the Cincinnati Historical Society, the Connecticut Historical Society, Cornell University Library, the Lilly Library at Indiana University, Lehigh University Li-

---

February 1869 letter to an autograph collector (formerly in the collection of Timothy F. McGillicuddy); his 30 April 1872 letter to Samuel Adams Drake (formerly in the collection of J. C. Pearson); and his 11 December 1887 letter to Rossiter Johnson (formerly in the collection of Estelle Doheny); for these, the features of the manuscripts that Davis and/or Gilman did describe have been included here, so identified, even though not verifiable at present, for possible future verification.

brary, Dawes Memorial Library at Marietta College (now sold), the New-York Historical Society, The Newberry Library, Firestone Library at Princeton University, Punahou School in Honolulu, Hawaii, Redwood Library, Social Law Library, and Cody Memorial Library at Southwestern University. Eleven of the new letters come from eight private collections: Cohen, Edmunds, Kennedy, Lisman, Manney (now sold), Reese, Shneidman, and Whitney; these collections were either unknown to Davis and Gilman or not yet formed at the time of their work. The texts of another nine of the new letters are taken from reproductions or transcriptions accompanying entries in dealers' and auction catalogues because the location of their original manuscripts could not be traced further.[15]

In addition to publishing newly discovered letters, the present edition builds upon the appended "Check List of Unlocated Letters" (by Melville) compiled by Davis and Gilman (pp. 309–19).[16] However, it places the 237 entries for these unlocated letters[17] in chronological order among the other entries, with a full discussion of the evidence establishing that Melville wrote them. Similarly, within the series of letters to Melville, the present edition also includes entries for letters that are now unlocated. Most of these unlocated letters, both to and from Melville, are specifically referred to or prom-

15.   In the case of three catalogue transcriptions (those of Melville's [23 or 30?] January 1847 letter to Harper & Brothers, his 9 October 1865 letter to an unidentified autograph collector, and his February 1869 letter to Miss H. I. True) where no indication is given of how Melville placed those letters on the page, their layout has been standardized according to Melville's general practice.

16.   Three of the 147 "unlocated letters" listed by Davis and Gilman have been located and included in this edition: Melville's October 1828 letter to his aunt Lucy Melvill and his 6 February and 31 October 1854 letters to George P. Putnam (Davis-Gilman Unlocated 272, 340a, and 341).

17.   If an apparently complete text is available, a letter is not considered "unlocated" for the purposes of the present edition even if the location of the original document is unknown; in these instances, the phrase "original document not located" is used in the textual report. Thus the term "Unlocated" at the beginning of an entry refers to the text, as distinguished from the complete physical document (which, of course, is also not located), and it is used both when no text is available or when no apparently complete text is available, as in the case of manuscript fragments (see footnote 19 below) or of brief quotations from letters (see footnote 20 below). This policy accounts for some differences in treatment from that of Davis and Gilman, who did not treat manuscript fragments and some partial quotations as "unlocated."

ised in his own correspondence and journals, in other contemporary letters or documents,[18] or in reminiscences. In a few instances a surviving fragment, envelope, or apparent enclosure provides evidence or even a few words of the unlocated letter.[19] For some dozen of the unlocated letters excerpts (ranging from a single word to several sentences) exist because they were quoted in other contemporary letters or publications or in subsequent auction or dealer catalogues.[20] The remaining entries for unlocated letters by or to Mel-

18. Those documents include Augusta Melville's record of correspondence, the diaries of Gansevoort Melville, Richard Brodhead, Sophia Hawthorne, and Catherine Gansevoort Lansing, and notations in letterbooks, on drafts, or in other letters, that letters had been written.

19. Entries for manuscript fragments include: a scrap bearing four partial lines and the closing and signature of Melville's letter to his son Stanwix tentatively dated July 1872; two pieces, bearing the heading and the closing and signature of Melville's 30 November 1872 letter to Susan Lansing Gansevoort; the cut dateline of a 13 November 1882 letter by Melville; a scrap bearing the closing and signature of an undated letter to Stanwix (see p. 537); and two scraps bearing closings and signatures (both undated, see pp. 536 and 539). In general, however, entries for manuscript fragments containing only Melville's signature are not included. Although, as discussed on pp. 786–88 above, many of these clipped autographs may be the only remnants of Melville's letters to his wife—probably cut from their envelopes addressed to "Mrs. Herman Melville"—some of them may have been taken from other documents. (One entry has been included on the basis of a Melville autograph, pasted into a copy of *John Marr*, that obviously came from an envelope addressed to his wife, since it also bears part of a postmark—enough to establish the place where Melville mailed it; see p. 539 above.)

20. See, for example, the entries for Melville's 1837 letter to Charles Van Loon, his 6 June 1846 letter to James K. Polk, his 14 December 1849 letter to N. P. Willis, his September 1867 letter to John Hoadley, his [December?] 1867 letter to the editors of *Putnam's Magazine*, his pre-15 July 1886 letter to his sister Helen Griggs, his 5 November 1888 letter to Peter [Past? Toft?], and his 10 August 1890 letter to T. Fisher Unwin. See also the entries for letters to Melville from Richard T. Greene (before 19 February 1847) and his sister Helen Griggs (31 January 1877). Melville's own replies also often quote briefly from the letters he is answering (for a convoluted example, see Melville's 5 September 1877 letter to his cousin Catherine Lansing, in which he quotes her quotation of the phrase *"people of leisure"* used in an earlier letter of his [now unlocated]). Letters whose texts survive in published forms that are substantial but abridged with ellipses points (such as Melville's 22 July 1851 letter to Nathaniel Hawthorne and his 7 June 1854 letter to George Putnam) are not, however, considered part of this category of unlocated letters. Also, manuscript letters that are missing a further page or from which pieces are cut or torn are not considered unlocated.

ville have been included (1) because an extant letter or other document was apparently written in response to or as a result of an unlocated one he wrote or received, even though that unlocated letter was not cited; (2) because a reply was necessary, firmly requested, and in some cases simply most likely; or (3) because in some instances, as in Melville's lecture arrangements, only a letter could have communicated the necessary information.[21]

21. The first category accounts for some twenty-five of the unlocated letters that can be inferred from other documents. See, for example, the entries for the letter Melville evidently wrote to his brother Gansevoort before 1 September 1845 and for the letter his brother Allan evidently wrote to him between 5 and 8 September 1857. See also the entry for Melville's letter to Louis A. Godey, written before December 1850, for an example of a letter that can be inferred from a published document. In the second category some twenty letters have been inferred. See, for example, the entries for Melville's replies to his sister Helen after 8 August 1832 and to Richard T. Greene after 16 June 1856. However, not all requests for a reply from Melville have been taken as cues to infer a letter. Allan's offhand request in his 23 December 1854 letter to their sister Augusta at Pittsfield—"Ask Herman to write what he is doing" (NYPL-GL)—has not been considered imperative enough to warrant an inferred reply. In all instances where a request for a letter is cited in an entry, but a reply seems dubious, the reasons for not inferring an answer are stated. See, for example, the entry for Henry Gansevoort's letter to Melville written before 3 November 1864, p. 695 above. The third category accounts for some forty-five inferred letters, primarily concerning Melville's lectures, as recorded in his lecture engagement notebook. Additional letters, such as one from Melville to his brother Gansevoort written before 20 December 1845 and one to his wife before 11 February 1863, have been inferred for the same reason—that only his letters could have allowed his brother and his wife to know information that they in turn conveyed to others in their letters. Such inferences have been made with caution and only when the evidence seems incontrovertible. In other instances, where the information could have been communicated by some other means—by another family member, for example—a letter has not been inferred. Thus, while it might seem logical to infer a letter from Melville to the Shaw family at the birth of his daughter Frances (Fanny)—since he had written such letters at the births of Malcolm and of Stanwix—there is no evidence to indicate that Melville did so. (See Helen Melville Griggs's 13 March 1855 letter to Augusta Melville in the *New Log*, ed. Jay Leyda and Hershel Parker [New York: Gordian Press, forthcoming], which reports that Hope Savage Shaw knew the baby's name, but gives no indication how she knew it.) Similarly, when a communication from or to Melville could have been made in person, no letter has usually been inferred; for example, two of Evert Duyckinck's requests that Melville write a book review—to which Melville replied on 14 November 1848 and 31 December 1863—could have been made by Duyckinck in person, and so no letters from him have been inferred.

This policy for including entries for letters not specifically cited in other sources is more conservative than that of Davis and Gilman, who, for example, inferred four letters as accompanying various publishing proposals and submissions, whereas these four have not been given entries in this volume (Davis-Gilman Unlocated 307, 386, 387, and 388). Although letters may well have accompanied Melville's review of Cooper's *The Sea Lions*, his poems published in *Harper's New Monthly Magazine* in 1866, and the submission of *Battle-Pieces* to the Harpers, it is also possible that Melville conveyed these items in person, or that his brother Allan did so on his behalf. Davis and Gilman also inferred a letter as accompanying Melville's gift of the manuscript poem "Philip" to Richard H. Stoddard (Davis-Gilman Unlocated 389); however, since this presentation could have easily been made in person while both were working in the Customs Service in New York, a letter cannot be inferred with a high degree of probability—as is the case with other Melville presentation copies, many of which may not have been accompanied by a letter for a number of reasons.[22]

22. In four further instances Davis-Gilman entries for unlocated letters have been dropped from the present edition. In the first instance, Davis and Gilman inferred from three letters concerning the negotiations for Melville's first book—his brother Gansevoort Melville's 26 September and 2 October 1845 letters to their mother (NYPL-GL) and 20 October letter to John Murray (Murray)—that Melville probably wrote his brother some instructions about it during September or October 1845 (Davis-Gilman Unlocated 281). Perhaps he did, but there is nothing in Gansevoort's letters or diary to indicate that he had received any. In the second instance, Davis and Gilman inferred from Wiley & Putnam's 7 October 1846 reply to Allan Melville (HCL-M) that Melville had written Allan asking him to make the inquiries he did about the costs and profits of *Typee* (Davis-Gilman Unlocated 296). However, the firm's letter in reply does not indicate that Allan had told them so, and on the back of it Allan noted "Called for by me | A. M". Third, similarly, Davis and Gilman inferred from Melville's 6 October 1849 letter to Lemuel Shaw that Melville had solicited a letter of introduction from a Mr. Baldwin (Davis-Gilman Unlocated 309); however, this is not stated by Melville, and it is equally if not more likely that Shaw rather than Melville initiated the request. Finally, Davis and Gilman inferred from Henry Gansevoort's remark in his 3 November 1864 letter to Allan Melville (NYPL-GL) that he hoped to hear from Melville in answer to his "last," that Melville did indeed reply (Davis-Gilman Unlocated 382); but given the care with which Henry Gansevoort saved the letters he received (see the headnote to Melville's 10 May 1864 letter to him), it seems unlikely that Melville wrote but his cousin did not keep such a letter.

TEXTUAL POLICY

T HE TEXTS presented in this volume, as in other volumes of
the Northwestern-Newberry Edition, are critical and unmodernized.[23] They are *critical* in that they do not aim to correspond
exactly to the documentary form of the texts but instead incorporate
some editorial alterations designed to bring the texts nearer to Melville's intention. They are *unmodernized* in that they do not aim to
bring spellings and punctuation into conformity with any presumed
modern usage or with the modern idea that consistency in such matters is desirable. Because the single source for most of the texts of
the letters is Melville's dispatched holograph (or holograph draft),
or those of his correspondents, and because these manuscript letters
are private writings, not intended for publication, the implications
of *critical* and *unmodernized*, however, are somewhat different from
those for the texts of the letters Melville wrote to editors of newspapers or other written material by him of the kinds normally intended for publication.[24] In the case of private writings such as manuscript letters, critical editors whose goal is a text reflecting the
author's intention at a particular time must use their judgment to
decide which features of the documentary text (or texts) were supplied by someone other than the author and without the author's full
concurrence and, in addition, which were slips made by the author.
In the case of Melville's letters, it is clear that no one but the author
was responsible for the bulk of the extant documentary texts, and
the central editorial problem becomes how to define the "slips" that
will be corrected.

Of course, one could argue that no such "slips" should be corrected and that the text should be presented *literatim,* without critical
editing (except for the compromises that are inevitable whenever
handwriting is transferred to print). Every text can usefully be presented either way—either as a literal transcription (or reprinting) of
an existing text (thus emphasizing the text of a document) or as a

23. The ensuing statement of textual policy closely follows the statement
written by G. Thomas Tanselle, as bibliographical editor of the Northwestern-
Newberry Edition, for the Note on the Text in the *Journals* volume (pp. 236–42).

24. See pp. 831–37 below for the textual policy governing Melville's letters to
editors, as well as those letters available only from a source other than a dispatched or
draft holograph, such as a publication, a scribal copy, or a later transcription.

critically edited text (and therefore emphasizing the intended text of the work, which is but imperfectly represented by the documentary text or texts). For private writings as well as those intended for publication, every feature of a document prepared by the author may be significant as psychological evidence; the difference between the two situations is that private writings are not subject to the same conventions of spelling, punctuation, and usage as are published writings, and all idiosyncrasies in them can be thought of as integral elements of the style, and therefore as features not merely of the document but of the work as well. This line of reasoning leads toward the production of noncritical texts. On the other hand, a distinction can be made between idiosyncrasies not intended by the author (such as the transposition of two letters) and those that can be regarded as private usages (such as spellings that would have been considered incorrect according to the conventions of the time and therefore would probably not have been tolerated by a publisher). This line of reasoning leads to the production of critical texts. The Northwestern-Newberry editors, cognizant of the merits of both these approaches, have decided to follow the latter as more compatible with the goal of the Edition as a whole to provide reading texts reflecting Melville's intentions.

The critical texts in this volume therefore attempt to present Melville's intentions in the act of writing: they aim to eliminate his slips of the pen but to retain other odd spellings that appear to have been what he intended at the time. In determining what falls into each category, the editors have had to expand the concept of an unmodernized text to include any spelling that seems intended. Unmodernized critical texts of works intended for publication normally alter spellings that do not conform to what was considered standard at the time (recognizing that some variations in the spelling of particular words were conventional in certain periods). But for private writings the standard of what was expected in print does not apply; the author was writing only for the recipient's eyes and was under little constraint to conform to any convention whatever. That the author may simply not have known the standard spellings for certain words is similarly irrelevant; the author may have wished to be "correct," but, if it is clear that an unconventional spelling was intended at the moment of writing, that spelling would be retained under the policy followed here. Implementing this policy requires two kinds of editorial decisions: (1) determining what spelling to adopt when the handwriting is either unclear or elided; (2) determining, when the handwriting is clear, which unconventional spellings are slips and which are intended.

Unclear handwriting and elided handwriting. In thinking about this problem, one must begin with the recognition that even the production of a noncritical transcription necessitates critical judgment in transferring a handwritten document into print. Although one's goal would be the exact transcription of the documentary text, subjective judgments are involved in deciding what in fact that text consists of, for the individual standard letterforms of a type design cannot reproduce all the ways in which words may be represented in handwriting—such as half-formed letters, extraneous strokes, or even indeterminate scrawls—and in any case the point of a transcription is to provide a specialist's interpretation of what is ambiguous in the document. How to transcribe unclear handwriting and elided handwriting must therefore be faced whether one's goal is a noncritical or a critical text. *Unclear handwriting*—here defined to mean the writing in those words where the author was attempting to form all the actual letters (as opposed to eliding some) but did not form them all completely or added extraneous strokes[25]—would probably be handled the same way in both kinds of editions: the context would suggest what letters were intended, and those letters would be placed in the text. Thus a letter that could be read as either *i* or *e* would be reported as one or the other depending on what seemed required by the context; and a superfluous stroke falling between *a* and *d*, but in the context not representing an additional letter, would be ignored. *Elided handwriting*—here defined to mean the writing in those words where the author, instead of forming or half-forming all the actual letters, used one or more strokes or a wavy line to stand for some of them—might be handled differently in the two kinds of editions: a noncritical text might attempt to suggest the nature of the elision, whereas a critical text would report the intended letters.

25. Extraneous strokes occur less frequently than elided letters in Melville's hand, but are nonetheless a feature of his hand. For one example, see the word "promenaded" in line 5 of the reproduction from his 3 March 1849 letter to Duyckinck (p. 842 below).

Thus the former might print *ig* and the latter *ing* where a wavy line vaguely resembling *ig* was obviously intended to mean *ing*. A good case could be made, however, for adopting *ing* under these circumstances even in a noncritical text, arguing that the goal of the edition is not the imitation of the strokes of the handwriting but the reporting of the letters they are meant to stand for. Certainly a critical text, like the one offered here, should take this approach.

Elisions are in fact one of the prominent characteristics of Melville's handwriting, often occurring in such combinations as *ance*, *ence*, *ment*, *ing*, *ion*, or *ious*, whether used medially or terminally (for examples, see the reproduction on p. 842 below: "leaving" at the end of line 6 and "Declaration of Independence" at the end of line 16). They must be distinguished from two other kinds of shortening also common to his hand—abbreviated words and fused letters. Abbreviated words by definition involve the intentional omission of one or more letters (the letters that are present may or may not be clearly formed), whereas elisions by definition are ambiguous strokes that presumably represent the unformed letter or letters in the word. In some instances it is not easy to distinguish an abbreviation from an elision, but the critical editor must make the attempt, because the distinction is important. An abbreviation, as an intended form of a word, has an existence independent of the fully spelled word it is linked with, and an author's choice of one or the other at a given point in a private piece of writing is a stylistic feature that should be respected by a critical editor. An elision, in contrast, does not signal an intended shortening of a word but is simply the paleographical evidence of a hurried attempt to represent the full word, and the critical editor should spell an elided word out in its conventional form (unless the author, when forming all the letters of the word, habitually used another spelling). Melville's habitual use of fused letters must also be distinguished from his elisions: fusions are instances where a single stroke does double duty as the ending stroke of one letter and the beginning stroke of the next. Although fusions often pose problems in reading Melville's hand, they do not—once they are identified—pose problems for transcription, because both letters in each instance are actually present (if sometimes only in part) and both would therefore be included in either a critical or a noncritical text.[26]

Unconventional spellings. Even when the handwriting is clear, critical editors still have a decision to make: whether the spelling that is clearly present is the one the writer intended. Melville's manuscripts are filled with peculiar spellings, and a noncritical text would incorporate all of them. But when the aim is to reflect his intention at the moment of writing, there is obviously a distinction to be made between, on the one hand, spellings like "tittle" (for "title" in Melville's 2 February 1850 letter to Evert Duyckinck), "antidtote" (for "antidote" in Melville's 17 July 1852 letter to Hawthorne), or "terrbily" (in Melville's 20 February 1849 letter to his brother Allan) and, on the other, those like "rememberances," "expence," or "feild" that occur repeatedly throughout Melville's letters. The former are examples of what are often called "slips of the pen," in which the writer, preoccupied by the idea being expressed, reverses two letters or mechanically repeats or anticipates one or more letters. The latter are examples of conceivable spellings: that is, whether or not they are justified by etymology or custom, they are conceivable in that they reflect pronunciation. The former could not have been intended by Melville; it is more accurate to call them "miswritten" than "misspelled," and a critical editor should correct them, as they have been corrected here. The latter may well (and in many instances one can say that they certainly do) represent Melville's intention at the time of writing, whether or not he spelled the same words in other ways at other times, and a critical editor should allow these spellings to stand.[27]

This policy has been applied conservatively in the present volume: the spellings that seem clearly to be instances of miswriting (there are 125 of them) are altered to standard (or Melville's standard) spellings, but all the other spellings are retained as they occur

26. The fullest description of the characteristics of Melville's handwriting is the one provided by Davis and Gilman in their 1960 edition (pp. xxi–xxv; reprinted on pp. 847–51 below). Further discussion of elision, fusion, and expansion (their term for the addition of superfluous strokes) may be found in their account.

27. Melville's intended form of particular words may vary from time to time; thus when Melville writes "past" for "passed" in his juvenile letter to his aunt Lucy (p. 4), this spelling is allowed to stand, as are other anomalous spellings in early letters up through 1837.

in the manuscripts.[28] The basic guideline for making these decisions is to treat as miswritten any spelling that seems inconceivable as Melville's intended spelling, either because its pronunciation would not resemble that of the intended word or because its sequence of letters is alien to any attempt to spell the word correctly. Although such decisions inevitably rest on editorial judgment, that judgment has operated within a framework established by a strict definition of the characteristics of miswriting. To be eligible for consideration as miswriting, a word must exhibit at least one of the following five features:

(1) *repetition*—The addition of one or more extraneous letters often takes the form of a mechanical repetition, as in "Hellen" (in Melville's 20 January 1845 letter to his sister Catherine), "possesss" (19 March 1846 to Lemuel Shaw), "possitive" (20 July 1849 to Bentley), "shee" (for "she"; 13 August 1852 to Hawthorne), and "L.R.R." (as an abbreviation for "Lightning-Rod"; 12 June 1854 to Putnam); sometimes the repetition is not consecutive, as in "overturers" (19 June [1847?] to Bentley) or "scence" (for "scene"; 2 September 1846 to Murray). It also may involve more than one letter, as in "addititional" (13 January 1872 to Miss Coffin), and sometimes even a whole word, as in "at, at" (28 May 1860 to Evert Duyckinck).

(2) *anticipation*—Another kind of miswriting results from the anticipation of letters that are to follow, either in the same word—as in "Truly" ([15?] July 1846 to Evert Duyckinck), "backswoodsmen" (20 July 1851 to Bentley), "carreer" (17 February 1863 to Catherine Gansevoort), and "archictect" (9 September 1868 to Catherine Gansevoort)—or in a succeeding word—as when "nod" is written for "not" in anticipation of the next word "add" (23 May 1846 to Alexander Bradford) or "another's" is written for "another" in anticipation of the next word "man's" (2 and 14 December 1849 to Evert Duyckinck). Other examples include "excellented" for "excellent" (the next word is "hearted"; 1 May 1850 to Dana), "obliges" for "oblige" (the next word is "Yours"; 21 August 1855 to G. P. Putnam & Co.), and "hastern" for "hasten" (the next word is "her"; 9 June 1869 to Peter Gansevoort).

---

28. Unlike many of his extant manuscript writings, Melville's letters have for the most part few cancellations, additions, and revisions in them, as well as relatively few miswritten words.

(3) *metathesis*—Transpositions of one or more letters, creating words that cannot possibly have been intended, occur in Melville's (as in nearly everyone's) handwriting: examples are "keens" (for "knees"; 14 November 1848 to Evert Duyckinck), "foregin" (20 February 1849 to Allan Melville), "childern" (24 February 1849 to Evert Duyckinck), "sinec" ("since"; 12 February 1851 to Evert Duyckinck), "Champange" (25 October 1852 to Hawthorne), "Magainze" (25 May 1854 to Harper & Brothers), "Pittsfiled" (27 March 1861 to Julius Rockwell), and "Genearl" (10 May 1864 to Henry Gansevoort).

(4) *omissions*—Some clear-cut omissions (that is, not instances of elision) create groups of letters that Melville cannot have intended as his spellings, such as "unintently" for "unintentionally" (3 July 1846 to Evert Duyckinck), "copright" for "copyright" (30 December 1846 to Brodhead), and "higer" for "higher" (5 June 1849 to Bentley). Uncompleted words such as "we" for "were" (2 September 1860 to Melville's daughter Bessie) also fall into this category.

(5) *misplaced familiar combinations of letters*—Several insertions, omissions, and substitutions seem to have resulted from a tendency to form familiar combinations of letters. For example, in writing the name "Abe" Melville added an *l*, unconsciously creating the common word "Able" (24 and 25 March 1861 to Elizabeth Shaw Melville); he also added a *y* to "am" (10, 13, and 14 November 1856 to Allan Melville), presumably because his hand automatically formed the common sequence of letters constituting "my". The same kind of automatic reaction may explain the *a* in "hundread" (5 June 1849 to Bentley) as well as the substitution of "that" for "than," which occurs in two letters (16 August 1850 to Evert Duyckinck and 24 and 25 March 1861 to Elizabeth Shaw Melville). In some cases only the context can indicate when this type of miswriting has occurred—as in Melville's 14 November 1848 letter to Evert Duyckinck where "books" is written for "book."

It is obvious that these five categories must be interpreted in the light of the general guidelines stated earlier, for not every word that falls into these categories is an example of miswriting. For instance, the repeated *e* in "shee" and *t* in "tittle" (noted above) make those words miswritten, whereas the repeated *l* in "untill" (14 November 1848 to Evert Duyckinck) and *g* in "Dagguerreotype" (16 May 1854 to George P. Putnam) do not, because the latter are (and the former are not) conceivable English combinations of letters for these words; and the metatheses in "Magainze" and "foregin" (noted above) produce miswritten words, whereas those in "beleive" and "feild" do not, because the latter are (and the former are not) pronounceable as the intended words. (It may be noted that "beleive" and "feild" were common lifelong spellings of Melville.) The characteristics placing words in one of the five categories enumerated here, therefore, are a necessary but not a sufficient condition for considering those words miswritten.[29]

There is one further way in which the present texts depart from Melville's inscriptions in his letters: they incorporate only his final wording at points where he made revisions at the time of his original inscription. The presence of canceled wording is one of the common characteristics of private documents, and a literal transcription would have to include this wording.[30] It is not part of what Melville intended, however, and is therefore not incorporated in these critical texts (though it is reported in notes).[31]

Since the texts of twenty-five of Melville's letters and thirty-one of the letters to him in this edition do not come from a dispatched holograph manuscript (or a holograph draft) but from one or more

29.   Applying these same guidelines, seven words are listed as miswritten in the letters written to Melville.

30.   The one exception to the omission of canceled material is the canceled 14 July 1852 note from John Clifford to Melville. Since the letter of Clifford's that ultimately replaced this canceled note is now unlocated, the note has here been included in lieu of the actual letter.

31.   Parts of words and punctuation marks that Melville did not actually strike through in his cancellation of the passages in which they stand are considered canceled in accordance with Melville's evident intention and are not included in the text or distinguished from other canceled matter in the textual notes. Similarly, several vestigial words, capital letters, and plurals which Melville let stand through incomplete revision are altered in the text to fit the revised context; these vestigial manuscript readings are reported in the textual notes. Words that Melville only partially revised have also been altered to follow his intention (see, for example, "gives" in Melville's draft letter to J. W. Henry Canoll, p. 495 above). In addition, words which can be inferred even though they were later obscured or effaced by either intended or accidental damage to the letter paper are included in the letter texts and recorded as such in the textual notes. Omitted words, however, are not supplied (though they are reported in the textual notes), nor are Melville's factual errors, such as incorrect dates or days, corrected; those that have been noted are identified in the headnotes.

printed or handwritten transcriptions, a different set of policies governing these texts must also be outlined. For four categories of letters such dispatched (or draft) holographs are not known to survive: (1) private letters inscribed for their authors and signed with their names, including the 26 March 1849 letter to the Harpers inscribed "per Allan Melville," the 22 May 1860 memoranda to Allan Melville that Elizabeth Shaw Melville inscribed for her husband, and the five letters to Melville that were inscribed by Herbert Russell for his father, William Clark Russell, as well as the part of the 7 August 1886 letter to her father that Frances Melville Thomas inscribed for her four-year-old daughter Eleanor; (2) private letters transcribed in the hands of the writers, such as Lemuel Shaw's copy of his 8 November 1858 letter to Melville enclosing a check for one hundred dollars or Abraham Lansing's letterbook copies of seven of his letters to Melville as executor of Frances Priscilla Melville's estate; (3) private letters published or transcribed by the recipients, their descendants, or others, such as Melville's letters to Hawthorne published by Julian Hawthorne and Rose Hawthorne Lathrop, Melville's 5 May 1870 letter to his mother copied by John Hoadley, and Bentley's and Murray's letterbook copies of letters sent to Melville (probably transcribed by clerks); and (4) letters intended for publication, such as Melville's letters to the *Albany Microscope*. Theoretically the first three categories might call for different editorial treatment from the fourth, since the intended form of private writing may contain more idiosyncratic spelling and punctuation than the intended form of writings aimed for publication. The present instances do not seem to provide any opportunities for making such a distinction, however, and for practical purposes all four categories can be treated alike, as cases where the goal is to reconstruct from these texts what the author intended. These letters can therefore be treated in the same way as the bulk of Melville's published writings.

All such Northwestern-Newberry texts are unmodernized critical texts, prepared according to the theory of copy-text formulated by Sir Walter Greg.[32] Central to that theory is the distinction be-

32. "The Rationale of Copy-Text," *Studies in Bibliography* 3 (1950–51), 19–36, reprinted in his *Collected Papers*, ed. J. C. Maxwell (Oxford: Clarendon Press, 1966), pp. 374–91. For an application of this method to the period of Melville, see the Center for Editions of American Authors, *Statement of Editorial Principles and Procedures* (rev. ed.; New York: Modern Language Association of America, 1972)

tween substantives (the words of a text) and accidentals (spelling and punctuation). Persons involved in the transcription, printing, and publishing of texts have often taken it upon themselves to alter accidentals; and authors, when examining or revising copied or printed forms of their work, have often been relatively unconcerned with accidentals.[33] An author's failure to change certain accidentals altered by a copyist, publisher, or compositor does not amount to an endorsement of those accidentals. When the aim of a critical edition, as here, is to establish a text that represents as nearly as possible the author's intentions, it follows that—in the absence of contrary evidence—the formal texture of the work will be most accurately reproduced by adopting as copy-text[34] the scribal copy or the first printing based on the dispatched holograph manuscript, when, as in the case of these letters, that manuscript has not been located. This basic text may then be emended with any later documentary variants (whether substantive or accidental) that are judged authorial and with other obvious corrections. Following this procedure maximizes the probability of keeping authorial readings when evidence is inconclusive as to the source of an alteration in a later document. Each resulting text is the product of critical judgment and (like the critical texts of the other letters) does not correspond exactly to any single surviving text; but its aim is to come closer to the author's intentions—insofar as they are recoverable—than any such text.

When more than one source was available (in only six cases), collations were made to check for differences in the transcriptions of the now unlocated original.[35] In the few cases of variation, the earli-

---

and the various discussions recorded in *The Center for Scholarly Editions: An Introductory Statement* (New York: Modern Language Association of America, 1977; also printed in *PMLA* 92 [1977], 586–97), along with G. Thomas Tanselle's *A Third Interim Supplement* to it (New York: Committee on Scholarly Editions, Modern Language Association of America, 1992).

33. Accidentals can affect the meaning (or substance) of a text, and Greg's distinction is not meant to suggest otherwise; rather, its purpose is to emphasize the fact that persons involved in the transmission of texts have habitually behaved differently in regard to the two categories.

34. "Copy-text" is the text accepted as the basis for an edition.

35. In the two instances where the sequence was uncertain—that of the two transcriptions of Melville's 29 June 1851 letter to Hawthorne (Julian Hawthorne's notebook transcription and his published one) and that of the three transcriptions of Melville's 22 July 1851 letter to him (an anonymous typescript transcription and

est printing or transcription was used as the copy-text, and the variants listed in textual notes. The principal source for emendations in these texts, however, was the editor's close reading of them—with only six emendations drawn from variant transcriptions.[36] The present edition incorporates twenty-six emendations of substantives, seventeen in Melville's letters and nine in the letters he received. Some, like the change from "scopes" to "tropes" in Melville's letter to the *Albany Microscope* published on 17 and 24 March 1838 or "hear" to "bear" in the 15 April 1837 letter from "R.," correct simple slips (authorial or compositorial). Some, however, correct errors that most likely arose from a misreading of Melville's hand. Examples of such misreadings include "fainting" for "painting" in the 29 June 1851 letter transcribed by Julian Hawthorne and "love" for "Jove" in the [17?] November 1851 letter to Hawthorne published by Rose Hawthorne Lathrop, an emendation which was first suggested by Harrison Hayford in his 1945 Yale dissertation.[37] Other emendations are based on matters of external fact, such as the correction of "July" to "June" in Melville's 7 June 1854 letter to George

Rose Lathrop's two published ones)—the collations were also used to determine the sequence of the transcriptions. Similarly, collations were made against reprintings of letters—such as the reprintings of Richard Greene's letters first published in the July 1846 *Buffalo Commercial Advertiser*—to determine whether variants in the reprintings were made through recourse to the original manuscript. When there was nothing to indicate such recourse (as in the Greene letters), NN considers the reprintings nonauthorial and does not list the variants.

36.   All occur in Melville's letters to Hawthorne; see the three emendations labeled with the symbol GL in his [16 April?] 1851 letter; the one labeled JH in his 29 June 1851 letter; and the two labeled L in his 22 July 1851 letter.

37.   Davis and Gilman did not adopt this reading for their 1960 edition. The NN symbol in the textual notes signifies only that the reading does not appear in the copy-text or in variant transcriptions; it does not imply that no one has ever thought of it before. Such substantive changes are of course made only when the copy-text reading is unsatisfactory. The emendation must produce wording that Melville would have used in the context (judging from his literary practice); it must improve the sense and fit the tone of the context; and, if a substitution, it must be a word that in Melville's hand could have been misread as the word in the copy-text (and such words may be spelled in an unusual form typical of Melville's habits, such as the emendation of "usable" to "visable" in Julian Hawthorne's transcription of Melville's [16 April?] 1851 letter). Other examples include the emendation of "revere" to "reverse" and "feeble" to "febrile" in Julian Hawthorne's transcriptions of Melville's [1 June?] and 29 June 1851 letters.

P. Putnam or the placement of Lotus Niles's name in Charles Van Loon's letter published in the 31 March and 7 April issues of the *Albany Microscope* (a correction Loon himself called for in a later letter to the newspaper).

In the absence of a dispatched or draft holograph manuscript, the degree to which the author was responsible for the accidentals—the spelling and punctuation—of a subsequent text is a matter impossible to settle conclusively. Even though some of the spelling and punctuation of the letters taken from these sources undoubtedly reflects the habits of the individuals who acted as scribes or the compositors who set them, they are nevertheless the only sources of the texts, and their accidentals, even when they may not be Melville's own, at least represent contemporary practice. Accordingly, the accidentals of these sources have been retained in the present edition, except in the instances outlined below, even when the spelling and punctuation may appear incorrect or inconsistent by late-twentieth-century standards. Certainly the texts of these letters contained inconsistencies. Some came from the scribes or compositors; but others were no doubt present in the manuscripts, and, although Melville may not have been aware of them, they constitute a suggestive part of his total expression, since patterns of accidentals do affect the texture of a piece of writing. Most of the inconsistencies probably reflect an indifference to consistency on Melville's part. In any event, to regularize the spelling and punctuation would mean taking the risk of choosing nonauthorial forms and imposing on the text a consistency alien to Melville. Completely to regularize the accidentals would involve making many changes, inevitably taking the text farther away from the manuscript and, in fact, producing a modernization. Therefore, no attempt has been made in these texts to impose general consistency on either spelling or punctuation,[38] and changes have been made sparingly (there are sixty-seven of them), according to the following guidelines:

38. No emendations are made to secure consistency in the use of capital letters; the insertion of hyphens in compounds; the use and placement of punctuation in association with quotation marks and parentheses; the punctuation of penultimate items in series; and the use of italics or of quotation marks (or both at once) for such items as quotations and paraphrases, foreign words, mottoes, titles of books, words cited as words, and the like. Likewise, since contemporary practice did not demand accuracy in the use of accent marks on foreign words (indeed,

Spelling. The general rule adopted here is to retain any spellings (even when inconsistent) that were acceptable by the standards during Melville's lifetime, as well as any obsolete variants that may have been intended by Melville or unusual spellings that reflect his habits; spellings are corrected only when they do not fall into these categories. Recourse to nineteenth-century dictionaries, such as the 1847 revision of Webster's *American Dictionary of the English Language* (Springfield, Mass., 1848) and Worcester's *A Universal and Critical Dictionary of the English Language* (Boston, 1847), as well as to sources for the historical study of spelling such as the *Oxford English Dictionary* and the *Dictionary of American English*, has provided the editor with sufficient contexts to justify the retention of some anomalous-appearing copy-text forms, such as "pugnancy" (an early form of "pungency") and "lounges" (a nineteenth-century spelling of "lunges") in Melville's letter published in the 17 and 24 March 1838 *Albany Microscope*, and "portrature" in Herbert Russell's 21 July 1886 letter inscribed for his father. A few other forms, not found in reliable parallels in such sources or not typical of Melville's spelling habits (or those of his correspondents), have been corrected, such as "chimearas" in Julian Hawthorne's transcription of Melville's 29 June 1851 letter, and "villifacation" and "falshoods" in Charles Van Loon's letter published in the 10 March 1838 *Microscope*.

Punctuation. Emendations in punctuation are made only to correct obvious typographical or scribal errors and evidently incorrect pointing; but when punctuation is not manifestly wrong no alterations are made to bring it into conformity with some presumed

---

contemporary dictionaries sometimes listed them without accents), such words as "expose" (in Charles Van Loon's letters published in the *Albany Microscope* on 31 March and 7 April and on 14 April 1838) are allowed to stand as they appear in the copy-text. In dealing with the letters available only in a publication, the effort has been to reconstruct what Melville or his correspondents wrote (and intended to write) in their manuscript submissions, eliminating from the published texts as many as possible of the typographical features for which the printer or publisher was responsible. Thus, for example, the small capitals in the *Microscope* letters, the published Hawthorne letters, and Richard T. Greene's letters in the *Buffalo Commercial Advertiser* have not been retained, since they most likely would not have appeared in the letter as submitted (since small capitals are considered nontextual, these changes are not listed as emendations; see footnote 44 below).

standard, except when consistency is clearly intended. Melville's punctuation generally conforms to the rhetorical style of punctuation common in the nineteenth century, rather than to the syntactical style that has been more common in the twentieth century. It is not normally feasible to consider questioning the choice of rhetorical punctuation at particular places, because the basis for rhetorical punctuation is too subjective to allow one to determine conclusively that the copy-text punctuation could not have been intended by Melville. Of course, when a period falls within a sentence or when missing end punctuation is required, correction is called for; four emendations of such errors are made in this edition. Similarly, missing or superfluous quotation marks have been supplied or deleted at six points; see, for example, the extra quotation mark after "means?" in John Hoadley's copy of Melville's 5 May 1870 letter to his mother. In this same letter, however, the practice of repeating an opening quotation mark at the beginning of each line of a quotation is not altered, since it was common at the time (see, for example, Melville's 6 June 1846 letter to James Buchanan and the enclosure to Giovanni Spaggiari's 9 April 1859 letter to Melville).

TEXTUAL APPARATUS

F OR THOSE LETTERS for which a text is printed in this edition, the textual apparatus consists of historical and biographical headnotes along with endnotes that enable readers to reconstruct certain features of the manuscripts and explain the reasoning that underlies the transcription at individual difficult points.

Headnotes. These notes give relevant biographical and historical background for the individual letters.[39] They point out Melville's

39. They follow standardized headings that identify the name of the recipient in the case of Melville's letters and the writer of the letter in the case of letters Melville received, the date of the letter, and the place from which the letter was written. This information is always based upon the letter's heading when it exists but is supplemented from other sources (including a universal calendar) and corrected for any errors in the document. Any part of the heading that is questionable is followed by a question mark and placed in square brackets.

errors in dating, call attention to other errors (such as mistaken identifications), identify sources and contexts for Melville's allusions,
and indicate the standard spellings for the names of persons and
places mentioned by Melville. They also discuss the basis for dating
undated or partially dated letters as well as certain conjectural readings. Throughout these headnotes Melville's name is spelled with a
final *e* even though his immediate family spelled the name "Melvill"
until sometime after the death of Allan Melvill on 28 January 1832,
as reflected in the fact that Melville signed his name without the *e* in
his childhood letters and continued to do so from time to time
throughout his life (see, for example, his 1 January 1848 letter to
John Murray [reproduced on p. 101 above], his 18 September 1855
letter to Peter and Susan Gansevoort, and his 17 November 1879
letter to Abraham Lansing). This policy is not applied to those other
members of the extended family who continued to spell their name
without the final *e*.

Textual Reports. These notes, printed below each letter, generally consist of four sections:

(1) When the original document was available, a description of
the manuscript, detailing the dimensions, pattern, and color of the
writing paper[40] (along with a record of how many pages were inscribed)[41] and of the envelope (if present), along with an account of
any extra-textual markings and notations by Melville himself, the
recipients, or other hands (except penciled notations that are clearly
librarians' cataloguing numbers); or, when the original document
was not located, the alternative source for the text is identified at this
point, and, if a manuscript, it is described.

(2) An indication of the present location of the manuscript letter or draft or copy (the phrase "at present unknown" means that

---

40. Since sunlight, age, and dirt have often altered the paper color in an indeterminate number of ways, no attempt has been made to describe the paper color in
anything but the most general terms—e.g., white, blue, pink. Thus, although the
paper of Melville's 3 October 1857 letter to William Cadwell could more accurately
be described at present as "buff" in color, it is called "white" here; similarly, that of
Melville's 20 February 1888 letter to Stedman now appears to be "light tan" in
color but is also called "white" here.

41. "Inscribed" means that some portion, not necessarily all, of the page was
written on.

the item is apparently now lost, in an undisclosed private collection, or at the time of publication of this volume in the hands of the last dealer listed under provenance). Then any known information regarding provenance is given as completely as possible, in sequential order.

(3) A record of the first publication of the letter (if the letter has been published), the first full appearance if the initial one was partial, and the Davis–Gilman number, if any.

(4) Textual notes, keyed to readings in the text, recording (a) any conjectural or alternative readings (also reproduced on pp. 843–46 below), (b) readings of the manuscript at those points where words are considered miswritten, (c) letters, words, or phrases canceled by Melville at the time of original inscription, (d) locations of words that Melville added (on the same line, above the line, below the line, or in a margin) and his means (if any) of showing where the words were intended to be read, (e) his marks of emphasis (such as circling, boxing, or underlining with flourishes), (f) his omission of words or quotation marks, and (g) any compound words hyphenated at line-ends in the copy-text.[42] If the original document has not been located, the textual notes record any differences between the alternative source and any later printings or transcriptions judged to be possibly authoritative (identified along with the alternative source in the initial section of the textual re-

---

42. For these words the form (hyphenated or unhyphenated) that Melville intended becomes a matter for editorial decision on the basis of his manuscript usage elsewhere. The following list is a guide to the established copy-text forms of compounds that happen to be hyphenated at the ends of lines in this edition; any word hyphenated at the end of a line in the present edition should be transcribed as one unhyphenated word unless it appears in this list. No editorial decisions are involved in this list, but the information recorded is essential for reconstructing the copy-text and making exact quotations from the present edition: "co-operated" (p. 16); "Red-Hill" (p. 96); "hundred-weight" (p. 116); "pen-&-ink" (p. 160); "New-Burlington" (p. 164); "wide-spreading" and "*garret-way*" (p. 167); "work-room" (p. 174); "exultation-breeding" (p. 212); "sea-lover" (p. 236); "fellow-citizens" (p. 244); "wood-house" (p. 291); "first-rate" (p. 346); "hail-storms" (pp. 347–48); "presentation-copy" (p. 377); "church-yard" (p. 381); "re-acknowledge" (p. 458); "flower-and-fruit" (p. 463); "two-faced" (p. 490); "co-operation" (p. 628); "Bash-Pish" (p. 641); "brother-in-law" (p. 644); "autograph-hunters" (p. 737). A break between the first and second stanzas of the "Ditty of Aristippus" is obscured by the page break on pp. 506–7 of the present edition.

port), as well as any Northwestern-Newberry emendations.[43] As discussed above, pp. 826–27, the textual notes do not attempt to describe unclear or elided handwriting.[44]

For those letters for which no full text has been located, the entries begin with the label "Unlocated" (referring, as explained in footnote 17 above, to the text of the letter [of course, the original document as well is not located, except in the case of the manuscript fragments]). The entries, preceded by standardized headings (see footnote 39 above), then provide in paragraph form evidence for the existence of the letter (with cross-references if, for example, a letter is cited within another entry), as much as is known about the contents of the letter and the circumstances surrounding its writing, and

43.   In the textual notes, the word(s) before the bracket identifies the NN reading being treated. Every word in italics after the bracket is editorial (the one- or two-letter abbreviations identifying the sources of texts are also editorial). Individual entries are separated by bullets. The following symbols may appear in the textual notes or in the descriptions of manuscripts: A wavy dash ($\sim$) stands for the word cited before the bracket and signals that only a punctuation mark is emended. The caret ($\wedge$) indicates the absence of a punctuation mark. Empty brackets ([ ]) indicate space where a mark of punctuation failed to print. A prefixed question mark before canceled words indicates a reading that is conjectural. A single vertical bar ($|$) in the transcriptions of addresses and hyphenated words indicates a line-break; a double vertical bar ($||$) (in the notes on draft letters) separates successively canceled words or phrases.

44.   The textual notes also do not report Northwestern-Newberry departures from the original documents or other copy-texts that are regarded as nontextual and that are therefore treated as purely matters of design in the present edition: the placement and spacing of datelines, salutations, and closings; the depth of paragraph indentations; the use of lines under superscript letters; unintended superscript letters; the length of hyphens, double-hyphens (here treated as ordinary hyphens), dashes, and lines (here given in five lengths: the ordinary hyphen, the en dash, the em dash, the two-em dash, and the three-em dash, with a few longer lines, as in the 13 August 1852 letter to Hawthorne); the space before and after dashes; the indeterminate placement of punctuation in relation to quotation marks (in such cases the punctuation has been uniformly placed outside the quotation marks in conformity with what appears to have been Melville's dominant practice); and the spacing of initials and abbreviations (which has been standardized to a single space between initials and no space within abbreviations). Features of printed texts that are regarded as nontextual include small capitals and ligatures (see footnote 38 above); thus, the elimination of these features is not noted in the lists of emendations (except when the copy-text reading must be cited to record an emendation of punctuation or spelling).

its number, if any, on Davis and Gilman's "Check List of Unlocated Letters."

To sum up, then, for the letters edited from sources other than dispatched or draft holographs, readers will find in the textual reports all the information needed to reconsider for themselves the textual decisions in the present edition. For the letters edited from dispatched or draft holographs, the texts attempt to reflect Melville's intention by expanding elisions, correcting miswritten words, and omitting canceled material in the manuscript letters. The guiding rule, as for the treatment of manuscript material in other volumes of the Northwestern-Newberry Edition, is that unclear, conjectural, and elided words are transcribed in standard spelling, but words that are clearly spelled unconventionally (except for those classified as miswritten) are retained as Melville wrote them.[45] Although the apparatus provides readers with evidence regarding miswritten words and cancellations, it cannot—short of offering a complete manuscript facsimile—make available all the evidence for the editor's decisions about how to read what is unclear and elided in the original manuscripts. Even a photofacsimile is not an adequate substitute for the original, and certainly no transcription can be. But transcriptions have contributions of their own to make, and the present critical transcription is offered as an attempt to establish the text Melville intended as he wrote his letters, along with information to help readers understand the nature of the documents and the private writings they contain.

45. This policy has resulted in differences in spellings from the Davis-Gilman edition, where the effort to render Melville's words *literatim* resulted in a greater number of nonstandard spellings.

Conjectural and Alternative Readings

R EPRODUCED HERE (some in reduced size) are those manuscript words for which the editor found no satisfactory reading (see p. 819 above). The Northwestern-Newberry readings in the second column are either conjectural as listed or have the possible alternative readings noted (this information also appears in the textual notes for each letter); adjacent words are also given when necessary to identify the specific occurrence of a word in the letter.

MELVILLE'S LETTERS

Date/Page	NN Reading	
8 Dec. 1846 p. 67	opinion (*possibly* opinions)	
25 March 1848 p. 106	feel (*possibly* find)	
	invincible (*possibly* incurible)	
	abandoning	

p. 106	continuously (*possibly* continually)	*continuously*
24 Feb. 1849 p. 118	every (*possibly* any)	*every*
3 March 1849 p. 122	full (*possibly* free)	*full*
5 April 1849 p. 128	morbid (*miswritten* morbib *with second* b *written* *over a wiped letter*)	*morbid*
	thing we (thing *possibly* why)	*why*
2 Dec. 1849 p. 148	inundative	*inundative*
2 Feb. 1850 p. 155	these old (these *possibly* those	*these*
13 Dec. 1850 p. 173	ship in (in *possibly* on)	*in*
p. 174	achieved	*achieved*
12 Feb. 1851 p. 180	plumb (*possibly* plump)	*plumb*
p. 181	had not read (not *possibly* nt)	*nt*
24 Aug. 1851 p. 202	over (*possibly* oer)	*over*
7 Nov. 1851 p. 209	Herman (*possibly* Norman)	*Norman*
	buy	*buy*
17 July 1852 p. 230	visit a (*possibly* meet a *or* wait on)	*visit a*
	brought (*possibly* bought)	*brought*
13 Aug. 1852 p. 235	There (*possibly* Here)	*There*

10 Nov. 1856 p. 302	generally (*possibly* usually)	
14 Sept. 1857 p. 312	Commissioner	
28 May 1860 p. 346	in sea (in *possibly* on)	
20 March 1861 p. 363	apprised (*possibly* apprized)	
24 March 1861 p. 367	shall (*possibly* still)	
17 Feb. 1863 p. 383	embarked in (in *possibly* on)	
9 June 1869 p. 410	letter (*possibly* letters)	
25 July 1876 p. 438	returning on (on *possibly* in)	
7 March 1877 p. 450	How about (How *possibly* Now)	
22 Jan. 1885 p. 485	faery (*possibly* fairy)	
After 23 Jan. 1886 p. 495	leave	
	Retaliate	
2 April 1886 p. 497	investing (*possibly* inverting)	
Between 7 April and 21 July 1886 p. 500	doubtlessly	
	various	
	marine	
	rendered	
	delineator	

| 12 Jan. 1890
p. 523 | Law in
(in *possibly* on) | *m* |
| Undated
p. 533 | received
(*possibly* rcvd) | |

LETTERS RECEIVED

Date/Page	*NN Reading*	
6 Feb. 1847 (enc.), p. 586	favorable judgement	
28 March 1851 p. 610	Rocborn	
p. 611	Now is it (Now *possibly* How)	
12 July [1856?] [M's notation], p. 647	Decline (*possibly* Dellins)	
19 Aug. 1886 p. 735	arranged (*possibly* annexed)	

Melville's Hand

THIS ANALYSIS, titled as above, by Merrell R. Davis and William H. Gilman
stood as the second of three sections of the introduction to their edition of *The
Letters of Herman Melville* (New Haven: Yale University Press, 1960), pp. xxi–xxv.
It is reprinted here for its continued relevance and some of its terminology, which is
adopted, with slight redefinitions, in the NOTE ON THE TEXT to the present edition
(and that of the *Journals*, vol. 15). (One evident misprint, "*Belvd*," is corrected to
"*Belev*" [p. 850].) The Northwestern-Newberry editors have applied the additional
term "miswritten," distinguishing such words from misspelled words (see pp. 828–
31 above). The Davis and Gilman textual notes went far in the attempt to report the
actual letters present in each word as seen in Melville's idiosyncratic hand, as it
appeared to depart from standard spelling; the Northwestern-Newberry editors,
however, in this and other volumes of the Edition, regard each of the many problematic words, unless clearly misspelled, as a representation of the word rather than
an approximate spelling in which all separate letters are discernible alike to every
reader. (Because of such differences in textual policy or variations in transcription,
some of the examples cited here do not appear in the present edition.)

Melville could write deliberately and carefully with an eye to clear
and understandable penmanship, but very often, even in formal or
business letters, haste or carelessness or enthusiasm produced characteristics of his hand that make his manuscripts difficult to read.
Recognizing that such difficulties existed, we early decided to make
transcripts as nearly literal as possible, copying the letters line by
line, indicating Melville's caret or marginal insertions, his false starts

and deletions, approximating the spacing of his headings, complimentary closes and signatures, and keeping his punctuation and spelling. Although photostats were to be obtained of as many letters as possible, the transcripts were to be made from the available original manuscripts. We have followed this practice consistently, with the additional safeguard of later rechecking transcripts against photostats and in most instances against the original manuscripts as well. In the letters that had previously been published, the transcripts were compared with the published versions and variations noted. The result was the establishment of as exact a transcript of each letter as possible upon which to base the text of the edition.

From the close and detailed study of the letters came also a recognition of three major characteristics of Melville's hand, perhaps best defined by the terms elision, fusion, and expansion. Much, if not all, of the difficulty in reading the letters was reduced by keeping in mind these three general peculiarities. Melville's characteristic elisions, for example, include the omission of certain letters of the alphabet singly or in groups (generally vowels) in numerous combinations. Occasionally, an actual abbreviation is intended and understood by an elimination of vowels in the writing of such words as *Edinbrgh* for Edinburgh, *Prce Albert* for Prince Albert, *acct* for account, *recvd* for received, or *Mondy Eveng* for Monday Evening. More often, the same or a similar process creates a word that is not intended as an abbreviation but is a condensed word that has resulted from haste or carelessness in the formation of letters. The distinction between actual abbreviations and condensed words with omitted letters or syllables, however, is not always clear, since there is no final consistency in Melville's elisions. It would be difficult to say, for example, whether Melville intended an abbreviation or simply produced a condensed word when he wrote *almst* for almost, *strngly* for strongly (clearly omitting the *o* in both), *mentned* for mentioned (omitting the *io*), *affectntly* for affectionately (omitting the vowels), *endeavrd* for endeavored (again omitting the vowels), or *frnd* for friend (omitting the *ie*). The habit of elision, then, may be either an intentional abbreviation or a kind of shorthand, but whichever it is, the habit is exhibited so often as to require special consideration both in transcribing and in reproducing such words typographically.

It is Melville's habit of combining or fusing individual strokes (either ascending or descending) that causes the most difficulty.

Here even a painstaking transcript cannot always distinguish between omitted letters and fused strokes of letters, but the recognition of both this and his habit of elision often permits an accurate transcript of a word that might otherwise be misinterpreted. Here also Melville's fused letters very often produce the same effect as an abbreviation, for example when he writes *every, never, send, leaves,* and *several* so that they appear to be *evry, nevr, snd, leavs, severl.* A close review will demonstrate that Melville has combined the ending stroke of one letter with the beginning stroke of another to make his characteristic fused letter. It should be emphasized that these are not condensations or elisions, they are actual fusions of strokes in the letter by which fewer strokes stand for the fully written-out letter through being combined with the strokes for the preceding or following letter. A careful examination will generally distinguish fused from elided letters.

Although not always as systematic as this description may imply, Melville's elisions and fusions of letters or syllables do represent a kind of method. On many occasions the same word or words in a similar group may illustrate the full word, the word with fused letters, or the word with elided letters. Examples are readily found, for instance, in the "Agatha" letter on the facsimile page [see p. 233 above], where in words ending with final -*ing* the different constructions appear in the word *talking* (spelled out with dotted *i*, full *n*, and final *g*); the words *visiting, concerning,* and *making* (fusion of the *n* with the open loop of final *g*), and the word *arriv[i]ng* (elision of undotted *i*) or the words *uncomplain[in]gly* and *hav[in]g* (elision of both *i* and *n*). A complete list of such words is unnecessary here, even if it were possible, but it may be useful to point out that examples of both elisions and fusions occur often in the following groups of words ending with:

-ance: acquaintance, advance, (dis)appearance, obeisance,
           remembrance(s)
-er: brother, dinner, ever(y), however, never, other,
           power(s), sincere(ly)
-ed: behaved, derived, furnished, happened, occurred,
           received
-est: earliest, earnest(ly), interest(ingly), request(ed)

-e(ie)nce: absence, coincidence, commence, conscience,
            experience(d), presence
-e(ie)nt: convenient, different, permanent, present, subsequent,
            sufficient
-ment: acknowledgment(s), agreement, arrangement(s),
            moment, punishment
-e(ie)nd: friend(ly), send
-ing: being, bring(s), evening, nothing, something, standing
-ion: affection(ately), attention, commission, imitation,
            invitation
-ious: curious, glorious(ly), obnoxious, previous(ly), serious(ly)
-out: about, out, without

For purposes of illustration this list emphasizes groups of words in which the terminal syllable is elided or fused. The same combination of letters, however, when they appear medially receive similar treatment from Melville's pen. In addition, the words containing diphthongs or digraphs *ou* (would, should), *ea* (great), *ua* (adequate), and the large group of *ei* and *ie* words may also be fused or elided. When Melville wrote out the word *believe* he consistently misspelled it by reversing the vowels, but he also elided or fused the letters in what appears to be an abbreviation (*Belev*), particularly in the complimentary close of a letter, so that it is not always possible to distinguish in each instance what his intention was.

A third characteristic, although not as frequent or misleading, is Melville's expansion of letters and gratuitous addition of strokes. Occasionally, as when he writes *possesss* with three final consonants, his pen has clearly misspelled the word through haste or carelessness. Melville also adds a stroke, especially before final *d*, *r*, or *rd*, in what is clearly a peculiarity of his penmanship. The words *apprised*, *aggravated, promenaded, paid,* and such words as *affair, regard, roads,* often have a clear but unnecessary stroke before the final consonant. Thus Melville's word *had* may appear to be written *hard*. If the sense of the context permits either meaning, as in Melville's comment on *Mardi*, "I had worked at it under an earnest ardor" [in his 25 March 1848 letter to John Murray, p. 106 above; NN reads "with" for "under"], the recognition of his habit of expansion is necessary to the accurate reading, *had* rather than *hard*.

Certain other characteristics in Melville's formation of letters need comment. He often leaves the letters *a* and *o* as well as the loop of his *g* open, failing to bring the stroke around to meet the preceding stroke. Although not an unusual characteristic of handwriting generally, it causes difficulty when combined with his fused or elided letters. Thus the open or unclosed *o* in *most* may produce what appears to be *must* and when fused with the last minim of the *m* will appear to be *mst*, which could be either word. Various other letters must be observed carefully. Melville does not always dot his *i*, so that in certain combinations confusion may exist between *i* and *o* (in account; on account) or between *i* and *u* (infatuate, unfortunate; immediate, unmerited). His medial *s* may appear to be *r* or *z* when written hastily, and his final *s* may be merely a return concave down-curl of the pen fused to the preceding letter and difficult to recognize at all (circumstance, circumstances). His final *g* and *y* may both be an unlooped or uncurled letter with a downstroke below the line (busy, being). His introductory *b* may be fragmented and fused with a following *r* to confuse the words *bought* and *brought*. His habit of fusing *e* on the final stroke of a preceding *v* may make for difficulty in differentiating between *instinctively* and *instinctually* or *effectively* and *effectually*. These and other combinations may produce such alternative readings as *feverishly-fervently, feel-find, invitation-imitation, pinions-powers*, and *rudely-widely*.

When the demons directed him, Melville's hand deteriorated, so that a direct correlation may be observed between a full and spontaneous flow of idea and the roughness of the hand that tried to keep up with his thought. The "Agatha" letter may serve as an illustration of this process (and consequently has been chosen for facsimile), for as the letter continues, Melville's fusions and elisions increase under the impact of writing what is uppermost in his mind. On the other hand, in the letters Melville wrote his brother Tom or his brother Allan, an informality of relationship is suggested by the casualness of the hand. Although Melville himself recognized the difficulties and occasionally inserted letters or rewrote a word to clarify it, still a general familiarity with his habits of eliding, fusing, or expanding strokes and a recognition of the peculiarities in his formation of letters will remove most doubtful readings even in those letters written hastily, casually, or spontaneously.

Manuscript leaf (recto, reduced), in an unidentified hand, possibly deriving from a letter by Melville. Courtesy of the Berkshire Athenaeum.

A Possible Melville Letter

T HE VOLUME editor, Lynn Horth, has identified one manuscript leaf of uncertain origin as possibly deriving from a Melville letter; Harrison Hayford
and Hershel Parker concur in her view.[1] This leaf is among the papers given by
Allan Melville's granddaughter Agnes Morewood to the Berkshire Athenaeum (see
the manuscript description below). It is not in Melville's hand, but either the un-

1.   For the record, two letters that might be mistaken as Melville's are reported here as
certainly not his. (1) A 20 December 1854 letter printed in Richard T. Greene's column in the
25 December 1854 Sandusky, Ohio, Mirror (see pp. 48–49 above), introduced as "from an old
friend in New York" and signed "YOUR OLD SHIPMATE," was adduced as possibly Melville's
by Clarence Gohdes in "Melville's Friend 'Toby,' " Modern Language Notes 59 (January 1944),
52–55; Gohdes concluded that "No one can say definitely that Melville wrote the letter . . . ,
but it is possible that he did so." However, the letter's gossipy style, which inquires, "Have
you seen Graham for January, yet?" and "Why not ask if I have seen Godey, or Peterson, or
Putnam, or any of the others? [New York and Philadelphia magazines]," is not typical of
Melville, who moreover was not living in New York but in Pittsfield at the time. It is also
most unlikely that in 1854 Melville was a regular subscriber to the paper, as was the letter
writer: "About the 1st of this present month I read in the Sandusky Morning Mirror, of which
you are one of the responsible editors, an article from your pen, entitled 'Jeremiah's Dream,
or the Effects of a Thanksgiving Dinner—being a warning to gormands.' " (2) An unsigned
manuscript letter, dated 25 January 1876, now in the Jay Family Papers, Rare Book and Manuscript Library, Columbia University, states "Mr Melville regrets very much" having to decline an invitation; it is not in Melville's hand and was written on "Royal Irish Linen" paper at
the Hotel Brunswick in New York. It was evidently written by some other "Mr Melville"
visiting in New York.

Manuscript leaf (verso, reduced), in an unidentified hand, possibly deriving from a letter by Melville. Courtesy of the Berkshire Athenaeum.

identified hand that inscribed it or a second hand wrote "Herman Melville" below the text—suggesting that it may have been copied from a letter Melville wrote. The letter sent several toasts meant to be given by its recipient in the writer's behalf at a wedding party at Broadhall, one which took place some while after the death, on 16 October 1863, of Sarah Morewood, who is remembered in the final toast.

Although the copyist did not replicate Melville's usual spelling "remember-ance," "Britton" is one of the spellings Melville used for Mrs. Ellen Brittain, Sarah Morewood's sister (see pp. 388–89 above). The reference to Rowland (here spelled "Roland") Morewood's surroundings as "like a Paradise" recalls Melville's ad-dressing Sarah Morewood as the "Lady of Paradise" in his [29 September 1856?] letter to her (p. 297 above); he also referred to books she had given him as "my Paradise in store" (p. 206 above). (Perhaps not coincidentally, Sarah Morewood and Ellen Brittain's mother's maiden name was Paradise.)

Hershel Parker suggests that the occasion may have been a family gathering at Broadhall for the wedding of the Morewoods' daughter Anne Rachel to Rich-ard Lathers, Jr., on 21 September 1882, a wedding Melville was unable to attend. (Melville had referred to Anne shortly after her birth in 1853 as the "infant Countess Hahn-Hahn" in his [20 December?] letter to her mother; for his rela-tionship with the Lathers family, see pp. 259–60 above.) Parker further points out that the "Pittsfield Beauty" toast was one Melville would have known: it had first been given in behalf of the absent Cornelius Mathews at a party at Broadhall, at which Melville most likely was present, and was reported in an article about the party in the 7 August 1851 *Boston Evening Transcript*, signed "Miantonowah" (J. E. A. Smith):

> He [Mathews], however, sent three toasts, two of which I omit, to spare the blushes of our hosts, whose praises they celebrated, and the other is so wicked I have half a mind to—but here it is:
>
> "*Pittsfield Beauty*—may it ever be in bloom, but never in bloomer."
>
> Fie upon you! Mr M, how could you? I couldn't drink but half your toast—but I drank that twice; so "it's all right."

Thus the toast, some thirty years old and perhaps also alluding to an earlier occa-sion involving bloomers during one of the summer gatherings so often organized by Sarah Morewood, would have needed some explanation, which the recipient of this letter either already knew or Melville had supplied.

P.S. Please present my best Respects & kind wishes to all of my summer acquaintances who may be with you: and, at the suitable moment (when you think the 'flowing bowl' will fully justify them) these sentments of remembrance from me.
(This Kiss to some suitable 3ᵈ Party)
Health & Happiness to Broad Hall:
The Fair Bride: Wherever fortune carries her may she remember Berkshire, beautiful and happy, as Berkshire will always remember *her*.

(after the 3ᵈ Bottle) *Pittsfield Beauty*: May it be ever in bloom, but never in Bloomer! (Please explain this to the Company)

With Special remembrances to Mrs. Britton, Mrs Fisher, Miss Allen, Miss Dillingham.

Please add —

Mr. Roland Morewood: He ought to be a Happy Man, for all he looks on without and within, is like a Paradise: and what is better, he *deserves* to be!

(*Final & Concluding Toast.*) If there be a Spirit in this Company who seeks the pleasure of others before her own, whose delight is in happy faces about her, who forgets not friends far away, and whom no acquaintance with the world can make worldly or selfish — as one who is distant from the scene now clearly sees there is — at this moment of parting be she now remembered by us all as we drink, from the heart, the *Health of Mr. Morewood*

Herman Melville —

Text inscribed, in ink, on both sides of a 12.6 × 20.9 cm part-sheet (torn along the left edge) of white laid paper, partially watermarked with the letters "R R I S".

TEXTUAL NOTES: *Health & Happiness to Broad Hall:*] *before canceled* Would that the Spirit of Enjoyment enter its vales here to night • beautiful] be *written over an* • Dillingham] *after* (over *in bottom margin* • like a] *possibly canceled or altered with short strokes* • of parting] *inserted above caret* • Herman Melville —] *possibly in a second hand*

Two Letters Concerning Melville

T HE FOLLOWING two letters are included in this volume because they are more directly and intimately concerned with Melville himself than any other known correspondence within his extended family. The letters were first published by Walter D. Kring and Jonathan S. Carey in the *Proceedings of the Massachusetts Historical Society* 87 (1975), 137–41. Donald Yannella and Hershel Parker later republished that article, along with eleven commentaries on the significance of the letters, in a pamphlet entitled *The Endless, Winding Way in Melville: New Charts by Kring and Carey* (Glassboro, N.J.: The Melville Society, 1981).

Both letters are to Dr. Henry Whitney Bellows (1814–82), minister of All Souls Unitarian Church in New York City; Melville and his wife were members of his congregation. The first letter, dated 6 May 1867, is from Samuel S. Shaw, Elizabeth Shaw Melville's half-brother (see the index for references to earlier connections between Melville and Shaw); Bellows's earlier letter to the Shaw brothers cited by Samuel Shaw is not known to survive. The second letter, dated 20 May 1867, is from Elizabeth Shaw Melville herself. No replies from Bellows, who was about to sail to Europe for a vacation, are known to survive. Both letters are transcribed here from photocopies of the original manuscripts, which are now in the Bellows papers at the Massachusetts Historical Society.

No further references to or documentation of the exact nature of the Melvilles' marital trouble or his psychological state at this time are known (see the pamphlet cited above). New troubles faced the family only a few months later, with the death of the oldest child, Malcolm (see pp. 115 and 399–400 above). For Dr. Augustus K. Gardner, see pp. 157–58 above.

SAMUEL S. SHAW TO HENRY W. BELLOWS
6 MAY 1867 · BOSTON

16 Court St.
May 6. 1867.

Dr. H. W Bellows
Dear Sir

Your letter to my brother and myself is just received. I thank you much for the interest which you have taken in my sisters case and am very glad to have your opinion and advice in the matter, which has been a cause of anxiety to all of us for years past. She will tell you that all the reasons set forth in your letter have been urged over and over again by me as a ground for a separation that we have offered to assist her to the best of our ability and that the Melvilles also, though not till quite recently, have expressed a willingness to lend their assistance. The whole family understands the case and the thing has resolved itself into the mere question of my sisters willingness to say the word. Of course we should not act against what we believed to be her *real* wishes, we should in any event act substantially under her direction and we must base our claim to act on what *she* knows and *not* on what *we* know. If I understand your letter it is proposed to make a sudden interference and carry her off, she protesting that she does not wish to go and that it is none of her doing. But I think that this would only obscure the real merits of the case in the eyes of the world, of which she has a most exaggerated dread.

I see no way in which she can throw off the responsibility of deciding for herself in this matter, and if it *is* her own act I do not see why she should wish it to appear to be the act of others, unauthorized by her.

The simplest way and the best way seems to me to be the one often talked about and once resolved upon viz that she should come to Boston as if on a visit, which will give her ample opportunity for preparation without exciting premature suspicion, and that when here her friends should inform her husband that a separation, for the present at least, has been decided on. That it should *not* appear to be the work of persons who urge her against her inclination but the deliberate decision of her judgment, which everybody believes to be good, assisted by the counsels of friends, and the professional advice of Dr. Gardner.

But if *we* are to seem to be the real putters asunder of man and wife and she is merely to acquiesce I do not think it could be managed better than by having her at our house and by keeping her there and carefully preventing her husband from seeing her, and telling him and everybody that we had made up our minds not to let her return.

But this might embarrass our subsequent relations with Mr. Melville and really injure my sister's case because if he should commence legal proceedings it would throw suspicion over her motives in acquiescing in a separation. It may well be said Here is a case of mischief making where the wife's relations have created all the trouble. "She says *now* that her husband ill treated her so that she could not live with him but why did she not say so before. She goes to Boston and by dint of argument and remonstrances and bad advice of all sorts is at last persuaded into thinking herself a much injured woman." &c &c &c

And her very patience and fortitude will be turned into arguments against her belief in the insanity of her husband.

I think that the safest course is to let her real position become apparent from the first, namely that of a wife, who, being convinced that her husband is insane *acts* as if she were so convinced and applies for aid and assistance to her friends and acts *with* them.

I think she would have done this long ago were it not for imaginary and groundless apprehensions of the censures of the world upon her conduct. If you can do anything to reassure her mind on that point I have no doubt it will contribute much to her future happiness and enable to do her hard duty more easily.

Or if you can suggest any plan of action by which the present lamentable state of things can be ended it will be most gratefully received. Our house will be as it always has been open to her as a home as long as we remain there. She shall have the best legal and medical advice that can be procured

I hope that your attention to this matter will not interfere with your many calls which must be very pressing just now.

Very truly yours
Samuel S. Shaw

ELIZABETH SHAW MELVILLE TO HENRY W. BELLOWS
20 MAY 1867 · NEW YORK

New York May 20. 1867

Rev. Dr. Bellows

My dear Sir,

I cannot refrain from writing to say how troubled I was at having missed seeing you on Saturday, and how much I appreciate your kind attention in calling in the busy moments of your departure. I had it in my heart to go to your house once more before you left, if only to bid you God speed on your voyage but refrained knowing how many and pressing must be the calls on your time and thoughts. I also wanted to thank you for the active interest you took in my behalf. I do so now — most sincerely — and whatever further trial may be before me, I shall feel that your counsel is a strong help to sustain, more perhaps than any other earthly counsel could. I think you will be glad to know that your long talk with me has been a very great comfort, both for its appreciative sympathy, and for other reasons. I lay to heart your encouraging words, and pray for submission and faith to *realize* the sustaining power of the Master's love, and to approach his Table in the very spirit of his last command.

I hesitate now to intrude myself and my griefs upon you, but feel impelled to express my gratitude for your kindness, since seas divide, and the opportunity may not be mine again.

And that you and yours may be held in Holy Keeping by land and by sea, and that you may return to us with renovated health and strength, shall be the earnest prayer of

yours sincerely & gratefully
Elizabeth S. Melville

Calendar of Melville's Correspondence

Bold type indicates letters for which texts have been located.

Index

P AGE NUMBERS in bold type indicate extant letters by Melville [M] to (or to Melville from) the person or organization indexed; numbers in italic type indicate subjects mentioned in a letter (and often in the preceding headnote as well; this page number is also italicized); all other numbers indicate editorial matter only. Melville's works (and Northwestern-Newberry [NN] editions) are indexed in a separate category under his name.

COLOPHON

THE TEXT *of the Northwestern-Newberry Edition of* THE WRITINGS OF HERMAN MELVILLE *is set in eleven-point Bembo, two points leaded. This exceptionally handsome type face is a modern rendering of designs made by Francesco Griffo for the office of Aldus Manutius in Venice and first used for printing, in 1495, of the tract* De Aetna *by Cardinal Pietro Bembo. The display face is Bruce Rogers's Centaur, a twentieth-century design based on and reflective of the late-fifteenth-century Venetian models of Nicolas Jenson.*

This volume was set in type by Alexander Typesetting, Inc., of Indianapolis, Indiana. It was printed and bound by BookCrafters, Inc., of Chelsea, Michigan. The typography and binding design of the edition are by Paul Randall Mize.